2002

BROOKMAN

UNITED STATES, UNITED NATIONS & CANADA
STAMPS & POSTAL COLLECTIBLES

INCLUDING
SPECIALIZED LISTINGS
OF
STATE DUCK & INDIAN RESERVATION STAMPS
PLATE NO. COILS & UNEXPLODED BOOKLETS
U.S. SOUVENIR CARDS • PAGES • PANELS
AND FEATURING
UNITED STATES FIRST DAY COVERS

Plus

**Confederate States
U.S. Possessions
U.S. Trust Territories
Canadian Provinces
U.N. First Day Covers**

PLUS SPECIAL
AUTOGRAPH SECTION

2002
BROOKMAN

TERMS AND INFORMATION

CONDITION - We price United States stamps issued prior to 1890 in two grades - Average and Fine. From 1890 to present we list a price for F-VF and VF quality. **FOR INFORMATION ON GRADING SEE PAGE vii.**

GUM AND HINGING

Original Gum (O.G.)
  Prior to 1882, Unused stamps may have partial or no gum. If you require o.g., add the percentage indicated in ( ). **Example** (OG + 25%). From 1882 to present, o.g. can be expected, but stamps may have been hinged or have hinge remnants.

Never Hinged
  Most issues are priced in F-VF, Never Hinged condition. Premiums for Average, NH usually run about half the F-VF premium. Prices for Never Hinged stamps on issues prior to 1882 will be quoted upon request.

SPECIAL PRICING INSTRUCTIONS

Average - From 1890-1934 **Average hinged perforated** stamps, when available, will be priced at 60-70% of the F-VF Hinged price depending upon the general quality of the issue.

  Average hinged imperforate stamps, when available, will be priced at 70-75% of the F-VF Hinged price depending upon the general quality of the issue.

  From 1935 to present, average quality, when available, will be priced at 20% below the F-VF price.

Very Fine NH, 1935-Date
  VF NH singles, plate blocks, line pairs, etc. are available (unless specifically priced at the following premiums:
  Add 10¢ to any item priced under 50¢. Add 20% to any item priced at 50¢ and up. Unless priced as Very Fine, sets are not available Very Fine and stamps should be listed individually with appropriate premium.

Very Fine Unused O.G. Plate Blocks & Line Pairs
  Very Fine Unused Plate Blocks and Line Pairs prior to #749 & 723 (and selected Back-of-the-Book Issues) are generally available at the respective F-VF NH price.

Very Fine Used
  From 1847-1934, Very Fine Used stamps, when available, are priced by adding the % indicated to the appropriate Fine or F-VF price.
  Example (VF + 50%).
  From 1935 to date, the premiums are the same as for VF NH copies.

MINIMUM ORDER OF $20 - Present day costs force us to require that mail orders total a minimum of $20.00. Send payment with order.

PRICES - Every effort will be made to maintain these prices throughout the life of this edition. However, prices are subject to change if market conditions require. We are not responsible for typographical errors.

SCOTT CATALOG NUMBERS ARE USED WITH THE EXPRESS PERMISSION OF THE SCOTT PUBLISHING CO.

The contents of this book are owned exclusively by
BROOKMAN/BARRETT & WORTHEN

and all rights thereto are reserved under the Pan American and Universal Copyright Conventions
Copyright 2001

BROOKMAN/BARRETT & WORTHEN
10 Chestnut Drive
Bedford, NH 03110
Phone (603) 472-5575
Fax (603) 472-8795
PRINTED IN USA

Edited By David S. Macdonald

First Day Covers Contributing Editors
Robert G. Driscoll
James McCusker
Bill Toutant
Autograph Contibuting Editors
Phillip Marks
Scott Winslow
Greg Tucker

TABLE OF CONTENTS
STAMPS

INDEX TO ADVERTISERS

Postal Reply Cards, Covers and Color Inserts

Featured Articles

We wish to thank the advertisers who help keep the Brookman Price Guide available at the lowest possible price. We urge you to support our advertisers and let them know their ads were helpful to you.

BROOKMAN GRADING GUIDE

The following guide is a simplified approach to stamp grading designed to help you better understand the quality you can expect to receive when you order a specific grade. All grades listed below are for undamaged stamps free of faults such as tears, thin spots, creases, straight edges, scrapes, etc. Stamps with those defects are considered "seconds" and sell for prices below those listed. The stamps you receive may not always match the criteria given since each stamp must be judged on its own special merits such as freshness, color, cancellation, etc. For example: a well centered stamp may be graded only as "Average" because of a very heavy cancellation. Grading stamps is an art, not a science, and frequently the cliche "beauty is in the eye of the beholder" applies. Stamps offered throughout this price list fall into the "Group A" category unless the heading contains a (B) or (C).

GROUP A - WELL CENTERED ISSUES

| Average | Average | Average | Average |

| F-VF | F-VF | F-VF | F-VF |

| Very Fine | Very Fine | Very Fine | Very Fine |

GROUP A	AVERAGE	F-VF	VERY FINE
PERFORATED STAMPS	Perforations touch or barely clear of design on one or two sides.	Perforations well clear of design on all sides.	Design very well centered within perforations.
IMPERFORATE STAMPS	One edge may touch design.	All four edges are clear of design.	Four edges are well clear of and well centered around design.
COILS AND BOOKLET PANES	Perforated and imperforate edge may touch design on one or two edges.	Perforated and imperforate edges are clear of the design.	Design very well centered within perforated and imperforate edges.

NOTE: Stamps of poorer centering than "Average" grade are considered seconds.

"EXTREMELY FINE" is a grading term used to desciibe stamps that are almost "Perfect" in centering, color, freshness, cancellations, etc. This grade, when available, is priced substantially higher than Very Fine quality.

GROUP B - MEDIAN CENTERED ISSUES

| Average | Average | Average | Average | Average |

| F-VF | F-VF | Very Fine | Very Fine | Very Fine |

GROUP B	AVERAGE	F-VF	VERY FINE
PERFORATED STAMPS	Perforations touch or barely cut into design on one or two sides.	Perforations clear of design on all four sides.	Design well centered within perforations.
IMPERFORATE STAMPS	One or two edges may touch or barely cut into design.	All four edges are clear of design as in "A".	Four edges are well clear of and well centered around design as in "A".
COILS AND BOOKLET PANES	Perforated and imperforate edge may touch or barely cut into design.	Perforated and imperforate edges are clear of design as in "A".	Design well centered within perforated and imperforated edges.

GROUP C - POORLY CENTERED ISSUES

| Average | Average | Average | Average | Average |

| Fine | Fine | Very Fine | Very Fine | Very Fine |

GROUP C	AVERAGE	FINE	VERY FINE
PERFORATED STAMPS	Perforations may cut into design on one or more sides.	Perforations touch or just clear of design on one or more sides.	Perforations will clear design on all four sides.
IMPERFORATE STAMPS	One or more edges may cut into design.	One or more edges touch the design.	All four edges clear of the design.
COILS AND BOOKLET PANES	Perforated and imp. edge may cut into design on one or more sides.	Perforated and imperforate edges may touch or just clear design.	Perfoforated and imperforated edges well clear of design on all four sides.

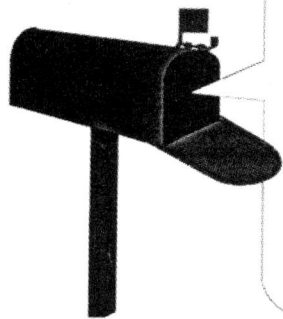

Welcome to Stamp Collecting!

Challenge....information....friendship.... and just plain fun are part of "the World's Most Popular Hobby," stamp collecting! For more than 150 years, stamp collecting has been the hobby of choice of royalty, movie stars, sport celebrities, and hundreds of thousands of other people. Why do so many different people like stamps? One reason is, the hobby of stamp collecting suits almost anybody -- it's very personal. You fit the hobby to yourself, instead of forcing yourself to fit rules, as with many hobbies. There is not much free choice about how to play golf or softball or square dance -- there are many rules.

But stamp collecting can be done in a very simple way using your stamps you find on your everyday mail and place on plain paper in a three-ring binder. Or you can give a "want list" to a stamp dealer. He will pull the stamps you want from his stock, and you mount them in the correct spaces in a custom-made album that you bought.

Or you can go to stamp shows or stamp shops and spend hours looking through boxes of stamps and envelopes in search of a particular stamp with a certain postal marking or a special first-day cover that has a meaning to suit your own interests.

Stamp collecting is a special mix of the structured and the unstructured, and you can make it a personal hobby that will not be like anyone else's. It's a world all its own, and anyone can find a comfortable place in it.

"Stamp Collector" or "Philatelist"?

Some people think that a "philatelist" (fi-LAT-uh-list) means someone who is more expert or serious than someone who is a "stamp collector." That is not true! But one advantage of using the word "philately" (fi-LAT-uh-lee) is that it includes all areas of the hobby -- not just stamps -- such as postal markings, postal history, postal stationery, and the postal items from the time before there were stamps, such as folder letters.

Finding Material for Your Collection

You can easily find everything for your stamp hobby by mail. Stamps, other philatelic material, catalogues, albums, and so on are easy to get by mail order. The philatelic press carries advertising for all these hobby needs, and stamp shows in your area also will have dealers there. If you are lucky, you also may have a retail stamp store nearby.

Stamps shows may be small one-or-two day events in your local area, or very large events in big city convention halls lasting several days and featuring hundreds of dealers and thousands of pages of exhibits to see. Stamp shows also provide chances to meet other collectors, some of whom you may have "met" only by mail before.

How to Learn About Your New Hobby

Organizations, publications, and other collectors can help you grow in the hobby. The hobbies/recreation section of your local library may have basic books about stamp collecting, and the free reference department may have a set of catalogs.

If your local library has no books on stamp collecting, you can borrow some from the huge collection of the American Philatelic Research Library through the interlibrary loan or by becoming a member of the American Philatelic Society.

The APS/APRL are the largest stamp club and library in the United States and offer many services to collectors, including a 100-page monthly magazine, insurance for stamp collections, and a Sale Division through which members can buy sell stamps by mail among themselves. The APS/APRL are at P.O. Box 8000, State College, PA 16803, or call (814) 237-3803.

There also are many newspapers and magazines in the stamp hobby, including Linn's Stamp News, Stamp Collector, Scott Monthly Journal, Mekeel's, Global Stamp News, and Stamps. Some can be found on a large newsstands.

Taking Care of Your Collection

Paper is very fragile and must be handled with care. Stamp collectors use special tools and materials to protect their collectibles. Stamp tongs may look like cosmetic tweezers, but they have special tips that will not damage stamps, so be sure to buy your tongs from a stamp dealer and not in the beauty section at the drugstore!

Stamp albums and other storage methods (temporary file folders and boxes, envelopes, etc.) should be archival quality and acid-free paper, and any plastic used on or near stamps and covers (postally-used envelopes of philatelic interest) also should be archival -- as used for safe storage by museums. Plastic that is not archivally safe has oil based softeners that can leach out and do much damage to the stamps. In recent years philatelic manufacturers have become more careful about their products, and it is easy to find safe paper and plastic for hobby use.

Never use cellophane or other tapes around your stamps. Even so-called "magic tape" will cause damage that can not be undone. Stamps should be put on pages either with hinges (small rectangles of special gummed paper) or with mounts (little self adhesive plastic envelopes in many sizes to fit stamps on covers). Mounts keep stamps in the condition in which you bought them. Also available are pages with strips of plastic attached to them; these are "self-mounting" pages, meaning all you have to do is slip your stamp into the plastic strip.

Other hobby tools include gauges, for measuring the perforations on the stamps, and watermark fluid, which makes the special marks in some stamp papers visible momentarily. "Perfs" and watermarks are important if you decide to do some types of specialized collecting.

A Stamp Is a Stamp?

Not really -- a stamp can be many things: a feast for the eye with beautiful design and color printing technique...a mystery story, as you try to find out about the person, place or event behind the stamp... a mystery story, as you try to find out how and why this stamp and envelope traveled and received certain postal markings. Collectors who enjoy postal history always want the stamp with its envelope, which is one reason why you should no be quick to soak stamps off their covers. If you find an old hoard of envelopes, get some advice before you take the stamps off!

Some collectors enjoy the "scientific" side of the hobby, studying production methods and paper and ink types. This also might include collecting stamps in which something went wrong in production: errors, freaks, and oddities. Studying watermarks takes special fluids and lighting

equipment, also needed to study the luminescent inks used on modern stamps to trigger high-tech canceling equipment in the post office.

Other branches of collecting includes first-day covers (FDCs), which carry a stamp on the first day it was sold with the day's postmark. Some FDCs have cachet (ca-SHAY), which is a design on the envelope that relates to the stamp and adds an attractive quality to the cover. Some clubs, catalogues, dealers specialize in FDCs.

Clubs, etc.

It is possible to collect for a lifetime and never leave home -- get everything you need by mail -- but a lot of enjoyment can be added if you join a club or go to stamp shows and exhibitions, and meet other collectors like yourself. Local clubs usually have a general focus, have meetings, and may organize stamp shows as part of their activities. Specialty-collecting groups, which may focus on stamps of one country or one type of stamp, will have a publication as the main service to members, but may have other activities and occasional meetings at large stamp shows. The American Philatelic Society, America's Stamp Club," is the oldest and largest stamp organization in the United States and has served hundreds of thousands of collectors since 1886.

Again, Welcome to Stamp Collecting!

The more you know about it, the more you will like it -- Happy Collecting!

This production was prepared by the American Philatelic Society, the oldest and largest national stamp organization in the United States. Information on member benefits and services is available from APS, P.O. Box 8000, State College, PA 16803; telephone 237-3803.

Commemorative, Special Issue & Air Mail Identifier

Commemorative, Special Issue & Air Mail Identifier

Commemorative, Special Issue & Air Mail Identifier

ix

Commemorative, Special Issue & Air Mail Identifier

Commemorative, Special Issue & Air Mail Identifier

DEFINITIVE ISSUE IDENTIFIER

The purpose of these listings is to aid the novice and intermediate collector in identifying U.S. definitive issues.

The first step in identification should be to note the stamp's denomination, color, and subject and then locate it on the list below. If that step does not provide you with a definitive Scott No., you will have to do some additional work.

If the identification can only be made by determining the stamp's "type", grill size or press from which the stamp was printed, it will be necessary to check the appropriate pages of the Brookman or Scott catalogs for this information.

If the identification can only be made by determining the stamp's perf measurements or watermark, you will then have to use your perf gauge and/or watermark detector. If you do not own these "tools," contact your favorite dealer.

    * With few exceptions, this list features major Scott Nos. and omits Reprints, Re-issues and Special Printings.
    * Watermark and Press notations are not listed when they do not contribute to the stamp's identification.
    * Scott nos. followed by "**" were also issued Bullseye Perf. 11.2
    * Scott nos. followed by a "*" were issued both Untagged and Tagged.
    * All bklt. singles are perforated on two or three sides only.

Den.	Color	Subject	Type / Comment	Press	Perf.	Wmk.	Scott #
½¢	olive brn	N. Hale		F	11		551
½¢	olive brn	N. Hale		R	11x10.5		653
½¢	dp orng	B. Franklin	1938 Prexie Issue		11x10.5		803
½¢	rd orng	B. Franklin	1954 Liberty Issue		11x10.5		1030
1¢	blue	B. Franklin	Ty I		Imperf		5
1¢	blue	B. Franklin	Ty Ib		Imperf		5A
1¢	blue	B. Franklin	Ty Ia		Imperf		6
1¢	blue	B. Franklin	Ty II		Imperf		7
1¢	blue	B. Franklin	Ty III		Imperf		8
1¢	blue	B. Franklin	Ty IIIa		Imperf		8A
1¢	blue	B. Franklin	Ty IV		Imperf		9
1¢	blue	B. Franklin	Ty I		15		18
1¢	brt. bl	B. Franklin	Ty I, reprint, w/o gum		12		40
1¢	blue	B. Franklin	Ty Ia		15		19
1¢	blue	B. Franklin	Ty II		15		20
1¢	blue	B. Franklin	Ty III		15		21
1¢	blue	B. Franklin	Ty IIIa		15		22
1¢	blue	B. Franklin	Ty IV		15		23
1¢	blue	B. Franklin	Ty V		15		24
1¢	blue	B. Franklin			12		63
1¢	blue	B. Franklin	"Z" Grill		12		85A
1¢	blue	B. Franklin	"E" Grill		12		86
1¢	blue	B. Franklin	"F" Grill		12		92
1¢	buff	B. Franklin	Issue of 1869 "G grill"		12		112
1¢	buff	B. Franklin	w/o grill, original gum		12		112b
1¢	buff	B. Franklin	Re-iss/wht crackly gum		12		123
1¢	buff	B. Franklin	Same, soft porous paper		12		133
1¢	brn. orng.	B. Franklin	Same, w/o gum		12		133a
1¢	ultra	B. Franklin	hard paper, w/grill		12		134
1¢	ultra	B. Franklin	Same, w/o grill		12		145
1¢	ultra	B. Franklin	Same, w/Secret mark		12		156
1¢	dk. ultra	B. Franklin	Soft porous paper		12		182
1¢	gray bl.	B. Franklin	Same, re-engraved		12		206
1¢	ultra	B. Franklin			12		212
1¢	dull bl.	B. Franklin	w/o Triangles		12		219
1¢	ultra	B. Franklin	w/ Tri. in Top corners		12	NW	246
1¢	blue	B. Franklin	w/ Tri. in Top corners		12	NW	247
1¢	blue	B. Franklin	w/ Tri. in Top corners		12	DL	264
1¢	dp. grn	B. Franklin	w/ Tri. in Top corners		12	DL	279
1¢	blue grn	B. Franklin	"Series 1902"		12	DL	300
1¢	blue grn	B. Franklin	"Series 1902"		Imperf	DL	314
1¢	blue grn	B. Franklin	"Series 1902" B. Pn./6		12	DL	300b
1¢	blue grn	B. Franklin	"Series 1902" Coil		12 Hz	DL	316
1¢	blue grn	B. Franklin	"Series 1902" Coil		12 Vert	DL	318
1¢	green	B. Franklin			12	DL	331
1¢	green	B. Franklin	Blue Paper		12	DL	357
1¢	green	B. Franklin			12	SL	374
1¢	green	B. Franklin			Imperf	DL	343
1¢	green	B. Franklin			Imperf	SL	383
1¢	green	B. Franklin	Bklt. Pn. of 6		12	DL	331a
1¢	green	B. Franklin	Bklt. Pn. of 6		12	SL	374a
1¢	green	B. Franklin	Coil		12 Hz	DL	348
1¢	green	B. Franklin	Coil		12 Hz	SL	385
1¢	green	B. Franklin	Coil		12 Vert	DL	352
1¢	green	B. Franklin	Coil		12 Vert	SL	387
1¢	green	B. Franklin	Coil		8.5 Hz	SL	390
1¢	green	B. Franklin	Coil		8.5 Vert	SL	392
1¢	green	Washington			12	SL	405
1¢	green	Washington			10	SL	424
1¢	green	Washington		F	10	NW	462
1¢	green	Washington		R	10	NW	543
1¢	green	Washington		F	11	NW	498
1¢	gray grn	Washington	Offset	F	11	NW	525
1¢	green	Washington	19mm x 22.5mm	R	11	NW	544
1¢	green	Washington	19.5-20mm x 22mm	R	11	NW	545
1¢	gray grn	Washington	Rossbach Press		12.5	NW	536
1¢	green	Washington		R	11x10	NW	538
1¢	green	Washington		R	10x11	NW	542
1¢	green	Washington			Imperf	SL	408
1¢	green	Washington			Imperf	NW	481
1¢	green	Washington	Offset		Imperf	NW	531
1¢	green	Washington	Bklt. Pn. of 6		12	SL	405b
1¢	green	Washington	Bklt. Pn. of 6		10	SL	424d
1¢	green	Washington	Bklt. Pn. of 6		10	NW	462a
1¢	green	Washington	Bklt. Pn. of 6		11	NW	498e
1¢	green	Washington	Bklt. Pn. of 30		11	NW	498f
1¢	green	Washington	Coil		8.5 Hz		410
1¢	green	Washington	Coil		8.5 Vert	SL	412
1¢	green	Washington	Coil	F	10 Hz	SL	441
1¢	green	Washington	Coil	R	10 Hz	SL	448
1¢	green	Washington	Coil	R	10 Hz	SL	441
1¢	green	Washington	Coil	R	10 Hz	NW	486
1¢	green	Washington	Coil	F	10 Vert	SL	443
1¢	green	Washington	Coil	R	10 Vert	SL	452
1¢	green	Washington	Coil	R	10 Vert	NW	490
1¢	deep grn	B. Franklin		F	11		552
1¢	green	B. Franklin	19¾ x 22¼mm	R	11		594
1¢	green	B. Franklin	19¼ x 22¾mm	R	11		596
1¢	green	B. Franklin		R	11x10		578
1¢	green	B. Franklin		R	10		581
1¢	green	B. Franklin		R	11x10.5		632
1¢	green	B. Franklin		F	Imperf		575
1¢	deep grn	B. Franklin	Bklt. Pn. of 6	F	11		552a
1¢	green	B. Franklin	Bklt. Pn. of 6	R	11x10.5		632a
1¢	green	B. Franklin	Coil		10 Vert		597
1¢	yel. grn.	B. Franklin	Coil	R	10 Hz		604
1¢	green	B. Franklin	Kansas Ovpt.		11x10.5		658
1¢	green	B. Franklin	Nebraska Ovpt.		11x10.5		669
1¢	green	Washington	1938 Prexie Issue		11x10.5		804
1¢	green	Washington	Bklt. Pn. of 6		11x10.5		804b
1¢	green	Washington	Coil		10 Vert		839
1¢	green	Washington	Coil		10 Hz		848
1¢	dk green	Washington	1954 Liberty Issue		11x10.5		1031
1¢	dk green	Washington	Coil		10 Vert		1054
1¢	green	A. Jackson			11x10.5		1209*
1¢	green	A. Jackson	Coil		10 Vert		1225*
1¢	green	T. Jefferson			11x10.5		1278
1¢	green	T. Jefferson	Bklt. Pn. of 8		11x10.5		1278a
1¢	green	T. Jefferson	B.Pn./4 + 2 labels		11x10.5		1278b
1¢	green	T. Jefferson	Coil		10 Vert		1299
1¢	dk blue	Inkwell & Quill			11x10.5		1581
1¢	dk blue	Inkwell & Quill	Coil		10 Vert		1811
1¢	black	Dorothea Dix			11		1844**
1¢	violet	Omnibus	Coil		10 Vert		1897
1¢	violet	Omnibus	Coil, re-engraved		10 Vert	B	2225
1¢	brnish verm	Margaret Mitchell			11		2168
1¢	multi	Kestrel	No "¢" Sign		11		2476
1¢	multi	Kestrel	'¢' sign added		11		2477
1¢	multi	Kestrel	Self-adhesive Coil "1999" Date		Die-cut 10.5 Vert		3031
1¢	multi	Kestrel	Self-adhesive Coil "2000" Date		Die-cut 10.5 Vert		3031A
1¢	multi	Kestrel	Coil		10 Vert		3044
1¼¢	turquoise	Palace of Governors			10.5x11		1031A
1¼¢	turquoise	Palace of Governors Coil			10 Hz		1054A
1¼¢	lt. grn	Albert Gallatin			11x10.5		1279
1½¢	yel brn	W.G. Harding		F	11		553
1½¢	yel brn	W.G. Harding		R	10		582
1½¢	yel brn	W.G. Harding		R	11x10.5		633
1½¢	brown	W.G. Harding	"Full Face"	R	11x10.5		684
1½¢	yel brn	W.G. Harding		F	Imperf		576
1½¢	yel brn	W.G. Harding		R	Imperf		631
1½¢	brown	W.G. Harding	Coil		10 Vert		598
1½¢	yel brn	W.G. Harding	Coil		10 Hz		605
1½¢	brown	W.G. Harding	"Full Face," Coil		10 Vert		686
1½¢	brown	W.G. Harding	Kansas Ovpt.		11x10.5		659
1½¢	brown	W.G. Harding	Nebraska Ovpt.		11x10.5		670
1½¢	bstr brn	M. Washington			11x10.5		805
1½¢	bstr brn	M. Washington Coil			10 Vert		840
1½¢	bstr brn	M. Washington Coil			10 Hz		849
1½¢	brn carm	Mount Vernon			10.5x11		1032
2¢	black	A. Jackson			12		73
2¢	black	A. Jackson	"D" Grill		12		84
2¢	black	A. Jackson	"Z" Grill		12		85B

xii

DEFINITIVE ISSUE IDENTIFIER

Den.	Color	Subject	Type / Comment	Press	Perf.	Wmk.	Scott #
2¢	black	A. Jackson	"E" Grill		12		87
2¢	black	A. Jackson	"F" Grill		12		93
2¢	brown	Horse & Rider	Issue of 1869 "G grill"		12		113
2¢	brown	Horse & Rider	w/o grill, original gum		12		113b
2¢	brown	Horse & Rider	Re-iss/wht crackly gum		12		124
2¢	red brown	A. Jackson	Hard paper, w/grill		12		135
2¢	red brown	A. Jackson	Hard paper, w/o grill		12		146
2¢	brown	A. Jackson	Same, w/secret mark		12		157
2¢	vermillion	A. Jackson	Yellowish wove (hard)		12		178
2¢	vermillion	A. Jackson	Soft porous paper		12		183
2¢	red brown	Washington			12		210
2¢	pl rd brn	Washington	Special Printing		12		211B
2¢	green	Washington			12		213
2¢	lake	Washington	w/o Triangles		12		219D
2¢	carmine	Washington	w/o Tri.		12		220
2¢	pink	Washington	Ty I Tri. in Top corners		12	NW	248
2¢	carm. lake	Washington	Ty I Tri. "		12	NW	249
2¢	carmine	Washington	Ty I Tri. "		12	NW	250
2¢	carmine	Washington	Ty I Tri. "		12	DL	265
2¢	carmine	Washington	Ty II Tri. "		12	NW	251
2¢	carmine	Washington	Ty II Tri. "		12	DL	266
2¢	carmine	Washington	Ty III Tri. "		12	NW	252
2¢	carmine	Washington	Ty III Tri. "		12	DL	267
2¢	red	Washington	Ty III Tri. "		12	DL	279B
2¢	carm rose	Washington	Ty III Tri. "		12	DL	279Bc
2¢	red	Washington	Bklt. Pn. of 6		12	DL	279Be
2¢	carmine	Washington	"Series 1902"		12	DL	301
2¢	carmine	Washington	"Series 1902" B.Pn./6		12	DL	301c
2¢	carmine	Washington	"Shield Design, Die I		12	DL	319
2¢	carmine	Washington	"Shield", Die II		12	DL	319i
2¢	carmine	Washington	"Shield", B.Pn./6, Die I		12	DL	319g
2¢	carmine	Washington	"Shield", B.Pn./6, Die II		12	DL	319h
2¢	lake	Washington	"Shield", B.Pn./6, Die II		12	DL	319q
2¢	carmine	Washington	"Shield" Design	Imperf		DL	320
2¢	lake	Washington	"Shield" Design	Imperf		DL	320a
2¢	carmine	Washington	"Shield" Coil		12 Hz	DL	321
2¢	carmine	Washington	"Shield" Coil		12 Vert	DL	322
2¢	carmine	Washington	"TWO CENTS" Design		12	DL	332
2¢	carmine	Washington	"TWO..." Blue Paper		12	DL	358
2¢	carmine	Washington	"TWO..."		12	SL	375
2¢	lake	Washington	"TWO..."		12	SL	375v
2¢	carmine	Washington	"TWO..."	F	11	DL	519
2¢	carmine	Washington	"TWO..."		Imperf	DL	344
2¢	carmine	Washington	"TWO..."		Imperf	SL	384
2¢	dark carm	Washington	"TWO..."		Imperf	SL	384v
2¢	carmine	Washington	"TWO..." Bklt. Pn. of 6		12	DL	332a
2¢	carmine	Washington	"TWO..." Bklt. Pn. of 6		12	SL	375a
2¢	carmine	Washington	"TWO..." Coil		12 Hz	DL	349
2¢	carmine	Washington	"TWO..." Coil		12 Hz	SL	386
2¢	carmine	Washington	"TWO..." Coil		12 Vert	DL	353
2¢	carmine	Washington	"TWO..." Coil		12 Vert	SL	388
2¢	carmine	Washington	"TWO..." Coil		8.5 Hz	SL	391
2¢	carmine	Washington	"TWO..." Coil		8.5 Vert	SL	393
2¢	carmine	Washington	"2 CENTS" Design		12	SL	406
2¢	lake	Washington	"2..."		12	SL	406v
2¢	carmine	Washington	"2..."		10	SL	425
2¢	carmine	Washington	"2..."		10	NW	463
2¢	carm rd	Washington	"2..."		11	SL	461
2¢	carmine	Washington	"2..." Ty I	F	11	NW	499
2¢	carmine	Washington	"2..." Ty Ia	F	11	NW	500
2¢	carmine	Washington	"2..." Offset Ty. IV		11	NW	526
2¢	carmine	Washington	"2..." Offset Ty. V		11	NW	527
2¢	carmine	Washington	"2..." Offset Ty. Va		11	NW	528
2¢	carmine	Washington	"2..." Offset Ty. VI		11	NW	528A
2¢	carmine	Washington	"2..." Offset Ty. VII		11	NW	528B
2¢	carm rose	Washington	"2..." Coil Waste:				
2¢	carm rose	Washington	Ty III	R	11	NW	546
2¢	carm rose	Washington	Ty I	R	11x10	NW	539
2¢	carm rose	Washington	Ty III	R	11x10	NW	540
2¢	carmine	Washington	"2 CENTS"	F	Imperf	SL	409
2¢	carmine	Washington	"2..."	F	Imperf	NW	482
2¢	carm rose	Washington	"2..." Offset Ty IV		Imperf	NW	532
2¢	carmine	Washington	"2..." Offset Ty V		Imperf	NW	533
2¢	carmine	Washington	"2..." Offset Ty Va		Imperf	NW	534
2¢	carmine	Washington	"2..." Offset Ty VI		Imperf	NW	534A
2¢	carmine	Washington	"2..." Offset Ty VII		Imperf	NW	534B
2¢	carmine	Washington	"2..." Bklt. Pn. of 6		12	SL	406a
2¢	carmine	Washington	"2..." Bklt. Pn. of 6		10	SL	425e
2¢	carmine	Washington	"2..." Bklt. Pn. of 6		10	NW	463a
2¢	carmine	Washington	"2..." Bklt. Pn. of 6	F	11	NW	499e
2¢	carmine	Washington	"2..." Bklt. Pn. of 30	F	11	NW	499f
2¢	carmine	Washington	"2 CENTS" Coil		8.5 Hz	SL	411
2¢	carmine	Washington	"2..." Coil		8.5 Vert	SL	413
2¢	carmine	Washington	"2..." Coil Ty I	F	10 Hz	SL	442
2¢	red	Washington	"2..." Coil Ty I	R	10 Hz	SL	449
2¢	carmine	Washington	"2..." Coil Ty II	R	10 Hz	NW	487
2¢	carmine	Washington	"2..." Coil Ty III	R	10 Hz	SL	450
2¢	carmine	Washington	"2..." Coil Ty III	R	10 Hz	NW	488
2¢	carmine	Washington	"2..." Coil Ty I	F	10 Vert	SL	444
2¢	carm red	Washington	"2..." Coil Ty I	R	10 Vert	SL	453
2¢	red	Washington	"2..." Coil Ty II	R	10 Vert	SL	454
2¢	carmine	Washington	"2..." Coil Ty II	R	10 Vert	NW	491
2¢	carmine	Washington	"2..." Coil Ty III	R	10 Vert	SL	455
2¢	carmine	Washington	"2..." Coil Ty III	R	10 Vert	NW	492
2¢	carmine	Washington	"2..." Hz Coil Ty I	F	Imperf	SL	459
2¢	deep rose	Washington	"2..." Hz Coil Ty Ia/ Shermack Ty IIPerfsF	F		*NW	482A
2¢	carmine	Washington		F	11		554
2¢	carmine	Washington	19¾ x 22¼ mm	R	11		595
2¢	carmine	Washington	19¾ x 22¼ mm	R	11x10		579
2¢	carmine	Washington	Die I	R	11x10.5		634
2¢	carmine	Washington	Die II	R	11x10.5		634A
2¢	carmine	Washington		R	10		583
2¢	carmine	Washington		F	Imperf		577
2¢	carmine	Washington	Bklt. Pn. of 6	F	11		554c
2¢	carmine	Washington	Bklt. Pn. of 6	R	10		583a
2¢	carmine	Washington	Bklt. Pn. of 6	R	11x10.5		634d
2¢	carmine	Washington	Coil		10 Vert		599
2¢	carmine	Washington	Coil Die II		10 Vert		599A
2¢	carmine	Washington	Coil		10 Hz		606
2¢	carmine	Washington	Kansas Ovpt.		11x10.5		660
2¢	carmine	J. Adams	Nebraska Ovpt.		11x10.5		671
2¢	rose carm	J. Adams			11x10.5		806
2¢	rose carm	J. Adams	Bklt. Pn. of 6		11x10.5		806b
2¢	rose carm	J. Adams	Coil		10 Vert		841
2¢	rose carm	J. Adams	Coil		10 Hz		850
2¢	carm rose	T. Jefferson			11x10.5		1033
2¢	carm rose	T. Jefferson	Coil		10 Vert		1055*
2¢	dk bl gray	Frank Lloyd Wright			11x10.5		1280
2¢	dk bl gray	Frank Lloyd Wright	B. Pn. of 5 + Label		11x10.5		1280a
2¢	dk bl gray	Frank Lloyd Wright	Booklet Pn. of 6		11x10.5		1280c
2¢	red brn	Speaker's Stand			11x10.5		1582
2¢	brn black	Igor Stravinsky			10.5x11		1845
2¢	black	Locomotive	Coil		10 Vert		1897A
2¢	black	Locomotive	Coil, "Re-engraved"	B	10 Vert		2226
2¢	brt blue	Mary Lyon			11		2169
2¢	multi	Red-headed Woodpecker			11.1		3032
2¢	multi	Red-headed Woodpecker	Coil		9¾ Vert		3045
2.5¢	**gray bl**	**Bunker Hill**			**11x10.5**		**1034**
2.5¢	gray bl	Bunker Hill	Coil		10 Vert		1056
3¢	**orng brn**	**Washington**	**Ty I**		**Imperf**		**10**
3¢	dull red	Washington	Ty I		Imperf		11
3¢	rose	Washington	Ty I		15		25
3¢	dull red	Washington	Ty II		15		26
3¢	dull red	Washington	Ty IIa		15		26a
3¢	pink	Washington			12		64
3¢	pgn bld pink	Washington			12		64a
3¢	rose pink	Washington			12		64b
3¢	rose	Washington			12		65
3¢	lake	Washington			12		66
3¢	scarlet	Washington			12		74
3¢	rose	Washington	"A" Grill		12		79
3¢	rose	Washington	"B" Grill		12		82
3¢	rose	Washington	"C" Grill		12		83
3¢	rose	Washington	"D" Grill		12		85
3¢	rose	Washington	"Z" Grill		12		85C
3¢	rose	Washington	"E" Grill		12		88
3¢	rose	Washington	"F" Grill		12		94
3¢	ultra	Locomotive	"G grill"		12		114
3¢	ultra	Locomotive	w/o grill, Original gum		12		114a
3¢	green	Washington	Hard paper, w/grill		12		136
3¢	green	Washington	Same, w/o grill		12		147
3¢	green	Washington	Same, w/secret mark		12		158
3¢	green	Washington	Same, Soft porous paper		12		184
3¢	blue grn	Washington	Same, re-engraved		12		207
3¢	vermillion	Washington			12		214
3¢	purple	A. Jackson	w/o Triangles		12		221
3¢	purple	A. Jackson	w/ Tri. in Top corners		12	NW	253
3¢	purple	A Jackson	w/ Tri. in Top corners		12	DL	268
3¢	violet	A. Jackson	"Series 1902"		12	DL	302
3¢	dp violet	Washington		F	12	DL	333
3¢	dp violet	Washington	Blue paper	F	12	DL	359
3¢	dp violet	Washington		F	12	SL	376
3¢	dp violet	Washington		F	10	SL	426
3¢	violet	Washington		F	10	NW	464
3¢	lt violet	Washington	Ty I	F	11	NW	501
3¢	dk violet	Washington	Ty II	F	11	NW	502
3¢	violet	Washington	Ty III Offset		11	NW	529
3¢	purple	Washington	Ty IV Offset		11	NW	530
3¢	violet	Washington	Ty II Coil Waste	R	11x10	NW	541

DEFINITIVE ISSUE IDENTIFIER

Den.	Color	Subject	Type/Comment	Press	Perf.	Wmk.	Scott #
3¢	dp violet	Washington		F	Imperf	DL	345
3¢	violet	Washington	Ty I	F	Imperf	NW	483
3¢	violet	Washington	Ty II	F	Imperf	NW	484
3¢	violet	Washington	Ty IV Offset		Imperf	NW	535
3¢	lt violet	Washington	B. Pn. of 6, Ty I	F	11	NW	501b
3¢	dk violet	Washington	B. Pn. of 6, Ty II	F	11	NW	502b
3¢	dp violet	Washington	Coil "Orangeburg"	F	12 Vert	SL	389
3¢	dp violet	Washington	Coil	F	8.5 Vert	SL	394
3¢	violet	Washington	Coil, Ty I	F	10 Vert	SL	445
3¢	violet	Washington	Coil, Ty I	R	10 Vert	SL	456
3¢	violet	Washington	Coil, Ty I	R	10 Hz	NW	489
3¢	dp violet	Washington	Coil, Ty I	R	10 Vert	NW	493
3¢	dull violet	Washington	Coil, Ty II	R	10 Vert	NW	494
3¢	violet	A. Lincoln		F	11		555
3¢	violet	A. Lincoln		R	10		584
3¢	violet	A. Lincoln		R	11x10.5		635
3¢	violet	A. Lincoln	Coil		10 Vert		600
3¢	violet	A. Lincoln	Kansas Ovpt.		11x10.5		661
3¢	violet	A. Lincoln	Nebraska Ovpt.		11x10.5		672
3¢	dp violet	Washington	Stuart Portrait		11x10.5		720
3¢	dp violet	Washington	Stuart B. Pn. of 6		11x10.5		720b
3¢	dp violet	Washington	Stuart Coil		10 Vert		721
3¢	dp violet	Washington	Stuart Coil		10 Hz		722
3¢	dp violet	T. Jefferson			11x10.5		807
3¢	dp violet	T. Jefferson	Bklt. Pn. of 6		11x10.5		807a
3¢	dp violet	T. Jefferson	Coil		10 Vert		842
3¢	dp violet	T. Jefferson	Coil		10 Hz		851
3¢	dp violet	Statue of Liberty			11x10.5		1035*
3¢	dp violet	Liberty	Bklt. Pn. of 6		11x10.5		1035a
3¢	dp violet	Liberty	Coil		10 Vert		1057*
3¢	violet	F. Parkman			10.5x11		1281
3¢	violet	F. Parkman	Coil		10 Vert		1297
3¢	olive	Early Ballot Box			11x10.5		1584
3¢	olive grn	Henry Clay			11x10.5		1846
3¢	dark grn	Handcar	Coil		10 Vert		1898
3¢	brt blue	Paul D. White MD			11		2170
3¢	claret	Conestoga Wagon	Coil		10 Vert		2252
3¢	multi	Bluebird			11		2478
3¢	multi	Eastern Bluebird			11.1		3033
3.1¢	**brn (yel)**	**Guitar**	**Coil**		**10 Vert**		**1613**
3.4¢	**dk blsh grn**	**School Bus**	**Coil**		**10 Vert**		**2123**
3.5¢	**prpl (yel)**	**Weaver Violins**	**Coil**		**10 Vert**		**1813**
4¢	**blue grn**	**A. Jackson**			**12**		**211**
4¢	carmine	A. Jackson			12		215
4¢	dk brn	A. Lincoln	w/ Triangles		12		222
4¢	dk brn	A. Lincoln	w/ Tri. in Top corners		12	NW	254
4¢	dk brn	A. Lincoln	w/ Tri. in Top corners		12	DL	269
4¢	rose brn	A. Lincoln	w/ Tri. in Top corners		12	DL	280
4¢	brown	U.S. Grant	"Series 1902"		12	DL	303
4¢	brown	U.S. Grant	Coil, Shermack Ty III	*		DL	314A
4¢	orng brn	Washington		F	12	DL	334
4¢	orng brn	Washington	Blue Paper	F	12	DL	360
4¢	brown	Washington		F	12	SL	377
4¢	brown	Washington		F	10	SL	427
4¢	orng brn	Washington		F	10	NW	465
4¢	brown	Washington		F	11	NW	503
4¢	orng brn	Washington		F	Imperf	DL	346
4¢	orng brn	Washington	Coil	F	12 Hz	DL	350
4¢	orng brn	Washington	Coil	F	12 Vert	DL	354
4¢	brown	Washington	Coil	F	8.5 Vert	SL	395
4¢	brown	Washington	Coil	F	10 Vert	SL	446
4¢	brown	Washington	Coil	R	10 Vert	SL	457
4¢	orng brn	Washington	Coil	R	10 Vert	NW	495
4¢	yel brn	M. Washington		F	11		556
4¢	yel brn	M. Washington		R	10		585
4¢	yel brn	M. Washington		R	11x10.5		636
4¢	yel brn	M. Washington	Coil		10 Vert		601
4¢	yel brn	M. Washington	Kansas Ovpt.		11x10.5		662
4¢	yel brn	M. Washington	Nebraska Ovpt.		11x10.5		673
4¢	brown	W.H. Taft			11x10.5		685
4¢	brown	W.H. Taft	Coil		10 Vert		687
4¢	red violet	J. Madison			11x10.5		808
4¢	red violet	J. Madison	Coil		10 Vert		843
4¢	red violet	A. Lincoln			11x10.5		1036*
4¢	red violet	A. Lincoln	Bklt. Pn. of 6		11x10.5		1036a
4¢	red violet	A. Lincoln	Coil		10 Vert		1058
4¢	black	A. Lincoln			11x10.5		1282*
4¢	black	A. Lincoln	Coil		10 Vert		1303
4¢	rose mag	"Books, etc."			11x10.5		1585
4¢	violet	Carl Schurz			10.5x11		1847
4¢	rdsh brn	Stagecoach	Coil		10 Vert		1898A
4¢	rdsh brn	Stagecoach	Coil, re-engr.	B	10 Vert		2228
4¢	bl violet	Father Flanagan			11		2171
4¢	claret	Steam Carriage	Coil		10		2451
4½¢	dark gray	White House			11x10.5		809

Den.	Color	Subject	Type/Comment	Press	Perf.	Wmk.	Scott #
4½¢	dark gray	White House	Coil		10 Vert		844
4½¢	blue grn	The Hermitage			10.5x11		1037
4½¢	blue grn	The Hermitage	Coil		10 Hz		1059
4.9¢	brn blk	Buckboard	Coil		10 Vert		2124
5¢	**rd brn**	**B. Franklin**			**Imperf**		**1**
5¢	rd brn	B. Franklin	Bluish paper (reprint)		Imperf		3
5¢	rd brn	T. Jefferson	Ty I		Imperf		12
5¢	brick red	T. Jefferson	Ty I		15		27
5¢	rd brn	T. Jefferson	Ty I		15		28
5¢	brt rd brn	T. Jefferson	Ty I		15		28b
5¢	Indian red	T. Jefferson	Ty I		15		28A
5¢	brown	T. Jefferson	Ty I		15		29
5¢	orng brn	T. Jefferson	Ty II		15		30
5¢	brown	T. Jefferson	Ty II		15		30A
5¢	buff	T. Jefferson			12		67
5¢	red brn	T. Jefferson			12		75
5¢	brown	T. Jefferson			12		76
5¢	brown	T. Jefferson	"A" Grill		12		80
5¢	brown	T. Jefferson	"F" Grill		12		95
5¢	blue	Z. Taylor	Yellowish wove (hard)		12		179
5¢	blue	Z. Taylor	Soft Porous Paper		12		185
5¢	yel brn	J. Garfield			12		205
5¢	indigo	J. Garfield			12		216
5¢	choc	U.S. Grant	w/o Triangles		12		223
5¢	choc	U.S. Grant	w/ Tri. in Top corners		12	NW	255
5¢	choc	U.S. Grant	w/ Tri. in Top corners		12	DL	270
5¢	dk blue	U.S. Grant	w/ Tri. in Top corners		12	DL	281
5¢	blue	A. Lincoln	"Series 1902"		12	DL	304
5¢	blue	A. Lincoln	"Series 1902"		Imperf	DL	315
5¢	blue	Washington			12	DL	335
5¢	blue	Washington	Blue Paper		12	DL	361
5¢	blue	Washington			12	SL	378
5¢	blue	Washington			10	SL	428
5¢	blue	Washington			10	NW	466
5¢	blue	Washington			11	NW	504
5¢	blue	Washington			Imperf	DL	347
5¢	blue	Washington	Coil		12 Hz	DL	351
5¢	blue	Washington	Coil		12 Vert	DL	355
5¢	blue	Washington	Coil		8.5 Vert	SL	396
5¢	blue	Washington	Coil	F	10 Vert	SL	447
5¢	blue	Washington	Coil	R	10 Vert	SL	458
5¢	blue	Washington	Coil	R	10 Vert	NW	496
5¢	carmine	Washington	Error of Color		10	NW	467
5¢	rose	Washington	Error of Color		11	NW	505
5¢	carmine	Washington	Error of Color		Imperf	NW	485
5¢	dk blue	T. Roosevelt		F	11		557
5¢	blue	T. Roosevelt		R	10		586
5¢	dk blue	T. Roosevelt	Coil	R	10 Vert		602
5¢	dk blue	T. Roosevelt		R	11x10.5		637
5¢	dp blue	T. Roosevelt	Kansas Ovpt.		11x10.5		663
5¢	dp blue	T. Roosevelt	Nebraska Ovpt.		11x10.5		674
5¢	brt blue	J. Monroe			11x10.5		810
5¢	brt blue	J. Monroe	Coil		10 Vert		845
5¢	blue	J. Monroe			11x10.5		1038
5¢	dk bl gray	Washington			11x10.5		1213*
5¢	dk bl gray	Washington	Bklt. Pn. of 5 + "Mailman" Label		11x10.5		1213a
5¢			"Use Zone Nos." Label		11x10.5		1213a*
5¢			"Use Zip Code" Label		11x10.5		1213a*
5¢	dk bl gray	Washington	Coil		10 Vert		1229*
5¢	blue	Washington			11x10.5		1283*
5¢	blue	Washington	Re-engr. (clean face)		11x10.5		1283B
5¢	blue	Washington	Coil		10 Vert		1304
5¢	henna brn	Pearl Buck			10.5x11		1848
5¢	gray grn	Motorcycle	Coil		10 Vert		1899
5¢	dk olv grn	Hugo Black			11		2172
5¢	carmine	Luis Munoz Marin			11		2173*
5¢	black	Milk Wagon	Coil		10 Vert		2253
5¢	red	Circus Wagon	Coil Engraved		10 Vert		2452
5¢	carmine	Circus Wagon	Coil Gravure		10 Vert		2452B
5¢	brown	Canoe	Coil Engraved		10 Vert		2453
5¢	red	Canoe	Coil Gravure		10 Vert		2454
5.2¢	**carmine**	**Sleigh**	**Coil**		**10 Vert**		**1900**
5.3¢	**black**	**Elevator**	**Coil**		**10 Vert**		**2254**
5.5¢	**dp mag**	**Star Rt Truck**	**Coil**		**10 Vert**		**2125**
5.9¢	**blue**	**Bicycle**	**Coil**		**10 Vert**		**1901**
6¢	**ultra**	**Washington**	**"G" Grill**		**12**		**115**
6¢	carmine	A. Lincoln	hard wh paper, w/grill		12		137
6¢	carmine	A. Lincoln	Same, w/o grill		12		148
6¢	dull pink	A. Lincoln	Same, secret mark		12		159
6¢	pink	A. Lincoln	Same, sft porous pap		12		186
6¢	rose	A. Lincoln	Same, re-engraved		12		208
6¢	brn red	A. Lincoln	Same, re-engraved		12		208a
6¢	brn red	J. Garfield	w/o Triangles		12		224
6¢	dull brn	J. Garfield	w/ Tri. in Top corners		12	NW	256

xiv

DEFINITIVE ISSUE IDENTIFIER

Den.	Color	Subject	Type / Comment	Press	Perf.	Wmk.	Scott #
6¢	dull brn	J. Garfield	w/ Tri. in Top corners		12	DL	271
6¢	dull brn	J. Garfield	w/ Tri. in Top corners		12	USIR	271a
6¢	lake	J. Garfield	w/ Tri. in Top corners		12	DL	282
6¢	claret	J. Garfield	"Series 1902"		12	DL	305
6¢	rd orng	Washington			12	DL	336
6¢	rd orng	Washington	Blue paper		12	DL	362
6¢	rd orng	Washington			12	SL	379
6¢	rd orng	Washington			10	SL	429
6¢	rd orng	Washington			10	NW	468
6¢	rd orng	Washington			11	NW	506
6¢	rd orng	J. Garfield		F	11		558
6¢	rd orng	J. Garfield		R	10		587
6¢	rd orng	J. Garfield		R	11x10.5		638
6¢	rd orng	J. Garfield	Kansas Ovpt.		11x10.5		664
6¢	rd orng	J. Garfield	Nebraska Ovpt.		11x10.5		675
6¢	dp orng	J. Garfield	Coil		10 Vert		723
6¢	red orng	J.Q. Adams			11x10.5		811
6¢	red orng	J.Q. Adams	Coil		10 Vert		846
6¢	carmine	T. Roosevelt			11x10.5		1039
6¢	gray brn	F.D. Roosevelt			10.5x11		1284*
6¢	gray brn	F.D. Roosevelt Bklt. Pn. of 8			11x10.5		1284b
6¢	gray brn	F.D. Roosevelt Bklt. Pn. of 5 + Label			xv11x10.5		1284c
6¢	gray brn	F.D. Roosevelt Coil			10 Hz		1298
6¢	gray brn	F.D. Roosevelt			10 Vert		1305
6¢	dk bl,rd & grn	Flag & White House			11		1338
6¢	dk bl,rd & grn	Flag & White House			11x10.5		1338D
6¢	dk bl,rd & grn	Flag & White House Coil			10 Vert		1338A
6¢	dk bl gray	D.D. Eisenhower			11x10.5		1393
6¢	dk bl gray	Eisenhower	Bklt. Pn of 8		11x10.5		1393a
6¢	dk bl gray	Eisenhower	Bklt. Pn of 5 + Label		11x10.5		1393b
6¢	dk bl gray	Eisenhower	Coil		10 Vert		1401
6¢	orng verm	Walter Lippmann			11		1849
6¢	multi	Circle of Stars Bklt. Single			11		1892
6¢	red brn	Tricycle	Coil		10 Vert		2126
6.3¢	brick red	Liberty Bell	Coil		10 Vert		1518
7¢	vermilion	E.M. Stanton	Hard wh paper, w/grill		12		138
7¢	vermilion	E.M. Stanton	Same, w/o grill		12		149
7¢	orng verm	E.M. Stanton	Same, w/secret mark		12		160
7¢	black	Washington			12	SL	407
7¢	black	Washington			10	SL	430
7¢	black	Washington			10	NW	469
7¢	black	Washington			11	NW	507
7¢	black	Wm. McKinley		F	11		559
7¢	black	Wm. McKinley		R	10		588
7¢	black	Wm. McKinley		R	11x10.5		639
7¢	black	Wm. McKinley	Kansas Ovpt.		11x10.5		665
7¢	black	Wm. McKinley	Nebraska Ovpt.		11x10.5		676
7¢	sepia	A. Jackson			11x10.5		812
7¢	rose carm	W. Wilson			11x10.5		1040
7¢	brt blue	B. Franklin			10.5x11		1393D
7¢	brt carm	Abraham Baldwin			10.5x11		1850
7.1¢	lake	Tractor	Coil		10 Vert		2127
7.4¢	brown	Baby Buggy	Coil		10 Vert		1902
7.6¢	brown	Carreta	Coil		10 Vert		2255
7.7¢	brn (brt yl)	Saxhorns	Coil		10 Vert		1614
7.9¢	carm (yl)	Drum	Coil		10 Vert		1615
8¢	lilac	W.T. Sherman w/o Triangles			12		225
8¢	violet brn	W.T. Sherman w/ Tri. in Top corners			12	NW	257
8¢	violet brn	W.T. Sherman w/ Tri. in Top corners			12	DL	272
8¢	violet brn	W.T. Sherman w/ Tri. in Top corners			12	USIR	272a
8¢	violet blk	M. Washington "Series 1902"			12	DL	306
8¢	olive grn	Washington			12	DL	337
8¢	olive grn	Washington	Blue Paper		12	DL	363
8¢	olive grn	Washington			12	SL	380
8¢	pl olv grn	B. Franklin			12	SL	414
8¢	pl olv grn	B. Franklin			10	SL	431
8¢	olv grn	B. Franklin			10	NW	470
8¢	olv grn	B. Franklin			11	NW	508
8¢	olv grn	U.S. Grant		F	11		560
8¢	olv grn	U.S. Grant		R	10		589
8¢	olv grn	U.S. Grant		R	11x10.5		640
8¢	olv grn	U.S. Grant	Kansas Ovpt.		11x10.5		666
8¢	olv grn	U.S. Grant	Nebraska Ovpt.		11x10.5		677
8¢	olv grn	M. Van Buren			11x10.5		813
8¢	dk viol bl & carm	Statue of Liberty		Flat	11		1041
		Statue of Liberty		Rotary	11		1041B
		Statue of Liberty Redrawn		Giori	11		1042
8¢	brown	Gen. J.J. Pershing		R	11x10.5		1042A
8¢	violet	Albert Einstein			11x10.5		1285*
8¢	multi	Flag & Wh House			11x10.5		1338F
8¢	multi	Flag & Wh House Coil			10 Vert		1338G
8¢	blk,rd & bl gry	Eisenhower			11		1394
8¢	dp claret	Eisenhower	Bklt. sgl./B.Pn. of 8		11x10.5		1395a
8¢	dp claret	Eisenhower	Bklt. Pn. of 6		11x10.5		1395b
8¢	dp claret	Eisenhower	Bklt. Pn. of 4 + 2 Labels		11x10.5		1395c

Den.	Color	Subject	Type / Comment	Press	Perf.	Wmk.	Scott #
8¢	dp claret	Eisenhower	Bklt. Pn. of 7 + Label		11x10.5		1395d
8¢	multi	Postal Service Emblem			11x10.5		1396
8¢	dp claret	Eisenhower	Coil		10 Vert		1402
8¢	olive blk	Henry Knox			10.5x11		1851
8.3¢	green	Ambulance	Coil		10 Vert		2128
8.3¢	green	Ambulance	Coil Precan.	B	10 Vert		2231
8.4¢	dk bl (yel)	Grand Piano	Coil		10 Vert		1615C
8.4¢	dp claret	Wheel Chair	Coil		10 Vert		2256
8.5¢	dk pris grn	Tow Truck	Coil		10 Vert		2129
9¢	salmn rd	B. Franklin			12	SL	415
9¢	salmn rd	B. Franklin			10	SL	432
9¢	salmn rd	B. Franklin			10	NW	471
9¢	salmn rd	B. Franklin			11	NW	509
9¢	rose	T. Jefferson		F	11		561
9¢	rose	T. Jefferson		R	10		590
9¢	orng red	T. Jefferson		R	11x10.5		641
9¢	lt rose	T. Jefferson	Kansas Ovpt.		11x10.5		667
9¢	lt rose	T. Jefferson	Nebraska Ovpt.		11x10.5		678
9¢	rose pink	W.H. Harrison			11x10.5		814
9¢	rose lilac	Alamo			10.5x11		1043
9¢	slate grn	Capitol Dome			11x10.5		1591
9¢	slate grn	Capitol Dome	Bklt. Single		11x10.5		1590
9¢	slate grn	Capitol Dome	Bklt. Single		10		1590a
9¢	slate grn	Capitol Dome	Coil		10 Vert		1616
9¢	dark grn	Sylvanus Thayer			10.5x11		1852
9.3¢	carm rose	Mail Wagon	Coil		10 Vert		1903
10¢	black	Washington			Imperf		2
10¢	black	Washington	Bluish paper (reprint)		Imperf		4
10¢	green	Washington	Ty I		Imperf		13
10¢	green	Washington	Ty II		Imperf		14
10¢	green	Washington	Ty III		Imperf		15
10¢	green	Washington	Ty IV		Imperf		16
10¢	green	Washington	Ty I		15		31
10¢	green	Washington	Ty II		15		32
10¢	green	Washington	Ty III		15		33
10¢	green	Washington	Ty IV		15		34
10¢	green	Washington	Ty V		15		35
10¢	dark grn	Washington	Premier Gravure, Ty I		12		62B
10¢	yel grn	Washington	Ty II		12		68
10¢	green	Washington	"Z" Grill		12		85D
10¢	green	Washington	"E" Grill		12		89
10¢	yel grn	Washington	"F" Grill		12		96
10¢	yellow	Eagle & Shield "G" Grill			12		116
10¢	brown	T. Jefferson	w/grill, Hard wh paper		12		139
10¢	brown	T. Jefferson	Same, w/o grill		12		150
10¢	brown	T. Jefferson	Same, w/secret mark		12		161
10¢	brown	T. Jefferson	Soft porous paper:				
			w/o secret mark		12		187
			w/secret mark		12		188
10¢	brown	T. Jefferson	Soft paper, re-engr.		12		209
10¢	green	D. Webster	w/o Triangles		12		226
10¢	dark grn	D. Webster	w/ Tri. in Top corners		12	NW	258
10¢	dark grn	D. Webster	w/ Tri. in Top corners		12	DL	273
10¢	brown	D. Webster	Ty I "		12	DL	282C
10¢	orng brn/brn	D. Webster	Ty II "		12	DL	283
10¢	pl rd brn	D. Webster	"Series 1902"		12	DL	307
10¢	yellow	Washington			12	DL	338
10¢	yellow	Washington	Blue Paper		12	DL	364
10¢	yellow	Washington			12	SL	381
10¢	yellow	Washington	Coil		12 Vert	DL	356
10¢	orng yel	B. Franklin			12	SL	416
10¢	orng yel	B. Franklin			10	SL	433
10¢	orng yel	B. Franklin			10	NW	472
10¢	orng yel	B. Franklin			11	NW	510
10¢	orng yel	B. Franklin	Coil	R	10 Vert	NW	497
10¢	yel orng	J. Monroe		F	11	NW	562
10¢	yel orng	J. Monroe		R	10	NW	591
10¢	orange	J. Monroe		R	11x10.5	NW	642
10¢	orange	J. Monroe	Coil	R	10 Vert	NW	603
10¢	orng yel	J. Monroe	Kansas Ovpt.		11x10.5	NW	668
10¢	orng yel	J. Monroe	Nebraska Ovpt.		11x10.5	NW	679
10¢	brn red	J. Tyler			11x10.5		815
10¢	brn red	J. Tyler	Coil		10 Vert		847
10¢	rose lake	Indep. Hall			10.5x11		1044*
10¢	lilac	A. Jackson			11x10.5		1286*
10¢	red & bl	Crossed Flags			11x10.5		1509
10¢	red & bl	Crossed Flags Coil			10 Vert		1519
10¢	blue	Jefferson Mem.			11x10.5		1510
10¢	blue	Jefferson Mem. Bklt. Pn. of 5 + Label			11x10.5		1510b
10¢	blue	Jefferson Mem. Bklt. Pn. of 8			11x10.5		1510c
10¢	blue	Jefferson Mem. Bklt. Pn. of 6			11x10.5		1510d
10¢	blue	Jefferson Mem. Coil			10 Vert		1520
10¢	multi	"Zip Code"			11x10.5		1511
10¢	violet	Justice			11x10.5		1592
10¢	violet	Justice	Coil		10 Vert		1617

DEFINITIVE ISSUE IDENTIFIER

Den.	Color	Subject	Type/Comment	Press	Perf.	Wmk.	Scott #
10¢	prus bl	Richard Russell			10.5x11		1853
10¢	lake	Red Cloud			11		2175
10¢	sky blue	Canal Boat	Coil		10 Vert		2257
10¢	green	Tractor Trailer Coil Intaglio			10 Vert		2457
10¢	green	Tractor Trailer Coil Gravure			10 Vert		2458
10¢	red&black	Joseph W. Stilwell			11		3420
10.1¢	slate blue	Oil Wagon	Coil		10 Vert		2130
10.9¢	purple	Hansom Cab	Coil		10 Vert		1904
11	dark grn	B. Franklin			10	SL	434
11¢	dark grn	B. Franklin			10	NW	473
11¢	light grn	B. Franklin			11	NW	511
11¢	lt bl/bl	R.B. Hayes		F	11		563
11¢	light blue	R.B. Hayes		R	11x10.5		692
11¢	ultra	J.K. Polk			11x10.5		816
11¢	carm & dk viol bl	Statue of Liberty			11		1044A*
11¢	orange	Printing Press			11x10.5		1593
11¢	dk blue	Alden Partridge			11		1854
11¢	red	RR Caboose	Coil		10 Vert		1905
11¢	dk green	Stutz Bearcat	Coil		10 Vert		2131
12¢	black	Washington			Imperf		17
12¢	black	Washington	Plate 1		15		36
12¢	black	Washington	Plate 3		15		36b
12¢	black	Washington			12		69
12¢	black	Washington	"Z" Grill		12		85E
12¢	black	Washington	"E" Grill		12		90
12¢	black	Washington	"F" Grill		12		97
12¢	green	S.S. Adriatic	"G grill"		12		117
12¢	dull violet	H. Clay	Hard wh paper, w/grill		12		140
12¢	dull violet	H. Clay	Same, w/o grill		12		151
12¢	blksh viol	H. Clay	Same, w/secret mark		12		162
12¢	claret brn	B. Franklin			12	SL	417
12¢	claret brn	B. Franklin			10	SL	435
12¢	copper rd	B. Franklin			10	SL	435a
12¢	claret brn	B. Franklin			10	NW	474
12¢	claret brn	B. Franklin			11	NW	512
12¢	brn carm	B. Franklin			11	NW	512a
12¢	brn violet	G. Cleveland		F	11		564
12¢	brn violet	G. Cleveland		R	11x10.5		693
12¢	bright viol	Z. Taylor			11x10.5		817
12¢	red	B. Harrison			11x10.5		1045*
12¢	black	Henry Ford			10.5x11		1286A*
12¢	rd brn (bge)	Liberty Torch	Coil		10 Vert		1816
12¢	dk blue	Stanley Stmr	Ty I Coil		10 Vert		2132
12¢	dk blue	Stanley Stmr	Ty II Coil, precanc.		10 Vert		2132b
12.5¢	olive grn	Pushcart	Coil		10 Vert		2133
13¢	purp blk	B. Harrison	"Series 1902"		12	DL	308
13¢	blue grn	Washington			12	DL	339
13¢	blue grn	Washington	Blue Paper		12	DL	365
13¢	apple grn	B. Franklin			11	NW	513
13¢	green	B. Harrison		F	11		622
13¢	yel grn	B. Harrison		R	11x10.5		694
13¢	bue grn	M. Fillmore			11x10.5		818
13¢	brown	J.F. Kennedy			11x10.5		1287*
13¢	brown	Liberty Bell			11x10.5		1595
13¢	brown	Liberty Bell	Bklt. Pn. of 6		11x10.5		1595a
13¢	brown	Liberty Brll	Bklt. Pn. of 7 + Label		11x10.5		1595b
13¢	brown	Liberty Bell	Bklt. Pn. of 8		11x10.5		1595c
13¢	brown	Liberty Bell	Bklt. Pn of 5 + Label		11x10.5		1595d
13¢	brown	Liberty Bell	Coil		10 Vert		1618
13¢	multi	Eagle & Shield	Bullseye Perfs		11x10.5		1596
13¢	multi	Eagle & Shield	Line Perfs		11		1596d
13¢	dk bl & rd	Flag Over Indep. Hall			11x10.5		1622
13¢	dk. bl & rd	Flag Over Indep. Hall			11		1622c
13¢	dk bl & rd	Flag Over Indep. Hall	Coil		10 Vert		1625
13¢	bl & rd	Flag Over Captl	Bklt. Single		11x10.5		1623
13¢	bl & rd	Flag Over Captl	Bklt. Single		10		1623b
13¢	bl & rd	Flag Over Captl	B. Pn. of 8 (7 #1623 (13¢) + 1 #1590 (9¢))		11X10.5		1623a
13¢	bl & rd	Flag Over Capt	B. Pn. of 8 (7 #1623b (13¢) + 1 #1590a (9¢))		10		1623c
13¢	brn & bl (grn bistr)	Indian Head Penny			11		1734
13¢	lt maroon	Crazy Horse			10.5x11		1855
13¢	black	Patrol Wagon	Coil		10 Vert		2258
13.2¢	slate grn	Coal Car	Coil		10 Vert		2259
14¢	blue	American Indian		F	11		565
14¢	dk blue	American Indian		R	11x10.5		695
14¢	blue	F. Pierce			11x10.5		819
14¢	gray brn	Fiorello LaGuardia			11x10.5		1397
14¢	slate grn	Sinclair Lewis			11		1856
14¢	sky blue	Iceboat	Coil, overall tag		10 Vert		2134
14¢	sky blue	Iceboat	Ty II Coil, block tag	B	10 Vert		2134b
14¢	crimson	Julia Ward Howe			11		2176
15¢	black	A. Lincoln			12		77
15¢	black	A. Lincoln	"Z" Grill		12		85F
15¢	black	A. Lincoln	"E" Grill		12		91
15¢	black	A. Lincoln	"F" Grill		12		98
15¢	brn & bl	Landing of Columbus:					
			Ty I Frame, "G grill"		12		118
			Same, w/o grill, o.g.		12		118a
			Ty II Frame, "G grill"		12		119
			Ty III, wh crackly gum		12		129
15¢	orange	D. Webster	Hard wh paper, w/grill		12		141
15¢	brt orng	D. Webster	Same, w/o grill		12		152
15¢	yel orng	D. Webster	Same, w/secret mark		12		163
15¢	red orng	D. Webster	Soft porous paper		12		189
15¢	indigo	H. Clay	w/o Triangles		12		227
15¢	dk blue	H. Clay	w/ Tri. in Top corners		12	NW	259
15¢	dk blue	H. Clay	w/ Tri. in Top corners		12	DL	274
15¢	olive grn	H. Clay	w/ Tri. in Top corners		12	DL	284
15¢	olive grn	H. Clay	"Series 1902"		12	DL	309
15¢	pl ultra	Washington			12	DL	340
15¢	pl ultra	Washington	Blue Paper		12	DL	366
15¢	pl ultra	Washington			12	SL	382
15¢	gray	B. Franklin			12	SL	418
15¢	gray	B. Franklin			10	SL	437
15¢	gray	B. Franklin			10	NW	475
15¢	gray	B. Franklin			11	NW	514
15¢	gray	Statue of Liberty		F	11		566
15¢	gray	Statue of Liberty		R	11x10.5		696
15¢	blue gray	J. Buchanan			11x10.5		820
15¢	rose lake	John Jay			11x10.5		1046*
15¢	maroon	O.W. Holmes			11x10.5		1288
15¢	dk rse clrt	O.W. Holmes	Type II		11x10.5		1288d
15¢	dk rse clrt	O.W. Holmes	Bklt. sgl./B.Pn. of 8		10		1288Bc
15¢	gray, dk bl & red	Ft McHenry Flag			11		1597
15¢		Ft McHenry Flag	Bklt. sgl./B. Pn. of 8		11x10.5		1598a
15¢		Ft McHenry Flag	Coil		10 Vert		1618C
15¢	multi	Roses	Bklt. sgl./B. Pn. of 8		10		1737a
15¢	sepia (yel)	Windmills	Bklt. Pn. of 10		11		1742a
15¢	rd brn & sepia	Dolley Madison			11		1822
15¢	claret	Buffalo Bill Cody			11		2177
15¢	violet	Tugboat	Coil		10 Vert		2260
15¢	multi	Beach Umbrella	Bklt. sgl./B. Pn. of 10		11.5x11		2443a
16¢	black	A. Lincoln			11x10.5		821
16¢	brown	Ernie Pyle			11x10.5		1398
16¢	blue	Statue of Liberty			11x10.5		1599
16¢	blue	Statue of Liberty	Coil		10 Vert		1619
16.7¢	rose	Popcorn Wagon	Coil		10 Vert		2261
17¢	black	W. Wilson		F	11		623
17¢	black	W. Wilson		R	10.5x11		697
17¢	rose red	A. Johnson			11x10.5		822
17¢	green	Rachel Carson			10.5x11		1857
17¢	ultra	Electric Auto	Coil		10 Vert		1906
17¢	sky blue	Dog Sled	Coil		10 Vert		2135
17¢	dk bl grn	Belva Ann Lockwood			11		2178
17.5¢	dk violet	Racing Car	Coil		10 Vert		2262
18¢	brn carm	U.S. Grant			11x10.5		823
18¢	violet	Dr. Elizabeth Blackwell			11x10.5		1399
18¢	dark bl	George Mason			10.5x11		1858
18¢	dark brn	Wildlife Animals Bklt. Pn. of 10			11		1889a
18¢	multi	Flag/Amber Waves...			11		1890
18¢	multi	Flag/Sea to...Sea	Coil		10 Vert		1891
18¢	multi	Flag/Purple Mtns...Bklt. Single			11		1893
18¢	multi	Flag/Purple Mnts...Bklt. Pn. of 8 (7 #1893 (18¢) + 1 #1892 (6¢))			11		1893a
18¢	dk brn	Surrey	Coil		10 Vert		1907
18¢	multi	Washington & Monument Coil			10 Vert		2149
19¢	brt violet	R.B. Hayes			11x10.5		824
19¢	brown	Sequoyah			10.5x11		1859
19¢	multi	Fawn			11.5x11		2479
19¢	multi	Fishing Boat	Coil Type I		10 Vert		2529
19¢	multi	Fishing Boat	Coil Type III		9.8 Vert		2529C
19¢	multi	Balloon	Bklt. sgl./B. Pn. of 10		10		2530,a
20¢	ultra	B. Franklin			12	SL	419
20¢	ultra	B. Franklin			10	SL	438
20¢	lt. ultra	B. Franklin			10	NW	476
20¢	lt. ultra	B. Franklin			11	NW	515
20¢	carm rse	Golden Rose		F	11		567
20¢	carm rse	Golden Gate		R	10.5x11		698
20¢	brt bl grn	J. Garfield			11x10.5		825
20¢	ultra	Monticello			10.5x11		1047
20¢	dp olive	George C. Marshall			11x10.5		1289*
20¢	claret	Ralph Bunche			10.5x11		1860
20¢	green	Thomas H. Gallaudet			10.5x11		1861
20¢	black	Harry S. Truman			11		1862**
20¢	blk, dk bl & red	Flag/Supreme Court			11		1894
		Flag/Sup. Ct. Coil			10 Vert		1895
20¢		Flag/Sup. Ct. Bklt. sgl./Pns. of 6 & 10			11x10.5		1896,a,b

DEFINITIVE ISSUE IDENTIFIER

Den.	Color	Subject	Type / Comment	Press	Perf.	Wmk.	Scott #
20¢	vermilion	Fire Pumper	Coil		10 Vert		1908
20¢	dk blue	Rocky Mtn. Bighorn	Bklt. sgl./Pn. of 10		11		1949a
20¢	sky blue	Consumer Ed.	Coil		10 Vert		2005
20¢	bl violet	Cable Car	Coil		10 Vert		2263
20¢	red brown	Virginia Agpar			11.1x11		2179
20¢	green	Cog Railway	Coil		10 Vert		2463
20¢	multi	Blue Jay	Bklt. Sgl./B. Pn. of 10		11x10		2483,a
20¢	multi	Blue Jay	Self-adhesive		Die-Cut		3048
20¢	multi	Blue Jay	Coil		11.6 Vert		3053
20¢	multi	Ring necked Pheasant Blkt. Sgl.	Die-cut		11.2		3050
20¢	multi	Ring necked Pheasant	Bklt.Sgle.Die-cut		10.5x11		3051
20¢	multi	Ring necked Pheasant Coil			Die-cut9.8 Vert		3055
20¢	dark carmine	George Washington	S.A. Booklet Stamp Die-cut 11.25x11				3482
20¢	dark carmine	George Washington	S.A. Booklet Stamp Die-cut 10.5x11				3483
20.5¢	rose	Fire Engine	Coil		10 Vert		2264
21¢	dull blue	Chester A. Arthur			11x10.5		826
21¢	green	Amadeo Giannini			11x10.5		1400
21¢	bl violet	Chester Carlson			11		2181
21¢	olive grn	RR Mail Car	Coil		10 Vert		2265
21¢	multi	Bison	Self-adhesive		Die-cut 11		3468
21¢	multi	Bison	Self-adhesive		Die-cut 8.5 Vert		3475
21.1¢	multi	Envelopes	Coil		10 Vert		2150
22¢	vermilion	G. Cleveland			11x10.5		827
22¢	dk chlky bl	John J. Audubon			11		1863**
22¢	bl rd blk	Flag/Capitol			11		2114
22¢	bl rd blk	Flag/Capitol	Coil		10 Vert		2115
22¢	bl rd blk	Flag/Capitol/"of the People"	Bklt. Sgl.		10 Hz		2116
22¢	bl rd blk	Flag/Capitol/"of the People"	B. Pn. of 5		10 Hz		2116a
22¢	blk & brn	Seashells	Bklt. Pn. of 10		10		2121a
22¢	multi	Fish	Bklt. Pn. of 5		10 Hz		2209a
22¢	multi	Flag & Fireworks			11		2276
22¢	multi	Flag & Fireworks	Bklt. Pn. of 20		11		2276a
22¢	multi	Uncle Sam	Self-adhesive	Die-cut	10.8		3259
22¢	multi	Uncle Sam	Self-adhesive Coil Die-cut9.9 Vert				3263
22¢	multi	Uncle Sam	Coil		9¾ Vert		3353
23¢	purple	Mary Cassatt			11		2181
23¢	dk blue	Lunch Wagon	Coil		10 Vert		2464
23¢	multi	Flag & Presorted First Class Coil			10 Vert		2605
23¢	multi	USA & Flag Presort First Cl Coil			10 Vert	ABNC	2606
23¢	multi	USA & Flag Presort First Cl Coil			10 Vert	BEP	2607
23¢	multi	USA & Flag Presort First Cl Coil			10 Vert	SVS	2608
24¢	gray lilac	Washington	"Twenty Four Cents"		15		37
24¢	red lilac	Washington	"24 Cents"		12		70
24¢	brn lilac	Washington			12		70a
24¢	steel blue	Washington			12		70b
24¢	violet	Washington			12		70c
24¢	grayish lil	Washington			12		70d
24¢	lilac	Washington			12		78
24¢	grayish lil	Washington			12		78a
24¢	gray	Washington			12		78b
24¢	blkish viol	Washington			12		78c
24¢	gray lilac	Washington	"F" Grill		12		99
24¢	grn & viol	Decl. of Indep.	"G grill"		12		120
24¢	grn & viol	Decl. of Indep.	w/o grill, original gum		12		120a
24¢	purple	Gen'l. W. Scott	Hard wh paper, w/grill		12		142
24¢	purple	Gen'l. W. Scott	Same, w/o grill		12		153
24¢	gray blk	B. Harrison			11x10.5		828
24¢	red (blue)	Old North Church			11x10.5		1603
24.1¢	dp ultra	Tandem Bicycle	Coil		10 Vert		2266
25¢	yel grn	Niagara Falls		F	11		568
25¢	blue grn	Niagara Falls		R	10.5x11		699
25¢	dp rd lil	Wm. McKinley			11x10.5		829
25¢	green	Paul Revere			11x10.5		1048
25¢	green	Paul Revere	Coil		10 Vert		1059A*
25¢	rose	Frederick Douglass			11x10.5		1290*
25¢	orng brn	Bread Wagon	Coil		10 Vert		2136
25¢	blue	Jack London			11		2182
25¢	blue	Jack London	Bklt. Pn. of 10		11		2182a
25¢	blue	Jack London	Bklt. Sgl./B. Pn. of 6		10		2197,a
25¢	multi	Flag & Clouds			11		2278
25¢	multi	Flag & Clouds	Bklt. Sgl./B. Pn. of 6		10		2285Ac
25¢	multi	Flag/Yosemite	Coil		10 Vert		2280
25¢	multi	Honeybee	Coil		10 Vert		2281
25¢	multi	Pheasant	Bklt. Sgl./B. Pn. of 10		11		2283,a
25¢	multi	Pheasant	Same, w/o red in sky		11		2283b,c
25¢	multi	Grossbeak	Bklt. Single		10		2284
25¢	multi	Owl	Bklt. Single		10		2285
25¢	multi	Grossbk & Owl	Bklt. Pn. of 10 (5 ea.)		10		2285b
25¢	multi	Eagle & Shield	Self-adhesive		Die cut		2431
25¢	dk rd & bl	Flag	Self-adhesive		Die cut		2475
28¢	brn (bl)	Ft. Nisqually			11x10.5		1604

Den.	Color	Subject	Type / Comment	Press	Perf.	Wmk.	Scott #
28¢	myrtle grn	Sitting Bull			11		2183
29¢	blue (bl)	Sandy Hook Lighthouse			11x10.5		1605
29¢	blue	Earl Warren			11		2184
29¢	dk violet	T. Jefferson			11		2185
29¢	multi	Red Squirrel	Self-adhesive		Die cut		2489
29¢	multi	Rose	Self-adhesive		Die cut		2490
29¢	multi	Pine Cone	Self-adhesive		Die cut		2491
29¢	blk & multi	Wood Duck	Bklt. sgl./B. Pn. of 10		10		2484,a
29¢	red & multi	Wood Duck	Bklt. sgl./B. Pn. of 10		11		2485,c
29¢	multi	African Violet	Bklt. sgl./B. Pn. of 10		10x11		2486,a
29¢	bl,rd,clar	Flag/Rushmore	Coil, Engraved		10		2523
29¢	bl,rd,brn	Flag/Rushmore	Coil, Gravure		10		2523A
29¢	multi	Tulip			11		2524
29¢	multi	Tulip			12.5x13		2524a
29¢	multi	Tulip	Coil	Roulette	10 Vert		2525
29¢	multi	Tulip	Coil		10 Vert		2526
29¢	multi	Tulip	Bklt. sgl./B. Pn. of 10		11		2527,a
29¢	multi	Flag/Rings	Bklt. sgl./B. Pn. of 10		11		2528
29¢	multi	Flags on Parade			11		2531
29¢	blk,gld,grn	Liberty/Torch	Self-adhesive		Die cut		2531A
29¢	multi	Flag & Pledge	blk. denom Bklt. sgl., Bklt. Pn. of 10		10		2593,a
29¢	multi	Flag & Pledge	red denom., Bklt. sgl., Bklt. Pn. of 10		10		2594,a
29¢	brn,multi	Eagle & Shield	Self-adhesive		Die cut		2595
29¢	grn,multi	Eagle & Shield	Self-adhesive		Die cut		2596
29¢	red,multi	Eagle & Shield	Self-adhesive		Die cut		2597
29¢	multi	Eagle	Self-adhesive		Die cut		2598
29¢	blue,red	Flag/White House	Coil		10 Vert		2609
29¢	multi	Liberty	Self-adhesive		Die cut		2599
30¢	orange	B. Franklin	Numeral at bottom		15		38
30¢	orange	B. Franklin	Numerals at Top		12		71
30¢	orange	B. Franklin	"A" Grill		12		81
30¢	orange	B. Franklin	"F" Grill		12		100
30¢	bl & carm	Eagle, Shield & Flags, "G" Grill			12		121
30¢			w/o grill, original gum		12		121a
30¢	black	A. Hamilton	Hard wh paper, w/grill		12		143
30¢	black	A. Hamilton	Same, w/o grill		12		154
30¢	gray blk	A. Hamilton	Same		12		165
30¢	full blk./grnish blk	A. Hamilton	Soft porous paper		12		190
30¢	orng brn	A. Hamilton			12		217
30¢	black	T. Jefferson			12		228
30¢	orng red	B. Franklin			12	SL	420
30¢	orng red	B. Franklin			10	SL	439
30¢	orng red	B. Franklin			10	NW	476A
30¢	orng red	B. Franklin			11	NW	516
30¢	olive brn	Buffalo		F	11		569
30¢	brown	Buffalo		R	10.5x11		700
30¢	dp ultra	T. Roosevelt			11x10.5		830
30¢	blue	T. Roosevelt			11x10.5		830 var
30¢	dp blue	T. Roosevelt			11x10.5		830 var
30¢	black	R.E. Lee			11x10.5		1049
30¢	red lilac	John Dewey			10.5x11		1291*
30¢	green	Morris School			11x10.5		1606
30¢	olv gray	Frank C. Laubach			11		1864**
30¢	multi	Cardinal			11		2480
32¢	blue	Ferryboat	Coil		10 Vert		2466
32¢	multi	Peach	Booklet Single		10x11		2487
32¢	multi	Peach	Self-adhesive		Die cut		2493
32¢	multi	Peach	Self-adhesive Coil		Die cut		2495
32¢	multi	Pear	Booklet Single		10x11		2488
32¢	multi	Pear	Self-adhesive		Die Cut		2494
32¢	multi	Pear	Self-adhesive Coil		Die cut		2495A
32¢	multi	Peach & Pear	Bklt. Pane of 10		10x11		2488A
32¢	multi	Peach & Pear	Self-adhesive Pane		Die cut		2494A
32¢	multi	Peach & Pear	Self-adhesive Coil		Die-cut		2495-95A
32¢	multi	Pink Rose	Self-adhesive		Die cut		2492
32¢	red-brown	James K. Polk			11.2		2587
32¢	multi	Flag over Porch			10.04		2897
32¢	multi	Flag over Porch Coil		BEP	9.9 Vert		2913
32¢	multi	Flag over Porch Coil		SVS	9.9 Vert		2914
32¢	multi	Flag over Porch Self-adhesive Coil			Die cut 8.7		2915
32¢	multi	Flag over Porch Self-adhesive Coil			Die cut 9.7		2915A
32¢	multi	Flag over Porch Self-adhesive Coil			Die cut 11.5		2915B
32¢	multi	Flag over Porch Self-adhesive Coil			Die cut 10.9		2915C
32¢	multi	Flag over Porch Self-adhesive Coil			Die cut 9.8		2915D
32¢	multi	Flag over Porch	Bklt.Sgle./P.P.n. of 10		11x10		2916a
32¢	multi	Flag over Porch Self-adhesive			Die-cut 8.8		2920,20b
32¢	multi	Flag over Porch Self-adhesive			Die-cut 11.3		2920d
32¢	multi	Flag over Porch Self-adhesive			Die-cut 9.8		2921a
32¢	multi	Flag over Porch Linerless SA Coil			Die-cut		3133
32¢	multi	Flag over Field Self-adhesive			Die cut		2919
32¢	lake	Henry R. Luce			11		2935
32¢	blue	Lila & DeWitt Wallace			11		2936
32¢	brown	Milton S. Hershey			11		2933

DEFINITIVE ISSUE IDENTIFIER

Den.	Color	Subject	Type/Comment	Press	Perf.	Wmk.	Scott #
32¢	green	Cal Farley		11			2934
32¢	multi	Yellow Rose	Self-adhesive	Die-cut 9.9 Vert			3049
32¢	multi	Yellow Rose	Self-adhesive Coil	Die-cut 9.8 Vert.			3054
32¢	multi	Statue of Liberty		Die-cut 11			3122
32¢	multi	Statue of Liberty		Die-cut 11.5x11.8			3122E
32¢	multi	Citron, Moth		Die-cut			3126,28a
32¢	multi	Flowering Pineapple, Cockroaches					
			Self-adhesive	Die-cut			3127,29a
33¢	**multi**	**Flag and City**		**11.2**			**3277**
33¢	multi	Flag and City	Self-adhesive	Die-cut 11.1			3278
33¢	multi	Flag and City SA Bklt.Single		Die-cut 11½x11¾			3278F
33¢	multi	Flag and City SA Bklt.Single		Die-cut 9.8			3279
33¢	multi	Flag and City Coil		9.9 Vert.			3280
33¢	multi	Flag and City SA Coil, square corner		Die-cut 9.8			3281
33¢	multi	Flag and City SA Coil, rounded corner		Die-cut 9.8			3282
33¢	multi	Flag and Chalkboard SA Bklt.Single		Die-cut 7.9			3283
33¢	multi	Fruit Berries SA Booklet Singles		Die-cut 11.2x11.7			3294-97
33¢	multi	Fruit Berries SA Booklet Singles		Die-cut 9.5x10			3298-3301
33¢	multi	Fruit Berries, SA Coils		Die-cut 8.5 Vert			3302-5
33¢	multi	Fruit Berries, SA Coils		Die-cut 8.5 Horiz.			3404-7
33¢	multi	Coral Pink Rose SA Bklt. Single		Die-cut 11½x11¼			3052
33¢	multi	Coral Pink Rose SA Bklt. Single		Die-cut10.75x10.5			3052E
33¢	red & black	Claude Pepper		11			3426
34¢	**multi**	**Statue of Liberty**	**S.A. Coil (rounded corners)**				
				Die-cut 9.75 Vert.			**3466**
34¢	multi	Statue of Liberty	Coil	9.75 Vert.			3476
34¢	multi	Statue of Liberty	S.A. Coil (square corners)				
				Die-cut 9.75 Vert.			3477
34¢	multi	Statue of Liberty S.A. Booklet Single		Die-cut			3484
34¢	multi	Statue of Liberty S.A. Single from Conv. Pane					
				Die-cut 11			3485
34¢	multi	Flag over Farm		11.25			3469
34¢	multi	Flag over Farm	Self-adhesive	Die-cut 11.25			3470
34¢	multi	Flowers	Self-adhesive Coils	Die-cut 8.5 Vert.			3478-81
34¢	multi	Flowers	S.A. Booklet Stamps				
				Die-cut 10.25x10.75			3487-90
34¢	multi	Apple & Orange S.A. Booklet Stamps		Die-cut 11.25			3491-92
35¢	**gray**	**Charles R. Drew M.D.**		**10.5x11**			**1865**
35¢	black	Dennis Chavez		11			2186
37¢	**blue**	**Robert Millikan**		**10.5x11**			**1866**
39¢	**rose lilac**	**Grenville Clark**		**11**			**1867****
40¢	**brn red**	**J. Marshall**		**11x10.5**			**1050**
40¢	bl black	Thomas Paine		11x10.5			1292*
40¢	dk grn	Lillian M. Gilbreth		11			1868**
40¢	dk blue	Claire Chennault		11			2187
45¢	**brt blue**	**Harvey Cushing, MD**		**11**			**2188**
45¢	multi	Pumpkinseed Fish		11			2481
46¢	**carmine**	**Ruth Benedict**		**11**			**2938**
50¢	**orange**	**T. Jefferson**	**w/ Tri. in Top corners**	**12**	**NW**		**260**
50¢	orange	T. Jefferson	w/ Tri. in Top corners	12	DL		275
50¢	orange	T. Jefferson	"Series 1902"	12	DL		310
50¢	violet	Washington		12	DL		341
50¢	violet	B. Franklin		12	SL		421
50¢	violet	B. Franklin		12	DL		422
50¢	violet	B. Franklin		10	SL		440
50¢	lt violet	B. Franklin		10	NW		477
50¢	rd violet	B. Franklin		11	NW		517
50¢	lilac	Arlington Amph	F	11			570
50¢	lilac	Arlington Amph	R	10.5x11			701
50¢	lt rd viol	W.H. Taft		11x10.5			831
50¢	brt prpl	S.B. Anthony		11x10.5			1051
50¢	rose mag	Lucy Stone		11x10.5			1293*
50¢	blk & orng	Iron "Betty" Lamp		11			1608
50¢	brown	Chester W. Nimitz		11			1869**
52¢	**purple**	**Hubert Humphrey**		**11**			**2189**
55¢	**green**	**Alice Hamilton**		**11**			**2940**
55¢	black	Justin Morrill		SA Die-cut 11½			2941
55¢	multi	Art-Deco Eagle	Self-adhesive	Die-cut 10.75			3471
56¢	**scarlet**	**John Harvard**		**11**			**2190**
65¢	**dk blue**	**"Hap" Arnold**		**11**			**2191**
75¢	**dp mag**	**Wendell Wilkie**		**11**			**2192**
76¢	**red & black**	**Hattie Caraway**	**Self-adhesive**	**Die-cut 11**			**3431**
77¢	**blue**	**Mary Breckenridge**		**11.8x11.6**			**2942**
78¢	**purple**	**Alice Paul**		**11.2**			**2943**
90¢	**blue**	**Washington**	**"Ninety Cents"**	**15**			**39**
90¢	blue	Washington	"90 Cents"	12			72
90¢	blue	Washington	Same, "F" Grill	12			101
90¢	carm & blk	A. Lincoln	"G grill"	12			122
90¢	carm & blk	A. Lincoln	w/o grill, o.g.	12			122a
90¢	carmine	Com. Perry	Hard wh paper, w/grill	12			144
90¢	carmine	Com. Perry	Same, w/o grill	12			155
90¢	rose carm	Com. Perry	Same	12			166
90¢	carmine	Com. Perry	Soft porous paper	12			191
90¢	purple	Com. Perry	Soft porous paper	12			218
90¢	orange	Com. Perry		12			229
$1.00	**black**	**Com. Perry**	**Ty I**	**12**	**NW**		**261**
$1.00	black	Com. Perry	Ty I	12	DL		276
$1.00	black	Com. Perry	Ty II	12	NW		261A
$1.00	black	Com. Perry	Ty II	12	DL		276A
$1.00	black	D.G. Farragut		12	DL		311
$1.00	violet brn	Washington		12	DL		342
$1.00	violet brn	B. Franklin		12	DL		423
$1.00	violet blk	B. Franklin		10	DL		460
$1.00	violet blk	B. Franklin		10	NW		478
$1.00	violet brn	B. Franklin		11	NW		518
$1.00	deep prus	B. Franklin		11	NW		518b
$1.00	violet blk	Lincoln Memorial		11			571
$1.00	prpl & blk	W. Wilson		11			832
$1.00	prpl & blk	W. Wilson		11		USIR	832b
$1.00	rd viol & blk	W. Wilson	Dry Print, smooth gum	11			832c
$1.00	purple	P. Henry		11x10.5			1052
$1.00	dl purple	Eugene O'Neill		11x10.5			1294*
$1.00	dl purple	Eugene O'Neill	Coil	10 Vert			1305
$1.00	brn,orng&yel (tan)	Rush Lamp & Candle Holder		11			1610
$1.00	dk prus grn	Bernard Revel		11			2193
$1.00	dk blue	Johns Hopkins		11			2194
$1.00	bl & scar	Seaplane	Coil	10 Vert			2468
$1.00	gold,multi	Eagle & Olympic Rings		11			2539
$1.00	blue	Burgoyne		11.5			2590
$1.00	multi	Red Fox		Die-cut 11.5x11.3			3036
$2.00	**brt blue**	**J. Madison**	**w/ Tri. in Top corners**	**12**	**NW**		**262**
$2.00	brt blue	J. Madison	w/ Tri. in Top corners	12	DL		277
$2.00	dk blue	J. Madison	"Series 1902"	12	DL		312
$2.00	dk blue	J. Madison	"Series 1902"	10	NW		479
$2.00	orng rd & blk	B. Franklin		11			523
$2.00	carm & blk	B. Franklin		11			547
$2.00	dp blue	U.S. Capitol		11			572
$2.00	yel grn&blk	W.G. Harding		11			833
$2.00	dk grn&rd (tan)	Kerosene Table Lamp		11			1611
$2.00	brt viol	William Jennings Bryan		11			2195
$2.00	multi	Bobcat		11			2482
$2.90	**multi**	**Eagle**		**11**			**2540**
$2.90	multi	Space Shuttle		11x10½			2543
$3.00	**multi**	**Challenger Shuttle**		**11.2**			**2544, 2544a**
$3.00	multi	Mars Pathfinder		Souv. Sheet			3178
$3.20	**multi**	**Space Shuttle Landing**					
			Self-adhesive	Die-cut 11.5			3261
$3.50	**multi**	**Capitol Dome**	Self-adhesive	Die-cut 11.25x11.5			3472
$5.00	**dk green**	**J. Marshall**	**w/ Tri. in Top corners**	**12**	**NW**		**263**
$5.00	dk green	J. Marshall	w/ Tri. in Top corners	12	DL		278
$5.00	dk green	J. Marshall	"Series 1902"	12	DL		313
$5.00	lt green	J. Marshall	"Series 1902"	10	NW		480
$5.00	dp grn & blk	B. Franklin		11			524
$5.00	carm & bl	Freedom Statue/Capitol		11			573
$5.00	carm & blk	C. Coolidge		11			834
$5.00	rd brn & blk	C. Coolidge		11			834a
$5.00	black	A. Hamilton		11			1053
$5.00	gray blk	John Bassett Moore		11x10.5			1295*
$5.00	rd brn,yel&orng (tan)	RR Conductors Lantern		11			1612
$5.00	copper rd	Bret Harte		11			2196
$5.00	slate grn	Washington & Jackson		11.5			2592
$8.75	**multi**	**Eagle & Moon**		**11**			**2394**
$9.35	**multi**	**Eagle & Moon**	Bklt. sgl./B. Pn. of 3	**10 Vert**			**1909,a**
$9.95	**multi**	**Eagle**		**11**			**2541**
$9.95	multi	Moon Landing		10.7x11.1			2842
$10.75	**multi**	**Eagle & Moon**	Bklt. sgl./B. Pn. of 3	**10 Vert**			**2122,a**
$10.75	multi	Endeavor Shuttle		11			2544A
$11.75	**multi**	**Piggyback Space Shuttle**					
			Self-adhesive	Die-cut 11.5			3262
$12.25	**multi**	**Washington Monument**					
			Self-adhesive	Die-cut 11.25x11.5			3473
$14.00	**multi**	**Spread winged Eagle**		**11**			**2542**
(1¢)	**multi**	**Weather Vane, Blue Date**		**11.2**			**3257**
(1¢)	multi	Weather Vane, Black Date		11.2			3258
(3¢)	**multi**	**Dove**	**ABN**	**11x10.8**			**2877**
(3¢)	multi	Dove	SVS	10.8x10.9			2878
* (4¢)	gold,carm	Text only	Make-up rate	11			2521
(5¢)	**multi**	**Butte**	Coil	**9.8 Vert**			**2902**
(5¢)	multi	Butte	Self-adhesive Coil	Die-cut 11.5			2902B
(5¢)	multi	Mountain	Coil	BEP 9.8 Vert			2903
(5¢)	multi	Mountain	Coil	SVS 9.8 Vert			2904
(5¢)	multi	Mountain	Self-adhesive Coil	Die-cut 11.5			2904A
(5¢)	multi	Mountain	Self-adhesive Coil	Die-cut 9.8			2904B
(5¢)	multi	Wetlands	Coil	10 Vert			3207
(5¢)	multi	Wetlands	Self-adhesive Coil	Die-cut 9.7 Vert			3207A
(10¢)	**multi**	**Automobile**	Coil	**9.8 Vert**			**2905**
(10¢)	multi	Automobile	Self-adhesive Coil	Die-cut 11.5			2907
(10¢)	multi	Eagle & Shield	Coil "Bulk Rate, USA"	10 Vert			2602
(10¢)	multi	Eagle & Shield	Coil "USA Bulk Rate"	10 Vert		BEP	2603
(10¢)	multi	Eagle & Shield	Coil "USA Bulk Rate"	10 Vert		SVS	2604

Den.	Color	Subject	Type / Comment	Press	Perf.	Wmk.	Scott #
(10¢)	multi	Eagle & Shield	Self-adhesive Coil		Die-cut 11.5		2906
(10¢)	multi	Eagle & Shield	Coil "Presorted"		9.9 Vert		3270
(10¢)	multi	Eagle & Shield	Self-adhesive Coil "Presorted"				
					Die-cut 9.9 Vert		3271
(10¢)	multi	Green Bicycle	Self-adhesive Coil		Die-cut 9.8 Vert		3228
(10¢)	multi	Green Bicycle	Coil		9.9 Vert		3229
(10¢)	multi	New York Public Library Lion					
			Self-adhesive Coil		Die-cut 11.5 Vert.		3447
A (15¢) orange		**Eagle**			**11**		**1735**
A (15¢)	orange	Eagle	Bklt. Sgl./Pn. of 8		11x10.5		1736,a
A (15¢)	orange	Eagle	Coil		10 Vert		1743
(15¢)	multi	Auto Tail Fin	Coil	BEP	9.8 Vert		2908
(15¢)	multi	Auto Tail Fin	Coil	SVS	9.8 Vert		2909
(15¢)	multi	Auto Tail Fin	Self-adhesive Coil		Die-cut 11.5		2910
B (18¢) violet		**Eagle**			**11x10.5**		**1818**
B (18¢)	violet	Eagle	Bklt. sgl./Pn of 8		10		1819,a
B (18¢)	violet	Eagle	Coil		10 Vert		1820
C (20¢) brown		**Eagle**			**11x10.5**		**1946**
C (20¢)	brown	Eagle	Coil		10 Vert		1947
C (20¢)	brown	Eagle	Bklt. sgl./Pn. of 10		11x10.5		1948,a
G (20¢) multi		**Flag Black "G"**		**BEP**	**11.2x11.1**		**2879**
G (20¢)	multi	Flag Red "G"		SVS	11x10.9		2880
D (22¢) green		**Eagle**			**11**		**2111**
D (22¢)	green	Eagle	Coil		10 Vert		2112
D (22¢)	green	Eagle	Bklt. sgl./Pn. of 10		11		2113,a
E (25¢) multi		**Earth**			**11**		**2277**
E (25¢)	multi	Earth	Coil		10 Vert		2279
E (25¢)	multi	Earth	Bklt. sgl./Pn. of 10		10		2282a
(25¢)	multi	Juke Box	Coil	BEP	9.8 Vert		2911
(25¢)	multi	Juke Box	Coil	SVS	9.8 Vert		2912
(25¢)	multi	Juke Box	Self-adhesive Coil		Die-cut 11.5		2912A
(25¢)	multi	Juke Box	Self-adhesive Coil		Die-cut 9.8		2912B
(25¢)	multi	Juke Box	Linerless SA Coil		Die-cut		3132
(25¢)	multi	Diner	Coil		10 Vert		3208
(25¢)	multi	Diner	Self-adhesive Coil		Die-cut 9.7 Vert		3208A
G (25¢)	multi	Flag, Black "G"	Coil	SVS	9.8 Vert		2888
F (29¢) multi		**Tulip**			**13**		**2517**
F (29¢)	multi	Tulip	Coil		10		2518
F (29¢)	multi	Tulip	Bklt. Stamp	BEP	11 bullseye		2519
F (29¢)	multi	Tulip	Bkt. Stamp	KCS	11		2520
F (29¢)	blk,dk bl,red	Flag	Self-adhesive		Die cut		2522
G (32¢) multi		**Flag, Black "G"**		**BEP**	**11.2x11.1**		**2881**
G (32¢)	multi	Flag, Red "G"		SVS	11x10.9		2882
G (32¢)	multi	Flag, Black "G"	Bklt. Stamp	BEP	10x9.9		2883
G (32¢)	multi	Flag, Blue "G"	Bklt. Stamp	ABN	10.9		2884
G (32¢)	multi	Flag, Red "G"	Bklt. Stamp	SVS	11x10.9		2885
G (32¢)	multi	Flag	Self-adhesive		Die cut		2886,87
G (32¢)	multi	Flag, Black "G"	Coil	BEP	9.8 vert.		2889
G (32¢)	multi	Flag, Blue "G"	Coil	ABN	9.8 vert.		2890
G (32¢)	multi	Flag, Red "G"	Coil	SVS	9.8 vert.		2891
G (32¢)	multi	Flag, Red "G"	Coil	Roulette	9.8 vert.		2892
H (33¢) multi		**Uncle Sam's Hat**			**11.2**		**3260**
H (33¢)	multi	Uncle Sam's Hat	Coil		9.8 Vert		3264
H (33¢)	multi	Uncle Sam's Hat					
			Self-adhesive Coil		Die-cut 9.9 Vert		3265
H (33¢)	multi	Uncle Sam's Hat					
			Self-adhesive Coil		Die-cut 9.7 Vert		3266
H (33¢)	multi	Uncle Sam's Hat, Small Date					
			S.A.Bklt. Stamp		Die-cut 9.9		3267
H (33¢)	multi	Uncle Sam's Hat, Large Date					
			S.A.Bklt. Stamp		Die-cut 11.2x11.1		3268
H (33¢)	multi	Uncle Sam's Hat					
			S.A. Bklt. Stamp		Die-cut 8		3269
(34¢)	**multi**	**Flag over Farm**			**11.25**		**3448**
(34¢)	multi	Flag over Farm	Self-adhesive		Die-cut 11.25		3449
(34¢)	multi	Flag over Farm	S.A. Booklet Stamp		Die-cut 8		3450
(34¢)	multi	Statue of Liberty	S.A. Booklet Stamp		Die-cut 11		3451
(34¢)	multi	Statue of Liberty	Coil		9.75 Vert.		3452
(34¢)	multi	Statue of Liberty	Self-adhesive Coil		Die-cut 10 Vert.		3453
(34¢)	multi	Flowers	S.A. Booklet Stamps				
					Die-cut10.25x10.75		3454-57
(34¢)	multi	Flowers	S.A. Booklet Stamp				
					Die-cut 11.25x11.75		3458-61
(34¢)	multi	Flower	Self-adhesive Coils				
					Die-cut 8.5 Vert.		3462-65

Adventures in Topicals

By George Griffenhagen
Editor of *Topical Time*

There is much more to topical stamp collecting than accumulating postage stamps picturing something or some one associated with a theme. To experience the adventure of topical collecting, you need to expand your horizons by including a variety of philatelic elements in your collection. We will review the variety of philatelic elements that awaits your discovery.

To most people, a postage stamp is something they stick on a envelope to mail a letter. However, stamp collectors know that postage stamps come in a variety of forms. There are Definitives (most 19th century stamps were definitives); Commemoratives (they made there appearance at the close of the 19th century); Semi-Postals (also called charity stamps); Provisionals (to fill an urgent need); and Locals (for use in a limited geographical area). The stamp design is generally limited to a single stamp, but Composites are those in which the design extends over two or more adjacent stamps differing in design or denomination, while Tete-beche is a term describing adjacent stamps, one of which is inverted.

Any of the above stamps can include a Surcharges (inscriptions that change the face value) or Overprints (inscription that change the purpose of the stamp); a classical example of the latter is the 1928 U.S. George Washington stamp with overprint for MOLLY PITCHER, Revolutionary War heroine.

Perfins and Watermarks offer interesting philatelic elements. Among the thousands of Perfins (named for PERForated INSignia), topical collectors can find designs for anchors, bells, coffee grinders, dancers, eagles, fish, flags, spinning wheels, swans, and windmills. Watermarks (patterns impressed into the paper during manufacture) also come in a variety of images including anchors, birds, coats-of-arms, flowers, lions, moons, posthorns, pyramids, stars, swans, and trees.

Marginal inscriptions frequently include more than plate numbers or other post office inscriptions. Design on tabs and margins (selvage) of stamps and souvenir sheets often supplement a theme as much as the design of the stamp itself. Equally interesting are the tabs and marginal advertisements attached to postage stamps.

The introduction of postage stamp booklets in 1895 offered opportunities for governmental promotional messages and commercial advertising on covers, interleaves, and labels required to make total face value of a booklet a convenient multiple of the local currency. Commercial advertising was introduced into the stamp booklets during the first decade of the 19th century. By the 1920s, entire stamp booklets were devoted to advertisements of a single firm.

There are, of course, many stamps that are not postage stamps. Revenues (also called fiscals or tax stamps) are stamps indicating the payment of a fee or collection of a tax. They predate postage stamps by several centuries, having been used in The Netherlands as early as 1627 and in Spain as early as 1637. Even though revenues are not postage stamps, they lay claim to being the "most historic stamp of all time." It was a 1765 revenue stamp imposing a tax on legal documents in the British colonies in America which ignited the American Revolutionary War. Cinderellas are virtually any item that looks like a postage stamp but is not a postage stamp. They include such material as advertising seals, bogus stamps, charity seals, fantasy stamps, food rationing stamps, political seals, poster stamps, and propaganda seals. There are even Test Stamps issued by various postal administrations for use in developing stamp vending machines.

Covers (envelopes that have passed through the mail bearing appropriate postal markings) were used centuries before the introduction of the postage stamp. Today they are classified either as Commercial or Philatelic. Many adventures lies ahead for the collector who searches for a particular stamp that belongs in a topical collection. By the second half of the 19th century, envelopes were imprinted with a wide range of colorful advertisements (called Corner Cards referring to the return address). Patriotic Cover became popular during the American Civil War, and Mourning Covers (with their black boarders) were widely used during the Victorian era. Other interesting covers include Balloon Mail (which preceded First Flight Covers), Paquebots (mail posted on the high seas), Crash/ Wreck Covers, Free Frank Covers, and censored Covers. First Day Covers (FDCs) comprise a great portion of philatelic covers.

Postal Stationary includes all forms of stationary bearing a printed stamp (indicium). Pre-stamped letter sheets were used as early as the 17th century, but it was British Mulready which was introduced in 1840 that popularized postal stationery. The first Postal card bearing an indicium was issued in Austria 1869, and the Aerogramme (air letter) led to subsequent use of the British Airgraph and American V-Mail during World War II.

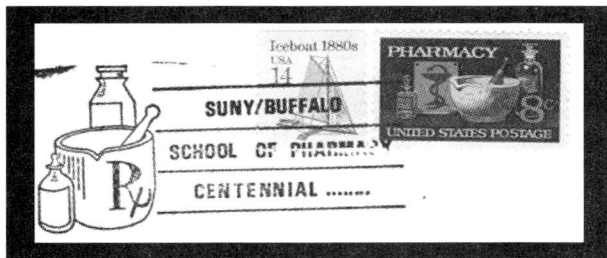

Cancellations (called postmarks when they include date and place of posting) come in variety of forms. The most desirable for the topical collector are Fancy Cancels applied by oblterators made of cork or wood. The rarest were produced in Waterbury, Connecticut, from 1865 to 1869. With the introduction of rapid cancelling machines, Slogan Cancels, Pictorial Cancels, and First Day of Issue Cancels were created. The introduction of the postage meter in the early 20th century also led to a variety of advertising slogans.

Other philatelic elements of interest to the topical collector are Maximum Cards (introduced around 1900); Autographs on stamps and covers; and the Telephone Card (which was used as early as the 1800s to prepay telephone calls). The scope of material for the topical collector is limited only by one's imagination.

SELECTED and ANNOTATED BIBLIOGRAPHY

The volumes listed below are recommended for the library of any collector who wishes to gain more knowledge in the areas covered by the *1996 Brookman*. While the main emphasis is on stamps, many of these volumes contain good postal history information. Check with your favorite dealer for availability and price. (To conserve space, some bibliographic notations have been abbreviated).

19th & 20th Century

Cummings, William W., ed., *Scott 1995 Specialized Catalogue of U.S. Stamps*
This annual publication offers a treasure trove of information on virtually every area of the postage and revenue stamps of the US, UN & US Possesstions. A "must have."

Sloane, George B., *Sloane's Column*, arr. by George Turner, 1961, (BIA 1980)
A subject by subject arrangement of Sloane's 1350 columns which appeared in "STAMPS" magazine from1932-1958 covering virtually every facet of U.S. philately.

White, Roy, *Encyclopedia of the Colors of U.S. Postage Stamps*, Vol 1-5, 1981, 86.
The first four volumes cover US stamps from 1847-1918 plus a few selected issues. Volume five covers the US Postage Dues from1879-1916. They are the finest available works for classifying the colors of U.S. postage stamps.

19th Century
General

Brookman, Lester G., *The United States Postage Stamps of the 19th Century*, 3 vol., 1966. (Reprinted in 1989 by D.G.Phillips Co.)
This is the finest and most informative work on 19th Century issues. Each stamp, from the 5¢ Franklin of 1847 thru the $2 Trans-Mississippi of 1898, is given separate, and often in-depth treatment. This is a must for any collector.

Luff, John N., *The Postage Stamps of the United States*, 1902.
While much of Luff's information has been superseded by Brookman, his treatment of Postmaster Provisionals and several Back-of-the-book sections make this a worthwhile volume. (The "Gossip Reprint", 1937, is more useful and recommended.)

Perry, Elliot, *Pat Paragraphs*, arr by George Turner & Thomas Stanton, BIA, 1981.
A subject by subject arrangement of Perry's 58 pamphlets which were published from 1931-1958. The emphasis is on the 19th century classics as well as carriers & locals.

Baker, Hugh J. and J. David, *Bakers' U.S. Classics*, 1985
An annotated compilation of the Bakers' columns from "STAMPS" magazine which appeared from 1962-1969. This major work provides extensive coverage of nearly all aspects of U.S. and Confederate philately.

By Issue or Subject

Ashbrook, Stanley B., *The United States One Cent Stamp of 1851-57*, 2 vol, 1938.
Although most of stamp and plating information in Volume 1 has been superseded by Mortimer Neinken's great work, Vol. 2 features an indispensible amount of information on the postal history of the period.

Neinken, Mortimer L., *The United States One Cent Stamp of 1851 to 1861*, 1972.
United States, The 1851-57 Twelve Cent Stamp, 1964.
The One cent book supplements and updates, but does not replace, Ashbrook's study. The Twelve cent booklet deals almost exclusively with the plating of this issue. Both are fundamental works.

Chase, Dr. Carroll, *The 3¢ Stamp of the U.S. 1851-57 Issue*, Rev. ed., 1942.
This outstanding work provides the most comprehensive information available in one place on this popular issue. (The Quarterman reprint, 1975, contains a new forward, corrections, additions and a selected bibliography of articles.)

Hill, Henry W., *The United States Five Cent Stamps of 1856-1861*, 1955.
This extensively illustrated volume is the only work dealing exclusively with this issue. It includes studies on stamps, plating, cancels, and postal history.

Neinken, Mortimer L., *The United States Ten Cent Stamps of 1855-1859*, 1960.
This work not only provides an indispensable amount of stamp and plating information, but it also reprints Chapters 50-53 from Ashbrook Vol. 2 dealing with California, Ocean and Western Mails.

Cole, Maurice F., *The Black Jacks of 1863-1867*, 1950.
A superb study of the issue with major emphasis on postal history.

Lane, Maryette B., *The Harry F. Allen Collection of Black Jacks, A Study of the Stamp and it's Use*, 1969
The title says it all. This book beautifully complements, but does not replace, Cole.

Ashbrook, Stanley B., *The U.S. Issues of 1869, Preceded by Some Additional Notes on "The premieres Gravures of 1861"*, 1943
This work concentrates on the design sources and production of the 1869 issue. Ashbrook concludes with his "Addendum" attacking Scott for listing the Premieres.

Willard, Edward L., *The U.S. Two Cent Red Brown of 1883-1887*, 2 vol., 1970.
Volume I deals with the background, production and varieties of the stamp. Vol. II deals exclusively with the cancellations found on the stamp. A good Banknote intro.

20th Century
General

King, Beverly S. and Johl, Max G. *The United States Postages Stamps of the Twentieth Century*, Vol. 1 revised, Vol. 2-4, 1934-38.
These volumes are still the standard work on 20th Century U.S. postage stamps from 1901 to 1937. (The 1976 Quarterman reprint contains only the regular issue, air mail and Parcel Post sections from the original volumes. It is highly recommended.)

By Issue or Subject

Armstrong, Martin A., *Washington-Franklins, 1908-1921*, 2nd Edition, 1979.
Armstrong, Martin A., *US Definitive Series, 1922-1938*, 2nd Edition, 1980.
Armstrong, Martin A., *United States Coil Issues, 1906-38*, 1977
Each of these volumes not only supplements the information found in Johl, but expands each area to include studies of essays, proofs, booklet panes, private perfs, Offices in China and the Canal Zone. One major plus is the wealth of illustrations, many of rare and unusual items, which were not included in Johl's work due to laws restricting the publication of stamp pictures prior to 1938.

20th Century
By Issue or Subject (cont.)

Schoen, DeVoss & Harvey, *Counterfeit Kansas-Nebraska Overprints on 1922-34 Issue plus First Day Covers of the Kansas-Nebraska Overprints*, 1973.
A fine pamphlet covering K-N varieties, errors and First Day covers, plus important information pointing out the differences between genuine and fake overprints.

Datz, Stephen, *U.S. Errors: Inverts, Imperforates, Colors Omitted*, 1992 Ed., 1991.
This volume does a superb job covering the subjects listed in its title, It is extensively illustrated and provides price, quantity and historical information.

Air Mail & Back-of-the-Book

Amercian Air Mail Society, *American Air Mail Catalog, Fifth Ed.*, 5 vols + 1990 Pricing Supplement, 1974-1990.
Virtually everything there is to know about air mail stamps and postal history.

Arfken, George B., *Postage Due, The United States Large Numeral Postage Due Stamps, 1879-1894*, 1991.
A Comprehensive study of virtually every aspect of these interesting stamps. Additionally, about half the book is devoted to their extensive usage which helps to clarify some of the more complex markings and routings found on "Due" covers.

Gobie, Henry M. *The Speedy, A History of the U.S. Special Delivery Service*, 1976
Gobie, Henry M., *U.S. Parcel Post, A Postal History*, 1979.
Each of these volumes includes information on the stamps, but their main thrust is on the postal history of the respective services. Official documents and Postal Laws & Regulations have been extensively reproduced and numerous covers illustrating the various aspects of the services are pictured.

Markovits, Robert L., *United States, The 10¢ Registry Stamp of 1911*, 1973.
This pamphlet provides a superb blueprint for the formation of specialized collection around a single stamp. It is extensively illustrated and concludes with an extensive bibliography which touches upon a multitude of additional subjects.

McGovern, Edmund C., ed, *Catalog of the 19th Century Stamped Envelopes and Wrappers of the United States*, USPSS 1984

Haller, Austin P., ed., *Catalog of the 20th Century Stamped Envelopes and Wrappers of the United States*, USPSS 1990

Beachboard, John H., ed., *United States Postal Card Catalog*, USPSS 1990
Each of the three previous volumes contains the finest available information in their respective fields. They are indispensable to the postal stationery collector.

First Day Covers & Related Collectibles

Planty, Dr. Earl & Mellone, Michael, *Planty's Photo Encyclopedia of Cacheted FDCs*, 1923-1939, Vol. 1-10, 1976-1984

Mellone, Mike, *Specialized Catalog of First Day Covers of the 1940's (2nd ed.)*, 1950's and 1960's, 2 vol., 2 vol., 3 vol. respectively, 1983-1985.

Pelcyger, Dr. Scott, *Mellone's Specialized Catalog of First Day Ceremony Programs & Events*, 1989
Each of these volumes illustrates virtually every known cachet and ceremony program for the stamps listed within. They each provide an invaluable resource.

Radford, Dr. Curtis D., *The Souvenir Card Collectors Society Numbering System for Forerunner and Modern Day Souvenir Card*, 1989.
The most informative work on this popular collecting area.

Revenues

Toppan, Deats and Holland, *'An Historical Reference List of the Revenue Stamps of the United States...'*, 1899.
The information in this volume, while almost 100 years old, still provides the collector with much of the basic knowledge available today on US Revenues and "Match and Medicines" from 1862-1898. (The "Gossip" reprint is recommended.)

Confederate States

Dietz, August, *The Postal Service of the Confederate States of America*, 1929
This monumental work has been the "Bible" for Confederate collectors. Covering virtually every aspect of Confederate philately, its content remains useful, even after 60+ years. (A 1989 reprint makes this work more affordable for the average collector.)

Skinner, Gunter and Sanders, *The New Dietz Confederate States Catalog and Handbook*, 1986.
This volume makes an effort to cover every phase of Confederate philately and postal history. Despite the presence of some flaws, it is highly recommended.

Possessions

Plass, Brewster and Salz, *Canal Zone Stamps*, 1986.
Published by the Canal Zone Study Group, this outstanding well written and extensively illustrated volume, is now the "bible" for these fascinating issues.

Meyer, Harris, et. at, *Hawaii, Its Stamps and Postal History*, 1948.
After 45 years, this volume, which deals with virtually every facet of Hawaiian stamps and postal history, remains the finest work written on the subject.

Palmer, Maj. F.L., *The Postal Issues of the Philippines*, 1912
An ancient, but still useful study, with interesting information on the U.S. overprints.

British North America

Boggs, Winthrop S., *The Postage Stamps and Postal History of Canada*, 2 vol., 1945. (Quarterman reprint, One vol., 1975.)
For almost 50 years the standard work on Canadian stamps and postal history. One of the "must have" books. (The reprint omits most of the Vol. 2 appendices.)

Lowe, Robson, *The Encyclopedia of British Empire Postage Stamps, Vol. 5, North America*, 1973
This work continues the fine tradition of Robson Lowe's earlier volumes dealing with the British Empire. Covering all of BNA, it is an essential tool for the collector.

PLEASE READ INFORMATION ABOUT CONDITION ON PAGES II AND IV

1847 General Issue, Imperforate VF + 50% (C)

1,3,948a

2,4,948b

Scott's No.		Unused Fine	Ave.	Used Fine	Ave.
1	5¢ Franklin, Red Brown	4250.00	2500.00	475.00	300.00
1	5¢ Red Brown, Pen Cancel	...	250.00	175.00	
2	10¢ Washington, Black		13000.00	1200.00	750.00
2	10¢ Black, Pen Cancel		...	700.00	475.00
3	5¢ Red Brown, 1875 Reproduction ...	750.00	550.00	...	...
4	10¢ Black, 1875 Reproduction	900.00	675.00	...	...

NOTE: SEE #948 FOR 5¢ BLUE AND 10¢ BROWN ORANGE.

1851-57 Issue, Imperf "U.S. Postage" at Top (VF, OG+150%, VF+75%,OG+75%) (C)

5A-9   **10-11**   **12**   **13-16**   **17**

Scott's No.		Unused Fine	Ave.	Used Fine	Ave.
5A	1¢ Franklin, Blue, Type Ib	...	...	3500.00	2000.00
6	1¢ Blue, Type Ia			6500.00	3750.00
7	1¢ Blue, Type I	450.00	275.00	130.00	75.00
8	1¢ Blue, Type III			1950.00	1200.00
8A	1¢ Blue, Type IIIa	2000.00	1200.00	750.00	450.00
9	1¢ Blue, Type IV	400.00	240.00	95.00	57.50
10	3¢ Wash., Orange Brown, Ty. I	1500.00	900.00	82.50	50.00
11	3¢ Dull Red, Type I	120.00	70.00	8.75	5.25
12	5¢ Jefferson, Red Brown, Ty. I	...		950.00	550.00
13	10¢ Wash., Green, Type I			675.00	400.00
14	10¢ Green, Type II	1600.00	975.00	190.00	135.00
15	10¢ Green, Type III	1600.00	975.00	190.00	135.00
16	10¢ Green, Type IV			1200.00	700.00
17	12¢ Washington, Black		1500.00	300.00	180.00

1857-61 Designs as above but Perf. 15 (VF,OG+200%,VF+100% OG+75%) (C)

18-24   **25-26**   **27-30A**   **31-35**

36   **37**   **38**   **39**

Scott's No.		Unused Fine	Ave.	Used Fine	Ave.
18	1¢ Franklin, Blue, Type I	700.00	425.00	375.00	225.00
19	1¢ Blue, Type Ia			3250.00	2000.00
20	1¢ Blue, Type II	475.00	275.00	190.00	115.00
21	1¢ Blue, Type III (Plate 4)		3500.00	1400.00	825.00
22	1¢ Blue, Type IIIa	800.00	500.00	350.00	200.00
23	1¢ Blue, Type IV	3000.00	1800.00	450.00	250.00
24	1¢ Blue, Type V	80.00	50.00	35.00	20.00
25	3¢ Washington, Rose, Type I	1000.00	600.00	55.00	35.00
26	3¢ Dull Red, Type II	55.00	31.50	4.75	2.75
26a	3¢ Dull Red, Type IIa	100.00	60.00	37.50	22.50
27	5¢ Jefferson, Brick Red, Type I	5500.00		900.00	550.00
28	5¢ Red Brown, Type I	1650.00	1000.00	425.00	250.00
28A	5¢ Indian Red, Type I			1950.00	1250.00
29	5¢ Brown, Type I	850.00	475.00	275.00	165.00
30	5¢ Orange Brown, Type II	525.00	325.00	750.00	450.00
30A	5¢ Brown, Type II	750.00	450.00	225.00	135.00
31	10¢ Washington, Green, Type I	4000.00		600.00	350.00
32	10¢ Green, Type II	2275.00	1300.00	210.00	130.00
33	10¢ Green, Type III	2275.00	1300.00	210.00	130.00
34	10¢ Green, Type IV			1750.00	950.00
35	10¢ Green, Type V	160.00	95.00	57.50	35.00
36	12¢ Washington, Black, Plate I	625.00	375.00	150.00	90.00
36b	12¢ Black, Plate III	375.00	200.00	140.00	80.00
37	24¢ Washington, Gray Lilac	550.00	325.00	270.00	160.00

Scott's No.		Unused Fine	Ave.	Used Fine	Ave.
38	30¢ Franklin, Orange	750.00	435.00	325.00	190.00
39	90¢ Washington, Blue	1200.00	750.00	...	...

NOTE: #5A THROUGH 38 WITH PEN CANCELS USUALLY SELL FOR 50-60% OF LISTED USED PRICES. USED EXAMPLES OF #39 SHOULD ONLY BE PURCHASED WITH, OR SUBJECT TO, A CERTIFICATE OF AUTHENTICITY.

#40-47 ARE 1875 REPRINTS OF THE 1857-60 ISSUE.

1861 New Designs, Perf.12, Thin Paper (VF,OG+150%, VF+75% OG+75%) (C)

62B	10¢ Wash., Dark Green	...	...	600.00	350.00

1861-62 Modified Designs, Perf. 12 (VF,OG+200%, VF+100% OG+75%) (C)

63,86,92   **73,84,85B,
87,93**   **65,79,83,85,
85C,88,94**   **67,75-76,
95**   **68,89,96**

69,85E,90,97   **77,91,98**   **70,78,99**   **71,100**   **72,101**

		Unused Fine	Ave.	Used Fine	Ave.
63	1¢ Franklin, Blue	125.00	75.00	23.50	14.00
64	3¢ Washington, Pink		2200.00	500.00	300.00
64b	3¢ Rose Pink	210.00	125.00	100.00	55.00
65	3¢ Rose	70.00	40.00	2.40	1.50
67	5¢ Jefferson, Buff	5000.00		550.00	325.00
68	10¢ Washington, Yellow Green	200.00	115.00	37.50	22.50
69	12¢ Washington, Black	475.00	275.00	70.00	40.00
70	24¢ Washington, Red Lilac	650.00	400.00	110.00	60.00
70b	24¢ Steel Blue		3000.00	400.00	225.00
70c	24¢ Violet, Thin Paper		3500.00	700.00	400.00
71	30¢ Franklin, Orange	525.00	300.00	110.00	65.00
72	90¢ Washington, Blue	1200.00	700.00	285.00	160.00

#66 3¢ LAKE IS CONSIDERED A TRIAL COLOR PROOF

1861-66 New Vals. or Designs, Perf. 12 (VF,OG+200%,VF+100% OG+75%) (C)

73	2¢ Jackson, Black (1863)	145.00	75.00	45.00	25.00
75	5¢ Jefferson, Red Brn.	1800.00	1075.00	325.00	190.00
76	5¢ Brown (1863)	415.00	260.00	80.00	50.00
77	15¢ Lincoln, Black (1866)	550.00	325.00	115.00	70.00
78	24¢ Washington, Lilac/Gray Lilac ..	425.00	250.00	70.00	45.00

#74 3¢ SCARLET IS CONSIDERED A TRIAL COLOR PROOF

1867 Designs of 1861-66 with Grills of Various Sizes
(VF,OG+200%, VF+100%OG+75%) (C)

Grills consist of small pyramids impressed on the stamp and are classified by area, shape of points and number of rows of points. On Grilled-All-Over and "C" Grills, points thrust upward on FACE of stamp; on all other grills points thrust upward on BACK of stamp. Points of "Z" grill show horizontal ridges (-); other grills from "D" through "I" show vertical (I) ridges or come to a point. It is important to see a Scott catalog for details of these interesting stamps.

1867 "A" Grill (Grill All Over)
79	3¢ Washington, Rose		1500.00	875.00	525.00

1867 "C" Grill 13 x 16mm Points Up
83	3¢ Washington, Rose		2500.00	1475.00	650.00	400.00

1867 "D" Grill 12 x 14mm Points Down
84	2¢ Jackson, Black		4500.00	1750.00	1100.00
85	3¢ Washington, Rose	2250.00	1300.00	600.00	350.00

1867 "Z" Grill 11 x 14mm
85B	2¢ Jackson, Black	3350.00	1950.00	775.00	450.00
85C	3¢ Washington, Rose		3000.00	1700.00	1100.00
85E	12¢ Washington, Black	5000.00	3000.00	825.00	500.00

1867 "E" Grill 11 x 13mm
86	1¢ Franklin, Blue	1100.00	675.00	325.00	200.00
87	2¢ Jackson, Black	400.00	250.00	90.00	52.50
88	3¢ Washington, Rose	300.00	165.00	13.50	8.00
89	10¢ Washington, Green	1700.00	1000.00	210.00	1210.00
90	12¢ Washington, Black	1800.00	1050.00	235.00	135.00
91	15¢ Lincoln, Black	1800.00	1600.00	465.00	275.00

1867 "F" Grill 9 x 13mm
92	1¢ Franklin, Blue	400.00	250.00	130.00	75.00
93	2¢ Jackson, Black	160.00	90.00	35.00	20.00
94	3¢ Washington, Red	140.00	80.00	5.00	3.00
95	5¢ Jefferson, Brown	1200.00	675.00	475.00	300.00
96	10¢ Wash., Yellow Green	1000.00	575.00	165.00	100.00
97	12¢ Washington, Black	1275.00	700.00	160.00	95.00
98	15¢ Lincoln, Black	1350.00	750.00	215.00	130.00
99	24¢ Washington, Gray Lilac	2000.00	1100.00	525.00	325.00
100	30¢ Franklin, Orange	2250.00	1300.00	500.00	300.00
101	90¢ Washington, Blue	3750.00	2000.00	835.00	475.00

#102-11 ARE 1875 RE-ISSUES OF THE 1861-66 ISSUE.

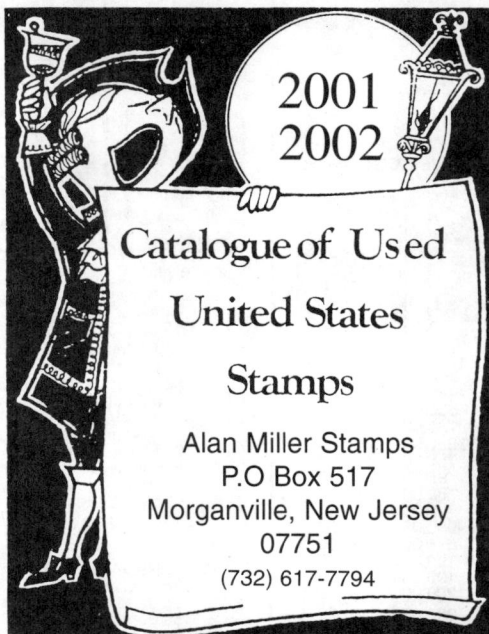

2

1869 Pictorial Issues-"G" Grill 9½ mm., Hard Wove Paper, Perf.12
(VF,OG+150%, VF+75%, OG+75%) (C)

112,123,133   113,124   114   115   116

117   118   119   120   121

Scott's		Unused		Used	
No.		Fine	Ave.	Fine	Ave.
112	1¢ Franklin, Buff	300.00	175.00	100.00	60.00
113	2¢ Horse & Rider, Brown	265.00	160.00	40.00	23.50
114	3¢ Locomotive, Ultramarine	160.00	90.00	16.50	10.00
115	6¢ Washington, Ultramarine	1150.00	700.00	150.00	90.00
116	10¢ Shield & Eagle, Yellow	800.00	475.00	110.00	65.00
117	12¢ "S.S. Adriatic", Green	800.00	475.00	115.00	70.00
118	15¢ Columbus, Brn & Blue,Ty.I	3100.00	1800.00	450.00	275.00
119	15¢ Brown & Blue, Type II	1375.00	825.00	195.00	120.00
120	24¢ Decl. of Indep., Grn & Vio	2500.00	1400.00	525.00	325.00
121	30¢ Shield, Eagle & Flags	2650.00	1500.00	400.00	240.00
122	90¢ Lincoln, Carm. & Black	4000.00	2300.00	1600.00	1000.00

1875 and 1880 Re-issues, without Grill (VF,OG+150%, VF+75%, OG+75%) (C)

123	1¢ Buff, Hard White Paper	275.00	160.00	240.00	140.00
124	2¢ Brown, Hard White Paper	365.00	200.00	350.00	210.00
133	1¢ Buff, Soft Porous Paper (1880)	140.00	85.00	165.00	95.00
133a	1¢ Brown Orange, w/o gum (1881)	160.00	110.00	135.00	75.00

#125-32 ARE 1875 RE-ISSUES OF THE 1869 ISSUE.

1870-71 National Bank Note Company Printing
-Grilled-Hard Paper (VF,OG+150%, VF+75%, OG+75%) (C)

134,145,156, 182,206   135,146,157, 178,183   136,147,158, 184,207,214   179,185   137,148,159, 186,208

138,149,160   139,150,161, 187-88,209   141,152,163, 189   143,154,165, 190,217   144,155,166, 191,218

134	1¢ Franklin, Ultramarine	675.00	400.00	90.00	55.00
135	2¢ Jackson, Red Brown	425.00	235.00	52.50	31.50
136	3¢ Washington, Green	300.00	170.00	14.00	8.50
137	6¢ Lincoln, Carmine	1600.00	900.00	350.00	210.00
138	7¢ Stanton, Vermilion (1871)	1250.00	750.00	325.00	200.00
139	10¢ Jefferson, Brown	2000.00	1200.00	500.00	300.00
140	12¢ Clay, Dull Violet	...	...	2100.00	1300.00
141	15¢ Webster, Orange	2250.00	1300.00	900.00	525.00
143	30¢ Hamilton, Black	...	3500.00	1500.00	975.00
144	90¢ Perry, Carmine	...	3500.00	1000.00	600.00

1870-72 Same as above but without Grill (VF,OG+150%, VF+75% OG+60%) (C)

145	1¢ Franklin, Ultramarine	200.00	120.00	11.00	6.50
146	2¢ Jackson, Red Brown	130.00	75.00	6.75	4.00
147	3¢ Washington, Green	130.00	75.00	1.00	.60
148	6¢ Lincoln, Carmine	250.00	145.00	16.50	9.75
149	7¢ Stanton, Vermilion (1871)	325.00	195.00	67.50	40.00
150	10¢ Jefferson, Brown	275.00	160.00	17.00	10.00
151	12¢ Clay, Dull Violet	675.00	375.00	100.00	60.00
152	15¢ Webster, Bright Orange	650.00	365.00	100.00	60.00
153	24¢ Scott, Purple	650.00	365.00	100.00	60.00
154	30¢ Hamilton, Black (1871)	1600.00	900.00	115.00	70.00
155	90¢ Perry, Carmine (1872)	1600.00	900.00	230.00	140.00

IMPORTANT NOTICE
PRIOR TO 1881, UNUSED PRICES ARE FOR STAMPS WITH PARTIAL OR NO GUM,
FOR ORIGINAL GUM, ADD % PREMIUM INDICATED IN ( ).

1870-71 National Printing - Without Secret Marks

1¢   2¢   3¢ 6¢   7¢   10¢   12¢

Arrows point to distinguishing characteristics: 1¢ ball is clear; 2¢ no spot of color; 3¢ light shading; 6¢ normal vertical lines; 7¢ no arcs of color cut around lines; 10¢ ball is clear; 12¢ normal 2.

1873 Continental Printing White Hard Paper (VF,OG+150%,VF+75%OG+60%)(C)
Same designs as preceding issue but with secret marks as shown below.

Arrows point to distinguishing characteristics: 1¢ dash in ball; 2¢ spot of color where lines join in scroll ornaments; 3¢ under part of ribbon heavily shaded; 6¢ first four vertical lines strengthened; 7¢ arcs of color cut around lines; 10¢ a crescent in the ball; 12¢ ball of 2 is crescent shaped.

Scott's		Unused		Used	
No.		Fine	Ave.	Fine	Ave.
156	1¢ Franklin, Ultramarine	100.00	62.50	2.75	1.65
157	2¢ Jackson, Brown	185.00	105.00	12.00	7.25
158	3¢ Washington, Green	55.00	30.00	.45	.30
159	6¢ Lincoln, Dull Pink	200.00	110.00	15.00	9.00
160	7¢ Stanton, Org. Vermilion	425.00	235.00	57.50	32.50
161	10¢ Jefferson, Brown	285.00	170.00	13.50	8.50
162	12¢ Clay, Blackish Violet	675.00	375.00	75.00	45.00
163	15¢ Webster, Yellow Orange	725.00	400.00	70.00	42.50
165	30¢ Hamilton, Gray Black	775.00	450.00	80.00	47.50
166	90¢ Perry, Rose Carmine	1300.00	775.00	185.00	110.00

1875 Continental Printing-Yellowish Hard Paper
(VF,OG+150%,VF+75% OG+60%) (C)

178	2¢ Jackson, Vermilion	160.00	95.00	7.50	4.50
179	5¢ Taylor, Blue	225.00	140.00	13.00	7.50

1879-87 American Printing - Continental Design, Soft Porous Paper
(VF,OG+150%, VF + 75% OG + 60%) (C)

Soft porous paper is less transparent than hard paper.
When held to the light it usually appears mottled, somewhat like newsprint.

182	1¢ Franklin, Dark Ultramarine	120.00	70.00	1.75	1.10
183	2¢ Jackson, Vermilion	60.00	33.50	1.75	1.10
184	3¢ Washington, Green	50.00	30.00	.40	.25
185	5¢ Taylor, Blue	240.00	130.00	9.75	5.75
186	6¢ Lincoln, Pink	400.00	225.00	15.00	9.00
187	10¢ Brown (no secret mark)	800.00	435.00	17.50	10.75
188	10¢ Brown (secret mark)	600.00	350.00	17.50	10.75
189	15¢ Webster, Red Orange (1881)	170.00	95.00	18.00	11.00
190	30¢ Hamilton, Full Black (1881)	450.00	250.00	42.50	25.00
191	90¢ Perry, Carmine (1887)	1000.00	575.00	190.00	110.00

#166-77,180-81,192-204 ARE 1875-80 RE-ISSUES.

212   210,213   211,215   205,216

1882 New Design (VF NH+75%, VF OG & Used+50%) (C)

Scott's		NH	Unused,OG		Used	
No.		Fine	Fine	Ave.	Fine	Ave.
205	5¢ Garfield, Yel. Brn.	375.00	175.00	100.00	5.75	3.50

1881-82 Re-engraved Designs (VF NH+75%, VF OG & Used+60%) (C)

206	1¢ Franklin, Gray Blue	115.00	55.00	33.50	.75	.45
207	3¢ Washington, Blue Grn	100.00	50.00	30.00	.45	.30
208	6¢ Lincoln, Rose (1882)	750.00	350.00	210.00	52.50	31.50
208a	6¢ Brown Red (1883)	625.00	300.00	180.00	80.00	47.50
209	10¢ Jefferson, Brown (1882)	225.00	110.00	65.00	3.75	2.25
209b	10¢ Black Brown	700.00	325.00	190.00	35.00	20.00

1883-87 New Designs (VF NH+75%, VF OG & Used + 60%) (C)

210	2¢ Washington Red Brn	65.00	32.50	19.00	.30	.20
211	4¢ Jackson, Blue Green	350.00	170.00	100.00	10.75	6.50
212	1¢ Franklin, Ultramarine (1887)	175.00	85.00	50.00	.95	.60

1887-88 Revised Colors (VF NH+75%, VF OG & Used +60%) (C)

213	2¢ Washington, Green (1887)	60.00	30.00	17.50	.35	.25
214	3¢ Wash., Vermilion (1887)	115.00	57.50	35.00	40.00	24.00
215	4¢ Jackson, Carmine (1888)	300.00	150.00	90.00	14.00	8.50
216	5¢ Garfield, Indigo (1888)	325.00	165.00	100.00	8.50	5.00
217	30¢ Hamilton, Org.Brn (1888)	650.00	325.00	195.00	75.00	43.50
218	90¢ Perry, Purple (1888)	1500.00	800.00	475.00	165.00	100.00

#205C, 211B and 211D are Special Printings

NOTE: Deduct 40% for unused, without gum on #205-218.

1890-1893 No Triangles (VF Used + 60%) (C)

219 | 219D,220 | 221 | 222

223 | 224 | 225 | 226

227 | 228 | 229

Scott's No.		NH		Unused		Used
		VF	F-VF	VF	F-VF	FVF
219	1¢ Franklin, Dull Blue	52.50	33.50	29.00	18.50	.30
219D	2¢ Washington, Lake	425.00	270.00	225.00	140.00	.65
220	2¢ Carmine	50.00	30.00	27.50	17.00	.30
220a	2¢ Cap on left "2"	160.00	100.00	85.00	52.50	2.00
220c	2¢ Cap on both "2's"	800.00	500.00	395.00	250.00	14.50
221	3¢ Jackson, Purple	160.00	100.00	80.00	50.00	5.25
222	4¢ Lincoln, Dark Brn	160.00	100.00	80.00	50.00	2.00
223	5¢ Grant, Chocolate	160.00	100.00	80.00	50.00	2.00
224	6¢ Garfield, Brn Red	170.00	105.00	85.00	52.50	16.00
225	8¢ Sherman, Lilac (1893)	130.00	80.00	65.00	40.00	9.50
226	10¢ Webster, Green	315.00	200.00	175.00	110.00	2.85
227	15¢ Clay, Indigo	425.00	260.00	215.00	130.00	16.50
228	30¢ Jefferson, Black	700.00	450.00	360.00	225.00	21.00
229	90¢ Perry, Orange	1075.00	675.00	535.00	335.00	90.00

1893 Columbian Issue (VF Used + 60%) (B)

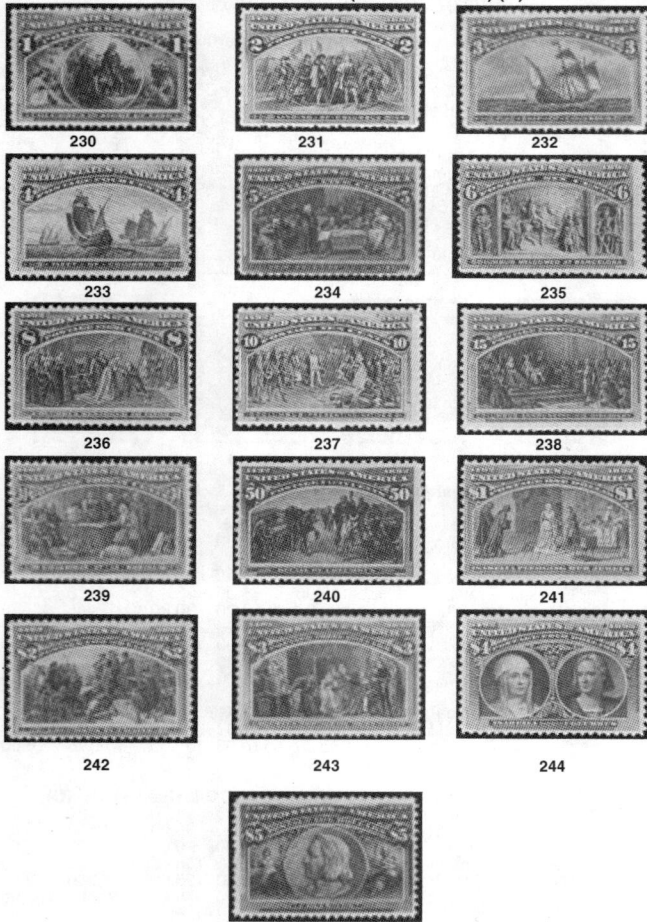

230 | 231 | 232

233 | 234 | 235

236 | 237 | 238

239 | 240 | 241

242 | 243 | 244

245

1893 Columbian Issue (VF Used + 60%) (B)

Scott's No.		NH		Unused		Used
		VF	F-VF	VF	F-VF	F-VF
230	1¢ Blue	55.00	35.00	27.50	17.50	.40
231	2¢ Violet	47.50	31.50	24.00	15.75	.25
231v	2¢ Violet, "Broken Hat" 3rd person to left of Columbus has a triangular "cut" in his hat	160.00	100.00	80.00	50.00	.80
232	3¢ Green	140.00	90.00	70.00	45.00	11.75
233	4¢ Ultramarine	210.00	130.00	105.00	65.00	6.75
234	5¢ Chocolate	225.00	140.00	110.00	70.00	6.50
235	6¢ Purple	210.00	135.00	105.00	67.50	18.50
236	8¢ Magenta	195.00	120.00	95.00	60.00	9.50
237	10¢ Black Brown	325.00	200.00	160.00	100.00	7.00
238	15¢ Dark Green	575.00	360.00	285.00	180.00	55.00
239	30¢ Orange Brown	775.00	475.00	380.00	240.00	70.00
240	50¢ Slate Blue	1450.00	900.00	725.00	450.00	135.00
241	$1 Salmon .... ……	3500.00	2200.00	1700.00	1100.00	500.00
242	$2 Brown Red	3800.00	2400.00	1900.00	1200.00	475.00
243	$3 Yellow Green	6350.00	4000.00	3150.00	2000.00	850.00
244	$4 Crimson Lake	8000.00	5000.00	4000.00	2500.00	1100.00
245	$5 Black	9250.00	5850.00	4650.00	2950.00	1200.00

1894 Issue - Triangles - No Watermark (VF Used + 75%) (C)

246-47,264 279 | 248-52,265-67, 279B | 253,268 | 254,269,280 | 255,270,281

256,271,282 | 257,272 | 258,273,282C-83 | 259,274,284

260,275 | 261-61A,276-76A | 262,277 | 263,278

246	1¢ Franklin, Ultramarine	67.50	40.00	35.00	21.00	3.95
247	1¢ Blue	145.00	85.00	75.00	45.00	2.00
248	2¢ Wash., Pink, Tri. A	57.50	35.00	30.00	18.50	3.00
249	2¢ Carmine Lake, Tri. A	315.00	190.00	165.00	100.00	2.10
250	2¢ Carmine, Triangle A	67.50	40.00	35.00	21.50	.50
251	2¢ Carmine, Triangle B	525.00	325.00	270.00	165.00	3.25
252	2¢ Carmine, TriC, Type III	235.00	145.00	130.00	80.00	3.50
253	3¢ Jackson, Purple	215.00	135.00	120.00	75.00	7.75
254	4¢ Lincoln, Dark Brown	280.00	170.00	145.00	90.00	3.75
255	5¢ Grant, Chocolate	200.00	125.00	110.00	70.00	4.00
256	6¢ Garfield, Dull Brown	315.00	200.00	175.00	110.00	18.00
257	8¢ Sherman, Violet Brn	290.00	180.00	160.00	100.00	12.50
258	10¢ Webster, Dark Grn	500.00	315.00	265.00	165.00	9.75
259	15¢ Clay, Dark Blue	595.00	380.00	315.00	200.00	40.00
260	50¢ Jefferson, Orange	900.00	575.00	475.00	300.00	80.00
261	$1 Perry, Black, Type I	1900.00	1175.00	1050.00	650.00	225.00
261A	$1 Black, Type II	4500.00	2850.00	2350.00	1500.00	475.00
262	$2 Madison, Bright Blue	6500.00	4000.00	3450.00	2100.00	675.00
263	$5 Marshall, Dark Green	9750.00	6250.00	5000.00	3250.00	1450.00

Triangle Varieties on the 2¢ Stamps

Triangle A | Triangle B | Triangle C

TRIANGLE A - The horizontal background lines run across the triangle and are of the same thickness within the triangle as the background lines.

TRIANGLE B - Horizontal lines cross the triangle but are thinner within the triangle than the background lines.

TRIANGLE C - The horizontal lines do not cross the triangle and the lines within the triangle are as thin as in Triangle B.

5

Circle Varieties on the $1 Stamps

Type I	Type II

Types of $1.00 stamps. Type I, the circles enclosing "$1" are broken where they meet the curved lines below "One Dollar." Type II, the circles are complete.

DOUBLE-LINE WATERMARK
This illustration shows a block of 15 with the Double Line watermark. Since only 90 letters were used per 100 stamps, they appear in various positions on the stamps.

1895 Same Designs - Double Line Wmk. (VF Used + 60%) (C)

Scott's No.		VF	NH F-VF	Unused VF	F-VF	Used F-VF
264	1¢ Franklin, Blue	13.50	8.50	7.50	4.75	.25
265	2¢ Wash., Carmine, Tri .A	65.00	43.50	35.00	23.00	.80
266	2¢ Carmine, Triangle B	67.50	45.00	37.50	24.00	3.00
267	2¢ Carmine,Triangle C Type III	11.50	7.25	6.25	4.00	.25
268	3¢ Jackson, Purple	75.00	47.50	42.50	27.50	1.00
269	4¢ Lincoln, Dark Brown	85.00	53.50	46.50	29.50	1.40
270	5¢ Grant, Chocolate	85.00	53.50	46.50	29.50	1.65
271	6¢ Garfield, Dull Brown	190.00	120.00	105.00	65.00	4.25
272	8¢ Sherman, Violet Brn	135.00	85.00	70.00	45.00	1.10
273	10¢ Webster, Dark Green	185.00	115.00	100.00	62.50	1.30
274	15¢ Clay, Dark Blue	450.00	275.00	240.00	150.00	7.50
275	50¢ Jefferson, Orange	635.00	395.00	330.00	210.00	17.50
276	$1 Perry, Black, Type I	1300.00	800.00	675.00	425.00	52.50
276A	$1 Black, Type II	2650.00	1700.00	1400.00	900.00	120.00
277	$2 Madison, Bright Blue	2150.00	1450.00	1150.00	800.00	275.00
278	$5 Marshall, Dark Green	5100.00	3250.00	2600.00	1650.00	375.00

1897-1903 NEW Colors - Double Line Wmk. (VF Used + 60%) (C)

279	1¢ Franklin, Green (1898)	21.00	13.50	11.75	7.50	.25
279B	2¢ Wash., Red Tri C, Ty IV,	21.00	13.50	11.75	7.50	.25
279Be	2¢ Booklet Pane of 6, Triangle C, Type IV	850.00	550.00	475.00	315.00	...
280	4¢ Lincoln,Rose Brown (1898)	70.00	45.00	38.50	24.50	.80
281	5¢ Grant, Dark Blue (1898)	77.50	49.00	45.00	27.50	.70
282	6¢ Garfield, Lake (1898)	90.00	57.50	50.00	32.50	2.00
282a	6¢ Purplish Lake	135.00	85.00	70.00	45.00	3.00
282C	10¢ Webster, Brown, Type I (1898)	425.00	260.00	225.00	140.00	2.25
283	10¢ Orange Brn.,Ty.II (1898)	250.00	160.00	130.00	85.00	1.90
284	15¢ Clay, Olive Green (1898)	315.00	200.00	175.00	110.00	6.50

1898 Trans-Mississippi Issue (VF Used + 60%) (B)

285	286	287

288	289	290

291	292	293

285	1¢ Marquette, Green	65.00	41.50	35.00	22.50	5.25
285	Arrow Block of 4	275.00	180.00	150.00	95.00	...
285	Plate Block of 4	515.00	325.00	280.00	180.00	...
286	2¢ Farming, Copper Red	55.00	35.00	31.00	20.00	1.30
286	Arrow Block of 4	250.00	160.00	140.00	90.00	...
286	Plate Block of 4	425.00	265.00	235.00	150.00	...
287	4¢ Indian, Orange	330.00	210.00	175.00	110.00	19.50
288	5¢ Fremont, Dull Blue	330.00	210.00	175.00	110.00	16.50
289	8¢ Wagon Train, Vio. Brn.	460.00	285.00	240.00	150.00	30.00
290	10¢ Emigration, Gray Vio.	460.00	285.00	240.00	150.00	17.50

1898 Trans-Mississippi Issue (VF Used + 60%) (B)

Scott's No.		VF	NH F-VF	Unused VF	F-VF	Used F-VF
291	50¢ Mining, Sage Green	1550.00	950.00	800.00	500.00	140.00
292	$1 Cattle in Storm, Black	2700.00	1750.00	1450.00	900.00	415.00
293	$2 Bridge, Orange Brn.	5200.00	3300.00	2600.00	1650.00	700.00

Note: See # 3209-3210 for multi-color issues

1901 Pan-American Issue VF Used + 60% (B)

294	295	296

297	298	299

294-99	Set of 6	1125.00	725.00	600.00	375.00	86.50
294	1¢ Steamship, Grn. & Blk.	47.50	28.50	26.00	16.00	3.25
294	Arrow Block of 4	200.00	135.00	115.00	75.00	...
294	Plate Block of 6	500.00	325.00	280.00	180.00	...
295	2¢ Train, Carmine & Blk.	38.50	25.00	21.00	13.50	.95
295	Arrow Block of 4	190.00	125.00	105.00	67.50	...
295	Plate Block of 6	550.00	350.00	300.00	190.00	...
296	4¢ Auto, Choc. & Blk.	200.00	125.00	105.00	65.00	14.00
297	5¢ Bridge, Ultra & Black	230.00	150.00	125.00	77.50	12.00
298	8¢ Canal, Brn. Vio & Blk.	290.00	185.00	150.00	95.00	40.00
299	10¢ Steamship, Brn. & Blk.	400.00	250.00	210.00	130.00	21.50

1902-03 Issue Perf. 12 VF Used + 60% (C)

300,314	301	302	303	304,315

305	306	307	308	309

310	311	312,479	313,480	319

300	1¢ Franklin, Blue Green	22.50	14.50	12.50	8.00	.25
300	Plate Block of 6	360.00	230.00	225.00	140.00	...
300b	1¢ Booklet Pane of 6	1150.00	700.00	675.00	425.00	...
301	2¢ Washington, Carmine	31.50	19.50	17.00	10.75	.25
301	Plate Block of 6	475.00	290.00	260.00	160.00	...
301c	2¢ Booklet Pane of 6	1100.00	700.00	600.00	375.00	...
302	3¢ Jackson, Bright Violet	120.00	75.00	65.00	40.00	2.50
303	4¢ Grant, Brown	130.00	80.00	67.50	42.50	1.25
304	5¢ Lincoln, Blue	130.00	80.00	67.50	42.50	1.35
305	6¢ Garfield, Claret	145.00	95.00	80.00	50.00	2.40
306	8¢ M. Wash., Violet Black	90.00	57.50	48.50	29.50	1.80
307	10¢ Webster, Red Brown	135.00	85.00	72.50	45.00	1.60
308	13¢ B. Harrison, Purp. Black	95.00	60.00	52.50	32.50	7.00
309	15¢ Clay, Olive Green	350.00	220.00	190.00	120.00	5.25
310	50¢ Jefferson, Orange	975.00	600.00	515.00	325.00	20.00
311	$1 Farragut, Black	1600.00	950.00	835.00	525.00	45.00
312	$2 Madison, Dark Blue	2600.00	1600.00	1300.00	800.00	150.00
313	$5 Marshall, Dark Green	6250.00	3850.00	3150.00	2000.00	525.00

1906-08 Same Designs, Imperforate VF Used + 30% (B)

314	1¢ Franklin, Blue Green	46.50	35.00	24.50	18.50	16.00
314	Arrow Block of 4	210.00	150.00	110.00	85.00	...
314	Center Line Block of 4	335.00	250.00	185.00	140.00	...
314	Plate Block of 6	350.00	260.00	195.00	150.00	...
315	5¢ Lincoln, Blue	750.00	525.00	435.00	300.00	400.00

* Genuinely used examples of #315 are rare. Copies should have contemporary cancels and be purchased with, or subject to, a certificate of authenticity.

1903 Shield Issue, Perforated 12 VF Used + 60% (C)

319	2¢ Carmine, Type I	14.50	9.00	8.00	5.00	.25
319	Plate Block of 6	190.00	125.00	110.00	70.00	...
319g	2¢ Booklet Pane of 6, Ty.I	250.00	155.00	160.00	95.00	...
319f	2¢ Lake, Type II	26.50	16.00	15.00	8.75	.50
319h	2¢ Booklet Pane of 6, Ty.II	575.00	365.00	315.00	200.00	...

1906 Shield Issue, Imperforate VF Used + 30% (B)

Scott's No.		NH VF	NH F-VF	Unused VF	Unused F-VF	Used F-VF
320	2¢ Carmine, Type I	47.50	35.00	26.50	20.00	14.75
320	Arrow Block of 4	215.00	160.00	120.00	90.00	...
320	Center Line Block of 4	325.00	235.00	180.00	135.00	...
320	Plate Block of 6	375.00	280.00	225.00	170.00	...
320a	2¢ Lake, Type II	130.00	95.00	70.00	52.50	40.00

1904 Louisiana Purchase Issue VF Used + 60% (B)

323

324

325

326

327

Scott's No.		NH VF	NH F-VF	Unused VF	Unused F-VF	Used F-VF
323-27	**Set of 5**	**865.00**	**560.00**	**465.00**	**295.00**	**73.50**
323	1¢ Livingston, Green	62.50	39.50	35.00	22.50	4.25
323	Arrow Block of 4	280.00	175.00	160.00	100.00	...
323	Plate Block of 4	365.00	235.00	215.00	135.00	...
324	2¢ Jefferson, Carmine	55.00	33.50	29.50	18.50	1.75
324	Arrow Block of 4	235.00	150.00	130.00	80.00	...
324	Plate Block of 4	375.00	240.00	215.00	135.00	...
325	3¢ Monroe, Violet	195.00	125.00	105.00	67.50	26.50
326	5¢ McKinley, Blue	210.00	135.00	110.00	70.00	18.50
327	10¢ Map, Brown	400.00	260.00	215.00	135.00	28.50

1907 Jamestown Issue VF Used + 100% (C)

328

329

330

Scott's No.		NH VF	NH F-VF	Unused VF	Unused F-VF	Used F-VF
328-30	**Set of 3**	**435.00**	**230.00**	**240.00**	**125.00**	**30.00**
328	1¢ John Smith, Green	62.50	31.50	35.00	17.50	3.25
328	Arrow Block of 4	275.00	140.00	150.00	75.00	...
328	Plate Block of 6	575.00	300.00	315.00	160.00	...
329	2¢ Jamestown, Carmine	80.00	40.00	45.00	22.50	3.25
329	Arrow Block of 4	365.00	190.00	195.00	100.00	...
329	Plate Block of 6	800.00	400.00	450.00	225.00	...
330	5¢ Pocahontas, Blue	325.00	170.00	175.00	90.00	25.00

1908-09 Washington-Franklins Double Line Wmk. - Perf. 12 VF Used + 60% (B)

331,343,348,352, 357,374,383,385, 387,390,392,519

332,344,349,353, 358,375,384,386, 388,391,393

333,345,359,376, 389,394,426,445, 456,464,483,489, 493-94,501-2, 529-30,535,541

334,346,350,354, 377,395,427,446, 457,465,495,503

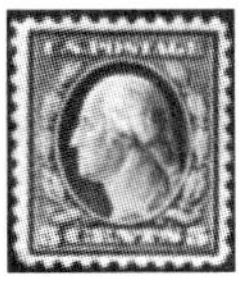
335,347,351.355, 361,378,396,428, 447,458,466,496, 504-5

336,362,379,429, 468,506

337,380

338,356,364,381

339,365

340,366,382

341

342

1908-09 Wash-Franklins Double Line Wmk. - Perf. 12 VF Used + 60% (B)

Scott's No.		NH VF	NH F-VF	Unused VF	Unused F-VF	Used F-VF
331	1¢ Franklin, Green	14.50	9.00	8.75	5.50	.15
331	Plate Block of 6	130.00	82.50	80.00	50.00	...
331a	1¢ Booklet Pane of 6	335.00	215.00	210.00	130.00	...
332	2¢ Washington, Carmine	14.50	9.00	8.00	5.00	.15
332	Plate Block of 6	140.00	82.50	80.00	50.00	...
332a	2¢ Booklet Pane of 6	290.00	190.00	180.00	115.00	...
333	3¢ Deep Violet	67.50	41.50	36.50	23.50	2.85
333	Plate Block of 6	700.00	450.00	395.00	250.00	...
334	4¢ Orange Brown	85.00	55.00	47.50	30.00	1.00
335	5¢ Blue	100.00	62.50	55.00	35.00	2.00
336	6¢ Red Orange (1909)	135.00	85.00	75.00	47.50	4.75
337	8¢ Olive Green	100.00	62.50	55.00	35.00	3.00
338	10¢ Yellow (1909)	145.00	90.00	79.50	49.50	1.35
339	13¢ Blue Green (1909)	90.00	55.00	48.50	31.00	18.00
340	15¢ Ultramarine (1909)	130.00	80.00	70.00	45.00	5.75
341	50¢ Violet (1909)	700.00	450.00	375.00	240.00	17.00
342	$1 Violet Brown (1909)	1100.00	675.00	600.00	375.00	65.00

1908-09 Series, Double Line Watermark - Imperforate VF Used + 30% (B)

Scott's No.		NH VF	NH F-VF	Unused VF	Unused F-VF	Used F-VF
343	1¢ Franklin, Green	14.00	10.50	7.95	6.00	3.50
343	Arrow Block of 4	62.50	45.00	36.00	27.50	...
343	Center Line Block or 4	75.00	55.00	42.50	32.50	...
343	Plate Block of 6	100.00	75.00	59.50	45.00	...
344	2¢ Washington, Carmine	20.00	14.00	12.00	8.50	3.25
344	Arrow Block of 4	95.00	65.00	55.00	40.00	...
344	Center Line Block of 4	110.00	75.00	60.00	45.00	...
344	Plate Block of 6	200.00	145.00	120.00	90.00	...
345	3¢ Deep Violet (1909)	41.50	31.50	25.00	18.50	19.50
345	Arrow Block of 4	185.00	140.00	110.00	85.00	...
345	Center Line Block of 4	210.00	165.00	130.00	100.00	...
345	Plate Block of 6	385.00	295.00	240.00	180.00	...
346	4¢ Orange Brown (1909)	57.50	42.50	33.50	25.00	22.50
346	Arrow Block of 4	270.00	195.00	160.00	120.00	...
346	Center Line Block of 4	325.00	250.00	195.00	150.00	...
346	Plate Block of 6	485.00	375.00	300.00	225.00	...
347	5¢ Blue	100.00	75.00	60.00	45.00	30.00
347	Arrow Block of 4	465.00	350.00	280.00	215.00	...
347	Center Line Block of 4	535.00	400.00	325.00	250.00	...
347	Plate Block of 6	775.00	575.00	475.00	350.00	...

1908-10 Coils, Double Line Watermark. - Perf. 12 Horiz. VF Used + 60% (C)

Scott's No.		NH VF	NH F-VF	Unused VF	Unused F-VF	Used F-VF
348	1¢ Franklin, Green	72.50	45.00	40.00	25.00	14.00
348	Pair	175.00	110.00	100.00	65.00	...
348	Line Pair	535.00	325.00	300.00	185.00	...
349	2¢ Wash.,Carmine(1909)	125.00	80.00	70.00	45.00	8.00
349	Pair	315.00	200.00	170.00	110.00	...
349	Line Pair	875.00	550.00	525.00	325.00	...
350	4¢ Orange Brown (1910)	290.00	180.00	160.00	100.00	80.00
350	Pair	725.00	450.00	385.00	250.00	...
351	5¢ Blue (1909)	325.00	210.00	180.00	115.00	110.00
351	Pair	750.00	500.00	450.00	285.00	...

1909 Coils, Double Line Watermark - Perf. 12 Vert. VF Used + 60% (C)

Scott's No.		NH VF	NH F-VF	Unused VF	Unused F-VF	Used F-VF
352	1¢ Franklin, Green	145.00	90.00	80.00	50.00	30.00
352	Pair	350.00	225.00	200.00	125.00	...
352	Line Pair	1150.00	700.00	650.00	400.00	...
353	2¢ Washington, Carmine	160.00	100.00	90.00	57.50	8.00
353	Pair	400.00	250.00	225.00	130.00	...
353	Line Pair	1050.00	650.00	565.00	365.00	...
354	4¢ Orange Brown	350.00	225.00	195.00	125.00	57.50
354	Pair	850.00	550.00	475.00	300.00	...
355	5¢ Blue	375.00	235.00	210.00	130.00	75.00
355	Pair	900.00	575.00	515.00	315.00	...
356	10¢ Yellow	4250.00	2650.00	2400.00	1500.00	875.00

(#348-56, should be purchased with, or subject to, a certificate of authenticity.)

1909 "Blue Papers", Double Line Wmk., Perf. 12 VF Used + 60% (B)

Scott's No.		NH VF	NH F-VF	Unused VF	Unused F-VF	Used F-VF
357	1¢ Franklin, Green	210.00	130.00	130.00	80.00	90.00
358	2¢ Washington, Carmine	210.00	130.00	130.00	80.00	90.00
359	3¢ Deep Violet	...	2500.00	2300.00	1450.00	...
361	5¢ Blue	...	5500.00	...	3350.00	...
362	6¢ Red Orange	...	1750.00	1850.00	1075.00	1200.00
364	10¢ Yellow	...	2000.00	2150.00	1250.00	1350.00
365	13¢ Blue Green	...	3500.00	...	2150.00	1700.00
366	15¢ Pale Ultramarine	...	1600.00	1700.00	1000.00	1200.00

#360 AND #363 WERE NOT REGULARLY ISSUED

*** Blue Papers, which were printed on experimental paper with approximately 35% rag content, actually have a grayish appearance which can best be observed by looking at the stamps from the gum side. Additionally, the watermark is more clearly visible than on the stamps printed on regular paper (#331-340). The stamps are also noted for having carbon specks imbedded in the texture of the paper. Blue papers should be purchased with, or subject to, a certificate of authenticity.**

1909 Commemoratives (Used Perf.VF+40%, Imperf.VF+30%) (B)

367-69

370-71

372-73

Scott's No.		NH VF	NH F-VF	Unused VF	Unused F-VF	Used F-VF
367	2¢ Lincoln, Perf. 12	10.50	7.50	6.00	4.25	1.75
367	Plate Block of 6	230.00	165.00	150.00	110.00	...
368	2¢ Lincoln, Imperf.	50.00	37.50	30.00	22.50	17.50
368	Arrow Block of 4	215.00	160.00	130.00	100.00	...
368	Center Line Block of 4	275.00	210.00	175.00	130.00	...
368	Plate Block of 6	340.00	250.00	215.00	160.00	...
369	2¢ Bluish Paper, Perf. 12	450.00	300.00	265.00	175.00	195.00

1909 Commemoratives (Used Perf.VF+40%, Imperf.VF+30%) (B)

Scott's No.		NH VF	NH F-VF	Unused VF	Unused F-VF	Used F-VF
370	2¢ Alaska-Yukon, Perf. 12	17.50	12.50	10.75	7.50	1.50
370	Plate Block of 6	365.00	250.00	220.00	165.00	...
371	2¢ Alaska-Yukon, Imperf.	80.00	57.50	45.00	33.50	21.50
371	Arrow Block of 4	335.00	240.00	200.00	150.00	...
371	Center Line Block of 4	385.00	300.00	240.00	190.00	...
371	Plate Block of 6	565.00	425.00	360.00	275.00	...
372	2¢ Hudson-Fulton, Perf. 12	24.00	17.50	14.00	10.00	3.50
372	Plate Block of 6	525.00	375.00	315.00	225.00	...
373	2¢ Hudson-Fulton, Imperf.	75.00	57.50	45.00	35.00	21.50
373	Arrow Block of 4	340.00	260.00	210.00	160.00	...
373	Center Line Block of 4	500.00	385.00	315.00	240.00	...
373	Plate Block of 6	525.00	400.00	330.00	250.00	...

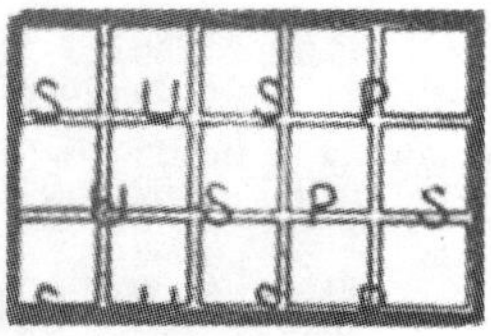

SINGLE-LINE WATERMARK
This illustration shows a block of 15 stamps with the Single Line Watermark. The watermark appears in various positions on the stamps.

1910-11 Single Line Watermark Perf 12, VF Used + 60% (B)

Scott's No.		NH VF	NH F-VF	Unused VF	Unused F-VF	Used F-VF
374	1¢ Franklin, Green	16.00	9.50	8.75	5.50	.20
374	Plate Block of 6	140.00	90.00	95.00	60.00	...
374a	1¢ Booklet Pane of 6	280.00	175.00	175.00	110.00	...
375	2¢ Washington, Carmine	14.50	9.00	8.25	5.25	.20
375	Plate Block of 6	155.00	100.00	100.00	65.00	...
375a	2¢ Booklet Pane of 6	240.00	150.00	150.00	95.00	...
376	3¢ Deep Violet (1911)	38.50	25.00	23.50	15.00	1.75
376	Plate Block of 6	335.00	210.00	220.00	140.00	...
377	4¢ Brown (1911)	57.50	37.50	35.00	22.50	.80
377	Plate Block of 6	415.00	265.00	275.00	175.00	...
378	5¢ Blue (1911)	57.50	37.50	35.00	22.50	.60
378	Plate Block of 6	475.00	300.00	315.00	200.00	...
379	6¢ Red Orange (1911)	70.00	45.00	41.50	26.50	.80
380	8¢ Olive Green (1911)	235.00	145.00	135.00	85.00	11.00
381	10¢ Yellow (1911)	240.00	150.00	145.00	90.00	4.00
382	15¢ Pale Ultramarine (1911)	525.00	325.00	325.00	200.00	14.50

1910 Single Line Wmk., Imperf. VF Used + 30% (B)

Scott's No.		NH VF	NH F-VF	Unused VF	Unused F-VF	Used F-VF
383	1¢ Franklin, Green	6.50	5.00	4.00	3.00	2.00
383	Arrow Block of 4	30.00	22.50	19.00	14.00	...
383	Center Line Block of 4	52.50	40.00	32.50	25.00	...
383	Plate Block of 6	80.00	60.00	52.50	40.00	...
384	2¢ Washington, Carmine	11.50	9.00	7.00	5.50	2.25
384	Arrow Block of 4	52.50	40.00	32.50	25.00	...
384	Center Line Block of 4	90.00	70.00	58.50	45.00	...
384	Plate Block of 6	225.00	170.00	145.00	110.00	...

1910 Coils S. Line Wmk. - Perf. 12 Horiz. VF Used + 60% (C)

Scott's No.		NH VF	NH F-VF	Unused VF	Unused F-VF	Used F-VF
385	1¢ Franklin, Green	57.50	37.50	35.00	22.50	12.00
385	Pair	150.00	100.00	90.00	60.00	...
385	Line Pair	700.00	450.00	425.00	275.00	...
386	2¢ Washington, Carmine	105.00	65.00	63.50	40.00	16.50
386	Pair	375.00	240.00	235.00	150.00	...

1910-11 Coils S. Line Wmk. - Perf. 12 Vert. VF Used + 60% (C)

Scott's No.		NH VF	NH F-VF	Unused VF	Unused F-VF	Used F-VF
387	1¢ Franklin, Green	240.00	150.00	145.00	90.00	40.00
387	Pair	575.00	375.00	350.00	225.00	...
387	Line Pair	1050.00	650.00	625.00	400.00	...
388	2¢ Washington, Carmine	1475.00	950.00	850.00	550.00	300.00
389	3¢ Washington, Deep Violet (1911)	...	**USED FINE**			**8500.00**

(Examples of #388 and 389 must be purchased with, or subject to, a certificate.)

1910 Coils S. Line Wmk. - Perf. 8½ Horizontally VF Used + 60% (B)

Scott's No.		NH VF	NH F-VF	Unused VF	Unused F-VF	Used F-VF
390	1¢ Franklin, Green	9.75	6.25	5.75	3.75	4.50
390	Pair	22.75	14.50	13.75	8.75	...
390	Line Pair	80.00	50.00	47.50	30.00	...
391	2¢ Washington, Carmine	67.50	43.50	41.50	26.50	10.50
391	Pair	160.00	105.00	100.00	65.00	...
391	Line Pair	435.00	275.00	260.00	165.00	...

1910-13 Coils S. Line Wmk. - Perf. 8½ Vertically VF Used + 60% (B)

Scott's No.		NH VF	NH F-VF	Unused VF	Unused F-VF	Used F-VF
392	1¢ Franklin, Green	43.50	28.50	27.50	17.50	16.50
392	Pair	110.00	72.50	67.50	43.50	...
392	Line Pair	280.00	180.00	170.00	110.00	...
393	2¢ Washington, Carmine	81.50	51.50	50.00	31.50	8.00
393	Pair	230.00	140.00	140.00	87.50	...
393	Line Pair	495.00	310.00	300.00	190.00	...
394	3¢ Deep Violet (1911)	105.00	65.00	62.50	40.00	42.50
394	Pair	270.00	165.00	160.00	100.00	...
394	Line Pair	700.00	450.00	425.00	275.00	...
395	4¢ Brown (1912)	105.00	65.00	62.50	40.00	42.50
395	Pair	270.00	165.00	160.00	100.00	...
395	Line Pair	700.00	450.00	425.00	275.00	...
396	5¢ Blue (1913)	105.00	65.00	62.50	40.00	42.50
396	Pair	270.00	165.00	160.00	100.00	...
396	Line Pair	700.00	450.00	425.00	275.00	...

1913 Panama-Pacific, Perf. 12 VF Used + 60% (B)

397,401

398,402

399,403

400,400A,404

1913 Panama-Pacific, Perf. 12 VF Used + 60% (B)

Scott's No.		NH VF	NH F-VF	Unused VF	Unused F-VF	Used F-VF
397-400A	**Set of 5**	**1000.00**	**635.00**	**575.00**	**365.00**	**41.50**
397	1¢ Balboa, Green	36.50	23.50	21.50	13.50	1.50
397	Plate Block of 6	315.00	210.00	200.00	130.00	...
398	2¢ Panama Canal, Carmine	39.50	25.00	23.50	15.00	.50
398	Plate Block of 6	500.00	325.00	325.00	210.00	...
399	5¢ Golden Gate, Blue	160.00	100.00	87.50	55.00	8.00
400	10¢ San Fran., Orange Yel	300.00	190.00	170.00	110.00	19.50
400A	10¢ Orange	535.00	335.00	315.00	195.00	15.00

1914-15 Panama-Pacific, Perf. 10 VF Used + 60% (B)

Scott's No.		NH VF	NH F-VF	Unused VF	Unused F-VF	Used F-VF
401-04	**Set of 4**	**2550.00**	**1625.00**	**1525.00**	**975.00**	**72.50**
401	1¢ Balboa, Green	51.50	32.50	31.50	20.00	5.50
401	Plate Block of 6	665.00	415.00	425.00	260.00	...
402	2¢ Panama, Carmine (1915)	155.00	105.00	90.00	57.50	1.70
403	5¢ Golden Gate, Blue(1915)	375.00	240.00	225.00	140.00	16.00
404	10¢ San Fran.,Orange(1915)	2100.00	1350.00	1250.00	800.00	52.50

1912-14 Single Line Wmk. - Perf. 12 VF Used + 50% (B)

405,408,410,412, 424,441,443,448, 452,462,481,486, 490,498,525,531, 536,538,542-45

406,409,411,413, 425,442,444, 449-50,453-55, 463,482,487-88, 491-92,499-500, 526-28B,532-34B, 539-40,546

407,430,469,507

414,431,470,508

415,432,471,509

416,433,472,497,

434,473,511

417,435,474,512

513

418,437,475,514

419,438,476,515

420,439,516

421-22,440,477,517

423,460,478,518

NOTE: THE 1¢ TO 7¢ STAMPS FROM 1912-21 PICTURE WASHINGTON. THE 8¢ TO $5 STAMPS PICTURE FRANKLIN.

Scott's No.		NH VF	NH F-VF	Unused VF	Unused F-VF	Used F-VF
405	1¢ Washington, Green	11.50	7.50	6.75	4.50	.20
405	Plate Block of 6	150.00	100.00	90.00	60.00	...
405b	1¢ Booklet Pane of 6	150.00	100.00	90.00	60.00	...
406	2¢ Carmine	11.50	7.50	6.75	4.50	.20
406	Plate Block of 6	200.00	125.00	120.00	75.00	...
406a	2¢ Booklet Pane of 6	150.00	100.00	90.00	60.00	...
407	7¢ Black (1914)	160.00	105.00	90.00	60.00	9.50

1912 Single Line Wmk. - Imperf. VF Used + 30% (B)

Scott's No.		NH VF	NH F-VF	Unused VF	Unused F-VF	Used F-VF
408	1¢ Washington, Green	2.80	2.10	1.65	1.25	.50
408	Arrow Block of 4	12.50	9.00	7.25	5.50	...
408	Center Line Block of 4	19.50	15.00	12.50	9.50	...
408	Plate Block of 6	30.00	22.50	21.00	15.75	...
409	2¢ Carmine	2.85	2.15	1.65	1.25	.65
409	Arrow Block of 4	13.50	9.50	7.25	5.50	...
409	Center Line Block of 4	22.75	16.50	13.00	10.00	...
409	Plate Block of 6	62.50	46.50	39.00	30.00	...

1912 Coils Single Line Wmk. - Perf. 8½ Horiz. VF Used + 60% (B)

Scott's No.		NH VF	NH F-VF	Unused VF	Unused F-VF	Used F-VF
410	1¢ Washington, Green	13.75	8.75	8.25	5.25	3.75
410	Pair	35.00	22.50	21.00	13.00	...
410	Line Pair	85.00	53.50	50.00	32.50	...
411	2¢ Carmine	19.50	12.50	11.75	7.50	3.50
411	Pair	48.50	31.50	29.00	18.75	...
411	Line Pair	110.00	70.00	67.50	42.50	...

1912 Coils Single Line Wmk. - Perf. 8½ Vert. VF Used + 60% (B)

Scott's No.		NH VF	NH F-VF	Unused VF	Unused F-VF	Used F-VF
412	1¢ Washington, Green	52.50	32.50	31.50	20.00	5.00
412	Pair	130.00	80.00	78.50	50.00	...
412	Line Pair	225.00	145.00	140.00	90.00	...
413	2¢ Carmine	85.00	53.50	51.50	32.50	1.50
413	Pair	210.00	130.00	125.00	80.00	...
413	Line Pair	465.00	300.00	285.00	185.00	...

NOTE: PRIOR TO 1935, TO DETERMINE VERY FINE USED PRICE, ADD VF% AT BEGINNING OF EACH SET TO THE APPROPRIATE FINE PRICE.
MINIMUM 10¢ PER STAMP

9

1912-14 Franklin Design. Single Line Wmk. - Perf. 12 VF Used + 50% (B)

Scott's No.		NH VF	NH F-VF	Unused VF	Unused F-VF	Used F-VF
414	8¢ Franklin, Olive Green	87.50	58.50	52.50	35.00	1.25
415	9¢ Salmon Red (1914)	100.00	67.50	60.00	40.00	10.75
416	10¢ Orange Yellow	87.50	58.50	52.50	35.00	.40
417	12¢ Claret Brown (1914)	100.00	67.50	60.00	39.50	3.95
418	15¢ Gray	165.00	110.00	100.00	65.00	3.50
419	20¢ Ultramarine (1914)	375.00	250.00	225.00	150.00	14.50
420	30¢ Orange Red (1914)	260.00	170.00	150.00	100.00	14.50
421	50¢ Violet (1914)	825.00	550.00	485.00	325.00	16.50

*** #421 usually shows an offset on the back; #422 usually does not.**

1912 Franklin Design. Double Line Wmk. - Perf. 12 VF Used + 50% (B)

Scott's No.		NH VF	NH F-VF	Unused VF	Unused F-VF	Used F-VF
422	50¢ Franklin, Violet	525.00	350.00	315.00	210.00	16.50
423	$1 Violet Brown	1000.00	675.00	600.00	400.00	57.50

1914-15 Flat Press Single Line Wmk., Perf. 10 VF Used + 50% (B)

Scott's No.		NH VF	NH F-VF	Unused VF	Unused F-VF	Used F-VF
424	1¢ Washington, Green	5.85	3.75	3.50	2.25	.20
424	Plate Block of 6	75.00	50.00	45.00	30.00	...
424	Pl.Bk. of 10 "COIL STAMPS"	270.00	180.00	165.00	110.00	...
424d	1¢ Booklet Pane of 6	10.50	6.50	6.50	4.00	...
425	2¢ Rose Red	5.00	3.25	3.00	2.00	.20
425	Plate Block of 6	47.50	31.50	30.00	20.00	...
425	Pl.Bk.of 10 "COIL STAMPS"	300.00	200.00	185.00	125.00	...
425e	2¢ Booklet Pane of 6	50.00	33.50	29.50	20.00	...
426	3¢ Deep Violet	30.00	19.50	17.50	11.50	1.35
426	Plate Block of 6	325.00	215.00	210.00	140.00	...
427	4¢ Brown	75.00	49.50	45.00	30.00	.60
427	Plate Block of 6	975.00	650.00	600.00	400.00	...
428	5¢ Blue	68.50	45.00	41.50	27.50	.60
428	Plate Block of 6	725.00	475.00	450.00	300.00	...
429	6¢ Red Orange	110.00	72.50	65.00	42.50	1.50
429	Plate Block of 6	7765.00	500.00	485.00	325.00	...
430	7¢ Black	165.00	110.00	100.00	67.50	4.75
431	8¢ Franklin, Olive Green	82.50	55.00	46.50	31.50	1.85
431	Plate Block of 6	950.00	625.00	565.00	375.00	...
432	9¢ Salmon Red	100.00	65.00	57.50	38.50	9.50
433	10¢ Orange Yellow	100.00	65.00	58.00	39.00	.60
434	11¢ Dark Green (1915)	55.00	35.00	32.50	21.50	7.50
434	Plate Block of 6	425.00	280.00	270.00	180.00	...
435	12¢ Claret Brown	55.00	36.50	32.50	21.50	6.50
435	Plate Block of 6	550.00	365.00	350.00	225.00	...
435a	12¢ Copper Red	60.00	40.00	37.50	25.00	6.75
435a	Plate Block of 6	595.00	395.00	375.00	250.00	...
437	15¢ Gray	240.00	160.00	145.00	97.50	7.00
438	20¢ Ultramarine	400.00	270.00	250.00	165.00	4.50
439	30¢ Orange Red	550.00	350.00	325.00	210.00	15.75
440	50¢ Violet (1915)	1250.00	825.00	750.00	495.00	17.50

1914 Coils Flat Press S.L Wmk. - Perf. 10 Horiz. VF Used + 60% (B)

Scott's No.		NH VF	NH F-VF	Unused VF	Unused F-VF	Used F-VF
441	1¢ Washington, Green	2.50	1.60	1.50	.95	.95
441	Pair	6.35	4.00	3.75	2.50	...
441	Line Pair	15.00	9.50	9.50	6.00	...
442	2¢ Carmine	21.50	13.50	12.50	8.00	6.50
442	Pair	55.00	33.50	31.50	19.75	...
442	Line Pair	105.00	65.00	65.00	40.00	...

1914 Coils Flat Press S.L. Wmk. - Perf. 10 Vert. VF Used + 60% (B)

Scott's No.		NH VF	NH F-VF	Unused VF	Unused F-VF	Used F-VF
443	1¢ Washington, Green	50.00	32.50	30.00	19.50	5.25
443	Pair	125.00	80.00	75.00	50.00	...
443	Line Pair	275.00	180.00	175.00	115.00	...
444	2¢ Carmine	75.00	47.50	45.00	28.50	1.40
444	Pair	210.00	135.00	125.00	80.00	...
444	Line Pair	450.00	285.00	270.00	175.00	...
445	3¢ Violet	550.00	335.00	325.00	200.00	110.00
445	Pair	1350.00	825.00	800.00	500.00	...
446	4¢ Brown	285.00	185.00	170.00	110.00	39.50
446	Pair	700.00	465.00	425.00	275.00	...
447	5¢ Blue	110.00	70.00	66.50	42.50	32.50
447	Pair	285.00	175.00	170.00	105.00	...
447	Line Pair	470.00	300.00	285.00	185.00	...

Perf. Horizontally **Perf. Vertically**

The two top stamps are Rotary Press While the underneath stamps are Flat Press. Note that the designs of the Rotary Press stamps are a little longer or Wider than Flat Press stamps. Flat Press Stamps usually show spots of color Back.

1915 Coils Rotary S.L. Wmk. - Perf. 10 Horiz. VF Used + 50% (B)

Scott's No.		NH VF	NH F-VF	Unused VF	Unused F-VF	Used F-VF
448	1¢ Washington, Green	14.75	9.50	9.00	6.00	3.25
448	Pair	36.50	23.50	22.50	15.00	...
448	Line Pair	90.00	56.50	52.50	35.00	...
449	2¢ Red, Type I	...	...	3000.00	1800.00	350.00
450	2¢ Carmine, Type III	21.00	14.00	12.75	8.50	3.75
450	Pair	55.00	35.00	32.50	21.50	...
450	Line Pair	135.00	90.00	85.00	55.00	...

1914-16 Coils Rotary S.L. Wmk. - Perf. 10 Vert. VF Used + 50% (B)

Scott's No.		NH VF	NH F-VF	Unused VF	Unused F-VF	Used F-VF
452	1¢ Washington, Green	27.50	18.50	16.50	11.00	2.25
452	Pair	68.50	46.50	41.50	27.50	...
452	Line Pair	145.00	95.00	87.50	57.50	...
453	2¢ Carm. Rose, Type I	250.00	160.00	150.00	95.00	3.75
453	Pair	625.00	395.00	375.00	235.00	...
453	Line Pair	1150.00	750.00	675.00	450.00	...
454	2¢ Red, Type II (1915)	250.00	165.00	135.00	90.00	9.75
454	Pair	600.00	375.00	325.00	215.00	...
454	Line Pair	975.00	625.00	575.00	375.00	...
455	2¢ Carmine, Type III (1915)	20.00	13.00	12.00	8.00	1.25
455	Pair	50.00	33.50	30.00	20.00	...
455	Line Pair	115.00	75.00	67.50	45.00	...
456	3¢ Violet (1916)	600.00	400.00	365.00	240.00	85.00
457	4¢ Brown (1916)	62.50	41.50	37.50	25.00	19.50
457	Pair	160.00	105.00	95.00	62.50	...
457	Line Pair	300.00	200.00	180.00	120.00	...

1914-16 Coils Rotary S.L. Wmk. - Perf. 10 Vert. VF Used + 50% (B)

Scott's No.		NH VF	NH F-VF	Unused VF	Unused F-VF	Used F-VF
458	5¢ Blue (1916)	70.00	47.50	42.50	28.50	19.50
458	Pair	185.00	120.00	110.00	70.00	...
458	Line Pair	350.00	230.00	210.00	140.00	...

1914 Imperf. Coil Rotary Press S.L. Wmk. - VF Used + 30% (B)

Scott's No.		NH VF	NH F-VF	Unused VF	Unused F-VF	Used F-VF
459	2¢ Washington, Carmine	650.00	500.00	450.00	350.00	775.00

*** Genuinely used examples of #459 are rare. Copies should have contemporary cancels and be purchased with, or subject to, a certificate of authenticity.**

1915 Flat Press Double Line Wmk. - Perf. 10 VF Used + 75% (B)

Scott's No.		NH VF	NH F-VF	Unused VF	Unused F-VF	Used F-VF
460	$1 Franklin, Violet Black	1800.00	1100.00	1100.00	675.00	75.00

1915 Flat Press S. Line Wmk. - Perf. 11 VF Used + 100% (B)

Scott's No.		NH VF	NH F-VF	Unused VF	Unused F-VF	Used F-VF
461	2¢ Pale Carmine Red	335.00	180.00	200.00	110.00	225.00

(Counterfeits of #461 are common. Purchase with, or subject to, a certificate.)

1916-17 Flat Press, No Wmk. - Perf. 10 (VF Used + 50%) (B)

Scott's No.		NH VF	NH F-VF	Unused VF	Unused F-VF	Used F-VF
462	1¢ Washington, Green	18.50	12.00	11.00	7.25	.40
462	Plate Block of 6	270.00	180.00	180.00	120.00	...
462a	1¢ Booklet Pane of 6	22.50	14.00	13.50	9.00	...
463	2¢ Carmine	9.75	6.50	6.00	4.00	.25
463	Plate Block of 6	225.00	150.00	150.00	100.00	...
463a	2¢ Booklet Pane of 6	175.00	115.00	110.00	75.00	...
464	3¢ Violet	170.00	100.00	100.00	60.00	12.50
465	4¢ Orange Brown	97.50	62.50	57.50	37.50	2.00
465	Plate Block of 6	1275.00	825.00	775.00	500.00	...
466	5¢ Blue	170.00	100.00	100.00	60.00	1.95
467	5¢ Carmine ERROR	1250.00	800.00	800.00	500.00	600.00
467	5¢ Single in Block of 9	1900.00	1250.00	1250.00	800.00	...
467	5¢ Pair in Block of 12	3300.00	2150.00	2100.00	1375.00	...
468	6¢ Red Orange	200.00	120.00	115.00	72.50	7.50
469	7¢ Black	235.00	150.00	140.00	90.00	11.50
470	8¢ Franklin, Olive Green	120.00	75.00	70.00	45.00	6.00
470	Plate Block of 6	1000.00	650.00	650.00	425.00	...
471	9¢ Salmon Red	120.00	75.00	70.00	45.00	13.00
471	Plate Block of 6	1400.00	900.00	900.00	575.00	...
472	10¢ Orange Yellow	225.00	135.00	135.00	82.50	1.30
473	11¢ Dark Green	85.00	55.00	50.00	32.50	16.50
473	Plate Block of 6	750.00	475.00	475.00	300.00	...
474	12¢ Claret Brown	105.00	70.00	62.50	41.50	5.50
474	Plate Block of 6	1150.00	725.00	725.00	475.00	...
475	15¢ Gray	385.00	250.00	230.00	150.00	10.75
476	20¢ Ultramarine	500.00	315.00	300.00	190.00	11.75
477	50¢ Light Violet (1917)	2100.00	1300.00	1275.00	795.00	62.50
478	$1 Violet Black	1600.00	1000.00	975.00	600.00	17.50

1917 Flat Press, No Wmk.-Perf. 10, Designs of 1902-3 VF used 35% (B)

Scott's No.		NH VF	NH F-VF	Unused VF	Unused F-VF	Used F-VF
479	$2 Madison, Dark Blue	750.00	500.00	450.00	300.00	40.00
480	$5 Marshall, Light Green	635.00	425.00	375.00	250.00	40.00

NOTE: #479 & 480 have the same designs as #312 & 313

1916-17 Flat Press, No Wmk. - Imperforate VF Used + 30% (B)

Scott's No.		NH VF	NH F-VF	Unused VF	Unused F-VF	Used F-VF
481	1¢ Washington, Green	1.95	1.50	1.20	.90	.90
481	Arrow Block of 4	9.25	6.50	5.75	4.25	...
481	Center Line Block of 4	15.00	11.00	9.00	7.00	...
481	Plate Block of 6	23.00	17.50	15.00	11.50	...
482	2¢ Carmine, Type I	3.35	2.50	2.00	1.50	1.20
482	Arrow Block of 4	15.00	11.00	8.75	6.75	...
482	Center Line Block of 4	19.00	14.00	11.50	8.75	...
482	Plate Block of 6	45.00	35.00	29.50	22.50	...
483	3¢ Violet, Type I (1917)	28.50	21.50	17.50	13.00	7.25
483	Arrow Block of 4	130.00	100.00	77.50	60.00	...
483	Center Line Block of 4	150.00	110.00	91.50	70.00	...
483	Plate Block of 6	230.00	170.00	150.00	115.00	...
484	3¢ Violet, Type II (1917)	22.00	16.00	13.50	10.00	5.00
484	Arrow Block of 4	100.00	70.00	60.00	45.00	...
484	Center Line Block of 4	120.00	90.00	80.00	60.00	...
484	Plate Block of 6	190.00	140.00	120.00	90.00	...

***3¢ Type I, the 5th line from the left of the toga rope is broken or missing; 3¢ Type II, the 5th line is complete. See Scott for more details.**

1916-19 Coils Rotary, No Wmk. - Perf. 10 Horiz. VF Used + 50% (B)

Scott's No.		NH VF	NH F-VF	Unused VF	Unused F-VF	Used F-VF
486	1¢ Washington, Green (1918) ...	2.00	1.35	1.30	.85	.25
486	Pair	4.35	2.90	2.75	1.85	...
486	Line Pair	10.00	6.75	6.50	4.25	...
487	2¢ Carmine, Type II	33.75	22.75	20.75	13.75	4.50
487	Pair	75.00	50.00	43.75	30.75	...
487	Line Pair	240.00	160.00	140.00	95.00	...
488	2¢ Carmine, Type III (1919)	7.50	4.95	4.50	2.95	1.50
488	Pair	17.50	11.50	10.50	7.00	...
488	Line Pair	43.50	27.50	26.50	17.50	...
489	3¢ Violet, Type I (1917)	10.00	6.75	6.00	4.00	1.65
489	Pair	22.75	15.00	13.75	9.00	...
489	Line Pair	70.00	45.00	42.50	27.50	...

1916-22 Coils, Rotary, No Wmk. - Perf. 10 Vert. VF Used + 50% (B)

Scott's No.		NH VF	NH F-VF	Unused VF	Unused F-VF	Used F-VF
490	1¢ Washington, Green	1.40	.90	.85	.55	.25
490	Pair	3.15	2.10	2.00	1.30	...
490	Line Pair	9.50	6.25	5.75	3.75	...
491	2¢ Carmine, Type II	...	...	2300.00	1500.00	500.00
492	2¢ Carmine, Type III	20.00	13.00	12.00	8.00	.25
492	Pair	45.00	30.00	27.00	18.00	...
492	Line Pair	110.00	77.50	70.00	47.50	...
493	3¢ Violet, Type I (1917)	36.50	24.50	22.00	14.50	3.25
493	Pair	80.00	53.50	48.50	32.50	...
493	Line Pair	240.00	160.00	140.00	95.00	...
494	3¢ Violet, Type II (1918)	22.50	15.00	13.50	9.00	.90
494	Pair	53.50	35.00	32.00	21.00	...
494	Line Pair	140.00	95.00	87.50	60.00	...
495	4¢ Orange Brown (1917)	24.00	15.75	14.00	9.50	3.75
495	Pair	55.00	37.50	32.50	22.75	...
495	Line Pair	165.00	110.00	100.00	70.00	...
496	5¢ Blue (1919)	8.00	5.50	4.75	3.25	.90
496	Pair	17.50	12.00	10.50	7.25	...
496	Line Pair	65.00	45.00	38.50	26.50	...
497	10¢ Franklin, Orng.Yel.(1922) .	43.50	29.00	26.00	17.50	9.50
497	Pair	95.00	65.00	57.50	38.75	...
497	Line Pair	265.00	175.00	160.00	110.00	...

1917-19 Flat Press, No Watermark - Perf. 11 VF Used + 50% (B)

Scott's No.		NH VF	NH F-VF	Unused VF	Unused F-VF	Used F-VF
498	1¢ Washington, Green	1.00	.70	.65	.45	.20
498	Plate Block of 6	30.00	20.00	19.00	13.50	...
498e	1¢ Booklet Pane of 6	5.75	3.75	3.75	2.50	...
499	2¢ Carmine, Ty. I	.90	.65	.55	.40	.20
499	Plate Block of 6	30.00	20.00	19.00	13.50	...
499e	2¢ Booklet Pane of 6	11.00	7.50	7.25	4.75	...
500	2¢ Deep Rose, Ty. Ia	550.00	350.00	325.00	210.00	160.00
501	3¢ Light Violet, Type I	27.50	18.50	16.50	11.00	.25
501	Plate Block of 6	230.00	155.00	150.00	100.00	...
501b	3¢ Booklet Pane of 6	140.00	95.00	90.00	60.00	...
502	3¢ Dark Violet, Type II	33.50	23.00	20.75	14.00	.50
502	Plate Block of 6	265.00	180.00	175.00	120.00	...
502b	3¢ Booklet Pane of 6 (1918)	100.00	70.00	62.50	45.00	...
503	4¢ Brown	25.00	16.50	15.00	10.00	.30
503	Plate Block of 6	295.00	120.00	185.00	125.00	...
504	5¢ Blue	19.50	13.00	12.00	8.00	.35
504	Plate Block of 6	240.00	160.00	145.00	100.00	...
505	5¢ Rose ERROR	850.00	600.00	525.00	375.00	450.00
505	5¢ ERROR in Block of 9	1350.00	950.00	850.00	600.00	...
505	5¢ Pair in Block of 12	2400.00	1750.00	1500.00	1100.00	...
506	6¢ Red Orange	27.00	18.50	16.00	11.00	.40
506	Plate Block of 6	350.00	230.00	220.00	150.00	...
507	7¢ Black	57.50	38.50	35.00	23.50	1.25
507	Plate Block of 6	500.00	350.00	325.00	225.00	...
508	8¢ Franklin, Olive Bistre	27.00	18.50	16.00	11.00	1.00
508	Plate Block of 6	300.00	210.00	195.00	135.00	...
509	9¢ Salmon Red	31.50	21.00	18.50	12.50	2.00
509	Plate Block of 6	300.00	210.00	195.00	135.00	...
510	10¢ Orange Yellow	38.75	25.00	24.00	15.75	.20
510	Plate Block of 6	335.00	230.00	220.00	150.00	...
511	11¢ Light Green	20.00	13.75	12.00	8.25	3.25
511	Plate Block of 6	260.00	180.00	165.00	115.00	...
512	12¢ Claret Brown	20.00	13.75	12.00	8.25	.55
512	Plate Block of 6	260.00	180.00	165.00	115.00	...
513	13¢ Apple Green (1919)	24.75	16.50	14.75	10.00	6.50
513	Plate Block of 6	250.00	170.00	160.00	110.00	...
514	15¢ Gray	90.00	60.00	52.50	35.00	.90
514	Plate Block of 6	1050.00	750.00	725.00	475.00	...
515	20¢ Light Ultramarine	105.00	70.00	65.00	42.50	.35
515	Plate Block of 6	1175.00	800.00	775.00	525.00	...
516	30¢ Orange Red	90.00	60.00	52.50	35.00	.90
516	Plate Block of 6	1075.00	725.00	700.00	475.00	...
517	50¢ Red Violet	160.00	110.00	95.00	65.00	.75
518	$1 Violet Brown	150.00	100.00	90.00	60.00	1.75
518b	$1 Deep Brown	...	2150.00	2000.00	1350.00	875.00

1917 Same Design as #332, D.L. Wmk. - Perf. 11 VF Used + 100% (C)

519	2¢ Washington, Carmine	975.00	500.00	550.00	300.00	675.00

(* Mint and used copies of #519 have been extensively counterfeited. Examples of either should be purchased with, or subject to, a certificate of authenticity.)

523,547

524

537

1918 Flat Press, No Watermark, Perf. 11 VF Used + 50% (B)

523	$2 Franklin,Orng. Red & Blk.	1400.00	950.00	900.00	600.00	225.00
524	$5 Deep Green & Black	500.00	350.00	315.00	210.00	32.50

1918-20 Offset Printing, Perforated 11 VF Used + 50% (B)

525	1¢ Washington, Gray Grn.	5.50	3.65	3.35	2.25	.80
525	Plate Block of 6	46.50	32.50	30.00	20.00	...
526	2¢ Carmine, Type IV (1920)	55.00	37.50	32.50	22.50	4.50
526	Plate Block of 6	415.00	280.00	275.00	185.00	...
527	2¢ Carmine, Type V (1920)	43.00	28.50	27.00	18.00	1.25
527	Plate Block of 6	300.00	200.00	195.00	130.00	...
528	2¢ Carmine, Type Va (1920)	18.50	12.50	12.00	8.00	.60
528	Plate Block of 6	160.00	110.00	105.00	70.00	...
528A	2¢ Carmine, Type VI (1920)	105.00	72.50	67.50	45.00	1.65
528A	Plate Block of 6	725.00	475.00	485.00	325.00	...
528B	2¢ Carmine, Type VII (1920)	45.00	31.00	28.50	19.50	.45
528B	Plate Block of 6	295.00	200.00	200.00	135.00	...
529	3¢ Violet, Type III	7.00	4.75	4.50	3.00	.30
529	Plate Block of 6	95.00	65.00	65.00	45.00	...
530	3¢ Purple, Type IV	3.50	2.35	2.25	1.50	.30
530	Plate Block of 6	37.50	25.00	25.00	17.00	...

1918-20 Offset Printing, Imperforate VF Used + 30% (B)

531	1¢ Washington, Green (1919)	19.50	15.00	12.00	9.00	8.50
531	Arrow Block of 4	85.00	65.00	53.50	39.50	...
531	Center Line Block of 4	110.00	85.00	68.50	52.50	...
531	Plate Block of 6	145.00	110.00	90.00	70.00	...
532	2¢ Carmine Rose, Type IV (20)	80.00	60.00	45.00	35.00	27.50
532	Arrow Block of 4	335.00	250.00	195.00	150.00	...
532	Center Line Block of 4	375.00	285.00	225.00	175.00	...
532	Plate Block of 6	550.00	400.00	350.00	265.00	...
533	2¢ Camine, Type V (1920)	365.00	275.00	230.00	175.00	95.00
534	2¢ Carmine, Type Va (1920)	27.00	21.00	17.00	13.00	7.00
534	Arrow Block of 4	115.00	90.00	75.00	60.00	...
534	Center Line Block of 4	130.00	100.00	85.00	65.00	...
534	Plate Block of 6	180.00	135.00	120.00	90.00	...
534A	2¢ Carmine, Type VI (1920)	77.50	57.50	45.00	35.00	27.50
534A	Arrow Block of 4	325.00	240.00	195.00	150.00	...
534A	Center Line Block of 4	365.00	270.00	225.00	170.00	...
534A	Plate Block of 6	575.00	425.00	360.00	275.00	...
534B	2¢ Carmine, Type VII (1920)	...	2300.00	1950.00	1500.00	700.00
535	3¢ Violet, Type IV	17.50	13.00	10.50	8.00	5.75
535	Arrow Block of 4	79.50	60.00	49.50	37.50	...
535	Center Line Block of 4	90.00	68.50	55.00	42.50	...
535	Plate Block of 6	125.00	95.00	80.00	62.50	...

1919 Offset Printing, Perforated 12½ VF Used + 75% (B)

Scott's No.		NH VF	NH F-VF	Unused VF	Unused F-VF	Used F-VF
536	1¢ Washington, Gray Green	39.50	23.50	24.75	15.00	17.00
536	Plate Block of 6	325.00	195.00	225.00	135.00	...

1919 Victory Issue VF Used + 50% (B)

537	3¢ Violet	17.50	11.50	11.50	7.50	3.50
537	Plate Block of 6	190.00	125.00	120.00	80.00	...
537a	3¢ Deep Red Violet	1700.00	1150.00	1100.00	750.00	...
537c	3¢ Red Violet	85.00	57.50	55.00	37.50	12.50

1919-21 Rotary Press Printing - Various Perfs. VF Used + 75% (C)

538	1¢ Wash. Perf. 11x10	26.50	15.00	16.50	9.50	8.50
538	Plate Block of 4	195.00	115.00	130.00	75.00	...
539	2¢ Car. Rose, Ty. II, Pf. 11x10	...	...	...	2500.00	...
540	2¢ Car. Rose,T.III, Pf.11x10	31.50	17.00	18.00	10.50	8.50
540	Plate Block of 4	210.00	120.00	140.00	80.00	...
541	3¢ Violet, Perf. 11x10	77.50	47.50	50.00	30.00	27.50
541	Plate Block of 4	675.00	400.00	450.00	265.00	...
542	1¢ Green, Perf. 10x11 (1920)	25.00	15.00	16.00	9.50	1.15
542	Plate Block of 6	300.00	185.00	200.00	120.00	...
543	1¢ Green, Perf. 10 (1921)	1.95	1.20	1.20	.75	.30
543	Plate Block of 4	30.00	18.00	20.00	12.00	...
543	Plate Block of 6	72.50	41.50	47.50	27.50	...
544	1¢ Perf. 11 (19x22½ mm) (1922)	...	...	...	...	2400.00
545	1¢ Pf.11 (19½x22 mm) (21)	325.00	195.00	200.00	120.00	125.00
546	2¢ Carmine Rose, Pf.11 (21)	220.00	130.00	135.00	80.00	135.00

1920 Flat Press, No Watermark, Perf. 11 VF Used + 50% (B)

547	$2 Franklin, Carm. & Blk.	415.00	270.00	265.00	175.00	35.00
547	Arrow Block of 4	1750.00	1175.00	1150.00	750.00	...
547	Center Line Block of 4	1850.00	1250.00	1200.00	800.00	...

1920 Pilgrim Issue VF Used + 40% (B)

548

549

550

548-50	**Set of 3**	**95.00**	**69.50**	**59.50**	**41.75**	**16.50**
548	1¢ Mayflower, Green	7.75	5.50	4.85	3.50	2.65
548	Plate Block of 6	71.50	51.50	48.50	35.00	...
549	2¢ Landing, Carmine Rose	12.50	8.75	7.75	5.50	1.75
549	Plate Block of 6	130.00	85.00	77.50	55.00	...
550	5¢ Compact, Deep Blue	80.00	57.50	50.00	35.00	13.00
550	Plate Block of 6	850.00	600.00	565.00	400.00	...

1922-25 Regular Issue, Flat Press, Perf. 11 VF Used + 40% (B)

551,653

552,575,578, 581,594,596, 597,604,632

553,576,582, 598,605,631, 633

554,577,579, 583,595,599-9A 606,634-34A

555,584,600, 635

556,585,601, 636

557,586,602, 637

558,587,638, 723

559,588,639

560,589,640

561,590,641

562,591,603, 642

563,692

564,693

565,695

566,696

567,698

568,699

569,700

1922-25 Regular Issue, Flat Press, Perf. 11 VF Used + 40% (B)

570,701

571

572

573

Scott's No.		NH VF	NH F-VF	Unused VF	Unused F-VF	Used F-VF
551-73	**Set of 23**	**1350.00**	**950.00**	**825.00**	**595.00**	**29.95**
551	½¢ Hale, Olive Brown ('25)	.40	.30	.30	.20	.15
551	Plate Block of 6	8.75	6.25	6.50	4.50	...
552	1¢ Franklin, Green ('23)	3.25	2.35	2.10	1.50	.15
552	Plate Block of 6	39.50	26.50	26.00	18.00	...
552a	1¢ Booklet Pane of 6	16.00	11.00	10.50	7.50	...
553	1½¢ Harding, Yel. Brn. ('25)	5.75	4.00	3.50	2.50	.30
553	Plate Block of 6	56.50	40.00	37.50	26.50	...
554	2¢ Wash. Carmine ('23)	3.65	2.50	2.40	1.70	.15
554	Plate Block of 6	39.50	26.50	26.00	18.00	...
554c	2¢ Booklet Pane of 6	21.00	15.00	12.50	8.75	...
555	3¢ Lincoln, Violet ('23)	37.50	26.50	22.75	16.50	1.00
555	Plate Block of 6	280.00	200.00	185.00	135.00	...
556	4¢ M.Wash.,Yellow Brown('23)	37.50	26.50	22.75	16.50	.40
556	Plate Block of 6	280.00	200.00	165.00	120.00	...
557	5¢ T. Roosevelt, Dark Blue	37.50	26.50	22.75	16.50	.30
557	Plate Block of 6	280.00	200.00	190.00	135.00	...
558	6¢ Garfield, Red Orange	67.50	47.50	41.50	30.00	.85
558	Plate Block of 6	625.00	450.00	420.00	300.00	...
559	7¢ McKinley, Black ('23)	18.50	13.00	11.00	8.00	.70
559	Plate Block of 6	115.00	82.50	77.50	55.00	...
560	8¢ Grant, Olive Green ('23)	85.00	60.00	52.50	37.50	.90
560	Plate Block of 6	900.00	650.00	625.00	450.00	...
561	9¢ Jefferson, Rose ('23)	31.50	21.50	18.75	13.50	1.30
561	Plate Block of 6	250.00	175.00	165.00	120.00	...
562	10¢ Monroe, Orange ('23)	41.50	29.00	25.75	18.50	.20
562	Plate Block of 6	365.00	265.00	250.00	180.00	...
563	11¢ Hayes, Greenish Blue	3.50	2.50	2.30	1.65	.45
563	Plate Block of 6	51.50	36.50	35.00	25.00	...
564	12¢ Cleveland, Brn.Violet ('23)	14.75	10.50	9.00	6.50	.20
564	Plate Block of 6	150.00	110.00	105.00	75.00	...
565	14¢ Indian, Blue ('23)	10.50	7.25	6.35	4.50	.90
565	Plate Block of 6	95.00	70.00	62.50	45.00	...
566	15¢ Liberty, Gray	47.50	35.00	29.75	21.75	.20
566	Plate Block of 6	400.00	290.00	280.00	200.00	...
567	20¢ Golden Gate,C.Rose ('23)	47.50	35.00	29.75	21.75	.20
567	Plate Block of 6	400.00	290.00	280.00	200.00	...
568	25¢ Niagara Falls, Yel. Grn.	40.00	28.00	25.00	17.50	.55
568	Plate Block of 6	365.00	260.00	250.00	175.00	...
569	30¢ Buffalo, Ol Brown ('23)	70.00	50.00	42.50	30.00	.50
569	Plate Block of 6	425.00	300.00	285.00	200.00	...
570	50¢ Amphitheater, Lilac	115.00	82.50	70.00	50.00	.25
570	Plate Block of 6	1050.00	750.00	700.00	500.00	...
571	$1 Lincoln Memorial, Violet Black (1923)	95.00	67.50	58.50	42.50	.50
571	Arrow Block of 4	415.00	285.00	265.00	185.00	...
571	Plate Block of 6	700.00	485.00	465.00	335.00	...
572	$2 Capitol, Blue (1923)	215.00	150.00	135.00	95.00	8.75
572	Arrow Block of 4	900.00	650.00	585.00	415.00	...
572	Plate Block of 6	1750.00	1250.00	1200.00	850.00	...
573	$5 Freedom Statue, Carmine & Blue (1923)	385.00	270.00	240.00	170.00	13.50
573	Arrow Block of 4	1650.00	1175.00	1035.00	735.00	...
573	Center Line Block of 4	1700.00	1225.00	1095.00	775.00	...
573	Plate Block of 8	4400.00	3200.00	3000.00	2200.00	...

1923-25 Flat Press - Imperforate VF Used + 30% (B)

Scott's No.		NH VF	NH F-VF	Unused VF	Unused F-VF	Used F-VF
575-77	**Set of 3**	**20.75**	**16.00**	**13.50**	**10.50**	**6.75**
575	1¢ Franklin, Green	15.00	11.75	9.75	7.50	4.00
575	Arrow Block of 4	70.00	53.50	45.00	35.00	...
575	Center Line Block of 4	85.00	63.50	52.50	40.00	...
575	Plate Block of 6	125.00	95.00	85.00	65.00	...
576	1½¢ Harding, Yel. Brn. (1925)	3.00	2.40	1.90	1.50	1.40
576	Arrow Block of 4	14.50	10.75	9.00	6.75	...
576	Center Line Block of 4	23.00	17.00	14.00	11.00	...
576	Plate Block of 6	35.00	27.00	23.00	17.50	...
577	2¢ Washington, Carmine	4.00	3.00	2.60	1.95	1.65
577	Arrow Block of 4	18.00	13.50	11.50	8.75	...
577	Center Line Block of 4	27.00	20.00	17.00	13.00	...
577	Plate Block of 6	55.00	42.50	36.50	27.50	...

1923 Rotary Press, Perforated 11 x 10 VF Used + 75% (C)

Scott's No.		NH VF	NH F-VF	Unused VF	Unused F-VF	Used F-VF
578	1¢ Franklin, Green	180.00	110.00	110.00	65.00	110.00
578	Plate Block of 4	1500.00	875.00	950.00	550.00	...
579	2¢ Washington, Carmine	155.00	92.50	97.50	57.50	100.00
579	Plate Block of 4	1050.00	685.00	675.00	425.00	...

1923-26 Rotary Press, Perforated 10 VF Used + 50% (B)

Scott's No.		NH VF	NH F-VF	Unused VF	Unused F-VF	Used F-VF
581-91	**Set of 11**	**300.00**	**240.00**	**220.00**	**145.00**	**18.50**
581	1¢ Franklin, Green	19.50	13.00	12.00	8.00	1.00
581	Plate Block of 4	175.00	120.00	120.00	80.00	...
582	1½¢ Harding, Brown (1925)	9.75	6.50	6.00	4.00	.80
582	Plate Block of 4	65.00	45.00	45.00	30.00	...
583	2¢ Wash., Carmine (1924)	4.15	2.75	2.60	1.75	.30
583	Plate Block of 4	50.00	34.00	32.50	21.50	...
583a	2¢ Booklet Pane of 6	165.00	110.00	105.00	70.00	...
584	3¢ Lincoln, Violet (1925)	55.00	35.00	32.50	21.50	2.25
584	Plate Block of 4	350.00	240.00	245.00	165.00	...
585	4¢ M. Wash., Yel Brn (1925)	33.50	22.50	21.00	14.00	.70
585	Plate Block of 4	350.00	240.00	225.00	150.00	...
586	5¢ T. Roosevelt, Blue (1925)	33.50	22.50	21.00	14.00	.45
586	Plate Block of 4	315.00	210.00	215.00	145.00	...
587	6¢ Garfield, Red Org. (1925)	15.75	10.50	9.75	6.50	.75
587	Plate Block of 4	145.00	95.00	97.50	65.00	...

1923-26 Rotary Press, Perforated 10 VF Used + 50% (B)

Scott's No.		NH VF	NH F-VF	Unused VF	Unused F-VF	Used F-VF
588	7¢ McKinley, Black (1926)	23.75	15.00	14.00	9.50	6.50
588	Plate Block of 4	150.00	105.00	105.00	70.00	...
589	8¢ Grant, Olive Green (1926)	48.50	31.50	30.00	20.00	3.85
589	Plate Block of 4	360.00	240.00	250.00	170.00	...
590	9¢ Jefferson, Rose (1926)	11.00	7.25	6.50	4.50	2.25
590	Plate Block of 4	77.50	52.50	52.50	35.00	...
591	10¢ Monroe, Orange (1925)	120.00	80.00	75.00	50.00	.70
591	Plate Block of 4	975.00	650.00	625.00	425.00	...

1923 Rotary Press, Perforated 11 VF Used + 100% (C)

Scott's No.		NH VF	NH F-VF	Unused VF	Unused F-VF	Used F-VF
594	1¢ Franklin, Green	...	...	FINE	USED	4750.00
595	2¢ Washington, Carmine	550.00	300.00	325.00	175.00	250.00

1923-29 Rotary Press Coils, VF Used + 30% (B), (599A VF Used + 75% (C))

Scott's No.		NH VF	NH F-VF	Unused VF	Unused F-VF	Used F-VF
597-99,600-06	**Set of 10**	**33.50**	**23.75**	**20.95**	**15.65**	**2.25**
597-99,600-06	**Set of 10 Line Pairs**	**200.00**	**145.00**	**127.50**	**95.00**	**...**
	Perforated 10 Vertically					
597	1¢ Franklin, Green	.60	.45	.40	.30	.20
597	Line Pair	3.65	2.70	2.35	1.80	...
598	1½¢ Harding, Brown (1925)	1.70	1.25	1.10	.80	.20
598	Line Pair	9.50	7.00	6.25	4.50	...
599	2¢ Washington, Car. Type I	.75	.55	.45	.35	.20
599	Line Pair	3.60	2.75	2.40	1.80	...
599A	2¢ Carmine, Type II (1929)	300.00	180.00	175.00	100.00	10.75
599A	2¢ Average Quality	...	100.00	...	60.00	7.50
599A	Line Pair	1300.00	750.00	850.00	500.00	...
599,599A	Combination Line Pair	1500.00	900.00	975.00	600.00	...
600	3¢ Lincoln, Violet (1924)	12.50	8.75	7.75	5.75	.25
600	Line Pair	52.50	38.50	33.50	25.00	...
601	4¢ M. Washington, Yel. Brn	7.50	5.50	4.75	3.50	.45
601	Line Pair	60.00	45.00	37.50	27.50	...
602	5¢ T. Roosevelt,Dk.Blue(1924)	3.35	2.50	2.20	1.65	.25
602	Line Pair	19.50	14.75	12.75	9.75	...
603	10¢ Monroe, Orange (1924)	7.00	5.00	4.25	3.25	.25
603	Line Pair	43.50	32.50	28.50	21.50	...
	Perforated 10 Horizontally					
604	1¢ Franklin, Green (1924)	.60	.45	.40	.30	.20
604	Line Pair	6.00	4.50	4.00	3.00	...
605	1½¢ Harding, Yel. Brn. (1925)	.60	.45	.40	.30	.25
605	Line Pair	6.75	5.25	4.50	3.50	...
606	2¢ Washington, Carmine	.60	.45	.40	.30	.20
606	Line Pair	4.50	3.50	3.00	2.35	...

NOTE: Type I, #599, 634 - No heavy hair lines at top center of head.
Type II, #599A, 634A - Three heavy hair lines at top center of head.

NOTE: From 1923 to date, Unused Coil Pairs are usually available at double the single stamp price.

1923 Harding Memorial (#610 VF Used + 30%(B), #612 VF Used + 50%(C)) #611 Imperf. VF Used + 25% (B)

610

611

612

Scott's No.		NH VF	NH F-VF	Unused VF	Unused F-VF	Used F-VF
610-12	**Set of 3**	**45.00**	**30.75**	**28.50**	**19.75**	**6.50**
610-12	**Set of 3 Plate Blocks**	**695.00**	**465.00**	**475.00**	**335.00**	**...**
610	2¢ Black, Flat Press, Perf. 11	1.20	.85	.75	.55	.20
610	Plate Block of 6	36.00	27.50	23.50	18.00	...
611	2¢ Black, Flat Press Imperf.	12.00	9.00	7.75	5.75	4.35
611	Arrow Block of 4	52.50	38.50	32.50	25.00	...
611	Center Line Block of 4	100.00	75.00	65.00	50.00	...
611	Plate Block of 6	170.00	130.00	110.00	85.00	...
612	2¢ Black, Rotary, Perf. 10	33.50	22.50	21.50	14.50	2.25
612	Plate Block of 4	525.00	350.00	360.00	240.00	...

1924 Huguenot - Walloon Issue VF Used + 30% (B)

614

615

616

Scott's No.		NH VF	NH F-VF	Unused VF	Unused F-VF	Used F-VF
614-16	**Set of 3**	**68.50**	**51.50**	**44.50**	**33.50**	**21.00**
614-16	**Set of 3 Plate Blocks**	**650.00**	**495.00**	**460.00**	**350.00**	**...**
614	1¢ "New Netherlands"	5.50	4.25	3.85	2.95	2.95
614	Plate Block of 6	63.50	47.50	42.50	32.50	...
615	2¢ Fort Orange	10.00	7.50	6.65	5.00	2.40
615	Plate Block of 6	110.00	80.00	75.00	57.50	...
616	5¢ Ribault Monument	56.50	41.50	36.50	27.00	16.00
616	Plate Block of 6	525.00	395.00	365.00	275.00	...

NOTE: PRIOR TO 1935, TO DETERMINE VERY FINE USED PRICE, ADD VF% AT BEGINNING OF EACH SET TO THE APPROPRIATE FINE PRICE. MINIMUM 10¢ PER STAMP.

NOTE: STAMP ILLUSTRATIONS INDICATE DESIGNS, PERFORATIONS AND TYPES MAY VARY

NOTE: PRICES THROUGHOUT THIS LIST ARE SUBJECT TO CHANGE WITHOUT NOTICE IF MARKET CONDITIONS REQUIRE. MINIMUM MAIL ORDER MUST TOTAL AT LEAST $20.00.

1925 Lexington - Concord Issue VF Used + 30% (B)

617   618   619

Scott's No.		VF	NH F-VF	Unused VF	F-VF	Used F-VF
617-19	Set of 3	65.00	48.50	43.50	32.75	18.50
617-19	Set of 3 Plate Blocks	625.00	475.00	435.00	325.00	...
617	1¢ Cambridge	6.00	4.50	3.95	3.00	2.25
617	Plate Block of 6	70.00	52.50	49.50	37.50	...
618	2¢ "Birth of Liberty"	10.00	7.50	6.65	5.00	4.00
618	Plate Block of 6	120.00	90.00	85.00	65.00	...
619	5¢ "Minute Man"	52.50	39.50	35.00	26.50	13.50
619	Plate Block of 6	475.00	350.00	325.00	250.00	...

620   621   622,694   623,697

1925 Norse American VF Used + 30% (B)

Scott's No.		VF	NH F-VF	Unused VF	F-VF	Used F-VF
620-21	Set of 2	32.50	24.50	21.75	17.00	14.00
620-21	Set of 2 Plate Blocks	1275.00	975.00	935.00	750.00	...
620	2¢ Sloop, Carmine & Blk.	8.00	6.00	5.35	4.00	3.50
620	Arrow Block of 4	35.00	27.00	23.50	18.00	...
620	Center Line Block of 4	48.50	36.50	32.00	24.00	...
620	Plate Block of 8	315.00	240.00	235.00	180.00	...
621	5¢ Viking Ship, Blue & Black ..	26.75	20.00	17.50	13.50	11.00
621	Arrow Block of 4	120.00	95.00	85.00	65.00	...
621	Center Line Block of 4	140.00	110.00	100.00	77.50	...
621	Plate Block of 8	975.00	750.00	725.00	550.00	...

1925-26 Designs of 1922-25, Flat Press, Perf. 11 VF Used + 40% (B)

622	13¢ Harrison, Green (1926) ...	27.00	19.50	18.00	13.00	.65
622	Plate Block of 6	250.00	190.00	180.00	130.00	...
623	17¢ Wilson, Black	31.50	23.50	20.00	15.00	.40
623	Plate Block of 6	295.00	225.00	225.00	160.00	...

1926 Commemoratives

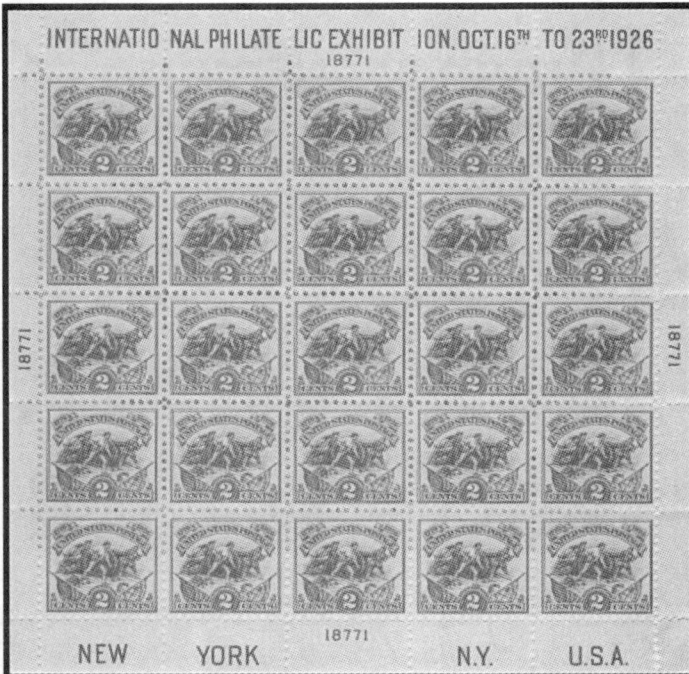

627   628   629

630

1926 Commemoratives VF Used + 30% (B)

Scott's No.		VF	NH F-VF	Unused VF	F-VF	Used F-VF
627-29,643-44	Set of 5	27.50	19.75	19.50	14.50	8.85
627	2¢ Sesquicentennial	5.00	3.75	3.75	2.75	.55
627	Plate Block of 6	60.00	47.50	47.50	35.00	...
628	5¢ Ericsson Memorial	11.50	8.50	8.00	5.75	3.35
628	Plate Block of 6	125.00	95.00	95.00	70.00	...
629	2¢ Battle of White Plains	3.75	2.75	2.60	1.95	1.75
629	Plate Block of 6	58.50	45.00	43.50	32.50	...

1926 International Philatelic Exhibition Souvenir Sheet

630	2¢ White Plains Sheet of 25 .	750.00	595.00	550.00	425.00	450.00
630v	2¢ "Dot over S" Var. Sheet ...	800.00	635.00	585.00	450.00	475.00

1926 Rotary Press, Imperforate VF Used + 25% (B)

631	1½¢ Harding, Brown	3.25	2.50	2.35	1.85	1.65
631	Arrow Block of 4	16.50	12.50	12.00	9.50	...
631	Center Line Block of 4	32.50	25.00	23.50	18.00	...
631	Plate Block of 4	100.00	80.00	70.00	55.00	...
631v	1½¢ Vert. Pair, Horiz. Gutter ...	8.50	7.00	6.50	5.50	...
631h	1½¢ Horiz. Pair, Vert. Gutter ...	8.50	7.00	6.50	5.50	...

1926-1928 Rotary. Pf. 11x10½, Same as 1922-25 VF Used +30% (B)
(634A VF Used +75% (C))

632-34,635-42	Set of 11	32.75	24.50	24.75	18.50	1.75
632	1¢ Franklin, Green (1927)	.35	.25	.30	.20	.15
632	Plate Block of 4	3.00	2.25	2.30	1.75	...
632a	1¢ Booklet Pane of 6	10.50	7.00	8.00	5.50	...
633	1½¢ Harding, Yel. Brn. (1927) ..	3.50	2.60	2.65	2.00	.20
633	Plate Block of 4	115.00	85.00	80.00	60.00	...
634	2¢ Wash., Carmine, Ty. I	.35	.25	.30	.20	.15
634	Plate Block of 4	3.25	2.50	2.30	1.75	...
634	Electric Eye Plate Block of 10	9.00	6.75	6.50	5.00	...
634d	2¢ Booklet Pane of 6 (1927)	3.35	2.15	2.50	1.65	...
634A	2¢ Carmine, Type II (1928) ...	650.00	400.00	415.00	250.00	14.50
635	3¢ Lincoln, Violet (1927)	.75	.60	.60	.45	.20
635	Plate Block of 4	14.50	11.00	10.75	8.00	...
636	4¢ M. Wash., Yel. Brown (1927)	4.25	3.25	3.25	2.50	.20
636	Plate Block of 4	130.00	95.00	90.00	67.50	...
637	5¢ T. Roos., Dark Blue (1927) ..	4.00	2.95	3.00	2.25	.20
637	Plate Block of 4	26.50	20.00	19.50	15.00	...
638	6¢ Garfield, Red Orge. (1927)	3.50	2.60	2.70	2.00	.20
638	Plate Block of 4	26.50	20.00	19.50	15.00	...
639	7¢ McKinley, Black (1927)	3.50	2.60	2.70	2.00	.20
639	Plate Block of 4	26.50	20.00	19.50	15.00	...
640	8¢ Grant, Olive Green (1927) ...	3.50	2.60	2.70	2.00	.20
640	Plate Block of 4	26.50	20.00	19.50	15.00	...
641	9¢ Jefferson, Orge. Red (1927)	3.50	2.60	2.70	2.00	.20
641	Plate Block of 4	26.50	20.00	19.50	15.00	...
642	10¢ Monroe, Orange (1927)	7.50	5.75	5.65	4.25	.20
642	Plate Block of 4	47.50	36.50	37.50	27.50	...

U.S. MINT SHEETS FINE TO VERY FINE, NEVER HINGED

Scott No. (Size)	F-VF NH	Scott No. (Size)	F-VF NH	Scott No. (Size)	F-VF NH	Scott No. (Size)	F-VF NH
610 (100)	130.00	620 (100)	825.00	633 (100)	315.00	638 (100)	285.00
614 (50)	260.00	627 (50)	225.00	634 (100)	22.50	639 (100)	285.00
615 (50)	450.00	628 (50)	550.00	635 (100)	65.00	640 (100)	285.00
617 (50)	265.00	629 (100)	350.00	636 (100)	375.00	641 (100)	285.00
618 (50)	435.00	632 (100)	25.00	637 (100)	300.00	642 (100)	585.00

643   644   645   646

647   648   649   650

1927 Commemoratives (cont.) VF Used + 30% (B)

643	2¢ Vermont Sesquicentennial ...	2.15	1.70	1.60	1.20	1.10
643	Plate Block of 6	65.00	48.50	50.00	37.50	...
644	2¢ Burgoyne Campaign	6.50	4.65	4.75	3.50	2.65
644	Plate Block of 6	68.50	52.50	51.50	39.50	...

1928 Commemoratives VF Used +30%, #646-48 VF Used +50% (B)

645-50	Set of 6	45.00	31.75	33.75	23.85	20.75
645	2¢ Valley Forge	1.65	1.30	1.30	1.00	.50
645	Plate Block of 6	46.50	35.00	33.50	25.00	...
646	2¢ "Molly Pitcher" ovpt (on #634)	2.25	1.50	1.65	1.10	1.10
646	Plate Block of 4	57.50	37.50	40.00	27.50	...
647	2¢ "Hawaii" ovpt. (on #634)	9.00	6.25	6.75	4.50	4.00
647	Plate Block of 4	240.00	160.00	165.00	110.00	...
648	5¢ "Hawaii" ovpt. (on #637)	25.00	16.50	18.50	12.50	12.00
648	Plate Block of 4	485.00	325.00	360.00	240.00	...
649	2¢ Aeronautics	2.10	1.60	1.60	1.20	.90
649	Plate Block of 6	21.00	16.00	15.75	12.00	...
650	5¢ Aeronautics	8.50	6.50	6.50	5.00	3.50
650	Plate Block of 6	105.00	77.50	75.00	55.00	...

We Buy All Stamp Collections

Valued from $200 to $2 Million and Up!

If the value of your stamp collection falls anywhere between $200 and $2 million or more, Mystic is ready to buy it.

U.S. or worldwide, rare or not so rare, topical or one of a kind, Mystic wants to buy your stamp collection.

Mystic Comes To You

Mystic travels for stamps worth $10,000 or more. Not sure of the value? Call today and speak with a Mystic buyer. We will give you honest advice on how best to proceed with selling your stamps.

Guaranteed payment

Free appraisals and prompt payments are hallmarks of dealing with Mystic. We back up our offers with a check "on the spot." No waiting months for an auction and months more to be paid when you sell direct to Mystic.

Stamps We Need Now...

• High-quality stamps, both U.S. and worldwide
• Rare stamps, both U.S. and worldwide
• Award-winning collections
• Entire stamp dealer stocks, store inventory, show dealer and mail order dealer stocks
• United States stamp collections
• Worldwide country or topical collections
• Error stamps
• Accumulations and mixed stamps (they don't need to be organized)
• Postage lots
• First Day Covers

Service to Collectors
Since 1923

Over 75 years of experience and fair dealing have given Mystic a spotless reputation money can't buy. If you want to get paid what your stamps are really worth, you owe it to yourself to contact Mystic. Call today and speak with a buyer.

Mystic Stamp Company
We Pay More For Your Stamps

We Pay More for Your Stamps
Call 1-800-835-3609

Name _____

Street _____

City _____ State _____ Zip _____

Phone Number (include area code) _____

❑ United States ❑ Worldwide ❑ Collection ❑ Accumulation

Approximate value _____

Based on _____

_____

Brief description of stamps _____

_____

_____

Mystic Stamp Company
Attention: Buying Department
9700 Mill Street, Camden, N.Y. 13316

Phone: 1-800-835-3609
Fax: 1-800-385-4919

BA277

15

651 654-656 657

1929 Commemorative VF Used + 30% (B)

Scott's No.		NH VF	NH F-VF	Unused VF	Unused F-VF	Used F-VF
651, 654-57, 680-81	**Set of 7**	**32.00**	**22.75**	**21.50**	**16.00**	**4.95**
651	2¢ George Rogers Clark	1.15	.85	.80	.60	.55
651	Arrow Block of 4	5.35	3.75	3.60	2.70	...
651	Plate Block of 6	17.50	12.50	13.50	9.50	...

1929 Rotary, Perf. 11x10½, Design of #551 VF Used + 30% (B)

653	½¢ Hale, Olive Brown	.35	.25	.30	.20	.15
653	Plate Block of 4	2.50	1.85	1.80	1.35	...

1929 Commemoratives VF Used + 30% (B)

654	2¢ Edison, Flat, Perf. 11	1.35	1.00	1.00	.75	.75
654	Plate Block of 6	42.75	33.50	33.75	25.75	...
655	2¢ Edison, Rtry, Perf. 11x10½	1.30	.85	.95	.65	.25
655	Plate Block of 4	62.50	45.00	46.50	32.50	...
656	2¢ Edison Coil, Perf. 10 Vert	26.50	19.50	18.00	13.50	1.95
656	Line Pair	125.00	95.00	85.00	65.00	...
657	2¢ Sullivan Expedition	1.20	.95	.90	.70	.60
657	Plate Block of 6	38.75	30.00	30.00	23.50	...

1929 KANSAS - NEBRASKA ISSUES

658 665 668 671 677

1929 "Kans." Overprints on Stamps #632-42 VF Used + 60% (C)

658-68	**Set of 11**	**495.00**	**310.00**	**350.00**	**225.00**	**150.00**
658	1¢ Franklin, Green	5.50	3.50	3.95	2.50	2.25
658	Plate Block of 4	70.00	42.50	50.00	30.00	...
659	1½¢ Harding, Brown	9.00	5.50	6.25	3.95	2.75
659	Plate Block of 4	83.50	52.50	58.50	37.50	...
660	2¢ Washington, Carmine	8.25	5.25	5.85	3.75	1.10
660	Plate Block of 4	75.00	47.50	53.50	33.50	...
661	3¢ Lincoln, Violet	45.00	28.00	31.50	20.00	13.50
661	Plate Block of 4	340.00	210.00	240.00	145.00	...
662	4¢ M. Washington, Yel. Brn	40.00	25.00	28.00	17.50	8.50
662	Plate Block of 4	340.00	210.00	240.00	145.00	...
663	5¢ T. Roosevelt, Deep Blue	25.00	16.00	18.00	11.00	8.75
663	Plate Block of 4	270.00	170.00	190.00	120.00	...
664	6¢ Garfield, Red Orange	55.00	35.00	39.00	25.00	16.50
664	Plate Block of 4	750.00	465.00	525.00	325.00	...
665	7¢ McKinley, Black	54.00	33.50	38.50	24.00	22.50
665	Plate Block of 4	790.00	495.00	565.00	350.00	...
666	8¢ Grant, Olive Green	210.00	125.00	145.00	90.00	60.00
666	Plate Block of 4	1500.00	900.00	1050.00	650.00	...
667	9¢ Jefferson, Light Rose	30.00	19.50	21.75	13.50	10.75
667	Plate Block of 4	335.00	210.00	240.00	150.00	...
668	10¢ Monroe, Orange Yellow	49.50	30.00	34.00	21.50	11.00
668	Plate Block of 4	550.00	350.00	400.00	250.00	...

1929 "Nebr." Overprints on Stamps #632-42 VF Used + 60% (C)

669-79	**Set of 11**	**660.00**	**415.00**	**470.00**	**290.00**	**137.50**
669	1¢ Franklin, Green	8.00	5.00	5.75	3.65	2.00
669	Plate Block of 4	80.00	49.50	56.50	35.00	...
670	1½¢ Harding, Brown	7.75	4.85	5.50	3.50	2.00
670	Plate Block of 4	85.00	52.50	60.00	37.50	...
671	2¢ Washington, Carmine	7.75	4.85	5.50	3.50	1.25
671	Plate Block of 4	75.00	45.00	52.50	32.50	...
672	3¢ Lincoln, Violet	32.50	20.00	23.00	14.50	10.50
672	Plate Block of 4	325.00	195.00	230.00	140.00	...
673	4¢ M. Washington, Yel. Brn	41.50	25.00	29.50	18.00	13.50
673	Plate Block of 4	375.00	240.00	265.00	165.00	...
674	5¢ T. Roosevelt, Deep Blue	37.50	24.00	26.00	16.50	13.50
674	Plate Block of 4	450.00	280.00	315.00	200.00	...
675	6¢ Garfield, Red Orange	85.00	55.00	60.00	38.50	22.50
675	Plate Block of 4	900.00	575.00	635.00	400.00	...
676	7¢ McKinley, Black	50.00	32.00	35.00	22.50	16.00
676	Plate Block of 4	535.00	315.00	350.00	225.00	...
677	8¢ Grant, Olive Green	73.50	45.00	51.50	31.50	21.75
677	Plate Block of 4	700.00	450.00	500.00	325.00	...
678	9¢ Jefferson, Light Rose	82.50	52.50	57.50	36.50	22.50
678	Plate Block of 4	900.00	575.00	625.00	400.00	...
679	10¢ Monroe, Orange Yellow	270.00	170.00	190.00	120.00	19.50
679	Plate Block of 4	1700.00	1100.00	1250.00	800.00	...

NOTE: IN 1929, SOME 1¢-10¢ STAMPS WERE OVERPRINTED "Kans." AND "Nebr." AS A MEASURE OF PREVENTION AGAINST POST OFFICE ROBBERIES IN THOSE STATES, THEY WERE USED ABOUT ONE YEAR, THEN DISCONTINUED.

Genuine unused, o.g. K-N's have either a single horiz. gum breaker ridge or two widely spaced horiz. ridges (21 mm apart). Unused, o.g. stamps with two horiz. ridges spaced 10 mm apart have counterfeit ovpts. Unused stamps without ridges are regummed and/or have a fake ovpt.

680 681 682 683

1929 Commemoratives (continued) VF Used + 30% (B)

Scott's No.		NH VF	NH F-VF	Unused VF	Unused F-VF	Used F-VF
680	2¢ Battle of Fallen Timbers	1.25	.95	1.00	.75	.70
680	Plate Block of 6	39.50	29.00	28.50	22.00	...
681	2¢ Ohio River Canal	.95	.75	.70	.55	.60
681	Plate Block of 6	30.00	22.50	22.00	16.50	...

1930 Commemoratives VF Used + 30% (B)

682-83,688-90,702-3	**Set of 7**	**6.75**	**5.25**	**4.75**	**3.50**	**3.30**
682	2¢ Massachusetts Bay	.95	.75	.70	.55	.45
682	Plate Block of 6	45.00	35.00	32.50	25.00	...
683	2¢ Carolina-Charleston	2.00	1.50	1.40	1.10	1.10
683	Plate Block of 6	67.50	52.50	52.00	40.00	...

684,686 685,687 688 689 690

1930 Regular Issues, Rotary Press Perf.11x10½ VF Used + 30% (B)

684	1½¢ Harding,Full Face, Brown,	.60	.45	.40	.30	.15
684	Plate Block of 4	3.95	2.95	2.70	2.10	...
685	4¢ Taft, Brown	1.75	1.30	1.20	.90	.15
685	Plate Block of 4	17.50	12.50	12.50	10.00	...

1930 Regular Issue Coils, Perf.10 Vertically VF Used + 30% (B)

686	1½¢ Harding,Full Face,Brown	3.25	2.50	2.30	1.75	.25
686	Line Pair	14.00	10.50	9.75	7.50	...
687	4¢ Taft, Brown	5.75	4.25	4.00	3.00	.65
687	Line Pair	27.50	20.75	19.50	15.00	...

1930-31 Commemoratives (cont.) VF Used + 30% (B)

688	2¢ Braddock's Field	1.60	1.20	1.25	.90	.85
688	Plate Block of 6	52.50	40.00	40.00	30.00	...
689	2¢ Baron Von Steuben	.85	.65	.60	.45	.45
689	Plate Block of 6	39.50	29.50	30.00	22.50	...
690	2¢ General Pulaski (1931)	.45	.35	.35	.25	.20
690	Plate Block of 6	17.50	13.00	13.50	10.00	...

U.S. MINT SHEETS FINE TO VERY FINE, NEVER HINGED

Scott No. (Size)	F-VF NH	Scott No. (Size)	F-VF NH	Scott No. (Size)	F-VF NH	Scott No. (Size)	F-VF NH
643 (100)	250.00	649 (50)	90.00	655 (100)	135.00	683 (100)	190.00
644 (50)	260.00	650 (50)	400.00	657 (100)	130.00	684 (100)	45.00
645 (100)	165.00	651 (50)	65.00	680 (100)	140.00	685 (100)	140.00
646 (100)	180.00	653 (100)	22.50	681 (100)	125.00	688 (100)	150.00
647 (100)	750.00	654 (100)	140.00	682 (100)	135.00	689 (100)	80.00
						690 (100)	45.00

1931 Rotary Press, Pf. 11x10½ or 10½x11 VF Used + 30% (B)
Designs of #563-70, 622-23

Scott's No.		NH VF	NH F-VF	Unused VF	Unused F-VF	Used F-VF
692-701	**Set of ten**	**175.00**	**130.00**	**128.00**	**96.50**	**2.25**
692	11¢ Hayes,Light Blue	4.50	3.35	3.35	2.50	.20
692	Plate Block of 4	23.50	16.00	15.75	12.00	...
693	12¢ Cleveland, Brown Violet	9.75	7.50	7.00	5.50	.20
693	Plate Block of 4	45.00	33.75	33.50	26.50	...
694	13¢ Harrison, Yel. Grn	3.95	3.00	2.80	2.15	.30
694	Plate Block of 4	22.50	17.00	16.00	12.50	...
695	14¢ Indian, Dark Blue	6.00	4.50	4.25	3.25	.50
695	Plate Block of 4	37.50	27.50	25.75	19.50	...
696	15¢ Liberty, Gray	14.00	10.50	10.00	7.50	.20
696	Plate Block of 4	66.50	48.50	47.50	36.50	...
697	17¢ Wilson, Black	9.00	6.75	6.25	4.75	.35
697	Plate Block of 4	48.50	35.00	33.00	25.75	...
698	20¢ Golden Gate, Car. Rose	16.00	11.75	12.00	9.00	.20
698	Plate Block of 4	80.00	57.50	58.50	45.00	...
699	25¢ Niagara Falls, Blue Green	17.50	12.75	13.00	10.00	.25
699	Plate Block of 4	77.50	60.00	60.00	47.50	...
700	30¢ Buffalo, Brown	28.00	21.50	21.00	16.00	.25
700	Plate Block of 4	110.00	85.00	87.50	67.50	...
701	50¢ Amphitheater, Lilac	77.50	57.50	55.00	41.50	.20
701	Plate Block of 4	360.00	275.00	260.00	200.00	...

702 703 704 705

| 706 | 707 | 708 | 709 | 710 |

| 711 | 712 | 713 | 714 | 715 |

1931 Commemoratives (cont.) VF Used + 30% (B)

Scott's No.		VF	NH F-VF	Unused VF	F-VF	Used F-VF
702	2¢ Red Cross	.35	.25	.30	.20	.20
702	Arrow Block of 4	1.50	1.10	1.30	.85	...
702	Plate Block of 4	3.95	2.95	2.80	2.25	...
703	2¢ Battle of Yorktown	.55	.45	.45	.35	.30
703	Arrow Block of 4	2.95	2.25	2.20	1.75	...
703	Center Line Block of 4	3.25	2.50	2.50	1.95	...
703	Plate Block of 4	4.25	3.25	3.25	2.50	...
703	Plate Block of 6	5.75	4.50	4.50	3.50	...

1932 Washington Bicentennial VF Used + 40% (B)

Scott's No.		VF	NH F-VF	Unused VF	F-VF	Used F-VF
704-15	Set of 12	46.50	34.75	32.95	23.95	2.50
704-15	Set of 12 Plate Blocks	615.00	435.00	475.00	340.00	...
704	½¢ Olive Brown	.35	.25	.30	.20	.15
704	Plate Block of 4	8.00	5.50	6.00	4.25	...
705	1¢ Green	.35	.25	.30	.20	.15
705	Plate Block of 4	7.75	5.50	6.00	4.25	...
706	1½¢ Brown	.70	.50	.55	.40	.20
706	Plate Block of 4	35.00	25.00	26.50	19.00	...
707	2¢ Carmine Rose	.35	.25	.30	.20	.15
707	Plate Block of 4	3.50	2.50	2.50	1.75	...
708	3¢ Deep Violet	1.00	.75	.75	.55	.20
708	Plate Block of 4	30.00	22.00	24.00	17.00	...
709	4¢ Light Brown	.50	.40	.40	.30	.20
709	Plate Block of 4	12.50	9.00	9.50	7.00	...
710	5¢ Blue	2.65	2.00	2.10	1.60	.20
710	Plate Block of 4	31.50	23.00	25.00	18.50	...
711	6¢ Red Orange	6.50	4.50	4.75	3.35	.20
711	Plate Block of 4	105.00	75.00	82.50	60.00	...
712	7¢ Black	.50	.40	.40	.30	.20
712	Plate Block of 4	13.50	9.75	10.75	7.75	...
713	8¢ Olive Bistre	6.00	4.00	4.50	3.15	.70
713	Plate Block of 4	110.00	75.00	82.50	60.00	...
714	9¢ Pale Red	4.85	3.30	3.50	2.50	.25
714	Plate Block of 4	85.00	57.50	62.50	45.00	...
715	10¢ Orange Yellow	19.00	17.50	17.50	12.50	.20
715	Plate Block of 4	210.00	150.00	165.00	120.00	...

U.S. MINT SHEETS FINE TO VERY FINE, NEVER HINGED

Scott No. (Size)	F-VF NH	Scott No. (Size)	F-VF NH	Scott No. (Size)	F-VF NH	Scott No. (Size)	F-VF NH
692 (100)	335.00	697 (100)	675.00	706 (100)	70.00	711 (100)	500.00
693 (100)	750.00	702 (100)	22.50	707 (100)	17.50	712 (100)	47.50
694 (100)	300.00	703 (50)	25.00	708 (100)	90.00	713 (100)	495.00
695 (100)	460.00	704 (100)	19.50	709 (100)	47.50	714 (100)	375.00
696 (100)	1075.00	705 (100)	22.50	710 (100)	225.00	715 (100)	1850.00

1932 Commemoratives VF Used + 30% (B)

| 716 | 717 | 718 | 719 |

Scott's No.		VF	NH F-VF	Unused VF	F-VF	Used F-VF
716-19, 724-25	Set of 6	8.75	6.50	6.75	5.15	1.30
716	2¢ Winter Olympics, Lake Placid	.75	.55	.60	.45	.25
716	Plate Block of 6	20.00	15.00	15.00	11.50	...
717	2¢ Arbor Day	.35	.25	.30	.20	.20
717	Plate Block of 4	12.50	9.50	9.75	7.50	...
718	3¢ Summer Olympics	2.65	2.00	2.10	1.60	.20
718	Plate Block of 4	28.00	21.75	21.00	16.00	...
719	5¢ Summer Olympics	4.15	3.15	3.25	2.50	.30
719	Plate Block of 4	47.50	36.50	37.50	28.50	...

| 720 | 721 | 722 | 723 |

1932 Regular Issue, Rotary Press VF Used + 30% (B)

Scott's No.		VF	NH F-VF	Unused VF	F-VF	Used F-VF
720	3¢ Washington, D. Violet	.35	.25	.30	.20	.15
720	Plate Block of 4	2.35	1.75	1.75	1.35	...
720b	3¢ Booklet Pane of 6	75.00	52.50	50.00	35.00	...

1932 Regular Issue Rotary Press Coils VF Used + 30%)B)

721	3¢ Washington, Perf. 10 Vert.	4.25	3.25	3.25	2.50	.20
721	Line Pair	11.50	8.75	9.25	7.00	...
722	3¢ Washington, Perf. 10 Horiz.	2.25	1.70	1.65	1.25	.70
722	Line Pair	8.50	6.50	6.50	5.00	...
723	6¢ Garfield, Orange, Pf.10 Vert.	16.00	13.00	11.75	9.00	.30
723	Line Pair	90.00	67.50	65.00	50.00	...

| 724 | 725 | 726 | 727,752 |

1932 Commemoratives (cont.) VF Used + 30% (B)

Scott's No.		VF	NH F-VF	Unused VF	F-VF	Used F-VF
724	3¢ William Penn	.65	.50	.45	.35	.25
724	Plate Block of 6	18.00	14.50	14.00	10.50	...
725	3¢ Daniel Webster	.75	.55	.55	.40	.35
725	Plate Block of 6	32.50	25.00	26.00	20.00	...

1933 Commemoratives VF Used + 30% (B)

726-29,732-34	Set of 7	3.50	2.70	2.90	2.10	1.60
726	3¢ Georgia, Oglethorpe	.65	.50	.45	.35	.25
726	Plate Block of 6	22.50	18.00	17.50	13.50	...
726	Plate Block of 10 with "CS"	31.50	25.00	25.00	19.50	...
727	3¢ Peace, Newburgh	.35	.25	.30	.20	.15
727	Plate Block of 4	8.25	6.50	6.65	5.00	...

| 728,730a, 766a | 729,731a, 767a | 732 | 733,735a, 753 | 734 |

730,766

731,767

1933 Commemoratives (cont.) VF Used + 30% (B)

Scott's No.		VF	NH F-VF	Unused VF	F-VF	Used F-VF
728	1¢ Chicago, Fort Dearborn	.35	.25	.30	.20	.15
728	Plate Block of 4	4.25	3.15	2.95	2.35	...
729	3¢ Chicago, Federal Bldg.	.35	.25	.30	.20	.15
729	Plate Block of 4	5.25	4.00	4.00	3.00	...

1933 American Philatelic Society Souvenir Sheets

730	1¢ Chicago, Imperf S/S of 25	...	...	...	35.00	32.50
730a	1¢ Single Stamp from sheet	...	...	.75	.65	.55
731	3¢ Chicago, Imperf. S/S of 25	...	...	...	32.50	30.00
731a	3¢ Single Stamp from Sheet	...	...	...	.65	.50

1933 Commemoratives (continued) VF Used + 30% (B)

732	3¢ Natl. Recovery Act (NRA)	.35	.25	.30	.20	.15
732	Plate Block of 4	2.50	2.00	2.10	1.60	...
733	3¢ Byrd Antarctic Expedition	.90	.70	.70	.55	.55
733	Plate Block of 6	22.75	17.50	18.00	14.50	...
734	5¢ General Kosciuszko	1.00	.75	.80	.60	.35
734	Plate Block of 6	55.00	42.50	45.00	35.00	...

1934 National Stamp Exhibition (Byrd Antarctic) Souvenir Sheet

735,768

| 735 | 3¢ Byrd, Imperf S/S of 6 | ... | ... | ... | 16.00 | 15.00 |
| 735a | 3¢ Single Stamp from sheet | ... | ... | 2.75 | 2.50 | 2.25 |

NOTE: #730, 731 AND 735 WERE ISSUED WITHOUT GUM.

1934 Commemoratives VF Used + 30% (B)

736   **737,738,754**   **739,755**

Scott's No.		VF	NH F-VF	Unused VF	F-VF	Used F-VF
736-39	Set of 4	1.60	1.15	1.20	.80	.75
736	3¢ Maryland Tercentary	.40	.30	.30	.20	.20
736	Plate Block of 6	16.00	12.50	12.75	10.00	...
737	3¢ Mother's Day, Rotary, Perf. 11x10½	.40	.30	.30	.20	.20
737	Plate Block of 4	1.85	1.50	1.60	1.25	...
738	3¢ Mother's Day, Flat Press, Perf. 11	.45	.35	.35	.25	.25
738	Plate Block of 6	7.50	6.00	6.50	5.00	...
739	3¢ Wisconsin Tercentary	.45	.35	.35	.25	.20
739	Plate Block of 6	5.75	4.50	4.75	3.50	...

U.S. MINT SHEETS FINE TO VERY FINE, NEVER HINGED

Scott No. (Size)	F-VF NH	Scott No. (Size)	F-VF NH	Scott No. (Size)	F-VF NH	Scott No. (Size)	F-VF NH
716 (100)	70.00	724 (100)	60.00	729 (100)	22.50	737 (50)	14.00
717 (100)	29.50	725 (100)	85.00	732 (100)	20.00	738 (50)	21.50
718 (100)	220.00	726 (100)	60.00	733 (50)	55.00	739 (50)	20.00
719 (100)	330.00	727 (100)	22.50	734 (100)	110.00		
720 (100)	27.50	728 (100)	18.00	736 (100)	35.00		

1934 National Parks Issue - Perf. 11 VF Used + 30% (B)

740,751,756   **744,760**   **747,763**   **749,765**

1934 National Parks Issue - Perf. 11 VF Used + 30% (B

741,757   **742,758**   **743,759**

745,761   **746,762**   **748,764**

Scott's No.		VF	NH F-VF	Unused VF	F-VF	Used F-VF
740-49	Set of 10	17.25	13.50	14.00	10.75	6.65
740-49	Set of 10 Plate Blocks	180.00	140.00	145.00	110.00	...
740	1¢ Yosemite, Green	.35	.25	.30	.20	.20
740	Plate Block of 6	2.10	1.65	1.70	1.35	...
741	2¢ Grand Canyon, Red	.35	.25	.30	.20	.20
741	Plate Block of 6	2.50	1.95	2.00	1.50	...
742	3¢ Mt. Rainier, Violet	.35	.25	.30	.20	.20
742	Plate Block of 6	3.25	2.50	2.60	2.00	...
743	4¢ Mesa Verde, Brown	.65	.50	.50	.40	.45
743	Plate Block of 6	14.00	10.75	11.00	8.50	...
744	5¢ Yellowstone, Blue	1.35	1.10	1.10	.90	.70
744	Plate Block of 6	15.00	12.00	12.00	9.50	...
745	6¢ Crater Lake, Dk. Blue	1.95	1.50	1.60	1.25	1.00
745	Plate Block of 6	28.75	22.50	23.00	18.00	...
746	7¢ Acadia, Black	1.15	.90	.90	.70	.70
746	Plate Block of 6	18.00	14.50	14.75	11.50	...
747	8¢ Zion, Sage Green	3.35	2.65	2.60	2.10	1.95
747	Plate Block of 6	32.50	25.00	26.00	20.00	...
748	9¢ Glacier, Red Orange	3.30	2.60	2.60	1.95	.65
748	Plate Block of 6	32.50	25.00	26.00	20.00	...
749	10¢ Great Smoky, Gray Blk	6.00	4.65	4.75	3.65	1.10
749	Plate Block of 6	45.00	35.00	35.00	27.50	...

1934 National Parks Souvenir Sheets

750,770

751,769

U.S. MINT SHEETS FINE TO VERY FINE, NEVER HINGED

Scott No. (Size)	F-VF NH	Scott No. (Size)	F-VF NH	Scott No. (Size)	F-VF NH	Scott No. (Size)	F-VF NH
740-49	**735.00**	742 (50)	13.50	745 (50)	100.00	748 (50)	140.00
740 (50)	9.75	743 (50)	37.50	746 (50)	55.00	749 (50)	245.00
741 (50)	11.00	744 (50)	57.50	747 (50)	150.00		

Scott's No.		VF	NH F-VF	Unused VF	F-VF	Used F-VF
750	3¢ Parks, Imperf. Sheet of 6		47.50	...	40.00	37.50
750a	3¢ Single Stamp from Sheet	5.75	5.25	5.00	4.50	3.75
751	1¢ Parks, Imperf. Sheet of 6		19.50	...	16.00	15.00
751a	1¢ Single Stamp from Sheet	2.50	2.25	2.15	1.90	1.75

1935 Farley Special Printing Issue

754   755   757

756   760   763   765

758   759   761

762   764   771

These stamps were issued imperforate (except #752 & 753) and without gum. For average quality on #752 and 753, deduct 20%. Horiz. and Vert. Gutter or Line Blocks are available at double the pair price.
NOTE: #752, 766A-70A HAVE GUTTERS INSTEAD OF LINES.

Scott's No.		F-VF Plate Blocks	Hz. Pair Vert.Line	Vert. Pr. Hz.Line	Singles Unused	Used
752-71	Set of 20 .... (15)	415.00	128.50	85.00	28.75	26.75
752	3¢ Newburgh, Pf.10½x11	19.50	7.00	4.00	.20	.20
753	3¢ Byrd, Perf. 11 .... (6)	17.50	39.50	1.95	.55	.50
754	3¢ Mother's Day, Imperf (6)	17.50	1.85	2.10	.60	.55
755	3¢ Wisconsin, Imperf. ... (6)	17.50	1.85	2.10	.60	.55

National Parks, Imperforate

Scott's No.		F-VF Plate Blocks	Hz. Pair Vert.Line	Vert. Pr. Hz.Line	Singles Unused	Used
756-65	Set of 10 .... (6)	285.00	42.50	41.50	15.00	14.50
756	1¢ Yosemite .... (6)	5.95	.55	.45	.20	.20
757	2¢ Grand Canyon .... (6)	6.50	.60	.60	.25	.25
758	3¢ Mt. Rainier .... (6)	15.00	1.50	1.60	.55	.55
759	4¢ Mesa Verde .... (6)	21.50	2.50	2.95	1.10	1.10
760	5¢ Yellowstone .... (6)	27.00	5.25	4.75	2.10	1.95
761	6¢ Crater Lake .... (6)	45.00	6.00	7.00	2.50	2.40
762	7¢ Acadia .... (6)	36.50	4.50	5.00	1.80	1.75
763	8¢ Zion .... (6)	47.50	6.75	5.35	2.15	1.95
764	9¢ Glacier .... (6)	50.00	5.50	6.00	2.25	2.00
765	10¢ Great Smoky .... (6)	55.00	13.00	11.00	4.15	4.00

Singles And Pairs From Souvenir Sheets, Imperforate

Scott's No.			Hz. Pair Vert.Line	Vert. Pr. Hz.Line	Singles Unused	Used
766a-70a	Set of 5	...	39.75	34.75	10.75	8.95
766a	1¢ Chicago.	...	8.75	6.00	1.10	.70
767a	3¢ Chicago.	...	9.00	6.50	1.10	.70
768a	3¢ Byrd	...	8.50	7.50	3.00	2.75
769a	1¢ Park	...	5.25	4.75	1.85	1.80
770a	3¢ Park	...	11.00	12.50	4.25	3.75

Airmail Special Delivery, Imperforate (Design of CE1)

771	16¢ Dark Blue .... (6)	75.00	6.75	8.50	2.75	2.50

Horizontal Pairs Vertical Gutters   **Vertical Pair Horizontal Line**

FARLEY SPECIAL PRINTING SHEETS AND POSTIION BLOCKS

Scott's No.		Stamps in Sheets	Uncut Sheet	Center Line Block	T or B Arrow Block	L or R Arrow Block
752-71	Set of 20	...	7750.00	440.00	...	...
752	3¢ Newburgh, Pf.10½x11	(400)	375.00	46.50	15.00	8.50
753	3¢ Byrd, Perf.11	(200)	595.00	90.00	85.00	4.25
754	3¢ Mother's Day	(200)	175.00	9.00	4.00	4.50
755	3¢ Wisconsin	(200)	175.00	9.00	4.00	4.50
756-65	Set of 10 Parks	...	3500.00	150.00	95.00	108.00
756	1¢ Yosemite	(200)	60.00	3.75	1.25	1.00
757	2¢ Grand Canyon	(200)	70.00	5.00	1.50	1.40
758	3¢ Mount Rainier	(200)	150.00	6.75	3.35	3.75
759	4¢ Mesa Verde	(200)	265.00	11.00	5.50	6.75
760	5¢ Yellowstone	(200)	485.00	18.00	11.50	10.50
761	6¢ Crater Lake	(200)	600.00	20.00	13.50	15.75
762	7¢ Acadia	(200)	450.00	17.00	10.00	11.50
763	8¢ Zion	(200)	550.00	22.50	15.00	12.50
764	9¢ Glacier	(200)	535.00	18.00	12.50	13.50
765	10¢ Great Smoky	(200)	850.00	32.50	28.00	24.00
766a-770a	Set of 5	...	2100.00	85.00	...	...
766a	1¢ Chicago	(225)	375.00	17.50	...	...
767a	3¢ Chicago	(225)	400.00	20.00	...	...
768a	3¢ Byrd	(150)	500.00	18.50	...	...
769a	1¢ Yosemite	(120)	225.00	10.75	...	...
770a	3¢ Mount Rainier	(120)	650.00	26.50	...	...
771	16¢ Airmail Special Del. ..	(200)	800.00	70.00	14.50	18.00

VERY FINE COPIES OF #752 TO THE PRESENT ARE AVAILABLE FOR THE FOLLOWING PREMIUMS:
ADD 10¢ TO ANY ITEM PRICED UNDER 50¢. ADD 20% TO ANY ITEM PRICED AT 50¢ & UP. UNLESS PRICED AS VERY FINE, SETS ARE NOT AVAILABLE VERY FINE AND STAMPS SHOULD BE LISTED INDIVIDUALLY WITH APPROPRIATE PREMIUM.

Cross Gutter Block   **Center Line Block**

Arrow Block

772, 778a   773, 778b   775, 778c

774   784   777

778

776, 778d   782   783

1935 Commemoratives

Scott's No.		Mint Sheet	Plate Block	F-VF NH	F-VF Used
772-75	Set of 4	...	...	.85	.55
772	3¢ Connecticut Tercentenary	14.50	2.25	.30	.15
773	3¢ California-Pacific Expo	12.00	1.70	.25	.15
774	3¢ Boulder Dam	9.00 (6)	2.10	.20	.15
775	3¢ Michigan Centenary	9.00	1.60	.20	.15

1936 Commemoratives

Scott's No.		Mint Sheet	Plate Block	F-VF NH	F-VF Used
776-78,782-84	Set of 6	...	...	3.50	3.00
776	3¢ Texas Centennial	8.75	1.50	.20	.15
777	3¢ Rhode Island Tercentenary	14.50	1.90	.30	.15
778	3¢ TIPEX Souvenir Sheet of 4 ...	...	...	2.65	2.50
778a	3¢ Connecticut, Imperforate	...	...	.65	.60
778b	3¢ California-Pacific, Imperforate .	...	...	.65	.60
778c	3¢ Michigan, Imperforate	...	...	.65	.60
778d	3¢ Texas, Imperforate	...	...	.65	.60
782	3¢ Arkansas Centennial	11.75	1.60	.25	.15
783	3¢ Oregon Territory	8.75	1.50	.20	.15
784	3¢ Susan B. Anthony .... (100)	17.50	1.00	.20	.15

1936-1937 Army - Navy Series

785   786   787

788   789

1936-1937 Army - Navy Series

790   791   792

793   794

Scott's No.		Mint Sheet	Plate Block	F-VF NH	F-VF Used
785-94	Set of 10	225.00	50.00	4.15	1.70
785-94	Very Fine Set of 10	...	59.50	5.15	2.50
785	1¢ Army-Washington & Greene ..	5.75	1.10	.20	.15
786	2¢ Army-Jackson & Scott (1937)	11.00	1.35	.25	.15
787	3¢ Army-Sherman,Grant,Sheridan (37)	21.00	1.95	.40	.15
788	4¢ Army-Lee & Jackson (1937) ..	37.50	11.00	.50	.25
789	5¢ Army-West Point (1937)	47.50	12.00	.80	.30
790	1¢ Navy-Jones & Barry	5.75	1.10	.20	.15
791	2¢ Navy-Decatur & MacDonough (37)	13.50	1.50	.30	.15
792	3¢ Navy-Farragut & Porter (1937)	18.00	1.85	.35	.15
793	4¢ Navy-Sampson, Dewey, Schley (37)	40.00	12.50	.55	.25
794	5¢ Navy-U.S. Naval Academy (37)	45.00	12.00	.80	.30

1937 Commemoratives

795   796   798

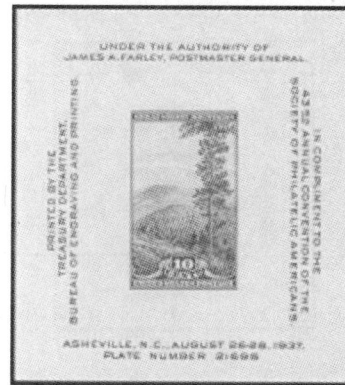   

797   799

800   801   802

Scott's No.		Mint Sheet	Plate Block	F-VF NH	F-VF Used
795-802	Set of 8	...	...	2.40	1.50
795	3¢ Ordinance of 1787	13.50	1.65	.30	.15
796	5¢ Virginia Dare .... (48)	22.50 (6)	9.50	.35	.20
797	10¢ Society of Philatelic Americans Souvenir Sheet..	...	...	.85	.65
798	3¢ Constitution Signing	13.75	1.80	.30	.15
799-802	Territorials Set of 4	38.75	5.95	.80	.50
799	3¢ Hawaii Territory	11.50	1.65	.25	.15
800	3¢ Alaska Territory	11.50	1.65	.25	.15
801	3¢ Puerto Rico Territory	8.75	1.50	.20	.15
802	3¢ Virgin Is. Territory	8.75	1.50	.20	.15

NOTE: FROM 1935 TO DATE, WITH FEW LISTED EXCEPTIONS, UNUSED PRICES ARE FOR NEVER HINGED STAMPS. HINGED STAMPS, WHEN AVAILABLE, ARE PRICED AT APPROXIMATELY 15% BELOW THE NEVER HINGED PRICE.

1938 Presidential Series

803	804,839,848	805,840,849	806,841,850	807,842,851

808,843	809,844	810,845	811,846	812

813	814	815,847	816	817

818	819	820	821	822

823	824	825	826	827

828	829	830	831

832	833	834

Scott's No.		Mint Sheet	Plate Block	F-VF NH	F-VF Used
803-34	Set of 32	...	850.00	185.00	14.95
803-34	Very Fine Set of 32	...	1025.00	220.00	19.75
803-31	Set of 29 (½¢-50¢)	...	175.00	36.00	5.25
803-31	Very Fine Set of 29	...	220.00	43.00	7.75
803	½¢ Franklin .... (100)	8.00	.45	.20	.15
804	1¢ Washington .... (100)	8.50	.45	.20	.15
804b	1¢ Booklet Pane of 6, 2½ mm (1942)	...	...	2.25	1.95
804bv	Same, 3 mm Gutter (1939)	...	...	6.50	...
805	1½¢ Martha Washington .... (100)	9.50	.45	.20	.15
806	2¢ John Adams .... (100)	12.75	.55	.20	.15
806	2¢ Electric Eye Plate	...(10)	7.50	...	...
806b	2¢ Booklet Pane of 6, 2½ mm (1942)	...	...	5.75	...
806bv	Same, 3 mm Gutter (1939)	...	...	8.95	...
807	3¢ Jefferson .... (100)	27.50	1.25	.30	.15
807	3¢ Electric Eye Plate	...(10)	35.00	...	...
807a	3¢ Booklet Pane of 6, 2½ mm (1942)	...	...	8.25	7.75
807av	Same, 3 mm Gutter (1939)	...	...	14.95	...
808	4¢ Madison .... (100)	110.00	4.50	1.00	.15
809	4½¢ White House .... (100)	25.00	1.50	.25	.15
810	5¢ Monroe .... (100)	28.00	1.20	.25	.15
811	6¢ John Quincy Adams .... (100)	36.50	1.70	.35	.15
812	7¢ Jackson .... (100)	49.50	2.40	.50	.15
813	8¢ Van Buren .... (100)	45.00	2.00	.40	.15
814	9¢ William H. Harrison .... (100)	52.50	2.25	.45	.15
815	10¢ Tyler .... (100)	42.50	1.75	.40	.15

Scott's No.		Mint Sheet	Plate Block	F-VF NH	F-VF Used
816	11¢ Polk .... (100)	72.50	4.00	.75	.15
817	12¢ Taylor .... (100)	135.00	6.75	1.40	.20
818	13¢ Fillmore .... (100)	200.00	9.00	2.00	.20
819	14¢ Pierce .... (100)	105.00	6.50	1.10	.20
820	15¢ Buchanan .... (100)	62.50	2.50	.55	.15
821	16¢ Lincoln .... (100)	125.00	7.00	1.30	.55
822	17¢ Andrew Johnson .... (100)	115.00	6.00	1.20	.20
823	18¢ Grant .... (100)	225.00	11.00	2.25	.20
824	19¢ Hayes .... (100)	160.00	7.95	1.70	.60
825	20¢ Garfield .... (100)	100.00	4.50	1.00	.15
826	21¢ Arthur .... (100)	230.00	11.50	2.30	.20
827	22¢ Cleveland .... (100)	165.00	12.50	1.75	.75
828	24¢ Benjamin Harrison .... (100)	425.00	18.50	4.25	.35
829	25¢ McKinley .... (100)	95.00	4.25	.95	.15
830	30¢ Theodore Roosevelt .... (100)	550.00	24.00	5.50	.20
831	50¢ Taft	...	37.50	8.00	.20
832	$1 Wilson, Purple. & Black	...	45.00	10.00	.20
832b	$1 Wtmk. "USIR" (1951)	...	1750.00	300.00	65.00
832c	$1 Dry Printing, Red Vlt/Blk (1954)	...	40.00	9.00	.20
833	$2 Harding	...	125.00	25.00	5.25
834	$5 Coolidge	...	550.00	125.00	5.00

	ARROW BLOCKS				CENTER LINE BLOCKS		
Scott #	NH VF	NH F-VF	Unused F-VF	Scott #	NH VF	NH F-VF	Unused F-VF
832	52.50	45.00	...	832	57.50	50.00	...
833	140.00	115.00	...	833	150.00	120.00	...
834	650.00	550.00	...	834	750.00	625.00	...

1938 Commemoratives

835	836	837	838

Scott's No.		Mint Sheet	Plate Block	F-VF NH	F-VF Used
835-38	Set of 4	...	...	1.30	.50
835	3¢ Constitution Ratification	27.50	4.50	.55	.15
836	3¢ Swedish-Finnish Terr .... (48)	13.50(6)	3.25	.30	.15
837	3¢ Northwest Territory .... (100)	35.00	10.50	.30	.15
838	3¢ Iowa Territory	18.50	7.50	.25	.15

1939 Presidential Coils

Scott's No.		Line Pairs NH	F-VF NH	F-VF Used
839-51	Set of 13	135.00	32.50	5.15
839-51	Very Fine Set of 13	165.00	40.00	6.65

Perforated 10 Vertically

839	1¢ Washington	1.35	.30	.15
840	1½¢ M. Washington	1.30	.30	.15
841	2¢ John Adams	1.40	.30	.15
842	3¢ Jefferson	1.75	.50	.20
843	4¢ Madison	30.00	7.25	.75
844	4½¢ White House	5.00	.60	.45
845	5¢ Monroe	27.50	5.00	.45
846	6¢ John Q. Adams	7.00	1.10	.25
847	10¢ Tyler	46.50	11.00	.85

Perforated 10 Horizontally

848	1¢ Washington	2.75	.75	.25
849	1½¢ M. Washington	4.00	1.35	.50
850	2¢ John Adams	7.50	3.00	.70
851	3¢ Jefferson	6.25	2.50	.70

1939 Commemoratives

852	853	854	857

855	856	858

Scott's No.		Mint Sheet	Plate Block	F-VF NH	F-VF Used
852-58	Set of 7	...	...	4.25	1.00
852	3¢ Golden Gate Expo	10.00	1.50	.20	.15
853	3¢ N.Y. World's Fair	14.50	2.50	.30	.15
854	3¢ Washington Inaugural	47.50 (6)	7.50	.95	.15
855	3¢ Baseball Centennial	120.00	11.00	2.25	.20
856	3¢ Panama Canal	22.00 (6)	4.00	.45	.20
857	3¢ Printing	9.00	1.60	.20	.15
858	3¢ 4 States to Statehood	9.00	1.60	.20	.15

1940 Famous Americans Series

859

860

861

862

863

864

865

866

867

868

869

870

871

872

873

874

875

876

877

878

879

880

881

882

883

884

885

886

887

888

889

890

891

892

893

Scott's No.		Mint Sheet	Plate Block	F-VF NH	F-VF Used
859-93	Set of 35	2750.00	395.00	33.50	17.50
859-93	Very Fine Set of 35	...	470.00	41.00	21.75
859/91	1¢,2¢,3¢ Values (21)	...	35.00	3.75	2.65
	Authors				
859	1¢ Washington Irving .... (70)	13.75	1.40	.25	.15
860	2¢ James F. Cooper .... (70)	18.50	1.65	.30	.15
861	3¢ Ralph W. Emerson .... (70)	15.00	1.60	.25	.15
862	5¢ Louisa M. Alcott .... (70)	40.00	11.75	.45	.30
863	10¢ Samuel L. Clemens .... (70)	190.00	47.50	2.25	1.90

Famous Americans (continued)

Scott's No.		Mint Sheet	Plate Block	F-VF NH	F-VF Used
	Poets				
864	1¢ Henry W. Longfellow ...... (70)	8.75	2.25	.20	.15
865	2¢ John G. Whittier .... (70)	16.50	2.50	.25	.15
866	3¢ James R. Lowell .... (70)	17.50	3.00	.25	.15
867	5¢ Walt Whitman .... (70)	50.00	12.00	.55	.30
868	10¢ James W. Riley .... (70)	200.00	49.50	2.25	2.00
	Educators				
869	1¢ Horace Mann .... (70)	13.50	2.75	.20	.15
870	2¢ Mark Hopkins .... (70)	8.75	1.60	.20	.15
871	3¢ Charles W. Eliot .... (70)	16.50	3.15	.25	.15
872	5¢ Frances E. Willard .... (70)	47.50	13.50	.45	.30
873	10¢ Booker T. Washington ...... (70)	160.00	39.50	2.00	1.85
	Scientists				
874	1¢ John James Audubon .... (70)	7.75	1.20	.20	.15
875	2¢ Dr. Crawford W. Long .... (70)	11.50	1.30	.25	.15
876	3¢ Luther Burbank .... (70)	10.50	1.30	.20	.15
877	5¢ Dr. Walter Reed .... (70)	29.50	8.75	.35	.30
878	10¢ Jane Addams .... (70)	115.00	27.50	1.65	1.50
	Composers				
879	1¢ Stephen C. Foster .... (70)	17.50	1.50	.30	.15
880	2¢ John Philip Sousa .... (70)	12.00	1.50	.20	.15
881	3¢ Victor Herbert .... (70)	11.50	1.60	.20	.15
882	5¢ Edward A. MacDowell .... (70)	46.50	12.50	.55	.30
883	10¢ Ethelbert Nevin .... (70)	335.00	47.50	4.50	2.00
	Artists				
884	1¢ Gilbert C. Stuart .... (70)	15.00	1.40	.25	.15
885	2¢ James A. Whistler .... (70)	7.00	1.10	.20	.15
886	3¢ Augustus Saint-Gaudens ... (70)	22.50	1.75	.35	.15
887	5¢ Daniel Chester French .... (70)	50.00	10.75	.65	.30
888	10¢ Frederic Remington .... (70)	180.00	35.00	2.10	1.75
	Inventors				
889	1¢ Eli Whitney .... (70)	15.00	2.50	.25	.15
890	2¢ Samuel F.B. Morse .... (70)	18.75	1.50	.30	.15
891	3¢ Cyrus H. McCormick .... (70)	25.00	2.00	.30	.15
892	5¢ Elias Howe .... (70)	105.00	16.50	1.25	.45
893	10¢ Alexander Graham Bell .... (70)	1050.00	85.00	15.00	3.25

1940 Commemoratives

894

895

896

897

898

899

900

901

902

Scott's No.		Mint Sheet	Plate Block	F-VF NH	F-VF Used
894-902	**Set of 9**	...	...	**1.85**	**1.30**
894	3¢ Pony Express	19.75	4.25	.35	.20
895	3¢ Pan American Union	17.00	3.65	.25	.15
896	3¢ Idaho Statehood	12.00	2.30	.20	.15
897	3¢ Wyoming Statehood	11.50	1.95	.20	.15
898	3¢ Coronado Expedition	10.75	1.95	.20	.15
899	1¢ Defense, Liberty .... (100)	10.75	.65	.20	.15
900	2¢ Defense, Anti-Aircraft ...... (100)	10.75	.65	.20	.15
901	3¢ Defense, Torch .... (100)	15.00	.85	.20	.15
902	3¢ Thirteenth Amendment	17.00	4.25	.30	.20

1941-1943 Commemoratives

903

904

905

906

907

908

1941-43 Commemoratives (continued)

Scott's No.		Mint Sheet	Plate Block	F-VF NH	F-VF Used
903-08	Set of 6	...	...	2.30	.90
903	3¢ Vermont Statehood	16.50	2.35	.30	.15
904	3¢ Kentucky (1942)	12.00	1.60	.25	.15
905	3¢ Win the War (1942) (100)	17.50	.60	.20	.15
906	5¢ China (1942)	75.00	17.50	1.35	.30
907	2¢ United Nations (1943) (100)	9.75	.50	.20	.15
908	1¢ Four Freedoms (1943) (100)	8.75	.65	.20	.15

1943-44 Overrun Nations (Flags)

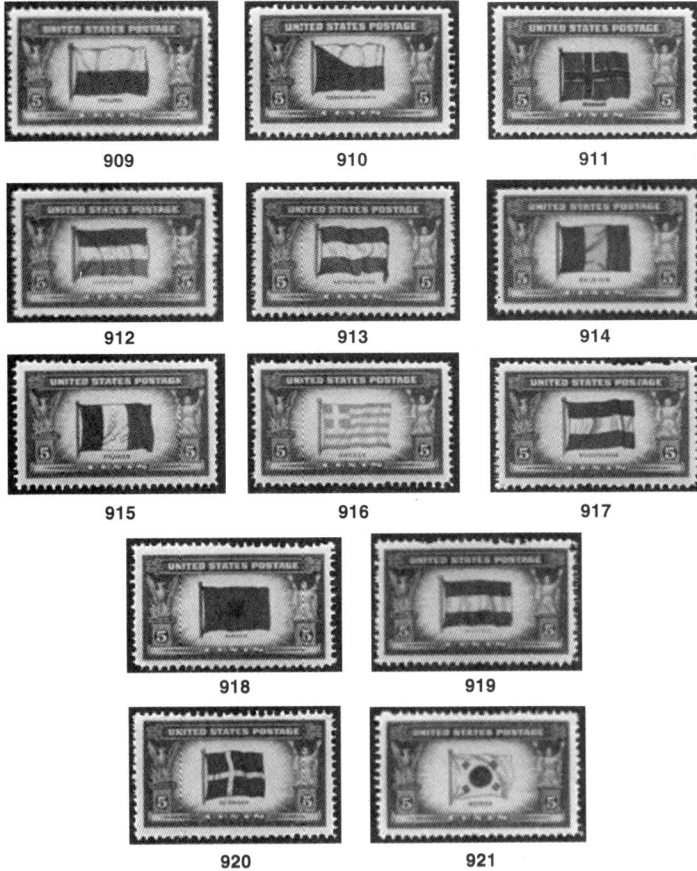

909

910

911

912

913

914

915

916

917

918

919

920

921

Scott's No.		Mint Sheet	Plate Block	F-VF NH	F-VF Used
909-21	Set of 13	215.00	65.00	3.65	2.75
909-21	Very Fine Set of 13	...	75.00	4.75	3.65
909	5¢ Poland	17.50	8.00	.25	.20
910	5¢ Czechoslovakia	16.50	3.75	.30	.20
911	5¢ Norway	10.75	2.00	.25	.20
912	5¢ Luxembourg	10.75	1.80	.25	.20
913	5¢ Netherlands	10.75	1.80	.25	.20
914	5¢ Belgium	12.00	1.80	.25	.20
915	5¢ France	10.75	1.80	.25	.20
916	5¢ Greece	37.50	16.00	.60	.40
917	5¢ Yugoslavia	24.00	7.50	.35	.25
918	5¢ Albania	24.00	7.50	.35	.25
919	5¢ Austria	22.50	6.00	.35	.25
920	5¢ Denmark	23.00	7.00	.35	.25
921	5¢ Korea (1944)	17.00	6.50	.25	.25
921v	5¢ "KORPA" Variety (1 per sheet)	45.00	...	25.00	...

(On #909-21, the country name rather than a plate number appears in the margin.)

1944 Commemoratives

922

923

924

925

926

Scott's No.		Mint Sheet	Plate Block	F-VF NH	F-VF Used
922-26	Set of 5	...	...	1.10	.60
922	3¢ Transcontinental Railroad	13.50	1.80	.25	.15
923	3¢ Steamship "Savannah"	13.50	2.00	.30	.15
924	3¢ Telegraph	11.50	1.25	.25	.15
925	3¢ Corregidor, Philippines	8.75	1.35	.20	.15
926	3¢ Motion Pictures	9.75	1.25	.20	.15

1945 Commemoratives

927

928

929

930

931

932

933

934

935

936

937

938

Scott's No.		Mint Sheet	Plate Block	F-VF NH	F-VF Used
927-38	Set of 12	...	...	1.90	1.25
927	3¢ Florida Statehood	7.50	.70	.20	.15
928	5¢ United Nations Conference	9.00	.70	.20	.15
929	3¢ Iwo Jima (Marines)	16.50	1.75	.35	.15
930-33	Set of 4	23.75	2.30	.70	.50
930	1¢ Roosevelt, Hyde Park	3.00	.45	.20	.15
931	2¢ Roosevelt, Warm Springs	5.00	.55	.20	.15
932	3¢ Roosevelt, White House	7.50	.70	.20	.15
933	5¢ Roosevelt, Map (1946)	9.75	.90	.20	.15
934	3¢ Army	10.50	.85	.20	.15
935	3¢ Navy	10.50	.85	.25	.15
936	3¢ Coast Guard	10.50	.85	.25	.15
937	3¢ Alfred E. Smith (100)	19.50	.85	.25	.15
938	3¢ Texas Statehood	10.50	.85	.25	.15

1946 Commemoratives

939

940

941

942

943

944

Scott's No.		Mint Sheet	Plate Block	F-VF NH	F-VF Used
939-44	Set of 6	...	...	1.10	.65
939	3¢ Merchant Marine	7.50	.70	.20	.15
940	3¢ Honorable Discharge (100)	14.50	.70	.20	.15
941	3¢ Tennessee Statehood	13.50	1.25	.30	.15
942	3¢ Iowa Centennial	7.50	.70	.20	.15
943	3¢ Smithsonian Institution	13.50	1.25	.30	.15
944	3¢ Santa Fe, Kearny Expedition	7.50	.70	.20	.15

NOTE: FROM 1935 TO DATE, WITH FEW LISTED EXCEPTIONS, UNUSED PRICES ARE FOR NEVER HINGED STAMPS. HINGED STAMPS, WHEN AVAILABLE, ARE PRICED AT APPROXIMATELY 15% BELOW THE NEVER HINGED PRICE.

1947 Commemoratives

 945

 946

 947

 948

 952

 949

 950

 951

Scott's No.		Mint Sheet	Plate Block	F-VF NH	F-VF Used
945-52	**Set of 8**	...	...	**1.90**	**1.35**
945	3¢ Thomas A. Edison .... (70)	15.00	1.10	.25	.15
946	3¢ Joseph Pulitzer	13.50	1.30	.30	.15
947	3¢ Postage Centenary	7.50	.70	.20	.15
948	5¢ & 10¢ CIPEX Souv. Sheet	...	...	.90	.80
948a	5¢ Franklin, Blue	...	...	.40	.30
948b	10¢ Wash., Brown Orange	...	...	.50	.40
949	3¢ Doctors	7.50	.70	.20	.15
950	3¢ Utah Settlement Centennial ...	7.50	.70	.20	.15
951	3¢ Frigate Constitution	7.50	.70	.20	.15
952	3¢ Everglades Park	7.50	.70	.20	.15

1948 Commemoratives

 953

 954

 955

 956

 957

 958

 959

 960

 961

 962

 963

 964

1948 Commemoratives (continued)

 965

 966

 967

 968

 969

 970

 971

 972

 973

 974

 975

 976

 977

 978

 979

 980

Scott's No.		Mint Sheet	Plate Block	F-VF NH	F-VF Used
953-80	**Set of 28**	...	...	**4.50**	**2.75**
953	3¢ George W. Carver .... (70)	10.50	.70	.20	.15
954	3¢ California Gold Rush	7.50	.70	.20	.15
955	3¢ Mississippi Territory	11.00	1.10	.25	.15
956	3¢ Four Chaplains	13.50	1.30	.30	.15
957	3¢ Wisconsin Centennial	7.50	.70	.20	.15
958	5¢ Swedish Pioneers	9.50	.75	.20	.15
959	3¢ Progress of Women	7.50	.70	.20	.15
960	3¢ William A. White .... (70)	10.50	.70	.20	.15
961	3¢ U.S. - Canada Friendship	7.50	.70	.20	.15
962	3¢ Francis Scott Key	13.50	1.30	.30	.15
963	3¢ American Youth	7.50	.70	.20	.15
964	3¢ Oregon Territory	7.50	.70	.20	.15
965	3¢ Harlan F. Stone .... (70)	15.00	1.10	.25	.15
966	3¢ Palomar Observatory .... (70)	11.00	1.35	.20	.15
967	3¢ Clara Barton, Red Cross	7.50	.70	.20	.15
968	3¢ Poultry Industry	13.50	1.30	.30	.15
969	3¢ Gold Star Mothers	7.50	.70	.20	.15
970	3¢ Fort Kearny, Nebraska	7.50	.70	.20	.15
971	3¢ Volunteer Firemen	14.00	1.35	.30	.15
972	3¢ Indian Centennial	7.50	.70	.20	.15
973	3¢ Rough Riders	7.50	.70	.20	.15
974	3¢ Juliette Low, Girl Scouts	13.50	1.30	.30	.15
975	3¢ Will Rogers, Humorist .... (70)	10.50	.70	.20	.15
976	3¢ Fort Bliss, Texas .... (70)	10.50	1.30	.20	.15
977	3¢ Moina Michael, Educator	13.50	1.30	.30	.15
978	3¢ Gettysburg Address	16.00	1.50	.35	.15
979	3¢ Turners Society	11.00	1.10	.25	.15
980	3¢ Joel Chandler Harris .... (70)	21.75	1.50	.35	.15

1949 Commemoratives

 981

 982

 983

984   985   986

Scott's No.		Mint Sheet	Plate Block	F-VF NH	F-VF Used
981-86	Set of 6	...	...	1.10	.60
981	3¢ Minnesota Territory	7.50	.70	.20	.15
982	3¢ Washington & Lee University	11.00	1.10	.25	.15
983	3¢ Puerto Rico Election	7.50	.70	.20	.15
984	3¢ Annapolis Tercentenary	11.00	1.10	.25	.15
985	3¢ Grand Army of the Republic ..	11.00	1.10	.25	.15
986	3¢ Edgar Allan Poe, Writer ...... (70)	19.50	1.30	.30	.15

1950 Commemoratives

987   988   990

991   989   992

993   994   995

996   997

Scott's No.					
987-97	Set of 11	...	...	1.70	1.15
987	3¢ Bankers Association	13.50	1.30	.30	.15
988	3¢ Samuel Gompers, Labor .... (70)	10.50	.70	.20	.15
989-92	National Capitol, Set of 4	32.50	3.00	.70	.45
989	3¢ Freedom Statue, Capitol	7.50	.70	.20	.15
990	3¢ Executive Mansion	7.50	.70	.20	.15
991	3¢ Supreme Court	11.00	1.10	.25	.15
992	3¢ U.S. Capitol	9.00	.70	.20	.15
993	3¢ Railroad Engineers	11.00	1.10	.25	.15
994	3¢ Kansas City Centenary	7.50	.70	.20	.15
995	3¢ Boy Scouts	7.50	.70	.20	.15
996	3¢ Indiana Territory	11.00	1.10	.25	.15
997	3¢ California Statehood	7.50	.70	.20	.15

1951 Commemoratives

998   999   1000

1001   1002   1003

Scott's No.		Mint Sheet	Plate Block	F-VF NH	F-VF Used
998-1003	Set of 6	...	...	.95	.55
998	3¢ Confederate Veterans	11.00	1.10	.25	.15
999	3¢ Nevada Settlement Centennial	7.50	.70	.20	.15
1000	3¢ Landing of Cadillac, Detroit ...	7.50	.70	.20	.15
1001	3¢ Colorado Statehood	7.50	.70	.20	.15
1002	3¢ Chemical Society	13.50	1.30	.30	.15
1003	3¢ Battle of Brooklyn	11.00	1.10	.25	.15

1952 Commemoratives

1004   1005   1006

1007   1008   1009   1011

1010   1012   1013

1014   1015   1016

Scott's No.					
1004-16	Set of 13	...	...	2.00	1.25
1004	3¢ Betsy Ross	11.00	1.10	.25	.15
1005	3¢ 4-H Clubs	11.00	1.10	.25	.15
1006	3¢ B & O Railroad	7.50	.70	.20	.15
1007	3¢ Amer. Automobile Assoc	7.50	.70	.20	.15
1008	3¢ N.A.T.O. .... (100)	14.50	.70	.20	.15
1009	3¢ Grand Coulee Dam	7.50	.70	.20	.15
1010	3¢ Marquis de Lafayette	16.00	1.50	.35	.15
1011	3¢ Mt. Rushmore Memorial	7.50	.70	.20	.15
1012	3¢ Civil Engineers Society	13.50	1.30	.30	.15
1013	3¢ Service Women	7.50	.70	.20	.15
1014	3¢ Gutenberg Bible	7.50	.70	.20	.15
1015	3¢ Newspaper Boys	7.50	.70	.20	.15
1016	3¢ Int'l. Red Cross	7.50	.70	.20	.15

1953 Commemoratives

1017   1018   1019

1020   1021   1022

Scott's No.					
1017-28	Set of 12	...	...	1.80	1.25
1017	3¢ National Guard	7.50	.70	.20	.15
1018	3¢ Ohio Statehood .... (70)	19.50	1.10	.30	.15
1019	3¢ Washington Territory	7.50	70	.20	.15
1020	3¢ Louisiana Purchase	13.50	1.10	.30	.15
1021	5¢ Opening of Japan, Perry	14.00	1.10	.30	.15
1022	3¢ American Bar Association	7.50	.70	.20	.15

1953 Commemoratives (cont.)

1023   1024   1025

1026   1027   1028

Scott's No.		Mint Sheet	Plate Block	F-VF NH	F-VF Used
1023	3¢ Sagamore Hill, T. Roosevelt ..	7.50	.70	.20	.15
1024	3¢ Future Farmers	7.50	.70	.20	.15
1025	3¢ Trucking Industry	7.50	.70	.20	.15
1026	3¢ General George S. Patton	7.50	.70	.20	.15
1027	3¢ New York City	11.00	1.10	.25	.15
1028	3¢ Gadsden Purchase	7.50	.70	.20	.15

1954 Commemoratives

1029   1060   1061

1062   1063

		Mint Sheet	Plate Block	F-VF NH	F-VF Used
1029,1060-63	Set of 5	...	...	.75	.50
1029	3¢ Columbia University	11.00	1.10	.25	.15

1954-1968 Liberty Series (B)
(Sheets of 100)

1030   1031,1054   1031A,1054A   1032   1033,1055

1034,1056   1035,1057   1036,1058   1037,1059   1038

1039   1040   1041,1041B   1042   1042A

		Mint Sheet	Plate Block	F-VF NH	F-VF Used
1030-53	Set of 27 (No #1041B)	...	525.00	127.50	11.50
1030-53	Very Fine Set of 27 (No #1041B)	...	635.00	155.00	14.00
1030-51	½¢-50¢ Values only (25) (No#1041B)	...	65.00	14.75	2.40
1030	½¢ B.Franklin, Dry (1958)	7.50	.70	.20	.15
1030a	½¢ Wet Printing (1955)	6.50	.45	.20	.15
1031	1¢ G.Washington, Dry (1956)	5.50	.40	.20	.15
1031b	1¢ Wet Printing (1954)	9.50	.95	.25	.15
1031A	1¼¢ Palace of Governors (1960) ...	7.00	.60	.20	.15
1032	1½¢ Mount Vernon (1956)	25.00	1.95	.30	.15
1033	2¢ T.Jefferson	10.00	.65	.20	.15
1034	2½¢ Bunker Hill (1959)	20.00	1.10	.25	.15
1035	3¢ Statue of Liberty, Dry	11.00	.50	.20	.15
1035f	3¢ Booklet Pane of 6, Dry Printing	...	...	7.25	3.50
1035b	3¢ Tagged, Dry Printing (1966) ...	40.00	9.00	.35	.30
1035e	3¢ Wet Printing	22.50	1.10	.25	.20
1035a	3¢ Booklet Pane of 6, Wet Printing	...	...	6.50	...

1954-1968 Liberty Series (B)
(Sheets of 100)

Scott's No.		Mint Sheet	Plate Block	F-VF NH	F-VF Used
1036	4¢ Abraham Lincoln, Dry	25.00	1.25	.30	.15
1036a	4¢ Booklet Pane of 6 (1958)	...	...	3.25	2.50
1036b	4¢ Tagged, Dry Printing (1963) ...	80.00	11.95	.70	.55
1036c	4¢ Wet Printing	22.50	1.10	.25	.20
1037	4½¢ The Hermitage (1959)	25.00	1.30	.30	.15
1038	5¢ James Monroe	26.50	1.25	.30	.15
1039	6¢ T. Roosevelt, Dry (1955)	42.50	1.95	.45	.15
1039a	6¢ Wet Printing	55.00	2.50	.55	.20
1040	7¢ Woodrow Wilson (1956)	32.50	1.50	.35	.15
1041	8¢ St. of Liberty, Original, Flat	33.50	2.75	.35	.15
1041B	8¢ Liberty, Original, Rotary	38.50	3.75	.40	.20

#1041B is slightly taller than #1041

| 1042 | 8¢ St. Liberty, Redrawn (1958) ... | 33.50 | 1.50 | .35 | .15 |

#1041,1041B: Torch Flame between "U.S." and "POSTAGE".
#1042: Torch Flame goes under "P" of "POSTAGE".

| 1042A | 8¢ J.J. Pershing ('61) .... | 34.50 | 1.50 | .35 | .15 |

1043   1044   1044A   1045   1046

1047   1048,1059A   1049   1050   1051

1052   1053

		Mint Sheet	Plate Block	F-VF NH	F-VF Used
1043	9¢ The Alamo (1956)	46.50	2.25	.50	.15
1044	10¢ Independence Hall (1956)	50.00	2.50	.55	.15
1044b	10¢ Tagged (1966)	...	45.00	3.75	2.50
1044A	11¢ Statue of Liberty (1961)	40.00	1.95	.40	.15
1044Ac	11¢ Tagged (1967)	...	47.50	2.25	1.75
1045	12¢ Ben. Harrison (1959)	55.00	2.50	.50	.15
1045a	12¢Tagged (1968)	65.00	5.00	.65	.35
1046	15¢ John Jay (1958)	100.00	4.50	1.00	.15
1046a	15¢ Tagged (1966)	...	11.75	1.50	.75
1047	20¢ Monticello (1956)	70.00	3.50	.70	.15
1048	25¢ Paul Revere (1958)	175.00	7.95	1.80	.15
1049	30¢ Robert E. Lee, Dry (1957) ...	180.00	8.50	1.85	.15
1049a	30¢ Wet Printing (1955)	...	11.50	2.75	1.25
1050	40¢ John Marshall (1958)	275.00	13.00	2.75	.15
1050a	40¢ Wet Printing (1955)	...	17.50	3.75	1.75
1051	50¢ S.B. Anthony, Dry (1958)	220.00	10.00	2.25	.15
1051a	50¢ Wet Printing (1955)	...	14.75	2.50	1.25
1052	$1 Patrick Henry, Dry (1958)	...	31.50	7.00	.20
1052a	$1 Wet Printing (1955)	36.50	8.50	2.95	...
1053	$5 Alex Hamilton ('56)	...	475.00	110.00	8.50

NOTE: SETS CONTAIN OUR CHOICE OF WET OR DRY, TAGGED OR UNTAGGED.

1954-80 Liberty Series Coil Stamps, Perf. 10 (B)

		Line Pairs	F-VF NH	F-VF Used
1054-59A	Set of 8	28.75	3.15	2.50
1054-59A	Very Fine Set of 8	33.75	3.90	3.25

#1054A and #1059 are Perforated Horizontally.

1054	1¢ Washington, Dry, Small Holes (1960)	1.10	.25	.15
1054l	1¢ Washington, Dry, Large Holes ('57)	5.50	2.25	.75
1054c	1¢ Wet Printing, Small Holes (1954) ..	3.75	.65	.25
1054A	1¼¢ Pal.of Governors, Sm.Holes ('60)	2.75	.20	.15
1054Al	1¼¢ Large Holes	285.00	19.50	.90
1055	2¢ Jefferson, Dry, Large Holes (1957)	1.50	.35	.25
1055s	2¢ Dry, Small Holes (1961)	30.00	10.00	1.00
1055a	2¢ Tagged, Shiny Gum (1968)	.70	.20	.15
1055av	2¢ Tagged, Dull Gum	1.95	.30	...
1055d	2¢ Wet Printing, Yellow Gum (1954) ..	5.00	.70	.50
1055dw	2¢ Wet Printing, White Gum	32.50	4.25	...
1056	2½¢ Bunker Hills, Large Holes ('59) ..	3.50	.25	.20
1057	3¢ Dry Printing, Small Holes (1958) ..	.60	.20	.15
1057l	3¢ Liberty, Dry, Large Holes (1956) ..	4.00	.50	.30
1057b	3¢ Tagged, Small Holes (1967)	37.50	2.00	1.75
1057c	3¢ Wet Printing, Large Holes (1954) ..	4.25	.75	.50
1058	4¢ Dry Printing, Small Holes	1.00	.30	.15
1058l	4¢ Lincoln, Dry, Large Holes (1958) ..	4.50	1.00	.40
1059	4½¢ Hermitage, Large Holes (1959) ..	15.00	1.60	1.50
1059s	4½¢ Small Holes	525.00	29.50	...
1059A	25¢ Paul Revere (1965)	2.50	.75	.30
1059Ab	25¢ Tagged, Shiny Gum (1973)	4.00	1.20	.50
1059Ad	25¢ Tagged, Dull Gum (1980)	6.50	1.85	...

NOTE: SETS INCLUDE OUR CHOICE OF LARGE OR SMALL HOLES.

Scott's No.		Mint Sheet	Plate Block	F-VF NH	F-VF Used
1060	3¢ Nebraska Territory	7.50	.70	.20	.15
1061	3¢ Kansas Territory	7.50	.70	.20	.15
1062	3¢ George Eastman .... (70)	15.00	1.10	.25	.15
1063	3¢ Lewis & Clark Expedition	7.50	.70	.20	.15

1955 Commemoratives

1064

1065

1068

1066

1067

1069

1070

1071

1072

1064-72	Set of 9	...	...	1.95	.95
1064	3¢ Penn. Academy of Fine Arts ..	15.00	1.50	.35	.15
1065	3¢ Land Grant Colleges	7.50	.70	.20	.15
1066	8¢ Rotary International	14.50	1.75	.30	.15
1067	3¢ Armed Forces Reserves	7.50	.70	.20	.15
1068	3¢ Old Man of the Mtns, NH	15.00	1.50	.35	.15
1069	3¢ Soo Locks Centennial	7.50	.70	.20	.15
1070	3¢ Atoms for Peace	7.50	.70	.20	.15
1071	3¢ Fort Ticonderoga, NY	13.50	1.30	.30	.15
1072	3¢ Andrew Mellon .... (70)	18.75	1.30	.30	.15

1956 Commemoratives

1073

1074

1076

1075

1073-85	Set of 13	...	...	4.25	3.50
1073	3¢ Franklin 250th Anniv	11.00	1.10	.25	.15
1074	3¢ Booker T. Washington	7.50	.70	.20	.15
1075	3¢ & 8¢ FIPEX Souvenir Sheet ..	...	...	2.50	2.40
1075a	3¢ Liberty Single	...	...	1.00	.90
1075b	8¢ Liberty Single	...	...	1.25	1.15
1076	3¢ FIPEX Stamp	7.50	.70	.20	.15

NOTE: WE HAVE ESTABLISHED A MINIMUM PRICE OF .20 FOR UNUSED STAMPS AND .15 PER USED STAMP. THIS INCLUDES THE VALUE OF THE STAMP PLUS THE COST INVOLVED IN PROCESSING. YOU CAN USUALLY SAVE SUBSTANTIALLY WHEN PURCHASING COMPLETE SETS.

1956 Commemoratives (continued)

1077

1078

1079

1080

1081

1082

1083

1084

1085

Scott's No.		Mint Sheet	Plate Block	F-VF NH	F-VF Used
1077	3¢ Wildlife - Wild Turkey	7.50	.70	.20	.15
1078	3¢ Wildlife - Antelope	7.50	.70	.20	.15
1079	3¢ Wildlife - King Salmon	11.00	1.10	.25	.15
1080	3¢ Pure Food & Drug Act	11.00	1.10	.25	.15
1081	3¢ Wheatland, Buchanan	11.00	1.10	.25	.15
1082	3¢ Labor Day	13.50	1.30	.30	.15
1083	3¢ Nassau Hall, Princeton	13.50	1.30	.30	.15
1084	3¢ Devils Tower, Wyoming	7.50	.70	.20	.15
1085	3¢ Children's Issue	7.50	.70	.20	.15

1957 Commemoratives

1086

1087

1088

1089

1090

1091

1092

1093

1094

1095

1096

1097

1098

1099

Scott's No.		Mint Sheet	Plate Block	F-VF NH	F-VF Used
1086-99	Set of 14	...	...	2.15	1.35
1086	3¢ Alexander Hamilton	7.50	.70	.20	.15
1087	3¢ Polio, March of Dimes	7.50	.70	.20	.15
1088	3¢ Coast & Geodetic Society	7.50	.70	.20	.15
1089	3¢ Architects Institute	7.50	.70	.20	.15
1090	3¢ Steel Industry	7.50	.70	.20	.15
1091	3¢ Naval Review, Jamestown	7.50	.70	.20	.15
1092	3¢ Oklahoma Statehood	7.50	.70	.20	.15
1093	3¢ School Teachers	10.75	1.20	.25	.15
1094	4¢ 48-Star U.S. Flag	7.50	.70	.20	.15
1095	3¢ Shipbuilding Anniv .... (70)	10.50	.70	.20	.15
1096	8¢ Ramon Magsaysay .... (48)	10.75	1.10	.25	.15
1097	3¢ Birth of Lafayette	13.50	1.30	.30	.15
1098	3¢ Wildlife - Whooping Crane	11.00	1.10	.25	.15
1099	3¢ Religious Freedom	7.50	.70	.20	.15

1958 Commemoratives

1100

1104

1105

1106

1107

1108

1109

1110

1112

1113

1114

1115

1116

1118

1119

1120

1121

1122

1123

Scott's No.		Mint Sheet	Plate Block	F-VF NH	F-VF Used
1100,1104-1123	Set of 21	...	...	3.25	1.95
1100	3¢ Gardening-Horticulture	7.50	.70	.20	.15
1104	3¢ Brussels World Fair	7.50	.70	.20	.15
1105	3¢ James Monroe .... (70)	10.50	.70	.20	.15
1106	3¢ Minnesota Centennial	7.50	.70	.20	.15
1107	3¢ Geophysical Year	7.50	.70	.20	.15
1108	3¢ Gunston Hall, Virginia	7.50	.70	.20	.15
1109	3¢ Mackinac Bridge, MI	7.50	.70	.20	.15
1110	4¢ Simon Bolivar .... (70)	10.50	.70	.20	.15
1111	8¢ Simon Bolivar .... (72)	17.50	1.75	.25	.15
1112	4¢ Atlantic Cable Centennial	7.50	.70	.20	.15

1958-59 Lincoln Commemoratives

1113-16	Set of 4	35.00	3.15	.80	.50
1113	1¢ Beardless Lincoln (1959)	3.00	.40	.20	.15
1114	3¢ Bust of Lincoln (1959)	13.50	1.30	.30	.15
1115	4¢ Lincoln-Douglas Debates	8.50	.85	.20	.15
1116	4¢ Statue of Lincoln (1959)	13.00	1.20	.25	.15

1958 Commemoratives (continued)

1117	4¢ Lajos Kossuth .... (70)	10.50	.70	.20	.15
1118	8¢ Lajos Kossuth .... (72)	17.50	1.45	.25	.15
1119	4¢ Freedom of Press	7.50	.70	.20	.15
1120	4¢ Overland Mail	11.00	1.10	.25	.15
1121	4¢ Noah Webster .... (70)	14.50	1.10	.25	.15
1122	4¢ Forest Conservation	7.50	.70	.20	.15
1123	4¢ Fort Duquesne, Pittsburgh	13.50	1.30	.30	.15

1959 Commemoratives

1124

1126

1127

1134

1128

1129

1130

1131

1132

1133

1124-38	Set of 15	...	...	2.60	1.60
1124	4¢ Oregon Statehood	7.50	.70	.20	.15
1125	4¢ Jose San Martin .... (70)	10.50	.70	.20	.15
1126	8¢ Jose San Martin .... (72)	17.50	1.20	.25	.15
1127	4¢ 10th Anniv. N.A.T.O. .... (70)	10.50	.70	.20	.15
1128	4¢ Arctic Explorations	13.50	1.30	.30	.15
1129	8¢ World Peace & Trade	14.50	1.40	.30	.15
1130	4¢ Silver Discovery	7.50	.70	.20	.15
1131	4¢ St. Lawrence Seaway	11.00	1.10	.25	.15
1132	4¢ 49-Star Flag	7.50	.70	.20	.15
1133	4¢ Soil Conservation	7.50	.70	.20	.15
1134	4¢ Petroleum Industry	13.50	1.30	.30	.15

1959 Commemoratives (continued)

1135

1136

1137

1138

Scott's No.		Mint Sheet	Plate Block	F-VF NH	F-VF Used
1135	4¢ Dental Health	11.00	1.10	.25	.15
1136	4¢ Ernst Reuter .... (70)	10.50	.70	.20	.15
1137	8¢ Ernst Reuter .... (72)	17.50	1.20	.25	.15
1138	4¢ Dr. Ephraim McDowell .... (70)	18.50	1.30	.30	.15

1960 Commemoratives

1139

1140

1141

1142

1143

1144

Scott's No.		Mint Sheet	Plate Block	F-VF NH	F-VF Used
1139-73	Set of 35	...	...	6.15	3.75
1139-44	Set of 6	60.00	6.25	1.40	.65
1139	4¢ Washington Credo	11.00	1.10	.25	.15
1140	4¢ Franklin Credo	11.00	1.10	.25	.15
1141	4¢ Jefferson Credo	11.00	1.10	.25	.15
1142	4¢ F.S. Key Credo	13.50	1.30	.30	.15
1143	4¢ Lincoln Credo	11.00	1.10	.25	.15
1144	4¢ Henry Credo (1961)	11.00	1.10	.25	.15

1145

1146

1147

1151

1149

1150

1152

1153

1154

1155

1156

1157

1158

1159

1960 Commemoratives (continued)

Scott's No.		Mint Sheet	Plate Block	F-VF NH	F-VF Used
1145	4¢ Boy Scout Jubilee	11.00	1.10	.25	.15
1146	4¢ Winter Olympics	7.50	.70	.20	.15
1147	4¢ Thomas G. Masaryk .... (70)	10.50	.70	.20	.15
1148	8¢ Thomas G. Masaryk .... (72)	17.50	1.20	.25	.15
1149	4¢ World Refugee Year	7.50	.70	.20	.15
1150	4¢ Water Conservation	7.50	.70	.20	.15
1151	4¢ Southeast Asia Treaty .... (70)	10.50	.70	.20	.15
1152	4¢ American Woman	7.50	.70	.20	.15
1153	4¢ 50-Star Flag	7.50	.70	.20	.15
1154	4¢ Pony Express Centennial	10.00	1.00	.25	.15
1155	4¢ Employ the Handicapped	7.50	.70	.20	.15
1156	4¢ World Forestry Congress	7.50	.70	.20	.15
1157	4¢ Mexican Independence	7.50	.70	.20	.15
1158	4¢ U.S. - Japan Treaty	7.50	.70	.20	.15
1159	4¢ Ignacy J. Paderewski .... (70)	10.50	.70	.20	.15
1160	8¢ Ignacy J. Paderewski .... (72)	19.75	1.40	.30	.15

1161

1162

1163

1167

1164

1165

1169

1170

1171

1172

1173

Scott's No.		Mint Sheet	Plate Block	F-VF NH	F-VF Used
1161	4¢ Robert A. Taft .... (70)	18.50	1.30	.30	.15
1162	4¢ Wheels of Freedom	7.50	.70	.20	.15
1163	4¢ Boys' Club of America	13.50	1.30	.30	.15
1164	4¢ Automated Post Office	13.50	1.30	.30	.15
1165	4¢ Gustaf Mannerheim .... (70)	10.50	.70	.20	.15
1166	8¢ Gustaf Mannerheim .... (72)	17.50	1.20	.25	.15
1167	4¢ Camp Fire Girls	7.50	.70	.20	.15
1168	4¢ Guiseppe Garibaldi .... (70)	10.50	.70	.20	.15
1169	8¢ Guiseppe Garibaldi .... (72)	17.50	1.20	.25	.15
1170	4¢ Walter F. George .... (70)	18.50	1.30	.30	.15
1171	4¢ Andrew Carnegie .... (70)	18.50	1.30	.30	.15
1172	4¢ John Foster Dulles .... (70)	18.50	1.30	.30	.15
1173	4¢ "Echo I" Satellite	15.00	1.50	.35	.15

1961 Commemoratives

1174

1175

1176

1177

1178

1179

1180

1181

1182

1183

29

Scott's No.		Mint Sheet	Plate Block	F-VF NH	F-VF Used
1174-1190	Set of 17		...	4.75	1.75
1174	4¢ Mahatma Gandhi .... (70)	10.50	.70	.20	.15
1175	8¢ Mahatma Gandhi .... (72)	17.50	1.20	.25	.15
1176	4¢ Range Conservation	7.50	.70	.20	.15
1177	4¢ Horace Greeley .... (70)	16.00	1.10	.25	.15

1961-1965 Civil War Centennial

		Mint Sheet	Plate Block	F-VF NH	F-VF Used
1178-82	Set of 5	110.00	10.95	2.25	.55
1178	4¢ Fort Sumter (1961)	22.50	2.15	.50	.15
1179	4¢ Battle of Shiloh (1962)	16.00	1.50	.35	.15
1180	5¢ Gettysburg (1963)	21.00	2.10	.45	.15
1181	5¢ Wilderness (1964)	18.75	1.85	.40	.15
1182	5¢ Appomattox (1965)	36.75	4.00	.75	.15

1184   1185   1186

1187   1188   1189   1190

1183	4¢ Kansas Statehood	7.50	.70	.20	.15
1184	4¢ George W. Norris	11.00	1.10	.25	.15
1185	4¢ Naval Aviation	7.50	.70	.20	.15
1186	4¢ Workmen's Compensation	7.50	.70	.20	.15
1186v	Plate Number Inverted	7.75	.75	...	...
1187	4¢ Frederic Remington	13.50	1.30	.30	.15
1188	4¢ Republic of China, Sun Yat-sen	11.00	1.00	.25	.15
1189	4¢ Basketball - James Naismith .	14.00	1.30	.30	.15
1190	4¢ Nursing	14.75	1.40	.30	.15

1962 Commemoratives (See also 1179)

1191   1192   1193

1195   1194   1196

1197   1198   1199

1200   1201

Scott's No.		Mint Sheet	Plate Block	F-VF NH	F-VF Used
1191-1207	Set of 17	...	...	2.50	1.85
1191	4¢ New Mexico Statehood	7.50	.70	.20	.15
1192	4¢ Arizona Statehood	7.50	.70	.20	.15
1193	4¢ Project Mercury	12.00	1.10	.25	.15
1194	4¢ Malaria Eradication	7.50	.70	.20	.15
1195	4¢ Charles Evans Hughes	7.50	.70	.20	.15
1196	4¢ Seattle World's Fair	7.50	.70	.20	.15
1197	4¢ Louisiana Statehood	11.00	1.10	.25	.15
1198	4¢ Homestead Act	7.50	.70	.20	.15
1199	4¢ Girl Scouts 50th Anniversary .	7.50	.70	.20	.15
1200	4¢ Brien McMahon	11.00	1.10	.25	.15
1201	4¢ Apprenticeship Act	7.50	.70	.20	.15

1202   1203   1205

1206   1207

1202	4¢ Sam Rayburn	7.50	.70	.20	.15
1203	4¢ Dag Hammarskjold	7.50	.70	.20	.15
1204	4¢ Hammarskjold "Error"	8.50	1.60	.20	.15

Note: The yellow background is inverted on #1204

1205	4¢ Christmas Wreath .... (100)	14.50	.70	.20	.15
1206	4¢ Higher Education	7.50	.70	.20	.15
1207	4¢ Winslow Homer Seascape	11.00	1.10	.25	.15

1962-1963 Regular Issues

1208   1209,1225   1213,1229

1208	5¢ Flag & White House ('63) ... (100)	18.50	.90	.20	.15
1208a	5¢ Flag Tagged (1966) .... (100)	28.50	2.00	.30	.20
1209	1¢ Andrew Jackson (1963) .... (100)	7.00	.40	.20	.15
1209a	1¢ Tagged (1966) .... (100)	7.50	.55	.20	.20
1213	5¢ George Washington .... (100)	18.50	.90	.20	.15
1213a	5¢ Pane of 5 "Mailman", Slogan I	...	...	5.75	4.75
1213a	5¢ Pane of 5 "Use Zone", Slogan II	...	...	25.75	12.50
1213a	5¢ Pane of 5 "Use Zip Code", Slogan III	...	...	3.25	2.50
1213b	5¢ Tagged (1963) .... (100)	60.00	8.00	.65	.50
1213c	5¢ Pane of 5 "Zone" Tagged, Slogan II	...	...	90.00	...
1213c	5¢ Pane of 5 "Zip" Tagged, Slogan III	...	...	1.50	...
1225	1¢ A.Jackson Coil	Line Pr.	2.75	.20	.15
1225a	1¢ Coil, Tagged (1966)	Line Pr.	.65	.20	.15
1229	5¢ Washington Coil	Line Pr.	3.25	1.10	.15
1229a	5¢ Coil, Tagged (1963)	Line Pr.	9.75	1.65	.25

1963 Commemoratives (See also 1180)

1230   1231   1232

1233   1234   1235

1230-41	Set of 12	...	...	2.15	1.20
1230	5¢ Carolina Charter	15.00	1.50	.35	.15
1231	5¢ Food for Peace	7.50	.70	.20	.15
1232	5¢ West Virginia Statehood	7.50	.70	.20	.15

1963 Commemoratives (continued)

1236

1237

1238

1239

1240

1241

Scott's No.		Mint Sheet	Plate Block	F-VF NH	F-VF Used
1233	5¢ Emancipation Proclamation ...	8.00	.85	.20	.15
1234	5¢ Alliance for Progress	7.50	.70	.20	.15
1235	5¢ Cordell Hull	13.50	1.30	.30	.15
1236	5¢ Eleanor Roosevelt	13.50	1.30	.30	.15
1237	5¢ The Sciences	7.50	.70	.20	.15
1238	5¢ City Mail Delivery	7.50	.70	.20	.15
1239	5¢ Int'l. Red Cross Centenary	7.50	.70	.20	.15
1240	5¢ Christmas Tree .... (100)	14.50	.70	.20	.15
1240a	5¢ Christmas, Tagged .... (100)	70.00	7.50	.70	.50
1241	5¢ Audubon-Columbia Jays	13.75	1.30	.30	.15

1964 Commemoratives (See also 1181)

1243

1242

1244

1245

1246

1247

1248

1249

1250

1251

1242-60	Set of 19	...	...	4.60	1.85
1242	5¢ Sam Houston	7.50	.70	.20	.15
1243	5¢ Charles M. Russell	7.50	.70	.20	.15
1244	5¢ N.Y. World's Fair	13.50	1.30	.30	.15
1245	5¢ John Muir, Naturalist	7.50	.70	.20	.15
1246	5¢ John F. Kennedy Memorial	21.00	1.90	.45	.15
1247	5¢ New Jersey Tercentenary	15.00	1.50	.35	.15
1248	5¢ Nevada Statehood	7.50	.70	.20	.15
1249	5¢ Register and Vote	7.50	.70	.20	.15
1250	5¢ William Shakespeare	7.50	.70	.20	.15
1251	5¢ Doctors Mayo	14.50	1.40	.30	.15

FOR INFORMATION CONCERNING VERY FINE SEE PAGE II

1964 Commemoratives (cont.)

1252

1254 1255
1256 1257

1253

1258

1259

1260

Scott's No.		Mint Sheet	Plate Block	F-VF NH	F-VF Used
1252	5¢ American Music	7.50	.70	.20	.15
1253	5¢ Homemakers, Sampler	7.50	.70	.20	.15
1254-7	5¢ Christmas, attached .... (100)	33.50	1.75	1.50	1.10
1254-7	Set of 4 Singles	...	...	1.30	.60
1254-7a	5¢ Christmas Tagged, attd ...... (100)	80.00	8.75	3.25	2.95
1254-7a	Set of 4 Singles	...	...	2.95	2.40
1258	5¢ Verrazano-Narrows Bridge	13.50	1.30	.30	.15
1259	5¢ Fine Arts - Stuart Davis	7.50	.70	.20	.15
1260	5¢ Amateur Radio	14.00	1.40	.30	.15

1965 Commemoratives

1262

1261

1263

1265

1264

1266

1267

1268

1269

1270

1261-76	Set of 16	...	...	2.95	2.00
1261	5¢ Battle of New Orleans	13.50	1.30	.30	.15
1262	5¢ Physical Fitness - Sokol	7.50	.70	.20	.15
1263	5¢ Crusade Against Cancer	7.50	.70	.20	.15
1264	5¢ Churchill Memorial	10.00	1.10	.25	.15
1265	5¢ Magna Carta	7.50	.70	.20	.15
1266	5¢ Int'l. Cooperation Year, U.N. ..	7.50	.70	.20	.15
1267	5¢ Salvation Army	7.50	.70	.20	.15
1268	5¢ Dante Alighieri	7.50	.70	.20	.15
1269	5¢ Herbert Hoover	7.50	.70	.20	.15
1270	5¢ Robert Fulton	7.50	.70	.20	.15

1965 Commemoratives (cont.)

1271   **1272**   **1273**

1274   **1276**   **1275**

Scott's No.		Mint Sheet	Plate Block	F-VF NH	F-VF Used
1271	5¢ 400th Anniv. of Florida	7.50	.70	.20	.15
1272	5¢ Traffic Safety	7.50	.70	.20	.15
1273	5¢ John S. Copley Painting	13.50	1.30	.30	.15
1274	11¢ Telecommunication Union	27.50	6.50	.50	.30
1275	5¢ Adlai Stevenson	7.50	.70	.20	.15
1276	5¢ Christmas Angel ....(100)	14.50	.70	.20	.15
1276a	5¢ Christmas, Tagged ....(100)	65.00	8.75	.65	.35

1965-79 Prominent Americans Series
(Sheets of 100)

1278,1299   **1279**   **1280**   **1281,1297**   **1282,1303**

1283,1304   **1283B,1304C**   **1284,1298**   **1285**   **1286**

1286A   **1287**   **1288/1305E**   **1289**   **1290**

Scott's No.		Mint Sheet	Plate Block	F-VF NH	F-VF Used
1278-88,1289-95	**Set of 20**	...	110.00	23.00	4.95
1278-88, 1289-95	**Very Fine Set of 20** ..	...	135.00	27.50	6.95

NOTE: SETS WILL CONTAIN OUR CHOICE OF TAGGED OR UNTAGGED.

1278	1¢ Thomas Jefferson (1968)	7.00	.50	.20	.15
1278a	1¢ Booklet Pane of 8	...	...	1.10	1.30
1278ae	1¢ Pane of 8, Dull Exp. Gum	...	...	1.75	...
1278b	1¢ Booklet Pane of 4 (1971)	...	...	.70	.80
1279	1¼¢ Albert Gallatin (1967)	16.50	10.75	.20	.15
1280	2¢ Frank Lloyd Wright (1968)	7.00	.40	.20	.15
1280a	2¢ Booklet Pane of 5 (S4 or S5) ('68)	...	...	1.10	1.10

S4 is "Mail Early", S5 is "Use Zip Code"

1280c	2¢ Booklet Pane of 6 ('71)	...	...	1.00	1.10
1280ce	2¢ Pane of 6, Dull Exp. Gum	...	...	1.00	...
1281	3¢ Francis Parkman ('67)	9.50	.50	.20	.15
1282	4¢ Abraham Lincoln	31.50	1.50	.35	.15
1282a	4¢ Lincoln, Tagged	27.50	1.30	.30	.15

S4 = Mail Early in the Day
S5 = Use Zip Code

1283	5¢ Washington, Dirty Face ('66) .	18.75	.75	.20	.15
1283a	5¢ Washington, Tagged	15.00	.65	.20	.15
1283B	5¢ Washington, Clean Face ('67) .	13.50	.80	.20	.15
1283Bv	5¢ Clean Face, Dull Gum	39.50	3.25	.40	...
1284	6¢ F.D.Roosevelt (1966)	24.00	.95	.25	.15
1284a	6¢ F.D.R., Tagged	20.00	.75	.20	.15
1284b	6¢ Booklet Pane of 8 (1967)	...	...	1.60	1.50
1284c	6¢ Pane of 5 (S4 or S5) (1968) ..	...	...	1.50	1.35
1285	8¢ Albert Einstein (1966)	36.50	1.70	.40	.15
1285a	8¢ Einstein, Tagged	32.50	1.50	.35	.20
1286	10¢ Andrew Jackson (1967)	36.50	1.65	.40	.15
1286A	12¢ Henry Ford (1968)	32.50	1.40	.35	.15
1287	13¢ John F. Kennedy (1967)	55.00	2.50	.60	.15
1288	15¢ O.W. Holmes, Die I (1968) ..	42.50	2.10	.45	.15
1288d	15¢ Holmes, Die II (1979)	95.00	15.00	1.00	.20

1965-79 Prominent Americans Series (Cont.)
(Sheets of 100)

Scott's No.		Mint Sheet	Plate Block	F-VF NH	F-VF Used
1288B	15¢ Bklt. Single, Pf. 10 Die III	...	...	.45	.15
1288Bc	15¢ Bk. Pane of 8, Die III (1978) ...	...	...	3.60	3.50
1289	20¢ George C. Marshall (1967) ..	72.50	3.25	.75	.15
1289a	20¢ Marshall, Tagged (1973)	62.50	2.75	.65	.30
1289ad	20¢ Dull Gum	140.00	7.50	1.50	...
1290	25¢ Fred.Douglass, Rose lake (1967)	97.50	4.25	1.10	.15
1290a	25¢ Douglass, Tagged (1973)	90.00	3.95	.95	.15
1290ad	25¢ Dull Gum	115.00	6.75	1.20	...
1290b	25¢ Douglass, Magenta	...	175.00	27.50	...

1291   **1292**   **1293**   **1294,1305C**   **1295**

1291	30¢ John Dewey (1968)	120.00	5.25	1.25	.15
1291a	30¢ Dewey, Tagged(1973)	105.00	4.75	1.10	.15
1292	40¢ Thomas Paine (1968)	125.00	5.95	1.35	.15
1292a	40¢ Paine, Tagged (1973)	100.00	4.75	1.10	.25
1292ad	40¢ Dull Gum	130.00	6.75	1.35	...
1293	50¢ Lucy Stone (1968)	165.00	7.50	1.75	.15
1293a	50¢ Stone, Tagged (1973)	140.00	6.25	1.50	.25
1294	$1 Eugene O'Neill (1967)	325.00	14.50	3.50	.15
1294a	$1 O'Neill, Tagged (1973)	275.00	12.50	3.00	.15
1295	$5 John B. Moore (1966)	...	72.50	16.50	2.95
1295a	$5 Moore, Tagged (1973)	...	57.50	13.00	2.75

#1288 and 1305E: Die I top bar of "5" is horiz., tie touches lapel.
#1288d and 1305Ei: Die II top bar of "5" slopes down to right, tie does not touch lapel.
#1288B and 1288Bc: Die III booklets only, design shorter than Die I or II.

1297   **1298**   **1304 Line Pair**   **1305**

1966-81 Prominent Americans, Coils, Perf. 10

Scott's No.	Line Pair	F-VF NH	F-VF Used
1297-1305C Prominent Am. Coils (9) ...	14.50	5.00	2.00
1297-1305C Very Fine Set of 9	17.00	6.00	2.80
1297 3¢ Francis Parkman (1975)	.60	.20	.15
1297b 3¢ Bureau Precancel	4.35	.50	.25
1297d 3¢ Dull Gum	5.00	.85	...
1298 6¢ F.D. Roosevelt, Pf. Horiz. ('67) ..	...	1.50	.25 .15
1299 1¢ Jefferson (1968)	.40	.20	.15
1299a 1¢ Bureau Precancel	225.00	17.50	.75
1303 4¢ Abraham Lincoln	.90	.35	.15
1303a 4¢ Bureau Precancel	160.00	10.00	.75
1304 5¢ Washington, Original	.50	.20	.15
1304a 5¢ Bureau Precancel	175.00	10.75	.75
1304d 5¢ Dull Gum	8.50	1.10	...
1304C 5¢ Redrawn, Clean Face (1981) ..	2.00	.25	.15
1305 6¢ F.D.Roosevelt, Pf. Vert. ('68) .	.75	.25	.15
1305b 6¢ Bureau Precancel	300.00	16.00	1.25
1305E 15¢ O.W.Holmes, Die I (1978) ...	1.30	.45	.15
1305Ed 15¢ Die I, Dull Gum	7.50	1.95	...
1305Ef 15¢ Bureau Precancel	...	37.50	3.95
1305Ei 15¢ Holmes, Die II (1979)	2.50	.70	.25
1305C $1 Eugene O'Neill (1973)	7.50	3.25	1.10
1305Cd $1 Dull Gum	8.75	3.85	...

NOTE: F.VF, NH Bureau Precancels have full original gum
and have never been used.

1966 Commemoratives

1306   **1307**

1308   **1309**   **1310**   **1312**

32

1966 Commemoratives

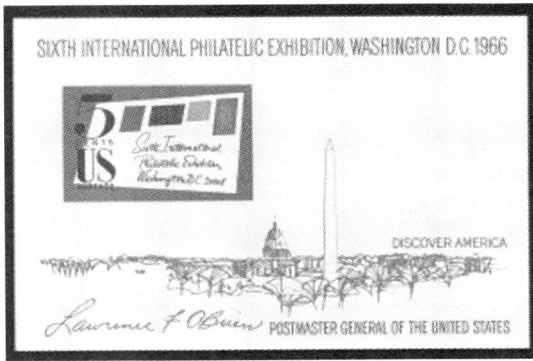

1311

Scott's No.		Mint Sheet	Plate Block	F-VF NH	F-VF Used
1306-22	Set of 17	...	...	3.00	1.85
1306	5¢ Migratory Bird Treaty	7.50	.70	.20	.15
1307	5¢ Humane Treatment Animals ..	7.50	.70	.20	.15
1308	5¢ Indiana Statehood	13.50	1.30	.30	.15
1309	5¢ American Circus (Clown)	11.00	1.10	.25	.15
1310	5¢ SIPEX Stamp	7.50	.70	.20	.15
1311	5¢ SIPEX Souvenir Sheet	...	...	.20	.20
1312	5¢ Bill of Rights	7.50	.70	.20	.15

1313   **1314**   **1315**

1316   **1317**   **1318**

1319   **1320**   **1321**   **1322**

1313	5¢ Polish Millenium		7.50	.70	.20	.15
1314	5¢ National Park Service		7.75	.70	.20	.15
1314a	5¢ Parks, Tagged		16.50	2.00	.35	.30
1315	5¢ Marine Corps Reserve		7.50	.70	.20	.15
1315a	5¢ Marines, Tagged		16.50	2.00	.35	.30
1316	5¢ Fed. of Women's Clubs		7.50	.70	.20	.15
1316a	5¢ Women's Clubs, Tagged		16.50	2.00	.35	.30
1317	5¢ Johnny Appleseed		13.50	1.30	.30	.15
1317a	5¢ Appleseed, Tagged		18.50	2.25	.40	.30
1318	5¢ Beautification of America		7.50	.70	.20	.15
1318a	5¢ Beautification, Tagged		16.50	2.00	.50	.30
1319	5¢ Great River Road		13.50	1.30	.30	.15
1319a	5¢ Great River, Tagged		18.50	2.25	.40	.30
1320	5¢ Savings Bond - Servicemen ..		7.50	.70	.20	.15
1320a	5¢ Savings Bonds, Tagged		16.50	2.00	.35	.30
1321	5¢ Christmas, Madonna and Child by Hemming	(100)	14.50	.85	.20	.15
1321a	5¢ Christmas, Tagged	(100)	32.50	2.25	.35	.30
1322	5¢ Mary Cassatt Painting		8.00	.75	.20	.15
1322a	5¢ Cassatt, Tagged		16.50	2.00	.35	.30

NOTE: FROM #752 TO DATE, AVERAGE QUALITY STAMPS, WHEN AVAILABLE, WILL BE PRICED AT APPROX. 20% BELOW THE APPROPRIATE FINE QUALITY PRICE. VERY FINE COPIES OF #752-DATE ARE AVAILABLE FOR THE FOLLOWING PREMIUMS: ADD 10¢ TO ANY ITEM PRICED UNDER 50¢. ADD 20% TO ANY ITEM PRICED AT 50¢ & UP. UNLESS PRICED AT VERY FINE, SETS ARE NOT AVAILABLE VERY FINE STAMPS SHOULD BE LISTED INDIVIDUALLY WITH APPROPRIATE PREMIUM.

1967 Commemoratives

1323   **1324**   **1325**

1326   **1327**   **1328**

1329   **1330**   **1333**   **1334**

1331   **1332**

1335   **1336**   **1337**

Scott's No.		Mint Sheet	Plate Block	F-VF NH	F-VF Used
1323-37	Set of 15	...	...	4.95	1.65
1323	5¢ National Grange	11.00	1.10	.25	.15
1324	5¢ Canada Centenary	7.50	.70	.20	.15
1325	5¢ Erie Canal	15.00	1.50	.35	.15
1326	5¢ Search for Peace - Lions	13.50	1.30	.30	.15
1327	5¢ Henry David Thoreau	15.00	1.50	.35	.15
1328	5¢ Nebraska Statehood	15.00	1.50	.35	.15
1329	5¢ Voice of America	7.50	.70	.20	.15
1330	5¢ Davy Crockett	13.50	1.30	.30	.15
1331-2	5¢ Space Twins, Attached	52.50	5.25	2.25	1.50
1331-2	Set of 2 Singles	...	...	1.50	.40
1333	5¢ Urban Planning	7.50	.70	.20	.15
1334	5¢ Finnish Independence	7.50	.70	.20	.15
1335	5¢ Thomas Eakins Painting	13.50	1.30	.30	.15
1336	5¢ Christmas, Madonna	7.50	.70	.20	.15
1337	5¢ Mississippi Statehood	15.00	1.50	.35	.15

1968-71 Regular Issues

1338   **1338A,D**   **1338F,G**

1338	6¢ Flag & White House	(100)	18.00	.85	.20	.15
1338D	6¢ Same, Huck Press ('70)	(100)	18.50	(20) 3.50	.20	.15
1338F	8¢ Flag & White House ('71) ..	(100)	22.50	(20) 4.50	.25	.15
1338A	6¢ Flag & W.H.-Huck Coil ('69) ... Full Line Pr.		6.50		.25	.15
1338A	6¢ Flag & W.H.-Huck Coil ('69) ... Partial Line Pr.		1.25		...	...
1338G	8¢ Flag & W.H.-Huck Coil ('71) ... Partial Line Pr.		2.75		.25	.15

NOTE: #1338 is 19mm x 22mm, #1338D is 18¼mm x 21 mm.

| 1339 | 1341 | 1340 |

1968 Commemoratives

Scott's No.		Mint Sheet	Plate Block	F-VF NH	F-VF Used
1339-40,42-64	Set of 25	...	...	7.75	4.50
1339	6¢ Illinois Statehood	11.00	1.10	.25	.15
1340	6¢ Hemis Fair '68, San Antonio ..	7.75	.70	.20	.15

1968 Airlift to Servicemen

| 1341 | $1 Eagle Holding Pennant .... | 150.00 | 12.75 | 3.00 | 1.95 |

1968 Commemoratives (cont.)

| 1342 | 1343 | 1344 |

| 1345 | 1346 | 1347 |

| 1348 | 1349 | 1350 |

| 1351 | 1352 | 1353 |

| 1354 | 1355 | 1356 |

1342	6¢ Support Our Youth - Elks	7.75	.70	.20	.15
1343	6¢ Law and Order	16.75	1.70	.35	.15
1344	6¢ Register and Vote	7.75	.70	.20	.15

1968 Historic American Flags

1345-54	Hist. Flag, Strip/10	19.50 (20)	8.95	4.25	4.00
1345-46	Plate Blk. of 4	...	1.75	...	...
1345-54	Set of 10 Singles	...	...	3.50	2.75
1345	6¢ Fort Moultrie	...	...	.45	.30
1346	6¢ Fort McHenry	...	...	.45	.30
1347	6¢ Washington Cruisers	...	...	.40	.30
1348	6¢ Bennington	...	...	.40	.30
1349	6¢ Rhode Island	...	...	.40	.30
1350	6¢ First Stars & Stripes	...	...	.40	.30
1351	6¢ Bunker Hill	...	...	.40	.30
1352	6¢ Grand Union	...	...	.40	.30
1353	6¢ Philadelphia Light Horse	...	...	.40	.30
1354	6¢ First Navy Jack	...	...	.40	.30

1968 Commemoratives (continued)

| 1355 | 6¢ Walt Disney .... | 25.00 | 2.50 | .50 | .15 |
| 1356 | 6¢ Father Marquette .... | 15.00 | 1.50 | .35 | .15 |

1968 Commemoratives (continued)

| 1357 | 1358 | 1359 |

| 1360 | 1362 |

| 1361 | 1363 | 1364 |

1357	6¢ Daniel Boone	11.00	1.10	.25	.15
1358	6¢ Arkansas River Navigation	11.00	1.10	.25	.15
1359	6¢ Leif Erikson	11.00	1.10	.25	.15
1360	6¢ Cherokee Strip	11.00	1.10	.25	.15
1361	6¢ John Trumbull Painting	18.50	1.70	.40	.15
1362	6¢ Waterfowl Conservation	11.75	1.25	.25	.15
1363	6¢ Christmas, Angel Gabriel	8.75 (10)	1.75	.20	.15
1363a	6¢ Christmas, Untagged	21.50 (10)	4.50	.45	.25
1364	6¢ American Indian - Joseph	13.50	1.30	.30	.15

1969 Commemoratives

| 1365 | 1366 |
| 1367 | 1368 |

| 1369 | 1370 | 1371 | 1373 |

| 1372 | 1374 | 1375 |

1365-86	Set of 22 (no precancels)	...	...	8.75	2.95
1365-8	6¢ Beautification, attached	27.00	2.65	2.30	2.25
1365-8	Set of 4 Singles	...	...	1.95	.75
1369	6¢ American Legion	7.50	.70	.20	.15
1370	6¢ Grandma Moses Painting	7.50	.70	.20	.15
1371	6¢ Apollo 8 Mission	13.75	1.35	.30	.15
1372	6¢ W.C. Handy	13.50	1.30	.30	.15
1373	6¢ California Settlement	7.50	.70	.20	.15
1374	6¢ John Wesley Powell	7.50	.70	.20	.15
1375	6¢ Alabama Statehood	13.50	1.30	.30	.15

1969 Commemoratives (continued)

1376 1377
1378 1379

1381

1380

1382

1383

1385

1386

1384

1384 Precancel

Scott's No.		Mint Sheet	Plate Block	F-VF NH	F-VF Used
1376-9	6¢ Botanical Congress, att'd.	32.75	3.25	2.95	2.95
1376-9	Set of Singles	...	...	2.75	.80
1380	6¢ Dartmouth College	15.00	1.50	.35	.15
1381	6¢ Professional Baseball	55.00	4.95	1.20	.20
1382	6¢ College Football	25.00	2.30	.55	.15
1383	6¢ D.D. Eisenhower Memorial . (32)	5.25	.75	.20	.15
1384	6¢ Christmas, Winter Sunday	8.25 (10)1.75		.20	.15
1384a	6¢ Precancelled (Set of 4 Cities)	200.00(10)110.00		2.65	2.50
1385	6¢ Crippled Children	7.50	.70	.20	.15
1386	6¢ William M. Harnett Painting (32)	5.25	.70	.20	.15

NOTE: #1384a EXISTS WITH "ATLANTA, GA"; "BALTIMORE, MD", MEMPHIS, TN"
   AND "NEW HAVEN, CT" PRECANCELS.

1970 Commemoratives

1387 1388
1389 1390

1391

1392

1970 Commemoratives

Scott's No.		Mint Sheet	Plate Block	F-VF NH	F-VF Used
1387-92,1405-22	Set of 24 (no prec.) ...	...	...	7.50	2.90
1387-90	6¢ Natural History, attached .. (32)	7.75	1.10	1.00	1.00
1387-90	Set of 4 Singles	...	...	.95	.70
1391	6¢ Maine Statehood	11.00	1.30	.25	.15
1392	6¢ Wildlife Conserv. - Buffalo	13.50	1.50	.30	.15

1970-74 Regular Issue

1393,1401

1393D

1394-95,1402

1396

1397

1398

1399

1400

Scott's No.		Mint Sheet	Plate Block	F-VF NH	F-VF Used
1393-94,1396-1400	Set of 8	...	...	2.95	.95
1393	6¢ Eisenhower .... (100)	17.50	.75	.20	.15
1393v	6¢ Dull Gum .... (100)	39.50	4.00	.40	...
1393a	6¢ Booklet Pane of 8	...	...	2.10	1.85
1393ae	6¢ Pane of 8, Dull Exper. Gum ...	...	...	1.80	...
1393b	6¢ Bklt. Pane of 5, (S4 or S5) ('71)	...	...	1.25	1.20
1393D	7¢ Benjamin Franklin ('72) ...... (100)	27.50	1.30	.30	.15
1393Dv	7¢ Dull Gum .... (100)	39.50	2.75	.40	...
1394	8¢ Ike, Multicolored ('71) ...... (100)	24.00	1.00	.25	.15
1395	8¢ Ike, Deep Claret, Bklt. Single .	...	...	.35	.15
1395v	8¢ Booklet Single, Dull Gum	...	...	.35	...
1395a	Booklet Pane of 8 (1971)	...	...	2.40	2.25
1395b	Booklet Pane of 6 (1971)	...	...	1.70	1.65
1395c	Booklet Pane of 4 Dull('72)	...	...	1.60	1.50
1395d	Booklet Pane of 7, Dull (S4) (1972)	...	...	3.25	2.75
1395d	Booklet Pane of 7, Dull (S5) (1972)	...	...	2.10	1.95

S4 is "Mail Early", S5 is "Use Zip Code"

1396	8¢ U.S. Postal Service ('71) ... (100)	22.50 (12)	3.00	.25	.15
1396	8¢ U.S. Postal Service	... (20)	4.75	...	...
1397	14¢ Fiorello La Guardia ('72) .. (100)	35.00	1.60	.40	.15
1398	16¢ Ernie Pyle ('71) .... (100)	52.50	2.35	.55	.15
1399	18¢ Dr. Eliz. Blackwell ('74) ... (100)	52.50	2.25	.55	.15
1400	21¢ Amadeo P. Giannini ('73) . (100)	62.50	2.75	.65	.25

NOTE: #1395 ONLY EXISTS WITH ONE OR MORE STRAIGHT EDGES SINCE IT COMES FROM BOOKLET PANES.

1970-71 Dwight D. Eisenhower, Coils, Perf. 10 Vertically

Scott's No.		Line Pair	F-VF NH	F-VF Used
1401	6¢ Gray.	.50	.20	.15
1401a	6¢ Bureau Precancel	150.00	9.50	.95
1401d	6¢ Dull Gum	2.25	.45	...
1402	8¢ Deep Claret ('71)	.60	.25	.15
1402b	8¢ Bureau Precancel	110.00	6.50	.95

1970 Commemoratives (continued)

1405

1406

1407

1408

1409

1419

1414

1414a

1420

1410 1411
1412 1413

1415 1416
1417 1418

1421 1422

Scott's No.		Mint Sheet	Plate Block	F-VF NH	F-VF Used
1405	6¢ Edgar Lee Masters - Poet	8.25	.75	.20	.15
1406	6¢ Women Suffrage	8.25	.75	.20	.15
1407	6¢ South Carolina Founding	15.00	1.50	.35	.15
1408	6¢ Stone Mountain Memorial	15.00	1.50	.35	.15
1409	6¢ Fort Snelling, Minnesota	11.00	1.10	.25	.15
1410-13	6¢ Anti-Pollution, Attached	18.75 (10)	4.75	1.75	1.70
1410-13	Set of 4 Singles	...	...	1.60	.65
1414	6¢ Christmas, Nativity, Ty. I	8.25 (8)	1.50	.20	.15
1414a	6¢ Christmas, Nativity, Precncl ...	11.00 (8)	2.50	.25	.20
1414d	6¢ Type II, Horiz. Gum Breakers	45.00 (8)	10.75	.95	.30
1414e	6¢ Type II, Precancelled	52.50 (8)	12.50	1.10	.35

Type I – blurry impression, snowflakes in sky, no gum breakers
Type II – sharper impression, no snowflakes in sky, with gum breakers

1415-18	6¢ Christmas Toys, attd	25.00 (8)	5.00	2.35	2.50
1415-18	Set of 4 Singles	...	...	1.95	.60
1415a-18a	6¢ Toys, Precan., attached ..	37.50 (8)	7.50	3.50	3.95
1415a-18a	Set of 4 Singles	...	...	2.75	1.00
1419	6¢ United Nations 25th Anniv	8.25	.75	.20	.15
1420	6¢ Landing of the Pilgrims	8.25	.75	.20	.15
1421-22	6¢ DAV - Servicemen, attd	9.00	1.40	.50	.45
1421-22	Set of 2 Singles	...	...	...	.45	.30

1971 Commemoratives

1423

1425

1424

1427 1428
1429 1430

1426

1432

1431

1433

1434 1435

1436

1437

1438

1439

1440 1441
1442 1443

1444

1445

1446

1447

Scott's No.		Mint Sheet	Plate Block	F-VF NH	F-VF Used
1423-45	**Set of 23**	...	...	5.95	2.85
1423	6¢ American Wool Industry	8.25	.75	.20	.15
1424	6¢ Gen. Douglas MacArthur	8.25	.75	.20	.15
1425	6¢ Blood Donor	8.25	.75	.20	.15
1426	8¢ Missouri Sesquicentennial	15.00 (12)	4.25	.35	.15
1427-30	8¢ Wildlife, attached .... (32)	8.75	1.20	1.10	1.00
1427-30	Set of 4 Singles	...	...	1.00	.70
1431	8¢ Antarctic Treaty	10.75	1.00	.25	.15
1432	8¢ Bicentennnial Emblem	13.00	1.25	.30	.15
1433	8¢ John Sloan Painting	10.75	1.00	.25	.15
1434-5	8¢ Space Achievement, attd	12.75	1.15	.55	.50
1434-5	Set of 2 Singles	...	...	.50	.30
1436	8¢ Emily Dickinson	15.00	1.50	.35	.15
1437	8¢ San Juan, Puerto Rico	10.75	1.00	.25	.15
1438	8¢ Prevent Drug Abuse	10.75 (6)	1.50	.25	.15
1439	8¢ CARE	10.75 (8)	1.95	.25	.15
1440-3	8¢ Historic Preservation, attd .. (32)	9.75	1.40	1.25	1.10
1440-3	Set of 4 Singles	...	...	1.20	.70
1444	8¢ Christmas, Adoration	10.75 (12)	2.75	.25	.15
1445	8¢ Christmas, Partridge	10.75 (12)	2.75	.25	.15

1972 Commemoratives

National Parks Centennial

1452

National Parks Centennial

National Parks Centennial

1448 1449
1450 1451

National Parks Centennial — Old Faithful, Yellowstone

1454

1453

Colonial American Craftsmen

1456 1457
1458 1459

Family Planning

1455

Scott's No.		Mint Sheet	Plate Block	F-VF NH	F-VF Used
1446-74	**Set of 29**	...	...	7.50	3.75
1446	8¢ Sidney Lanier	18.00	1.70	.40	.15
1447	8¢ Peace Corps	11.75 (6)	1.60	.25	.15
1448-54,C84	Parks Set of 8	65.00	6.00	1.65	1.15
1448-51	2¢ Cape Hatteras, attached . (100)	9.75	.75	.60	.50
1448-51	Set of 4 Singles	...	...	.55	.45
1452	6¢ Wolf Trap Farm	13.50	1.30	.30	.15
1453	8¢ Old Faithful (32)	7.50	1.00	.25	.15
1454	15¢ Mt. McKinley	20.00	1.75	.45	.25
	See #C84 for 11¢ City of Refuge National Park Issue				
1455	8¢ Family Planning	10.75	1.10	.25	.15
1456-9	8¢ Colonial Craftsmen, attd	12.50	1.20	1.10	.95
1456-9	Set of 4 Singles	...	...	.90	.60

1460

1461

1462

Wildlife Conservation

1464 1465
1466 1467

P.T.A. Parent Teacher Association

1463

Osteopathic Medicine

1469

100th Anniversary of Mail Order

1468

Tom Sawyer

1470

1460-62,C85	Olympics Set of 4	52.50	11.75	1.25	.70
1460	6¢ Olympics - Bicycling	8.50 (10)	1.85	.20	.15
1461	8¢ Olympics - Bobsledding	10.75 (10)	2.50	.25	.15
1462	15¢ Olympics - Running	21.00 (10)	4.50	.45	.35
	See #C85 for 11¢ Olympics				

1973 Commemoratives (continued)

Scott's No.		Mint Sheet	Plate Block	F-VF NH	F-VF Used
1463	8¢ Parent Teacher Assn	10.75	1.00	.25	.15
1463r	8¢ P.T.A. Error Plate # Reversed	11.00	1.10	...	...
1464-7	8¢ Wildlife Conserv., attd (32)	8.25	1.25	1.10	1.00
1464-7	Set of 4 Singles	...	...	1.00	.70
1468	8¢ Mail Order Business	10.75 (12)	2.80	.25	.15
1469	8¢ Osteopathic Medicine	10.75 (6)	1.60	.25	.15
1470	8¢ Tom Sawyer	15.00	1.50	.35	.15

Christmas

1471

Twas the Night before Christmas

1472

Pharmacy — United States Postage

1473

Stamp Collecting

1474

1471	8¢ Christmas Angel	10.75 (12)	2.80	.25	.15
1472	8¢ Christmas, Santa Claus	13.75 (12)	3.50	.30	.15
1473	8¢ Pharmacy	18.75	2.00	.40	.15
1474	8¢ Stamp Collecting (40)	8.50	1.00	.25	.15

1973 Commemoratives

1475

Rise of the Spirit of Independence

1476

Rise of the Spirit of Independence

1477

Rise of the Spirit of Independence

1478

Rise of the Spirit of Independence

1479

Copernicus 1473-1973

1488

The Boston Tea Party

1480 1481
1482 1483

George Gershwin

1484

Robinson Jeffers

1485

Henry Tanner

1486

Willa Cather

1487

Scott's No.		Mint Sheet	Plate Block	F-VF NH	F-VF Used
1475-1508	**Set of 34**	...	...	8.50	4.25
1475	8¢ Love	10.75 (6)	1.50	.25	.15
1476-79	Communications in Colonial America (4)	39.75	3.85	.95	.50
1476	8¢ Printers and Patriots	10.75	1.00	.25	.15
1477	8¢ Posting a Broadside	10.75	1.00	.25	.15
1478	8¢ Postrider	10.75	1.00	.25	.15
1479	8¢ Drummer	10.75	1.00	.25	.15
1480-83	8¢ Boston Tea Party, attd	12.00	1.30	1.10	1.00
1480-83	Set of 4 Singles	...	...	1.00	.60
1484-87	Arts Set of 4	32.75	11.95	.95	.50
1484	8¢ Arts - George Gershwin (40)	9.00 (12)	3.25	.25	.15
1485	8¢ Arts - Robinson Jeffers (40)	9.00 (12)	3.25	.25	.15
1486	8¢ Arts - Henry Tanner (40)	9.00 (12)	3.25	.25	.15
1487	8¢ Arts - Willa Cather (40)	11.00 (12)	3.75	.30	.15
1488	8¢ Nicolaus Copernicus	11.50	1.00	.25	.15

VERY FINE COPIES OF #752-DATE ARE AVAILABLE FOR THE FOLLOWING PREMIUMS:
ADD 10¢ TO ANY ITEM PRICED UNDER 50¢. ADD 20% TO ANY ITEM PRICED AT 50¢ & UP.

1973 Postal Service Employees

1488   1490   1491   1492   1493

1494   1495   1496   1497   1498

Scott's No.		Mint Sheet	Plate Block	F-VF NH	F-VF Used
1489-98	8¢ Postal Employees, strip, attd ..	14.50 (20)	6.00	2.75	2.50
1489-98	8¢ Set of 10 Singles	...	...	2.60	1.80

1973 Commemoratives (continued)

1500   1499   1501

1502   1503   1504

1505

1506   1507   1508

1499	8¢ Harry S Truman .... (32)	7.25	1.00	.25	.15
1500-2,C86	Electronics Set of 4	52.50	4.95	1.15	.70
1500	6¢ Electronics - Marconi	8.25	.85	.20	.15
1501	8¢ Electronics - Transistors	10.75	1.00	.25	.15
1502	15¢ Electronics - Inventions	21.75	1.85	.45	.35
See #C86 for 11¢ Electronics					
1503	8¢ Lyndon B. Johnson .... (32)	7.75 (12)	3.25	.25	.15
1504	8¢ Rural America - Cattle	10.75	1.00	.25	.15
1505	10¢ Rural America - Tent ('74)	13.50	1.30	.30	.15
1506	10¢ Rural America - Wheat ('74) ..	13.50	1.30	.30	.15
1507	8¢ Christmas, Madonna	10.75 (12)	3.00	.25	.15
1508	8¢ Christmas, Needlepoint	10.75 (12)	3.00	.25	.15

1973-1974 Regular Issues

1509,1519   1510,1520   1511   1518

Scott's No.		Mint Sheet	Plate Block	F-VF NH	F-VF Used
1509	10¢ Crossed Flags .... (100)	28.50 (20)	6.50	.30	.15
1510	10¢ Jefferson Memorial .... (100)	28.50	1.35	.30	.15
1510b	Booklet Pane of 5	...	...	1.75	1.85
1510c	Booklet Pane of 8	...	...	2.25	2.25
1510d	Booklet Pane of 6 (1974)	...	...	8.75	4.75
1511	10¢ Zip Code (1974) .... (100)	28.00 (8)	2.50	.30	.15

1973-74 Regular Issue Coils, Perf. 10 Vert.

Scott's No.		Line Pair	F-VF NH	F-VF Used
1518	6.3¢ Liberty Bell Coil ('74)	.60	.20	.15
1518a	6.3¢ Bureau Precancel	1.65	.35	.20
1519	10¢ Crossed Flags Coil .... Full 5.75 Part 2.25		.35	.15
1520	10¢ Jefferson Memorial Coil	.70	.30	.15
1520a	10¢ Bureau Precancel	110.00	6.00	1.00

1974 Commemoratives (See also 1505-06)

1525   1526   1527

1528   1529

1530   1531   1532   1533
1534   1535   1536   1537

Scott's No.		Mint Sheet	Plate Block	F-VF NH	F-VF Used
1525-52	Set of 28	...	...	8.95	3.95
1525	10¢ Veterans of Foreign Wars	13.50	1.30	.30	.15
1526	10¢ Robert Frost	21.00	1.90	.45	.15
1527	10¢ Expo '74, Spokane .... (40)	11.00 (12)	3.75	.30	.15
1528	10¢ Horse Racing	21.00 (12)	5.50	.45	.15
1529	10¢ Skylab I	13.50	1.30	.30	.15
1530-37	10¢ U.P.U. Centenary blk, attd . (32)	11.50 (10)	3.50	2.75	2.50
1530-37	Strip of 8	...	...	2.75	2.50
1530-37	Plate Block of 16	...	(16)	5.95	...
1530-37	Set of 8 Singles	...	...	2.65	2.00

1538   1540
1539   1541

1542

1543   1544
1545   1546

1547

1548

1549

1551

1550

1552

Scott's No.		Mint Sheet	Plate Block	F-VF NH	F-VF Used
1538-41	10¢ Mineral Heritage blk, attd .. (48)	15.00	1.50	1.35	1.00
1538-41	Strip of 4	...	...	1.30	1.00
1538-41	Set of 4 Singles	...	...	1.20	.60
1542	10¢ Kentucky Settlement	18.00	1.70	.40	.15
1543-46	10¢ First Continental Congress, attd	15.00	1.40	1.30	1.10
1543-46	Set of 4 Singles	...	...	1.20	.60
1547	10¢ Energy Conservation	13.50	1.30	.30	.15
1548	10¢ Sleepy Hollow	13.50	1.30	.30	.15
1549	10¢ Retarded Children	13.50	1.30	.30	.15
1550	10¢ Christmas, Angel	13.50 (10)	3.25	.30	.15
1551	10¢ Christmas, Currier & Ives	13.50 (12)	3.75	.30	.15
1552	10¢ Christmas, Peace on Earth, Self-adhesive	16.00 (20)	7.25	.35	.25
1552	Same - Plate Block of 12	... (12)	4.50	...	...

NOTE: MOST UNUSED COPIES OF #1552 ARE DISCOLORED FROM THE ADHESIVE. PRICE IS FOR DISCOLORED COPIES.

1975 Commemoratives

1553

1555

1554

1556

1557

1558

1559

1560

1561

1562

1563

1564

1567   1568
1565   1566

1569
1570

1571

1573   1572
1575   1574

Scott's No.		Mint Sheet	Plate Block	F-VF NH	F-VF Used
1553-80	Set of 28 (No #1580B)			8.95	3.75
1553-55	American Arts Issue				
1553	10¢ Benjamin West Portrait	20.75 (10)	4.75	.45	.15
1554	10¢ Paul Laurence Dunbar - Poet	20.75 (10)	4.75	.45	.15
1555	10¢ D.W. Griffith	20.75	1.90	.45	.15
1556	10¢ Space Pioneer - Jupiter	16.00	1.50	.35	.15
1557	10¢ Space Mariner 10	16.00	1.50	.35	.15
1558	10¢ Collective Bargaining	13.50 (8)	2.50	.30	.15
1559-62	Contributors to the Cause (4)	59.75	14.50	1.30	.75
1559	8¢ Sybil Ludington	10.75 (10)	2.50	.25	.20
1560	10¢ Salem Poor	15.00 (10)	3.75	.35	.15
1561	10¢ Haym Salomon	13.50 (10)	3.25	.30	.15
1562	18¢ Peter Francisco	25.00 (10)	6.25	.55	.35
1563	10¢ Lexington-Concord	15.00 (40) 12	4.95	.40	.15
1564	10¢ Battle of Bunker Hill	13.50 (40) 12	4.50	.35	.15
1565-68	10¢ Military Uniforms, attd	16.00 (12)	4.75	1.40	1.10
1565-68	Set of 4 Singles	...	...	1.30	.60
1569-70	10¢ Apollo Soyuz, attd	(24) 7.25 (12)	4.00	.65	.50
1569-70	Set of 2 Singles	...	...	.60	.30
1571	10¢ Int'l. Women's Year	13.50 (6)	1.90	.30	.15
1572-75	10¢ Postal Service Bicent., attd	14.50 (12)	4.25	1.30	1.10
1572-75	Set of 4 Singles	...	...	1.20	.60

1975 Commemoratives (cont.)

1576   1577   1578

1579   1580

Scott's No.		Mint Sheet	Plate Block	F-VF NH	F-VF Used
1576	10¢ World Peace through Law	16.00	1.60	.35	.15
1577-78	10¢ Banking Commerce, attd ... (40)	15.00	1.95	.85	.50
1577-78	Set of 2 Singles	...	...	.80	.30
1579	10¢ Christmas, Madonna and				
	Child by Ghirlandaio	13.50 (12)	3.75	.30	.15
1580	10¢ Christmas Card, Perf. 11.2	17.50 (12)	5.00	.40	.20
1580c	10¢ Christmas, Perf. 10.9	13.50 (12)	3.75	.30	.15
1580B	10¢ Christmas (P. 10½ x 11)	45.00 (12)	14.50	.85	.50

1975-1981 Americana Issue (Perf. 11 x 10½)

1581,1811   1582   1584   1585

1590,91,1616   1592,1617   1593   1594,1816

1595,1618   1596   1597/1618C   1599,1619

1603   1604   1605   1606

1608   1610   1611   1612

Scott's No.		Mint Sheet	Plate Block	F-VF NH	F-VF Used
1581-85,91-94,96-97,99-1612 Set of 19 ..		...	133.50	28.00	5.75
1581	1¢ Ability to Write (1977)	5.00	.50	.20	.15
1581v	1¢ Dry Gum	7.00	1.25	.20	...
1582	2¢ Freedom/Speak Out ('77)	6.75	.50	.20	.15
1582v	2¢ Dry Gum, white paper	29.50	2.50	.30	...
1582b	2¢ Dry Gum, cream paper (1981) .	18.50	2.75	.25	.20
1584	3¢ Cast a Free Ballot ('77)	11.00	.50	.20	.15
1584v	3¢ Dry Gum	19.50	1.30	.25	...
1585	4¢ Public That Reads ('77)	12.50	.60	.20	.15
1585v	4¢ Dry Gum	23.75	1.50	.25	...
1590	9¢ Assem., Bklt.Sngl Pf.11x10½ ('77)	...	...	.70	.60
1590 & 1623 attached Pair (from 1623a)		...	...	1.20	1.50
1590A	9¢ Booklet Single, Perf. 10	...	...	25.00	22.50
1590A & 1623B attd. Pair (from 1623c)		...	...	27.00	25.00

1975-1981 Americana Issue (continued)
(Sheets of 100)

Scott's No.		Mint Sheet	Plate Block	F-VF NH	F-VF Used
1591	9¢ Assemble, Large Size	27.50	1.25	.30	.15
1591v	9¢ Dry Gum	97.50	8.95	1.00	...
1592	10¢ Right to Petition ('77)	28.50	1.40	.30	.15
1592v	10¢ Dry Gum	67.50	3.75	.70	...
1593	11¢ Freedom of Press	32.50	1.50	.35	.15
1594	12¢ Freedom of Conscience ('81) ...	33.50	1.85	.35	.15
1595	13¢ Liberty Bell, Bklt. Single	...	...	.40	.15
1595a	13¢ Booklet Pane of 6	...	...	2.35	2.00
1595b	13¢ Booklet Pane of 7	...	...	2.50	2.50
1595c	13¢ Booklet Pane of 8	...	...	2.75	2.65
1595d	13¢ Booklet Pane of 5 (1976)	...	...	2.25	2.10
1596	13¢ Eagle & Shield, Bullseye Perfs.	38.50 (12)	5.00	.40	.15
1596d	13¢ Line Perfs *	... (12)	595.00	40.00	...
1597	15¢ McHenry Flag, Pf. 11 ('78)	47.50 (20)	10.50	.50	.15
1598	15¢ McHenry Flag, Bklt. Sgl. ('78) ..	...	...	.70	.15
1598a	15¢ Booklet Pane of 8	...	...	5.50	2.75
1599	16¢ Statue of Liberty (1978)	47.50	2.25	.50	.20
1603	24¢ Old North Church	65.00	3.25	.70	.20
1604	28¢ Fort Nisqually (1978)	75.00	3.75	.80	.20
1604v	28¢ Dry Gum	160.00	13.50	1.70	...
1605	29¢ Lighthouse (1978)	85.00	4.25	.90	.65
1605v	29¢ Dry Gum	190.00	17.50	2.00	...
1606	30¢ Schoolhouse (1979)	90.00	4.50	.95	.15
1608	50¢ Iron "Betty" (1979)	140.00	6.50	1.50	.25
1610	$1 Rush Lamp (1979)	295.00	13.00	3.00	.25
1611	$2 Kerosene Table Lamp ('78)	535.00	23.00	5.50	.75
1612	$5 Railroad Lantern (1979)	1300.00	60.00	13.75	2.75

* #1596 Bullseye Perforations line up perfectly where horiz. and vertical rows meet. Pf 11.2   #1596d Line Perfs. do not meet evenly. Perforated 11:
Note: #1608-1612 are Perforated 11.

1975-79 Americana Coil Issues - Perf. 10 Vert.

1613   1614   1615   1615C

Scott's No.		Line Pair	F-VF NH	F-VF Used
1613-19,1811-16 Americana Coils (12) .... (11)		11.85	3.25	1.95
1613	3.1¢ Guitar (1979)	.85	.20	.15
1613a	3.1¢ Bureau Precancel, Lines Only	6.50	.30	.25
1614	7.7¢ Saxhorns (1976)	1.20	.30	.20
1614a	7.7¢ Bureau Precancel	3.75	.70	.45
1615	7.9¢ Drum Shiny Gum (1976)	1.20	.30	.20
1615a	7.9¢ Bureau Precancel Shiny Gum	3.25	.40	.25
1615va	7.9¢ Dry Gum	4.00	.45	...
1615vb	7.9¢ Bureau Precancel, Dry Gum	4.75	.50	...
1615C	8.4¢ Steinway Grand Piano Shiny Gum (1978)	2.50	.30	.20
1615Cd	8.4¢ Bureau Precancel, Shiny Gum	6.75	.55	.30
1615Cdv	8.4¢ Precancel, Dry Gum	3.75	.50	...
1616	9¢ Right to Assemble (1976)	.75	.30	.20
1616b	9¢ Bureau Precancel, Shiny Gum	30.00	1.50	.50
1616bv	9¢ Bureau Precancel, Dry Gum	30.00	1.50	...
1617	10¢ Right to Petition, Shiny Gum (1977)	.95	.30	.15
1617a	10¢ Bureau Precancel, Dry Gum	37.50	1.75	.25
1617v	10¢ Dry Gum	2.50	.45	...
1618	13¢ Liberty Bell, Shiny Gum	.95	.35	.15
1618a	13¢ Bureau Precancel	79.50	8.50	1.00
1618v	13¢ Dry Gum	2.25	.65	...
1618va	13¢ Bureau Precancel, Dry Gum	21.75	1.40	...
1618C	15¢ Fort McHenry Flag (1978) (No Lines)	...	.35	.15
1619	16¢ Statue of Liberty Overall Tagging (1978)	1.40	.50	.35
1619a	16¢ Block Tagging (No Lines)	...	.90	.75

Note: Also see #1811-1816 for 1980-81 issues.

1975-77 Regular Issue

1622,1625   1623

Scott's No.		Mint Sheet	Plate Block	F-VF NH	F-VF Used
1622	13¢ Flag/Ind. Hall, Pf. 11x10½ ... (100)	37.50 (20)	8.25	.40	.15
1622C	13¢ Perf. 11 (1981) .... (100)	175.00 (20)	90.00	1.10	.95
* Plate Blocks of #1622 have Pl. #'s at Top or Bottom.					
* Plate Blocks of #1622C have Pl. #'s at Left or Right.					
1623	13¢ Flag over Capitol, Bklt. Sgl.				
	Pf. 11 x 10½ (1977)	...	...	.40	.15
1623a	13¢ & 9¢ Bklt. Pn./8 (7#1623,1#1590)	...	...	2.75	2.75
1623B	13¢ B. Sgl., Pf. 10 (1977)	...	...	.60	.55
1623c	13¢ & 9¢ B.P./8 (7#1623b,1#1590a)	...	...	32.75	20.00
1625	13¢ Flag over Ind. Hall, Coil .... (Partial Line)	4.75	...	.40	.15
1625	Full Line Pair	...	19.75	...	...

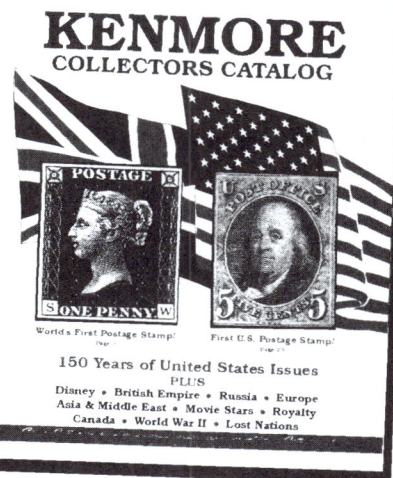

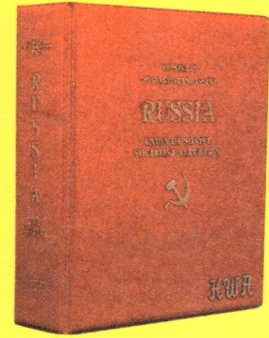

No serious collector should be without Linn's Stamp News.

Miss an issue of Linn's and you miss plenty:

- All the latest-breaking news from Linn's exclusive national and international sources.

- In-depth analysis from top authors on all aspects of collecting, including pricing trends, values, news issues, forgeries, security and more.

- Regular features you can't afford to miss — *Stamp Market Tips and Tip of the Week, Collectors' Forum, Editor's Choice, Readers' Opinions, Postmark Pursuit, Collectors' Workshop, Refresher Course* and much more

- The world's largest stamp marketplace. Listings of events, auctions and sales. Classified ads and readers' notices for buying, selling and trading.

Right now you can receive Linn's at the special introductory rate of only $19.95... plus get a bonus refresher manual to help jump start your own collection. *Linn's Stamp Collecting Made Easy…* is yours FREE with your paid, introductory subscription.

Your FREE refresher course will take you on a simplified tour of the techniques, terms and intricacies of stamp collecting. We'll show you how to buy stamps, how to sort, soak, catalog, store and mount them.

We'll explain terms like roulette, souvenir sheet, overprint and surcharge. You'll learn the right way to use a perforation gauge.

Linn's is researched, written and published by stamp collectors like you. And we understand you want to get the most fun and satisfaction from your collecting.

To order Linn's by phone call 1-800-448-7293

Be sure to give our Customer Service Representatives the code T010BR to get this special introductory rate

Subscribe at the special introductory rate of 26 issues for $19.95. You'll save over 69% off the regular price plus get our money back guarantee. We'll also send you FREE, Linn's 96-page, all illustrated: *STAMP COLLECTING MADE EASY* with your paid order.

Linn's Stamp News

P.O. Box 29, Sidney, OH 45365
www.linns.com

Guarantee: Receive a complete refund if you are not completely satisfied at any time.

40D

1976 Commemoratives

| | 1629 | 1630 | 1631 | | 1632 |

Scott's No.	Mint Sheet	Plate Block	F-VF NH	F-VF Used
1629-32,83-85,90-1703 Set of 21	...	...	**9.75**	**2.95**
1629-31 13¢ Spirit of '76, attd	20.75 (12)	5.50	1.35	.90
1629-31 Set of 3 Singles	...	...	1.25	.50
1632 13¢ Interphil '76, Philadelphia	18.50	1.70	.40	.15

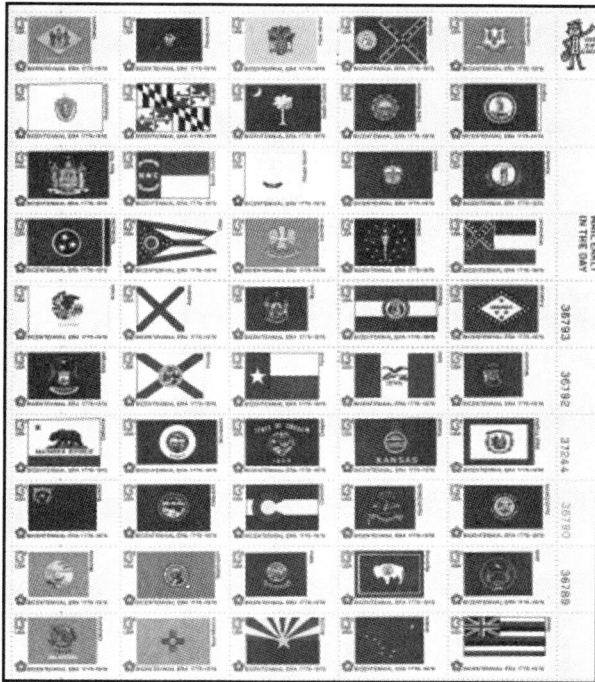

1633-82 Sheet

1976 State Flags Issue

	Mint Sheet	Plate Block	F-VF NH	F-VF Used
1633-82 13¢ State Flags attd	24.75 (12)	6.75	...	...
1633-82 Set of 50 Singles	...	...	23.75	14.50
1633-82 13¢ Individual Singles	...	...	.65	.35

1633	DE	1646	VT	1659	FL	1671	ND
1634	PA	1647	KY	1660	TX	1672	SD
1635	NJ	1648	TN	1661	IA	1673	MT
1636	GA	1649	OH	1662	WI	1674	WA
1637	CT	1650	LA	1663	CA	1675	ID
1638	MA	1651	IN	1664	MN	1676	WY
1639	MD	1652	MS	1665	OR	1677	UT
1640	SC	1653	IL	1666	KS	1678	OK
1641	NH	1654	AL	1667	WV	1679	NM
1642	VA	1655	ME	1668	NV	1680	AZ
1643	NY	1656	MO	1669	NE	1681	AK
1644	NC	1657	AR	1670	CO	1682	HI
1645	RI	1658	MI				

1976 Commemoratives (continued)

| 1683 | 1684 | 1685 |

		Mint Sheet	Plate Block	F-VF NH	F-VF Used
1683	13¢ Telephone Centennial	20.00	1.85	.45	.15
1684	13¢ Commercial Aviation	17.50 (10)	4.65	.40	.15
1685	13¢ Chemistry	22.50 (12)	6.25	.50	.15

1976 American Bicentennial Souvenir Sheets

1686

1687

1688

1689

Scott's No.	Mint Sheet	Plate Block	F-VF NH	F-VF Used
1686-89 Set of Four Souvenir Sheets	...	...	**28.75**	**25.00**
1686a-89e Set of 20 Singles	...	...	**28.00**	**23.75**
1686 13¢ Surrender of Cornwallis	...	...	4.75	4.00
1686a-e Any Single	...	...	1.10	.90
1687 18¢ Decl. of Independence	...	...	6.75	5.75
1687a-e Any Single	...	...	1.50	1.30
1688 24¢ Washington Crossing Delaware	...	...	9.25	8.00
1688a-e Any Single	...	...	1.95	1.70
1689 31¢ Washington at Valley Forge ...	...	...	12.00	10.50
1689a-e Any Single	...	...	2.50	2.15

1976 Commemoratives (continued)

1691 1692 1693 1694

1699

1690

1700

1695 1696
1697 1698

1701

1702,1703

1690	13¢ Ben Franklin and Map		17.50	1.60	.40	.15
1691-94	13¢ Dec. of Independence, attd ..		32.50 (16)	13.00	3.00	1.25
1691-94	Set of 4 Singles		...	...	2.90	.70
1695-98	13¢ Winter Olym. Games, attd		22.50 (12)	6.50	1.90	1.80
1695-98	Set of 4 Singles		...	...	1.80	.70
1699	13¢ Clara Mass	(40)	19.50 (12)	6.50	.50	.15
1700	13¢ Adolph S. Ochs	(32)	15.00	2.10	.50	.15
1701	13¢ Christmas, Nativity		17.50 (12)	4.75	.40	.15
1702	13¢ Christmas Winter Pastime, Andriotti Press		17.50 (10)	3.95	.40	.15
1703	13¢ Same, Gravure-Intaglio		17.50 (20)	7.75	.40	.15

#1702: Andriotti Press, lettering at Base is Black, No Snowflakes in Sky.
#1703: Intaglio-Gravure, lettering at Base is Gray Black, Snowflakes in Sky.

1977 Commemoratives

1704

1706 1707
1708 1709

1977 Commemoratives (continued)

1705

1710

1711

1712 1713
1714 1715

1716

1717 1718
1718 1719

1721

1722

1725

1723
1724

1726

Scott's No.		Mint Sheet	Plate Block	F-VF NH	F-VF Used
1704-1730	Set of 27	...	...	10.50	3.35
1704	13¢ Washington at Princeton .... (40)	14.00 (10)	3.95	.50	.15
1705	13¢ Sound Recording	22.50	2.10	.50	.15
1706-09	13¢ Pueblo Art, block, attd .... (40)	15.75 (10)	4.50	1.65	1.25
1706-09	Strip of 4	...	...	1.65	1.25
1706-09	Set of 4 Singles	...	...	1.50	.70
1710	13¢ Lindbergh's Flight	17.50 (12)	4.75	.40	.15
1711	13¢ Colorado Sthd., Line Perfs	17.50 (12)	4.75	.40	.15
1711c	Bullseye Perfs	57.50 (12)	19.50	1.15	.95
#1711 Perforated 11, #1711c Perf. 11.2					
1712-15	13¢ American Butterflies, attd	18.50 (12)	5.50	1.65	1.25
1712-15	Set of 4 Singles	...	...	1.50	.70
1716	13¢ Lafayette's Landing .... (40)	18.00	2.10	.50	.15
1717-20	13¢ Revolutionary War Civilian Skills, attd	18.50 (12)	5.50	1.65	1.25
1717-20	Set of 4 Singles	...	...	1.50	.70
1721	13¢ Peace Bridge 50th Ann.	21.00	1.85	.45	.15
1722	13¢ Herkimer at Oriskany .... (40)	14.00 (10)	3.95	.40	.15
1723-24	13¢ Energy Conservation, attd (40)	15.00 (12)	5.00	.85	.60
1723-24	Set of 2 Singles	...	...	.80	.30
1725	13¢ Alta California Settlement	17.50	1.60	.40	.15
1726	13¢ Articles of Confederation	19.50	1.85	.45	.15

NOTE: MODERN BOOKLET PANES ARE GLUED INTO BOOKLETS AND PRICES LISTED ARE FOR PANES WITHOUT SELVEDGE AND, USUALLY, FOLDED. LIMITED QUANTITIES EXIST UNFOLDED WITH FULL SELVEDGE—THESE ARE USUALLY PRICED ANYWHERE FROM 1½ TO 4 TIMES THESE PRICES WHEN AVAILABLE.

NOTE: PRICES THROUGHOUT THIS LIST ARE SUBJECT TO CHANGE WITHOUT NOTICE IF MARKET CONDITIONS REQUIRE. MIN. MAIL ORDER MUST TOTAL AT LEAST $20.00.

1977 Commemoratives (continued)

1727   1728   1729   1730

Scott's No.		Mint Sheet	Plate Block	F-VF NH	F-VF Used
1727	13¢ Talking Pictures	17.50	1.60	.40	.15
1728	13¢ Surrender at Saratoga .... (40)	14.00 (10)	4.00	.40	.15
1729	13¢ Christmas, Washington at Valley Forge .... (100)	34.50 (20)	8.00	.40	.15
1730	13¢ Christmas - Mailbox .... (100)	33.50 (10)	4.00	.40	.15

1731   1732   1733   1734   1735-36,1743

1737   1738   1739   1740   1741   1742

1978 Commemoratives

1731-33,44-69	**Set of 29**	...	...	14.50	6.25
1731	13¢ Carl Sandburg, Poet	17.50	1.60	.40	.15
1732-33	Captain Cook, attached	17.50 (20)	9.50	.95	.75
1732	13¢ Captain Cook Portrait	...	1.60	.40	.15
1733	13¢ Hawaii Seascape	...	1.60	.40	.15

1978-80 Regular Issues

1734	13¢ Indian Head Penny .... (150)	55.00	1.70	.40	.15
1735	(15¢) "A" & Eagle, Perf. 11 .... (100)	42.50	1.90	.45	.15
1735c	(15¢) Bullseye Perf. 11.2 .... (100)	52.50	2.75	.55	.35
1736	(15¢) "A" & Eagle, Perf. 11x10½ Booklet Single	...	...	.55	.15
1736a	15¢ Booklet Pane of 8	...	...	3.75	3.00
1737	15¢ Roses, Perf. 10, Bklt. Single .	...	...	.45	.15
1737a	15¢ Booklet Pane of 8	...	...	3.25	3.00
1738-42	15¢ Windmills, Strip of 5 (1980) .	...	...	2.35	2.25
1738-42	15¢ Set of 5 Singles	...	...	2.25	.90
1742a	15¢ Booklet Pane of 10 (2 ea. #1738-42) (1980)	...	...	4.50	4.25
1743	(15¢) "A" & Eagle, Coil, Pf. Vert. ... Line Pr.		1.15	.45	.15

1978 Commemoratives (continued)

1744

1745   1746
1747   1748

1978 Commemoratives (continued)

1749   1750   1753
1751   1752

1754   1755   1756

1757

Scott's No.		Mint Sheet	Plate Block	F-VF NH	F-VF Used
1744	13¢ Harriet Tubman	23.50 (12)	6.25	.50	.15
1745-48	13¢ Quilts, attd .... (48)	19.00 (12)	5.50	1.65	1.25
1745-48	Set of 4 Singles	...	...	1.50	.70
1749-52	13¢ American Dance, attd .... (48)	19.00 (12)	5.50	1.65	1.25
1749-52	Set of 4 Singles	...	...	1.50	.70
1753	13¢ French Alliance .... (40)	14.00	1.60	.40	.15
1754	13¢ Cancer Detection,Pap Test	20.00	1.85	.45	.15
#1755-56 Performing Arts					
1755	13¢ Jimmie Rodgers	25.00 (12)	7.00	.55	.15
1756	15¢ George M. Cohan	27.50 (12)	7.50	.60	.15

1978 Canadian International Philatelic Exhibition Souvenir Sheet

1757	13¢x8 ($1.04) CAPEX Souvenir Sheet .... (6)	17.50		3.00	2.75
1757	S.Sh. with Plate No	...	3.25	...	...
1757a-h	Set of 8 Singles	...	...	2.95	2.00
	Strip of Four (a-d)	...	...	1.60	1.50
	Strip of Four (e-h)	...	...	1.60	1.50
	Block of 8, attached	...	...	3.50	3.25

1757a Cardinal	1757d Blue Jay	1757g Red Fox
1757b Mallard	1757e Moose	1757h Raccoon
1757c Canada Goose	1757f Chipmunk	

NOTE: PRICES THROUGHOUT THIS LIST ARE SUBJECT TO CHANGE WITHOUT NOTICE IF MARKET CONDITIONS REQUIRE. MINIMUM ORDER MUST TOTAL AT LEAST $20.00.

1978 Commemoratives (continued)

1758

1759

1760 1761
1762 1763

1764 1765
1766 1767

1768

1769

Scott's No.		Mint Sheet	Plate Block	F-VF NH	F-VF Used
1758	15¢ Photography .... (40)	15.75 (12)	5.75	.45	.15
1759	15¢ Viking Mission to Mars	18.50	2.10	.45	.15
1760-63	15¢ American Owls, attd	21.00	2.00	1.80	1.65
1760-63	Set of 4 Singles	...	...	1.70	.70
1764-67	15¢ American Trees, attd ..... (40)	17.50 (12)	6.00	1.80	1.65
1764-67	Set of 4 Singles	...	...	1.70	.70
1768	15¢ Christmas Madonna .... (100)	41.50 (12)	5.50	.45	.15
1769	15¢ Christmas Hobbyhorse .... (100)	41.50 (12)	5.50	.45	.15

1979 Commemoratives

1770

1771

1772

1774

1775 1776
1777 1778

1773

1979 Commemoratives (continued)

Scott's No.		Mint Sheet	Plate Block	F-VF NH	F-VF Used
1770-1802	Set of 33 (No#1789A,B,1795A-98A)...		...	15.50	4.95
1770	15¢ R.F. Kennedy .... (48)	22.00	2.10	.50	.15
1771	15¢ Martin Luther King, Jr.	24.00 (12)	6.75	.55	.15
1772	15¢ Int'l. Year of the Child	19.50	1.80	.45	.15
1773	15¢ John Steinbeck	19.00	1.80	.45	.15
1774	15¢ Albert Einstein	27.50	2.50	.60	.15
1775-78	15¢ PA Toleware, attd .... (40)	18.00 (10)	5.00	1.90	1.50
1775-78	Set of 4 Singles	...	...	1.80	.80

1779 1780
1781 1782

1783 1784
1785 1786

1787

1788

1789

1790

1791 1792
1793 1794

1795 1796
1797 1798

1799

1800

Scott's No.		Mint Sheet	Plate Block	F-VF NH	F-VF Used
1779-82	15¢ Architecture, attd .... (48)	25.00	2.75	2.25	2.00
1779-82	Set of 4 Singles	...	...	2.15	.80
1783-86	15¢ Endangered Flowers, attd	22.75 (12)	6.50	1.90	1.50
1783-86	Set of 4 Singles	...	...	1.80	.80
1787	15¢ Seeing Eye Dog	27.50 (20)	12.00	.60	.15
1788	15¢ Special Olympics	19.50 (10)	4.50	.45	.15
1789	15¢ John P. Jones, Perf. 11x12	19.50 (10)	4.50	.45	.15
1789A	15¢ Perforated 11	32.50 (10)	7.25	.65	.25
1789B	15¢ Perforated 12			1600.00	...
1790	10¢ Olympics - Decathalon	14.50 (12)	4.50	.30	.20
1791-94	15¢ Summer Olympics, attd	21.00 (12)	6.50	2.10	1.75
1791-94	Set of 4 Singles	...	...	1.95	.80

1979 Commemoratives (continued)

1801

1802

Scott's No.		Mint Sheet	Plate Block	F-VF NH	F-VF Used
1795-98	15¢ Winter Olympics, Perf. 11 x 10½, attd. (1980)	21.00 (12)	6.50	2.10	1.50
1795-98	Set of 4 Singles			1.95	.80
1795A-98A	15¢ Perforated 11 attd	47.50 (12)	14.00	4.00	3.95
1795A-98A	Set of 4 Singles			3.75	3.60
1799	15¢ Christmas Madonna ...... (100)	39.50 (12)	5.50	.45	.15
1800	15¢ Christmas Ornament ..... (100)	39.50 (12)	5.50	.45	.15
1801	15¢ Will Rogers	21.00 (12)	6.00	.45	.15
1802	15¢ Vietnam Veterans	26.50 (10)	5.95	.55	.15

1980 Commemoratives (See also 1795-98)

1803

1804

1805	1807	1809
1806	1808	1810

Scott's No.		Mint Sheet	Plate Block	F-VF NH	F-VF Used
1803-10,21-43	Set of 31	...	...	15.95	4.85
1803	15¢ W.C. Fields	21.00 (12)	6.00	.45	.15
1804	15¢ Benjamin Banneker	25.00 (12)	6.75	.55	.15
1805-10	15¢ Letter Writing, attd	(60) 33.75	(36) 21.50	3.50	3.25
1805-10	Set of 6 Singles	...	...	3.25	1.40

1811	1813	1816	1818-1820

1980-81 Americana Coils, Perf. 10 Vert.

Scott's No.		Line Pair	F-VF NH	F-VF Used
1811	1¢ Inkwell & Quill, Shiny Gum	.50	.20	.15
1811v	1¢ Dry Gum	.65	.20	...
1813	3.5¢ Two Violins, Coil	.95	.20	.15
1813a	3.5¢ Bureau Precancel	2.50	.30	.25
1816	12¢ Conscience, Coil (1981)	1.95	.35	.20
1816a	12¢ Bureau Precancel	43.50	1.65	.95

1981 "B" Eagle Regular Issue

Scott's No.		Mint Sheet	Plate Block	F-VF NH	F-VF Used
1818	(18¢) Perf. 11x10½ .... (100)	47.50	2.25	.50	.15
1819	(18¢) Perf. 10, Booklet Single	...	...	.65	.15
1819a	(18¢) Booklet Pane of 8	...	...	4.95	3.75
1820	(18¢) Coil	Line Pr.	1.50	.55	.15

1980 Commemoratives (continued)

 1821

 1822

 1823

 1824

 1825

 1826

1827	1828
1829	1830

1834	1835
1836	1837

 1831

 1832

 1833

 1842

1838	1837
1840	1841

 1843

Scott's No.		Mint Sheet	Plate Block	F-VF NH	F-VF Used
1821	15¢ Frances Perkins	21.00	1.95	.45	.15
1822	15¢ Dolley Madison .... (150)	67.50	2.25	.50	.15
1823	15¢ Emily Bissell	27.50	2.50	.60	.15
1824	15¢ H. Keller/A. Sullivan	19.50	1.80	.45	.15
1825	15¢ Veterans Administration	19.50	1.80	.45	.15
1826	15¢ Gen. Bernardo de Galvez	19.50	1.80	.45	.15
1827-30	15¢ Coral Reefs, attd	20.50 (12)	6.00	1.85	1.35
1827-30	Set of 4 Singles	...	...	1.70	.80
1831	15¢ Organized Labor	19.50 (12)	5.50	.45	.15

45

1980 Commemoratives (continued)

Scott's No.		Mint Sheet	Plate Block	F-VF NH	F-VF Used
1832	15¢ Edith Wharton	21.75	2.00	.45	.15
1833	15¢ Education in America	26.00	(6) 3.25	.55	.15
1834-37	15¢ Pacific Northwest Indian Masks, attd	(40) 26.50	(10) 7.50	2.75	1.85
1834-37	Set of 4 Singles	...	...	2.65	.80
1838-41	15¢ Am. Architecture, attd	(40) 22.50	2.50	2.25	2.15
1838-41	Set of 4 Singles	...	...	2.00	.80
1842	15¢ Christmas Madonna	19.50	(12) 5.50	.45	.15
1843	15¢ Christmas Toys	21.50	(20)10.00	.45	.15

1980-85 Great Americans Series

1844 — Dorothea Dix USA 1c
1845 — Igor Stravinsky USA 2c
1846 — Henry Clay USA 3c
1847 — Carl Schurz 4c USA

1848 — Pearl Buck USA 5c
1849 — Walter Lippmann 6 USA
1850 — Abraham Baldwin USA 7c
1851 — Henry Knox USA 8

1852 — Sylvanus Thayer USA 9
1853 — Richard Russell USA 10c
1854 — Alden Partridge USA 11
1855 — Crazy Horse usa 13c

1856 — Sinclair Lewis USA 14
1857 — Rachel Carson USA 17c
1858 — George Mason USA 18c
1859 — Sequoyah USA 19c

1860 — Ralph Bunche USA 20c
1861 — Thomas H. Gallaudet USA 20c
1862 — Harry S. Truman USA 20c
1863 — John J. Audubon USA 22

1864 — Frank C. Laubach USA 30c
1865 — Charles R. Drew MD USA 35c
1866 — Robert Millikan 37c USA
1867 — Grenville Clark USA 39

1868 — Lillian M. Gilbreth USA 40c
1869 — Chester W. Nimitz USA 50

Perf. 11 x 10½ (Sheets of 100)

Scott's No.		Mint Sheet	Plate Block	F-VF NH	F-VF Used
1844-69	Set of 26	...	...	12.95	3.95
1844	1¢ Dix, Bullseye Perfs. Pf.11.2 ('83)	8.75 (20)	2.75	.20	.15
1844c	1¢ Line Perfs.10.8, Small Block Tagging (1983)	6.75 (20)	2.00	.20	.15
1844d	1¢ Perf.10.8, Large Block Tagging('85)	6.75 (20)	2.00	.20	.15
1845	2¢ Igor Stravinsky (1982)	6.75	.60	.20	.15
1846	3¢ Henry Clay (1983)	9.75	.65	.20	.15
1847	4¢ Carl Schurz (1983)	12.50	.65	.20	.15
1848	5¢ Pearl Buck (1983)	15.00	.70	.20	.15
1849	6¢ Walter Lippmann Perf. 11 (1985)	18.00 (20)	4.15	.20	.15
1850	7¢ Abraham Baldwin Perf. 11 (1985)	27.50 (20)	6.25	.30	.15
1851	8¢ Gen. Henry Knox Perf. 11 (1985)	21.50	1.25	.25	.15
1852	9¢ Sylvanus Thayer Perf. 11 (1985)	32.50 (20)	7.25	.35	.20
1853	10¢ R. Russell Perf. 11, Small Block Tagging (1984)	37.50 (20)	8.50	.40	.15
1853a	10¢ Large Block Tagging	37.50 (20)	8.50	.40	.15
1854	11¢ Alden Partridge Perf. 11 (1985)	40.00	1.90	.45	.15
1855	13¢ Crazy Horse (1982)	42.00	2.10	.45	.25

1980-85 Great Americans Series (continued)

Scott's No.		Mint Sheet	Plate Block	F-VF NH	F-VF Used
1856	14¢ Sinclair Lewis, Perf. 11, Small Block Tagging (1985)	42.00 (20)	9.75	.45	.15
1856a	14¢ Large Block Tagging	42.00 (20)	9.75	.45	.15
1857	17¢ Rachel Carson (1981)	47.50	2.15	.50	.15
1858	18¢ George Mason (1981)	47.50	2.50	.50	.20
1859	19¢ Sequoyah	60.00	2.85	.65	.25
1860	20¢ Dr. Ralph Bunche (1982)	65.00	3.50	.70	.15
1861	20¢ Thomas Gallaudet (1983)	70.00	3.75	.75	.15
1862	20¢ Truman, Line Perf. 11, Small Block Tagging,Dull Gum (1984)	62.50 (20)	13.00	.65	.15
1862a	20¢ Bullseye, Perf 11.2, Large Block Tagging,Dull Gum	67.50 (4)	4.50	.70	.30
1862b	20¢ Pf.11.2,Overall Tag,Dull (1990)	72.50	5.75	.75	.50
1862d	20¢ Perf. 11.2, Mottled Tagging, Shiny Gum (1993)	77.50	5.50	.80	.70
1863	22¢ J.Audubon, Line Perf 11, Small Block Tagging (1985)	72.50 (20)	16.50	.75	.15
1863a	22¢ Perf.11, Large Block Tagging	72.50 (20)	16.50	.75	.15
1863b	22¢ Bullseye Perfs, Perf. 11.2('87)	72.50 (4)	5.75	.75	.20
1864	30¢ F.C. Laubach, Line Perf. 11,Small Block Tagging (1984)	85.00 (20)	19.75	.90	.15
1864a	30¢ Bullseye Perf. 11.2, Large Block Tagging	87.50	5.75	.90	.20
1864b	30¢ Perf. 11.2, Overall Tagging	...	39.50	2.50	2.00
1865	35¢ Dr. Charles Drew ('81)	100.00	5.00	1.10	.20
1866	37¢ R. Millikan ('82)	100.00	4.75	1.10	.20
1867	39¢ Gren Clark, Line Perf 10.9, Small Block Tagging (1985)	100.00 (20)	24.50	1.10	.20
1867c	39¢ Perf.10.9, Large Block Tagging	100.00 (20)	24.50	1.10	.20
1867d	39¢ Bullseye Perf 11.2, Large Block Tagging	100.00 (4)	6.75	1.10	.20
1868	40¢ L. Gilbreth, Line Perf. 11, Small Block Tagging (1984)	110.00 (20)	25.00	1.20	.20
1868a	40¢ Bullseye Perf.11.2, Large Block Tagging	110.00	6.75	1.20	.20
1869	50¢ C.Nimitz, Line Perf. 11, Overall Tagging, Shiny Gum (1985)	160.00 (4)	10.00	1.50	.20
1869a	50¢ Bullseye Perf. 11.2, Large Block Tagging, Dull Gum	150.00	8.25	1.60	.25
1869d	50¢ Perf.11.2,Overall Tagging, Dull Gum	195.00	12.50	2.10	.35
1869e	50¢ Pf.11.2,Mottled Tagging, Shiny Gum (1993)	165.00	10.00	1.75	.50

TAGGING VARIATIONS

Tagging is a usually invisible coating applied to postage stamps which can be "read" by the automated mail-handling equipment used by the post office. After a period of years of testing, tagging has since been applied to most stamps. This tagging can be detected by use of a short-wave ultra-violet lamp.

Overall Tagging: The tagging has been applied to the entire surface of the stamp.

Block Tagging: The tagging is applied over the center area of the stamp with the outside edges untagged. Comes in small or large sized block tagging.

Solid Tagging: The tagging is applied as part of the process of coating prephosphored paper making it very smooth. Also known as surface tagging.

Mottled Tagging: Also applied to prephosphored paper without a coating. Appears to have a mottled or blotchy appearance. Experts disagree on details of mottled tagging.

1981 Commemoratives

1874 — USA 15c Everett Dirksen
1875 — Whitney Moore Young, Black Heritage USA 15c
1876 — Rose USA 18c
1877 — Camellia USA 18c
1878 — Dahlia USA 18c
1879 — Lily USA 18c

ZIP, MAIL EARLY & COPYRIGHT BLOCKS

Due to space limitations, we do not list individual prices for Zip Code, Mail Early, Copyright and other inscription blocks. With the exception of those items listed below, these are priced at the total price for the single stamps plus one additional stamp. For example, if the single stamp retailed for 45¢, a zip block of 4 would retail for $2.25 (5x.45). Se-tenants should be based on the attached price plus 25%. (blocks of 6 would be 75% over attached block prices)

Scott's No.		Copyright Block	Mail Early Block	Zip Code Block
1274	1965 11¢ Telecommunication	...	...	3.75
1284	1966 6¢ F. D. Roosevelt	...	4.50	3.75
1284a	Same, tagged	...	2.25	1.75
1347-49	1968, 6¢ Historic Flags	...	2.35	
1353-54	1968, 6¢ Historic Flags	...		1.70
C72	1968, 10¢ 50 State Runway	...	5.50	4.50
C95-96	1979, 25¢ Wiley Post	7.50	...	7.50

1981 Commemoratives (continued)

Scott's No.	Mint Sheet	Plate Block	F-VF NH	F-VF Used
1874-79,1910-45 Set of 42	...	...	24.95	6.50
1874 15¢ Everett Dirksen	19.50	1.80	.45	.15
1875 15¢ Whitney Young	22.50	2.00	.50	.15
1876-79 18¢ Flowers, attd .... (48)	28.75	2.75	2.50	2.00
1876-79 Set of 4 Singles	...	...	2.30	.80

1981-82 Regular Issues

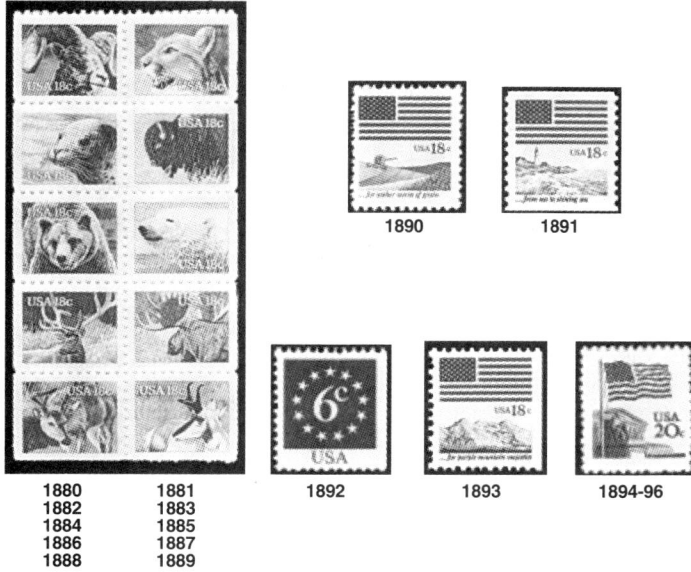

1890 **1891**

1880 1881
1882 1883
1884 1885
1886 1887
1888 1889

1892 **1893** **1894-96**

	Mint Sheet	Plate Block	F-VF NH	F-VF Used
1880-89 18¢ Wildlife Booklet Singles	...	...	9.00	2.00
1889a Wildlife Bklt., Pane of 10	...	...	9.75	7.50
1890 18¢ Flag & "Amber Waves" .... (100)	52.50 (20)	11.50	.55	.15
1891 18¢ Flag "Sea", Coil .... (Pl. # Strip)	6.75 (5)	5.00 (3)	.55	.15
1892 6¢ Circle of Stars, Bklt. Single ..	...	...	.85	.30
1893 18¢ Flag & "For Purple" Bklt. Sgl	...	...	.50	.15
1892-93 6¢ & 18¢, Vertical Pair	...	...	1.35	1.50
1893a Bklt Pn of 8 (2 #1892, 6 #1893) ..	...	...	4.00	3.75
1894 20¢ Flag over Supreme Court, Line Pf. 11, Dry Gum .... (100)	95.00 (20)	21.00	1.00	.25
1894e 20¢ Bullseye Pf. 11.2 .... (100)	62.50 (20)	13.50	.65	.15
1895 20¢ Flag over S.C., Coil .... Pl. # Strip	5.00 (5)	3.50 (3)	.60	.15
1895b 20¢ Flag, Precancelled .... Pl. # Strip	95.00 (5)	90.00 (3)	1.30	.75
1896 20¢ Flag over S.C., Bklt. Single ..	...	...	.70	.15
1896a 20¢ Booklet Pane of 6	...	...	3.95	3.50
1896b 20¢ Booklet Pane of 10 (1982) ...	...	...	6.50	5.25

1981-91 Transportation Coil Series

1897 **1897A** **1898** **1898A**

1899 **1900** **1901** **1902**

1903 **1904** **1905** **1906**

1907 **1908 Plate Number Strip of 3**

11¢ RR Untagged Issue not included in Set.
Pl. #s must appear on center stamp

1981-91 Transportation Coils (continued)

Scott's No.	Pl# Strip of 5	Pl# Strip of 3	F-VF NH	F-VF Used
1897-1908 Mint (14 values)	115.00	58.50	3.85	1.85
1897 1¢ Omnibus (1983)	.60	.50	.20	.15
1897A 2¢ Locomotive (1982)	.65	.55	.20	.15
1898 3¢ Handcar (1983)	.85	.75	.20	.15
1898A 4¢ Stagecoach (1982)	1.60	1.25	.20	.15
1899 5¢ Motorcycle (1983)	1.50	1.10	.20	.15
1900 5.2¢ Sleigh (1983)	11.75	5.95	.25	.15
1901 5.9¢ Bicycle (1982)	18.50	7.50	.25	.20
1902 7.4¢ Baby Buggy (1984)	14.50	7.00	.30	.20
1903 9.3¢ Mail Wagon (1981)	16.50	6.75	.30	.20
1904 10.9¢ Hansom Cab (1982)	45.00	15.00	.50	.20
1905 11¢ RR Caboose (1984)	5.25	3.50	.35	.15
1905b 11¢ Untagged, not precanc. ('91) .	3.75	3.00	.35	.25
1906 17¢ Electric Car	3.25	2.25	.50	.15
1907 18¢ Surrey	4.25	3.00	.60	.15
1908 20¢ Fire Pumper	4.00	2.75	.60	.15

#1897-97A: See #2225-26 for designs without "¢" signs.
#1898A: See #2228 for "B" Press

1981-91 Transportation Coil Series Precancelled Stamps

1898Ab **1900a** **1901a** **1902a**

1903a **1904a** **1905a** **1906a**

	Pl# Strip of 5	Pl# Strip of 3	F-VF NH	F-VF Used
1898Ab/1906a Precancelled (8 values) .	127.50	115.00	2.85	1.75
1898Ab 4¢ Stagecoach (1982)	7.50	6.75	.30	.20
1900a 5.2¢ Sleigh (1983)	15.00	13.50	.25	.20
1901a 5.9¢ Bicycle (1982)	47.50	42.50	.40	.25
1902a 7.4¢ Baby Buggy (1984)	6.50	5.95	.35	.25
1903a 9.3¢ Mail Wagon	4.00	3.25	.40	.25
1904a 10.9¢ Hansom Cab (1982)	45.00	42.50	.55	.25
1905a 11¢ RR Caboose (1984)	5.25	4.25	.40	.25
1906a 17¢ Electric Car, Type "A"	6.50	5.75	.50	.35
1906ab 17¢ Type "B"	37.50	35.00	1.50	.75
1906ac 17¢ Type "C"	17.00	14.00	1.00	.50

Type "A" - "Presorted" 11.5mm Length
Type "B" - "Presorted" 12.5mm Length
Type "C" - "Presorted" 13.5mm Length

1983 Express Mail Issue

1909

Scott's No.	Mint Sheet	Plate Block	F-VF NH	F-VF Used
1909 $9.35 Eagle & Moon, Booklet Single	...	...	30.00	22.50
1909a $9.35 Booklet Pane of 3	...	...	88.50	...

1981 Commemoratives (continued)

1912	1913	1914	1915
1916	1917	1918	1919

47

1910

1911

1920

1921 1922

1923 1924

1937 1938

1940

1941

1942 1943 1945
1944

Scott's No.		Mint Sheet	Plate Block	F-VF NH	F-VF Used
1925	18¢ Disabled Persons	25.00	2.40	.55	.15
1926	18¢ Edna St. Vincent Millay	25.00	2.40	.55	.15
1927	18¢ Alchoholism	55.00 (20)	40.00	.60	.15
1928-31	18¢ Architecture, attd .... (40)	27.50	3.00	2.75	2.25
1928-31	Set of 4 Singles	...	...	2.50	.70
1932	18¢ Babe Didrikson Zaharias	37.50	4.00	.80	.15
1933	18¢ Bobby Jones	75.00	8.50	1.60	.15
1934	18¢ F. Remington Sculpture	25.00	2.40	.55	.15
1935	18¢ James Hoban	25.00	2.40	.55	.15
1936	20¢ James Hoban	26.00	2.50	.55	.15
1937-38	18¢ Yorktown - Capes, attd	28.75	3.00	1.40	.90
1937-38	Set of Singles	...	...	1.30	.40
1939	(20¢)Christmas Madonna .... (100)	50.00	2.50	.55	.15
1940	(20¢)Christmas-Teddy Bear	26.00	2.50	.55	.15
1941	20¢ John Hanson	28.50	2.75	.60	.15
1942-45	20¢ Desert Plants, attached ... (40)	26.00	3.25	2.75	1.50
1942-45	Set of 4 Singles	...	...	2.50	.70

1981-82 Regular Issues

1946-1948

1949

1946	(20¢) "C" & Eagle, Pf. 11x10½ .. (100)	52.50	2.50	.55	.15
1947	(20¢) "C" & Eagle, Coil		Line Pr.1.95	.75	.15
1948	(20¢) "C" & Eagle,Perf.10,Bklt. Sgl.	...	...	.60	.15
1948a	(20¢)Booklet Pane of 10	...	...	5.95	5.00
1949	20¢ Ty. I,Bighorn Sheep,Bklt. Sgl .	...	...	.70	.15
1949a	20¢ Ty. I, Booklet Pane of 10	...	...	7.25	4.50
1949c	20¢ Type II, Bklt Single	...	...	1.75	.50
1949d	20¢ Ty. II, Booklet Pane of 10	...	...	16.50	...

* Ty. I is 18¾ mm wide and has overall tagging.
  Ty. II is 18½ mm wide and has block tagging.

1982 Commemoratives

1950

1951

1952

1950-52,2003-4,2006-30 Set of 30 (No #1951A) ...		...	21.50	4.25
1950	20¢ Franklin D. Roosevelt .... (48)	26.50	2.50	.55	.15
1951	20¢ "LOVE", Perf. 11	29.50	2.75	.60	.15
1951A	20¢ Perf. 11x 10½	45.00	5.50	.95	.35
1952	20¢ George Washington	28.50	2.75	.60	.15

1925

1926

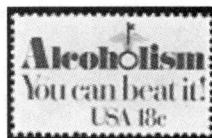

1927

1928 1929
1930 1931

Scott's No.		Mint Sheet	Plate Block	F-VF NH	F-VF Used
1910	18¢ American Red Cross	26.50	2.80	.55	.15
1911	18¢ Savings & Loan	25.00	2.50	.55	.15
1912-19	18¢ Space Achievement, attd .. (48)	32.50 (8)	6.00	5.50	3.25
1912-19	Set of 8 Singles	...	...	5.25	2.00
1920	18¢ Professional Management	25.00	2.40	.55	.15
1921-24	18¢ Wildlife Habitats, attd	26.50	2.50	2.30	1.60
1921-24	Set of 4 Singles	...	...	2.10	.70

1932

1934

1933

1935

1936

1939

1982 State Birds & Flowers Issue

1953-2002 Sheet

1957	1961	1966	1972
California	Florida	Indiana	Maryland

Scott's No.		Mint Sheet	Plate Block	F-VF NH	F-VF Used
1953-2002	20¢ 50 States, attd, Perf. 10½ x 11	41.50	...	...	...
1953-2002	Set of Singles, ...	...	...	39.50	23.50
1953-2002	20¢ Individual Singles ...	...	...	1.10	.60
1953A-2002A	20¢ 50 States, attd., Pf. 11	47.50	...	...	...

NOTE: Sets of singles may contain mixed perforation sizes.

1953	Alabama	1970	Louisiana	1987	Ohio
1954	Alaska	1971	Maine	1988	Oklahoma
1955	Arizona	1972	Maryland	1989	Oregon
1956	Arkansas	1973	Massachusetts	1990	Pennsylvania
1957	California	1974	Michigan	1991	Rhode Island
1958	Colorado	1975	Minnesota	1992	South Carolina
1959	Connecticut	1976	Mississippi	1993	South Dakota
1960	Delaware	1977	Missouri	1994	Tennessee
1961	Florida	1978	Montana	1995	Texas
1962	Georgia	1979	Nebraska	1996	Utah
1963	Hawaii	1980	Nevada	1997	Vermont
1964	Idaho	1981	New Hampshire	1998	Virginia
1965	Illinois	1982	New Jersey	1999	Washington
1966	Indiana	1983	New Mexico	2000	West Virginia
1967	Iowa	1984	New York	2001	Wisconsin
1968	Kansas	1985	North Carolina	2002	Wyoming
1969	Kentucky	1986	North Dakota		

2003	2004	2005

1982 Commemoratives (continued)

2003	20¢ U.S. & Netherlands	32.50 (20)	13.95	.60	.15
2004	20¢ Library of Congress	27.50	2.50	.55	.15

1982 Consumer Education Coil

2005	20¢ Clothing Label .... (Pl# Strip)	140.00(5)	27.50(3)	1.00	.15

1982 Commemoratives (continued)

2006	2007	2010
2008	2009	

2012	2011	2013

2015	2014	2016

2019	2020	2017
2021	2022	
		2018

2023	2024	2025

Scott's No.		Mint Sheet	Plate Block	F-VF NH	F-VF Used
2006-09	20¢ Knoxville Fair, attd	37.50	3.65	3.15	1.50
2006-09	Set of 4 Singles	...	...	3.10	.80
2010	20¢ Horatio Alger	26.50	2.50	.55	.15
2011	20¢ "Aging Together"	26.50	2.50	.55	.15
2012	20¢ Arts - The Barrymores	26.50	2.50	.55	.15
2013	20¢ Mary Walker, Surgeon	28.75	2.75	.60	.15
2014	20¢ Peace Garden	28.75	2.75	.60	.15
2015	20¢ Libraries of America	26.50	2.50	.55	.15
2016	20¢ Jackie Robinson	95.00	8.95	2.00	.20
2017	20¢ Touro Synagogue	38.50 (20)	16.75	.80	.15
2018	20¢ Wolf Trap Farm Park	26.50	2.50	.55	.15
2019-22	20¢ Architecture, attached ... (40)	32.50	4.50	3.50	2.50
2019-22	Set of 4 Singles	...	...	3.25	.80
2023	20¢ St. Francis of Assisi	28.50	2.75	.60	.15
2024	20¢ Ponce de Leon	35.00 (20)	16.00	.75	.15
#2025-30	Christmas Issues				
2025	13¢ Christmas, Kitten & Puppy	21.75	2.00	.45	.15

1982 Commemoratives (continued)

2026

| 2027 | 2028 |
| 2029 | 2030 |

Scott's No.		Mint Sheet		Plate Block	F-VF NH	F-VF Used
2026	20¢ Christmas, Tiepolo Madonna	29.50	(20)	13.75	.60	.15
2027-30	20¢ Christmas Winter Scenes, attd	41.50		4.50	3.75	1.75
2027-30	Set of 4 Singles	...		...	3.60	.80

1983 Commemoratives

| 2032 | 2033 | 2035 |
| | 2034 | |

2036

2031

2037

2039

2038

2040

2041

2042

2043

2044

2045

2046

2047

1983 Commemoratives (continued)

Scott's No.		Mint Sheet		Plate Block	F-VF NH	F-VF Used
2031-65	Set of 35	...		...	22.95	5.15
2031	20¢ Sciences & Industry	26.50		2.50	.55	.15
2032-35	20¢ Ballooning, attached	(40) 26.00		3.00	2.75	1.50
2032-35	Set of 4 Singles	...		...	2.50	.80
2036	20¢ Sweden, B. Franklin	26.50		2.50	.55	.15
2037	20¢ Civilian Conservation Corp	26.50		2.50	.55	.15
2038	20¢ Joseph Priestley	29.00		2.75	.60	.15
2039	20¢ Voluntarism	29.00	(20)	13.95	.60	.15
2040	20¢ German Immigration	26.50		2.50	.55	.15
2041	20¢ Brooklyn Bridge	26.50		2.50	.55	.15
2042	20¢ Tennessee Valley Authority	31.75	(20)	14.95	.65	.15
2043	20¢ Physical Fitness	29.75	(20)	13.95	.60	.15
2044	20¢ Scott Joplin	32.50		3.00	.70	.15
2045	20¢ Medal of Honor	(40) 29.50		3.25	.75	.15
2046	20¢ Babe Ruth	105.00		9.75	2.25	.20
2047	20¢ Nathaniel Hawthorne	31.50		2.95	.65	.15

| 2048 | 2049 |
| 2050 | 2051 |

2052

2053

2054

| 2055 | 2056 |
| 2057 | 2058 |

| 2059 | 2060 |
| 2061 | 2062 |

Scott's No.		Mint Sheet		Plate Block	F-VF NH	F-VF Used
2048-51	13¢ Summer Olympics, attd	29.50		3.50	3.00	1.50
2048-51	Set of 4 Singles	...		...	2.90	.80
2052	20¢ Treaty of Paris	(40) 23.50		2.75	.60	.15
2053	20¢ Civil Service	29.75	(20)	13.95	.60	.15
2054	20¢ Metropolitan Opera	29.50		2.75	.60	.15
2055-58	20¢ Inventors, attd	39.50		4.50	3.75	1.60
2055-58	Set of 4 Singles	...		...	3.00	.80
2059-62	20¢ Streetcars, attd	31.50		4.00	3.00	1.60
2059-62	Set of 4 Singles	...		...	2.90	.80

1983 Commemoratives (continued)

2063

2064

2065

Scott's No.		Mint Sheet	Plate Block	F-VF NH	F-VF Used
2063	20¢ Christmas, Raphael Madonna	26.50	2.50	.55	.15
2064	20¢ Christmas, Santa Claus	30.00 (20)	13.95	.60	.15
2065	20¢ Martin Luther	26.50	2.50	.55	.15

1984 Commemoratives

2067
2069
2068
2070

2066

2071

2072

2073

2074

2075

2076
2078
2077
2079

2066-2109	**Set of 44**	...	...	**32.95**	**6.50**
2066	20¢ Alaska Statehood	26.50	2.50	.55	.15
2067-70	20¢ Winter Olympics, attd	38.50	4.25	3.50	1.75
2067-70	Set of 4 Singles	...	...	3.25	.80
2071	20¢ Fed. Deposit Insurance	26.50	2.50	.55	.15
2072	20¢ Love, Hearts	29.50 (20)	14.50	.60	.15
2073	20¢ Carter G. Woodson	29.50	2.75	.60	.15
2074	20¢ Soil & Water Conservation	26.50	2.50	.55	.15
2075	20¢ Credit Union Act	26.50	2.50	.55	.15
2076-79	20¢ Orchids, attached .... (48)	30.00	3.50	2.75	1.60
2076-79	Set of 4 Singles	...	...	2.50	.80

1984 Commemoratives (cont.)

2080

2081

2082
2084

2083
2085

2086

2087

2091

2092

2088

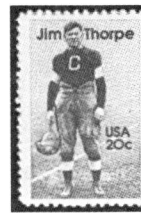

2089

2090

2093

2094

2095

2096

2097

Scott's No.		Mint Sheet	Plate Block	F-VF NH	F-VF Used
2080	20¢ Hawaii Statehood	29.50	2.75	.65	.15
2081	20¢ National Archives	29.50	2.75	.65	.15
2082-85	20¢ Summer Olympics, attd	47.50	5.50	4.65	2.25
2082-85	Set of 4 Singles	...	...	4.50	.90
2086	20¢ Louisiana World's Fair .... (40)	26.50	3.25	.70	.15
2087	20¢ Health Research	31.50	3.00	.65	.15
2088	20¢ Douglas Fairbanks	35.00 (20)	17.50	.65	.15
2089	20¢ Jim Thorpe	37.50	3.50	.80	.15
2090	20¢ John McCormack	26.50	2.50	.55	.15
2091	20¢ St. Lawrence Seaway	26.50	2.50	.55	.15
2092	20¢ Waterfowl Preservation	42.50	4.50	.90	.15
2093	20¢ Roanoke Voyages	35.00	3.25	.75	.15
2094	20¢ Herman Melville	26.50	2.50	.55	.15
2095	20¢ Horace Moses	40.00 (20)	18.75	.85	.15
2096	20¢ Smokey Bear	32.50	3.00	.70	.15
2097	20¢ Roberto Clemente	130.00	12.75	2.75	.20

NOTE: PRICES THROUGHOUT THIS LIST ARE SUBJECT TO CHANGE WITHOUT NOTICE IF MARKET CONDITIONS REQUIRE. MINIMUM ORDER MUST TOTAL AT LEAST $20.00.

1984 Commemoratives (continued)

2098
2100

2099
2101

2102

2103

2104

2105

2106

2107

2108

2110

2109

Scott's No.		Mint Sheet	Plate Block	F-VF NH	F-VF Used
2098-2101	20¢ Dogs, attd .... (40)	29.50	4.75	3.50	2.50
2098-2101	Set of 4 Singles	...	...	3.00	.80
2102	20¢ Crime Prevention	26.50	2.50	.55	.15
2103	20¢ Hispanic Americans .... (40)	21.50	2.50	.55	.15
2104	20¢ Family Unity .... (20)	40.00	17.75	.85	.15
2105	20¢ Eleanor Roosevelt .... (48)	26.50	2.75	.60	.15
2106	20¢ Nation of Readers	32.50	2.95	.70	.15
#2107-8	Christmas Issues				
2107	20¢ Madonna & Child	26.50	2.50	.55	.15
2108	20¢ Santa Claus	26.50	2.50	.55	.15
2109	20¢ Vietnam Memorial .... (40)	35.00	4.25	.90	.15

1985 Commemoratives

2110,2137-47,52-66 Set of 27		...	...	36.25	5.15
2110	22¢ Jerome Kern	31.50	3.00	.65	.15

1985-87 Regulars

2111-2113

2114-2115

2115b

2116

2111	(22¢) "D" Stamp Perf 11 .... (100)	100.00	(20) 32.50	.85	.15
2113	(22¢) "D" Booklet Single	...	...	1.00	.15
2113a	(22¢) "D" Bklt. Pane of 10	...	...	9.75	4.50
2114	22¢ Flag over Capitol ..... (100)	60.00	3.00	.65	.15
2116	22¢ Flag over Cap. Bklt. Sgl ...	...	...	.85	.15
2116a	22¢ Booklet Pane of 5	...	...	4.25	2.25

Scott's No.		Pl/ # Strip of 5	Pl # Strip of 3	F-VF NH	F-VF Used
2112	(22¢) "D" Coil, Perf 10 Vert. ...	9.50	6.50	.70	.15
2115	22¢ Flag over Cap. Coil Perf 10 Vert.	4.50	3.50	.65	.15
2115b	Flag "T" Test Coil ('87)	5.50	4.25	.65	.15
#2115b has a tiny "T" below capitol building					

1985-89 Regulars

2117
2118
2119
2120
2121

2122

Scott's No.		Mint Sheet	Plate Block	F-VF NH	F-VF Used
2117-21	22¢ Seashells, Strip of 5	...	...	3.50	2.50
2117-21	Set of 5 Singles	...	...	3.35	1.00
2121a	22¢ Bklt. Pane of 10	...	...	6.50	5.75
2122	$10.75 Express Mail, Eagle & Moon, Booklet Single, Type I	...	...	29.50	10.75
2122a	$10.75 Bklt. Pane of 3 (Pl. #11111)	...	...	87.50	...
2122b	$10.75 Type II, Bklt. Sgl (1989) .	...	...	37.50	13.95
2122c	$10.75 Ty. II Bklt.Pane of 3(Pl.#22222)...	...	...	110.00	...

* Ty. I: washed out appearance; "$10.75" is grainy.
* Ty. II: brighter colors; "$10.75" is smoother and less grainy.

1985-89 TRANSPORTATION COIL SERIES II

2123
2124
2125
2126

2127
2128
2129
2130

2131
2132
2133
2134

2135

2136

* Pl. #s must appear on center stamp. Sets do not include "B" press issue.

Scott's No.		Pl.# Strip of 5	Pl.# Strip of 3	F-VF NH	F-VF Used
2123-36	Mint (14 values)	39.75	30.00	4.80	2.25
2123	3.4¢ School Bus	1.30	1.00	.20	.15
2124	4.9¢ Buckboard	1.30	1.00	.20	.15
2125	5.5¢ Star Route Truck (1986) ...	2.65	2.10	.25	.15
2126	6¢ Tricycle	2.15	1.75	.25	.15
2127	7.1¢ Tractor (1987)	2.95	2.50	.35	.20
2128	8.3¢ Ambulance	2.20	1.65	.35	.20
2129	8.5¢ Tow Truck (1987)	3.60	3.00	.35	.20
2130	10.1¢ Oil Wagon	3.25	2.65	.35	.20
2131	11¢ Stutz Bearcat	2.50	1.95	.35	.15
2132	12¢ Stanley Steamer, Type I	3.50	2.50	.55	.20
2133	12.5¢ Pushcart	3.50	3.00	.35	.25
2134	14¢ Iceboat, Type I	2.85	2.25	.40	.20
2134b	14¢ "B" Press, Type II (1986) ...	6.75	5.50	.55	.25
	#2134 17½mm Wide, Overall Tagging, Line in Plate Strip				
	#2134b 17¼mm Wide, Block Tagging, No line in Plate Strip				
2135	17¢ Dog Sled (1986)	4.65	3.50	.65	.20
2136	25¢ Bread Wagon (1986)	4.95	3.75	.75	.15

1985-89 TRANSPORTATION COIL SERIES II
PRECANCELLED COILS

| 2123a | 2124a | 2125a | 2126a | 2127a |

| 2127b | 2128a | 2129a | 2130a | 2130b |

| 2132a | 2132b | 2133a |

Scott's No.		Pl.# Strip of 5	Pl.# Strip of 3	F-VF NH	Used
2123a/33a	Prec. (12 values) (No#2132b)	37.95	31.75	3.60	2.50
2123a	3.4¢ School Bus	5.75	5.00	.25	.20
2124a	4.9¢ Buckboard	2.25	1.85	.25	.20
2125a	5.5¢ Star Route Truck (1986)	2.50	2.10	.25	.20
2126a	6¢ Tricycle	2.40	1.95	.25	.20
2127a	7.1¢ Tractor (1987)	4.15	3.50	.35	.20
2127b	7.1¢ Zip + 4 Precancel (1989)	2.85	2.25	.35	.25
2128a	8.3¢ Ambulance	2.25	1.65	.35	.25
2129a	8.5¢ Tow Truck (1987)	3.75	3.15	.35	.25
2130a	10.1¢ Oil Wagon,Red Prec.('88)	3.35	2.75	.35	.25
2130av	10.1¢ Oil Wagon, Black Precan.	3.35	2.75	.35	.25
2132a	12¢ Stanley Steamer, Type I	3.50	2.50	.55	.25
2132b	12¢ "B" Press,Type II (1987)	29.50	26.50	1.80	.75

#2132, 2132a "Stanley Steamer 1909" 18mm, Line in Plate Strip
#2132b "Stanley Steamer 1909" 17½ mm, No line in Plate Strip

| 2133a | 12.5¢ Pushcart | 3.50 | 3.40 | .35 | .30 |

1985 Commemoratives (cont.)

| 2137 |
| 2138 / 2140 | 2139 / 2141 |

| 2142 | 2143 | 2144 |

| 2145 | 2146 | 2147 |

Scott's No.		Mint Sheet	Plate Block	F-VF NH	F-VF Used
2137	22¢ Mary Mcleod Bethune	39.50	3.75	.85	.15
2138-41	22¢ Duck Decoys, attached	95.00	11.50	8.75	5.50
2138-41	Set of 4 Singles	...	...	8.25	1.00
2142	22¢ Winter Spec. Olympics ... (40)	25.00	2.95	.65	.15

1985 Commemoratives (continued)

Scott's No.		Mint Sheet	Plate Block	F-VF NH	F-VF Used
2143	22¢ Love	33.50	3.25	.70	.15
2144	22¢ Rural Electrification Ad.	55.00 (20)	32.50	.80	.15
2145	22¢ Ameripex '86, Chicago ... (48)	28.75	2.75	.60	.15
2146	22¢ Abigail Adams	28.50	3.25	.70	.15
2147	22¢ Fredic A. Bartholdi	28.50	2.75	.60	.15

1985 Regular Issue Coil Stamps Perf. 10 Vertically

| 2149 | 2149a | 2150 | 2150a |

Scott's No.		Pl# Strip of 5	Pl# Strip of 3	F-VF NH	F-VF Used
2149	18¢ Washington, Pre-Sort	4.65	3.25	.75	.20
2149a	18¢ Precancelled	4.95	3.95	.55	.35
2149d	18¢ Precancelled, Dry Gum	6.25	5.50	.80	...
2150	21.1¢ Envelope	4.75	3.50	.70	.25
2150a	21.1¢ Zip + 4 Precancel	5.00	4.00	.75	.50

1985 Commemoratives (continued)

| 2152 | 2159 | 2153 |

| 2154 |
| 2155 / 2157 | 2156 / 2158 |

| 2160 / 2162 | 2161 / 2163 | 2165 |

| 2164 | 2166 | 2167 |

Scott's No.		Mint Sheet	Plate Block	F-VF NH	F-VF Used
2152	22¢ Korean War Vetrans	39.50	3.95	.85	.15
2153	22¢ Social Security Act	28.50	2.75	.60	.15
2154	22¢ World War I Vetrans	39.50	3.95	.85	.15
2155-58	22¢ Horses, attached ... (40)	115.00	15.00	13.00	7.00
2155-58	Set of 4 Singles	...	...	12.00	1.60
2159	22¢ Public Education	67.50	6.50	1.35	.15
2160-63	22¢ Int'l. Youth Year, attd	59.50	7.95	5.25	3.00
2160-63	Set of 4 Singles	...	...	4.00	1.20

1985 Commemoratives (continued)

Scott's No.		Mint Sheet	Plate Block	F-VF NH	F-VF Used
2164	22¢ Help End Hunger	31.50	3.00	.65	.15
#2165-66 Christmas					
2165	22¢ Madonna and Child	28.50	2.75	.60	.15
2166	22¢ Poinsettia Plants	28.50	2.75	.60	.15

1986 Commemoratives

2167,2202-04,2210-11,					
2220-24,2235-45 Set of 22 (1986)		...	...	18.50	3.50
2167	22¢ Arkansas Statehood	31.50	3.00	.65	.15

1986-94 Great Americans, Perforated 11, Tagged
(Sheets of 100)

2168	2169	2170	2171	
2172	2173	2175	2176	
2177	2178	2179	2180	2181
2182,2197	2183	2184	2185	2186
2187	2188	2189	2190	2191
2192	2193	2194	2195	2196

Scott's No.		Mint Sheet	Plate Block	F-VF NH	F-VF Used
2168/96	Set of 28	...	170.00	37.50	6.25
2168	1¢ Margaret Mitchell	11.00	.90	.25	.15
2169	2¢ Mary Lyon, Block Tagging (1987)	6.75	.45	.20	.15
2169a	2¢ Untagged (1996)	7.75	.90	.20	.20
2170	3¢ Dr.Paul Dudley White,Dull Gum	10.00	.60	.20	.15
2170a	3¢ Untagged, Dull Gum	10.00	.60	.20	.15
2170v	3¢ Untagged, Shiny Gum (1995) ...	10.00	.70	.20	...
2171	4¢ Father Flanagan, Blue Violet .	11.75	.75	.20	.15
2171a	4¢ Untagged, Grayish Violet	12.95	.85	.25	.20
2171b	4¢ Untagged,Deep Grayish Blue('93)	12.95	.85	.25	.20
2172	5¢ Hugo Black	14.50	.85	.20	.15
2173	5¢ Luis Munoz Marin (1990)	16.50	.90	.20	.15
2173	5¢ Marin, Pl No &Zip Blk of 4 Combo,LL or LR	1.25	...	...	
2173a	5¢ Marin, Untagged (1991)	18.00	.95	.20	.20
2175	10¢ Red Cloud, Block Tagging, Lake, Dull Gum (1987)	40.00	1.95	.45	.20
2175a	10¢ Overall Tagging, Dull Gum ('90)	67.50	4.00	.70	.35
2175c	10¢ Solid Tagging, Dull Gum(1991)	...	9.95	1.75	.50
2175d	10¢ Mottled Tagging, Shiny Gum('93)	...	9.95	1.75	.50
2175e	10¢ Carmine, Mottled Tagging, Shiny Gum (1994)	32.50	1.65	.35	.20
2176	14¢ Julia Ward Howe (1987)	40.00	2.10	.45	.15
2177	15¢ Buffalo Bill Cody, Large Block Tagging (1988)	60.00	3.95	.65	.25
2177a	15¢ Overall Tagging (1990)	37.50	2.30	.40	.15
2177b	15¢ Solid Tagging	...	6.50	1.00	.40
2178	17¢ Belva Ann Lockwood	47.50	2.50	.50	.15

1986-94 Great Americans, Perforated 11 (continued)
(Sheets of 100)

Scott's No.		Mint Sheet	Plate Block	F-VF NH	F-VF Used
2179	20¢ Virginia Agpar, Red Brown, Perf. 11 x 11.1 (1994)	47.50	3.00	.50	.15
2179a	20¢ Orange Brown	47.50	3.00	.50	.15
2180	21¢ Chester Carlson (1988)	57.50	3.25	.60	.25
2181	23¢ Mary Cassatt, Large Block Tagging, Dull Gum (1988)	60.00	3.50	.65	.20
2181a	23¢ Overall Tagging, Dull Gum	75.00	4.75	.80	.30
2181b	23¢ Solid Tagging, Dull Gum	65.00	3.85	.70	.20
2181c	23¢ Mottled Tagging, Shiny Gum	75.00	4.95	.80	.50
2182	25¢ Jack London, Perf. 11	70.00	3.50	.65	.15
2182v	25¢ Booklet Single,Perf.11(1988)	...	...	.75	.20
2182a	25¢ Booklet Pane of 10, Perf. 11 (1988)...	...	...	6.75	4.50
2183	28¢ Sitting Bull (1989)	75.00	4.00	.80	.20
2184	29¢ Earl Warren (1992)	75.00	4.00	.80	.20
2185	29¢ Jefferson Pf 11½ x 11 (1993)	75.00	4.00	.80	.20
2185	Jefferson, Plate Block of 8	...	7.50	...	...
2186	35¢ Dennis Chavez (1991)	95.00	5.00	1.00	.25
2187	40¢ C.Chennault, Overall Tagging, Dull Gum (1990)	105.00	5.50	1.10	.20
2187a	40¢ Solid Tagging, Dull Gum	120.00	6.00	1.25	.35
2187v	40¢ Grainy Solid Tagging, Low Gloss	105.00	5.50	1.10	...
2187b	40¢ Mottled Tagging, Shiny Gum	125.00	6.50	1.25	.35
2188	45¢ Dr. H. Cushing, Bright Blue, Large Block Tagging (1988)	125.00	6.00	1.30	.20
2188a	45¢ Blue, Overall Tagging (1990)	220.00	11.75	2.35	.75
2189	52¢ Hubert Humphrey, Solid Tagging, Dull Gum (1991)	150.00	7.75	1.60	.20
2189a	52¢ Mottled Tagging, Shiny('93) .	170.00	8.75	1.80	.50
2190	56¢ John Harvard	150.00	7.50	1.60	.25
2191	65¢ Gen. "Hap" Arnold (1988)	160.00	8.75	1.75	.25
2192	75¢ Wendell Willkie, Solid Tagging, Dull Gum (1992)	185.00	9.75	1.95	.20
2192a	75¢ Mottled Tagging, Shiny Gum	185.00	9.75	1.95	.20
2193	$1 Dr. Bernard Revel	375.00	17.50	4.00	.30
2194	$1 Johns Hopkins, Intense Deep Blue, Large Block Tagging, Dull Gum (1989) .... (20)	55.00	12.95	2.85	.25
2194b	$1 Deep Blue, Overall Tagging, Dull Gum (1990) .... (20)	55.00	12.95	2.85	.25
2194d	$1 Dark Blue, Solid Tagging, Dull Gum (1992) .... (20)	55.00	12.95	2.85	.25
2194e	$1 Blue, Mottled Tagging, Shiny Gum (1993) .... (20)	57.50	13.75	3.00	.35
2194f	$1 Blue, Grainy Solid Tagging, Low Gloss Gum (1998) .... (20)	57.50	13.75	3.00	.35
2195	$2 William Jennings Bryan	500.00	23.00	5.25	.55
2196	$5 Bret Harte, Large Block Tagging (1987) .... (20)	235.00	53.50	12.50	2.25
2196b	$5 Solid Tagging (1992) .... (20)	240.00	55.00	12.75	2.25
2197	25¢ J. London Booklet Single, Perf.10 (1988)	...	...	.75	.15
2197a	25¢ Booklet Pane of 6 (1988)	...	...	4.50	3.00

NOTE: SETS CONTAIN OUR CHOICE OF TAGGED OR UNTAGGED, ETC.

1986 Commemoratives (continued)

2198	2199	2200	2201
2202	2203	2204	2211
2205	2206	2207	
2208	2209	2210	

1986 Commemoratives (continued)

Scott's No.		Mint Sheet	Plate Block	F-VF NH	F-VF Used
2198-2201	22¢ Stamp Coll. Bklt.	...	...		
	Set of 4 Singles			2.60	1.20
2201a	22¢ Booklet Pane of 4	...	...	2.75	2.75
2202	22¢ Love, Puppy	32.50	2.95	.70	.15
2203	22¢ Sojourner Truth	37.50	3.50	.80	.15
2204	22¢ Texas, 150th Anniv	32.50	2.95	.70	.15
2205-09	22¢ Fish Set of 5 Booklet Singles	...	...	9.50	1.00
2209a	22¢ Booklet Pane of 5	...	...	9.75	3.75
2210	22¢ Public Hospitals	33.50	3.25	.70	.15
2211	22¢ Duke Ellington	31.50	3.00	.65	.15

1986 Presidents Miniature Sheets of 9

2216a George Washington
2216b John Adams
2216c Thomas Jefferson
2216d James Madison
2216e James Monroe
2216f John Quincy Adams
2216g Andrew Jackson
2216h Martin Van Buren
2216i William H. Harrison
2217a John Tyler
2217b James Knox Polk
2217c Zachary Taylor
2217d Millard Fillmore
2217e Franklin Pierce
2217f James Buchanan
2217g Abraham Lincoln
2217h Andrew Johnson
2217i Ulysses S. Grant
2218a Rutherfor B. Hayes
2218b James A. Garfield
2218c Chester A. Arthur
2218d Grover Cleveland
2218e Benjamin Harrison
2218f William McKinley
2218g Theodore Roosevelt
2218h William H. Taft
2218i Woodrow Wilson
2219a Warren G. Harding
2219b Calvin Coolidge
2219c Herbert Hoover
2219d Franklin Roosevelt
2219e White House
2219f Harry S Truman
2219g Dwight Eisenhower
2219h John F. Kennedy
2219i Lyndon B. Johnson

2216-2219

2216-19	22¢ Ameripex '86, Set of 4	...	...	25.75	24.75
2216a-19i	Presidents, Set of 36 Singles ...	...	...	24.75	15.75

1986 Commemoratives (continued)

2220 **2221** **2224**
2222 **2223**

2220-23	22¢ Arctic Explorers, attd	60.00	8.00	5.50	3.75
2220-23	Set of 4 Singles	...	...	4.50	.90
2224	22¢ Statue of Liberty	36.50	3.25	.75	.15

1986-96 Transportation "B" Press Coils

2225 **2226** **2228** **2231**

1986-96 Transportation "B" Press Coils (continued)

Scott's No.		Pl.# Strip of 5	Pl.# Strip of 3	F-VF NH	F-VF Used
2225-31	Set of 4	12.50	9.50	1.80	.65
2225	1¢ Omnibus, Large Block				
	Tagging, Dull Gum	.80	.70	.20	.15
2225a	1¢ Mottled Tagging, Shiny Gum	9.50	8.75	.25	.20
2225b	1¢ Untagged, Dull Gum	1.30	1.00	.20	.20
2225s	1¢ Untagged, Shiny Gum (1996)	.80	.70	.20	...
2225l	1¢ Untagged, Low Gloss Gum ..	1.50	1.40	.30	...
2226	2¢ Locomotive, Tagged, Dull (1987)	.95	.75	.20	.15
2226a	2¢ Untagged, Dull Gum (1994) .	1.15	.85	.20	.20
2226d	2¢ Untagged, Dull Gum	.95	.75	.20	...
2228	4¢ Stagecoach, Block Tagging .	1.50	1.15	.20	.20
2228a	4¢ Overall Tagging (1990)	17.50	16.50	.70	.25
1898A:	"Stagecoach 1890s" is 19½ mm. long				
2228:	"Stagecoach 1890s" is 17 mm. long				
2231	8.3¢ Ambulance, Precancel	9.75	7.50	1.40	.25

2128: "Ambulance 1860s" is 18½ mm. long   2231: "Ambulance 1860s" is 18 mm. Long

1986 Commemoratives (continued)

2235 **2236** **2240** **2241**
2237 **2238** **2242** **2243**

2239 **2244** **2245**

Scott's No.		Mint Sheet	Plate Block	F-VF NH	F-VF Used
2235-38	22¢ Navajo Art, attd	50.00	5.50	4.50	3.50
2235-38	Set of 4 Singles			4.00	.80
2239	22¢ T.S. Eliot	28.50	2.75	.60	.15
2240-43	22¢ Woodcarved Figurines., attd	42.50	4.75	3.75	3.00
2240-43	Set of 4 Singles			3.50	.80
2244-45	Christmas Issues				
2244	22¢ Madonna & Child .... (100)	57.50	2.75	.60	.15
2245	22¢ Village Scene .... (100)	57.50	2.75	.60	.15

1987 Commemoratives

2246 **2247** **2248**

2249 **2250** **2251**

2246-51,75,2336-38,2349-54,2360-61,2367-68	Set of 20	...		16.50	3.00
2246	22¢ Michigan Statehood	28.50	2.75	.60	.15
2247	22¢ Pan American Games	28.50	2.75	.60	.15
2248	22¢ Love, Heart .... (100)	55.00	2.75	.60	.15

1987 Commemoratives (continued)

1987-93 TRANSPORTATION COILS III

2252 — 2253 — 2254 — 2255

2256 — 2257 — 2258 — 2259

2260 — 2261 — 2262 — 2262a

2263 — 2264 — 2265 — 2266

Scott's No.		Pl.# Strip of 5	Pl.# Strip of 3	F-VF NH	Used
2252-66	Set of 15 Different Values	66.75	51.75	7.00	3.25
2252	3¢ Conestoga Wagon,Dull ('88)	1.15	.95	.20	.15
2252a	3¢ Untagged, Dull Gum (1992)	1.80	1.50	.20	.20
2252s	3¢ Untagged, Shiny Gum	2.25	1.80	.25	...
2252l	3¢ Untagged, Low Gloss Gum ..	10.75	9.75	.35	...
2253	5¢ Milk Wagon	1.50	1.20	.20	.15
2254	5.3¢ Elevator, Precancel (1988)	2.30	1.85	.30	.20
2255	7.6¢ Carretta, Precancel (1988)	3.15	2.65	.30	.20
2256	8.4¢ Wheelchair, Precancel (1986)	3.00	2.50	.30	.20
2257	10¢ Canal Boat, Large Block Tagging, Dull Gum	2.75	2.25	.35	.15
2257a	10¢ Overall Tagging,Dull (1993)	6.25	5.75	.45	.30
2257v	10¢ Overall Tagging,Shiny(1994)	5.25	4.75	.45	...
2257b	10¢ Mottled Tagging,Shiny	5.25	4.75	.35	.30
2258	13¢ Police Wagon, Prec. ('88) ..	5.75	4.75	.60	.25
2259	13.2¢ R.R. Coat Car, Prec. ('88)	4.25	3.65	.40	.20
2260	15¢ Tugboat, Large Block Tag.('88)	3.25	2.50	.45	.20
2260a	15¢ Overall Tagging (1990)	5.00	4.00	.60	.25
2260b	15¢ Untagged	200.00	190.00	4.25	...
2261	16.7¢ Popcorn Wagon, Prec.('88)	4.25	3.50	.50	.25
2262	17.5¢ Marmon Wasp	5.75	4.75	.60	.30
2262a	17.5¢ Precancelled, Untagged .	5.75	4.75	.65	.35
2263	20¢ Cable Car,Block Tagging ('88)	4.75	3.75	.60	.20
2263b	20¢ Overall Tagged (1990)	11.00	8.75	1.30	.35
2264	20.5¢ Fire Engine, Prec. (1988)	8.95	6.95	1.20	.35
2265	21¢ R.R. Mail Car, Prec. (1988)	7.00	5.25	.65	.35
2266	24.1¢ Tandem Bic., Prec. (1988)	6.50	5.25	.75	.35

1987 Special Occasions Issue

2267 — 2268 — 2269 — 2270

2271 — 2272 — 2273 — 2274

2275 — 2276 — 2277,79,82

2278,2285A — 2280 — 2281 — 2283

2284 — 2285

Scott's No.		Mint Sheet	Plate Block	F-VF NH	F-VF Used
	1987 Special Occasions Issue				
2267-74	22¢ Spec. Occ. Bklt. Sgls. (8) ...	...	...	14.50	2.95
2274a	22¢ Bklt. Pane of 10	...	...	16.50	12.00
	Booklet Pane contains 2 each of # 2267 and # 2272				
	1987 Commemoratives (cont)				
2275	22¢ United Way	28.50	2.75	.60	.15
	1987-89 Regular Issues				
2276	22¢ Flag & Fireworks .... (100)	57.50	3.00	.60	.15
2276a	22¢ Fireworks Booklet Pane of 20	...	...	12.50	11.00
2276v	22¢ Flag, Booklet Single	...	...	.70	.20
2277	(25¢) "E" Earth Issue ('88) ..... (100)	80.00	3.85	.85	.15
2278	25¢ Flag & Clouds ('88) .... (100)	75.00	3.25	.70	.15
2279	(25¢) "E" Earth Coil ('88) ... Pl# Strip	4.50 (5)	3.50 (3)	.70	.15
2280	25¢ Yosemite Coil. Large Block Tagging (1988) .... Pl# Strip	4.75 (5)	3.50 (3)	.80	.15
2280a	25¢ Mottled Tagging ('89) .. Pl# Strip	4.95 (5)	3.95 (3)	.80	.15
2281	25¢ Honeybee Coil .... Pl# Strip	4.50 (5)	3.50 (3)	.85	.15
2282	(25¢) "E" Booklet Single (1988) ..	...	...	.80	.20
2282a	(25¢) Booklet Pane of 10	...	...	7.75	5.25
2283	25¢ Pheasant Booklet Single, **red & blue sky** (1988)	...	...	.80	.15
2283a	25¢ Booklet Pane of 10	...	...	7.75	5.25
2283b	25¢ Blue Sky, **(red omitted)**, bklt. sgl. ('89)	...	...	8.75	2.00
2283c	25¢ Bklt. Pn. 10 **(Pl# A3111,A3222)**	...	...	85.00	...
2284	25¢ Grosbeak Booklet Single (1988)	...	...	.70	.20
2285	25¢ Owl Booklet Single (1988) ...	...	...	.70	.20
2284-85	Attached Pair	...	...	1.40	.95
2285b	25¢ Booklet Pane (5 ea. #2284,2285)	...	...	6.75	5.75
2285A	25¢ Flag/Cloud Booklet Single (1988)	...	...	.85	.15
2285Ac	25¢ Booklet Pane of 6	...	...	4.75	4.00

1987 North American Wildlife Series

2286-2335 Sheet

1987 North American Wildlife Series (continued)

2287   2288   2289

Scott's No.		Mint Sheet	Plate Block	F-VF NH	F-VF Used
2286-2335	22¢ American Wildlife	69.50	...	...	...
2286-2335	Set of 50 Singles	...	...	65.00	22.50
2286-2335	22¢ Individual Singles	...	...	1.50	.55

2286 Barn Swallow	2303 Blackbird	2320 Bison	
2287 Monarch Butterfly	2304 Lobster	2321 Snowy Egret	
2288 Bighorn Sheep	2305 Jack Rabbit	2322 Gray Wolf	
2289 Hummingbird	2306 Scarlet Tanager	2323 Mountain Goat	
2290 Cottontail	2307 Woodchuck	2324 Deer Mouse	
2291 Osprey	2308 Spoonbill	2325 Prairie Dog	
2292 Mountain Lion	2309 Bald Eagle	2326 Box Turtle	
2293 Luna Moth	2310 Brown Bear	2327 Wolverine	
2294 Mule Deer	2311 Iiwi	2328 American Elk	
2295 Gray Squirrel	2312 Badger	2329 Sea Lion	
2296 Armadillo	2313 Pronghorn	2330 Mockingbird	
2297 Eastern Chipmunk	2314 River Otter	2331 Raccoon	
2298 Moose	2315 Ladybug	2332 Bobcat	
2299 Black Bear	2316 Beaver	2333 Ferret	
2300 Tiger Swallowtail	2317 Whitetailed Deer	2334 Canada Goose	
2301 Bobwhite	2318 Blue Jay	2335 Red Fox	
2302 Ringtail	2319 Pika		

2336   2337   2338   2339

2340   2341   2342   2343

2344   2345   2346   2347

2348   2349   2350

1987-90 Ratification of the Constitution Bicentennial

		Mint Sheet	Plate Block	F-VF NH	F-VF Used
2336-48	Set of 13	560.00	55.00	11.75	2.35
2336	22¢ Delaware.	43.50	4.50	.95	.20
2337	22¢ Pennsylvania	43.50	4.50	.95	.20
2338	22¢ New Jersey	43.50	4.50	.95	.20
2339	22¢ Georgia ('88)	43.50	4.50	.95	.20
2340	22¢ Connecticut ('88)	43.50	4.50	.95	.20
2341	22¢ Massachusetts ('88)	43.50	4.50	.95	.20
2342	22¢ Maryland ('88)	47.50	4.75	1.00	.20
2343	25¢ South Carolina ('88)	46.50	4.50	.95	.20
2344	25¢ New Hampshire ('88)	46.50	4.50	.95	.20
2345	25¢ Virginia ('88)	46.50	4.50	.95	.20

1987-90 Ratification of the Constitution Bicentennial (continued)

Scott's No.		Mint Sheet	Plate Block	F-VF NH	F-VF Used
2346	25¢ New York ('88)	46.50	4.50	.95	.20
2347	25¢ North Carolina ('89)	46.50	4.50	.95	.20
2348	25¢ Rhode Island ('90)	52.50	5.25	1.10	.20

1987 Commemoratives (cont.)

2351   2352
2353   2354

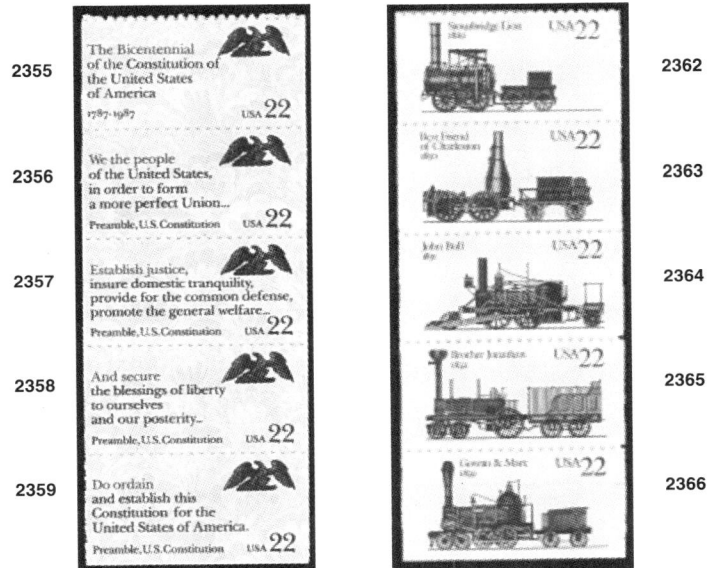

2355   2356   2357   2358   2359

2362   2363   2364   2365   2366

2360   2361   2367   2368

		Mint Sheet	Plate Block	F-VF NH	F-VF Used
2349	22¢ U.S.-Morocco Relations	28.50	2.75	.60	.15
2350	22¢ William Faulkner	36.50	3.50	.75	.15
2351-54	22¢ Lacemaking, attd .... (40)	35.00	5.00	3.50	3.00
2351-54	Set of 4 Sgls	...	...	3.35	1.00
2355-59	22¢ Drafting of Constitution, Bklt. Sgls. (5)	...	...	4.95	1.10
2359a	22¢ Bklt. Pane of 5	...	...	5.25	3.50
2360	22¢ Signing the Constitution	39.75	4.00	.85	.15
2361	22¢ Cert. Public Accounting	160.00	15.00	3.25	.20
2362-66	22¢ Locomotives Bklt. Sgls. (5)	...	...	4.25	1.10
2366a	22¢ Bklt. Pane of 5	...	...	4.50	3.50
#2367-68	Christmas Issues				
2367	22¢ Madonna & Child .... (100)	57.50	2.75	.60	.15
2368	22¢ Ornaments .... (100)	57.50	2.75	.60	.15

1988 Commemoratives

| 2369 | 2370 | 2371 |

| 2372 | 2373 | 2376 |
| 2374 | 2375 | |

| 2377 | 2378 | 2379 | 2380 |

Scott's No.		Mint Sheet	Plate Block	F-VF NH	F-VF Used
2339-46,69-80,86-93,99-2400	**Set of 30**	...	...	26.85	5.25
2369	22¢ 1988 Winter Olympics	32.50	3.25	.75	.15
2370	22¢ Australia Bicent .... (40)	24.00	2.75	.60	.15
2371	22¢ J.W. Johnson	31.50	3.00	.70	.15
2372-75	22¢ Cats, attd .... (40)	37.50	5.75	3.75	2.50
2372-75	Set of 4 Sgls	...	...	3.50	1.00
2376	22¢ Knute Rockne	38.50	3.95	.80	.15
2377	25¢ Francis Ouimet	52.50	5.75	1.10	.20
2378	25¢ Love, Roses .... (100)	67.50	3.25	.70	.15
2379	45¢ Love, Roses	65.00	5.75	1.35	.20
2380	25¢ Summer Olympics	37.50	3.50	.80	.15

| 2381 | 2382 |

| 2383 | 2384 |

| 2385 |

2381-85	25¢ Classic Cars, Bklt. Sgls.	...	...	9.50	1.25
2385a	25¢ Bk. Pn. 5	...	...	10.00	4.75

1988 Commemoratives (continued)

| 2386 | 2387 | 2390 | 2391 |
| 2388 | 2389 | 2392 | 2393 |

Scott's No.		Mint Sheet	Plate Block	F-VF NH	F-VF Used
2386-89	25¢ Antarctic Exp., attd	56.75	7.95	5.25	3.00
2386-89	Set of 4 Singles	...	...	4.75	1.00
2390-93	25¢ Carousel, attd	55.00	6.00	5.25	3.00
2390-93	Set of 4 Singles	...	...	4.75	1.00

| 2394 | 2399 | 2400 |

| 2395 | 2396 |

| 2397 | 2398 |

1988 Express Mail Issue

2394	$8.75 Eagle & Moon .... (20)	500.00	115.00	26.50	8.75

1988 Special Occasions Issue

2395-98	25¢ Special Occasions, Bklt. Sgls.	...	...	3.75	1.00
2396a	25¢ Happy Birthday & Best Wishes				
	B. Pn. of 6 (3&3) w/gutter	...	...	5.00	4.00
2398a	25¢ Thinking of You & Love You				
	B. Pn. of 6 (3&3) w/gutter	...	...	5.00	4.00

1988 Commemoratives (cont.)

2399	25¢ Madonna & Child	31.50	3.00	.65	.15
2400	25¢ Horse & Sleigh	31.50	3.00	.65	.15

| 2401 | 2402 | 2403 |

1989 Commemoratives

2347,2401-4,10-18,20-28,34-37 **Set of 27**		...	...	25.00	4.25
2401	25¢ Montana Sthd. Cent	40.00	4.00	.90	.15
2402	25¢ A. Philip Randolph	39.50	3.75	.85	.15
2403	25¢ North Dakota Sthd. Cent ...	39.50	3.75	.85	.15

2404

2410

2405

2406

2407

2411

2416

2408

2409

Scott's No.		Mint Sheet	Plate Block	F-VF NH	F-VF Used
2404	25¢ Washington Sthd. Cent	35.00	3.50	.75	.15
2405-09	25¢ Steamboats, Bklt. Sgls	...	...	4.75	1.10
2409a	25¢ Bklt. Pane of 5	(Unfolded 7.00)	...	4.95	3.50
2410	25¢ World Stamp Expo	35.00	3.50	.75	.15
2411	25¢ Arturo Toscanini	35.00	3.50	.75	.15
2412-15	Constitution Bicent., Set of 4 ...	155.00	16.00	3.50	.55
2412	25¢ House of Representatives .	42.50	4.15	.90	.15
2413	25¢ U.S. Senate	45.00	4.35	.95	.15
2414	25¢ Exec. Branch/G.W. Inaug ..	40.00	4.25	.90	.15
2415	25¢ U.S. Supreme Court (1990)	38.50	4.00	.85	.15
2416	25¢ South Dakota Sthd. Cent ...	35.00	3.50	.75	.15
2417	25¢ Lou Gehrig	52.50	5.25	1.10	.20
2418	25¢ Ernest Hemingway	37.50	3.75	.80	.15
1989 Priority Mail Issue					
2419	$2.40 Moon Landing .... (20)	150.00	33.50	7.75	3.25
1989 Commemoratives (cont.)					
2420	25¢ Letter Carriers .... (40)	25.00	3.00	.65	.15
2421	25¢ Drafting Bill of Rights	45.00	4.75	.95	.15
2422-25	25¢ Prehistoric Animals, attd (40)	53.50	6.50	5.75	2.75
2422-25	Set of 4 Singles	...	...	5.50	1.00
2426	25¢ Pre-Columbian Customs	31.50	3.00	.65	.15

2427

2428, 2429

2431

1989 Christmas Issues

2427	25¢ Madonna & Child	31.50	3.00	.65	.15
2427v	Madonna, Booklet Single	...	...	.75	.20
2427a	25¢ Bklt. Pane of 10	(Unfolded 15.00)	...	7.50	5.50
2428	25¢ Sleigh & Presents	31.50	3.00	.65	.15
2429	25¢ Sleigh, Bklt. Single	...	...	.90	.20
2429a	25¢ Bklt. Pane of 10	(Unfolded 19.50)	...	8.25	5.50
1989 Regular Issue					
2431	25¢ Eagle & Shield, self adhesive	...	...	1.00	.30
2431a	25¢ Pane of 18	...	...	17.50	...
2431v	25¢ Eagle & Shield, Coil (No#) Plain Strip of 3	2.70		.90	...

1989 World Stamp Expo '89, Washington, DC

2433

2438

2412

2413

2414

2415

2417

2418

2419

2420

2421

2422
2424
2433
2425

2426

| | 2434 | | 2435 |
| 2436 | | 2437 | |

Scott's No.		Mint Sheet	Plate Block	F-VF NH	F-VF Used
2433	90¢ World Stamp Expo S/S of 4 .	...	...	19.50	15.00
2434-37	25¢ Traditional Mail Deliv., attd (40)	45.00	6.00	5.00	3.25
2434-37	Set of 4 Singles	...	...	4.70	1.20
2438	25¢ Traditional Mail S/S of 4	...	...	7.25	5.00
	Also see #C122-26				

2439 2440,2441 2442 2443

2444

2449

2445 2447 2446 2448

1990 Commemoratives
2348,2439-40,2442,44-49,96-2500,2506-15 Set of 25

Scott's No.		Mint Sheet	Plate Block	F-VF NH	F-VF Used
	Set of 25	...	...	27.50	3.95
2439	25¢ Idaho Sthd. Centenary	31.50	3.00	.65	.15
2440	25¢ Love, Doves	31.50	3.00	.65	.15
2441	25¢ Love, Bklt. Single	...	...	1.10	.20
2441a	25¢ Booklet Pane of 10 .... (Unfolded 42.50)...		10.75	9.50
2442	25¢ Ida B. Wells	31.50	4.50	.95	.15
	1990 Regular Issue				
2443	15¢ Beach Umbrella, Bklt. Sgl .	...	...	.45	.15
2443a	15¢ Booklet Pane of 10 .... (Unfolded 8.95)...		4.35	3.50
	1990 Commemoratives (continued)				
2444	25¢ Wyoming Sthd. Centenary ...	36.50	3.50	.75	.15
2445-48	25¢ Classic Films, attd .... (40)	85.00	10.00	9.00	5.00
2445-48	Set of 4 Singles	...	...	8.75	1.00
2449	25¢ Marianne Moore	31.50	3.00	.65	.15

1990-95 Transportation Coils IV

2451 2452,2452B 2452D 2453,2454

2457 2458 2463

2464 2466 2468

Scott's No.		Pl# Strip of 5	Pl# Strip of 3	F-VF NH	FVF Used
2451/2468	Set of 12 values	43.50	33.50	5.50	2.10
2451	4¢ Steam Carriage (1991)	1.30	1.00	.20	.15
2451b	4¢ Untagged	1.50	1.25	.20	.20
2452	5¢ Circus Wagon, Engraved,Dull	1.50	1.25	.20	.15
2452a	5¢ Untagged, Dull Gum	2.00	1.60	.25	.20
2452l	5¢ Untagged, Low Gloss Gum				
2452B	5¢ Circus Wagon, Gravure ('92)	1.90	1.50	.25	.15
2452Bf	5¢ Circus Wagon, Hibrite	3.85	3.25	.30	
	Circus Wagon:#2452 Short letters and date,#2452B Taller, thinner letters & date				
2452D	5¢ Circus Wagon(¢ sign) Low Gloss Gum (1995)	1.80	1.60	.20	.15
2452Dg	5¢ Circus Wagon, Hibrite, Shiny	2.75	2.25	.40	
2453	5¢ Canoe, Brown (1991)	1.80	1.50	.20	.15
2454	5¢ Canoe, Red, Shiny (1991) ...	1.90	1.60	.20	.15
2454l	5¢ Low Gloss Gum	12.75	11.50	.65	...
2457	10¢ Tractor Trailer, Intaglio ('91)	3.00	2.50	.30	.20
	#2457"Additional Presort Postage Paid" In Gray.				
2458	10¢ Tractor Trailer, Gravure ('94)	4.25	3.50	.40	.20
	#2458 "Additional, etc." in black. Whiter paper.				
2463	20¢ Cog Railway (1995)	5.50	4.75	.50	.20
2464	23¢ Lunch Wagon, Overall Tagging, Dull Gum (1991)	5.00	3.95	.65	.15
2464a	23¢ Mottled Tagging, Dull Gum('93)	7.25	5.75	1.00	.35
2464s	23¢ Mottled Tagging, Shiny Gum('93)	7.00	5.75	.90	
2466	32¢ Ferryboat,Blue,Shiny Gum (1995)	8.00	6.75	.80	.15
2466l	32¢ Mottled Tagging, Low Gloss Gum	8.75	7.50	.95	.35
2466b	32¢ Bright "Bronx" blue	150.00	130.00	7.50	...
2468	$1 Seaplane, Overall Tagging, Dull Gum	16.00	11.00	2.65	.60
2468b	$1 Mottled Tagging, Shiny Gum('93)	17.00	11.50	2.80	.70
2468c	$1 Grainy Solid Tagging, Low Gloss Gum (1998)	17.00	11.50	2.80	.70

2470 2471 2472 2473 2474

2475

1990 Commemorative Booklet Pane

Scott's No.		Mint Sheet	Plate Block	F-VF NH	F-VF Used
2470-74	25¢ Lighthouse Bklt. Singles	...	...	7.25	1.00
2474a	25¢ Booklet Pane of 5 .... (Unfolded 11.75)		7.50	3.95
	1990 Flag Regular Issue				
2475	25¢ ATM Self Adhesive, Plastic Stamp ...	...	...	.85	.50
2475a	25¢ Pane of 12	...	...	9.95	...

1990-95 Flora and Fauna

2476 2477 2478 2479

2480 2481 2482

Scott's No.		Mint Sheet	Plate Block	F-VF NH	F-VF Used
2476-82	Set of 7	...	31.50	7.00	1.75
2476	1¢ Kestrel (1991) .... (100)	5.50	.60	.20	.15
2477	1¢ Redesign with "¢" sign (1995)(100)	5.50	.60	.20	.15
2478	3¢ Bluebird (1991) .... (100)	9.50	.65	.20	.15
2479	19¢ Fawn (1991) .... (100)	47.50	2.50	.50	.15
2480	30¢ Cardinal (1991) .... (100)	70.00	3.75	.75	.20
2481	45¢ Pumpkinseed Sunfish('92) (100)	115.00	5.95	1.20	.30
2482	$2.00 Bobcat .... (20)	85.00	19.50	4.50	.85

1991-95 Flora and Fauna Booklet Stamps

2483	2484,2485	2486	2487,2493, 2495	2488,2494, 2495A

Scott's No.		F-VF NH	F-VF Used
2483	20¢ Blue Jay, Booklet Single ('95)	.70	.15
2483a	20¢ Booklet Pane of 10 .... (Unfolded 8.95) ...	6.50	4.95
2484	29¢ Wood Duck, BEP bklt sgl Pf 10	.90	.20
2484a	29¢ BEP Bklt Pane of 10 ('91) ... (Unfolded 9.95) ...	7.95	6.95
2485	29¢ Wood Duck, KCS bklt sgl Pf 11	1.00	.20
2485a	29¢ KCS Bklt Pane of 10 ('91) ... (Unfolded 10.95)...	8.75	8.75
2486	29¢ African Violet	1.00	.20
2486a	29¢ Booklet Pane of 10 (1993) .. (Unfolded 10.75)...	9.25	6.50
2487	32¢ Peach, booklet single	.95	.20
2488	32¢ Pear, booklet single	.95	.20
2487-88	32¢ Peach & Pear, Attached Pair	1.90	1.50
2488a	32¢ Booklet Pane of 10 (1995) ... (Unfolded 9.95) ...	9.00	7.50

1993-96 Self Adhesive Booklets & Coils

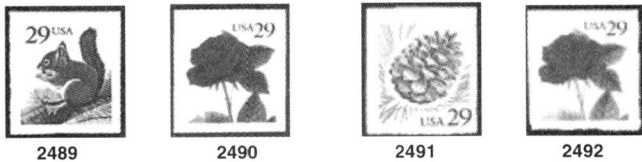

2489	2490	2491	2492

2489	29¢ Red Squirrel, ...	...	...	1.00	.40
2489a	29¢ Pane of 18	...	...	16.50	...
2489v	Squirrel Coil (No Plate #) .... Plain Strip of 3 2.70	.90	...
2490	29¢ Rose	...	...	1.00	.40
2490a	29¢ Pane of 18	...	...	16.50	...
2490v	Rose coil (No Plate #) .... Plain Strip of 3 2.70	.90	...
2491	29¢ Pine Cone	...	...	1.00	.40
2491a	29¢ Pane of 18 ('93)	...	...	16.50	...
2491v	Pine Cone coil .... Pl. #Strip (5) 8.00 (3) 6.75	.90	...
2492	32¢ Pink Rose	...	...	1.00	.30
2492a	32¢ Pane of 20 (1995)	...	...	16.50	...
2492r	32¢ Pane of 20 with Die-cut "Time to Reorder" (1995)	...	17.75	...
2492v	32¢ Pink Rose, Coil ...... Pl.#Strip (5) 6.75 (3) 5.50	.90	...
2492b	32¢ Pink Rose, Folded Pane of 15 ('96)...	...	12.95	...
2492e	32¢ Pink Rose, Folded Pane of 14 ('96)...	...	29.95	...
2492f	32¢ Pink Rose, Folded Pane of 16 ('96)...	...	34.95	...
2493	32¢ Peach, Self-adhesive single	...	...	.90	.30
2494	32¢ Pear, Self-adhesive single ...	...	...	.90	.30
2493-94	32¢ Peach & Pear, Attached Pair...	...	...	1.90	...
2494a	32¢ Pane of 20, Self-adhesive ('95)	...	16.50	...
2495	32¢ Peach, Coil, Self-adhesive ..	...	...	1.25	...
2495A	32¢ Pear, Coil, Self-adhesive	...	...	1.25	...
2495-95A	32¢ Peach & Pear, Coil Pair ('95) Pl # Strip(5)9.00 (3) 7.00 2.50	...

1990 Commemoratives (continued)

2496	2497	2498

2499	2500

Scott's No.		Mint Sheet	Plate Block	F-VF NH	F-VF Used
2496-2500	25¢ Olympians,Strip of 5 ...... (35) 38.50	(10)12.50	5.75	3.75
2496-2500	Set of 5 Singles	...	...	5.50	1.00
2496-2500	Tab singles, attd, Top or Bottom	...	...	6.75	5.75

1990 Commemoratives (continued)

2501	2502	2503

2504	2505

2506	2607

2508 2510	2509 2511

2512	2513

2514, 2514v	2515,2516

Scott's No.		Mint Sheet	Plate Block	F-VF NH	F-VF Used
2501-05	25¢ Indian Headdresses bklt. sgls.	...	...	5.50	1.00
2505a	25¢ Booklet Pane of 10 (2 ea.) .. (Unfolded 16.50)...		10.95	7.50
2506-07	25¢ Micronesia/Marshall Isl., attd	39.50	3.85	1.75	.80
2506-07	Set of 2 Singles	...	...	1.60	.40
2508-11	25¢ Sea Creatures, attd. .... (40)	38.50	4.50	4.00	2.50
2508-11	Set of 4 Singles	...	...	3.75	1.00
2512	25¢ America, Grand Canyon	38.50	3.75	.80	.15
2513	25¢ Dwight Eisenhower .... (40)	42.50	5.00	1.10	.15
2514	25¢ Christmas Madonna & Child	31.50	3.00	.65	.15
2514v	25¢ Madonna, Booklet Single	...	...	.90	.20
2514a	25¢ Booklet Pane of 10 .... (Unfolded 14.95)...		8.75	5.95
2515	25¢ Christmas Tree, Perf. 11	33.75	3.25	.70	.15
2516	25¢ Tree, Bklt. Sgl., Perf. 11½x11	...	...	1.15	.20
2516a	25¢ Booklet Pane of 10 .... (Unfolded 18.95)...		10.95	5.95

1991-94 Regular Issues

2517-2520

2521

2522

2523

2523A

2524-27

2528

2529

2529C

2530

2531

2531A

1991 Regular Issues

Scott's No.		Mint Sheet	Plate Block	F-VF NH	F-VF Used
2517	(29¢) "F" Flower Stamp .... (100)	80.00	4.00	.85	.15
2519	(29¢) "F" Flower, BEP booklet single	...	...	1.15	.20
2519a	(29¢) Bklt.Pane of 10,BEP,bullseye perfs...			11.50	6.75
2520	(29¢) "F" Flower, KCS booklet single	...	...	2.75	.35
2520a	(29¢) Booklet Pane of 10, KCS			26.95	19.95

#2519: Bullseye perforations (11.2). Horizontal and vertical perforations meet exactly in stamp corners.
#2520: Normal (line) perforations, Perf. 11

2521	(4¢) Non-Denom. "make-up" ... (100)	12.50	.70	.20	.15
2522	(29¢) "F" Flag Stamp, ATM self adhesive...	...	...	1.10	.60
2522a	(29¢) Pane of 12			10.95	...
2524	29¢ Flower, Perf. 11 .... (100)	75.00	4.25	.80	.20
2524a	29¢ Flower, Perf. 12½x13 ... (100)	90.00	5.50	.95	.25
2527	29¢ Flower booklet single	...	...	.85	.20
2527a	29¢ Booklet Pane of 10 ..... (Unfolded 9.75)			8.25	5.25
2528	29¢ Flag with Olympic Rings, booklet single...			.85	.20
2528a	29¢ Booklet Pane of 10 ..... (Unfolded 9.75)			8.50	5.25
2530	19¢ Hot-Air Balloons, booklet single ...			.55	.20
2530a	19¢ Booklet Pane of 10 ..... (Unfolded 6.75)			5.25	4.00
2531	29¢ Flags/Mem. Day Anniv ..... (100)	80.00	3.95	.85	.20
2531A	29¢ Liberty & Torch, ATM self adhesive ...			.95	.30
2531Ab	29¢ Pane of 18, Original back	...	...	16.75	...
2531Av	29¢ Pane of 18, Revised back ...	...	...	16.75	...

1991-94 Coil Stamps, Perforated Vertically

Scott's No.		Pl. Strip of 5	Pl. Strip of 3	F-VF NH	F-VF Used
2518	(29¢) "F" Flower Coil	5.00	3.75	.80	.15
2523	29¢ Flag & Mt. Rushmore, Blue, Red, Claret, Intaglio, Mottled Tagging	5.75	4.50	.80	.25
2523d	29¢ Solid Tagging	...	...	6.00	...
2523c	29¢ Blue, Red, Brown (Toledo Brown) Mottled Tagging	200.00	190.00	4.25	...
2523A	29¢ Flag, Gravure	6.25	4.95	.80	.25

* On # 2523A, "USA" & "29" are not outlined in white.

2525	29¢ Flower Coil, rouletted	6.75	5.25	.90	.20
2526	29¢ Flower Coil, perf (1992)	6.75	5.25	.90	.15
2529	19¢ Fishing Boat Coil, Ty. I	4.50	3.75	.55	.15
2529a	19¢ Boat Coil, Ty. II (1993)	4.50	3.75	.55	.30
2529b	19¢ Type II, Untagged (1993)	12.50	10.00	.90	.40
2529C	19¢ Boat Coil, Ty. III (1994)	8.75	7.50	.85	.30

*Type I: Darker color & large color cells, Perf. 10
Type II: Lighter color & small color cells, Perf. 10
Type III: Numerals & U.S.A. taller & thinner, only 1 loop of rope around piling, Perf.9.8

2533

1991 Commemoratives

2532

2534

Scott's No.		Mint Sheet	Plate Block	F-VF NH	F-VF Used
2532-35,37-38,50-51,53-58,60-61, 2567,78-79 Set of 19 (No #2535A)			...	17.00	3.35
2532	50¢ Switzerland joint issue ...... (40)	60.00	7.25	1.60	.35
2533	29¢ Vermont Bicentennial	45.00	4.50	.95	.20
2534	29¢ Savings Bond, 50th Anniv ...	39.50	3.75	.80	.20

1991 Commemoratives (continued)

2535,2536

2537

2538

Scott's No.		Mint Sheet	Plate Block	F-VF NH	F-VF Used
2535	29¢ Love Stamp, Pf. 12½x13	37.50	3.75	.80	.15
2535a	Same, Perf. 11	47.50	5.00	1.00	.25
2536	29¢ Booklet Single, Pf. 11 on 2-3 sides...	...		.85	.20
2536a	Booklet Pane of 10 .... (Unfolded 9.50)	...		8.50	4.95

NOTE: "29" is further from edge of design on #2536 than on #2535.

2537	52¢ Love Stamp, two ounces	70.00	6.50	1.45	.35
2538	29¢ William Saroyan	36.50	3.50	.75	.20

1991-96 Regular Issues

2539

2540

2541

2542

2543

2544

2544A

			Mint Sheet	Plate Block	F-VF NH	F-VF Used
2539	$1.00 USPS Logo&Olympic Rings	(20)	52.50	12.50	2.75	.75
2540	$2.90 Priority Mail, Eagle	(20)	160.00	37.00	8.50	3.00
2541	$9.95 Express Mail, Eagle and Olympic Rings, Domestic Rate ..	(20)	495.00	115.00	26.50	10.75
2542	$14.00 Express Mail, Eagle in Flight, International Rate.	(20)	675.00	150.00	35.00	21.50
2543	$2.90 Priority Mail, Space ('93) ..	(40)	285.00	33.50	7.50	2.75
2544	$3 Challenger Shuttle, Priority Mail (1995)	(20)	145.00	33.50	7.50	2.75
2544b	$3 with 1996 Date ('96)	(20)	145.00	33.50	7.50	3.00
2544A	$10.75 Endeavor Shuttle, Express Mail(1995)	(20)	475.00	110.00	25.00	8.95

1991 Commemoratives (continued)

2545

2546

2547

2548

2549

2545-49	29¢ Fishing Flies, bklt. singles. ..	...	...	8.00	1.10
2549a	29¢ Booklet Pane of 5 .... (Unfolded 13.75)...			8.50	3.75

2550

2551, 2552

2553

2554

2555

2556

2557

2558

2561

2560

Scott's No.		Mint Sheet	Plate Block	F-VF NH	F-VF Used
2550	29¢ Cole Porter	45.00	4.25	.95	.20
2551	29¢ Desert Shield/Desert Storm .	35.00	3.50	.75	.20
2552	29¢ Desert Storm, Bklt. Sgl., ABNCo		…	.95	.20
2552a	29¢ Booklet Pane of 5 .... (Unfolded 6.50)			4.75	4.25
2553-57	29¢ Summer Olympics, attd .... (40)	35.00	(10) 9.75	4.75	3.00
2553-57	Set of 5 Singles	…	…	4.50	1.00
2558	29¢ Numismatics	47.50	4.50	1.00	.20

1991 World War II Souvenir Sheet of 10

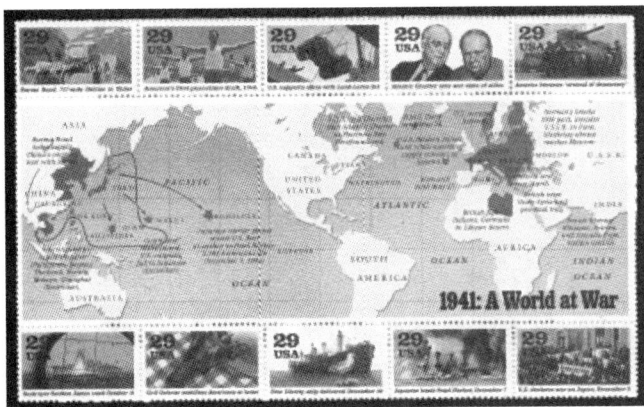
2559

2559	29¢ 1941 World War II Events (20)	21.50	…	10.75	7.75
2559a-j	Set of 10 Singles	…	…	10.50	5.50
2559s	Se-Tenant Center Block of 10	…	…	11.75	11.50

2559a Burma Road	2559e Arsenal of	2559h Liberty Ship
2559b Recruits	Democracy	2559i Pearl Harbor
2559c Lend-Lease Act	2559f Reuben James	2559j U.S.Declares War
2559d Atlantic Charter	2559g Gas Mask, Helmet	

2562

2563

2564

2565

2566

2568

2569

2570

2571

2572

2573

2574

2575

2576

2577

2567

2578

2579

2580
2581

2582

2583

2584

2585

Scott's No.		Mint Sheet	Plate Block	F-VF NH	F-VF Used
2560	29¢ Basketball, 100th Anniversary	47.50	4.50	1.00	.20
2561	29¢ District of Columbia Bicent ..	35.00	3.50	.75	.20
2562-66	29¢ Comedians, booklet singles	…	…	4.75	1.10
2566a	29¢ Booklet Pane of 10 (2 each) (Unfolded 11.75)			9.50	6.95
2567	29¢ Jan Matzeliger	40.00	4.25	.85	.20
2568-77	29¢ Space Exploration booklet singles…			11.50	3.25
2577a	29¢ Booklet Pane of 10 .... (Unfolded 15.75)…			11.75	7.95
1991 Christmas Issues					
2578	(29¢) Christmas, Madonna & Child	35.00	3.50	.75	.15
2578v	(29¢) Madonna, Booklet single ...	…		.85	.20
2578a	(29¢) Booklet Pane of 10 .... (Unfolded 10.75)			8.50	6.50
2579	(29¢) Christmas, Santa & Chimney	35.00	3.50	.75	.15
2580-85	(29¢) Santa & Chimney,				
	Set of 6 Booklet Singles	…	…	12.50	1.95
2580-81	(29¢) Booklet singles, Type I & II, attd ..	…	…	10.00	
* Ty. II, the far left brick from the top row of the chimney is missing from #2581					
2582-85	Booklet singles, Set of 4	…	…	3.00	.80
2581b-2585a	Booklet Panes of 4, Set of 5 (Unfolded 31.75)			24.95	22.50

1994-95 Definitives Designs of 1869 Essays

2587

2590

2592

Scott's No.		Mint Sheet	Plate Block	F-VF NH	F-VF Used
2587	32¢ James S. Polk (1995) ...... (100)	75.00	3.75	.80	.20
2590	$1 Surrender of Burgoyne .... (20)	47.50	11.00	2.50	1.25
2592	$5 Washington & Jackson ...... (20)	215.00	55.00	11.75	3.95

2593,2594

2595-97

2598

2599

1992-93 Pledge of Allegiance

2593	29¢ **black** denom. booklet single,Perf.10	...	.85	.15
2593a	29¢ Booklet Pane of 10, Perf. 10 (Unfolded 9.75) ...	8.25	5.95	
2593B	29¢ Black denom.,booklet single,Perf.11x10		1.55	.85
2593Bc	29¢ Bklt. Pane of 10, Perf. 11x10	...	14.95	8.50
2594	29¢,**red** denomination booklet single (1993)	...	1.00	.20
2594a	29¢ Booklet Pane of 10 .... (Unfolded 11.75)...	9.75	6.75	

1992 Eagle & Shield Self-Adhesive Stamps

2595	29¢ "Brown" denomination	...	1.00	.30
2595a	29¢ "Brown" denomination, Pane of 17...	15.00	...	
2596	29¢ "Green" denomination	...	1.00	.30
2596a	29¢ "Green" denomination, Pane of 17...	15.00	...	
2597	29¢ "Red" denomination	...	1.00	.30
2597a	29¢ "Red" denomination, Pane of 17 ...	15.00	...	

1992 Eagle & Shield Self-Adhesive Coils

2595v	29¢ "Brown" denomination .... Strip of 3	2.70	.90	...
2596v	29¢ "Green" denomination .... Strip of 3	2.70	.90	...
2597v	29¢ "Red" denomination .... Strip of 3	2.70	.90	...

NOTE: #2595v-2597v do not have plate numbers.

1994 Eagle Self-Adhesive Issue

2598	29¢ Eagle, self-adhesive	...	1.00	.30
2598a	29¢ Pane of 18	...	15.00	...
2598v	29¢ Eagle Coil, self-adhesive Pl#Strip(5)8.00	(3)6.75	.95	...

1994 Statue of Liberty Self-Adhesive Issue

2599	29¢ Statue of Liberty, self-adhesive	...	1.00	.30
2599a	29¢ Pane of 18	...	16.00	...
2599v	29¢ Liberty Coil,Self-adhesive Pl#Strip(5)8.00	(3)6.75	.95	...

1991-93 Coil Issues

2602

2603,2604,2907

2605

2606, 2607, 2608

2609

1991-93 Coil Issues (continued)

Scott's No.		Pl# Strip of 5	Pl# Strip of 3	F-VF NH	Used
2602	(10¢) Eagle, Bulk rate **ABNCo**	3.25	2.75	.30	.20
2603	(10¢) Eagle,Bulk rate,Shiny, **BEP** (1993)	3.65	3.00	.30	.20
2603l	(10¢) Low Gloss Gum	4.25	3.50	.35	...
2603b	(10¢) Tagged, Shiny Gum	17.75	15.75	1.10	.95
2604	(10¢) Eagle, Bulk rate,Shiny,**SVS** .	3.95	3.25	.30	.20
2604l	(10¢) Low Gloss Gum	3.95	3.25	.30	...

#2603 Orange yellow & multicolored, #2604 Gold & multicolored.

2605	23¢ Flag, Pre-sort First Class	5.25	4.00	.65	.30
2606	23¢ USA, Pre-sort 1st Cl., **ABNCo** ('92)	6.00	4.75	.65	.30
2607	23¢ USA, Pre-sort 1st Cl.,Shiny **BEP**(92)	6.25	5.00	.70	.30
2607l	23¢ Low Gloss Gum	6.50	5.25	.75	...
2608	23¢ USA, Pre-sort 1st Cl., **S.V.** (1993)	7.50	6.00	.85	.30

#2606 Light blue at bottom, "23" 6 mm wide, "First Class" 9½ mm wide.
#2607 Dark blue at bottom, "23" 7 mm wide, "First Class" 9½ mm wide.
#2608 Violet blue, "23" 6 mm wide, "First Class" 8½ mm wide.

2609	29¢ Flag & White House (1992)	6.25	4.75	.90	.15

1992 Commemoratives

2611

2612

2613

2614

2615

2616

2617

2618

2619

Scott's No.		Mint Sheet	Plate Block	F-VF NH	F-VF Used
2611-23,2630-41,2698-2704,2710-14,2720 Set of 38			...	34.50	9.50
2611-15	29¢ Winter Olympics, attd .... (35)	35.00	(10) 9.75	4.75	3.50
2611-15	Set of 5 Singles	...	...	4.50	1.25
2616	29¢ World Columbian Expo	35.00	3.50	.75	.20
2617	29¢ W.E.B. DuBois, Black Heritage	45.00	4.50	.95	.20
2618	29¢ Love, Envelope	35.00	3.50	.75	.20
2619	29¢ Olympic Baseball	56.50	5.50	1.20	.20

2596a Sample of Self-Adhesive Pane

2620
2622

2621
2623

2624

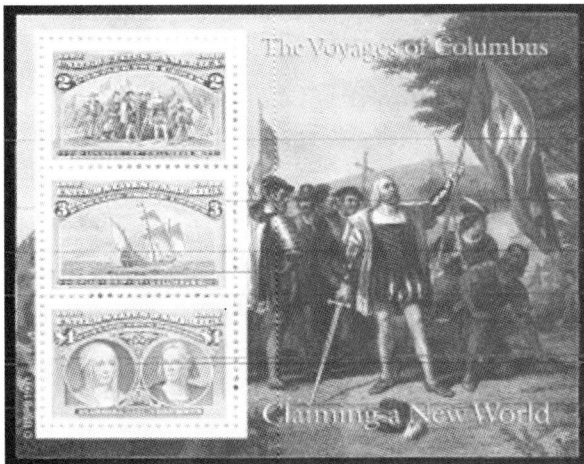

2625

2626

2627

2628

2629

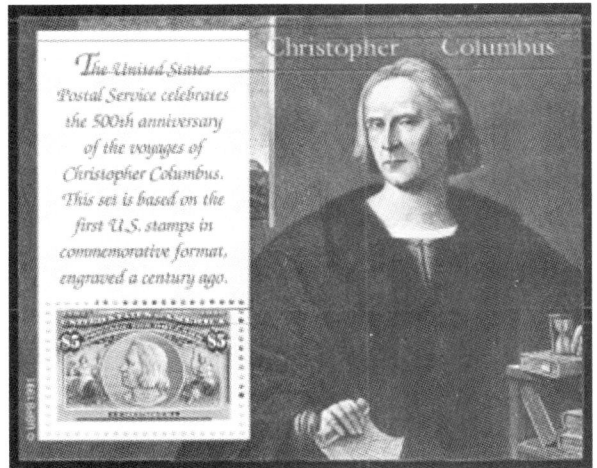

Scott's No.		Mint Sheet	Plate Block	F-VF NH	F-VF Used
2620-23	29¢ Voyage of Columbus, attd (40)	35.00	4.35	3.95	2.75
2620-23	Set of 4 Singles	...	...	3.75	1.10
2624-29	1¢-$5 Columbian Expo S/S, Set of 6	...	...	42.50	39.50
2624a-29	1¢-$5 Set of 16 Singles	...	...	41.50	37.50

2624a 1¢ Deep Blue	2626a 5¢ Chocolate	2628a 10¢ Black Brown
2624b 4¢ Ultramarine	2626b 30¢ Orange Brown	2628b 15¢ Dark Green
2624c $1 Salmon	2626c 50¢ Slate Blue	2628c $2 Brown Red
2625a 2¢ Brown Violet	2627a 6¢ Purple	2629 $5 Black
2625b 3¢ Green	2627b 8¢ Magenta	
2625c $4 Crimson Lake	2627c $3 Yellow Green	

1992 Commemoratives (cont.)

2631 2632
2633 2634

2630

2635

2636

2637

2638

2639

2640

2641

2642   2643   2644   2645   2646

Scott's No.		Mint Sheet	Plate Block	F-VF NH	F-VF Used
2630	29¢ New York Stock Exchange (40)	28.00	3.50	.75	.20
2631-34	29¢ Space Accomplishments, attd	47.50	4.65	4.25	3.00
2631-34	Set of 4 Singles	...	...	4.15	1.10
2635	29¢ Alaska Highway	35.00	3.50	.75	.20
2636	29¢ Kentucky Statehood	35.00	3.50	.75	.20
2637-41	29¢ Summer Olympics, attd .... (35)	31.50	(10) 10.00	4.75	3.50
2637-41	Set of 5 Singles	...	...	4.35	1.30
2642-46	29¢ Hummingbirds, Set of 5 bklt. sgls....	...	...	4.35	1.10
2646a	29¢ Booklet Pane of 5 .... (Unfolded 5.50)			4.50	3.50

1992 Wildflowers of American (continued)

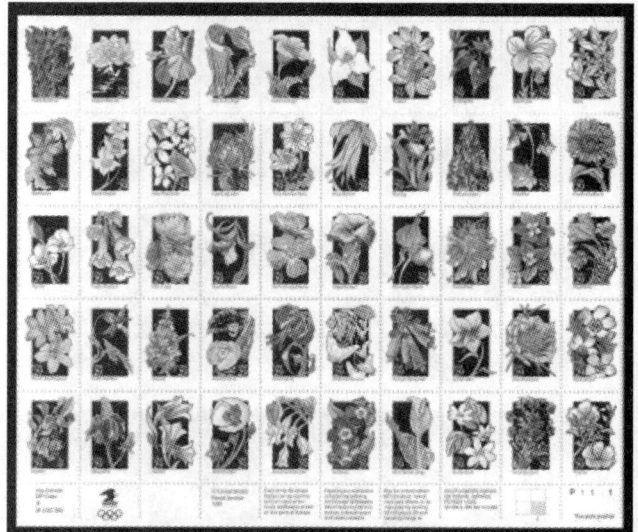

2647-96 Sheet

Scott's No.		Mint Sheet	Plate Block	F-VF NH	F-VF Used
2647-96	29¢ Wildflowers, Pane of 50 diff	47.50	...	...	...
2647-96	Set of 50 Singles	...	...	45.00	24.75
2647-96	29¢ Individual Singles	...	...	1.25	.60

2647 Indian Paintbrush
2648 Fragrant Water Lily
2649 Meadow Beauty
2650 Jack-in-the-Pulpit
2651 California Poppy
2652 Large-Flowered Trillium
2653 Tickseed
2654 Shooting Star
2655 Stream Violet
2656 Bluets
2657 Herb Robert
2658 Marsh Marigold
2659 Sweet White Violet
2660 Claret Cup Cactus
2661 White Mountain Avens
2662 Sessile Beltwort
2663 Blue Flag
2664 Harleguin Lupine

2665 Twinflower
2666 Common Sunflower
2667 Sego Lily
2668 Virginia Bluebells
2669 Ohi'a Lehua
2670 Rosebud Orchid
2671 Showy Evening Primrose
2672 Fringed Gentian
2673 Yellow Lady's Slipper
2674 Passionflower
2675 Bunchberry
2676 Pasqueflower
2677 Round-lobed Hepatica
2678 Wild Columbine
2679 Fireweed
2680 Indian Pond Lily
2681 Turk's Cap Lily

2682 Dutchmans' Breeches
2683 Trumpet Honeysuckle
2684 Jacob's Ladder
2685 Plains Prickly Pear
2686 Moss Campion
2687 Bearberry
2688 Mexican Hat
2 689 Harebell
2690 Desert Five-spot
2691 Smooth Solomon's Seal
2692 Red Maids
2693 Yellow Skunk Cabbage
2694 Rue Anemone
2695 Standing Cypress
2696 Wild Flax

1992 World War II Souvenir Sheet of 10

2697

		Mint Sheet		F-VF NH	F-VF Used
2697	29¢ 1942 World War II Events (20)	21.50	...	10.75	7.75
2697a-j	Set of 10 Singles	...	...	10.50	5.00
2697s	Se-Tenant Center Block of 10	...	...	11.75	11.50

2697a Raid on Tokyo
2697b Ration Coupons
2697c Coral Sea
2697d Corregidor

2697e Aleutian Islands
2697f Enemy Codes
2697g Midway
2697h Women in War

2697i Guadalcanal
2697j North Africa Landings

2698

2699

2704

2700

2701

2702

2703

2719

2705

2706

2707

2708

2709

2710

2711, 2715
2713, 2717

2712, 2716
2714, 2718

2720

Scott's No.		Mint Sheet	Plate Block	F-VF NH	F-VF Used
2698	29¢ Dorothy Parker, Literary Arts	35.00	3.50	.75	.20
2699	29¢ Dr. Theodore von Karman ...	35.00	3.50	.75	.20
2700-03	29¢ Minerals, attd .... (40)	37.50	4.50	4.00	2.75
2700-03	29¢ Strip of 4	...	...	4.00	2.75
2700-03	29¢ Set of 4 Singles	...	...	3.75	1.10
2704	29¢ Juan Rodriguez Cabrillo	35.00	3.50	.75	.20
2705-09	29¢ Wild Animals, booklet singles	...	...	4.50	1.10
2709a	29¢ Booklet Pane of 5 .... (Unfolded 6.00)			4.75	3.50
#2710-19a Christmas Issues					
2710	29¢ Madonna & Child	35.00	3.50	.75	.15
2710v	29¢ Madonna, booklet single	...	...	.85	.20
2710a	29¢ Booklet Pane of 10 .... (Unfolded 10.75)			7.95	7.50
2711-14	29¢ Toys, **offset**, attd.	45.00	4.75	4.00	3.00
2711-14	Set of 4 Singles	...	...	3.75	1.00
2715-18	29¢ Toys, **gravure**, 4 booklet singles	...	...	4.25	1.00
2718a	29¢ Booklet Pane of 4 .... (Unfolded 5.50)			4.50	3.50
2719	29¢ Locomotive, ATM, self adhesive single...		...	1.00	.40
2719a	29¢ Locomotive, ATM, pane of 18	...	...	16.50	...
2720	29¢ Happy New Year .... (20)	19.50	4.50	1.00	.20

2721

2722

2723

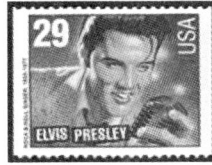
2724, 31

2725, 32

2726, 33

2727, 34

2728, 35

2729, 36

2730, 37

Scott's No.		Mint Sheet	Plate Block	F-VF NH	F-VF Used
2721-30,2746-59,2766,2771-74,2779-89,2791-94,					
2804-06	Set of 47(No #2723A)	...	...	43.95	9.75
2721	29¢ Elvis Presley .... (40)	36.50	4.25	.95	.20
2722	29¢ "Oklahoma!" .... (40)	28.00	3.50	.75	.25
2723	29¢ Hank Williams, Perf. 10 .... (40)	28.00	3.50	.75	.20
2723A	Same, Perf. 11.2 x 11.4	...	150.00	23.95	14.95
2724-30	29¢ Rock 'n Roll, Rythum & Blues, attached .... (35)	40.00	(8)9.50	8.75	6.50
2724-30	Top Horiz. Plate Block of 10	...	11.75	...	...
2724-30	Rock 'n Roll, R & B, set of 7 singles.	...	...	...	2.10
2731-37	29¢ Rock 'n Roll, R & B, 7 booklet singles...	...	...	6.25	2.40
2737a	29¢ Booklet Pane of 8 (Unfolded 8.95)	...	...	6.75	6.50
2737b	29¢ Booklet Pane of 4 (Unfolded 4.95)	...	...	4.00	3.85

2741

2742

2743

2744

2745

2747

2746

2748

2741-45	29¢ Space Fantasy, booklet singles	...	...	4.35	1.30
2745a	29¢ Booklet Pane of 5 .... (Unfolded 5.50)			4.50	3.75
2746	29¢ Percy Lavon Julian	37.50	3.75	.80	.20
2747	29¢ Oregon Trail	35.00	3.50	.75	.20
2748	29¢ World University Games	37.50	3.75	.80	.20

1993 Commemoratives (cont.)

| 2749 | 2754 | 2755 |

| 2752 | 2753 |
| 2750 | 2751 |

| 2756 | 2757 |
| 2758 | 2759 |

| 2760 | 2761 | 2762 | 2763 | 2764 |

Scott's No.		Mint Sheet	Plate Block	F-VF NH	F-VF Used
2749	29¢ Grace Kelly	35.00	3.50	.75	.20
2750-53	29¢ Circus, attd .... (40)	40.00 (6)	7.50	4.25	3.00
2750-53	Set of 4 Singles	...	...	4.15	1.10
2754	29¢ Cherokee Strip .... (20)	15.75	3.50	.80	.20
2755	29¢ Dean Acheson	35.00	3.50	.75	.20
2756-59	29¢ Sporting Horses, block of 4 (40)	37.50	4.65	4.00	3.00
2756-59	Set of 4 Singles	...	...	3.80	1.10
2760-64	29¢ Spring Garden Flowers, 5 booklet singles...	...	...	4.35	1.30
2764a	29¢ Booklet Pane of 5 .... (Unfolded 5.50)...	...	...	4.50	3.50

1993 World War II Souvenir Sheet of 10

2765

Scott's No.		Mint Sheet	Plate Block	F-VF NH	F-VF Used
2765	29¢ 1943 WWII Events .... (20)	21.50	...	10.75	7.75
2765a-j	Set of 10 Singles	...	...	10.50	5.00
2765s	Se-Tenant Center Block of 10	...	...	11.75	11.50

2765a Destroyers/U-Boats	2765d B-24's hit Ploesti	2765g Bonds & Stamps
2765b Military Medics	2765e V-Mail Delivers Letters	2765h "Willie & Joe"
2765c Sicily Attacked	2765f Italy Invaded	2765i Gold Stars
		2765j Marines at Tarawa

1993 Commemoratives (cont.)

2766

| 2771, 2775 | 2773, 2776 |
| 2772, 2777 | 2774, 2778 |

| 2767 |
| 2768 |
| 2769 |
| 2770 |

| 2779 | 2780 |
| 2781 | 2782 |

2766	29¢ Joe Louis	47.50	4.75	1.00	.20
2767-70	29¢ Broadway Musicals, 4 booklet singles...	...	...	3.75	1.00
2770a	29¢ Booklet Pane of 4 .... (Unfolded 4.95)...	...	...	3.85	3.35
2771-74	29¢ Country Music, Block attd .. (20)	21.75	4.95	4.50	3.00
2771-74	Horizontal Strip of 4	...	...	4.50	3.00
2771-74	Horiz. Pl. Block of 8 with Label	...	9.50	...	...
2771-74	Set of 4 Singles	...	...	4.35	1.00
2775-78	29¢ Country Music, 4 booklet singles	...	...	3.90	1.00
2778a	29¢ Booklet Pane of 4 .... (Unfolded 5.50)...	...	...	4.00	3.35
2779-82	29¢ Nat'l. Postal Museum, Block (20)	20.00	4.75	4.25	3.00
2779-82	Horizontal Strip of 4	...	...	4.25	3.00
2779-82	Set of 4 Singles	...	...	4.15	1.00

2783   2784   2789, 2790   2803

2785   2786   2793,96,2799   2794,95,2800
2787   2788   2791,98,2801   2792,97,2802

2804   2805   2806

Scott's No.		Mint Sheet	Plate Block	F-VF NH	F-VF Used
2783-84	29¢ Deaf Communication, pair ... (20)	16.50	3.95	1.80	1.15
2783-84	Set of 2 Singles	...	...	1.70	.40
2785-88	29¢ Children's Classics, Block .. (40)	37.50	4.50	4.00	3.00
2785-88	Horizontal Strip of 4	...	...	4.00	3.00
2785-88	Set of 4 Singles	...	...	3.80	1.00
2789	29¢ Christmas Madonna	35.00	3.50	.75	.15
2790	29¢ Madonna, Booklet Single	...	...	.80	.20
2790a	29¢ Booklet Pane of 4 .... (Unfolded 4.95)			3.50	2.75
2791-94	29¢ Christmas Designs, block of 4 ..	45.00	4.50	4.00	3.50
2791-94	Strip of 4	...	...	4.00	3.50
2791-94	Set of 4 Singles	...	...	3.85	.80
2795-98	29¢ Christmas Designs, set of 4 booklet singles ...			4.50	.90
2798a	29¢ Booklet Pane of 10 (3 Snowmen)(Unfolded 12.75)			10.50	7.50
2798b	29¢ Booklet Pane of 10 (2 Snowmen)(Unfolded 12.75)			10.50	7.50
2799-2802	29¢ Christmas Designs, self adhesive,4 singles...			5.00	1.80
2802a	29¢ Pane of 12, self-adhesive	...	...	13.75	...
2799-2802 var.	Coil, self-adhesive Plate Strip of 8 11.95			5.00	...
2803	29¢ Christmas Snowman, self adhes.			1.10	.45
2803a	29¢ Pane of 18, self adhesive	...	...	17.50	...
2804	29¢ No. Mariana Is. Comm'nwlth. .. (20)	15.75	3.75	.80	.20
2805	29¢ Columbus at Puerto Rico	36.50	3.50	.75	.20
2806	29¢ AIDS Awareness, Perf.11.2	40.00	3.95	.85	.20
2806a	29¢ AIDS Booklet Single, Perf.11	...	...	.90	.20
2806b	29¢ Booklet Pane of 5 .... (Unfolded 5.75)			4.50	3.25

1994 Commemoratives

2807   2808   2809   2810   2811

2807-12,2814C-28,2834-36,2839,
2848-68,2871-72,2876 Set of 49 (No #2871A) 30.75 12.50
2807-11   29¢ Winter Olympics, attd .... (20)16.75 (10)9.50   4.50   4.00
2807-11   Set of 5 Singles 4.35   1.40

2812   2813   2814,2814C   2815

2816   2817   2818

2819   2820   2821   2822   2823
2824   2825   2826   2827   2828

2829   2830   2831   2832   2833

Scott's No.		Mint Sheet	Plate Block	F-VF NH	F-VF Used
2812	29¢ Edward R. Murrow	36.50	3.50	.75	.20
2813	29¢ Love & Sunrise, self adhesive .	...	...	1.00	.30
2813a	29¢ Pane of 18	...	...	16.50	...
2813v	29¢ Love Coil, self adhesive Plate # Strip .... (5)	8.00 (3)	6.75	.85	...
2814	29¢ Love & Dove, booklet single	...	...	.90	.20
2814a	29¢ Booklet Pane of 10 .... (Unfolded 9.95)			8.75	5.25
2814C	29¢ Love & Dove, sheet stamp	42.50	4.00	.90	.20
2815	52¢ Love & Doves	72.50	7.25	1.50	.35
2816	29¢ Dr. Allison Davis .... (20)	16.00	4.00	.85	.20
2817	29¢ Chinese New Year, Dog ...... (20)	29.50	7.00	1.50	.20
2818	29¢ Buffalo Soldiers .... (20)	16.00	4.00	.85	.20
2819-28	29¢ Silent Screen Stars, attd .... (40)	32.50 (10)	8.95	8.50	6.25
2819-28	Half-Pane of 20 with selvedge	...	...	16.75	14.75
2819-28	Set of 10 singles	...	...	8.25	3.00
2829-33	29¢ Summer Garden Flowers, set of 5 booklet singles...			4.15	1.20
2833a	29¢ Booklet Pane of 5 .... (Unfolded 5.50)			4.25	3.00

2834   2835   2836

1994 Commemoratives (cont.)

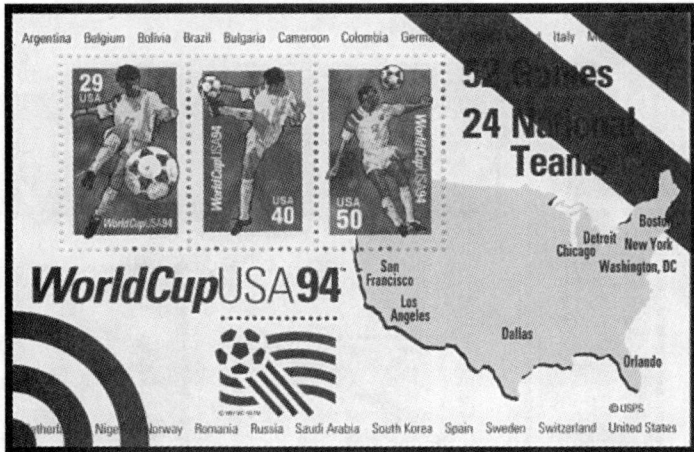

2837

Scott's No.		Mint Sheet	Plate Block	F-VF NH	F-VF Used
2834	29¢ World Cup Soccer .... (20)	16.50	4.25	.90	.20
2835	40¢ World Cup Soccer .... (20)	21.50	5.25	1.10	.35
2836	50¢ World Cup Soccer .... (20)	27.75	6.75	1.45	.50
2837	29¢,40¢,50¢ World Cup Soccer, Souvenir Sheet of 3	...	...	4.75	3.50

1994 World War II Souvenir Sheet of 10

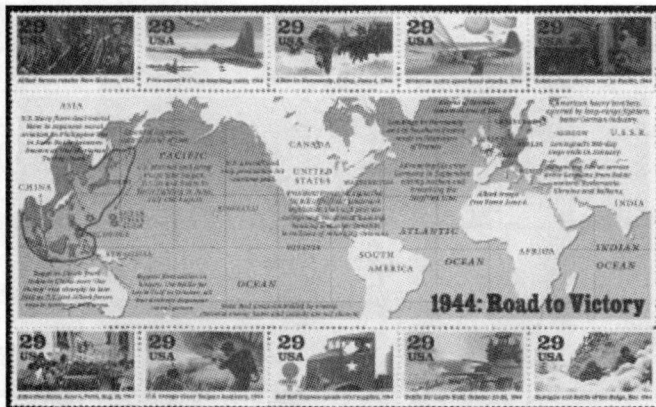

2838

2838	29¢ 1944 WWII Events .... (20)	21.50	...	10.75	7.75
2838a-j	Set of 10 Singles	...	...	10.50	6.00
2838v	Se-Tenant Center Block of 10	...	...	11.75	11.50

2838a Retake New Guinea	2838d Airborne Units	2838g Saipan Bunkers
2838b P51's and B-17's	2838e Submarines in Pacific	2838h Red Ball Express
2838c Normandy	2838f Allies Free Rome	2838i Battle Leyte Gulf
		2838j Battle of the Bulge

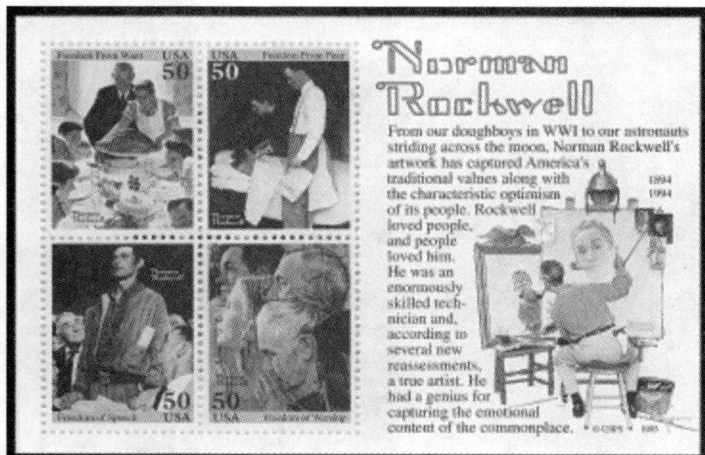

2840

	2839	2841a	284	2848

	2843	2844	2845

	2846	2847

Scott's No.		Mint Sheet	Plate Block	F-VF NH	F-VF Used
1994 Commemoratives (continued)					
2839	29¢ Norman Rockwell	42.50	4.25	.90	.20
2840	50¢ Norman Rockwell, Souvenir Sheet of 4 ...	...	...	5.95	4.95
	2840a Freedom from Want 2840b Freedom from Fear				
	2840c Freedom of Speech 2840d Freedom of Religion				
1994 Moon Landing, 25th Anniversary					
2841	29¢ Moon Landing Miniature Sheet of 12	...	...	12.95	9.50
2841a	29¢ Single Stamp from sheet	...	...	1.15	.30
2842	$9.95 Moon Landing Express Mail .... (20)	495.00	115.00	26.50	11.50
1994 Commemoratives (continued)					
2843-47	29¢ Locomotives, set of 5 booklet singles...	...	...	4.65	1.20
2847a	29¢ Booklet Pane of 5 .... (Unfolded 6.00)			4.75	3.50
2848	29¢ George Meany	36.50	3.50	.75	.20

2849	2850	2851

2852	2853

2854	2855	2856

2857	2858	2859

2860	2861

Scott's No.		Mint Sheet	Plate Block	F-VF NH	F-VF Used
2849-53	29¢ Popular Singers, attd .... (20)	23.50	(6)8.25	6.00	2.95
2849-53	Top Plate Block of 12	...	16.50	...	...
2849-53	Set of 5 Singles	...	...	5.75	2.00
2854-61	29¢ Blues & Jazz Artists, attd. ..... (35)	42.50	(10)13.50	(10)12.50	7.95
2854-61	Top Plate Block of 10 with Label	...	14.50	...	...
2854-61	Set of 8 Singles	...	...	9.50	3.20

NOTE: BECAUSE OF SHEET LAYOUT THERE ARE NO BLOCKS OF EIGHT POSSIBLE.

2862

2867

2868

2863

2864

2865

2866

2862	29¢ James Thurber	36.50	3.50	.75	.20
2863-66	29¢ Wonders of the Sea, attd. ..... (24)	27.50	4.25	3.75	2.25
2863-66	Set of 4 Singles	...	...	3.60	1.00
2867-68	29¢ Cranes, attd. .... (20)	18.95	4.75	2.00	1.10
2867-68	Set of 2 Singles	...	...	1.90	.45

1994 Legends of the West Miniature Sheet

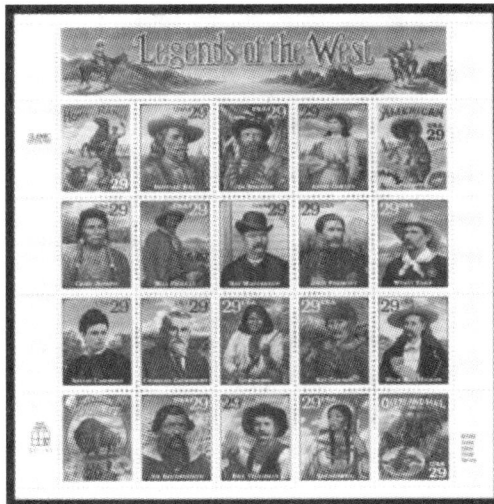

2869

2869	29¢ Revised Sheet of 20	...	...	19.95	13.95
2869a-t	Set of 20 Singles	...	...	19.75	9.95

2869a Home on the Range	2869h Bat Masterson	2869o Wild Bill Hickok
2869b Buffalo Bill Cody	2869i John C. Fremont	2869p Western Wildlife
2869c Jim Bridger	2869j Wyatt Earp	2869q Jim Beckwourth
2869d Annie Oakley	2869k Nellie Cashman	2869r Bill Tilghman
2869e Native American	2869l Charles Goodnight	2869s Sacagawea
2869f Chief Joseph	2869m Geronimo	2869t Overland Mail
2869g Bill Pickett	2869n Kit Carson	

Legends of the West Miniature Sheet (continued)

2870

Scott's No.		Mint Sheet	Plate Block	F-VF NH	F-VF Used
2870	29¢ Original (recalled) sheet of 20 with blue envelope..			350.00	...
2870	29¢ Without original blue envelope ..	...	...	325.00	...

NOTE; #2870 was the original sheet-it contained an incorrect picture of Bill Pickett (second stamp in second row). It was withdrawn and released in quantities via lottery. #2869 contains the correct picture of Bill Pickett.

1994 Commemoratives (continued)

2871

2872

2873

2874

2875

2876

#2871-74a Christmas Issues

2871	29¢ Madonna & Child, Perf.11¼	36.50	3.50	.75	.15
2871A	29¢ Madonna & Child, booklet single, Perf.9 3/4x11	...		.90	.20
2871Ab	29¢ Booklet Pane of 10 (Unfolded 9.95)			8.50	5.75
2872	29¢ Christmas Stocking	36.50	3.50	.75	.15
2872v	29¢ Stocking Booklet Single	...	...	.85	.20
2872a	29¢ Booklet Pane of 20 .... (Unfolded 21.50)			16.50	10.75
2873	29¢ Santa Claus, self-adhesive	...	...	1.00	.25
2873a	29¢ Pane of 12, self-adhesive	...	...	11.50	7.50
2873v	29¢ Santa Claus Coil, self-adhesive Pl# Strip	(5) 8.25	(3) 7.00	.85	...
2874	29¢ Cardinal in Snow, self-adhesive	...	...	1.00	.40
2874a	29¢ Pane of 18, self-adhesive	...	...	16.50	11.00
2875	$2 Bureau of Engraving Centennial Souvenir Sheet of 4	...	...	21.75	14.50
2875a	$2 Madison, Single Stamp from Souvenir Sheet...	...	...	5.50	3.50
2876	29¢ Year of the Boar, New Year .... (20)	18.75	4.35	.95	.25

1994 Interim Regular Issues

2877,2878 **2879,2880** **2881-87,2889-92** **2888** **2893**

Scott's No.		Mint Sheet	Plate Block	F-VF NH	F-VF Used
2877	(3¢) Dove, ABN, Light Blue .... (100)	8.50	.75	.20	.15
2878	(3¢) Dove, SVS, Darker Blue .... (100)	10.75	.95	.25	.15
	#2877 Thin, taller letters. #2878 Heavy, shorter letters.				
2879	(20¢) "G",Postcard Rate,BEP,Red "G:(100)	57.50	5.50	.60	.15
2880	(20¢) "G",Postcard Rate,SVS, Red "G"(100)	55.00	7.95	.55	.15
2881	(32¢) "G",BEP, Black "G" .... (100)	210.00	89.95	1.35	.25
2881v	(32¢) Black "G" booklet single	...	...	1.25	.20
2881a	(32¢) Booklet Pane of 10, Perf. 11.2 x 11.1	...	...	11.50	8.95
2882	(32¢) "G", SVS, Red "G" .... (100)	82.50	4.95	.90	.20
2883	(32¢) "G", BEP, Black "G", booklet single	...	...	1.15	.20
2883a	(32¢) Bklt Pane of 10, BEP, Perf. 10 x 9.9	...	...	10.95	7.95
2884	(32¢) "G", ABN, Blue "G" booklet single	...	...	1.15	.20
2884a	(32¢) Booklet Pane of 10, ABN	...	...	10.95	7.95
2885	(32¢) "G", KCS, Red "G" booklet single	...	...	1.25	.20
2885a	(32¢) Booklet Pane of 10, KCS	...	...	11.95	7.95
2886	(32¢) "G", Surface Tagged, self-adhesive	...	...	1.15	.30
2886a	(32¢) Pane of 18, self-adhesive, AD	...	...	19.00	...
2886v	(32¢) "G", Coil, self-adhesive Pl.# Strip	(5)7.50	(3) 6.00	1.00	...
2887	(32¢) "G", Overall Tagging, self-adhesive, AD	...	...	1.15	.35
2887a	(32¢) Pane of 18, self-adhesive, thin paper	...	...	19.00	...
	#2886 Limited amount of blue shading in the whitestripes below field of stars.				
	#2887 Stronger blue shading in the white stripes.				

1994-95 Interim Coil Stamps, Perf. Or Roul. 9.8 Vert.

Scott's No.		Pl.Strip of 5	Pl.Strip of 3	F-VF NH	F-VF Used
2888	(25¢) "G" Presort, Coil, SVS	8.25	6.75	.85	.25
2889	(32¢) "G" Coil, BEP, Black "G"	11.75	9.75	1.25	.25
2890	(32¢) "G" Coil, ABN, Blue "G"	8.25	6.75	.90	.20
2891	(32¢) "G" Coil, SVS, Red "G"	14.75	12.50	1.50	.30
2892	(32¢) "G" Coil, SVS, Rouletted	9.00	7.50	.90	.20
2893	(5¢) "G" Non-Profit, green ABN (1995) .	2.95	2.50	.25	.25

BEP=Bureau of Engraving and Printing ABN=American Bank-Note Co. SVS=Stamp Venturers KCS=KCS Industries   AD = Avery Dennison

1995-97 Regular Issues

2897,2913-16 **2902,2902B** **2903-4B** **2905,7**

2908-10 **2911-12B** **2919**

Scott's No.		Mint Sheet	Plate Block	F-VF NH	F-VF Used
2897	32¢ Flag over Porch, Shiny gum.....(100)	80.00	4.25	.85 .15
2897l	32¢ Low Gloss Gum...........................(100)	80.00	4.25	.85 ...
2897v	Folded Block of 15 in Booklet (BK243) .	...	...	14.95 ...

1995-97 Coil Stamps, Perf. Or Die-cut Vertically
Note: S.A. indicates Self-adhesive. Otherwise, stamps are moisture activated.

Scott's No.		Pl.Strip of 5	Pl.Strip of 3	F-VF NH	F-VF Used
2902	(5¢) Butte, Perf. 9.8	2.10	1.75	.20	.20
2902B	(5¢) Butte, SA, Die-cut 11.5 (1996) ...	2.65	2.25	.25	.25
2903	(5¢) Mountain, BEP, Perf. 9.8 (1996) ..	2.25	1.95	.20	.15
2904	(5¢) Mountain, SVS, Perf. 9.8 (1996) ..	2.65	2.25	.20	.15
2904A	(5¢) Mountain, SA Die-cut 11.5 (1996) .	2.65	2.25	.25	.25
2904B	(5¢) Mountain, SA Die-cut 9.8 (1997) ...	2.70	2.25	.25	.20
	NOTE: #2903, 2904B Letters outlined in purple.				
	#2904, 2904A No outline on letters.				
2905	(10¢) Automobile, Perf. 9.8	3.25	2.75	.30	.20
2906	(10¢) Automobile, SA, Die-cut 11.5 (1996)	2.95	2.65	.35	.25
2907	(10¢) Eagle & Shield, SA, (Design of 1993) Die-cut 11.5 (1996)	3.85	3.25	.35	.25
2908	(15¢) Auto Tail Fin, BEP, Perf. 9.8	3.75	3.00	.40	.35
2909	(15¢) Auto Tail Fin, SVS, Perf. 9.8	3.75	3.00	.40	.35
	Note: #2908 has darker colors and heavier shading than #2909				
2910	(15¢) Auto Tail Fin, SA Die-cut 11.5 (1996)	3.95	3.25	.45	.30
2911	(25¢) Juke Box, BEP, Perf. 9.8	6.25	5.25	.70	.40
2912	(25¢) Juke Box, SVS, Perf. 9.8	5.75	4.75	.70	.40
	Note: #2911 has darker colors and heavier shading than #2912				
2912A	(25¢) Juke Box, SA, Die-cut 11.5 (1996)	5.75	4.75	.70	.40
2912B	(25¢) Juke Box, SA, Die-cut 9.8 (1997)	5.75	4.75	.70	.40
2913	32¢ Flag-Porch, BEP, Perf. 9.8, Shiny gum	6.25	5.25	.90	.15
2913l	32¢ Low Gloss Gum	7.75	6.50	.90	...
2914	32¢ Flag over Porch, SVS, Perf. 9.8 ...	7.00	5.75	.90	.25
	Note: #2913 has Red "1995" Date. #2914 has Blue "1995" Date.				

1995-97 Regular Issue Coils (continued)

Scott's No.		Pl.Strip of 5	Pl.Strip of 3	F-VF NH	F-VF Used
2915	32¢ Flag over Porch, SA, Die-cut 8.7 ..	8.25	6.75	1.00	.30
2915A	32¢ Flag over Porch, SA, Die-cut 9.8 .. Red "1996", multiple stamps touch (1996)	8.95	7.50	1.10	.30
2915B	32¢ Flag-Porch, SA, Die-cut 11.5(1996)	8.25	6.50	.90	.30
2915C	32¢ Flag-Porch,SA,Die-cut 10.9(1996)	21.00	17.50	2.00	.65
2915D	32¢ Flag over Porch, SA, Die-cut 9.8, Red "1997" Stamps separate on backing (1997)	6.95	5.75	1.00	.30
	Note: See #3133 for Blue "1996" Date Die-cut 9.9				

1995-97 Booklets and Panes

Scott's No.		Mint Sheet	Plate Block	F-VF NH	F-VF Used
2916	32¢ Flag over Porch, booklet single ...	...	...	1.00	.20
2916a	32¢ Booklet Pane of 10 .... (Unfolded 11.75)		9.50	5.95
2919	32¢ Flag over Field, self-adhesive single	...	...	1.00	.30
2919a	32¢ Pane of 18, Self-adhesive	...	...	15.75	...
2920	32¢ Flag over Porch, self-adhesive single large Blue "1995" date Die-cut 8.8	...	...	1.00	.30
2920a	32¢ Pane of 20, self-adhesive, large "1995" ...	...	...	17.50	...
2920f	32¢ Flag over Porch, folded bklt of 15(1996)...	...	...	14.50	...
2920h	32¢ Flag over Porch, folded bklt of 16 with lower right stamp removed (1996)	...	...27.50	...
	Note: #2920f and 2920h have large "1995" dates like #2920				
2920b	32¢ Flag over Porch, self-adhesive single, small Blue "1995" date Die-cut 8.8			6.50	.75
2920c	32¢ Pane of 20, self-adhesive,small "1995" ...	...	...	120.00	...
2920D	32¢ Flag over Porch, self-adhesive, Blue "1996" date (1996) Die-cut 11.3			1.00	.35
2920De	32¢ Booklet Pane of 10, self-adhesive			9.50	...
2921	32¢ Flag over Porch, self-adhesive booklet single, Red "1996" Date (1996)	...	...	1.10	.30
2921a	32¢ Flag over Porch, self-adhesive Die-cut 9.8 Red "1996" Date (1996) ..... (Unfolded 10.75)		9.50	...
2921b	32¢ Flag over Porch, self-adhesive booklet single, Red "1997" Date (1997)	...	...	1.10	.30
2921c	32¢ Booklet Pane of 10, self-adhesive Die-cut 9.8 Red "1997" Date (1997)			9.50	...
2921d	32¢ Booklet Pane of 5, self-adhesive Die-cut 9.8 Red "1997" Date (1997) ..... (Unfolded 6.50)		4.95	...

1995-99 Great American Series

2933 **2934** **2935** **2936**

2938 **2940** **2941** **2942** **2943**

Scott's No.		Mint Sheet	Plate Block	F-VF NH	F-VF Used
2933-43	Set of 9	...	45.00	9.25	2.35
2933	32¢ Milton S. Hershey .... (100)	75.00	3.95	.80	.20
2934	32¢ Cal Farley (1996) .... (100)	75.00	3.95	.80	.20
2935	32¢ Henry R.Luce (1998) .... (20)	15.50	3.50	.80	.30
2936	32¢ Lila & DeWitt Wallace (1998) . (20)	15.50	3.50	.80	.30
2938	46¢ Ruth Benedict .... (100)	100.00	5.25	1.10	.25
2940	55¢ Alice Hamilton, MD .... (100)	115.00	5.75	1.20	.25
2941	55¢ Justin S. Morrill (1999) .... (20)	22.50	5.50	1.20	.30
2942	77¢ Mary Breckenridge, SA (1998) (20)	31.50	7.50	1.65	.40
2943	78¢ Alice Paul, Bright Violet, Solid Tagging .... (100)	165.00	8.25	1.70	.40
2943a	78¢ Dull Violet, Grainy Solid Tag... (100)	165.00	8.25	1.70	.40
2943b	78¢ Pale Violet,Grainy Solid Tag... (100)	165.00	8.25	1.70	.40

1995 Commemoratives

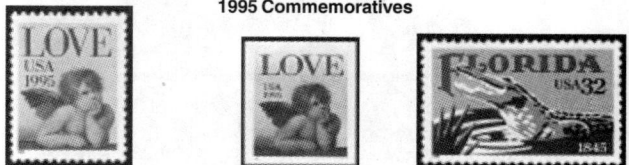

2948 **2949** **2950**

Scott's No.		Mint Sheet	Plate Block	F-VF NH	F-VF Used
	2948,2950-58,2961-68,2974,2976-80, 2982-92,2998-99,3001-7,3019-23				
	Set of 49 No #3003A	...	...	46.50	11.75
2948	(32¢) Love & Cherub	37.50	3.75	.80	.20
2949	(32¢) Love & Cherub, Self-adhesive ...	...	...	1.00	.25
2949a	(32¢) Pane of 20, Self-adhesive	...	...	18.75	...
2950	32¢ Florida Statehood .... (20)	17.50	4.25	.95	.20

2951
2953

2952
2954

2955

2956

2957,2959

2958

2960

2965

2961

2962

2963

2964

2966

2967

2968

2969

2970

2971

2972

2973

Scott's No.		Mint Sheet	Plate Block	F-VF NH	F-VF Used
2951-54	32¢ Earth Day/Kids Care, attd. ...... (16)	15.75	4.50	4.00	2.00
2951-54	Set of 4 Singles	...	...	3.75	1.00
2955	32¢ Richard Nixon	37.50	3.75	.80	.20
2956	32¢ Bessie Coleman, Black Heritage ..	37.50	3.75	.80	.20
2957	32¢ Love Cherub	37.50	3.75	.80	.20
2957v	Folded Block of 15 in Booklet (EK244)	...	...	14.95	...
2958	55¢ Love Cherub	72.50	6.75	1.50	.50
2959	32¢ Love Cherub, booklet single	...	...	.90	.20
2959a	32¢ Booklet Pane of 10 .... (Unfolded 9.95)	...	8.75	5.95
2960	55¢ Love Cherub, Self-Adhesive single	...	...	1.50	.65
2960a	55¢ Pane of 20, Self-Adhesive	...	...	27.50	...
2960v	55¢ Pane of 20 with Die-cut "Time to Reorder" (1996)	...	...	27.50	...
2961-65	32¢ Recreational Sports Strip .... (20)20.00 (10)11.00	5.25	3.25
2961-65	Set of 5 Singles	...	...	5.00	1.50

Scott's No.		Mint Sheet	Plate Block	F-VF NH	F-VF Used
2966	32¢ POW & MIA .... (20)	15.00	3.50	.80	.20
2967	32¢ Marilyn Monroe .... (20)	24.95	5.95	1.30	.25
2968	32¢ Texas Statehood .... (20)	17.50	4.25	.95	.20
2969-73	32¢ Great Lakes Lighthouses 5 booklet singles	...		4.85	1.25
2973a	32¢ Booklet Pane of 5 .... (Unfolded 5.75)	...	5.00	3.50

2974

2980

2975

2977
2979

2976
2978

		Mint Sheet	Plate Block	F-VF NH	F-VF Used
2974	32¢ United Nations .... (20)	15.00	3.50	.80	.20

1995 Civil War Miniature Sheet

				F-VF NH	F-VF Used
2975	32¢ Civil War, Miniature Sheet of 20	...	...	24.95	15.95
2975a-t	Set of 20 Singles	...	...	24.75	12.95

2975a Monitor & Virginia	2975h Frederick Douglass	2975o Mary Chesnut
2975b Robert E. Lee	2975i Raphael Semmes	2975p Chancellorsville
2975c Clara Barton	2975j Abraham Lincoln	2975q William T. Sherman
2975d Ulysses S. Grant	2975k Harriet Tubman	2975r Phoebe Pember
2975e Battle of Shiloh	2975l Stand Watie	2975s "Stonewall" Jackson
2975f Jefferson Davis	2975m Joseph E. Johnston	2975t Gettysburg
2975g David Farragut	2975n Winfield Hancock	

1995 Commemoratives (cont.)

		Mint Sheet	Plate Block	F-VF NH	F-VF Used
2976-79	32¢ Carousel Horses, attd .... (20)	19.50	4.50	4.00	3.00
2976-79	Set of 4 Singles	...	...	3.85	1.00
2980	32¢ Woman Suffrage .... (40)	30.00	3.75	.80	.20

1995 World War II Souvenir Sheet of 10

2981

		Mint Sheet		F-VF NH	F-VF Used
2981	32¢ 1945 WWar II Events .... (20)	21.50	...	10.75	7.75
2981a-j	Set of 10 Singles	...	...	10.50	5.50
2981v	Se-Tenant Center Block of 10...	...	...	11.75	11.50

2981a Iwo Jima	2981d U.S. & Soviets Meet	2981g Refugees
2981b Manila	2981e Holocaust	2981h Japan Surrender
2981c Okinawa	2981f German Surrender	2981i Victory Hits Home
		2981j Returning Veterans

1995 Commemoratives (continued)

2982   2983   2984

2985   2986   2987

2988   2989   2990

2991   2992   2999

2993   2994   2995   2996   2997

2998   3000

Scott's No.		Mint Sheet	Plate Block	F-VF NH	F-VF Used
2982	32¢ Louis Armstrong .... (20)	19.50	4.75	1.10	.20
2983-92	32¢ Jazz Musicians, attd .... (20)26.50 (10)		14.75	13.75	8.95
2983-92	Set of 10 Singles	...	...	13.00	4.00
2993-97	32¢ Fall Garden Flowers, 5 booklet singles...	...	...	4.35	1.25
2997a	32¢ Booklet Pane of 5 .... (Unfolded 5.75)	...	...	4.50	2.95
2998	60¢ Eddie Rickenbacker, original	82.50	7.50	1.70	.50
2998r	Rickenbacker, reprint (1999)	67.50	6.35	1.40	.50

Note: The original as a small "1995" date while the reprint "1995" is larger. The 1999 reprint is less sharp than the original and has paler colors.

| 2999 | 32¢ Republic of Palau .... | 37.50 | 3.75 | .80 | .20 |

1995 Comic Strips Miniature Sheet

Scott's No.		Mint Sheet	Plate Block	F-VF NH	F-VF Used
3000	32¢ Comic Strips, Min. Sheet of 20 ...	...	...	16.95	13.95
3000a-t	Set of 20 Singles	...	...	16.75	11.95

3000a The Yellow Kid	3000g Toonerville Folks	3000n Alley Oop
3000b Katzenjammer Kids	3000h Gasoline Alley	3000o Nancy
3000c Little Nemo	3000i Barney Google	3000p Flash Gordon
3000d Bringing Up Father	3000j Little Orphan Annie	3000q Li'l Abner
3000e Krazy Kat	3000k Popeye	3000r Terry and the Pirates
3000f Rube Goldberg	3000l Blondie	3000s Prince Valiant
	3000m Dick Tracy	

1995 Commemoratives (continued)

3001   3003   3002

3004,3010,3016   3005,3009,3015   3006,3011,3017   3007,3008,3014

3012,3018   3013

3001	32¢ U.S. Naval Academy .... (20)	15.00	3.50	.80	.20
3002	32¢ Tennessee Williams .... (20)	17.50	4.25	.95	.20
#3003-18 Christmas Issues					
3003	32¢ Madonna and Child, Perf.11.2	37.50	3.75	.80	.20
3003A	32¢ Madonna and Child, booklet.single, Pf.9.8x10.9 ...			1.00	.20
3003Ab	32¢ Booklet Pane of 10 .... (Unfolded 10.95)			9.50	5.95
3004-7	32¢ Santa & Children	39.50	3.95	3.50	2.50
3004-7	Strip of 4	...	...	3.50	2.50
3004-7	Set of 4 Singles	...	...	3.35	1.00
3004v-7v	32¢ Set of 4 Booklet Singles	...	...	4.00	1.20
3007b	32¢ Booklet Pane of 10, 3 each #3004-5, 2 each #3006-7 .... (Unfolded 11.75)			9.50	5.95
3007c	32¢ Booklet Pane of 10, 2 each #3004-5, 3 each #3006-7 .... (Unfolded 11.75)			9.50	5.95
Self-Adhesive Stamps					
3008-11	32¢ Santa & Children, Block of 9	...	...	9.75	...
3008-11	Set of 4 Singles	...	...	4.50	1.40
3011a	32¢ Pane of 20	...	...	19.50	...
3012	32¢ Midnight Angel	...	...	1.10	.35
3012a	32¢ Pane of 20	...	...	18.00	...
3012c	Folded Block of 15 in Booklet	...	...	14.50	...
3012d	Folded Pane of 16 with one stamp missing (15)...	...	...	15.95	...
3013	32¢ Children Sledding	...	...	1.10	.45
3013a	32¢ Pane of 18	...	...	16.50	...
Self-Adhesive Coil Stamps					
3014-17	32¢ Santa & Children .... Pl.Strip 8	...	9.75	3.75	...
3014-17	Set of 4 Singles	...	...	3.50	1.60
3018	32¢ Midnight Angel .... Pl.# Strip (5) 8.35 (3)		6.50	1.10	.40

3019   3020   3021

3022   3023

3019-23	32¢ Antique Automobiles, Strip ..... (25)	20.75 (10)	9.75	4.25	3.00
3019-23	Set of 5 Singles	...	...	4.15	1.25

1996 Commemoratives

3024   3030

3025   3026   3027   3028   3029

Scott's No.		Mint Sheet	Plate Block	F-VF NH	F-VF Used
3024,3030,3058-67,3069-70,3072-88					
3090-3104,3106-11,3118 Set of 53		...	...	48.50	12.25
3024	32¢ Utah Statehood	37.50	3.75	.80	.25
3024v	Folded Block of 15 in Booklet(BK 245)	...	...	17.95	...
3025-29	32¢ Winter Garden Flowers, 5 booklet singles	...	...	4.35	1.25
3029a	32¢ Booklet Pane of 5 .... (Unfolded 5.50)	...	...	4.50	3.25
3030	32¢ Love Cherub, Self-adhesive single	...	...	1.00	.30
3030a	32¢ Pane of 20, Self-adhesive	...	...	18.00	...
3030b	32¢ Folded Pane of 15 + Label	...	...	13.95	...

1996-2000 Flora and Fauna Series

3031,31A,44   3032,3045   3033   3036

3048,3053   3049,3054   3050-51,3055   3052

3031	1¢ Kestrel,SA, Black 1999 Date	4.50	.50	.20	.15
3031A	1¢ Kestrel,SA,Blue 2000 Date	2.50	.50	.20	.15
3032	2¢ Red-headed Woodpecker ....(100)	5.25	.55	.20	.15
3033	3¢ Eastern Bluebird ....(100)	7.50	.65	.20	.15
3036	$1 Red Fox, Self-adhesive (1998) ..(20)	40.00	9.25	2.10	.50
3036v	$1 Reprint, lighter colors (2000) .....(20)	40.00	9.25	2.10	.50
3048	20¢ Blue Jay, Self-adhesive Single ...	...	...	.55	.25
3048a	20¢ Pane of 10	...	...	5.25	...
3048b	20¢ Booklet Pane of 4	...	...	3.00	...
3048c	20¢ Booklet Pane of 6	...	...	4.50	...
3049	32¢ Yellow Rose, Self-adhesive Single	...	...	.95	.25
3049a	32¢ Pane of 20	...	...	17.50	...
3049b	32¢ Booklet Pane of 4	...	...	4.75	...
3049c	32¢ Booklet Pane of 5 + Label	...	...	5.95	...
3049d	32¢ Booklet Pane of 6	...	...	5.25	...
3050	20¢ Ringnecked Pheasant, SA Single, Die-cut 11¼ ...	...	...	.55	.20
3050a	20¢ Pane of 10 (1998)	...	...	4.95	...
3051	20¢ Ringnecked Pheasant, Die-cut 10½x11 on 3 sides, booklet single, SA (1999)	...	...	.85	.20
3051a	20¢ Die-cut 10½ on 3 sides, bklt single, SA	...	...	1.50	.30
3051b	20¢ Pheasant, Booklet Pane of 5 with 4 #3051 and 1 #3051a turned sideways at top, SA	...	...	4.50	...
3051c	20¢ Booklet Pane of 5 with 4 #3051 and 1 #3051a turned sideways at bottom, SA	...	...	4.50	...
3052	33¢ Coral Pink Rose, booklet single, SA (1999)	...	...	.80	.30
3052a	33¢ Rose Booklet Pane of 4	...	...	3.75	...
3052b	33¢ Rose Booklet Pane of 5	...	...	4.50	...
3052c	33¢ Rose Booklet Pane of 6	...	...	5.50	...
3052d	33¢ Rose Pane of 20	...	...	14.75	...
3052E	33¢ Coral Pink Rose, Bklt Sgl, Die-cut 11½ x 113/4	...	...	.80	.30
3052E	33¢ Double-sided Block of 8	...	...	6.50	...
3052Ef	33¢ Rose Double-sided Pane of 20, D-cut 11½ x 113/4 (2000)	14.75	...		

1996-99 Flora and Fauna Coils

Scott's No.		Pl.Strip of 5	Pl.Strip of 3	F-VF NH	F-VF Used
3044	1¢ Kestrel, Lighter Shade, Small "1996"	1.00	.80	.20	.15
3044a	1¢ Reprint, Deeper Shade,Large"1996"(1999)	1.35	1.20	.20	.15
3045	2¢ Woodpecker Coil (1999)	.90	.70	.20	.15
3053	20¢ Blue Jay Coil	5.25	4.35	.50	.20
3054	32¢ Yellow Rose Coil, SA (1997)	6.50	4.95	.90	.20
3055	20¢ Ringnecked Pheasant Coil, SA (1998)	5.25	4.35	.50	.20

1996 Commemoratives (continued)

3059   3058   3060

3061   3062   3065
3063   3064

3066   3067

Scott's No.		Mint Sheet	Plate Block	F-VF NH	F-VF Used
3058	32¢ Ernest E. Just ....(20)	17.50	4.25	.95	.25
3059	32¢ Smithsonian Institution ....(20)	15.00	3.50	.80	.25
3060	32¢ Year of the Rat ....(20)	18.50	4.25	.95	.25
3061-64	32¢ Pioneers of Communication ....(20)	17.00	4.00	3.50	2.25
3061-64	32¢ Strip of 4	...	...	3.50	2.25
3061-64	Set of 4 singles	...	...	3.40	1.00
3065	32¢ Fulbright Scholarships	37.50	4.00	.80	.25
3065v	Folded Block of 15 in Booklet (BK246)	...	...	15.95	...
3066	50¢ Jacqueline Cochran	63.50	5.95	1.30	.40
3067	32¢ Marathon ....(20)	15.00	3.50	.80	.25

1996 Atlanta '96 Summer Olympics Miniature Sheet

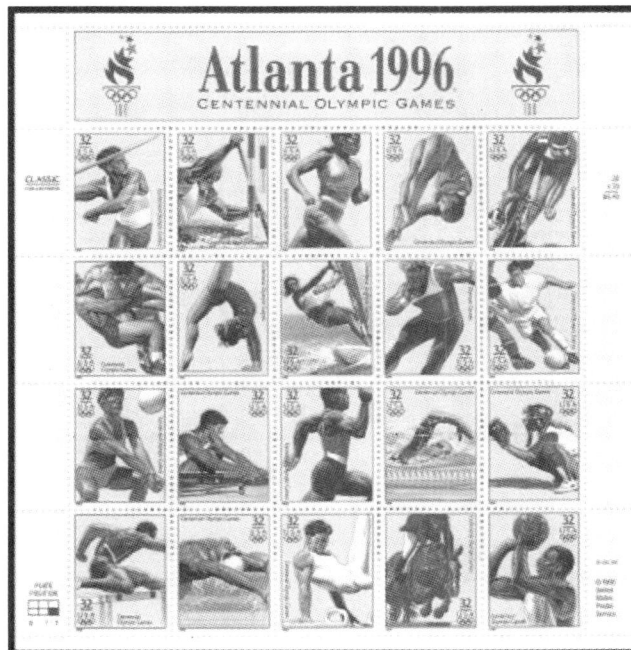

3068

75

Scott's No.	Mint Sheet	Plate Block	F-VF NH	F-VF Used
3068 32¢ Centen. Olympic Games, Mini Sht/20	…	…	19.95	15.75
3068a-t Olympics Set of 20 Singles	…	…	19.75	10.95

3068a Decathlon	3068h Women's Sailboarding	3068n Women's Swimming
3068b Men's Canoeing	3068i Men's Shot Put	3068o Women's Softball
3068c Women's Running	3068j Women's Soccer	3068p Men's Hurdles
3068d Women's Diving	3068k Beach Volleyball	3068q Men's Swimming
3068e Men's Cycling	3068l Men's Rowing	3068r Men's Gymnastics
3068f Freestyle Wrestling	3068m Men's Sprints	3068s Equestrian
3068g Women's Gymnastic		3068t Men's Basketball

1996 Commemoratives (continued)

3069   3070, 3071

3072   3073   3074   3075   3076

3079   3078
3077   3080   3081

3082   3083   3084   3087
          3085   3086

Scott's No.		Mint Sheet	Plate Block	F-VF NH	F-VF Used
3069	32¢ Georgia O'Keeffe ....(15)	12.50	3.75	.85	.25
3069v	Folded Block of 15 in Booklet (BK247)	…	…	15.95	…
3070	32¢ Tennessee Statehood	37.50	4.00	.80	.25
3070v	Folded Block of 15 in Booklet (BK248)	…	…	16.50	…
3071	Tennessee Self-adhesive single	…	…	1.00	.30
3071a	Tennessee Self-adhesive Pane of 20	…	…	18.95	…
3072-76	32¢ American Indian Dances, 5 Designs, Strip. ....(20) 17.00 (10)9.75			4.50	2.95
3072-76	Set of 5 singles	…	…	4.35	1.50
3072-76v	Folded Block of 15 in Booklet (BK249)	…	…	15.75	…

1996 Commemoratives (continued)

Scott's No.		Mint Sheet	Plate Block	F-VF NH	F-VF Used
3077-80	32¢ Prehistoric Animals, 4 Designs, attached, Block. ....(20)	18.00	4.15	3.75	2.25
3077-80	32¢ Strip of 4	…	…	3.75	2.25
3077-80	Set of 4 singles	…	…	3.65	1.00
3081	32¢ Breast Cancer ....(20)	20.75	4.75	1.10	.25
3082	32¢ James Dean ....(20)	20.75	4.75	1.10	.25
3082v	Folded Block of 15 in Booklet (BK250)	…	…	17.95	…
3083-86	32¢ Folk Heroes, 4 Designs, Block. (20)	18.50	4.50	4.00	2.25
3083-86	32¢ Strip of 4	…	…	4.00	2.25
3083-86	Folk Heroes Set of 4 singles	…	…	3.90	1.00
3083-86v	Folded Block of 15 in Booklet (BK251)	…	…	14.95	…
3087	32¢ Olympic Games, Discobolus ......(20)	18.50	4.50	1.00	.25
3087v	Folded Block of 15 in Booklet (BK252)	…	…	19.95	…

3090   3088-89   3104

3096   3097
3098   3099

3095
3091
3092
3093   3102   3103
3094   3100   3101

Scott's No.		Mint Sheet	Plate Block	F-VF NH	F-VF Used
3088	32¢ Iowa Statehood	37.50	3.75	.80	.25
3088v	Folded Block of 15 in Booklet (BK253)	…	…	15.95	…
3089	Iowa Self-Adhesive single	…	…	1.00	.30
3089a	Iowa Self-Adhesive Pane of 20	…	…	18.75	…
3090	32¢ Rural Free Delivery ....(20)	15.00	3.50	.80	.25
3090v	Folded Block of 30 in Booklet (BK254)	…	…	31.95	…
3091-95	32¢ Riverboats, self-adhesive, attd.(20)18.50 (10)10.95			4.95	2.95
3091-95	Riverboats, Set of 5 singles	…	…	4.85	1.25
3091-95v	Folded Block of 15 in Booklet (BK255)	…	…	17.95	…
3091-95b	32¢ Riverboats, self-adhesive attd, with "missing 3 perforations" special die cutting. ....(20)295.00(10)160.00			79.50	…
3096-99	32¢ Big Band Leaders, Block ....(20)	21.50	5.00	4.50	2.25
3096-99	32¢ Strip of 4	…	…	4.50	2.25
3096-99	32¢ Horiz. Pl. Block of 8 with selvedge	…	9.75	…	…
3096-99	Big Band Leaders set of 4 singles	…	…	3.90	1.00
3100-3	32¢ Songwriters Block ....(20)	21.50	5.00	4.50	2.25
3100-3	32¢ Strip of 4	…	…	4.50	2.25
3100-3	32¢ Horiz. Pl. Block of 8 with selvedge	…	9.75	…	…
3100-3	Songwriters set of 4 singles	…	…	3.90	1.00
3104	23¢ F. Scott Fitzgerald	31.50	3.25	.65	.25

NOTE: S.A.=SELF ADHESIVE STAMPS WHICH DON'T REQUIRE MOISTURE-ACTIVATION

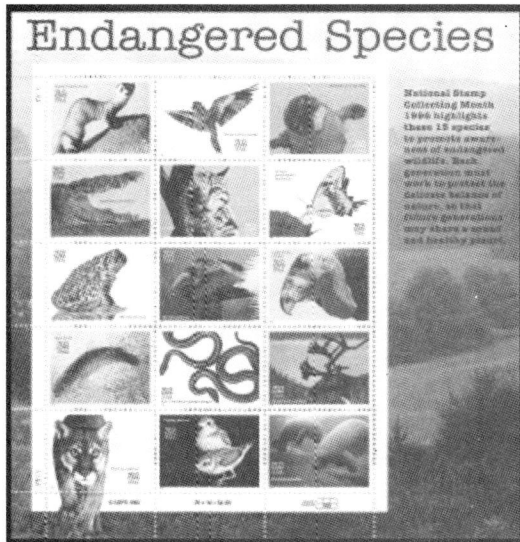

3105

Scott's No.		Mint Sheet	Plate Block	F-VF NH	F-VF Used
3105	32¢ Endangered Species,Miniature Sheet of 15	...	...	12.75	10.75
3105a-o	Set of 15 singles	...	...	12.50	8.95
3105v	Folded Block of 15 in Booklet (BK256)	...	...	13.95	...

3105a Black-footed Ferret	3105f Schaus	3105j Gila Trout
3105b Thick-Billed Parrot	Swallowtail Butterfly	3105k San Francisco
3105h Brown Pelican	3105g Wyoming Toad	Garter Snake
3105c Hawaiian Monk Seal	3105i California Condor	3105m Florida Panther
3105d American Crocodile	3105l Woodland Caribou	3105n Piping Plover
3105e Ocelot		3105o Florida Manatee

1996 Commemoratives (cont.)

3106

3108,3113
3110,3115

3109,3114
3111,3116

3107,3112   3118

3106	32¢ Computer Technology	(40) 30.95	3.75	.80	.25
#3107-3117a Christmas Issues					
3107	32¢ Madonna and Child	37.50	3.95	.80	.25
3107v	Folded Block of 15 in Booklet (BK257)	...	...	14.95	...
3108-11	32¢ Family Scenes, Block	47.50	4.75	4.00	2.25
3108-11	32¢ Strip of 4	...	...	4.00	2.25
3108-11	Family Scenes set of 4 singles	...	...	3.90	1.00
Self-Adhesive Booklet Stamps					
3112	32¢ Madonna and Child Single	...	...	1.00	.30
3112a	32¢ Pane of 20	...	...	17.75	...
3113-16	32¢ Family Scenes	...	...	4.25	1.40
3116a	32¢ Pane of 20	...	...	19.50	...
3117	32¢ Skaters single	...	...	1.00	.45
3117a	32¢ Pane of 18	...	...	16.95	...
1996 Commemoratives (cont.)					
3118	32¢ Hanukkah, Self-adhesive	(20) 15.00	3.50	.80	.25
3118v	Folded Block of 15 in Booklet (BK258)	...	...	14.95	...
3118b	32¢ Hanukkah, revised backing SA (1997)	(20) 15.00	3.50	.80	...

3119

Scott's No.		Mint Sheet	Plate Block	F-VF NH	F-VF Used
3119	50¢ Cycling Souvenir Sheet of 2	...	...	3.00	2.25
3119a-b	Set of 2 Singles	...	...	2.90	1.95
	3119a Orange & Multicolored, 3119b Blue Green & Multicolored				

3120   3121   3122

1997 Commemoratives
3120-21, 3125, 3130-31, 3134-35, 3141, 3143-50, 3152-75

				F-VF NH	F-VF Used
	Set of 40	...		35.00	9.95
3120	32¢ Chinese Year of the Ox	(20) 17.50	3.95	.90	.25
3121	32¢ Benjamin O. Davis, Sr, S.A.	(20) 17.50	4.25	.95	.25

1997 Statue of Liberty Self-Adhesive Regular Issue

3122	32¢ Liberty, Single, die-cut 11	...	...	1.10	.25
3122a	32¢ Pane of 20	...	...	18.50	...
3122b	32¢ Booklet Pane of 4	...	...	4.75	...
3122c	32¢ Booklet Pane of 5 + Label	...	...	5.50	...
3122d	32¢ Booklet Pane of 6, die-cut 11	...	...	5.25	...
3122E	32¢ Die-cut 11.5x11.8	...	...	1.50	...
3122Ef	32¢Bklt.Pane of 20, 11.5x11.8	...	...	45.00	...
3122Eg	32¢Bklt.Pane of 6, 11.5x11.8	...	...	7.50	...

1997 Commemoratives (continued)

3123   3124   3125

3123	32¢ Love, Swans, SA Single	...	...	1.00	.25
3123a	32¢ Pane of 20, SA	...	...	16.50	...
3124	55¢ Love, Swans, SA Single	...	...	1.35	.40
3124a	55¢ Pane of 20, SA	...	...	24.75	...
3125	32¢ Helping Children Learn, SA	(20) 18.00	4.25	.95	.25

UNCUT SHEETS AND POSITION PIECES
Many modern issues are released by the Postal Service in complete uncut sheets as they appear before being cut down to the panes normally available to the public.

The gutters between the panes create a variety of position pieces. The uncut sheets and position pieces are offered in special listings on page 110.?

Plate Number Coil Strips (pgs. 103-105),
Unfolded Booklet Panes with Plate Number (pg. 105),
Self-adhesive Panes (pg 106),
Unexploded Booklets (pgs. 107-109),
and Modern Errors (pgs. 111-112).

1997 Merian Botanical Prints Booklets, Self-Adhesive

3127   3126   3129   3128

Scott's No.		Mint Sheet	Plate Block	F-VF NH	F-VF Used
#3126-27a Serpentine Die Cut 10.9 x 10.2 on 2,3,4 sides					
3126	32¢ Citron Moth, booklet single	...	...	.90	.25
3127	32¢ Flowering Pineapple, Cockroaches, booklet single...	...	...	.90	.25
3127a	32¢ Booklet Pane of 20	...	...	16.50	...
#3128-29b Serpentine Die Cut 11.2 x 10.8 on 2 or 3 sides					
3128	32¢ Citron Moth, booklet single	...	...	.95	.25
3128a	32¢ Large perforation on right side .	...	...	1.40	.50
3128b	32¢ Booklet Pane of 5, 2-#3128-29, 1-#3128a	...	...	4.95	...
3129	32¢ Flowering Pineapple, Cockroaches, booklet single...	...	...	.95	.25
3129a	32¢ Large Perforations on right side	...	...	2.40	.60
3129b	32¢ Booklet Pane of 5, 2-#3128-29, 1-#3129a	...	...	5.95	...
3128-29	32¢ Attached Pair	...	...	1.90	...

1997 Pacific '97 Commemoratives

3130   3131

				F-VF NH	F-VF Used
3130	32¢ Clipper Ship	...	...	.90	.30
3131	32¢ Stagecoach	...	...	.90	.30
3130-31	32¢ Pair	(16) 13.95	4.00	1.80	1.00

1997 Linerless Coil Stamps

3132   3133

Scott's No.		Pl.Strip of 5	Pl.Strip of 3	F-VF NH	F-VF Used
3132	(25¢) Juke Box, SA, Imperf.	6.50	5.25	.75	.35
3133	32¢ Flag over Porch, SA, Die-cut 9.9	8.75	7.50	.90	.35

NOTE: #3133 has Blue "1996" Date at bottom

1997 Commemoratives (continued)

3134   3135

3136

1997 Commemoratives (continued)

Scott's No.		Mint Sheet	Plate Block	F-VF NH	F-VF Used
3134	32¢ Thornton Wilder	(20) 15.00	3.50	.80	.25
3135	32¢ Raoul Wallenberg	(20) 15.00	3.50	.80	.25

1997 World of Dinosaurs Miniature Sheet

3136	32¢ World of Dinosaurs, Miniature Pane of 15...	...	...	14.50	10.00
3136a-o	Dinosaurs Set of 15 singles	...	...	14.25	9.50

3136a Ceratosaurus	3136f Stegosaurus	3136k Daspletosaurus
3136b Camptosaurus	3136g Allosaurus	3136l Paleosaniwa
3136c Camarasaurus	3136h Opisthias	3136m Corythosaurus
3136d Brachiosaurus	3136i Edmontonia	3136n Ornithominus
3136e Goniopholis	3136j Einiosaurus	3136o Parasaurolophus

1997 Bugs Bunny Self-Adhesive Souvenir Sheet

3137

3137	32¢ Souvenir Sheet of 10	...	...	7.50	7.25
3137a	32¢ Single stamp	...	...	.80	.25
3137b	32¢ Booklet Pane of 9 (left side) ...	...	...	6.25	...
3137c	32¢ Booklet Pane of 1 (right side) ...	...	...	1.75	...
3138	32¢ Souvenir Sheet of 10 with special Die-cut that extends thru paper backing	...	...	250.00	...
3138a	32¢ Single stamp	...	...	3.00	...
3138b	32¢ Booklet Pane of 9 (left side)	...	...	27.50	...
3138c	32¢ Booklet Pane of 1 imperf (right side)	...	...	235.00	...

NOTE: Souvenir sheets from the uncut sheet do not have vertical roulette lines dividing the two halves of the souvenir sheet. They are listed with the Uncut Sheets.

1997 Pacific '97 Souvenir Sheets

3139

3140

Scott's No.		Mint Sheet	Plate Block	F-VF NH	F-VF Used
3139	50¢ Benjamin Franklin Sheet of 12 .	...	...	16.50	13.95
3139a	50¢ single stamp from souvenir sheet	...	...	1.50	.80
3140	60¢ George Washington Sheet of 12	...	...	19.50	14.95
3140a	60¢ single stamp from souvenir sheet	...	...	1.75	.95

1997 Commemoratives (continued)

3141

3141	32¢ Marshall Plan	(20)	15.00	3.50	.80	.25

1997 Classic American Aircraft Miniature Sheet

3142

3142	32¢ Classic Am. Aircraft, Mini Sht of 20	...	...	16.95	14.50
3142a-t	Aircraft Set of 20 Singles	...	...	16.50	10.95

3142a Mustang	3142h Stratojet	3142o Peashooter
3142b Model B	3142i GeeBee	3142p Tri-Motor
3142c Cub	3142j Staggerwing	3142q DC-3
3142d Vega	3142k Flying Fortress	3142r 314 Clipper
3142e Alpha	3142l Stearman	3142s Jenny
3142f B-10	3142m Constellation	3142t Wildcat
3142g Corsair	3142n Lightning	

1997 Commemoratives (continued)

3143, 3148

3144, 3149

3145, 3147

3146, 3150

3152

3153

3143-46	32¢ Legendary Football Coaches, attached	(20)	18.50	4.50	4.00	2.50
3143-46	32¢ Coaches, strip of 4	...	...	4.00	2.50
3143-46	Set of 4 singles	...	...	3.85	1.20
3143-46	Top Plate Block of 8 with Label ..	...	8.50	...	...
3147	32¢ Vince Lombardi	(20)	19.50	5.00	1.10	.35
3148	32¢ Bear Bryant	(20)	17.50	4.50	.95	.35
3149	32¢ Pop Warner	(20)	17.50	4.50	.95	.35

Scott's No.		Mint Sheet	Plate Block	F-VF NH	F-VF Used
3150	32¢ George Halas	(20) 17.50	4.50	.95	.35

NOTE: #3147-50 HAVE A RED BAR ABOVE THE COACHES NAME. THIS BAR IS MISSING ON THE SE-TENANT ISSUE #3143-46

1997 American Dolls Miniature Sheet

3151

3151	32¢ American Dolls, Miniature Sht of 15	...	...	17.50	14.50
3151a-o	32¢ American Dolls, set of 15 singles	...	...	17.00	9.00
3151v	Folded Block of 15 in Booklet (BK266)	...	...	14.95	...

3151a "Alabama Baby"	3151g Plains Indian	3151l "Betsy McCall"
3151b "Columbian Doll"	3151h Izannah Walker Doll	3151m "Skippy"
3151c "Raggedy Ann"	3151i "Babyland Rag"	3151n "Maggie Mix-up"
3151d Martha Chase Doll	3151j "Scootles"	3151o Albert Schoenhut Doll
3151e "American Child"	3151k Ludwig Greiner Doll	
3151f "Baby Coos"		

1997 Commemoratives (continued)

3152	32¢ Humphrey Bogart	(20)	17.50	4.35	.95	.25
3152v	Folded Block of 15 in Booklet (BK267)	...	...	14.95	...
3153	32¢ Stars and Stripes Forever	...	38.75	3.75	.80	.25
3153v	Folded Block of 15 in Booklet (BK268)	...	...	13.95	...

3154 3155
3156 3157

3158

3159

3160

3161

3162

3163

3164

3165

3166

3167

3173

3168

3169

3170

3171

3172

Scott's No.		Mint Sheet	Plate Block	F-VF NH	F-VF Used
3154-57	32¢ Opera Singers, Block	(20) 20.75	5.00	4.50	2.50
3154-57	32¢ Strip of 4	...	...	4.50	2.50
3154-57	TopPlate Block of 8 with Label ...	...	9.50	...	...
3154-57	Set of 4 singles	...	...	4.35	1.00
3158-65	32¢ Conductors & Composers attd	(20)20.75	(8) 10.50	9.50	5.75
3158-65	Set of 8 singles	...	...	9.25	2.75
3166	32¢ Padre Felix Varela	(20) 15.00	3.50	.80	.30
3167	32¢ U.S. Air Force 50th Anniv. ...	(20) 15.00	3.50	.80	.25

1997 Classic Movie Monsters

3168-72	32¢ Movie Monsters, attd.	(20) 18.75	(10)10.75	5.00	3.25
3168-72	Set of 5 singles	...	...	4.90	1.30
3168/72v	Folded Block of 15 in Booklet(BK 269)	...	...	15.95	...

1997 Commemoratives (continued)

3173	32¢ First Supersonic Flight 1947 self-adhesive	(20) 15.00	3.50	.80	.25

3174

3175

3176

3177

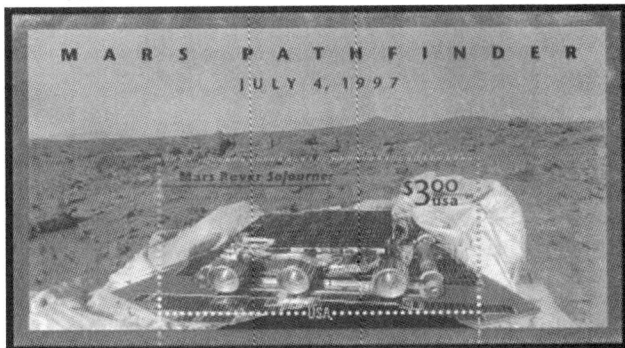
3178

3174	32¢ Women in the Military	(20) 15.00	3.50	.80	.25
3175	32¢ Kwanza, self-adhesive	38.50	3.75	.80	.25
3176	32¢ Madonna & Child, self-adhesive	...	...	.80	.25
3176a	32¢ Madonna , Pane of 20	...	...	15.00	...

Scott's No.		Mint Sheet	Plate Block	F-VF NH	F-VF Used
3177	32¢ American Holly , self-adhesive	...	...	.80	.20
3177a	32¢ Holly, Pane of 20	...	...	15.00	...
3177b	32¢ Holly, Booklet Pane of 4	...	...	4.25	...
3177c	32¢ Holly, Booklet Pane of 5 plus label	...	...	5.25	...
3177d	32¢ Holly, Booklet Pane of 6	...	...	4.95	...

1997 Priority Rate Souvenir Sheet

3178	$3 Mars Rover Sojourner	...	...	7.25	6.75

NOTE: #3178 IS IMPERFORATE ON ALL 4 SIDES AND MEASURES 146mm WIDE BY 82mm TALL. #3178v IS AN UNCUT SHEET OF 18 WITH VERTICAL PERFORATIONS BETWEEN THE SOUVENIR SHEETS AND WIDE HORIZONTAL GUTTERS. AN INDIVIDUAL SOUVENIR SHEET MEASURES APPROX. 152mm WIDE BY 87mm TALL. See uncut sheet listings.

1998 Commemoratives

3179

3180

3181

3179-81, 3192-3203, 3206, 3211-27, 3230-35, 3237-43, 49-52 Set of 51		...	...	38.50	10.95
3179	32¢ Happy New Year, Year of the Tiger	(20) 16.75	4.00	.90	.25
3180	32¢ Alpine Skiing	(20) 17.50	4.25	.95	.25
3181	32¢ Madam C.J. Walker, SA	(20) 17.50	4.25	.95	.25

1998-2000 Celebrate the Century Souvenir Sheets

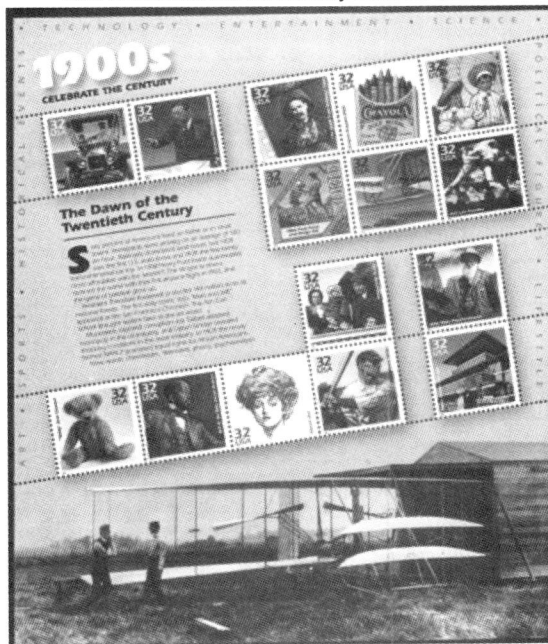
3182

3182-91	Set of 10 Souvenir Sheets			110.00	...
3182	32¢1900's, Sheet of 15			11.50	...
3182a-o	Set of 15 singles	...	...	11.50	8.95

3182a Model T Ford	3182e St.Louis World's Fair	3182j John Muir
3182b Theodore Roosevelt	3182f Pure Food & Drug Act	3182k "Teddy" Bear
3182c "Great Train Robbery"	3182g Wright Brothers	3182l W.E.B.DuBois
3182d Crayola Crayons	3182h Boxing Match	3182m Gibson Girl
	3182i Immigrants Arrive	3182n Baseball World Series
		3182o Robie House

3183	32¢1910's, Sheet of 15			11.50	...
3183a-o	Set of 15 singles	...	...	11.50	8.95

3183a Charlie Chaplin	3183f Panama Canal	3183l Crossword Puzzle
3183b Federal Reserve	3183g Jim Thorpe	3183m Jack Dempsey
3183c George W. Carver	3183h Grand Canyon	3183n Construction Toys
3183d Avant-Garde Art	3183i World War I	3183o Child Labor Reform
3183e Transcontinental Telephone Line	3183j Boy & Girl Scouts	
	3183k Woodrow Wilson	

Scott's No.		Mint Sheet	Plate Block	F-VF NH	F-VF Used
3184	32¢1920's, Sheet of 15			11.50	...
3184a-o	Set of 15 singles	...	...	11.50	8.95

3184a Babe Ruth	3184g Margaret Mead	3184l Four Horsemen of
3184b The Gatsby Style	3184h Flappers	Notre Dame
3184c Prohibition	3184i Radio Entertains	3184m Lindbergh Flies the
3184d Electric Toy Trains	3184j Art Deco	Atlantic
3184e 19th Amendment	3184k Jazz Flourishes	3184n American Realism
3184f Emily Post		

Scott's No.		Mint Sheet	Plate Block	F-VF NH	F-VF Used
3185	32¢1930's, Sheet of 15			11.50	...
3185a-o	Set of 15 singles	...	...	11.50	8.95

3185a F. D.Roosevelt	3185f Superman	3185j Jesse Owens
3185b Empire State Bldg	3185g Household	3185k Streamline Design
3185c Life Magazine	Conveniences	3185l Golden Gate Bridge
3185d Eleanor Roosevelt	3185h "Snow White and	3185m The Depression
3185e New Deal	the Seven Dwarfs"	3185n Bobby Jones
	3185i "Gone with the Wind"	

Scott's No.		Mint Sheet	Plate Block	F-VF NH	F-VF Used
3186	33¢1940's, Sheet of 15 (1999) ...			11.75	...
3186a-o	Set of 15 singles	...	...	11.75	8.95

3186a World War II	3186f TV Entertains America	3186k UN Headquarters
3186b Antibiotics	3186g Jitterbug	3186l Postwar Baby Boom
3186c Jackie Robinson	3186h Jackson Pollock	3186m Slinky
3186d Harry S Truman	3186i GI Bill	3186n "A Streetcar named
3186e Women War Effort	3186j Big Band Sound	Desire"
		3186o "Citizen Kane"

Scott's No.		Mint Sheet	Plate Block	F-VF NH	F-VF Used
3187	33¢1950's, Sheet of 15 (1999) ...			11.75	...
3187a-o	Set of 15 singles	...	...	11.75	8.95

3187a Polio Vaccine	3187e Korean War	3187i Drive-In Movies
3187b Teen Fashions	3187f Desegrating Public	3187j World Series
3187c The "Shot Heard	Schools	3187k Rocky Marciano
Round the World"	3187g Tail Fins	3187l "I Love Lucy"
3187d Satellites Launched	3187h "The Cat in the Hat"	3187m Rock n'Roll
		3187n Stock Car Racing

Scott's No.		Mint Sheet	Plate Block	F-VF NH	F-VF Used
3188	33¢ 1960's, Sheet of 15 (1999) ..			11.75	...
3188a-o	Set of 15 singles	...	...	11.75	8.95

3188a M. L. King, Jr.	3188f The Peace Corps	3188l Super Bowl
3188b Woodstock	3188g Viet Nam War	3188m Peace Symbol
3188c Man Walks - Moon	3188h Ford Mustang	3188n Roger Maris
3188d Green Bay Packers	3188i Barbie Doll	3188o The Beatles
3188e Star Trek	3188j Integrated Circuit	"Yellow Submarine"
	3188k Lasers	

Scott's No.		Mint Sheet	Plate Block	F-VF NH	F-VF Used
3189	33¢ 1970's, Sheet of 15 (2000) ..			11.75	...
3189a-o	Set of 15 singles	...	...	11.75	8.95

3189a Earth Day	3189f U.S. 200th Birthday	3189l Monday Night
3189b "All in the Family"	3189g Secretariat	Football
3189c "Seasame Street"	3189h VCR's	3189m Smiley Face
3189d Disco Music	3189iPioneer 10	3189n Jumbo Jets
3189e Pittsburgh Steelers	3189k 1970's Fashion	3189o Medical Imaging

Scott's No.		Mint Sheet	Plate Block	F-VF NH	F-VF Used
3190	33¢ 1980's, Sheet of 15 (2000) ..			11.75	...
3190a-o	Set of 15 singles	...	...	11.75	8.95

3190a Space Shuttle	3190f Cable TV	3190k Fall of Berlin Wall
3190b "Cats" Broadway	3190g Viet Nam Veterans	3190l Video Games
3190c San Francisco 49ers	Memorial	3190m "E.T."
3190d Hostages in Iran	3190h Compact Dics	3190n Personal
Come Home	3190i Cabbage Patch Kids	Computers
3190e Figure Skating	3190j "The Crosby Show"	3190o Hip-Hop Culture

Scott's No.		Mint Sheet	Plate Block	F-VF NH	F-VF Used
3191	33¢ 1990's, Sheet of 15 (2000) ..			11.75	...
3191a-o	Set of 15 Singles	...	...	11.75	8.95

3191a Baseball Records	3191f Computer Art and	3191k "Jurassic Park"
3191b Gulf War	Graphics	3191l "Titanic"
3191c "Seinfeld"	3191g Species Recovery	3191m Sports Utility
3191d Extreme Sports	3191h Space Exploration	Vehicle
3191e Education	3191i Special Olympics	3191n World Wide Web
	3191j Virtual Reality	3191o Cellular Phones

1998 Commemoratives (continued)

3192

3193

3194

3195

3196

3197

3198

3199

3200

3201

3202

3203

Scott's No.		Mint Sheet	Plate Block	F-VF NH	F-VF Used
3192	32¢ Remember the Maine	(20) 17.50	4.25	.95	.25
3193-97	32¢ Flowering Trees, SA, attd. ...	(20) 15.00	(10) 8.75	4.00	2.75
3193-97	32¢ Trees, Set of 5 Singles	...	...	3.90	1.35
3198-3202	32¢ Alexander Calder, attd.	(20) 17.50	(10)10.50	4.75	2.75
3198-3202	32¢ Calder, Set of 5 Singles	...	...	4.65	1.35
3203	32¢ Cinco de Mayo, SA.	(20) 17.50	(10) 4.25	.95	.25

1998 Tweety & Sylvester Self-Adhesive Souvenir Sheets

3204

1998 Tweety & Sylvester Self-Adhesive Souvenir Sheets

Scott's No.		Mint Sheet	Plate Block	F-VF NH	F-VF Used
3204	32¢ Souvenir Sheet of 10	...	...	7.50	...
3204a	32¢ Single Stamp	...	...	.80	.25
3204b	32¢ Booklet Pane of 9 (left side)	...	...	6.25	...
3204c	32¢ Booklet Pane of 1(right side)	...	...	1.75	...
3205	32¢ Souvenir Sheet of 10 with special Die-cut that extends thru paper backing	...	...	10.75	...
3205a	32¢ Single Stamp	...	...	1.00	...
3205b	32¢ Booklet Pane of 9 (left side)	...	...	7.95	...
3205c	32¢ Imperf Bklt. Pane of 1(right side)	...	...	3.50	...

NOTE: Souvenir sheets from the uncut sheet do not have vertical roulette lines dividing the two halves of the souvenir sheet. See uncut sheet listings.

3206　　　　3207　　　　3208

1998 Commemoratives (continued)

		Mint Sheet	Plate Block	F-VF NH	F-VF Used
3206	32¢ Wisconsin Statehood SA (20)	15.00	3.50	.80	.25

1998 Nondenominated Coil Stamps

Scott's No.		Pl.Strip of 5	Pl.Strip of 3	F-VF NH	F-VF Used
3207	(5¢) Wetlands, Non-Profit	2.40	2.10	.20	.15
3207A	(5¢) Wetlands, Self Adhesive	2.40	2.10	.20	.15
3208	(25¢) Diner, Water-Activated	5.75	4.75	.60	.30
3208A	(25¢) Diner, Self-Adhesive	5.75	4.75	.60	.30

1998 Trans-Mississippi Centennial Souvenir Sheets

3209

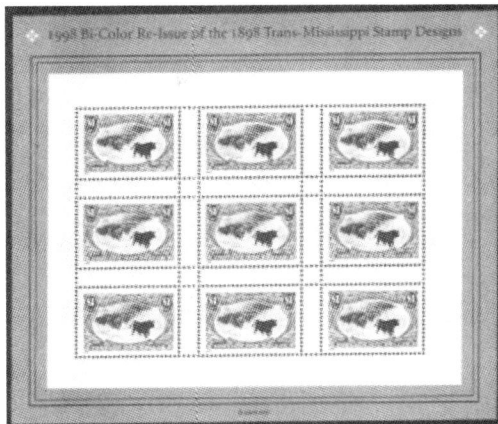

3210

Scott's No.		Mint Sheet	Plate Block	F-VF NH	F-VF Used
3209	1c-$2 Souvenir Sheet of 9	...	...	9.95	7.75
3209a-i	Set of 9 singles	...	...	9.75	7.25
3210	$1 Cattle in Storm, Souvenir Sheet of 9	...	...	21.50	17.75
3210a	Single from Souvenir Sheet	...	...	2.50	1.75

NOTE: #3209-10 contain bicolored versions of the designs of the 1898 Trans-Mississippi issue. (#285-93)

3209a 1¢ Green & Black	3209d 5¢ Blue & Black	3209g 50¢ Green & Black
3209b 2¢ Red Brown & Black	3209e 8¢ Dark Lilac & Black	3209h $1 Red & Black
3209c 4¢ Orange & Black	3209f 10¢ Purple & Black	3209i $2 Red Brown & Black

1998 Commemoratives (continued)

3211

3214　　3215
3212　　3213

3219　　3218　　　　　3220
3216　　3217

3221　　3224　3225　　　3226　　3227　　3228-29
　　　　3222　3223

Scott's No.		Mint Sheet	Plate Block	F-VF NH	F-VF Used
3211	32¢ Berlin Airlift	(20) 15.00	3.50	.80	.25
3212-15	32¢ Folk Musicians, block attd. .	(20) 18.00	4.25	3.75	2.25
3212-15	32¢ Strip of 4	...	...	3.75	2.25
3212-15	32¢ Folk, Set of 4 Singles	...	...	3.65	1.10
3216-19	32¢ Gospel Singers, block attd.	(20) 18.00	4.25	3.75	2.25
3216-19	32¢ Strip of 4	...	...	3.75	2.25
3216-19	32¢ Gospel, Set of 4 Singles	...	...	3.65	1.10
3220	32¢ Spanish Settlement of Southwest in 1598	(20) 15.00	3.50	.80	.25
3221	32¢ Stephen Vincent Benet	(20) 15.00	3.50	.80	.25
3222-25	32¢ Tropical Birds, attd.	(20) 16.75	3.95	3.50	2.25
3222-25	32¢ Birds, Set of 4 Singles	...	...	3.40	1.10
3222-25v	Folded Block of 15 in Booklet (BK272)	...	...	14.95	...

Scott's No.		Mint Sheet	Plate Block	F-VF NH	F-VF Used
3226	32¢ Alfred Hitchcock	(20) 15.00	3.50	.80	.25
3227	32¢ Organ & Tissue Donation, SA	(20) 15.00	3.50	.80	.25

1998-2000 Nondenominated Coil Stamps

Scott's No.		Pl.Strip of 5	Pl.Strip of 3	F-VF NH	F-VF Used
3228	(10¢) Green Bicycle, Small 1mm "1998" Date, Self-adhesive	3.65	3.00	.30	.15
3228a	(10¢) Large 1½mm "1998" Date, SA(2000)-2000	...	...	...	...
3229	(10¢) Green Bicycle, Water-Activated	3.65	3.00	.30	.15

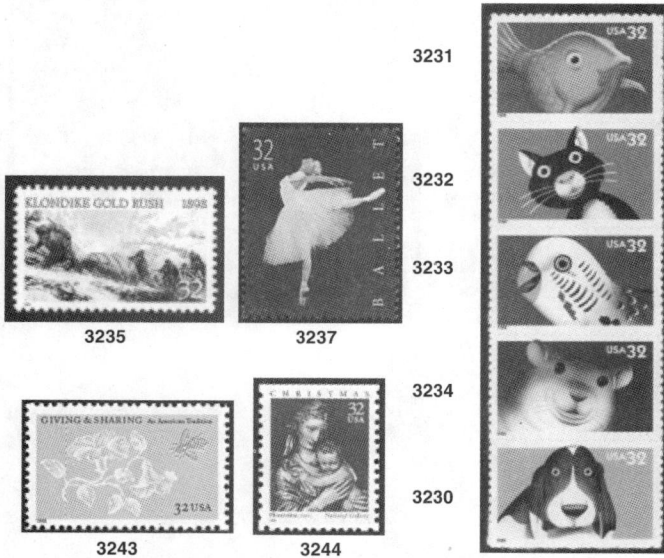

3231
3232
3233
3234
3230

3235

3237

3243

3244

3238   3239   3240   3241   3242

3245   3246

3249   3250

3251   3252

3247   3248

Scott's		Mint Sheet	Plate Block	F-VF NH	F-VF Used
3237	32¢ Ballet .... (20)	16.00	3.75	.85	.25
3237v	Folded Block of 15 in Booklet (BK273)	...	...	14.95	...
3238-42	32¢ Space Discovery, attd	16.00	(10)9.25	4.25	2.75
3238-42	32¢ Space, Set of 5 singles	...	...	3.40	1.40
3238-42v	Folded Block of 15 in Booklet (BK274)	...	...	14.95	...
3243	32¢ Giving and Sharing .... (20)	15.00	3.50	.80	.25
3244	32¢ Madonna & Child, Self-adhesive	...	...	.90	.20
3244a	32¢ Madonna, Pane of 20	...	...	16.50	...
3245-48	32¢ Christmas Wreaths, set of 4 singles ...	...	...	3.65	1.00
3248a	32¢ Wreaths, Booklet Pane of 4	...	...	3.75	...
3248b	32¢ Wreaths, Booklet Pane of 5	...	...	4.75	...
3248c	32¢ Wreaths, Booklet Pane of 6	...	...	5.50	...
3249-52	32¢ Christmas Wreaths, SA, att. (20)	15.00	3.75	3.25	...
3249-52	32¢ Wreaths, Set of 4 Singles ...	...	...	3.20	1.10
3249v-52v	32¢ Wreaths, from #3252b booklet of 20…	...	...	3.65	...
3252b	32¢ Wreaths, Booklet of 20	...	...	17.50	...

NOTE: #3245-48 are considerably smaller designs than #3249-52.

1998 Regular Issues

3257-58   3259,3263   3260,3264-69   3270-71

3261   3262

1998 Four Centuries of American Art Miniature Sheets

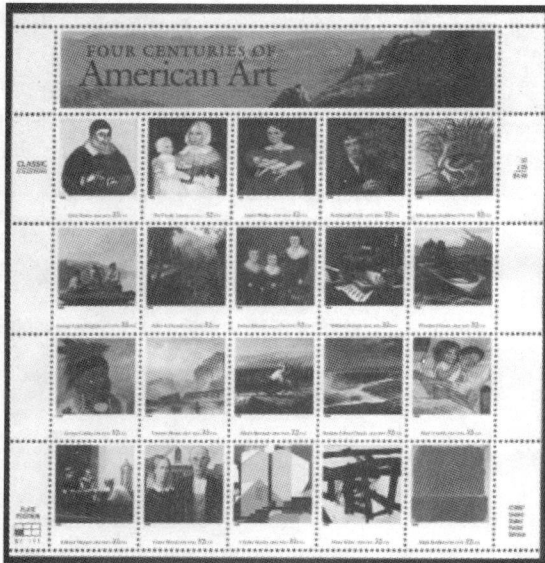

3236

Scott's No.		Mint Sheet	Plate Block	F-VF NH	F-VF Used
3230-34	32¢ Bright Eyes, SA, attd. .... (20)	15.00	(10) 8.50	4.00	2.75
3230-34	32¢ Bright Eyes, St of 5 Singles	...	...	3.90	1.40
3235	32¢ Klondike Gold Rush .... (20)	15.00	3.50	.80	.25

1998 Four Centuries of American Art Miniature Sheets

3236	32¢ American Art, Pane of 20	...	...	18.75	13.50
3236-a-t	32¢ Art, Set of 20 Singles	...	...	18.50	10.95

3236a John Foster Church
3236b The Freake Limner
3236c Ammi Phillips
3236d Rembrandt Peale
3236e John James Audubon
3236f George Caleb Bingham
3236g Asher B. Durand
3236h Joshua Johnson
3236i William Harnett
3236j Winslow Homer
3236k George Catlin
3236l Thomas Moran
3236m Alfred Bierstadt
3236n Frederic Edwin
3236o Mary Cassatt
3236p Edward Hopper
3236q Grant Wood
3236r Charles Sheelet
3236s Franz Kline
3236t Mark Rothko

1998 Regular Issue Sheet Stamps

3257	(1¢) Weather Vane, Make-Up Stamp, White "USA," Black 1998 Date, BCA	3.00	.45	.20	.15
3258	(1¢) Weather Vane, Pale blue "USA," Blue "1998" Date, AP	3.00	.45	.20	.15
3259	22¢ Uncle Sam, self-adhesive .... (20)	9.75	2.75	.50	.20
3260	(33¢) Hat, water-activated	37.50	3.75	.80	.15
3261	$3.20 Space Shuttle Landing, Priority Mail .... (20)	135.00	29.50	6.95	2.00
3262	$11.75 Piggyback Space Shuttle, Express Mail .... (20)	485.00	110.00	25.00	9.75

1998-2000 Regular Issue Coil Stamps

Scott's No.		Pl. Strip of 5	Pl. Strip of 3	F-VF NH	F-VF Used
3263	22¢ Uncle Sam, Self-adhesive ...	5.25	4.25	.50	.20
3264	(33¢) Hat, water-activated	7.00	5.75	.75	.25
3264d	(33¢) Duller Gum	7.50	6.00	.85	...
3265	(33¢) Hat, SA, Die-cut 9.9 vert.ical	7.00	5.75	.75	.25
3266	(33¢) Hat, SA, Die-cut 9.7 vert.ical	7.00	5.75	.75	.25

Note: Unused #3266 is on paper larger than stamp, #3265 is same size as stamp

3270	(10¢) Eagle & Shield, Water-activated, Small 1¼mm "1998" Date	3.00	2.50	.25	.20
3270a	(10¢) Large 1 3/4mm "1998" Date(2000)	6.50	6.00	.50	.40
3271	(10¢) Eagle & Shield, Self-adhesive, Small 1¼mm "1998" Date	3.00	2.50	.25	.20
3271b	(10¢) Large 1 3/4mm "1998"Date(2000)	...	...	...	...

Note: See #2602-4 for varieties with "Bulk Rate"

1998 Regular Issue Booklet Stamps and Panes

Scott's No.				F-VF NH	F-VF Used
3267	(33¢) Hat, Booklet single, SA, BEP, Small "1998" Date, Die-cut 9.9	...	...	.90	.25
3267a	(33¢) Hat, Booklet Pane of 10	...	...	8.50	...
3268	(33¢) Hat, single from pane of 10 SA, AV, Large "1998" Date, Die-cut 11.2 x 11.1	...	...	.90	.25
3268a	(33¢) Hat, Pane of 10	...	...	8.50	...
3268b	(33¢) Hat, single from pane of 20, SA, AV, Large "1998" Date, Die-cut 11	...	...	.90	.25
3268c	(33¢) Hat, Pane of 20	...	...	16.75	...
3269	(33¢) Hat, single from pane of 18,SA, AV	...	...	.90	.25
3269a	(33¢) Hat, Pane of 18	...	...	15.00	...

3273

3274

3275

3276

3272   3277-82   3283

1999 Commemoratives

Scott's No.		Mint Sheet	Plate Block	F-VF NH	F-VF Used
3272-73,75-76,86-92,3308-9,14-50,56-59, 3368-69 (58)		...	...	42.50	16.95
3272	33¢ Year of the Rabbit .... (20)	16.00	3.75	.85	.25
3273	33¢ Malcolm X, Black Heritage, SA (20)	18.95	4.50	.95	.25
3274	33¢ Victorian-Love Self-adhesive single	...	...	.80	.25
3274a	33¢ Victorian-Love Pane of 20 ...	...	...	15.00	...
3275	55¢ Victorian-Love SA .... (20)	25.00	5.75	1.30	.50
3276	33¢ Hospice-Care, SA .... (20)	14.00	3.25	.75	.25

1999 Flag over City Regular Issues

Scott's No.		Mint Sheet	Plate Block	F-VF NH	F-VF Used
3277	33¢ Red date, Water-activated .. (100)	72.50	3.75	.75	.15
3278	33¢ Black date, SA, Die-cut 11.1 (20)	14.00	3.25	.75	.20
3278v	33¢ Black date, Booklet Single, SA, Die-cut 11.1			.85	.20
3278vs	33¢ Bklt Sgl., Die-cut on 4 sides, from booklet of 20			1.20	.35
3278a	33¢ Booklet Pane of 4			3.50	...
3278b	33¢ Booklet Pane of 5			4.25	...
3278c	33¢ Booklet Pane of 6			5.25	...
3278d	33¢ Convertible Booklet of 10			8.25	...
3278e	33¢ Self-adhesive Pane of 20. BEP			16.50	...
3278F	33¢ Booklet single from Reprint Pane			.85	.20
3278Fv	33¢ Bklt.sgl.,Die-cut on 4 sides, from Reprint Pane			1.20	.35
3278Fg	33¢ Pane of 20, Reprint, SA, AVR			16.50	...

Note: The reprint is a bluer shade than the original - slight die-cutting differences.

3279	33¢ Red date, Booklet Single, SA, Die-cut 9.8			.85	.20
3279a	33¢ Red date, Booklet Pane of 10	...	...	8.25	...

1999-2000 Flag over City Regular Issue Coils

Scott's No.		Pl. Strip of 5	Pl. Strip of 3	F-VF NH	F-VF Used
3280	33¢ Red date, Water Activated, Small 1¼mm "1999" Date	6.00	4.75	.75	.20
3280a	33¢ Large 1 3/4mm "1999" Date(2000)	8.00	5.75	.75	.20
3281	33¢ Red date, SA Square, large 1 3/4mm date	6.00	4.75	.75	.20
3281c	33¢ Reprint with smaller 1¼m date	6.35	5.00	.80	.20
3282	33¢ Red date, SA, Rounded	6.00	4.75	.75	.20

Note: #3281 has square corners with backing same size as stamp.
#3282 has rounded corners with backing larger than the stamp.

1999 Flag Over Chalkboard

Scott's No.		Mint Sheet	Plate Block	F-VF NH	F-VF Used
3283	33¢ Flag. Self-adhesive single ...	...	...	.75	.25
3283a	33¢ Self-adhesive Pane of 18	...	...	13.95	...

1999 Commemoratives (continued)

3286   3287

3288   3289   3290   3291   3292

Scott's No.		Mint Sheet	Plate Block	F-VF NH	F-VF Used
3286	33¢ Irish Immigrants .... (20)	14.00	3.25	.75	.25
3287	33¢ Alfred Lunt & Lynn Fontaine (20)	14.00	3.25	.75	.25
3288-92	33¢ Arctic Animals, Strip of 5 .... (15)	11.75	(10) 8 50	3.95	3.00
3288-92	33¢ Arctic, Set of 5 Singles	...	...	3.85	1.50

1999 Sonoran Desert Miniature Sheet

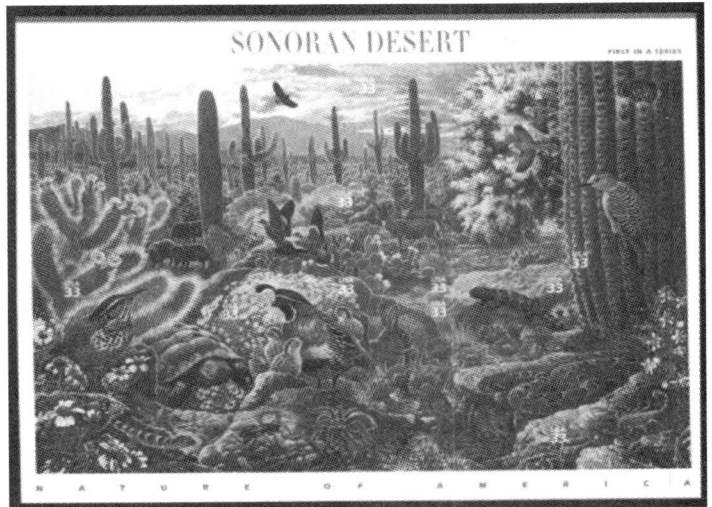

3293

3293	33¢ Sonoran Desert, Self-adh. Min.Sheet of 10...	...	...	7.95	...
3293a-j	33¢ Desert, Set of 10 Singles	...	...	7.85	5.00

3293a Cactus Wren, Brittlebush,Teddy Bear Cholla 3293b Desert Tortoise 3293c White-winged Dove Prickly Pear	3293d Gambel Quail 3293e Saguaro Cactus 3293f Desert Mule Deer 3293g Desert Cottontail Hedgehog Cactus	3293h Gila Monster 3293i W. Diamondback Rattlesnake, Cactus Mouse 3293j Gila Woodpecker

1999 Fruit Berries Self-Adhesive Regular Issues

3296,99,3305   3294,98,3302   3295,3300,3303   3297,3301,3304

3294-97	33¢ Bklt Sngls, Die-cut 11.2 x 11.7 (1999 Dates)	...		3.00	.80
3297b	33¢ Convertible Pane of 20 (1999 Dates)	...		14.50	...
3294a-97a	33¢ Booklet Singles (2000 Dates)	...		3.00	.80
3294-97a	33¢ Double-sided Block of 8 (2000 Dates)	...		6.00	...
3297d	33¢ Double-sided Pane of 20 (2000 Dates)	...		14.50	...
3298-3301	33¢ Booklet Singles, Die-cut 9.5 x 10	...		3.50	1.00
3301a	33¢ Booklet Pane of 4			3.50	
3301b	33¢ Booklet Pane of 5			4.25	...
3301c	33¢ Booklet Pane of 6			5.25	...
3302-5	33¢ Coils, Die-Cut 8.5 Vert., attd. (PS9)8.50 (PS5) 6.50			3.20	...
3302-5	33¢ Set of 4 Coil Singles			3.15	.90

1999 Daffy Duck Self-adhesive Souvenir Sheets

3306

Scott's No.		Mint Sheet	Plate Block	F-VF NH	F-VF Used
3306	33¢ Souvenir Sheet of 10	...	...	7.50	...
3306a	33¢ Single Stamp	...	...	.80	.25
3306b	33¢ Booklet Pane of 9 (left side)	...	...	6.25	...
3306c	33¢ Booklet Pane of 1 (right side)	...	...	1.75	...
3307	33¢ Souvenir Sheet of 10 with Special Die-cut that extends through paper backing...	...	...	10.75	...
3307a	33¢ Single stamp with special Die-cut	...	...	1.00	...
3307b	33¢ Booklet Pane of 9, Special Die-cut (left side)	...	...	7.95	...
3307c	33¢ Imperforate Bklt. Pane of 1 (right side)	...	...	3.50	...

1999 Commemoratives (continued)

3308   **3309**

3310   3311
3312   3313

3308	33¢ Ayn Rand, Literary	(20) 14.00	3.25	.75	.25
3309	33¢ Cinco de Mayo	(20) 14.00	3.25	.75	.25
3310-13	33¢ Tropical Flowers, SA, block .	...	...	3.50	...
3313b	33¢ Flowers, Self Adhesive Pane of 20	...	...	16.50	...
3310-13	33¢ Flowers, set of 4 singles	...	...	3.40	1.20
3313v	33¢ Flowers, 2 blocks of 4 back–to–back .	...	...	6.95	...

3314   **3315**   **3316**

1999 Commemoratives (continued)

3317   3318   3319   3320

3321   3322   3328   3327
3323   3324   3326   3325

Scott's No.		Mint Sheet	Plate Block	F-VF NH	F-VF Used
3314	33¢ John & William Bartram, SA	(20) 14.00	3.25	.75	.25
3315	33¢ Prostate Cancer, SA	(20) 14.00	3.25	.75	.25
3316	33¢ California Gold Rush	(20) 14.00	3.25	.75	.25
3317-20	33¢ Aquarium Fish, attd; SA	(20) 14.00	(8) 6.50	3.00	...
3317-20	33¢ Fish, set of 4 singles	...	...	2.95	1.20
3321-24	33¢ Xtreme Sports, block, SA ...	(20) 14.00	3.25	3.00	...
3321-24	33¢ Sports, strip of 4	...	...	3.00	...
3321-24	33¢ Sports, Set of 4 singles	...	...	2.95	1.20
3325-28	33¢ American Glass, block	(15) 11.00	...	3.00	2.25
3325-28	33¢ Glass, strip of 4	...	...	3.00	2.25
3325-28	33¢ Glass, Set of 4 singles	...	...	2.95	1.20
3325-28v	Folded Block of 15 in Booklet (BK277)	...	...	14.75	...

3329   **3330**   **3331**   **3332**

3334

3335

3336

3337

3333

3343   3344
3339   3340
3341   3342

3345 3346
3347 3348
3349 3350

3338

Scott's No.		Mint Sheet	Plate Block	F-VF NH	F-VF Used
3329	33¢ James Cagney, Legends of Hollywood Series	(20) 14.00	3.25	.75	.25
3330	55¢ William "Billy" Mitchell, SA	(20) 23.50	5.35	1.25	.50
3331	33¢ Honoring Those Who Served	(20) 14.00	3.25	.75	.25
3332	45¢ Universal Postal Union	(20) 18.75	5.50	1.00	.50
3333-37	33¢ All Aboard, 5 Trains, attd.	(20) 14.00	(10) 8.00	3.75	...
3333-37	33¢ Trains, Set of 5 singles.............	...	...	3.70	1.50
3333-37v	Folded Block of 15 in Booklet (BK278)	...	...	14.75	...
3338	33¢ Frederick Law Olmstead	(20) 14.00	3.25	.75	.25
3339-44	33¢ Hollywood Composers, attd.	(20) 14.50	(6) 5.25	4.50	3.95
3339-44	33¢ Composers, Top Plate Block of 8	...	6.75		
3339-44	33¢ Composers, set of 6 singles	...	...	4.40	2.40
3345-50	33¢ Broadway Songwriters, attd.	(20) 14.50	(6) 5.25	4.50	3.95
3345-50	33¢ Broadway, Top Plate Block of 8	...	6.75		
3345-50	33¢ Broadway, set of 6 singles	...	...	4.40	2.40

1999 Insects and Spiders Miniature Sheet

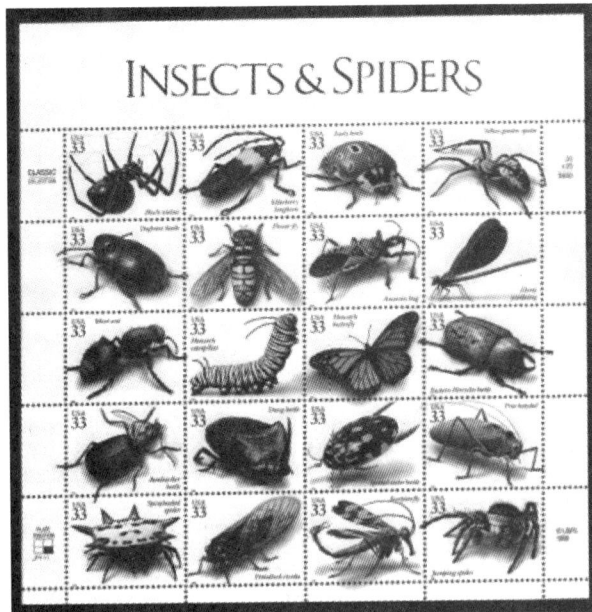

INSECTS & SPIDERS

3351

3351	33¢ Insects and Spiders Miniature Sheet of 20	...	...	14.95	10.95
3351a-t	33¢ Insects, set of 20 singles	...	...	14.85	9.95

3351a Black widow	3351g Assassin bug	3351n Dung beetle
3351b Elderberry longhorn	3351h Ebony jewelwing	3351o Spotted water
3351c Lady beetle	3351i Velvet ant	beetle
3351d Yellow garden spider	3351j Monarch caterpillar	3351p True katydid
3351e Dogbane beetle	3351k Monarch butterfly	3351q Spinybacked spider
3351f Flower fly	3351l Eastern hercules	3351r Periodical cicada
	beetle	3351s Scorpionfly
	3351m Bombantler beetle	3351t Jumping spider

3352

3353

3354

Scott's No.		Mint Sheet	Plate Block	F-VF NH	F-VF Used
	1999 Commemoratives (continued)				
3352	33¢ Hanukkah, #3318 design, SA	(20) 14.00	3.25	.75	.25
	1999 Regular Issue Coil Stamp				
3353	22¢ Uncle Sam, Perf 9 3/4	(PS5) 5.00	(PS3) 4.00	.50	.20
	1999 Commemoratives (continued)				
3354	33¢ North Atlantic Treaty Organ.	(20) 14.00	3.25	.75	.25

3355

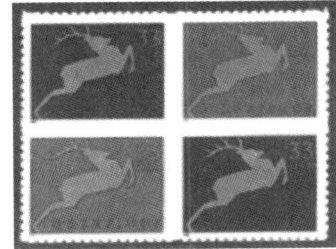

3356, 60 Red   3357,61 Blue
3358, 62 Purple   3359, 63 Green

3368

3369

3364 Red   3365 Blue   3366 Purple   3367 Green

3355	33¢ Madonna, booklet single, SA	...	...	.75	.20
3355v	33¢ Madonna, back-to-back booklet single, SA	...	...	1.50	...
3355a	33¢ Madonna, Pane of 20	...	...	14.00	...
3356-59	33¢ Deer, 4 designs, attd., SA ...	(20) 14.00	3.25	3.00	...
3356-59	33¢ Deer, strip of 4 from Sheet ...	...	...	3.00	...
3356-59	33¢ Deer, set of 4 singles from Sheet	...	...	2.95	1.00
3360-63	33¢ Deer, block of 4 from Pane of 20	...	...	3.00	...
3360-63	33¢ Deer, strip of 4 from Pane of 20	...	...	3.00	...
3360-63	33¢ Deer, set of 4 singles from Pane of 20	...	...	2.95	1.00
3360v-63v	33¢ set of 4 singles die-cut on 4 sides	...	...	4.00	1.60
3363a	33¢ Deer, Convertible Pane of 20, SA	...	...	14.00	...
	Note: 3356-59 have narrow borders. 3360-63 borders are much wider.				
3364-67	33¢ Deer, set of singles from Booklet of 15	...	...	3.50	1.20
3367a	33¢ Booklet Pane of 4	...	...	3.50	...
3367b	33¢ Booklet Pane of 5	...	...	4.25	...
3367c	33¢ Booklet Pane of 6	...	...	5.25	...
	Note: Designs of stamps in Deer Booklet of 15 are considerably Smaller than those in Sheet of 20 or Convertible Pane of 20				
3368	33¢ Kwanzaa, #3175 design, SA	(20) 14.00	3.25	.75	.25
3369	33¢ Millennium Baby, SA	(20) 14.00	3.25	.75	.25

2000 Commemoratives

3370

3371

3370-72,79-90,93-3402,14-17,38-46 (38)		...	...	23.95	...
3370	33¢ Year of the Dragon	(20) 14.00	3.25	.75	.25
3371	33¢ Black Heritage, Patricia Roberts Harris, SA	(20) 14.00	3.25	.75	.25

2000 U.S. Navy Submarines

3377a2

Scott's No.		Mint Sheet	Plate Block	F-VF NH	F-VF Used
3372	33¢ U.S. Navy Submarines	(20) 14.00	3.25	.75	.25
3377a1	22¢,33¢,55¢,60¢,$3.20 Booklet Pane of 5, Selvedge 1			11.50	...
3377a2	22¢,33¢,55¢,60¢,$3.20 Booklet Pane of 5, Selvedge 2			11.50	...
3377a	Prestige Booklet with 2 Panes (Selvedge 1 & 2)	...	...	22.75	...
Note: Selvedge 1 "THE DOLPHIN PIN", Selvedge 2 "THE SUBMARINE STAMPS"					
3373-77	22¢-$3.20 set of 5 Booklet Singles	...	...	11.50	6.25
3373	22¢ S Class Submarines	...	...	.55	.35
3374	33¢ Los Angeles Class	...	...	.80	.35
3375	55¢ Ohio Class	...	...	1.30	.65
3376	60¢ USS Holland	...	...	1.50	.75
3377	$3.20 Gato Class	...	...	7.65	4.50

2000 Pacific Coast Rain Forest Miniature Sheet of 10

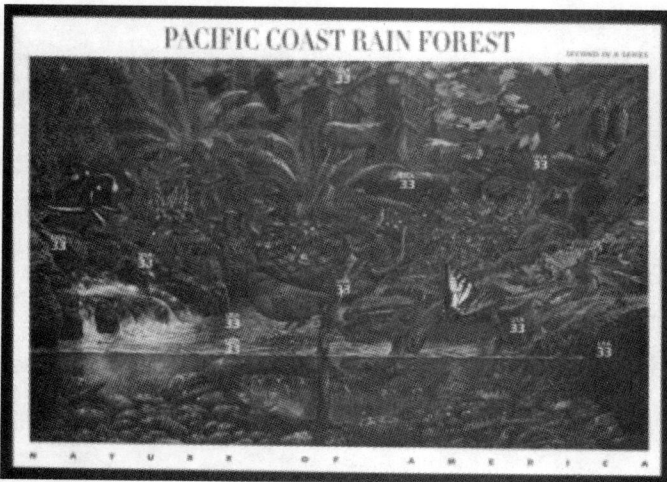

3378

3378	33¢ Rain Forest Miniature Sheet of 10	...	...	7.50	...
3378a-j	33¢ Rain Forest, set of 10 singles	...	...	7.50	4.95

3378a Harlequin Duck	3378g Pacific Giant	3378i Douglas Squirrel,
3378b Dwarf Oregongrape	Salamander, Rough	Foloise Lichen
3378c American Dipper	Skinned Newt	3378j Foloise Lichen,
3378d Cutthroat Trout	3378h Western Tiger	Banana slug
3378e Roosevelt Elk	Swallowtail	
3378f Winter Wren		

2000 Commemoratives (continued)

3379   3380   3381   3382   3383

3386   3387   3388   3384   3385

Scott's No.		Mint Sheet	Plate Block	F-VF NH	F-VF Used
3379-83	33¢ Lousie Nevelson, Wood Sculptures	(20) 14.00	(10) 8.25	3.75	2.75
3379-83	33¢ Nevelson, set of 5 singles	...	...	3.70	1.50
3384-88	33¢ Edwin Powell Hubble, Hubble Space Telescope Images	(20) 14.00	(10) 8.25	3.75	2.75
3384-88	33¢ Hubble, set of 5 singles	...	...	3.70	1.50

3389   3390   3397

3393   3394
3395   3396

3398

3391

3389	33¢ American Samoa	(20) 14.00	3.25	.75	.25
3390	33¢ Library of Congress	(20) 14.00	3.25	.75	.25

2000 Wile E. Coyote and Road Runner Souvenir Sheet of 10

3391	33¢ Souvenir Sheet of 10	...	...	7.50	...
3391a	33¢ Single stamp	...	...	.80	.25
3391b	33¢ Booklet Pane of 9 (left side)	...	...	6.25	...
3391c	33¢ Booklet Pane of 1 (right side)	...	...	1.75	...
3392	33¢ Souvenir Sheet of 10 with Special Die-cut that extends through paper backing + imperf.single	...	...	10.75	...
3392a	33¢ Single stamp with special die-cut from left side	...	...	1.00	...
3392b	33¢ Booklet Pane of 9 with special die-cut (left-side)	...	...	7.95	...
3392c	33¢ Imperforate Booklet Pane of 1 (right side)	...	...	3.50	...

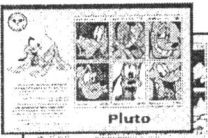

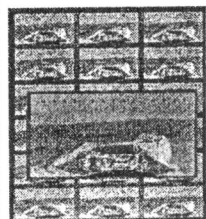

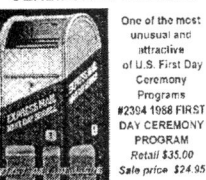

Scott's No.		Mint Sheet	Plate Block	F-VF NH	F-VF Used
3393-96	33¢ Distinguished Soldiers: John L. Hines, Omar Bradley, Alvin York, Audie Murphy, Block (20)	14.00	3.25	3.00	2.25
3393-96	33¢ Strip of 4	...	...	3.00	2.25
3393-96	33¢ Soldiers, set of 4 singles			2.95	1.20
3397	33¢ Summer Sports (20)	14.00	3.25	.75	.25
3398	33¢ Adoption (20)	14.00	3.25	.75	.25

| | 3399 | 3400 | 3401 | 3402 |

3399-3402	33¢ Youth Team Sports, Block (20)	14.00	3.25	3.00	2.25
3399-3402	33¢ Strip of 4	...	...	3.00	2.25
3399-3402	33¢ Team Sports, set of 4 singles	...	...	2.95	1.20

THE STARS AND STRIPES

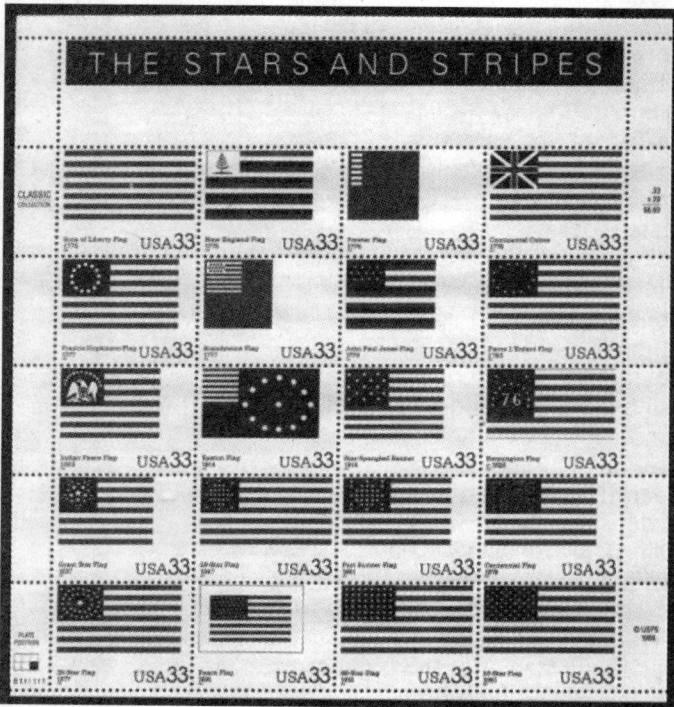

3403

2000 The Stars and Stripes

3403	33¢ Historic American Flags, Sheetlet of 20	...	14.50	...
3403a-t	33¢ Historic Flags, set of 20 singles	...	14.50	9.95

3403a Sons of Liberty	3403h Pierre L'Enfant	3403o Fort Sumter
3403b New England Flag	3403i Indian Peace Flag	3403p Centennial
3403c Forster Flag	3403j Easter Flag	3403q 38-Star FLag
3403d Continental Colors	3403k Star-Spangled Banner	3403r Peace Flag
3403e Francis Hopkinson	3403l Bennington Flag	3403s 48-Star Flag
3403f Brandywine Flag	3403m Great Star Flag	3403t 50-Star Flag
3403g John Paul Jones	3403n 29-Star Flag	

| 3404 | 3405 | 3406 | 3407 |

2000 Fruit Berries Self-adhesive Linerless Coils with "2000" Date

3404-7	33¢ Blueberry,Raspberry, Strawberry,Blackberry,Strip of 4 (PS9)8.50 (PS5) 6.50	3.00	...
3404-7	33¢ Berries, set of 4 singles	... ...	1.00

2000 Legends of Baseball

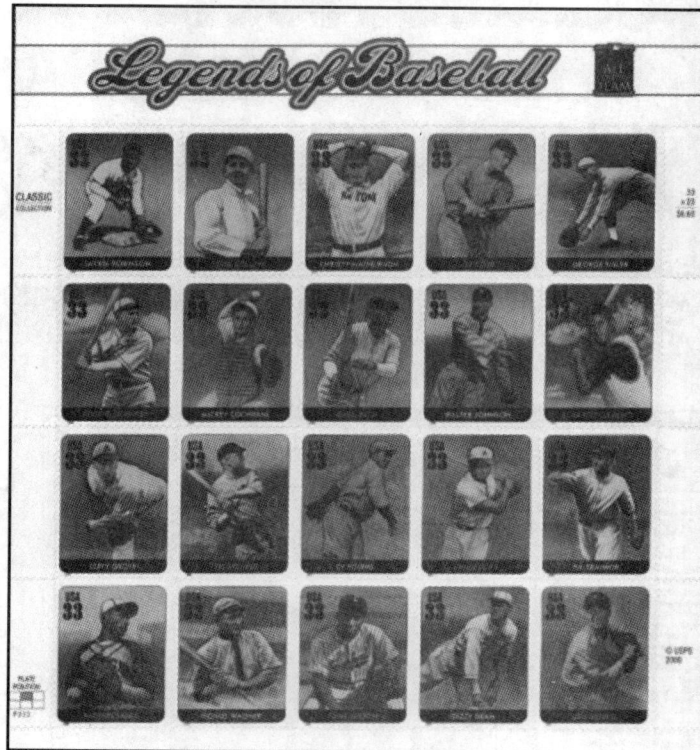

3408

Scott's No.		Mint Sheet	Plate Block	F-VF NH	F-VF Used
3408	33¢ Legends of Baseball Sheet of 20	...	...	13.50	12.50
3408a-t	33¢ Baseball, Set of 20 Singles	...	...	13.35	9.95

3408a Jackie Robinson	3408h Babe Ruth	3408o Pie Traynor
3408b Eddie Collins	3408i Walter Johnson	3408p Satchel Paige
3408c Christy Mathewson	3408j Roberto Clemente	3408q Honus Wagner
3408d Ty Cobb	3408k Lefty Grove	3408r Josh Gibson
3408e George Sisler	3408l Tris Speaker	3408s Dizzy Dean
3408f Rogers Hornsby	3408m Cy Young	3408t Lou Gehrig
3408g Mickey Cochrane	3408n Jimmie Foxx	

2000 Space Achievement and Exploration Souvenir Sheets

3409-13	60¢-$11.75 set of 5 souvenir sheets	...	86.50	...
3409	60¢ Probing the Vastness of Space, sheet of 6	...	8.25	...
3410	$1 Exploring the Solar System, sheet of 5	...	11.50	...
3411	$3.20 Escaping the Gravity of Earth, sheet of 2	...	14.50	...
3412	$11.75 Space Achievement and Exploration, sheet of 1	...	26.95	...
3413	$11.75 Landing on the Moon, hologram sheet of 1	...	26.95	...

PROBING THE VASTNESS OF SPACE

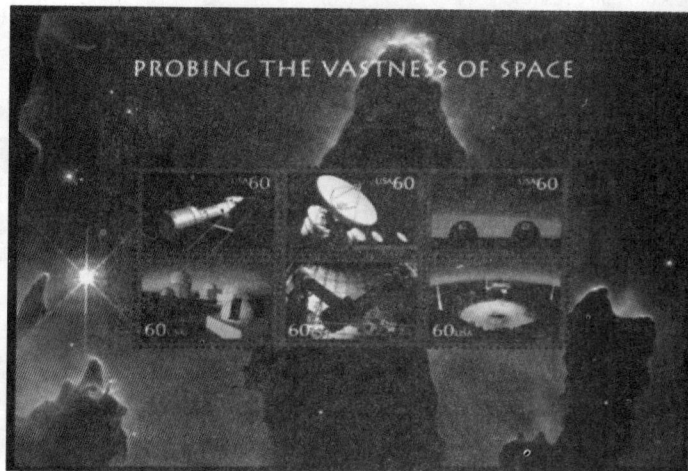

3409

3410

3411

3412

3413

| 3414 | 3415 | 3416 | 3417 |

Scott's No.		Mint Sheet	Plate Block	F-VF NH	F-VF Used
	2000 Commemoratives (continued)				
3414-17	33¢ "Stampin' the Future,Strip-4, SA	13.50	3.15	2.80	..
3414-17	33¢ "Stampin' the Future, set of 4 singles	...	...	2.75	1.20
	2000-2001 Distinguished Americans, Bi-Color				

3420   3426   3431

3420	10¢ General Joseph W. Stillwell	(50) 9.85	1.25	.20	.20
3426	33¢ Claude Pepper	12.95	2.95	.65	.20
3431	76¢ Hattie W. Caraway (2001)	28.75	6.50	1.50	.40

3439

3440

3441

3442

3443

3438

3445

3444

3446

3447

Scott's No.		Mint Sheet	Plate Block	F-VF NH	F-VF Used
3438	33¢ California Statehood, SA	12.95	2.95	.65	.25
3439-43	33¢ Deep Sea Creatures, attd.	(15) 9.75	(10) 6.75	3.25	2.75
3439-43	33¢ Sea Creatures, set of 5 singles	...	...	3.20	1.50
3444	33¢ Thomas Wolfe	12.95	2.95	.65	.25
3445	33¢ The White House, SA	12.95	2.95	.65	.25
3446	33¢ Edward G. Robinson	12.95	2.95	.65	.25

2000 Presorted Standard Coil

3447	(10¢) New York Public Library Lion	(PS5)2.40 (PS3) 1.95		.45	.20

2000 Non-Denominated Regular Issues

3448-50   3451   3452-53

3448	(34¢) Flag over Farm, Perf.11	12.75	2.85	.65	.20
3449	(34¢) Flag over Farm, SA, Die-cut 11.5, Small "2000" Date	18.75	4.50	.95	.30
3450	(34¢) Flag over Farm, SA Booklet Single, Die-cut 8, Large "2000" Date	...	...	.65	.20
3450a	(34¢) Flag over Farm, ATM Pane of 18	...	...	11.50	...
3451	(34¢) Statue of Liberty, SA, Booklet Single, Die-cut 11			.65	.20
3451v	(34¢) Liberty, Die-cut on 4 sides from Pane of 20			.95	.35
3451a	(34¢) Statue of Liberty, Convertible Pane of 20...			12.75	...
3451b	(34¢) Statue of Liberty, Booklet Pane of 4	...		2.60	...
3451c	(34¢) Statue of Liberty, Booklet Pane of 6	...		3.90	...
3452	(34¢) Liberty, Perforated Coil	(PS5) 5.25 (PS3)3.95		.65	.20
3453	(34¢) Liberty, SA Die-cut Coil	(PS5) 5.25 (PS3)3.95		.65	.20

3454,58,65   3455,59,64   3456,60,62   3457,61,63

3454-57	(34¢) Flowers, Block of 4 from #3457b, Die-cut 10½x10 3/4 Pane of 20	...	...	2.60	...
3454-57	(34¢) Flowers, Double-sided Block of 8 from #3457b	...	...	5.20	...
3454-57	(34¢) Flowers, set of 4 singles	...	...	2.55	1.00
3457b	(34¢) Flowers, Die-cut 10½ x 10 3/4, Double-sided Pane of 20	...	...	12.75	...

Scott's No.		Mint Sheet	Plate Block	F-VF NH	F-VF Used
3454v-57v	(34¢) Flowers, from Booklet BK281,Die-cut 10½x10 3/4			2.60	...
3457c	(34¢) Flowers, Booklet Pane of 4	...	...	2.60	...
3457d	(34¢) Flowers, Booklet Pane of 6 #3456-57 (1), #3454-55 (2)	...	...	3.90	...
3457e	(34¢) Flowers, Booklet Pane of 6 #3454-55 (1), #3456-57 (2)	...	...	3.90	...
3458-61	(34¢) Flowers, Block of 4 from #3461b or c, Die-cut 11½x11 3/4	...	...	9.95	...
3454-61	(34¢) Flowers, Back-to-Back Block of 8 with both #3454-57 and #3458-61	...	...	14.75	...
3461b	(34¢) Double-sided Pane of 20 (3-#3454-57, 2-#3458-61)	...	...	24.75	...
3461c	(34¢_ Double-sided Pane of 20 (2-#3454-57, 3-#3458-61)	...	...	32.75	...
3462-65	(34¢) Flowers, SA Die-cut Coils	(PS9)11.75 (PS5)7.75		3.90	1.50

2001 Regular Issues, With Denominations

3466,76-77,84-85   3468,3475   3469-70   3471

3472   3473

3466	34¢ Liberty, SA Die-cut 9 3/4 Coil, Rounded corners, stamps separate on rolls	(PS5) 5.25 (PS3) 3.95		.65	.15
3468	21¢ Bison, SA	7.85	1.85	.40	.20
3469	34¢ Flag over Farm, Perforated	(100)63.50	2.95	.65	.15
3470	34¢ Flag over Farm, SA Die-cut	12.75	2.95	.65	.15
3471	55¢ Art-Deco Eagle, SA	20.95	4.75	1.10	.40
3472	$3.50 U.S. Capitol, SA	130.00	30.00	6.75	2.95
3473	$12.25 Washington Monument, SA	450.00	100.00	23.50	11.95
3475	21¢ Bison, SA Die-cut Coil	(PS5) 3.15 (PS3)		.40	.20
3476	34¢ Liberty, Perforated Coil	(PS5) 5.25 (PS3)		.65	.15
3477	34¢ Liberty, SA Die-cut Coil, Square corners, stamps together on roll	(PS5) 5.25 (PS3) 3.95		.65	.15

3478,89   3479,90   3480,88   3481,87

3482-83   3491   3492

3478-81	34¢ Flowers, SA Die-cut Coil	(PS9) 7.75 (PS5) 5.25		2.60	1.00

Note: #3478,3489 Green Background #3479,3490 Red Background
#3480,3488 Tan Background #3481,3487 Purple Background

3482	20¢ G. Washington, Die-cut 11 1/4x11 SA Single Convertible Pane (3482a)	...		.40	.20
3482a	20¢ G. Wash., Die-cut 11 1/4x11 Conv. Pane of 10	...		3.85	...
3482v	20¢ G. Wash., Die-cut 11 1/4x11 SA Single from Booklet Panes 4 and 6 (3482b and c)	...		.40	.20
3482b	20¢ G. Wash., Die-cut 11 1/4x11 Booklet Pane of 4	...		1.60	...
3482c	20¢ G. Wash., Die-cut 11 1/4x11 Booklet Pane of 6	...		2.40	...
3483	20¢ G. Washington, Die-cut 11 1/4x11, SA Single from Convertible Pane (3483c)	...		1.60	...
3482-83	20¢ Horiz. Pair from Covert. Pane (3483c)	...		2.00	...
3483c	20¢ G. Wash., Covert. Pane of 10 (3483c)	...		9.75	...
3483v	20¢ G. Wash., Die-cut 10 1/2x11 SA Single from Booklet Panes 4 and 6 (3483a or b)			2.75	...
3482v-83v	20¢ Horiz. Pair from Bk. Pane 4 or 6 (3483a or b)	...		3.15	...
3483a	20¢ G. Wash., Bklt. Pane of 4 (2-#3482v, 2-#3483v)			6.00	...
3483b	20¢ G. Wash., Bklt. Pane of 6 (3-#3482v, 3-#3483v)			9.00	...
3484	34¢ Liberty, SA Single from Booklet Panes			.65	...

2000 Non-Denominated Regular Issues (continued)

Scott's No.		Mint Sheet	Plate Block	F-VF NH	F-VF Used
3484a	34¢ Liberty, Booklet Pane of 4	...	...	...	2.60 ...
3484b	34¢ Liberty, Booklet Pane of 6	...	...	3.90	...
3485	34¢ Statue of Liberty, SA Single from Convertible Pane			.65	.15
3485a	34¢ Liberty, Convertible Pane of 10	...	...	6.50	...
3485b	34¢ Liberty, Convertible Pane of 20	...	...	12.75	...
3487-90	34¢ Flowers, Block of 4 from Pane of 20	...	...	2.60	...
3487-90	34¢ Flowers, Double-sided Block of 8	...	...	5.20	...
3487-90	34¢ Flowers, set of 4 singles	...	...	2.55	1.00
3490e	34¢ Flowers, Double-sided Pane of 20	...	...	12.75	...

2001 Regular Issues, With Denominations (continued)

Scott's No.		Mint Sheet	Plate Block	F-VF NH	F-VF Used
3487v-90v	34¢ Flowers, Block of 4 from Booklet of 20	...	...	2.60	...
3490b	34¢ Flowers, Booklet Pane of 4	...	...	2.60	...
3490c	34¢ Flowers, Booklet Pane of 6, #3489-90 (1), #3487-88 (2)	...	...	3.90	...
3490d	34¢ Flowers, Booklet Pane of 6, #3487-88 (1), #3489-90 (2)	...	...	3.90	...
3491-92	34¢ Apple & Orange Booklet Pair	...	...	1.30	...
3491-92	34¢ Apple & Orange set of 2 singles	...	...	...	.50
3492b	34¢ Apple & Orange Convertible Pane of 20	...	...	12.75	...

Note: Prices on 2000 Non-denominated and 2001 Denominated Regular Issues are subject to change due to lack of information on availability of some varieties.

2001 Rose and Love Letters, Self-Adhesive

3496   3497-98   3499

Scott's No.		Mint Sheet	Plate Block	F-VF NH	F-VF Used
3496	(34¢) Booklet Single	...	...	.65	.20
3496a	(34¢) Convertible Pane of 20	...	...	12.75	...
3497	34¢ Single from Convertible Pane, Die-cut 11¼	...	...	.65	.20
3497a	34¢ Convertible Pane of 20	...	...	12.75	...
3498	34¢ Single from Booklet of 20, Die-cut 11½x10 3/4	...	...	1.00	.20
3498a	34¢ Booklet Pane of 4	...	...	3.85	...
3498b	34¢ Booklet Pane of 6	...	...	5.75	...
3499	55¢ Rose & Love Letters	20.95	4.75	1.10	.40

2001 Commemoratives

3500   3501

Scott's No.		Mint Sheet	Plate Block	F-VF NH	F-VF Used
3500	34¢ Year of the Snake	12.95	2.95	.65	.25
3501	34¢ Roy Wilkins, SA	12.95	2.95	.65	.25

2001 American Illustrators Miniature Sheet of 20

3502

2001 American Illustrators Miniature Sheet of 20 (continued)

Scott's No.		Mint Sheet	Plate Block	F-VF NH	F-VF Used
3502	34¢ Illustrators, Sheetlet of 20, SA	...	...	12.95	...
3502a-t	34¢ Illustrators, set of 20 singles	...	...	12.85	10.95

3502a James Montgomery Flagg
3502b Maxfield Parrish
3502c J.C.Leyendecker
3502d Robert Fawcett```
3502e Coles Phillips
3502f Al Parker
3502g A. B.Frost
3502h Howard Pyle
3502i Rose O'Neill
3502j Dean Cornwell

3502k Edwin Austin Abbey
3502l Jessie Wilcox Smith
3502m Neysa McMein
3502n Jon Whitcomb
3502o Harvey Dunn
3502p Frederic Remington
3502q Rockwell Kent
3502r N.C.Wyeth
3502s Norman Rockwell
3502t John Held Jr.

2001 Commemoratives (continued)

3503   3504

Scott's No.		Mint Sheet	Plate Block	F-VF NH	F-VF Used
3503	34¢ Diabetes Awareness, SA	12.95	2.95	.65	.25
3504	34¢ Nobel Prize Centennial	12.95	2.95	.65	.25

2001 Pan-American Inverts Souvenir Sheet

3505

Scott's No.		Mint Sheet	Plate Block	F-VF NH	F-VF Used
3505	1¢,2¢,4¢,80¢ (4) Souvenir Sheet of 7	...	...	6.50	...
3505a	1¢ Pan-American Invert single	...	...	.20	.20
3505b	2¢ Pan-American Invert single	...	...	.20	.20
3505c	4¢ Pan-American Invert single	...	...	.20	.20
3505d	80¢ Pan-American Exposition	...	...	1.60	.95

2001 Great Plains Prairie Miniature Sheet

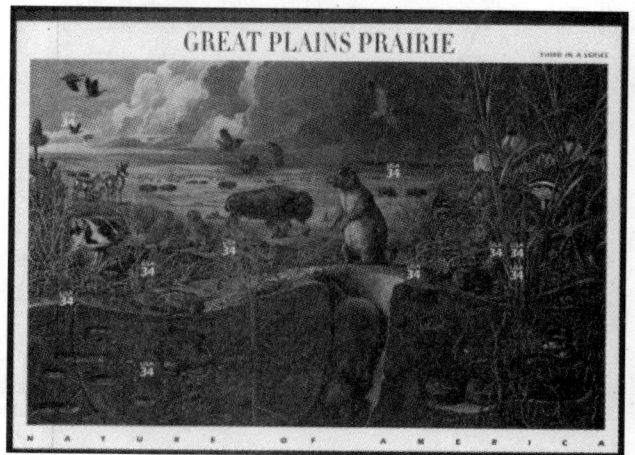

3506

Scott's No.		Mint Sheet	Plate Block	F-VF NH	F-VF Used
3506	34¢ Prairie Miniature Sheet of 10	...	...	6.50	...
...	34¢ Prairie set of 10 singles	...	...	6.50	...
3506a-j					4.95

2001 Commemoratives (continued)

Snoopy

U.S. Veterans

Scott's No.		Mint Sheet	Plate Block	F-VF NH	F-VF Used
...	34¢ "Peanuts", Snoopy World War I Flying Ace, SA	12.95	2.95	.65	.25
...	34¢ U.S. Veterans, Flag, SA	12.95	2.95	.65	.25
...	34¢ Frida Kahlo	12.95	2.95	.65	.25

2001 Legendary Major League Baseball Fields

...	34¢ Legendary Baseball Fields	12.95 (10)	7.00	6.50	...
...	34¢ Baseball Fields, set of 10 singles	...	...	6.50	4.50

2001 Commemoratives (continued)

...	34¢ Leonard Bernstein	12.95	2.95	.65	.25
...	34¢ Lucille Ball	12.95	2.95	.65	.25
...	34¢ Amish Quilts, 4 designs, SA	12.95	2.95	2.60	...
...	34¢ Amish Quilts, set of 4 singles	...	...	2.55	1.20
...	34¢ Carnivorous Plants, 4 designs, SA	12.95	2.95	2.60	...
...	34¢ Carnivorous Plants, set of 4 singles	...	...	2.55	1.20
...	34¢ Islamic Festival, Eid	12.95	2.95	.65	.25
...	34¢ Enrico Fermi	12.95	2.95	.65	.25

Note: Listings for stamps issued after editing is complete are tentative and subject to change.

SEMI POSTAL STAMPS
1998 Breast Cancer Research

B1

		Mint Sheet	Plate Block	F-VF NH	F-VF Used
B1	(32¢ + 8¢) Breast Cancer, 1st Class Rate (20)	19.00	4.50	1.00	.50

MINT COMMEMORATIVE YEAR SETS

Year	Scott's No.	Qty.	F-VF NH
1926-27	627-29, 43-44 ... 5		19.75
1928	645-50 6		31.75
1929	651, 54-57, 80-81	7	22.75
1930-31	682-3,88-90,702-3	7	5.25
1932	716-19, 24-25 6		6.50
1933	726-29, 32-34 7		2.70
1934	736-39 4		1.15
1935	772-75 4		.85
1936	776-84 6		3.50
1937	795-802 8		2.40
1938	835-38 4		1.30
1939	852-58 7		4.25
1940	894-902 9		1.85
1941-3	903-08 6		2.30
1944	922-26 5		1.10
1945	927-38 12		1.90
1946	939-44 6		1.10
1947	945-52 8		1.90
1948	953-80 28		4.50
1949	981-86 6		1.10
1950	987-97 11		1.70
1951	998-1003 6		.95
1952	1004-16 13		2.00
1953	1017-28 12		1.80
1954	1029,60-63 5		.75
1955	1064-72 9		1.95
1956	1073-85 13		4.25
1957	1086-99 14		2.15
1958	1100,04-23 21		3.25
1959	1124-38 15		2.60

Year	Scott's No.	Qty.	F-VF NH
1960	1139-73 35		6.15
1961	1174-90 17		4.75
1962	1191-1207 17		2.50
1963	1230-41 12		2.15
1964	1242-60 19		4.60
1965	1261-76 16		2.95
1966	1306-22 17		3.00
1967	1323-37 15		4.95
1968	1339-40,42-64 25		7.75
1969	1365-86 22		8.75
1970	1387-92,1405-22	24	7.50
1971	1423-45 23		5.95
1972	1446-74 29		7.50
1973	1475-1508 34		8.50
1974	1525-52 28		8.95
1975	1553-80 28		8.95
1976	1629-32,83-85		
	1690-1703 21		9.75
1977	1704-30 27		10.50
1978	1731-33,44-69 29		14.50
1979	1770-1802 33		15.50
1980	1803-10,21-43 31		15.95
1981	1874-79,1910-45	42	24.95
1982	1950-52,2003-4,955		
	2006-30 30		21.50
1983	2031-65 35		22.95
1984	2066-2109 44		32.95
1985	2110,37-47,52-66	27	36.25

Year	Scott's No.	Qty.	F-VF NH
1986	2167,2202-4,10-11,		
	2220-24,2235-2245		18.50
1987	2246-51,75,		
	2336-38,2349-54,		
	2360-61,2367-68	20	16.50
1988	2339-46,69-80,		
	86-93,2399-2400	30	26.85
1989	2347,2401-04,		
	10-18,20-28,34-37..27		25.00
1990	2348,2349-40,2442,		
	44-49,96-2500,		
	2506-15 25		27.50
1991	2532-35,37-38,50-51,		
	2553-58,60-61,67,		
	2578-79 19		17.00
1992	2611-23,30-41,98-99,		
	2700-04,10-14,20		
	 38		34.50
1993	2721-30,46-59,66,		
	2771-74,79-89,91-94,		
	2804-06 47		43.95
1994	2807-12,14C-28,2834-36,		
	39,48-68,2871-72,		
	76 49		30.75

Year	Scott's No.	Qty.	F-VF NH
1995	2948,50-58,61-68,74		
	76-80,82-92,98-99		
	3001-7,19-23 49		46.50
1996	3024,30,58-67,69-70		
	3072-88,90-3104,		
	3106-11,18 53		48.50
1997	3120-21,3125,30-31,		
	3134-35,3141,43-50,		
	3152-75 40		35.00
1998	3179-81,3192-3203,3206		
	3211-27,30-35,37-48		
	 51		38.50
1999	3272-73, 75-76, 86-92,		
	3308-9, 14-50, 54,		
	3356-59, 68-69 .. 58		42.50
2000	3370-72, 79-90, 93-2402,		
	3414-17, 38-46 ... 38		23.95

UNITED STATES POSTAL SERVICE MINT SETS
Commemoratives and Definitives
These are complete with folder or hard cover albums as produced by the U.S. Postal Service

Year	Scott's Nos.	# Stamps	Price
	Commemoratives		
1968 (1)	"Cover #334-890", #1339-40,		
	1342-64,C74 26		175.00
1968 (2)	"Cover #369-245", Contents		
	same as (1)		150.00
1969	#1365-86,C76 23		120.00
1970	#1387-92,1405-22 24		175.00
1971 (1)	"Mini Album" #1396,1423-45 .. 24		40.00
1971 (2)	Black strips, Contents same as (1)		120.00
1972	#1446-74,C84-85 31		22.50
1973	#1475-1504,1507-08,C86 33		18.00
1974	#1505-06,1525-51 29		15.00
1975	#1553-80 28		17.50
1976	#1629-32,1633/82 (1 single),		
	1683-85,1690-1702 21		29.50
1977	#1704-30 27		15.00
1978	#1731-33,44-56,58-69 28		17.50
1979	#1770-94,1799-1802,C97 30		18.50
1980	#1795-98,1803-04,21,23-43 ... 28		23.50
1981	#1874-79,1910-26,28-45 41		30.00
1982	#1950,52,1953/2002 (1 single),		
	2003-04,06-24,26-30 29		26.50
1983	#2031-65,C101-12 47		45.00
1984	#2066-71,73-2109 43		26.75
1985	#2110,37-47,52-66 27		35.00
1986	#2167,2201a,2202-04,2209a,		
	2210-11,2216a-9i (1 single),		
	2220-24,35-45 25		27.50
1987	Soft Cover, #2246-51,2274a,75,		
	2286/2335 (1 single), 2336-38,		
	2349-54,59a,60-61,66a,67-68 . 24		39.50
1987	Hard Cover, Same contents		57.50
1988	Soft Cover, #2339-46,69-80,		
	85a,86-93,95-99,2400,C117 37		42.50
1988	Hard Cover, Same contents		57.50
1989	#2347,2401-04,09a,10-14,		
	2416-18,20-28 22		45.00

Year	Scott's Nos.	# Stamps	Price
1990	#2348,2415,39-40,42,44-49,74a,		
	2496-2515 32		50.00
1991	#2532-35,37-38,49a,50-51,53-67,		
	2577a,78,80 or 81,82-85,		
	C130-31 33		57.50
1992	Hard Cover, #2611-23,30-41,46a,		
	2647/96 (1 single), 2697-99,		
	2700-04,2709a,10-14 41		57.50
1993	Hard Cover, #2721-23,31-37,45a,		
	2746-59,64a,65-66,70a,78a,79-89,		
	2791-94,2804-05 47		59.50
1994	Hard Cover, #2807-12,2814-28,		
	2833a,34-36,38-40,2841a,2847a,		
	2848-69,71-72 52		69.50
1995	Hard Cover, #2587,2876,2948,		
	2950-58,61-68,73a,74-92,97a,		
	2999-3007,3019-23 55		79.50
1996	Hard Cover #3024-29,58-65,67-70		
	3072-88,90-3111,3118-19 59		69.50
1996	Soft Cover,#3024,3025-29(1),3058-60		
	,61-64(1),65,67,68a-t(1),3069-70,72-76(1),		
	77-80(1),81-82, 3083-86(1),87-88,90,		
	91-95(1),3096-99(1),3100-3(1),3104,		
	3105a-o(1)3106-7, 3108-11(1),18,		
	19a-b(1) 29		45.00
1997	Hard Cover #3120-21, 23-27,		
	3130-31, 34-37, 39a, 40a		
	3141-46, 51-52, 54-77..... 47		65.00
1998	Hard Cover #3179-81, 92-3204,		
	3206 10a, 11-19, 21-27, 30-44,		
	3249-52 52		59.95
1999	Hard Cover #3272-76, 86-93		
	3306, 3308, 10-29, 37-51, 54,		
	3355(4), 3356-59 59		79.95

Year	Scott's Nos.	# Stamps	Price
2000	Hard Cover #3369-72,78-91,		
	3393-3402,3408,14-17,38-46	78	39.50
	Definitives & Stationery		
1980	#1738-42,1805-11,13,22,59,C98-100,		
	U590,U597-99,UC53,UX82-86 .. 27		55.00
1981	#1582b,1818,1819-20 PRS,57-58,		
	65,89a,90,91 PR,93a,94,95 PR,		
	96a,1903 PR,1906-08 PRS,1927,		
	46,47-48 PRS 22		37.50
1982	#1615v PR,1845,55,60,66,97A PR,		
	1698A PR,1901 PR,1904 PR,49a,		
	1951,2005 PR,2025,U591,U602-03,		
	UC55,UX94-97,UXC20 22		22.50
1983	#1844,46-48,61,97 PR,98 PR,99 PR,		
	1900 PR,O127-29,O130,32,35 PR,		
	U604-05,UC56-57,UO73,UX98-100,		
	UXC21,UZ2 25		17.50
1984	#1853,62,64,68,1902 PR,1905 PR,		
	2072,U606,UX101-04 12		12.50
1987-88	#2115b,2127,29,30av,69,76-78,80,		
	2182,83,88,92,2226,52-66,C118-19,		
	O138A-B,40-41 35		50.00
1989-90	#2127av,73,84,86,94A,2280v,2419,		
	2431 (6),43a,52,75a,76,O143,U611,		
	U614-18,UC62,UO79-80,UX127-38,		
	UX143-48,UX150-52 44		62.50

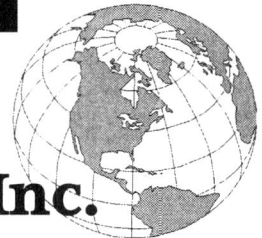

AIR MAIL STAMPS

C1-3   C4   C5   C6

1918 First Issue VF Used + 35% (B)

Scott's No.			NH		Unused		Used
		VF	F-VF	VF	F-VF		F-VF
C1-3	Set of 3	485.00	360.00	325.00	240.00		95.00
C1	6¢ Curtiss Jenny, Orange	135.00	100.00	87.50	65.00		28.50
C1	Arrow Block of 4	595.00	425.00	380.00	285.00		...
C1	Center Line Block of 4	650.00	485.00	435.00	325.00		...
C1	Plate Block of 6	1350.00	1000.00	950.00	700.00		...
C2	16¢ Green	180.00	135.00	125.00	90.00		35.00
C2	Arrow Block of 4	825.00	585.00	550.00	395.00		...
C2	Center Line Block of 4	950.00	700.00	650.00	475.00		...
C2	Plate Block of 6	2200.00	1650.00	1500.00	1150.00		...
C3	24¢ Carmine Rose & Blue	200.00	150.00	135.00	100.00		40.00
C3	Arrow Block of 4	875.00	650.00	600.00	450.00		...
C3	Center Line Block of 4	1050.00	775.00	700.00	525.00		...
C3	Plate Block of 12	2600.00	1975.00	1800.00	1350.00		...

1923 Second Issue VF Used + 35% (B)

		VF	F-VF	VF	F-VF		F-VF
C4-6	Set of 3	415.00	300.00	270.00	200.00		65.00
C4	8¢ Propeller, Dark Green	51.50	37.50	33.50	25.00		13.00
C4	Plate Block of 6	485.00	365.00	325.00	250.00		...
C5	16¢ Emblem, Dark Blue	195.00	140.00	125.00	90.00		27.50
C5	Plate Block of 6	3600.00	2700.00	2450.00	1850.00		...
C6	24¢ Biplane, Carmine	210.00	150.00	135.00	100.00		28.50
C6	Plate Block of 6	4000.00	3000.00	2750.00	2100.00		...

C7-9   C10

1926-27 Map & Mail Planes VF Used + 30% (B)

		VF	F-VF	VF	F-VF		F-VF
C7-9	Set of 3	29.75	22.50	19.75	14.95		4.25
C7-9	Plate Blocks set of 3	330.00	250.00	230.00	175.00		...
C7	10¢ Map, Dark Blue	5.65	4.25	3.75	2.85		.40
C7	Plate Block of 6	78.50	60.00	52.50	40.00		...
C8	15¢ Map, Brown	6.25	4.75	4.25	3.25		2.25
C8	Plate Block of 6	85.00	65.00	58.50	45.00		...
C9	20¢ Map, Green (1927) ...	19.50	14.50	12.75	9.75		1.90
C9	Plate Block of 6	185.00	140.00	130.00	100.00		...

1927 Lindbergh Tribute VF + 30% (B)

Scott's No.		NH VF	NH F-VF	Unused VF	Unused F-VF	Used F-VF
C10	10¢ Lindbergh, Dark Blue	14.00	10.50	9.00	7.00	2.25
C10	Plate Block of 6	250.00	190.00	175.00	135.00	...
C10a	10¢ Booklet Pane of 3	175.00	125.00	120.00	85.00	...

C11   C12,C16-17,C19

1928 Beacon VF Used + 40% (B)

C11	5¢ Carmine & Blue	8.50	6.00	6.00	4.25	.65
C11	Arrow Block of 4	36.50	27.00	26.75	19.00	...
C11	Plate Block of 6	75.00	52.50	51.50	40.00	...
C11	Pl.Block of 6 Double "TOP"	185.00	125.00	125.00	90.00	...
C11	Pl.Block of 8 No "TOP"	325.00	225.00	225.00	175.00	...

1930 Winged Globe, Flat Press, Perf. 11 VF Used + 30% (B)

C12	5¢ Violet	17.00	13.00	11.75	8.75	.40
C12	Plate Block of 6	295.00	225.00	215.00	160.00	...

1930 GRAF ZEPPELIN ISSUE VF Used + 25% (B)

C13   C14

C15   C18

C13-15	Set of 3	2850.00	2300.00	2000.00	1650.00	1275.00
C13	65¢ Zeppelin, Green	435.00	350.00	340.00	270.00	210.00
C13	Plate Block of 6	3900.00	3100.00	2900.00	2300.00	...
C14	$1.30 Zeppelin, Brown	975.00	800.00	700.00	575.00	425.00
C14	Plate Block of 6	9500.00	7500.00	6800.00	5500.00	...
C15	$2.60 Zeppelin, Blue	1575.00	1250.00	1100.00	875.00	700.00
C15	Plate Block of 6	15000.00	11500.00	10700.00	8500.00	...

Scott's No.	NH VF	F-VF	Unused VF	F-VF	Used F-VF

1931-32 Rotary Press, Perf. 10½x11, Designs of #C12 VF Used + 30% (B)

	NH VF	F-VF	Unused VF	F-VF	Used F-VF
C16 5¢ Winged Globe, Violet	10.50	8.00	7.00	5.25	.50
C16 Plate Block of 4	140.00	110.00	100.00	75.00	...
C17 8¢ Winged Globe (1932)	3.75	2.85	2.70	2.00	.35
C17 Plate Block of 4	56.50	42.50	39.00	30.00	...

1933 Century of Progress VF Used + 20% (B)

	NH VF	F-VF	Unused VF	F-VF	Used F-VF
C18 50¢ Graf Zeppelin, Green	150.00	120.00	105.00	85.00	77.50
C18 Plate Block of 6	1275.00	1050.00	925.00	750.00	...

1934 Winged Globe, Design of #C12 VF Used + 30% (B)

	NH VF	F-VF	Unused VF	F-VF	Used F-VF
C19 6¢ Orange	4.00	3.00	3.25	2.40	.20
C19 Plate Block of 4	37.50	28.50	29.50	21.75	...

C20

C21-22

C23

C24

1935-37 Trans-Pacific Issue (VF Used + 25%)

	NH VF	F-VF	Unused VF	F-VF	Used F-VF
C20-22 Clipper Set of 3	29.50	23.00	23.00	18.50	6.50
C20-22 Plate Block set of 3	360.00	285.00	295.00	230.00	...
C20 25¢ China Clipper	2.00	1.60	1.60	1.25	1.10
C20 Plate Block of 6	35.00	27.50	28.00	22.50	...
C21 20¢ China Clipper (1937) ...	13.50	10.75	10.50	8.50	1.50
C21 Plate Block of 6	170.00	135.00	140.00	110.00	...
C22 50¢ China Clipper ('37) ...	15.00	12.00	11.75	9.50	4.50
C22 Plate Block of 6	185.00	145.00	145.00	120.00	...

1938 Eagle (VF Used + 30%)

	NH VF	F-VF	Unused VF	F-VF	Used F-VF
C23 6¢ Dark Blue & Carmine ...	.70	.50	.55	.40	.15
C23 Arrow Block of 4	3.00	2.50	2.60	2.00	...
C23 Center Line Block of 4	3.35	2.75	2.90	2.25	...
C23 Plate Block of 4	12.50	9.50	9.75	7.50	...
C23 Top Plate Block o f10	22.00	16.50	17.00	12.50	...

1939 Trans-Atlantic Issue (VF Used + 30%)

	NH VF	F-VF	Unused VF	F-VF	Used F-VF
C24 30¢ Winged Globe, Blue .	14.50	11.00	11.50	8.75	1.35
C24 Plate Block of 6	235.00	185.00	195.00	150.00	...

U.S. AIRMAIL MINT SHEETS F-VF, NH

Scott No. (Size)	F-VF NH	Scott No. (Size)	F-VF NH	Scott No. (Size)	F-VF NH	Scott No. (Size)	F-VF NH
C7 (50)	275.00	C11 (50)	335.00	C19 (50)	175.00	C23 (50)	30.00
C8 (50)	295.00	C12 (50)	700.00	C20 (50)	95.00	C24 (50)	675.00
C9 (50)	850.00	C16 (50)	435.00	C21 (50)	600.00		
C10 (50)	700.00	C17 (50)	175.00	C22 (50)	675.00		

C25-31

C32

C33,C37,C39,C41

1941-44 Transport Plane

Scott's No.	Mint Sheet	Plate Block	F-VF NH	F-VF Used
C25-31 Set of 7	...	132.50	23.50	4.50
C25 6¢ Carmine	9.75	1.00	.20	.15
C25a 6¢ Booklet Pane of 3	...	...	3.35	3.00
C26 8¢ Olive Green (1944) ...	11.50	1.85	.25	.15
C27 10¢ Violet	75.00	10.00	1.50	.20
C28 15¢ Brown Carmine	150.00	13.50	3.00	.35
C29 20¢ Bright Green	115.00	10.75	2.30	.30
C30 30¢ Blue	135.00	12.75	2.75	.35
C31 50¢ Orange	700.00	80.00	13.00	3.50

1946-1948 Issues

	Mint Sheet	Plate Block	F-VF NH	F-VF Used
C32 5¢ DC-4 Skymaster	7.50	.65	.20	.15
C33 5¢ Small Plane (1947) .... (100)	15.00	.65	.20	.15

C34

C35

C36

Scott's No.	Mint Sheet	Plate Block	F-VF NH	F-VF Used
C34 10¢ Pan-Am Building (1947)	13.75	1.50	.30	.15
C34a 10¢ Dry Printing	21.75	2.10	.45	.25
C35 15¢ New York Skyline (1947)	21.50	2.00	.45	.15
C35b 15¢ Dry Printing	29.50	2.75	.60	.25
C36 25¢ Oakland Bay Bridge (1947) ..	52.50	4.75	1.10	.15
C36a 25¢ Dry Printing	65.00	5.75	1.35	.30

C38

C40

C42

C43

C44

C45

1948-49 Issues

	Line Pair		
C37 5¢ Small Plane, Coil	8.50	.95	.90

	Plate Blocks	F-VF NH	F-VF Used
C38 5¢ New York City Jubilee .... (100) 21.50	4.75	.25	.15
C39 6¢ Plane (Design of C33) ('49) (100) 18.50	.80	.25	.15
C39a 6¢ Booklet Pane of 6	...	10.75	7.50
C39b 6¢ Dry Printing .... (100) 115.00	7.50	1.25	.50
C39c 6¢ Bk. Pane of 6, Dry Printing ...	...	25.00	...
C40 6¢ Alexandria Bicentennial ('49) .	10.75	1.00	.25	.15

	Line Pair		
C41 6¢ Small Plane, Coil (1949)	14.50	3.25	.15

	Plate Blocks	F-VF NH	F-VF Used
C42-44 Univ. Postal Un., Set of 3 (1949)	...	9.50	1.40	1.00
C42 10¢ Post Office Building	14.50	1.50	.30	.25
C43 15¢ Globe & Doves	21.75	2.00	.45	.35
C44 25¢ Stratocruiser & Globe	36.50	6.50	.75	.50
C45 6¢ Wright Brothers Flight (1949) .	13.75	1.35	.30	.15

C46

1952 Hawaii Issue

	Mint Sheet	Plate Block	F-VF NH	F-VF Used
C46 80¢ Diamond Head	325.00	32.50	6.75	1.35

1953-58 Issues

C47

C48, C50

C49

C51,C52,C60,C61

	Mint Sheet	Plate Block	F-VF NH	F-VF Used
C47 6¢ Anniv. of Powered Flight	8.75	.80	.20	.15
C48 4¢ Eagle in Flight (1954) .... (100)	12.75	1.75	.20	.15
C49 6¢ Air Force 50th (1957)	9.75	.95	.20	.15
C50 5¢ Eagle (as C48) (1958) .... (100)	16.50	1.60	.20	.15
C51 7¢ Jet Silhouette, Blue (1958) (100)	17.50	.90	.20	.15
C51a 7¢ Booklet Pane of 6	...	...	11.75	6.75

	Line Pair		
C52 7¢ Jet Blue Coil, LargeHoles (1958)	...	17.00	2.10	.15
C52s 7¢ Small Holes	...	125.00	9.75	...

1959-61 Issues

C54

C53

C56

C55

C57

C58

1959-61 Issues (continued)

C59

C62

C63

Scott's No.		Mint Sheet	Plate Block	F-VF NH	F-VF Used
C53	7¢ Alaska Statehood	11.75	1.10	.25	.15
C54	7¢ Balloon Jupiter	13.75	1.30	.30	.15
C55	7¢ Hawaii Statehood	11.75	1.10	.25	.15
C56	10¢ Pan-Am Games, Chicago	13.75	1.40	.30	.25
C57	10¢ Liberty Bell (1960)	70.00	6.75	1.50	.90
C58	15¢ Statue of Liberty (1959)	21.50	1.95	.45	.20
C59	25¢ Abraham Lincoln	35.00	3.50	.75	.15
C59a	25¢ Tagged (1966)	40.00	3.75	.80	.35
C60	7¢ Jet Silhouette, Carmine ..... (100)	17.50	.90	.20	.15
C60a	7¢ Bk. Pane of 6	...	...	13.50	7.75
C61	7¢ Jet, Carmine Coil	Line Pair 40.00		4.00	.30
C62	13¢ Liberty Bell (1961)	21.00	1.80	.40	.15
C62a	13¢ Tagged (1967)	65.00	12.00	1.20	.65
C63	15¢ Liberty, Re-engraved (1961)	22.50	2.10	.45	.15
C63a	15¢ Tagged (1967)	24.00	2.35	.50	.25

#C58 has wide border around statue, #C63 is divided in center.

1962-67 Issues

C64,C65

C66

C67

C68

C69

C70

C71

C64	8¢ Jet over Capitol (1962) ...... (100)	22.75	1.00	.25	.15
C64a	8¢ Tagged (1963) .... (100)	27.50	1.20	.30	.20
C64b	8¢ B. Pane of 5, Sl. 1, "Your Mailman" ...	...		4.95	2.75
C64b	8¢ B. Pane of 5, Sl. 2, "Use Zone Numbers"	...		65.00	...
C64b	8¢ B. Pane of 5, Sl. 3, "Always Use Zip"...	...		12.75	...
C64c	8¢ Booklet Pane of 5, Tagged, Slogan 3...	...		1.50	1.25
C65	8¢ Capitol & Jet Coil (1962)	Line Pair 6.50		.50	.15
C65a	8¢ Tagged	Line Pair 2.75		.35	.15
C66	15¢ Montgomery Blair	35.00	3.50	.75	.55
C67	6¢ Bald Eagle .... (100)	18.50	1.75	.20	.15
C67a	6¢ Tagged (1967)	...	75.00	3.50	3.00
C68	8¢ Amelia Earhart (1963)	15.00	1.30	.30	.20
C69	8¢ Robert H. Goddard (1964)	24.50	2.10	.50	.20
C70	8¢ Alaska Purchase (1967)	14.50	1.60	.30	.20
C71	20¢ Columbia Jays (1967)	45.00	4.25	.90	.15

1968-73 Issues

C72,C73

C74

C75

C76

C77

C78,C82

C79,C83

C80

C81

1968-73 Issues (continued)

Scott's No.		Mint Sheet	Plate Block	F-VF NH	F-VF Used
C72	10¢ 50-Star Runway (1968) .... (100)	28.75	1.30	.30	.15
C72b	10¢ Booklet Pane of 8	...	...	2.35	2.25
C72c	10¢ B. Pane of 5 with Sl. 4 or Sl. 5	...	...	3.75	3.50
C72v	10¢ Congressional Precancel	...	110.00	2.00	...
C73	10¢ 50-Star Runway Coil (1968) .	Line Pair 1.95		.35	.15
C74	10¢ Air Mail Service 50th Anniv ('68)	15.00	2.50	.30	.20
C75	20¢ "USA" and Jet (1968)	27.00	2.65	.55	.20
C76	10¢ Moon Landing (1969) ...... (32)	13.75	1.95	.45	.20
C77	9¢ Delta Wing Plane Silh. ('71) . (100)	24.50	1.10	.25	.20
C78	11¢ Jet Airliner Silhouette ('71) . (100)	32.50	1.60	.35	.15
C78a	11¢ Booklet Pane of 4	...	...	1.35	1.15
C78b	11¢ Congressional Precancel	...	25.75	.65	.40
C79	13¢ Winged Envelope (1973) .... (100)	33.50	1.50	.35	.15
C79a	13¢ Booklet Pane of 5	...	...	1.60	1.50
C79b	13¢ Congressional Precancel	...	9.50	.50	.35
C80	17¢ Statue of Lib. Head (1971) ...	22.50	2.10	.45	.25
C81	21¢ "USA" and Jet (1971)	26.75	2.50	.55	.15
C82	11¢ Jet Silhouette Coil (1971)	Line Pair	.90	.35	.15
C83	13¢ Winged Env. Coil (1973)	Line Pair	1.25	.40	.15

1972-1979 Issues

C85

C84

C86

C87

C88

C89

C90

C91

C93

C95

C92

C94

C96

C87

C84	11¢ City of Refuge Park ('72)	16.50	1.60	.35	.20
C85	11¢ Olympic Games - Skiing ('72)	16.50	(10) 3.95	.35	.20
C86	11¢ Electronics (1973)	16.50	1.60	.35	.20
C87	18¢ Statue of Liberty (1974)	24.50	2.30	.50	.40
C88	26¢ Mt. Rushmore Memorial (1974)	34.50	3.25	.70	.15
C89	25¢ Plane & Globes (1976)	34.50	3.25	.70	.20
C90	31¢ Plane, Globe and Flag (1976)	41.50	3.75	.85	.20
C91-92	31¢ Wright Brothers, attd .... (100)	85.00	4.00	1.75	1.60
C91-92	Set of 2 Singles	...	...	1.70	.80
C93-94	21¢ Octave Chanute, attd. ('79) (100)	90.00	4.75	1.90	1.60
C93-94	Set of 2 Singles	...	...	1.85	.90
C95-96	25¢ Wiley Post, attd. ('79) .... (100)	145.00	10.75	2.95	2.00
C95-96	Set of 2 Singles	...	...	2.85	1.20
C97	31¢ Olympics - High Jump ('79)	45.00	(12) 11.50	.90	.35

1980 Issues

C99   C98   C100

Scott's No.		Mint Sheet	Plate Block	F-VF NH	F-VF Used
C98	40¢ Philip Mazzei, Perf. 11	58.50	(12)14.50	1.20	.25
C98A	40¢ Perf. 10½x11 (1982)	...	(12)110.00	5.50	2.00
C99	28¢ Blanche Scott (1980)	41.50	(12)11.00	.85	.25
C100	35¢ Glenn Curtiss	47.50	(12)13.50	1.00	.25

1983 Los Angeles Summer Olympic Issues

C101   C102
C103   C104

C105   C106
C107   C108

C109   C110
C111   C112

C101-4	28¢ Summer Olympics, attd	62.50	6.00	5.50	3.00
C101-4	Set of 4 Singles	...	...	4.75	1.20
C105-8	40¢ Summer Olympics, Bullseye Perfs Pf. 11.2, attd	60.00	5.75	5.25	4.00
C105-8	Set of 4 Singles	...	....	5.00	1.60
C105a-8a	40¢ Line Perfs Pf. 11, attd	110.00	12.75	8.75	7.50
C105a-8a	Set of 4 Singles	...	...	8.00	3.00
C109-12	35¢ Summer Olympics, attd	67.50	8.75	5.25	4.50
C109-12	Set of 4 Singles	...	...	4.75	2.40

1985-1989 Issues

C113   C114   C115

C116   C117   C118

C119   C120   C121

Scott's No.		Mint Sheet	Plate Block	F-VF NH	F-VF Used
C113	33¢ Alfred Verville	45.00	4.35	.95	.25
C114	39¢ Sperry Brothers	52.50	5.00	1.10	.35
C115	44¢ Transpacific Airmail	57.50	5.50	1.20	.30
C116	44¢ Father Junipero Serra	67.50	9.00	1.35	.40
C117	44¢ New Sweden (1988)	73.50	9.00	1.50	.75
C118	45¢ Samuel Langley, Block Tagging (1988)	65.00	6.00	1.35	.30
C118a	45¢ Overall Tagging (1988)	165.00	33.50	3.00	2.00
C119	36¢ Igor Sikorsky (1988)	48.50	4.65	1.00	.35
C120	45¢ French Revolution ('89) .. (30)	37.50	5.75	1.30	.55
C121	45¢ Pre-Columbian Customs ('89)	62.50	5.75	1.30	.40

1989 Universal Postal Congress Issues

C122   C123
C124   C125

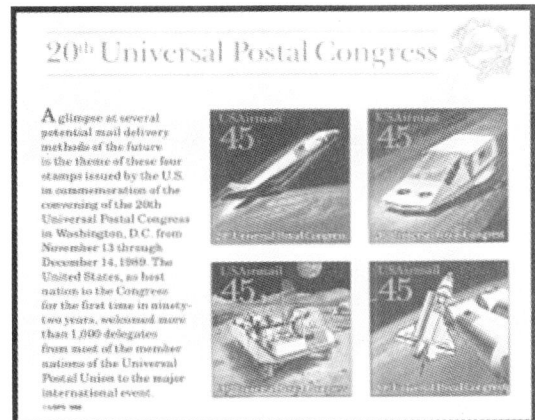

C126

C122-25	45¢ Futuristic Mail Deliv., Attd (40)	63.50	7.50	6.50	4.50
C122-25	Set of 4 Singles	...	...	6.25	2.00
C126	$1.80 Future Mail Delivery Souvenir Sheet, Imperforate			6.50	5.75

1990-1993 Airmail Issues

C127 · C128 · C129 · C130 · C131 · C132

Scott's No.		Mint Sheet	Plate Block	F-VF NH	F-VF Used
C127	45¢ America, Caribbean Coast ...	65.00	6.75	1.35	.50
C128	50¢ Harriet Quimby, Pf. 11 (1991)	70.00	7.00	1.50	.45
C128b	H.Quimby, Perf. 11.2 ('93)	75.00	7.50	1.60	.50
C129	40¢ William T. Piper (1991)	60.00	5.75	1.25	.45
C130	50¢ Antarctic Treaty (1991)	67.50	6.75	1.40	.65
C131	50¢ America (1991)	67.50	6.75	1.40	.55
C132	40¢ W.T. Piper, new design ('93)	97.50	19.75	1.80	.60

#C129: Blue sky clear along top of design, Perf. 11
#C132: Piper's hair is touching top of design, Bullseye Perf. 11.2

1999-2001 American Landmarks International Rate Regular Issues

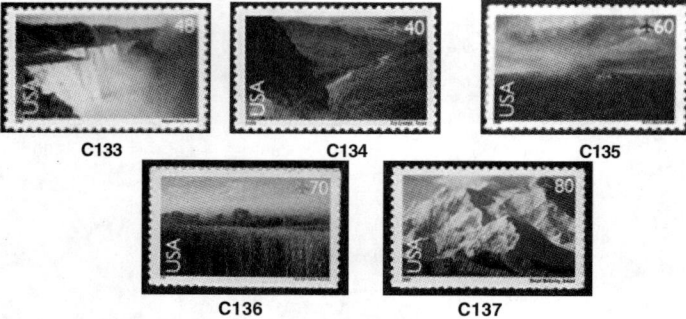

C133 · C134 · C135 · C136 · C137

Scott's No.			Plate Block	F-VF NH	F-VF Used
C134	40¢ Rio Grande, SA	(20) 17.00	3.95	.90	.30
C133	48¢ Niagara Falls, SA	(20) 20.75	5.00	1.10	.35
C135	60¢ Grand Canyon, SA (2000) ...	(20) 23.50	5.75	1.25	.35
C136	70¢ Nine Mile Prairie, SA (2001)	(20) 27.00	5.95	1.40	.50
C137	80¢ Mount McKinley, SA (2001) ..	(20) 30.75	6.95	1.60	.50
...	60¢ Acadia, SA (2001)	(20) 23.50	5.75	1.25	.35

1934-36 AIR MAIL SPECIAL DELIVERY VF Used + 20%

CE1,CE2

Scott's No.		NH VF	NH F-VF	Unused VF	Unused F-VF	F-VF Used
CE1	16¢ Great Seal, Dark Blue	1.10	.90	.95	.70	.70
CE1	Plate Block of 6	27.00	22.50	22.00	18.00	...
CE2	16¢ Seal, Red & Blue	.70	.55	.55	.45	.25
CE2	Arrow Block of 4	3.00	2.50	2.50	2.00	...
CE2	Center Line Block of 4	3.35	2.75	2.80	2.35	...
CE2	Plate Block of 4	10.50	8.50	8.65	6.75	...
CE2	Top Plate Block of 10	18.50	15.00	14.50	12.50	...

Mint Sheets of 50 F-VF, NH #CE1 60.00; #CE2 35.00

SPECIAL DELIVERY STAMPS

E1 · E2,E3 · E4,E5

1885 "At A Special Delivery Office", Unwatermarked, Perf. 12 (VF+60%)(C)

Scott's No.		NH Fine	Unused Fine	Unused Ave.	Used Fine	Used Ave.
E1	10¢ Messenger, Blue	415.00	235.00	140.00	35.00	20.75

1888-93 "At Any Post Office", No Line Under "TEN CENTS"
Unwatermarked, Perf. 12 VF + 60% (C)

E2	10¢ Blue	385.00	215.00	135.00	13.50	8.25
E3	10¢ Orange (1893)	235.00	135.00	80.00	16.50	10.50

1894 Line Under "TEN CENTS", Unwatermarked, Perf. 12 VF + 60% (C)

E4	10¢ Blue	875.00	500.00	315.00	25.00	16.00

1895 Line Under "TEN CENTS, Double Line Watermark, Perf. 12 VF + 60% (C)

E5	10¢ Blue	190.00	110.00	70.00	3.00	1.85

E6,E8-11 · E7

Scott No.		NH VF	NH F-VF	Unused VF	Unused F-VF	Used F-VF
	1902-08 Double Line Watermark, VF Used + 50% (B)					
E6	10¢ Ultramarine, Perf. 12	195.00	125.00	105.00	70.00	2.75
E7	10¢ Mercury, Green (1908) ...	120.00	77.50	67.50	45.00	29.50
	1911-14 Single Line Watermark VF Used + 50% (B)					
E8	10¢ Ultramarine, Perf. 12	195.00	130.00	115.00	75.00	4.25
E9	10¢ Ultra., Perf. 10 (1914)	350.00	230.00	200.00	135.00	5.00
	1916 Unwatermarked, Perf.10 VF Used + 50% (B)					
E10	10¢ Pale Ultramarine	575.00	375.00	340.00	225.00	22.50
	1917 Unwatermarked, Perf. 11 VF Used +40% (B)					
E11	10¢ Ultramarine	31.75	21.50	18.00	12.75	.45
E11	Plate Block of 6	320.00	215.00	210.00	150.00	...

E12-13,E15-18 · E14,E19

E12	**1922-1925 Flat Press Printings, Perf. 11 VF Used + 30% (B)** 10¢ Motorcycle, Gray Violet ...	50.00	37.50	31.50	23.50	.35
E12	Plate Block of 6	500.00	385.00	365.00	275.00	...
E13	15¢ Deep Orange (1925)	40.00	30.00	26.00	19.50	1.10
E13	Plate Block of 6	400.00	315.00	295.00	225.00	...
E14	20¢ P.O. Truck, Black (1925) ...	4.50	3.35	2.95	2.25	1.50
E14	Plate Block of 6	60.00	47.50	45.00	32.50	...
	1927-1951 Rotary Press Printings, Perf. 11x10½ VF Used + 20%					
E15-19	Set of 5	9.35	7.50	7.65	5.75	2.95
E15	10¢ Motorcycle, Gray Violet	1.35	1.10	1.10	.85	.15
E15	Plate Block of 4	7.50	5.75	5.75	4.25	...
E16	15¢ Orange (1931)	1.50	1.15	1.15	.90	.20
E16	Plate Block of 4	7.00	5.50	5.50	4.25	...
E17	13¢ Blue (1944)	1.00	.80	.80	.65	.20
E17	Plate Block of 4	5.00	4.00	4.00	3.25	...
E18	17¢ Orange Yellow (1944)	4.35	3.50	3.50	2.75	2.50
E18	Plate Block of 4	33.50	26.50	27.00	19.50	...
E19	20¢ P.O. Truck, Black (1951) ..	2.30	1.85	1.85	1.50	.20
E19	Plate Block of 4	11.50	8.75	8.75	7.00	...

MINT SHEETS OF 50, F-VF, NH
#E14 150.00, E15 50.00, E16 55.00, E17 36.50, E18 175.00, E19 95.00

E20,E21 · E22,E23

1954-1971

Scott's No.		Mint Sheet	Pl. Block NH	F-VF NH	F-VF Used
E20-23	Set of 4	...	19.50	4.15	.75
E20	20¢ Letter & Hands	30.00	2.85	.60	.15
E21	30¢ Letter & Hands (1957)	40.00	4.00	.85	.20
E22	45¢ Arrows (1969)	67.50	6.50	1.40	.30
E23	60¢ Arrows (1971)	72.50	7.00	1.50	.20

F1

FA1

1911 REGISTRATION VF Used + 40% (B)

Scott's No.		NH VF	NH F-VF	Unused VF	Unused F-VF	Used F-VF
F1	10¢ Eagle, Ultramarine	130.00	90.00	77.50	55.00	5.75

1955 CERTIFIED MAIL

Scott's No.		Mint Sheet	Pl.Block NH	F-VF NH	F-VF Used
FA1	15¢ Postman, Red	22.50	5.00	.45	.30

POSTAGE DUE STAMPS

J1-J28

J29-J67

J68

1879 Perforated 12 (NH + 100%, VF OG & Used + 60%, VF NH + 175%) (C)

Scott's No.		Unused Fine	Unused Ave.	Used Fine	Used Ave.
J1	1¢ Brown	37.50	22.50	6.50	3.75
J2	2¢ Brown	210.00	125.00	6.00	3.50
J3	3¢ Brown	33.50	20.00	3.50	2.10
J4	5¢ Brown	375.00	230.00	32.50	19.50
J5	10¢ Brown	400.00	250.00	18.75	11.50
J6	30¢ Brown	210.00	130.00	39.50	25.00
J7	50¢ Brown	300.00	185.00	46.50	27.50
	1884-89, Same Design Perf. 12 (NH + 100%, VF OG & Used + 60%, VF NH + 175%)				
J15	1¢ Red Brown	35.00	21.00	3.75	2.30
J16	2¢ Red Brown	43.50	26.00	4.00	2.50
J17	3¢ Red Brown	650.00	400.00	120.00	70.00
J18	5¢ Red Brown	325.00	190.00	17.50	10.75
J19	10¢ Red Brown	315.00	180.00	13.50	8.50
J20	30¢ Red Brown	125.00	75.00	37.50	22.50
J21	50¢ Red Brown	1100.00	650.00	135.00	82.50

*** Red Brown issues can be distinguished from Bright Claret issues by placing the stamps under long wave UV light. Bright Clarets give off a warm orange glow, Red Browns do not.**

1891-93 Same Design Perf. 12 (NH + 75%, VF OG & Used + 60%, VF NH + 150%)

Scott's No.		Unused Fine	Unused Ave.	Used Fine	Used Ave.
J22	1¢ Bright Claret	17.50	11.00	.85	.50
J23	2¢ Bright Claret	22.50	13.50	.90	.55
J24	3¢ Bright Claret	40.00	24.00	6.00	3.65
J25	5¢ Bright Claret	50.00	31.50	6.00	3.65
J26	10¢ Bright Claret	85.00	50.00	13.75	8.25
J27	30¢ Bright Claret	325.00	195.00	110.00	65.00
J28	50¢ Bright Claret	350.00	210.00	110.00	65.00

1894-95 Unwatermarked, Perforated 12 VF Used + 60% (C)

Scott's No.		NH VF	NH F-VF	Unused VF	Unused F-VF	Used F-VF
J29	1¢ Vermilion	3000.00	1950.00	1800.00	1150.00	275.00
J30	2¢ Vermilion	1100.00	700.00	675.00	425.00	85.00
J31	1¢ Claret	80.00	51.50	47.50	30.00	4.95
J32	2¢ Claret	67.50	42.50	40.00	25.00	3.00
J33	3¢ Claret (1895)	310.00	190.00	175.00	110.00	25.00
J34	5¢ Claret (1895)	465.00	275.00	260.00	160.00	27.50
J35	10¢ Claret	465.00	275.00	260.00	160.00	20.00
J36	30¢ Claret (1895)	700.00	435.00	400.00	250.00	70.00
J36b	Pale Rose	585.00	365.00	335.00	210.00	65.00
J37	50¢ Claret (1895)	2100.00	1400.00	1250.00	800.00	195.00
J37a	Pale Rose	2000.00	1350.00	1200.00	750.00	185.00
	1895-97, Double Line Watermark, Perf. 12 VF Used + 60% (C)					
J38	1¢ Claret	15.50	9.50	8.75	5.50	.55
J39	2¢ Claret	15.50	9.50	8.75	5.50	.55
J40	3¢ Claret	115.00	65.00	65.00	37.50	1.75
J41	5¢ Claret	125.00	72.50	70.00	41.50	1.65
J42	10¢ Claret	130.00	80.00	75.00	45.00	2.75
J43	30¢ Claret (1897)	1000.00	625.00	575.00	350.00	37.50
J44	50¢ Claret (1896)	625.00	390.00	360.00	225.00	30.00
	1910-12, Single Line Watermark, Perf. 12 VF Used + 60% (C)					
J45	1¢ Claret	55.00	33.50	32.50	20.00	2.50
J46	2¢ Claret	55.00	33.50	32.50	20.00	.75
J47	3¢ Claret	1000.00	625.00	600.00	375.00	22.50
J48	5¢ Claret	160.00	100.00	95.00	60.00	5.25
J49	10¢ Claret	210.00	125.00	125.00	75.00	9.75
J50	50¢ Claret (1912)	1600.00	1000.00	975.00	600.00	90.00
	1914 Single Line Watermark, Perf. 10 VF Used + 50% (C)					
J52	1¢ Carmine	100.00	67.50	60.00	40.00	8.75
J53	2¢ Carmine	85.00	55.00	50.00	32.50	.50
J54	3¢ Carmine	1475.00	975.00	850.00	575.00	29.50
J55	5¢ Carmine	65.00	41.50	38.00	25.00	2.00
J56	10¢ Carmine	97.50	62.50	57.50	37.50	1.50

POSTAGE DUES (continued)

Scott's No.		NH VF	NH F-VF	Unused VF	Unused F-VF	Used F-VF
J57	30¢ Carmine	450.00	300.00	265.00	175.00	13.50
J58	50¢ Carmine				6500.00	600.00
	1916 Unwatermarked, Perf. 10 VF Used + 50% (B)					
J59	1¢ Rose	...	...	2500.00	1650.00	250.00
J60	2¢ Rose	295.00	195.00	175.00	115.00	16.00
	1917-25 Unwatermarked, Perf. 11 VF Used + 50% (B)					
J61	1¢ Carmine Rose	4.50	3.00	2.75	1.85	.20
J61	Plate Block of 6	75.00	50.00	48.50	32.50	...
J62	2¢ Carmine Rose	4.25	2.75	2.50	1.65	.25
J62	Plate Block of 6	67.50	45.00	43.50	28.50	...
J63	3¢ Carmine Rose	19.00	12.00	11.50	7.75	.25
J63	Plate Block of 6	165.00	110.00	105.00	70.00	...
J64	5¢ Carmine Rose	19.00	12.00	11.50	7.75	.25
J64	Plate Block of 6	165.00	110.00	105.00	70.00	...
J65	10¢ Carmine Rose	29.50	18.50	17.00	11.50	.40
J66	30¢ Carmine Rose	150.00	100.00	90.00	60.00	.60
J67	50¢ Carmine Rose	200.00	125.00	120.00	75.00	.30
J68	½¢ Dull Red (1925)	1.60	1.10	1.10	.75	.30

J69,J79

J77,J87

J88

J101

1930-31 Flat Press, Perf. 11 VF Used + 40% (B)

Scott's No.		NH VF	NH F-VF	Unused VF	Unused F-VF	Used F-VF
J69	½¢ Carmine	8.00	5.50	5.25	3.75	1.10
J69	Plate Block of 6	70.00	50.00	50.00	35.00	...
J70	1¢ Carmine	5.25	3.75	3.50	2.50	.30
J70	Plate Block of 6	50.00	35.00	35.00	25.00	...
J71	2¢ Carmine	6.00	4.50	4.00	3.00	.30
J71	Plate Block of 6	70.00	50.00	50.00	35.00	...
J72	3¢ Carmine	40.00	27.50	25.00	17.50	1.50
J73	5¢ Carmine	35.00	25.00	22.50	16.00	2.00
J74	10¢ Carmine	80.00	55.00	50.00	35.00	.95
J75	30¢ Carmine	195.00	135.00	120.00	85.00	1.50
J76	50¢ Carmine	260.00	180.00	160.00	115.00	.55
J77	$1 Carmine or Scarlet	43.50	31.50	27.50	20.00	.30
J78	$5 Carmine or Scarlet, Dry	60.00	42.50	38.50	27.50	.35
J78b	$5 Scarlet, Wet Printing	65.00	45.00	42.50	30.00	.40

1931-56 Rotary Press, Perf. 11x10½ or 10½x11 (VF+25%)

Scott's No.			Mint Sheet	Pl.Blk NH	F-VF NH	F-VF Used
J79-87	**Set of 9**		**...**	**...**	**62.50**	**1.40**
J79	½¢ Carmine	(100)	110.00	27.50	.95	.20
J80	1¢ Carmine, dry printing	(100)	16.50	2.00	.20	.15
J80b	1¢ Carmine, wet printing	(100)	17.00	2.25	.20	.20
J81	2¢ Carmine, dry printing	(100)	17.50	2.00	.20	.15
J81b	2¢ Carmine, wet printing	(100)	18.00	2.25	.20	.20
J82	3¢ Carmine, dry printing	(100)	27.50	3.00	.30	.20
J82b	3¢ Carmine, wet printing	(100)	29.50	3.25	.35	.20
J83	5¢ Carmine, dry printing	(100)	42.50	4.50	.45	.20
J83b	5¢ Carmine, wet printing	(100)	50.00	5.50	.50	.20
J84	10¢ Carmine, dry printing	(100)	110.00	8.50	1.20	.20
J84b	10¢ Carmine, wet printing	(100)	120.00	9.00	1.25	.20
J85	30¢ Carmine		...	57.50	8.00	.25
J86	50¢ Carmine		...	70.00	12.50	.20
J87	$1 Scarlet (1956)		...	225.00	42.50	.30
	1959-85 Rotary Press, Perf. 11x10½					
J88-104	**Set of 17**		**...**	**...**	**18.50**	**4.50**
J88	½¢ Carmine Rose & Black	(100)	375.00	195.00	1.40	1.30
J89	1¢ Carmine Rose & Black	(100)	5.00	.50	.20	.15
J89v	1¢ Dull Gum	(100)	7.50	.75	.25	...
J90	2¢ Carmine Rose & Black	(100)	6.50	.50	.20	.20
J90v	2¢ Dull Gum	(100)	9.00	.75	.25	...
J91	3¢ Carmine Rose & Black	(100)	8.75	.50	.20	.15
J91v	3¢ Dull Gum	(100)	12.75	.75	.25	...
J92	4¢ Carmine Rose & Black	(100)	11.50	.90	.20	.15
J93	5¢ Carmine Rose & Black	(100)	13.75	.85	.20	.15
J93v	5¢ Dull Gum	(100)	22.75	1.25	.25	...
J94	6¢ Carmine Rose & Black	(100)	15.75	1.10	.20	.20
J94v	6¢ Dull Gum	(100)	...	...	165.00	...
J95	7¢ Carmine Rose & Black	(100)	22.50	2.00	.25	.15
J95v	7¢ Dull Gum	(100)	...	...	375.00	...
J96	8¢ Carmine Rose & Black	(100)	19.75	1.40	.25	.15
J97	10¢ Carmine Rose & Black	(100)	25.00	1.50	.25	.20
J97v	10¢ Dull Gum	(100)	29.50	1.85	.30	...
J98	30¢ Carmine Rose & Black	(100)	72.50	3.95	.75	.20
J98v	30¢ Dull Gum	(100)	87.50	4.95	.90	...
J99	50¢ Carmine Rose & Black	(100)	120.00	5.75	1.15	.15
J99v	50¢ Dull Gum	(100)	130.00	6.25	1.25	...
J100	$1 Carmine Rose & Black	(100)	240.00	12.00	2.50	.15
J100v	$1 Dull Gum	(100)	265.00	13.50	2.75	...
J101	$5 Carmine Rose & Black		...	50.00	10.75	.30
J101v	$5 Dull Gum		...	55.00	11.75	...
J102	11¢ Carmine Rose & Blk. ('78)	(100)	28.50	3.50	.30	.40
J103	13¢ Carmine Rose & Blk. ('78)	(100)	33.50	2.25	.35	.40
J104	17¢ Carmine Rose & Blk. ('85)	(100)	79.50	39.50	.45	.50

U.S. OFFICES IN CHINA

K2

K4

K7

1919 U.S. Postal Agency in China
VF Used + 50% (B)

Scott's No.		NH VF	NH F-VF	Unused VF	Unused F-VF	Used F-VF
K1	2¢ on 1¢ Green (on #498)	46.50	31.50	26.00	18.00	22.50
K2	4¢ on 2¢ Rose (on #499)	46.50	31.50	26.00	18.00	22.50
K3	6¢ on 3¢ Violet (#502)	82.50	55.00	47.50	32.50	50.00
K4	8¢ on 4¢ Brown (#503)	95.00	62.50	55.00	37.50	50.00
K5	10¢ on 5¢ Blue (#504)	105.00	70.00	62.50	42.50	50.00
K6	12¢ on 6¢ Red Orange(#506)	130.00	87.50	77.50	52.50	75.00
K7	14¢ on 7¢ Black (#507)	140.00	95.00	82.50	55.00	85.00
K8	16¢ on 8¢ Olive Bister (#508)	110.00	70.00	65.00	42.50	55.00
K8a	16¢ on 8¢ Olive Green	105.00	67.50	60.00	40.00	45.00
K9	18¢ on 9¢ Salmon Red (#509)	110.00	70.00	65.00	42.50	55.00
K10	20¢ on 10¢ Or. Yellow (#510)	105.00	67.50	60.00	40.00	50.00
K11	24¢ on 12¢ Brn. Carm. (#512)	115.00	75.00	67.50	45.00	57.50
K11a	24¢ on 12¢ Claret Brown	165.00	110.00	95.00	65.00	90.00
K12	30¢ on 15¢ Gray (#514)	140.00	95.00	82.50	55.00	95.00
K13	40¢ on 20¢ Deep Ultra (#515)	210.00	140.00	125.00	85.00	140.00
K14	60¢ on 30¢ Or. Red (#516)	200.00	135.00	120.00	80.00	125.00
K15	$1 on 50¢ Lt. Violet (#517)	875.00	575.00	525.00	350.00	425.00
K16	$2 on $1 Vlt. Brown (#518)	675.00	465.00	400.00	275.00	360.00

1922 Surcharged in Shanghai, China

K17	2¢ on 1¢ Green (#498)	225.00	150.00	135.00	90.00	85.00
K18	4¢ on 2¢ Carmine (#528B)	195.00	125.00	115.00	75.00	70.00

OFFICIAL DEPARTMENTAL STAMPS

O1-9,O94-5

O15-24,O96-103

O25-34,O106-7

O35-45

1873 Continental Bank Note Co. - Thin Hard Paper
(NH + 100%, VF OG & Used + 60%, VF NH + 175%) (C)

NOTE: Unused stamps without gum sell for about 30% less

DESIGNS: Busts are the same as 1873 Regular Issue with the exception of Post Office Dept.

AGRICULTURE DEPARTMENT

Scott's No.		Unused Fine	Unused Ave.	Used Fine	Used Ave.
O1	1¢ Franklin, Yellow	110.00	67.50	100.00	60.00
O2	2¢ Jackson	85.00	50.00	39.50	23.75
O3	3¢ Washington	80.00	47.50	7.75	4.75
O4	6¢ Lincoln	90.00	55.00	35.00	21.50
O5	10¢ Jefferson	170.00	100.00	120.00	70.00
O6	12¢ Clay	225.00	135.00	150.00	90.00
O7	15¢ Webster	190.00	45.00	130.00	80.00
O8	24¢ Scott	190.00	115.00	120.00	70.00
O9	30¢ Hamilton	260.00	155.00	160.00	95.00

EXECUTIVE DEPARTMENT

O10	1¢ Franklin, Carmine	400.00	230.00	265.00	160.00
O11	2¢ Jackson	275.00	165.00	135.00	80.00
O12	3¢ Washington	310.00	185.00	135.00	80.00
O13	6¢ Lincoln	475.00	285.00	325.00	195.00
O14	10¢ Jefferson	450.00	270.00	375.00	225.00

INTERIOR DEPARTMENT

O15	1¢ Franklin, Vermilion	22.50	13.50	5.25	3.15
O16	2¢ Jackson	20.00	12.50	6.25	3.75
O17	3¢ Washington	33.50	20.00	3.50	2.10
O18	6¢ Lincoln	23.00	13.50	3.50	2.10
O19	10¢ Jefferson	24.00	14.00	10.75	6.50
O20	12¢ Clay	31.75	18.50	5.25	3.00
O21	15¢ Webster	60.00	35.00	12.00	7.50
O22	24¢ Scott	42.50	25.00	9.00	5.50
O23	30¢ Hamilton	60.00	37.50	9.50	6.00
O24	90¢ Perry	135.00	80.00	33.50	14.00

JUSTICE DEPARTMENT

O25	1¢ Franklin, Purple	75.00	45.00	60.00	35.00
O26	2¢ Jackson	130.00	75.00	60.00	35.00
O27	3¢ Washington	130.00	75.00	13.50	8.00
O28	6¢ Lincoln	135.00	80.00	21.00	12.75
O29	10¢ Jefferson	130.00	75.00	45.00	27.00
O30	12¢ Clay	110.00	70.00	30.00	17.75
O31	15¢ Webster	210.00	125.00	100.00	60.00
O32	24¢ Scott	525.00	315.00	225.00	135.00
O33	30¢Hamilton	465.00	280.00	170.00	100.00
O34	90¢ Perry	700.00	425.00	335.00	195.00

NAVY DEPARTMENT

O35	1¢ Franklin, Ultramarine	52.50	30.00	25.00	16.00
O36	2¢ Jackson	42.50	25.00	12.00	7.00
O37	3¢ Washington	42.50	25.00	6.00	3.50
O38	6¢ Lincoln	42.50	25.00	9.50	5.75
O39	7¢ Stanton	275.00	165.00	120.00	70.00
O40	10¢ Jefferson	52.50	31.50	19.50	11.75
O41	12¢ Clay	65.00	37.50	20.00	12.00
O42	15¢ Webster	125.00	75.00	40.00	23.75

OFFICIAL DEPARTMENTAL STAMPS (continued)

Scott's No.		Unused Fine	Unused Ave.	Used Fine	Used Ave.
O43	24¢ Scott	125.00	75.00	45.00	26.75
O44	30¢ Hamilton	95.00	55.00	23.50	14.00
O45	90¢ Perry	475.00	275.00	140.00	85.00

O47-56,O108

O57-67

O68-71

O72-82,O109-13

O83-93,O114-20

POST OFFICE DEPARTMENT

O47	1¢ Black	8.25	5.00	5.00	3.00
O48	2¢	11.00	6.50	4.50	2.85
O49	3¢	3.50	2.10	.90	.50
O50	6¢	11.00	6.50	4.00	2.50
O51	10¢	45.00	27.00	27.50	16.50
O52	12¢	25.00	15.00	5.50	3.00
O53	15¢	32.50	20.00	9.50	5.50
O54	24¢	42.50	25.00	11.50	7.00
O55	30¢	42.50	25.00	11.50	7.00
O56	90¢	60.00	35.00	10.00	6.00

STATE DEPARTMENT

O57	1¢ Franklin, Green	77.50	47.50	35.00	20.00
O58	2¢ Jackson	150.00	90.00	50.00	30.00
O59	3¢ Washington	60.00	35.00	11.50	6.75
O60	6¢ Lincoln	52.50	30.00	15.00	9.00
O61	7¢ Stanton	110.00	65.00	32.50	19.50
O62	10¢ Jefferson	85.00	50.00	25.00	15.00
O63	12¢ Clay	135.00	85.00	62.50	37.50
O64	15¢ Webster	145.00	90.00	45.00	27.50
O65	24¢ Scott	300.00	180.00	120.00	70.00
O66	30¢ Hamilton	265.00	160.00	90.00	55.00
O67	90¢ Perry	500.00	300.00	190.00	120.00
O68	$2 Seward Green & Black	575.00	335.00	450.00	270.00
O69	$5 Green & Black	4250.00	2600.00	2500.00	1575.00
O70	$10 Green & Black	2800.00	1575.00	1650.00	1000.00
O71	$20 Green & Black	2250.00	1300.00	1250.00	750.00

TREASURY DEPARTMENT

O72	1¢ Franklin, Brown	26.00	16.00	3.15	1.85
O73	2¢ Jackson	32.50	19.50	3.15	1.85
O74	3¢ Washington	22.50	13.50	1.25	.75
O75	6¢ Lincoln	30.00	18.00	2.50	1.50
O76	7¢ Stanton	60.00	36.50	15.00	9.00
O77	10¢ Jefferson	60.00	36.50	5.25	3.00
O78	12¢ Clay	60.00	36.50	4.25	2.50
O79	15¢ Webster	55.00	32.50	5.50	3.25
O80	24¢ Scott	295.00	180.00	45.00	26.50
O81	30¢ Hamilton	105.00	65.00	6.00	3.50
O82	90¢ Perry	100.00	60.00	6.50	3.75

WAR DEPARTMENT

O83	1¢ Frankin, Rose	100.00	60.00	6.00	3.50
O84	2¢ Jackson	90.00	55.00	6.75	4.00
O85	3¢ Washington	95.00	57.50	2.00	1.20
O86	6¢ Lincoln	300.00	180.00	4.00	2.25
O87	7¢ Stanton	80.00	47.50	47.50	28.50
O88	10¢ Jefferson	27.50	16.50	9.75	5.75
O89	12¢ Clay	110.00	65.00	6.75	4.00
O90	15¢ Webster	26.75	16.00	7.50	4.50
O91	24¢ Scott	26.75	16.00	4.50	2.65
O92	30¢ Hamilton	26.50	16.00	4.50	2.65
O93	90¢ Perry	60.00	36.50	27.50	16.00

1879 American Bank Note Co. - Soft Porous Paper
(NH + 75%, VF OG & Used + 60%, VF NH + 150%) (C)

O94	1¢ **Agric. Dept.** (Issued w/o gum)	2250.00	1400.00	...	...
O95	3¢ Washington	200.00	120.00	45.00	27.50
O96	1¢ **Interior Department,** Franklin	170.00	100.00	150.00	90.00
O97	2¢ Jackson	2.75	1.60	1.00	.60
O98	3¢ Washington	2.50	1.50	.75	.40
O99	6¢ Lincoln	3.50	2.10	3.50	2.10
O100	10¢ Jefferson	45.00	27.00	40.00	24.00
O101	12¢ Clay	87.50	50.00	62.50	38.50
O102	15¢ Webster	200.00	120.00	160.00	100.00
O103	24¢ Scott	2175.00	1300.00	...	...
O106	3¢ **Justice Department**	67.50	40.00	45.00	28.00
O107	6¢ Lincoln	150.00	90.00	120.00	72.50
O108	3¢ **Post Office Department**	10.00	6.00	3.50	2.10
O109	3¢ **Treasury Department**	29.50	17.00	4.50	2.50
O110	6¢ Lincoln	60.00	35.00	25.00	15.00
O111	10¢ Jefferson	100.00	60.00	35.00	21.50
O112	30¢ Hamilton	850.00	500.00	200.00	120.00
O113	90¢ Perry	1400.00	850.00	200.00	120.00
O114	1¢ **War Department,** Franklin	2.50	1.50	1.80	1.10
O115	2¢ Jackson	3.35	2.00	2.25	1.35
O116	3¢ Washington	3.35	2.00	.95	.55
O117	6¢ Lincoln	3.00	1.65	.90	.50
O118	10¢ Jefferson	25.00	15.00	25.00	15.00
O119	12¢ Clay	20.00	12.00	7.00	4.25
O120	30¢ Hamilton	55.00	32.50	46.50	28.50

OFFICIAL POSTAL SAVINGS

O121, 25	O124	O126

1910-11 Double-line Watermark VF Used + 50% (B)

Scott's No.		VF	NH F-VF	Unused VF	F-VF	Used F-VF
O121	2¢ Black	23.00	15.00	14.75	9.75	1.35
O122	50¢ Dark Green	235.00	150.00	145.00	95.00	30.00
O123	$1 Ultramarine	225.00	145.00	135.00	90.00	9.75

1911 Single-line Watermark VF Used + 50% (B)

O124	1¢ Dark Violet	13.00	8.50	8.25	5.50	1.15
O125	2¢ Black	77.50	57.50	50.00	32.50	4.00
O126	10¢ Carmine	29.00	19.50	19.00	12.50	1.25

MODERN OFFICIAL ISSUES

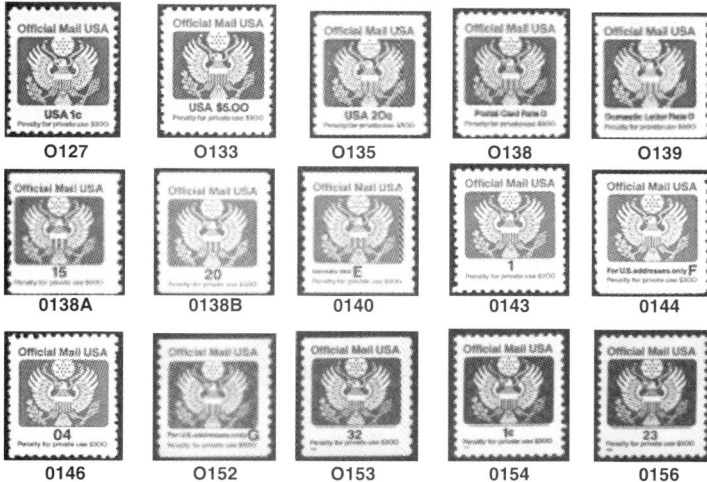

O127	O133	O135	O138	O139
O138A	O138B	O140	O143	O144
O146	O152	O153	O154	O156

1983-85 Official Sheet Stamps

Scott's No.		Mint Sheet	Pl# Blk. F-VF NH	F-VF NH	F-VF Used
O127-33, O138 set of 8		...	...	20.75	...
O127	1¢ Eagle (100)	7.50	.50	.20	.15
O128	4¢ Eagle (100)	12.50	.70	.20	.25
O129	13¢ Eagle (100)	42.50	2.10	.45	.80
O129A	14¢ Eagle (No Pl.#) (1985) (100)	42.50		.45	.50
O130	17¢ Eagle (100)	50.00	2.95	.55	.45
O132	$1 Eagle($1.00) (100)	285.00	13.50	3.00	1.50
O133	$5 Eagle	...	55.00	12.75	5.50
O138	(14¢) "D" Postcard rate ('85) (100)	385.00	35.00	4.00	4.25

1983-88 Official Coil Stamps

O135-36, O138A-B, O139-41 set of 7		...	8.65	...
O135	20¢ Eagle (with ¢ sign) (Pl.# Strip)75.00(5)	12.50(3)	.95	1.50
O136	22¢ Eagle (No Plate #) (1985)		1.10	1.50
O138A	15¢ Eagle (1988)		.50	.50
O138B	20¢ Eagle (No ¢ sign) (1988)		.60	.65
O139	(22¢) "D" Eagle (1985) (Pl.# Strip)90.00(5)	47.50(3)	3.75	2.75
O140	(25¢) "E" Eagle (1988)		1.25	1.85
O141	25¢ Eagle (1988)		.90	.50

1989-1995 Official Sheet Stamps

O143,O146-48,O151,O154-56 set of 9		...	...	5.95	...
O143	1¢ Offset (No ¢ sign) (1989) (100)	9.50	...	.20	.20
O146	4¢ Make-up rate (1991) (100)	12.75	...	.20	.30
O146A	10¢ Eagle (1993) (100)	27.50	...	.30	.50
O147	19¢ Postcard rate (1991) (100)	52.50	...	.55	.55
O148	23¢ 2nd Ounce rate (1991) (100)	65.00	...	.70	.50
O151	$1 Eagle ($1)(1993) (100)	280.00	...	3.00	1.75
O154	1¢ "¢" Sign added,No "USA"('95)(100)	8.75	...	.20	.20
O155	20¢ Sheet Stamp (1995) (100)	47.50	...	.50	.50
O156	23¢ Reprint,Line above "23"('95)(100)	57.50	...	.60	.60

1991-2001 Official Coil Stamps

O144-45, O152-53, O157-58 set of 6		...	...	5.85	...
O144	(29¢) "F" Eagle (1991)			1.60	.75
O145	29¢ Eagle (1991)			.95	.45
O152	(32¢) "G" Eagle (1994)			1.00	1.00
O153	32¢ Eagle (1995)			1.20	.95
O157	33¢ Eagle (1999)			.75	.70
O158	34¢ Great Seal (2001)			.70	...

1913 PARCEL POST STAMPS VF Used + 40% (B)

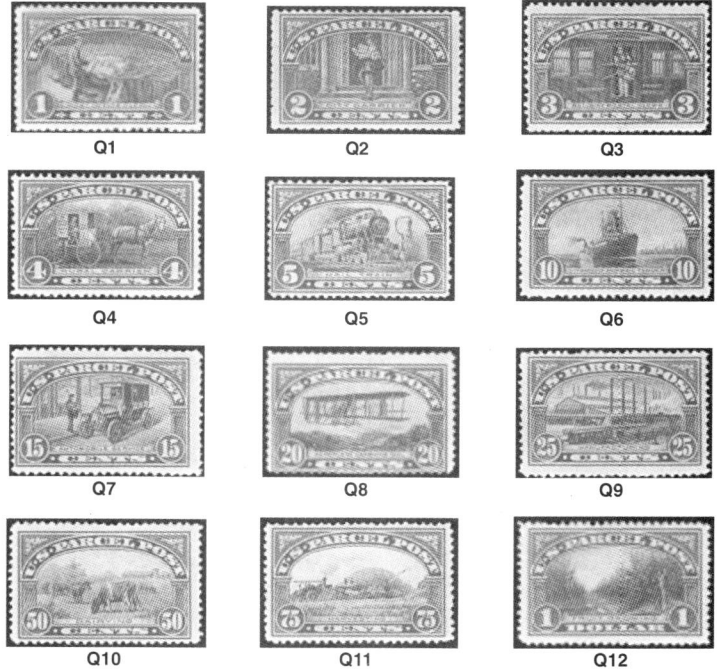

Q1	Q2	Q3
Q4	Q5	Q6
Q7	Q8	Q9
Q10	Q11	Q12

Scott's No.		VF	NH F-VF	Unused VF	F-VF	Used F-VF
Q1	1¢ Post Office Clerk	8.50	6.00	5.00	3.50	1.20
Q1	Plate Block of 6	170.00	120.00	110.00	75.00	...
Q2	2¢ City Carrier	11.00	7.50	6.50	4.50	.90
Q2	Plate Block of 6	180.00	125.00	120.00	85.00	...
Q3	3¢ Railway Clerk	22.50	16.00	13.50	9.50	4.75
Q3	Plate Block of 6	365.00	250.00	240.00	170.00	...
Q4	4¢ Rural Carrier	62.50	45.00	37.50	26.50	2.25
Q5	5¢ Mail Train	52.50	37.50	31.50	22.50	1.80
Q6	10¢ Steamship & Tender	85.00	60.00	50.00	35.00	2.25
Q7	15¢ Automobile Service	110.00	75.00	65.00	45.00	8.75
Q8	20¢ Airplane Carrying Mail	230.00	160.00	135.00	95.00	18.50
Q9	25¢ Manufactured	115.00	80.00	65.00	47.50	5.50
Q10	50¢ Dairying	465.00	330.00	280.00	200.00	32.50
Q11	75¢ Harvesting	160.00	110.00	95.00	65.00	26.50
Q12	$1 Fruit Growing	585.00	425.00	350.00	250.00	25.00

JQ1	QE1

QE2	QE3	QE4

1912 PARCEL POST DUE VF + 40% (B)

JQ1	1¢ Dark Green	17.50	12.50	10.50	7.50	3.75
JQ2	2¢ Dark Green	145.00	100.00	85.00	60.00	13.00
JQ3	5¢ Dark Green	23.50	16.50	14.00	10.00	4.25
JQ4	10¢ Dark Green	285.00	200.00	170.00	120.00	40.00
JQ5	25¢ Dark Green	180.00	125.00	105.00	75.00	3.75

1925-1955 SPECIAL HANDLING STAMPS VF + 30% (B)

QE1	10¢ Yellow Green, Dry (1955)	2.35	1.75	1.60	1.25	1.00
QE1	Plate Block of 6	23.75	17.50	17.50	13.50	...
QE1a	10¢ Wet Printing (1928)	4.00	3.15	2.75	2.25	1.10
QE1a	Plate Block of 6	40.00	29.50	27.50	22.50	...
QE2	15¢ Yellow Green, Dry (1955)	2.65	2.00	1.85	1.40	1.00
QE2	Plate Block of 6	42.50	31.50	29.50	22.50	...
QE2a	15¢ Wet Printing (1928)	5.15	3.90	3.65	2.75	1.10
QE2a	Plate Block of 6	62.50	47.50	45.00	35.00	...
QE3	20¢ Yellow Green, Dry (1955)	3.75	2.80	2.60	2.00	1.50
QE3	Plate Block of 6	42.50	32.50	31.50	25.00	...
QE3a	20¢ Wet Printing (1928)	5.75	4.25	4.00	3.00	1.65
QE3a	Plate Block of 6	77.50	57.50	55.00	42.50	...
QE4	25¢ Yellow Green (1929)	31.50	23.50	22.00	16.50	7.50
QE4	Plate Block of 6	385.00	290.00	275.00	210.00	...
QE4a	25¢ Deep Green (1925)	42.50	31.50	29.50	22.50	5.25
QE4a	Plate Block of 6	465.00	340.00	325.00	250.00	...

U.S. AUTOPOST ISSUES
Computer Vended Postage

Washington, DC

Kensington, MD

Washington, D.C., Machine 82
CV1a	25¢ First Class, Ty. 1	
CV2a	$1.00 3rd Class, Ty. 1	
CV3a	$1.69 Parcel Post, Ty. 1	
CV4a	$2.40 Priority Mail, Ty. 1	
CV5a	$8.75 Express Mail, Ty. 1	
	Set of 5	95.00

Washington, D.C., Machine 83
CV6a	25¢ First Class, Ty. 1	
CV7a	$1.00 3rd Class, Ty. 1	
CV8a	$1.69 Parcel Post, Ty. 2	
CV9a	$2.40 Priority Mail, Ty. 1	
CV10a	$8.75 Express Mail, Ty. 1	
	Set of 5	77.50

Kensington, MD, Machine 82
CV11a	25¢ First Class, Ty. 1	
CV12a	$1.00 3rd Class, Ty. 1	
CV13a	$1.69 Parcel Post, Ty. 2	
CV14a	$2.40 Priority Mail, Ty. 1	
CV15a	$8.75 Express Mail, Ty. 1	
	Set of 5	77.50

Kensington, MD, Machine 83
CV16a	25¢ First Class, Ty. 1	
CV17a	$1.00 3rd Class, Ty. 1	
CV18a	$1.69 Parcel Post, Ty. 2	
CV19a	$2.40 Priority Mail, Ty. 1	
CV20a	$8.75 Express Mail, Ty. 1	
	Set of 5	77.50

CV31,31a,31b,31c

CV32, CV33

1992-96 Variable Rate Coils (Computer Vending)

Scott's No.		Pl# Strip of 5	Pl# Strip of 3	F-VF NH	F-VF Used
CV31	29¢ Shield, horiz.design, Dull Gum	15.00	12.75	1.50	.50
CV31a	29¢ Shield, Shiny Gum	15.00	12.75	1.50	...
CV31b	32¢ Shield, Dull Gum (1994)	14.75	12.75	1.50	.65
CV31c	32¢ Shield, Shiny Gum (1995)	14.75	12.75	1.50	...
CV32	29¢ Shield, vertical design (1994)	11.00	9.75	1.00	.50
CV33	32¢ Shield, Vertical Design ('96)	11.00	9.75	1.10	.50

NOTE: VARIABLE RATE COILS COME IN A NUMBER DIFFERENT DENOMINATIONS BUT THE FIRST CLASS RATE OF 29¢ AND 32¢ ARE THE ONLY RATES REGULARLY AVAILABLE.

U.S. TEST COILS

11 etc.   **31etc.**   **41 etc.**   **SV1**

Scott's No.		Line Pair	Pair	F-VF NH

BUREAU OF ENGRAVING & PRINTING TEST COILS

Blank Coils
T11	Imperforate	...	57.50	27.50
T15	Perforated 10, Shiny Gum	...	1.80	.90
T17	Perforated 11	...	9.00	4.50
T18	Perf. 10, Tagged, Dull Gum (1980)	65.00	11.50	5.75
T21	Perf. 10, Two Horiz. Red Lines	...	12.00	6.00

1938-60 Solid Design Coil
T31	Purple	30.00	11.00	5.50
T32	Carmine (1954)	...	...	...
T33	Red Violet, Small Holes (1960)	35.00	7.50	3.75
T33l	Red Violet, Large Holes	140.00	25.00	12.50

1962-98 "FOR TESTING PURPOSES ONLY"
T41	Black, untagged, shiny gum	25.00	3.50	1.75
T41a	Black, tagged, shiny gum	5.50	1.60	.80
T41b	Black, tagged, pebble-surfaced gum	25.00	3.50	1.75
T41d	Black, tagged, dull gum	22.50	7.50	3.75
T41e	Black, untagged, dull gum	12.75	2.20	1.10
T42	Carmine, tagged (1970)	...	...	...
T43	Green, tagged	...	300.00	150.00
T43c	Green, untagged	...	300.00	150.00
T44	Brown, untagged	52.50	5.50	2.75
T45	Orange, tagged	...	...	...
T46	Black, "B" Press, 19mm wide (1988)	...	1.70	.85
T46a	Black, on white paper,Self-adhesive(1998)..	...	1.40	.70
T46a	Same, Plate #V1, Strip of 5	...	12.95	...
T46b	Black,on blue paper, self-adhesive	...	1.40	.70
T46b	Same, Plate #1111, Strip of 5	...	12.95	...

STAMP VENTURERS TEST COILS
SV1	Eagle, Perforated	...	2.20	1.10
SV2	Eagle, Rouletted	...	6.50	3.25

SAVINGS STAMPS

PS8   **PS14**   **S1**   **S7**   **WS8**

1911-36 Postal Savings Stamps VF Used + 30% (B)

Scott's No.		VF	NH F-VF	Unused VF	F-VF	Used F-VF
PS1	10¢ Orange	12.50	9.50	9.00	6.75	1.25
PS2	10¢ Orange Imprint on Deposit Card	...	...	175.00	140.00	37.50
PS4	10¢ Blue, Single-line Wk.,Pf.12	8.25	6.00	5.50	4.00	1.10
PS5	10¢ Blue Imprint on Deposit Card	...	...	175.00	140.00	25.00
PS6	10¢ Blue, Unwmk.,Perf.11(1936)	7.75	6.00	6.00	4.75	1.15

1940 Postal Savings - Numerals VF +30% (B)

Scott's No.		Plate Block	F-VF NH	F-VF Used
PS7	10¢ Deep Ultramarine	225.00	14.75	5.00
PS8	25¢ Dark Carmine Rose	250.00	16.50	8.00
PS9	50¢ Dark Blue Green	...	15.00	15.00
PS10	$1 Gray Black	...	125.00	15.00

1941 Postal Savings - Minute Man VF + 20%

PS11	10¢ Rose Red	7.50	.60	...
PS11b	10¢ Booklet Pane of 10	...	45.00	...
PS12	25¢ Blue Green	18.75	1.75	...
PS12b	25¢ Booklet Pane of 10	...	55.00	...
PS13	50¢ Ultramarine	50.00	6.50	...
PS14	$1 Gray Black	75.00	11.00	...
PS15	$5 Sepia, Size 36mm x 46mm	...	37.50	...

1954-61 Savings Stamps - Minute Man VF + 20%

S1	10¢ Rose Red	3.00	.45	...
S1a	10¢ Booklet Pane of 10 (1955) ...	...	140.00	...
S2	25¢ Blue Green	32.50	6.75	...
S2a	25¢ Booklet Pane of 10 (1955) ...	...	775.00	...
S3	50¢ Ultramarine (1956)	47.50	8.00	...
S4	$1 Gray Black (1957)	...	21.50	...
S5	$5 Sepia (1956)	...	85.00	...
S6	25¢ 48 Star Flag, Blue & Carmine (1958)	8.75	1.75	...
S6a	25¢ Booklet Pane of 10	...	67.50	...
S7	25¢ 50 Star Flag, Blue & Carmine (1961)	10.00	1.35	...

1917 War Savings Thrift Stamps VF Used + 40% (B)

Scott's No.		VF	NH F-VF	Unused VF	F-VF	Used F-VF
WS1	25¢ Deep Green	31.75	21.50	20.75	14.50	2.00

1917-19 War Savings Certificate Stamps VF Used + 40% (B)

WS2	$5 Washington, Green,Pf.11 .	150.00	110.00	100.00	75.00	22.50
WS4	$5 Franklin, Deep Blue (1919)	565.00	400.00	375.00	270.00	140.00
WS5	$5 Washington, Carmine('1919)...	...	...	950.00	650.00	225.00

1942-45 War Savings Stamps VF + 20%

Scott's No.		Plate Block	F-VF NH	F-VF Used
WS7	10¢ Rose Red	4.75	.45	.20
WS7b	10¢ Booklet Pane of 10	...	45.00	...
WS8	25¢ Blue Green	8.00	1.00	.30
WS8b	25¢ Booklet Pane of 10	...	45.00	...
WS9	50¢ Deep Ultramarine	21.50	3.75	1.15
WS10	$1 Gray Black	65.00	11.00	3.25
WS11	$5 Violet Brown (1945)	...	50.00	15.00

1943 War Savings Coil Stamps Perf.10 Vert. VF + 20%

WS12	10¢ Rose Red .... Line Pair	9.50	2.50	.80
WS13	25¢ Dark Blue Green .... Line Pair	18.50	4.50	1.50

1945 POSTAL NOTE STAMPS

PN1-18 Examples

PN1-18	set of 18	...	28.50	2.50
PN1	1¢ Black	2.50	.20	.15
PN2	2¢ Black	2.50	.20	.15
PN3	3¢ Black	2.75	.20	.15
PN4	4¢ Black	3.00	.25	.15
PN5	5¢ Black	4.25	.30	.15
PN6	6¢ Black	5.00	.35	.15
PN7	7¢ Black	7.00	.50	.15
PN8	8¢ Black	8.50	.60	.15
PN9	9¢ Black	9.00	.65	.15
PN10	10¢ Black	11.00	.75	.15
PN11	20¢ Black	20.00	1.40	.15
PN12	30¢ Black	27.00	1.80	.15
PN13	40¢ Black	32.50	2.35	.15
PN14	50¢ Black	42.50	2.95	.15
PN15	60¢ Black	57.50	3.95	.15
PN16	70¢ Black	62.50	4.35	.15
PN17	80¢ Black	75.00	5.25	.15
PN18	90¢ Black	85.00	5.95	.15

PLATE NUMBER COIL STRIPS

1897

2127

Scott No.	F-VF,NH	Pl.Strip of 5	Pl.Strip of 3
	1981		
1891	**18¢ Flag**		
	Pl# 1	375.00	100.00
	Pl# 2	57.50	19.50
	Pl# 3	875.00	250.00
	Pl# 4	10.75	6.50
	Pl# 5	6.75	5.00
	Pl# 6	P.O.R.	P.O.R.
	Pl# 7	42.50	32.50
1895	**20¢ Flag**		
	Pl# 1	90.00	6.50
	Pl# 2,11,12	10.75	7.00
	Pl# 3,5,9-10,13-14	5.00	3.50
	Pl# 4	675.00	35.00
	Pl# 6	210.00	80.00
	Pl# 8	16.00	5.00
1895b	Pl# 14	95.00	90.00
	1981-91 Transportation Coils		
1897	**1¢ Omnibus**		
	Pl# 1,2,5,6	.60	.50
	Pl# 3,4	1.00	.80
1897A	**2¢ Locomotive**		
	Pl# 2,6	.75	.60
	Pl# 3,4,8,10	.65	.55
1898	**3¢ Handcar**		
	Pl# 1-4	.85	.75
1898A	**4¢ Stagecoach**		
	Pl# 1,2,3,4	1.60	1.25
	Pl# 5,6	3.25	2.50
1898Ab	Pl# 3,4,5,6	7.50	6.75
1899	**5¢ Motorcycle**		
	Pl# 1-4	1.50	1.10
1900	**5.2¢ Sleigh**		
	Pl# 1,2	11.75	5.95
	Pl# 3	400.00	225.00
	P1#5	240.00	165.00
1900a	Pl# 1-3, 5	15.00	13.50
	P1#4,6	18.50	17.00
1901	**5.9¢ Bicycle**		
	Pl# 3,4	18.50	7.50
1901a	Pl# 3,4	47.50	42.50
	Pl# 5,6	110.00	95.00
1902	**7.4¢ Baby Buggy**		
	Pl# 2	14.50	7.00
1902a	Pl# 2	6.50	5.95
1903	**9.3¢ Mail Wagon**		
	Pl# 1,2	16.50	6.75
	Pl# 3,4	45.00	21.50
	Pl# 5,6	375.00	350.00
1903a	Pl# 1,2	14.50	13.00
	Pl# 3	47.50	39.50
	Pl# 4	22.50	17.50
	Pl# 5,6	4.00	3.25
	Pl# 8	325.00	300.00
1904	**10.9¢ Hansom Cab**		
	Pl# 1,2	45.00	15.00
1904a	Pl# 1,2	45.00	42.50
	Pl# 3,4	525.00	500.00
1905	**11¢ Caboose**		
	Pl# 1	5.25	3.50
1905b	Pl# 2, untagged	3.75	3.00
1905a	Pl# 1	5.25	4.25
1906	**17¢ Electric Car**		
	Pl# 1-5	3.50	2.50
	Pl# 6	18.75	17.50
	Pl# 7	7.75	7.00
1906a	Pl# 3A-5A	6.50	5.75
	Pl# 6A,7A	16.50	15.00
1906ab	Pl# 3B,4B	37.50	35.00
	Pl# 5B,6B	42.50	39.50
1906ac	Pl# 1C,2C,3C,4C	17.00	14.00
	Pl# 5C,7C	43.50	40.00
1907	**18¢ Surrey**		
	Pl# 1	120.00	67.50
	Pl# 2,5,6,8	4.25	3.00
	Pl# 3,4	100.00	65.00
	Pl# 7	40.00	35.00
	Pl# 9,10	20.00	15.00
	Pl# 11,12,	18.00	16.00
	Pl# 13-14,17-18	7.50	5.25
	Pl# 15-16	35.00	30.00

Scott No.	F-VF,NH	Pl.Strip of 5	Pl.Strip of 3
1908	**20¢ Fire Pumper**		
	Pl# 1	185.00	25.00
	Pl# 2	1150.00	180.00
	Pl# 3,4,13,15,16	5.25	4.25
	Pl# 5,9,10	4.00	2.75
	Pl# 6	50.00	35.00
	Pl# 7,8	210.00	65.00
	Pl# 11	100.00	25.00
	Pl# 12,14	8.75	7.50
	1982-1987		
2005	**20¢ Consumer**		
	Pl# 1,2	200.00	30.00
	Pl# 3,4	140.00	27.50
2112	**(22¢) "D" Eagle Coil**		
	Pl# 1,2	9.50	6.50
2115	**22¢ Flag/Capitol**		
	Pl# 1,7,13	15.00	10.00
	Pl# 2,8,10,12	4.50	3.50
	Pl# 3	75.00	13.00
	Pl# 4,5,6,11	8.75	7.50
	Pl# 14	43.50	40.00
	Pl# 15,19,22	4.50	3.50
	Pl# 16,17,18,20,21	8.75	7.50
2115b	22¢ Flag Test Coil		
	Pl# T1	5.50	4.25
	1985-89 Transportation Coils		
2123	**3.4¢ School Bus**		
	Pl# 1,2	1.30	1.00
2123a	Pl# 1,2	5.75	5.00
2124	**4.9¢ Buckboard**		
	Pl# 3,4	1.30	1.00
2124a	Pl# 1-6	2.25	1.85
2125	**5.5¢ Star Route Truck**		
	Pl# 1	2.65	2.10
2125a	Pl# 1,2	2.50	2.35
2126	**6¢ Tricycle**		
	Pl# 1	2.15	1.75
2126a	Pl# 1	2.40	1.95
	Pl# 2	9.75	9.00
2127	**7.1¢ Tractor**		
	Pl# 1	2.95	2.50
2127a	Pl# 1	4.15	3.50
2127b	Zip + 4		
	Pl# 1	2.85	2.25
2128	**8.3¢ Ambulance**		
	Pl# 1,2	2.20	1.65
2128a	Pl# 1,2	2.25	1.65
	Pl# 3,4	6.50	5.50
2129	**8.5¢ Tow Truck**		
	Pl# 1	3.60	3.00
2129a	Pl# 1	3.75	3.15
	Pl# 2	14.50	13.50
2130	**10.1¢ Oil Wagon**		
	Pl# 1	3.25	2.65
2130a	Pl# 2,3 Red Prec.	3.35	2.50
2130av	Pl# 1,2 Black Prec.	3.35	2.75
2131	**11¢ Stutz Bearcat**		
	Pl# 1-4	2.50	1.95
2132	**12¢ Stanley Steamer**		
	Pl# 1,2	3.50	2.50
2132a	Pl# 1,2	3.00	2.50
2132b	12¢ "B" Press, Prec.		
	Pl# 1	29.50	26.50
2133	**12.5¢ Pushcart**		
	Pl# 1	3.50	3.00
	P1#2	6.00	5.25
2133a	Pl# 1	3.50	3.00
	P1#2	5.00	4.25
2134	**14¢ Iceboat**		
	Pl# 1-4	2.85	2.25
2134b	"B" Press		
	Pl# 2	6.75	5.50
2135	**17¢ Dog Sled**		
	Pl# 2	4.65	3.50
2136	**25¢ Bread Wagon**		
	Pl# 1-5	4.95	3.75
	1985		
2149	**18¢ GW Monument**		
	Pl# 1112,3333	4.65	3.25
2149a	Pl# 11121,33333	4.95	3.95
2149d	Pl# 33333 Dry Gum	6.75	5.50
	Pl# 43444 Dry Gum	8.75	7.50

Scott No.	F-VF,NH	Pl.Strip of 5	Pl.Strip of 3
2150	**21.1¢ Pre-Sort**		
	Pl# 111111	4.75	3.50
	Pl# 111121	6.50	5.25
2150a	Pl# 111111	5.00	4.00
	Pl# 111121	6.25	5.25
	1986-96 Transportation Coils		
2225	**1¢ Omnibus "B" Press**		
	Pl# 1,2	.80	.70
2225a	Pl# 3 mottled tagging	9.50	8.75
2225b	Pl# 2,3 untagged, Dull	1.30	1.00
2225s	Pl# 3 Shiny, untagged	.80	.70
2225l	Pl# 3 Low gloss,untagged	1.50	1.40
2226	**2¢ Locomotive "B" Press**		
	Pl# 1 Tagged, Dull	.95	.75
2226a	Pl# 2 untagged, Dull	1.15	.85
2226s	Pl# 2, untagged,Shiny	1.50	1.30
2228	**4¢ Stagecoach "B"**		
	Pl# 1, block tagging	1.50	1.15
2228a	Pl# 1, overall tagging	19.50	18.50
2231	**8.3¢ Ambul."B" Press,Precancel**		
	Pl# 1	9.75	7.50
	Pl# 2	10.50	9.50
	1987-94 Transportation Coils		
2252	**3¢ Conestoga Wagon**		
	Pl# 1	1.15	.95
2252a	Pl# 2,3 untagged, Dull	1.85	1.50
2252s	Pl# 3 untagged, Shiny	2.25	1.80
	Pl# 5,6 untagged,Shiny	3.50	3.00
2252l	Pl# 3 untagged,Low gloss	10.75	9.75
2253	**5¢ Milk Wagon**		
	Pl# 1	1.50	1.20
2254	**5.3¢ Elevator, Precancel**		
	Pl# 1	2.30	1.85
2255	**7.6¢ Carreta, Precancel**		
	Pl# 1,2	3.15	2.65
	Pl# 3	6.50	6.00
2256	**8.4¢ Wheel Chair, Precancel**		
	Pl# 2	3.00	2.50
	Pl# 3	18.00	16.50
2257	**10¢ Canal Boat**		
	Pl# 1 block tagging,Dull	2.75	2.25
2257a	Pl# 1 overall tagging,Dull	6.25	5.75
2257b	Pl# 1-4 mottled tagging, Shiny gum	5.25	4.75
2257v	Pl# 5 overall tag,Shiny	5.25	4.75
2258	**13¢ Patrol Wagon, Precancel**		
	Pl# 1	5.75	4.75
2259	**13.2¢ Coal Car, Precancel**		
	Pl# 1,2	4.25	3.65
2260	**15¢ Tugboat**		
	Pl# 1,2 large block tagging	3.25	2.50
2260a	Pl# 2, overall tagging	5.00	4.00
2260b	Pl# 2 untagged	200.00	190.00
2261	**16.7¢ Popcorn Wagon, Precancel**		
	Pl# 1	4.25	3.50
	P1# 2	5.75	5.25
2262	**17.5¢ Marmon Wasp**		
	Pl# 1	5.75	4.75
2262a	Pl# 1	5.75	4.75
2263	**20¢ Cable Car**		
	Pl# 1,2 block tag	4.75	3.75
2263b	Pl# 2, overall tag	11.00	8.75
2264	**20.5¢ Fire Engine, Prec.**		
	Pl# 1	8.95	6.95
2265	**20.5¢ RR Mail Car, Prec.**		
	Pl# 1,2	7.00	5.25
2266	**24.1¢ Tandem Bike, Prec.**		
	Pl# 1	6.50	5.25
	1988		
2279	**(25¢) "E" Series**		
	Pl# 1111,1222	4.50	3.50
	Pl# 1211, 2222	6.00	5.00
2280	**25¢ Yosemite Block tagged**		
	Pl# 1,7	8.50	7.50
	Pl# 2-5,8	4.75	3.50
	Pl# 9	15.00	13.75
2280a	25¢ Yosemite mottled tagging		
	Pl# 1	45.00	42.50
	Pl# 3,7-11,13-14	4.95	3.95
	Pl# 5,15	8.50	7.50
	Pl# 6	15.75	14.00

PLATE NUMBER COIL STRIPS

2518

2904B

Scott No.	F-VF,NH	Pl.Strip of 5	Pl.Strip of 3
2281	25¢ Honeybee		
	Pl# 1,2	4.50	3.50
	1990-95 Transportation Coils		
2451	4¢ Steam Carriage		
	Pl# 1	1.30	1.00
2451b	Pl# 1, untagged	1.50	1.25
2452	5¢ Circus Wagon, Engraved, Dull gum		
	Pl# 1	1.50	1.25
2452a	Pl# 1, untagged, Dull	2.00	1.60
2452l	Pl# 2 untagged,Low gloss	2.00	1.60
2452B	5¢ Circus Wagon, Gravure		
	Pl# A1,A2	1.90	1.50
2452Bf	Pl# A3 Hi-brite	3.85	3.25
2452D	5¢ Circus Wagon (¢ sign)		
	Pl# S1,S2, Low gloss	1.80	1.60
2452Dg	Pl# S2 Hi-brite, Shiny	2.75	2.25
2453	5¢ Canoe, Brown, Engraved		
	Pl# 1,2,3	1.80	1.50
2454	5¢ Canoe, Red, Gravure		
	Pl# S11	1.90	1.60
2454l	Pl# S11 Low gloss	12.75	11.50
2457	10¢ Tractor Trailer,intaglio		
	Pl# 1	3.00	2.50
2458	10¢ Tractor Trailer, Gravure		
	Pl#11	6.00	5.00
	Pl# 22	4.25	3.50
2463	20¢ Cog Railway		
	Pl# 1,2	5.50	4.75
2464	23¢ Lunch Wagon		
	Pl# 2,3 overall tagging	5.00	3.95
2464a	23¢ Dull Gum		
	Pl# 3, 4 mottled tagging	7.25	5.75
2464s	23¢ Shiny Gum		
	Pl# 3, 4, 5 mottled tag	7.00	5.75
2466	32¢ Ferry Boat,Shiny gum		
	Pl# 2,3,4	8.00	6.75
	Pl# 5	14.50	13.50
2466l	32¢ Mottled tagging, Low gloss Gum		
	Pl# 3,5	8.75	7.50
	Pl# 4	22.75	21.75
2466b	32¢ Bronx Blue		
	P1# 5	150.00	130.00
2468	$1 Seaplane, Overall tag, Dull Gum		
	Pl# 1	16.00	11.00
2468b	$1 mottled tagging, Shiny Gum		
	Pl# 3	17.00	11.50
2468c	$1 solid tagging, Low gloss Gum		
	P1# 3	17.00	11.50
	1993-95 Flora & Fauna		
2491v	29¢ Pine Cone, SA		
	Pl# B1	8.00	6.75
2492v	32¢ Pink Rose, SA		
	Pl# S111	6.75	5.50
2495-95Av	32¢ Peach & Pear, SA		
	Pl# V11111	9.00	7.00
	1991-1994		
2518	(29¢) "F" Flower		
	Pl# 1111,1222,2211,2222	5.00	3.75
	Pl# 1211	16.50	15.00
2523	29¢ Flag/Mt. Rushmore		
	Pl# 1-8 mottled tagging	5.75	4.50
	Pl# 9	14.00	12.75
2523c	29¢ Toledo Brown		
	P1# 7	200.00	190.00
2523A	29¢ Rushmore/Gravure		
	Pl# A11111,A22211	6.25	4.95
2525	29¢ Flower, rouletted		
	Pl# S1111,S2222	6.75	5.25
2526	29¢ Flower, perforated		
	Pl# S2222	6.75	5.25
2529	19¢ Fishing Boat, Type I		
	Pl# A1111,A1212,A2424	4.50	3.75
	Pl# A1112	8.75	7.75
2529a	Type II, Andreotti Gravure		
	Pl# A5555,A5556, A6667	4.50	3.75
	P1# A7667, A7679 A7766, A7779	5.95	4.95
2529b	Type II,untagged A5555	12.50	10.00
2529C	Type III, S111	8.75	7.50
2598v	29¢ Eagle, SA		
	Pl# 111	8.00	6.75

Scott No.	F-VF,NH	Pl.Strip of 5	Pl.Strip of 3
2599v	Statue of Liberty, SA		
	Pl# D1111	8.00	6.75
2602	(10¢) Eagle &Shield		
	A11111,A11112,A21112, A22112,A22113,A33333, A43334,A43335,A53335	3.25	2.75
	A12213	18.00	16.50
	A21113,A33335, A43324,A43325,A43326, A43426,A54444,A54445	3.25	2.75
	A34424,A34426,	6.50	5.75
	A32333	395.00	375.00
	A33334	120.00	110.00
	A77777,A88888,A88889, A89999,A99998,A99999	3.50	2.65
	A1010101010,A1110101010, A1011101011,etc.	4.50	3.50
	A111010101011	12.00	11.00
2603	(10¢) Eagle & Shield (BEP)		
	Pl# 11111,22221, 22222	3.65	3.00
2603l	(10¢) Low Gloss Gum, Pl# 22222, 44444, 33333	4.25	3.50
2603b	(10¢) Tagged, Shiny Pl# 11111, 22221	17.75	15.75
2604	(10¢) Eagle & Shield (SV)		
	Pl# S11111,S22222	3.95	3.25
2604l	(10¢) Low Gloss Gum, Pl# S11111,S22222 .	3.95	3.25
2605	23¢ Flag, Bulk Rate		
	Pl# A111,A212, A222 (FAT)	5.25	4.00
	Pl# A112,A122,A333, A222(THIN)	5.25	4.00
2606	23¢ USA Pre-sort, ABNCo.		
	Pl# A1111,A2222,A2232,	6.00	4.75
	P1# A2233,A3333,A4443, A4444,A4453,A4364	6.50	5.25
2607	23¢ USA Pre-sort, BEP, Shiny		
	Pl# 1111	6.25	5.00
2607l	23¢ Low gloss Gum #1111	6.25	5.25
2608	23¢ USA Pre-sort, S.V.		
	Pl# S1111	7.50	6.00
2609	29¢ Flag/White House		
	Pl# 1-11	6.25	4.75
	Pl# 13-16,18	7.50	6.25
	1993 Self-Adhesive		
2799-2802v	29¢ Christmas		
	Pl#V1111111 .... (8)	11.95	...
2813v	29¢ Love		
	Pl# B1	8.00	6.75
2873v	29¢ Santa Claus		
	Pl# V1111	8.25	7.00
2886v	(32¢) "G"		
	Pl# V11111	7.50	6.00
	1994-95 "G" Coils		
2888	(25¢) "G"		
	Pl# S11111	8.25	6.75
2889	(32¢) Black "G"		
	Pl# 1111, 2222	11.75	9.75
2890	(32¢) Blue "G"		
	Pl# A1111,A1112,A1113, A1211,A1212,A1311, A1324,A1417,A1433 A2211,A2212,A2213,A2214, A2223,A2313,A3113,A3314, A3315,A3323,A3324,A3423, A3433,A3435,A3436,A4426, A4427,A5327,A5417,A5427, A5437	8.25	6.75
	P1#A1113, A1222, A1313, A1314	12.75	9.75
	Pl# A3114, A3426	9.00	7.75
	Pl# A4435	210.00	195.00
2891	(32¢) Red "G"		
	Pl# S1111	14.75	12.50
2892	(32¢) "G" Rouletted		
	Pl# S1111,S2222	9.00	7.50
2893	(5¢) "G" Non-Profit		
	Pl# A11111,A21111	2.95	2.50
	1995-97 Non Denominated Coils		
2902	(5¢) Butte,		

Scott No.	F-VF,NH	Pl.Strip of 5	Pl.Strip of 3
	Pl# S111,S222, S333 ..	2.10	1.75
2902B	(5¢) Butte, SA		
	Pl# S111	2.65	2.25
2903	(5¢) Mountain, BEP		
	Pl# 11111	2.25	1.95
2904	(5¢) Mountain, SVS		
	Pl# S111	2.65	2.25
2904A	(5¢) Mountain, 11.5		
	Pl# V222222, V333323, V333333, V333342, V333343	2.65	2.25
2904B	(5¢) Mountain, 9.8		
	Pl# 1111	2.70	2.25
2905	(10¢) Automobile		
	Pl# S111,S222,S333	3.25	2.75
2906	(10¢) Automobile		
	Pl# S111	2.95	2.65
2907	(10¢) Eagle & Shield		
	Pl# S11111	3.85	3.25
2908	(15¢) Auto Tail Fin, BEP		
	Pl# 11111	3.75	3.00
2909	(15¢) Auto Tail Fin, SVS		
	Pl# S11111	3.75	3.00
2910	(15¢) Auto Tail Fin, SA		
	Pl# S11111	3.95	3.25
2911	(25¢) Juke Box, BEP		
	Pl# 111111,212222, 222222,332222	6.25	5.25
2912	(25¢) Juke Box, SVS		
	Pl# S11111,S22222	5.75	4.75
2912A	(25¢) Juke Box, 11.5, SA		
	Pl# S11111, S22222	5.75	4.75
2912B	(25¢) Juke box, 9.8, SA		
	Pl# 111111,222222	5.75	4.75
	1995-97 Flag over Porch		
2913	32¢ Flag over Porch, BEP, Shiny		
	Pl# 11111,22221,22222	6.25	5.25
2913l	32¢ Low Gloss Gum		
	Pl# 11111,22221,22222, 33333, 34333, 44444, 45444, 66646, 77767, 78767 91161, 99969	7.75	6.50
	Pl# 22322	48.50	45.00
	P1#66666	17.50	12.50
2914	32¢ Flag over Porch, SVS		
	Pl# S11111	7.00	5.75
2915	32¢ Flag over Porch, 8.7, SA		
	Pl# V11111	8.25	6.75
2915A	32¢ Flag over Porch, 9.7,SA		
	Pl#11111,22222,23222, 33333,44444,45444, 55555,66666,78777, 88888,89878,97898 99999,11111A,13231A, 22222A,33333A,44444A, 55555A,66666A,77777A, 78777A,88888A	8.95	7.50
	P1#87898,89888, 89898,	19.75	18.50
	P1#87888,99899 ...	45.00	42.50
	P1#88898, 89899 ...	POR	POR
	P1#13211A	95.00	90.00
2915B	32¢ Flag over Porch, 11.5, SA		
	Pl# S11111	8.25	6.50
2915C	32¢ Flag over Porch, 10.9, SA		
	PL# 55555,66666 ...	21.00	17.50
2915D	32¢ Flag over Porch, 9.8,SA Stamps Separate		
	Pl# 11111	6.95	5.75
	1995-99		
3014-17	32¢ Santa & Children, SA		
	Pl# V1111 .... (8)	9.75	...
3018	32¢ Midnight Angel, SA		
	Pl# B1111	8.35	6.50
3044	1¢ Kestrel		
	Pl # 1111	1.00	.80
3044a	1¢ Kestrel, Reprint		
	Pl# 1111,2222,3333	1.35	1.20
3045	2¢ Woodpecker		
	Pl# 11111	.90	.70
	Pl# 22222	2.75	2.50
3053	20¢ Blue Jay, SA		
	Pl# S1111	5.25	4.35

PLATE NUMBER COIL STRIPS

3132

0135

Scott No.	F-VF, NH	Pl. Strip of 5	Pl. Strip of 3
3054	32¢ Yellow Rose, SA		
	Pl # 1111, 1112, 1122 2222, 2223, 2233, 2333, 3344, 3444, 4455, 5455, 5555, 5556, 5566, 5666,	6.50	4.95
	Pl# 6666, 6677, 6777, 7777, 8888	10.50	9.75
3055	20¢ Ringnecked Pheasant, SA		
	Pl#1111, 2222	5.25	4.35
3132	(25¢) Juke Box, SA		
	Linerless Pl #M11111	6.50	5.25
3133	32¢ Flags over Porch, SA		
	Linerless Pl #M11111	8.75	7.50
3207	(5¢) Wetlands		
	Pl#S111	2.40	2.10
3207A	(5¢) Wetlands, SA		
	Pl#1111, 2222, 3333, 4444	2.40	2.10
3208	(25¢) Diner, SA		
	Pl#S11111	5.75	4.75
3208A	(25¢) Diner, SA		
	Pl#11111, 22211, 22222, 33333, 44444	5.75	4.75
3228	(10¢) Green Bicycle, SA		
	Pl# 111, 221, 222, 333, 344, 444, 555, 666, 777, 888, 999	3.65	3.00
3229	(10¢) Green Bicycle		
	Pl#S111	3.65	3.00
	1998 Regular Issues		
3263	22¢ Uncle Sam, SA		
	Pl#1111	5.25	4.25
3264	(33¢) Hat		
	Pl#1111, 3333, 3343, 3344, 3444	7.00	5.75
3264d	(33¢) Duller Gum		
	Pl# 1111	7.50	6.00
3265	(33¢) Hat, SA, Die-cut 9.9		
	Pl#1111, 1131, 2222, 3333	7.00	5.75
3266	(33¢) Hat, SA Die-cut 9.7		
	Pl# 1111	7.00	5.75

Scott No.	F-VF, NH	Pl. Strip of 5	Pl. Strip of 3
3270	(10¢) Eagle, Pre-sorted, Small Date		
	Pl#11111	3.00	2.50
3270a	(10¢) Eagle, Pre-sorted, Large Date		
	Pl#22222	6.50	6.00
3271	(10¢) Eagle, Pre-sorted, SA		
	Pl#11111, 22222	3.00	2.50
	1999-2000		
3280	33¢ Flag over City, WA, Small Date		
	Pl# 1111, 2222	6.00	4.75
3280a	33¢ Flag over City, WA, Large Date		
	Pl# 3333	8.00	5.75
3281	33¢ Flag over City, SA, Square Corners, 1 3/4 mm date		
	Pl# 1111A, 2222A, 3333A, 4444, 6666, 7777, 8888, 9999	6.00	4.75
3281c	33¢ Smaller 1¼ mm date		
	Pl# 1111, 2222, 3333, 3433, 4443, 4444, 5555	6.35	5.00
3282	33¢ Flag over City, SA, Rounded Corners		
	Pl# 1111, 2222	6.00	4.75
3302-5	33¢ Fruit Berries		
	Pl# B1111, B1112, B2221, B2221, B2222	8.50	6.50
3353	22¢ Uncle Sam		
	Pl# 1111	5.00	4.00
3404-7	33¢ Fruit Berries		
	Pl# G1111 .... (9) 8.00 (5)		5.75
3447	(10¢) N.Y.Public Library Lion		
	Pl# S11111	2.40	1.95
3452	(34¢) Statue of Liberty, Perforated		
	Pl# 1111	5.25	3.95
3453	(34¢) Statue of Liberty, SA, Die-cut		
	Pl# 1111	5.25	3.95
	2000-2001 Regular Issue Coils		
3462-65	(34¢) Flowers, SA Die-cut		
	Pl# B1111 ...... (9)11.75 (5)		7.75

Scott No.	F-VF, NH	Pl. Strip of 5	Pl. Strip of 3
3466	34¢ Liberty, SA Die-cut, Rounded Corners		
	Pl# 1111	5.25	3.95
3475	21¢ Bison, SA		
	Pl# V1111	3.15	2.40
3476	34¢ Liberty, Perforated		
	Pl# 1111	5.25	3.95
3477	34¢ Liberty, Die-cut, Square Corners		
	Pl# 1111	5.25	3.95
3478-81	34¢ Flowers, SA Die-cut		
	Pl# B1111	7.75	5.25
	1983-85 Official Stamps		
O135	20¢ Official		
	Pl# 1111	75.00	12.50
O139	(22¢) "D" Official		
	Pl# 1111	90.00	47.50
	VARIABLE RATE COILS		
CV31	29¢ Shield, Dull Gum		
	Pl# 1	15.00	12.75
CV31a	29¢ Shiny Gum		
	Pl# 1	15.00	12.75
CV31b	32¢ Dull Gum		
	Pl# 1	14.75	12.75
CV31c	32¢ Shiny Gum		
	Pl# 1	14.75	12.75
CV32	29¢ Vertical Design		
	Pl# A11	11.00	9.75
CV33	32¢ Vertical Design		
	Pl# 11	11.00	9.75

UNFOLDED BOOKLET PANES WITH PLATE NUMBERS

Scott No.	Description	FVF,NH
2409a	25¢ Steamboats, Pl#1	7.00
	Pl# 2	22.50
2427a	25¢ Madonna (10) Pl# 1	15.00
2429a	25¢ Sleigh (10) Pl# 1111	19.50
	Pl#2111	25.75
2441a	25¢ Love (10), Pl# 1211	42.50
2474a	25¢ Lighthouse (5) Pl# 1,3,5	11.75
	Pl# 2	13.95
2484a	29¢ Wood Duck, BEP(10) Pl#1111	9.95
2485a	29¢ Wood Duck, KCS (10)	
	Pl#K11111	10.95
2486a	29¢ African Violet (10) Pl# K1111	10.75
2505a	25¢ Indian Headresses (10)	
	Pl# 1,2	16.50
2516a	25¢ Christmas Tree (10) Pl#1211	18.95
2527a	29¢ Flower (10) Pl# K1111	9.75
2530a	19¢ Hot-Air Balloons (10) Pl# 1111	6.75
2536a	29¢ Love (10) Pl# 1111, 1112	9.50
2549a	29¢ Fishing Flies (5) Pl# A23213	13.75
	Pl# A23133	15.00
	Pl# A23124	57.50
	pl# A33225, A33233	27.50
2552a	29¢ Desert Storm (5)	
	Pl# A11121111	6.50
2566a	29¢ Comedians (10) Pl#1	11.75
2577a	29¢ Space (10) Pl# 111111	15.75
2581b-85a	(29¢) Santa, set of 5 Panes of 4, Pl# A11111	31.75
2593a	29¢ Pledge, black (10) Pl# 1111	9.75
2646a	29¢ Hummingbirds (5)	
	Pl# A2212112, A2212122, A2222222	5.50
	Pl# A1111111, A2212222	9.95
2718a	29¢ Toys (4) Pl# A111111, A222222	5.50
2737a	29¢ Rock'n Roll (8) Pl#A222228	8.95
2737b	29¢ Rock'n Roll (4) Pl#A222224	4.95
2745a	29¢ Space Fantasy (5)	
	Pl# 1111, 1211	5.50
	Pl# 2222	6.75
2764a	29¢ Garden Flowers (5) Pl# 1	5.50
2770a	29¢ Broadway Musicals (4)	
	Pl# A11111, A11121, A22222	4.95
2778a	29¢ Country Music (4)	
	Pl# A222222	5.50

2552a

Scott No.	Description	FVF,NH
2790a	29¢ Madonna (4)	
	Pl# K1-11111, K1-44444	4.95
	Pl# K1-33333	7.50
2798a	29¢ 3 Snowmen (10) Pl#111111	12.75
2798b	29¢ 2 Snowmen (10) Pl#111111	12.75
2814a	29¢ Love & Dove (10) Pl# A11111	9.95
2833a	29¢ Garden Flowers (5) Pl# 2	5.50
2871Ab	29¢ Madonna (10) Pl# 1,2	9.95
2872a	29¢ Stocking (20)	
	Pl# P11111, P44444	21.50
	Pl# P22222	27.50
2916a	32¢ Flag over Porch (10)	
	Pl# 11111	11.75
2921a	32¢ Flag over Porch SA, (10)	
	Pl# 21221, 22221, 22222	10.75
2921d	32¢ Flag over porch, (5)	
	P1# 11111	6.50
3007b	32¢ Santa (10) Pl# P11111	11.75
3007c	32¢ Santa (10) Pl# P11111	11.75
3049c	32¢ Yellow Rose (5), SA	
	Pl#S1111	5.95
3049d	32¢ Yellow Rose (6) SA	
	Pl# S1111	6.25

Scott No.	Description	FVF,NH
3122c	32¢ Liberty (5), SA	
	Pl# V1111	5.50
3122d	32¢ Liberty (6), #V1111, SA	5.25
3128b	32¢ Merian Botanical (5) (2 ea. 3128-29, 1-3128a)	
	Pl# S11111	4.95
3129b	32¢ Merian Botanical (5) (2 ea. 3128-29, 1-3129a)	
	Pl# S11111	5.95
3177d	32¢ Holly (6) Pl# B11111, SA	4.95
3248b	32¢ Wreaths (5) #B11111	4.75
3278b	33¢ Flag over City (5) #V1111, V1112, V1212, V2212, SA	4.25
3301c	33¢ Fruit Berries(6)#B1112, B2212, B2221, B2222, SA	5.25
3367c	33¢ Deer (6) #B111111, SA	5.25

CONVERTIBLE SELF-ADHESIVE PANES (Complete Unfolded Booklets)

2960a

2490a

3116a

Scott No.	Description	F-VF,NH
3117a	32¢ Skaters (18)	
	Pl# V1111, V2111	16.95
3122a	32¢ Liberty & Torch, Die-cut 11 (20)	
	Pl# V1111, V1211, V1311, V2122, V2222, V2311, V2331, V3233, V3333, V3532, V4532	18.50
3122Ef	32¢ Liberty & Torch, Die-cut 11.5x11.8(20)	
	Pl# V1111, V1211, V2122, V2222	45.00
3123a	32¢ Love & Swans (20)	
	Pl# B1111, B2222, B3333, B4444, B5555, B6666, B7777	16.50
3124a	55¢ Love & Swans (20)	
	Pl#B1111, B2222, B3333, B4444	24.75
3127a	32¢ Merian Botanical, SA	
	Prints (20) Pl#S11111, S22222, S33333	16.50
3176a	32¢ Madonna (20)	
	Pl# 1111, 2222, 3333	15.00
3177a	32¢ American Holly (20)	
	Pl# B1111, B2222, B3333	15.00
3244a	32¢ Madonna (20)	
	Pl# 1111, 2222, 3333	16.50
3268a	(33¢) Hat (10)	
	Pl# V1111, V1211, V2211, V2222	8.50
3268b	(33¢) Hat (20)	
	Pl# V1111, V1112, V1113, V1122, V1213, V1222, V2113, V2122, V2213, V2222, V2223	16.75
3269a	(33¢) Hat (18)	
	Pl# V1111	15.00
3274a	33¢ Victorian-Love (20)	
	Pl #V1111, V1112, V1117, V1118, V1211, V1212, V1213, V1233, V1313, V1314, V1333, V1334, V1335, V2123, V2221, V2222, V2223, V2424, V2425, V2426, V2324, V3123, V3124, V3125, V3133, V3134, V3323, V3327, V3333, V3334, V3336, V4529, V5650	15.00
3278d	33¢ Flag over City (10)	
	Pl# V1111, V1112, V1113, V2222, V2322, V3434	8.25
3278e	33¢ Flag over City (20)	
	Pl#V1111, V1211, V2122, V2222, V2223, V3333, V4444	16.50
3278Fg	33¢ Flag over City, Reprint (20)	
	Pl# V1111, V1131, V2222, V2223, V2323, V2423, V2443, V3333, V4444, V5445, V5576, V5578, V6423, V6456, V6546, V6556, V6575, V7567, V7667	12.95
3283a	33¢ Flag over Chalkboard (20)	
	Pl# V1111	13.95
3297b	33¢ Fruit Berries (20)	
	Pl# B1111, B1112, B2211, B2222, B3331, B3332, B3333, B4444 B5555	14.50
3297d	33¢ Fruit Berries (20)	
	Pl# B1111	14.50
3313b	33¢ Tropical Flowers (20)	
	Pl# S11111, S22222, S22244, S22344, S22444, S22452, S22462, S23222, S24222, S24224, S24242, S24244, S24422, S24442, S24444, S26462, S32323, S32333, S32444, S33333, S44444, S45552, S46654, S55452, S55552, S56462, S62544, S62562, S64452, S64544, S65552, S66462, S66544, S66552, S66562, S66652	16.50
3355a	33¢ Madonna (20)	
	Pl# B1111, B2222, B3333	14.00
3363a	33¢ Deer (20)	
	Pl# B444444, B555555, B666666	12.95
3450a	(34¢) Flag over Farm (18)	
	Pl# V1111	11.50
3451a	(34¢) Statue of Liberty (20)	
	Pl# V1111	12.75
3457b	(34¢) Flowers, Die-cut 10¼x10 3/4 (20)	
	Pl# S1111	12.75
3482a	20¢ G. Washington, Die-cut 11¼x11 (10)	
	Pl# P1	3.85
3483c	20¢ G. Washington, Die-cut 11¼x11(5) and 10 1/2 x 11(5)	
	Pl# P1	9.75
3485a	34¢ Statue of Liberty (10)	
	Pl# V1111	6.50
3485b	34¢ Statue of Liberty (20)	
	Pl# V1111	12.75
3490e	34¢ Flowers (20)	
	Pl# S1111	12.75
3492b	34¢ Apples & Oranges (20)	
	Pl# B1111	12.75
3496a	(34¢) Rose & Love Letters (20)	
	Pl# B1111	12.75
3497a	34¢ Rose & Love Letters (20)	
	Pl# B1111	12.75

Scott No.	Description	F-VF,NH
2431a	25¢ Eagle & Shield (18)	
	Pl# A1111	17.50
2475a	25¢ Flag, Plastic (12) No #	9.95
2489a	29¢ Red Squirrel (18)	
	Pl# D11111, D22211	16.50
	Pl#D22221, D22222, D23133	19.75
2490a	29¢ Rose (18)	
	Pl# S111	16.50
2491a	29¢ Pine Cone (18)	
	Pl# B2-3, B5-11, B13-16	16.50
	Pl# B1, B4, B12	18.75
2492a	32¢ Pink Rose (20)	
	Pl# S111, S112, S333	16.50
2492r	32¢ Die-Cut "Time to Reorder" S444, S555	17.75
2494a	32¢ Peach & Pear (20)	
	Pl# V11111, V11122, V11132, V12132, V12211, V22212, V22221, V22222, V33333, V33353, V33363, V44424, V44454	16.50
	Pl# V11131, V12131, V12221, V33142, V33143, V33243, V33343, V33453, V44434, V45434, V45464, V54565, V55365	19.75
	Pl# V33323	25.00
2522a	(29¢) "F" Flag (12) No Pl#	10.95
2531Ab	29¢ Liberty & Torch (18) No Pl#	16.75
2531Av	29¢ Revised back No Pl#	16.75
2595a	29¢ Eagle, Brown (17)	
	Pl# B1111-1, B1111-2, B3434-1	15.00
	Pl# B2222-1, B2222-2, B3333-1, B3333-3, B3434-3, B4344-1, B4444-1, B4444-3	24.75
2596a	29¢ Eagle, Green (17)	
	Pl# D21221, D22322, D32322,	15.00
	Pl# D11111, D23322, D43352, D43452, D43453, D54563, D54571, D54573, D65784	15.95
	Pl# D54561, D54673, D61384	23.50
	Pl# D32342, D42342	35.00
2597a	29¢ Eagle, Red (17)	
	Pl# S1111	15.00
2598a	29¢ Eagle (18)	
	Pl# M1111, M1112	15.00
2599a	29¢ Statue of Liberty (18)	
	Pl# D1111, D1212	16.00
2719a	29¢ Locomotive (18)	
	Pl# V11111	16.50
2802a	29¢ Christmas (12)	
	Pl# V111-1111, V222-1222, V222-2112, V222-2122, V222-2221, V222-2222,	13.75
	Pl# V333-3333	16.75
2803a	29¢ Snowman (18)	
	Pl# V11111, V22222	17.50
2813a	29¢ Love & Sunrise (18)	
	Pl# B111-1, B111-2, B111-3, B111-4, B222-4, B222-5, B222-6, B333-9, B333-10, B333-11, B333-12, B333-17, B344-12, B344-13, B444-10, B444-13, B444-15, B444-17, B444-18, B444-19, B555-20, B555-21	16.50
	Pl# B121-5, B221-3, B444-7, B444-8, B444-9, B444-14, B444-16	18.75
	Pl# B333-5, B333-7, B333-8	22.50
	Pl# B344-11	50.00
2873a	29¢ Santa Claus (12)	
	Pl# V1111	11.50

Scott No.	Description	F-VF,NH
2874a	29¢ Cardinal in Snow (18)	
	Pl# V1111, V2222	16.50
2886a	(32¢) "G" Surface (18)	
	Pl# V11111, V22222	19.00
2887a	(32¢) "G" Overall (18)	
	No Plate Number	19.50
2919a	32¢ Flag over Field (18)	
	Pl# V1111, V1311, V1433, V2141, V2222, V2322	15.75
2920a	32¢ Flag over Porch, Large "1995"(20)	
	Pl# V12211, V12212, V12312, V12321, V12322, V12331, V13322, V13831, V13834, V13836, V22211, V23322, V34743, V34745, V36743, V42556, V45554, V56663, V56665, V56763, V57663, V65976, V78989	17.50
	Pl# V23422	27.50
	Pl# V23522	45.00
2920c	32¢ Flag over Porch, Small "1995"(20)	
	Pl# V11111	120.00
2920De	32¢ Flag over Porch, 11.3 (10)	
	Pl# V11111, V12111, V23222, V31121, V32111, V32121, V44322, V44333, V44444, V55555, V66666, V66886, V67886, V68886, V68896, V76989, V77666, V77668, V77766, V78698, V78886, V78896, V78898, V78986, V78989, V89999	9.50
2949a	(32¢) Love & Cherub (20)	
	Pl# B1111-1, B2222-1 B2222-2, B3333-2	18.75
2960a	55¢ Love Cherub (20)	
	Pl# B1111-1, B2222-1	27.50
3011a	32¢ Santa & Children (20)	
	Pl# V1111, V1211, V3233, V3333, V4444	19.50
	Pl# V1212	25.00
3012a	32¢ Midnight Angel (20)	
	Pl# B1111, B2222, B3333	18.00
3013a	32¢ Children Sledding (20)	
	Pl# V1111	16.50
3030a	32¢ Love Cherub (20)	
	Pl#B1111-1, B1111-2 B2222-1, B2222-2	18.00
3048a	20¢ Blue Jay (10) SA	
	Pl# S1111, S2222	5.50
3049a	32¢ Yellow Rose)20)	
	Pl# S1111, S2222, S3333	17.50
3050a	20¢ Ringnecked Pheasant (10) SA	
	Pl# V1111, V2222, V2232, V2333, V2342, V2343, V3232, V3243, V3333	4.95
3052d	33¢ Rose, Die-cut 11½x11¾ (20)	
	Pl# S222	14.75
3052Ef	33¢ Rose, Die-cut 11½x11¼ (20)	
	Pl# S111	14.75
3071a	32¢ Tennessee (20)	
	Pl# S11111	18.95
3089a	32¢ Iowa (20), Pl# B11111	18.75
3112a	32¢ Madonna (20)	
	Pl# 11111, 12111, 22121, 22221, 23231, 33231, 33331, 33341, 44441, 55441, 55562, 56562, 66661, 66662, 67661, 78871, 78872, 78882, 79882	17.75
	Pl# 6656-2	25.00
	Pl# 5556-1	30.00
	Pl# 5555-1	70.00
3116a	32¢ Family Scenes (20)	
	Pl# B1111, B2222, B3333,	19.50

COMPLETE BOOKLETS

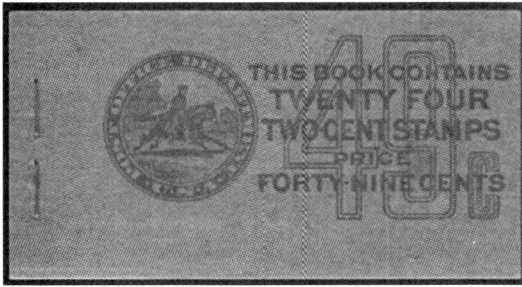

BK81

BK115

Scott No.	Cover Value, Pane No. and Description(Number of Panes)	F-VF NH
1914 Flat Press, Perf. 10, Single-Line Wtmk.		
BK41	25¢ #424d,1¢ Washington (4)	275.00
BK42	97¢ #424d,1¢ Washington (16)	125.00
BK43	73¢ #424d,1¢(4) + #425e,2¢ (4)	350.00
BK44	25¢ #425e,2¢ Washington (2)	500.00
1916 Flat Press, Perf. 10, Unwatermarked		
BK47	25¢ #462a,1¢ Washington(4)	700.00
BK48	97¢ #462a,1¢ Washington (16)	450.00
BK50	25¢ #463a,2¢ Washington(2)	550.00
1917-23 Flat Press, Perforated 11		
BK53	25¢ #498e,1¢ Wash.,"POD"(4)	450.00
BK54	97¢ #498e,1¢ Washington(16)	75.00
BK55	25¢ #498e,1¢ "City Carrier"(4)	85.00
BK56	73¢ #498e,1¢(4) + #499e,2¢(4)	77.50
BK57	73¢ #498e,1¢(4) + #554c,2¢(4)	125.00
BK58	25¢ #499e,2¢ Washington(2)	225.00
BK59	49¢ #499e,2¢ Washington(4)	525.00
BK60	97¢ #499e,2¢ Washington(8)	675.00
BK62	37¢ #501b,3¢ Wash.,Type I(2)	575.00
BK63	37¢ #502b,3¢ Wash., Type II(2)	225.00
1923 Flat Press, Perforated 11		
BK66	25¢ #552a,1¢ Franklin(4)	70.00
BK67	97¢ #552a,1¢ Franklin(16)	625.00
BK68	73¢ #552a,1¢(4) + #554c,2¢(4)	125.00
BK69	25¢ #554a,2¢ Washington(2)	400.00
1926 Rotary Press, Perforated 10		
BK72	25¢ #583a,2¢ Washington(2)	500.00
BK73	49¢ #583a,2¢ Washington(4)	600.00
1927-32 Rotary Press, Perf. 11 x 10½		
BK75	25¢ #632a,1¢ Franklin(4)	92.50
BK76	97¢ #632a,1¢ "P.O.D."cvr.(16)	565.00
BK77	97¢ #632a,1¢ "Postrider"cvr.(16)	675.00
BK79	73¢ #632a,1¢(4) + #634a,2¢(4) "Postrider" Cover	85.00
BK80	25¢ #634d,2¢ Washington(4)	10.00
BK81	49¢ #634d,2¢ Washington(4)	16.50
BK82	97¢ #634d,2¢ "Postrider"cvr.(8)	57.50
BK84	37¢ #720b,3¢ Washington(2)	140.00
BK85	73¢ #720b,3¢ Washington(4)	335.00
1939 Presidential Series - 3mm Gutters		
BK86	25¢ #804bv,1¢ Washington(4)	75.00
BK87	97¢ #804bv,1¢ Washington(16)	600.00
BK89	73¢ #804bv,1¢(4) + #806bv,2¢(4)	180.00
BK94	97¢ #806bv,2¢ John Adams(8)	550.00
BK100	37¢ #807av,3¢ Jefferson(2)	95.00
1942 Presidential Series - 2½mm Gutters		
BK90	25¢ #804b,1¢ Washington(4)	9.75
BK91	97¢ #804b,1¢ "P.O.D."cover(16)	550.00
BK92	73¢ #804b,1¢(4) + #806b,2¢(4) "Postrider" cover	35.00
BK93	73¢ #804b,1¢(4) + #806b,2¢(4)] "P.O. Seal" cover	42.50
BK96	25¢ #806b,2¢ Adams "Postrider"(2)	18.50
BK97	25¢ #806b,2¢ Adams "P.O.Seal"(2)	110.00
BK98	49¢ #806b,2¢ Adams "Postrider"(4)	60.00
BK99	49¢ #806b,2¢ Adams "P.O. Seal"(4)	65.00
BK102	37¢ #807a,3¢ Jefferson(2)	25.00
BK103	73¢ #807a,3¢ Jefferson(4)	45.00
1954-58 Liberty Series		
BK104	37¢ #1035a,3¢ Liberty, Wet(2)	21.75
BK104a	37¢ #1035f,3¢ Dry Printing(2)	25.00
BK105	73¢ #1035a,3¢ Liberty, Wet(4)	29.75
BK105a	73¢ #1035f,3¢ Dry Printing(4)	38.50
BK106	97¢ on 37¢ #1036a,4¢ Lincoln(4)	75.00
BK107	97¢ on 73¢ #1036a,4¢ Lincoln(4)	42.50
BK108	97¢ "Yellow" paper #1036a(4)	125.00
BK109	97¢ "Pink" paper #1036a(4)	15.00

Scott No.	Cover Value, Pane No. and Description(Number of Panes)	F-VF NH
1962-64 George Washington Issue		
BK110	$1 #1213a,5¢ Slog.1 "Mailman"(4)	37.50
BK111	$1 #1213a,5¢ Slogan 2 "Zone"(4) "Postrider" Cover	150.00
BK112	$1 #1213a,5¢ Slogan 2 "Zone"(4) "Mr. Zip" Cover	150.00
BK113	$1 #1213a,5¢ Slogan 3 "Zip"(4)	16.50
BK114	$1 #1213c,5¢ Tagged, Slogan 2(4)	350.00
BK115	$1 #1213c,5¢ Tagged, Slogan 3(4)	6.50
1967-78 Regular Issues		
BK116	$2 #1278a,1¢(1) + 1284b,6¢(4)	7.50
BK117	$1 #1280c,2¢(1) + #1284c,6¢(3)	6.00
BK117A	$3.60 #1288Bc,15¢ Holmes(3)	11.00
BK117B	$2 #1278a,1¢(1) + #1393a,6¢(4) "P.O. Seal" Cover	14.75
BK118	$2 #1278a,1¢(1) + #1393a,6¢(4) "Eisenhower" Cover	8.50
BK119	$2 #1278ae,1¢(1) + #1393ae,6¢(4) Dull Gum,"Eisenhower"Cover	9.00
BK120	$1 #1280a,2¢(1) + #1393b,6¢(3)	5.95
BK121	$1.92 #1395a,8¢ Eisenhower-8(3)	7.75
BK122	$1 #1278b,1¢(1) + #1395b,8¢(3)	5.75
BK123	$2 #1395c,8¢(1) + #1395d,8¢(3)	8.50
BK124	$1 #1510b,10¢ Jeff. Meml. - 5(2)	3.50
BK125	$4 #1510c,10¢ Jeff. Meml. - 8(5)	13.00
BK126	$1.25 #1510d,10¢(1)+#C79a,13¢(1)	10.75
1975-80 Regular Issues		
BK127	90¢ #1280c,2¢(1) +1595a,13¢(1)	3.75
BK128	$2.99 #1595b,13¢(1)+#1595c,13¢(2)	7.95
BK129	$1.30 #1595d,13¢ Liberty Bell-5(2)	6.00
BK130	$1.20 #1598a,15¢ Fort McHenry Flag-8(1)	5.75
BK131	$1 #1623a,9¢ + 13¢, Pf. 11x10½(1)	3.25
BK132	$1 #1623c,9¢ + 13¢, Perf. 10(1)	33.75
BK133	$3.60 #1736a,(15¢) "A"(3)	12.00
BK134	$2.40 #1737a,15¢ Roses(2)	6.50
BK135	$3 #1742a,15¢ Windmills(2)	9.50
BK136	$4.32 #1819a,(18¢) "B"(3)	15.00
1981-83 Regular Issues		
BK137	$3.60 #1889a,18¢ Wildlife(2)Pl#1-10	20.00
BK137	Pl# 11-13	50.00
BK137	Pl# 14-16	45.00
BK138	$1.20 #1893a,6¢ + 18¢ Flag(1)Pl# 1	4.00
BK139	$1.20 #1896a,20¢ Flag - S.C. -6(1)	
	Pl# 1	4.25
BK140	$2 #1896b,20¢ Flag-S. Court-10(1)	
	Pl#1	7.50
BK140	Pl#4	52.50
BK140A	$4 #1896b,20¢ Flag-S. Court-10(2)	
	Pl#1	13.50
BK140A	Pl#3	17.50
BK140B	$28.05#1909a,$9.35 Exp.Mail(1) #1111	89.50
BK141	$4#1948a,(20¢) "C"(2)No Pl#	11.95
BK142	$4 #1949a,20¢ Bighorn Sheep(2) Pl#1-6, 9-10	14.50
BK142	Pl# 11,12,15	37.50
BK142	Pl# 14	30.00
BK142	Pl# 16	85.00
BK142	Pl# 17-19	70.00
BK142	Pl# 20, 22-24	110.00
BK142	Pl# 25-26	175.00
BK142a	$4 #1949d,20¢ Sheep, Type II(2) Pl# 34	33.50

Scott No.	Cover Value, Pane No. and Description(Number of Panes)	F-VF NH
1985-89 Regular Issues		
BK143	$4.40 #2113a,(22¢) "D"(2)Pl#1,3,4	21.50
BK144	$1.10 #2116a,22¢ Flag - Capitol(1) Pl# 1,3	5.00
BK145	$2.20 #2116a,22¢ Flag - Capitol(2) Pl# 1,3	10.00
BK146	$4.40 #2121a,22¢ Seashells(2) Multi-Seashells Cover (7 covers needed for all 25 shells)Pl#1,3	13.95
BK146	Pl# 2	15.75
BK147	$4.40 #2121a,22¢(2)"Beach"Cover Pl#1,3,5,7,10	12.95
BK147	Pl# 8	15.00
BK148	$32.25 #2122a,$10.75 Express Mail Type I(1) Pl#11111	89.50
BK149	$32.25 #2122c, Type II(1) Pl# 22222	115.00
BK150	$5 #2182a, 25¢ Jack London-10(2) Pl# 1,2	13.50
BK151	$1.50 #2197a,25¢ Jack London-6(1) Pl# 1	4.75
BK152	$3 #2197a,25¢ Jack London-6(2) Pl#1	9.25
1986 Commemoratives		
BK153	$1.76 #2201a,22¢ Stamp Coll(2) Pl# 1	5.50
BK154	$2.20 #2209a,22¢ Fish(2) Pl# 11111,22222	19.75
1987-88 Regular Issues		
BK155	$2.20 #2274a,22¢ Sp. Occasions(1) Pl# 111111,222222	16.50
BK156	$4.40 #2276a,22¢ Flag-Fireworks(1) No Pl#	13.00
BK156	Pl# 1111,2222	15.75
BK156	Pl# 2122	22.50
BK157	$5 #2282a,(25¢) "E"(2) Pl#111111,222222	16.00
BK157	Pl# 2122	18.75
BK158	$5 #2283a,25¢ Pheasant(2) Pl# A1111	16.00
BK159	$5 #2283c Bluer sky(2) Pl# A3111,A3222	190.00
BK160	$5 #2285b,25¢ Owl-Grosbeak(2) Pl#1111,1112,1211,1433,1434 1734,2121,2321,3333,5955	13.50
BK160	Pl# 1133,2111,2122,2221,2222, 3133,3233,3412,3413,3422,3521 4642,4644,4911,4941	22.75
BK160	Pl# 1414	100.00
BK160	Pl# 1634,3512,3822	47.50
BK160	Pl# 5453	150.00
BK161	$3 #2285Ac,25¢ Flag-Clouds(2) Pl# 1111	9.50
1987-90 Commemoratives		
BK162	$4.40 #2359a,22¢ Constitution (4) Pl# 1111,1112	20.95
BK163	$4.40 #2366a,22¢ Locomotives (4) Pl# 1,2	17.95
BK164	$5 #2385a,25¢ Classic Cars(4) Pl#1	39.95
BK165	$3 #2396a(1),2398a(1), 25¢ Special OccasionsPl# A1111	10.00
BK166	$5 #2409a,25¢ Steamboats(4) Pl#1,2	19.75
BK167	$5 #2427a,25¢ 1989 Madonna(2) Pl#1	15.00
BK168	$5 #2429a,25¢ Sleigh(2) Pl# 1111,2111	16.50
BK169	$5 #2441a,25¢ Love,Doves(2) Pl# 1211	21.50
BK169	Pl# 2111,2222	29.50
BK169	Pl# 2211	35.00

BK215

BK191

BK176

BK202A

Scott No.	Cover Value, Pane No. and Description(Number of Panes)	F-VF NH
1990 Regular Issue		
BK170	$3 #2443a,15¢ Beach Umbrella(2) Pl#111111	8.75
BK170	Pl# 221111	11.75
1990 Commemorative		
BK171	$5 #2474a,25¢ Lighthouses(4) Pl#1-5	29.75
1991-96 Flora and Fauna Regular Issues		
BK172	$2 #2483a,20¢ Blue Jay(1)Pl# S1111	6.75
BK173	$2.90 #2484a,29¢ Duck,BEP(1) Pl# 4444	8.50
BK174	$5.80 #2484a,29¢ Duck,BEP(2) Pl# 1111,2222,4444	15.95
BK174	Pl# 1211,3221	115.00
BK174	Pl# 2122,3222,3333	22.50
BK175	$5.80 #2485a,29¢ Duck,KCS(2) Pl# K11111	17.50
BK176	$2.90 #2486a,29¢ African Violet(1) Pl# K11111	9.25
BK177	$5.80 #2486a,29¢ African Violet(2 Pl# K11111	18.50
BK178	$6.40 #2488a,32¢ Peach-Pear(2) Pl# 11111	17.95
BK178A	$4.80 #2492b,32¢ Pink Rose(1)	14.95
BK178B	$4.80 #2492f (1) 32¢ Pink Rose	..
BK178C	$9.60 #2492b,32¢ Pink Rose (2) No Pl#	29.75
BK178D	$9.60 #2492f,32¢ Pink Rose (2) 2 Panes of #2492f with missing stamp (15 stamps) No Pl#	69.50
BK178E	$9.60 #2492e (1), 2492f (1) 32¢ Pink Rose No Pl#	64.95
BK178F	$9.60 #2492b (1), 2492f (1) 32¢ Pink Rose No Pl#	195.00
1990 Commemoratives		
BK179	$5 #2505a,25¢ Indian Headdress(2) Pl# 1,2	21.75
BK180	$5 #2514a,25¢ Madonna(2) Pl# 1	17.50
BK181	$5 #2516a,25¢ Christmas Tree(2) Pl# 1211	21.75
1991 Regular Issues		
BK182	$2.90 #2519a,(29¢) "F",BEP(1) Pl # 2222	11.50
BK183	$5.80 #2519a,(29¢) "F",BEP(2) Pl#1111,2121,2222	23.00
BK183	Pl#1222,2111,2212	30.00
BK184	$2.90 #2520a,(29¢) "F",KCS(1) Pl# K1111	27.50
BK185	$5.80 #2527a,29¢ Flower(2) Pl# K1111,K2222,K3333	16.50
BK186	$2.90 #2528a,29¢ Olympic(1) Pl# K11111 (Blue Cover)	8.50
BK186A	$2.90 #2528a, 29¢ Olympic (1) Pl# K11111 (Red Cover)	10.75
BK186Ab	$2.90 #2528a, WCSE Ticket Cover	18.95
BK187	$3.80 #2530a,19¢ Balloons(2) Pl#1111,2222	10.50
BK187	Pl# 1222	35.00
1991 Commemoratives		
BK188	$5.80 #2536a,29¢ Love(2) Pl# 1111,1112	16.95
BK188	Pl#1113,1123,2223	18.95
BK188	Pl# 1212	45.00

Scott No.	Cover Value, Pane No. and Description(Number of Panes)	F-VF NH
BK189	$5.80 #2549a,29¢ Fishing Flies(4) Pl# A22122,A23123,A23124,A33235 A44446,A45546,A45547	33.75
BK189	Pl# A11111,A22113,A23133, A23313	47.50
BK189	Pl#A22132,A32224,A32225, A33233	39.50
BK190	$5.80 #2552a,29¢ Desert Storm(2) Pl# A11111111,A11121111	18.95
BK191	$5.80 #2566a,29¢ Comedians(2) Pl# 1,2	18.95
BK192	$5.80 #2577a,29¢ Space(2) Pl#111111,111112	23.50
BK193	$5.80 #2578a,(29¢) Madonna(2) Pl# 1	16.95
BK194	$5.80 #2581b-85a,(29¢) Santa & Chimney(5 Panes, 1 each) Pl# A11111,A12111	25.00
1992-93 Regular Issues		
BK195	$2.90 #2593a,29¢ Pledge,Pf.10(1) Pl# 1111,2222	10.95
BK196	$5.80 #2593a,29¢ Pledge,Pf.10(2) Pl# 1111,2222	16.50
BK197	$5.80 #2593Bc,29¢ Perf. 11x10(2) Pl# 1111,2222,3333	29.95
BK197	Pl# 1211,2122,2232	31.95
BK197	Pl#4444	52.50
BK198	$2.90 #2594a,29¢ Pledge, Red(1) Pl# K1111	11.95
BK199	$5.80 #2594a,29¢ Pledge, Red(2) Pl# K1111	19.50
1992 Commemoratives		
BK201	$5.80 #2646a 29¢ Hummingbirds(4) Pl# A1111111,A2212112,A2212222 A2222222	17.95
BK201	Pl# A2212122	21.95
BK202	$5.80 #2709a,29¢ Wild Animals(4) Pl# K1111	18.95
BK202A	$5.80 #2710a,29¢ Madonna(2)Pl# 1	15.95
BK203	$5.80 #2718a,29¢ Toys(5) Pl# A111111,A112211,A222222	22.50
1993 Commemoratives		
BK204	$5.80 #2737a(2),2737b(1) 29¢ Rock'n Roll, Rythym & Blues Pl# A11111,A22222	17.50
BK204	Pl# A13113,A44444	19.75
BK207	$5.80 #2745a,29¢ Space Fantasy(4) Pl# 1111,1211,2222	17.95
BK208	$5.80 #2764a,29¢ Garden Flowers(4) Pl# 1,2	17.95
BK209	$5.80 #2770a,29¢ Broadway(5) Pl# A11111,A11121,A22222, A23232,A23233	18.95
BK210	$5.80 #2778a,29¢ Country Music(5) Pl# A111111,A222222,A333333 A422222	19.75
BK211	$5.80 #2790a,29¢ Madonna(5) Pl# K111111,K133333,K144444 K255555,K266666	17.50
BK211	Pl# 222222	35.00
BK212	$5.80 #2798a(1),2798b(1) 29¢ Christmas Designs Pl# 111111,222222	20.95
BK213	$2.90 #2806b,29¢ AIDS(2) Pl# K111	8.95

Scott No.	Cover Value, Pane No. and Description(Number of Panes)	F-VF NH
1994 Commemoratives		
BK214	$5.80 #2814a,29¢ Love & Dove(2) Pl# A11111,A11311,A12112 A21222,A22112,A22222,A22332	17.50
BK214	Pl# A12111,A12211,A12212, A21311	27.50
BK215	$5.80 #2833a,29¢ Garden Flowers(4) Pl# 1,2	16.95
BK216	$5.80 #2847a,29¢ Locomotives(4) Pl# S11111	18.95
BK217	$5.80 #2871Ab,29¢ Madonna(2)Pl#1,2	16.95
BK218	$5.80 #2872a,29¢ Stocking(4) Pl# P11111,P22222,P44444	16.50
1994 "G" Regular Issues		
BK219	$3.20 #2881a,(32¢) BEP,Pf.11(1) Pl# 1111	14.50
BK220	$3.20 #2883a,(32¢) BEP,Pf.10(1) Pl# 1111,2222	10.95
BK221	$6.40 #2883a,(32¢)BEP,Pf.10(2) Pl# 1111,2222	21.75
BK222	$6.40 #2884a,(32¢)ABN,Blue(2) Pl# A1111,A1211,A2222 A3333,A4444	21.75
BK223	$6.40 #2885a,(32¢)KCS,Red(2) Pl# K1111	23.75
1995-97 Regular Issues		
BK225	$3.20 #2916a,32¢ Flag-Porch(1) Pl# 11111,22222,33332	9.95
BK226	$6.40 #2916a,32¢ Flag-Porch(2) Pl# 11111,22222,23222,33332, 44444	18.95
BK226A	$4.80#2920f 32¢ Flag-Porch (1)No Pl#	14.50
BK226B	$4.80#2920h 32¢ Flag-Porch(1)No Pl#	27.50
BK227	$9.60#2920f 32¢ Flag-Porch(2)No Pl#	28.95
BK227A	$4.80#2921c(1), 2921d(1) 32¢ Flag-Porch Pl# 11111	14.50
BK228	$6.40 #2921a 32¢ Flag-Porch (2) Pl# 11111,13111,21221,22221,22222, 44434,44444,55555,66666,77777, 88788,88888,99999	18.95
BK228A	$9.60 2921c 32¢ Flag-Porch (3) Pl# 11111	28.50
1995 Commemoratives		
BK229	$6.40 #2959a,32¢ Love (2) Pl#1	17.50
BK230	$6.40 #2973a,32¢ Great Lakes Lighthouses(4) Pl# S11111	19.95
BK231	$6.40 #2997a,32¢ Garden Flowers(4) Pl #2	17.95
BK232	$6.40 #3003Ab,32¢ Madonna(2) Pl# 1	18.95
BK233	$6.40 #3007b(1),3007c(1), 32¢ Santa & Children Pl# P1111,P2222	18.95
BK233A	$4.80 #3012c,32¢ Midnight Angel(1) Pl# B1111,B2222,B3333	14.50
BK233B	$4.80 #3012d 32¢ Midnight Angel (1)	...
BK233C	$9.60 #3012c,32¢ Midnight Angel(2) Pl# B1111,B2222,B3333	28.50
BK233D	$9.60 #3012d,32¢ Midnight Angel(2) No Pl#	31.95
BK233E	$9.60 #3012c,3012d	49.50

COMPLETE BOOKLETS

BK246

BKC19

QI2

BK264

Scott No.	Cover Value, Pane No. and Description(Number of Panes)	F-VF NH
	1996 Commemoratives	
BK234	$6.40 #3029a,32¢ Winter Garden Flowers(4) Pl# 1	17.95
BK235	$4.80 3030b 32¢ Love (1)	13.95
BK236	$9.60 3030b 32¢ Love (2)	27.95
	1996-97 Issues	
BK237	$2 3048b (1), 3048c (1) 20¢ Ring-necked Pheasant Pl# S1111	7.50
BK241	$4.80 3049b (1), 3049c (1), 3049d (1) 32¢ Yellow Rose Pl# S1111	15.75
BK242	$9.60 3049d 32¢ Yellow Rose (5) Pl# S1111	29.75
	1999 Flora & Fauna Issues	
BK242A	$4 3051b (2) 20¢ Ringnecked Pheasant Pl# V1111	8.50
BK242B	$4.95 3052a (1), 3052b (12), 3052c (1) 33¢ Coral Pink Rose Pl# S111	13.50
	1996 Makeshift Vending Machine Booklets	
BK243	$4.80 2897 32¢ Flag Over Porch(15)	14.95
BK244	$4.80 2957 32¢ Love Cherub (15)	14.95
BK245	$4.80 3024 32¢ Utah Statehood (15)	17.95
BK246	$4.80 3065 32¢ Fulbright (15)	15.95
BK247	$4.80 3069 32¢ Geo. O'Keefe (15)	15.95
BK248	$4.80 3070 32¢ Tennessee (15)	16.50
BK249	$4.80 3072-76 32¢Indian Dances(15)	15.75
BK250	$4.80 3082 32¢ James Dean (15)	17.95
BK251	$4.80 3083-86 32¢ Folk Heroes (15)	14.95
BK252	$4.80 3087 32¢ Discobolus (15)	19.95
BK253	$4.80 3088 32¢ Iowa (15)	15.95
BK254	$4.80 3090 32¢ Rural Free (30)	31.95
BK255	$4.80 3091-95 32¢ Riverboats (15)	17.95
BK256	$4.80 3105a/o 32¢ End Species (15)	15.75
BK257	$4.80 3107 32¢ Madonna (15)	14.95
BK258	$4.80 3118 32¢ Hanukkah (15)	14.95
	1997 Issues	
BK259	$4.80 3122b (1), 3122c (1), 3122d (1) 32¢ Statue of Liberty Pl# V1111	15.00
BK260	$9.60 3122d 32¢ Statue of Liberty(5) Pl# V1111	25.75
BK260A	$9.60 3122Eg32¢ Stat. of Liberty(5)	37.50
BK261	$4.80 3128b (2), 3129b (1), 32¢ Merian Botanical Prints Pl#S11111	15.75
BK264	$4.80 3177b (1) 3177c (1) 3177d (1) 32¢ Holly, Pl# B1111	14.50
BK265	$9.60 3177d (5) 32¢ Holly,Pl# B1111	24.75

Scott No.	Cover Value, Pane No. and Description(Number of Panes)	F-VF NH
	1997 Makeshift Vending Machine Booklets	
BK266	$4.80 3151a-o 32¢ Dolls	14.95
BK267	$4.80 3152 32¢ Bogart	14.95
BK268	$4.80 3153 32¢ Stars & Stripes	14.95
BK269	$4.80 3168-72 32¢ Monsters	15.95
	1998 Issues	
BK270	$4.80 3248a(1), 3248b(1) 3248c(1) 32¢ Wreaths Pl# B111111	13.95
BK271	$6.60 3267a (33¢) Hat (2) Pl.#1111, 2222,3333	16.95
	1998 Makeshift Vending Booklets	
BK272	$4.80 3222-25 32¢ Tropical Birds	14.95
BK273	$4.80 3237 32¢ Ballet	14.95
BK274	$4.80 3238-42 32¢ Space Discovery	14.95
	1999 Flag and City	
BK275	$4.95 3278a (1), 3278b (1), 3278c (1) 33¢ Flag, Pl.# V1111,V1112,V1121, V1212,V2212	11.95
BK276	$6.60 3279a (2) Pl.# 1111,1121	16.50
	1999 Fruits and Berries	
BK276A	$4.95 3301a (1), 3301b (1), 3301c(1)33¢ Pl.#B1112,B2222	12.95
	1999 Christmas Deer	
BK276B	$4.95 3367a (1), 3367b (1), 3367c (1) 33¢ Deer Pl.# B111111	12.95
	1999 Makeshift Vending Booklets	
BK277	$4.95 3325,27-28 (4 each), 3326 (3) 33¢ Glass	14.75
BK278	$4.95 3333-37 (3 each) 33¢ Trains	14.75
	2000 U.S. Navy Submarines Prestige Booklet	
BK279	$9.80 3377a (2) 22¢-$3.20	22.75
	2000-2001 Regular Issues	
BK280	$6.80 3451b (2), 3451c (2) (34¢) Statue of Liberty Pl#V1111	12.75
BK281	$6.80 3457c (2), 3457d(1),3457e(1) 34¢ Flowers Pl# S1111	12.75
BK282	$2 3483a (1), 3483b (1) 20¢ G. Washington Pl# P2	14.75
BK282A	$2 3482b(1) 3482c(1) 20¢ G. Washington Pl# P1	3.95
BK283	$6.80 3484a (2), 3484b (2) 34¢ Liberty Pl# V1111	12.75
BK284	$6.80 3490c (2),3490d (1),3490e(1), 34¢ Flowers Pl# S1111	12.75

Scott No.	Cover Value, Pane No. and Description(Number of Panes)	F-VF NH
BK285	$6.80 3498a (2), 3498b (2), 34¢ Rose & Love Letter Pl# B1111	18.95
	1927-60 Airmail Issues	
BKC1	61¢ #C10a.10¢ Lindbergn(2)	295.00
BKC2	37¢ #C25a,6¢ Transport(2)	9.50
BKC3	73¢ #C25a,6¢ Transport(4)	18.75
BKC4	73¢ #C39a,6¢ Small Plane, Wet(2)	25.00
BKC4a	73¢ #C39a,6¢ Small Plane, Dry(2)	50.00
BKC5	85¢ on 73¢ #C51a,7¢ Blue Jet(2)	45.00
BKC6	85¢ #C51a,7¢ Blue Jet(2)	29.50
BKC7	85¢ #C60a,7¢ Red Jet(2),Blue Cvr.	39.50
BKC8	85¢ #C60a,7¢ Red Jet (2),Red Cvr.	40.00
	1962-64 Jet over Capitol	
BKC9	80¢ #C64b,8¢ Slog.1,"Mailman"(2)	20.00
BKC10	$2 #C64b,8¢ Slog.1,"Mailman"(5)	30.00
BKC11	80¢ #C64b,8¢ Slogan 3, "Zip"(2)	31.50
BKC12	$2 #C64b,8¢ Slogan 2, "Zone"(5) "Wings" Cover	450.00
BKC13	$2 #C64b,8¢ Slog.2(5) Mr. Zip Cvr.	435.00
BKC15	$2 #C64b,8¢ Slogan 3, "Zip"(5)	100.00
BKC16	80¢ #C64c,8¢ Tagged Slogan 3(2)	41.75
BKC18	$2 #C64c,8¢ Tagged, Sl.3,Pink(5)	395.00
BKC19	$2 #C64c,8¢ Tagged, Sl 3,Red(5)	7.75
	1968-73 Airmail Issues	
BKC20	$4 #C72b,10¢ 50-Star Runway-8(5)	12.00
BKC21	$1 #C72c,10¢ 50-Star Runway-5(2)	8.95
BKC22	$1 #1280c,2¢(1) + #C78a,11¢(2)	5.25
BKC23	$1.30 #C79a,13¢ Envelope (2)	3.50
	1965-81 Postal Insurance Booklets	
QI1	(10¢) "Insured P.O.D. V"	165.00
QI2w	(20¢) "Insured U.S.Mail" White Cvr.	6.00
QI2b	(20¢) "Insured U.S.Mail" Black Cvr.	3.50
QI3	(40¢) "Insured U.S.Mail" Black	3.50
QI4	(50¢) "Insured U.S.Mail" Green	2.50
QI5	(45¢) "Insured U.S.Mail" Red	2.50

UNCUT PRESS SHEETS AND POSITION PIECES

Scott No.	Description	F-VF,NH
2869	**1994 29¢ Legends of the West**	
	Uncut Sheet of 120 (6 Panes of 20)	110.00
	Block of 10 with Horizontal Gutter	16.50
	Block of 8 with Vertical Gutter	11.95
	4 Pairs with Vertical Gutters	10.95
	5 Pairs with Horizontal Gutters	13.95
	Center Gutter Block of 4	17.50
	Cross Gutter Block of 20	27.75
2967	**1995 32¢ Marilyn Monroe**	
	Uncut Sheet of 120 (6 Panes of 20)	175.00
	Block of 8 with Vertical Gutter	57.50
	Cross Gutter Block of 8	70.00
	Vertical Pair with Horizontal Gutter	4.95
	Horizontal Pair with Vertical Gutter	8.95
2975	**1995 32¢ Civil War**	
	Uncut Sheet of 120 (6 Panes of 20)	175.00
	Block of 10 with Horizontal Gutter	24.95
	Block of 8 with Vertical Gutter	21.75
	4 Pairs with Vertical Gutters	19.50
	5 Pairs with Horizontal Gutters	23.95
	Center Gutter Block of 4	21.50
	Cross Gutter Block of 20	43.50
3000	**1995 32¢ Comic Strips**	
	Uncut Sheet of 120 (6 Panes of 20)	135.00
	Block of 8 with Horizontal Gutter ..	21.75
	Block of 10 with Vertical Gutter	26.75
	5 Pairs with Vertical Gutters	24.95
	4 Pairs with Horizontal Gutters	19.50
	Center Gutter Block of 4	19.50
	Cross Gutter Block of 20	47.50
3068	**1996 32¢ Atlanta Olympic Games**	
	Uncut Sheet of 120 (6 Panes of 20)	150.00
	Block of 8 with Vertical Gutter	21.75
	Block of 10 with Horizontal Gutter	25.75
	4 Pairs with Vertical Gutters	19.50
	5 Pairs with Horizontal Gutters	23.95
	Center Gutter Block of 4	21.50
	Cross Gutter Block of 20	42.50
3082	**1996 32¢ James Dean**	
	Uncut Sheet of 120 (6 Panes of 20)	140.00
	Block of 8 with Vertical Gutter	22.75
	Cross Gutter Block of 8	29.50
	Vertical Pair with Horizontal Gutter	3.25
	Horizontal Pair with Vertical Gutter	5.25
3130-31	**1997 Pacific'97 Triangles**	
	Uncut Sheet of 96 (6 Panes of 16)	95.00
	Block of 32 (2Panes)	33.50
	Vertical Pair with Horizontal Gutter	11.75
	Horizontal Pair with Vertical Gutter	6.75
	Cross Gutter Block of 16	34.50
3137v	**1997 32¢ Bugs Bunny**	
	Top Uncut Sheet of 60 (6 Panes of 10)	450.00
	Bottom Uncut Sheet of 60 with Plate Number (6 Panes of 10)	750.00
	Souvenir Sheet from uncut sheet .	80.00
	Souvenir Sheet with plate number	395.00
	Vertical Pair with Horizontal Gutter	30.00
	Horizontal Pair with Vertical Gutter	60.00
3142	**1997 32¢ Classic American Aircraft**	
	Uncut Sheet of 120 (6 Panes of 20)	120.00
	Block of 10 with Vertical Gutter	14.50
	Block of 8 with Horizontal Gutter ..	12.50
	5 Pairs with Vertical Gutters	12.75
	4 Pairs with Horizontal Gutters	10.75
	Center Gutter Block of 4	19.95
	Center Gutter Block of 20	26.50
3152	**1997 32¢ Humphrey Bogart**	
	Uncut Sheet of 120 (6 Panes of 20)	120.00
	Block of 8 with Vertical Gutter	16.75
	Cross Gutter Block of 8	21.50
	Vertical Pair with Horizontal Gutter	3.00
	Horizontal Pair with Vertical Gutter	4.25
3168-72	**1997 32¢ Classic Movie Monsters**	
	Uncut Sheet of 180 (9 Panes of 20)	165.00
	Block of 8 with Vertical Gutter	10.50
	Block of 10 with Horizontal Gutter	13.50
	4 Pairs with Vertical Gutters	10.75
	5 Pairs with Horizontal Gutters	12.75
	Center Gutter Block of 8	17.50
3175	**1997 32¢ Kwanza**	
	Uncut Sheet of 250 (5 Panes of 50)	700.00
	Horizontal Pair with Vertical Gutter	13.50
3178	**1997 $3 Mars Pathfinder, Rover Sojourner..** Uncut Sht of 18 Souvenir Sheets	175.00
	Vertical Pair with Horizontal Gutter	20.00
	Horizontal Pair with Vertical Gutter	20.00
	Block of 6 (3 wide by 2 tall)	75.00
3178c	Souvenir Sheet perforated 2 sides	12.50
3178c	Vertical Pair with Horiz. Gutter	25.00
3178l	Souv.Sheet perforated on left side	12.50
3178l	Vertical Pair with Horiz. Gutter	25.00
3178r	Souv.Sheet perforated on right side	12.50
3178r	Vertical Pair with Horiz. Gutter	25.00
3182	**1998 32¢ Celebrate the Century 1900's**	
	Uncut Sheet of 60 (4 Panes of 15)	49.50
3183	**1998 32¢ Celebrate the Century 1910's**	
	Uncut Sheet of 60 (4 Panes of 15)	49.50
3184	**1998 32¢ Celebrate the Century 1920's**	
	Uncut Sheet of 60 (4 Panes of 15)	49.50
3185	**1998 32¢ Celebrate the Century 1930's**	
	Uncut Sheet of 60 (4 Panes of 15)	49.50
3186	**1999 33¢ Celebrate the Century 1940's**	
	Uncut Sheet of 60 (4 Panes of 15)	51.50
3187	**1999 33¢ Celebrate the Century 1950's**	
	Uncut Sheet of 60 (4 Panes of 15)	51.50
3188	**1999 33¢ Celebrate the Century 1960's**	
	Uncut Sheet of 60 (4 Panes of 15)	51.50
3189	**1999 33¢ Celebrate the Century 1970's**	
	Uncut Sheet of 60 (4 Panes of 15)	51.50
3190	**2000 33¢ Celebrate the Century 1980's**	
	Uncut Sheet of 60 (4 Panes of 15)	51.50
3191	**2000 33¢ Celebrate the Century 1990's**	
	Uncut Sheet of 60 (4 Panes of 15)	51.50
3198-3202	**1998 32¢ Alexander Calder**	
	Uncut Sheet of 120 (6 Panes of 20)	130.00
	5 Pairs with Horizontal Gutters	23.50
	Block of 10 with Horizontal Gutter	26.50
	Block of 8 with Vertical Gutter	29.50
	Cross Gutter Block of 20	45.00
3203	**1998 32¢ Cinco de Mayo**	
	Uncut Sheet of 180 (9 Panes of 20)	110.00
	Cross Gutter Block of 4	15.00
	Vertical Pair with Horizontal Gutter	2.50
	Horizontal Pair with Vertical Gutter	2.50
3204v	**1998 32¢ Tweety & Sylvester**	
	Top Uncut Sheet of 60 (6 Panes of 10)	95.00
	Bottom Uncut Sheet of 60 with Plate Number (6 Panes of 10)	135.00
	Souvenir Sheet from uncut sheet .	17.50
	Souvenir Sheet with plate number	60.00
	Vertical Pair with Horizontal Gutter	7.50
	Horizontal Pair with Vertical Gutter	15.00
3209-10	**1998 1¢-$2 Trans-Mississippi**	
	Uncut Sheet of 54 (3 each #3209 & 3210)	130.00
	Block of 18 with Vertical Gutter between & selvage on 4 sides	59.50
	Block of 9 with Horizontal Gutter ..	49.50
	Block of 12 with Vertical Gutter	39.50
	Cross Gutter Block of 12	67.50
	4 Pairs with Horizontal Gutters	42.50
	3 Pairs with Vertical Gutters	30.00
3226	**1998 32¢ Alfred Hitchcock**	
	Uncut Sheet of 120 (6 Panes of 20)	105.00
	Block of 8 with Vertical Gutter	16.50
	Cross Gutter Block of 8	21.50
	Horizontal Pair with Vertical Gutter	4.00
	Vertical Pair with Horizontal Gutter	2.75
3236	**1998 32¢ American Art**	
	Uncut Sheet of 120 (6 Panes of 20)	125.00
	Block of 8 with Vertical Gutter	11.50
	Block of 10 with Horizontal Gutter	14.50
	Cross Gutter Block of 20	27.50
	5 Pairs with Horizontal Gutters	12.50
	4 Pairs with Vertical Gutters	10.00
3237	**1998 32¢ Ballet**	
	Uncut Sheet of 120 (6 Panes of 20)	110.00
	Cross Gutter Block of 4	14.50
	Vertical Pair with Horizontal Gutter	2.50
	Horizontal Pair with Vertical Gutter	2.50
3238-42	**1998 32¢ Space Discovery**	
	Uncut Sheet of 180 (9 Panes of 20)	145.00
	Cross Gutter Block of 10	20.00
	Block of 10 with Horizontal Gutter	14.00
	Horizontal Pair with Vertical Gutter	2.50
	5 Pairs with Horizontal Gutters	13.00
3293	**1999 33¢ Sonoran Desert**	
	Uncut Sheet of 60 (6 Panes of 10)	45.00
3306v	**1999 33¢ Daffy Duck**	
	Top Uncut Sheet of 60 (6 Panes-10)	55.00
	Bottom Uncut Sheet of 60 with Plate Number (6 Panes of 10)	77.50
	Souvenir Sheet from uncut sheet .	11.50
	Souvenir Sheet with plate number	25.00
	Vertical Pair with Horizontal Gutter	2.50
	Horizontal Pair with Vertical Gutter	5.00
3317-20	**1999 33¢ Aquarium Fish**	
	Uncut Sheet of 120 (6 Panes of 20)	110.00
	Block of 8 with Horizontal Gutter ..	11.00
	Cross Gutter Block of 8	17.50
	Horizontal Pair with Vertical Gutter	2.50
	4 Pairs with Horizontal Gutters	10.00
3321-24	**1999 33¢ Xtreme Sports**	
	Top Uncut Sheet of 80 (4 Panes-20)	70.00
	Bottom Uncut Sheet of 80 with Plate Number (4 Panes of 20)	85.00
	Cross Gutter Block of 8	17.50
	2 Pairs with Horizontal Gutters	5.50
	4 Pairs with Vertical Gutters	11.00
	Block of 4 with Horizontal Gutter ..	6.00
	Block of 8 with Vertical Gutter	11.00
3329	**1999 33¢ James Cagney**	
	Uncut Sheet of 120 (6 Panes of 20)	110.00
	Block of 8 with Vertical Gutter	13.50
	Cross Gutter Block of 8	20.00
	Horizontal Pair with Vertical Gutter	3.50
	Vertical Pair with Horizontal Gutter	2.50
3333-37	**1999 33¢ All Aboard, Trains**	
	Uncut Sheet of 120 (6 Panes of 20)	110.00
	Block of 10 with Vertical Gutter	13.75
	Block of 8 with Horizontal Gutter ..	11.50
	Cross Gutter Block of 8	17.50
	4 Pairs with Horizontal Gutters	10.00
	5 Pairs with Vertical Gutters	12.50
3351	**1999 33¢ Insects and Spiders**	
	Uncut Sheet of 80 (4 Panes of 20)	59.95
	Block of 10 with Vertical Gutter	12.00
	Block of 8 with Horizontal Gutter ..	10.00
	Cross Gutter Block of 20	22.50
	5 Pairs with Horizontal Gutters	10.00
	4 Pairs with Vertical Gutters	8.00
3378	**2000 33¢ Pacific Coast Rain Forest**	
	Uncut Sheet of 60 (6 Panes of 10)	45.00
	Cross Gutter Block of 4	16.50
	Pair with Vertical Gutter	7.50
	Pair with Horizontal Gutter	7.50
3391	**2000 33¢ Wile E. Coyote and Road Runner**Top Uncut Sheet of 60 (6 Panes of 10)	65.00
	Bottom Uncut Sheet of 60 with Plate Number (6 Panes of 10)	95.00
	Souvenir Sheet from uncut sheet .	11.50
	Souvenir Sheet with plate number	42.50
	Vertical Pair with Horizontal Gutter	2.50
	Horizontal Pair with Vertical Gutter	5.00
3403	**2000 33¢ Stars and Stripes**	
	Uncut Sheet of 120 (6 Panes of 20)	85.00
	Blockof 10 with Vertical Gutter	13.75
	Block of 8 with Horizontal Gutter ..	11.50
	Center Gutter Block of 20	26.50
	5 Pairs with Vertical Gutters	12.50
	4 Pairs with Horizontal Gutters	10.50
3408	**2000 33¢ Legends of Baseball**	
	Uncut Sheet of 120 (6 Panes of 20)	95.00
	Block of 10 with Horizontal Gutter	13.50
	Block of 8 with Vertical Gutter	11.50
	Center Gutter Blockof 20	26.50
	5 Pairs with Horizontal Gutters	12.50
	4 Pairs with Vertical Gutters	10.50
3409-13	**2000 60¢-$11.75 Space Achievement and Exploration ....**	
	Uncut Sheet of 15 designs (5 Souvenir Sheets)	99.50
3339-43	**2000 33¢ Deep Sea Creatures**	
	Uncut Sheet of 135 (9 Panes of 15)	110.00
3446	**2000 33¢ Edward G. Robinson**	
	Uncut Sheet of 120 (6 Panes of 20)	89.50
3502	**2001 34¢ American Illustrators**	
	Uncut Sheet of 80 (4 Panes of 20)	62.50
3505	**2001 1¢,2¢,4¢,80¢ Pan-Am Inverts**	
	Uncut Sheet of 28 (4 Panes of 7) .	32.50
3506	**2001 34¢ Great Plains Prairie**	
	Uncut Sheet of 60 (6 Panes o f 10)	45.00
...	**2001 34¢ Legendary Baseball Fields**	
	Uncut Sheet of 160 (8 Panes of 20)	120.00

MODERN ERRORS

The following listings include the most popular and affordable errors and are not intended to be complete. New listings are added each year to bring this section up-to-date.

1519a

1895a

IMPERFORATE MAJOR ERRORS

Scott's No.		F-VF NH
498a	1¢ Washington, Vertical Pair, Imperforate Horizontally	195.00
498b	1¢ Washington, Horizontal Pair, Imperforate Between	90.00
499a	2¢ Washington, Vertical Pair, Imperforate Horizontally	150.00
501c	3¢ Washington, Vertical Pair, Imperforate Horizontally	375.00
502c	3¢ Washington, Vertical Pair, Imperforate Horizontally	300.00
525c	1¢ Washington, Horiz. Pair, Imperf. Between	95.00
538a	1¢ Washington, Vert. Pair, Imperf. Horiz.	75.00
540a	2¢ Washington, Vert. Pair, Imperf. Horiz.	75.00
554a	2¢ Washington, Horiz. Pair, Imperf. Vert	225.00
639a	7¢ McKinley, Vert. Pair, Imperf. Between	200.00
720c	3¢ Washington, Vert Pair, Imperf. Between	375.00
739a	3¢ Wisconsin, Vert. Pair, Imperf. Horiz.	350.00
739b	3¢ Wisconsin, Horiz. Pair, Imperf. Vert.	450.00
740a	1¢ Yosemite, Vertical Pair, Imperforate Horizontally	500.00
741a	2¢ Grand Canyon, Vertical Pair, Imperf. Horizontally	550.00
741b	2¢ Grand Canyon, Horizontal Pair, Imperforate Vertically	650.00
742a	3¢ Mount Rainier, Vertical Pair, Imperf. Horizontally	525.00
805b	1.5¢ M. Washington, Horiz. Pair, Imperf. Between	170.00
805b	1.5¢ M. Washington, Horiz. Pair, Imperf. Between, precancelled	25.00
899a	1¢ Defense, Vert. Pair, Imperf. Between	550.00
899b	1¢ Defense, Horizontal Pair, Imperf. Between	45.00
900a	2¢ Defense, Horizontal Pair, Imperf. Between	47.50
901a	3¢ Defense, Horizontal Pair, Imperf. Between	32.50
966a	3¢ Palomar, Vert. Pair, Imperf. Between	625.00
1055b	2¢ Jefferson, Coil Pair, Imperf., precancelled	625.00
1055c	2¢ Jefferson, Coil Pair, Imperf.	675.00
1058a	4¢ Lincoln, Coil Pair, Imperf	115.00
1058a	4¢ Same, Line Pair	225.00
1059Ac	25¢ Revere, Coil Pair, Imperf.	45.00
1059Ac	Same, Line Pair	90.00
1125a	4¢ San Martin, Horizontal Pair, Imperf. Between	1650.00
1138a	4¢ McDowell, Vert. Pair, Imperf. Between	450.00
1138b	4¢ McDowell, Vert. Pair, Imperf. Horizontal	325.00
1151a	4¢ SEATO, Vertical Pair, Imperf. Between	175.00
1229b	5¢ Washington, Coil Pair, Imperf	450.00
1297a	3¢ Parkman, Coil Pair, Imperf	27.50
1297a	Same, Line Pair	55.00
1297c	Same, Precancelled	7.50
1297c	Same, Precancelled, Line Pair	22.50
1299a	1¢ Jefferson, Coil Pair, Imperf	30.00
1299b	Same, Line Pair	65.00
1303b	4¢ Lincoln, Coil Pair, Imperf	975.00
1304b	5¢ Washington, Coil Pair Imperf	200.00
1304e	Same, Precancelled	425.00
1304Cd	5¢ Washington, Redrawn, Coil Pair, Imperf.	8.25
1305a	6¢ FDR, Coil Pair, Imperf	95.00
1305a	Same, Line Pair	150.00
1305Eg	15¢ Holmes, Shiny Gum, Coil Pair, Imperf	40.00
1305Eg	Same, Line Pair	100.00
1305Ej	Holmes, Type II, Dry Gum, Coil Pair, Imperf	95.00
1305Ej	Same, Line Pair	300.00
1305Eh	Same, Horizontal Pair, Imperf. Between	195.00
1338k	6¢ Flag, Vert. Pair, Imperf. Between	550.00
1338Ab	6¢ Flag, Coil Pair, Imperf	500.00
1338De	6¢ Flag, Horiz. Pair, Imperf. Between	165.00
1338Fi	8¢ Flag, Vert. Pair, Imperf. Between	50.00
1338Fj	8¢ Flag, Horiz. Pair, Imperf. Between	60.00
1338Gh	8¢ Flag, Coil Pair	60.00
1355b	6¢ Disney, Vert. Pair, Imperf. Horiz	675.00
1355c	6¢ Disney, Imperf. Pair	700.00
1362a	6¢ Waterfowl, Vertical Pair, Imperf. Between	525.00
1363b	6¢ Christmas, Imperf. Pair, tagged	225.00
1363d	6¢ Christmas, Imperf. Pair, untagged	295.00
1370a	6¢ Grandma Moses, Horiz. Pair, Imperf. Between	225.00
1402a	8¢ Eisenhower, Coil Pair, Imperf	60.00
1402a	Same, Line Pair	95.00
1484a	8¢ Gershwin, Vert. Pair, Imperf. Horiz	235.00
1485a	8¢ Jeffers, Vert. Pair, Imperf. Horiz	275.00
1487a	8¢ Cathers, Vert. Pair, Imperf. Horiz	275.00
1503a	8¢ Johnson, Horiz. Pair, Imperf. Vert	375.00
1508a	8¢ Christmas, Vert. Pair, Imperf. Between	350.00
1509a	10¢ Flags, Horiz. Pair, Imperf. Between	55.00
1510e	10¢ Jefferson Memorial, Vert. Pair, Imperf. Horiz	550.00
1518b	6.3¢ Bell Coil Pair, Imperf	200.00
1518c	Same, Precancelled Pair	125.00
1518c	Same, Line Pair	250.00
1519a	10¢ Flag Coil Pair, Imperf	42.50

IMPERFORATE MAJOR ERRORS (cont.)

Scott's No.		F-VF NH
1520b	10¢ Jefferson Memorial, Coil Pair, Imperf	45.00
1520b	Same, Line Pair	80.00
1563a	10¢ Lexington-Concord, Vert. Pair, Imperf. Horiz	450.00
1579a	10¢ Madonna, Imperf. Pair	110.00
1580a	10¢ Christmas Card, Imperf. Pair	110.00
1596a	13¢ Eagle & Shield, Imperf. Pair	50.00
1597a	15¢ Flag (from Sheet), Imperf. Pair	20.00
1615a	7.9¢ Drum, Coil, Pair, Imperf.	650.00
1615Ce	8.4¢ Piano, Coil, Precancelled Pr., Imperf. Between	55.00
1615Ce	Same, Line Pair	120.00
1615Cf	8.4¢ Piano, Coil, Precancelled Pair, Imperf	20.00
1615Cf	Same, Line Pair	35.00
1616a	9¢ Capitol, Coil Pair, Imperf.	160.00
1616a	Same, Line Pair	375.00
1616c	9¢ Capitol, Coil, Precancelled Pair, Imperf.	750.00
1617b	10¢ Petition, Coil Pair, Imperf	75.00
1617b	Same, Line Pair	150.00
1617bd	Same, Pair, dull finish gum	75.00
1618b	13¢ Liberty Bell, Coil Pair, Imperf	30.00
1618b	Same, Line Pair	75.00
1618Cd	15¢ Flag, Coil Pair, Imperf	25.00
1618Ce	Same, Coil Pair, Imperf. Between	175.00
1622a	13¢ Flag, Horiz. Pair, Imperf. Between	60.00
1622Cd	Same, Imperf. Pair	175.00
1625a	13¢ Flag, Coil Pair, Imperf	25.00
1695-98b	13¢ Winter Olympics, Imperf. Block of 4	850.00
1699a	13¢ Maass, Horiz. Pair, Imperf. Vert	525.00
1701a	13¢ Nativity, Imperf. Pair	110.00
1702a	13¢ Currier & Ives, Overall Tagging, Imperf. Pair	115.00
1703a	13¢ Currier & Ives, Block Tagging, Imperf. Pair	120.00
1704a	13¢ Princeton, Horiz. Pair, Imperf. Vert.	650.00
1711a	13¢ Colorado, Horiz. Pair, Imperf. Between	675.00
1711b	13¢ Colorado, Horizontal Pair, Imperf. Vertically	950.00
1729a	13¢ G.W. at Valley Forge, Imperf. Pair	80.00
1730a	13¢ Christmas Mailbox, Imperf. Pair	325.00
1734a	13¢ Indian Head Penny, Horiz. Pair, Imperf. Vert	325.00
1735a	(15¢) "A" Eagle, Vert. Pair, Imperf	100.00
1735b	(15¢) "A" Eagle, Vert. Pair, Imperf. Horiz.	775.00
1743a	(15¢) "A" Eagle, Coil Pair, Imperf	100.00
1743a	Same, Line Pair	225.00
1768a	15¢ Christmas Madonna, Imperf. Pair	100.00
1769a	15¢ Hobby Horse, Imperf. Pair	110.00
1783-86b	15¢ Flora, Block of 4, Imperf	625.00
1787a	15¢ Seeing Eye Dog, Imperf. Pair	475.00
1789c	15¢ J.P.Jones, Perf. 12, Vert. Pair, Imperf. Horiz	195.00
1789Ad	Same, Perf. 11, Vert. Pair, Imperf. Horiz	165.00
1799a	15¢ 1979 Madonna & Child, Imperf. Pair	100.00
1801a	15¢ Will Rogers, Imperf. Pair	250.00
1804a	15¢ B. Banneker, Horiz. Pair, Imperf. Vert.	850.00
1811a	1¢ Quill Pen, Coil Pair, Imperf	200.00
1811a	Same, Line Pair	325.00
1813b	3.5¢ Violin, Coil Pair, Imperf.	275.00
1813b	Same, Line Pair	450.00
1816b	12¢ Torch, Coil Pair, Imperf	200.00
1816b	Same, Line Pair	375.00
1820a	(18¢) "B" Eagle, Coil Pair, Imperf	120.00
1820a	Same, Line Pair	210.00
1823a	15¢ Bissell, Vert. Pair, Imperf. Horiz	450.00
1825a	15¢ Veterans, Horiz. Pair, Imperf. Vert	525.00
1831a	15¢ Organized Labor, Imperf. Pair	400.00
1833a	15¢ Learning, Horiz. Pair, Imperf. Vert	265.00
1842a	15¢ 1980 Madonna, Imperf. Pair	80.00
1843a	15¢ Toy Drum, Imperf. Pair	80.00
1844a	1¢ Dorothea Dix, Imperf. Pair	500.00
1856b	14¢ S. Lewis, Vert. Pair, Imperf. Horiz	150.00
1856c	14¢ S. Lewis, Horizontal Pair, Imperf. Between	10.00
1867a	39¢ Clark, Horiz. Pair, Imperf. Horiz	675.00
1890a	18¢ "Amber" Flag, Imperf. Pair	120.00
1890b	18¢ "Amber" Flag, Vertical Pair, Imperf. Horiz.	875.00
1891a	18¢ "Shining Sea", Coil Pair, Imperf	25.00
1893b	6¢/18¢ Booklet, Imperf. Vertical Between, Perfs at Left	85.00
1894a	20¢ Flag, Vert. Pair, Imperf	40.00
1894b	20¢ Flag, Vert.Pair, Imperf. Horiz.	550.00
1895a	20¢ Flag, Coil Pair, Imperf	11.00
1897b	1¢ Omnibus, Imperf. Pair	750.00
1897Ae	2¢ Locomotive, Coil Pair, Imperf	60.00
1898Ac	4¢ Stagecoach, Imperf. Pair, Precancelled	850.00
1898Ad	4¢ Stagecoach, Imperf. Pair	950.00
1901b	5.9¢ Bicycle, Precancelled Coil Pair, Imperf	200.00
1903b	9.3¢ Mail Wagon, Precancelled Coil Pair, Imperf	130.00
1904b	10.9¢ Hansom Cab, Prec. Coil Pair, Imperf	160.00
1906b	17¢ Electric Car, Coil Pair, Imperf	170.00
1906c	Same, Precancelled Pair, Imperf	675.00
1907a	18¢ Surrey, Coil Pair, Imperf	135.00
1908a	20¢ Fire Pumper, Coil Pair, Imperf	125.00
1927a	18¢ Alcoholism, Imperf. Pair	475.00
1934a	18¢ Remington, Vert. Pair, Imperf. Between	295.00
1939a	20¢ 1981 Madonna, Imperf. Pair	130.00
1940a	20¢ Teddy Bear, Imperf. Pair	275.00
1949b	20¢ Ram Bklt. Booklet Pane Vert. Imperf. Btwn., Perfs. at Left	110.00
1951b	20¢ Love, Imperf. Pair	300.00

2115e

2603a

2913a

IMPERFORATE MAJOR ERRORS (cont.)

Scott's No.		F-VF NH
2003a	20¢ Netherlands, Imperf. Pair	325.00
2005a	20¢ Consumer, Coil Pair, Imperf	110.00
2015a	20¢ Libraries, Vert. Pair, Imperf. Horiz	300.00
2024a	20¢ Ponce de Leon, Imperf. Pair	550.00
2025a	13¢ Puppy & Kitten, Imperf. Pair	650.00
2026a	20¢ Madonna & Child, Imperf. Pair	175.00
2039a	20¢ Voluntarism, Imperf. Pair	750.00
2044a	20¢ Joplin, Imperf. Pair	500.00
2064a	20¢ 1983 Santa Claus, Imperf. Pair	185.00
2072a	20¢ Love, Horiz. Pair, Imperf. Vert	200.00
2092a	20¢ Waterfowl, Horiz. Pair, Imperf. Vert	425.00
2096a	20¢ Smokey Bear, Horiz. Pair, Imperf. Between	350.00
2096b	Same, Vert. Pair, Imperf. Between	250.00
2104a	20¢ Family Unity, Horiz. Pair, Imperf. Vert	600.00
2111a	(22¢) "D" Eagle, Vert. Pair, Imperf	55.00
2112a	(22¢) "D" Eagle, Coil Pair, Imperf	52.50
2112b	(22¢) "D" Eagle, Coil Pair, Tagging Omitted, Imperf.	175.00
2115e	22¢ Flag, Coil Pair, Imperf	14.00
2115e	same, Plate Number Strip of 5	200.00
2121c	22¢ Seashells Booklet Pane, Imperf. Vert.	750.00
2126b	6¢ Tricycle, Precancelled Coil Pair, Imperf	225.00
2130bv	10.1¢ Oil Wagon, Black Precancel, Coil Pair, Imperf	100.00
2130bv	same, Plate Number 1 Strip of 5	500.00
2130b	10.1¢ Oil Wagon, Red Precancel, Coil Pair, Imperf	17.50
3130b	same, Plate Number 3 Strip of 5	225.00
2133b	12.5¢ Pushcart, Precancelled Coil Pair, Imperf	60.00
2133b	same, Plate Number 1 Strip of 5	275.00
2134a	14¢ Iceboat, Coil Pair, Imperf	110.00
2135a	17¢ Dogsled, Coil Pair, Imperf. Miscut	525.00
2136a	25¢ Bread Wagon, Coil Pair, Imperf	12.50
2136a	same, Plate Number Strip of 5	250.00
2136b	25¢ Bread Wagon, Imperf. Between	750.00
2142a	22¢ Winter Special Olympics, Vert. pair, Imperf. Horiz	600.00
2146a	22¢ A. Adams, Imperf. Pair	300.00
2165a	22¢ 1985 Madonna, Imperf. Pair	100.00
2166a	22¢ Poinsettia, Imperf. Pair	135.00
2210a	22¢ Public Hospitals, vert. pair, imperf. horiz	335.00
2228b	4¢ Stagecoach "B" Press, Coil Pair, Imperf	325.00
2256a	8.4¢ Wheel Chair, Coil Pair, Imperf.	700.00
2259a	13.2¢ Coal Car, Coil Pair, Imperf	110.00
2259a	same, Plate Number 1 Strip of 5	375.00
2260c	15¢ Tugboat, Coil Pair, Imperf	900.00
2261a	16.7¢ Popcorn Wagon Pair, Imperf	210.00
2263a	20¢ Cable Car, Coil Pair, Imperf	75.00
2263a	same, Plate Number 2 Strip of 5	350.00
2265a	21¢ Railway Car, Coil Pair, Imperf	65.00
2265a	same, Plate Number 1 Strip of 5	350.00
2279a	(25¢) "E" Earth, Coil Pair, Imperf	90.00
2280b	25¢ Flag Over Yosemite, Coil Pair, Block Tagged, Imperf	35.00
2280c	25¢ Flag Over Yosemite, Coil Pair, Prephosphor paper, Impf	15.00
2280c	same, Plate Number Strip of 5	225.00
2281a	25¢ Honeybee Coil, Imperf. Pair	60.00
2281a	same, Plate Number Strip of 5	300.00
2419b	$2.40 Moon Landing, Imperf. Pair	850.00
2431b	25¢ Eagle & Shield Pair, Die-cut Omitted	375.00
2440a	25¢ Love, Imperf. Pair	900.00
2451a	4¢ Steam Carriage, Imperf. Pair	750.00
2452c	5¢ Circus Wagon, Coil Pair, Imperf	875.00
2453a	5¢ Canoe, Coil Pair, Imperf	350.00
2457a	10¢ Tractor Trailer, Coil Pair, Imperf	300.00
2457a	same, Plate Number 1 Strip of 5	750.00
2463a	20¢ Cog Railway, Coil Pair, Imperf	140.00
2463a	same, Plate Number 1 Strip of 5	350.00
2464b	23¢ Lunch Wagon, Coil Pair, Imperf	185.00
2485b	29¢ Wood Duck, Vert. Pair, Imperf.Horiz.	250.00
2517a	(29¢) Flower, Imperf. Pair	800.00
2518a	(29¢) "F" Coil, Imperf. Pair	42.50
2518a	same, Plate Number Strip of 5	250.00
2521a	4¢ Non-denominated, Vert. Pair, Imperf. Horiz	110.00
2521b	4¢ Non-denominated Imperf. Pair	100.00
2523b	29¢ Mt. Rushmore, Coil Pair, Imperf	25.00
2523b	same, Plate Number Strip of 5	300.00
2527c	29¢ Flower, Horiz. Pair, Imperf. Vert.	350.00
2550a	29¢ Cole Porter, Vert. Pair, Imperf. Horiz	675.00

IMPERFORATE MAJOR ERRORS (cont.)

Scott's No.		F-VF NH
2579a	(29¢) Santa in Chimney, Horiz. Pair, Imperf. Vertically	350.00
2579b	(29¢) Santa in Chimney, Vert. Pair, Imperf. Horiz	550.00
2594b	29¢ Flag, Imperf. Pair	950.00
2595b	29¢ Eagle & Shield Pair, Die-cut Omittted	225.00
2603a	(10¢) Eagle & Shield, Coil Pair, Imperf	35.00
2603a	same, Plate Number Strip of 5	160.00
2607c	23¢ USA Pre-sort, Coil Pair, Imperf	110.00
2609a	29¢ Flag over White House, Coil Pair, Imperf	20.00
2609a	same, Plate Number Strip of 5	200.00
2609b	same, Pair, Imperf. Between	110.00
2618a	29¢ Love, Horizontal Pair, Imperf. Vertically	800.00
2877a	(3¢) Dove, Imperf. Pair	210.00
2889a	(32¢) & Black "G", Imperf. Pair	350.00
2897a	32¢ Flag over Porch, Imperf. Pair	150.00
2902a	(5¢) Butte Coil Imperf. Pair	800.00
2904c	(5¢) Mountain Imperf. Pair	550.00
2913a	32¢ Flag over Porch Coil, Imperf. Pair	50.00
2913a	same, Plate Number Strip of 5	400.00
2915Ah	32¢ Flag over Porch, Imperf. Pair	50.00
2915Ah	same, Plate Number Strip of 5	200.00
2967a	32¢ Marilyn Monroe, Imperf. Pair	700.00
3004-7d	32¢ Santa & Children, Imperf. Block	750.00
3054a	32¢ Yellow Rose Pair, Die-cut Omitted	110.00
3069a	32¢ Georgia O'Keeffe, Imperf. Pair	210.00
3082a	32¢ James Dean, Imperf. Pair	425.00
3112b	32¢ Madonna Pair, Die-cut Omitted	95.00
3123b	32¢ Love Pair, Die-cut Omitted	235.00

AIRMAILS & SPECIAL DELIVERY

C23a	6¢ EagleVertical Pair, Imperf. Horizontal	385.00
C73a	10¢ Stars, Coil Pair, Imperf	650.00
C82a	11¢ Jet, Coil Pair, Imperf	325.00
C82a	Same, Line Pair	500.00
C83a	13¢ Winged Env., Coil Pair, Imperf	90.00
C83a	Same, Line Pair	165.00
C113	33¢ Verville, Imperf. Pair	950.00
C115	44¢ Transpacific, Imperf. Pair	950.00
E15c	10¢ Motorcycle, horiz. pair, imperf. between	325.00
O148a	23¢ Official Mail, Imperf. Pair	250.00

COLOR ERRORS & VARIETIES

Scott's No.		F-VF NH
499 var.	2¢ Washington, "Boston Lake", with PFC	175.00
1895 var.	20¢ Flag, Blue "Supreme Court" color var	175.00
2115 var.	22¢ Flag, Blue "Capitol Bldg." color var	12.00
C23c	6¢ Ultramarine & Carmine	200.00

COLOR OMITTED - MAJOR ERRORS

1271a	5¢ Florida, ochre omitted	350.00
1331-32 var.	5¢ Space Twins, red stripes of capsule flag omitted, single in block of 9	225.00
1338Fp	8¢ Flag and White House, Slate green omitted	500.00
1355a	6¢ Disney, ochre omitted	750.00
1362b	6¢ Waterfowl, red & dark blue omitted	900.00
1363c	6¢ Christmas, 1968, light yellow omitted	75.00
1370b	6¢ Grandma Moses, black and prussian blue omitted	850.00
1381a	6¢ Baseball, black omitted	1100.00
1384c	6¢ Christmas, 1969, light green omitted	30.00
1414b	6¢ Christmas, 1970, black omitted	600.00
1420a	6¢ Pilgrims, orange & yellow omitted	975.00
1432a	8¢ Revolution, gray & black omitted	700.00
1436a	8¢ Emily Dickinson, black & olive omitted	800.00
1444a	8¢ Christmas, gold omitted	575.00
1471a	8¢ Christmas, 1972, pink omitted	175.00
1473a	8¢ Pharmacy, blue & orange omitted	800.00
1474a	8¢ Stamp Collecting, black omitted	750.00
1501a	8¢ Electronics, black omitted	550.00
1509b	10¢ Crossed Flags, blue omitted	175.00
1511a	10¢ Zip, yellow omitted	60.00
1528a	10¢ Horse Racing, blue omitted	950.00
1542a	10¢ Kentucky, dull black omitted	950.00
1547a	10¢ Energy Conservation, blue & orange omitted	975.00
1547b	10¢ Energy Conservation, orange & green omitted	750.00
1547c	10¢ Energy Conservation, green omitted	875.00
1551a	10¢ Christmas, buff omitted	27.50
1555a	10¢ D.W. Griffith, brown omitted	700.00
1556b	10¢ Pioneer 10, dark blues omitted	900.00
1557a	10¢ Mariner, red omitted	550.00
1559a	8¢ Ludington, green inscription on gum omitted	300.00
1560a	10¢ Salem Poor, green inscription on gum omitted	275.00
1561a	10¢ Salomon, green inscription on gum omitted	275.00
1561b	10¢ Salomon, red color omitted	275.00
1596b	13¢ Eagle & Shield, yellow omitted	170.00
1597b	15¢ McHenry Flag, gray omitted	625.00
1608a	50¢ Lamp, black color omitted	325.00
1610a	$1.00 Lamp, dark brown color omitted	300.00
1610b	$1.00 Lamp, tan, yellow & orange omitted	375.00
1618Cf	15¢ Flag Coil, grey omitted	45.00
1690a	13¢ Franklin, light blue omitted	275.00
1800a	15¢ Christmas, green & yellow omitted	650.00
1800b	15¢ Christmas, yellow, green & tan omitted	775.00
1826a	15¢ de Galvez, red, brown & blue omitted	850.00
1843b	15¢ Wreath, buff omitted	30.00
1894c	20¢ Flag, dark blue omitted	85.00
1894d	20¢ Flag, black omitted	350.00
1895f	20¢ Flag Coil, blue omitted	55.00
1926a	18¢ Millay, black omitted	375.00
1934b	18¢ Remington, brown omitted	500.00
1937-38b	18¢ Yorktown, se-tenant pair, black omitted	425.00
1951c	20¢ Love, blue omitted	240.00
1951d	20¢ Love, yellow omitted	950.00
2014a	20¢ Peace Garden, black, green & brown omitted	270.00
2045a	20¢ Medal of Honor, red omitted	285.00
2055-58b	20¢ Inventors, Block of 4, black omitted	425.00
2059-62b	20¢ Streetcars, Block of 4, black omitted	450.00
2145a	22¢ Ameripex, black, blue & red omitted	200.00
2201b	22¢ Stamp Collecting Pane of 4, black omitted	70.00
2201b	22¢ Stamp Collecting, cplt. bklt. of 2 panes, black omitted	140.00
2235-38b	22¢ Navajo Art, black omitted	375.00
2281b	25¢ Honeybee, black (engraved) omitted	65.00
2281c	25¢ Honeybee, Black (litho) omitted	500.00
2349a	22¢ U.S./Morocco, black omitted	300.00
2361a	22¢ CPA, black omitted	800.00
2399a	25¢ Christmas, 1988, gold omitted	35.00
2421a	25¢ Bill of Rights, black (engraved) omitted	325.00
2422-25b	25¢ Prehistoric Animals, black omitted	1100.00
2427b	25¢ Christmas, red omitted	850.00
2434-37b	25¢ Traditional Mail Delivery, dark blue omitted	1000.00
2441c	25¢ Love, Booklet Single, bright pink omitted	225.00

COLOR OMITTED (continued)

Scott's No.		F-VF NH
2443c	15¢ Beach Umbrella, Booklet Single, blue omitted	180.00
2474b	25¢ Lighthouse bklt., white omitted, cplt. bklt. of 4 panes	350.00
	Same, Individual Pane	90.00
2479b	19¢ Fawn, red omitted	875.00
2481b	45¢ Sunfish, black omitted	550.00
2482a	$2 Bobcat, black omitted	300.00
2508-11b	25¢ Sea Creatures, black omitted	900.00
2561a	29¢ Washington, DC Bicentennial, black "USA 29¢" omitted	135.00
2562-66b	29¢ Comedians, Booklet Pane, red & violet omitted	825.00
2595a	29¢ Eagle & Shield, brown omitted	475.00
2635a	29¢ Alaska Highway, black omitted	950.00
2764a	29¢ Garden Flowers, booklet pane, black omitted	325.00
2833c	29¢ Garden Flowers, booklet pane, black omitted	375.00
2980a	32¢ Women's Suffrage, black omitted	475.00
3003c	32¢ Madonna, black omitted	275.00
3066a	50¢ Jacqueline Cochran, black omitted	75.00
C76a	10¢ Man on the Moon, red omitted	550.00
C76 var.	10¢ Man on the Moon, patch only omitted	250.00
C84a	11¢ City of Refuge, blue & green omitted	975.00
C91-92b	31¢ Wright Bros., ultramarine & black omitted	850.00
C122-25b	45¢ Future Mail Delivery, light blue omitted	975.00
J89a	Postage Due, Black Numeral omitted	315.00

POSTAL STATIONERY ENTIRES

U571a	10¢ Compass, brown omitted	130.00
U572a	13¢ Homemaker, brown omitted	130.00
U573a	13¢ Farmer, brown omitted	130.00
U575a	13¢ Craftsman, brown omitted	130.00
U583a	13¢ Golf, black omitted	800.00
U583b	13¢ Golf, black & blue omitted	700.00
U584a	13¢ Conservation, red & yellow omitted	275.00
U584b	13¢ Conservation, yellow omitted	200.00
U584c	13¢ Conservation, black omitted	200.00
U584d	13¢ Conservation, black & red omitted	450.00
U586a	13¢ Star, black surcharge omitted	225.00
U587a	15¢ Auto Racing, black omitted	130.00
U587c	15¢ Auto Racing, red omitted	130.00
U595a	15¢ Veterinarians, gray omitted	675.00
U595b	15¢ Veterinarians, brown omitted	975.00
U596a	15¢ Olympics, red & green omitted	250.00
U596b	15¢ Olympics, black omitted	250.00
U596c	15¢ Olympics, black & green omitted	250.00
U596d	15¢ Olympics, red omitted	450.00
U597a	15¢ Bicycle, blue omitted	110.00
U599a	15¢ Honeybee, brown omitted	125.00
U602a	20¢ Great Seal, blue omitted	170.00
U605c	20¢ Paralyzed Veterans, red & black omitted	150.00
U605d	20¢ Paralyzed Veterans, blue & black omitted	150.00
U605e	20¢ Paralyzed Veterans, black omitted	275.00
U611a	25¢ Stars, dark red omitted	80.00
U612a	8.4¢ Constellation, black omitted	625.00
U617a	25¢ Space Station, ultramarine omitted	625.00
U619a	29¢ Star, rose omitted	425.00
U621a	29¢ Love, bright rose omitted	525.00
U632a	32¢ Liberty Bell, greenish blue omitted	525.00
U632b	32¢ Liberty Bell, blue omitted	150.00
UC39a	13¢ J.F.Kennedy, red omitted	500.00
UC39b	13¢ J.F.Kennedy, dark blue omitted	500.00
UC42b	13¢ Human Rights, brown omitted	425.00
UC53a	30¢ "USA", red omitted	75.00
UX44b	2¢ FIPEX, dark violet blue omitted	575.00
UX50a	4¢ Customs, blue omitted	650.00
UX51a	4¢ Social Security, blue omitted	700.00
UX57a	5¢ Weather Vane, yellow & black omitted	750.00
UX57b	5¢ Weather Vane, blue omitted	600.00
UX57c	5¢ Weather Vane, black omitted	650.00
UX60a	6¢ Hospital, blue & yellow omitted	750.00

MINT POSTAL STATIONERY ENTIRES

U 350

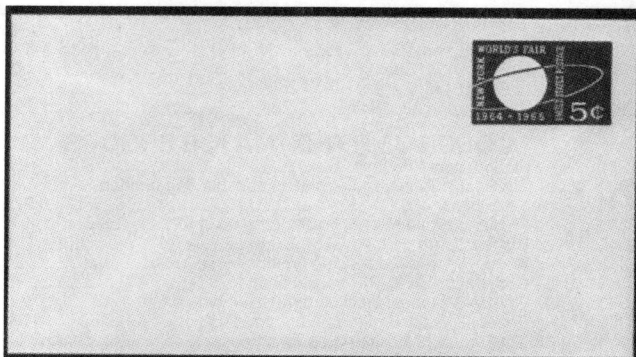

U546

Scott's No.		Mint Entire
	1886 Grant Letter Sheet	
U293	2¢ Green, folded	25.00
	1887-94 Issues	
U294	1¢ Blue	.85
U295	1¢ Dark blue	10.00
U296	1¢ Blue, amber	5.50
U297	1¢ Dk. blue, amber	52.50
U300	1¢ Blue, manila	1.10
W301	1¢ Blue, wrapper	1.50
U302	1¢ Dk. blue, manila	35.00
W303	1¢ Dk. blue, wrapper	25.00
U304	1¢ Blue, amber manila	8.25
U305	2¢ Green, die 1	22.50
U306	2¢ Green, amber	29.50
U307	2¢ Green, oriental buff	100.00
U311	2¢ Green, die 2	.65
U312	2¢ Green, amber	.70
U313	2¢ Green, oriental buff	1.10
U314	2¢ Green, blue	1.15
U315	2¢ Green, manila	3.00
W316	2¢ Green, wrapper	8.50
U317	2¢ Green,amber manila	5.25
U324	4¢ Carmine	4.75
U325	4¢ Carmine, amber	5.75
U326	4¢ Carmine,oriental buff	11.00
U327	4¢ Carmine, blue	8.75
U328	4¢ Carmine, manila	9.00
U329	4¢ Carmine,amber manila	9.00
U330	5¢ Blue, die 1	6.75
U331	5¢ Blue, amber	9.00
U332	5¢ Blue, oriental buff	13.00
U333	5¢ Blue, blue	15.00
U334	5¢ Blue, die 2	15.00
U335	5¢ Blue, amber	17.00
U336	30¢ Red brown	57.50
U337	30¢ Red brown,amber	57.50
U338	30¢ Red brown, oriental buff	52.50
U339	30¢ Red brown,blue	52.50
U340	30¢ Red brown,manila	55.00
U341	30¢ Red brown, amber manila	57.50
U342	90¢ Purple	80.00
U343	90¢ Purple, amber	110.00
U344	90¢ Purple,oriental buff	110.00
U345	90¢ Purple, blue	115.00
U346	90¢ Purple, manila	120.00
U347	90¢ Purple, amber manila	125.00
	1893 Columbian Issue	
U348	1¢ Deep Blue	2.75
U349	2¢ Violet	3.25
U350	5¢ Chocolate	13.50
U351	10¢ Slate Brown	60.00
	1899 Issues	
U352	1¢ Green	1.25
U353	1¢ Green, amber	7.75
U354	1¢ Green, or. buff	13.50
U355	1¢ Green, blue	14.00
U356	1¢ Green, manila	6.00
W357	1¢ Wrapper	11.00
U358	2¢ Carmine	7.00
U359	2¢ Carmine, amber	26.75
U360	2¢ Carmine, or. buff	29.75
U361	2¢ Carmine, blue	75.00
U362	2¢ Carmine	.60
U363	2¢ Carmine, amber	3.25
U364	2¢ Carmine, or. buff	2.75
U365	2¢ Carmine, blue	3.50
W366	2¢ Wrapper	12.50
U367	2¢ Carmine	8.50
U368	2¢ Carmine, amber	15.00
U369	2¢ Carmine, or. buff	30.00
U370	2¢ Carmine, blue	22.50
U371	4¢ Brown	26.75

Scott's No.		Mint Entire
U372	4¢ Brown, amber	32.50
U374	4¢ Brown	22.50
U375	4¢ Brown, amber	50.00
W376	4¢ Wrapper	26.75
U377	5¢ Blue	15.75
U378	5¢ Blue, amber	20.75
	1903-04 Issues	
U379	1¢ Green	1.10
U380	1¢ Green, amber	18.75
U381	1¢ Green, or. buff	18.50
U382	1¢ Green, blue	25.00
U383	1¢ Green, manila	4.85
W384	1¢ Wrapper	2.50
U385	2¢ Carmine	.75
U386	2¢ Carmine, amber	3.50
U387	2¢ Carmine, or. buff	2.25
U388	2¢ Carmine, blue	3.25
W389	2¢ Wrapper	21.50
U390	4¢ Chocolate	25.00
U391	4¢ Chocolate, amber	23.50
W392	4¢ Wrapper	25.00
U393	5¢ Blue	22.50
U394	5¢ Blue, amber	25.00
U395	2¢ Carmine (1904)	1.00
U396	2¢ Carmine, amber	11.75
U397	2¢ Carmine, or. buff	7.50
U398	2¢ Carmine, blue	5.75
W399	2¢ Wrapper	22.50
	1907-16 Issues	
U400	1¢ Green	.45
U401	1¢ Green, amber	1.10
U402	1¢ Green, or. buff	5.95
U403	1¢ Green, blue	5.95
U404	1¢ Green, manila	4.50
W405	1¢ Wrapper	.75
U406	2¢ Brown red	1.65
U407	2¢ Brown red, amber	7.50
U408	2¢ Brown red, or. buff	10.75
U409	2¢ Brown red, blue	5.75
W410	2¢ Wrapper	57.50
U411	2¢ Carmine	.60
U412	2¢ Carmine, amber	.85
U413	2¢ Carmine, or. buff	.65
U414	2¢ Carmine, blue	1.00
W415	2¢ Wrapper	8.50
U416	4¢ Black	8.75
U417	4¢ Black, amber	10.50
U418	5¢ Blue	11.50
U419	5¢ Blue, amber	18.00
	1916-32 Issues	
U420	1¢ Green	.40
U421	1¢ Green, amber	.55
U422	1¢ Green, or. buff	2.60
U423	1¢ Green, blue	.70
U424	1¢ Green, manila	8.50
W425	1¢ Wrapper	.35
U426	1¢ Green (Glazed)	40.00
W427	1¢ Green (Glazed)	75.00
U428	1¢ Green, brown	12.50
U429	2¢ Carmine	.35
U430	2¢ Carmine, amber	.50
U431	2¢ Carmine, or. buff	4.50
U432	2¢ Carmine, blue	.60
W433	2¢ Wrapper	.50
U436	3¢ Dark violet	.70
U436f	3¢ Purple (1932)	.60
U437	3¢ Dark violet, amber	7.75
U437a	3¢ Purple, amber (1932)	1.10
U438	3¢ Dark violet, buff	32.50
U439	3¢ Dark violet, blue	12.50
U439a	3¢ Purple, blue (1932)	.80
U440	4¢ Black	2.75
U441	4¢ Black, amber	4.50
U442	4¢ Black, blue	5.00
U443	5¢ Blue	5.50
U444	5¢ Blue, amber	5.00

Scott's No.		Mint Entire
U445	5¢ Blue, blue	7.75
	1920-21 Surcharge Issues	
U446	2¢ on 3¢ (U436)	18.00
U447	2¢ on 3¢ (U436)	9.50
U448	2¢ on 3¢ (U436)	3.25
U449	2¢ on 3¢ (U437)	8.00
U450	2¢ on 3¢ (U438)	21.50
U451	2¢ on 3¢ (U439)	19.75
U458	2¢ on 3¢ (U436)	.70
U459	2¢ on 3¢ (U437)	4.25
U460	2¢ on 3¢ (U438)	3.75
U461	2¢ on 3¢ (U439)	6.75
U468	2¢ on 3¢ (U436)	.90
U469	2¢ on 3¢ (U437)	4.50
U470	2¢ on 3¢ (U438)	7.75
U471	2¢ on 3¢ (U439)	9.50
U472	2¢ on 4¢ (U390)	25.00
U473	2¢ on 4¢ (U391)	23.50
	1925 Issues	
U481	1½¢ Brown	.55
U482	1½¢ Brown, amber	1.60
U483	1½¢ Brown, blue	2.25
U484	1½¢ Brown, manila	12.50
W485	1½¢ Wrapper	1.35
U490	1½¢ on 1¢ (U400)	6.50
U491	1½¢ on 1¢ (U401)	14.50
U495	1½¢ on 1¢ (U420)	.85
U496	1½¢ on 1¢ (U421)	25.00
U497	1½¢ on 1¢ (U422)	5.25
U498	1½¢ on 1¢ (U423)	2.25
U499	1½¢ on 1¢ (U424)	18.50
U500	1½¢ on 1¢ (U428)	70.00
U501	1½¢ on 1¢ (U426)	75.00
U508	1½¢ on 1¢ (U353)	70.00
U509	1½¢ on 1¢ (U380)	25.00
U509B	1½¢ on 1¢ (U381)	65.00
U510	1½¢ on 1¢ (U400)	3.75
U512	1½¢ on 1¢ (U402)	12.00
U513	1½¢ on 1¢ (U403)	8.50
U514	1½¢ on 1¢ (U404)	35.00
U515	1½¢ on 1¢ (U420)	.60
U516	1½¢ on 1¢ (U421)	57.50
U517	1½¢ on 1¢ (U422)	6.50
U518	1½¢ on 1¢ (U423)	6.50
U519	1½¢ on 1¢ (U424)	32.50
U521	1½¢ on 1¢ (U420)	5.00
	1926-32 Issues	
U522	2¢ Sesquicentennial	2.25
U522a	Same, Die 2	11.75
U523	1¢ Washington Bicentennial (1932)	2.25
U524	1½¢ Wash. Bicent	3.25
U525	2¢ Wash. Bicent	.70
U526	3¢ Wash. Bicent	4.00
U527	4¢ Wash. Bicent	30.00
U528	5¢ Wash. Bicent	6.50
U529	6¢ Circle, Orange	9.00
U530	6¢ Orange, amber	15.00
U531	6¢ Orange, blue	15.00
	1950-58 Issues	
U532	1¢ Franklin (1950)	7.75
U533	2¢ Washington	1.35
U534	3¢ Washington	.55
U535	1½¢ Washington (1952)	6.25
U536	2¢ Franklin (1958)	.95
U537	2¢ + 2¢ Surch., Circle	3.95
U538	2¢ + 2¢ Surch., Oval	1.00
U539	3¢ + 1¢ Surch., Circle	16.00
U540	3¢ + 1¢ Surch., Oval	.65
	1960-74 Issues	
U541	1¼¢ Franklin	.90
U542	2½¢ Washington	.95
U543	4¢ Pony Express	.70
U544	5¢ Lincoln (1962)	.95
U545	4¢ + 1¢ Surch., Franklin	1.65
U546	5¢ NY World's Fair ('64)	.70

Scott's No.		Mint Entire
U547	1¼¢ Liberty Bell (1965)	.90
U548	1-4/10¢ Liberty Bell ('68)	1.00
U548A	1-6/10¢ Liberty Bell ('69)	.90
U549	4¢ Old Ironsides ('65)	.95
U550	5¢ Eagle	.90
U551	6¢ Liberty Head (1968)	.90
U552	4¢ + 2¢ Surcharge	4.50
U553	5¢ + 1¢ Surcharge	4.25
U554	6¢ Moby Dick (1970)	.65
U555	6¢ Brotherhood (1971)	.80
U556	1-7/10¢ Liberty Bell	.40
U557	8¢ Eagle	.50
U561	6¢ + 2¢ Liberty	1.15
U562	6¢ + 2¢ Brotherhood	3.00
U563	8¢ Bowling	.65
U564	8¢ Aging	.65
U565	8¢ Transpo. '72 (1972)	.75
U566	8¢ + 2¢ Sur., Eagle ('73)	.50
U567	10¢ Liberty Bell	.45
U568	1-8/10¢ Volunteer ('74)	.35
U569	10¢ Tennis	.55
	1975-82 Issues	
U571	10¢ Seafaring	.50
U572	13¢ Homemaker (1976)	.50
U573	13¢ Farmer (1976)	.50
U574	13¢ Doctor (1976)	.50
U575	13¢ Craftsman (1976)	.50
U576	13¢ Liberty Tree (1975)	.45
U577	2¢ Star & Pinwheel ('76)	.35
U578	2.1¢ Hexagon (1977)	.35
U579	2.7¢ U.S.A (1978)	.40
U580	(15¢) "A" & Eagle	.55
U581	15¢ Uncle Sam	.55
U582	13¢ Bicentennial (1976)	.50
U583	13¢ Golf (1977)	.95
U584	13¢ Conservation	.50
U585	13¢ Development	.50
U586	15¢ on 16¢ Surch ('78)	.55
U587	15¢ Auto Racing	.75
U588	15¢ on 13¢ Tree	.55
U589	3.1¢ Non Profit	.35
U590	3.5¢ Violins	.35
U591	5.9¢ Circle (1982)	.35
U592	(18¢) "B" & Eagle (1981)	.55
U593	18¢ Star	.55
U594	(20¢) "C" & Eagle	.55
U595	15¢ Veterinary (1979)	.55
U596	15¢ Soccer	.80
U597	15¢ Bicycle (1980)	.55
U598	15¢ America's Cup	.55
U599	15¢ Honeybee	.55
U600	18¢ Blinded Veteran	.60
U601	20¢ Capitol Dome	.55
U602	20¢ Great Seal (1982)	.55
U603	20¢ Purple Heart	.60
	1983-89 Issues	
U604	5.2¢ Non Profit	.45
U605	20¢ Paralyzed Vets	.55
U606	20¢ Small Business ('84)	.70
U607	(22¢) "D" & Eagle (1985)	.65
U608	22¢ Bison	.60
U609	6¢ Old Ironsides	.35
U610	8.5¢ Mayflower (1986)	.35
U611	25¢ Stars (1988)	.70
U612	8.4¢ USS Const	.35
U613	25¢ Snowflake	.90
U614	25¢ Philatelic Env. ('89)	.65
U615	25¢ Stars Security Env	.65
U616	25¢ Love	.65
U617	25¢ WSE Space Station Hologram	.75
	1990-94 Issues	
U618	25¢ Football	.65
U619	29¢ Star (1991)	.85
U620	11.1¢ Non Profit	.40
U621	29¢ Love	.75

U 597

UC17

Scott's No.		Mint Entire
U622	29¢ Magazine Industry	.75
U623	29¢ Stars & Bars	.75
U624	29¢ Country Geese	.75
U625	29¢ Space Station ('92)	.75
U626	29¢ Western Americana	.75
U627	29¢ Environmen	.75
U628	19.8¢ Bulk Rate	.55
U629	29¢ Disabled Americans	.75
U630	29¢ Kitten (1993)	.75
U631	29¢ Football (1994)	.75
1995-96 Issues		
U632	32¢ Liberty Bell	.80
U633	(32¢) "G" #6 ¾	.80
U634	(32¢) "G", Security Envelope #10	.80
U635	(5¢) Sheep	.35
U636	(10¢) Eagle	.45
U637	(32¢) Spiral Heart	.80
U638	32¢ Liberty Bell, Security Envelope	.80
U639	32¢ Space Shuttle	.80
U640	32¢ Environment ('96)	.80
U641	32¢ Paralympics ('96)	.80
1999-2001 Issues		
U642	33¢ Flag	.80
U643	33¢ Flag, Security Env.	.80
U644	33¢ Love	.80
U645	33¢ Lincoln	.80
U646	34¢ Federal Eagle	.80
U647	34¢ Lovebirds	.80
U648	34¢ Community Colleges	.80

AIR MAIL ENTIRES

1929-44 Issues

Scott's No.		Mint Entire
UC1	5¢ Blue, Die 1	4.25
UC2	5¢ Blue, Die 2	16.50
UC3	6¢ Orange, Die 2a (1934)	2.00
UC3v	6¢ No Border	2.65
UC4	6¢ Orange, Die 2b (1942)	57.50
UC4v	6¢ No Border	4.50
UC5	6¢ No Border, Die 2c (1944)	1.25

Scott's No.		Mint Entire
UC6	6¢ Orange, Die 3 ('42)	1.75
UC6v	6¢ Die 3, No Border	2.75
UC7	8¢ Olive Green ('32)	17.00
1945-47 Issues		
UC8	6¢ on 2¢ Surcharge, Washington	1.65
UC9	6¢ on 2¢ Wash. Bicent.	110.00
UC10	5¢ on 6¢ Orange Die 2a (1946)	4.50
UC11	5¢ on 6¢ Orge. Die 2b	11.00
UC12	5¢ on 6¢ Orge. Die 2c	1.50
UC13	5¢ on 6¢ Orge. Die 3	1.25
UC14	5¢ Plane, Die 1	1.00
UC15	5¢ Plane, Die 2	1.00
UC17	5¢ CIPEX (1947)	.55
1950-58 Issues		
UC18	6¢ Skymaster	.65
UC19	6¢ on 5¢, Die 1 ('51)	1.30
UC20	6¢ on 5¢, Die 2	1.30
UC21	6¢ on 5¢, Die 1 ('52)	35.00
UC22	6¢ on 5¢, Die 2	5.50
UC25	6¢ FIPEX (1956)	1.00
UC26	7¢ Skymaster (1958)	1.00
UC27	6¢ + 1¢ Orge., Die 2a	300.00
UC28	6¢ + 1¢ Orge., Die 2b	90.00
UC29	6¢ + 1¢ Orge., Die 2c	45.00
UC30	6¢ + 1¢ Skymaster	1.25
UC31	6¢ + 1¢ FIPEX	1.50
UC33	7¢ Jet, Blue	.80
1960-73 Issues		
UC34	7¢ Jet, Carmine	.70
UC36	8¢ Jet Airliner (1962)	.80
UC37	8¢ Jet, Triangle (1965)	.55
UC37a	same, Tagged (1967)	2.00
UC40	10¢ Jet, Triangle ('68)	.80
UC41	8¢ + 2¢ Surcharge	.90
UC43	1¢ Three Circles ('71)	.65
UC45	10¢ + 1¢ Triangle	2.00
UC47	13¢ Bird in Flight ('73)	.65

Scott's No.		Mint Entire
AIRLETTER SHEETS		
1947-71 Issues		
UC16	10¢ DC3, 2 Lines, "Air Letter"	7.50
UC16a	10¢ 4 Lines, "Air Letter" (1951)	15.00
UC16c	10¢ "Aerogramme, 4 Lines (1953)	52.50
UC16d	10¢ Aero., 3 Lines (1955)	7.50
UC32	10¢ Jet, 2 Lines ('59)	6.50
UC32a	10¢ Jet, 3 Lines ('58)	10.75
UC35	11¢ Jet & Globe ('61)	2.70
UC38	11¢ J.F. Kennedy (1965)	3.75
UC39	13¢ J.F. Kennedy (1967)	3.25
UC42	13¢ Human Rights (1968)	7.50
UC44	15¢ Birds, Letter ('71)	1.50
UC44a	15¢ w/"Aerogramme"	1.50
1973-81 Issues		
UC46	15¢ Ballooning	.85
UC48	18¢ "USA" (1974)	.80
UC49	18¢ NATO	.95
UC50	22¢ "USA" (1976)	.95
UC51	22¢ "USA" (1978)	.85
UC52	22¢ Moscow Olympics (1979)	1.65
UC53	30¢ "USA", Blue, Red & Brown (1980)	.85
UC54	30¢ "USA", Yellow, Blue & Black (1981)	.85
1982-99 Issues		
UC55	30¢ World Trade	.85
UC56	30¢ Communication Year (1983)	.85
UC57	30¢ Olympics	.85
UC58	36¢ Landsat Satellite (85)	.85
UC59	36¢ Travel	.85
UC60	36¢ Mark Twain/ Halley's Comet	.85
UC61	39¢ Stylyized Aero ('88)	1.00
UC62	39¢ Montgomery Blair (1989)	1.00

Scott's No.		Mint Entire
UC63	45¢ Eagle, blue paper (1991)	1.10
UC63a	Eagle, white paper	1.10
UC64	50¢ T.Lowe (1995)	1.20
UC65	60¢ Voyaguers Park (1999)	1.25

POSTAL SAVINGS OFFICIAL ENVELOPES

U070	1¢ Green (1911)	85.00
U071	1¢ Green, Oriental buff (1911)	225.00
U072	2¢ Carmine (1911)	20.00

OFFICIAL MAIL ENTIRES

UO73	20¢ Eagle (1983)	1.15
UO74	22¢ Eagle (1985)	.90
UO75	22¢ Bond Envel. (1987)	.90
UO76	(25¢) "E" Bond Env ('88)	1.10
UO77	25¢ Eagle	.80
UO78	25¢ Bond Envelope	1.00
UO79	45¢ Passport 2 oz (90)	1.50
UO80	65¢ Passport env.3 oz	1.80
UO81	45¢ Self-sealing Passport 2 oz	1.30
UO82	65¢ Self-sealing 3 oz	1.80
UO83	(29¢) "F" Savings Bond (1991)	1.25
UO84	29¢ Official Mail	.85
UO85	29¢ Sav. Bond Env	.85
UO86	52¢ Consular Service (1992)	2.50
UO87	75¢ Consular Service	4.25
UO88	32¢ Official Mail (1995)	1.10
UO89	33¢ Great Seal (1999)	.90
UO90	34¢ Great Seal (2001)	.80

MINT POSTAL CARDS

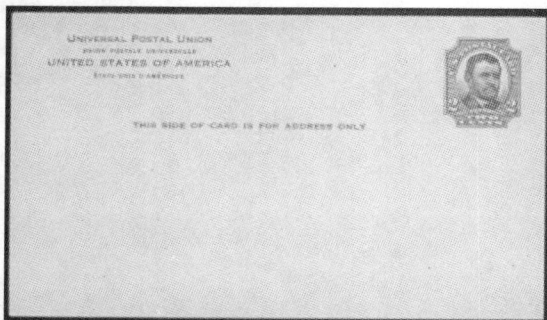

UX25

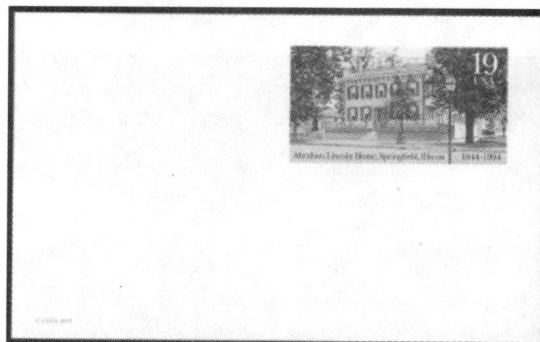

UX174

Scott's No.		Mint Card
1873-98 Issues		
UX1	1¢ Liberty, brown, large watermark	335.00
UX1	Preprinted	60.00
UX3	Same, small watermark	75.00
UX3	Preprinted	20.00
UX5	1¢ Liberty, black, "Write" (1875)	65.00
UX5	Preprinted	8.00
UX6	2¢ Liberty, blue on buff (1879)	28.50
UX6	Preprinted	11.00
UX7	1¢ Liberty, black, "Nothing" (1881)	67.50
UX7	Preprinted	7.50
UX8	1¢ Jefferson,brown (85)	50.00
UX8	Preprinted	9.50
UX9	1¢ Jeff., black (1886)	18.50
UX9	Preprinted	1.95
UX10	1¢ Grant, black (1891)	32.50
UX10	Preprinted	8.00
UX11	Same, blue	15.00
UX11	Preprinted	3.25
UX12	1¢ Jefferson, black, small wreath (1894)	40.00
UX12	Preprinted	3.25
UX13	2¢ Liberty, blue on cream (1897)	155.00
UX13	Preprinted	80.00
UX14	1¢ Jefferson, black, large wreath	27.50
UX14	Preprinted	3.00
UX15	1¢ Adams, black (1898)	42.50
UX15	Preprinted	12.75
UX16	2¢ Liberty, black, "No Frame" (1898)	11.50
UX16	Preprinted	6.50
1902-18 Issues		
UX18	1¢ McKinley, oval	13.00
UX18	Preprinted	2.25
UX19	1¢ McKinley ('07)	40.00
UX19	Preprinted	2.75
UX20	1¢ Correspond Space at Left (1908)	50.00
UX20	Preprinted	9.50
UX21	1¢ McKinley,shaded('10)	100.00
UX21	Preprinted	19.50
UX22	Same, White background	15.00
UX22	Preprinted	2.00
UX23	1¢ Lincoln, red ('11)	9.50
UX23	Preprinted	3.75
UX24	1¢ McKinley, red	12.00
UX24	Preprinted	1.75
UX25	2¢ Grant, red	1.65
UX25	Preprinted	.85
UX26	1¢ Lincoln, green ('13)	11.50
UX26	Preprinted	3.50
UX27	1¢ Jeffer, Die 1 (1914)	.35
UX27	Preprinted	.20
UX28	1¢ Lincoln, green ('17)	.75
UX28	Preprinted	.35
UX29	2¢ Jefferson, Die 1	45.00
UX29	Preprinted	8.00
UX30	2¢ Jeff, Die 2 (1918)	28.50
UX30	Preprinted	5.50
1920-64 Issues		
UX32	1¢ on 2¢ red, die 1	52.50
UX32	Preprinted	18.00
UX33	1¢ on 2¢ red, die 2	13.50
UX33	Preprinted	3.50
UX37	3¢ McKinley (1926)	5.00
UX37	Preprinted	2.50
UX38	2¢ Franklin (1951)	.40
UX38	Preprinted	.30
UX39	2¢ on 1¢ Jeff, green ('52)	.65

Scott's No.		Mint Card
UX39	Preprinted	.40
UX40	2¢ on 1¢ Lincoln, green	.85
UX40	Preprinted	.60
UX41	2¢ on 1¢ Jeff, dark green	5.50
UX41	Preprinted	2.50
UX42	2¢ on 1¢ Lincoln, dk grn	5.75
UX42	Preprinted	3.00
UX43	2¢ Lincoln, carmine	.30
UX43	Preprinted	.25
UX44	2¢ FIPEX (1956)	.30
UX45	4¢ Liberty	1.60
UX46	3¢ Liberty (1958)	.50
UX46c	Precancelled (1961)	5.00
UX48	4¢ Lincoln, precan (1962)	.30
UX48a	Same, Tagged ('66)	.65
UX49	7¢ "USA" (1963)	4.50
UX50	4¢ Customs (1964)	.55
UX51	4¢ Social Security	.50
1965-73 Issues		
UX52	4¢ Coast Guard	.40
UX53	4¢ Census	.40
UX54	8¢ "USA" (1967)	4.75
UX55	5¢ Lincoln (1968)	.35
UX56	5¢ Women Marines	.40
UX57	5¢ Weather (1970)	.35
UX58	6¢ Paul Revere (1971)	.35
UX59	10¢ "USA"	4.75
UX60	6¢ Hospitals	.35
UX61	6¢ Constellation ('72)	1.00
UX62	6¢ Monument Valley	.50
UX63	6¢ Gloucester	.50
UX64	6¢ John Hanson	.30
UX64a	Coarse Paper	1.25
UX65	6¢ Liberty (1973)	.30
UX66	8¢ Samuel Adams	.40
1974-79 Issues		
UX67	12¢ Visit USA	.40
UX68	7¢ Thomson (1975)	.35
UX69	9¢ Witherspoon	.35
UX70	9¢ Rodney (1976)	.35
UX71	9¢ Galveston (1977)	.45
UX72	9¢ Nathan Hale	.45
UX73	10¢ Music Hall (1978)	.40
UX74	(10¢) John Hancock	.40
UX75	10¢ John Hancock	.35
UX76	14¢ Cutter "Eagle"	.45
UX77	10¢ Molly Pitcher	.45
UX78	10¢ G.R. Clark (1979)	.35
UX79	10¢ Pulaski	.35
UX80	10¢ Olympics	.65
UX81	10¢ Iolani Palace	.35
1980-83 Issues		
UX82	14¢ Winter Olympics	.70
UX83	10¢ Salt Lake Temple	.35
UX84	10¢ Rochambeau	.35
UX85	10¢ King's Mt	.35
UX86	19¢ Golden Hinde	.80
UX87	10¢ Cowpens (1981)	.35
UX88	(12¢) Eagle	.40
UX89	12¢ Isaiah Thomas	.40
UX90	12¢ N. Greene	.35
UX91	12¢ Lewis & Clark	.35
UX92	(13¢) Morris	.35
UX93	13¢ Morris	.35
UX94	13¢ F. Marion (1982)	.35
UX95	13¢ LaSalle	.35
UX96	13¢ Music Academy	.35
UX97	13¢ St. Louis P.O.	.35
UX98	13¢ Georgia (1983)	.35
UX99	13¢ Old P. Office	.35
UX100	13¢ Yachting	.35
1984-88 Issues		
UX101	13¢ Ark & Dove,Maryland	.35
UX102	13¢ Olympics	.35
UX103	13¢ Father Baraga	.35
UX104	13¢ Rancho San Pedro	.35

Scott's No.		Mint Card
UX105	(14¢) Charles Carroll(85)	.35
UX106	14¢ Charles Carroll	.55
UX107	25¢ Flying Cloud	.75
UX108	14¢ George Wythe	.35
UX109	14¢ Connecticut Anniv	.35
UX110	14¢ Stamp Collecting ('86)	.35
UX111	14¢ Francis Vigo	.35
UX112	14¢ Rhode Island	.35
UX113	14¢ Wisconsin Terr.	.35
UX114	14¢ National Guard	.35
UX115	14¢ Steel Plow (1987)	.35
UX116	14¢ Constitution Conv	.35
UX117	14¢ U.S. Flag	.35
UX118	14¢ Pride in America	.35
UX119	14¢ Timberline Lodge	.35
UX120	15¢ Amercia the Beautiful (1988)	.35
UX121	15¢ Blair House	.35
UX122	28¢ Yorkshire	.70
UX123	15¢ Iowa Territory	.35
UX124	15¢ NW/Ohio Territory	.35
UX125	15¢ Hearst Castle	.35
UX126	15¢ Federalist Papers	.35
1989-92 Issues		
UX127	15¢ The Desert	.35
UX128	15¢ Healy Hall	.35
UX129	15¢ Wetlands	.35
UX130	15¢ Oklahoma	.35
UX131	21¢ Canada Geese/Mtns	.60
UX132	15¢ Seashore	.35
UX133	15¢ Woodlands	.35
UX134	15¢ Hull House	.35
UX135	15¢ Independence Hall	.35
UX136	15¢ Baltimore Inner Harbor	.35
UX137	15¢ 59th St.Bridge,NY	.35
UX138	15¢ Capitol Bldg	.35
UX139-42	15¢ Cityscape sheet of 4 postcards	16.50
UX143	15¢ The White House	1.40
UX144	15¢ Jefferson Memorial	1.40
UX145	15¢ Papermaking ('90)	.35
UX146	15¢ World Literacy Year.	.35
UX147	15¢ Geo. Bingham Art	1.25
UX148	15¢ Isaac Royall House	.45
UX150	15¢ Stanford Univ	.45
UX151	15¢ DAR/Const. Hall	1.25
UX152	15¢ Chicago Orch.Hall	.45
UX153	19¢ Flag (1991)	.50
UX154	19¢ Carnegie Hall	.50
UX155	19¢ "Old Red", U of TX	.50
UX156	19¢ Bill of Rights Bicent	.50
UX157	19¢ Notre Dame	.50
UX158	30¢ Niagara Falls	.90
UX159	19¢ Old Mill, U of VT	.50
UX160	19¢ Wadsworth Atheneum,Hartford (92)	.50
UX161	19¢ Cobb Hall, Chicago	.50
UX162	19¢ Waller Hall	.50
UX163	19¢ America's Cup	1.40
UX164	19¢ Columbia River	.50
UX165	19¢ Great Hall,Ellis Island	.50
1993-94 Issues		
UX166	19¢ National Cathedral	.50
UX167	19¢ Wren Building	.50
UX168	19¢ Holocaust Memorial	1.40
UX169.	19¢ Fort Recovery	.50
UX170	19¢ Playmaker's Theater	.50
UX171	19¢ O'Kane Hall	.50
UX172	19¢ Beecher Hall	.50
UX173	19¢ Massachusetts Hall	.50
UX174	19¢ Lincoln Home ('94)	.50
UX175	19¢ Myers Hall	.50
UX176	19¢ Canyon de Chelly	.50
UX177	19¢ St. Louis Station	.50
UX178-97	19¢ Legends of the West (20)	29.50

Scott's No.		Mint Card
1995-96 Issues		
UX198	20¢ Red Barn	.50
UX199	(20¢) "G"	.60
UX200-19	20¢ Civil War (20)	32.50
UX220	20¢ Clipper Ship	.50
UX221-40	20¢ Comic Strips (20)	29.50
UX241	20¢ Winter Farm Scene (1996)	.60
UX242-61	20¢ Atlanta Olympics (20)(1996)	32.50
UX262	20¢ McDowell Hall (96)	.50
UX263	20¢ Alexander Hall (96)	.50
UX264-78	20¢ Endangered Species (15) (1996)	35.00
1997-98 Issues		
UX279	20¢ Love-Swans	1.95
UX279a	Same, Package of 12	19.95
Note: UX279 is sold in packages of 12 with 8 different stamp designs without values.		
UX280	20¢ City College of New York	.50
UX281	20¢ Bugs Bunny	1.60
UX281a	20¢ Bugs Bunny Booklet of 10	14.95
UX282	20¢ Golden Gate Bridge	.50
UX283	50¢ Golden Gate Bridge	1.25
UX284	20¢ Fort McHenry	.50
UX285-89	20¢ Movie Monsters(5)	4.75
UX289a	Same, booklet of 20	18.50
UX290	20¢ University of Mississippi (1998)	.50
UX291	20¢ Tweety & Sylvester (1998)	1.60
UX291a	20¢ Tweety & Sylvester Booklet of 10	14.95
UX292	20¢ Girard College	.50
UX293-96	20¢ Tropical Birds (4)	4.25
UX296a	same, booklet of 10	17.50
UX297	20¢ Ballet	1.50
UX297a	same, booklet of 10	14.50
UX298	20¢ Northeastern Univ	.50
UX299	20¢ Brandeis Univ	.50
1999 Commemoraives		
UX300	20¢ Love	.95
UX300a	Love Booklet of 20	16.50
UX301	20¢ Univ. of Wisconsin	.50
UX302	20¢ Wash. & Lee Univ.	.50
UX303	20¢ Redwood Library	.50
UX304	20¢ Daffy Duck	1.60
UX304a	Daffy Duck Pack-10	14.95
UX305	20¢ Mount Vernon	.50
UX306	20¢ Block Island Light House	.50
UX307-11	20¢ Famous Trains (5)	4.75
UX311a	20¢ Famous Trains Booklet of 20 (4 each)	16.50
2000 Commemoratives		
UX312	20¢ University of Utah	.45
UX313	20¢ Ryman Auditorium	.45
UX314	20¢ Wile E. Coyote & Road Runner	1.60
UX314a	Wile E. Coyote & Road Runner Pack of 10	14.95
UX315	20¢ Adoption	1.60
UX315	Adoption Pack of 10	14.95
UX316	20¢ Middlebury College	.45
UX317-36	20¢ Stars & Stripes in 5 Sheets of 4 (20)	20.95
UX337-56	20¢ Legends of Baseball 5 sheets of 4 (20)	20.95

MINT POSTAL CARDS

UXC24

UZ2

UY29

Scott's No. .... MintCard		Scott's No.	Mint Card	Scott's No.	Mint Card	Scott's No.	Mint Card
2000-2001 Commemoratives		**OFFICIAL POSTAL CARDS**		**POSTAL REPLY CARDS**		**1924-68 (cont.)**	
UX357-60 20¢ Christmas Deer (4)	3.65	UZ2 13¢ Great Seal (1983) ..	.70	**1892-1920 Issues**		UY15 2¢ on 1¢ + 2¢ on 1¢,	
UX360a 20¢ Christmas Deer,		UZ3 14¢ Great Seal (1985) ..	.70	Unsevered Cards-Folded		M&G Wash., green	150.00
Booklet of 20 (5 each) .	17.95	UZ4 15¢ Great Seal (1988) ..	.70	Unfolded +50%		UY15 Preprinted	60.00
UX361 20¢ Yale University(2001)	.40	UZ5 19¢ Great Seal (1991) ..	.65	UY1 1¢ Grant, black	37.50	UY16 4¢ + 4¢ Liberty (1956) ..	1.50
UX362 20¢ Un.of South Carolina	.40	UZ6 20¢ Great Seal (1995) ..	.60	UY1 Preprinted	17.50	UY17 3¢ + 3¢ Liberty (1958) ..	5.25
UX363 20¢ Northwestern Univ. .	.40			UY2 2¢ Liberty, blue ('93)	18.50	UY18 4¢ + 4¢ Lincoln (1962) ..	6.00
UX364 20¢ Univ.of Portland	.40	**"POSTAL BUDDY" CARDS**		UY2 Preprinted	14.50	UY19 7¢ + 7¢ "USA" (1963)	3.75
		CVUX1 15¢ (1990) Eagle	8.00	UY3 1¢ Grant, no frame(98) .	70.00	UY20 8¢ + 8¢ "USA" (1967)	3.50
AIRMAIL POSTAL CARDS		Sheet of 4	32.50	UY3 Preprinted	16.50	UY21 5¢+5¢ Lincoln (1968)	2.00
UXC1 4¢ Eagle	.50	CVUX2 19¢ (1991) Eagle	4.25	UY4 1¢ + 1¢ Sherman			
UXC2 5¢ Eagle (1958)	1.75	Sheet of 4	17.00	and Sheridan (1904)	55.00	**1971-99**	
UXC3 5¢ Eagle, redrawn (60) .	6.50	CVUX3 19¢ (1992) Plain, star ..	10.00	UY4 Preprinted	12.50	Unsevered Cards-Unfolded	
UXC4 6¢ Bald Eagle (1963)	.65	Sheet of 4	42.50	UY5 1¢ + 1¢ Martha &George		UY22 6¢ + 6¢ Revere	1.25
UXC5 11¢ SIPEX, Travel (66) .	.60	CVUX3a With Logo	11.00	Washington,Blue (1910)	170.00	UY23 6¢ + 6¢ Hanson (1972) ..	1.35
UXC6 6¢ Virgin Islands ('67) ...	.50	CVUX3b New Back	75.00	UY5 Preprinted	50.00	UY24 8¢ + S. Adams (1973) ...	1.10
UXC7 6¢ Boy Scouts	.50	Sheet of 4	300.00	UY6 Same, Green (1911)	170.00	UY25 7¢ + 7¢ Thomson (1975)	1.10
UXC8 13¢ Travel USA	1.60	CVUX3c New Back w\ Logo	135.00	UY6 Preprinted	65.00	UY26 9¢ + 9¢ Witherson	1.10
UXC9 8¢ Eagle, Precan ('68) ..	.70			UY7 Same,single frame		UY27 9¢ + 9¢ Rodney (1976) ..	1.10
UXC9a Same, Tagged (1969)	2.65			line (1915)	1.50	UY28 9¢ + 9¢ Hale (1977)	1.30
UXC10 9¢ Eagle, Precan ('71) ..	.60			UY7 Preprinted	.60	UY29 (10¢+10¢) Hancock (78)	10.75
UXC11 15¢ Travel USA	1.75			UY8 2¢ + 2¢ Martha &George		UY30 10¢ + 10¢ Hancock	1.25
UXC12 9¢ Grand Canyon ('72) .	.55			Washington,red (1918) .	90.00	UY31 (12¢ + 12¢) Eagle ('81) .	1.25
UXC13 15¢ Niagara Falls	.70			UY8 Preprinted	35.00	UY32 12¢ + 12¢ Thomas	1.75
UXC14 11¢ Mail Early (1974)	.75			UY9 1¢ on 2¢ + 1¢ on 2¢,		UY33 (13¢ + 13¢) Morris	2.25
UXC15 18¢ Visit USA	.90			Martha & George		UY34 13¢ + 13¢ Morris	1.25
UXC16 14¢ Visit USA (1975) ...	.85			Washington, red (1920)	20.00	UY35 (14¢ + 14¢) Carroll ('85)	3.25
UXC17 21¢ Curtiss Jenny ('78) ..	.80			UY9 Preprinted	11.50	UY36 14¢ + 14¢ Carroll	1.25
UXC18 21¢ Olympics (1979)	1.10					UY37 14¢ + 14¢ Wythe	1.25
UXC19 28¢ Trans-Pacific ('81) .	1.00			**1924-68**		UY38 14¢ + 14¢ U.S. Flag ('87)	1.25
UXC20 28¢ Soaring (1982)	1.00			Unsevered cards-Unfolded		UY39 15¢ + 15¢ America the	
UXC21 28¢ Speedskating ('83) .	.90			UY11 2¢ + 2¢ Liberty, red	3.00	Beautiful (1988)	1.25
UXC22 33¢ China Clipper ('85) .	1.00			UY11 Preprinted	1.50	UY40 19¢ + 19¢ Flag (1991) ..	1.25
UXC23 33¢ Ameripex (1986)	.85			UY12 3¢ + 3¢ McKinley ('26) ..	15.00	UY41 20¢ + 20¢ Red Barn ('95)	1.25
UXC24 36¢ DC-3 (1988)	.85			UY12 Preprinted	6.50	UY42 20¢ + 20¢ Block Island	
UXC25 40¢ Yankee Clipper (91)	.90			UY13 2¢ + 2¢ Martha &George		Light House (1999)	1.25
UXC26 50¢ Eagle (1995)	1.15			Washington (1951)	1.75		
UXC27 55¢ Mt. Rainier (1999) ..	1.20			UY13 Preprinted	.80		
UXC28 70¢ Badlands (2001)	1.40			UY14 2¢ on 1¢ + 2¢ on 1¢			
				M&G Wash (1952)	1.75		
				UY14 Preprinted	1.00		

UNITED STATES REVENUES

R5a

R25a

R37b

R46a

R60c

1862-71 (All Used) (C) (VF + 60%)

Scott's No.		Imperforate(a) Fine	Ave.	Part Perforate(b) Fine	Ave.	Perforated(c) Fine	Ave.
R1	1¢ Express	52.50	27.50	37.50	21.00	1.25	.75
R2	1¢ Play Cards	975.00	575.00	800.00	500.00	150.00	90.00
R3	1¢ Proprietary	650.00	375.00	110.00	60.00	.50	.30
R4	1¢ Telegraph	375.00	200.00	...	...	10.75	6.50
R5	2¢ Bank Check,Blue	1.10	.70	1.50	.90	.25	.20
R6	2¢ Bank Ck.,Orange	...	...	65.00	37.50	.25	.20
R7	2¢ Certificate,Blue	12.00	7.00	...	...	25.00	14.00
R8	2¢ Certif.,Orange	...	...	...	...	27.50	16.50
R9	2¢ Express,Blue	12.00	7.00	19.50	11.00	.40	.30
R10	2¢ Express,Orange	...	...	...	...	7.50	4.50
R11	2¢ Playing Cards,Blue	...	...	160.00	95.00	3.75	2.25
R12	2¢ Ply.Cds.,Orange	...	...	...	...	35.00	20.00
R13	2¢ Proprietary, Blue	325.00	225.00	110.00	65.00	.40	.25
R14	2¢ Propriet.,Orange	...	...	...	...	35.00	20.00
R15	2¢ U.S.I.R.	...	...	...	...	.20	.15
R16	3¢ Foreign Exchange	...	...	230.00	130.00	3.15	1.75
R17	3¢ Playing Cards	...	...	...	...	110.00	65.00
R18	3¢ Proprietary	...	...	275.00	175.00	3.00	1.80
R19	3¢ Telegraph	55.00	30.00	19.50	11.50	2.65	1.50
R20	4¢ Inland Exchange	...	...	...	...	1.65	1.10
R21	4¢ Playing Cards	...	...	...	...	465.00	250.00
R22	4¢ Proprietary	...	...	185.00	110.00	5.75	3.50
R23	5¢ Agreement	...	...	...	...	.30	.20
R24	5¢ Certificate	2.50	1.40	10.00	5.75	.30	.20
R25	5¢ Express	4.35	2.65	5.50	3.50	.30	.20
R26	5¢ Foreign Exchange	...	...	...	...	.30	.20
R27	5¢ Inland Exchange	4.50	2.65	3.50	2.10	.25	.20
R28	5¢ Playing Cards	...	...	...	...	18.00	11.00
R29	5¢ Proprietary	...	...	...	...	22.50	13.00
R30	6¢ Inland Exchange	...	...	...	...	1.60	.95
R32	10¢ Bill of Lading	42.50	25.00	210.00	130.00	.95	.55
R33	10¢ Certificate	110.00	60.00	250.00	150.00	.25	.20
R34	10¢ Contract,Blue	...	...	150.00	85.00	.35	.25
R35	10¢ Foreign Exchange,Blue	...	...	...	...	6.50	4.00
R36	10¢ Inland Exchange	150.00	85.00	3.25	1.95	.25	.20
R37	10¢ Power of Attorney	425.00	250.00	20.00	12.00	.60	.40
R38	10¢ Proprietary	...	...	...	...	14.00	8.50
R39	15¢ Foreign Exchange	...	...	...	...	13.50	8.00
R40	15¢ Inland Exchange	27.50	16.00	11.00	6.00	1.10	.65
R41	20¢ Foreign Exchange	38.50	21.50	...	...	30.00	15.00
R42	20¢ Inland Exchange	14.00	8.00	16.50	9.50	.35	.25
R43	25¢ Bond	130.00	75.00	5.75	3.50	2.25	1.30
R44	25¢ Certificate	9.25	5.25	5.50	3.25	.25	.20
R45	25¢ Entry Goods	16.50	9.50	57.50	32.50	.70	.45
R46	25¢ Insurance	9.00	5.50	9.00	5.00	.25	.20
R47	25¢ Life Insurance	32.50	18.50	225.00	135.00	6.00	4.00
R48	25¢ Power of Attorney	5.50	3.25	25.00	15.00	.30	.20
R49	25¢ Protest	27.50	16.50	265.00	160.00	6.50	4.00
R50	25¢ Warehouse Receipt	40.00	23.00	225.00	130.00	21.50	11.75
R51	30¢ Foreign Exchange	65.00	40.00	900.00	500.00	47.50	26.50
R52	30¢ Inland Exchange	46.50	25.00	58.50	35.00	3.00	1.80
R53	40¢ Inland Exchange	500.00	285.00	6.50	3.75	3.25	1.95
R54	50¢ Conveyance,Blue	12.00	6.75	1.50	.95	.20	.15
R55	50¢ Entry of Goods	...	...	11.00	6.50	.40	.25
R56	50¢ Foreign Exchange	42.50	24.00	40.00	23.00	4.75	3.00
R57	50¢ Lease	22.50	13.00	55.00	32.50	7.75	4.75
R58	50¢ Life Insurance	27.50	16.00	47.50	26.00	1.10	.65
R59	50¢ Mortgage	13.00	7.50	2.25	1.35	.45	.30
R60	50¢ Original Process	2.65	1.50	525.00	375.00	.55	.35
R61	50¢ Passage Ticket	67.50	37.50	130.00	75.00	1.15	.70
R62	50¢ Probate of Will	32.50	18.00	55.00	30.00	17.00	10.00
R63	50¢ Surety Bond,Blue	135.00	80.00	2.35	1.30	.30	.20
R64	60¢ Inland Exchange	80.00	45.00	45.00	25.00	5.25	3.00
R65	70¢ Foreign Exchange	300.00	170.00	95.00	55.00	7.25	4.25
R66	$1 Conveyance	11.00	6.00	395.00	225.00	14.00	8.50
R67	$1 Entry of Goods	29.50	17.00	...	...	1.75	1.00
R68	$1 Foreign Exchange	55.00	30.00	...	...	.65	.40
R69	$1 Inland Exchange	11.50	6.75	300.00	170.00	.50	.30
R70	$1 Lease	32.50	18.00	...	...	2.00	1.25
R71	$1 Life Insurance	140.00	85.00	...	...	5.75	3.50
R72	$1 Manifest	45.00	25.00	...	...	25.00	14.50
R73	$1 Mortgage	18.50	11.00	...	...	160.00	95.00
R74	$1 Passage Ticket	230.00	135.00	...	...	180.00	110.00
R75	$1 Power of Attorney	67.50	40.00	...	...	2.00	1.20
R76	$1 Probate of Will	65.00	35.00	...	...	35.00	20.00
R77	$1.30 Foreign Exchange	...	...	...	...	50.00	30.00
R78	$1.50 Inland Exchange	21.50	12.50	...	...	2.85	1.75
R79	$1.60 Foreign Exchange	850.00	475.00	...	...	90.00	50.00
R80	$1.90 Foreign Exchange	...	2000.00	...	...	80.00	47.50

1862-71 Issue (continued) (All Used) (C)

R78a

R85c

R91a

Scott's No.		Imperforate(a) Fine	Ave.	Part Perforate(b) Fine	Ave.	Perforated(c) Fine	Ave.
R81	$2 Conveyance	100.00	55.00	1300.00	750.00	2.50	1.40
R82	$2 Mortgage	90.00	50.00	...	...	2.65	1.50
R83	$2 Probate of Will	...	1750.00	...	...	50.00	28.50
R84	$2.50 Inland Exchange	2500.00	1500.00	...	...	5.75	3.50
R85	$3 Charter Party	95.00	55.00	...	...	4.65	2.75
R86	$3 Manifest	100.00	60.00	...	...	22.50	12.50
R87	$3.50 Inland Exchange	...	1500.00	...	...	45.00	27.50
R88	$5 Charter Party	225.00	130.00	...	...	5.75	3.50
R89	$5 Conveyance	33.00	18.50	...	...	5.75	3.50
R90	$5 Manifest	100.00	55.00	...	...	75.00	41.50
R91	$5 Mortgage	100.00	55.00	...	...	17.00	9.50
R92	$5 Probate of Will	425.00	250.00	...	...	17.00	9.50
R93	$10 Charter Party	500.00	285.00	...	...	25.00	14.00
R94	$10 Conveyance	85.00	50.00	...	...	55.00	32.50
R95	$10 Mortgage	350.00	210.00	...	...	22.50	12.50
R96	$10 Probate of Will	950.00	600.00	...	...	25.00	14.00
R97	$15 Mortgage,Blue	1050.00	650.00	...	...	100.00	65.00
R98	$20 Conveyance	110.00	65.00	...	...	60.00	37.50
R99	$20 Probate of Will	1075.00	600.00	...	...	975.00	625.00
R100	$25 Mortgage	850.00	485.00	...	...	100.00	60.50
R101	$50 U.S.I.R.	180.00	110.00	...	...	80.00	45.00
R102	$200 U.S.I.R.	1300.00	750.00	...	...	575.00	325.00

1ST ISSUE HANDSTAMPED CANCELLATIONS ARE GENERALLY AVAILABLE FOR A 20% PREMIUM.

1871 SECOND ISSUE (C) (VF + 60%)

R103

R107, R137

R112

R118, R144

Scott's No.		Used Fine	Ave.	Scott's No.		Used Fine	Ave.
R103	1¢	37.50	19.50	R118	$1	2.75	1.50
R104	2¢	1.10	.65	R119	$1.30	280.00	160.00
R105	3¢	17.50	11.00	R120	$1.50	11.50	7.00
R106	4¢	55.00	30.00	R121	$1.60	350.00	195.00
R107	5¢	1.30	.70	R122	$1.90	160.00	90.00
R108	6¢	90.00	50.00	R123	$2	14.50	8.00
R109	10¢	.95	.55	R124	$2.50	27.50	16.00
R110	15¢	25.00	15.00	R125	$3	30.00	18.00
R111	20¢	5.50	3.00	R126	$3.50	140.00	80.00
R112	25¢	.60	.35	R127	$5	17.00	10.00
R113	30¢	65.00	37.50	R128	$10	95.00	55.00
R114	40¢	40.00	23.50	R129	$20	335.00	200.00
R115	50¢	.55	.35	R130	$25	335.00	200.00
R116	60¢	87.50	52.50	R131	$50	365.00	225.00
R117	70¢	35.00	21.50				

R103 through R131 have blue frames and a black center.

1871-72 Third Issue - Same Designs as Second Issue (C) (VF + 60%)

R134	1¢ Claret	28.50	16.50	R143	70¢ Green	45.00	25.00
R135	2¢ Orange	.20	.15	R144	$1 Green	1.35	.75
R136	4¢ Brown	35.00	19.50	R145	$2 Vermillion	20.00	11.00
R137	5¢ Orange	.25	.20	R146	$2.50 Claret	33.50	19.00
R138	6¢ Orange	40.00	23.50	R147	$3 Green	33.50	19.00
R139	15¢ Brown	10.50	6.50	R148	$5 Vermillion	20.00	12.00
R140	30¢ Orange	15.00	9.50	R149	$10 Green	75.00	45.00
R141	40¢ Brown	35.00	21.00	R150	$20 Orange	425.00	235.00
R142	60¢ Orange	65.00	40.00				

R134 through R150 have black centers.

Note : Cut cancels are priced at 40% to 60% of the above prices.

1874 Fourth Issue (C) (VF+60%)

Scott's No.		Uncancelled Fine	Ave.	Used Fine	Ave.
R151	2¢ Orange and Black, Green Paper	...	...	.20	.15

1875-78 Fifth Issue (C)(VF + 60%)

R152a	2¢ Liberty, Blue, Silk Paper	1.50	.90	.20	.15
R152b	2¢ Blue, Watermarked	1.50	.90	.20	.15
R152c	2¢ Blue, Rouletted, Watermarked	...	...	28.50	14.50

* 1898 Postage Stamps Overprinted "I.R." (C) (VF + 50%)

Scott's No.		Uncancelled Fine	Uncancelled Ave.	Used Fine	Used Ave.
R153	1¢ Green, Small I.R. (#279)	2.80	1.70	2.75	1.65
R154	1¢ Green, Large I.R. (#279)	.25	.20	.20	.15
R154a	1¢ Green, Inverted Surcharge	19.50	11.00	15.00	8.50
R155	2¢ Carmine, Large I.R. (#267)	.25	.20	.20	.15
*** 1898 Newspaper Stamps Surcharged "INT. REV./$5/DOCUMENTARY" (C)**					
R159	$5 Blue, Surcharge down (#PR121)	300.00	190.00	140.00	85.00
R160	$5 Blue, Surcharge up (#PR121)	90.00	50.00	60.00	35.00

*** Used prices are for stamps with contemporary cancels.**

R170

R174

R195, R206

R217

1898 Documentary "Battleship" Designs (C) (VF +40%) (Rouletted 5½)

R161	½¢ Orange	2.35	1.50	6.50	4.00
R162	½¢ Dark Gray	.30	.20	.20	.15
R163	1¢ Pale Blue	.25	.20	.20	.15
R163p	1¢ Hyphen Hole Perf. 7	.35	.22	.30	.20
R164	2¢ Carmine	.25	.20	.20	.15
R164p	2¢ Hyphen Hole Perf. 7	.35	.22	.30	.20
R165	3¢ Dark Blue	1.70	1.00	.20	.15
R165p	3¢ Hyphen Hole Perf. 7	17.00	10.00	.90	.55
R166	4¢ Pale Rose	1.10	.70	.20	.15
R166p	4¢ Hyphen Hole Perf. 7	6.00	3.50	1.25	.75
R167	5¢ Lilac	.25	.20	.20	.15
R167p	5¢ Hyphen Hole Perf. 7	6.25	4.00	.30	.20
R168	10¢ Dark Brown	1.30	.80	.20	.15
R168p	10¢ Hyphen Hole Perf. 7	4.25	2.60	.30	.20
R169	25¢ Purple Brown	2.15	1.25	.20	.15
R169p	25¢ Hyphen Hole Perf. 7	7.00	4.25	.35	.25
R170	40¢ Blue Lilac (cut .25)	110.00	70.00	1.80	1.00
R170p	40¢ Hyphen Hole Perf. 7	160.00	100.00	32.50	20.00
R171	50¢ Slate Violet	16.00	10.00	.20	.15
R171p	50¢ Hyphen Hole Perf. 7	30.00	18.00	.65	.40
R172	80¢ Bistre (cut .15)	82.50	50.00	.35	.25
R172p	80¢ Hyphen Hole Perf. 7	170.00	100.00	38.50	23.50

Commerce Design (C) (Rouletted 5½) (VF + 40%)

R173	$1 Commerce, Dark Green	7.00	4.25	.20	.15
R173p	1¢ Hyphen Hole Perf. 7	14.50	9.00	.70	.45
R174	$3 Dark Brown (cut .20)	20.00	12.50	.75	.45
R174p	3¢ Hyphen Hole Perf. 7(cut .30) .	26.50	16.50	2.50	1.50
R175	$5 Orange Red Perf. 7 (cut .20)	26.50	16.50	1.35	.80
R176	$10 Black Perf. 7 (cut .60)	70.00	45.00	2.80	1.70
R177	$30 Red Perf. 7 (cut 40.00)	215.00	125.00	95.00	57.50
R178	$50 Gray Brown Perf.7(cut 1.80)	110.00	65.00	5.50	3.50

1899 Documentary Stamps Imperforated (C) (VF + 40%)

R179	$100 Marshall, Brn. & Blk.(cut 17.50)	115.00	70.00	30.00	19.00
R180	$500 Hamilton,Car.Lk/Blk(cut 210.00)	800.00	500.00	500.00	300.00
R181	$1000 Madison,Grn&Blk (cut 95.00)	650.00	400.00	300.00	240.00

1900 Documentary Stamps (C) (Hyphen Hole Perf 7) (VF + 40%)

R182	$1 Commerce, Carmine (cut .20)	16.00	10.00	.50	.30
R183	$3 Lake (cut 7.50)	110.00	65.00	40.00	24.50

1900 Surcharged Large Black Numerals (C) (VF + 40%)

R184	$1 Gray (cut .15)	10.00	5.75	.20	.15
R185	$2 Gray (cut .15)	10.50	6.00	.20	.15
R186	$3 Gray (cut 2.50)	57.50	32.50	10.00	5.50
R187	$5 Gray (cut 1.00)	38.50	23.50	6.50	3.95
R188	$10 Gray (cut 3.35)	70.00	42.50	15.00	9.00
R189	$50 Gray (cut 80.00)	650.00	375.00	375.00	225.00

1902 Surcharged Ornamental Numerals (C) (VF + 40%)

R190	$1 Green (cut .25)	18.50	10.75	3.25	1.95
R191	$2 Green (cut .25)	16.00	9.50	1.30	.80
R192	$5 Green (cut $4.00)	125.00	75.00	26.50	16.50
R193	$10 Green (cut 45.00)	300.00	175.00	130.00	70.00
R194	$50 Green (cut 210.00)	975.00	565.00	725.00	400.00

1914 Documentary Single Line Watermark "USPS" (VF + 50%) (B)

Scott's No.		Unused Fine	Unused Ave.	Used Fine	Used Ave.
R195	½¢ Rose	6.75	4.25	3.00	1.85
R196	1¢ Rose	1.25	.70	.20	.15
R197	2¢ Rose	1.65	.95	.20	.15
R198	3¢ Rose	45.00	25.00	25.00	14.50
R199	4¢ Rose	12.50	7.50	1.75	1.00
R200	5¢ Rose	3.50	1.95	.20	.15
R201	10¢ Rose	3.00	1.65	.20	.15
R202	25¢ Rose	27.50	18.00	.60	.35
R203	40¢ Rose	15.00	9.00	.85	.50
R204	50¢ Rose	5.50	3.25	.20	.15
R205	80¢ Rose	85.00	50.00	9.00	5.50

1914 Documentary Double Line Watermark "USIR" (VF + 50%) (B)

Scott's No.		Unused Fine	Unused Ave.	Used Fine	Used Ave.
R206	½¢ Rose	1.35	.75	.50	.30
R207	1¢ Rose	.25	.20	.20	.15
R208	2¢ Rose	.25	.20	.20	.15
R209	3¢ Rose	1.35	.70	.20	.15
R210	4¢ Rose	3.25	1.85	.40	.25
R211	5¢ Rose	1.60	.90	.25	.20
R212	10¢ Rose	.70	.45	.20	.15
R213	25¢ Rose	4.50	2.70	1.10	.65
R214	40¢ Rose (cut .50)	65.00	38.50	11.00	6.50
R215	50¢ Rose	14.00	9.00	.25	.20
R216	80¢ Rose (cut .90)	95.00	55.00	16.00	8.75
R217	$1 Liberty, Green (cut .15)	26.50	16.00	.30	.20
R218	$2 Carmine (cut .15)	40.00	24.00	.45	.30
R219	$3 Purple (cut .40)	50.00	28.50	2.30	1.25
R220	$5 Blue (cut .60)	47.50	26.50	2.50	1.50
R221	$10 Orange (cut .90)	110.00	65.00	4.50	2.65
R222	$30 Vermillion (cut 2.00)	225.00	140.00	9.75	6.00
R223	$50 Violet (cut 300.00)	1100.00	650.00	700.00	385.00

1914-15 Documentary stamps - Perforated 12, without gum (VF+40%) (B)

R224	$60 Lincoln, Brown (cut 42.50) ...	...	...	100.00	60.00
R225	$100 Wash., Green (cut 16.50) ..	50.00	32.50	37.50	20.00
R226	$500 Hamilton, Blue (cut 185.00)	...	...	450.00	250.00
R227	$1000 Madison, Orange (cut 165.00)	...	...	400.00	225.00

R239

R244

R734

1917-33 Documentary Stamps - Perf. 11 (VF + 40%) (B)

R228	1¢ Rose	.25	.20	.20	.15
R229	2¢ Rose	.25	.20	.20	.15
R230	3¢ Rose	1.20	.70	.35	.25
R231	4¢ Rose	.50	.30	.20	.15
R232	5¢ Rose	.25	.20	.20	.15
R233	8¢ Rose	1.65	1.00	.30	.20
R234	10¢ Rose	.35	.25	.20	.15
R235	20¢ Rose	.80	.50	.20	.15
R236	25¢ Rose	1.00	.60	.20	.15
R237	40¢ Rose	1.35	.80	.35	.25
R238	50¢ Rose	1.75	1.10	.20	.15
R239	80¢ Rose	4.25	2.25	.20	.15
R240	$1 Green, Without Date	5.75	3.50	.20	.15
R241	$2 Rose	9.50	5.75	.20	.15
R242	$3 Violet (cut .15)	31.50	19.00	.65	.35
R243	$4 Brown (cut .15)	23.00	14.00	1.50	.90
R244	$5 Blue (cut .15)	15.00	8.50	.25	.20
R245	$10 Orange (cut .15)	27.50	16.50	.85	.50

1917 Documentary Stamps - Perforated 12, Without Gum (VF+40%) (B)

R246	$30 Grant, Orange (cut 1.25)	40.00	25.00	8.50	5.25
R247	$60 Lincoln, Brown (cut .85)	47.50	30.00	6.50	4.00
R248	$100 Wash., Green (cut .40)	28.00	17.00	1.10	.65
R249	$500 Hamilton, Blue (cut 9.00)	200.00	135.00	30.00	17.50
R250	$1000 Madison, Orange (cut 4.25)	110.00	62.50	13.00	7.50

1928-29 Documentary Stamps - Perf. 10 (30%) (B)

R251	1¢ Carmine Rose	1.90	1.15	1.30	.80
R252	2¢ Carmine Rose	.55	.35	.20	.15
R253	4¢ Carmine Rose	5.50	3.00	3.75	2.25
R254	5¢ Carmine Rose	1.15	.65	.55	.35
R255	10¢ Carmine Rose	1.70	1.10	1.10	.70
R256	20¢ Carmine Rose	5.75	3.25	5.00	3.00
R257	$1 Green (cut 4.50)	92.50	57.50	27.50	16.50
R258	$2 Rose	35.00	21.50	2.25	1.30
R259	$10 Orange (cut 22.50)	110.00	70.00	37.50	22.50

1929-30 Documentary Stamps - Perf. 11x10 (VF + 30%) (B)

R260	2¢ Carmine Rose	2.75	1.50	2.50	1.40
R261	5¢ Carmine Rose	2.00	1.25	1.75	1.10
R262	10¢ Carmine Rose	7.50	4.00	6.50	4.00
R263	20¢ Carmine Rose	16.50	10.00	8.50	5.00

#R264-R732 1940-1958 Documentary Stamps (Dated)
We will be glad to quote prices on any of these items we have in stock.

1962-1963 Documentary Stamps

Scott's No.		Plate Block	F.VF NH	F.VF Used
R733	10¢ Internal Revenue Bldg	14.75	1.75	.45
R734	10¢ Bldg., Without Date (1963)	30.00	4.25	.45

RB1	RB12	 RB32, RB44	RB65

1871-74 Proprietary (All Used) (VF+60%) (C)

Scott's No.		Violet Paper(a) Fine	Ave.	Green Paper(b) Fine	Ave.
RB1	1¢ Green and Black	4.25	2.65	7.50	4.50
RB2	2¢ Green and Black	5.25	3.00	17.00	10.00
RB3	3¢ Green and Black	15.00	9.00	45.00	25.00
RB4	4¢ Green and Black	9.00	5.50	16.50	10.00
RB5	5¢ Green and Black	135.00	80.00	135.00	85.00
RB6	6¢ Green and Black	30.00	18.00	85.00	50.00
RB7	10¢ Green and Black	215.00	130.00	45.00	26.50
RB8	50¢ Green and Black	525.00	300.00	825.00	450.00

1875-81 Proprietary (All Used) (VF+60%) (C)

Scott's No.		Silk Paper(s) Fine	Ave.	Watermarked(b) Fine	Ave.	Rouletted(c) Fine	Ave.
RB11	1¢ Green	1.65	1.00	.40	.25	70.00	40.00
RB12	2¢ Brown	2.25	1.30	1.35	.75	90.00	55.00
RB13	3¢ Orange	10.75	5.75	4.00	2.50	90.00	55.00
RB14	4¢ Red Brown	5.25	3.00	5.25	2.95	…	…
RB15	4¢ Red	…	…	4.00	2.25	130.00	80.00
RB16	5¢ Black	95.00	55.00	80.00	45.00	…	…
RB17	6¢ Violet Blue	21.50	13.00	18.00	11.00	235.00	140.00
RB18	6¢ Violet	…	…	27.50	17.00	…	…
RB19	10¢ Blue	…	…	265.00	160.00	…	…

1898 Proprietary Stamps (Battleship) (C) (40%) (Roulette 5½)

Scott's No.		Uncancelled Fine	Ave.	Used Fine	Ave.
RB20	1/8¢ Yellow Green	.25	.20	.20	.15
RB20p	1/8¢ Hyphen Hole Perf 7	.25	.20	.20	.15
RB21	1/4¢ Pale Brown	.25	.20	.20	.15
RB21p	1/4¢ Hyphen Hole Perf 7	.25	.20	.20	.15
RB22	3/8¢ Deep Orange	.25	.20	.20	.15
RB22p	3/8¢ Hyphen Hole Perf 7	.30	.20	.20	.15
RB23	5/8¢ Deep Ultramarine	.25	.20	.20	.15
RB23p	5/8¢ Hyphen Hole Perf 7	.30	.20	.20	.15
RB24	1¢ Dark Green	1.30	.80	.30	.20
RB24p	1¢ Hyphen Hole Perf 7	23.50	14.75	14.50	9.00
RB25	1¼¢ Violet	.25	.20	.20	.15
RB25p	1¼¢ Hyphen Hole Perf 7	.30	.20	.20	.15
RB26	1 1/8¢ Dull Blue	10.00	6.25	1.35	.90
RB26p	1 1/8¢ Hyphen Hoe Perf 7	26.50	16.50	6.50	4.25
RB27	2¢ Violet Brown	.85	.55	.20	.15
RB27p	2¢ Hyphen Hole Perf 7	5.25	3.25	.65	.40
RB28	2½¢ Lake	2.65	1.50	.25	.20
RB28p	2½¢ Hyphen Hole Perf 7	4.50	2.85	.30	.20
RB29	3¾¢ Olive Gray	35.00	22.00	8.75	5.75
RB29p	3¾¢ Hyphen Hole Perf 7	65.00	37.50	17.50	10.75
RB30	4¢ Purple	11.00	6.50	.85	.50
RB30p	4¢ Hyphen Hole Perf 7	55.00	32.50	16.00	9.50
RB31	5¢ Brown Orange	11.00	6.50	.85	.50
RB31p	5¢ Hyphen Hole Perf 7	55.00	32.50	18.00	11.00

1914 Black Proprietary Stamps - S.L. Wmk. "USPS" (VF + 50%) (B)

Scott's No.		Unused Fine	Ave.	Used Fine	Ave.
RB32	1/8¢ Black	.25	.20	.20	.15
RB33	¼¢ Black	1.75	1.10	1.10	.65
RB34	3/8¢ Black	.25	.20	.20	.15
RB35	5/8¢ Black	3.75	2.25	2.25	1.35
RB36	1¼¢ Black	2.65	1.75	1.10	.70
RB37	1 7/8¢ Black	35.00	21.00	15.00	9.50
RB38	2½¢ Black	8.25	5.00	2.35	1.50
RB39	3 1/8¢ Black	80.00	50.00	47.50	27.50
RB40	3¼¢ Black	35.00	21.50	20.00	12.50
RB41	4¢ Black	52.50	31.50	26.50	16.00
RB42	4 3/8¢ Black	…	695.00	…	…
RB43	5¢ Black	95.00	57.50	60.00	35.00

1914 Black Proprietary Stamps - D.L. Wmk. "USIR" (50%) (B)

Scott's No.		Unused Fine	Ave.	Used Fine	Ave.
RB44	1/8¢ Black	.25	.20	.20	.15
RB45	¼¢ Black	.25	.20	.20	.15
RB46	3/8¢ Black	.55	.33	.30	.20
RB47	½¢ Black	3.25	1.95	2.25	1.40
RB48	5/8¢ Black	.25	.20	.20	.15
RB49	1¢ Black	4.50	2.50	4.00	2.25
RB50	1¼¢ Black	.40	.25	.35	.25
RB51	1½¢ Black	3.25	1.90	2.00	1.10
RB52	1 7/8¢ Black	1.10	.65	.75	.45
RB53	2¢ Black	5.50	3.50	3.75	2.35
RB54	2½¢ Black	1.10	.65	1.10	.65
RB55	3¢ Black	3.75	2.10	2.50	1.50
RB56	3 1/8¢ Black	5.00	3.00	2.75	1.65
RB57	3¾¢ Black	10.00	6.00	8.00	4.75
RB58	4¢ Black	.50	.30	.20	.15
RB59	4 3/8¢ Black	12.00	7.00	7.00	4.25
RB60	5¢ Black	2.65	1.50	2.50	1.40
RB61	6¢ Black	47.50	29.50	36.50	21.75
RB62	8¢ Black	15.00	9.00	11.00	6.75
RB63	10¢ Black	10.00	6.00	7.50	4.50
RB64	20¢ Black	20.00	12.50	16.00	9.75

1919 Proprietary Stamps (VF + 40%) (B)

Scott's No.		Unused Fine	Ave.	Used Fine	Ave.
RB65	1¢ Dark Blue	.25	.20	.20	.15
RB66	2¢ Dark Blue	.25	.20	.20	.15
RB67	3¢ Dark Blue	1.10	.65	.65	.40
RB68	4¢ Dark Blue	1.10	.65	.55	.30
RB69	5¢ Dark Blue	1.35	.80	.65	.40
RB70	8¢ Dark Blue	13.00	8.00	9.00	5.50
RB71	10¢ Dark Blue	4.25	2.75	2.10	1.30
RB72	20¢ Dark Blue	7.00	4.50	3.25	1.95
RB73	40¢ Dark Blue	40.00	25.00	10.50	6.50

1918-34 Future Delivery Stamps (VF + 40%) (B)
1917 Documentary Stamps overprinted "FUTURE DELIVERY" in black or red

Horizontal Overprints

Scott's No.		Unused Fine	Ave.	Used Fine	Ave.
RC1	2¢ Carmine Rose	3.85	2.50	.20	.15
RC2	3¢ Carmine Rose (cut 10.75)	28.00	17.00	20.00	12.50
RC3	4¢ Carmine Rose	6.75	4.00	.20	.15
RC3A	5¢ Carmine Rose	67.50	40.00	6.50	3.75
RC4	10¢ Carmine Rose	11.50	7.25	.20	.15
RC5	20¢ Carmine Rose	16.00	9.50	.20	.15
RC6	25¢ Carmine Rose (cut .20)	35.00	21.00	.75	.45
RC7	40¢ Carmine Rose (cut .20)	40.00	25.00	.85	.50
RC8	50¢ Carmine Rose	9.00	5.50	.35	.20
RC9	80¢ Carmine Rose (cut .85)	77.50	50.00	9.00	5.50

Vertical Overprints

RC10	$1 Green (cut .20)	31.50	18.00	.25	.20
RC11	$2 Rose (cut .20)	35.00	21.00	.25	.20
RC12	$3 Violet (cut .20)	82.50	50.00	2.25	1.30
RC13	$5 Dark Blue (cut .20)	62.50	37.50	.50	.25
RC14	$10 Orange (cut .20)	82.50	50.00	1.00	.60
RC15	$20 Olive Bistre (cut .50)	150.00	90.00	5.00	3.00

Horizontal Overprints, Without Gum

RC16	$30 Vermillion (cut 1.50)	65.00	40.00	3.25	1.95
RC17	$50 Olive Green (cut .55)	50.00	28.50	1.10	.65
RC18	$60 Brown (cut .80)	65.00	35.00	2.10	1.30
RC19	$100 Yellow Green (cut 5.75)	95.00	55.00	25.00	15.00
RC20	$500 Blue (cut 4.50)	75.00	45.00	10.50	6.25
RC21	$1000 Green (cut 1.65)	85.00	50.00	5.25	3.25
RC22	1¢ Carm. Rose, Narrow Overprt.	1.10	.70	.20	.15
RC23	80¢ Narrow Overprint (cut .30)	67.50	42.50	2.50	1.50

Horizontal Serif Overprints

RC25	$1 Green (cut .20)	30.00	18.50	.75	.45
RC26	$10 Orange (cut 8.75)	90.00	55.00	15.00	10.00

1918-22 Stock Transfer Stamps, Perf. 11 or 12 (VF +40%) (B)
1917 Documentary Stamps overprinted "STOCK TRANSFER" in black or red

Horizontal Overprints

RD1	1¢ Carmine Rose	.80	.45	.20	.15
RD2	2¢ Carmine Rose	.25	.20	.20	.15
RD3	4¢ Carmine Rose	.25	.20	.20	.15
RD4	5¢ Carmine Rose	.25	.20	.20	.15
RD5	10¢ Carmine Rose	.25	.20	.20	.15
RD6	20¢ Carmine Rose	.50	.35	.20	.15
RD7	25¢ Carmine Rose (cut .15)	1.40	.80	.25	.20
RD8	40¢ Carmine Rose	1.25	.70	.20	.15
RD9	50¢ Carmine Rose	.55	.35	.20	.15
RD10	80¢ Carmine Rose (cut .15)	2.75	1.65	.30	.20

Vertical Overprints

RD11	$1 Green, Red Overprint (cut 4.00)	75.00	45.00	18.00	11.00
RD12	$1 Green, Black Overprint	2.10	1.25	.25	.20
RD13	$2 Rose	2.10	1.25	.20	.15
RD14	$3 Violet (cut .25)	16.50	9.50	3.75	2.30
RD15	$4 Brown (cut .15)	8.50	5.00	.25	.20
RD16	$5 Blue (cut .15)	5.00	3.00	.25	.20
RD17	$10 Orange (cut .15)	14.50	9.00	.30	.20
RD18	$20 Bistre (cut 3.00)	65.00	40.00	18.00	11.00

Horizontal Serif Overprints, Without Gum

RD19	$30 Vermillion (cut 2.00)	16.00	9.75	4.25	2.50
RD20	$50 Olive Green (cut 17.50)	95.00	52.50	52.50	28.75
RD21	$60 Brown (cut 7.75)	95.00	52.50	20.00	13.00
RD22	$100 Green (cut 2.00)	21.50	13.00	5.25	3.00
RD23	$500 Blue (cut 60.00)	285.00	190.00	100.00	65.00
RD24	$1000 Orange (cut 26.75)	150.00	95.00	65.00	40.00

1928 Stock Transfer, Perf.10 (VF + 40%) (B)

RD25	1¢ Carmine rose	2.10	1.40	.25	.20
RD26	4¢ Carmine rose	2.10	1.40	.25	.20
RD27	10¢ Carmine rose	1.80	1.20	.25	.20
RD28	20¢ Carmine rose	2.50	1.60	.25	.20
RD29	50¢ Carmine rose	3.00	2.00	.25	.20
RD30	$1 Green	28.00	19.50	.25	.20
RD31	$2 Carmine rose	28.00	19.50	.25	.20
RD32	$10 Orange (cut .20)	30.00	21.00	.35	.25

1920 Stock Transfers, Serif Overprints, Perf.11 (VF+ 40%) (B)

RD33	2¢ Carmine rose	6.75	4.25	.60	.40
RD34	10¢ Carmine rose	1.15	.75	.30	.20
RD35	20¢ Carmine rose	1.00	.65	.25	.20
RD36	50¢ Carmine rose	2.75	1.75	.25	.20
RD37	$1 Green (cut .25)	40.00	25.00	8.50	5.50
RD38	$2 Rose (cut .25)	35.00	22.50	8.50	5.50

1920 Stock Transfers, Serif Overprints, Perf .10 (VF+ 40%) (B)

RD39	2¢ Carmine rose	6.00	.45		.30
RD40	10¢ Carmine rose	1.35	.90	.45	.30
RD41	20¢ Carmine rose	2.25	1.50	.25	.20

We will be glad to quote on any of the following Revenue categories:
1940-58 Dated Documentaries

CORDIAL AND WINE STAMPS (VF + 40%)

 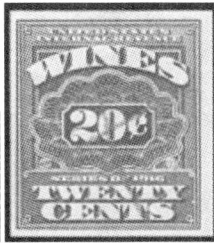

RE27   RE41

Scott's No.		Fine Unused	Used
1914 Single-line Wtmk."USPS",Perf.10			
RE1	¼¢ Green	.70	.50
RE2	½¢ Green	.45	.25
RE3	1¢ Green	.40	.30
RE4	1½¢ Green	2.00	1.35
RE5	2¢ Green	2.75	2.75
RE6	3¢ Green	3.00	1.15
RE7	4¢ Green	2.50	1.50
RE8	5¢ Green	1.00	.55
RE9	6¢ Green	5.75	3.25
RE10	8¢ Green	3.50	1.40
RE11	10¢ Green	3.00	2.65
RE12	20¢ Green	4.00	1.65
RE13	24¢ Green	13.00	7.50
RE14	40¢ Green	3.00	1.00
RE15	$2 Imperf	6.50	.20
1914 Double-Line Wtmk."USIR",Perf.10			
RE16	¼¢ Green	5.50	4.50
RE17	½¢ Green	3.50	2.75
RE18	1¢ Green	.25	.20
RE19	1½¢ Green	40.00	30.00
RE20	2¢ Green	.20	.20
RE21	3¢ Green	2.50	2.25
RE22	4¢ Green	.95	.95
RE23	5¢ Green	11.75	10.00
RE24	6¢ Green	.50	.30
RE25	8¢ Green	1.80	.45
RE26	10¢ Green	.50	.25
RE27	20¢ Green	.70	.45
RE28	24¢ Green	12.50	.75
RE29	40¢ Green	27.50	9.50
RE30	$2 Imperf	28.00	2.95
RE31	$2 Perf.11	72.50	80.00
1916 Rouletted 3½			
Inscribed "Series of 1916"			
RE32	1¢ Green	.35	.30
RE33	3¢ Green	4.25	4.00
RE34	4¢ Green	.30	.30
RE35	5¢ Green	1.40	.75
RE36	7½¢ Green	6.75	3.75
RE37	10¢ Green	1.10	.40
RE38	12¢ Green	2.75	3.75
RE39	15¢ Green	1.60	1.75
RE40	18¢ Green	23.00	21.00
RE41	20¢ Green	.30	.30
RE42	24¢ Green	3.75	2.75
RE43	30¢ Green	2.00	2.35
RE44	36¢ Green	18.50	14.00
RE45	50¢ Green	.55	.40
RE46	60¢ Green	3.50	2.00
RE47	72¢ Green	32.50	25.00
RE48	80¢ Green	.75	.55
RE49	$1.20 Green	6.50	5.50
RE50	$1.44 Green	8.00	2.75
RE51	$1.60 Green	23.50	16.50
RE52	$2 Green	1.65	1.35
RE53	$4 Green	.90	.20
RE54	$4.80 Green	3.50	2.75
RE55	$9.60 Green	1.15	.25
RE56	$20 Pf. 12	80.00	37.50
RE57	$40 Pf. 12	160.00	45.00
RE58	$50 Pf. 12	55.00	42.50
RE59	$100 Pf. 12	225.00	130.00
1933 Rouletted 7			
RE60	1¢ Lt. green	2.50	.30
RE61	3¢ Lt. green	6.50	2.25
RE62	4¢ Lt. green	1.40	.20
RE63	6¢ Lt. green	10.00	4.50
RE64	7½¢ Lt. green	2.75	.50
RE65	10¢ Lt. green	1.75	.20
RE66	12¢ Lt. green	8.50	4.25
RE67	15¢ Lt. green	3.50	.25
RE69	20¢ Lt. green	4.50	.20
RE70	24¢ Lt. green	4.50	.20
RE71	30¢ Lt. green	4.50	.25
RE72	36¢ Lt. green	10.00	.55
RE73	50¢ Lt. green	4.25	.25
RE74	60¢ Lt. green	6.75	.20
RE75	72¢ Lt. green	11.50	.30
RE76	80¢ Lt. green	11.50	.20
RE77	$1.20 Lt. green ..	9.00	1.50
RE78	$1.44 Lt. green ..	11.50	4.00
RE79	$1.60 Lt. green ..	...	170.00
RE80	$2 Lt. green	35.00	6.25
RE81	$4 Lt. green	27.50	6.25

Scott No.		Fine Unused	Used
RE82	$4.80 Lt. green ..	27.50	13.75
RE83	$9.60 Lt. green ..	130.00	75.00

RE83A

1934-40 "Series of 1934" Rouletted 7			
RE83A	1/5¢ Green	.65	.20
RE84	½¢ Green	.50	.35
RE85	1¢ Green	.60	.20
RE86	1¼¢ Green	1.00	.70
RE87	1½¢ Green	6.00	4.75
RE88	2¢ Green	1.75	.60
RE89	2½¢ Green	1.75	.50
RE90	3¢ Green	4.50	3.75
RE91	4¢ Green	2.25	.20
RE92	5¢ Green	.55	.20
RE93	6¢ Green	1.65	.50
RE94	7½¢ Green	2.00	.20
RE95	10¢ Green	.45	.20
RE96	12¢ Green	1.50	.20
RE96A	14 2/5¢ Green ...	150.00	3.00
RE97	15¢ Green	.75	.20
RE98	18¢ Green	1.40	.20
RE99	20¢ Green	1.10	.20
RE100	24¢ Green	1.80	.20
RE101	30¢ Green	1.30	.20
RE102	40¢ Green	3.00	.25
RE102A	43 1/5¢ Green ...	12.50	2.00
RE103	48¢ Green	12.75	1.50
RE104	$1 Green	16.00	10.00
RE105	$1.50 Green	26.50	13.50
RE105	Perforated Initial	..	4.75
RE106	$2.50 Green	32.50	15.00
RE106	Perforated Initial	..	7.75
RE107	$5 Green	28.75	6.75
RE107	Perforated Initial	..	2.25
1942 "Series of 1941" Rouletted 7			
RE108	1/5¢ Green & Bk..	.60	.40
RE109	¼¢ Green & Bk.	2.00	1.60
RE110	½¢ Green & Bk.	2.75	1.80
RE111	1¢ Green & Bk. .	1.15	.75
RE112	2¢ Green & Bk. .	5.50	5.00
RE113	3¢ Green & Bk. .	5.25	4.25
RE114	3¾¢ Green & Bk.	9.50	6.00
RE115	3¾¢ Green & Bk.	9.50	6.00
RE116	4¢ Green & Bk. .	3.75	2.75
RE117	5¢ Green & Bk. .	2.75	2.00
RE118	6¢ Green & Bk. .	3.25	2.50
RE119	7¢ Green & Bk. .	6.75	4.75
RE120	7½¢ Green & Bk.	9.75	5.00
RE121	8¢ Green & Bk. .	5.00	3.50
RE122	9¢ Green & Bk. .	11.00	8.00
RE123	10¢ Green & Bk.	5.00	1.00
RE124	11¼¢ Green & Bk.	5.50	4.50
RE125	12¢ Green & Bk.	7.50	5.50
RE126	14¢ Green & Bk.	26.50	22.50
RE127	15¢ Green & Bk.	5.25	2.75
RE128	16¢ Green & Bk.	12.50	8.00
RE129	19 1/5¢ Grn & Bk.	160.00	7.50
RE130	20¢ Green & Bk.	6.50	1.75
RE131	24¢ Green & Bk.	4.75	.20
RE132	30¢ Green & Bk.	1.40	.20
RE133	30¢ Green & Bk.	1.40	.20
RE134	32¢ Green & Bk.	160.00	7.00
RE135	36¢ Green & Bk.	3.25	.20
RE136	40¢ Green & Bk.	2.75	.20
RE137	45¢ Green & Bk.	6.50	.25
RE138	48¢ Green & Bk.	18.00	6.50
RE139	50¢ Green & Bk.	10.75	6.75
RE140	60¢ Green & Bk.	3.75	.20
RE141	72¢ Green & Bk.	10.75	1.00
RE142	80¢ Green & Bk.	...	9.00
RE143	84¢ Green & Bk.	...	55.00
RE144	90¢ Green & Bk.	17.00	.20
RE145	96¢ Green & Bk.	13.50	.20
RE146-RE172 Denomination in 2 lines			
RE146	$1.20 Yellow Green and Black	6.25	.20

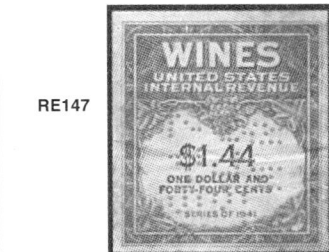

RE147

RE147	$1.44 Y.G. & Bk.	1.50	.20
RE148	$1.50 Y.G. & Bk.	115.00	60.00
RE149	$1.60 Y.G. & Bk.	9.00	1.00
RE150	$1.68 Y.G. & Bk.	110.00	45.00
RE151	$1.80 Y.G. & Bk.	2.75	.20
RE152	$1.92 Y.G. & Bk.	55.00	35.00
RE153	$2.40 Y.G. & Bk.	9.25	1.00

Scott No.		Fine Unused	Used
RE154	$3 Y. green & Bk.	75.00	35.00
RE155	$3.36 Y.G. & Bk.	80.00	25.00
RE156	$3.60 Y.G. & Bk.	140.00	5.50
RE157	$4 Y. green & Bk.	26.50	5.00
RE158	$4.80 Y.G. & Bk.	140.00	3.00
RE159	$5 Y.green & Bk.	13.50	9.00
RE160	$7.20 Y.G. & Bk.	17.50	.45
RE161	$10 Y.G. & Bk. ..	215.00	160.00
RE162	$20 Y.G. & Bk. ..	115.00	70.00
RE163	$50 Y.G. & Bk. ..	115.00	70.00
RE163	Perforated Initial	...	17.50
RE164	$100 Y.G. & Bk.	275.00	27.50
RE164	Perforated Initial	...	17.50
RE165	$200 Y.G. & Bk.	170.00	18.50
RE165	Perforated Initial	...	7.50
RE166	$500 Y.G. & Bk.	...	140.00
RE166	Perforated Initial	...	30.00
RE167	$600 Y.G. & Bk.	...	120.00
RE169	$1000 Y.G. & Bk.	...	185.00
RE171	$3000 Y.G. & Bk.	...	180.00
1949 "Series of 1941" Rouletted 7			
#RE173-RE182 Denominations in one line.			
RE173	$1 Y.green & Bk.	4.00	1.40
RE175	$2 Y.green & Bk.	6.50	1.85
RE176	$4 Y.green & Bk.	...	350.00
RE177	$5 Y.green & Bk.	...	75.00
RE178	$6 Y.green & Bk.	...	450.00
RE179	$7 Y.green & Bk.	...	50.00
RE179	$8 Y.green & Bk.	...	385.00
RE179	Perforated Initial	...	75.00
RE180	$10 Y.green & Bk.	8.75	5.00
RE180	Perforated Initial	...	1.75
RE181	$20 Y.green & Bk.	18.00	3.50
RE181	Perforated Initial	...	1.60
1951-54 "Series of 1941" Rouletted 7			
RE183	3 2/5¢ Grn. & Bk.	50.00	45.00
RE184	8½¢ Green & Bk.	27.50	18.50
RE185	13 2/5¢ Grn. & Bk.	90.00	70.00
RE186	17¢ Green & Bk.	14.00	13.50
RE187	20 2/5¢ Gr. & Bk.	100.00	55.00
RE188	33½¢ Green & Bk.	80.00	65.00
RE189	38¼¢ Green & Bk.	110.00	80.00
RE190	40 4/5¢ Grn. & Bk.	3.50	.60
RE191	51¢ Green & Bk.	3.50	1.00
RE192	67¢ Green & Bk.	10.75	3.50
RE193	68¢ Green & Bk.	3.50	.60
RE194	80 2/5¢ Grn. & Bk.	110.00	90.00
#RE195-RE197 Denominations in two lines in smaller letters. Yellow Green & Black			
RE195	$1.50¾	45.00	35.00
RE196	$1.60 4/5	4.00	.55
RE197	$1.88 3/10	275.00	70.00
RE198	$1.60 4/5	27.50	5.50
#RE198-RE204 Denominations in two lines in large letters as #RE146-72			
RE199	$2.01 Y.green & Bk.	3.50	.75
RE200	$3.28 Y.green & Bk.	3.50	1.20
RE201	$4.08 Y.gn. & Bk.	70.00	30.00
RE202	$5.76 Y.& Bk.	225.00	100.00
RE203	$8.16 Y.green & Bk.	16.00	6.00

PLAYING CARD STAMPS (VF+ 40%)

RF1    RF16

1894-1902 Rouletted			
RF1	2¢ Lake "On Hand"	.60	.40
RF2	2¢ Ultramarine, "Act of.", Unwmk.16.00		2.50
RF3	2¢ Blue, Wmtk. ..	5.25	.50
RF4	2¢ Blue, Perf. 12	...	46.50
1917 Various Surcharges			
RF6	7¢ on 2¢ Blue "17"	...	45.00
RF9	7¢ on 2¢ "7 CENTS"	...	8.75
RF10	7¢ on 2¢ Blue "7¢"	...	55.00
1918-1929			
RF11	Blue, Imperf.	37.50	27.50
RF12	Blue, Roul. 14	...	200.00
RF13	7¢ Blue, Roul. 9½	...	37.50
RF14	8¢ on 2¢ Roul. 7	...	90.00
RF16	8¢ on 2¢ Blue ...	130.00	1.00
RF17	(8¢) Blue, Roul. 7	16.50	1.25
RF18	8¢ Blue, Roul. 7	...	32.50
RF19	10¢ Blue, Roul. 7	11.50	.40
RF20	10¢ Perf. 10 Coil	...	.25
RF21	10¢ Flat, Perf. 11	21.00	5.00
RF22	10¢ Blue, Perf. 10	13.00	4.00
1929-1940			

RF27

Scott No.		Fine Unused	Used
RF23	10¢ Perf. 10 Coil	...	.20
RF24	10¢ Flat, Perf. 10	11.50	1.25
RF25	10¢ Flat, Perf. 11	11.50	1.25
RF26	Blue, Perf. 10 Coil	...	.40
RF27	Blue, Perf. 10 Coil	2.75	.20
RF28	Blue, Flat. Pf. 11	5.00	.75
RF29	Blue, Perf. 10x11	160.00	...

SILVER TAX STAMPS (VF + 30%)

RG 6   RG 108

1934 Documentary Stamps of 1917 Overprinted, D.L. Wmk., Perf. 11

Scott's No.		Fine Unused	Used
RG1	1¢ Carm rose	1.00	.75
RG2	2¢ Carm rose	1.25	.50
RG3	3¢ Carm rose	1.50	.75
RG4	4¢ Carm rose	2.00	1.50
RG5	5¢ Carm rose	2.95	1.50
RG6	8¢ Carm rose	4.25	2.75
RG7	10¢ Carm rose ..	4.50	2.50
RG8	20¢ Carm rose ..	5.75	3.00
RG9	25¢ Carm rose ..	6.00	4.00
RG10	40¢ Carm rose ..	7.25	5.00
RG11	50¢ Carm rose ..	7.00	6.00
RG12	80¢ Carm rose ..	13.75	8.50
RG13	$1 Green	23.50	11.50
RG14	$2 Rose	27.50	13.50
RG15	$3 Violet	52.50	28.50
RG16	$4 Yellow brn	45.00	20.00
RG17	$5 Dark blue	55.00	20.00
RG18	$10 Orange	75.00	18.50
Without Gum, Perf. 12			
RG19	$30 Vermillion	130.00	47.50
RG19	Cut cancel	...	17.50
RG20	$60 Brown	150.00	70.00
RG20	Cut cancel	...	25.00
RG21	$100 Green	150.00	31.50
RG22	$500 Blue	435.00	225.00
RG22	Cut cancel	...	95.00
RG23	$1000 Orange	...	100.00
RG23	Cut cancel	...	52.50
1936 Same Ovpt., 11 mm between words "SILVER TAX"			
RG26	$100 Green	275.00	60.00
RG27	$1000 Orange	...	600.00

1940 Documentary Stamps of 1917 D.L. Wmk., Perf. 11, Overprinted

SERIES 1940

SILVER TAX

RG37	1¢ Rose pink	18.50	...
RG38	2¢ Rose pink	18.50	...
RG39	3¢ Rose pink	18.50	...
RG40	4¢ Rose pink	20.00	...
RG41	5¢ Rose pink	12.00	...
RG42	8¢ Rose pink	20.00	...
RG43	10¢ Rose pink	18.50	...
RG44	20¢ Rose pink	20.00	...
RG45	25¢ Rose pink	18.50	...
RG46	40¢ Rose pink	27.50	...
RG47	50¢ Rose pink	27.50	...
RG48	80¢ Rose pink	27.50	...
RG49	$1 Green	125.00	...
RG50	$2 Rose	195.00	...
RG51	$3 Violet	265.00	...
RG52	$4 Yellow brn	525.00	...
RG53	$5 Dark blue	625.00	...
RG54	$10 Orange	700.00	...
Ovpt in Blk. SERIES OF 1941 Perf.11 (Gray)			
RG58	1¢ Hamilton	3.50	...
RG59	2¢ Wolcott, Jr	3.50	...
RG60	3¢ Dexter	3.50	...
RG61	4¢ Gallatin	5.50	...
RG62	5¢ Campbell	7.00	...
RG63	8¢ Dallas	7.50	...
RG64	10¢ Crawford	8.50	...
RG65	20¢ Rush	16.00	...
RG66	25¢ Ingham	19.00	...
RG67	40¢ McLane	30.00	...
RG68	50¢ Duane	40.00	...
RG69	80¢ Taney	67.50	...
RG70	$1 Woodbury	85.00	30.00
RG71	$2 Ewing	210.00	60.00
RG72	$3 Forward	175.00	75.00
RG73	$4 Spencer	260.00	70.00
RG74	$5 Bibb	210.00	85.00
RG75	$10 Walker	375.00	85.00
RG76	$20 Meredith	525.00	265.00

Scott No.		Fine Unused	Used
Without Gum, Perf. 12			
RG77	$30 Corwin	295.00	185.00
RG77	Cut cancel	...	85.00
RG79	$60 Cobb	...	215.00
RG79	Cut cancel	...	100.00
RG80	$100 Thomas	...	300.00
RG80	Cut cancel	...	125.00
#RG58-82 Overprinted SERIES OF 1942			
RG83	1¢ Hamilton	2.00	...
RG84	2¢ Wolcott, Jr	2.00	...
RG85	3¢ Dexter	2.00	...
RG86	4¢ Gallatin	2.00	...
RG87	5¢ Campbell	2.00	...
RG88	8¢ Dallas	4.50	...
RG89	10¢ Crawford	5.00	...
RG90	20¢ Rush	7.50	...
RG91	25¢ Ingham	15.00	...
RG92	40¢ McLane	20.00	...
RG93	50¢ Duane	22.50	...
RG94	80¢ Taney	55.00	...
RG95	$1 Woodbury	80.00	...
RG96	$2 Ewing	80.00	...
RG97	$3 Forward	150.00	...
RG98	$4 Spencer	160.00	...
RG99	$5 Bibb	160.00	...
RG100	$10 Walker	475.00	...
RG101	$20 Meredith	600.00	...
1944 Silver Stamps of 1941 w/o ovpt.			
RG108	1¢ Hamilton	.85	...
RG109	2¢ Wolcutt, Jr	.90	...
RG110	3¢ Dexter	1.00	...
RG111	4¢ Gallatin	1.20	...
RG112	5¢ Campbell	2.10	...
RG113	8¢ Dallas	3.15	...
RG114	10¢ Crawford	3.15	...
RG115	20¢ Rush	6.50	...
RG116	25¢ Ingham	9.00	...
RG117	40¢ McLane	13.75	...
RG118	50¢ Duane	13.75	...
RG119	80¢ Taney	25.00	...
RG120	$1 Woodbury	47.50	17.50
RG121	$2 Ewing	70.00	40.00
RG122	$3 Forward	80.00	30.00
RG123	$4 Spencer	110.00	70.00
RG124	$5 Bibb	125.00	32.50
RG125	$10 Walker	175.00	50.00
RG125	Cut cancel	...	16.00
RG126	$20 Meredith	550.00	475.00
RG126	Cut cancel	...	250.00
Without Gum, Perf. 12			
RG127	$30 Corwin	290.00	130.00
RG127	Cut cancel	...	60.00
RG128	$50 Gutherie	650.00	550.00
RG128	Cut cancel	...	285.00
RG129	$60 Cobb	...	400.00
RG129	Cut cancel	...	175.00
RG130	$100 Thomas	...	32.50
RG130	Cut cancel	...	14.00
RG131	$500 Dix	...	450.00
RG131	Cut cancel	...	225.00
RG132	$1000 Chase	...	150.00
RG132	Cut cancel	...	75.00

CIGARETTE TUBE STAMPS
(Very Fine + 40%)

RH 1

Doc. Stamp of 1917 ovpt., D.L. Wmk.

RH1	1¢ Carm rose (1919)	.50	.25
Perf. 11			
RH2	1¢ Carm rose (1929)	27.50	9.50

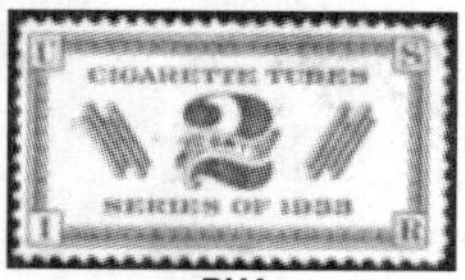

RH4

RH3	1¢ Rose (1933)	2.25	.90
RH4	2¢ Rose (1933)	6.75	1.75

POTATO TAX STAMPS (VF + 30%)

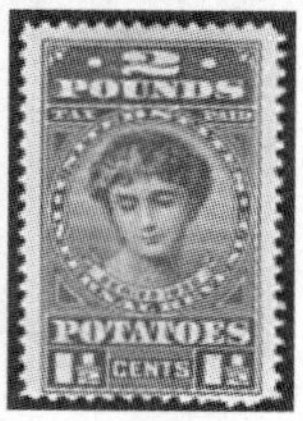

RI 1

1935 Tax Paid Potato Stamps

Scott's No.		F-VF Unused
RI1	¾¢ Carm rose	.30
RI2	1¼¢ Black brn	.50
RI3	2¼¢ Yellow grn	.50
RI4	3¢ Light Violet	.50
RI5	3¾¢ Olive Bistre	.50
RI6	7½¢ Orange brn	1.35
RI7	11¼¢ Deep orange	1.65
RI8	18¾¢ Violet brn	4.50
RI9	37½¢ Red orange	4.00
RI10	75¢ Blue	4.50
RI11	93¾¢ Rose lake	6.50
RI12	$1.12½¢ Green	12.75
RI13	$1.50 Yellow brn	12.00
1935 Tax Exempt Potato Stamps		
RI14	2 lb Black brown	.90
RI15	5 lb Black brown	20.00
RI16	10 lb Black brown	20.00
RI17	25 lb Black brown	110.00
RI18	50 lb Black brown	1.00

TOBACCO SALE TAX STAMPS
1934 Doc. Issue of 1917, Ovpt. D.L. Wmk., pf. 11 (VF + 30%)

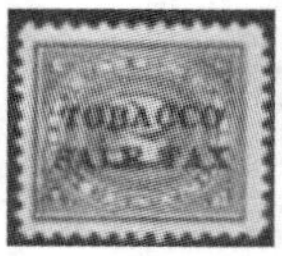

RJ 1

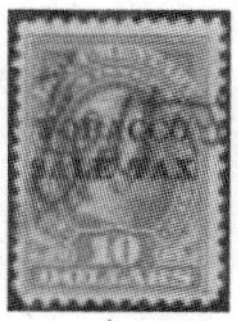

RJ 10

Scott's No.		Fine Unused	Used
RJ1	1¢ Carm rose	.35	.20
RJ2	2¢ Carm rose	.35	.20
RJ3	5¢ Carm rose	1.25	.35
RJ4	10¢ Carm rose	1.50	.35
RJ5	25¢ Carm rose	4.00	1.50
RJ6	50¢ Carm rose	4.00	1.50
RJ7	$1 Green	8.50	1.75
RJ8	$2 Rose	16.00	1.75
RJ9	$5 Dark blue	22.50	3.75
RJ10	$10 Orange	32.50	10.00
RJ11	$20 Olive bistre	80.00	12.50

NARCOTIC TAX STAMPS (VF + 30%)

1919 Doc. Issue of 1914, D.L. Wmk., pf. 10, Handstamped "NARCOTIC" in Magenta, Blue or Black

RJA1	1¢ Rose	75.00	70.00

1919 Doc. Issue of 1917, D.L. Wmk., Perf. 11, Handstamped "NARCOTIC," "Narcotic," "NARCOTICS," or "ACT/NARCOTIC/1918" in Magenta, Blue, Black, Violet or Red

RJA9	1¢ Carm rose	1.75	1.70
RJA10	2¢ Carm rose	4.50	3.75
RJA11	3¢ Carm rose	25.00	25.00
RJA12	4¢ Carm rose	9.00	8.00
RJA13	5¢ Carm rose	14.50	14.00
RJA14	8¢ Carm rose	10.50	10.00
RJA15	10¢ Carm rose	45.00	18.50
RJA16	20¢ Carm rose	55.00	55.00
RJA17	25¢ Carm rose	37.50	30.00
RJA18	40¢ Carm rose	95.00	95.00
RJA19	50¢ Carm rose	17.50	15.00
RJA20	80¢ Carm rose	95.00	85.00
RJA21	$1 Green	85.00	45.00

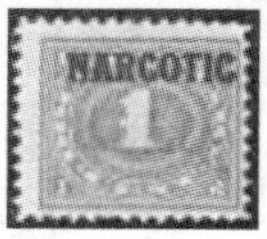

RJA 33

1919 Doc. Issue of 1917, D.L. Wmk., perf. 11, Overprinted NARCOTIC 17½ mm wide

RJA33	1¢ Carm rose	1.00	.60
RJA34	2¢ Carm rose	1.50	1.00
RJA35	3¢ Carm rose	32.50	22.50
RJA36	4¢ Carm rose	5.00	3.00
RJA37	5¢ Carm rose	12.00	9.00
RJA38	8¢ Carm rose	21.50	16.50
RJA39	10¢ Carm rose	3.00	3.00
RJA40	25¢ Carm rose	24.00	16.50
Overprint Reading Up			
RJA41	$1 Green	40.00	17.50

Narcotic Issues of 1919-64, D.L. Wmk.

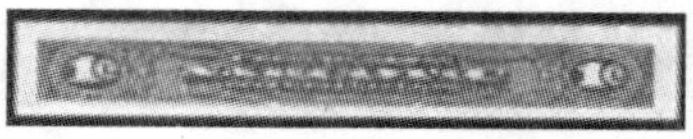

RJA43

NARCOTICS TAX (cont.)

Scott's No.		Fine Used a.Impf.	b.roult
RJA42	1¢ Violet	4.50	.25
RJA43	1¢ Violet	.50	.25
RJA44	2¢ Violet	1.00	.50
RJA45	3¢ Violet	...	115.00
RJA46	1¢ Violet	2.25	.75
RJA47	2¢ Violet	1.75	.75
RJA49	4¢ Violet	...	8.00
RJA50	5¢ Violet	38.50	5.00
RJA51	6¢ Violet	...	1.00
RJA52	8¢ Violet	45.00	3.00
RJA53	9¢ Violet	75.00	18.50
RJA54	10¢ Violet	27.50	.50
RJA55	16¢ Violet	52.50	4.00
RJA56	18¢ Violet	100.00	8.50
RJA57	19¢ Violet	135.00	22.50
RJA58	20¢ Violet	350.00	175.00
"Cents" below value			
RJA59	1¢ Violet	50.00	10.00
RJA60	2¢ Violet	...	18.50
RJA61	4¢ Violet	42.50	47.50
RJA62	5¢ Violet	...	25.00
RJA63	6¢ Violet	65.00	22.50
RJA64	8¢ Violet	...	40.00
RJA65	9¢ Violet	21.50	17.00
RJA66	10¢ Violet	12.50	14.00
RJA67	16¢ Violet	15.00	12.50
RJA68	18¢ Violet	350.00	400.00
RJA69	19¢ Violet	11.50	...
RJA70	20¢ Violet	350.00	195.00
RJA71	25¢ Violet	...	23.50
RJA72	40¢ Violet	425.00	...
RJA73	$1 Green	...	1.25
RJA74	$1.28 Green	27.50	10.50

Imperforate
1963 Denom. added in blk. by rubber plate (similar to 1959 Postage Dues)

		Fine Unused	Used
RJA105	1¢ Violet	85.00	75.00

1964 Denomination on Stamp Plate

RJA106	1¢ Violet	80.00	5.50

CONSULAR SERVICE FEE STAMPS
(Very Fine + 40%)

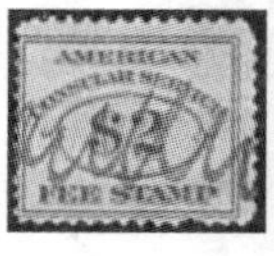

RK 4

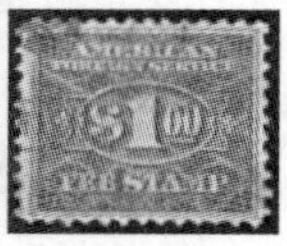

RK 34

1906 "Consular Service" Pf. 12

Scott No.		Fine Used
RK1	25¢ Dark green	45.00
RK2	50¢ Carmine	62.50
RK3	$1 Dark violet	6.75
RK4	$2 Brown	4.75
RK5	$2.50 Dark blue	1.50
RK6	$5 Brown red	19.50
RK7	$10 Orange	55.00
Perf. 10		
RK8	25¢ Dark green	50.00
RK9	50¢ Carmine	60.00
RK10	$1 Dark violet	300.00
RK11	$2 Brown	70.00
RK12	$2.50 Dark blue	18.50
RK13	$5 Brown red	95.00
Consular Service, Perf. 11		
RK14	25¢ Dark green	52.50
RK15	50¢ Carmine	85.00
RK16	$1 Dark violet	1.70
RK17	$2 Brown	2.25
RK18	$2.50 Dark blue	.75
RK19	$5 Brown red	3.75
RK20	$9 Gray	14.00
RK21	$10 Orange	28.50
1924 "Foreign Service" Pf. 11		
RK22	$1 Dark violet	65.00
RK23	$2 Brown	77.50
RK24	$2.50 Dark blue	9.75
RK25	$5 Brown red	52.50
RK26	$9 Gray	185.00
Issue of 1925-52 Perf. 10		
RK27	$1 Violet	22.50
RK28	$2 Brown	55.00
RK29	$2.50 Ultramarine	1.35
RK30	$5 Carmine	9.75
RK31	$9 Gray	39.50
Perf. 11		
RK32	25¢ Green	65.00
RK33	50¢ Orange	65.00
RK34	$1 Violet	2.75
RK35	$2 Brown	2.75
RK36	$2.50 Blue	.50
RK37	$5 Carmine	3.25
RK38	$9 Gray	14.00
RK39	$10 Blue gray	75.00
RK40	$20 Violet	80.00

1887 CUSTOMS FEES (VF + 40%)

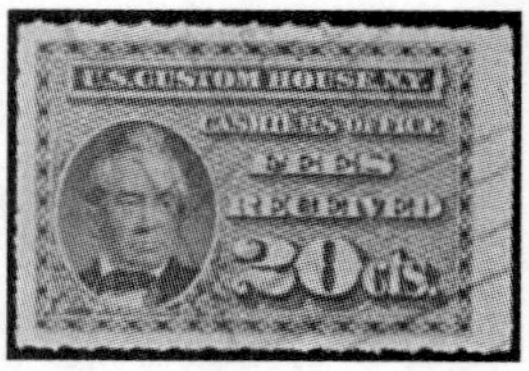

RL 1

Scott No.		Fine Used
RL1	20¢ Dull Rose	1.00
RL2	30¢ Orange	1.75
RL3	40¢ Green	2.00
RL4	50¢ Dark blue	4.25
RL5	60¢ Red violet	1.75
RL6	70¢ Brown violet	27.50
RL7	80¢ Brown	67.50
RL8	90¢ Black	80.00

MOTOR VEHICLE USE STAMPS
(Very Fine + 30%)

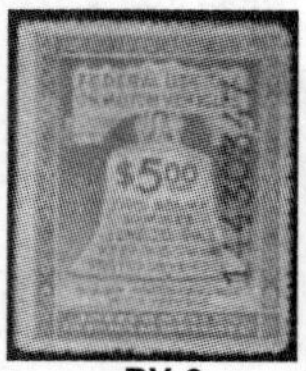

RV 6

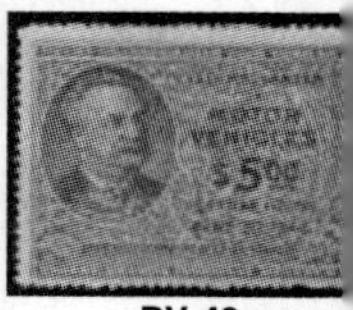

RV 42

Scott No.		F-VF Unused
1942 Gum on Back		
RV1	$2.09 Lt.green (used .50)	1.25
Gum on Face, Inscription on Back		
RV2	$1.67 Light green	17.00
RV3	$1.25 Light green	12.00
RV4	84¢ Light green	14.50
RV5	42¢ Light green	14.50
1942 Gum and Control # on Face		
RV6	$5.00 Rose red (used .90)	2.50
RV7	$4.59 Rose red	27.50
RV8	$4.17 Rose red	31.50
RV9	$3.75 Rose red	27.50
RV10	$3.34 Rose red	27.50
RV11	$2.92 Rose red	27.50
1943		
RV12	$2.50 Rose red	33.50
RV13	$2.09 Rose red	22.50
RV14	$1.67 Rose red	19.50
RV15	$1.25 Rose red	19.50
RV16	84¢ Rose red	19.50
RV17	42¢ Rose red	15.00
RV18	$5.00 Yellow (used .75)	2.75
RV19	$4.59 Yellow	33.50
RV20	$4.17 Yellow	45.00
RV21	$3.75 Yellow	45.00
RV22	$3.34 Yellow	47.50
RV23	$2.92 Yellow	60.00
1944		
RV24	$2.50 Yellow	65.00
RV25	$2.09 Yellow	40.00
RV26	$1.67 Yellow	33.50
RV27	$1.25 Yellow	33.50
RV28	84¢ Yellow	27.50
RV29	42¢ Yellow	27.50
Gum on Face Control # and Inscription on Back		
RV30	$5.00 Violet (used .75)	2.50
RV31	$4.59 Violet	47.50
RV32	$4.17 Violet	37.50
RV33	$3.75 Violet	37.50
RV34	$3.34 Violet	33.50
RV35	$2.92 Violet	33.50
1945		
RV36	$2.50 Violet	27.50
RV37	$2.09 Violet	25.00
RV38	$1.67 Violet	25.00
RV39	$1.25 Violet	25.00
RV40	84¢ Violet	19.00
RV41	42¢ Violet	16.50
1945 Bright blue green & Yellow green		
RV42	$5.00 (used .75)	2.50
RV43	$4.59	38.50
RV44	$4.17	38.50
RV45	$3.75	33.50
RV46	$3.34	27.50
RV47	$2.92	22.50
1946 Bright blue green & Yellow green		
RV48	$2.50	25.00
RV49	$2.09	25.00
RV50	$1.67	18.50
RV51	$1.25	16.00
RV52	84¢	16.00
RV53	42¢	11.50

BOATING STAMPS (VF+20%)

RVB 1

		NH F-VF
1960 Rouletted		
RVB1	$1.00 Rose red,blk.# ..	35.00
	Plate Blk. of 4	160.00
RVB2	$3.00 Blue, red #	50.00
	Plate Blk. of 4	225.00

DISTILLED SPIRITS (VF + 30%)

RX3

1950
Inscribed
"STAMP FOR SERIES 1950"
Yellow, Green & Black

Scott's No.		Fine Unused	Used
RX1	1¢	27.50	22.50
RX2	3¢	90.00	85.00
RX3	5¢	18.50	15.00
RX4	10¢	16.50	13.50
RX5	25¢	9.50	7.50
RX6	50¢	9.50	7.50
RX7	$1	2.50	2.00
RX8	$3	20.00	16.50
RX9	$5	6.50	5.00
RX10	$10	3.00	2.50
RX11	$25	13.50	11.50
RX12	$50	7.50	6.50
RX13	$100	5.00	3.50
RX14	$300	25.00	22.50
RX15	$500	16.50	12.50
RX16	$1000	9.50	7.50
RX17	$1500	52.50	42.50
RX18	$2000	5.50	4.50

DISTILLED SPIRITS (continued)

Scott's No.		Fine Unused	Used
RX19	$3000	23.50	17.50
RX20	$5000	23.50	17.50
RX21	$10,000	27.50	22.50
RX22	$20,000	35.00	28.50
RX23	$30,000	75.00	55.00
RX24	$40,000	800.00	600.00
RX25	$50,000	85.00	75.00

1952
DISTILLED SPIRITS
Inscription
"STAMP FOR SERIES 1950"
omitted
Yellow, Green & Black

		Fine Punch Cancel
RX28	5¢	35.00
RX29	10¢	4.00
RX30	25¢	15.00
RX31	50¢	11.50
RX32	$1	1.50
RX33	$3	21.50
RX34	$5	23.50
RX35	$10	1.75
RX36	$25	9.50
RX37	$50	23.50
RX38	$100	2.25
RX39	$300	7.50
RX40	$500	32.50
RX41	$1000	6.50
RX43	$2000	65.00
RX44	$3000	800.00
RX45	$5000	45.00
RX46	$10,000	75.00

FIREARMS TRANSFER TAX STAMPS
(VF + 30%)
Documentary Stamp of 1917
Overprinted Vertically in Black

National Firearms Act

	Without Gum	Fine Unused
RY1	$1 Green (1934)	300.00

RY 2,4,6

FIREARM TRANSFER TAX (continued)

	Without Gum	Fine Unused
	$200 Face Value	
	1934-1974	
RY2	Dark blue & red Serial #1-1500 (1934) .	1250.00
RY4	Dull blue & red Serial #1501-3000 (1950)	500.00
RY6	Dull blue & red Serial #3001 & up (1974)	225.00
	With Gum	
RY3	$1 Green (1938)	75.00
RY5	$5 Red (1960)	22.50

1946 RECTIFICATION TAX STAMPS
(VF+20%)

Rectification Tax Stamps were for the use of rectifiers in paying tax on liquor in bottling tanks. **Used stamps have staple holes.**

RZ1

		Fine Unused	Used
RZ1	1¢	7.50	3.00
RZ2	3¢	25.00	8.50
RZ3	5¢	16.50	2.50
RZ4	10¢	16.50	2.50
RZ5	25¢	16.50	3.00
RZ6	50¢	20.00	5.00
RZ7	$1	20.00	5.00
RZ8	$3	90.00	17.50
RZ9	$5	37.50	10.00
RZ10	$10	30.00	3.25
RZ11	$25	90.00	10.50
RZ12	$50	90.00	8.00
RZ13	$100	...	9.50
RZ14	$300	...	9.50
RZ15	$500	...	9.50
RZ16	$1000	...	15.00
RZ17	$1500	...	40.00
RZ18	$2000	...	75.00

U.S. HUNTING PERMIT STAMPS

RW1

RW2

RW12

RW16

On each stamp the words "Void After ..." show a date 1 year later than the actual date of issue. Even though RW1 has on it "Void After June 30, 1935," the stamp was issued in 1934.
RW1-RW25, RW31 Plate Blocks of 6 Must Have Margins on Two Sides

RW1-RW10 VF Used + 50% (B)

Scott's No.		Never Hinged VF	F-VF	Unused VF	F-VF	Used F-VF
RW1	1934, $1 Mallards	825.00	595.00	525.00	375.00	120.00
RW2	1935, $1 Canvasbacks	775.00	550.00	450.00	350.00	140.00
RW3	1936, $1 Canada Geese	420.00	320.00	260.00	190.00	65.00
RW4	1937, $1 Scaup Ducks	340.00	265.00	190.00	150.00	45.00
RW5	1938, $1 Pintails	525.00	325.00	250.00	175.00	45.00
RW6	1939, $1 Teal	250.00	160.00	130.00	95.00	40.00
RW6	Plate Block of 6	2000.00	1800.00	1650.00	1400.00	...
RW7	1940, $1 Mallards	250.00	160.00	130.00	95.00	40.00
RW7	Plate Block of 6	2000.00	1800.00	1650.00	1400.00	...
RW8	1941, $1 Ruddy Ducks	250.00	160.00	130.00	95.00	40.00
RW8	Plate Block of 6	2000.00	1800.00	1650.00	1400.00	...
RW9	1942, $1 Baldplates	250.00	170.00	140.00	110.00	40.00
RW9	Plate Block of 6	2000.00	1800.00	1650.00	1400.00	...
RW10	1943, $1 Ducks	95.00	70.00	65.00	45.00	40.00
RW10	Plate Block of 6	695.00	525.00	575.00	395.00	...

RW1-RW12 VF Used + 50% RW13-RW15 VF Used + 40%

Scott's No.		Never Hinged VF	F-VF	Unused VF	F-VF	Used F-VF
RW11	1944, $1 Geese	110.00	70.00	70.00	55.00	25.00
RW11	Plate Block of 6	795.00	525.00	595.00	395.00	...
RW12	1945, $1 Shovellers	75.00	55.00	45.00	30.00	24.00
RW12	Plate Block of 6	450.00	350.00	375.00	250.00	...
RW13	1946, $1 Redheads	55.00	38.00	35.00	30.00	13.00
RW13	Plate Block of 6	350.00	300.00	275.00	225.00	...
RW14	1947, $1 Snow Geese	55.00	38.00	35.00	30.00	13.00
RW14	Plate Block of 6	350.00	300.00	275.00	225.00	...
RW15	1948, $1 Buffleheads	65.00	45.00	40.00	30.00	13.00
RW15	Plate Block of 6	395.00	300.00	295.00	225.00	...
	1949-52 Issues VF Used + 40%					
RW16	1949, $2 Goldeneyes	70.00	50.00	45.00	35.00	13.00
RW16	Plate Block of 6	425.00	350.00	325.00	275.00	...
RW17	1950, $2 Swans	90.00	65.00	55.00	45.00	10.00
RW17	Plate Block of 6	560.00	400.00	400.00	295.00	...
RW18	1951, $2 Gadwalls	90.00	65.00	60.00	45.00	10.00
RW18	Plate Block of 6	560.00	400.00	400.00	295.00	...
RW19	1952, $2 Harlequins	90.00	65.00	55.00	45.00	8.00
RW19	Plate Block of 6	560.00	400.00	400.00	295.00	...

U.S. HUNTING PERMIT STAMPS

On each stamp the words "Void After ..." show a date 1 year later than the actual date of issue. Even though RW1 has on it "Void After June 30, 1935," the stamp was issued in 1934.
RW1-RW25, RW31 Plate Blocks of 6 Must Have Margins on Two Sides

RW21   RW25

Scott's No.		Never Hinged VF	F-VF	Unused VF	F-VF	Used F-VF
1953-58 Issues VF Used + 40%						
RW20	1953, $2 Teal	90.00	65.00	55.00	45.00	8.00
RW20	Plate Block of 6	575.00	400.00	400.00	325.00	...
RW21	1954, $2 Ring-neckeds	95.00	65.00	60.00	45.00	8.00
RW21	Plate Block of 6	560.00	400.00	400.00	325.00	...
RW22	1955, $2 Blue Geese	95.00	65.00	60.00	45.00	8.00
RW22	Plate Block of 6	575.00	400.00	400.00	325.00	...
RW23	1956, $2 Merganser	95.00	65.00	60.00	45.00	8.00
RW23	Plate Block of 6	590.00	400.00	425.00	325.00	...
RW24	1957, $2 Eider	95.00	65.00	60.00	45.00	8.00
RW24	Plate Block of 6	560.00	400.00	400.00	325.00	...
RW25	1958, $2 Canada Geese	95.00	65.00	60.00	45.00	8.00
RW25	Plate Block of 6	560.00	400.00	400.00	325.00	...

RW27   RW32

1959-71 Issues VF Used + 30%

Scott's No.		Pl# Blocks F-VF NH	VF NH	F-VF NH	Unus.	F-VF Used
RW26	1959, $3 Retriever	475.00	130.00	100.00	70.00	8.00
RW27	1960, $3 Redhead Ducks	400.00	100.00	80.00	55.00	8.00
RW28	1961, $3 Mallard	425.00	100.00	85.00	55.00	8.00
RW29	1962, $3 Pintail Ducks	475.00	110.00	90.00	67.00	8.00
RW30	1963, $3 Brant Landing	475.00	110.00	90.00	67.00	8.00
RW31	1964, $3 Hawaiian Nene (6)	2000.00	110.00	90.00	60.00	8.00
RW32	1965, $3 Canvasback Ducks	475.00	110.00	90.00	60.00	9.00

RW33   RW35

RW33	1966, $3 Whistling Swans	475.00	110.00	90.00	67.00	8.00
RW34	1967, $3 Old Squaw Ducks	495.00	125.00	90.00	67.00	8.00
RW35	1968, $3 Hooded Mergansers	280.00	75.00	60.00	38.00	8.00
RW36	1969, $3 White-wing Scooters	280.00	75.00	60.00	38.00	7.00
RW37	1970, $3 Ross's Geese	280.00	75.00	60.00	40.00	6.00
RW38	1971, $3 Cinnamon Teals	170.00	45.00	35.00	25.00	6.00

RW38   RW46

1972-79 Issues VF Used + 25%

Scott's No.		VF Pl# Blk	VF	NH F-VF	Used F-VF
RW39	1972, $5 Emperor Geese	135.00	35.00	25.00	6.00
RW40	1973, $5 Steller's Eiders	120.00	28.00	20.00	6.00
RW41	1974, $5 Wood Ducks	95.00	25.00	17.00	6.00
RW42	1975, $5 Decoy & Canvasbacks	70.00	20.00	12.00	6.00
RW43	1976, $5 Canada Geese	60.00	20.00	14.00	6.00
RW44	1977, $5 Pair of Ross's Geese	65.00	20.00	14.00	6.00
RW45	1978, $5 Hooded Merganser Drake	60.00	16.00	11.00	6.00
RW46	1979, $7.50 Green-winged Teal	70.00	19.00	14.00	7.00

RW51   RW54

Scott's No.		VF Pl# Blk	VF	NH F-VF	Used F-VF
1980-89 Issues VF Used + 25%					
RW47	1980, $7.50 Mallards	70.00	18.00	14.00	7.00
RW48	1981, $7.50 Ruddy Ducks	70.00	18.00	14.00	7.00
RW49	1982, $7.50 Canvasbacks	70.00	18.00	13.00	6.00
RW50	1983, $7.50 Pintails	70.00	18.00	13.00	6.00
RW51	1984, $7.50 Wigeon	80.00	22.00	14.00	7.00
RW52	1985, $7.50 Cinnamon Teal	70.00	18.00	12.00	7.00
RW53	1986, $7.50 Fulvous Whistling Duck	70.00	18.00	12.00	7.00
RW54	1987, $10 Red Head Ducks	90.00	20.00	16.00	9.00
RW55	1988, $10 Snow Goose	90.00	20.00	16.00	9.00
RW56	1989, $12.50 Lesser Scaups	95.00	21.00	17.00	10.00

RW57   RW62

1990-98 Issues VF Used + 25%					
RW57	1990, $12.50 Blk-Bellied Whistl. Duck	90.00	21.00	17.00	11.00
RW58	1991, $15.00 King Eiders	125.00	30.00	23.00	12.00
RW59	1992, $15.00 Spectacled Eider	125.00	30.00	23.00	12.00
RW60	1993, $15.00 Canvasbacks	125.00	30.00	23.00	12.00
RW61	1994, $15.00 Redbreasted Merganser	125.00	30.00	23.00	12.00
RW62	1995, $15.00 Mallards	120.00	26.00	23.00	12.00

RW63   RW64

RW63	1996, $15.00 Surf Scoter	120.00	26.00	23.00	12.00
RW64	1997, $15.00 Canada Goose	120.00	26.00	23.00	12.00

RW65   RW66

RW65	1998, $15.00 Barrow's Goldeneye	120.00	26.00	23.00	...
RW65A	1998, Same, Self-Adhesive	...	26.00	23.00	12.00
RW66	1999, $15.00 Greater Scaup	120.00	26.00	23.00	...
RW66A	1999, Same, Self-Adhesive	...	26.00	23.00	12.00

RW67

RW67	2000, $15.00 Mottled Duck	120.00	26.00	23.00	...
RW67A	2000, Same, Self-Adhesive	...	26.00	23.00	12.00
RW68	2001, $15.00 Northern Pintail	120.00	26.00	23.00	...
RW68A	2001, Same, Self-Adhesive	...	26.00	23.00	12.00

129

The Beginning of State Duck Stamps

One of the main purposes of the state waterfowl stamp programs have been to generate revenue for waterfowl conservation and restoration project. In addition, waterfowl stamps validate hunting licenses and often serve as a control to limit the harvest within a specific geographical area.

The federal government recognized the need to protect waterfowl in the U.S. with Migratory Bird Treaty Act of 1918. On March 16, 1934 President Franklin Roosevelt signed the Migratory Bird Hunting Stamp Act into law. Sale of federal waterfowl stamps provided funding for the purchase and development of federal waterfowl areas.

Soon, state and local governments began requiring hunters to purchase waterfowl hunting stamps. Since these agencies did not have collectors in mind, most of the early stamps are printed text only. These include Pymatuning, Marion County, Honey Lake and the states of California, Illinois, North and South Dakota as well as several Indian Reservations.

Pictorial state waterfowl stamps saw their beginning in 1971, when California commissioned Paul Johnson to design the state's first duck stamp, a relatively simple rendition of a pair of pintails in flight. California's decision to issue pictorial stamps were prompted by the growing number of collectors interested in fish and game stamps. State officials estimated that any added production costs could be more than made up through the increased sale of stamps to collectors. In 1971, Iowa became the second state to initiate a pictorial waterfowl stamp program.

The appearance of new pictorial issues, combined with the publication of E.L. Vanderford's *Handbook of Fish and Game Stamps* in 1973, led to a surge in waterfowl stamp collecting.

Maryland and Massachusetts began to issue their stamps in 1974. All of Massachusetts stamps depict waterfowl decoys by famous carvers. Illinois started a pictorial stamp program in 1975. The face value of this stamp was $5, and half of the revenue obtained through its sale went to Ducks Unlimited, a private conservation organization which has done much to aid in waterfowl restoration throughout North America.

These pictorial stamp programs were so successful in raising funds for waterfowl conservation projects that many additional states adopted similar stamp programs. Between 1976 and 1980, 13 additional states began issuing pictorial waterfowl stamps. Tennessee became the first state to issue separate pictorial waterfowl stamps for nonresidents. These non-resident stamps were discontinued after only two years.

In response to an increasing demand for waterfowl stamps on the part of stamp collectors, many states started to print there stamps in two different formats in the 1980's. There was one type, usually printed in booklet panes, for license agents to issue to hunters, and a second type, usually printed in sheets, that was sold to collectors.

The 1981 Arkansas stamp was printed in booklet panes of thirty and issued with protective booklet covers to license agents. Sheets of thirty, without protective covers, were kept in Little Rock for sale to collectors. South Carolina issued their first stamp in 1981. They were printed in sheets of thirty. Starting with their second issues in 1982, a portion of the stamps were serially numbered on the reverse and distributed to license agents. Collectors who bought stamps directly from the state were sold stamps from sheets lacking the serial numbers. The agent, or "hunter type" stamps as they are often called, were only sold to those collectors who specially requested them.

When North Dakota introduced their first pictorial stamps in 1982, the first 20,000 stamps were set aside to be sold with prints or to be signed by the artist. These were printed in sheets of ten. Stamp numbered 20,001-150,000 were printed in booklet panes of five and distributed to license agents. Stamps with serial numbers higher than 150,000 were printed in sheets of thirty and reserved for sale to collectors. The stamps that were distributed to license agents were available to collectors for a brief period of time following the end of the hunting season and then destroyed. The collector type stamps, on the other hand were kept on sale for three years. This accounts for the relative difficulty in obtaining unused examples of early North Dakota Booklet-type (hunter stamps).

New Hampshire's first stamp was printed in two different formats. When collectors placed their orders, they were asked whether they wanted stamps with straight edges on three sides (booklet type) or fully perforated (from sheets printed for collectors). Not understanding the difference between the two types, the majority of collectors requested fully perforated stamps.

Collector interest in state duck stamps exploded in the mid 1980's. This can be attributed to the large number of states issuing stamps by this time and the fact that an album containing spaces for federal and state waterfowl stamps was published in 1987. In the years since, every state has initiated a waterfowl program.

Nearly half of the states print their stamps in two formats today. Hunter stamps from Montana are printed in booklet panes of ten (2x5) with selvage on both sides. These are most often collected in horizontal pairs. (Connecticut 1993-1996 and Virginia 1988-1995 issued stamps in the same format). The selvage on each side of the pair makes it easy to differentiate them from collectors-type stamps, which are printed in sheets of thirty. When the 1986 Montana stamps were issued, some representatives at the state agency did not recognize a difference between the booklet and sheet type stamps. Therefore, only a small number of booklet-type stamps were obtained by collectors.

There have been some occasions when the waterfowl season was ready to begin and the state license sections had not yet received their stamps from the printer. This occurred in 1989 for Oregon and in 1991 for Idaho. In these instances "temporary" non-pictorial stamps were printed and distributed to license agents for issue to hunters until the regular pictorial stamps were received.

In the late 1980's the U.S. Fish and Wildlife Service encouraged many tribal governments to formally organize their fish and wildlife programs. Many of these programs were made to include stamp and license requirements in their general provisions. In 1989 the Crow Creek Sioux of South Dakota became the first tribal government to issue pictorial waterfowl stamps. These stamps were not printed with collectors in mind. Rather, tribal Department of Natural Resources officials were simply attempting to conform to standards set by South Dakota Game, Fish and Parks Commission for their pictorial stamps. Separate stamps were printed for reservations residents, South Dakota residents who did not live on the reservation and nonresidents of the state. For each classification only 200 stamps were printed.

In the last few years, several tribal governments have issued waterfowl stamps that are more readily available to collectors.

-Michael Jaffe

STATE DUCK STAMPS

State Duck Stamps provide a natural area for the person who wishes to expand his or her field of interest beyond the collecting of Federal Ducks. In 1971, California became the first state to issue a pictorial duck stamp. Other states followed with the sales providing a much needed source of revenue for wetlands. By 1994, all 50 states will have issued duck stamps.

Similar to Federal policy, many states hold an art competition to determine the winning design. Other states commission an artist. Beginning in 1987, some states started to issue a "Governor's" stamp. These stamps with high face values were designed to garner additional wetland funds. In 1989, the Crow Creek Sioux Tribe of South Dakota became the first Indian Reservation to issue a pictorial duck stamp.

Hunter or Agent stamps generally come in booklets with a tab attached to the stamp, or specific serial numbers on the stamp issued in sheet format that allows collectors' orders to be filled more easily. Many of these stamps exist with plate numbers in the margin. The items illustrated below represent just a sampling of the interesting varieties which have been produced by the various states.

FL 15T SURVEY TAB

OR 3A HUNTER TYPE WITH TAB

WA 6A MINI SHEET

MT 4A HZ. PAIR WITH SIDE MARGINS

AR 16 PROOF PAIR, IMPERF.

TN 1A NON-RES. LICENSE

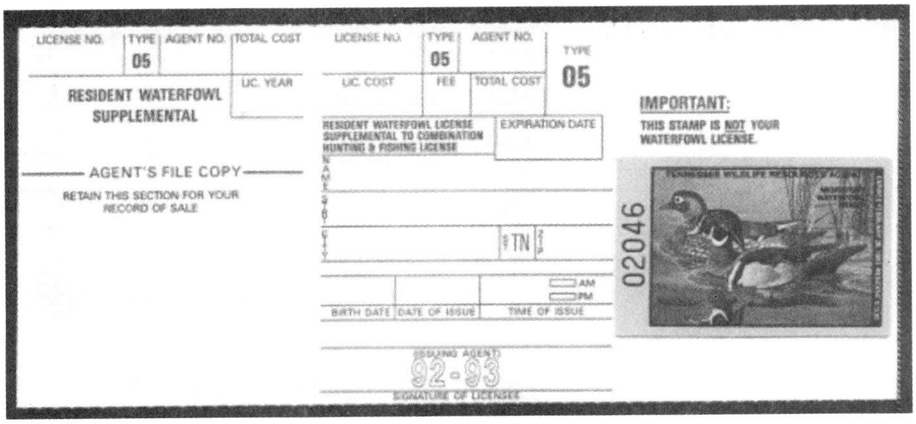

TN 14B 3 PART CARD

STATE HUNTING PERMIT STAMPS

ALABAMA

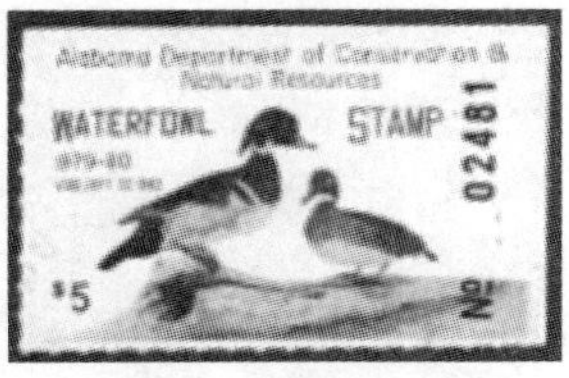

WATERFOWL STAMP
$5
02481

AL 1

No.	Description	F-VF NH
AL 1	'79 $5 Wood Ducks	10.00
AL 2	'80 $5 Mallards	10.00
AL 3	'81 $5 Canada Geese	10.00
AL 4	'82 $5 Grn Winged Teal .	10.00
AL 5	'83 $5 Widgeon	10.00
AL 6	'84 $5 Buffleheads	10.00
AL 7	'85 $5 Wood Ducks	14.00
AL 8	'86 $5 Canada Geese	14.00
AL 9	'87 $5 Pintails	15.00
AL 10	'88 $5 Canvasbacks	10.00
AL 11	'89 $5 Hooded Mergan ...	10.00
AL 12	'90 $5 Wood Ducks	10.00
AL 13	'91 $5 Redheads	10.00
AL 14	'92 $5 Cinnamon Teal	10.00
AL 15	'93 $5 Grn Winged Teal ..	10.00
AL 16	'94 $5 Canvasbacks	10.00
AL 17	'95 $5 Canda Geese	10.00
AL 18	'96 $5 Wood Ducks	10.00
AL 19	'97 $5 Snow Goose	10.00
AL 20	'98 $5 Barrow's goldeneye	10.00
AL 21	'99 $5 Redheads	10.00
AL 22	'00 $5 Buffleheads	10.00
AL 23	'01 $5 Ruddy Duck	10.00

Alabama Set 1979-2000 (22) 213.00

ALASKA

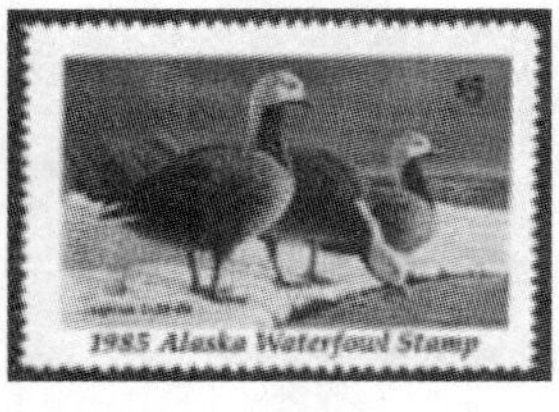

$5
1985 Alaska Waterfowl Stamp

AK 1

No.	Description	F-VF NH
AK 1	'85 $5 Emperor Geese ...	10.00
AK 2	'86 $5 Steller's Elders	10.00
AK 3	'87 $5 Spectacled Elders	10.00
AK 3A	'87 $5 Hunted Full Tab ...	10.00
AK 4	'88 $5 Trumpeter Swan ..	10.00
AK 4A	'88 $5 Hunter/Full Tab	10.00
AK 5	'89 $5 Goldeneyes	9.00
AK 5A	'89 $5 Hunter/Full Tab	10.00
AK 6	'90 $5 Oldsquaw	9.00
AK 6A	'90 $5 Hunter/Full Tab	9.50
AK 7	'91 $5 Snowgeese	9.00
AK 7A	'91 $5 Hunter/Full Tab	9.50
AK 8	'92 $5 Canvasbacks	9.00
AK 8A	'92 $5 Hunter/Full Tab	9.50
AK 9	'93 $5 Wh. Fronted Geese	9.00
AK 9A	'93 $5 Hunter/Full Tab	9.50
AK 10	'94 $5 Harlequin	10.00
AK 10A	'94 $5 Hunter/Full Tab	9.50
AK 11	'95 $5 Pacific Brant	10.00
AK 11A	'95 $5 Hunter w/ Full Tab .	9.50
AK 12	'96 $5 Aleutian Ca. Geese	10.00
AK 12A	'96 $5 Hunter w/ Full Tab	9.50
AK 13	'97 $5 King Eiders	10.00
AK 13A	'97 $5 Hunter w/ Full Tab	9.50
AK 14	'98 $5 Barrow's Goldeneye	9.00
AK 14A	'98 $5 Hunter w/ Full Tab	9.50
AK 15	'99 $5 Northern Pintails ...	9.00
AK 15A	'99 $5 Hunter with Full Tab	9.50
AK 16	'00 $5 Common Eiders	9.00
AK 16A	'00 $5 Hunter with Full Tab	9.50
AK 17	'01 $5 Buffleheads	9.00

Alaska Set 1985-2000 (16) 140.00
Alaska Hunter type, cplt. set (14) 96.00
NOTE: Governor's stamps available upon request.

ARIZONA

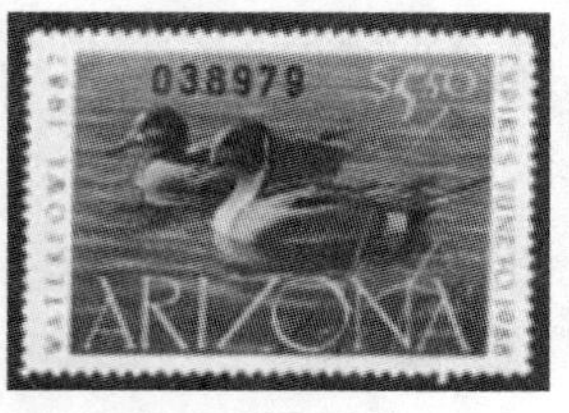

038979
$5.50
ARIZONA

AZ 1

No.	Description	F-VF NH
AZ 1	'87 $5.50 Pintails	11.00
AZ 1A	'87 $5.50 Hunter w/tab ...	11.00
AZ 2	'88 $5.50 Grn. Winged Teal	11.00
AZ 2A	'88 $5.50 Hunter w/tab ...	11.00
AZ 3	'89 $5.50 Cinnamon Teal	11.00
AZ 3A	'89 $5.50 Hunter w/tab ...	11.00
AZ 4	'90 $5.50 Canada Geese	11.00
AZ 4A	'90 $5.50 Hunter w/tab ...	11.00
AZ 5	'91 $5.50 Bl. Winged Teal	9.50
AZ 5A	'91 $5.50 Hunter w/tab ...	11.00
AZ 6	'92 $5.50 Buffleheads	9.50
AZ 6A	'92 $5.50 Hunter w/tab ...	11.00
AZ 7	'93 $5.50 Mexican Duck	9.50
AZ 7A	'93 $5.50 Hunter w/tab ...	9.50
AZ 8	'94 $5.50 Mallards	9.50
AZ 8A	'94 $5.50 Hunter w/tab ...	9.50
AZ 9	'95 $5.50 Wigeon	9.50
AZ 9A	'95 $5.50 Hunter w/tab ...	9.50
AZ 10	'96 $5.50 Canvasback ...	9.50
AZ 10A	.'96 $5.50 Hunter w/ Tab	9.50
AZ 11	'97 $5.50 Gadwall	9.50
AZ 11A	'97 $5.50 Hunter w/ Tab .	9.50
AZ 12	'98 $5.50 Wood Duck	9.50
AZ 12 A	'98 $5.50 Hunter w/ tab	9.50
AZ 13	'99 $5.50 Snow Goose	9.50
AZ 13A	'99 $5.50 Hunter with Tab	9.50
AZ 14	'00 $7.50 Ruddy Ducks ...	11.50
AZ 14A	'00 $7.50 Hunter with Tab	11.50
AZ 15	'01 $7.50	11.50
AZ 15A	'01 $7.50 Hunter with Tab	11.50

Arizona Set 1987-2000 (14) 123.00
Arizona Hunter type, cplt. set . 128.00
NOTE: Gov. stamps avail upon req.

ARKANSAS

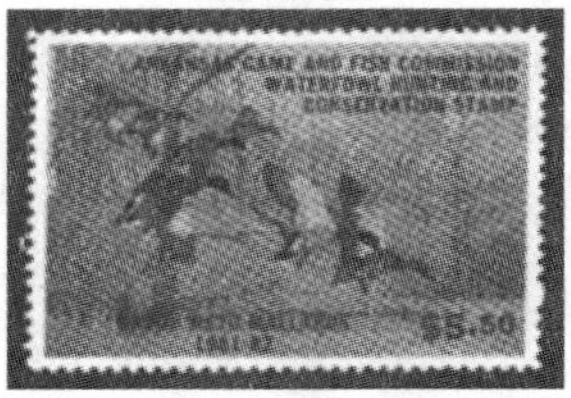

AR 1

No.	Description	F-VF NH
AR 1	'81 $5.50 Mallards	40.00
AR 1B	'81 Hunter (S# 110,001-200,000)	55.00
AR 1P	'81 Imperf Proof Pair	20.00
AR 2	'82 $5.50 Wood Ducks ...	40.00
AR 2B	'82 Hunter (S# 110,001-200,000)	55.00
AR 2P	'82 Imperf Proof Pair	25.00
AR 3	'83 $5.50 Grn.Wngd Teal	55.00
AR 3B	'83 Hunter (S# 70,001-160,000)	1000.00
AR 3P	'83 Imperf Proof Sgl	70.00
AR 4	'84 $5.50 Pintails	25.00
AR 4B	'84 Hunter (S# 25,001-100,000)	35.00
AR 4P	'84 Imperf Proof Pair	20.00
AR 5	'85 $5.50 Mallards	14.00
AR 5B	'85 Hunter (S# 25,001-100,000)	28.00
AR 5P	'85 Imperf Proof Pair	20.00
AR 6	'86 $5.50 Blk. Swamp Mallards	12.00
AR 6B	'86 Hunter (S# 25,001-100,000)	17.00
AR 6P	'86 Imperf Proof Pair	20.00
AR 7	'87 $7 Wood Ducks	12.00
AR 7A	'87 $5.50 Wood Ducks ...	13.00
AR 7B	'87 Hunter (S# 25,001-100,000)	14.00
AR 7P	'87 Imperf Proof Pair	20.00
AR 8	'88 $7 Pintails	11.00
AR 8A	'88 $5.50 Pintails	13.00
AR 8B	'88 Hunter (S# 25,001-100,000)	14.00
AR 8P	'88 Imperf Proof Pair	23.00
AR 9	'89 $7 Mallards	11.00
AR 9B	'89 Hunter (S# 30,001-100,000)	12.00
AR 9P	'89 Imperf Proof Pair	23.00
AR 10	'90 $7 Blk Duck/Mallards	11.00
AR 10B	'90 Hunter (S# 30,001-100,000)	12.00
AR 10P	'90 Imperf Proof Pair	23.00
AR 11	'91 $7 Widgeons	11.00
AR 11B	'91 Hunter (S# 30,001-100,000)	11.00
AR 11P	'91 Imperf Proof Pair	17.00
AR 12	'92 $7 Shovelers	11.00
AR 12B	'92 Hunter (S# 30,001-100,000)	11.00
AR 12P	'92 Imperf Proof Pair	17.00
AR 13	'93 $7 Mallards	11.00
AR 13B	'93 Hunter (S# 30,001-100,000)	11.00
AR 13P	'93 Imperf Proof Pair	17.00
AR 14	'94 $7 Canada Geese	11.00
AR 14B	'94 Hunter (S# 25,001-100,000)	11.00
AR 14P	'94 Imperf Proof Pair	16.00
AR 15	'95 $7 Mallard	11.00
AR 15B	'95 Hunter (S# 25,001-100,000)	11.00
AR 15P	'95 Imperf Proof Pair .	16.00
AR 16	'96 $7.00 Black Lab ..	11.00
AR 16B	Hunter (SN# 13,001-100,000).	11.00
AR 16P	'96 Imperf Proof Pair ..	16.00
AR 17	'97 $7.00 Chocolate Lab	11.00
AR 17B	Hunter (SN# 13,001-100,000).	11.00
AR 17P	'97 Imperf Proof Pair	16.00
AR 18	'98 Mallards / Yellow Lab	11.00
AR 18B	Hunter (13,001-100,000)	11.00
AR 18P	'98 Imperf Proof Pair	16.00
AR 19	'99 $7.00 Wood Ducks .	11.00
AR 19B	Hunter (13,001-100,000)	11.00
AR 19P	'99 Imperf Proof Pair	16.00
AR 20	'00 $7.00 Mallards/Dog .	11.00
AR 20B	Hunter (13,001-100,000)	11.00
AR 20P	'00 Imperf.Proof Pair	16.00
AR 21	'01 $7.00 Canvas back .	11.00
AR 21B	Hunter (13,001-100,000)	11.00

Arkansas Set 1981-2000 (22) .. 340.00
Arkansas Hunter, cplt (20) 1280.00
Arkansas Imperfs, cplt (20) 365.00

CALIFORNIA

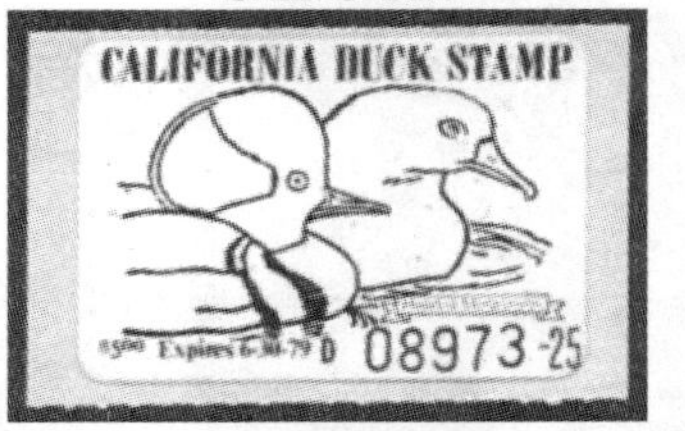

CALIFORNIA DUCK STAMP
08973-25

CA 8

No.	Description	F-VF NH
CA 1	'71 $1 Pintails Original Backing	825.00
CA 1	'71 $1 Unsigned w/o Orig. Backing	165.00
CA 2	'72 $1 Canvasback Original Backing	3200.00
CA 2	'72 $1 Unsigned w/o Orig. Backing	300.00
CA 3	'73 $1 Mallards	12.00
CA 4	'74 $1 Wh. Fronted Geese	3.00
CA 5	'75 $1 Grn. Winged Teal Clear Wax Back	165.00
CA 5R	'75 $1 Same,Ribbed Back	40.00
CA 6	'76 $1 Widgeon	20.00
CA 7	'77 $1 Cinnamon Teal ..	45.00
CA 7A	'78 $5 Cinnamon Teal ..	10.00
CA 8	'78 $5 Hooded Mergans	150.00
CA 9	'79 $5 Wood Ducks	9.00
CA 9P	'79 Imperf Proof Pair	55.00
CA 10	'80 $5 Pintails	9.00
CA 10P	'80 Imperf Proof Pair	55.00
CA 11	'81 $5 Canvasbacks	9.50
CA 12	'82 $5 Widgeon	9.50
CA 13	'83 $5 Grn.Winged Teal	9.50
CA 14	'84 $7.50 Mallard Decoy	12.00
CA 15	'85 $7.50 Ring Neck Duck	12.00
CA 16	'86 $7.50 Canada Goose	12.00
CA 17	'87 $7.50 Redheads	12.00
CA 18	'88 $7.50 Mallards	12.00
CA 19	'89 $7.50 Cinnamon Teal	12.00
CA 20	'90 $7.50 Canada Goose	12.00
CA 21	'91 $7.90 Gadwalls	12.00
CA 22	'92 $7.90 Wh.Frntd Goose	12.00
CA 23	'93 $10.50 Pintails	14.50
CA 24	'94 $10.50 Wood Ducks	14.50
CA 25	'95 $10.50 Snow Geese	14.50
CA 25a	Strip of 4 designs	58.00
CA 25m	Mini sheet of 4	150.00
CA 26	'96 $10.50 Mallard	14.50
CA 27	'97 $10.50 Pintails	14.50
CA 28	'98 $10.50 Green Winged teal (Pair)	32.00
CA 29	'99 $10.50 Wood Ducks Pr.	32.00
CA 30	'00 $10.50 Canada Goose & Mallard	15.00
CA 31	'01 $10.50 Redheads	15.00

California Set 1973-2000 (28) . 635.00

COLORADO

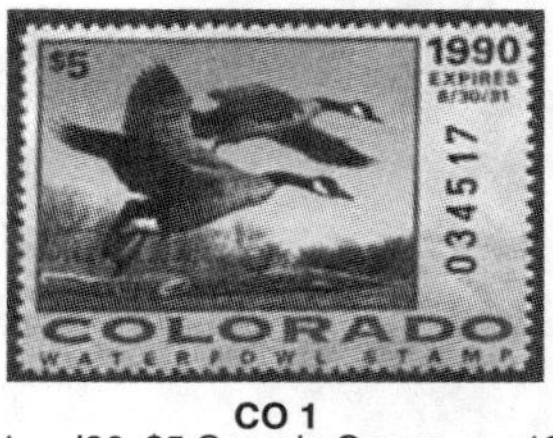

$5
1990
034517
COLORADO
WATERFOWL STAMP

CO 1

No.	Description	F-VF NH
CO 1	'90 $5 Canada Geese ..	12.00
CO 1A	'90 $5 Hunter w/tab	12.00
CO 2	'91 $5 Mallards	20.00
CO 2A	'91 $5 Hunter w/tab	12.00
CO 3	'92 $5 Pintails	9.00
CO 3A	'92 $5 Hunter w/tab	11.00
CO 4	'93 $5 Grn. Winged Teal	9.00
CO 4A	'93 $5 Hunter w/tab	9.50
CO 5	'94 $5 Wood Ducks	9.00
CO 5A	'94 $5 Hunter w/tab	9.50
CO 6	'95 $5 Buffleheads	9.00
CO 6A	'95 $5 Hunter w/tab	9.50
CO 7	'96 $5 Cinnamon Teal ...	9.00
CO 7A	'96 $5 Hunter w/Tab	9.50
CO 8	'97 $5 Widgeon	9.00
CO 8A	'97 $5 Hunter w/tab	9.50
CO 9	'98 $5 Cinnamon Teal ...	9.00
CO 9 A	'98 $5 Hunter w/ tab	9.50
CO 10	'99 $5 Blue Winged Teal	9.00
CO 10A	'99 $5 Hunter with tab .	9.00
CO 11	'00 $5 Gadwell	9.00
CO 11A	'00 $5 Hunter with tab ...	9.50
CO 12	'01 $5 Ruddy Duck	9.00
CO 12A	'01 $5 Hunter with tab ...	9.50

Colorado Set 1990-2000 (11)... 102.00
Colorado Hunter Set (11) 101.00
NOTE: Governor's stamps available upon request.

CONNECTICUT

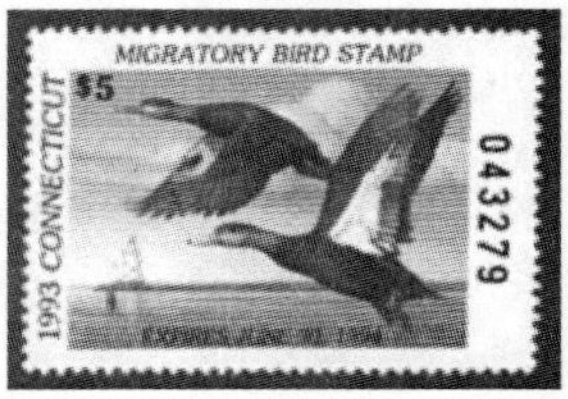

MIGRATORY BIRD STAMP
$5
1993 CONNECTICUT
043279

CT 1

No.	Description	F-VF NH
CT 1	'93 $5 Black Ducks	10.00
CT 1A	'93 $5 Hunter Hz. Pair .	20.00
CT 1M	'93 Commem. Sht. of 4	80.00
CT 2	'94 $5 Canvasbacks	10.00
CT 2A	'94 $5 Hunter Horiz. Pair	20.00
CT 2M	'94 Commem Sheet of 4	50.00
CT 3	'95 $5 Mallards	10.00
CT 3A	'95 $5 Hunter Horiz. Pair	20.00
CT 4	'96 $5 Old Squaw	10.00
CT 4A	'96 $5 Hunter Horiz. Pair.	20.00
CT 5	'97 $5 Green Winged Teal	10.00
CT 5A	'97 $5 Hunter "H" Prefix	10.00
CT 6	'98 $ 5 Mallards	10.00
CT 6A	'98 $ 5 Hunter "H" prefix	10.00
CT 7	'99 $5 Canada Goose ..	10.00
CT 7A	'99 $5 Hunter "H" Prefix	10.00
CT 8	'00 $5 Wood Ducks	10.00
CT 8A	'00 $5 Hunter "H" Prefix	10.00

Connecticut Set 1993-2000 (8) .. 75.00
Ct. Hunter Set (8)...................... 115.00
NOTE: Governor's stamps available upon request.

DELAWARE

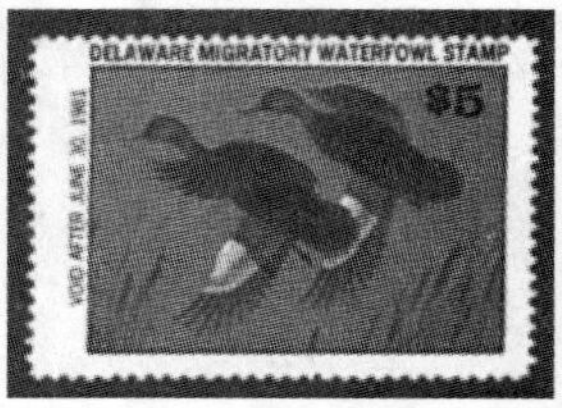

DELAWARE MIGRATORY WATERFOWL STAMP
$5

DE 1

No.	Description	F-VF NH
DE 1	'80 $5 Black Ducks	95.00
DE 2	'81 $5 Snow Geese	70.00
DE 3	'82 $5 Canada Geese ..	70.00
DE 4	'83 $5 Canvasbacks	45.00
DE 5	'84 $5 Mallards	15.00
DE 6	'85 $5 Pintail	12.00
DE 7	'86 $5 Widgeon	12.00
DE 8	'87 $5 Redheads	12.00
DE 9	'88 $5 Wood Ducks	10.00
DE 10	'89 $5 Buffleheads	9.50
DE 11	'90 $5 Green Winged Teal	9.50
DE 12	'91 $5 Hooded Mergans	9.50
DE 12A	'91 Hunter-SN# on Back	11.00
DE 13	'92 $5 Bl. Wngd. Teal...	9.50
DE 13A	'92 Hunter-SN# on Back	9.50
DE 14	'93 $5 Goldeneyes	9.50
DE 14A	'93 Hunter-SN# on Back	9.50
DE 15	'94 $5 Blue Geese	9.50
DE 15A	'94 Hunter-SN# on back	9.50
DE 16	'95 $5 Scaup	9.00
DE 16A	'95 Hunter-SN# on back	9.50
DE 17	'96 $6 Gadwall	9.00
DE 17A	'96 Hunter-SN# on back	9.50
DE 18	'97 $6 Wh. Winged Scoter	9.00
DE 18A	'97 Hunter-SN# on back	9.50

Note: Hunting Permit Illustrations can be found at the following website:
www.duckstamps.com

STATE HUNTING PERMIT STAMPS

No.	Description	F-VF NH
	DELAWARE (continued)	
DE 19	'98 Blue Winged Teal	9.00
DE 19A	'98 Hunter SN# on back	9.50
DE 20	'99 $6 Tundra Swan	9.00
DE 20A	'99 Hunter SN# on back	9.50
DE 21	'00 $6 American Brandt	9.00
DE 21A	'00 Hunter SN# on back	9.50
DE 22	'01 $6 Old Squaw	9.00
DE 22A	'01 Hunter SN# on back	9.50
Delaware Set 1980-2000 (21)		**423.00**
Delaware Hunters (10)		**91.00**

NOTE: Governor's stamps available upon request.

FLORIDA

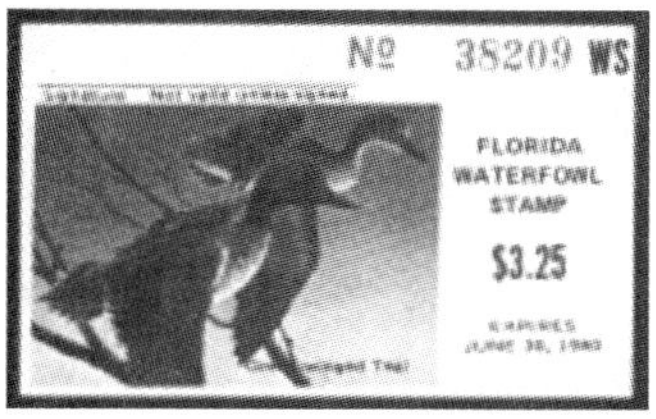

FL 1

No.	Description	F-VF NH
FL 1	'79 $3.25 Grn Wngd Teal	185.00
FL 1T	'79 $3.25 Full Tab Attd.	210.00
FL 2	'80 $3.25 intails	20.00
FL 2T	'80 $3.25 Full Tab Attd	24.00
FL 3	'81 $3.25 Widgeon	17.00
FL 3T	'81 $3.25 Full Tab Attd	24.00
FL 4	'82 $3.25 Ring-Neck Duck	24.00
FL 4T	'82 $3.25Full Tab Attd	35.00
FL 5	'83 $3.25 Buffleheads	50.00
FL 5T	'83 $3.25Full Tab Attd	60.00
FL 6	'84 $3.25 Hooded Merg	13.00
FL 6T	'84 $3.25 Full Tab Attd	18.00
FL 7	'85 $3.25 Wood Ducks	13.00
FL 7T	'85 $3.25 Full Tab Attd	10.00
FL 8	'86 $3.00 Canvasbacks	11.00
FL 8T	'86 $3.00 Survey Tab Attd	18.00
FL 9	'87 $3.50 Mallards	9.50
FL 9T	'87 $3.50 Survey Tab Attd	25.00
FL 10	'88 $3.50 Redheads	9.50
FL 10T	'88 $3.50 Survey Tab Attd	23.00
FL 11	'89 $3.50 Bl. Winged Teal	7.50
FL 11T	'89 $3.50 Survey Tab Attd	23.00
FL 12	'90 $3.50 Wood Ducks	7.50
FL 12T	'90 $3.50 Survey Tab Attd	23.00
FL 13	'91 $3.50 Northern Pintail	7.50
FL 13T	'91 $3.50 Survey Tab Attd	17.00
FL 14	'92 $3.50 Ruddy Duck	7.50
FL 14T	'92 $3.50 Survey Tab Attd	14.00
FL 15	'93 $3.50 Amer. Widgeon	7.00
FL 15T	'93 $3.50 Survey Tab Attd	14.00
FL 16	'94 $3.50 Mottled Duck	6.50
FL 16T	'94 $3.50 Survey Tab Attd.	14.00
FL 17	'95 $3.50 Fulvous Whistling Duck	6.50
FL 17T	'95 $3.50 Survey Tab Attd.	14.00
FL 18	'96 $3.50 Goldeneyes	6.50
FL 18T	'96 $3.50 Survey Tab Attchd	15.00
FL 19	'97 $3.50 Hooded Mergansers	6.50
FL 19T	'97 $3.50 Survey Tab Attd	15.00
FL 20	'98 $3.50 Shoveler	15.00
FL 20T	'98 $3.50 Survey Tab Attd	35.00
FL 21	'99 $3.50 Northern Pintail	6.50
FL 21T	'99 $3.50 Survey Tab Attd	15.00
FL 22	'00 $3.50 Ring necked Duck	6.50
FL 22T	'00 $3.50 Survey Tab Attd.	15.00
FL 23	'01 $3.50 Canvas back	6.50
FL 23T	'01 $3.50 Survey Tab Attd.	15.00
Florida Set 1979-2000 (22)		**415.00**
Florida Tabs Set 1979-2000(20)		**625.00**

GEORGIA

GA 1

No.	Description	F-VF NH
GA 1	'85 $5.50 Wood Ducks	15.00
GA 2	'86 $5.50 Mallards	8.50
GA 3	'87 $5.50 Canada Geese	8.50
GA 4	'88 $5.50 Ring Neck Ducks	8.50
GA 5	'89 $5.50 Duckling/uppy	11.00
GA 6	'90 $5.50 Wood Ducks	8.50
GA 7	'91 $5.50 Grn. Winged Teal	8.50
GA 8	'92 $5.50 Buffleheads	8.50
GA 9	'93 $5.50 Mallards	11.00
GA 10	'94 $5.50 Ringnecks	11.00
GA 11	'95 $5.50 Widgeons/Blk Lab	11.00
	GEORGIA (continued)	
GA 12	'96 $5.50 Black Ducks	11.00
GA 13	'97 $5.50 Lesser Scaup	11.00
GA 14	'98 $5.50 Black Labrador w/ Ringnecks	10.00
GA 15	'99 $5.50 Pintails	10.00
Georgia Set 1985-99 (15)		**141.00**

HAWAII

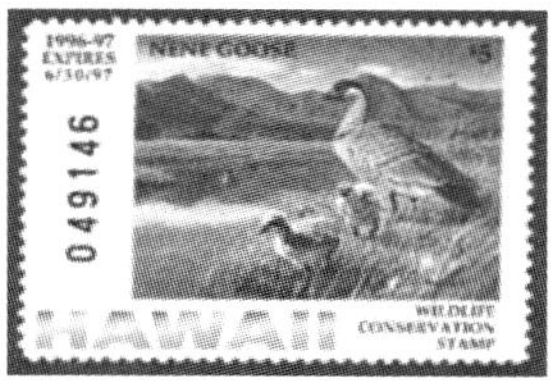

HI 1

No.	Description	F-VF NH
HI 1	'96 $5 Nene Geese	11.00
HI 1A	'96 $5 Hunter Type	11.00
HI 1B	'96 $5 Booklet	13.00
H1 1M	'96 $5 Mini Sheet of 4	50.00
HI 2	'97 $5 Hawaiian Duck	10.00
HI 2A	'97 $5 Hunter Type	11.00
HI 2B	'97 $5 Booklet	13.00
HI 2M	'97 $5 Mini Sheet of 4	45.00
HI 3	'98 $5 Wild Turkey	9.00
HI 3A	'98 $5 Hunter Type	9.00
HI 4	'99 $5 Pheasant	8.50
HI 4A	'99 $5 Hunter Type	9.00
HI 5	'00 $5 Erckels Francolin	8.50
HI 5A	'00 $5 Hunter Type	9.00
HI 6	'01 $5 Japanese Green Pheasant	8.50
HI 6A	'01 $5 Hunter Type	9.00
Hawaii set 1996-2000 (5)		**45.00**
Hawaii Hunter set (5)		**45.00**

IDAHO

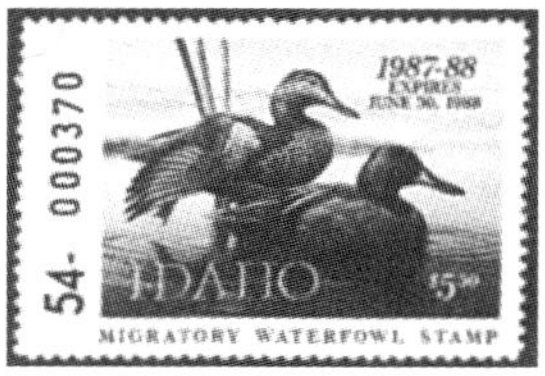

ID 1

No.	Description	F-VF NH
ID 1	'87 $5.50 Cinnamon Teals	15.00
ID 1A	'87 $5.50 Bklt. sgl. w/Tab	11.00
ID 2	'88 $5.50 Grn. Winged Teal	13.00
ID 2A	'88 $5.50 Bklt. sgl. w/Tab	13.00
ID 3	'89 $6 Bl. Winged Teal	11.00
ID 3A	'89 $6 Bklt. sgl. w/Tab	11.00
ID 4	'90 $6 Trumpeter Swan	20.00
ID 4A	'90 $6 Bklt. sgl. w/Tab	11.00
ID 5	'91 $6 Amer. Widgeons	9.50
ID 5A	'91 $6 Bklt. sgl. w/Tab	11.00
ID 5V	'91 $6 Provisional.	135.00
ID 6	'92 $6 Canada Geese	9.50
ID 6A	'92 $6 Bklt. sgl. w/Tab	9.50
ID 7	'93 $6 Com'n Goldeneye	10.00
ID 7A	'93 $6 Bklt. sgl. w/Tab	9.50
ID 8	'94 $6 Harlequin	10.00
ID 8A	'94 $6 Bklt. sgl. w/Tab	9.50
ID 9	'95 $6 Wood Ducks	10.00
ID 9A	'95 $6 Bklt. Sgl. w/tab	9.50
ID 10	'96 $6 Mallard	10.00
ID 11	'97 $6.50 Shovelers	10.00
ID 12	'98 $6.50 Canada Geese	10.00
Idaho Set 1987-98 (12)		**130.00**
Idaho Bklt. Set 1987-95 (9)		**90.00**

ILLINOIS

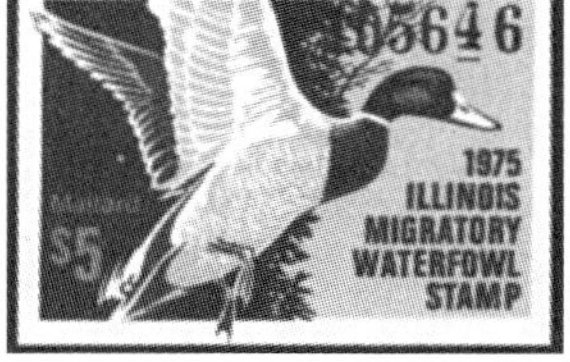

IL 1

No.	Description	F-VF NH
IL 1	'75 $5 Mallard	550.00
IL 2	'76 $5 Wood Ducks	250.00
IL 3	'77 $5 Canada Goose	195.00
IL 4	'78 $5 Canvasbacks	110.00
IL 5	'79 $5 Pintail	110.00
IL 6	'80 $5 Grn. Winged Teal	110.00
IL 7	'81 $5 Widgeon	110.00
IL 7A	'81 $5 G.W. Teal Error	595.00
IL 8	'82 $5 Black Ducks	67.50
	ILLINOIS (continued)	
IL 9	'83 $5 Lesser Scaup	70.00
IL 10	'84 $5 Bl. Winged Teal	70.00
IL 11	'85 $5 Red Head	15.00
IL 11T	'85 $5 Full Tab Attd	20.00
IL 12	'86 $5 Gadwalls	15.00
IL 12T	'86 $5 Full Tab Attd	17.00
IL 13	'87 $5 Buffleheads	12.00
IL 13T	'87 $5 Full Tab Attd	14.00
IL 14	'88 $5 Com'n Goldeneye	12.00
IL 14T	'88 $5 Full Tab Attd	14.00
IL 15	'89 $5 Ring Neck Duck	10.00
IL 15T	'89 $5 Full Tab Attd	11.00
IL 16	'90 $10 Lesser Snow Gs	16.00
IL 16T	'90 $10 Full Tab Attd	17.00
IL 17	'91 $10 Blk. Lab/Can. Gs	15.00
IL 17T	'91 $10 Full Tab Attd	17.00
IL 18	'92 $10 Retvr./Mallards	20.00
IL 18T	'92 $10 Full Tab Attd	22.00
IL 19	'93 $10 Puppy/Decoy	20.00
IL 19T	'93 $10 Full Tab Attd	22.00
IL 20	'94 $10 Chessies & Canvasbacks	20.00
IL 20T	'94 $10 Full Tab Attd	22.00
IL 21	'95 $10 Green Winged Teal/C. Lab	20.00
IL 21T	'95 $10 Full Tab Attd.	22.00
IL 22	'96 $10 Wood Ducks	15.00
IL 23	'97 $10 Canvasbacks	15.00
IL 24	'98 $10 Canada Geese	15.00
IL 25	'99 $10 Canada Geese/Lab	15.00
IL 26	'00 $10 Mallard/Gold Retrv.	15.00
IL 27	'01 $10 Canvasback/ Yellow Labrador	15.00
Illinois Set 1975-2000 Without Error (26)		**1795.00**

NOTE: Governor's stamps available upon request.

INDIANA

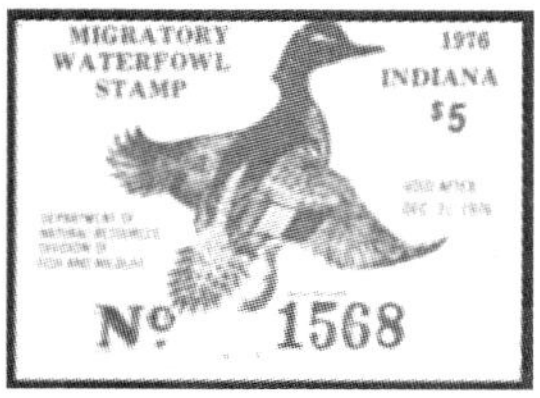

IN 1

No.	Description	F-VF NH
IN 1	'76 $5 Green Winged Teal	9.00
IN 2	'77 $5 Pintail	9.00
IN 3	'78 $5 Canada Geese	9.00
IN 4	'79 $5 Canvasbacks	9.00
IN 5	'80 $5 Mallard Ducklings	9.00
IN 6	'81 $5 Hooded Mergans	9.00
IN 7	'82 $5 Bl. Winged Teal	9.00
IN 8	'83 $5 Snow Geese	9.00
IN 9	'84 $5 Redheads	9.00
IN 10	'85 $5 Pintail	9.00
IN 10T	'85 $5 Full Tab Attd	12.00
IN 11	'86 $5 Wood Duck	9.00
IN 11T	'86 $5 Full Tab Attd	12.00
IN 12	'87 $5 Canvasbacks	9.00
IN 12T	'87 $5 Full Tab Attd	12.00
IN 13	'88 $6.75 Redheads	11.00
IN 13T	'88 $6.75 Full Tab Attd	12.00
IN 14	'89 $6.75 Canada Goose	11.00
IN 14T	'89 $6.75 Full Tab Attd	12.00
IN 15	'90 $6.75 Bl. Winged Teal	11.00
IN 15T	'90 $6.75 Full Tab Attd	12.00
IN 16	'91 $6.75 Mallards	11.00
IN 16T	'91 $6.75 Full Tab Attd	12.00
IN 17	'92 $6.75 Grn. Winged Tl	11.00
IN 17T	'92 $6.75 Full Tab Attd	12.00
IN 18	'93 $6.75 Wood Ducks	11.00
IN 18T	'93 $6.75 Full Tab Attd	12.00
IN 19	'94 $6.75 Pintail	11.00
IN 19T	'94 $6.75 Full Tab Attd	12.00
IN 20	'95 $6.75 Goldeneyes	11.00
IN 20T	'95 $6.75 Full Tab Attd.	12.00
IN 21	'96 $6.75 Black Ducks	11.00
IN 21T	'96 $6.75 Full Tab Attd.	12.00
IN 22	'97 $6.75 Canada Geese	11.00
IN 22T	'97 $6.75 Full Tab Attd.	12.00
IN 23	'98 $6.75 Widgeon	11.00
IN 23T	'98 $6.75 Full Tab Attd.	12.00
IN 24	'99 $6.75 Bluebills	11.00
IN 24T	'99 $6.75 Full Tab Attd	12.00
IN 25	'00 $6.75 Hood'd Merganser	11.00
IN 25T	'00 $6.75 Full Tab Attd	12.00
IN 26	'01 $6.75 Green Winged Teal	11.00
IN 26T	'01 $6.75 Full Tab Attd.	12.00
Indiana Set 1976-2000 (23)		**230.00**

Note: Hunting Permit Illustrations can be found at the following website:
www.duckstamps.com

IOWA

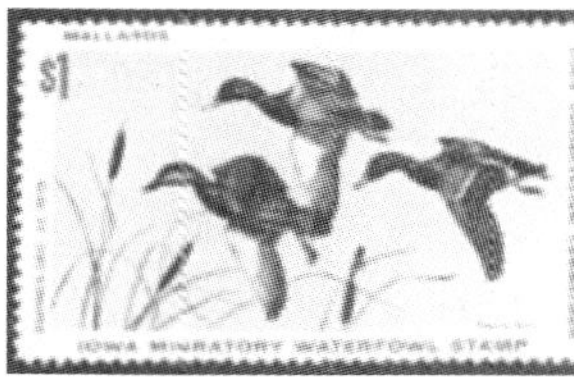

IA 9

No.	Description	F-VF NH
IA 1	'72 $1 Mallards	195.00
IA 2	'73 $1 Pintails	45.00
IA 3	'74 $1 Gadwalls	100.00
IA 4	'75 $1 Canada Geese	125.00
IA 5	'76 $1 Canvasbacks	25.00
IA 6	'77 $1 Lesser Scaup	25.00
IA 7	'78 $1 Wood Ducks	50.00
IA 8	'79 $5 Buffleheads	420.00
IA 9	'80 $5 Redheads	30.00
IA 10	'81 $5 Grn. Winged Teal	30.00
IA 11	'82 $5 Snow Geese	18.00
IA 12	'83 $5 Widgeon	20.00
IA 13	'84 $5 Wood Ducks	40.00
IA 14	'85 $5 Mallard & Decoy	24.00
IA 15	'86 $5 Bl. Wngd. Teal	16.00
IA 16	'87 $5 Canada Goose	14.00
IA 17	'88 $5 Pintails	12.00
IA 18	'89 $5 Bl. Winged Teal	12.00
IA 19	'90 $5 Canvasback	8.00
IA 19A	'90 Serial #26001-80000	12.00
IA 20	'91 $5 Mallards	8.00
IA 21	'92 $5 Blk. Lab/Ducks	9.50
IA 22	'93 $5 Mallards	9.50
IA 23	'94 $5 Grn. Winged Teal	9.00
IA 24	'95 $5 Canada Geese	9.00
IA 25	'96 $5 Canvasbacks	12.00
IA 26	'97 $5 Canada Geese	9.00
IA 27	'98 $5 Pintails	9.00
IA 28	'99 $5.50 Trumpeter Swans	9.00
IA 29	'00 $5.50 Hooded Merganser	9.00
IA 30	'01 $6 Snow Goose	10.00
Iowa Set 1972-2000 (29)		**1215.00**

KANSAS

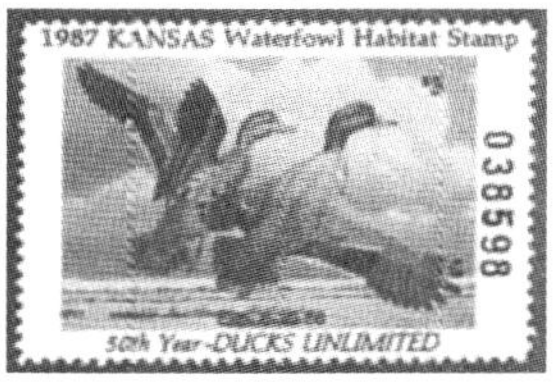

KS 1

No.	Description	F-VF NH
KS 1	'87 $3 Grn. Winged Teal	9.00
KS 1	'87 $3 Horiz. Pair	18.00
KS 1AD	'87 Hunter sgl. with DD in Serial Number	8.50
KS 1AD	'87 Horiz. Pair with DD in Serial Number	18.00
KS 1AS	'87 Hunter sgl. with SS in Serial Number	8.50
KS 1AS	'87 Horiz. Pair with SS in Serial Number	18.00
KS 2	'88 $3 Canada Geese	6.50
KS 2A	'88 Hunter sgl.	8.50
KS 2A	'88 $3 Horiz. Pair	18.00
KS 3	'89 $3 Mallards	6.50
KS 3A	'89 Hunter sgl.	7.00
KS 3A	'89 $3 Horiz. Pair	14.00
KS 4	'90 $3 Wood Ducks	6.50
KS 4A	'90 Hunter sgl.	7.00
KS 4A	'90 $3 Horiz. Pair	12.50
KS 5	'91 $3 Pintail	6.00
KS 5A	'91 Hunter sgl.	7.00
KS 5A	'91 $3 Horiz. Pair	12.50
KS 6	'92 $3 Canvasbacks	6.00
KS 7	'93 $3 Mallards	6.00
KS 8	'94 $3 Blue Winged Teal	6.00
KS 9	'95 $3 Barrow's Goldeneyes	6.00
KS 10	'96 $3 Wigeon	6.00
KS 11	'97 $3 Mallard (Blue)	6.00
KS 12	'98 $3 Mallard (Green)	8.00
KS 13	'99 $3 Mallard (Red)	6.00
KS 14	'00 S3 Mallard (Purple)	6.00
Kansas Set 1987-2000 (14)		**85.00**
Kansas Hunters Pairs Set 1987-91 (5)		**85.00**

KENTUCKY

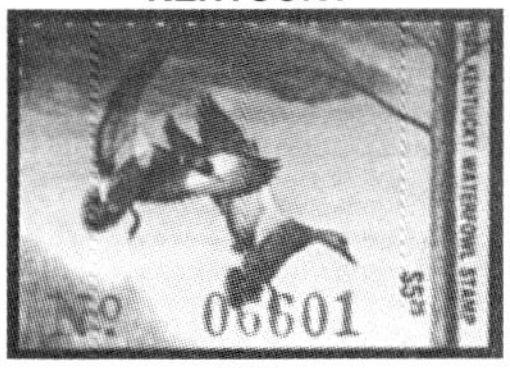

KY1

STATE HUNTING PERMIT STAMPS

KENTUCKY (cont.)

No.	Description	F-VF NH
KY 1	'85 $5.25 Mallards	14.00
KY 1T	'85 $5.25 Full Tab Attd	15.00
KY 2	'86 $5.25 Wood Ducks	9.50
KY 2T	'86 $5.25 Full Tab Attd	12.00
KY 3	'87 $5.25 Black Ducks	9.50
KY 3T	'87 $5.25 Full Tab Attd	12.00
KY 4	'88 $5.25 Canada Goose	9.50
KY 4T	'88 $5.25 Full Tab Attd	12.00
KY 5	'89 $5.25 Cnvsbk/Retrvr	9.50
KY 5T	'89 $5.25 Full Tab Attd	12.00
KY 6	'90 $5.25 Widgeons	9.50
KY 6T	'90 $5.25 Full Tab Attd	12.00
KY 7	'91 $5.25 Pintails	9.50
KY 7T	'91 $5.25 Full Tab Attd	12.00
KY 8	'92 $5.25 Grn.Winged Teal	12.00
KY 8T	'92 $5.25 Full Tab Attd	15.00
KY 9	'93 $5.25 Canvasbk/Decoy	15.00
KY 9T	'93 $5.25 Full Tab Attd	16.00
KY 10	'94 $5.25 Canada Goose	12.00
KY 10T	'94 $5.25 Full Tab Attd	10.00
KY 11	'95 $7.50 Ringnecks/ Black Lab	11.50
KY 11T	'95 $7.50 Full tab attd.	12.00
KY 12	'96 $7.50 Bl. Winged Teal	11.50
KY 13	'97 $7.50 Shovelers	11.50
KY 14	'98 $7.50 Gadwalls	11.50
KY 15	'99 $7.50 Goldeneyes	11.50
KY 16	'00 $7.50 Redheads	11.50

Kentucky Set 1985-2000 (16) .. 169.00

LOUISIANA

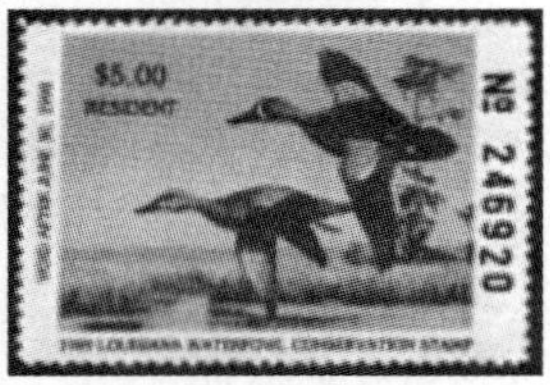

LA 1

No.	Description	F-VF NH
LA 1	'89 $5 Bl. Winged Teal	12.00
LA 1A	'89 $7.50 Non-Resident	16.00
LA 2	'90 $5 Grn. Winged Teal	9.00
LA 2A	'90 $7.50 Non-Resident	13.00
LA 3	'91 $5 Wood Ducks	9.50
LA 3A	'91 $7.50 Non-Resident	13.00
LA 4	'92 $5 Pintails	8.50
LA 4A	'92 $7.50 Non-Resident	11.75
LA 5	'93 $5 Amer. Widgeons	8.50
LA 5A	'93 $7.50 Non-Resident	11.75
LA 6	'94 $5 Mottled Duck	8.50
LA 6A	'94 $7.50 Non-Resident	11.50
LA 7	'95 $5 Speckled Belly Goose	8.50
LA 7A	'95 $7.50 Non-Resident	11.50
LA 8	'96 $5 Gadwall	8.50
LA 8A	'96 $7.50 Non-Resident Gadwall	11.50
LA 9	'97 $5 Ring Necked Duck	8.50
LA 9A	'97 $13.50 Ring Neck Duck	17.50
LA 10	'98 $5 Mallard	8.50
LA 10A	'98 $13.50 Non-Resident Mallard	17.50
LA 11	'99 $5.50 Snow Goose	9.00
LA 11A	'99 $13.50 Non-Resident Lesser Scaup	17.50
LA 12	'00 $5.50 Lesser Scaup	9.00
LA 12A	'00 $25.00 Non-Resident	33.00
LA 13	'01 $5.50 Northern Shoveler	8.50
LA 13A	'01 $25.00 Non-Resident	32.00

Louisiana Set Resident & Non-Res. 1989-2000 (24) 245.00

NOTE: Governor's stamps available upon request.

MAINE

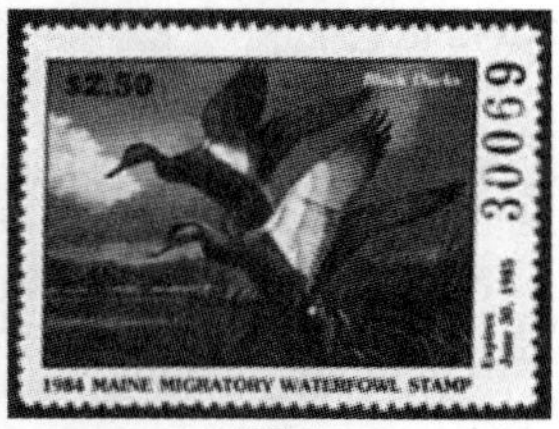

ME 1

No.	Description	F-VF NH
ME 1	'84 $2.50 Black Ducks	25.00
ME 2	'85 $2.50 Common Eiders	55.00
ME 3	'86 $2.50 Wood Ducks	10.00
ME 4	'87 $2.50 Buffleheads	8.50
ME 5	'88 $2.50 Grn Winged Teal	8.50
ME 6	'89 $2.50 Goldeneyes	6.00
ME 7	'90 $2.50 Canada Geese	6.00
ME 8	'91 $2.50 Ring Neck Duck	6.00
ME 9	'92 $2.50 Old Squaw	6.00
ME 10	'93 $2.50 Hooded Mergans	6.00

MAINE (cont.)

No.	Description	F-VF NH
ME 11	'94 $2.50 Mallards	6.00
ME 12	'95 $2.50 White Winged Scoter	6.00
ME 13	'96 $2.50 Blue Winged Teal	6.00
ME 14	'97 $2.50 Greater Scaup	6.00
ME 15	'98 $2.50 Surf Scoter	6.50
ME 16	'99 $2.50 Black Duck	6.00
ME 17	'00 $2.50 Common Eider	6.00
ME 18	'01 $2.50	6.00

Maine Set 1984-2000 (17) 150.00

MARYLAND

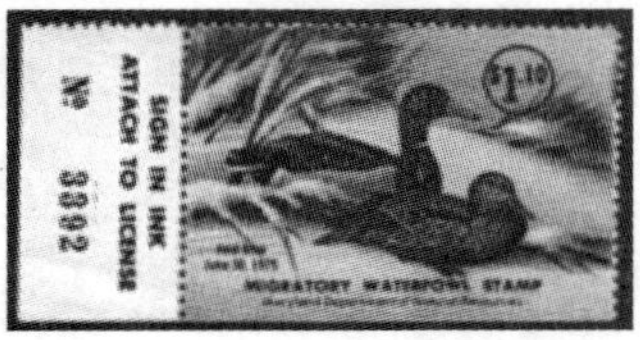

MD 1

No.	Description	F-VF NH
MD 1	'74 $01.10 Mallards	12.00
MD 2	'75 $1.10 Canada Geese	12.00
MD 3	'76 $1.10 Canvasbacks	12.00
MD 4	'77 $1.10 Greater Scaup	12.00
MD 5	'78 $1.10 Redheads	12.00
MD 6	'79 $1.10 Wood Ducks	12.00
MD 7	'80 $1.10 Pintail Decoy	12.00
MD 8	'81 $3 Widgeon	7.00
MD 9	'82 $3 Canvasbacks	10.00
MD 10	'83 $3 Wood Duck	14.00
MD 11	'84 $6 Black Duck	12.00
MD 12	'85 $6 Canada Geese	11.00
MD 13	'86 $6 Hooded Mergan	11.00
MD 14	'87 $6 Redheads	11.00
MD 15	'88 $6 Ruddy Duck	11.00
MD 16	'89 $6 Bl. Wngd. Teal	12.00
MD 17	'90 $6 Lesser Scaup	10.00
MD 18	'91 $6 Shovelers	10.00
MD 19	'92 $6 Bufflehead	10.00
MD 20	'93 $6 Canvasbacks	10.00
MD 21	'94 $6 Redheads	10.00
MD 22	'95 $6 Mallards	10.00
MD 23	'96 $6 Canada Geese	10.00
MD 24	'97 $6 Canvasbacks	10.00
MD 25	'98 $6 Pintail	10.00
MD 26	'99 $6 Wood Ducks	10.00
MD 27	'00 $6 Old Squaws	10.00
MD 28	'01 $6 American Widgeon	10.00

Maryland Set 1974-2000 (27) .. 267.00

MASSACHUSETTS

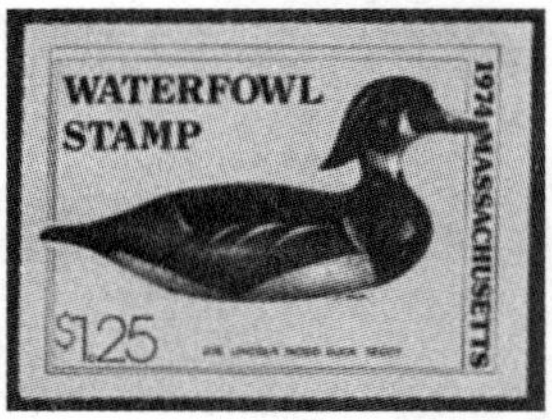

MA 1

No.	Description	F-VF NH
MA 1	'74 $1.25 Wood Duck	16.00
MA 2	'75 $1.25 Pintail	16.00
MA 3	'76 $1.25 Canada Goose	16.00
MA 4	'77 $1.25 Goldeneye	16.00
MA 5	'78 $1.25 Black Duck	16.00
MA 6	'79 $1.25 Ruddy Turnstone	16.00
MA 7	'80 $1.25 Old Squaw	16.00
MA 8	'81 $1.25 Rd Brstd Mrgnsr	16.00
MA 9	'82 $1.25 Grtr. Yellowlegs	16.00
MA 10	'83 $1.25 Redhead	16.00
MA 11	'84 $1.25 Wh. Ringed Scooter	16.00
MA 12	'85 $1.25 Ruddy Duck	15.00
MA 13	'86 $1.25 Preening Bluebill	15.00
MA 14	'87 $1.25 Amer. Widgeon	15.00
MA 15	'88 $1.25 Mallard Drake	15.00
MA 16	'89 $1.25 Brant	10.00
MA 17	'90 $1.25 Whistler Hen	10.00
MA 18	'91 $5 Canvasback	11.00
MA 19	'92 $5 Blk-Bellied Plover	11.00
MA 20	'93 $5 Rd Breasted Merg	11.00
MA 21	'94 $5 Wh. Winged Scoter	11.00
MA 22	'95 $5 Hooded Merganser	10.00
MA 23	'96 $5 Eider Decoy	10.00
MA 24	'97 $5 Curlew Shorebird	10.00
MA 25	'98 $5 Canada Goose	10.00
MA 26	'99 $5 Old Squaw	10.00
MA 27	'00 $5 Merganser	10.00
MA 28	'01 $5 Black Duck	9.00

Massachusetts Set 1974-2000 (27) 340.00

MICHIGAN

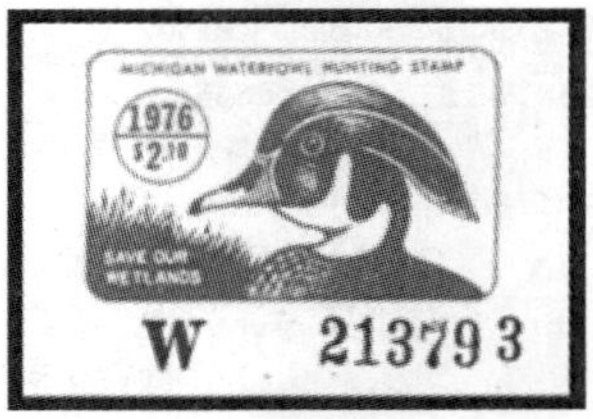

MI 1

No.	Description	F-VF NH
MI 1	'76 $2.10 Wood Duck	5.00
MI 2	'77 $2.10 Canvasbacks	350.00
MI 3	'78 $2.10 Mallards	28.00
MI 3T	'78 $2.10 Full Tab	50.00
MI 4	'79 $2.10 Canada Geese	50.00
MI 4T	'79 $2.10 Full Tab	67.50
MI 5	'80 $3.75 Lesser Scaup	23.00
MI 5T	'80 $3.75 Full Tab	34.00
MI 6	'81 $3.75 Buffleheads	28.00
MI 7	'82 $3.75 Redheads	28.00
MI 8	'83 $3.75 Wood Ducks	28.00
MI 9	'84 $3.75 Pintails	28.00
MI 10	'85 $3.75 Ring Neck Duck	28.00
MI 11	'86 $3.75 Com'n Gldneyes	21.00
MI 12	'87 $3.85 Grn. Winged Teal	12.00
MI 13	'88 $3.85 Canada Goose	10.00
MI 14	'89 $3.85 Widgeon	8.00
MI 15	'90 $3.85 Wood Ducks	8.00
MI 16	'91 $3.85 Bl. Wngd. Teal	7.00
MI 17	'92 $3.85 Rd Breasted Merg	7.00
MI 18	'93 $3.85 Hooded Mergan	7.00
MI 19	'94 $3.85 Black Duck	7.00
MI 20	'95 $4.35 Blue Winged Teal	8.00
MI 21	'96 $4.35 Canada Geese	8.00
MI 22	'97 $5 Canvasbacks	8.00
MI 23	'98 $5 Pintail	8.00
MI 24	'99 $5 Northern Shoveler	8.00
MI 25	'00 $5 Mallard	8.00
MI 26	'01 $5 Ruddy Duck	8.00

Michigan Set 1976-2000 (25) ... 675.00

MINNESOTA

MN 1

No.	Description	F-VF NH
MN 1	'77 $3 Mallards	17.00
MN 2	'78 $3 Lesser Scaup	11.00
MN 3	'79 $3 Pintails	11.00
MN 4	'80 $3 Canvasbacks	11.00
MN 5	'81 $3 Canada Geese	10.00
MN 6	'82 $3 Redheads	11.00
MN 7	'83 $3 Bl & Snow Geese	11.00
MN 8	'84 $3 Wood Ducks	11.00
MN 9	'85 $3 Wh. Front Geese	9.00
MN 10	'86 $5 Lesser Scaup	10.00
MN 11	'87 $5 Goldeneyes	12.00
MN 11T	'87 $5 Full Tab	14.50
MN 12	'88 $5 Buffleheads	11.00
MN 12T	'88 $5 Full Tab	14.50
MN 13	'89 $5 Amer. Widgeons	11.00
MN 13T	'89 $5 Full Tab	14.50
MN 14	'90 $5 Hooded Mergan	25.00
MN 14T	'90 $5 Full Tab	35.00
MN 15	'91 $5 Ross' Goose	9.00
MN 15T	'91 $5 Full Tab	9.50
MN 16	'92 $5 Barrow's Gold'eye	9.00
MN 16T	'92 $5 Full Tab	9.50
MN 17	'93 $5 Bl. Winged Teal	9.00
MN 17T	'93 $5 Full Tab	9.50
MN 18	'94 $5 Ring Necked Duck	9.00
MN 18T	'94 $5 Full Tab	9.50
MN 19	'95 $5 Gadwalls	9.00
MN 19T	'95 $5 Full Tab	9.50
MN 20	'96 $5 Scaup	9.00
MN 20T	'96 $5 Full Tab	9.50
MN 21	'97 $5 Shoveler w/Decoy	9.00
MN 21T	'97 $5 Full Tab	9.50
MN 22	'98 $5 Harlequin Ducks	9.00
MN 22T	'98 $5 Full Tab	9.50
MN 23	'99 $5 Green Winged Teal	9.00
MN 23T	'99 $5 Full Tab	9.50
MN 24	'00 $5 Mallards	9.00
MN 25	'01 $5 Black Duck	9.00

Minnesota Set 1977-2000 (24). 245.00

Note: Hunting Permit Illustrations can be found at the following website: **www.duck-stamps.com**

MISSISSIPPI

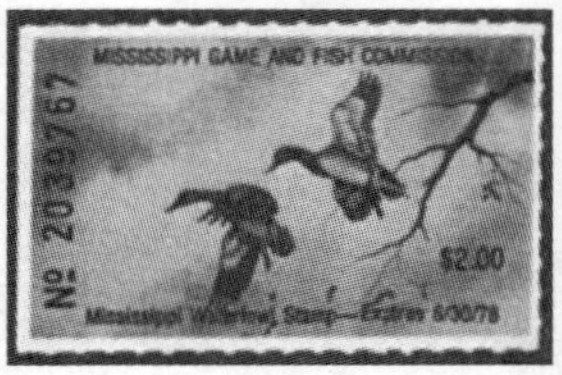

MS 2

No.	Description	F-VF NH
MS 1	'76 $2 Wood Duck	23.00
MS 1B	'76 $2 Full Comput. Card	28.00
MS 2	'77 $2 Mallards	9.00
MS 3	'78 $2 Grn. Winged Teal	9.00
MS 4	'79 $2 Canvasbacks	9.00
MS 5	'80 $2 Pintails	9.00
MS 6	'81 $2 Redheads	9.00
MS 7	'82 $2 Canada Geese	8.00
MS 7A	'82 $2 Canada Geese	9.00
MS 8	'83 $2 Lesser Scaup	9.00
MS 9	'84 $2 Black Ducks	9.00
MS 10	'85 $2 Mallards	9.00
MS 10A	'85 Serial # Error-No Hz#	165.00
MS 10B	'85 Serial # Var.- No Silver Bar	600.00
MS 11	'86 $2 Widgeon	9.00
MS 12	'87 $2 Ring Neck Ducks	9.00
MS 13	'88 $2 Snow Geese	9.00
MS 14	'89 $2 Wood Ducks	6.50
MS 15	'90 $2 Snow Geese	14.00
MS 16	'91 $2 Blk. Lab/ Canvasbk Decoy	6.50
MS 17	'92 $2 Grn. Winged Teal	5.00
MS 18	'93 $5 Mallards	8.00
MS 19	'94 $5 Canvasbacks	8.00
MS 20	'95 $5 Blue Winged Teal	8.00
MS 21	'96 $5 Hooded Merganser	8.00
MS 22	'97 $5 Wood Duck	9.00
MS 23	'98 $5 Pin Tails	9.00
MS 24	'99 $5 Ring necked Duck	9.00
MS 25	'00 $5 Mallards	9.00
MS26	'01 $10 Gadwall	14.00

Mississippi Set 1976-2000 (25) 220.00

NOTE: Governor's stamps available upon request.

MISSOURI

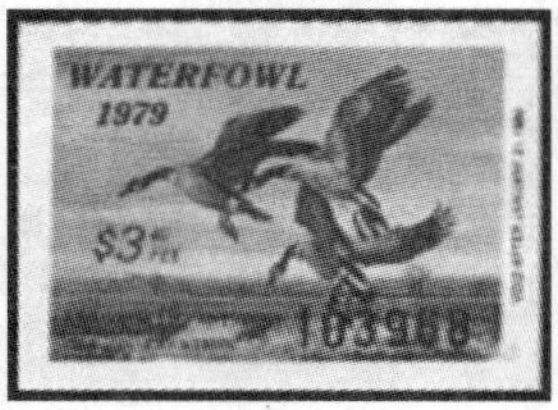

MO 1

No.	Description	F-VF NH
MO 1	'79 $3.40 Canada Geese	695.00
MO 1T	'79 $3.40 Full Tab Attd	895.00
MO 2	'80 $3.40 Wood Ducks	120.00
MO 2T	'80 $3.40 Full Tab Attd	145.00
MO 3	'81 $3 Lesser Scaup	65.00
MO 3T	'81 $3 Full Tab Attd	80.00
MO 4	'82 $3 Buffleheads	60.00
MO 4T	'82 $3 Full Tab Attd	75.00
MO 5	'83 $3 Bl. Wngd. Teal	50.00
MO 5T	'83 $3 Full Tab Attd	60.00
MO 6	'84 $3 Mallards	40.00
MO 6T	'84 $3 Full Tab Attd	60.00
MO 7	'85 $3 Widgeon	25.00
MO 7T	'85 $3 Full Tab Attd	25.00
MO 8	'86 $3 Hooded Mergans	15.00
MO 8T	'86 $3 Full Tab Attd	18.00
MO 9	'87 $3 Pintails	12.00
MO 9T	'87 $3 Full Tab Attd	15 00
MO 10	'88 $3 Canvasbacks	11.00
MO 10T	'88 $3 Full Tab Attd	12.00
MO 11	'89 $3 Ring Neck Ducks	8.50
MO 11T	'89 $3 Full Tab Attd	9.50
MO 12	'90 $3 Redheads	8.00
MO 12T	'90 $3 Full Tab Attd	10.00
MO 13	'91 $5 Snow Geese	8.00
MO 13T	'91 $5 Full Tab Attd	11.00
MO 14	'92 $5 Gadwalls	8.00
MO 14T	'92 $5 Full Tab Attd	11.00
MO 15	'93 $5 Grn. Winged Teal	8.00
MO 15T	'93 $5 Full Tab Attd	10.00
MO 16	'94 $5 Wh Fronted Geese	8.00
MO 16T	'94 $5 Full Tab Attd	9.00
MO 17	'95 $5 Goldeneyes	10.00
MO 17T	'95 $5 Full Tab Attached	11.00
MO 18	'96 $5 Black Duck	10.00

Missouri Set 1979-96 (18) 1100.00

Missouri Tab Set 1979-95 (17) 1450.00

NOTE: Governor's stamps available upon request.

STATE HUNTING PERMIT STAMPS

MONTANA

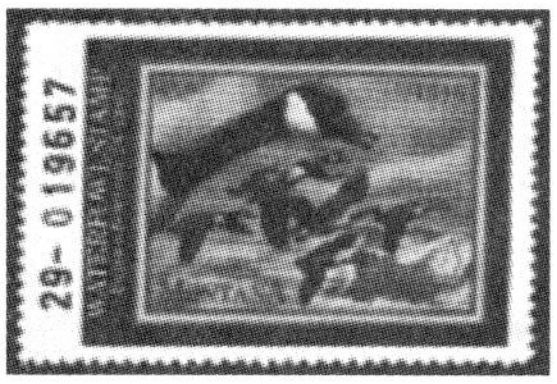

MT 1

No.	Description	F-VF NH
MT 1	'86 $5 Canada Geese	13.00
MT 1A	'86 $5 Horiz. Pair w/ Side Margins	2800.00
MT 2	'87 $5 Redheads	17.00
MT 2A	'87 $5 Hz.Pr./side mgns	35.00
MT 3	'88 $5 Mallards	14.00
MT 3A	'88 $5 Hz.Pr./side mgns	25.00
MT 4	'89 $5 Blk. Lab & Pintail	1.00
MT 4A	'89 $5 Hz.Pr./side mgns	34.00
MT 5	'90 $5 Cinn & Bl.Wng.Teal	8.50
MT 5A	'90 $5 Hz.Pr./side mgns	22.00
MT 6	'91 $5 Snow Geese	8.50
MT 6A	'91 $5 Hz.Pr./side mgns	23.00
MT 7	'92 $5 Wood Ducks	8.50
MT 7A	'92 $5 Hz.Pr./side mgns	23.00
MT 8	'93 $5 Harlequin	8.50
MT 8A	'93 $5 Hz.Pr./side mgns	23.00
MT 9	'94 $5 Widgeon	8.50
MT 9A	'94 $5 Hz.Pr./side mgns.	23.00
MT 10	'95 $5 Tundra Swans ...	8.50
MT 10A	'95 $5 Hor.Pr/side mgns.	23.00
MT 11	'96 $5 Canvasbacks ...	8.50
MT 11A	'96 $5 Hor.Pr./side Mgns	23.00
MT 12	'97 $5 Golden Retriever	10.00
MT 12A	'97 $5 Horz.Pr./side Mgns	23.00
MT 13	'98 $5 Gadwalls	8.50
MT 13A	'98 $5 Horz. Pr./side Mgns	18.00
MT 14	'99 $5 Goldeneyes	8.50
MT 14A	'99 $5 Hoz.Pr./side Mgns	18.00
MT 15	'00 $5 Mallard Decoy ...	8.50
MT 15A	'00 $5 Hor.Pr./side Mgns.	18.00
MT 16	'01 $5 Canada Geese/ Steamboat	8.50

Montana Set 1986-2000 (15) 131.00

NOTE: Governor's stamps available upon request.

NEBRASKA

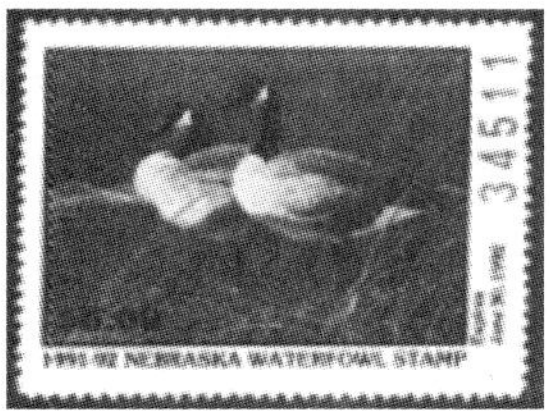

NE 1

No.	Description	F-VF NH
NE 1	'91 $6 Canada Goose ..	11.00
NE 2	'92 $6 Pintails	10.00
NE 3	'93 $6 Canvasbacks	10.00
NE 4	'94 $6 Mallard	10.00
NE 5	'95 $6 Wood Ducks	10.00

Nebraska Set 1991-95 (5) 49.00

NOTE: Governor's stamps available upon request.

NEVADA

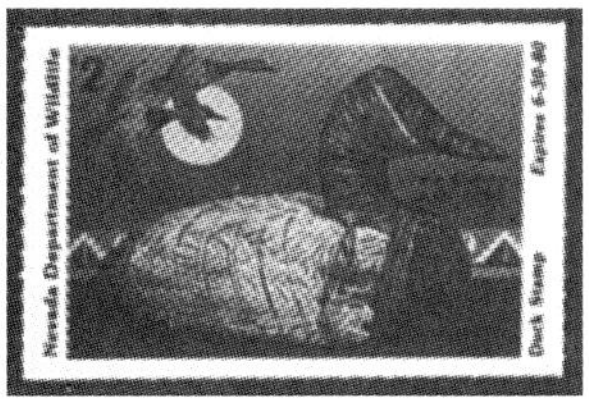

NV1

No.	Description	F-VF NH
NV1	'79 $2 Canvasbks/Decoy	45.00
NV 1T	'79 $2 Serial # Tab Attd	55.00
NV 2	'80 $2 Cinnamon Teal ...	8.00
NV 2T	'80 $2 Serial # Tab Attd	9.00
NV 3	'81 $2 Whistling Swans	10.00
NV 3T	'81 $2 Serial # Tab Attd	12.00
NV 4	'82 $2 Shovelers	10.00
NV 4T	'82 $2 Serial # Tab Attd	12.00
NV 5	'83 $2 Gadwalls	12.00
NV 5T	'83 $2 Serial # Tab Attd	14.00
NV 6	'84 $2 Pintails	12.00
NV 6T	'84 $2 Serial # Tab Attd	14.00
NV 7	'85 $2 Canada Geese ..	17.00
NV 7T	'85 $2 Serial # Tab Attd	19.00
NV 8	'86 $2 Redheads	15.00
NV 8T	'86 $2 Serial # Tab Attd	16.00

NEVADA (cont.)

No.	Description	F-VF NH
NV 9	'87 $2 Buffleheads	12.00
NV 9T	'87 $2 Serial # Tab Attd	14.00
NV 10	'88 $2 Canvasback	12.00
NV 10T	'88 $2 Serial # Tab Attd	14.00
NV 11	'89 $2 Ross' Geese	8.00
NV 11T	'89 $2 Serial # Tab Attd	11.00
NV 11A	'89 Hunter Tab #50,001-75,000	21.00
NV 12	'90 $5 Grn. Winged Teal	9.00
NV 12T	'90 $5 Serial # Tab Attd	12.00
NV 12A	'90 Hunter Tab #50,001-75,000	16.00
NV 13	'91 $5 Wh. Faced Ibis ..	19.00
NV 13T	'91 $5 Serial # Tab Attd	12.00
NV 13A	'91 Hunter Tab #50,001-75,000	13.00
NV 14	'92 $5 Amer. Widgeon .	8.50
NV 14T	'92 $5 Serial # Tab Attd	9.00
NV 14A	'92 Hunter Tab #50,001-75,000	12.00
NV 15	'93 $5 Com'n Goldeneye	8.50
NV 15T	'93 $5 Serial # Tab Attd	9.00
NV 15A	'93 Hunter Tab #50,001-75,000	9.00
NV 16	'94 $5 Mallard	8.50
NV 16T	'94 $5 Serial # Tab Attd	9.00
NV 16A	'94 Hunter Tab #50,001-75,000	9.00
NV 17	'95 $5 Wood Ducks	8.50
NV 17T	'95 $5 Serial # Tab Attd.	9.00
NV17A	'95 Hunter Tab #50,001-75,000	9.00
NV 18	'96 $5 Ring Necked Duck	8.50
NV 18T	'96 $5 Serial # Tab Attd.	9.00
NV 18A	'96 Hunter Tab #50,001-75,000	9.00
NV 19	'97 $5 Ruddy Duck	8.50
NV 19T	'97 $5 Serial # Tab Attd.	9.00
NV 19A	'97 Hunter Tab #50,001-75,000	9.00
NV 20	'98 $5 Hooded Merganser	8.50
NV 20T	'98 Serial # Tab Attd.	9.00
NV 20A	'98 Hunter Tab	9.00
NV 21	'99 $5 Tule Decoy	8.50
NV 21T	'99 Serial # Tab Attd.	9.00
NV 21A	'99 Hunter Tab #40,001-75,000	9.00
NV 22	'00 $5 Canvasback	8.50
NV 22T	'00 Serial # Tab Attd.	9.00
NV 22A	'00 Hunter Tab #40,001-75,000	9.00
NV 23	'01 $5	8.50
NV 23T	'01 Serial # Tab Attd.	9.00
NV23A	'01 Hunter Tab #40,001-75,000	9.00

Nevada Set 1979-2000 (22) 240.00
Nevada Tab Set 1979-2000 (22) 270.00

NEW HAMPSHIRE

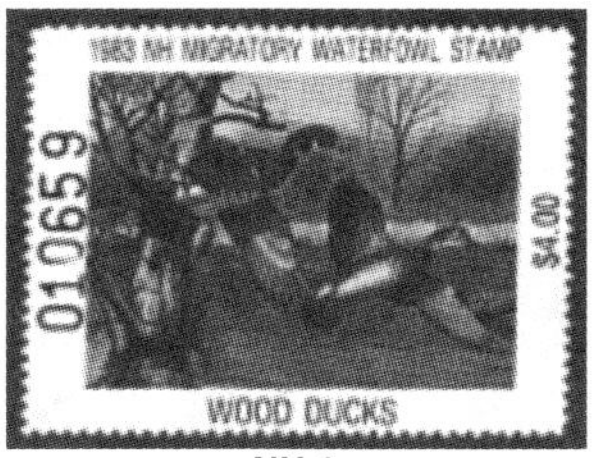

NH 1

No.	Description	F-VF NH
NH 1	'83 $4 Wood Ducks	150.00
NH 1A	'83 3 Part Bklt. Type	150.00
NH 2	'84 $4 Mallards	105.00
NH 2A	'84 3 Part Bklt. Type	200.00
NH 3	'85 $4 Bl. Wngd. Teal ...	110.00
NH 3A	'85 3 Part Bklt. Type	110.00
NH 4	'86 $4 Mergansers	25.00
NH 4A	'86 3 Part Bklt. Type	30.00
NH 5	'87 $4 Canada Geese ..	15.00
NH 5A	'87 3 Part Bklt. Type ...	14.00
NH 6	'88 $4 Buffleheads	8.50
NH 6A	'88 3 Part Bklt. Type ...	12.00
NH 7	'89 $4 Black Ducks	8.50
NH 7A	'89 3 Part Bklt. Type ...	12.00
NH 8	'90 $4 Grn. Winged Teal	8.00
NH 8A	'90 3 Part Bklt. Type ...	9.00
NH 9	'91 $4 Gldn Retr/Mallard	12.00
NH 9A	'91 3 Part Bklt. Type ...	15.00
NH 10	'92 $4 Ring Neck Ducks	8.00
NH 10A	'92 3 Part Bklt. Type ...	9.00
NH 11	'93 $4 Hooded Mergans	8.00
NH 11A	'93 3 Part Bklt. Type ...	8.00
NH 12	'94 $4 Common Gldneyes	8.00
NH 12A	'94 3 Part Bklt. Type ...	8.00
NH 13	'95 $4 Pintails	8.00
NH 13A	'95 3 Part Bklt. Type ...	8.00
NH 14	'96 $4 Surf Scoters	8.00
NH 14A	'96 3 Part Booklet Type	8.00
NH 15	'97 $4 Old Squaws	8.00
NH 15A	'97 $4 -3 Part Booklet Type	8.00
NH 16	'98 $4 Canada Goose .	8.00
NH 16A	'98 $4 3 Part Booklet Type	8.00

NEW HAMPSHIRE (cont.)

No.	Description	F-VF NH
NH 17	'99 $4 Mallards	8.00
NH 17A	'99 $4 3 Part Booklet Type	8.00
NH 18	'00 $4 Black Ducks	8.00
NH 18A	'00 $4 3 Part Booklet Type	8.00
NH 19	'01 $4	8.00
NH 19A	'01 $4 3 Part Booklet Type	8.00

New Hampshire Set 1983-2000 (18) 480.00
NH Bklt. Type Set '83-'2000 (16) 599.00

NOTE: Governor's stamps available upon request.

NEW JERSEY

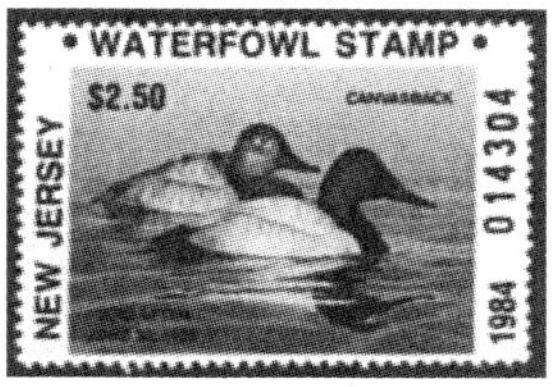

NJ 1

No.	Description	F-VF NH
NJ 1	'84 $2.50 Canvasbacks	50.00
NJ 1A	'84 $5.00 Non-Resident	60.00
NJ 1B	'84 $2.50 Hunter Bklt. Sgl	65.00
NJ 2	'85 $2.50 Mallards	15.00
NJ 2A	'85 $5.00 Non-Resident	20.00
NJ 2B	'85 $2.50 Hunter Bklt. Sgl	30.00
NJ 3	'86 $2.50 Pintails	12.00
NJ 3A	'86 $5.00 Non-Resident	15.00
NJ 3B	'86 $2.50 Hunter Bklt. Sgl	12.00
NJ 4	'87 $2.50 Canada Geese	15.00
NJ 4A	'87 $5.00 Non-Resident	15.00
NJ 4B	'87 $2.50 Hunter Bklt. Sgl	12.00
NJ 4AB	'87 $5.00 Hunter Bklt. Sgl	12.00
NJ 5	'88 $2.50 Grn.Winged Teal	8.50
NJ 5A	'88 $5.00 Non-Resident	10.00
NJ 5B	'88 $2.50 Hunter Bklt. Sgl	10.00
NJ 5AB	'88 $5.00 Hunter Bklt. Sgl	12.00
NJ 6	'89 $2.50 Snow Geese	6.00
NJ 6A	'89 $5.00 Non-Resident	10.00
NJ 6B	'89 $2.50 Hunter Bklt. Sgl	7.00
NJ 6AB	'89 $5.00 Hunter Bklt. Sgl	10.00
NJ 7	'90 $2.50 Wood Ducks	6.00
NJ 7A	'90 $5.00 Non-Resident	9.50
NJ 7B	'90 $2.50 Hunter Bklt. Sgl	6.00
NJ 7AB	'90 $5.00 Hunter Bklt. Sgl	10.00
NJ 8	'91 $2.50 Atlantic "Brandt"	6.00
NJ 8A	'91 $5.00 Non-Resident	9.50
NJ 8B	'91 $2.50 Hunter Bklt. Sgl	6.00
NJ 8AB	'91 $5.00 Hunter Bklt. Sgl	10.00
NJ 8AV	'91 $5.00 Atlantic"Brandt"	35.00
NJ 8V	'91 $2.50 Atlantic"Brandt"	22.00
NJ 9	'92 $2.50 Bluebills	6.00
NJ 9A	'92 $5.00 Non-Resident	8.50
NJ 9B	'92 $2.50 Hunter Bklt. Sgl	6.00
NJ 9AB	'92 $5.00 Hunter Bklt. Sgl	10.00
NJ 10	'93 $2.50 Buffleheads .	6.00
NJ 10A	'93 $5.00 Non-Resident	8.50
NJ 10B	'93 $2.50 Hunter Bklt. Sgl	6.00
NJ 10AB	'93 $5.00 Hunter Bklt. Sgl	10.00
NJ 11	'94 $2.50 Black Ducks	6.00
NJ 11A	'94 $5.00 Black Ducks	8.00
NJ 11B	'94 $2.50 Hunter Bklt. Sgl	6.00
NJ 11AB	'94 $5.00 Hunter Bklt. Sgl	10.00
NJ 12	'95 $2.50 Widgeon	6.00
NJ 12A	'95 $5 Widgeon	8.00
NJ 12B	'95 $2.50 Hunter Bklt. Sgl.	6.00
NJ 12AB	'95 $5 Hunter Bklt. Sgl.	10.00
NJ 13	'96 $2.50 Goldeneyes .	8.00
NJ 13A	'96 $5 Goldeneyes	15.00
NJ 13B	'96 $2.50 Hunter Bklt.Sgl.	10.00
NJ 13AB	'96 $5 Hunter Bklt.Single.	15.00
NJ 13C	'96 $2.50 Goldeneyes .	7.00
NJ 14	'97 $5 Old Squaws	8.50
NJ 14A	'97 $10 Old Squaws	15.00
NJ 14B	'97 $5 Hunter Bklt Single	8.50
NJ 14AB	'97 $10 HunterBklt Single	15.00
NJ 15	'98 $5 Mallards	8.50
NJ 15A	'98 $10 Mallards	15.00
NJ 15B	'98 $5 Hunter Bklt Single	8.50
NJ 15AB	'98 $10 Hunter Bklt Single	15.00
NJ 16	'99 $5 Redheads	8.50
NJ 16A	'99 $10 Redheads Non-res.	15.00
NJ 16B	'99 $5 Hunter Bklt.Single	8.50
NJ 16AB	'99 $10 Hunter Bklt.Single	15.00
NJ 17	'00 $5 Canvasbacks	8.50
NJ 17A	'00 $10 Canvasbacks NR	15.00
NJ 17B	'00 $5 Hunter Bklt.Single	8.50
NJ 17AB	'00 $10 Hunter Bklt.Single	15.00
NJ 18	'01 $5 Tundra Swans	8.00
NJ 18A	'01 $10 Tundra Swans NR	15.00
NJ 18B	'01 $5 Hunter Bklt.Single	8.00
NJ 18AB	'01 $10 Hunter Bklt.Sing.	15.00

New Jersey Set 1984-2000 (35) 400.00
NJ Bklt. Type Set '84-2000 (31) 370.00

NOTE: Governor's stamps available upon request.

NEW MEXICO

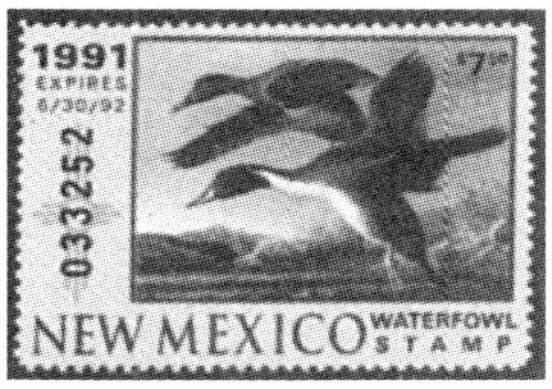

NM 1

No.	Description	F-VF NH
NM 1	'91 $7.50 Pintails	11.00
NM 1A	'91 $7.50 Booklet sgl ...	12.00
NM 2	'92 $7.50 Amer. Widgeon	11.00
NNM 2A	'92 $7.50 Booklet sgl ...	12.00
NM 3	'93 $7.50 Mallards	11.00
NM 3A	'93 $7.50 Booklet sgl ...	12.00
NM 3M	'93 Commem. Sheet of 4	60.00
NM 3MI	'93 Imperf. Commem. Sheet of 4	85.00
NM 4	'94 $7.50 Grn.Wngd.Teal	15.00
NM 4A	'94 $7.50 Booklet sgl ...	16.00
NM 4A	'94 Strip of 4 diff. attd .	64.00
NM 4M	'94 Commem. Sheet of 4	95.00
NM 4MI	'94 Imperf. Commem. Sheet of 4	200.00

New Mexico Set 1991-94 (7) ... 89.00
N.M. Hunter Set 1991-94 (7) 99.00

NOTE: Governor's stamps available upon request.

NEW YORK

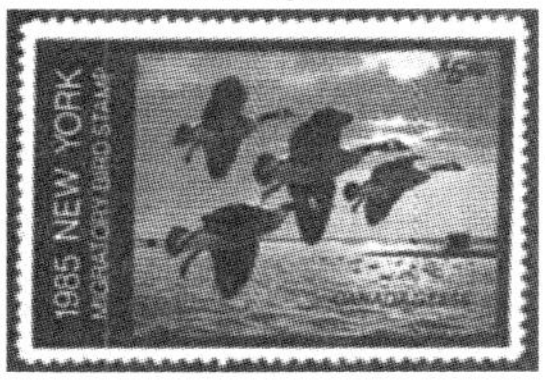

NY 1

No.	Description	F-VF NH
NY 1	'85 $5.50 Canada Geese	15.00
NY 2	'86 $5.50 Mallards	10.00
NY 3	'87 $5.50 Wood Ducks	9.00
NY 4	'88 $5.50 Pintails	9.00
NY 5	'89 $5.50 Greater Scaup	9.00
NY 6	'90 $5.50 Canvasbacks	9.00
NY 7	'91 $5.50 Redheads	9.00
NY 8	'92 $5.50 Wood Duck ..	9.00
NY 9	'93 $5.50 Bl. Wngd. Teal	9.00
NY 10	'94 $5.50 Canada Geese	9.00
NY 11	'95 $5.50 Canada Geese	9.00
NY 12	'96 $5.50 Common Loon	9.00
NY 13	'97 $5.50 Hood.Merganser	9.00
NY 14	'98 $5.50 Osprey	9.00
NY 15	'99 $5.50 Buffleheads .	9.00
NY 16	'00 $5.50 Wood Duck ..	9.00
NY 17	'01 $5.50 Pintails	9.00

New York Set 1985-2000(16) 131.00

NORTH CAROLINA

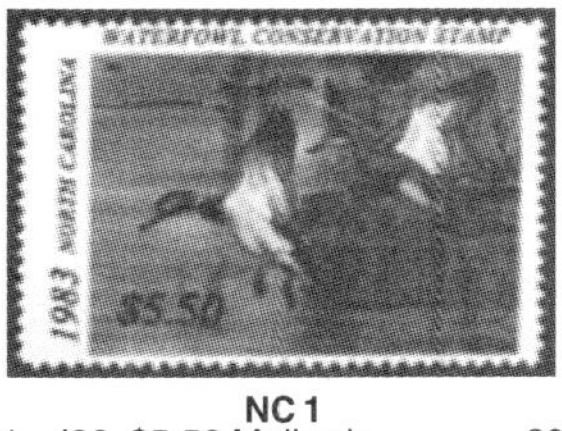

NC 1

No.	Description	F-VF NH
NC 1	'83 $5.50 Mallards	80.00
NC 2	'84 $5.50 Wood Ducks	55.00
NC 3	'85 $5.50 Canvasbacks ...	25.00
NC 4	'86 $5.50 Canada Geese .	18.00
NC 5	'87 $5.50 Pintails	15.00
NC 6	'88 $5 Grn. Winged Teal ...	10.00
NC 7	'89 $5 Snow Geese	10.00
NC 8	'90 $5 Redheads	10.00
NC 9	'91 $5 Bl. Wngd. Teal	10.00
NC 10	'92 $5 Amer. Widgeon	13.00
NC 11	'93 $5 Tundra Swan	10.00
NC 12	'94 $5 Buffleheads	10.00
NC 13	'95 $5 Brant	10.50
NC 14	'96 $5 Pintails	8.50
NC 15	'97 $5 Wood Ducks	8.50
NC 15B	'97 $5 Self Adhesive	20.00
NC 16	'98 $5 Canada Geese	8.50
NC 16B	'98 $5 Self Adhesive	10.00
NC 17	'99 $5 Green Winged Teal	8.50
NC 17B	'99 $5 Self Adhesive	10.00
NC 18	'00 $10 Canvasbacks	15.00
NC 18B	'00 $10 Self Ahhesive	15.00
NC 19	'01 $10 Black Duck/Lighths.	15.00
NC 19B	'01 $10 Self-Adhesive	15.00

North Carolina Set '83-'00 (18) 290.00

STATE HUNTING PERMIT STAMPS

NORTH DAKOTA

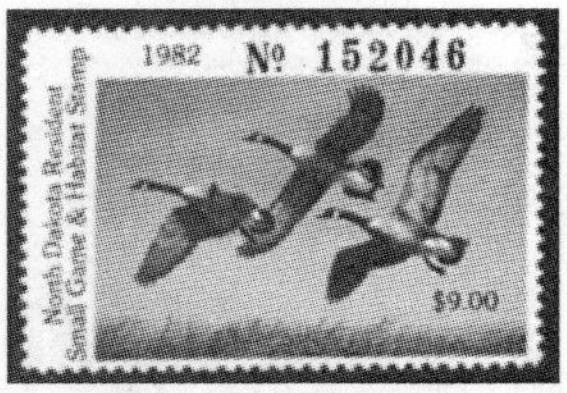

ND 1

North Dakota Hunter Stamps have the following serial #'s:
1982-86 #20,001-150,000
1987-95 #20,001-140,000

No.	Description	F-VF NH
ND 1	'82 $9 Canada Geese	140.00
ND 1A	'82 $9 Hunter Type with Selvedge	1750.00
ND 2	'83 $9 Mallards	75.00
ND 2A	'83 $9 Hunter Type with Selvedge	3000.00
ND 3	'84 $9 Canvasbacks	35.00
ND 3A	'84 $9 Hunter Type	3000.00
ND 4	'85 $9 Blue Bills	24.00
ND 4A	'85 $9 Hunter Type	4000.00
ND 5	'86 $9 Pintails	20.00
ND 5A	'86 $9 Hunter Type	900.00
ND 6	'87 $9 Snow Geese	20.00
ND 6A	'87 $9 Hunter Type	60.00
ND 7	'88 $9 Wh.Wngd.Scooter	15.00
ND 7A	'88 $9 Hunter Type	35.00
ND 8	'89 $6 Redheads	12.00
ND 8A	'89 $6 Hunter Type	17.00
ND 9	'90 $6 Blk Labs/Mallards	12.00
ND 9A	'90 $6 Hunter Type	17.00
ND 10	'91 $6 Grn. Winged Teal	11.00
ND 10A	'91 $6 Hunter Type	14.50
ND 11	'92 $6 Bl. Winged Teal	9.00
ND 11A	'92 $6 Hunter Type	14.00
ND 12	'93 $6 Wood Ducks	9.00
ND 12A	'93 $6 Hunter Type	11.00
ND 13	'94 $6 Canada Geese	9.00
ND 13A	'94 $6 Hunter Type	12.00
ND 14	'95 $6 Widgeon	9.00
ND 14A	'95 $6 Hunter Type	12.00
ND 15	'96 $6 Mallards	9.00
ND 15A	'96 $6 Hunter Type	12.00
ND 16	'97 $6 White Frnted Geese	9.00
ND 16A	'97 $6 Hunter Type	12.00
ND 17	'98 $6 Blue Winged Teal	9.00
ND 17A	'98 $6 Hunter Type	12.00
ND 18	'99 $6 Gadwall	9.00
ND 18A	'99 $6 Hunter Type	12.00
ND 19	'00 $6 Pintails	9.00
ND 19A	'00 $6 Hunter Type	12.00
ND 20	'01 $6 Canada Geese	9.00
ND 20A	'01 $6 Hunter Type	12.00

North Dakota Set 1982-2000(19) 416.00

OHIO

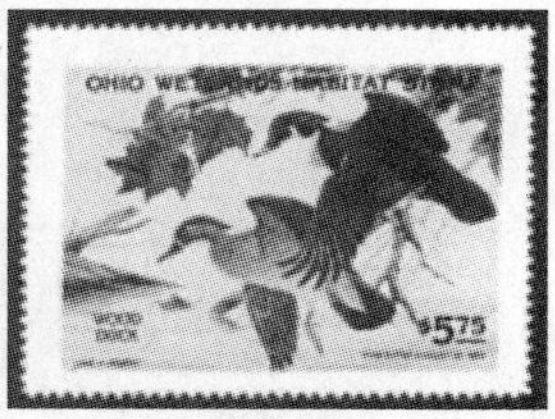

OH 1

No.	Description	F-VF NH
OH 1	'82 $5.75 Wood Ducks	75.00
OH 2	'83 $5.75 Mallards	75.00
OH 3	'84 $5.75 Grn.Winged Teal	75.00
OH 4	'85 $5.75 Redheads	35.00
OH 5	'86 $5.75 Canvasbacks	30.00
OH 6	'87 $5.75 Bl.Winged Teal	12.00
OH 7	'88 $5.75 Goldeneyes	12.00
OH 8	'89 $5.75 Canada Geese	12.00
OH 9	'90 $9 Black Ducks	14.00
OH 10	'91 $9 Lesser Scaup	14.00
OH 11	'92 $9 Wood Ducks	13.00
OH 12	'93 $9 Buffleheads	13.00
OH 13	'94 $11 Mallard	16.00
OH 14	'95 $11 Pintails	16.00
OH 15	'96 $11 Hooded Merganser	16.00
OH 16	'97 $11 Widgeons	16.00
OH 17	'98 $11 Gadwall	16.00
OH 18	'99 $11 Mallard Hen	16.00
OH 19	'00 $11 Buffleheads	16.00
OH 20	'01 $11 Canvas back	16.00

Ohio Set 1982-99 (18) 462.00

Note: Hunting Permit Illustrations can be found at the following website:
www.duck-stamps.com

OKLAHOMA

OK 1

No.	Description	F-VF NH
OK 1	'80 $4 Pintails	70.00
OK 2	'81 $4 Canada Goose	25.00
OK 3	'82 $4 Grn.Wngd.Teal	10.00
OK 4	'83 $4 Wood Ducks	10.00
OK 5	'84 $4 Ring Neck Ducks	9.00
OK 5T	'84 $4 Same, with Tab	10.00
OK 6	'85 $4 Mallards	7.50
OK 6T	'85 $4 Full Tab Attd	9.00
OK 7	'86 $4 Snow Geese	7.50
OK 7T	'86 $4 Full Tab Attd	9.00
OK 8	'87 $4 Canvasbacks	7.50
OK 8T	'87 $4 Full Tab Attd	9.00
OK 9	'88 $4 Widgeons	7.50
OK 9T	'88 $4 Full Tab Attd	9.00
OK 9TV	'88 $4 Full Tab Attd. Serial #>30,000	18.00
OK 10	'89 $4 Redheads	7.50
OK 10A	'89 $4 Hunter Ty., w/Tab	9.00
OK 11	'90 $4 Hood'd Mergans'r	7.50
OK 11A	'90 $4 Hunter Ty., w/Tab	9.00
OK 12	'91 $4 Gadwalls	7.50
OK 12A	'91 $4 Hunter Ty., w/Tab	9.00
OK 13	'92 $4 Lesser Scaup	7.00
OK 13A	'92 $4 Hunter Ty.,w/ Tab	9.00
OK 14	'93 $4 Wh. Frnt'd Geese	7.00
OK 14A	'93 $4 Hunter Ty.,w/ Tab	8.00
OK 15	'94 $4 Widgeon	7.00
OK 15A	'94 $4 Hunter Ty.,w/ Tab	7.00
OK 16	'95 $4 Ruddy Ducks	7.00
OK 16A	'95 $4 Hunter Ty.,w/ Tab	7.00
OK 17	'96 $4 Buffleheads	7.00
OK 17A	'96 $4 Hunter Type w/Tab	7.00
OK 18	'97 $4 Goldeneyes	7.00
OK 18A	'97 $4 Hunter Type w/Tab	7.00
OK 19	'98 $4 Shoveler	7.00
OK 20	'99 $4 Canvasbacks	7.00
OK 21	'00 $4 Pintail	7.00
OK 22	'01 $4 Canada Goose	7.00

Oklahoma Set 1980-2000 (21). 214.00
NOTE: Governor's stamps available upon request.

OREGON

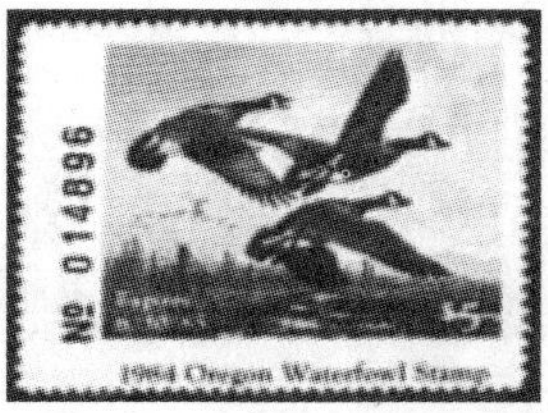

OR 1

No.	Description	F-VF NH
OR 1	'84 $5 Canada Geese	30.00
OR 2	'85 $5 Snow Geese	42.00
OR 2A	'85 $5 Hunter Ty. w/Tab	675.00
OR 2A	'85 $5 Same, w/o Tab	105.00
OR 3	'86 $5 Pacific Brant	15.00
OR 3A	'86 $5 Hunter Ty. w/Tab	20.00
OR 3A	'86 $5 Same, w/o Tab	11.00
OR 4	'87 $5 Wh. Frnt'd Geese	10.00
OR 4A	'87 $5 Hunter Ty. w/Tab	14.00
OR 4A	'87 $5 Same, w/o Tab	10.00
OR 5	'88 $5 Grt. Basin Geese	10.00
OR 5A	'88 $5 Hunter Ty (89X197mm)	17.00
OR 6	'89 $5 Blk. Lab/Pintail	10.00
OR 6A	'89 $5 Hunter Ty (89X197mm)	14.00
OR 6VB	'89 $5 Provisional Issue, Black Serial #	30.00
OR 6VR	'89 $5 Provisional Issue, Red Serial #	12.50
OR 7	'90 $5 Gldn. Retr/Mallard	12.00
OR 7A	'90 $5 Hunter Ty (89X197mm)	12.00
OR 8	'91 $5 Ch'pk Bay Retrvr	10.00
OR 8A	'91 $5 Hunter Ty. w/Tab	12.00
OR 9	'92 $5 Grn. Winged Teal	10.00
OR 9A	'92 $5 Hunter Ty(216X152mm)	11.00
OR 10	'93 $5 Mallards	10.00
OR 10A	'93 $5 Hunter Type	12.00
OR 10M	'93 Mini. Sheet of 2	25.00
OR 10MI	'93 Same, Imperf.	180.00
OR 11	'94 $5 Pintails	10.00
OR 11A	'94 $5 Hunter Ty(216X152mm)	12.00
OR 11AN	'94 $25 Hunter Type	50.00

OREGON(cont.)

No.	Description	F-VF NH
OR 12	'95 $5 Wood Ducks	11.00
OR 12A	'95 $5 Hunter Type	12.00
OR 12AN	'95 $25 Hunter Booklet	60.00
OR 13	'96 $5 Mallard/Widgeon/ Pintail	11.00
OR 13A	'96 $5 Hunter Booklet	12.00
OR 13AN	'96 $25 NR Hunter Bklt	60.00
OR 14	'97 $5 Canvasbacks	11.00
OR 14A	'97 $5 Hunter Booklet	12.00
OR 14AN	'97 $25 NR Hunter Bklt	45.00
OR 15	'98 $5 Pintail	11.00
OR 15A	'98 $5 Hunter Booklet	12.00
OR 15AN	'98 $25 NR Hunter Bklt	35.00
OR 16	'99 $5 Canada Geese	11.00
OR 16A	'99 $5 Hunter Booklet	12.00
OR 16AN	'99 $25 NR in booklet	35.00
OR 17	'00 $7.50 Mallard	12.00
OR18	'01 $7.50 Canvasbacks	12.00

Oregon Set 1984-2000 (17) 220.00
NOTE: Governor's stamps available upon request.

PENNSYLVANIA

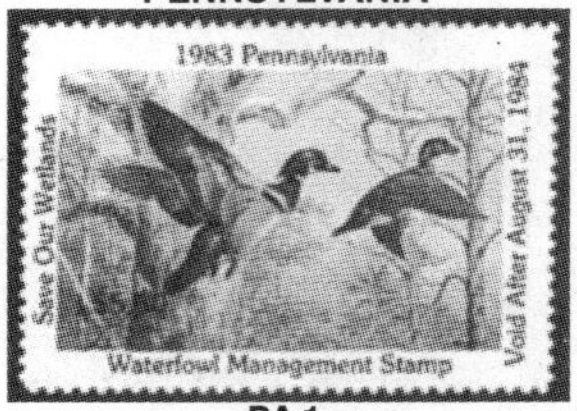

PA 1

No.	Description	F-VF NH
PA 1	'83 $5.50 Wood Ducks	18.00
PA 2	'84 $5.50 Canada Geese	15.00
PA 3	'85 $5.50 Mallards	10.00
PA 4	'86 $5.50 Bl. Winged Teal	10.00
PA 5	'87 $5.50 Pintails	10.00
PA 6	'88 $5.50 Wood Ducks	10.00
PA 7	'89 $5.50 Hood Mergans'r	10.00
PA 8	'90 $5.50 Canvasbacks	9.00
PA 9	'91 $5.50 Widgeon	9.00
PA 10	'92 $5.50 Canada Geese	9.00
PA 11	'93 $5.50 North'n Shovelers	9.00
PA 12	'94 $5.50 Pintails	8.50
PA 13	'95 $5.50 Buffleheads	8.50
PA 14	'96 $5.50 Black Ducks	8.50
PA 15	'97 $5.50 Hood Mergans'r	8.50
PA 16	'98 $5.50 Wood Ducks	8.50
PA 17	'99 $5.50 Ring Necked Duck	8.50
PA 18	'00 $5.50 Green winged Teal	8.50
PA 19	'01 $5.50 Pintails	8.50

Pennsylvania Set '83-2000 (18) 168.00

RHODE ISLAND

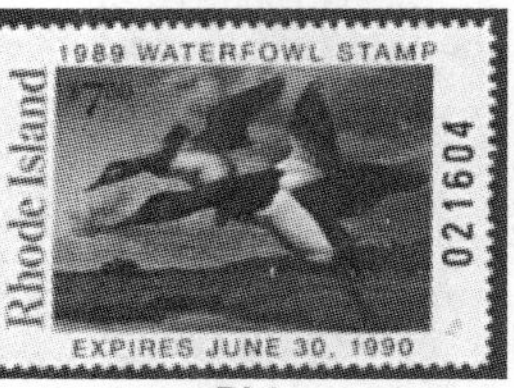

RI 1

No.	Description	F-VF NH
RI 1	'89 $7.50 Canvasbacks	12.00
RI 1A	'89 $7.50 Hunter Type	17.00
RI 2	'90 $7.50 Canada Geese	12.00
RI 2A	'90 $7.50 Hunter Type	15.00
RI 3	'91 $7.50 Blk. Lab/Wd Dks	13.00
RI 3A	'91 $7.50 Hunter Type	14.50
RI 4	'92 $7.50 Bl. Winged Teal	12.00
RI 4A	'92 $7.50 Hunter Type	12.00
RI 5	'93 $7.50 Pintails	11.00
RI 5A	'93 $7.50 Hunter Type	12.00
RI 5M	'93 Commem. Sheet of 4	55.00
RI 5MI	'93 Same, Imperf.	85.00
RI 6	'94 $7.50 Wood Duck	11.00
RI 6A	'94 $7.50 Hunter Type	12.00
RI 7	'95 $7.50 Hooded Mergan.	11.00
RI 7A	'95 $7.50 Hunter Type	12.00
RI 8	'96 $7.50 Harlequin	11.00
RI 8A	'96 $7.50 Hunter Type	12.00
RI 9	'97 $7.50 Greater Scaup	11.00
RI 9A	'97 $7.50 Hunter Type	12.00
RI 10	'98 $7.50 Black Ducks	11.00
RI 10A	'98 $7.50 Hunter Type	12.00
RI 11	'99 $7.50 Common Eider & Lighthouse	11.00
RI 11A	'99 $7.50 Hunter Type	12.00
RI 12	'00 $7.50 Canvasback & Lighthouse	11.00
RI 12A	'00 $7.50 Hunter Type	12.00
RI 13	'01 $7.50	11.00
RI 13A	'01 $7.50 Hunter Type	12.00

Rhode Island Set 1989-2000(12) 128.00
RI Hunter Type Set 1989-00 (12) 140.00
NOTE: Governor's stamps available upon request.

SOUTH CAROLINA

SC 1

No.	Description	F-VF NH
SC 1	'81 $5.50 Wood Ducks	65.00
SC 2	'82 $5.50 Mallards	115.00
SC 2A	'82 Hunter-Ser'l # on Rev	565.00
SC 3	'83 $5.50 Pintails	100.00
SC 3A	'83 Hunter-Ser'l # on Rev	525.00
SC 4	'84 $5.50 Canada Geese	65.00
SC 4A	'84 Hunter-Ser'l # on Rev	230.00
SC 5	'85 $5.50 Grn. Winged Teal	65.00
SC 5A	'85 Hunter Ser'l # on Rev	130.00
SC 6	'86 $5.50 Canvasbacks	25.00
SC 6A	'86 Hunter-Ser'l # on Rev	45.00
SC 7	'87 $5.50 Black Ducks	20.00
SC 7A	'87 Hunter-Ser'l # on Rev	25.00
SC 8	'88 $5.50 Spaniel/Widg'n	20.00
SC 8A	'88 Hunter-Ser'l # on Rev	40.00
SC 9	'89 $5.50 Bl. Wingd. Teal	10.00
SC 9A	'89 Hunter-Ser'l # on Rev	15.00
SC 10	'90 $5.50 Wood Ducks	10.00
SC 10A	'90 Hunter-Ser'l # on Rev	10.00
SC 11	'91 $5.50 Blk. Lab/Pintails	10.00
SC 11A	'91 Hunter-Ser'l # on Rev	9.00
SC 12	'92 $5.50 Buffleheads	12.00
SC 12A	'92 Hunter-Ser'l # on Front	9.00
SC 13	'93 $5.50 Lesser Scaup	12.00
SC 13A	'93 Hunter-Ser'l # on Front	9.00
SC 14	'94 $5.50 Canvasbacks	12.00
SC 14A	'94 Hunter-Ser'l # on Front	9.00
SC 15	'95 $5.50 Shovelers	12.00
SC 15A	'95 Hunter, Serial # on Front	9.00
SC 16	'96 $5.50 Redheads/ Lighthouse	12.00
SC 16A	'96 Hunter-Serial# on Front	9.00
SC 17	'97 $5.50 Old Squaws	12.00
SC 17A	'97 Hunter-Serial# on Front	9.00
SC 18	'98 $5.50 Ruddy Ducks	12.00
SC 18A	'98 Hunter-Serial # on Front	9.00
SC 19	'99 $5.50 Goldeneyes/ Light house	11.00
SC 20	'00 $5.50 Wood Duck/Dog	10.00
SC 21	'01 $5.50 Mallard/Decoy/ Dog	10.00

So. Carolina Set 1981-2000(18) 560.00
SC Hunter Type Set '82-'98 (17) 1560.00
NOTE: Governor's stamps available upon request.

SOUTH DAKOTA

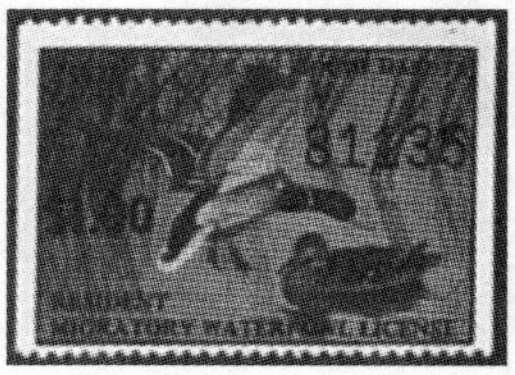

SD 1

No.	Description	F-VF NH
SD 1	'76 $1 Mallards	35.00
SD 1V	'76 Small Serial # Variety	75.00
SD 2	'77 $1 Pintails	24.00
SD 3	'78 $1 Canvasbacks	14.00
SD 4	'86 $2 Canada Geese	10.00
SD 5	'87 $2 Blue Geese	8.00
SD 6	'88 $2 Wh. Fronted Geese	6.00
SD 7	'89 $2 Mallards	6.00
SD 8	'90 $2 Bl. Winged Teal	5.00
SD 9	'91 $2 Pintails	5.00
SD 10	'92 $2 Canvasbacks	5.00
SD 11	'93 $2 Lesser Scaup	5.00
SD 12	'94 $2 Redhead	5.00
SD 13	'95 $2 Wood Ducks	5.00
SD 14	'96 $2 Canada Goose	5.00
SD 15	'97 $2 Widgeons	5.00
SD 16	'98 $2 Green Winged Teal	5.00
SD 17	'99 $3 Tundra Swan	7.00
SD 18	'00 $3 Buffleheads	7.00
SD 19	'01 $3 Mallards	7.00

South Dakota Set 1976-2000(18) 140.00

STATE HUNTING PERMIT STAMPS

TENNESSEE

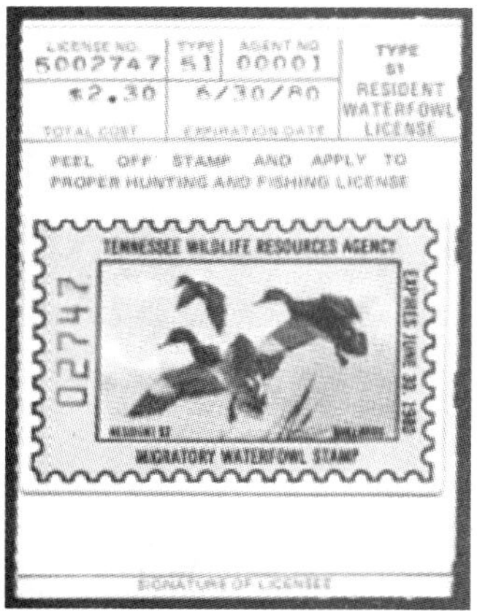

TN 1

No.	Description	F-VF NH
TN 1	'79 $2.30 Mallards	160.00
TN 1A	'79 $5.30 Non-Resident	1050.00
TN 2	'80 $2.30 Canvasbacks	60.00
TN 2A	'80 $5.30 Non-Resident	400.00
TN 2B	'80 $2.30 3 Part Card	925.00
TN 3	'81 $2.30 Wood Ducks	45.00
TN 3B	'81 $2.30 3 Part Card	...
TN 4	'82 $6.50 Canada Geese	60.00
TN 5	'83 $6.50 Pintails	60.00
TN 5B	'83 $6.50 3 Part Card	75.00
TN 6	'84 $6.50 Black Ducks	60.00
TN 6B	'84 $6.50 3 Part Card	75.00
TN 7	'85 $6.50 Bl. Winged Teal	25.00
TN 7B	'85 $6.50 3 Part Card	50.00
TN 8	'86 $6.50 Mallards	15.00
TN 8B	'86 $6.50 3 Part Card	50.00
TN 9	'87 $6.50 Canada Geese	12.00
TN 9B	'87 $6.50 3 Part Card	18.00
TN 10	'88 $6.50 Canvasbacks	14.00
TN 10B	'88 $6.50 3 Part Card	23.00
TN 11	'89 $6.50 Grn Wngd Teal	12.00
TN 11B	'89 $6.50 3 Part Card	14.00
TN 12	'90 $13 Redheads	18.00
TN 12B	'90 $13 3 Part Card	22.00
TN 13	'91 $13 Mergansers	18.00
TN 13B	'91 $13 3 Part Card	22.00
TN 14	'92 $14 Wood Ducks	18.50
TN 14B	'92 $14 3 Part Card	22.00
TN 15	'93 $14 Pintail/Decoy	18.50
TN 15B	'93 $14 3 Part Card	22.00
TN 16	'94 $16 Mallard	21.00
TN 16B	'94 $16 3 Part Card	22.50
TN 17	'95 $16 Ring Nckd Ducks	22.00
TN 17B	'95 $16 3 Part Card	22.50
TN 18	'96 $18 Black Ducks	24.00
TN 18B	'96 $18 3 Part Card	25.00
TN 19	'99 $10 Mallard	15.00
TN 20	'00 $10 Bufflehead	15.00
TN 21	'01 $10 Wood Ducks	15.00
Tennessee Set 1979-2000 (22)		**1995.00**
Tennessee Set 1979-96 (20) w/o Non-Res		**624.00**

TEXAS

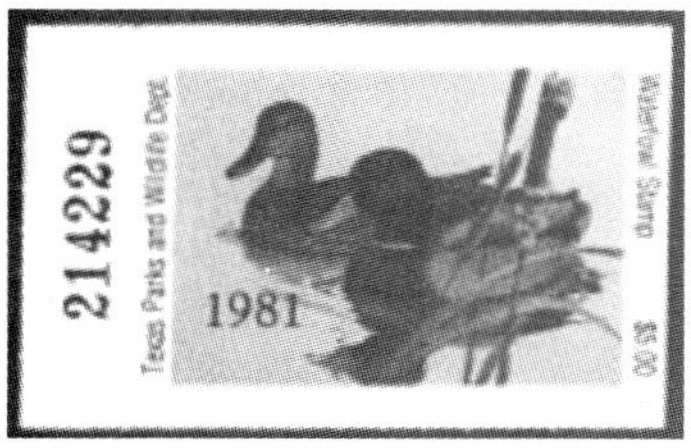

TX 1

No.	Description	F-VF NH
TX 1	'81 $5 Mallards	50.00
TX 2	'82 $5 Pintails	30.00
TX 3	'83 $5 Widgeon	175.00
TX 4	'84 $5 Wood Ducks	30.00
TX 5	'85 $5 Snow Geese	10.00
TX 6	'86 $5 Grn. Winged Teal	10.00
TX 7	'87 $5 Wh. Frnt'd Geese	10.00
TX 8	'88 $5 Pintails	10.00
TX 9	'89 $5 Mallards	10.00
TX 10	'90 $5 Widgeons	10.00
TX 11	'91 $7 Wood Duck	10.00
TX 12	'92 $7 Canada Geese	10.00
TX 13	'93 $7 Bl. Wngd. Teal	10.00
TX 14	'94 $7 Shovelers	10.00
TX 15	'95 $7 Buffleheads	10.00
TX 16	'96 $20 Book of 8 Different	20.00
TX 17	'97 $20 Book of 8 Different	20.00
TX 18	'98 $20 Book of 8 Different	20.00
TX 19	'99 $3 Canvasback in book	20.00
TX 20	'00 $3 Hooded Merganser	20.00
Texas Set 1981-2000 (20)		**460.00**

UTAH

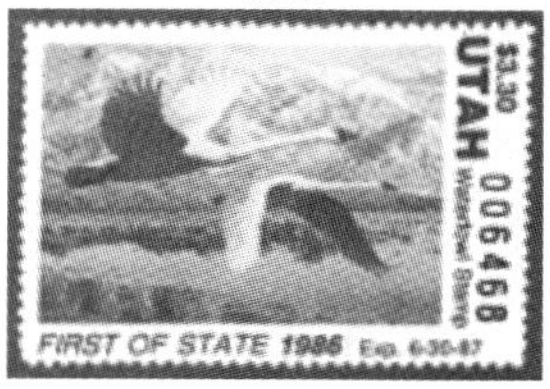

UT 1

No.	Description	F-VF NH
UT 1	'86 $3.30 Whistling Swans	10.00
UT 2	'87 $3.30 Pintails	8.00
UT 3	'88 $3.30 Mallards	8.00
UT 4	'89 $3.30 Canada Geese	7.00
UT 5	'90 $3.30 Canvasbacks	7.00
UT 5A	'90 $3.30 Bklt, sgl. w/Tab	8.00
UT 6	'91 $3.30 Tundra Swans	6.50
UT 6A	'91 $3.30 Bklt. sgl w/Tab	7.00
UT 7	'92 $3.30 Pintails	6.50
UT 7A	'92 $3.30 Bklt. sgl w/Tab	7.00
UT 8	'93 $3.30 Canvasbacks	6.50
UT 8A	'93 $3.30 Bklt. sgl w/Tab	7.00
UT 9	'94 $3.30 Chesepeake	65.00
UT 9A	'94 $3.30 Bklt. sgl. w/Tab	60.00
UT10	'95 $3.30 Grn Winged Teal	6.50
UT 10A	'95 $3.30 Bklt. Sgl. w/Tab	7.00
UT 11	'96 $7.50 Wh.FrontedGoose	13.00
UT 12	'97 $7.50 Redheads PR(2)	30.00
Utah Set 1986-97 (13)		**170.00**
Utah Set Bklt. Sgl. 1990-95 (6)		**91.00**

NOTE: Governor's stamps available upon request.

VERMONT

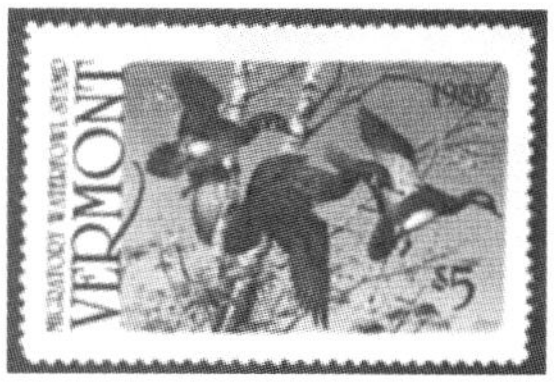

VT 1

No.	Description	F-VF NH
VT 1	'86 $5 Aut'mn Wd Ducks	12.00
VT 2	'87 $5 Wintr Goldeneyes	10.00
VT 3	'88 $5 Spring Blk. Ducks	9.00
VT 4	'89 $5 Summer Canada Geese	9.00
VT 5	'90 $5 Grn Wngd Teal	9.00
VT 6	'91 $5 H'ded Mergans'r	9.00
VT 7	'92 $5 Snow Geese	9.00
VT 8	'93 $5 Mallards	9.00
VT 9	'94 $5 Ring Necked Duck	9.00
VT 10	'95 $5 Bufflehead	9.00
VT 11	'96 $5 Bluebills	9.00
VT 12	'97 $5 Pintail	9.00
VT 13	'98 $5 Blue Winged Teal	9.00
VT 14	'99 $5 Canvasbacks	9.00
VT 15	'00 $5 Widgeon	9.00
VT 16	'01 $5 Old Squaw	9.00
Vermont Set 1986-2000 (15)		**115.00**

VIRGINIA

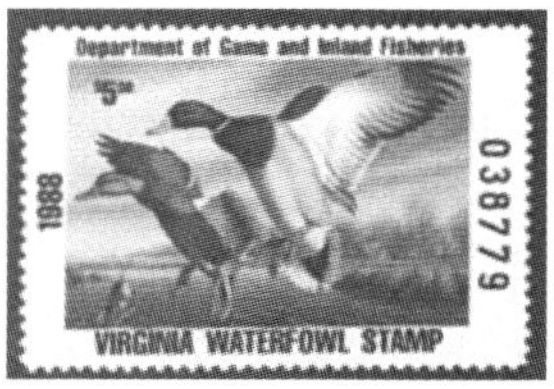

VA 1

No.	Description	F-VF NH
VA 1	'88 $5 Mallards	12.00
VA 1A	'88 $5 Bklt. Single	15.00
VA 1A	'88 $5 Hz. pr./side mgns	25.00
VA 2	'89 $5 Canada Geese	12.00
VA 2A	'89 $5 Bklt. Single	14.50
VA 2A	'89 $5 Hz. pr./side mgns	28.00
VA 3	'90 $5 Wood Ducks	9.00
VA 3A	'90 $5 Bklt. Single	12.00
VA 3A	'90 $5 Hz. pr./side mgns	23.00
VA 4	'91 $5 Canvasbacks	9.00
VA 4A	'91 $5 Bklt. Single	12.00
VA 4A	'91 $5 Hz. pr./side mgns	23.00
VA 5	'92 $5 Buffleheads	9.00
VA 5A	'92 $5 Bklt. Single	12.00
VA 5A	'92 $5 Hz. pr./side mgns	23.00
VA 6	'93 $5 Black Ducks	8.50
VA 6A	'93 $5 Bklt. Single	8.50
VA 6A	'93 $5 Hz. pr./side mgns	17.00
VA 7	'94 $5 Lesser Scaup	8.00
VA 7A	'94 $5 Bklt. Single	17.00
VA 7A	'94 $5 Hz. pr./side mgns.	17.00

VIRGINIA (cont.)

No.	Description	F-VF NH
VA 8	'95 $5 Snow Geese	8.00
VA 8A	'95 $5 hz. pr./side Mgns.	17.00
VA 9	'96 $5 Hooded Merganser	9.00
VA 10	'97 $5 Lab/Pintail	10.00
VA 11	'98 $5 Mallards	9.00
VA 12	'99 $5 Green Winged Teal	9.00
VA 13	'00 $5 Mallards	9.00
VA 14	'01 $5	9.00
Virginia Set 1988-2000 (13)		**115.00**
VA Hunter Pairs Set 1988-95 (8)		**165.00**

WASHINGTON

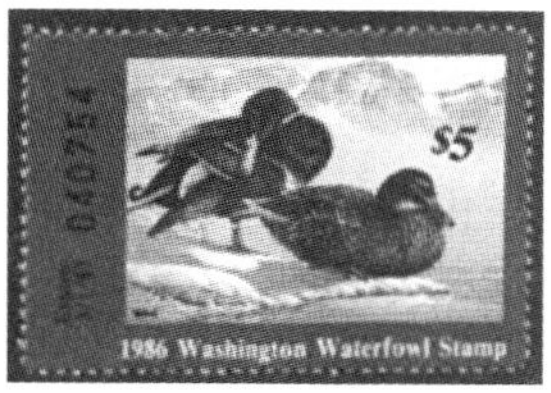

WA 1

No.	Description	F-VF NH
WA 1	'86 $5 Mallards	9.00
WA 1A	'86 $5 Hunter Type (77X82MM)	15.00
WA 2	'87 $5 Canvasbacks	15.00
WA 2A	'87 $5 Hunter Type (77X82MM)	10.00
WA 3	'88 $5 Harlequin	9.00
WA 3A	'88 $5 Hunter Type (77X82MM)	10.00
WA 4	'89 $5 Amer. Widgeon	9.00
WA 4A	'89 $5 Hunter Type (77X82MM)	10.00
WA 5	'90 $5 Pintails/Sour Duck	9.00
WA 5A	'90 $5 Hunter Type (77X82MM)	10.00
WA 6	'91 $5 Wood Duck	9.00
WA 6A	'91 $5 Hunter Type (77X82MM)	10.00
WA 6V	'91 $6 Wood Duck	12.00
WA 6AN	'91 $6 Mini Sheet/ No Staple Holes	45.00
WA 6AV	'91 $6 Hunter Type (77X82MM)	10.00
WA 7	'92 $6 Puppy/Can. Geese	10.00
WA 7N	'92 $6 Mini Sheet/ No Staple Holes	40.00
WA 7A	'92 $6 Hunter Type (77X82MM)	10.00
WA 8	'93 $6 Snow Geese	10.00
WA 8N	'93 $6 Mini Sheet/ No Staple Holes	20.00
WA 8A	'93 $6 Hunter Type (77X82MM)	10.00
WA 9	'94 $6 Black Brant	10.00
WA 9A	'94 $6 Hunter Type (77X82MM)	10.00
WA 9N	'94 $6 Mini Sheet, No staple holes	20.00
WA 10	'95 $6 Mallards	10.00
WA 10A	'95 $6 Hunter Type (77 x 82 MM)	10.00
WA 10N	'95 $6 Mini Sheet No staple holes	17.00
WA 11	'96 $6 Redheads	9.00
WA 11A	'96 $6 Hunter Type (77x82MM)	10.00
WA 11N	'96 $6 Mini Sheet No staple holes	17.00
WA 12	'97 $6 Canada Geese	9.00
WA 12A	'97 $6 Hunter Type (77x82MM)	9.00
WA 12AN	'97 $6 Mini Sheet No staple holes	18.00
WA 13	'98 $6 Goldeneye	9.00
WA 13A	'98 $6 Hunter Type (61x137mm)	9.00
WA 13N	'98 $6 Mini Sheet No staple holes	15.00
WA 14	'99 $6 Buffleheads/Pintails	9.00
WA 14A	'99 $6 Hunter type (61mm x 137mm)	9.00
WA 14N	'99 $6 Mini Sheet No staple holes	12.00
WA 15	'00 $6 Widgeon/Canada Goose	9.00
WA 15A	'00 $6 Hunter type (61mm x 137mm)	9.00
WA 15N	'00 $6 Mini Sheet No staple holes	12.00
WA 16	'01 $6 Mallards	9.00
WA 16A	'01 $6 Hunter type (61mm x 137mm)	9.00
Washington Set 1986-2000 (16)		**143.00**
WA Hunter Set 1986-2000 (15)		**140.00**

WEST VIRGINIA

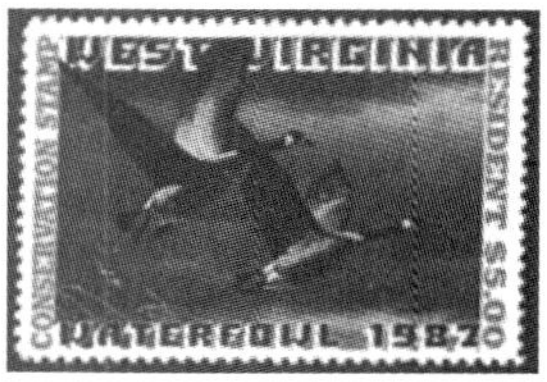

WV 1

No.	Description	F-VF NH
WV 1	'87 $5 Can. Geese/Res	16.00
WV 1A	'87 $5 Non-Resident	16.00
WV 1B	'87 $5 Bklt. sgl-Resident	45.00
WV 1AB	'87 Same, Non-Res	45.00
WV 2	'88 $5 Wood Ducks/Res	12.00
WV 2A	'88 $5 Non-Resident	12.50
WV 2B	'88 $5 Bklt. sgl-Resident	28.00
WV 2AB	'88 Same, Non-Res	28.00
WV 3	'89 $5 Decoys/Res	12.50
WV 3A	'89 $5 Non-Resident	12.50
WV 3B	'89 $5 Bklt. sgl-Resident	13.00
WV 3AB	'89 Same, Non-Res	13.00
WV 4	'90 Lab/Decoys/Res	12.00
WV 4A	'90 $5 Non-Resident	12.00
WV 4B	'90 $5 Bklt. sgl-Resident	12.00
WV 4AB	'90 Same, Non-Res	12.00
WV 5	'91 $5 Mallards/Res	8.50
WV 5A	'91 $5 Non-Resident	8.50
WV 5B	'91 $5 Bklt. sgl-Resident	12.00
WV 5AB	'91 Same, Non-Res	12.00
WV 5S	'91 WV Ohio Riv. Sht of 6	55.00
WV 6	'92 $5 Can. Geese/Res	9.50
WV 6A	'92 $5 Non-Resident	9.50
WV 6B	'92 $5 Bklt. sgl-Resident	9.50
WV 6AB	'92 Same, Non-Res	9.50
WV 7	'93 $5 Pintails/Res	9.00
WV 7A	'93 $5 Non-Resident	9.00
WV 7B	'93 $5 Bklt. sgl-Resident	9.00
WV 7AB	'93 Same, Non-Res	9.00
WV 8	'94 $5 Grn. Winged Teal	8.50
WV 8A	'94 Same, Non-Res	8.50
WV 8B	'94 $5 Pintails-Hunter	9.00
WV 8AB	'94 Same, Non-Res	9.00
WV 9	'95 $5 Wood Duck	8.50
WV 9A	'95 Same, Non-Resident	8.50
WV 9B	'95 $5 Hunter Type	9.00
WV 9AB	'95 Same, Non-Resident	9.00
WV 10	'96 $5 American Widgeons	8.50
WV 10A	'96 $5 Widgeon Non-Res.	8.50
WV 10B	'96 $5 Widgeon Hunter Typ	9.00
WV 10AB	'96 $5 Widgeon NR Hunter	9.00
West Virginia Set 1987-96 (20)		**210.00**
WV Hunter Ty. Set 1987-96 (20)		**275.00**

NOTE: Governor's stamps available upon request.

WISCONSIN

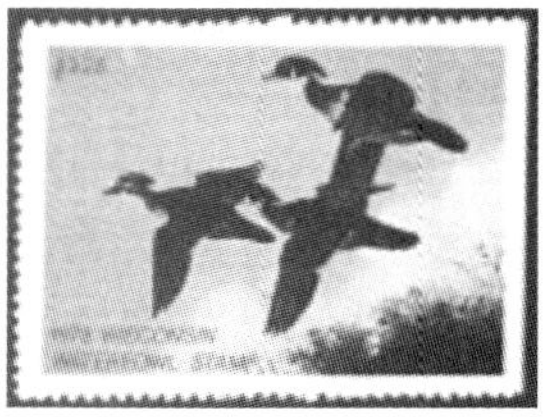

WI 1

No.	Description	F-VF NH
WI 1	'78 $3.25 Wood Ducks	115.00
WI 2	'79 $3.25 Buffleheads	30.00
WI 3	'80 $3.25 Widgeon	12.00
WI 4	'81 $3.25 Lesser Scaup	10.00
WI 5	'82 $3.25 Pintails	8.00
WI 5T	'82 $3.25 Full Tab Attd	10.00
WI 6	'83 $3.25 Bl. Winged Teal	8.50
WI 6T	'83 $3.25 Full Tab Attd	12.00
WI 7	'84 $3.25 Hd'd Mergans'r	8.50
WI 7T	'84 $3.25 Full Tab Attd	12.00
WI 8	'85 $3.25 Lesser Scaup	10.00
WI 8T	'85 $3.25 Full Tab Attd	12.00
WI 9	'86 $3.25 Canvasbacks	10.00
WI 9T	'86 $3.25 Full Tab Attd	12.00
WI 10	'87 $3.25 Canada Geese	6.50
WI 10T	'87 $3.25 Full Tab Attd	8.00
WI 11	'88 $3.25 Hd'd Mergans'r	6.50
WI 11T	'88 $3.25 Full Tab Attd	8.00
WI 12	'89 $3.25 Cm'n Gldneye	6.50
WI 12T	'89 $3.25 Full Tab Attd	8.00
WI 13	'90 $3.25 Redheads	6.50
WI 13T	'90 $3.25 Full Tab Attd	8.00
WI 14	'91 $5.25 Grn. Wngd. Teal	8.50
WI 14T	'91 $5.25 Full Tab Attd	9.50
WI 15	'92 $5.25 Tundra Swans	8.50
WI 15T	'92 $5.25 Full Tab Attd	9.50
WI 16	'93 $5.25 Wood Ducks	8.50
WI 16T	'93 $5.25 Full Tab Attd	9.50
WI 17	'94 $5.25 Pintails	8.50
WI 17A	'94 $5.25 Full Tab Attd	9.50

STATE HUNTING PERMIT STAMPS

WISCONSIN (cont.)

No.	Description	F-VF NH
WI 18	'95 $5.25 Mallards	8.50
WI 18A	'95 $5.25 Full Tab Attd ..	9.50
WI 19	'96 $5.25 Gr. Winged Teal	8.50
WI 19T	'96 $5.25 Full Tab Attchd.	9.50
WI 20	'97 $7 Canada Goose	10.00
WI 20T	'97 $7 Full Tab Attchd. ..	11.00
WI 21	'98 $7 Snow Goose	10.00
WI 21T	'98 Full Tab Attached	11.00
WI 22	'99 $7 Greater Scaup	10.00
WI 22T	'99 $7 Full Tab Attached .	11.00
WI 23	'00 $7 Canvasbacks	10.00
WI 23T	'00 $7 Full Tab Attached .	11.00
WI 24	'01 $7 Common Goldeneye	10.00
WI 24T	'01 $7 Full Tab Attached .	11.00
Wisconsin Set 1978-2000 (23)		**305.00**

WYOMING

WY 1

WYOMING (cont.)

No.	Description	F-VF NH
WY 1	'84 $5 Meadowlark	50.00
WY 2	'85 $5 Canada Geese	45.00
WY 3	'86 $5 Prnghrn Antelope	55.00
WY 4	'87 $5 Sage Grouse	55.00
WY 5	'88 $5 Cut-Throat Trout ..	60.00
WY 6	'89 $5 Mule Deer	95.00
WY 7	'90 $5 Grizzly Bear	40.00
WY 8	'91 $5 Big Horn Sheep ...	40.00
WY 9	'92 $5 Bald Eagle	25.00
WY 10	'93 $5 Elk	20.00
WY 11	'94 $5 Bobcat	15.00
WY 12	'95 $5 Moose	12.00
WY 13	'96 $5 Turkey	12.00
WY 14	'97 $5 Rocky Mntn Goats	12.00
WY 15	'98 $5 Thunder Swans ...	12.00
WY 16	'99 $5 Brown Trout	12.00
WY 17	'00 $5 Buffalo	12.00
WY 18	'01 $10 Whitetailed Deer .	10.00
Wyoming Set 1984-2000 (17) ..		**525.00**

NOTE: SEE END OF CANADIAN LISTINGS FOR CANADA FEDERAL AND PROVINCIAL DUCK STAMPS.

NATIONAL FISH AND WILDLIFE

NF1

No.	Description	F-VF NH
NFW 1	'87 $5 Canada Goose	10.00
NFW 2	'88 $5 Mallards	10.00
NFW 3	'89 $5 Wood Ducks	10.00
NFW 4	'90 $7.50 Tundra Swans .	12.50
NFW 5	'91 $7.50 Pintails	12.50
NFW 6	'92 $7.50 Snow Geese	12.50
NFW 7	'93-4 $7.50 Canvasbacks	12.50
NFW 8	'95 $7.50 Green Winged Teal	12.50
NFW 9	'96 $7.50 Pintails	12.50
NFW 10	'97 $7.50 Common Loon	12.50
NFW 11	'98 $7.50 Barrow's Goldeneyes	12.50

JUNIOR DUCKS

JR2

No.	Description	F-VF NH
JR 1	'92 $10 Sheet of 9	35.00
JR 2	'93 $5 Redhead	25.00
JR 3	'94 $5 Hooded Merganser	25.00
JR 4	'95 $5 Pintail	25.00
JR 5	'96 $5 Canvasback	10.00
JR 6	'97 $5 Canada Goose	10.00
JR 7	'98 $5 Black Ducks	10.00
JR 8	'99 $5 Wood Ducks	10.00
JR 9	'00 $5 Northern Pintails ..	10.00
JR10	'01 $5 Trumpeter Swan ...	10.00

INDIAN RESERVATION STAMPS

MONTANA - CROW

MONTANA - FLATHEAD

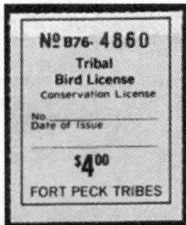

MONTANA - FORT PECK TRIBES

MONTANA-FORT BELKNAP

NEW MEXICO - JICARILLA

NORTH DAKOTA STANDING ROCK SIOUX

S.D. -CHEYENNE RIVER SIOUX

S.D.-CROW CREEK SIOUX

S.D.-LOWER BRULE SIOUX TRIBE

S.D.-LAKE TRAVERSE

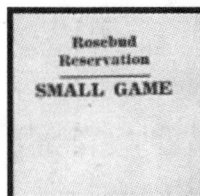

S.D.-ROSEBUD

S.D.-PINE RIDGE - OGLALA SIOUX

INDIAN RESERVATION STAMPS

No.	Description	F-VF NH
	ARIZONA	
	NAVAJO	
NA 1	1991 Habitat	65.00
NA 2	1992 Habitat	12.00
NA 3	1993 Habitat	12.00
NA 4	1994 Habitat	10.00
NA 5	1995 Habitat	10.00
NA 6	1996 Habitat	12.00
NA 6A	1996 2nd Printing	12.00
NA 7	1997 Habitat	10.00
	MONTANA	
	CROW	
CW 2	1992 Upland Game	60.00
CW 2v	1993 Upland, undated	12.00
CW 3	1992 Waterfowl	110.00
CW 3v	1993 Waterfowl, undated	12.00
	FLATHEAD	
FH 1	1987 Bird	1450.00
FH 3	1988 Bird/Fish	1500.00
FH 4	1989 Bird/Fish Pr w/Dupe	18.00
FH 5	1989 Shiny Paper	55.00
FH 7	1990 Shiny Paper	575.00
FH 8	1990 Bird/Fish "Fasson" Backing	40.00
FH 9	1990 Bird/Fish Pr w/Dupe	18.00
FH 10	1991 Joint Bird	11.00
FH 12	1992 Bird Annual	10.00
FH 13	1992 Bird 3-Day	9.00
FH 16	1993 Bird Annual	9.00
FH 17	1993 Bird 3-Day	9.00
FH 20	1994 Bird Annual	9.00
FH 21	1994 Bird 3-Day	8.00
FH 24	1995 Bird Resident	10.00
FH 25	1995 Bird Non-Resident	15.00
FH 28	1996 Bird Resident	12.00
FH 29	1996 Bird Non-Resident	16.00
FH 33	1997 Bird Resident	12.00
FH 34	1997 Bird Non-Resident	16.00
FH 38	1998 Bird Resident	12.00
FH 39	1998 Bird Non-Resident	15.00
FH 43	1999 Bird Resident	12.00
FH 44	1999 Bird Non-Resident	12.00
FH 48	2000 Bird Resident	12.00
FH 49	2000 Bird Non-Resident	12.00
	FORT BELKNAP	
FB 4	1996 Waterfowl	50.00
FB 8	1997 Waterfowl	50.00
FB 11	1998 Waterfowl	30.00
FB 15	1999 Waterfowl	75.00
	FORT PECK	
FP 3	1975 Bird	1550.00
FP 5	1976 Bird	110.00
FP 9	1978 Bird	350.00
FP 14	1988 $25 Upland Game (yellow)	40.00
FP 15	1988 $50 Upland Game (yellow)	75.00
FP 16	1988 $10 Upland Game (yellow)	25.00
FP 16a	1988 $10 Plate Flaw	125.00
FP 17	1994 $40 Upland Game (yellow)	75.00

No.	Description	F-VF NH
	FORT PECK (continued)	
FP 18	1994 $15 Upland Game (drawing)	22.00
FP 19	1994 $45 Upland Game (drawing)	60.00
FP 20	1995 $45 Upland Game (white brown)	60.00
FP 25	1996 $25 Upland Game (blue)	25.00
FP 26	1996 $65 Upland Game (brn)	55.00
FP 27	1997 $10 Waterfowl (orange)	20.00
FP 28	1997 $40 Waterfowl (green)	35.00
FP 31	1997 $25 Upland (blue)	25.00
FP 32	1997 $40 Upland (plum)	45.00
	NEW MEXICO	
	JICARILLA	
JI 2	1988 Wildlife Stamp	15.00
	ZUNI	
ZU 1	1995 Habitat	25.00
ZU 2	1996 Habitat	20.00
ZU 3	1997 Habitat	15.00
ZU 4	1998 Habitat	15.00
ZU 5	1999 Habitat	15.00
ZU 6	2000 Habitat	15.00
	NORTH DAKOTA	
	FORT BERTHOLD	
TT 12	1990 Small Game	85.00
TT 14	1990 Upland Game	140.00
TT 15	1990 Waterfowl	2500.00
TT 19	1991 Small Game	80.00
TT 21	1991 Upland Game	105.00
TT 22	1991 Waterfowl	900.00
TT 26	1992 Small Game	80.00
TT 28	1992 Upland Game	85.00
TT 33	1993 Small Game	175.00
TT 35	1993 Upland Game	85.00
TT 36	1993 Waterfowl	600.00
TT 39	1994 Small Game	70.00
TT 41	1994 Upland Game	295.00
TT 42	1994 Waterfowl	615.00
TT 45	1995 Small Game	100.00
TT 47	1995 Upland Bird	85.00
TT 48	1995 Waterfowl	275.00
TT 51	1996 Small Game	55.00
TT 53	1996 Upland Game	85.00
TT 54	1996 Waterfowl	225.00
TT58	1997 Sand Hill Crane #1-30	975.00
TT 59	1997 Small Game	50.00
TT 62	1997 Waterfowl	260.00
TT61	1997 Upland Game	50.00
TT68	1998 Sand Hil Crane #31-60	852.00
TT 69	196998 Small Game	40.00
TT 72	199872 Waterfowl	300.00
TT71	1998 Up71land Game	50.00
TT76	1999 Small76 Game	35.00
TT80	1999 Waterfo80wl	325.00
TT79	1999 Upland Ga79me	40.00
TT84	2000 Small Game	35.00

No.	Description	F-VF NH
	FORT BERTHOLD	
TT86	2000 Upland Game	150.00
TT87	2000 Waterfowl	250.00
	STANDING ROCK SIOUX TRIBE	
SR 10	1992 Waterfowl	17.00
SR 20	1993 Waterfowl	12.00
SR 30	1994 Waterfowl	11.00
SR 39	1995 Waterfowl	15.00
SR 48	1996 Waterfowl	15.00
SR 57	1997 Waterfowl	15.00
SR 73	1998 Waterfowl	15.00
SR73a	1998 Waterfowl (Green backing)	50.00
SR 74	1998 Waterfowl (orange)	110.00
SR94	1999 Waterfowl	12.00
SR103	2001 Waterfowl	12.00
	SOUTH DAKOTA	
	CHEYENNE RIVER SIOUX TRIBE	
CR 2	1984-91 Birds&Small Game, Member	
CR 7	1984-91 Same,Non-Member	
CR 12	1989-94 Birds & Small Game Member, Shiny Paper	30.00
CR 18	Non-Member,Shiny Paper	55.00
CR 29	1989-94 Birds & Small Game Member	15.00
CR 34	Same, Non-Member	30.00
CR 32	1994 Waterfowl, Member	20.00
CR 42	1994 Same, Non-Member	30.00
	CROW CREEK SIOUX TRIBE	
CC 27	1989 $10 Canada Geese Reservation	600.00
CC 28	1989 $30 SD Resident	
CC 29	1989 $65 Non-Resident	1500.00
CC 30	1990 $10 Canada Geese Reservation	425.00
CC 31	1990 $30 SD Resident	350.00
CC 32	1990 $65 Non-Resident	1400.00
1989-1990 Sportsman Set (8 stamps)		
CC 33-40	($770 Face Val.)	4200.00
1989-1990 Upland Game Set		
CC 15-20	(6 stamps)	1050.00
CC 61	1994 $5 Tribal Member	55.00
CC 62	1994 $15 Resident	80.00
CC 63	1994 $30 Non-Res. Daily	115.00
CC 64	1994 $75 Non-Resident	195.00
CC 91-94	1995 Set of 4	295.00
CC 121-124	1996 Set of 4	295.00
CC 152-155	1997 Set of 4	295.00
CC 170-73	'98 Spring Goose (3)	135.00
CC 187-90	1998 Set of 4	295.00
	LAKE TRAVERSE INDIAN RESERVATION (SISSETON-WAHPETON)	
LT 5	1986 Game Bird	180.00
LT 9	1986 Upland Game	500.00
LT 24	1991 Small Game	50.00
LT 26	1991 Upland Bird	70.00
LT 27	1991 Waterfowl-Br.Green	125.00
LT 31	1992 Sm. Game-Orange	12.50
LT 32	1992 Sm. Game-Green	25.00
LT 34	1992 Upland Game	4.00

No.	Description	F-VF NH
	LAKE TRAVERSE (continued)	
LT 35	1992 Wood Duck	17.00
LT 40	1993 Small Game	12.00
LT 42	1993 Upland Bird	12.00
LT 43	1993 Waterfowl-Bright Rd	25.00
LT 52	1994 Small Game	6.00
LT 55	1994 Upland Bird	6.00
LT 56	1994 Waterfowl-Yel. Or.	10.00
LT 59	1995 Small Game	8.00
LT 62	1995 Waterfowl	12.00
LT 65	1996 Small Game	8.00
LT 67	1996 Upland Bird	7.00
LT 68	1996 Waterfowl	225.00
LT 71	1997 Small Game	8.00
LT 72	1997 Sportsman	35.00
LT 73	1997 Upland Bird	7.00
LT 74	1997 Waterfowl	10.00
LT 77	1998 Small Game	7.00
LT 78	1998 Sportsman	35.00
LT 79	1998 Upland Bird	6.00
LT 80	1998 Waterfowl	40.00
LT 85	1999 Sportsman	10.00
LT 86	1999 Upland Bird	6.00
LT 87	1999 Waterfowl	10.00
LT	2000 Sportsman	8.00
LT	2000 Upland Game	10.00
LT	2000 Waterfowl	
	LOWER BRULE	
LB 26-30	1995 Set of 5 Waterfowl	50.00
LB 31-33	1996 Set of 3 Waterfowl	35.00
LB 34-36	1997 Set of 3 Waterfowl	35.00
LB 37-39	1998 Set of 3 Waterfowl	35.00
LB 40-42	1999 Set of 3 Waterfowl	35.00
	PINE RIDGE (OGLALA SIOUX)	
PR 11	1988-92 $4 Waterfowl, Rouletted	375.00
PR 30	1988-92 $4 Waterfowl, Perforated	30.00
PR 47	1992 $4 Canada Geese	12.50
PR 48	1993 $6 Canada Geese	12.50
PR 49	1994 $6 '94 ovrprt on '93	15.00
	ROSEBUD	
RB 10	1970's Sm. Game Ser.#	1750.00
RB 11	1980's Sm.l Game Ser.#	275.00
RB 52	1988 $10 Small Game	45.00
RB 53	1989 $45 Small Game	190.00
RB	1996-99 Small Game, Tribal	30.00
RB	1996-99 Small Game, Resident	85.00
	1999-96 Small Game, Non Res.	
	2000 $10 Small Game, Tribal (red)	
RB	2000 $30 Small Game, Resident (Red)	400.00
RB	2000 $85.00 Small Game, Non-Resident (Red)	125.00

The American First Day Cover Society

. . . is the best source of information, fellowship, education and authority on First Day Cover Collecting. Most importantly, the AFDCS is a nonprofit, non-commercial, international society and the world's largest society devoted to First Day Cover collecting!

A First Day Cover (FDC) is an envelope or card with a new stamp issue that is postmarked on the first day the stamp is sold.

A cachet (pronounced ka-shay) is the design on the envelope. It usually shows something more about the new stamp and is usually on the left side of the envelope. Some cachets cover the entire face of the envelope with the design.

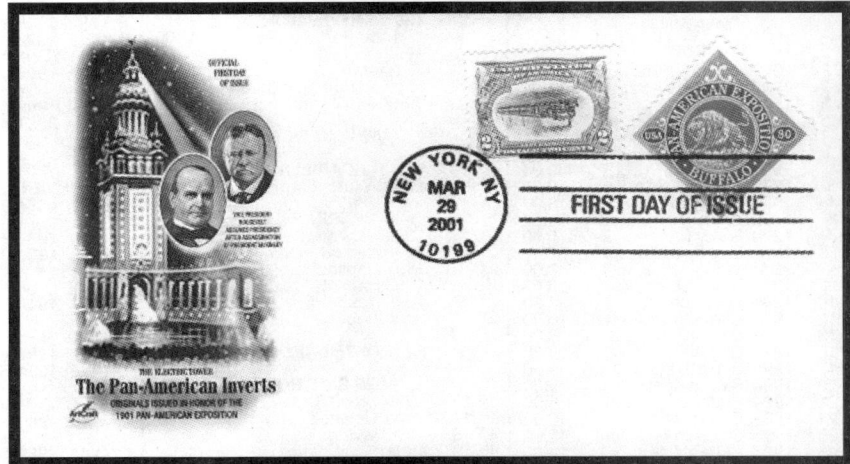

FDC Collecting is a hobby of personal involvement limited only by your own creativity. This FDC has a 50¢ Ben Franklin stamp added to another Franklin FDC made over 40 years earlier. These are called "dual" FDCs. The "AFDCS Glossary of Terms" comes in your FDC collecting package when you join the AFDCS! See the membership information on the opposite page.

A Joint Issue First Day Cover has two or more stamps issued by different countries to commemorate the same person, place or event. You will learn more about Joint Issues when you read *FIRST DAYS,* the award winning journal of the AFDCS. This popular area of collecting has expanded to include dozens of new issues and countries all around the world each year.

Welcome to First Day Cover Collecting!

by Barry Newton, Editor *FIRST DAYS*, the official journal of the American First Day Cover Society

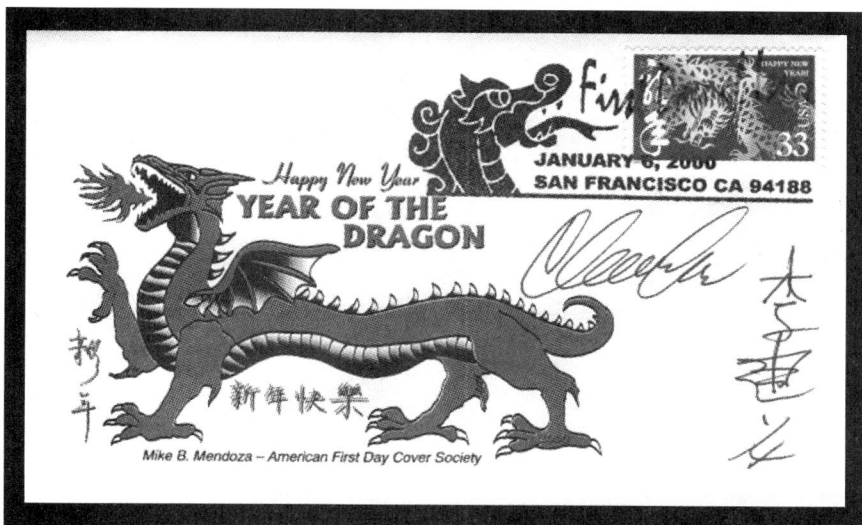

First Day Cover (FDC) Collecting is a hands-on hobby much more than simple collecting. It encourages the individual collector to fully develop a range of interests through cachetmaking, autographs and combo FDCs so that the final collection is a reflection of personal taste. In FDCs, uniqueness is the rule, not the exception. This Chinese New Year FDC was autographed by the stamp designer, Clarence Lee.

Join the American First Day Cover Society Today!

When you join the American First Day Cover Society you will receive a FDC collecting package featuring publications, free FDCs and a coupon book worth over $850 for FDCs and other hobby merchandise.

The 55-page Coupon Book offers 83 coupons from 67 *FIRST DAYS* advertisers for FDCs, FDC catalogs and publications, collecting supplies, auction services and much more! The total value of this Coupon Book is over $850.00!

Four Publications valued at over $10.00 to get you started on FDC Collecting, including a *Cram Course in FDC Collecting, The AFDCS Current Cachetmakers Directory, Mini-Adventures in FDC Collecting* and *The AFDCS New Members Handbook.*

Five Free FDCs!

All you need to do to join is send your name, address and membership fee to the address below. You will immediately receive your FDC Collecting package, your AFDCS membership card and your first issue of FIRST DAYS. Every six weeks you will get another issue full of information on FDC collecting. (Submission of membership dues means that you agree to abide by the rules and bylaws of the AFDCS.)

Membership Dues ... $20 per year
Junior Membership (age 17 or under) ... $13.00 per year
Foreign (including Canada and Mexico) ... $8.00 additional
The above three membership classes include eight great issues of *FIRST DAYS*
Please make money orders or checks payable in US funds. Credit cards also accepted.
Applicant must submit dues with Membership Application.

AFDCS Central Office, PO Box 65960, Tucson, AZ 85728, USA

Visit us on the Web at www.AFDCS.org

FIRST CACHETS

by Marjory J. Sente

Stamp collectors are always interested in the oldest, first, best, rare, most expensive items. So it is not unusual for First Day Cover enthusiasts to search for earliest known cachets by a particular manufacturer or designer. First cachets are fascinating and challenging speciality. They have been researched and documented for thousands of artists and cachet makers. Yet, the search for other first cachets continue.

A first cachet is the initial design commercially produced by a cachet maker. To qualify as commercially produced, the cacheted First Day Cover is made and sold in a quantity greater than maker's personal needs. As an example is the design prepared by Colorano "Silk" cachets for the 1971 American Wool Industry commemorative, issued Janruary 19 at Las Vegas, NV. Ray

Novak had seen silk cachets produced by french firm, Ceres, and decided to market the same type of cachet for United States postal issues. For the first Colorano "Silk" cachet, Ray produced 1200 covers. The press run increased to 2400 in 1972 and by the cachet line's tenth anniversary, production had increased to 10,000 per issue.

Sometimes it is difficult to identify a cachetmaker's initial production, because it is not signed. So researchers need to rely on philatelic publications released about the time the cachet was produced and advertised for distribution. Stuffers in the FDCs also provide good clues as to the cachet's producer. The first Fleetwood cachet, prepared for the Vermont Statehood commemorative, released on March 4, 1941, was not signed, but a stuffer identifies Staehle as the

designer and Fleetwood as the producer. The line has undergone many changes over the years, and today, the colorful Fleetwood designs produced by Unicover are likely the most mass-marketed Firs Day Covers.

Other cachets are relatively easy to identify, because most designs including the first one are signed. Fluegel cachets, produced from the mid-1940's until 1960's, are nearly always signed "Fluegel." Herman "Cap" Fleugel prepared his first commercial venture for the 3-cent Roosevelt commemorative issued on June 27, 1945. Known for their brilliant colors, his early cachets were printed in letterpress in five o six colors.

Addresses on FDCs are sometimes a tip to their origin. Cachet makers frequently send covers to themselves or relatives. Ernest J.

Weschcke produced his first and only cachet for the Norse-American Centennial commemorative pair, released May 18, 1925. The distinctive red cachet printed on Norwegian Blue envelopes is unsigned but most of the FDCs are addressed to him. It is estimated that Weschcke made about 200 of these FDCs, but few were sold. The others were treasured by the family and kept in pristine condition.

Sometimes a first cachet gives birth to a line with a formal trademark. Of the four major cachet lines that are marked today-- Artcraft, Artmaster, House of Farnam and Fleetwood--only the first Artmaster cachet appeared with its well known script trademark. The other three cachet lines adopted trademarks later.

Robert Schmidt of Louisville, Kentucky, prepared the first Artmaster cachet for the Honor Discharge issue released on May 9, 1946. For this initial cachet 15,000 covers were sold and 10,000 distributed free for advertising and publicity purposes.

Dabbling or creating multiple cachet lines are other confusing issues for the positive identification cachets. Cachetmakers frequently will dabble at making cachets before launching into commercial production. They will design a cachet as an experiment for their own amusement, or as a favor for an organization. Do these for runners qualify as first cachets? Part of the answer is whether you collect first cachets by artist or designer or cachetmaker or the cachet line.

Sometimes the artist will prepare cachets for earlier FDCs than the one that is considered to be first because it is defined by cachetmaker or the name of the cachet line. For example, Ludwig Staehle prepared his first cachet for the Swedish-Finnish Tercentenary commemorative issued in 1938, several years earlier than the first Fleetwood cachet that he had designed for the 1941 Vermont Statehood issue.

Doris Gold's cachet making career provides another example. She began making one-of-a-kind handrawn/handpainted covers. Her first endeavor for a U.S. issue was for 1975 Benjamin West issue. Her first commercial special events cover was prepared for the 1976 Writer's day INTERPHIL show cancellation. Her first commercial handrawn/handpainted FDC was made for the 1976 Olympics block of four commemorative. The release of the 1977 Lindbergh Transatlantic commemorative was the birth of the DG series. And in 1987 she started the DGHC series beginning with Enrico Caruso commemorative. With this series an outline is printed in black outline, and then the cover is painted by hand. The first cachet for the DGX series, which employs laser color printing was prepared for the 1990 Movie Classics issue.

Sometimes a cachetmaker is involved in commercially producing event covers before making FDCs. This is true for John Adlen, producer of Pilgrim cachets. He started making event covers in the early 1930s. His first cachet on an FDC was for 1937 Constitution commemorative. Most of his covers are signed and include a return address at the bottom of the cachet.

Along with the first cachets come one-time cachets. These designs are the works of cachetmakers who produce only one cachet in their lifetime. Some collectors call them one-timers, first cachets. Others say to have a cachet, you must have second. An excellent discussion on "Collecting First Day Cachets" appeared in September/October 1980 *First Days*.

The systematic compilation of data on first cachets resulted in the publication of *Mellone's First Cachets A FDC Reference Catalog* by Hal Ansink, Lois Hamilton and Dr. Richard A. Monty in 1980. Three years later an updated version was published, followed by a third in 1989. A fourth edition, *First Cachets Revisited*, is the latest comprehensive update of the list. In the interim, *First Days*, the official journal of the American First Day Cover Society, publishes an ongoing column updating research.

Marjory Sente has written about First Day Covers for more than two decades. Her monthly column appears in Mekeel's Weekly and Stamps. *She also teach an independent learning course on* FDCs *offered through* Penn. State.

370

569

FDC's will be addressed from #5A-952 and unaddressed from 953 to date
Cacheted prices are for FDC's with common printed cachets. From #704 all FDC's will be cacheted. Multiples are generally priced @ 1.25x for blocks & 2x for plate blks. or line pairs

Scott #	Description	Uncacheted
	1851-1890	
5A	1¢ Franklin, Blue, Type 1b, 7/1/1851 Any City	135,000.00
7	1¢ Franklin, Blue, Type II 7/1/1851 Any City	6,500.00
10	3¢ Washington, Orange Brown 7/1/1851 Any City	17,500.00
64B	3¢ Washington, Rose Pink 8/17/1861 Any City	30,000.00
79	3¢ Washington "A" Grill 8/13/1867 Any City	15,000.00
210	2¢ Washington, Red Brown 10/1/1883 Any City	2,700.00
210-211	2¢ Wash., 4¢ Jackson on one cvr, 10/1/1883	40,000.00
219D	2¢ Washington, Lake 2/22/1890 Any City	20,000.00
	1893 COLUMBIAN ISSUE	
230	1¢ Columbian 1/2/1893 Any City	8,000.00
	Salem, MA 12/31/1892	15,000.00
231	2¢ Columbian 1/2/1893 Any City	5,000.00
	New York, NY or Boston, MA 1/1/1893	7,500.00
	Salem, MA 12/31/1892	15,000.00
232	3¢ Columbian 1/2/1893 Any City	15,000.00
233	4¢ Columbian 1/2/1893 Any City	15,000.00
234	5¢ Columbian 1/2/1893 Any City	20,000.00
235	6¢ Columbian 1/2/1893 Any City	22,500.00
237	10¢ Columbian 1/2/1893 Any City	25,000.00
	East Lexington, MA 12/31/92 bkstp	25,000.00
242	$2.00 Columbian 1/2/1893 New York, NY	65,000.00
265	2¢ Washington 5/2/1895 Any City	9,500.00

* Since Jan. 1, 1893 was a Sunday and few post offices were open, both Jan. 1 and Jan. 2 covers are considered FDC's by collectors.

	1898 TRANS-MISSISSIPPI ISSUE	
285	1¢ Trans-Mississippi 6/17/1898 Any City	14,500.00
286	2¢ Trans-Mississippi 6/17/1898 DC	12,000.00
	6/17/1898 Pittsburgh, PA	13,000.00
287	4¢ Trans-Mississippi 6/17/1898 Any City	20,000.00
288	5¢ Trans-Mississippi 6/17/1898 DC	20,000.00
289	8¢ Trans-Mississippi 6/17/1898 DC	25,000.00
290	10¢ Trans-Mississippi 6/17/1898 Any City	30,000.00
291	50¢ Trans-Mississippi 6/17/1898 DC	35,000.00
292	$1 Trans-Mississippi 6/17/1898 DC	60,000.00
	1901 PAN AMERICAN ISSUE	
294	1¢ Pan-American 5/1/01 Any City	6,000.00
	294,296, 297 on one cover,Boston, MA	30,000.00
295	2¢ Pan-American 5/1/01 Any City	3,500.00
296	4¢ Pan-American 5/1/01 Any City	15,000.00
297	5¢ Pan-American 5/1/01 Any City	19,500.00
298	8¢ Pan-American 5/1/01 Any City	19,500.00
298,296	4¢ & 8¢ on one FDC Boston, MA	22,500.00
294-299	1¢-10¢ Pan-American, cplt. set on one FDC, Any City	47,500.00
	1904 LOUISIANA PURCHASE 1907 JAMESTOWN ISSUES	
323	1¢ Louisiana Purchase 4/30/04 Any City	7,500.00
324	2¢ Louisiana Purchase 4/30/04 Any City	6,000.00
325	3¢ Louisiana Purchase 4/30/04 Any City	18,000.00
326	5¢ Louisiana Purchase 4/30/04 Any City	26,000.00
327	10¢ Louisiana Purchase 4/30/04 Any City	27,500.00
323-327	1¢-10¢ Louisiana Purchase, complete set on 1 FDC	100,000.00
328	1¢ Jamestown Expedition 4/26/07 Any City	12,500.00
329	2¢ Jamestown Expedition 4/26/07 Any City	15,000.00
330	5¢ Jamestown Expedition 5/10/07 Norfolk, VA (eku)	20,000.00
328-30	On one cover, 5/10/07 Norwalk, VA (eku)	22,000.00
331a	1¢ Franklin, bklt. sgl. 12/2/08 DC	25,000.00
332a	2¢ Washington, bklt. sgl. 11/16/08 DC	35,000.00
	1909 COMMEMORATIVES	
367	2¢ Lincoln 2/12/09 Any City	400.00
367	2¢ Lincoln 2/12/09 Any City on Lincoln-related post-card	600.00
368	2¢ Lincoln Imperf. 2/12/09 Canton, OH	25,000.00
370	2¢ Alaska-Yukon 6/1/09 Any City	5,000.00
370	On related card	6,000.00
370	On card, Any City	5,500.00

Scott #	Description	Uncacheted
	1909 COMMEMORATIVES (cont.)	
372	2¢ Hudson-Fulton, 9/25/09, Any City, (100-200 Known)	800.00
372	2¢ Hudson-Fulton, 9/25/09, Any City on related post-card	1,500.00
373	2¢ Hudson-Fulton Imperf. 9/25/09 Any City	12,000.00
	1913 PAN-PACIFIC ISSUE	
397	1¢ Pan-Pacific Expo 1/1/13 Any City	5,000.00
398	2¢ Pan-Pacific Expo 1/18/13 Washington, D.C.	2,000.00
399	5¢ Pan-Pacific Expo 1/1/13 Any City	22,000.00
400	10¢ Pan-Pacific Expo 1/1/13 Any City	17,500.00
403	5¢ Pan-Pacific Expo, Perf. 10, 2/6/15 Chicago, Ill	7,500.00
397,399,400	1¢,5¢ & 10¢ Pan-Pacific on one FDC, SF, CA	30,000.00
497	10¢ Franklin Coil 1/31/22 DC (all are Hammelman cvrs)	5,500.00
526	2¢ Offset Ty. IV 3/15/20 Any City (eku)	1,250.00
537	3¢ Victory 3/3/19 Any City	800.00
542	1¢ Rotary Perf. 10 x 11 5/26/20 Any City	2,500.00
	1920 PILGRIM TERCENTENARY	
548	1¢ "Mayflower" Pair 12/21/20 DC	1,500.00
549	2¢ "Landing of the Pilgrims" 12/21/20 DC	1,200.00
	12/21/20 Philadelphia, PA	4,000.00
	12/21/20 Plymouth, MA	5,000.00
548-50	1¢-5¢ Complete set on one cover, Phila., PA	3,200.00
	Complete set on one cover, DC	3,200.00
	1922-25 FLAT PLATE PERF. 11	
551	½¢ Hale (Block of 4) 4/4/25 DC	18.00
551 cont.	New Haven, CT	23.00
	Unofficial City	175.00
	551 & 576 on one FDC 4/4/25 DC	125.00
552	1¢ Franklin 1/17/23 DC	22.50
	Philadelphia, PA	45.00
	Unofficial City	200.00
553	1½¢ Harding 3/19/25 DC	25.00
554	2¢ Washington 1/15/23 DC	35.00
555	3¢ Lincoln 2/12/23 DC	35.00
	Hodgenville, KY	200.00
	Unofficial City	300.00
556	4¢ Martha Washington 1/15/23 DC	70.00
557	5¢ Teddy Roosevelt 10/27/22 DC	115.00
	New York, NY	175.00
	Oyster Bay, NY	2,500.00
558	6¢ Garfield 11/20/22 DC	250.00
559	7¢ McKinley 5/1/23 DC	150.00
	Niles, OH	210.00
560	8¢ Grant 5/1/23 DC	160.00
	559-560 on one FDC, DC	750.00
	565 & 560 on one FDC, DC	2,500.00
561	9¢ Jefferson 1/15/23 DC	160.00
	556-561 on one FDC, DC	900.00
562	10¢ Monroe 1/15/23 DC	160.00
	562,554,556 & 561 on one FDC	2,000.00
562 & 554	On one FDC	800.00
563	11¢ Hayes 10/4/22 DC	650.00
	Fremont, OH	3,750.00
564	12¢ Cleveland 3/20/23 DC	175.00
	Boston, MA	250.00
	Caldwell, NJ	175.00
	Lynn, MA	4,500.00
565	14¢ Indian 5/1/23 DC	325.00
	Muskogee, OK	2,000.00
566	15¢ Statue of Liberty 11/11/22 DC	550.00
567	20¢ Golden Gate 5/1/23 DC	550.00
	Oakland, CA	8,000.00
	San Francisco, CA	3,750.00
568	25¢ Niagara Falls 11/11/22 DC	650.00
569	30¢ Bison 3/20/23 DC	800.00
	569 & 564 on one FDC, DC	6,000.00
570	50¢ Arlington 11/11/22 DC	1,500.00
	570,566 & 568 on one FDC	7,500.00
571	$1 Lincoln Memorial 2/12/23 DC	6,500.00
	Springfield, IL	6,500.00
	571 & 555 on one FDC, DC	9,500.00
572	$2 U.S. Capitol 3/20/23 DC	17,500.00
573	$5 Freedom Statue 3/20/23 DC	32,500.00

*EKU: Earliest Known Use

U.S. First Day Covers

610

Scott #	Description	Uncacheted
	1925-26 ROTARY PRESS PERF. 10	
576	1½¢ Harding Imperf. 4/4/25 DC	50.00
581	1¢ Franklin, unprecancelled 10/17/23 DC	7,500.00
582	1½¢ Harding 3/19/25 DC	45.00
583a	2¢ Washington bklt pane of 6, 8/27/26 DC	1,400.00
584	3¢ Lincoln 8/1/25 DC	60.00
585	4¢ Martha Washington 4/4/25 DC	60.00
585-587	On one FDC	750.00
586	5¢ T. Roosevelt 4/4/25 DC	65.00
587	6¢ Garfield 4/4/25 DC	65.00
588	7¢ McKinley 5/29/26 DC	70.00
589	8¢ Grant 5/29/26 DC	80.00
590	9¢ Jefferson 5/29/26 DC	80.00
	590, 588 & 589 on one FDC	350.00
591	10¢ Monroe 6/8/25 DC	100.00

Scott #	Description	Uncacheted	Line Pairs
	1923-25 Coil Issues		
597	1¢ Franklin 7/18/23 DC	750.00	1,750.00
598	1½¢ Harding 3/19/25 DC	55.00	175.00
*599	2¢ Washington 1/15/23 DC (37 known)	2,250.00	3,500.00
	1/10/23 Lancaster, PA (1 known)	4,000.00	...

*** These are the eku from DC and prepared by Phil Ward.
Other covers are known date 1/10, 1/11 & 1/13.**

Scott #	Description	Uncacheted	Line Pairs
600	3¢ Lincoln 5/10/24 DC	125.00	275.00
602	5¢ T. Roosevelt 3/5/24 DC	100.00	275.00
603	10¢ Monroe 12/1/24 DC	110.00	350.00
604	1¢ Franklin 7/19/24 DC	85.00	225.00
605	1½¢ Harding 5/9/25 DC	75.00	175.00
606	2¢ Washington 12/31/23 DC	150.00	450.00

Scott #	Description	Uncacheted	Line Pairs
	1923 Issues		
610	2¢ Harding 9/1/23 DC	30.00	...
	Marion, OH	20.00	...
	George W. Linn cachet (1st modern cachet)	...	875.00
611	2¢ Harding Imperf. 11/15/23 DC	90.00	...
612	2¢ Harding Perf. 10 9/12/23 DC	110.00	...

Scott #	Description	Uncacheted	Line Pairs
	1924 HUGENOT-WALLOON ISSUE		
614	1¢ Hugenot-Walloon 5/1/24 DC	40.00	...
	Albany, NY	40.00	...
	Allentown, PA	40.00	...
	Charleston, SC	40.00	...
	Jacksonville, FL	40.00	...
	Lancaster, PA	40.00	...
	Mayport, FL	40.00	...
	New Rochelle, NY	40.00	...
	New York, NY	40.00	...
	Philadelphia, PA	40.00	...
	Reading, PA	40.00	...
	Unofficial City	100.00	...
615	2¢ Hugenot-Walloon 5/1/24 DC	60.00	...
	Albany, NY	60.00	...
	Allentown, PA	60.00	...
	Charleston, SC	60.00	...
	Jacksonville, FL	60.00	...
	Lancaster, PA	60.00	...
	Mayport, FL	60.00	...
	New Rochelle, NY	60.00	...
	New York, NY	60.00	...
	Philadelphia, PA	60.00	...
	Reading, PA	60.00	...
	Unofficial City	125.00	...
616	5¢ Hugenot-Walloon 5/1/24 DC	85.00	...
	Albany, NY	85.00	...
	Allentown, PA	85.00	...
	Charleston, SC	85.00	...
	Jacksonville, FL	85.00	...
	Lancaster, PA	85.00	...
	Mayport, FL	85.00	...
	New Rochelle, NY	85.00	...
	New York, NY	85.00	...
	Philadelphia, PA	85.00	...
	Reading, PA	85.00	...
	Unofficial City	150.00	...
614-16	1¢-5¢ Comp. set on 1 cover, any official city	175.00	...
614-16	Same, Any Unofficial City	400.00	...

Scott #	Description	Uncacheted	Line Pairs
	1925 LEXINGTON-CONCORD ISSUE		
617	1¢ Lexington-Concord 4/4/25 DC	30.00	125.00
	Boston, MA	30.00	125.00
	Cambridge, MA	30.00	125.00
	Concord, MA	30.00	125.00
	Concord Junction, MA	35.00	...
	Lexington, MA	35.00	125.00
	Unofficial City	75.00	...
618	2¢ Lexington-Concord 4/4/25 DC	35.00	125.00
	Boston, MA	35.00	125.00
	Cambridge, MA	35.00	125.00
	Concord, MA	35.00	125.00
	Concord Junction, MA	40.00	...
	Lexington, MA	40.00	125.00
	Unofficial City	100.00	...
619	5¢ Lexington-Concord 4/4/25 DC	80.00	175.00
	Boston, MA	80.00	175.00
	Cambridge, MA	80.00	175.00
	Concord, MA	80.00	175.00
	Concord Junction, MA	90.00	...
	Lexington, MA	90.00	175.00
	Unofficial City	125.00	...
617-19	1¢-5¢ **1st Jackson cachet**		
	(see above listings for prices except #619 which is $750.)		
617-19	1¢-5¢ Lexington-Concord, cplt. set on one cover	150.00	...
	Same, Concord-Junction or Lexington	175.00	...
	Same, Any Unofficial City	250.00	...

Scott #	Description	Uncacheted	Line Pairs
	1925 NORSE-AMERICAN ISSUE		
620	2¢ Norse-American 5/18/25 DC	20.00	...
	Algona, IA	20.00	...
	Benson, MN	20.00	...
	Decorah, IA	20.00	...
	Minneapolis, MN	20.00	...
	Northfield, MN	20.00	...
	St. Paul, MN	20.00	...
	Unofficial City	60.00	...
621	5¢ Norse-American 5/18/25 DC	30.00	...
	Algona, IA	30.00	...
	Benson, MN	30.00	...
	Decorah, IA	30.00	...
	Minneapolis, MN	30.00	...
	Northfield, MN	30.00	...
	St. Paul, MN	30.00	...
	Unofficial City	90.00	...
620-21	2¢ Norse-Amer., one cover 5/18/25 DC	50.00	275.00
	2¢-5¢ Algona, IA	50.00	275.00
	2¢-5¢ Benson, MN	50.00	275.00
	2¢-5¢ Decorah, IA	50.00	275.00
620-1 cont	2¢-5¢ Minneapolis, MN	50.00	275.00
	2¢-5¢ Northfield, MN	50.00	275.00
	2¢-5¢ St. Paul, MN	50.00	275.00
	Unofficial City	150.00	...
	1st Ernest J. Weschcke cachet	...	275.00
	1st A.C. Roessler cachet	...	300.00
622	13¢ Harrison 1/11/26 DC	15.00	...
	Indianapolis, IN	25.00	...
	North Bend, OH	150.00	...
	Unofficial City	200.00	...
623	17¢ Wilson 12/28/25	20.00	275.00
	New York, NY	20.00	275.00
	Princeton, NJ	30.00	275.00
	Staunton, VA	25.00	275.00
	Unofficial City	175.00	...
	1st Nickles cachet	...	275.00
627	2¢ Sesquicentennial 5/10/26 DC	10.00	65.00
	Boston, MA	10.00	65.00
	Philadelphia, PA	10.00	65.00
	1st Griffin cachet	...	150.00
	1st Baxter cachet	...	75.00
628	5¢ Ericsson Memorial 5/29/26 DC	25.00	450.00
	Chicago, IL	25.00	450.00
	Minneapolis, MN	25.00	450.00
	New York, NY	25.00	450.00
629	2¢ White Plains 10/18/26 New York, NY	8.00	70.00
	New York, NY Int. Phil. Ex. Agency	8.00	70.00
	White Plains, NY	8.00	70.00
630a	2¢ White Plains S/S, sgl. 10/18/26 NY, NY	12.00	75.00
	New York, NY Int. Phil. Ex. Agency	12.00	75.00
	White Plains, NY	12.00	75.00
	Block of 10 with selvage	250.00	...
630	Complete Sheet 10/18/26	1700.00	...
630	10/28/26	1300.00	...
631	1½¢ Harding Rotary Imperf. 8/27/26 DC	50.00	...

Scott #	Description	Uncacheted	Line Pairs
	1926-27 ROTARY PRESS PERF. 11 X 10½		
632	1¢ Franklin 6/10/27 DC	42.50	...
632a	Bklt. Pane of 6 11/27	4500.00	...
633	1½¢ Harding 5/17/27 DC	42.50	...
634	2¢ Washington 12/10/26 DC	45.00	...
634EE	Experimental Electric Eye 3/28/35	1200.00	...
635	3¢ Lincoln 2/3/27 DC	45.00	...
635a	3¢ Lincoln Re-issue 2/7/34 DC	25.00	45.00
636	4¢ Martha Washington 5/17/27 DC	55.00	...
637	5¢ T. Roosevelt 3/24/27 DC	55.00	...
638	6¢ Garfield 7/27/27 DC	65.00	...
639	7¢ McKinley 3/24/27 DC	60.00	...

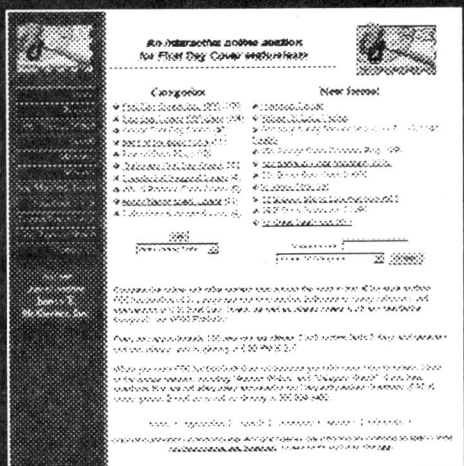

658

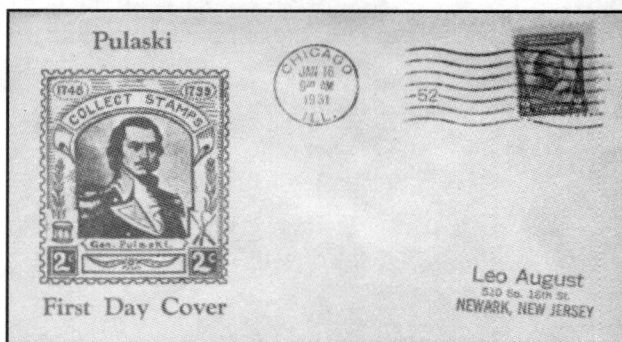

Scott #	Description	Uncacheted	Cacheted
	1926-27 ROTARY PRESS PERF. 11 X 10½ (Cont.)		
639, 637	on one FDC	300.00	...
640	8¢ Grant 6/10/27 DC	65.00	...
	640, 632 on one FDC	300.00	...
641	9¢ Jefferson 5/17/27 DC	70.00	...
	641, 633, & 636 on one FDC	450.00	...
642	10¢ Monroe 2/3/27 DC	85.00	...
	632-42, set of 12	700.00	...
643	2¢ Vermont 8/3/27 DC	8.00	60.00
	Bennington, VT	8.00	60.00
	1st Joshua Gerow cachet	...	200.00
	1st Harris Hunt cachet	...	150.00
	1st Kirkjian cachet	...	275.00
644	2¢ Burgoyne 8/3/27 DC	12.00	75.00
	Albany, NY	12.00	75.00
	Rome, NY	12.00	75.00
	Syracuse, NY	12.00	75.00
	Utica, NY	12.00	75.00
	1st Ralph Dyer cachet	...	300.00
	Unofficial City	40.00	125.00
	1928		
645	2¢ Valley Forge 5/26/28 DC	5.00	60.00
	Cleveland, OH	60.00	140.00
	Lancaster, PA	5.00	60.00
	Norristown, PA	5.00	60.00
	Philadelphia, PA	5.00	60.00
	Valley Forge, PA	5.00	60.00
	West Chester, PA	5.00	60.00
	Cleveland Midwestern Phil. Sta	5.00	60.00
	1st J.W. Stoutzenberg cachet	...	275.00
	1st Adam K. Bert cachet	...	75.00
	1st Egolf cachet		90.00
646	2¢ Molly Pitcher 10/20/28 DC	12.50	85.00
	Freehold, NJ	12.50	85.00
	Red Bank, NJ	12.50	85.00
647	2¢ Hawaii 8/13/28 DC	25.00	125.00
	Honolulu, HI	25.00	125.00
648	5¢ Hawaii 8/13/28 DC	25.00	150.00
	Honolulu, HI	30.00	150.00
647-48	Hawaii on one cover	50.00	250.00
	1st F.W. Reid Cachet	...	325.00
	1st Best Cachet	...	325.00
649	2¢ Aeronautics Conf., green pmk. 12/12/28 DC	6.00	40.00
	Black pmk.	10.00	40.00
650	5¢ Aeronautics Conf., green pmk. 12/12/28 DC	10.00	50.00
	Black pmk	12.50	50.00
649-50	Aero. Conf., one cover, green pmk	15.00	70.00
	One cover, black pmk	17.50	75.00
	1929		
651	2¢ Clark 2/25/29 Vinncennes, in	5.00	30.00
	1st Harry loor cachet	...	175.00
653	½¢ Hale (block of 4) 5/25/29 DC	40.00	...
	Unofficial City	175.00	...
654	2¢ Electric Lt., flat press 6/5/29 Menlo Park, NJ	10.00	45.00
	1st Klotzbach cachet	...	225.00
655	2¢ Electric Light, rotary press 6/11/29 DC	100.00	250.00
656	2¢ Electric Light, coil 6/11/29 DC	100.00	250.00
656	Coil Line Pair	150.00	275.00
655-56	Rotary & Coil sgls. on one FDC	175.00	375.00
657	2¢ Sullivan 6/17/29 Auburn, NY	4.00	30.00
	Binghamton, NY	4.00	30.00
	Canajoharie, NY	4.00	30.00
	Canandaigua, NY	4.00	30.00
	Elmira, NY	4.00	30.00
	Geneva, NY	4.00	30.00
	Geneseo, NY	4.00	30.00
	Horseheads, NY	4.00	30.00
	Owego, NY	4.00	30.00
	Penn Yan, NY	4.00	30.00
	Perry, NY	4.00	30.00
	Seneca Falls, NY	4.00	30.00
	Waterloo, NY	4.00	30.00
	Watkins Glen, NY	4.00	30.00
	Waverly, NY	4.00	30.00
	1st Robert Beazell cachet	...	400.00
	1st A.C. Elliot cachet	...	75.00

690

Scott #	Description	Uncacheted	Cacheted
	KANSAS OVERPRINTS		
658	1¢ Franklin 5/1/29 DC	50.00	...
	4/15/29 Newton, KS	500.00	...
659	1½¢ Harding 5/1/29 DC	60.00	...
660	2¢ Washington 5/1/29 DC	60.00	75.00
661	3¢ Lincoln 5/1/29 DC	75.00	...
662	4¢ Martha Washington 5/1/29 DC	100.00	...
663	5¢ T. Roosevelt 5/1/29 DC	100.00	200.00
664	6¢ Garfield 5/1/29 DC	125.00	...
	4/15/29 Newton, KS	900.00	...
665	7¢ McKinley 5/1/29 DC	150.00	...
666	8¢ Grant 5/1/29 DC	150.00	...
	4/15/29 Newton, KS	900.00	...
667	9¢ Jefferson 5/1/29 DC	150.00	...
668	10¢ Monroe 5/1/29 DC	200.00	...
658-68	1¢-10¢ Kansas cplt. set on one FDC 5/1/29 DC	1,300.00	2,000.00
658-68	Kansas Set of 11 covers	1,250.00	2,000.00
658,664,666	4/15/29 Newton, KS	1,900.00	
	NEBRASKA OVERPRINTS		
669-79	Nebraska Set of 11 Covers	1250.00	2000.00
669	1¢ Franklin 5/1/29 DC	50.00	...
	4/15/29 Beatrice, NE	400.00	...
670	1½¢ Harding 5/1/29 DC	60.00	...
	4/15/29 Hartington, NE	350.00	...
671	2¢ Washington 5/1/29 DC	60.00	...
	4/15/29 Auburn, NE	350.00	...
	4/15/29 Beatrice, NE	350.00	...
	4/15/29 Hartington, NE	350.00	...
672	3¢ Lincoln 5/1/29 DC	75.00	...
	4/15/29 Beatrice, NE	450.00	...
	4/15/29 Hartington, NE	450.00	...
673	4¢ Martha Washington 5/1/29 DC	100.00	...
	4/15/29 Beatrice, NE	500.00	...
	4/15/29 Hartington, NE	500.00	...
674	5¢ T. Roosevelt 5/1/29 DC	100.00	200.00
	4/15/29 Beatrice, NE	500.00	...
	4/15/29 Hartington, NE	500.00	...
675	6¢ Garfield 5/1/29 DC	125.00	...
676	7¢ McKinley 5/1/29 DC	150.00	...
677	8¢ Grant 5/1/29 DC	150.00	...
678	9¢ Jefferson 5/1/29 DC	150.00	...
679	10¢ Monroe 5/1/29 DC	200.00	...
669-79	1¢-10¢ Nebraska cplt. set on one FDC 5/1/29 DC	1300.00	1700.00
658-79	all 22 values on 1 cover (2 known)	4500.00	...
680	2¢ Fallen Timbers 9/14/29 Erie, PA	3.00	35.00
	Maumee, OH	3.00	35.00
	Perrysburgh, OH	3.00	35.00
	Toledo, OH	3.00	35.00
	Waterville, OH	3.00	35.00
681	2¢ Ohio River 10/19/29 Cairo, IL	3.00	35.00
	Cincinnati, OH	3.00	35.00
	Evansville, IN	3.00	35.00
	Homestead, PA	3.00	35.00
	Louisville, KY	3.00	35.00
	Pittsburgh, PA	3.00	35.00
	Wheeling, WV	3.00	35.00
	1930-31		
682	2¢ Mass. Bay Colony 4/8/30 Boston, MA	3.00	35.00
	Salem, MA	3.00	35.00
683	2¢ Carolina-Charleston 4/10/30 Charleston, SC	3.00	35.00
684	1½¢ Harding 12/1/30 Marion, OH	4.00	45.00
685	4¢ Taft 6/4/30 Cincinnati, OH	6.00	60.00
686	1½¢ Harding, coil 12/1/30 Marion, OH	5.00	60.00
686	Coil Line Pair	15.00	90.00
687	4¢ Taft, coil 9/18/30 DC	40.00	150.00
687	Coil Line Pair	75.00	250.00
688	2¢ Braddock 7/9/30 Braddock, PA	4.00	35.00
689	2¢ Von Steuben 9/17/30 New York, NY	4.00	35.00
690	2¢ Pulaski 1/16/31 Brooklyn, NY	4.00	35.00
	Buffalo, NY	4.00	35.00
	Chicago, IL	4.00	35.00
	Cleveland, OH	4.00	35.00
	Detroit, MI	4.00	35.00

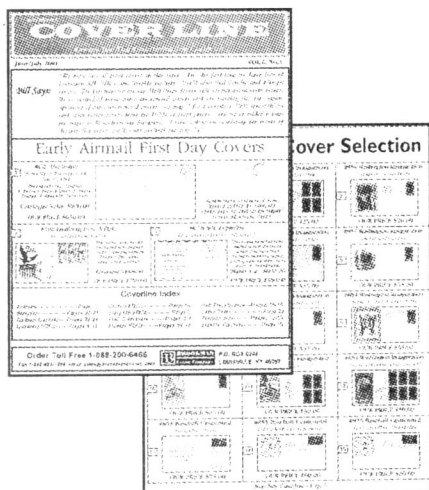

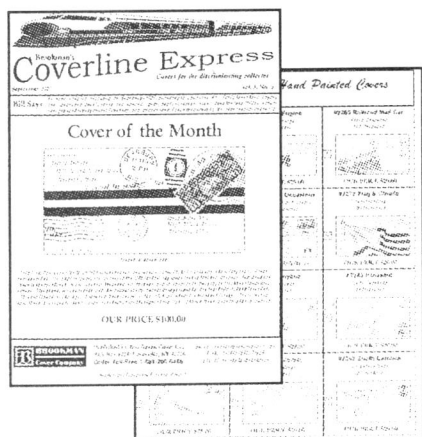

149

U.S. First Day Covers

737

Scott #	Description	Uncacheted	Cacheted
690	Gary, IN	4.00	35.00
	Milwaukee, WI	4.00	35.00
	New York, NY	4.00	35.00
	Pittsburgh, PA	4.00	35.00
	Savannah, GA	4.00	35.00
	South Bend, IN	4.00	35.00
	Toledo, OH	4.00	35.00
	1st Truby cachet	...	125.00

1931 ROTARY PRESS HI-VALUES

Scott #	Description	Uncacheted
692	11¢ Hayes 9/4/31 DC	125.00
693	12¢ Cleveland 8/25/31 DC	125.00
694	13¢ Harrison 9/4/31 DC	125.00
695	14¢ Indian 9/8/31 DC	125.00
696	15¢ Statue of Liberty 8/27/31 DC	140.00
697	17¢ Wilson 7/27/31 DC	400.00
	7/25/31 Brooklyn, NY	3,000.00
698	20¢ Golden Gate 9/8/31 DC	300.00
699	25¢ Niagara Falls 7/27/31 DC	400.00
	7/25/31 Brooklyn, NY	1,500.00
	697, 699 on one FDC, Brooklyn, NY	4,000.00
700	30¢ Bison 9/8/31 DC	300.00
701	50¢ Arlington 9/4/31 DC	450.00

1931

Scott #	Description	Uncacheted	Cacheted
702	2¢ Red Cross 5/21/31 DC	3.00	35.00
	Dansville, NY	3.00	35.00
	1st Edward Hacker cachet	...	150.00
703	2¢ Yorktown 10/19/31 Wethersfield, CT	3.00	45.00
	Yorktown, VA	3.00	45.00
	Any Predate	200.00	...
	Unofficial City	45.00	...
	1st Crosby cachet	...	400.00
	1st Aeroprint cachet	...	150.00

1932 WASHINGTON BICENTENNIAL ISSUE

Scott #	Description	Cacheted
704-15	Bicentennial Set of 12 Covers	220.00
704	½¢ olive brown 1/1/32 DC	20.00
705	1¢ green 1/1/32 DC	20.00
706	1½¢ brown 1/1/32 DC	20.00
707	2¢ carmine rose 1/1/32 DC	20.00
708	3¢ deep violet 1/1/32 DC	20.00
709	4¢ light brown 1/1/32 DC	20.00
710	5¢ blue 1/1/32 DC	20.00
711	6¢ red orange 1/1/32 DC	20.00
712	7¢ black 1/1/32 DC	20.00
713	8¢ olive bistre 1/1/32 DC	20.00
714	9¢ pale red 1/1/32 DC	20.00
715	10¢ orange yellow 1/1/32 DC	20.00
	1st Rice cachet (on any single)	25.00
	1st Raley cachet (on any single)	40.00
704-15	Wash. Bicent. on one cover	250.00

1932

Scott #	Description	Cacheted
716	2¢ Winter Olympic Games 1/25/32 Lake Placid, NY	35.00
	1st Beverly Hills cachet	250.00
717	2¢ Arbor Day 4/22/32 Nebraska City, NE	25.00
	1st Linnprint cachet	40.00
718	3¢ Summer Olympics 6/15/32 Los Angeles, CA	40.00
719	5¢ Summer Olympics 6/15/32 Los Angeles, CA	40.00
718-19	Summer Olympics cplt. set on one FDC	60.00
720	3¢ Washington 6/16/32 DC	40.00
720b	3¢ Booklet Pane 7/25/32 DC	200.00
721	3¢ Washington, coil, vert. 6/24/32 DC	50.00
721	Coil Line Pair	90.00
722	3¢ Washington, coil, horiz. 10/12/32 DC	50.00
722	Coil Line Pair	90.00
723	6¢ Garfield, coil 8/18/32 Los Angeles, CA	60.00
723	Coil Line Pair	95.00
724	3¢ William Penn 10/24/32 New Castle, DE	25.00
	Chester, PA	25.00
	Philadelphia, PA	25.00
725	3¢ Daniel Webster 10/24/32 Franklin, NH	25.00
	Exeter, NH	25.00
	Hanover, NH	25.00
726	3¢ Gen'l Oglethorpe 2/12/33 Savannah, GA	25.00
	1st Anderson cachet	150.00

Scott #	Description	Cacheted
727	3¢ Peace Proclamation 4/19/33 Newburgh, NY	25.00
	1st Grimsland cachet	**350.00**
728	1¢ Century of Progress 5/25/33 Chicago, IL	20.00
729	3¢ Century of Progress 5/25/33 Chicago, IL	20.00
728-29	Progress on one cover	25.00
730	1¢ Amer. Phil. Soc., sht. of 25 8/25/33 Chicago, IL	200.00
730a	1¢ Amer. Phil. Soc., single 8/25/33 Chicago, IL	20.00
731	3¢ Amer. Phil. Soc., sht. of 25 8/25/33 Chicago, IL	200.00
731a	3¢ Amer. Phil. Soc., single 8/25/33 Chicago, IL	20.00
730-731	On one Uncacheted Cover	850.00
730a-31a	Amer. Phil. Soc. on one cover	25.00
732	3¢ National Recovery Act 8/15/33 DC	20.00
	Nira, IA 8/17/33, unofficial	25.00
733	3¢ Byrd Antarctic 10/9/33 DC	30.00
734	5¢ Kosciuszko 10/13/33 Boston, MA	20.00
	Buffalo, NY	20.00
	Chicago, NY	20.00
	Detroit, MI	20.00
	Pittsburgh, PA	50.00
	Kosciuszko, MS	20.00
	St. Louis, MO	20.00
735	3¢ Nat'l Exhibition, sht. of 6 2/10/34 New York, NY	75.00
735a	3¢ National Exhibition, single 2/10/34 New York NY	20.00
736	3¢ Maryland 3/23/34 St. Mary's City, MD	20.00
	1st Torkel Gundel cachet	**300.00**
	1st Don Kapner cachet	**25.00**
	1st Louis Nix cachet	**250.00**
	1st Top Notch cachet	**25.00**
737	3¢ Mothers of Am., rotary 5/2/34 any city	15.00
738	3¢ Mothers of Am., flat 5/2/34 any city	15.00
737-38	Mothers of Am. on one cover	35.00
739	3¢ Wisconsin 7/7/34 Green Bay, WI	20.00

1934 NATIONAL PARKS ISSUE

Scott #	Description	Cacheted
740-49	National Parks set of 10 covers	125.00
740-49	On 1 Cover 10/8/34	150.00
740	1¢ Yosemite 7/16/34 Yosemite, CA	12.50
	DC	12.50
741	2¢ Grand Canyon 7/24 34 Grand Canyon, AZ	12.50
	DC	12.50
742	3¢ Mt. Rainier 8/3/34 Longmire, WA	12.50
	DC	12.50
743	4¢ Mesa Verde 9/25/34 Mesa Verde, CO	12.50
	DC	12.50
744	5¢ Yellowstone 7/30/34 Yellowstone, WY	12.50
	DC	12.50
745	6¢ Crater Lake 9/5/34 Crater Lake, OR	12.50
	DC	12.50
746	7¢ Acadia 10/2/34 Bar Harbor, ME	12.50
	DC	12.50
747	8¢ Zion 9/18/34 Zion, UT	12.50
	DC	12.50
748	9¢ Glacier Park 8/27/34 Glacier Park, MT	12.50
	DC	12.50
749	10¢ Smoky Mts. 10/8/34 Sevierville, TN	12.50
	DC	12.50
750	3¢ Amer. Phil. Soc., sheet of 6 8/28/34 Atlantic City, NJ	75.00
750a	3¢ Amer. Phil. Soc., single 8/28/34 Atlantic City, NJ	20.00
751	1¢ Trans-Miss. Phil. Expo., sht. of 6 10/10/34 Omaha, NE	75.00
751a	1¢ Trans-Miss. Phil. Expo., single 10/10/34 Omaha, NE	20.00

Scott #	Description	Center Gutter or Line Blk	Cacheted Gutter or Line Pair	Singles
	1935 FARLEY SPECIAL PRINTING			
752-71	Set of 20 covers	...	...	500.00
752-71	Set on 1 cover 3/15/35	...	...	450.00
752-55,766a-71	10 varieties on 1 cover 3/15/35	...	...	250.00
752	3¢ Peace Proclamation 3/15/35 DC	150.00	50.00	35.00
753	3¢ Byrd 3/15/35 DC	175.00	50.00	35.00
754	3¢ Mothers of America 3/15/35 DC	150.00	45.00	35.00
755	3¢ Wisconsin 3/15/35 DC	150.00	45.00	35.00
756-65	Parks set of 10 covers	1,750.00	400.00	300.00
756-65	Set on 1 cover 3/15/35	...	...	175.00
756	1¢ Yosemite 3/15/35 DC	150.00	40.00	30.00
757	2¢ Grand Canyon 3/15/35 DC	150.00	40.00	30.00
758	3¢ Mount Rainier 3/15/35 DC	150.00	40.00	30.00
759	4¢ Mesa Verde 3/15/35 DC	150.00	40.00	30.00
760	5¢ Yellowstone 3/15/35 DC	150.00	40.00	30.00
761	6¢ Crater Lake 3/15/35 DC	150.00	40.00	30.00
762	7¢ Acadia 3/15/35 DC	150.00	40.00	30.00
763	8¢ Zion 3/15/35 DC	150.00	40.00	30.00
764	9¢ Glacier Park 3/15/35 DC	150.00	40.00	30.00
765	10¢ Smoky Mountains 3/15/35 DC	150.00	40.00	30.00
766	1¢ Century of Progress 3/15/35, DC Imperf, pane of 25,		600.00	...
766a	Strip of 3	150.00	50.00	40.00
767	3¢ Century of Progress 3/15/35, DC Imperf, pane of 25	...	600.00	...
767a	Single	150.00	50.00	40.00
768	3¢ Byrd 3/15/35 DC Imperf, pane of 25	...	600.00	...
768a	Single	175.00	70.00	40.00
769	1¢ Yosemite 3/15/35 DC Imperf, pane of 6	...	600.00	...
769a	Strip of 3	150.00	55.00	40.00
770	3¢ Mount Rainier 3/15/35 Imperf, pane of 6	...	600.00	...
770a	Single	150.00	55.00	40.00
771	16¢ Air Mail-Spec. Del. 3/15/35 DC	175.00	60.00	40.00

U.S. First Day Covers

794

Scott #	Description	Cacheted
	1935-36	
772	3¢ Connecticut 4/26/35 Hartford, CT	17.50
	1st Winfred Grandy cachet	**30.00**
773	3¢ Calif. Exposition 5/29/35 San Diego, CA	17.50
	1st W. Espenshade cachet	**30.00**
774	3¢ Boulder Dam 9/30/35 Boulder City, NV	20.00
775	3¢ Michigan 11/1/35 Lansing, MI	17.50
	1st Risko Art Studio cachet	**200.00**
776	3¢ Texas 3/2/36 Gonzales, TX	20.00
	1st John Sidenius cachet	**60.00**
	1st Walter Czubay cachet	**75.00**
777	3¢ Rhode Island 5/4/36 Providence, RI	17.50
	1st J.W. Clifford cachet	**30.00**
778	3¢ TIPEX sheet 5/9/36 New York, NY	17.50
	1st House of Farnam cachet	**500.00**
778a-78d	Single from sheet	10.00
782	3¢ Arkansas 6/15/36 Little Rock, AK	15.00
783	3¢ Oregon 7/14/36 Astoria, OR	12.50
	Daniel, WY	12.50
	Lewiston, ID	12.50
	Missoula, MT	12.50
	Walla Walla, WA	12.50
784	3¢ Susan B. Anthony 8/26/36 DC	17.50
	1st Historic Arts cachet	**25.00**

Scott #	Description	Price
	1936-37 ARMY - NAVY	
785-94	Army-Navy set of 10 covers	75.00
785	1¢ Army 12/15/36 DC	7.50
786	2¢ Army 1/15/37 DC	7.50
787	3¢ Army 2/18/37 DC	7.50
	1st William Von Ohlen cachet	**75.00**
788	4¢ Army 3/23/37 DC	7.50
789	5¢ Army 5/26/37 West Point, NY	7.50
	#785-89, Army set on one cover, 5/26/37	35.00
790	1¢ Navy 12/15/36 DC	7.50
791	2¢ Navy 1/15/37 DC	7.50
792	3¢ Navy 2/18/37 DC	7.50
793	4¢ Navy 3/23/37 DC	7.50
794	5¢ Navy 5/26/37 Annapolis, MD	7.50
	#790-94, Navy set on one cover, 5/26/37	35.00
	#785-94, Army-Navy set on one cover, 5/26/37	75.00

	1937	
795	3¢ Ordinance of 1787 7/13/37 Marietta, OH	12.00
	New York, NY	12.00
	1st Cachet Craft cachet	**60.00**
	1st Linto cachet	**150.00**
796	5¢ Virginia Dare 8/18/37 Manteo, NC	15.00
797	10¢ S.P.A. sheet 8/26/37 Asheville, NC	12.00
798	3¢ Constitution 9/17/37 Philadelphia, PA	12.00
	1st Pilgrim cachet	**90.00**
	1st Fidelity Stamp Co. cachet	**15.00**
799-802	Territory set of 4 covers	60.00
799-802	On 1 Cover 12/15/37	40.00
799	3¢ Hawaii 10/18/37 Honolulu, HI	20.00
800	3¢ Alaska 11/12/37 Juneau, AK	15.00
801	3¢ Puerto Rico 11/25/37 San Juan, PR	15.00
802	3¢ Virgin Islands 12/15/37 Charlotte Amalie, VI	15.00

	1938-1954 PRESIDENTIAL SERIES	
803-34	Presidents set of 32 covers	450.00
803-31	Presidents set of 29 covers	110.00
803	½¢ Franklin 5/19/38 Philadelphia, PA	3.00
804	1¢ Washington 4/25/38 DC	3.00
804b	booklet pane 1/27/39 DC	15.00
805	1½¢ Martha Washington 5/5/38 DC	3.00
806	2¢ J. Adams 6/3/38 DC	3.00
806b	booklet pane 1/27/39 DC	15.00
807	3¢ Jefferson 6/16/38 DC	3.00
807a	booklet pane 1/27/39 DC	15.00
	#804b, 806b, 807a Bklt. set on one cover, 1/27/38 DC	60.00
808	4¢ Madison 7/1/38 DC	3.00
809	4½¢ White House 7/11/38 DC	3.00
810	5¢ Monroe 7/21/38 DC	3.00
811	6¢ J.Q. Adams 7/28/38 DC	3.00
812	7¢ Jackson 8/4/38 DC	3.00

834

Scott #	Description	Cacheted
	1938-1954 PRESIDENTIAL SERIES (cont.)	
813	8¢ Van Buren 8/11/38 DC	3.00
814	9¢ Harrison 8/18/38 DC	3.00
815	10¢ Tyler 9/2/38 DC	3.00
816	11¢ Polk 9/8/38 DC	5.00
817	12¢ Taylor 9/14/38 DC	5.00
818	13¢ Fillmore 9/22/38 DC	5.00
819	14¢ Pierce 10/6/38 DC	5.00
820	15¢ Buchanan 10/13/38 DC	5.00
821	16¢ Lincoln 10/20/38 DC	6.00
822	17¢ Johnson 10/27/38 DC	6.00
823	18¢ Grant 11/3/38 DC	6.00
824	19¢ Hayes 11/10/38 DC	6.00
825	20¢ Garfield 11/10/38 DC	6.00
	#824-825 on one FDC	40.00
826	21¢ Arthur 11/22/38 DC	7.00
827	22¢ Cleveland 11/22/38 DC	7.00
	#826-827 on one FDC	40.00
828	24¢ Harrison 12/2/38 DC	8.00
829	25¢ McKinley 12/2/38 DC	8.00
	#828-829 on one FDC	40.00
830	30¢ Roosevelt 12/8/38 DC	10.00
831	50¢ Taft 12/8/38 DC	15.00
	#830-831 on one FDC	40.00
832	$1 Wilson 8/29/38 DC	65.00
832c	$1 Wilson, dry print 8/31/54 DC	30.00
833	$2 Harding 9/29/38 DC	125.00
834	$5 Coolidge 11/17/38 DC	210.00

	PRESIDENTIAL ELECTRIC EYE FDC's	
803-31EE	Presidents set of 29 Covers	550.00
803EE	½¢ Electric Eye 9/8/41 DC	10.00
804EE	1¢ Electric Eye 9/8/41 DC	10.00
	#803, 804, E15 on one FDC	30.00
805EE	1½¢ Electric Eye 1/16/41 DC	10.00
806EE	2¢ Electric Eye (Type I) 6/3/38 DC	15.00
806EE	2¢ Electric Eye (Type II) 4/5/39 DC	8.00
807EE	3¢ Electric Eye 4/5/39 DC	8.00
	#806-807 on one FDC 4/5/39	15.00
807EE	3¢ Electric Eye convertible 1/18/40	12.50
808EE	4¢ Electric Eye 10/28/41 DC	17.50
809EE	4½¢ Electric Eye 10/28/41 DC	17.50
810EE	5¢ Electric Eye 10/28/41 DC	17.50
811EE	6¢ Electric Eye 9/25/41 DC	15.00
812EE	7¢ Electric Eye 10/28/41 DC	17.50
813EE	8¢ Electric Eye 10/28/41 DC	17.50
814EE	9¢ Electric Eye 10/28/41 DC	17.50
815EE	10¢ Electric Eye 9/25/41 DC	15.00
	#811, 815 on one FDC	25.00
816EE	11¢ Electric Eye 10/8/41 DC	20.00
817EE	12¢ Electric Eye 10/8/41 DC	20.00
818EE	13¢ Electric Eye 10/8/41 DC	20.00
819EE	14¢ Electric Eye 10/8/41 DC	20.00
820EE	15¢ Electric Eye 10/8/41 DC	20.00
	#816-820 on one FDC	30.00
821EE	16¢ Electric Eye 1/7/42 DC	25.00
822EE	17¢ Electric Eye 10/28/41 DC	25.00
	#808-10, 812-14, 822 on one FDC	60.00
823EE	18¢ Electric Eye 1/7/42 DC	25.00
824EE	19¢ Electric Eye 1/7/42 DC	25.00
825EE	20¢ Electric Eye 1/7/42 DC	25.00
	#824-825 on one FDC	30.00
826EE	21¢ Electric Eye 1/7/42 DC	25.00
	#821, 823-26 on one FDC	60.00
827EE	22¢ Electric Eye 1/28/42 DC	35.00
828EE	24¢ Electric Eye 1/28/42 DC	35.00
829EE	25¢ Electric Eye 1/28/42 DC	40.00
830EE	30¢ Electric Eye 1/28/42 DC	40.00
831EE	50¢ Electric Eye 1/28/42 DC	50.00
	#827-831 on one FDC	75.00

	1938	
835	3¢ Ratification 6/21/38 Philadelphia, PA	15.00
836	3¢ Swedes and Finns 6/27/38 Wilmington, DE	15.00
	1st Staehle cachet	**50.00**
837	3¢ NW Territory 7/15/38 Marietta, OH	15.00
838	3¢ Iowa Territory 8/24/38 Des Moines, IA	15.00

U.S. First Day Covers

924

1939 PRESIDENTIAL COILS

Scott #	Description	Line Pr	Price
839-51	Presidents set of 13 covers	...	65.00
839	1¢ Washington, pair 1/20/39 DC	12.00	5.00
840	1½¢ M. Wash., pair 1/20/39 DC	12.00	5.00
841	2¢ J. Adams, pair 1/20/39 DC	12.00	5.00
842	3¢ Jefferson 1/20/39 DC	12.00	5.00
842	Same, pair	...	7.00
843	4¢ Madison 1/20/39 DC	12.00	6.00
844	4½¢ White House 1/20/39 DC	12.00	6.00
845	5¢ Monroe 1/20/39 DC	15.00	6.00
846	6¢ J.Q. Adams, vert. 1/20/39 DC	17.50	7.00
847	10¢ Tyler 1/20/39 DC	20.00	10.00
839-847	On 1 Cover	125.00	60.00
848	1¢ Washington, pair, vert. coil 1/27/39 DC	12.00	6.00
849	1½¢ M. Wash., pair, vert. coil 1/27/39 DC	12.00 ea	6.00
850	2¢ J. Adams, pair, vert. coil 1/27/39 DC	12.00	6.00
851	3¢ Jefferson 1/27/39 DC, Vert coil	12.00	6.00
848-51	On 1 Cover	75.00	40.00
839-51	On 1 cover	200.00	110.00

1939

Scott #	Description	Cacheted
852	3¢ Golden Gate 2/18/39 San Francisco, CA	17.50
853	3¢ World's Fair 4/1/39 New York, NY	17.50
	1st Artcraft cachet unaddressed	300.00
854	3¢ Wash. Inauguration 4/30/39 NY, NY	17.50
855	3¢ Baseball 6/12/39 Cooperstown, NY	40.00
856	3¢ Panama Canal 8/15/39 USS Charleston	25.00
857	3¢ Printing Tercent. 9/25/39 NY, NY	17.50
858	3¢ 50th Anniv. 4 States 11/2/39 Bismarck, ND	15.00
	11/2/39 Pierre, SD	15.00
	11/8/39 Helena, MT	15.00
	11/11/39 Olympia, WA	15.00

1940 FAMOUS AMERICANS

Scott #	Description	Cacheted
859-93	**Famous Americans set of 35 covers**	175.00
859	1¢ Washington Irving 1/29/40 Terrytown, NY	4.00
860	2¢ James Fenimore Cooper 1/29/40 Cooperstown, NY	4.00
861	3¢ Ralph Waldo Emerson 2/5/40 Boston, MA	4.00
862	5¢ Louisa May Alcott 2/5/40 Concord, MA	5.00
863	10¢ Samuel Clemens 2/13/40 Hannibal, MO	10.00
859-63	Authors on one cover 2/13/40	40.00
864	1¢ Henry W. Longfellow 2/16/40 Portland, ME	4.00
865	2¢ John Greenleaf Whittier 2/16/40 Haverhill, MA	4.00
866	3¢ James Russell Lowell 2/20/40 Cambridge, MA	4.00
867	5¢ Walt Whitman 2/20/40 Camden, NJ	5.00
868	10¢ James Whitcomb Riley 2/24/40 Greenfield, IN	6.00
864-68	Poets on one cover 2/24/40	40.00
869	1¢ Horace Mann 3/14/40 Boston, MA	4.00
870	2¢ Mark Hopkins 3/14/40 Williamstown, MA	4.00
871	3¢ Charles W. Eliot 3/28/40 Cambridge, MA	4.00
872	5¢ Frances E. Willard 3/28/40 Evanston, IL	5.00
873	10¢ Booker T. Washington 4/7/40 Tuskegee Inst., AL	13.00
869-73	Educators on one cover 4/7/40	45.00
874	1¢ John James Audubon 4/8/40 St. Francesville, LA	5.00
875	2¢ Dr. Crawford W. Long 4/8/40 Jefferson, GA	5.00
876	3¢ Luther Burbank 4/17/40 Santa Rosa, CA	4.00
877	5¢ Dr. Walter Reed 4/17/40 DC	5.00
878	10¢ Jane Addams 4/26/40 Chicago, IL	6.00
874-78	Scientists on one cover 4/26/40	40.00
879	1¢ Stephen Collins Foster 5/3/40 Bardstown, KY	4.00
880	2¢ John Philip Sousa 5/3/40 DC	4.00
881	3¢ Victor Herbert 5/13/40 New York, NY	4.00
882	5¢ Edward A. MacDowell 5/13/40 Peterborough, NH	5.00
883	10¢ Ethelbert Nevin 6/10/40 Pittsburgh, PA	6.00
879-83	Composers on one cover 6/10/40	40.00
884	1¢ Gilbert Charles Stuart 9/5/40 Narragansett, RI	4.00
885	2¢ James A. McNeill Whistler 9/5/40 Lowell, MA	4.00
886	3¢ Augustus Saint-Gaudens 9/16/40 New York, NY	4.00
887	5¢ Daniel Chester French 9/16/40 Stockbridge, MA	5.00
888	10¢ Frederic Remington 9/30/40 Canton, NY	6.00
884-88	Artists on one cover 9/30/40	40.00
889	1¢ Eli Whitney 10/7/40 Savannah, GA	4.00
890	2¢ Samuel F.B. Morse 10/7/40 NY, NY	4.00
891	3¢ Cyrus Hall McCormick 10/14/40 Lexington, VA	4.00
892	5¢ Elias Howe 10/14/40 Spencer, MA	5.00
893	10¢ Alexander Graham Bell 10/28/40 Boston, MA	7.00
889-93	Inventors on one cover 10/28/40	40.00
859-93	Famous American set on one cover 10/28/40	200.00

Scott #	Description	Cacheted
	1940-43	
894	3¢ Pony Exxpress 4/3/40 St. Joseph, MO	9.00
	Sacramento, CA	9.00
	1st Aristocrats cachet	15.00
895	3¢ Pan American Union 4/14/40 DC	7.00
896	3¢ Idaho Statehood 7/3/40 Boise, ID	7.00
897	3¢ Wyoming Statehood 7/10/40 Cheyenne, WY	7.00
	1st Spartan cachet	40.00
898	3¢ Coronado Expedition 9/7/40 Albuquerque, NM	7.00
899	1¢ National Defense 10/16/40 DC	6.00
900	2¢ National Defense 10/16/40 DC	6.00
901	3¢ National Defense 10/16/40 DC	6.00
899-901	National Defense on one cover	10.00
902	3¢ 13th Amend. 10/20/40 World's Fair, NY	12.00
903	3¢ Vermont Statehood 3/4/41 Montpelier, VT	10.00
	1st Fleetwood cachet	90.00
	1st Dorothy Knapp hand painted cachet	1,750.00
904	3¢ Kentucky Statehood 6/1/42 Frankfort, KY	7.00
	1st Signed Fleetwood cachet	75.00
905	3¢ Win the War 7/4/42 DC	7.00
906	5¢ China Resistance 7/7/42 Denver, CO	15.00
907	2¢ United Nations 1/14/43 DC	7.00
908	1¢ Four Freedoms 2/12/43 DC	7.00

1943-44 OVERRUN NATIONS (FLAGS)

Scott #	Description	Name Blks.	Singles
909-21	**Flags set of 13 covers**	130.00	40.00
909	5¢ Poland 3/22/43 Chicago, IL	10.00	6.00
	DC	10.00	6.00
	1st Penn Arts cachet	...	20.00
	1st Smartcraft cachet	...	15.00
910	5¢ Czechoslovakia 7/12/43 DC	10.00	5.00
911	5¢ Norway 7/27/43 DC	10.00	5.00
912	5¢ Luxembourg 8/10/43 DC	10.00	5.00
913	5¢ Netherlands 8/24/43 DC	10.00	5.00
914	5¢ Belgium 9/14/43 DC	10.00	5.00
915	5¢ France 9/28/43 DC	10.00	5.00
916	5¢ Greece 10/12/43 DC	10.00	5.00
917	5¢ Yugoslavia 10/26/43 DC	10.00	5.00
918	5¢ Albania 11/9/43 DC	10.00	5.00
919	5¢ Austria 11/23/43 DC	10.00	5.00
920	5¢ Denmark 12/7/43 DC	10.00	5.00
	#909-920 on one cover, 12/7/43	...	70.00
921	5¢ Korea 11/2/44 DC	10.00	6.00
	#909-921 on one cover, 11/2/44	...	85.00

Scott #	Description	Cacheted
	1944	
922	3¢ Railroad 5/10/44 Ogden, UT	9.00
	Omaha, NE	9.00
	San Francisco, CA	9.00
923	3¢ Steamship 5/22/44 Kings Point, NY	8.00
	Savannah, GA	8.00
924	3¢ Telegraph 5/24/44 DC	8.00
	Baltimore, MD	8.00
925	3¢ Corregidor 9/27/44 DC	9.00
926	3¢ Motion Picture 10/31/44 Hollywood, CA	8.00
	10/31/44 New York, NY	8.00
	1945	
927	3¢ Florida 3/3/45 Tallahassee, FL	7.00
928	5¢ UN Conference 4/25/45 San Francisco, CA	10.00
929	3¢ Iwo Jima 7/11/45 DC	17.50
930	1¢ Roosevelt 7/26/45 Hyde Park, NY	5.00
931	2¢ Roosevelt 8/24/45 Warm Springs, GA	5.00
932	3¢ Roosevelt 6/27/45 DC	5.00
	1st Fluegel cachet	75.00
933	5¢ Roosevelt 1/30/46 DC	5.00
	#930-933 on one cover 1/30/46 DC	12.00
934	3¢ Army 9/28/45 DC	10.00
935	3¢ Navy 10/27/45 Annapolis, MD	10.00
936	3¢ Coast Guard 11/10/45 New York, NY	10.00
937	3¢ Alfred E. Smith 11/26/45 New York, NY	6.00
938	3¢ Texas Centennial 12/29/45 Austin, TX	9.00
	1946	
939	3¢ Merchant Marine 2/26/46 DC	10.00
	#929, 934-36, 939 on one cover 2/26/46	30.00
940	3¢ Honorable Discharge 5/9/46 DC	10.00
	1st Artmaster cachet	20.00
	#929, 934-36, 939-940 on one cover 5/9/46	35.00
941	3¢ Tennessee Sthd. 6/1/46 Nashville, TN	4.00
942	3¢ Iowa Statehood 8/3/46 Iowa City, IA	4.00
943	3¢ Smithsonian 8/10/46 DC	4.00
944	3¢ New Mexico 10/16/46 Santa Fe, NM	4.00
	1947	
945	3¢ Thomas A. Edison 2/11/47 Milan, OH	4.50
946	3¢ Joseph Pulitzer 4/10/47 New York, NY	4.00
947	3¢ Stamp Centenary Sheet 5/17/47 New York, NY	4.00
	1st Fulton cachet (10 different)	30.00
948	5c-10¢ Stamp Centenary Sheet 5/19/47 New York, NY	4.50
949	3¢ Doctors 6/9/47 Atlantic City, NJ	8.00
950	3¢ Utah Cent. 7/24/47 Salt Lake City, UT	4.00
951	3¢ Constitution 10/21/47 Boston, MA	7.50
	1st C.W. George cachet	75.00
	1st Suncraft cachet	25.00

U.S. First Day Covers

963

Scott #	Description	Cacheted
	1948	
952	3¢ Everglades 12/5/47 Florida City, FL	4.00
953	3¢ G. Washington Carver 1/5/48 Tuskegee Inst., AL	6.00
	1st Jackson cachet	**35.00**
954	3¢ Discovery of Gold 1/24/48 Coloma, CA	3.00
955	3¢ Mississippi 4/7/48 Natchez, MS	3.00
956	3¢ Four Chaplains 5/28/48 DC	5.00
957	3¢ Wisconsin Cent. 5/29/48 Madison, WI	2.00
958	5¢ Swedish Pioneers 6/4/48 Chicago, IL	2.00
959	3¢ Women's Prog. 7/19/48 Seneca Falls, NY	2.00
960	3¢ William A. White 7/31/48 Emporia, KS	2.00
961	3¢ US-Canada 8/2/48 Niagara Falls, NY	2.00
962	3¢ Francis Scott Key 8/9/48 Frederick, MD	2.25
963	3¢ Youth of America 8/11/48 DC	2.00
964	3¢ Oregon Terr. 8/14/48 Oregon City, OR	2.00
965	3¢ Harlan Fisk Stone 8/25/48 Chesterfield, NH	2.00
966	3¢ Palomar Observatory 8/30/48 Palomar Mt., CA	3.50
967	3¢ Clara Barton 9/7/48 Oxford, MA	3.50
968	3¢ Poultry Industry 9/9/48 New Haven, CT	2.00
969	3¢ Gold Star Mothers 9/21/48 DC	2.00
970	3¢ Fort Kearny 9/22/48 Minden, NE	2.00
971	3¢ Fireman 10/4/48 Dover, DE	5.00
972	3¢ Indian Centennial 10/15/48 Muskogee, OK	2.00
973	3¢ Rough Riders 10/27/48 Prescott, AZ	2.00
974	3¢ Juliette Low 10/29/48 Savannah, GA	7.50
975	3¢ Will Rogers 11/4/48 Claremore, OK	2.00
	1st Kolor Kover cachet	**125.00**
976	3¢ Fort Bliss 11/5/48 El Paso, TX	3.50
977	3¢ Moina Michael 11/9/48 Athens, GA	2.00
978	3¢ Gettysburgh Address 11/19/48 Gettysburg, PA	4.00
979	3¢ Amer. Turners 11/20/48 Cincinnati, OH	2.00
980	3¢ Joel Chandler Harris 12/9/48 Eatonton, GA	2.00
	1949	
981	3¢ Minnesota Terr. 3/3/49 St. Paul, MN	3.00
982	3¢ Washington & Lee Univ. 4/12/49 Lexington, VA	3.00
983	3¢ Puerto Rico 4/27/49 San Juan, PR	4.00
984	3¢ Annapolis 5/23/49 Annapolis, MD	4.00
985	3¢ G.A.R. 8/29/49 Indianapolis, IN	4.00
986	3¢ Edgar Allan Poe 10/7/49 Richmond, VA	4.00
	1950	
987	3¢ Bankers 1/3/50 Saratoga Springs, NY	3.00
988	3¢ Samuel Gompers 1/27/50 DC	2.00
989	3¢ Statue of Freedom 4/20/50 DC	2.00
990	3¢ White House 6/12/50 DC	2.00
991	3¢ Supreme Court 8/2/50 DC	2.00
992	3¢ Capitol 11/22/50 DC	2.00
	#989-992 on one cover 11/22/50	7.50
993	3¢ Railroad Engineers 4/29/50 Jackson, TN	5.00
994	3¢ Kansas City 6/3/50 Kansas City, MO	2.00
995	3¢ Boy Scouts 6/30/50 Valley Forge, PA	7.50
996	3¢ Indiana Terr. 7/4/50 Vincennes, IN	2.00
997	3¢ California Sthd. 9/9/50 Sacramento, CA	3.00
	1951	
998	3¢ Confederate Vets. 5/30/51 Norfolk, VA	4.00
999	3¢ Nevada Territory 7/14/51 Genoa, NV	2.00
1000	3¢ Landing of Cadillac 7/24/51 Detroit, MI	2.00
1001	3¢ Colorado Statehood 8/1/51 Minturn, CO	2.50
1002	3¢ Amer. Chem. Soc. 9/4/51 New York, NY	2.00
1003	3¢ Battle of Brooklyn 12/10/51 Brooklyn, NY	2.00
	1st Velvatone cachet	**75.00**
	1952	
1004	3¢ Betsy Ross 1/2/52 Philadelphia, PA	2.50
	1st Steelcraft cachet	**30.00**
1005	3¢ 4-H Clubs 1/15/52 Springfield, OH	7.50
1006	3¢ B. & O. Railroad 2/28/52 Baltimore, MD	5.00
1007	3¢ Am. Automobile Assoc. 3/4/52 Chicago, IL	2.00
1008	3¢ NATO 4/4/52 DC	2.00
1009	3¢ Grand Coulee Dam 5/15/52 Grand Coulee, WA	2.00
1010	3¢ Lafayette 6/13/52 Georgetown, SC	2.00
1011	3¢ Mount Rushmore 8/11/52 Keystone, SD	2.00
1012	3¢ Civil Engineers 9/6/52 Chicago, IL	2.00
1013	3¢ Service Women 9/11/52 DC	2.50
1014	3¢ Gutenberg Bible 9/30/52 DC	2.00
1015	3¢ Newspaper Boys 10/4/52 Phila., PA	2.00

Scott #	Description	Cacheted
	1953	
1016	3¢ Red Cross 11/21/52 New York, NY	3.00
1017	3¢ National Guard 2/23/53 DC	2.00
1018	3¢ Ohio Statehood 3/2/53 Chillicothe, OH	2.00
	1st Boerger cachet	**25.00**
1019	3¢ Washington Terr. 3/2/53 Olympia, WA	2.00
1020	3¢ Louisiana Pur. 4/30/53 St. Louis, MO	2.00
1021	3¢ Opening of Japan 7/14/53 DC	3.00
	1st Overseas Mailers cachet	**75.00**
1022	3¢ Amer. Bar Assoc. 8/24/53 Boston, MA	6.00
1023	3¢ Sagamore Hill 9/14/53 Oyster Bay. NY	2.00
1024	3¢ Future Farmers 10/13/53 KS City, MO	2.00
1025	3¢ Trucking Ind. 10/27/53 Los Angeles, CA	3.00
1026	3¢ General Patton 11/11/53 Fort Knox, NY	3.00
1027	3¢ Founding of NYC 11/20/53 New York, NY	2.00
1028	3¢ Gadsden Purchase 12/30/53 Tucson, AZ	2.00
	1954	
1029	3¢ Columbia Univ. 1/4/54 New York, NY	2.00
	1954-61 LIBERTY SERIES	
1030-53	Liberty set of 27	100.00
1030	½¢ Franklin 10/20/55 DC	1.75
1031	1¢ Washington 8/26/54 Chicago, IL	1.75
1031A	1¼¢ Palace 6/17/60 Santa Fe, NM	1.75
1032	1½¢ Mt. Vernon 2/22/56 Mt. Vernon, VA	1.75
1033	2¢ Jefferson 9/15/54 San Francisco, CA	1.75
1034	2½¢ Bunker Hill 6/17/59 Boston, MA	1.75
1035	3¢ Statue of Liberty 6/24/54 Albany, NY	1.75
1035a	booklet pane 6/30/54 DC	4.00
1035b	Luminescent 7/6/66 DC	50.00
1035b & 1225a	Luminescent, combo	60.00
1036	4¢ Lincoln 11/19/54 New York, NY	1.75
1036a	booklet pane 7/31/58 Wheeling, WV	3.00
1036b	Luminescent 11/2/63 DC	100.00
1037	4½¢ Hermitage 3/16/59 Hermitage, TN	1.75
1038	5¢ Monroe 12/2/54 Fredericksburg, VA	1.75
1039	6¢ Roosevelt 11/18/55 New York, NY	1.75
1040	7¢ Wilson 1/110/56 Staunton, VA	1.75
1041	8¢ Statue of Liberty 4/9/54 DC	1.75
1042	8¢ Stat. of Lib. (Giori Press) 3/22/58 Cleveland, OH	1.75
1042A	8¢ Pershing 11/17/61 New York, NY	2.25
1043	9¢ The Alamo 6/14/56 San Antonio, TX	2.00
1044	10¢ Independence Hall 7/4/56 Phila., PA	2.00
1044b	Luminescent 7/6/66	50.00
1044A	11¢ Statue of Liberty 6/15/61 DC	2.50
1044Ac	Luminescent 1/11/67	50.00
1045	12¢ Harrison 6/6/59 Oxford, OH	2.00
1045a	Luminescent 5/6/68	40.00
1045a & 1055a	Luminescent, combo	40.00
1046	15¢ John Jay 12/12/58 DC	2.50
1046a	Luminescent 5/6/68	50.00
1047	20¢ Monticello 4/13/56 Charlottesville, VA	2.50
1048	25¢ Paul Revere 4/118/58 Boston, MA	2.50
1049	30¢ Robert E. Lee 9/21/55 Norfolk, VA	4.00
1050	40¢ John Marshall 9/24/55 Richmond, VA	4.00
1051	50¢ Susan Anthony 8/25/55 Louisville, KY	6.00
1052	$1 Patrick Henry 10/7/55 Joplin, MO	10.00
1053	$5 Alex Hamilton 3/19/56 Patterson, NJ	50.00
	1954-65 LIBERTY SERIES COILS	
1054	1¢ Washington 10/8/54 Baltimore, MD	1.75
1054A	1¼¢ Palace 6/17/60 Santa Fe, NM	1.75
1055	2¢ Jefferson 10/22/54 St. Louis, MO	1.75
1055a	Luminescent 5/6/68 DC	40.00
1055a & 1045a	Luminescent, combo	50.00
1056	2½¢ Bunker Hill 9/9/59 Los Angeles, CA	1.75
1057	3¢ Statue of Liberty 7/20/54 DC	1.75
1057b	Luminescent 5/12/67 DC	60.00
1058	4¢ Lincoln 7/31/58 Mandan, ND	1.75
1059	4½¢ Hermitage 5/1/59 Denver, CO	1.75
1059A, & 1289-95	1973 Regular Tagged Issues, set of 8, 4/3/73, NY	450.00
1059A, & 1289-95	1973 Regular Tagged Issues, all 8 on 1 cover, 4/3/73, NY	250.00
1059A	25¢ Paul Revere 2/25/65 Wheaton, MD	2.50
1059b	Luminescent 4/3/73 NY, NY	40.00
1060	3¢ Nebraska Ter. 5/7/54 Nebraska City, NE	1.75
1061	3¢ Kansas Terr. 5/31/54 Fort Leavenworth, KS	1.75
1062	3¢ George Eastman 7/12/54 Rochester, NY	1.75
1063	3¢ Lewis & Clark 7/28/54 Sioux City, IA	1.75
	1955	
1064	3¢ Fine Arts 1/15/55 Philadelphia, PA	1.75
1065	3¢ Land Grant Colleges 2/12/55 East Lansing, MI	3.00
1066	3¢ Rotary Int. 2/23/55 Chicago, IL	4.00
1067	3¢ Armed Forces Reserve 5/21/55 DC	2.00
1068	3¢ New Hampshire 6/21/55 Franconia, NH	1.75
1069	3¢ Soo Locks 6/28/55 Sault St. Marie, MI	1.75
1070	3¢ Atoms for Peace 7/28/55 DC	1.75
1071	3¢ Fort Ticonderoga 9/18/55 Ticonderoga, NY	1.75
1072	3¢ Andrew W. Mellon 12/20/55 DC	1.75
	1956	
1073	3¢ Benjamin Franklin 1/17/56 Phila., PA	1.75
	Poor Richard Station	1.75
1074	3¢ Booker T. Washington 4/5/56	
	Booker T. Washington Birthplace, VA	4.00

U.S. First Day Covers

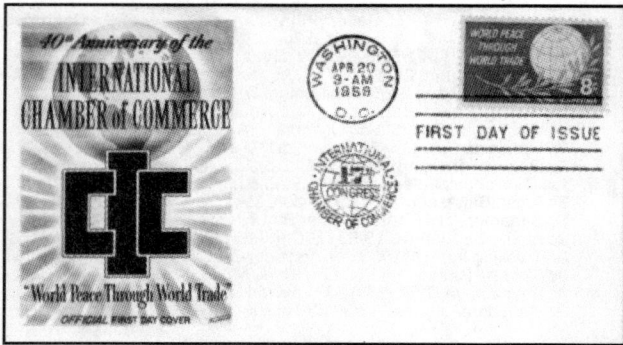

1129

Scott #	Description	Cacheted
	1956 (cont.)	
1075	11¢ FIPEX Sheet 4/28/56 New York, NY	4.50
1076	3¢ FIPEX 4/30/56 New York, NY	1.75
1077	3¢ Wild Turkey 5/5/56 Fond du Lac, WI	3.00
1078	3¢ Antelope 6/22/56 Gunnison, CO	3.00
1079	3¢ King Salmon 11/9/56 Seattle, WA	3.00
1080	3¢ Pure Food and Drug Laws 6/27/56 DC	1.75
1081	3¢ Wheatland 8/5/56 Lancaster, PA	1.75
1082	3¢ Labor Day 9/3/56 Camden, NJ	1.75
1083	3¢ Nassau Hall 9/22/56 Princeton, NJ	1.75
1084	3¢ Devils Tower 9/24/56 Devils Tower, NY	1.75
1085	3¢ Children 12/15/56 DC	1.75
	1957	
1086	3¢ Alex Hamilton 1/11/57 New York, NY	1.75
1087	3¢ Polio 1/15/57 DC	2.50
1088	3¢ Coast & Geodetic Survey 2/11/57 Seattle, WA	1.75
1089	3¢ Architects 2/23/57 New York, NY	2.25
1090	3¢ Steel Industry 5/22/57 New York, NY	1.75
1091	3¢ Naval Review 6/10/57 USS Saratoga, Norfolk, VA ..	1.75
1092	3¢ Oklahoma Statehood 6/14/57 Oklahoma City, OK	1.75
1093	3¢ School Teachers 7/1/57 Phila., PA	2.50
	"Philadelpia" error cancel	7.50
1094	4¢ American Flag 7/4/57 DC	1.75
1095	3¢ Shipbuilding 8/15/57 Bath, ME	1.75
1096	8¢ Ramon Magsaysay 8/31/57 DC	1.75
1097	3¢ Lafayette 9/6/57 Easton, PA	1.75
	Fayetteville, NC	1.75
	Louisville, KY	1.75
1098	3¢ Whooping Crane 11/22/57 New York, NY	2.50
	New Orleans, LA	2.50
	Corpus Christi, TX	2.50
1099	3¢ Religious Freedom 12/27/57 Flushing, NY	1.75
	1958-59	
1100	3¢ Horticulture 3/15/58 Ithaca, NY	1.75
1104	3¢ Brussels Exhibit. 4/17/58 Detroit, MI	1.75
1105	3¢ James Monroe 4/28/58 Montross, VA	1.75
1106	3¢ Minnesota Sthd. 5/11/58 St. Paul, MN	1.75
1107	3¢ Int'l. Geo. Year 5/31/58 Chicago, IL	1.75
1108	3¢ Gunston Hall 6/12/58 Lorton, VA	1.75
1109	3¢ Mackinaw Bridge 6/25/58 Mackinaw Bridge, MI	1.75
1110	4¢ Simon Bolivar 7/24/58 DC	1.75
1111	8¢ Simon Bolivar 7/24/58 DC	1.75
1110-11	Bolivar on one cover	2.50
1112	4¢ Atlantic Cable 8/15/58 New York, NY	1.75
1113	1¢ Lincoln 2/12/59 Hodgenville, NY	1.75
1114	3¢ Lincoln 2/27/59 New York, NY	1.75
1115	4¢ Lincoln & Douglas 8/27/58 Freeport, IL	1.75
1116	4¢ Lincoln Statue 5/30/59 DC	1.75
1113-16	On 1 Cover	8.00
1117	4¢ Lajos Kossuth 9/19/58 DC	1.75
1118	8¢ Lajos Kossuth 9/19/58 DC	1.75
1117-18	Kossuth on one cover	2.50
1119	4¢ Freedom of Press 9/22/58 Columbia, MO	1.75
1120	4¢ Overland Mail 10/10/58 San Fran., CA	1.75
	1958	
1121	4¢ Noah Webster 10/16/58 W. Hartford, CT	1.75
1122	4¢ Forest Conserv. 10/27/58 Tucson, AZ	1.75
1123	4¢ Fort Duquesne 11/25/58 Pittsburgh, PA	1.75
1124	4¢ Oregon Sthd. 2/14/59 Astoria, OR	1.75
1125	4¢ Jose de San Martin 2/25/59 DC	1.75
1126	8¢ Jose de San Martin 2/25/59 DC	1.75
1125-26	San Martin on one cover	2.50
1127	4¢ NATO 4/1/59 DC	1.75
1128	4¢ Arctic Explorers 4/6/59 Cresson, PA	1.75
1129	8¢ World Trade 4/20/59 DC	1.75
1130	4¢ Silver Cent. 6/8/59 Virginia City, NV	1.75
1131	4¢ St. Lawrence Seaway 6/26/59 Massena, NY	2.00
1131	Joint issue w/Canada	10.00
1131	Joint issue w/Canada, dual cancel	250.00
1132	4¢ 49-Star Flag 7/4/59 Auburn, NY	1.75
1133	4¢ Soil Conserv. 8/26/59 Rapid City, SD	1.75
1134	4¢ Petroleum Ind. 8/27/59 Titusville, PA	3.00
1135	4¢ Dental Health 9/14/59 New York, NY	5.00

Scott #	Description	Cacheted
	1959 (cont.)	
1136	4¢ Ernst Reuter 9/29/59 DC	1.75
1137	8¢ Ernst Reuter 9/29/59 DC	1.75
1136-37	Reuter on one cover	2.50
1138	4¢ Dr. McDowell 12/3/59 Danville, KY	1.75
	1960	
1139	4¢ Washington Credo 1/20/60 Mt. Vernon, VA	1.75
1140	4¢ Franklin Credo 3/31/60 Phila., PA	1.75
1141	4¢ Jefferson Credo 5/18/60 Charlottesville, VA	1.75
1142	4¢ Francis Scott Key Credo 9/14/60 Baltimore, MD	1.75
1143	4¢ Lincoln Credo 11/19/60 New York, NY	1.75
1144	4¢ Patrick Henry Credo 1/11/61 Richmond, VA	1.75
	#1139-1144 on one cover, 1/11/61	6.00
1145	4¢ Boy Scouts 2/8/60 DC	7.50
1146	4¢ Winter Olympics 2/18/60 Olympic Valley, CA	1.75
1147	4¢ Thomas G. Masaryk 3/7/60 DC	1.75
1148	8¢ Thomas G. Masaryk 3/7/60 DC	1.75
1147-48	Masaryk on one cover	2.50
1149	4¢ World Refugee Year 4/7/60 DC	1.75
1150	4¢ Water Conservation 4/18/60 DC	1.75
1151	4¢ SEATO 5/31/60 DC	1.75
1152	4¢ American Women 6/2/60 DC	2.00
1153	4¢ 50-Star Flag 7/4/60 Honolulu, HI	1.75
1154	4¢ Pony Express Centennial 7/19/60 Sacramento, CA ...	3.00
1155	4¢ Employ the Handicapped 8/28/60 New York, NY	3.00
1156	4¢ World Forestry Co. 8/29/60 Seattle, WA	1.75
1157	4¢ Mexican Indep. 9/16/60 Los Angeles, CA	1.75
1157	Joint issue w/Mexico	20.00
1157	Joint issue w/Mexico, dual cancel	375.00
1158	4¢ US-Japan Treaty 9/28/60 DC	1.75
1159	4¢ Paderewski 10/8/60 DC	1.75
1160	8¢ Paderewski 10/8/60 DC	1.75
1159-60	Paderewski on one cover	2.50
1161	4¢ Robert A. Taft 10/10/60 Cincinnati, OH	1.75
1162	4¢ Wheels of Freedom 10/15/60 Detroit, MI	1.75
1163	4¢ Boys Clubs 10/18/60 New York, NY	2.00
1164	4¢ Automated P.O. 10/20/60 Providence, RI	1.75
1165	4¢ Gustav Mannerheim 10/26/60 DC	1.75
1166	8¢ Gustav Mannerheim 10/26/60 DC	1.75
1165-66	Mannerheim on one cover	2.50
1167	4¢ Camp Fire Girls 11/1/60 New York, NY	4.00
1168	4¢ Giuseppe Garibaldi 11/2/60 DC	1.75
1169	8¢ Giuseppe Garibaldi 11/2/60 DC	1.75
1168-69	Garibaldi on one cover	2.50
1170	4¢ Walter F. George 11/5/60 Vienna, GA	1.75
1171	4¢ Andrew Carnegie 11/25/60 New York, NY	1.75
1172	4¢ John Foster Dulles 12/6/60 DC	1.75
1173	4¢ Echo 1 12/15/60 DC	3.00
	1961-65	
1174	4¢ Mahatma Gandhi 1/26/61 DC	1.75
1175	8¢ Mahatma Gandhi 1/26/61 DC	1.75
1174-75	Gandhi on one cover	2.50
1176	4¢ Range Cons. 2/2/61 Salt Lake City, UT	1.75
1177	4¢ Horace Greeley 2/3/61 Chappaqua, NY	1.75
1178	4¢ Fort Sumter 4/12/61 Charleston, SC	6.00
1179	4¢ Battle of Shiloh 4/7/62 Shiloh, TN	6.00
1180	5¢ Battle of Gettysburg 7/1/63 Gettysburg, PA	6.00
1181	5¢ Battle of Wilderness 5/5/64 Fredericksburg, VA	6.00
1182	5¢ Appomattox 4/9/65 Appomattox, VA	6.00
1178-82	Civil War on 1 cover 4/9/65	12.00
1183	4¢ Kansas Statehood 5/10/61 Council Grove, KS	1.75
1184	4¢ George Norris 7/11/611 DC	1.75
1185	4¢ Naval Aviation 8/20/61 San Diego, CA	2.00
1186	4¢ Workmen's Comp. 9/4/61 Milwaukee, WI	1.75
1187	4¢ Frederic Remington 10/4/61 DC	2.00
1188	4¢ Sun Yat-Sen 10/10/61 DC	6.00
1189	4¢ Basketball 11/6/61 Springfield, MA	8.00
1190	4¢ Nursing 12/28/61 DC	12.00
	1962	
1191	4¢ New Mexico Sthd. 1/6/62 Santa Fe, NM	2.25
1192	4¢ Arizona Sthd. 2/14/62 Phoenix, AZ	2.25
	1st Glory cachet	**35.00**
1193	4¢ Project Mercury 2/20/62 Cape Canaveral, FL	4.00
	1st Marg cachet	**25.00**
1194	4¢ Malaria Eradication 3/30/62 DC	2.00
1195	4¢ Charles Evans Hughes 4/11/62 DC	1.75
1196	4¢ Seattle Fair 4/25/62 Seattle, WA	1.75
1197	4¢ Louisiana 4/30/62 New Orleans, LA	1.75
1198	4¢ Homestead Act 5/20/62 Beatrice, NE	1.75
1199	4¢ Girl Scouts 7/24/62 Burlington, VT	6.00
1200	4¢ Brien McMahon 7/28/62 Norwalk, CT	1.75
1201	4¢ Apprenticeship 8/31/62 DC	1.75
1202	4¢ Sam Rayburn 9/16/62 Bonham, TX	3.00
1203	4¢ Dag Hammarskjold 10/23/62 NY, NY	1.75
1204	4¢ Hammarskjold Invert. 11/16/62 DC	5.00
1205	4¢ Christmas 11/1/62 Pittsburgh, PA	2.00
1206	4¢ Higher Education 11/14/62 DC	2.25
1207	4¢ Winslow Homer 12/15/62 Gloucester, MA	2.25
	1962-63 REGULAR ISSUES	
1208	5¢ 50-Star Flag 1/9/63 DC	1.75
1208a	5¢ Luminescent 8/25/66 DC	35.00
1209	1¢ Andrew Jackson 3/22/63 New York, NY	1.75
1209a	Luminescent 7/6/66 DC	35.00

U.S. First Day Covers

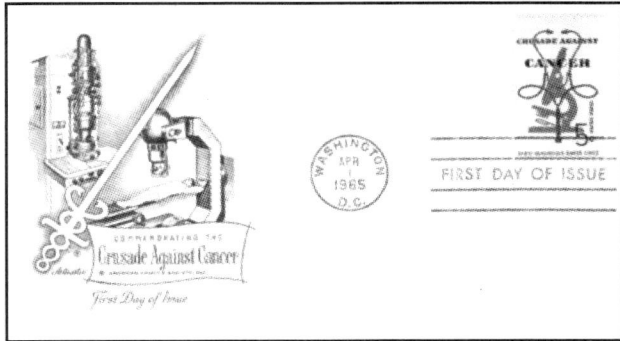

1263

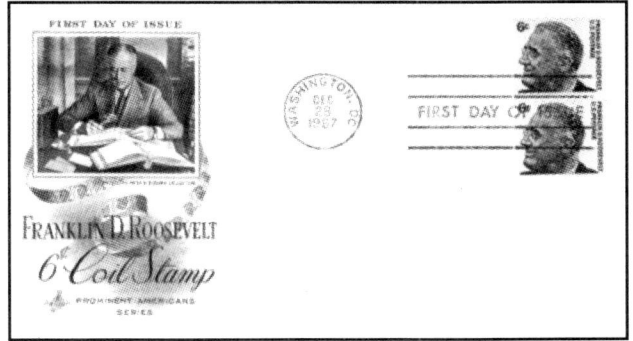

1298

Scott #	Description	Cacheted
	1962-63 REGULAR ISSUES (cont.)	
1213	5¢ Washington 11/23/62 New York, NY	1.75
1213a	Booklet Pane 11/23/62 New York, NY	3.00
1213b	Luminescent 10/28/63 Dayton, OH	35.00
1213c	Luminescent bklt. pair 10/28/63 Dayton, OH	40.00
1213c	Luminescent bklt. pane 10/28/63 Dayton, OH	100.00
	DC	125.00
1225	1¢ Jackson, coil 5/31/63 Chicago, IL	1.75
1225a	Luminescent 7/6/66 DC	35.00
1225a & 1035b Luminescent combo		40.00
1229	5¢ Washington, coil 11/23/62 New York, NY	1.75
1229a	Luminescent 10/28/63 Dayton, OH	35.00
	DC	35.00
1229a,1213b, & 1213c On one FDC 10/28/63 Dayton, OH		60.00
	1963	
1230	5¢ Carolina Charter 4/6/63 Edenton, NC	1.75
1231	5¢ Food for Peace 6/4/63 DC	1.75
1232	5¢ W. Virginia Sthd. 6/20/63 Wheeling, WV	1.75
1233	5¢ Emancipation Proc. 8/16/63 Chicago, IL	4.00
1234	5¢ Alliance for Progress 8/17/63 DC	1.75
1235	5¢ Cordell Hull 10/5/63 Carthage, TN	1.75
1236	5¢ Eleanor Roosevelt 10/11/63 DC	1.75
1237	5¢ Science 10/14/63 DC	2.00
1238	5¢ City Mail Delivery 10/26/63 DC	2.00
1239	5¢ Red Cross 10/29/63 DC	2.50
1240	5¢ Christmas 11/1/63 Santa Claus, IN	2.00
1240a	5¢ Luminescent 11/2/63 DC	60.00
1241	5¢ Audobon 12/7/63 Henderson, KY	2.00
	1964	
1242	5¢ Sam Houston 1/10/64 Houston, TX	4.00
1243	5¢ Charles Russell 3/19/64 Great Falls, MT	2.50
1244	5¢ NY World's Fair 4/22/64 World's Fair, NY	2.00
	1st Sarzin Metallic cachet	**20.00**
1245	5¢ John Muir 4/29/64 Martinez, CA	3.00
1246	5¢ John F. Kennedy 5/29/64 Boston, MA	2.50
	1st Cover Craft cachet	**40.00**
1247	5¢ New Jersey Terc. 6/15/64 Elizabeth, NJ	1.75
1248	5¢ Nevada Sthd. 7/22/64 Carson City, NV	1.75
1249	5¢ Register & Vote 8/1/64 DC	2.00
1250	5¢ Shakespeare 8/14/64 Stratford, CT	2.00
1251	5¢ Doctors Mayo 9/11/64 Rochester, MN	5.00
1252	5¢ American Music 10/15/64 New York, NY	2.50
1253	5¢ Homemakers 10/26/64 Honolulu, HI	1.75
1254-57	5¢ Christmas attd. 11/9/64 Bethlehem, PA	4.00
1254-57	Christmas set of 4 singles	10.00
1254-57a	Luminescent Christmas attd 11/10/64 Dayton, OH	60.00
1254-57a	Luminescent Christmas set of 4 singles	80.00
1258	5¢ Verrazano-Narrows Bridge 11/21/64 Stat. Is., NY	1.75
1259	5¢ Fine Arts 12/2/64 DC	1.75
1260	5¢ Amateur Radio ˙ 2/15/64 Anchorage, AK	7.50
	1965	
1261	5¢ Battle of New Orleans 1/8/65 New Orleans, LA	1.75
1262	5¢ Physical Fitness 2/15/65 DC	2.00
1263	5¢ Cancer Crusade 4/1/65 DC	3.50
1264	5¢ Winston Churchill 5/13/65 Fulton, MO	2.00
1265	5¢ Magna Carta 6/15/65 Jamestown, VA	1.75
1266	5¢ Int'l. Cooperation Year 6/26/65 San Francisco, CA	1.75
1267	5¢ Salvation Army 7/2/65 New York, NY	3.00
1268	5¢ Dante 7/17/65 San Francisco, CA	1.75
1269	5¢ Herbert Hoover 8/10/65 West Branch, IA	1.75
1270	5¢ Robert Fulton 8/19/65 Clermont, NY	1.75
1271	5¢ 400th Anniv. of FL 8/28/65 St. Augustine, FL	1.75
1271	Combo w/Spain	90.00
1271	Combo w/Spain, dual cancel	450.00
1272	5¢ Traffic Safety 9/3/65 Baltimore, MD	1.75
1273	5¢ John Copley 9/17/65 DC	1.75
1274	11¢ Int'l. Telecomm. Union 10/6/65 DC	1.75
1275	5¢ A. Stevenson 10/23/65 Bloomington, IL	1.75
1276	5¢ Christmas 11/2/65 Silver Bell, AZ	1.75
1276a	Luminescent 11/16/65 DC	50.00
	1965-68 PROMINENT AMERICANS SERIES	
1278	1¢ Jefferson 1/12/68 Jeffersonville, IN	1.75

Scott #	Description	Cacheted
	1965-68 PROMINENT AMERICANS SERIES (cont.)	
1278a	bklt. pane of 8 1/12/68 Jeffersonville, IN	2.00
1278a	bklt. pane of 8, dull gum 3/1/71 DC	90.00
1278a & 1393a Combo, 3/1/71		150.00
1278b	booklet pane of 4 5/10/71 DC	15.00
1279	1¼¢ Gallatin 1/30/67 Gallatin, MO	1.75
1280	2¢ Wright 6/8/66 Spring Green, WI	1.75
1280a	booklet pane of 5 1/8/68 Buffalo, NY	3.00
1280c	booklet pane of 6 5/7/71 Spokane, WA	15.00
1280c var.	bklt. pane of 6, dull gum 10/31/75 Cleveland, OH	100.00
1281	3¢ Parkman 9/16/67 Boston, MA	1.75
1282	4¢ Lincoln 11/19/65 New York, NY	1.75
1282a	Luminescent 12/1/65 Dayton, OH	40.00
	DC	45.00
1283	5¢ Washington 2/22/66 DC	1.75
1283a	Luminescent 2/23/66 Dayton, OH	100.00
	DC	27.50
1283B	5¢ Washington, redrawn 11/17/67 New York, NY	1.75
1284	6¢ Roosevelt 1/29/66 Hyde Park, NY	1.75
1284a	Luminescent 12/29/66	40.00
1284b	booklet pane of 8 12/28/67 DC	2.50
1284bs	booklet single	1.75
1284c	booklet pane of 5 1/9/68 DC	125.00
1285	8¢ Einstein 3/14/66 Princeton, NJ	4.50
1285a	Luminescent 7/6/66 DC	40.00
1286	10¢ Jackson 3/15/67 Hermitage, TN	1.75
1286A	12¢ Ford 7/30/68 Greenfield Village, MI	3.00
1287	13¢ Kennedy 5/29/67 Brookline, MA	2.50
1288	15¢ Holmes 3/8/68 DC	1.75
1288B	booklet single 6/14/78 Boston, MA	1.75
1288Bc	15¢ bklt. pane of 8 6/14/78 Boston, MA	3.50
1289	20¢ Marshall 10/24/67 Lexington, VA	2.00
1289a	Luminescent 4/3/73 New York, NY	40.00
1290	25¢ Douglass 2/14/67 DC	4.50
1290a	Luminescent 4/3/73 DC	45.00
1291	30¢ Dewey 10/21/68 Burlington, VT	2.50
1291a	Luminescent 4/3/73 New York, NY	45.00
1292	40¢ Paine 1/29/68 Philadelphia, PA	3.00
1292a	Luminescent 4/3/73 New York, NY	45.00
1293	50¢ Stone 8/13/68 Dorchester, MA	4.00
1293a	Luminescent 4/3/73 New York, NY	50.00
1294	$1 O'Neill 10/16/67 New London, CT	7.00
1294a	Luminescent 4/3/73 New York, NY	65.00
1295	$5 Moore 12/3/66 Smyrna, DE	40.00
1295a	Luminescent 4/3/73 New York NY	125.00
#1295 & 1295a on one cover 4/3/73		250.00
	1966-81 PROMINENT AMERICAN COILS	
1297	3¢ Parkman 11/4/75 Pendleton, OR, Vertical coil	1.75
1298	6¢ Roosevelt, vert. coil 12/28/67 DC	1.75
1299	1¢ Jefferson 1/12/68 Jeffersonville, IN	1.75
1303	4¢ Lincoln 5/28/66 Springfield, IL	1.75
1304	5¢ Washington 9/8/66 Cinncinati, OH	1.75
1304C	5¢ Washington re-engraved 3/31/81 DC	25.00
1305	6¢ Roosevelt, horiz. coil 2/28/68 DC	1.75
1305E	15¢ Holmes 6/14/78 Boston, MA	1.75
1305C	$1 O'Neill 1/12/73 Hampstead, NY	4.00
	1966	
1306	5¢ Migratory Bird 3/16/66 Pittsburgh, PA	2.50
1307	5¢ Humane Treatment 4/9/66 New York, NY	2.00
1308	5¢ Indiana Sthd. 4/16/66 Corydon, IN	1.75
1309	5¢ Circus 5/2/66 Delevan, WI	4.00
1310	5¢ SIPEX 5/21/66 DC	1.75
1311	5¢ SIPEX sheet 5/23/66 DC	2.00
1312	5¢ Bill of Rights 7/1/66 Miami Beach, FL	3.00
1313	5¢ Polish Millenium 7/30/66 DC	1.75
1314	5¢ Nat'l. Park Service 8/25/66 Yellowstone Nat'l. Park	2.00
1314a	Luminescent 8/26/66	50.00
1315	5¢ Marine Corps Reserve 8/29/66 DC	2.50
1315a	Luminescent 8/29/66 DC	50.00
1316	5¢ Women's Clubs 9/12/66 New York, NY	2.00
1316a	Luminescent 9/13/66 DC	50.00
1317	5¢ Johnny Appleseed 9/24/66 Leominster, MA	1.75
1317a	Luminescent 9/26/66 DC	50.00
1318	5¢ Beautification 10/5/66 DC	1.75

U.S. First Day Covers

1365-68

1425

Scott #	Description	Cacheted
	1966 (cont.)	
1318a	Luminescent 10/5/66 DC	50.00
1319	5¢ Great River Road 10/21/66 Baton Rouge, LA	1.75
1319a	Luminescent 10/22/66 DC	50.00
1320	5¢ Savings Bonds 10/26/66 Sioux City, IA	1.75
1320a	Luminescent 10/27/66 DC	50.00
1321	5¢ Christmas 11/1/66 Christmas, MI	1.75
1321a	Luminescent 11/2/66	50.00
1322	5¢ Mary Cassatt 11/17/66 DC	2.00
1322a	Luminescent 11/17/66 DC	50.00
	1967	
1323	5¢ National Grange 4/17/67 DC	1.75
1324	5¢ Canada Centenary 5/25/67 Montreal, CAN	1.75
1325	5¢ Erie Canal 7/4/67 Rome, NY	1.75
1326	5¢ Search for Peace 7/5/67 Chicago, IL	1.75
1327	5¢ Henry Thoreau 7/12/67 Concord, MA	1.75
1328	5¢ Nebraska Statehood. 7/29/67 Lincoln, NE	1.75
1329	5¢ Voice of America 8/1/67 DC	4.00
1330	5¢ Davy Crockett 8/17/67 San Antonio, TX	3.00
1331-32	5¢ Space Twins attd. 9/29/67 Kennedy Space Ctr., FL	8.00
1331-32	Space Twins set of 2 singles	8.00
1333	5¢ Urban Planning 10/2/67 DC	1.75
1334	5¢ Finland Indep. 10/6/67 Finland, MI	1.75
1335	5¢ Thomas Eakins 11/2/67 DC	2.00
1336	5¢ Christmas 11/6/67 Bethlehem, GA	2.00
1337	5¢ Mississippi Statehood 12/11/67 Natchez, MS	1.75
	1968-71 REGULAR ISSUES	
1338	6¢ Flag & White House 1/24/68 DC	1.75
1338A	6¢ Flag & W.H., coil 5/30/69 Chicago, IL	1.75
1338D	6¢ Flag & W.H. (Huck Press) 8/7/70 DC	1.75
1338F	8¢ Flag & White House 5/10/71 DC	1.75
1338G	8¢ Flag & White House, coil 5/10/71 DC	1.75
	1968	
1339	6¢ Illinois Statehood 2/12/68 Shawneetown, IL	1.75
1340	6¢ Hemis Fair '68 3/30/68 San Antonio, TX	1.75
1341	$1 Airlift 4/4/68 Seattle, WA	7.50
1342	6¢ Support Our Youth 5/1/68 Chicago, IL	1.75
1343	6¢ Law and Order 5/17/68 DC	4.00
1344	6¢ Register and Vote 6/27/68 DC	2.50
1345-54	6¢ Historic Flags attd. 7/4/68 Pittsburgh, PA	8.50
1345-54	Historic Flags set of 10 singles	30.00
1355	6¢ Walt Disney 9/11/68 Marceline, MO	40.00
1356	6¢ Marquette 9/20/68 Sault Ste. Marie, MI	1.75
1357	6¢ Daniel Boone 9/26/68 Frankfort, KY	1.75
1358	6¢ Arkansas River 10/1/68 Little Rock, AR	1.75
1359	6¢ Leif Ericson 10/9/68 Seattle, WA	1.75
1360	6¢ Cherokee Strip 10/15/68 Ponca, OK	1.75
1361	6¢ John Trumbull 10/18/66 New Haven, CT	4.00
1362	6¢ Waterfowl Cons. 10/24/68 Cleveland, OH	2.00
1363	6¢ Christmas, tagged 11/1/68 DC	2.00
1363a	6¢ Not tagged 11/2/68 DC	15.00
1364	6¢ American Indian 11/4/68 DC	2.00
	1969	
1365-68	6¢ Beautification attd. 1/16/69 DC	5.00
1365-68	Beautification set of 4 singles	10.00
1369	6¢ American Legion 3/15/69 DC	1.75
1370	6¢ Grandma Moses 5/1/69 DC	2.00
1371	6¢ Apollo 8 5/5/69 Houston, TX	3.00
1372	6¢ W.C. Handy 5/17/69 Memphis, TN	4.00
1373	6¢ California 7/16/69 San Diego, CA	1.75
1374	6¢ John W. Powell 8/1/69 Page, AZ	1.75
1375	6¢ Alabama Sthd. 8/2/69 Huntsville, AL	1.75
1376-79	6¢ Botanical Congress attd. 8/23/69 Seattle, WA	6.00
1376-79	Botanical Congress set of 4 singles	10.00
1380	6¢ Dartmouth Case 9/22/69 Hanover, NH	1.75
1381	6¢ Baseball 9/24/69 Cincinnati, OH	12.00
1382	6¢ Football 9/26/69 New Brunswick, NJ	6.00
1383	6¢ Eisenhower 10/14/69 Abilene, KS	1.75
1384	6¢ Christmas 11/3/69 Christmas, FL	2.00
1384a	6¢ Christmas - Precancel 11/4/69 Atlanta, GA	200.00
	Baltimore, MD	200.00
	Memphis, TN	225.00
	New Haven, CT	200.00

Scott #	Description	Cacheted
	1970	
1385	6¢ Hope for Crippled 11/20/69 Columbus, OH	2.00
1386	6¢ William Harnett 12/3/69 Boston, MA	1.75
1387-90	6¢ Natural History attd. 5/6/70 NY, NY	4.00
1387-90	Natural History set of 4 singles	8.00
1391	6¢ Maine Statehood 7/9/70 Portland, ME	1.75
1392	6¢ Wildlife - Buffalo 7/20/70 Custer, SD	1.75
	1970-74 REGULAR ISSUES	
1393	6¢ Eisenhower 8/6/70 DC	1.75
1393a	booklet pane of 8 8/6/70 DC	2.50
1393a	booklet pane of 8, dull gum 3/1/71 DC	75.00
1393a & 1278a	Combo, 3/1/71	150.00
1393b	booklet pane of 5 8/6/70 DC	3.00
1393bs	booklet single, 8/6/70	1.75
1393D	7¢ Franklin 10/20/72 Philadelphia, PA	1.75
1394	8¢ Eisenhower 5/10/71 DC	1.75
1395	8¢ Eisenhower, claret 5/10/71 DC	2.00
1395a	booklet pane of 8 5/10/71 DC	2.50
1395b	booklet pane of 6 5/10/71 DC	2.50
1395c	bklt. pane of 4 1/28/72 Casa Grande, AZ	2.00
1395cs	Booklet Single 1/28/72 Casa Grande, AZ	1.75
1395d	bklt. pane of 7 1/28/72 Casa Grande, AZ	2.00
1395ds	Booklet Single 1/28/72 Casa Grande, AZ	1.75
1396	8¢ Postal Service Emblem 7/1/71 any city	1.75
1397	14¢ LaGuardia 4/24/72 New York, NY	1.75
1398	16¢ Ernie Pyle 5/7/71 DC	2.50
1399	18¢ Eliz. Blackwell 1/23/74 Geneva, NY	2.00
1400	21¢ Giannini 6/27/73 San Mateo, CA	2.25
1401	6¢ Eisenhower, coil 8/6/70 DC	1.75
1402	8¢ Eisenhower, coil 5/10/71 DC	1.75
1405	6¢ Edgar Lee Masters 8/22/70 Petersburg, IL	1.75
1406	6¢ Woman Suffrage 8/26/70 Adams, MA	1.75
1407	6¢ South Carolina 9/12/70 Charleston, SC	1.75
1408	6¢ Stone Mountain 9/19/70 Stone Mt., GA	1.75
1409	6¢ Ft. Snelling 10/17/70 Ft. Snelling, MT	1.75
1410-13	6¢ Anti-Pollution attd. 10/28/70 San Clemente, CA	5.00
1410-13	Anti-Pollution set of 4 singles	8.00
1414	6¢ Christmas - Religious 11/5/70 DC	1.75
1414a	6¢ Christmas Precancel 11/5/70 DC	3.00
1415-18	6¢ Christmas Toys attd. 11/5/70 DC	6.00
1415-18	Christmas Toys set of 4 singles	10.00
1415a-18a	Christmas Toys-Precancel attd. 11/5/70 DC	15.00
1415a-18a	Christmas Toys-Precancel set of 4 singles	50.00
1414a-18a	Religious & Toys (5) on one FDC 11/5/70 DC	30.00
1419	6¢ UN 25th Anniv. 11/20/70 New York, NY	1.75
1420	6¢ Pilgrims' Landing 11/21/70 Plymouth, MA	1.75
1421-22	6¢ Disabled Vets - US Servicemen attd.	
	11/24/70 Cincinnati or Montgomery	2.00
1421-22	D.A.V. - Serv. set of 2 singles	3.50
	1971	
1423	6¢ Wool Industry 1/19/71 Las Vegas, NV	1.75
	1st Bazaar cachet	30.00
	1st Colorano Silk cachet	300.00
1424	6¢ MacArthur 1/26/71 Norfolk, VA	2.00
1425	6¢ Blood Donor 3/12/71 New York, NY	1.75
1426	6¢ Missouri 5/8/71 Independence, MO	1.75
1427-30	8¢ Wildlife Conservation attd. 6/12/71 Avery Island, LA	4.00
1427-30	Wildlife set of 4 singles	8.00
1431	8¢ Antarctic Treaty 6/23/71 DC	1.75
1432	8¢ American Revolution Bic. 7/4/71 DC	1.75
	1st Medallion cachet	30.00
1433	8¢ John Sloan 8/2/71 Lock Haven, PA	1.75
1434-35	8¢ Space Achievement Decade attd. 8/2/71	
	Kennedy Space Center, FL	2.50
	Houston, TX	2.50
	Huntsville, AL	2.50
1434-35	Space Achievement set of 2 singles	
	Kennedy Space Center, FL	3.50
	Houston, TX	3.50
	Huntsville, AL	3.50
1436	8¢ Emily Dickinson 8/28/71 Amherst, MA	1.75
1437	8¢ San Juan 9/12/71 San Juan, PR	1.75
1438	8¢ Drug Abuse 10/4/71 Dallas, TX	1.75
1439	8¢ CARE 10/27/71 New York, NY	1.75
1440-43	8¢ Historic Preservation attd. 10/29/71 San Diego, CA	4.00

U.S. First Day Covers

Scott #	Description	Cacheted
	1972	
1440-43	Historic Preservation set of 4 singles	8.00
1444	8¢ Christmas - Religious 11/10/71 DC	2.00
1445	8¢ Christmas - Partridge 11/10/71 DC	2.00
1444-45	Christmas on one cover	2.50
1446	8¢ Sidney Lanier 2/3/72 Macon, GA	1.75
1447	8¢ Peace Corps 2/11/72 DC	1.75
1448-51	2¢ Cape Hatteras 4/5/72 Hatteras, NC	1.75
1452	6¢ Wolf Trap Farm 6/26/72 Vienna, VA	1.75
1453	8¢ Yellowstone 3/1/72 DC	1.75
	Yellowstone Nat'l. Park, WY	1.75
1454	15¢ Mt. McKinley 7/28/72 Mt. McKinley Nat'l. Park, AK ..	1.75
1448-54,C84	Parks on one cover 7/28/72	6.00
1455	8¢ Family Planning 3/18/72 New York, NY	1.75
1456-59	8¢ Colonial Craftsmen attd. 7/4/72 Williamsburg, VA	4.00
1456-59	Colonial Craftsmen set of 4 singles	8.00
1460	6¢ Olympic - Bicycling 8/17/72 DC	1.75
1461	8¢ Olympic - Bobsledding 8/17/72 DC	1.75
1462	15¢ Olympic - Runners 8/17/72 DC	1.75
1460-62,C85	Olympics on one cover	4.00
1463	8¢ P.T.A. 9/15/72 San Francisco, CA	1.75
1464-67	8¢ Wildlife attd. 9/20/72 Warm Springs, OR	4.00
1464-67	Wildlife set of 4 singles	8.00
1468	8¢ Mail Order 9/27/72 Chicago, IL	1.75
1469	8¢ Osteopathic Medicine 10/9/72 Miami, FL	2.50
1470	8¢ Tom Sawyer 10/13/72 Hannibal, MO	2.50
1471	8¢ Christmas - Religious 11/9/72 DC	1.75
1472	8¢ Christmas - Santa Claus 11/9/72 DC	1.75
1471-72	Christmas on one cover	2.50
1473	8¢ Pharmacy 11/10/72 Cincinnati, OH	10.00
1474	8¢ Stamp Collecting 11/17/72 NY, NY	2.00
	1973	
1475	8¢ Love 1/26/73 Philadelphia, PA	2.25
1476	8¢ Pamphleteer 2/16/73 Portland, OR	1.75
1477	8¢ Broadside 4/13/73 Atlantic City, NJ	1.75
1478	8¢ Post Rider 6/22/73 Rochester, NY	1.75
1479	8¢ Drummer 9/28/73 New Orleans, LA	1.75
1480-83	8¢ Boston Tea Party attd. 7/4/73 Boston, MA	4.00
1480-83	Boston Tea Party set of 4 singles	8.00
1484	8¢ Geo. Gershwin 2/28/73 Beverly Hills, CA	1.75
1485	8¢ Robinson Jeffers 8/13/73 Carmel, CA	1.75
1486	8¢ Henry O. Tanner 9/10/73 Pittsburgh, PA	4.00
1487	8¢ Willa Cather 9/20/73 Red Cloud, NE	1.75
1488	8¢ Nicolaus Copernicus 4/23/73 DC	2.00
1489-98	8¢ Postal People attd. 4/30/73 any city	7.00
1489-98	Postal People set of 10 singles	20.00
1499	8¢ Harry Truman 5/8/73 Independence, MO	2.00
1500	6¢ Electronics 7/10/73 New York, NY	1.75
1501	8¢ Electronics 7/10/73 New York, NY	1.75
1502	15¢ Electronics 7/10/73 New York, NY	1.75
1500-2,C86	Electronics on one cover	7.00
1500-2,C86	Electronics set of 4	8.00
1503	8¢ Lyndon B. Johnson 8/27/73 Austin, TX	1.75
1504	8¢ Angus Cattle 10/5/73 St. Joseph, MO	1.75
1505	10¢ Chautauqua 8/6/74 Chautauqua, NY	1.75
1506	10¢ Wheat 8/16/74 Hillsboro, KS	1.75
1507	8¢ Christmas - Madonna 11/7/73 DC	1.75
1508	8¢ Christmas - Tree 11/7/73 DC	1.75
1507-08	Christmas on one cover	2.75
	1973-74 REGULAR ISSUES	
1509	10¢ Crossed Flags 12/8/73 San Fran., CA	1.75
1510	10¢ Jefferson Memorial 12/14/73 DC	1.75
1510b	booklet pane of 5 12/14/73 DC	2.00
1510bs	booklet pane single, 12/14/73	1.75
1510c	booklet pane of 8 12/14/73 DC	2.25
1510d	booklet pane of 6 8/5/74 Oakland, CA	5.25
1510ds	booklet pane single, 8/5/74	1.75
1511	10¢ Zip Code 1/4/74 DC	1.75
1518	6.3¢ Liberty Bell, coil 10/1/74 DC	1.75
1518	Untagged, 10/2/74 DC	5.00
1519	10¢ Crossed Flags, coil 12/8/73 San Francisco, CA	1.75
1520	10¢ Jefferson Memorial, coil 12/14/73 DC	1.75
	1974	
1525	10¢ Veterans of Foreign Wars 3/11/74 DC	1.75
1526	10¢ Robert Frost 3/26/74 Derry, NH	1.75
1527	10¢ EXPO '74 4/18/74 Spokane, WA	1.75
1528	10¢ Horse Racing 5/4/74 Louisville, KY	5.00
1529	10¢ Skylab 5/14/74 Houston, TX	2.00
1530-37	10¢ UPU Centenary attd. 6/6/74 DC	5.00
1530-37	UPU Centenary set of 8 singles	20.00
1538-41	10¢ Mineral Heritage attd. 6/13/74 Lincoln, NE	4.00
1538-41	Mineral Heritage set of 4 singles	8.00
1542	10¢ Fort Harrod 6/15/74 Harrodsburg, KY	1.75
1543-46	10¢ Continental Congr. attd. 7/4/74 Philadelphia, PA	4.00
1543-46	Continental Congress set of 4 singles	8.00
1547	10¢ Energy Conserv. 9/23/74 Detroit, MI	1.75
1548	10¢ Sleepy Hollow 10/10/74 North Tarrytown, NY	2.00
1549	10¢ Retarded Children 10/12/74 Arlington, TX	1.75
1550	10¢ Christmas - Angel 10/23/74 NY, NY	1.75
1551	10¢ Christmas - Currier & Ives 10/23/74 NY, NY	1.75
1550-51	Christmas on one cover	2.25
1552	10¢ Christmas - Dove 11/15/74 New York, NY	3.00
1550-52	Christmas, dual cancel	5.00

1577-78

Scott #	Description	Cacheted
	1975	
1553	10¢ Benjamin West 2/10/75 Swarthmore, PA	1.75
1554	10¢ Paul Dunbar 5/1/75 Dayton, OH	3.00
1555	10¢ D.W. Griffith 5/27/75 Beverly, Hills, CA	1.75
1556	10¢ Pioneer - Jupiter 2/28/75 Mountain View, CA	1.75
1557	10¢ Mariner 10 4/4/75 Pasadena, CA	1.75
1558	10¢ Collective Bargaining 3/13/75 DC	1.75
1559	8¢ Sybil Ludington 3/25/75 Carmel, NY	1.75
1560	10¢ Salem Poor 3/25/75 Cambridge, MA	3.00
1561	10¢ Haym Salomon 3/25/75 Chicago, IL	1.75
1562	18¢ Peter Francisco 3/25/75 Greensboro, NC	1.75
1559-62	Contributions on one cover, any city	8.00
1563	10¢ Lexington-Concord 4/19/75 Lexington, MA	1.75
	Concord, MA	1.75
1564	10¢ Bunker Hill 6/17/75 Charlestown, MA	1.75
1565-68	10¢ Military Uniforms attd. 7/4/75 DC	4.00
1565-68	Military Uniforms set of 4 singles	8.00
1569-70	10¢ Apollo-Soyuz attd. 7/15/75 Kennedy Sp. Ctr., FL	3.00
1569-70	Apollo-Soyuz set of 2 singles	4.00
1569-70	Apollo-Soyuz, combo, dual cancel	450.00
1571	10¢ Women's Year 8/26/75 Seneca Falls, NY	1.75
1572-75	10¢ Postal Serv. Bicent. attd. 9/3/75 Philadelphia, PA	4.00
1572-75	Postal Service set of 4 singles	8.00
1576	10¢ World Peace through Law 9/29/75 DC	2.00
1577-78	10¢ Banking - Commerce attd. 10/6/75 New York, NY	2.00
1577-78	Banking-Commerce set of 2 singles	3.00
1579	(10¢) Christmas - Madonna 10/14/75 DC	1.75
1580	(10¢) Christmas - Card 10/14/75 DC	1.75
1579-80	Christmas on one cover	2.50
	1975-81 AMERICANA SERIES REGULAR ISSUES	
1581	1¢ Inkwell & Quill 12/8/77 St. Louis, MO	1.75
1582	2¢ Speaker's Stand 12/8/77 St. Louis, MO	1.75
1584	3¢ Ballot Box 12/8/77 St. Louis, MO	1.75
1585	4¢ Books & Eyeglasses 12/8/77 St. Louis, MO	1.75
1581-85	4 values on one cover	3.00
1590	9¢ Capitol Dome, bklt. single	
	perf. 11 x 10½ 3/11/77 New York, NY	10.00
1590a	9¢ Capitol Dome, bklt. single	
	perf. 10 3/11/77 New York, NY	15.00
1591	9¢ Capitol Dome 11/24/75 DC	1.75
1592	10¢ Justice 11/17/77 New York, NY	1.75
1593	11¢ Printing Press 11/13/75 Phila., PA	1.75
1594	12¢ Liberty's Torch 4/8/81 Dallas, TX	1.75
1595	13¢ Liberty Bell, bklt. sgl. 10/31/75 Cleveland, OH	1.75
1595a	bklt. pane of 6 10/31/75 Cleveland, OH	2.25
1595b	bklt. pane of 7 10/31/75 Cleveland, OH	2.50
1595c	bklt. pane of 8 10/31/75 Cleveland, OH	2.75
1595d	bklt. pane of 5 4/2/76 Liberty, MO	2.00
1595ds	bklt. pane single, 4/2/76	1.75
1596	13¢ Eagle & Shield 12/1/75 Juneau, AK	1.75
1597	15¢ Ft. McHenry Flag 6/30/78 Baltimore, MD	1.75
1598	15¢ Ft. McHenry Flag,bklt. sgl. 6/30/78 Baltimore, MD ...	1.75
1598a	booklet pane of 8 6/30/78 Baltimore, MD	2.75
1599	16¢ Statue of Liberty 3/31/78 NY, NY	1.75
1603	24¢ Old North Church 11/14/75 Boston, MA	1.75
1604	28¢ Ft. Nisqually 8/11/78 Tacoma, WA	1.75
1605	29¢ Lighthouse 4/14/78 Atlantic City, NJ	1.75
1606	30¢ School House 8/27/79 Devils Lake, ND	1.75
1608	50¢ Betty Lamp 9/11/79 San Jaun, PR	2.00
	1975-81 AMERICANA SERIES REGULAR ISSUES	
1610	$1 Rush Lamp 7/2/79 San Francisco, CA	3.50
1611	$2 Kerosene Lamp 11/16/78 New York, NY	7.00
1612	$5 Railroad Lantern 8/23/79 Boston, MA	15.00
	1975-79 AMERICANA SERIES COILS	
1613	3.1¢ Guitar 10/25/79 Shreveport, LA	1.75
1614	7.7¢ Saxhorns 11/20/76 New York, NY	1.75
1615	7.9¢ Drum 4/23/76 Miami, FL	1.75
1615C	8.4¢ Grand Piano 7/13/78 Interlochen, MI	1.75
1616	9¢ Capitol Dome 3/5/76 Milwaukee, WI	1.75
1617	10¢ Justice 11/4/77 Tampa, FL	1.75
1618	13¢ Liberty Bell 11/25/75 Allentown, PA	1.75
1618C	15¢ Ft. McHenry Flag 6/30/78 Baltimore, MD	1.75
1619	16¢ Statue of Liberty 3/31/78 NY, NY	1.75

U.S. First Day Covers

1685

1760-63

Scott #	Description	Cacheted
	1975-77 Regular Series (cont.)	
	1975-77 REGULAR SERIES	
1622	13¢ Flag over Ind. Hall 11/15/75 Philadelphia, PA	1.75
1623	13¢ Flag over Capitol, bklt. single	
	perf. 11 x 10½ 3/11/77 NY, NY	2.50
1623a	13¢ & 9¢ booklet pane of 8 (7 #1623 & 1 #1590)	
	perf. 11 x 10½ 3/11/77 NY, NY	25.00
1623b	13¢ Flag over Capitol, bklt. single	
	perf. 10 3/11/77 New York, NY	2.00
1623c	13¢ & 9¢ booklet pane of 8 (7 #1623b & 1 #1590a)	
	perf. 10 3/11/77 New York, NY	15.00
1625	13¢ Flag over Ind. Hall, coil 11/15/75 Phila., PA	1.75
	1976	
1629-31	10¢ Spirit of '76 attd. 1/1/76 Pasadena, CA	3.00
1629-31	Spirit of '76 set of 3 singles	5.75
1632	13¢ Interphil '76 1/17/76 Phila., PA	1.75
	1976 STATE FLAGS	
1633-82	13¢ State Flags 2/23/76 set of 50 DC	75.00
	State Capitals	80.00
	State Capital & DC cancels, set of 50 combo FDC's	150.00
1682a	Full sheet on one FDC (In Folder)	40.00
1683	13¢ Telephone 3/10/76 Boston, MA	1.75
1684	13¢ Aviation 3/19/76 Chicago, IL	2.00
1685	13¢ Chemistry 4/6/76 New York, NY	2.50
1686-89	13¢-31¢ Bicent. Souv. Shts. 5/29/76 Philadelphia, PA	30.00
1686a-89e	Set of 20 singles from sheets	90.00
1686a-89e	Set of 20 singles on 4 covers	40.00
1690	13¢ Franklin 6/1/76 Philadelphia, PA	1.75
1690	Joint issue w/ Canada	5.00
1690	Joint issue w/ Canada, dual cancel	15.00
1691-94	13¢ Decl. of Indep. attd. 7/4/76 Philadelphia, PA	4.00
1691-94	Decl. of Indep. set of 4 singles	8.00
1695-98	13¢ Olympics attd. 7/16/76 Lake Placid, NY	4.00
1695-98	Olympics set of 4 singles	8.00
1699	13¢ Clara Maass 8/18/76 Belleville, NJ	2.00
1700	13¢ Adolph S. Ochs 9/18/76 New York, NY	1.75
1701	13¢ Nativity 10/27/76 Boston, MA	1.75
1702	13¢ "Winter Pastime" 10/27/76 Boston, MA	1.75
1701-02	Christmas on one cover	2.00
1701,03	13¢ "Winter Pastime", Grav.-Int. 10/27/76 Boston, MA ..	2.00
1703	Christmas on one cover	2.25
1702-03	Christmas on one cover	2.50
1701-03	Christmas on one cover	3.00
	1977	
1704	13¢ Washington 1/3/77 Princeton, NJ	1.75
	1st Carrollton cachet	**20.00**
1705	13¢ Sound Recording 3/23/77 DC	2.00
1706-09	13¢ Pueblo Pottery attd. 4/13/77 Santa Fe, NM	4.00
1706-09	Pueblo Pottery set of 4 singles	8.00
1710	13¢ Lindbergh 5/20/77 Roosevelt Field Sta., NY	3.00
	1st Doris Gold cachet	**65.00**
	1st GAMM cachet	**50.00**
	1st Spectrum cachet	**25.00**
	1st Tudor House cachet	**20.00**
	1st Z-Silk cachet	**20.00**
1711	13¢ Colorado Sthd. 5/21/77 Denver, CO	1.75
1712-15	13¢ Butterflies attd. 6/6/77 Indianapolis, IN	4.00
1712-15	Butterflies set of 4 singles	8.00
	1st Ham cachet	**450.00**
1716	13¢ Lafayette 6/13/77 Charleston, SC	1.75
1717-20	13¢ Skilled Hands attd. 7/4/77 Cincinnati, OH	4.00
1717-20	Skilled Hands set of 4 singles	8.00
1721	13¢ Peace Bridge 8/4/77 Buffalo, NY	1.75
	US and Canadian stamps on one cover	2.50
	Dual US & Canadian FD cancels	7.50
1722	13¢ Herkimer 8/6/77 Herkimer, NY	1.75
1723-24	13¢ Energy Conservation attd. 10/20/77 DC	2.50
1723-24	Energy Conservation set of 2 singles	3.00
1725	13¢ Alta California 9/9/77 San Jose, CA	1.75
1726	13¢ Articles of Confed. 9/30/77 York, PA	1.75
1727	13¢ Talking Pictures 10/6/77 Hollywood, CA	2.25
1728	13¢ Surrender at Saratoga 10/7/77 Schuylerville, NY	1.75
1729	13¢ Christmas - Valley Forge 10/21/77 Valley Forge, PA	1.75
1730	13¢ Christmas - Mailbox 10/21/77 Omaha, NE	1.75

Scott #	Description	Cacheted
	1978	
1729-30	Christmas on one cover, either city	2.50
1729-30	Christmas on one cover, dual FD cancels	4.00
1731	13¢ Carl Sandburg 1/6/78 Galesburg, IL	1.75
	1st Western Silk cachet	**35.00**
1732-33	13¢ Captain Cook attd. 1/20/78 Honolulu, HI	2.00
	Anchorage, AK	2.00
1732-33	Captain Cook set of 2 singles Honolulu, HI	3.50
	Anchorage, AK	3.50
1732-33	Set of 2 on one cover with dual FD cancels	15.00
	1st K.M.C. Venture cachet (set of 3)	**70.00**
1734	13¢ Indian Head Penny 1/11/78 Kansas City, MO	1.75
	1978-80 REGULAR ISSUES	
1735	(15¢) "A" & Eagle 5/22/78 Memphis, TN	1.75
1736	(15¢) "A", booklet single 5/22/78 Memphis, TN	1.75
1736a	(15¢) Booklet Pane of 8 5/22/78 Memphis, TN	3.00
1737	15¢ Roses, booklet single 7/11/78 Shreveport, LA	1.75
1737a	Booklet Pane of 8 7/11/78 Shreveport, LA	3.50
1738-42	15¢ Windmills set of 5 singles 2/7/80 Lubbock, TX	10.00
1742av	15¢ Windmills, strip of 5	5.00
1742a	Windmills booklet pane of 10	5.00
1743	(15¢) "A" & Eagle, coil 5/22/78 Memphis, TN	1.75
	1st Kribbs Kover cachet	**40.00**
1744	13¢ Harriet Tubman 2/1/78 DC	3.00
1745-48	13¢ American Quilts attd. 3/8/78 Charleston, WV	4.00
1745-48	American Quilts set of 4 singles	8.00
	1st Collins cachet	**450.00**
1749-52	13¢ American Dance attd. 4/26/78 New York, NY	4.00
1749-52	American Dance set of 4 singles	8.00
	1st Andrews cachet	**40.00**
1753	13¢ French Alliance 5/4/78 York, PA	1.75
1754	13¢ Dr. Papanicolaou 5/18/78 DC	1.75
1755	13¢ Jimmie Rodgers 5/24/78 Meridian, MS	1.75
1756	15¢ George M. Cohan 7/3/78 Providence, RI	1.75
1757	15¢ CAPEX Sheet 6/10/78 Toronto, Canada	3.50
1757a-h	CAPEX set of 8 singles	16.00
1758	15¢ Photography 6/26/78 Las Vegas, NV	1.75
1759	15¢ Viking Mission 7/20/78 Hampton, VA	1.75
1760-63	15¢ American Owls attd. 8/26/78 Fairbanks, AK	4.00
1760-63	American Owls set of 4 singles	8.00
1764-67	15¢ Amer. Trees attd. 10/9/78 Hot Springs Nat'l. Park, AR	4.00
1764-67	American Trees set of 4 singles	8.00
1768	15¢ Christmas - Madonna 10/18/78 DC	1.75
1769	15¢ Christmas - Hobby Horse 10/18/78 Holly, MI	1.75
1768-69	Christmas on one cover, either City	2.50
1768-69	Dual Cancel	3.00
	1979	
1770	15¢ Robert F. Kennedy 1/12/79 DC	2.00
	1st DRC cachet	**75.00**
1771	15¢ Martin Luther King 1/13/79 Atlanta, GA	3.00
1772	15¢ Int'l. Yr. of the Child 2/15/79 Philadelphia, PA	1.75
1773	15¢ John Steinbeck 2/27/79 Salinas, CA	1.75
1774	15¢ Albert Einstein 3/4/79 Princeton, NJ	3.00
1775-78	15¢ Toleware attd. 4/19/79 Lancaster, PA	4.00
1775-78	Toleware set of 4 singles	8.00
1779-82	15¢ Architecture attd. 6/4/79 Kansas City, MO	4.00
1779-82	Architecture set of 4 singles	8.00
1783-86	15¢ Endangered Flora attd. 6/7/79 Milwaukee, WI	4.00
1783-86	Endangered Flora set of 4 singles	8.00
1787	15¢ Seeing Eye Dogs 6/15/79 Morristown, NJ	1.75
1788	15¢ Special Olympics 8/9/79 Brockport, NY	1.75
1789	15¢ John Paul Jones, perf. 11x12 9/23/79 Annapolis, MD	2.00
1789a	15¢ John Paul Jones, perf. 11 9/23/79 Annapolis, MD	2.00
1789,89a	Both Perfs. on 1 Cover	12.00
1790	10¢ Olympic Javelin 9/5/79 Olympia, WA	1.75
1791-94	15¢ Summer Olympics attd. 9/28/79 Los Angeles, CA ...	4.00
1791-94	Summer Olympics set of 4 singles	8.00
1795-98	15¢ Winter Olympics attd. 2/1/80 Lake Placid, NY	4.00
1795-98	Winter Olympics set of 4 singles	8.00
1799	15¢ Christmas - Painting 10/18/79 DC	1.75
1800	15¢ Christmas - Santa Claus 10/18/79 North Pole, AK	1.75
1799-1800	Christmas on one cover, either city	2.50
1799-1800	Christmas, dual cancel	2.50
1801	15¢ Will Rogers 11/4/79 Claremore, OK	1.75
1802	15¢ Vietnam Vets 11/11/79 Arlington, VA	3.50

FIRST DAY COVER COLLECTING MADE EASY!

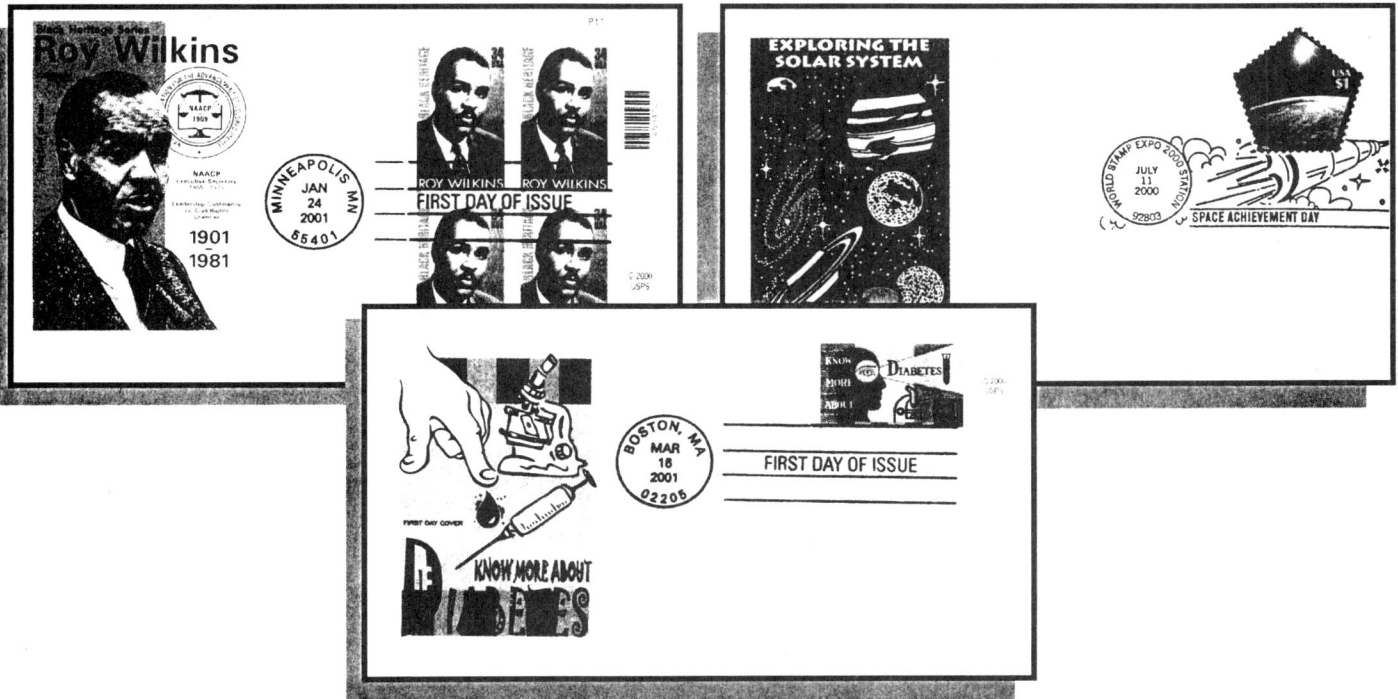

U.S. First Day Covers

1833

1906

Scott #	Description	Cacheted
	1980	
1803	15¢ W.C. Fields 1/29/80 Beverly Hills, CA	2.50
	1st Gill Craft cachet	30.00
	1st Kover Kids cachet	20.00
1804	15¢ Benj. Banneker 2/15/80 Annapolis, MD	3.00
1805-06	15¢ Letters - Memories attd. 2/25/80 DC	2.00
1805-06	Letters - Memories set of 2 singles	3.00
1807-08	15¢ Letters - Lift Spirit attd. 2/25/80 DC	2.00
1807-08	Letters - Lift Spirit set of 2 singles	3.00
1809-10	15¢ Letters - Opinions attd. 2/25/80 DC	2.00
1809-10	Letters - Opinions set of 2 singles	3.00
1805-10	15¢ Letter Writing attd. 2/25/80 DC	4.00
1805-10	Letter Writing set of 6 singles	7.50
1805-10	Letters, Memories, 6 on 3	5.00
	1980-81 REGULAR ISSUES	
1811	1¢ Inkwell, coil 3/6/80 New York, NY	1.75
1813	3½¢ Violins, coil 6/23/80 Williamsburg, PA	1.75
1816	12¢ Liberty's Torch, coil 4/8/81 Dallas, TX	1.75
1818	(18¢) "B" & Eagle 3/15/81 San Fran., CA	2.00
1819	(18¢) "B" & Eagle, bklt. sngl. 3/15/81 San Francisco, CA	1.75
1819a	(18¢) Bklt. Pane of 8 3/15/81 San Francisco, CA	4.00
1820	(18¢) "B" & Eagle, coil 3/15/81 San Francisco, CA	1.75
1818-20	No One Cover	2.50
	1980	
1821	15¢ Frances Perkins 4/10/80 DC	1.75
1822	15¢ Dolly Madison 5/20/80 DC	1.75
	1st American Postal Arts Society cachet (Post/Art)	35.00
1823	15¢ Emily Bissell 5/31/80 Wilmington, DE	1.75
1824	15¢ Helen Keller 6/27/80 Tuscumbia, AL	2.00
1825	15¢ Veterans Administration 7/21/80 DC	2.50
1826	15¢ Bernardo de Galvez 7/23/80 New Orleans, LA	1.75
1827-30	15¢ Coral Reefs attd. 8/26/80 Charlotte Amalie, VI	4.00
1827-30	Coral Reefs set of 4 singles	8.00
1831	15¢ Organized Labor 9/1/80 DC	1.75
1832	15¢ Edith Wharton 9/5/80 New Haven, CT	1.75
1833	15¢ Education 9/12/80 Franklin, MA	2.00
1834-37	15¢ Indian Masks attd. 9/25/80 Spokane, WA	4.00
1834-37	Indian Masks set of 4 singles	8.00
1838-41	15¢ Architecture attd. 10/9/80 New York, NY	4.00
1838-41	Architecture set of 4 singles	8.00
1842	15¢ Christmas - Madonna 10/31/80 DC	1.75
1843	15¢ Christmas - Wreath & Toys 10/31/80 Christmas, MI	1.75
1842-43	Christmas on one cover	2.50
1842-43	Christmas, dual cancel	3.00
	1980-85 GREAT AMERICANS SERIES	
1844	1¢ Dorothea Dix 9/23/83 Hampden, ME	1.75
1845	2¢ Igor Stravinsky 11/18/82 New York, NY	1.75
1846	3¢ Henry Clay 7/13/83 DC	1.75
1847	4¢ Carl Shurz 6/3/83 Watertown, WI	1.75
1848	5¢ Pearl Buck 6/25/83 Hillsboro, WV	1.75
1849	6¢ Walter Lippman 9/19/85 Minneapolis, MN	1.75
1850	7¢ Abraham Baldwin 1/25/85 Athens, GA	1.75
1851	8¢ Henry Knox 7/25/85 Thomaston, ME	1.75
1852	9¢ Sylvanus Thayer 6/7/85 Braintree, MA	2.00
1853	10¢ Richard Russell 5/31/84 Winder, GA	1.75
1854	11¢ Alden Partridge 2/12/85 Norwich Un., VT	2.00
1855	13¢ Crazy Horse 1/15/82 Crazy Horse, SD	1.75
1856	14¢ Sinclair Lewis 3/21/85 Sauk Centre, MN	1.75
1857	17¢ Rachel Carson 5/28/81 Springdale, PA	1.75
1858	18¢ George Mason 5/7/81 Gunston Hall, VA	1.75
1859	19¢ Sequoyah 12/27/80 Tahlequah, OK	1.75
1860	20¢ Ralph Bunche 1/12/82 New York, NY	3.00
1861	20¢ Thomas Gallaudet 6/10/83 West Hartford, CT	2.00
1862	20¢ Harry S. Truman 1/26/84 DC	2.00
1863	22¢ John J. Audubon 4/23/85 New York, NY	2.00
1864	30¢ Frank Laubach 2/2/84 Benton, PA	1.75
1865	35¢ Charles Drew 6/3/81 DC	3.00
1866	37¢ Robert Millikan 1/26/82 Pasadena, CA	1.75
1867	39¢ Grenville Clark 3/20/85 Hanover, NH	2.00
1868	40¢ Lillian Gilbreth 2/24/84 Montclair, NJ	2.00
1869	50¢ Chester W. Nimitz 2/22/85 Fredericksburg, TX	2.00
	1981	
1874	15¢ Everett Dirksen 1/4/81 Pekin, IL	1.75
1875	15¢ Whitney Moore Young 1/30/81 NY, NY	3.00
1876-79	15¢ Flowers attd. 4/23/81 Ft. Valley, GA	4.00

Scott #	Description	Cacheted
	1981 (cont.)	
1876-79	Flowers set of 4 singles	8.00
1880-89	18¢ Wildlife set of 10 sgls. 5/14/81 Boise, ID	17.50
1889a	Wildlife booklet pane of 10	6.00
	1981-82 REGULAR ISSUES	
1890	18¢ Flag & "Waves of Grain" 4/24/81 Portland, ME	1.75
1891	18¢ Flag & "Sea" coil 4/24/81 Portland, ME	1.75
1892	6¢ Circle of Stars, bklt. sngl. 4/24/81 Portland, ME	2.00
1893	18¢ Flag & "Mountain", bklt. sgl. 4/24/81 Portland, ME	1.75
1892-93	6¢ & 18¢ Booklet Pair 4/24/81 Portland, ME	3.75
1893a	18¢ & 6¢ B. Pane of 8 (2 #1892 & 6 #1893) 4/24/81 Portland, ME	5.00
1894	20¢ Flag over Supreme Court 12/17/81 DC	1.75
1895	20¢ Flag, coil 12/17/81 DC	1.75
1896	20¢ Flag, bklt. single 12/17/81 DC	1.75
1896a	Flag, bklt. pane of 6 12/17/81 DC	4.00
	#1894, 1895 & 1896a on one FDC	7.00
1896b	Flag, bklt. pane of 10 6/1/82 DC	6.00
1896bv	Reissue-Flag bklt single, 11/17/83, NY	2.50
1896bv	Reissue-Flag, pane of 10, 11/17/83, NY	20.00
	1981-84 TRANSPORTATION COIL SERIES	
1897	1¢ Omnibus 8/19/83 Arlington, VA	2.00
1897A	2¢ Locomotive 5/20/82 Chicago, IL	2.50
1898	3¢ Handcar 3/25/83 Rochester, NY	2.00
1898A	4¢ Stagecoach 8/19/82 Milwaukee, WI	2.00
1899	5¢ Motorcycle 10/10/83 San Francisco, CA	2.50
1900	5.2¢ Sleigh 3/21/83 Memphis, TN	2.00
1900a	Precancelled	150.00
1901	5.9¢ Bicycle 2/17/82 Wheeling, WV	2.00
1901a	Precancelled	200.00
1902	7.4¢ Baby Buggy 4/7/84 San Diego, CA	2.00
1902a	Precancelled	300.00
1903	9.3¢ Mail Wagon 12/15/81 Shreveport, LA	2.00
1903a	Precancelled	300.00
1904	10.9¢ Hansom Cab 3/26/82 Chattanooga, TN	2.00
1904a	Precancelled	300.00
1905	11¢ Caboose 2/3/84 Rosemont, IL	2.50
1906	17¢ Electric Car 6/25/81 Greenfield Village, MI	2.00
1907	18¢ Surrey 5/18/81 Notch, MO	2.00
1908	20¢ Fire Pumper 12/10/81 Alexandria, VA	2.00
1909	$9.35 Express Mail, single 8/12/83 Kennedy Sp. Ctr., FL	60.00
1909a	Express Mail, booklet pane of 3	175.00
	1981 Commemoratives (continued)	
1910	18¢ American Red Cross 5/1/81 DC	2.00
1911	18¢ Savings and Loans 5/8/81 Chicago, IL	1.75
1912-19	18¢ Space Ach. attd. 5/21/81 Kennedy Sp. Ctr., FL	6.00
1912-19	Space Achievement set of 8 singles	16.00
1920	18¢ Professional Management 6/18/81 Philadelphia, PA	1.75
1921-24	18¢ Wildlife Habitats attd. 6/26/81 Reno, NV	4.00
1921-24	Wildlife Habitats set of 4 singles	8.00
1925	18¢ Disabled Persons 6/29/81 Milford, MI	1.75
1926	18¢ Edna St. Vincent Millay 7/10/81 Austeritz, NY	1.75
1927	18¢ Alcoholism 8/19/81 DC	4.00
1928-31	18¢ Architecture attd. 8/28/81 DC	4.00
1928-31	Architecture set of 4 singles	8.00
1932	18¢ Babe Zaharias 9/22/81 Pinehurst, NC	8.00
1933	18¢ Bobby Jones 9/22/81 Pinehurst, NC	12.00
1932-33	Zaharias & Jones on one cover	15.00
1934	18¢ Frederic Remington 10/9/81 Oklahoma City, OK	2.00
1935	18¢ James Hoban 10/13/81 DC	1.75
1936	20¢ James Hoban 10/13/81 DC	1.75
1935-36	Hoban on one cover	3.50
1935-36	Joint issue w/ Ireland	3.00
1935-36	Joint issue w/ Ireland dual cancel	15.00
1937-38	18¢ Battle of Yorktown 10/16/81 Yorktown, VA	2.00
1937-38	Battle of Yorktown set of 2 singles	3.00
1939	(20¢) Christmas - Madonna 10/28/81 Chicago, IL	1.75
1940	(20¢) Christmas - Teddy Bear 10/28/81 Christmas Valley, OR	1.75
1939-40	Christmas on one cover	2.50
1939-40	Christmas, dual cancel	3.00
1941	20¢ John Hanson 11/5/81 Frederick, MD	1.75
1942-45	20¢ Desert Plants attd. 12/11/81 Tucson, AZ	4.00
1942-45	Desert Plants set of 4 singles	8.00
	1st Pugh cachet	100.00

U.S. First Day Covers

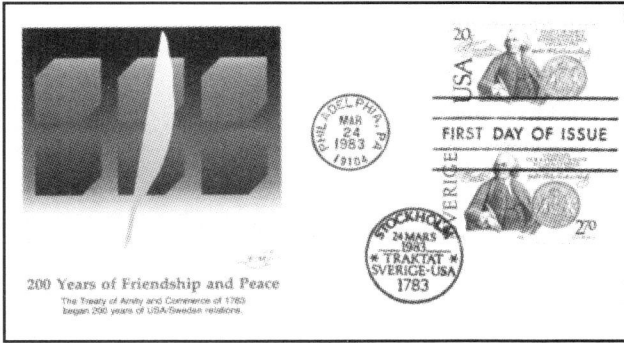

2036

Scott #	Description	Cacheted
	1981-82 REGULAR ISSUES	
1946	(20¢) "C" & Eagle 10/11/81 Memphis, TN	1.75
1947	(20¢) "C" Eagle, coil 10/11/81 Memphis, TN	1.75
1948	(20¢) "C" Eagle, bklt. single 10/11/81 Memphis, TN	1.75
1948a	(20¢) "C" Booklet Pane of 10	5.50
1949	20¢ Bighorn Sheep, bklt. single 1/8/82 Bighorn, MT	1.75
	1st New Direxions cachet	**25.00**
1949a	20¢ Booklet Pane of 10	6.00
	1982 Commemoratives	
1950	20¢ Franklin D. Roosevelt 1/30/82 Hyde Park, NY	1.75
1951	20¢ Love 2/1/82 Boston, MA	1.75
1952	20¢ George Washington 2/22/82 Mt. Vernon, VA	2.00
	1982 STATE BIRDS AND FLOWERS	
1953-2002	20¢ Birds & Flowers 4/14/82 Set of 50 DC	70.00
	Set of 50 State Capitals	75.00
2002a	Complete pane of 50 (Uncacheted)	45.00
	1982 Commemoratives (continued)	
2003	20¢ US & Netherlands 4/20/82 DC	1.75
2003	Joint issue w/ Netherlands	7.50
...	Joint issue w/ Netherlands, dual cancel	15.00
2004	20¢ Library of Congress 4/21/82 DC	1.75
2005	20¢ Consumer Education, coil 4/27/82 DC	1.75
2006-09	20¢ Knoxville World's Fair, attd. 4/29/82 Knoxville, TN	4.00
2006-09	20¢ Knoxville World's Fair, Knoxville, TN, set of 4 sngls	8.00
2010	20¢ Horatio Alger 4/30/82 Willow Grove, PA	1.75
2011	20¢ "Aging Together" 5/21/82 Sun City, AZ	1.75
2012	20¢ The Barrymores 6/8/82 New York, NY	1.75
2013	20¢ Dr. Mary Walker 6/10/82 Oswego, NY	1.75
2014	20¢ Peace Garden 6/30/82 Dunseith, ND	1.75
2015	20¢ Libraries 7/13/82 Philadelphia, PA	1.75
2016	20¢ Jackie Robinson 8/2/82 Cooperstown, NY	7.00
2017	20¢ Touro Synagogue 8/22/82 Newport, RI	3.00
2018	20¢ Wolf Trap 9/1/82 Vienna, VA	1.75
2019-22	20¢ Architecture attd. 9/30/82 DC	4.00
2019-22	Architecture set of 4 singles	8.00
2023	20¢ St. Francis of Assisi 10/7/82 San Francisco, CA	1.75
2024	20¢ Ponce de Leon 10/12/82 San Juan, PR	1.75
2025	13¢ Christmas - Kitten & Puppy 11/3/82 Danvers, MA	2.00
2026	20¢ Christmas - Madonna & Child 10/28/82 DC	1.75
2027-30	20¢ Christmas - Winter Scene, attd. 10/28/82 Snow, OK	4.00
2027-30	Christmas set of 4 singles	8.00
2026-30	Christmas on one cover either city	3.00
2026-30	Christmas, dual cancel	3.50
	1983 Commemoratives	
2031	20¢ Science & Industry 1/19/83 Chi., IL	1.75
2032-35	20¢ Ballooning 3/31/83 DC	4.00
	Ballooning Albuquerque, NM	4.00
2032-35	Ballooning set of 4 singles DC	8.00
	Ballooning Albuquerque, NM	8.00
2036	20¢ Sweden, 3/24/83 Philadelphia, PA	1.75
2036	20¢ US & Sweden, joint Issue, dual cancel	15.00
2036	20¢ US & Sweden, joint issue	5.00
2036	**1st Panda Cachet**	**25.00**
2037	20¢ Civilian Conservation Corps 4/5/83 Luray, VA	1.75
2038	20¢ Joseph Priestley 4/13/83 Northumberland, PA	1.75
2039	20¢ Voluntarism 4/20/83 DC	1.75
2040	20¢ German Immigration 4/29/83 Germantown, PA	1.75
2040	Joint issue w/Germany, dual cancel	15.00
2041	20¢ Brooklyn Bridge 5/17/83 Brooklyn, NY	3.00
2042	20¢ Tennessee Valley Authority 5/18/83 Knoxville, TN	1.75
2043	20¢ Physical Fitness 5/14/83 Houston, TX	2.00
2044	20¢ Scott Joplin 6/9/83 Sedalia, MO	3.00
2045	20¢ Medal of Honor 6/7/83 DC	6.00
2046	20¢ Babe Ruth 7/6/83 Chicago, IL	6.00
2047	20¢ Nathaniel Hawthorne 7/8/83 Salem, MA	1.75
2048-51	13¢ Summer Olympics attd. 7/28/83 South Bend, IN	4.00
2048-51	Summer Olympics set of 4 singles	8.00
2052	20¢ Treaty of Paris 9/2/83 DC	1.75
2052	Joint issue w/France, dual cancel	8.00
2052	French issue only	3.50
2053	20¢ Civil Service 9/9/83 DC	1.75

Scott #	Description	Cacheted
	1983 Commemoratives (cont.)	
2054	20¢ Metropolitan Opera 9/14/83 NY, NY	1.75
2055-58	20¢ Inventors attd. 9/21/83 DC	4.00
2055-58	Inventors set of 4 singles	8.00
2059-62	20¢ Streetcars attd. 10/8/83 Kennebunkport, ME	4.00
2059-62	Streetcars set of 4 singles	8.00
2063	20¢ Christmas - Madonna & Child 10/28/83 DC	1.75
2064	20¢ Christmas - Santa Claus 10/28/83 Santa Claus, IN	1.75
2063-64	Christmas on one cover either city	2.50
2063-64	Christmas, dual cancel	3.00
2065	20¢ Martin Luther 11/11/83 DC	1.75
2065	Joint issue w/Germany, dual cancel	15.00
	1984 Commemoratives	
2066	20¢ Alaska Sthd. 1/3/84 Fairbanks, AK	1.75
2067-70	20¢ Winter Olympics attd. 1/6/84 Lake Placid, NY	4.00
2067-70	Winter Olympics set of 4 singles	8.00
2071	20¢ Fed. Deposit Ins. Corp. 1/12/84 DC	1.75
2072	20¢ Love 1/31/84 DC	1.75
2073	20¢ Carter Woodson 2/1/84 DC	3.00
2074	20¢ Soil & Water Cons. 2/6/84 Denver, CO	1.75
2075	20¢ Credit Union Act 2/10/84 Salem, MA	1.75
2076-79	20¢ Orchids attd. 3/5/84 Miami, FL	4.00
2076-79	Orchids set of 4 singles	8.00
2080	20¢ Hawaii Sthd. 3/12/84 Honolulu, HI	2.00
2081	20¢ National Archives 4/16/84 DC	1.75
2082-85	20¢ Summer Olympics attd. 5/4/84 Los Angeles, CA	4.00
2082-85	Summer Olympics set of 4 singles	8.00
2086	20¢ Louisiana World's Fair 5/11/84 New Orleans, LA	1.75
2087	20¢ Health Research 5/17/84 New York, NY	1.75
2088	20¢ Douglas Fairbanks 5/23/84 Denver, CO	1.75
2089	20¢ Jim Thorpe 5/24/84 Shawnee, OK	5.00
2090	20¢ John McCormack 6/6/84 Boston, MA	1.75
2090	Joint issue w/Ireland, dual cancel	15.00
2091	20¢ St. Lawrence Swy. 6/26/84 Massena, NY	1.75
	Joint issue w/Canada, dual cancel	15.00
2092	20¢ Waterfowl Preservation 7/2/84 Des Moines, IA	1.75
	1st George Van Natta cachet	**40.00**
2093	20¢ Roanoke Voyages 7/13/84 Manteo, NC	1.75
2094	20¢ Herman Melville 8/1/84 New Bedford, MA	1.75
2095	20¢ Horace Moses 8/6/84 Bloomington, IN	1.75
2096	20¢ Smokey the Bear 8/13/84 Capitan, NM	2.00
2097	20¢ Roberto Clemente 8/17/84 Carolina, PR	10.00
2098-2101	20¢ Dogs attd. 9/7/84 New York, NY	4.00
2098-2101	Dogs set of 4 singles	8.00
2102	20¢ Crime Prevention 9/26/84 DC	2.00
2103	20¢ Hispanic Americans 10/31/84 DC	3.00
2104	20¢ Family Unity 10/1/84 Shaker Heights, OH	1.75
2105	20¢ Eleanor Roosevelt 10/11/84 Hyde Park, NY	1.75
2106	20¢ Nation of Readers 10/16/84 DC	1.75
2107	20¢ Christmas - Madonna & Child 10/30/84 DC	1.75
2108	20¢ Christmas - Santa 10/30/84 Jamaica, NY	1.75
2107-08	Christmas on one cover, either city	2.50
2107-08	Christmas, dual cancel	3.00
2109	20¢ Vietnam Memorial 11/10/84 DC	4.50
	1985 REGULARS & COMMEMS.	
2110	22¢ Jerome Kern 1/23/85 New York, NY	1.75
2111	(22¢) "D" & Eagle 2/1/85 Los Angeles, CA	1.75
2112	(22¢) "D" coil 2/1/85 Los Angeles, CA	1.75
2113	(22¢) "D" bklt. single 2/1/85 L.A., CA	1.75
2111-13	(22¢) "D" Stamps on 1	5.00
2113a	(22¢) Booklet Pane of 10	7.00
2114	22¢ Flag over Capitol 3/29/85 DC	1.75
2115	22¢ Flag over Capitol, coil 3/29/85 DC	1.75
2115b	Same, Phosphor Test Coil 5/23/87 Secaucus, NJ	2.50
2116	22¢ Flag over Capitol, bklt. single 3/29/85 Waubeka, WI	1.75
2116a	Booklet Pane of 5	3.00
2117-21	22¢ Seashells set of 5 singles 4/4/85 Boston, MA	10.00
2121a	Seashells, booklet pane of 10	7.00
2122	$10.75 Express Mail, bklt. sgl. 4/29/85 San Francisco, CA	25.00
2122a	Express Mail, booklet pane of 3	135.00
2122b	$10.75 Re-issue, bklt. sgl. 6/19/89 DC	250.00
2122c	Re-issue, booklet pane of 3	700.00
	1985-89 TRANSPORTATION COILS	
2123	3.4¢ School Bus 6/8/85 Arlington, VA	1.75
2123a	Precancelled 6/8/85 (earliest known use)	250.00
2124	4.9¢ Buckboard 6/21/85 Reno, NV	1.75
2124a	Precancelled 6/21/85 (earliest known use)	250.00
2125	5.5¢ Star Route Truck 11/1/86 Fort Worth, TX	1.75
2125a	Precancelled 11/1/86 DC	5.00
2126	6¢ Tricycle 5/6/85 Childs, MD	1.75
2127	7.1¢ Tractor 2/6/87 Sarasota, FL	1.75
2127a	Precancelled 2/6/87 Sarasota, FL	5.00
2127av	Zip + 4 Prec., 5/26/89 Rosemont, IL	1.75
2128	8.3¢ Ambulance 6/21/85 Reno, NV	1.75
2128a	Precancelled 6/21/85 DC (earliest known use)	250.00
2129	8.5¢ Tow Truck 1/24/87 Tucson, AZ	1.75
2129a	Precancelled 1/24/87 DC	5.00
2130	10.1¢ Oil Wagon 4/18/85 Oil Center, NM	1.75
2130a	Black Precancel 4/18/85 DC (earliest known use)	250.00
2130av	Red. Prec. 6/27/88 DC	1.75
2131	11¢ Stutz Bearcat 6/11/85 Baton Rouge, LA	1.75
2132	12¢ Stanley Steamer 4/2/85 Kingfield, ME	1.75
2132b	"B" Press cancel 9/3/87 DC	60.00

U.S. First Day Covers

2155-58

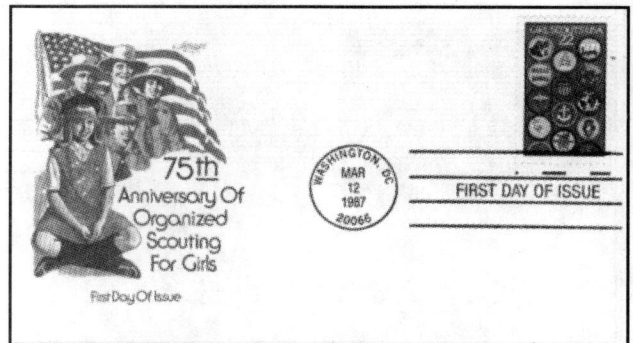

2251

Scott #	Description	Cacheted
	1985-89 TRANSPORTATION COILS (cont.)	
2133	12.5¢ Pushcart 4/18/85 Oil Center, NM	1.75
2134	14¢ Iceboat 3/23/85 Rochester, NY	1.75
2135	17¢ Dog Sled 8/20/86 Anchorage, AK	1.75
2136	25¢ Bread Wagon 11/22/86 Virginia Bch., VA	1.75
2137	22¢ Mary McLeod Bethune 3/5/85 DC	3.00
2138-41	22¢ Duck Decoys attd. 3/22/85 Shelburne, VT	4.00
2138-41	Duck Decoys set of 4 singles	8.00
2142	22¢ Winter Special Olympics 3/25/85 Park City, UT	1.75
2143	22¢ Love 4/17/85 Hollywood, CA	1.75
2144	22¢ Rural Electrification Admin. 5/11/85 Madison, SD	1.75
2145	22¢ Ameripex '86 5/25/85 Rosemont, IL	1.75
2146	22¢ Abigail Adams 6/14/85 Quincy, MA	1.75
2147	22¢ Frederic A. Bartholdi 7/18/85 NY, NY	1.75
2149	18¢ Washington Pre-Sort, coil 11/6/85 DC	1.75
2149a	18¢ Washington, Precanceled, pair w/2149	5.00
2150	21.1¢ Zip + 4, coil 10/22/85 DC	1.75
2150a	21.1¢ Zip + 4, Precanceled, pair w/2150	5.00
2152	22¢ Korean War Veterans 7/26/85	3.00
2153	22¢ Social Security Act 8/14/85 Baltimore, MD	1.75
2154	22¢ World War I Vets 8/26/85 Milwaukee, WI	2.00
2155-58	22¢ Horses attd. 9/25/85 Lexington, KY	4.00
2155-58	Horses set of 4 singles	8.00
2159	22¢ Public Education 10/1/85 Boston, MA	2.00
2160-63	22¢ Int'l. Youth Year attd. 10/7/85 Chicago, IL	4.00
2160-63	Set of 4 singles	8.00
2164	22¢ Help End Hunger 10/15/85 DC	1.75
2165	22¢ Christmas - Madonna 10/30/85 Detroit, MI	1.75
2166	22¢ Christmas - Poinsettia 10/30/85 Nazareth, MI	1.75
2165-66	Christmas on one cover, either city	2.50
2165-66	On One Cover, dual cancel	3.00
	1986	
2167	22¢ Arkansas Sthd. 1/3/86 Little Rock, AR	1.75
	1986-94 GREAT AMERICANS SERIES	
2168	1¢ Margaret Mitchell 6/30/86 Atlanta, GA	4.00
2169	2¢ Mary Lyon 2/28/87 South Hadley, MA	1.75
2170	3¢ Dr. Paul Dudley White 9/15/86 DC	1.75
2171	4¢ Father Flanagan 7/14/86 Boys Town, NE	1.75
2172	5¢ Hugo L. Black 2/27/86 DC	1.75
2173	5¢ Luis Munoz Marin 2/18/90 San Juan, PR	1.75
2175	10¢ Red Cloud 8/15/87 Red Cloud, NE	2.00
2176	14¢ Julia Ward Howe 2/12/87 Boston, MA	1.75
2177	15¢ Buffalo Bill Cody 6/6/88 Cody, WY	1.75
2178	17¢ Belva Ann Lockwood 6/18/86 Middleport, NY	1.75
2179	20¢ Virginia Agpar 10/24/94 Dallas, TX	1.75
2180	21¢ Chester Carlson 10/21/88 Rochester, NY	1.75
2181	23¢ Mary Cassatt 11/4/88 Phila., PA	1.75
2182	25¢ Jack London 1/11/86 Glen Ellen, CA	2.00
2182a	Bklt. Pane of 10 Perf, 11 5/3/88 San Francisco, CA	8.00
2182as	Perf. 11 bklt. single 5/3/88 San Francisco, CA	2.00
2183	28¢ Sitting Bull 9/14/89 Rapid City, SD	2.25
2184	29¢ Earl Warren 3/9/92 DC	2.00
2185	29¢ Thomas Jefferson 4/13/93 Charlottesville, VA	2.00
2186	35¢ Dennis Chavez 4/3/91 Albuquerque, NM	2.00
2187	40¢ General Claire Chennault 9/6/90 Monroe, LA	3.00
2188	45¢ Dr. Harvey Cushing 6/17/88 Cleveland, OH	2.00
2189	52¢ Hubert H. Humphrey 6/3/91 Minneapolis, MN	2.00
2190	56¢ John Harvard 9/3/86 Cambridge, MA	3.00
2191	65¢ General "Hap" Arnold 11/5/88 Gladwyne, PA	3.00
2192	75¢ Wendell Wilkie 2/16/92 Bloomington, IN	3.00
2193	$1 Dr. Bernard Revel 9/23/86 NY, NY	6.00
2194	$1 Johns Hopkins 6/7/89 Baltimore, MD	5.00
2195	$2 William Jennings Bryan 3/19/86 Salem, IL	8.00
2196	$5 Bret Harte 8/25/87 Twain Harte, CA	17.50
2197	25¢ Jack London, perf. 10 bklt. sgl. 5/3/88 San Fran., CA	1.75
2197a	Bklt. Pane of 6	4.00
2198-2201	22¢ Stamp Coll. set of 4 1/23/86 State College, PA	8.00
	Joint issue, US + Swedish Panes on one Cover	15.00
2201a	Stamp Collecting, Bklt. pane of 4	5.00
2201b	Color error, Black omitted on #2198 & 2201	300.00
2201b	Same, set of 4 singles	300.00
2202	22¢ Love 1/30/86 New York, NY	1.75
2203	22¢ Sojourner Truth 1/4/86 New Paltz, NY	3.00
2204	22¢ Texas 3/2/86 San Antonio, TX	3.00
	Washington-on-the-Brazos, TX	3.00

Scott #	Description	Cacheted
	1986-94 GREAT AMERICAN SERIES (cont.)	
2205-09	22¢ Fish set of 5 singles 3/21/86 Seattle, WA	10.00
2209a	Fish, booklet pane of 5	6.00
2210	22¢ Public Hospitals 4/11/86 NY, NY	1.75
2211	22¢ Duke Ellington 4/29/86 New York, NY	4.00
2216-19	22¢ U.S. Presidents 4 sheets of 9 5/22/86 Chicago, IL	24.00
2216a-19a	US President set of 36 singles	60.00
2220-23	22¢ Explorers attd. 5/28/86 North Pole, AK	6.00
2220-23	22¢ Explorers set of 4 singles	12.00
2224	22¢ Statue of Liberty 7/4/86 NY, NY	2.00
2224	Joint issue w/France	5.00
2224	Joint issue w/France, dual cancel	15.00
2225	1¢ Omnibus Coil Re-engraved 11/26/86 DC	1.75
2226	2¢ Locomotive Coil Re-engraved 3/6/87 Milwaukee, WI	1.75
2228	4¢ Stagecoach Coil "B" Press 8/15/86 DC (eku)	150.00
2231	8.3¢ Ambulance Coil "B" Press 8/29/86 DC (eku)	150.00
2235-38	22¢ Navajo Art attd. 9/4/86 Window Rock, AZ	4.00
2235-38	Set of 4 singles	8.00
2239	22¢ T.S. Eliot 9/26/86 St. Louis, MO	1.75
2240-43	22¢ Woodcarved Figurines attd. 10/1/86 DC	4.00
2240-43	Set of 4 singles	8.00
2244	22¢ Christmas - Madonna & Child 10/24/86 DC	2.00
2245	22¢ Christmas Village Scene 10/24/86 Snow Hill, MD	2.00
	1987	
2246	22¢ Michigan Statehood 1/26/87 Lansing, MI	1.75
2247	22¢ Pan American Games 1/29/87 Indianapolis, IN	1.75
2248	22¢ Love 1/30/87 San Francisco, CA	1.75
2249	22¢ Jean Baptiste Point du Sable 2/20/87 Chicago, IL	3.00
2250	22¢ Enrico Caruso 2/27/87 NY, NY	1.75
2244-45	Christmas on one Cover, either City	2.50
2244-45	Christmas on one Cover, either City	3.00
2251	22¢ Girl Scouts 3/12/87 DC	4.00
	1987-88 TRANSPORTATION COILS	
2252	3¢ Conestoga Wagon 2/29/88 Conestoga, PA	1.75
2253	5¢ Milk Wagon 9/25/87 Indianapolis, IN	1.75
2254	5.3¢ Elevator, Prec. 9/16/88 New York, NY	1.75
2255	7.6¢ Carretta, Prec. 8/30/88 San Jose, CA	1.75
2256	8.4¢ Wheelchair, Prec. 8/12/88 Tucson, AZ	1.75
2257	10¢ Canal Boat 4/11/87 Buffalo, NY	1.75
2258	13¢ Police Patrol Wagon, Prec. 10/29/88 Anaheim, CA	2.50
2259	13.2¢ RR Car, Prec. 7/19/88 Pittsburgh, PA	1.75
2260	15¢ Tugboat 7/12/88 Long Beach, CA	1.75
2261	16.7¢ Popcorn Wagon, Prec. 7/7/88 Chicago, IL	1.75
2262	17.5¢ Marmon Wasp 9/25/87 Indianapolis, IN	1.75
2262a	Precancelled	5.00
2263	20¢ Cable Car 10/28/88 San Francisco, CA	1.75
2264	20.5¢ Fire Engine, Prec. 9/28/88 San Angelo, TX	2.00
2265	21¢ R.R. Mail Car, Prec. 8/16/88 Santa Fe, NM	1.75
2266	24.1¢ Tandem Bicycle, Prec. 10/26/88 Redmond, WA	1.75
	1987-88 REGULAR & SPECIAL ISSUES	
2267-74	22¢ Special Occasions, bklt. sgls. 4/20/87 Atlanta, GA	16.00
2274a	Booklet Pane of 10	7.00
2275	22¢ United Way 4/28/87 DC	1.75
2276	22¢ Flag and Fireworks 5/9/87 Denver, CO	1.75
2276a	Booklet Pane of 20 11/30/87 DC	12.00
2277	(25¢) "E" Earth Issue 3/22/88 DC	1.75
2278	25¢ Flag & Clouds 5/6/88 Boxborough, MA	1.75
2279	(25¢) "E" Earth Coil 3/22/88 DC	1.75
2280	25¢ Flag over Yosemite Coil 5/20/88 Yosemite, CA	1.75
2280 var.	Phosphor paper 2/14/89 Yosemite, CA	1.75
2281	25¢ Honeybee Coil 9/2/88 Omaha, NE	1.75
2282	(25¢) "E" Earth Bklt. Sgl. 3/22/88 DC	1.75
2282a	Bklt. Pane of 10	7.50
2283	25¢ Pheasant Bklt. Sgl. 4/29/88 Rapid City, SD	1.75
2283a	Bklt. Pane of 10	8.00
2284	25¢ Grosbeak Bklt. Sgl. 5/28/88 Arlington, VA	1.75
2285	25¢ Owl Bklt. Sgl. 5/28/88 Arlington, VA	1.75
2284-85	attached pair	3.50
2285b	Bklt. Pane of 10 (5 of ea.)	8.00
2285A	25¢ Flag & Clouds bklt. sgl. 7/5/88 DC	1.75
2285Ac	Bklt. Pane of 6	4.50
2286-2335	22¢ American Wildlife 6/13/87 Toronto, Canada Set of 50 singles	75.00
2335a	Complete Pane of 50	40.00

U.S. First Day Covers

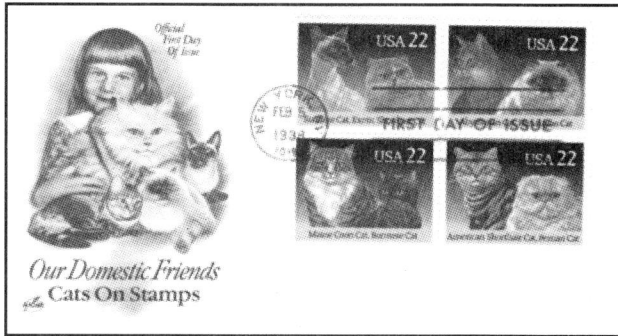

2372-75

2452

RATIFICATION OF CONSTITUTION
STATE BICENTENNIAL ISSUES 1987-90

Scott #	Description	Cacheted
2336-48	Set of 13 State Bicent. Issues on one cover each w/ a different First Day cancel	100.00
2336	22¢ Delaware Statehood Bicent. 7/4/87 Dover, DE	2.00
2337	22¢ Pennsylvania Bicent. 8/26/87 Harrisburg, PA	2.00
2338	22¢ New Jersey Bicent. 9/11/87 Trenton, NJ	2.00
2339	22¢ Georgia Bicent. 1/6/88 Atlanta, GA	2.00
2340	22¢ Connecticut Bicent. 1/9/88 Hartford, CT	2.00
2341	22¢ Massachusetts Bicent. 2/6/88 Boston, MA	2.00
2342	22¢ Maryland Bicent. 2/15/88 Annapolis, MD	2.00
2343	25¢ South Carolina Bicent. 5/23/88 Columbia, SC	2.00
2344	25¢ New Hampshire Bicent. 6/21/88 Concord, NH	2.00
2345	25¢ Virginia Bicent. 6/25/88 Williamsburg, VA	2.00
2346	25¢ New York Bicent. 7/26/88 Albany, NY	2.00
2347	25¢ North Carolina Bicent. 8/22/89 Fayetteville, NC	2.00
2348	25¢ Rhode Island Bicent. 5/29/90 Pawtucket, RI	2.00
2349	22¢ U.S.-Morocco Relations 7/17/87 DC	1.75
2349	Morocco issue only	5.00
2349	Joint issue w/Morocco, dual cancel	15.00
2349	**1st Anagram cachet**	25.00
2350	22¢ William Faulkner 8/3/87 Oxford, MS	1.75
2351-54	22¢ Lacemaking attd. 8/14/87 Ypsilanti, MI	4.00
2351-54	Set of 4 singles	8.00
2355-59	22¢ Drafting of Constitution bklt. sgls. (5) 8/28/87 DC	10.00
2359a	Booklet Pane of 5	5.00
2360	22¢ Signing the Constitution 9/17/87 Philadelphia, PA	2.00
2361	22¢ Certified Public Accounting 9/21/87 NY, NY	12.00
2362-66	22¢ Locomotives, bklt. sgls. (5) 10/1/87 Baltimore, MD	10.00
2366a	Booklet Pane of 5	4.00
2367	22¢ Christmas - Madonna & Child 10/23/87 DC	2.00
2368	22¢ Christmas Ornaments 10/23/87 Holiday, CA	2.00
2367-68	Christmas on one cover, either city	3.00
2367-68	Christmas on one cover, dual cancel	4.00

1988

Scott #	Description	Cacheted
2369	22¢ 1988 Winter Olympics 1/10/88 Anchorage, AK	1.75
2370	22¢ Australia Bicentennial 1/26/88 DC	3.00
2370	Joint issue w/Australia, dual cancel	15.00
2370	Australia issue only	5.00
2371	22¢ James Weldon Johnson 2/2/88 Nashville, TN	3.00
2372-75	22¢ Cats 2/5/88 New York, NY	8.00
2372-75	Set of 4 singles	15.00
2376	22¢ Knute Rockne 3/9/88 Notre Dame, IN	4.00
2377	25¢ Francis Ouimet 6/13/88 Brookline, MA	7.50
2378	25¢ Love, 7/4/88 Pasadena, CA	1.75
2379	45¢ Love, 8/8/88 Shreveport, LA	2.00
2380	25¢ Summer Olympics 8/19/88 Colo. Springs, CO	1.75
2381-85	25¢ Classic Cars, Bklt. Sgls. 8/25/88 Detroit, MI	10.00
2385a	Bklt. Pane of 5	4.00
2386-89	25¢ Antarctic Explorers attd. 9/14/88 DC	4.00
2386-89	Set of 4 singles	8.00
2390-93	25¢ Carousel Animals attd. 10/1/88 Sandusky, OH	4.00
2390-93	Set of 4 singles	8.00
2394	$8.75 Eagle 10/4/88 Terra Haute, IN	30.00
2395-98	25¢ Sp. Occasions Bklt. Sgls. 10/22/88 King of Prussia, PA	7.00
2396a	Happy Birthday & Best Wishes, Bklt. Pane of 6	5.00
2398a	Thinking of You & Love You, Bklt. Pane of 6	5.00
2399	25¢ Christmas Madonna & Child 10/20/88 DC	2.00
2400	25¢ Christmas Sleigh & Village 10/20/88 Berlin, NH	2.00
2399-00	Christmas on one Cover	2.50
2399-00	Christmas on one Cover, dual cancel	3.00

1989

Scott #	Description	Cacheted
2401	25¢ Montana Statehood 1/15/89 Helena, MT	2.00
2402	25¢ A. Philip Randolph 2/3/89 New York, NY	3.00
2403	25¢ North Dakota Statehood 2/21/89 Bismarck, ND	1.75
2404	25¢ Washington Statehood 2/22/89 Olympia, WA	1.75
2405-09	25¢ Steamboats, Bklt. Sgls. 3/3/89 New Orleans, LA	10.00
2409a	Bklt. Pane of 5	4.00
2410	25¢ World Stamp Expo 3/16/89 New York, NY	1.75
2411	25¢ Arturo Toscanini 3/25/89 New York, NY	1.75
2412	25¢ U.S. House of Representatives 4/4/89 DC	2.00
2413	25¢ U.S. Senate 4/6/89 DC	2.00
2414	25¢ Exec. Branch & George Washington Inaugural	

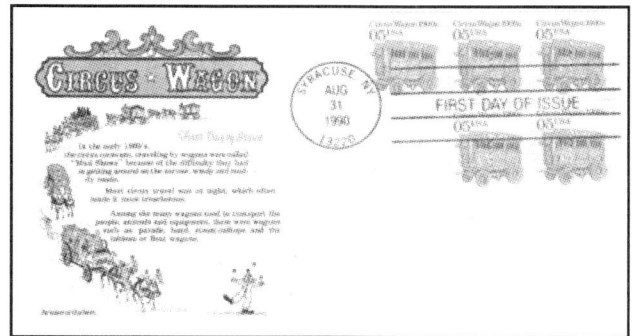

Scott #	Description	Cacheted
	1989 (cont.)	
	4/16/89 Mt. Vernon, VA	2.00
2412-15	Government combo 2/2/90 Washington, DC	3.50
2415	25¢ U.S. Supreme Court 2/2/90 DC	2.00
2416	25¢ South Dakota Statehood 5/3/89 Pierre, SD	1.75
2417	25¢ Lou Gehrig 6/10/89 Cooperstown, NY	5.50
2418	25¢ Ernest Hemingway 7/17/89 Key West, FL	1.75
2419	$2.40 Moon Landing, Priority Mail, 7/20/89 DC	7.00
2420	25¢ Letter Carriers 8/30/89 Milwaukee, WI	1.75
2421	25¢ Drafting the Bill of Rights 9/25/89 Philadelphia, FA	1.75
2422-25	25¢ Prehistoric Animals attd. 10/1/89 Orlando, FL	5.00
2422-25	Set of 4 singles	10.00
2426, C21(1)	25¢ Pre-Columbian w/45¢ Air Combo	7.50
2426	25¢ Pre-Columbian Customs 10/12/89 San Juan, PR	1.75
2427	25¢ Christmas Madonna & Child 10/19/89 DC	1.75
2427a	Madonna booklet single	1.75
2427a	Booklet Pane of 10	8.00
2428	25¢ Christmas Sleigh & Presents 10/19/89 Westport, CT	1.75
2427-28	Christmas on one Cover, either City	2.50
2427-28	Christmas on one Cover, dual cancel	3.00
2429	25¢ Christmas Sleigh, bklt. sgl. Westport, CT	1.75
2429a	Booklet Pane of 10	8.00
2431	25¢ Eagle & Sheild, pair on backing paper	4.00
2431	25¢ Eagle & Sheild, pane of 6	8.00
2431	25¢ Eagle & Shield, self-adhes. 11/10/89 Virginia Bch., VA	1.75
2431a	Booklet Pane of 18	30.00
2433	90¢ World Stamp Expo S/S of 4 11/17/89 DC	14.50
2434-37	25¢ Traditional Mail Transportation attd. 11/19/89 DC	4.00
2434-37	Set of 4 singles	8.00
2438	25¢ Traditional Mail Transportation, S/S of 4 11/28/89 DC	4.50

1990

Scott #	Description	Cacheted
2439	25¢ Idaho Statehood 1/6/90 Boise, ID	2.00
2440	25¢ Love 1/18/90 Romance, AR	2.00
2441	25¢ Love, bklt. sgl. 1/18/90 Romance, AR	1.75
2441a	Booklet Pane of 10	8.00
2442	25¢ Ida B. Wells 2/1/90 Chicago, IL	3.00
2443	15¢ Beach Umbrella, bklt. sgl. 2/3/90 Sarasota, FL	1.75
2443a	Booklet Pane of 10	6.00
2444	25¢ Wyoming Statehood 2/23/90 Cheyenne, WY	1.75
2445-48	25¢ Classic Films attd. 3/23/90 Hollywood, CA	7.50
2445-48	Set of 4 singles	12.00
2449	25¢ Marianne Moore 4/18/90 Brooklyn, NY	2.00

1990-95 TRANSPORTATION COILS

Scott #	Description	Cacheted
2451	4¢ Steam Carriage 1/25/91 Tucson, AZ	1.75
2452	5¢ Circus Wagon 8/31/90 Syracuse, NY	2.50
2452B	5¢ Circus Wagon, Gravure 12/8/92 Cincinnati, OH	2.50
2452D	5¢ Circus Wagon, Reissue (5¢) 3/20/95, Kansas City MO	3.00
2453	5¢ Canoe, brown 5/25/91 Secaucus, NJ	1.75
2454	5¢ Canoe, red, Gravure print 10/22/91 Secaucus, NJ	1.75
2457	10¢ Tractor Trailer,Intaglio 5/25/91 Secaucus, NJ	1.75
2458	10¢ Tractor Trailer, Gravure 5/25/94 Secaucus, NJ	1.75
2463	20¢ Cog Railway Car 6/9/95 Dallas, TX	1.90
2464	23¢ Lunch Wagon 4/12/91 Columbus, OH	1.75
2466	32¢ Ferry Boat 6/2/95 McLean, VA	1.90
2468	$1.00 Seaplane 4/20/90 Phoenix, AZ	3.00

1990-93

Scott #	Description	Cacheted
2470-74	25¢ Lighthouse bklt. sgls. 4/26/90 DC	10.00
2474a	Booklet Pane of 5	4.00
2475	25¢ Flag Stamp, ATM self-adhes. 5/18/90 Seattle, WA	1.75
2475a	Pane of 12	10.00
2476	1¢ Kestrel 6/22/91 Aurora, CO	1.75
2477	1¢ Reprint 5/10/95 Aurora,CO w "¢" sign	1.75
2478	3¢ Bluebird 6/22/91 Aurora, CO	1.75
2479	19¢ Fawn 3/11/91 DC	1.75
2480	30¢ Cardinal 6/22/91 Aurora, CO	1.75
2481	45¢ Pumpkinseed Sunfish 12/2/92 DC	2.50
2482	$2 Bobcat 6/1/90 Arlington, VA	7.00
2483	20¢ Blue Jay, Bklt.sgl. 6/15/95 Kansas City, MO	2.00
2483a	Booklet Pane of 10	8.50
2484	29¢ Wood Duck, BEP single 4/12/91 Columbus, OH	1.75
2484a	BEP Booklet Pane of 10	9.00
2485	29¢ Wood Duck, KCS bklt. single 4/12/91 Columbus, OH	1.75

U.S. First Day Covers

Scott #	Description	Cacheted
	1993-95 SELF ADHESIVE BOOKLETS & COILS	
2485a	KCS Booklet Pane of 10	9.00
2486	29¢ African Violet, Bklt. Sgl. 10/8/93 Beaumont, TX	1.75
2486a	Booklet Pane of 10	8.00
2487	32¢ Peach, Bklt. sgl. 7/8/95 Reno, NV	2.00
2488	32¢ Pear, Bklt. sgl. 7/8/95 Reno, NV	2.00
2487-88	32¢ Peach & Pear, Attached Pair	2.50
2488A	Booklet Pane of 10	8.50
	1993-95 SELF ADHESIVE BOOKLETS & COILS	
2489	29¢ Red Squirrel, Self adhesive,sgl. 6/25/93 Milwaukee, WI	1.75
2489	29¢ Red Squirrel, pair on backing paper	3.00
2489a	Pane of 18	14.00
2490	29¢ Rose, pair on backing paper	3.00
2490	29¢ Rose, Self adhesive sgl. 8/19/93 Houston, TX	1.75
2490a	Pane of 18	14.00
2491	29¢ Pine Cone, pair on backing paper	3.00
2491	29¢ Pine Cone, Self adhesive sgl. 11/5/93 Kansas City, MO	1.75
2491a	Pane of 18	14.00
2492	29¢ Pink Rose, pair on backing paper	3.00
2492	32¢ Pink Rose, Self-adhesive 6/2/95 McLean, VA	2.00
2492a	Pane of 20, Self-adhesive	15.50
2493	32¢ Peach, self-adhesive 7/8/95 Reno, NV	2.00
2494	32¢ Pear, self-adhesive 7/8/95 Reno, NV	2.00
2493-94	32¢ Peach & Pear, attd	2.50
2494a	Pane of 20, self-adhesive	15.50
2495	32¢ Peach, Coil, Self adhesive 7/8/95 Reno, NV	2.00
2495A	32¢ Pear, Coil, Self-adhesive 7/8/95 Reno, NV	2.00
2495-95A	Peach & Pear, Coil Pair	2.50
	1990 COMMEMORATIVES (cont.)	
2496-2500	25¢ Olympians attd. 7/6/90 Minneapolis, MN	7.50
2496-2500	Set of 5 singles	15.00
2496-2500	Olympians with Tab singles attd.	8.00
2496-2500	Set of 5 singles with Tabs	12.00
2501-05	25¢ Indian Headdresses bklt. singles 8/17/90 Cody, WY	10.00
2505a	Booklet Pane of 5	8.00
2506-07	25¢ Micronesia & Marshall Isles 9/28/90 DC	3.00
2506-07	Set of 2 singles	4.00
2506-07	Joint issue w/Micronesia & Marshal Isles.	5.00
2506-07	Joint issue w/Micronesia & Marshal Isles, Triple Cancel .	15.00
2506	Micronesia issue only	3.00
2507	Marshal Island issue only, strip of 3	4.00
2508-11	25¢ Sea Creatures attd. 10/3/90 Baltimore, MD	5.00
2508-11	Set of 4 singles	10.00
2508-11	Joint issue w/USSR, attd	5.00
2508-11	Joint issue w/USSR attd, dual cancel	15.00
2508-11	Joint issue w/USSR, set of 4 singles	20.00
2512&C127	Combination on one Cover	4.00
2512	25¢ Pre-Columbian Customs 10/12/90 Grand Canyon, AZ	2.00
2513	25¢ Dwight D. Eisenhower 10/13/90 Abilene, KS	2.00
2514	25¢ Christmas Madonna & Child 10/18/90 DC	2.00
2514	Madonna booklet single	2.00
2514a	Booklet Pane of 10 10/18/90 DC	6.50
2515	25¢ Christmas Tree 10/18/90 Evergreen, CO	2.00
2514-15	Christmas on one Cover, dual cancel	3.00
2516	25¢ Christmas Tree bklt. sgl. 10/18/90 Evergreen, CO ...	2.00
2516a	Booklet Pane of 10 10/18/90	6.50
	1991-94 COMMEMORATIVES	
2517	(29¢) "F" Flower stamp 1/22/91 DC	1.75
2518	(29¢) "F" Flower coil 1/22/91 DC	1.75
2519	(29¢) "F" Flower, BEP bklt. single 1/22/91 DC	1.75
2519a	Bklt. Pane of 10, BEP	7.50
2517-19	Combination on one Cover	3.00
2520	(29¢) "F" Flower, KCS bklt. single 1/22/91 DC	3.50
2520a	Bklt. Pane of 10, KCS	9.50
2521	(4¢) Make-up rate stamp 1/22/91 DC, non-denom	1.75
2522	(29¢) "F" Flag stamp, ATM self-adhes. 1/22/91 DC	1.75
2522a	Pane of 12	10.00
2523	29¢ Flag over Mt. Rushmore Coil 3/29/91 Mt. Rushmore, SD	1.75
2523A	Same, Gravure print 7/4/91 Mt. Rushmore, SD	1.75
	* On #2523A "USA" and "29" are **not** outlined in white	
2524	29¢ Flower 4/5/91 Rochester, NY	1.75
2525	29¢ Flower coil, rouletted 8/16/91 Rochester, NY	1.75
2526	29¢ Flower coil, perforated 3/3/92 Rochester, NY	1.75
2527	29¢ Flower, bklt. single 4/5/91 Rochester, NY	1.75
2527a	Booklet Pane of 10	7.50
2528	29¢ Flag with Olympic Rings, bklt. sgl. 4/21/91 Atlanta, GA	1.75

Scott #	Description	Cacheted
	1991-94 COMMEMORATIVES (cont.)	
2528a	Booklet Pane of 10	7.50
2529	19¢ Fishing Boat, coil 8/8/91 DC	2.50
2529C	19¢ Fishing Boat, coil, Type III 6/25/94 Arlington, VA	2.50
2530	19¢ Ballooning, bklt. sgl. 5/17/91 Denver, CO	2.00
2530a	Booklet Pane of 10	9.00
2531	29¢ Flags/Memorial Day, 125th Anniv. 5/30/91 Waterloo,NY	1.75
2531A	29¢ Liberty Torch, ATM self-adhes. 6/25/91 New York, NY	1.75
2531Ab	Pane of 18	14.00
	1991 COMMEMORATIVES	
2532	50¢ Switzerland, joint issue 2/22/91 DC	2.00
2532	Joint issue w/Switzerland, dual cancel	15.00
2532	Swiss issue only	3.00
2533	29¢ Vermont Statehood 3/1/91 Bennington, VT	2.25
2534	29¢ Savings Bonds 4/30/91 DC	1.75
2535	29¢ Love 5/9/91 Honolulu, HI	1.75
2536	29¢ Love, Booklet Sgl. 5/9/91 Honolulu, HI	1.75
2536a	Booklet Pane of 10	7.50
2537	52¢ Love, 2 ounce rate 5/9/91 Honolulu, HI	2.00

Scott #	Description	Cacheted
	1991 COMMEMORATIVES (CONT.)	
2538	29¢ William Saroyan 5/22/91 Fresno, CA	2.25
2538	Joint issue w/USSR, dual cancel	15.00
	1991-95 REGULAR ISSUES	
2539	$1.00 USPS & Olympic Rings 9/29/91 Orlando, FL	3.00
2540	$2.90 Priority Mail 7/7/91 San Diego, CA	9.00
2541	$9.95 Express Mail,Domestic rate 6/16/91 Sacramento,CA ..	25.00
2542	$14.00 Express Mail,Internat'l rate 8/31/91 Hunt Valley MD ..	32.50
2543	$2.90 Priority Mail, Space 6/3/93 Kennedy Space Center FL	7.50
2544	$3 Challenger Shuttle, Priority Mail 6/22/95 Anaheim, CA ...	7.75
2544A	$10.75 Endeavor Shuttle Express Mail 8/4/95 Irvine, CA	25.00
	1991 COMMEMORATIVES (cont.)	
2545-49	29¢ Fishing Flies, bklt. sgls. 5/31/91 Cudlebackville, NY	10.00
2549a	Booklet Pane of 5	5.00
2550	29¢ Cole Porter 6/8/91 Peru, IN	2.50
2551	29¢ Desert Shield / Desert Storm 7/2/91 DC	2.00
2552	29¢ Desert Shield / Desert Storm bklt. sgl. 7/2/91 DC	2.00
2552a	29¢ Booklet Pane of 5	4.50
2553-57	29¢ Summer Olympics,strip of 5 7/12/91 Los Angeles, CA	4.50
2553-57	Set of 5 singles	10.00
2558	29¢ Numismatics 8/13/91 Chicago, IL	2.00
2559	29¢ World War II S/S of 10 9/3/91 Phoenix, AZ	12.00
2559a-j	Set of 10 singles	30.00
2560	29¢ Basketball 8/28/91 Springfield, MA	3.00
2561	29¢ District of Columbia Bicent. 9/7/91 DC	1.75
2562-66	29¢ Comedians ,set of 5 8/29/91 Hollywood, CA	10.00
2562-66	Set of 5 on 1	4.50
2566a	Booklet Pane of 10	7.50
2567	29¢ Jan Matzeliger 9/15/91 Lynn, MA	3.00
2568-77	29¢ Space Exploration bklt. sgls. 10/1/91 Pasadena, CA	20.00
2577a	Booklet Pane of 10	8.00
2578	(29¢) Christmas, Madonna & Child 10/17/91 Houston,TX	1.75
2578a	Booklet Pane of 10	8.00
2579	(29¢) Christmas, Santa & Chimney 10/19/91 Santa, ID	1.75
2580-85	(29¢) Christmas, bklt. pane sgls. 10/17/91 Santa, ID	12.00
2581b-85a	Booklet Panes of 4, set of 5	20.00
	1994-95 DEFINITIVES DESIGNS OF 1869 ESSAYS	
2587	32¢ James S. Polk 11/2/95 Columbia, TN	1.90
2590	$1 Surrender of Burgoyne 5/5/94 New York, NY	4.00
2592	$5 Washington & Jackson 8/19/94 Pittsburgh, PA	20.00
	1992-93 REGULAR ISSUES	
2593	29¢ "Pledge" Black denom., bklt. sgl. 9/8/92 Rome, NY	1.75
2593a	Booklet Pane of 10	7.00
	1992 Eagle & Shield Self-Adhesives Stamps (9/25/92 Dayton, OH)	
2595	29¢ "Brown" denomination, sgl	2.00
2595a	Pane of 17 + label	12.00
2596	29¢ "Green" denomination, sgl	2.00
2596a	Pane of 17 + label	12.00
2597	29¢ "Red" denomination, sgl	2.00
2597a	Pane of 17 + label	12.00
	1992 Eagle & Shield Self-Adhesive Coils	
2595v	29¢ "Brown" denomination, pair with paper backing	2.25
2596v	29¢ "Green" denomination, pair with paper backing	2.25
2597v	29¢ "Red" denomination, pair with paper backing	2.25
	1994 Eagle Self-Adhesive Issues	
2598	29¢ Eagle, single 2/4/94 Sarasota, FL	1.75
2598a	Pane of 18	12.50
2598v	29¢ Coil Pair with paper backing	2.25
	1994 Statue of Liberty Self-Adhesive Issue	
2599	29¢ Statue of Liberty, single 6/24/94 Haines, FL	1.75
2599a	Pane of 18	12.50
2599v	29¢ Coil pair with paper backing	2.25

U.S. First Day Covers

2721

2833

Scott #	Description	Cached
	1991-93 Coil Issues	
2602	(10¢) Eagle & Shield, bulk-rate 12/13/91 Kansas City, MO	1.75
2603	(10¢) Eagle & Shield, **BEP** 5/29/93 Secaucus, NJ	1.75
2604	(10¢) Eagle & Shld., **Stamp Venturers** 5/29/93 Secaucus, NJ	1.75
2605	23¢ Flag, First Class pre-sort 9/27/91 DC	1.75
2606	23¢ USA, 1st Cl, pre-sort, **ABNCo.** 7/21/92 Kansas City, MO	1.75
2607	23¢ USA, 1st Cl, pre-sort, **BEP** 10/9/92 Kansas City, MO	1.75
2608	23¢ USA, 1st Cl, p.s., **Stamp Venturers** 5/14/93 Denver, CO	1.75
2609	29¢ Flag over White House 4/23/92 DC	1.75
	1992 Commemoratives	
2611-15	29¢ Winter Olympics, strip of 5 1/11/92 Orlando, FL	5.00
2611-15	Set of 5 singles	10.00
2616	29¢ World Columbian Expo 1/24/92 Rosemont, IL	1.75
2617	29¢ W.E.B. DuBois 1/31/92 Atlanta, GA	3.00
2618	29¢ Love 2/6/92 Loveland. CO	1.75
2619	29¢ Olympic Baseball 4/3/92 Atlanta, GA	3.50
	1992 Columbus Commemoratives	
2620-23	29¢ First Voyage of Columbus 4/24/92 Christiansted, VI	4.00
2620-23	Set of 4 singles	8.00
2620-23	Joint issue w/Italy, dual cancel	15.00
2620-23	Joint Issue w/Italy, Dual with blue cancel	450.00
2620-23	Joint Issue w/Italy, set of 4	30.00
2620-23	Italian issue only block of 4	4.00
2624-29	1¢-$5.00 Voyages of Columbus 6 S/S's 5/22/92 Chicago, IL	50.00
2624a-29	Set of 16 singles	90.00
2624-29	Italian issue only, set of 6	35.00
2624-29	Spanish issue only, set of 6	15.00
2624-29	Portugal issue only, set of 6	35.00
	1992 Commemoratives (cont.)	
2630	29¢ New York Stock Exchange 5/17/92 New York, NY	4.00
2631-34	29¢ Space: Accomplishments 5/29/92 Chicago, IL	4.00
2631-34	Set of 4 singles	10.00
2631-34	Joint issue w/Russia,dual cancel, blocks of 4	15.00
2631-34	Joint issue w/Russia, dual cancel, set of 4	20.00
2631-34	Russian issue only, block of 4	3.25
2631-34	Russian issue only, set of 4	12.00
2635	29¢ Alaska Highway 5/30/92 Fairbanks, AK	1.75
2636	29¢ Kentucky Statehood Bicent. 6/1/92 Danville, KY	1.75
2637-41	29¢ Summer Olympics, strip of 5 6/11/92 Baltimore, MD	5.00
2637-41	Set of 5 singles	10.00
2642-46	29¢ Hummingbirds, bklt. sgls. 6/15/92 DC	10.00
2646a	Booklet Pane of 5	5.00
2647-96	29¢ Wildflowers, set of 50 singles 7/24/92 Columbus, OH	87.50
2697	29¢ World War II S/S of 10 8/17/92 Indianapolis, IN	10.00
2697a-j	Set of 10 singles	25.00
2698	29¢ Dorothy Parker 8/22/92 West End, NJ	2.50
2699	29¢ Dr. Theodore von Karman 8/31/92 DC	2.50
2700-03	29¢ Minerals 9/17/92 DC	4.00
2700-03	Set of 4 singles	8.00
2704	29¢ Juan Rodriguez Cabrillo 9/28/92 San Diego, CA	1.75
2705-09	29¢ Wild Animals, bklt. sgls. 10/1/92 New Orleans, LA	10.00
2709a	Booklet Pane of 5	5.00
2710	29¢ Christmas, Madonna & Child 10/22/92 DC	2.00
2710	Madonna booklet single	
2710a	Booklet Pane of 10 10/22/92 DC	8.00
2710-14	Christmas on one Cover, dual cancel	4.50
2710-14	Christmason 4 Covers, dual cancel	9.00
2711-14	29¢ Christmas Toys,offset, 10/22/92 Kansas City, MO	4.00
2711-14	Set of 4 singles	10.00
2715-18	29¢ Christmas Toys,gravure,bklt.sgls.10/22/92 Kansas City,MO	10.00
2715-18	Set of 4 booklet single	
2718a	Booklet Pane of 4	4.00
2719	29¢ Christmas Train self-adhes. ATM 10/28/92 NY, NY	1.75
2719a	Pane of 18	14.00
2720	29¢ Happy New Year 12/30/92 San Francisco, CA	3.00
	1993 Commemoratives	
2721	29¢ Elvis Presley 1/8/93 Memphis, TN	2.00
2722	29¢ Oklahoma! 3/30/93 Oklahoma City, OK	1.75
2723	29¢ Hank Williams 6/9/93 Nashville, TN	1.75
2724-30	29¢ R 'n' R/R & B 6/16/93 on one cover Cleveland, OH & Santa Monica, CA (same cancel ea. city)	10.50
2724-30	Set of 7 singles on 2 covers	12.00

Scott #	Description	Cacheted
	1993 Commemoratives (cont.)	
2724-30	Set of 7 singles	21.00
2731-37	29¢ R 'n' R/R & B, Set/7 bklt. sgls. 6/16/93 Cleveland, OH & Santa Monica, CA (same cancel ea. city)	21.00
2731-37	Set of 7 singles on 2 covers	12.00
2737a	Booklet Pane of 8	9.00
2737b	Booklet Pane of 4	5.50
2737a,b	Booklet Panes on 1 cover	14.00
2741-45	29¢ Space Fantasy, bklt. sgls. 1/25/93 Huntsville, AL	10.00
2745a	Booklet Pane of 5	5.00
2746	29¢ Percy Lavon Julian 1/29/93 Chicago, IL	3.00
2747	29¢ Oregon Trail 2/12/93 Salem, OR	1.75
2748	29¢ World University Games 2/25/93 Buffalo, NY	2.00
2749	29¢ Grace Kelly 3/24/93 Hollywood, CA	3.50
2749	Joint issue w/Monaco, dual cancel	15.00
2749	Monaco issue only	2.50
2750-53	29¢ Circus 4/6/93 DC	5.00
2750-53	Set of 4 singles	12.00
2754	29¢ Cherokee Strip 4/17/93 Enid, OK	1.75
2755	29¢ Dean Acheson 4/21/93 DC	1.75
2756-59	29¢ Sport Horses 5/1/93 Louisville, KY	6.00
2756-59	Set of 4 singles	15.00
2760-64	29¢ Garden Flowers, bklt. sgls. 5/15/93 Spokane, WA	10.00
2764a	Booklet Pane of 5	5.00
2765	29¢ World War II S/S of 10 5/31/93 DC	10.00
2765a-j	Set of 10 singles	25.00
2766	29¢ Joe Louis 6/22/93 Detroit, MI	4.00
2767-70	29¢ Broadway Musicals, bkt. sgls. 7/14/93 New York, NY	12.00
2770a	Booklet Pane of 4	6.00
2771-74	29¢ Country Music attd. 9/25/93 Nashville, TN	5.00
2771-74	Set of 4 singles	10.00
2775-78	29¢ Country Music, bklt. sgls. 9/25/93 Nashville, TN	10.00
2778a	Booklet Pane of 4	5.00
2779-82	29¢ National Postal Museum 7/30/93 DC	4.00
2779-82	Set of 4 singles	10.00
2783-84	29¢ Deaf Communication, pair 9/20/93 Burbank, CA	3.00
2783-84	Set of 2 singles	5.00
2785-88	29¢ Children's Classics, block of 4 10/23/93 Louisville, KY	4.00
2785-88	Set of 4 singles	10.00
2789	29¢ Madonna & Child 10/21/93 Raleigh, NC	1.75
2790	Booklet Single	1.75
2790a	Booklet Pane of 4	4.00
2789+91-94	Christmas on one Cover, dual cancel	4.50
2789+91-94	Christmas on 4 Covers, dual cancel	9.00
2791-94	29¢ Christmas Designs attd. 10/21/93 New York, NY	4.00
2791-94	Set of 4 singles	10.00
2795-98	29¢ Contemp. Christmas, 4 bklt.singles 10/21/93 NY, NY	10.00
2798a	Booklet Pane of 10 (3 snowmen)	8.00
2798b	Booklet Pane of 10 (2 snowmen)	8.00
2799-2802	29¢ Contemp. Christmas, self-adhes. Set of 4 10/28/93 NY, NY	9.00
2802a	Pane of 12	10.00
2803	29¢ Snowman, self-adhesive 10/28/93 New York, NY	1.75
2803a	Booklet Pane of 18	14.00
2804	29¢ Northern Mariana Isles 11/4/93 DC	1.75
2805	29¢ Columbus-Puerto Rico 11/19/93 San Juan, PR	1.75
2806	29¢ AIDS Awareness 12/1/93 New York, NY	3.00
2806a	29¢ AIDS, booklet single 12/1/93 New York, NY	3.00
2806b	Booklet Pane of 5	8.00
	1994 Commemoratives	
2807-11	29¢ Winter Olympics, Strip of 5, 1/6/94 Salt Lake City, UT	5.00
2807-11	Set of 5 Singles	10.00
2812	29¢ Edward R. Murrow 1/21/94 Pullman, WA	1.75
2813	29¢ Love & Sunrise, self-adhesive sgl. 1/27/94 Loveland, OH	1.75
2813a	Pane of 18	14.00
2813v	Coil Pair with paper backing	2.25
2814	29¢ Love & Dove, booklet single 2/14/94 Niagara Falls, NY	1.75
2814a	Booklet Pane of 10	7.00
2814C	29¢ Love & Dove, Sheet Stamp 6/11/94 Niagara Falls, NY	1.75
2815	52¢ Love & Doves 2/14/94 Niagara Falls, NY	2.00
2816	29¢ Dr. Allison Davis 2/1/94 Williamstown, MA	3.00
2817	29¢ Chinese New Year, Dog 2/5/94 Pomona, CA	2.50
2818	29¢ Buffalo Soldiers 4/22/94 Dallas, TX	4.00
2819-28	29¢ Silent Screen Stars, attd. 4/27/94 San Francisco, CA	8.00
2819-28	Set of 10 Singles	20.00

U.S. First Day Covers

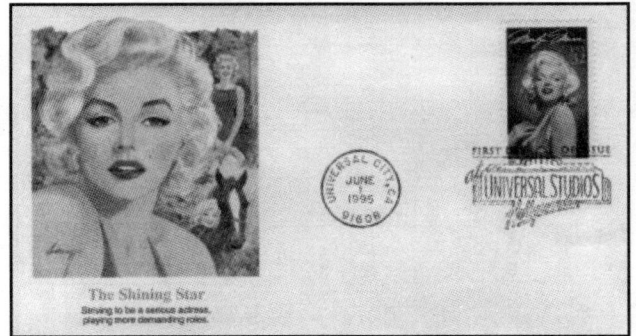

The Shining Star

2967

166

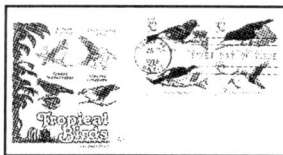

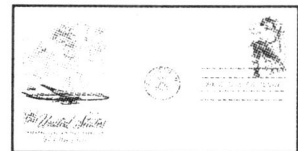

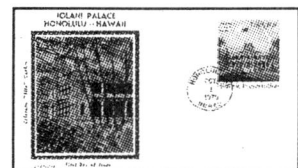

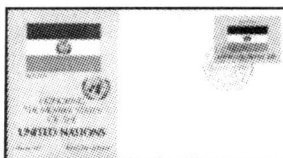

167

U.S. First Day Covers

1995 Commemoratives (cont.)

Scott #	Description	Cacheted
2974	32¢ United Nations 6/26/95 San Francisco, CA	3.00
2975	32¢ Civil War, Miniature Sht. of 20, 6/29/95 Gettysburg, PA	30.00
2975a-t	Set of 20 singles	60.00
2975a-t	Set of 20 on 4 covers	20.00
2976-79	32¢ Carousel Horses attd. 7/21/95 Lahaska, PA	4.35
2976-79	Set of 4 singles	8.00
2980	32¢ Women's Suffrage 8/26/95 DC	2.00
2981	32¢ World War II S/S of 10 9/2/95 Honolulu, HI	10.00
2981a-j	Set of 10 singles	25.00
2982	32¢ Louis Armstrong 9/1/95 New Orleans, LA	3.00

1995 Commemoratives (cont.)

Scott #	Description	Cacheted
2983-92	32¢ Jazz Musicians 9/16/95 Monterey, CA	12.00
2983-92	Set of 10 singles	30.00
2993-97	32¢ Fall Garden Flowers, bklt. sgles. 9/19/95 Encinitas, CA	10.00
2997a	Booklet Pane of 5	5.50
2998	60¢ Eddie Rickenbacker 9/25/95 Columbus, OH	3.00
2999	32¢ Republic of Palau 9/29/95 Agana, Guam	2.00
3000	32¢ Comic Strips, Min. Sheet of 20 10/2/95 Boca Raton, FL	25.00
3000a-t	Set of 20 Singles	50.00
3000a-t	Set of 5 combos (incl. Plate Block)	15.00
3001	32¢ U.S. Naval Academy, 150 Anniv. 10/10/95 Annapolis, MD	3.00
3002	32¢ Tennessee Williams 10/13/95 Clarksdale, MS	2.00
3003	32¢ Madonna and Child 10/19/95 Washington, DC	2.00
3003a	Booklet Single	2.00
3003b	Booklet Pane of 10	8.50
3004-7	32¢ Santa + Children 9/30/95 North Pole, NY, set of 4	8.00
3007a	32¢ Christmas (secular) sheet, 9/30/95, North Pole, NY	3.50
3007b	32¢ Santa & Children, Pane of 10 w/3 of #3004	8.50
3007c	32¢ Santa & Children, Pane of 10 w/2 of #3004	8.50

1995 Self-Adhesive Stamps

Scott #	Description	Cacheted
3008-11	32¢ Santa + Children 9/30/95 North Pole, NY	3.50
3008-11	Set of 4 Singles	7.00
3011a	Pane of 20	15.50
3012	32¢ Midnight Angel 10/19/95 Christmas, FL	2.00
3012a	Pane of 20	15.50
3013	32¢ Children Sledding 10/19/95 Christmas, FL	2.00
3013a	Pane of 18	14.00

1995 Self-Adhesive Coil Stamps

Scott #	Description	Cacheted
3014-17	32¢ Santa + Children 9/30/95 North Pole, NY	3.50
3014-17	Set of 4 Singles	7.00
3018	32¢ Midnight Angel 10/19/95 Christmas, FL	2.00
3018	32¢ Midnight Angle, Pair on backing paper	3.00

1995 Commemoratives (cont.)

Scott #	Description	Cacheted
3019-23	32¢ Antique Automobiles 11/3/95 New York, NY	3.75
3019-23	Set of 5 Singles	8.50

1996 Commemoratives

Scott #	Description	Cacheted
3024	32¢ Utah Statehood 1/4/96 Salt Lake City, UT	2.00
3025-29	32¢ Winter Garden Flowers Bklt.Singles 1/19/96 Kennett Sq,PA	10.00
3029a	Booklet Pane of 5	5.50
3030	32¢ Love Cherub, Self-adhesive 1/20/96 New York, NY	2.00
3030a	Booklet Pane of 20	15.50

1996 Flora and Fauna Series

Scott #	Description	Cacheted
3031	1¢ Kestrel S/A, 11/19/99, NY,NY	2.00
3032	2¢ Red-headed Woodpecker 2/2/96 Sarasota, FL	2.00
3033	3¢ Eastern Bluebird 4/3/96 DC	2.00
3036	$1.00 Red Fox, 8/14/98	5.00
3044	1¢ Kestrel, Coil 1/20/96 New York, NY	2.00
3045	2¢ Woodpecker coil, 6/22/99, Wash., DC	2.00
3048	20¢ Blue Jay, S/A, 8/2/96 St. Louis, MO	2.00
3048a	Booklet Pane of 10	8.50
3048 + 53	Combo - Blue Jays, 8/2/96, St. Louis, MO	5.00
3049	32¢ Yellow Rose, single, 10/24/96, Pasadena, Ca.	2.00
3049a	Booklet Pane of 20, S/A	15.50
3050	20¢ Ring-Neck Pheasant S/A, 7/31/98, Somerset, NJ	2.00
3050	20¢ Ring-Neck Pheasant, S/A BP10, 7/31/98	8.50
3050+3055	Combo	3.00
3052	33¢ Pink Coral Rose S/A 8/13/99, Indy, IN	2.00
3052	Convert. BP 20	15.00
3052	Booklet Pane of 4	4.00
3052	Booklet Pane of 5 & Label	4.50
3052	Booklet Pane of 6	5.00
3052E	33c Pink Coral Rose, 4/7/00 New York, NY	2.00
	Pane of 8	8.00
3053	20¢ Blue Jay, Coil, S/A, 8/2/96, St. Louis, MO	2.00
3054	32¢ Yellow Rose, S/A Coil 8/1/97	2.00
3055	20¢ Ring-Neck Pheasant, S/A Coil, 7/31/98, Somerset, NJ	2.00

1996 Commemoratives (cont.)

Scott #	Description	Cacheted
3058	32¢ Ernest E. Just 2/1/96 DC	3.00
3059	32¢ Smithsonian Institution 2/5/96 DC	2.00
3060	32¢ Year of the Rat 2/8/96 San Francisco, CA	2.50
3061-64	32¢ Pioneers of Communication Set of 4 2/22/96 NY, NY	7.00
3061-64a	Block of 4 on one cover	3.50
3065	32¢ Fulbright Scholarship 2/28/96 Fayetteville, AR	2.00
3066	50¢ Jacqueline Cochran 3/9/96 Indio, CA	2.25
3067	32¢ Marathon 4/11/96 Boston, MA	3.00
3068	32¢ Centennial Olympic Games, Min. Sheet of 20 5/2/96 DC	20.00
3068a-t	Set of 20 Singles	40.00
3068a-t	Set of 20 on 4 covers	13.00
3069	32¢ Georgia O'Keeffe 5/23/96 Santa Fe, NM	2.00

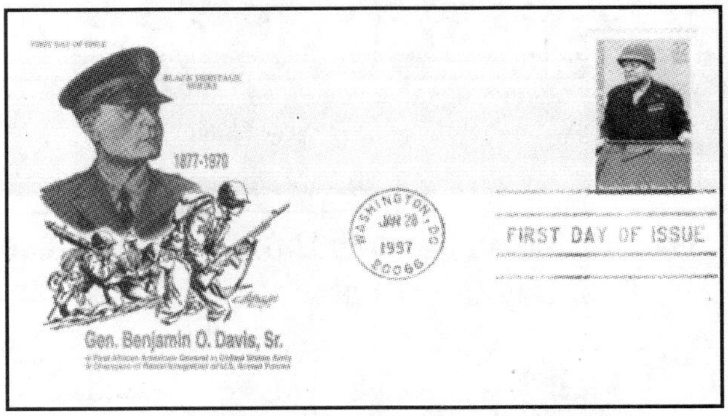

3121

1996 Commemoratives (cont.)

Scott #	Description	Cacheted
3069	Souvenir Sheet of 15	11.50
3070	32¢ Tennessee Statehood 5/31/96 Nashville, Knoxville or Memphis, TN	2.00
3071	32¢ Tennessee Statehood, Self-adhesive single	2.00
3071a	Booklet Pane of 20	13.00
3076a	32¢ American Indian Dances, 5 designs attached 6/7/96 Oklahoma City, OK	4.00
3072-76	Set of 5 Singles	8.50
3077-80	32¢ Prehistoric Animals, 4 designs attached 6/8/96 Toronto, Canada	4.00
3077-80	Set of 4 Singles	8.00
3081	32¢ Breast Cancer Awareness 6/15/96 DC	2.00
3082	32¢ James Dean 6/24/96 Hollywood, CA	3.00
3082	Pane of 20	17.50
3083-86	32¢ Folk Heroes, 4 designs attached 7/11/96 Anaheim, CA	4.00
3083-86	Set of 4 Singles	8.00
3087	32¢ Olympic Games, Discobolus 7/19 /96	2.00
3088	32¢ Iowa Statehood 8/1/96 Dubuque, IA	2.00
3089	Self-adhesive Single	2.00
3089a	Self-adhesive Pane of 20	15.50
3090	32¢ Rural Free Delivery 8/6/96 Charleston, WV	2.00
3091-95	32¢ River Boats, S/A, 8/22/96, set of 5, Orlando, Fl.	10.00
3095a	Strip of 5	5.50
3096-99	32¢ Big Band Leaders, set of 4, 9/11/96, New York, NY	12.00
3099a	32¢ Big Band Leaders, attd., 9/11/96, New York, NY	6.00
3100-03	32¢ Songwriters, set of 4, 9/11/96, New York, NY	10.00
3103a	32¢ Songwriters, att'd., 9/11/96, New York	5.00
3104	23¢ F. Scott Fitzgerald, 9/27/96, St. Paul, MN	2.00
3105	32¢ Endangered Species, pane of 15,10/2/96, San Diego, Ca.	14.50
3105a-o	Set of 15 covers	30.00
3106	32¢ Computer Tech., 10/8/96, Aberdeen Proving Ground, MD	3.00
3107	32¢ Madonna & Child, 11/1/96, Richmond, Va.	2.00
3107-11	Christmas on one Cover, dual cancel	4.50
3108-11	32¢ Christmas Family Scenes,set of 4,10/8/96,North Pole,AK	8.00
3111a	Block or strip of 4	4.25
3112	32¢ Madonna & Child, single, 11/1/96, Richmond, Va.	2.00
3112a	Pane of 20, S/A	15.50
3116a	Booklet Pane of 20, S/A	15.50
3113-16	32¢ Christmas Family Scene, set of 4, Bklt Pane Singles	8.00
3108-11 + 3117	Combination on one Cover	4.50
3117	32¢ Skaters - for ATM, 10/8/96, North Pole, AK	2.00
3117a	Booklet Pane of 18, S/A	14.75
3118	32¢ Hanukkah, S/A, 10/22/96, Washington, DC	3.00
3118	Joint issue w/Israel, dual cancel	15.00
3118	Israel issue only	4.00
3119	50¢ Cycling, sheet of 2, 11/1/96, New York, NY	3.75
3119	50¢ Cycling, sheet of 2, 11/1/96, Hong Kong	3.75
3119	50¢ Cycling, set of 2, 11/1/96, New York, NY	4.50
3119	50¢ Cycling, set of 2, 11/1/96, Hong Kong	4.50
3119	Joint issue w/Hong Kong, dual cancel, S/S	15.00

1997 Commemoratives

Scott #	Description	Cacheted
3120	32¢ Lunar New Year (Year of the Ox), 1/5/97	2.50
3121	32¢ Benjamin O' Davis Sr., S/A, 1/28/97, Wash. DC	3.00
3122	32¢ Statue of Liberty, S/A, Bklt Single, 2/1/97	2.00
3122a	Pane of 20 w/Label	15.50
3122c	Pane of 5 w/Label	5.50
3122d	Pane of 6	6.00
3123	32¢ Love Swan, S/A, Single, 2/4/97	2.00
3123a	Booklet Pane of 20 w/Label	15.50
3124	55¢ Love Swan, S/A, Single, 2/4/97	2.00
3124a	Booklet Pane of 20 w/Label	15.50
3125	32¢ Helping Children Learn, S/A, 2/18/97	2.00
3123+3124	Combo	3.00
3126-27	Citron Moth & Flowering Pineapple, attd, 3/3/97, Wash. DC	2.50
3126-27	Pane of 20	15.50
3126-27	Set of 2	5.00
3128-29	Slightly smaller than 3126-27, set of 2	5.00
3128-29b	Booklet pane of 5, Vendor Bklt, From booklet of 15	5.50
3128a-29a	(2) Mixed die-cut	6.00
3130-31	32¢ Pacific '97 Stagecoach & Ship, 3/13/97, New York, NY	2.50
3130-31	Set of Singles	4.00
3132	25¢ Jukebox (Linerless Coil) 3/14/97 NY,NY	2.00
3133	32¢ Flag over Porch (LInerless Coil) 3/14/97 NY,NY	2.00

U.S. First Day Covers

3204a

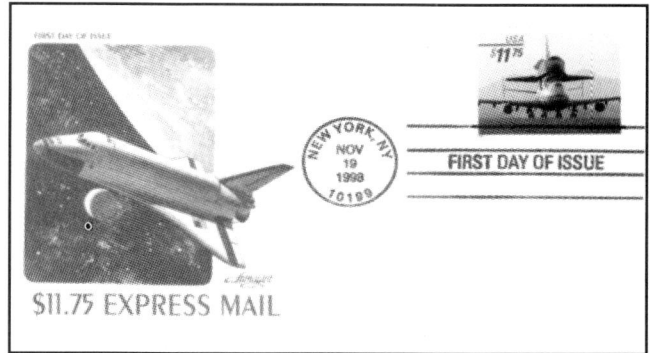

3262

Scott #	Description	Cacheted
	1997 Commemoratives (cont.)	
3132+3132	Combo	3.00
3134	32¢ Thornton Wilder, 4/17/97, Hamden, Ct.	2.00
3135	32¢ Raoul Wallenberg, 4/24/97, Wash. DC	3.50
3136	32¢ The World of Dinosaurs, set of 15, 5/1/97	30.00
3136a-o	15 on 1 miniature pane	12.00
3137	32¢ Bugs Bunny, S/A, pane of 10, 5/22/97	11.00
3137a	32¢ Bugs Bunny, S/A, Single, 5/22/97, Burbank CA	2.50
3137c	32¢ Bugs, single pane (right side) 5/22/97, Burbank,CA	5.00
3138	32¢ Bugs, Pane of 10 (9/1) imperf, 5/22/97, Burbank,CA	275.00
3138c	32¢ Bugs, Pane of 1, imperf, 5/22/97, Burbank,CA	250.00
3139	50¢ Pacific '97 - 1847 Franklin, S/S, 5/29/97, S.F., Ca.	24.00
3139a	50¢ single from S/S	4.00
3140	60¢ Pacific '97 - 1847 Washington, 5/30/97, S.F., Ca.	24.00
3140a	60¢ single from S/S	4.00
3141	32¢ Marshall Plan 6/4/97 Cambridge, MA	2.00
3142a-t	32¢ Classic American Aircraft,set of 20,7/19/97,Dayton, OH .	40.00
3142	Sheet of 20	15.50
3143-46	32¢ Legendary Football Coaches, att'd., 7/25/97	4.00
3146a	Set of 4 singles	8.00
3147-50	32¢ Legendary Football Coaches,set of 4 w/red bar	8.00
3147	32¢ Vince Lombardi,single, Green Bay WI,8/5/97	2.00
3148	32¢ Paul (Bear) Bryant, single, 8/7/97, Tuscaloosa, AL	2.00
3149	32¢ Glenn (Pop) Warner,single, 8/8/97, Phil. PA	2.00
3150	32¢ George Halas, single, 8/16/97, Chicago, IL	2.00
3151a-o	32¢ Classic American Dolls, set of 15, 7/28/97, Anaheim, Ca.	30.00
3151	Sheet of 15	12.00
3152	Pane of 20	17.50
3152	32¢ Humphrey Bogart, Legends of Hollywood series, 7/31/97	2.50
3153	32¢ Stars & Stripes Forever, 8/21/97, Milwaukee, WI	2.00
3154-57	Set of 4	8.00
3157a	32¢ Opera Singers, att'd., 9/10/97 New York, NY	4.25
3158-65	Set of 8	16.00
3165a	32¢ Conductors & Composers, Set of 2, 9/12 /97 Cincinnati, OH	11.00
3166	32¢ Padre Felix Varela 9/15/97 Miami, FL	2.00
3167	32¢ U.S. Air Force, 9/18/97 Washington, DC	3.00
3172a	32¢ Classic Movie Monsters, att'd., 9/30/97 Universal City, CA	5.50
3168-72	Set of 5	10.00
3173	32¢ 1st Supersonic Flight, S/A, 10/14/97,Edwards AF Base,CA	2.50
3174	32¢ Women in the Military, 10/18/97 Wash. DC	2.50
3175	32¢ Kwanzaa 10/22/97, LA,CA	3.00
3176	32¢ Madonna & Child, 10/27/97, Wash. DC	2.00
3176a	32¢ Madonna & Child, Pane of 20, Wash. DC	15.00
3177	32¢ American Holly, S/A, 10/30/97,NY,NY	2.00
3177a	32¢ American Holly, S/A, Pane of 20, 10/30/97,NY,NY	15.50
3177b	32¢ American Holly, S/A, Pane of 6, 10/30/97,NY,NY	6.00
3177b	Pane of 4	4.00
3177c	32¢ American Holly, S/A, Pane of 5&Label,10/30/97,NY,NY	5.50
3177c	Pane of 5	5.00
3177d	Pane of 6	6.00
3176-77	Madonna & Holly on one Cover, dual cancel	3.00
3178	$3 Mars Rover Sojourner, S/S, 12/10/97,Pasadena,CA	12.00
	1998 Commemoratives	
3179	32¢ Year of the Tiger, 1/5/98, Seattle WA	2.50
3180	32¢ Alpine Skiing, 1/22/98, Salt Lake City UT	2.00
3181	32¢ Madam C.J. Walker, 1/28/98, Ind., IN	3.00
	2000 Celebrate The Century Series	
3182	1900's 32¢ Celebrate the Century,	
	Pane of 15,2/3/98, Wash.DC	15.00
3182a-o	1900's 32¢ Celebrate the Century,	
	Set of 15,2/3/98, Wash.DC	35.00
3183	1910's 32¢ Celebrate the Century,	
	Pane of 15,2/3/98, Wash.DC	15.00
3183a-o	1910's 32¢ Celebrate the Century,	
	Set of 15,2/3/98, Wash.DC	35.00
3184	1920's 32¢ Celebrate the Century,	
	Pane of 15, 5/28/98, Chicago, IL	15.00
3184a-o	1920's 32¢ Celebrate the Century,	
	Set of 15, 5/28/98, Chicago, IL	35.00
3185	1930's 32¢ Celebrate the Century,	
	Pane of 15, 9/10/98, Cleveland, OH	15.00

Scott #	Description	Cacheted
	1998-2000 Celebrate The Century Series (cont.)	
3185a-o	1930's 32¢ Celebrate the Century,	
	Set of 15, 9/10/98, Cleveland, OH	35.00
3186	1940's 33¢ Celebrate the Century,	
	Pane of 15, 2/18/99, Dobins AFB, GA	15.00
3186a-o	1940's 33¢ Celebrate the Century	
	Set of 15, 2/18/99, Dobins AFB, GA	35.00
3187	1950's 33¢ Celebrate the Century,	
	Pane of 15, 5/26/99, Springfield, MA	15.00
3187a-o	1950's 33¢ Celebrate the Century,	
	Set of 15, 5/26/99, Springfield, MA	35.00
3188	1960's 33¢ Celebrate the Century,	
	Pane of 15, 9/17/99, Green Bay, WI	15.00
3188a-o	1960's 33¢ Celebrate the Century	
	Set of 15, 9/17/99, Green Bay, WI	35.00
3189	1970's 33¢ Celebrate the Century,	
	Pane of 15, 11/18/99, NY, NY	15.00
3189a-o	1970's 33¢ Celebrate the Century,	
	Set of 15, 11/18/99, NY, NY	35.00
3190	1980's 33¢ Celebrate the Century,	
	Pane of 15, 1/12/00, Titusville, FL	15.00
3190a-o	1980's 33¢ Celebrate the Century	
	Set of 15, 1/12/00, Titusville, FL	35.00
3191	1990's 33¢ Celebrate the Century,	
	Pane of 15, 5/2/00, Escondido, CA	15.00
3191a-o	1990's 33¢ Celebrate the Century,	
	Set of 15, 5/2/00, Escondido, CA	35.00
	1998 Commemoratives (cont.)	
3192	32¢ Remember the Maine, 2/15/98, Key West FL	3.00
3193-97	32¢ Flowering Trees, S/A, Set of 5, 3/19/98, NY,NY	10.00
3197a	32¢ Flowering Trees, S/A, Strip of 5, 3/19/98, NY,NY	5.50
3198-3202	32¢ Alexander Calder, S/A, Set of 5, 3/25/98, Wash, DC	10.00
3202a	32¢ Alexander Calder, S/A, Strip of 5, 3/25/98, Wash, DC	5.50
3203	32¢ Cinco de Mayo, S/A, 4/16/98, San Antonio, TX	2.00
3203	Joint issue w/Mexico, dual cancel	15.00
3203	Mexican issue only	3.00
3204	32¢ Tweety&Sylvester, S/S of 10, perf. 4/27/98, NY, NY	10.00
3204a	32¢ Tweety&Sylvester, single, perf. 4/27/98, NY, NY	2.00
3204c	32¢ Tweety&Sylvester, pane of 1, perf. 4/27/98, NY, NY	5.00
3205	32¢ Tweety&Sylvester, S/S of 10, imperf. 4/27/98, NY, NY	15.00
3205c	Tweety&Sylvester, imperf single	10.00
3205c	32¢ Tweety&Sylvester, pane of 1, imperf. 4/27/98, NY, NY	12.00
3205c	Tweety&Sylvester, perf and imperf Pane on 1 Cover	20.00
3206	32¢ Wisconsin Statehood, 5/29/98, Madison WI	2.25
3207	5¢ Wetlands, Coil, 6/5/98, McLean, VA	2.00
3208	25¢ Diner, coil, 6/5/98, McLean, VA	2.20
3207+3208	Combo	3.00
3209	1¢-$2 Trans Mississippi Cent. 9 diff., 6/18/98, Anaheim,CA	25.00
3209a	1¢-$2 Trans Mississippi Cent. 9 diff., plus pair of $1 issue	30.00
3209	1¢-$2 Trans Mississippi Cent. Full sheet, 6/18/98, Anaheim,CA	10.75
3209	1¢-$2 Trans Mississippi Cent. Full sheet, plus Pair of $1 issue	15.00
3210	$1 Cattle in Storm, pane of 9, 6/18/98, Anaheim,CA	16.50
3211	32¢ Berlin Airlift, 6/26/98, Berlin Station, APOAE	2.00
3215a	32¢ Folk Musicians, 7 designs attd., 6/26/98, (1) Wash. DC .	6.00
3212-15	32¢ Set of 4 Wash. DC	12.00
3219a	32¢ Gospel Singers, att'd., 7/15/98, New Orleans, LA	6.00
3216-19	32¢ Gospel Singers, Set of 4 7/15/98,	16.00
3220	32¢ Spanish Settlement of SW 1598, 7/11/98 Espanola, NM	2.00
3221	32¢ Stephen Vincent Benet, 7/22/98, Harper's Ferry, WV	2.00
3225a	32¢ Tropical Birds, 7/29/98, Puerto Rico. Block 4	5.50
3222-25	32¢ Tropical Birds, 7/29/98, Set of 4	10.00
3226	32¢ Alfred Hitchcock, 8/3/98, LA, CA	2.00
3226	Pane of 20	17.50
3227	32¢ Organ & Tissue Donation, 8/5/98 coumbus, oh	2.00
3228	(10¢) Bicycle, S/A coil, 8/14/98, Wash. DC	
	(American Transportation)	2.00
3229	(10¢) Bicycle, W/A coil,8/14/98, Wash., DC	
	(American Transporation)	2.00
3228-29	On one FDC	3.00
3234a	32¢ Bright Eyes, strip of 5, 8/20/98, Boston, MA	5.50
3230-34	32¢ Bright Eyes, Set of 5, 8/20/98,	10.00
3235	32¢ Klondike Gold Rush, 8/21/98, Nome, AK	2.50
3236	32¢ Four Centuries of American Art,	

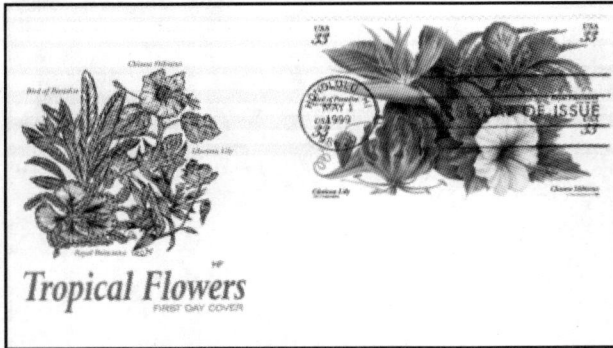

Tropical Flowers
FIRST DAY COVER

3313a

3337a

Scott #	Description	Cacheted
	1998 Commemoratives (cont.)	
	pane of 20 8/27/98, Santa Clara, CA	15.50
3236a-t	32¢ Four Centuries of American Art on 4 Covers	20.00
3236a-t	32¢ Four Centuries of American Art,	
	(20), 8/27/98, Santa Clara, CA	40.00
3237	32¢ Ballet, 9/16/98, NY, NY	2.00
3242a	32¢ Space Discovery, Strip of 5, 10/1/98	6.00
3238-42	32¢ Space Discovery, Set of 5, 10/1/98	12.00
3243	32¢ Giving & Sharing, 10/7/98, Atlanta GA	2.00
3244	32¢ Madonna and Child, 10/15/98, Wash. DC	2.00
3244a	Pane of 20	15.50
3245-48	32¢ Wreath Set of 4 Vending Bklt sgls, S/A, 10/15/98,	
	Christmas, MI	8.00
3248a	Pane of 4	4.00
3248b	Pane of 5	4.50
3248c	Pane of 6	5.25
3249-52	32¢ Wreathes, set of 4 sheet singles, S/A, (larger than vending)	
	S/A, 10/15/98, Christmas, MI	8.00
3249-52	32¢ Wreathes, attd.	4.00
3252b	32¢ Wreathes, Bklt of 20	15.50
3257	(1¢) Make up Rate – Weathervane, A.P., 11/9/98, Troy, NY	1.90
3258	(1¢) Make up Rate – Weathervane, BCA, 11/9/98, Troy, NY	1.90
3257 &58	On one FDC	2.00
3259	22¢ Uncle Sam, S/A from sheet, 11/9/98, Troy, NY	2.00
3260	(33¢) "H" Hat, W/A from sheet, 11/9/98, Troy, NY	2.00
3261	$3.20 Space Shuttle, Priority Mail, 11/9/98, Troy, NY	8.00
3262	$11.75 Piggyback Space Shuttle, Exp. Mail 11/19/98 NY NY	30.00
3263	22¢ Uncle Sam, coil, pair, S/A, 11/9/98, Troy, NY	2.00
3264	(33¢) "H" Hat, Coil, 11/9/98, Troy, NY	2.00
3265	(33¢) "H" Hat, S/A, single, 11/9/98, Troy, NY	2.00
3266	(33¢) "H" Hat, S/A (w/gaps between stamps) 11-9-98, Troy,NY	2.00
3267	(33¢) "H" Hat, Folded Bklt, Pane of 10, 10/9/98, Troy, NY	8.50
3268	(33¢) "H" Hat, Convertible Bklt, Pane of 10, 10/9/98, Troy, NY	8.50
3268a	Single from Convertible Pane of 10	3.00
3268b	Convertible Pane of 20	15.50
3269	(33¢) "H" Hat, ATM, Pane 18, 11/9/98, Troy, NY	14.00
3269a	Single from ATM Pane 18	3.00
3270	(10¢) Eagle & Shield, W/A, 12/14/98, Wash. DC	2.00
3271	(10¢) Eagle & Shield, S/A Coil, Presort; 12/14/98, Wash. DC	2.00
3270-71	(10¢) Eagle & Shield, Both W/A & S/A on 1	2.20
	1999 Commemoratives	
3272	33¢ Year of the Rabbit, 1/5/99, LA, CA	2.50
3273	33¢ Malcolm X, BH Series, 1/20/99NY, NY	3.00
3274	33¢ Love, S/A, 1/28/99, Loveland, CO	2.00
3274a	33¢ Love, Bklt of 20, 1/28/99	15.50
3274+3275	Combo	3.00
3275	55¢ Love, S/A, 1/28/99, Loveland, CO	2.25
3276	33¢ Hospice Care, 2/9/99, Largo, FL	2.25
3277	33¢ Flag & City, Single W/A sheet, 2/25/99, Orlando, FL	2.00
3278	33¢ Flag & City, S/A Sheet, 2/25/99, Orlando, FL	2.00
3278 a-c	33¢ Flag & City, (3) Convertible Bklts, 2/25/99, Orlando, FL	10.50
3278d	33¢ Flag & City, Convertible Bklt of 10	8.50
3278e	33¢ Flag & City, Convertible Bklt of 20	15.50
3279	33¢ Flag & City, S/A Bklt Stamp, 2/25/99, Orlando, FL	2.00
3279a	33¢ Flag & City, S/A Bklt Pane of 10, 2/25/99, Orlando, FL	8.50
3280	33¢ Flag & City, W/A coil, 2/25/99, Orlando, FL	2.00
3281	33¢ Flag & City, S/A Coil Square die-cut corners, 2/25/99,	
	Orlando, FL	2.00
3282	33¢ Flag & City, S/A Coil Rounded die-cut corners, 2/25/99,	
	Orlando, FL	2.00
3283s	33¢ Flag & Chalkboard, S/A, Cleveland, OH, 3/13/99.	2.00
3283	33¢ Flag & Chalkboard, S/A, Pane of 18 OH, 3/13/99	14.50
3286	33¢ Irish Immigration, 2/26/99, Boston, MA	2.50
3286	Joint issue w/Ireland, dual cancel	15.00
3286	Irish issue only	4.25
3287	33¢ Alfred Hunt & Lynn Fontanne, 3/2/99	2.00
3292	33¢ Arctic Animals, strip of 5, 3/12/99, Barrow, AK	5.50
3288-92	33¢ Arctic Animals, set of 5, 3/12/99, Barrow, AK	10.00
3293	33¢ Sonora Dessert, pane of 10, 4/6/99	10.00
3294a-3297c	33¢ Fruit Berries S/A booklet, 3/15/00 Ponchatoula, LA	
	Pane of 8	8.00
	Set of 4 singles	8.00
3293a-j	33¢ Sonora Dessert, set of 10, 4/6/99	25.00

Scott #	Description	Price
	2000 Commemoratives (cont.)	
3297a	33¢ Fruits & Berries, S/A Pane of 20, 4/10/99	15.50
3294-97	33¢ Fruits & Berries, S/A set of 4, 4/10/99	8.00
3294-97	33¢ Fruits & Berries on one cover	5.50
3301a	33¢ Fruits & Berries, S/A vend. Bklt of 15, 4/10/99	12.50
3302-5	33¢ Fruits & Berries, strip of 4, 4/10/99	4.00
	set of 4 singles from coil, 4/10/99	8.00
3306	Is perf variety	
3306	33¢ Daffy Duck, S/A Imperf Pane of 10, 4/16/99, LA, CA	15.00
3306a	33¢ Daffy Duck, S/A Imperf single, 4/16/99, LA, CA	6.00
3306c	33¢ Daffy Duck, S/A Imperf Pane(right side), 4/16/99, LA, CA	10.00
3307	Is imperf variety	
3307	33¢ Daffy Duck, S/A Perf Pane of 10, 4/16/99, LA, CA	15.00
3307a	33¢ Daffy Duck, S/A Perf Single, 4/16/99, LA, CA	2.50
3307c	33¢ Daffy Duck, S/A Perf Pane (right side), 4/16/99	6.00
3306c&07c	33¢ Daffy Duck combo	15.00
3308	33¢ Ayn Rand, 4/22/99	2.00
3309	33¢ Cinco de Mayo, 4/27/99	2.00
3313a	33¢ Tropical Flowers (1), 5/1/99	5.50
3313b	33¢ Tropical Flowers Bklt Pane of 8 plus label	7.50
3310-13	Set of 4	10.00
3314	33¢ John & William Bartram, 5/18/99	2.00
3315	33¢ Prostrate Cancer Awarenedss, 5/28/99, Austin, TX	2.00
3316	33¢ Cal. Gold Rush, 6/18/99, Sacremento, CA	2.00
3320a	33¢ Aquarium Fish, 6/24/99, Anaheim, CA	4.50
3317-20	Set of 4	8.00
3324a	33¢ Extreme Sports, 6/25/99, SF., CA	4.25
3321-24	Set of 4	8.00
3328a	33¢ American Glass, 6/29/99, Corning, NY	5.50
3325-28	Set of 4	10.00
3329	33¢ James Cagney, 7/17/99, Burbank, CA	2.00
3329	Sheet of 20	16.00
3330	55¢ Bill Mitchell, 7/30/99, Strafford, VT	2.25
3331	33¢ Honoring Those Who Served, 8/16/99, Kansas City, MO	2.00
3332'	45¢ Universal Postal Union, 8/25/99, Beijing, China	2.00
3337a	33¢ Trains (1), 8/26/99, Cleveland, OH	5.50
3333-7	Set of 5	10.00
3338	33¢ F.L. Olmstead,, 9/12/99, Boston, MA	2.00
3344a	33¢ Hollywood Composers, 9/16/99, LA, CA	5.50
3339-44	Set of 6	12.00
3350a	33¢ Broadway Songwriters, 9/21/99, NY, NY	5.50
3345-50	Set of 6	12.00
3351	33¢ Insects & Spiders, sheet of 20, 10/1/99, Ind. IN	16.00
3351a-t	Set of 20	40.00
3352	33¢ Hannukkah, 10/8/99, Wash., DC	2.50
3353	22¢ Uncle Sam, W/A Coil, 10/8/99, Wash., DC	2.00
3354	33¢ NATO, 10/13/99, Kansas City, MO	2.00
3355	33¢ Madonna & Child, 10/20/99, Wash., DC	2.00
3355	Pane of 20	15.00
3356-9	33¢ Holiday Deer, S/A Sheet Block, 10/20/99,Rudolph, WI	4.25
3356-9	Set of 4	8.00
3360-3	33¢ Holiday Deer, CB Pane 20, 10/20/99, Rudolph, WI	16.00
3360-3	Set of 4	8.00
3368	33¢ Kwanzaa, 10/29/99, LA, CA	3.00

Scott #	Description	Price
	2000 Commemoratives (cont.)	
3369	33¢ Year 2000, 12/27/99, Wash., DC and Nation Wide	2.00
3370	33¢ Year of the Dragon, 1/6/00, SF, CA	2.50
3371	33¢ Patricia R. Harris, 1/27/00, Wash., DC	3.00
	33¢ Fruits & Berries S/A Pane of 8,3/15/00, Ponchatoula, LA	8.00
	Set of 4	8.00
3372	33¢ LA Class Submarines,3/27/00, Groton, CT	2.00
3377a	$4.90 US Navy Submarines, BP of 5, Groton, CT	12.00
3373-77	Set of 5	15.00
3378	33¢ Pacific Coast Rain Forest, full sheet, 3/29/00, Seattle, WA	10.00
3378a-j	Set of 10	25.00
3383a	33¢ Louise Nevelson, strip of 5, 4/6/00, NY, NY	5.50
3379-83	Set of 5	10.00
	33¢ Pink Coral Rose, S/A, 4.7/00, NY, NY	2.00
	Pane of 8	8.00
3388a	33¢ Edwin Hubble, strip of 5, 4/10/00, NY, NY	5.50
3384-88	Set of 5	10.00
3389	33¢ American Samoa, 4/17/00, Pago, Pago, AS	2.00

#

U.S. First Day Covers

3391

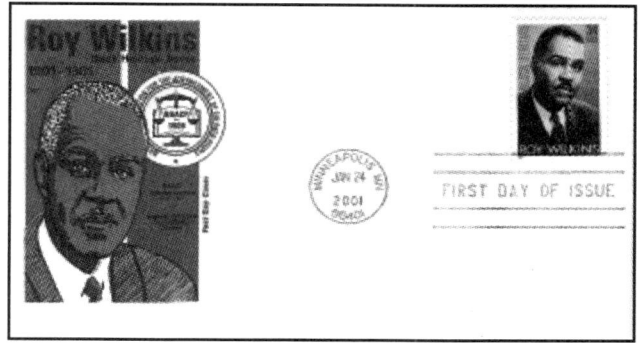

3501

Scott #	Description	Price
	2000 Commemoratives (cont.)	
3390	33¢ Library of Congress, 4/24/00, Wash., DC	2.00
3391	33¢ Wile E. Coyote & Roadrunner, Perf. Pane 10, 4/26/00	
	Phoenix, AZ	10.00
	Perf. Single	2.50
	Perf. Pane (right side)	5.00
3392	33¢ Wile E. Coyote & Roadrunner Imperf. Pane 10, 4/26/00	
	Phoenix, AZ	12.00
	Imperf. Single	5.00
	Imperf. Pane (right side)	6.00
3391&92	Perf & Imperf Pane Combo	10.00
3396a	33¢ Distinguished Soldiers, block of 4, 5/3/00, Wash., DC	4.25
3393-96	Set of 4	8.00
3397	33¢ Summer Sports, 5/5/00, Spokane, WA	2.00
3398	33¢ Adoption, 5/10/00, LA, CA	2.00
3402a	33¢ Youth Team Sports, block of 4, 5/ /00	4.25
3999-02	Set of 4	8.00
3403	33¢ Stars & Stripes, sheet of 20, 6/14/00, Baltimore, MD	16.00
3403a-t	Set of 20	40.00
3404-07	33¢ Fruits & Berries, Coil Strip of 4, 6/16/00, Buffalo,NY	4.00
3404-07	Set of 4	8.00
3408	33¢ Legends of Baseball, Sheet of 20, 7/6/00, Atlanta, Ga	16.00
3408a-t	Set of 20	45.00
3409	60¢ x 6 Probing the Vastness of Space, 7/10/00, Anaheim, CA	9.00
3409a-f	Set of 6	15.00
3409	Full Souvenir Sheet	12.50
3410	$1.00 x 5 Exploring the Solar System, 7/11/00, Anaheim, CA	12.50
3410	Full Souvenir Sheet	13.50
3410a-e	Set of 5	17.50
3411	$3.20 x 2 Escaping the Gravity of Earth, 7/9/00, Anaheim,CA	13.50
3411a-b	Set of 2	15.00
3411	Full Souvenir Sheet	18.00
3412	$11.75 Achievements in Exploration, 7/6/00, Anaheim, CA	25.00
3412	Full Souvenir Sheet	30.00
3413	$11.75 Landing on the Moon, 7/8/00, Anaheim, CA	25.00
3413	Full Souvenir Sheet	30.00
3417a	33¢ x4 Stampin' the Future, 7/13/00, Anaheim, CA	4.25
3414-17	Set of 4	8.00
3420	10¢ Gen. Joseph Stilwell, Great Amer. Series, 8/24/00, Prov. RI	2.00
3426	33¢ Claude Pepper, 9/ 7/00, Tallahassee, FL	2.00
3431	76¢ Hattie Caraway S/A, 2/21/01, Little Rock,AR	2.50
3438	33¢ California Statehood, 9/8 /00, Sacramento, CA	2.00
3439-43	33c Deep Sea Creatures set 5, 10/2/00, Monterey, CA	10.00
3443a	Strip of 5	5.50
3444	33c Thomas Wolfe, 10/3/00, Asheville, NC	2.00
3445	33c White House, 10/18/00, Washington, DC	2.00
3446	33¢Edward G. Robinson, 10/24/00 Los Angeles, CA	2.00
3446	Full Sheet of 20	14.00
3447	(10c) Lion State S/A coil 11/9/00, New York, NY	2.00
3448	(34c) Farm Flag W/A, 12/15/00, Washington, DC	2.00
3449	(34c) Farm Flag S/A, 12/15/00, Washington, DC	2.00
3450	(34c) Farm Flag ATM, 12/15/00, Washington, DC	2.00
	Pane of 18	13.50
3451	(34c) Statue of Liberty S/A booklet single	2.00
	Covertible booklet pane of 10	14.50
	Vending booklet pane of 4 w/plate #	5.50
3452	(34c) Statue of Liberty W/A coil, 12/15/00, New York, NY	2.00
3453	(34c) Statue ofLiberty S/A coil, 12/15/00, New York, NY	2.00
3454-57	(34c) Flowers S/A set of 4, 12/15/00, Washington, DC	8.00
	On one Cover	4.50
	Convertible booklet pane of8	8.00
	Perf. variety set of 4	16.00
	Perf. variety block of 4	9.00
3458-61	(34c) Flowers S/A coil strip of 4, 12/15/00, Washington, DC ..	4.50
	Set of 4 coil singles	8.00

2001 Commemoratives

Scott #	Description	Price
3466	34c Statueof Liberty S/A coil, 1/1/01, Washington, DC	2.00
3468	21c Bison S/A, 2/23/01, Wall, SD	2.25
3469	34c Farm Flag W/A, 2/7/01, New York, NY	2.00
3470	34c Farm Flag S/A, 3/6/01, Lincoln, NE	2.00
3471	55c Art Deco Eagles S/A, 2/22/01, Wall, SC	2.25
3472	$3.50 Capitol Dome S/A, 1/29/01, Washington, DC	8.00
3473	$12.25 Washington Monument S/A, 1/29/01, Washington, DC	30.00

Scott #	Description	Price
	2001 Commemoratives (cont.)	
3475	21c Bison S/A coil, 2/2201, Wall, SD	2.25
3476	34c Statue of Liberty W/A coil, 2/7/01, New York, NY	2.00
3477	34c Statue of Liberty S/A coil, 2/7/01, New York, NY	2.00
3478-81	34c Flowers S/A coil strip, 2/7/01, New York, NY	4.50
	Set of 4 singles	8.00
3482	20c G. Washington S/A, 2/22/01, Little Rock, AR	2.25
	Convertible booklet pane of 10	6.00
3483	20c G. Washington S/A, 2/22/01 LR, AR (perf 10.5x11)	2.25
	Vending booklet pane of 10	6.00
3485	34c Statue of Liberty S/A booklet, 2/7/01, New York, NY	2.00
	Convertible booklet pane of 20	14.50
	Pane of 10	8.50
3487-90	34c Flowers set 4 booklet singles, 2/7/01, New York, NY	8.00
	Convertible booklet pane of 12	10.50
	Vending booklet pane of 20 (split on #10 envelope)	17.50
3491-92	34c Apple& Orange S/A pair, 3/6/01, Lincoln, NE	2.50
	Set of 2 singles	4.00
	Block of 10 w/pl# from Convertible booklet	8.50
3496	(34c) Love Letter S/A, 1/19/01, Tucson, AZ	2.00
	Convertible booklet paneof 20	14.50
3497	34c Love Letter S/A, 2/14/01, Lovejoy, GA	2.00
	Convertible booklet pane of 20	14.50
3498	34c Love VB single, 2/14/01, Lovejoy, GA	2.00
	Pane of 4 w/pl# from Vending booklet	5.00
3499	55c Love LetterS/A, 2/14/01, Lovejoy, GA	2.25
	Convertible booklet pane of 20	20.00
3497-99	Love combination on one Cover	3.00
3500	34c Year of the Snake, 1/20/01, Oakland, CA	2.50
3501	34c Roy Wilkins, 1/24/01, Minneapolis, MN	3.00
3502	34c American Illustrators Pane 20, 2/1/01, New York, Ny	15.00
3502a-t	Set of 20 singles	45.00
	Set on 4 Covers	13.50
	34c Diabetes Awareness, 3/16/01, Boston, MA	2.00
	34c Noble Prize, 3/22/01, Washington, DC	2.00
	Joint issue w/Sweden, dual cancel	12.00
	Swedish stamp & cancel only	4.00
	1c, 2c & 4c Pan American inverts & 80c Buffalo, 3/29/01	
	Set of 4 singles, New York, NY	12.00
	Full Souvenir Sheet	10.00
	34c Great Plains Prairie Full Sheet, 4/19/01, Lincoln, NE	10.00
	Set of 10 singles	20.00
	34c Peanuts, 5/17/01, Santa Rosa, CA	2.50
	34c U.S. Veterans, 5/23/01, Washington, DC	2.50
	34c Frida Kahlo, 6/21/01, Phoenix, AZ	2.00
	34c Baseball's Legendary Playing Fields pane 20, 6/27/01 ...	17.50
	Set of 10 singles	25.00
	(10c) Atlas Statue S/A coil, 6/29/01, New York, NY	2.00
	34c Leonard Bernstein, 7/10/01, New York, NY	2.00
	(10c) Lion Statue W/A coil	2.00

Semi-Postal Stamps

Scott #	Description	Price
B1	1st Class Rate+8¢ Breast Cancer	
	Research,8/13/98, Wash,DC	2.25

1906

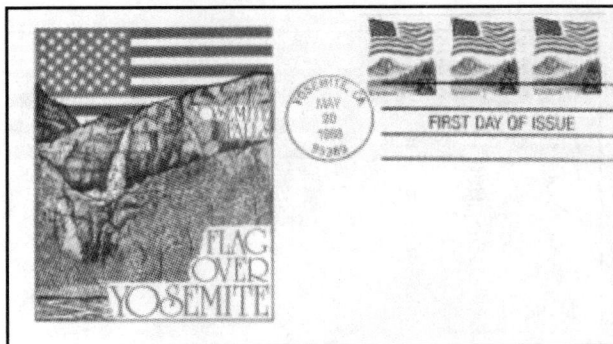

2280

The listing below omits prices on FDC's which are extremely rare or where sufficient pricing information is not available. *Due to market volatility, prices are subject to change without notice.* **Prices are for unaddressed FDC's with common cachets and cancels which do not obscure the Pl. #. Strips of 3 must have a plate # on the center stamp.**

Scott #	Description	Pl# Pr.	Pl# Str of 3
1891	18¢ Flag 4/24/81		
	Pl# 1	75.00	120.00
	Pl# 2	180.00	340.00
	Pl# 3	260.00	420.00
	Pl# 4	160.00	280.00
	Pl# 5	125.00	...
1895	20¢ Flag 12/17/81		
	Pl# 1	17.50	36.00
	Pl# 2	100.00	160.00
	Pl# 3	160.00	320.00
1897	1¢ Omnibus 8/19/83		
	Pl # 1,2	7.00	10.50
1897A	2¢ Locomotive 5/20/82		
	Pl# 3,4	10.50	17.00
1898	3¢ Handcar 3/25/83		
	Pl# 1,2,3,4	8.00	17.00
1898A	4¢ Stagecoach 8/19/82		
	Pl# 1,2,3,4	8.00	16.00
1899	5¢ Motorcycle 10/10/83		
	Pl# 1,2	9.00	13.50
	Pl# 3,4	...	...
1900	5.2¢ Sleigh 3/21/83		
	Pl# 1,2	13.50	27.00
1900a	Pl# 1,2	...	...
1901	5.9¢ Bicycle 2/17/82		
	Pl# 3,4	13.50	22.50
1901a	Pl# 3,4	...	...
1902	7.4¢ Baby Buggy 4/7/84		
	Pl# 2	8.50	18.00
1903	9.3¢ Mail Wagon 12/15/81		
	Pl# 1,2	18.00	34.00
	Pl# 3,4	...	...
1904	10.9¢ Hansom Cab 3/26/82		
	Pl# 1,2	14.50	32.50
1904a	Pl# 1,2	....	....
1905	11¢ Caboose 2/3/84, Pl# 1	13.50	32.50
1905a	11¢ Caboose, "B" Press 9/25/91		
	Pl#2	...	...
1906	17¢ Electric Car 6/25/82		
	Pl# 1,2	14.50	27.00
1907	18¢ Surrey 5/18/81		
	Pl# 1	27.00	...
	Pl# 2	17.50	40.00
	Pl# 3,4,7,9,10	100.00	...
	Pl# 5	100.00	...
	Pl# 6,8	...	...
1908	20¢ Fire Pumper 12/10/81		
	Pl# 1,7,8	...	...
	Pl# 2	150.00	240.00
	Pl# 3,4	13.50	36.00
	Pl# 5,6	100.00	175.00
2005	20¢ Consumer 4/27/82		
	Pl# 1,2,3,4	22.50	...
2112	(22¢) "D" Coil 2/1/85		
	Pl# 1,2	8.50	16.00
2115	22¢ Flag over Capitol 3/29/85		
	Pl# 1	32.50	57.50
	Pl# 2	13.50	20.00
2115b	22¢ Test Coil 5/23/87		
	Pl# T1	...	11.00
2123	3.4¢ School Bus 6/8/85		
	Pl# 1,2	5.50	8.50
2124	4.9¢ Buckboard 6/21/85		
	Pl# 3,4	6.00	11.50
2125	5.5¢ Star Route Truck 11/1/86		
	Pl# 1	6.00	11.50
2125a	Pl# 1	...	36.00
2126	6¢ Tricycle 5/6/85		
	Pl# 1	5.50	8.50
2126a	Pl# 1		
2127	7.1¢ Tractor Coil 2/6/87, Pl# 1	6.50	11.50
2127a	Pl# 1	...	32.50
2127a	7.1¢ Zip + 4 Pl# 1 5/26/89	...	6.50
2128	8.3¢ Ambulance 6/21/86		
	Pl# 1,2	6.50	11.00
2128a	Pl# 1,2	...	...
2129	8.5¢ Tow Truck 1/24/87		
	Pl# 1	5.50	8.50

Scott #	Description	Pl# Pr.	Pl# Str of 3
2129a	Pl# 1	...	15.50
2130	10.1¢ Oil Wagon 4/18/85		
	Pl# 1	6.50	10.50
2130a	10.1¢ Red Prec. Pl# 2 6/27/88	...	7.50
2131	11¢ Stutz Bearcat 6/11/85		
	Pl# 3,4	...	11.00
2132	12¢ Stanley Steamer 4/2/85		
	Pl# 1,2	6.50	11.00
2132a	Pl# 1	...	...
2133	12.5¢ Pushcart 4/18/85		
	Pl# 1	6.50	11.00
2134	14¢ Iceboat 3/23/85		
	Pl# 1,2	8.50	13.50
2135	17¢ Dog Sled 8/20/86		
	Pl# 2	6.50	10.50
2136	25¢ Bread Wagon 11/22/86		
	Pl# 1	6.50	11.00
2149	18¢ GW Monument 11/6/85		
	Pl# 1112,3333	17.50	32.50
2149a	Pl# 11121	40.00	...
	Pl# 33333	40.00	...
2150	21.1¢ Pre-Sort 10/22/85		
	Pl# 111111	13.50	22.50
2150a	Pl# 111111	35.00	...
2225	1¢ Omnibus Re-engraved 11/26/86		
	Pl# 1	5.50	11.00
2226	2¢ Locomotive Re-engraved 3/6/87		
	Pl# 1	...	7.00
2228	4¢ Stagecoach, "B" Press 8/15/86 **(eku)**		
	Pl# 1	...	260.00
2231	8.3¢ Ambulance, "B" Press 8/29/86 **(eku)**		
	Pl# 1	...	...
2252	3¢ Conestoga Wagon 2/29/88		
	Pl# 1	...	6.00
2253	5¢ Milk Wagon 9/25/87		
	Pl# 1	...	6.00
2254	5.3¢ Elevator 9/16/88		
	Pl# 1	...	6.00
2255	7.6¢ Carreta 8/30/88		
	Pl# 1	...	6.50
2256	8.4¢ Wheelchair 8/12/88		
	Pl# 1	...	6.50
2257	10¢ Canal Boat 4/11/87		
	Pl# 1	...	7.50
2258	13¢ Patrol Wagon 10/29/88		
	Pl# 1	...	6.50
2259	13.2¢ Coal Car 7/19/88		
	Pl# 1	...	6.50
2260	15¢ Tugboat 7/12/88		
	Pl# 1	...	6.50
2261	16.7¢ Popcorn Wagon 7/7/88		
	Pl# 1	...	6.50
2262	17.5¢ Racing Car 9/25/87		
	Pl# 1	...	7.50
2263	20¢ Cable Car 10/28/88		
	Pl# 1	...	6.50
	Pl# 2	...	60.00
2264	20.5¢ Fire Engine 9/28/88		
	Pl# 1	...	6.50
2265	21¢ Railroad Mail Car 8/16/88		
	Pl# 1	...	6.50
	Pl# 2	...	...
2266	24.1¢ Tandem Bicycle 10/26/88		
	Pl# 1	...	6.50
2279	(25¢) "E" & Earth 3/22/88		
	Pl# 1111,1222	...	6.50
	Pl# 1211	...	8.50
	Pl# 2222	...	22.50
2280	25¢ Flag over Yosemite 5/20/88		
	Pl# 1,2	...	8.50
	Pl# 3,4	...	125.00
2280v	Pre-Phosphor Paper 2/14/89		
	Pl# 5	...	16.00
	Pl# 6,9	...	32.50
	Pl# 7,8	...	7.50
	Pl# 10	...	...
2281	25¢ Honeybee 9/2/88		
	Pl# 1	...	8.50
	Pl# 2	...	27.00
2451	4¢ Steam Carriage 1/25/91, Pl# 1	...	5.50
2452	5¢ Circus Wagon 8/31/90, Pl# 1	...	5.50
2452B	5¢ Circus Wagon, Gravure 12/8/92, Pl# A1,A2	...	5.50
2452D	5¢ Circus Wagon, SV 3/20/95, Pl# S1	...	5.50
2453	5¢ Canoe 5/25/91, Pl# 1	...	5.50

U.S. Plate No. Coil First Day Covers

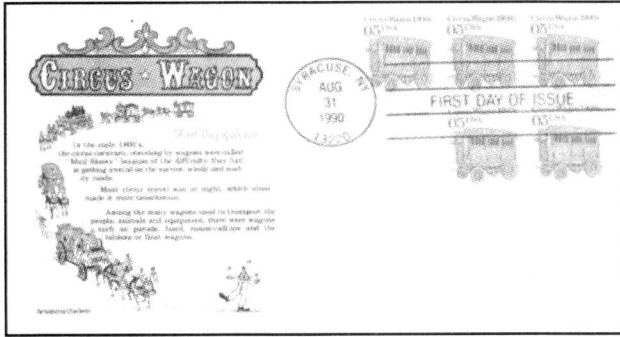

2452

2468

Scott #	Description	Pl# Pr.	Pl# Str of 3
2454	5¢ Canoe, Gravure Print 10/22/91, Pl# S11	...	5.50
2457	10¢ Tractor Trailer 5/25/91, Pl# 1	...	5.50
2458	Tractor Trailer 5/25/91, a1 Pl# 1 & 2	...	
2463	20¢ Cog Railroad 6/9/95, Pl#1		6.50
2464	23¢ Lunch Wagon 4/12/91		
	Pl# 2	...	7.50
	Pl# 3	...	6.50
2466	32¢ Ferryboat 6/2/95		
	Pl# 2-3		6.50
	Pl# 4		13.50
	Pl# 5		32.50
2468	$1.00 Seaplane 4/20/90, Pl# 1		8.50
2491	29¢ Pine Cone (self-adhesive)11/5/93, Pl# B1		8.50
2492	32¢ Rose (self-adhesive) 6/2/95, Pl# S111		8.50
2495A	32¢ Peaches and Pears (self-adhesive) 7/8/95		
	Pl# A11111		8.50
2518	(29¢) "F" & Flower 1/22/91		
	Pl# 1111,1222,2222,1211	...	8.50
	Pl# 2211	...	22.50
2523	29¢ Flag over Mt. Rushmore 3/29/91, Pl# 1-7	6.50	...
2523A	29¢ Mt. Rushmore, Gravure Print 7/4/91		
	Pl# 11111	...	6.50
2525	29¢ Flower, rouletted 8/16/91, Pl# S1111, S2222	...	6.50
2526	29¢ Flower, perforated 3/3/92, Pl# 2222	6.50	...
2529	(19¢) Fishing Boat 8/8/91		
	Pl# 1111,1212	...	6.50
2529c	(19¢) Fishing Boat 6/25/94, Pl# S111	...	6.50
2599	29¢ Statue of Liberty (self-adhesive) 6/24/94		
	Pl# D1111	...	8.50
2602	10¢ Eagle & Shield, ABNCo 12/13/91	...	5.50
	Any Pl# (except A12213 & A32333)	...	5.50
	Pl# A12213	...	24.00
	Pl# A32333	...	125.00
2603	10¢ Eagle & Shield, BEP 5/29/93, Pl# 11111	...	5.50
2604	10¢ Eagle & Shield, SV, Pl# S11111	...	5.50
2607	23¢ Flag, First Class pre-sort 9/27/91	...	6.50
2608	23¢ "USA" First Class pre-sort ABNCo, 7/21/92		
	Pl# A1111, A2222	...	6.50
2608A	23¢ "USA" First Class pre-sort BEP, 10/9/92		
	Pl# 1111	...	6.50
2608B	23¢ "USA" First Class pre-sort SV, 5/14/93		
	Pl# S111	...	6.50
2609	29¢ Flag over White House 4/23/92	...	5.25
	Pl# 1-7	...	5.25
	Pl# 8	...	...
2799-2809	29¢ Christmas (self-adhesive) 10/28/93		
	Pl# V1111111	...	8.50
2813	29¢ Love (self-adhesive) 1/27/94		
	Pl# B1	...	8.50
2873	29¢ Santa (self-adhesive) 10/20/94		
	Pl# V1111	...	8.50
2886	(32¢) "G" Flag (self-adhesive) 12/13/94		
	Pl# V11111	...	6.50
2888	(32¢) "G" Flag 12/13/94, Pl# S11111	...	6.50
2889	(32¢) "G" Flag 12/13/94		
	Pl# 1111, 2222	...	6.50
2890	(32¢) "G" Flag 12/13/94		
	Pl# A1111, A1112, A1113, A1211, A1212,		
	A1222, A1311, A1313, A1314, A1324, A1417,		
	A1433, A2211, A2212, A2213, A2214, A2223,		
	A2313, A3113, A3114, A3315, A3323, A3423,		
	A3324, A3426, A3433, A3435, A3536, A4426,		
	A4427, A5327, A5417, A5427, A5437	...	8.50
2890	(32¢) "G" Flag 12/13/94 ,Pl# A4435	...	200.00
2891	(32¢) "G" Flag 12/13/94, Pl# S1111	...	6.50
2892	(32¢) "G" Flag 12/13/94, Pl# S1111,S2222	...	6.50
2893	(32¢) "G" Flag 12/13/94, Pl# A11111, A21111	...	6.50
2902	5¢ Butte 3/10/95, Pl# S111	...	5.50
2902b	5¢ ButteSV, self-adhesive 6/15/96		
	Pl# S111	...	5.50
2903	5¢ Mountains, BEP, 3/16/96, Pl# 11111	...	5.50

Scott #	Description	Pl# Pr.	Pl# Str of 3
2904	5¢ Mountains,SV, 3/16/96, Pl# S11	...	5.50
2904a	5¢ Mountains,SA, 6/15/96		
	Pl# V222222,V333333,V333323		
	V333342,V333343	...	5.50
	Pl# S11111		6.50
2911	25¢ Juke Box, BEP 3/17/95		
	Pl# S111111	...	6.50
2905	10¢ Auto, 3/10/95, Pl # S111	...	6.50
2906	10¢ Auto,SA 6/15/96, Pl # S111	...	5.50
2907	10¢ Eagle & Shield, SA 5/21/96, Pl # S1111	...	5.50
2908	15¢ Auto Tail Fin, BEP, 3/17/95, Pl# 11111	...	6.50
2909	15¢ Auto Tail Fin, SV, 3/17/95, Pl# S11111	...	6.50
2912	25¢ Juke Box, 3/17/95, Pl# 111	...	6.50
2912a	25¢ Juke Box,SV,SA 6/15/96, Pl# S11111	...	6.50
2912b	25¢ Juke Box, BEP,SA 6/15/96, Pl# 11111	...	6.50
2913	32¢ Flag over Porch 4/18/95		
	Pl# 11111,22222,33333,44444,S11111	...	6.50
	Pl# 22221	...	13.50
	Pl# 45444,66646	...	30.00
2914	32¢ Flag over Porch SV 5/19/95, Pl# S11111	...	8.50
2915A	32¢ Flag over Porch BEP (self-adhesive) 5/21/96		
	Pl# 55555,66666,78777	...	8.50
	Pl# 87888	...	50.00
	Pl# 87898,88888	...	8.50
	Pl# 88898	...	500.00
	Pl# 89878	...	8.50
	Pl# 89888	...	50.00
	Pl# 89898	...	17.50
	Pl# 97898,99999	...	8.50
2915B	32¢ Flag over Porch SV 6/15/96		
	Pl# S11111	...	8.50
2915C	32¢ Flag over Porch BEP 5/21/96		
	serpentine die-cut Pl# 66666		22.50
3017	32¢ Christmas (self-adhesive) 9/30/95		
	Pl# V1111	...	8.50
3018	32¢ Christmas Angel (self-adhesive) 10/31/95		
	Pl# B1111	...	8.50
3044	1¢ Kestrel 1/20/96, Pl# 1111	...	5.50
3045	2¢ Woodpecker, 6/22/99, Pl#11111	...	5.50
3053	20¢ Blue Jay (self-adhesive)8/2/96, Pl# S111	...	6.50
3054	32¢ Yellow Rose, S/A, 8/1/97		
	Pl# 1111,1112,1122,2222,2223,2333,3344,		
	3444,4455,5455,5555,5556,5566,5666		8.00
3055	20¢ Ring-Necked Pheasant, 7/31/98, Pl#1111		7.00
3207	(5¢) Wetlands, 6/5/98, Pl#S1111		6.50
3207A	(5¢) Welands S/A, 121/14/98, Pl#1111		6.50
3208	(25¢) Diner, 6/5/98, Pl#S11111		7.00
3208A	(25¢) Diner, 9/30/98, Pl#1111		7.00
3228	(10¢) Bicycle S/A, 8/14/98, Pl#111,221,222,333		7.00
3229	(10¢) Bicycle, 8/14/98, Pl#S111		7.00
3263	22¢ Uncle Sam, 11/9/98, Pl#111		7.50
3264	(33¢) "H" Hat, 11/9/98, Pl#1111,3333,3343,3344,3444		8.00
3265	(33¢) "H" Hat S/A, 11/9/98, Pl#1111,1131,2222,3333		8.00
3266	(33¢) "H" Hat S/A w/gaps, 11/9/98, Pl#1111		8.00
3270	(10¢) Eagle & Shield, 12/14/98, Pl#1111		6.50
3271	(10¢) Eagle & Shield S/A, 12/14/98, Pl#11111		6.50
3280	33¢ Flag & City, 2/25/99, Pl#1111,2222		8.00
3281	33¢ Flag & City S/A, 2/25/99, Pl#1111,2222,3333,3433,		
	4443,4444,5555		8.00
3281	33¢ Flag & City S/A w/gaps, 2/25/99, Pl#1111,1222	...	8.00
3404-07	34¢ Fruit Berries, 6/16/00, Pl#S1111		8.00
3447	(10¢) Lion Statue, 11/9/00,Pl#S11111		6.50
3452	(34c) Statue of Liberty W/A, 12/15/00, Pl#1111		7.00
3453	(34c) Statue of Liberty S/A, 21/15/00, Pl#1111		7.00
3458-61	(34c) Flowers S/A, 12/15/00, Pl#B1111		8.00
3466	34c Statue of Liberty S/A, 1/7/01, Pl#1111		7.00
3467	34c Statue of Liberty W/A, 2/7/01, Pl#1111		7.00
3468	34c Statue of Liberty S/A, 27/01, Pl#3333		7.00
3475	21c Bison S/A, 2/22/01, Pl#V1111		6.50

OFFICIAL STAMPS

Scott #	Description	Pl# Pr.	Pl# Str of 3
O135	20¢ Official, Pl# 1	25.00	75.00
O139	(22¢) "D" Official, Pl# 1	30.00	75.00

COMPUTER VENDED POSTAGE

Scott #	Description	Pl# Pr.	Pl# Str of 3
CV31	29¢ Variable Rate Coil 8/20/92		
	Pl# 1		7.00
CV31	29¢ Variable Rate 8/20/92, 1st Print		
	Pl# 1		7.00
CV31b	29¢ Variable Rate 8/20/92, 2nd Print		
	Pl# 1		22.50
CV32	29¢ Variable Rate 8/20/92		
	Pl# A11	...	7.00

U.S. First Day Covers

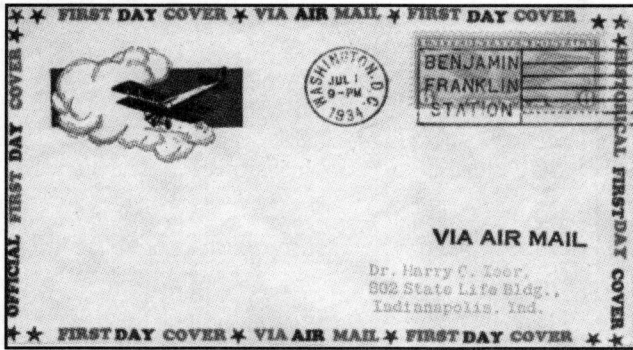

AIR MAIL FIRST DAY COVERS

Cacheted prices are for FDC's with common printed cachets.
From #C4 - C31, FDC's will usually be addressed.
Prices and Dates for #C1-3 are for First Flight Covers, AND FDC's.

Scott #	Description	Uncacheted	Cacheted
C1	6¢ Jenny 12/10/18 Washington, DC FDC	25,000.00	...
C1	6¢ Jenny 12/16/18 NYC; Phila.,PA; DC FFC	2,750.00	...
C2	16¢ Jenny 7/11/18 Washington, DC FDC	25,000.00	...
C2	16¢ Jenny 7/15/18 NYC; Phila.,PA; DC FFC	850.00	...
C3	24¢ Jenny 5/15/18 NYC; Phila.,PA; DC FFC	800.00	...
C4	8¢ Propeller 8/15/23 DC	350.00	...
C5	16¢ Air Service Emblem 8/17/23 DC	525.00	...
C6	24¢ DeHavilland Biplane 8/21/23 DC	650.00	...
C7	10¢ Map 2/13/26 DC	80.00	...
	Chicago, IL	90.00	...
	Detroit, MI	90.00	...
	Cleveland, OH	120.00	...
	Dearborn, MI	120.00	...
	Unofficial city	175.00	...
C8	15¢ Map 9/18/26 DC	90.00	...
C9	20¢ Map 1/25/27 DC	100.00	...
	New York, NY	110.00	...
	1st Albert E. Gorham cachet	...	**250.00**
C10	10¢ Lindbergh 6/18/27 DC	30.00	175.00
	St. Louis, MO	30.00	175.00
	Detroit, MI	40.00	175.00
	Little Falls, MN	40.00	175.00
	Air Mail Field, Chicago, unofficial	150.00	...
	Unofficial city (other than AMF Chicago) ..	175.00	...
	1st Milton Mauck cachet	...	**250.00**
C10a	10¢ **Booklet Single** 5/26/28 DC	100.00	175.00
	Booklet Sgl., Cleveland Midwest Phil. Sta. ...	100.00	175.00
	#C10a sgl. & 645 Cleveland Midwest Sta	150.00	200.00
C10a	10¢ **Booklet Pane of 3** 5/26/28 DC	875.00	1000.00
	B. Pane of 3, Cleveland Midwest Sta.	825.00	1000.00
	#C10a & 645 on one FDC, Clev. Midwst.	900.00	1100.00
	Booklet Pane w/o tab, DC or Cleveland	425.00	750.00
C11	5¢ Beacon, pair 7/25/28 DC	60.00	250.00
	Single on FDC	200.00	...
	Single on FDC with postage due	250.00	...
	Unofficial city (pair)	250.00	...
	Predate 7/24/28	1,500.00	...
C12	5¢ Winged Globe 2/10/30 DC	15.00	90.00
C13	65¢ Graf Zeppelin 4/19/30 DC	1,100.00	2,500.00
	On flight cover, any date	250.00	...
C14	$1.30 Graf Zeppelin 4/19/30 DC	800.00	2,500.00
	On flight cover, any date	400.00	...
C15	$2.60 Graf Zeppelin 4/19/30 DC	950.00	2,500.00
	On flight cover, any date	600.00	...
C13-15	Graf Zeppelin, cplt. set on one cover	16,000.00	...
	Complete set on one Flight Cover, any date .	2,400.00	...
C16	5¢ Winged Globe, Rotary 8/19/31 DC	175.00	...
C17	8¢ Winged Globe 9/26/32 DC	16.50	50.00
	Combo with UC7	60.00	...
C18	50¢ Zeppelin 10/2/33 New York, NY	175.00	250.00
	Akron, OH 10/4/33	250.00	400.00
	DC 10/5/33	225.00	425.00
	Miami, FL 10/6/33	250.00	325.00
	Chicago, IL 10/7/33	250.00	400.00
	On flight cover, any date	110.00	150.00
C19	6¢ Winged Globe 6/30/34 Baltimore, MD	200.00	600.00
	New York, NY	1,250.00	1,750.00
	First Day of Rate 7/1/34 DC	20.00	40.00
	Combo with UC3	60.00	...

Scott #	Description 1935-39	Cacheted
C20	25¢ China Clipper 11/22/35 DC	45.00
	San Francisco, CA	45.00
C21	20¢ China Clipper 2/15/37 DC	55.00

Scott #	Description 1935-39	Cacheted
C22	50¢ China Clipper 2/15/37 DC	60.00
C21-22	China Clipper on one cover	125.00
C23	6¢ Eagle Holding Shield 5/14/38 Dayton, OH	17.50
	St. Petersburg, FL	17.50
C24	30¢ Winged Globe 5/16/39 New York, NY	60.00
C25	6¢ Plane 6/25/41 DC	7.50
C25a	Booklet Pane of 3 (3/18/43) DC	30.00
	Booklet single	10.00
C26	8¢ Plane 3/21/44 DC	6.00
C27	10¢ Plane 8/15/41 Atlantic City, NJ	9.00
C28	15¢ Plane 8/19/41 Baltimore, MD	9.00
C29	20¢ Plane 8/27/41 Philadelphia, PA	12.00
C30	30¢ Plane 9/25/41 Kansas City, MO	20.00
C31	50¢ Plane 10/29/41 St. Louis, MO	30.00
C25-31,C25a	Transport Plane set of 8 covers	95.00

From #C32 - Date, prices are for unaddressed FDC's & common cachets.

	1946-59	
C32	5¢ DC-4 Skymaster 9/25/46 DC	1.75
C33	5¢ Small Plane (DC-4) 3/26/47 DC	1.75
C34	10¢ Pan Am. Building 8/30/47 DC	1.75
C35	15¢ New York Skyline 8/20/47 NY, NY	2.00
C36	25¢ Bay Bridge 7/30/47 San Francisco, CA	2.50
C37	5¢ Small Plane, coil 1/15/48 DC	1.75
C38	5¢ NY City Jubilee 7/31/48 New York, NY	2.00
C39	6¢ DC-4 Skymaster 1/18/49 DC	1.75
C39a	Booklet Pane of 6 11/18/49 NY, NY	12.00
C39as	Booklet Pane, single, ...	4.00
C40	6¢ Alexandria 5/11/49 Alexandria, VA	2.00
C41	6¢ DC-4 Skymaster, coil 8/25/49 DC	1.75
C42	10¢ Post Office Bldg. 11/18/49 New Orleans, LA	1.75
C43	15¢ Globe & Doves 10/7/49 Chicago, IL	3.00
C44	25¢ Boeing 11/30/49 Seattle, WA	4.00
C45	6¢ Wright Brothers 12/17/49 Kitty Hawk, NC	3.00
C46	80¢ Diamond Head 3/26/52 Honolulu, HI	15.00
C47	6¢ Powered Flight 5/29/53 Dayton, OH	2.50
C48	4¢ Eagle in Flight 9/3/54 Phila., PA	1.75
C49	6¢ Air Force 8/1/57 DC	2.00
C50	5¢ Eagle 7/31/58 Colorado Springs, CO	1.75
C51	7¢ Blue Jet 7/31/58 Philadelphia, PA	1.75
C51a	Booklet Pane of 6 7/31/58 San Antonio, TX	7.00
C51as	Booklet Pane, single, ...	4.00
C52	7¢ Blue Jet, coil 7/31/58 Miami, FL	1.75
C53	7¢ Alaska 1/3/59 Juneau, AK	2.00
C54	7¢ Balloon 8/17/59 Lafayette, IN	3.00
C55	7¢ Hawaii Sthd. 8/21/59 Honolulu, HI	2.00
C56	10¢ Pan Am Games 8/27/59 Chicago, IL	2.00

	1959-68	
C57	10¢ Liberty Bell 6/10/60 Miami, FL	1.75
C58	15¢ Statue of Liberty 11/20/59 NY, NY	1.75
C59	25¢ Lincoln 4/22/60 San Francisco, CA	1.75
C59a	Luminescent 12/29/66 DC	60.00
C60	7¢ Red Jet 8/12/60 Arlington, VA	1.75
C60a	Booklet Pane of 6 8/19/60 St. Louis, MO	8.00
C60as	Booklet Pane, single, ...	4.00
C61	7¢ Red Jet, coil 10/22/60 Atlantic City, NJ	1.75
C62	13¢ Liberty Bell 6/28/61 New York, NY	1.75
C62a	Luminescent 2/15/67 DC	60.00
C63	15¢ Statue of Liberty 1/31/61 Buffalo, NY	1.75
C63a	Luminescent 1/11/67 DC	60.00
C64	8¢ Jet over Capitol, single 12/5/62 DC	1.75
C64a	Luminescent 8/1/63 Dayton, OH	1.75
C64b	Booklet Pane of 5 12/5/62 DC	1.75
C64bs	Booklet Pane, single, ...	4.00
C65	8¢ Jet over Capitol, 12/5/62 DC, single	1.75
C65a	Luminescent 1/14/65 New Orleans, LA	60.00
C66	15¢ Montgomery Blair 5/3/63 Silver Springs, MD	2.50
C67	6¢ Bald Eagle 7/12/63 Boston, MA	1.75
C67a	Luminescent 2/15/67 DC	60.00
C68	8¢ Amelia Earhart 7/24/63 Atchinson, KS	4.00
C69	8¢ Robert Goddard 10/5/64 Roswell, NM	3.00
C70	8¢ Alaska Purchase 3/30/67 Sitka, AK	2.00
C71	20¢ Columbia Jays 4/26/67 New York, NY	2.50
C72	10¢ 50-Star Runway 1/5/68 San Fran., CA	1.75
C72	Precancelled, 5/19/71, Wash, DC	75.00

U.S. First Day Covers

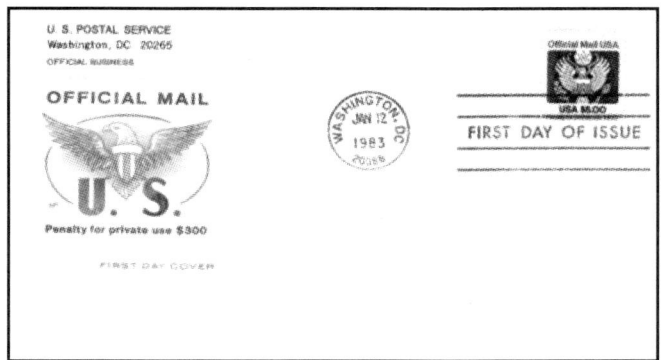

Scott #	Description	Cacheted
	1969-91	
C72b	Bklt. Pane of 8 1/5/68 San Fran., CA	3.00
C72bs	Booklet Pane, single,	4.00
C72c	Bklt. Pane of 5 1/6/68 DC	125.00
C73	10¢ 50-Star Runway, coil 1/5/68 San Francisco, CA	1.75
C74	10¢ Jenny 5/15/68 DC	2.00
C75	20¢ "USA" & Jet 11/22/68 New York, NY	1.75
C76	10¢ First Man on Moon 9/9/69 DC	5.00
C77	9¢ Delta Plane 5/15/71 Kitty Hawk, NC	1.75
C78	11¢ Jet Silhouette 5/7/71 Spokane, WA	1.75
C78	Precancel, 5/19/71, Wash, DC	75.00
C78a	Booklet Pane of 4 5/7/71 Spokane, WA	3.00
C78as	Booklet Pane Single	4.00
C79	13¢ Winged Envelope 11/16/73 NY, NY	1.75
C79	Precancel, 3/4/74, Wash, DC	75.00
C79a	Bklt. Pane of 5 12/27/73 Chicago, IL	3.00
C79as	Blklt.Pane, single	4.00
C80	17¢ Statue of Liberty 7/13/71 Lakehurst, NJ	1.75
C81	21¢ "USA" & Jet 5/21/71 DC	1.75
C82	11¢ Jet Silhouette, coil 5/7/71 Spokane, WA	1.75
C83	13¢ Winged Envelope, coil 12/27/73 Chicago, IL	1.75
C84	11¢ City of Refuge 5/3/72 Honaunau, HI	1.75
C85	11¢ Olympics 8/17/72 DC	1.75
C86	11¢ Electronics 7/10/73 New York, NY	1.75
C87	18¢ Statue of Liberty 1/11/74 Hampstead, NY	1.75
C88	26¢ Mt. Rushmore 1/2/74 Rapid City, SD	1.75
C89	25¢ Plane and Globe 1/2/76 Honolulu, HI	1.75
C90	31¢ Plane, Globe & Flag 1/2/76 Honolulu, HI	1.75
C89-90	On one FDC	3.00
C91-92	31¢ Wright Bros. attd. 9/23/78 Dayton, OH	2.50
C91-92	Wright Bros. set of 2 singles	3.50
C93-94	21¢ Octave Chanute attd. 3/29/79 Chanute, KS	2.50
C93-94	Octave Chanute set of 2 singles	3.50
C95-96	25¢ Wiley Post attd. 11/20/79 Oklahoma City, OK	2.50
C95-96	Wiley Post set of 2 singles	3.50
C97	31¢ Olympic - High Jump 11/1/79 Col. Springs, CO	2.50
C98	40¢ Philip Mazzei 10/13/80 DC	2.50
C99	28¢ Blanche Scott 12/30/80 Hammondsport, NY	2.50
C100	35¢ Glenn Curtiss 12/30/80 Hammondsport, NY	2.50
C99-100	Scott & Curtiss on one cover	3.50
C101-04	28¢ Olympics attd. 6/17/83 San Antonio, TX	4.00
C101-04	Olympics set of 4 singles	10.00
C105-08	40¢ Olympics attd. 4/8/83 Los Angeles, CA	4.50
C105-08	Olympics set of 4 singles	10.00
C109-12	35¢ Olympics attd. 11/4/83 Colorado Springs, CO	4.50
C109-12	Olympics set of 4 singles	10.00
C113	33¢ Alfred Verville 2/13/85 Garden City, NY	2.50
C114	39¢ Sperry Bros. 2/13/85 Garden City, NY	2.50
C115	44¢ Transpacific Airmail 2/15/85 San Francisco, CA	3.00
C116	44¢ Junipero Serra 8/22/85 San Diego, CA	2.50
C117	44¢ New Sweden, 350th Anniv. 3/29/88 Wilmington, DE	2.50
C117	Joint issue w/Sweden, dual cancel	15.00
C117	Swedish issue only, pane of 6	8.00
C118	45¢ Samuel P. Langley 5/14/88 San Diego, CA	2.50
C119	36¢ Igor Sikorsky 6/23/88 Stratford, CT	2.50
C120	45¢ French Revolution 7/14/89 DC	2.50
C121	45¢ Pre-Columbian Customs 10/12/89 San Juan, PR	2.50
C122-25	45¢ Future Mail Transportation attd. 11/27/89 DC	8.00
C122-25	Set of 4 singles	12.00
C126	$1.80 Future Mail Trans. S/S of 4, imperf. 11/24/89 DC	8.00
C127	45¢ America, Caribbean Coast 10/12/90 Grand Canyon, AZ	2.50
C128	50¢ Harriet Quimby 4/27/91 Plymouth, MI	2.50
C129	40¢ William T. Piper 5/17/91 Denver, CO	2.50
C130	50¢ Antarctic Treaty 6/21/91 DC	2.50
C131	50¢ America 10/12/91 Anchorage, AK	2.50
C133	48¢ Niagara Falls, 5/12/99, Niagara Falls, NY	2.00
C134	40¢ Rio Grande, 7/30/99, Milwaukee, WI	2.00
C135	60¢ Grand Canyon, 1/20/00, Grand Canyon, AZ	2.25
C136	70¢ Nine Mile Prairie, 3/6/01, Lincoln, NE	2.50
	80¢ Mt. McKinley, 4/17/01, Fairbanks, AK	2.50
	60¢ Acadia National Park, 5/30/01, Bar Harbor, ME	2.50

1934-36 AIRMAIL SPECIAL DELIVERY ISSUES

CE1	16¢ Great Seal, blue 8/30/34 Chic., IL (AAMS Conv. Sta.)	30.00
CE2	16¢ Great Seal, red & blue 2/10/36 DC	25.00

Scott #	Description	Uncacheted	Cacheted
	1885-1931 SPECIAL DELIVERY (cont.)		
E1	10¢ Messenger 10/1/85 Any City	12,500.00	...
E12	10¢ Motorcycle,Flat plate,perf.11 7/12/22 DC	375.00	...
E13	15¢ Motorcycle,Flat plate,perf.11 4/11/25 DC	225.00	...
E14	20¢ Truck, Flat plate, perf.11 4/25/25 DC	110.00	...
E15	10¢ Motorcycle, Rotary 11/29/27 DC	95.00	...
E15EE	Electric Eye 9/8/41 DC		25.00
E16	15¢ Motorcycle, Rotary 8/6/31 Easton, PA	2300.00	...
	Motorcycle, Rotary 8/13/31 DC	125.00	...

SPECIAL SERVICE FIRST DAY COVERS

1944-1971 SPECIAL DELIVERY

E17	13¢ Motorcycle 10/30/44	...	10.00
E18	17¢ Motorcycle 10/30/44	...	10.00
E17-18	Motorcycles on one cover	...	15.00
E19	20¢ Post Office Truck, Rotary 11/30/51 DC	...	4.50
E20	20¢ Letter & Hands 10/13/54 Boston, MA	...	2.00
E21	30¢ Letter & Hands 9/3/57 Indpls., IN	...	2.00
E22	45¢ Arrows 11/21/69 New York, NY	...	2.25
E23	60¢ Arrows 5/10/71 Phoenix, AZ	...	2.50

1911 REGISTERED MAIL

F1	10¢ Eagle, blue 12/1/11 Any City	19,500.00	...
	10¢ Eagle, blue 11/28/11 Pre Date	22,000.00	...

1955 CERTIFIED MAIL

FA1	15¢ Postman, red 6/6/55 DC	...	2.00

POSTAGE DUE
1925

J68	½¢ P. Due (4/15/25 EKU) Phil., PA	900.00	
	Rahway, NJ	2200.00	

1959

J88	½¢ Red & Black 6/19/59 Any city	75.00	...
J89	1¢ Red & Black 6/19/59 Any city	75.00	...
J90	2¢ Red & Black 6/19/59 Any city	75.00	...
J91	3¢ Red & Black 6/19/59 Any city	75.00	...
J92	4¢ Red & Black 6/19/59 Any city	75.00	...
J93	5¢ Red & Black 6/19/59 Any city	115.00	...
J94	6¢ Red & Black 6/19/59 Any city	115.00	...
J95	7¢ Red & Black 6/19/59 Any city	115.00	...
J96	8¢ Red & Black 6/19/59 Any city	115.00	...
J97	10¢ Red & Black 6/19/59 Any city	115.00	...
J98	30¢ Red & Black 6/19/59 Any city	115.00	...
J99	50¢ Red & Black 6/19/59 Any city	115.00	...
J100	$1 Red & Black 6/19/59 Any city	125.00	...
J101	$5 Red & Black 6/19/59 Any city	125.00	...

1978-85

J102	11¢ Red & Black 1/2/78 Any city	...	5.00
J103	13¢ Red & Black 1/2/78 Any city	...	5.00
	#J102-103 on one FDC	...	7.50

1978-85

J104	17¢ Red & Black 6/10/85 Any city	...	5.00

1983-95 OFFICIAL STAMPS

O74	3¢ Treasury 7/1/1873 Washington, DC	5,000.00	...
O127	1¢ Eagle 1/12/83 DC	...	1.75
O128	4¢ Eagle 1/12/83 DC	...	1.75
O129	13¢ Eagle 1/12/83 DC	...	1.75
O129A	14¢ Eagle 5/15/85 DC	...	2.00
O130	17¢ Eagle 1/12/83 DC	...	1.75
O132	$1 Eagle 1/12/83 DC	...	5.00
O133	$5 Eagle 1/12/83 DC	...	15.00
O136	22¢ Eagle 5/15/85 DC	...	1.75
O138	(14¢) "D" Eagle 2/4/85 DC	...	1.75
O143	1¢ Eagle, Offset Printing, No ¢ sign 7/5/89 DC	...	1.75
O146	4¢ Official Mail 4/6/91 Oklahoma City, OK	...	1.75
O146A	10¢ Official Mail 10/19/93	...	1.75
O147	19¢ Official Postcard rate 5/24/91 Seattle, WA	...	1.75
O148	23¢ Official 2nd oz. rate 5/24/91 Seattle, WA	...	1.75
O151	$1 Eagle Sept 1993	...	7.00
O154	1¢ Eagle, with ¢ sign 5/9/95 DC	...	1.90

Scott #	Description	Uncacheted	Cacheted
	1983-95 OFFICIAL STAMPS (cont.)		

U.S. First Day Covers

O155	20¢ Eagle, postcard rate 5/9/95 DC	...	1.90
O156	23¢ Eagle, 2nd oz. rate 5/9/95 DC	...	1.90
O154-56	1¢, 20¢, 23¢, 32¢ Coil Combo cover, 5/9/95 DC (1)	...	2.50

1983-95 OFFICIAL COILS

O135	20¢ Eagle, with ¢ sign 1/12/83 DC	...	1.75
	#O127-129,O130-135 on one FDC	...	15.00
O138A	15¢ Official Mail 6/11/88 Corpus Christi, TX	...	1.75
O138B	20¢ Official Mail, No ¢ sign 5/19/88 DC	...	1.75

1988-95 Official Stamps

O139	(22¢) "D" Eagle 2/4/85 DC	...	1.75
O140	(25¢) "E" Official 3/22/88 DC	...	1.75
O141	25¢ Official Mail 6/11/88 Corpus Christi, TX	...	1.75
O144	(29¢) "F" Official 1/22/91 DC	...	1.75
O145	29¢ Official Mail 5/24/91 Seattle, WA	...	1.75
O152	(32¢) "G" Official 12/13/94 DC	...	1.90
O153	32¢ Official Mail 5/9/95 DC	...	1.90
O158	34c Eagle coil, 2/27/01, Washington, DC	...	2.00

POSTAL NOTES

PN1-18	1¢-90¢ Black, cplt. set on 18 forms	750.00	...
PN1	1¢ Black 2/1/45 on cplt 3 part M.O. form, any city	45.00	...
PN2	2¢ 2/1/45 on cplt 3 part M.O. form, any city	45.00	...
PN3	3¢ 2/1/45 on cplt 3 part M.O. form, any city	45.00	...
PN4	4¢ 2/1/45 on cplt 3 part M.O. form, any city	45.00	...
PN5	5¢ 2/1/45 on cplt 3 part M.O. form, any city	45.00	...
PN6	6¢ 2/1/45 on cplt 3 part M.O. form, any city	45.00	...
PN7	7¢ 2/1/45 on cplt 3 part M.O. form, any city	45.00	...
PN8	8¢ 2/1/45 on cplt 3 part M.O. form, any city	45.00	...
PN9	9¢ 2/1/45 on cplt 3 part M.O. form, any city	45.00	...
PN10	10¢ 2/1/45 on cplt 3 part M.O. form, any city ...	45.00	...
PN11	20¢ 2/1/45 on cplt 3 part M.O. form, any city ...	45.00	...
PN12	30¢ 2/1/45 on cplt 3 part M.O. form, any city ...	45.00	...
PN13	40¢ 2/1/45 on cplt 3 part M.O. form, any city ...	45.00	...
PN14	50¢ 2/1/45 on cplt 3 part M.O. form, any city ...	45.00	...
PN15	60¢ 2/1/45 on cplt 3 part M.O. form, any city ...	45.00	...
PN16	70¢ 2/1/45 on cplt 3 part M.O. form, any city ...	45.00	...
PN17	80¢ 2/1/45 on cplt 3 part M.O. form, any city ...	45.00	...
PN18	90¢ 2/1/45 on cplt 3 part M.O. form, any city ...	45.00	...

POSTAL SAVINGS

PS11	10¢ Minuteman, red 5/1/41 Any city .,............	175.00	...

PARCEL POST

Scott #	Description	4th Class (1/1/13)	1st Class (7/1/13)
Q1	1¢ Post Office Clerk, any city	3500.00	2500.00
Q2	2¢ City Carrier, any city	4500.00	2500.00
Q3	3¢ Railway Postal Clerk, any city	...	4500.00
Q4	4¢ Rural Carrier, any city	...	5500.00
Q5	5¢ Mail Train, any city	4000.00	7000.00

1925-28 SPECIAL HANDLING

Scott #	Description	Uncacheted	Cacheted
QE1-3	Set of 3 on one FDC	300.00	
QE1	10¢ Yellow Green 6/25/28 DC	50.00	...
QE2	15¢ Yellow Green 6/25/28 DC	50.00	...
QE3	20¢ Yellow Green 6/25/28 DC	50.00	...
QE4a	25¢ Deep Green 4/11/25 DC	225.00	...

REVENUE STAMPS

R155	2¢ Carmine, 7/1/98	1000.00	...
R733	10¢ Documentary	200.00	...

1981 Duck Stamp First Day Cover
The amazing Ruddy Ducks swim America's lakes and marshes from Atlantic to Pacific coasts.

RW48

FEDERAL DUCK STAMP FIRST DAY COVERS

Scott #	Description	Uncacheted	Cacheted
RW47	$7.50 Mallards 7/1/80 DC		150.00
RW48	$7.50 Ruddy Ducks 7/1/81 DC		75.00
RW49	$7.50 Canvasbacks 7/1/82 DC		55.00
RW50	$7.50 Pintails 7/1/83 DC		55.00
RW51	$7.50 Widgeons 7/2/84 DC		60.00
RW52	$7.50 Cinnamon Teal 7/1/85		45.00
RW53	$7.50 Fulvous Whistling Duck 7/1/86		45.00
RW54	$10.00 Red Head Ducks 7/1/87		45.00
RW55	$10.00 Snow Goose 7/1/88 Any city		45.00
RW56	$12.50 Lesser Scaups 6/30/89 DC		45.00
RW57	$12.50 Black-Bellied Whistling Duck 6/30/90 DC		45.00
RW58	$15.00 King Eiders 6/30/91 DC		45.00
RW59	$15.00 Spectacled Eiders 6/30/92 DC		45.00
RW60	$15.00 Canvasbacks 6/30/93 DC		37.50
RW60	Same, Mound, MN		37.50
RW61	$15.00 Redbreasted Merganser 6/30/94 DC		37.50
RW62	$15.00 Mallard 6/30/95 DC		37.50
RW63	$15.00 Surf Scoter 6/27/96 DC		37.50
RW64	$15.00 Canada Goose 6/21/97 DC		37.50
RW65	$15.00 Barrow's Goldeneye W/A 7/1/98 DC		37.50
RW65A	$15.00 Barrow's Goldeneye S/A 7/1/98		37.50
RW66	$15.00 Greater Scaup W/A 7/1/99 DC		37.50
RW66A	$15.00 Greater Scaup S/A 7/1/99 DC		37.50
RW67	$15.00 Mottled Duck W/A 7/1/00 DC		37.50
RW67A	$15.00 Mottled Duck S/A 7/1/00 DC		37.50
RW68	$15.00 Northern Pintail W/A 6/29/2001		40.00
RW68A	$15.00 Northern Pintail S/A 6/29/2001		40.00

POSTAL STATIONERY FIRST DAY COVERS
Prices are for standard 6¾ size envelopes, unless noted otherwise.

Scott #	Description	Uncacheted	Cacheted
	1925-32		
U436a	3¢ G. Washington, white paper, extra quality 6/16/32 DC, size 5, die 1, wmk. 29	75.00	...
	Size 8, die 1, wmk. 29	18.00	...
U436e	3¢ G. Washington, white paper, extra quality 6/16/32 DC, size 5, die 7, wmk. 29	12.00	30.00
U436f	3¢ G. Washington, white paper, extra quality 6/16/32 DC, size 5, die 9, wmk. 29	12.00	50.00
	Size 12, die 9, wmk. 29	18.00	...
U437a	3¢ G. Washington, amber paper, standard qual. 7/13/32 DC, size 5, wmk. 28	50.00	...
	7/19/32 DC, size 5, wmk. 29, extra qual.	35.00	...
U439	3¢ G. Washington, blue paper, standard qual. 7/13/32, size 5, wmk. 28	40.00	...
	Size 13, die 9, wmk. 28	65.00	...
	9/9/32 DC, size 5, wmk. 28	85.00	...
U439a	3¢ G. Washington, blue paper, extra quality 7/19/32 DC, size 5, die 29	40.00	...
U481	1½¢ G. Wash. 3/19/25 DC, size 5, wmk. 27 .	35.00	...
	Size 8, wmk. 27	70.00	...
	Size 13, wmk. 26	50.00	...
	Size 5, wmk. 27 with Sc#553, 582 & 598	150.00	...
	Size 8, wmk. 27 with Sc#553, 582 & 598	125.00	...
	Size 13, wmk. 26 with Sc#553	60.00	...
U495	1½¢ on 1¢ B. Franklin 6/1/25 DC, size 5	50.00	...
	6/3/25 DC, size 8	65.00	...
	6/2/25 DC, size 13	60.00	...
U515	1½¢ on 1¢ B. Franklin 8/1/25 Des Moines, IA size 5, die 1	50.00	
U521	1½¢ on 1¢ B. Franklin 10/22/25 DC size 5, die 1, watermark 25	100.00	...
U522a	2¢ Liberty Bell 7/27/26 Philadelphia, PA		
	Size 5, wmk. 27	20.00	30.00
	Size 5, wmk. 27 DC	22.50	32.50
	Unofficial city, Size 5, wmk. 27	35.00	45.00

WASHINGTON BICENTENNIAL ISSUE

U523	1¢ Mount Vernon 1/1/32 DC, size 5, wmk. 29	10.00	32.50
	Size 8, wmk. 29	12.50	37.50
	Size 13, wmk. 29	10.00	32.50
U524	1½¢ Mount Vernon 1/1/32 DC, size 5, wmk.29	10.00	32.50

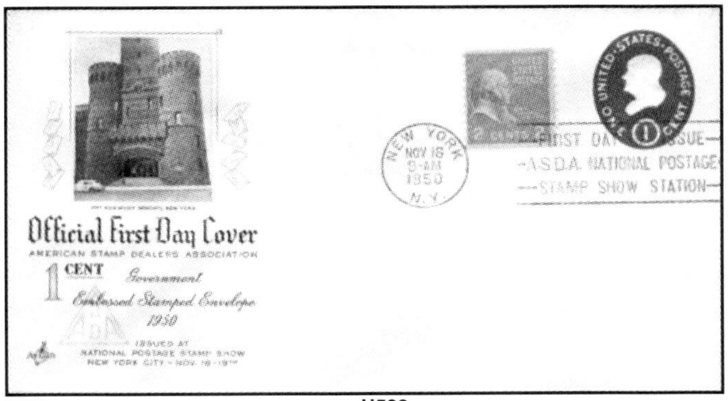

U532

Scott #	Description	Uncacheted	Cacheted
	WASHINGTON BICENTENNIAL ISSUE (cont.)		
	Size 8, wmk. 29	12.50	37.50
	Size 13, wmk. 29	10.00	32.50
U525	2¢ Mount Vernon 1/1/32 DC, size 5, wmk. 29	8.00	30.00
	Size 8, wmk. 29	10.00	30.00
	Size 13, wmk. 29	8.00	30.00
U526	3¢ Mount Vernon 6/16/32 DC, size 5, wmk.29	18.00	40.00
	Size 8, wmk. 29	25.00	80.00
	Size 13, wmk. 29	20.00	60.00
U527	4¢ Mount Vernon 1/1/32 DC, size 5, wmk. 29	30.00	80.00
U528	5¢ Mount Vernon 1/1/32 DC, size 5, wmk. 29	18.00	40.00
	Size 8, wmk. 29	20.00	45.00
	Size 13, wmk. 29	10.00	32.50
	1932-71		
U529	6¢ G. Washington, white paper, 8/18/32		
	Los Angeles, CA, size 8, wmk 29	15.00	...
	8/19/32 DC, size 7, wmk 29	20.00	...
	8/19/32 DC, size 9, wmk 29	20.00	...
U530	6¢ G. Washington, amber paper, 8/18/32		
	Los Angeles, CA, size 8, wmk 29	15.00	...
U530	8/19/32 DC, size 7, wmk 29	20.00	...
	8/19/32 DC, size 9, wmk 29	20.00	...
	size 8, wmk 29 with Sc#723 pair	40.00	...
U531	6¢ G. Washington, blue paper, 8/18/32		
	Los Angeles, CA, size 8, wmk 29	15.00	...
	8/19/32 DC, size 7, wmk 29	20.00	...
	8/19/32 DC, size 9, wmk 29	20.00	...
U532	1¢ Franklin 11/16/50 NY, NY, size 13, wmk 42	...	1.75
U533a	2¢ Wash. 11/17/50 NY, NY, size 13, wmk 42 ...	...	1.75
U534a	3¢ Wash.,die 1 11/18/50 NY,NY,size 13,wmk 42	...	1.75
U534b	3¢ Wash.,die 2 11/19/50 NY,NY,size 8,wmk 42...	4.00	

POSTAL STATIONERY FIRST DAY COVERS

Scott #	Description	Uncacheted	Cacheted
U536	4¢ Franklin 7/31/58 Montpelier, VT	...	1.75
	Size 8, wmk 46	60.00	...
	Size 12, wmk 46	60.00	...
	Size 13, window	25.00	...
	Wheeling, WV, size 6¾, wmk 46, w/#1036a ...	35.00	...
U540	3¢+1¢ G.Washington (U534c) 7/22/58 Kenvil, NJ		
	Size 8, wmk 46, die 3 (earliest known use)	50.00	...
U541	1¼¢ Franklin 6/25/60 Birmingham, AL		1.75
U542	2½¢ Washington 5/28/60 Chicago, IL		1.75
U543	4¢ Pony Express 7/19/60 St. Joseph, MO		1.75
	Sacramento, CA		3.50
U544	5¢ Lincoln 11/19/62 Springfield, IL		1.75
U546	5¢ World's Fair 4/22/64 World's Fair, NY		1.75
U547	1¼¢ Liberty Bell 1/6/65 DC		1.75
	1/8/65 DC, size 10, wmk 48		15.00
U548	1.4¢ Liberty Bell 3/26/68 Springfield, MA		1.75
	3/27/68 DC, size 10, wmk 48		8.00
U548A	1.6¢ Liberty Bell 6/16/69 DC		1.75
	Size 10, wmk 49		1.75
U549	4¢ Old Ironsides 1/6/65 DC		1.75
	1/8/65, window		15.00
	Size 10		15.00
	Size10, window		15.00
U550	5¢ Eagle 1/5/65 Williamsburg, PA		1.75
	1/8/65, window		15.00
	Size 10		15.00
	Size 10, window		15.00
U550a	5¢ Eagle, tagged 8/15/67 DC, wmk 50		3.50
	Dayton, OH		15.00
	Wmk 48		5.00
	Size 10, wmk 48		5.00
	Size 10, wmk 49, Dayton, OH only		7.50
	Size 10, wmk 49, window		5.00
U551	6¢ Liberty 1/4/68 New York, NY		1.75
	1/5/68 DC, window		3.00
	Size 10, wmk 47		3.00
	Size 10, window, wmk 49		3.00
	11/15/68 DC, shiny plastic window, wmk 48		5.00
U552	4 + 2¢ Old Ironsides, revalued 2/5/68 DC, wmk 50		7.50
	Window, wmk 48		7.50

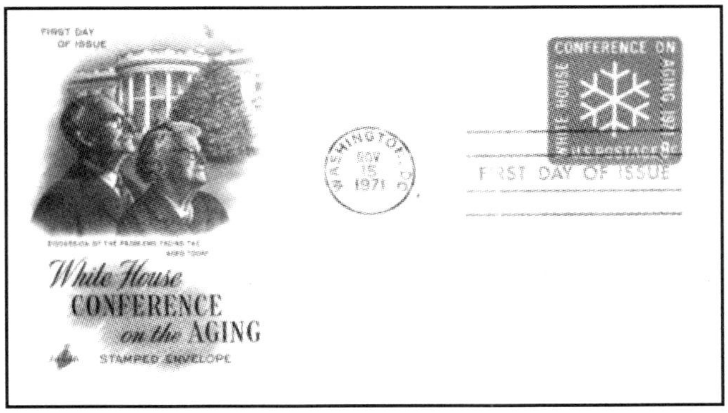

U564

POSTAL STATIONERY FIRST DAY COVERS

Scott #	Description	Cacheted
	Size 10, wmk 47	7.50
	Size 10, window, wmk 49	7.50
U553	5 + 1¢ Eagle, revalued 2/5/68 DC	7.50
	Size 10, window	7.50
U553a	5 + 1¢ Eagle, revalued, tagged 2/5/68 DC, wmk 48	15.00
	Size 10, wmk 47 or 49	7.50
	Size 10, window, wmk 49	7.50
U554	6¢ Moby Dick 6/7/70 New Bedford, MA	1.75
U554	**1st Colonial Cachet**	**30.00**
U555	6¢ Youth Conf. 2/24/71 DC	1.75
U556	1.7¢ Liberty Bell 5/10/71 Balt., MD, wmk 48A	1.75
	5/10/71 DC, wmk 49 with #1394	15.00
	5/10/71 Phoenix, AZ, wmk 48A with #E23	30.00
	5/10/71 DC, with #1283	3.00
	5/11/71 DC, size 10, wmk 47 or 49	12.00
	5/11/71 DC, size 10, wmk 48A	6.00
	1971-78	
U557	8¢ Eagle 5/6/71 Williamsburg, PA, wmk 48A	1.75
	Wmk 49	2.50
	5/7/71 DC, window, wmk 48A	3.50
	Size 10, wmk 49	3.50
	Size 10, window, wmk 47	3.50
U561	6 + 2¢ Liberty Bell, revalued 5/16/71 DC, wmk 47	3.00
	Wmk 48A	25.00
	Wmk 49	4.00
	Window, wmk 47	3.00
	Size 10, wmk 48A	3.00
	Size 10, wmk 49	6.00
	Size 10, window, wmk 47	3.00
	Size 10, window, wmk 49	5.00
U562	6 + 2¢ Youth Conf., revalued 5/16/71 DC, wmk 49	3.00
	Wmk 47	30.00
U563	8¢ Bowling 8/21/71 Milwaukee, WI	2.50
	Size 10	2.00
U564	8¢ Aging Conference 11/15/71 DC	1.75
U565	8¢ Transpo '72 5/2/72 DC, wmk 49	1.75
	Wmk 47	3.00
U566	8 + 2¢ Eagle, revalued 12/1/73 DC	2.50
	Window, wmk 48A **(uncacheted)**	7.50
	Window, wmk 49	4.50
	Size 10, wmk 47	4.50
	Size 10, window, wmk 47	4.50
U567	10¢ Liberty Bell 12/5/73 Phila., PA knife depth 58 mm ..	1.75
	Knife depth 51 mm	1.75
U568	1.8¢ Volunteer 8/23/74 Cincinnati, OH	1.75
	Size 10	1.75
U569	10¢ Tennis 8/31/74 Forest Hills, NY	3.00
	Size 10	3.00
	9/3/74 DC, window	4.00
	Size 10, window	4.00
U571	10¢ Seafaring 10/13/75 Minneapolis, MN	1.75
	Size 10	1.75
U572	13¢ Homemaker 2/2/76 Biloxi, MS	1.75
	Size 10	1.75
U573	13¢ Farmer 3/15/76 New Orleans, LA	1.75
	Size 10	1.75
U574	13¢ Doctor 3/30/76 Dallas, TX	2.50
	Size 10	3.00
U575	13¢ Craftsman 8/6/76 Hancock, MA	1.75
	Size 10	1.75
U576	13¢ Liberty Tree 11/8/75 Memphis, TN	1.75
	Size 10	1.75
U577	2¢ Star & Pinwheel 9/10/76 Hempstead, NY	1.75
	Size 10	1.75
U578	2.1¢ Non-Profit 6/3/77 Houston, TX	1.75
	Size 10	1.75
U579	2.7¢ Non-Profit 7/5/78 Raleigh, NC	1.75
	Size 10	1.75
U580	(15¢) "A" Eagle 5/22/78 Memphis, TN, wmk 47	2.00
	Wmk 48A	1.75
	Window, wmk 47 or 48A	2.50
	Size 10	1.75
	Size 10, window	2.50
	Size 6¾, wmk 48A with sheet, coil & bklt. pane	10.00
U581	15¢ Uncle Sam 6/3/78 Williamsburg, PA	1.75

U.S. First Day Covers

U603

Scott #	Description	Cacheted
	1971-78	
	Window	2.50
	Size 10	1.75
	Size 10, window	2.50
U582	13¢ Bicentennial 10/15/76 Los Angeles, CA, wmk 49	1.75
	Wmk 49, dark green	7.50
	Wmk 48A	3.00
	Size 10	1.75
U583	13¢ Golf 4/7/77 Augusta, GA	7.00
	Size 10	7.50
	4/8/77 DC, Size 6¾, window	9.50
	Size 10, window	9.50
	1977-85	
U584	13¢ Conservation 10/20/77 Ridley Park, PA	1.75
	Window	2.50
	Size 10	1.75
	Size 10, window	2.50
U585	13¢ Development 10/20/77 Ridley Park, PA	1.75
	Window	2.50
	Size 10	1.75
	Size 10, window	2.50
U586	15¢ on 16¢ Surcharged USA 7/28/78 Williamsburg, PA	1.75
	Size 10	1.75
U587	15¢ Auto Racing 9/2/78 Ontario, CA	1.75
	Size 10	1.75
U588	13 + 2¢ Lib. Tree, revalued 11/28/78 Williamsburg, PA	1.75
	Size 10	1.75
	11/29/78 DC, size 6¾, window	2.00
	Size 10, window	2.00
U589	3.1¢ Non-Profit 5/18/79 Denver, CO	1.75
	Size 6¾, window	2.00
	Size 10	1.75
	Size 10, window	2.00
U590	3.5¢ Non-Profit 6/23/80 Williamsburg, PA	1.75
	Size 10	1.75
U591	5.9¢ Non-Profit 2/17/82 Wheeling, WV	1.75
	Size 6¾, window	2.00
	Size 10	1.75
	Size 10, window	2.00
U592	(18¢) "B" Eagle 3/15/81 Memphis, TN	1.75
	Size 6¾, window	2.00
	Size 10	1.75
	Size 10, window	2.00
U593	18¢ Star 4/2/81 Star City, IN	1.75
	Size 10	1.75
U594	(20¢) "C" Eagle 10/11/81 Memphis, TN	1.75
	Size 10	1.75
U595	15¢ Veterinary Med. 7/24/79 Seattle, WA	1.75
	Size 10	1.75
	7/25/79 Seattle, WA, size 6¾, window, (uncacheted)	4.00
	Size 10, window (uncacheted)	4.00
U596	15¢ Olympics 12/10/79 E. Rutherford, NJ	1.75
	Size 10	1.75
U597	15¢ Bicycle 5/16/80 Baltimore, MD	1.75
	Size 10	1.75
U598	15¢ America's Cup 9/15/80 Newport, RI	1.75
	Size 10	1.75
U599	15¢ Honey Bee 10/10/80 Paris, IL	1.75
	Size 10	1.75
U600	18¢ Blinded Veteran 8/13/81 Arlington, VA	1.75
	Size 10	1.75
U601	20¢ Capitol Dome 11/13/81 Los Angeles, CA	1.75
	Size 10	1.75
U602	20¢ Great Seal 6/15/82 DC	1.75
	Size 10	1.75
U603	20¢ Purple Heart 8/6/82 DC	2.00
	Size 10	2.00
U604	5.2¢ Non-Profit 3/21/83 Memphis, TN	1.75
	Size 6¾, window	1.75
	Size 10	1.75
	Size 10, window	1.75
U605	20¢ Paralyzed Vets 8/3/83 Portland, OR	1.75
	Size 10	1.75
U606	20¢ Small Business 5/7/84 DC	1.75
	Size 10	1.75

UC25

Scott #	Description	Cacheted
	1977-85 (cont.)	
U607	(22¢) "D" Eagle 2/1/85 Los Angeles, CA	1.75
	Size 6¾, window	1.75
	Size 10	1.75
	Size 10, window	1.75
U608	22¢ Bison 2/25/85 Bison, SD	1.75
	Size 6¾, window	1.75
	Size 10	1.75
	Size 10, window	1.75
	1985-96	
U609	6¢ Old Ironsides, Non-Profit 5/3/85 Boston, MA	1.75
	Size 10	2.00
U610	8.5¢ Mayflower 12/4/86 Plymouth, MA	1.75
	Size 10	2.00
U611	25¢ Stars 3/26/88 Star, MS	1.75
	Size 10	2.00
U612	9.4¢ USS Constellation 4/12/88 Baltimore, MD	1.75
	Size 10	2.00
U613	25¢ Snowflake 9/8/88 Snowflake, AZ	1.75
U614	25¢ Philatelic Mail Return Env. 3/10/89 Cleveland, OH size 9	1.75
U615	25¢ Security Envelope 7/10/89 DC size 9	3.00
U616	25¢ Love 9/22/89 McLean, VA size 10	3.50
U617	25¢ Space Hologram, World Stamp Expo 12/3/89 DC size 10	1.75
U618	25¢ Football 9/9/90 Green Bay, WI size 10	4.00
U619	29¢ Star 1/24/91 DC	1.75
	Size 10	2.00
U620	11.1¢ Non-Profit 5/3/91 Boxborough, MA	1.75
	Size 10	2.00
	Size 10	2.25
U621	29¢ Love 5/9/91 Honolulu, HI	1.75
	Size 10	2.00
U622	29¢ Magazine Industry 10/7/91 Naples, FL size 10	1.75
U623	29¢ USA & Star, Security Envelope 7/20/91 DC size 10	1.75
U624	29¢ Country Geese 11/8/91 Virginia Beach, VA	1.75
	Size 10 1/21/92	2.00
U625	29¢ Space Station Hologram 1/21/92 Virginia Beach, VA size 10	1.75
U626	29¢ Western Americana 4/10/92 Dodge City, KS size 10	1.75
U627	29¢ Protect the Environment 4/22/92 Chicago, IL size 10	1.75
U628	19.8¢ Bulk-rate, third class 5/18/92 Las Vegas, NV size 10	1.75
U629	29¢ Disabled Americans 7/22/92 DC	1.75
	Size 10	2.00
U630	29¢ Kitten 10/2/93 King of Prussia, PA	1.75
	Size 10	2.00
U631	29¢ Football size 10 9/17/94 Canton, OH	3.00
U632	32¢ Liberty Bell 1/3/95 Williamsburg, VA	2.00
	Size 10	2.00
U633	(32¢) Old Glory 12/13/94 Cancel, released 1/12/95	2.00
U634	(32¢) Old Glory, Security Envelope	2.00
U635	(5¢) Sheep 3/10/95 State College, PA size 10	2.00
U636	(10¢) Eagle 3/10/95 State College, PA size 10	2.00
U637	32¢ Spiral Heart 5/12/95 Lakeville, PA	2.00
U638	32¢ Liberty Bell Security Size 9 5/15/95 DC	2.00
U639	32¢ Space Hologram (Legal size only) 9/22/95 Milwaukee, WI	2.00
U640	32¢ Environment 4/20/96 Chicago, IL size 10	2.00
U641	32¢ Paralympics 5/2/96 DC size 10	2.00
U642	33¢ Flag, 3 colors, 1/11/99, Washington DC	2.00
	Size 10	2.25
U643	33¢ Flag, 2 colors, 1/11/99, Washington DC size 9	2.00
U644	33¢ Love, 1/28/99, Loveland, CO	2.00
	Size 10	2.25
U645	33¢ Lincoln, 6/5/99	2.00
	Size10	2.25
U646	34c Federal Eagle, 1/7/01, Washington, DC size 6-3/4	2.00
	Size 10	2.25
	Size 9, security envelope	2.25
U647	34c Lovebirds, 2/14/01, Lovejoy, GA	2.00
	Size 10	2.25
U648	34c Community Colleges, 2/20/01, Joilet, IL 6-3/4	2.00
	Size 10	2.25

AIRMAIL POSTAL STATIONARY

Scott #	Description	Uncacheted
	1929-71	
UC1	5¢ Blue 1/12/29 DC, size 13	40.00
	2/1/29, DC, size 5	75.00

U.S. First Day Covers

U089

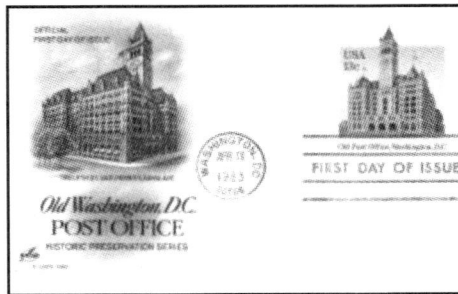

UX99

Scott #	Description 1929-71 (cont.)	Cacheted
	2/1/29, DC, size 8	75.00
UC3	6¢ Orange 7/1/34, size 8	25.00
	Size 13	14.00
UC3	Combo with C19	60.00
UC7	8¢ Olive green 9/26/32, size 8	30.00
	Size 13	11.00
UC7	Combo with C17	60.00
UC10	5¢ on 6¢ Orange 10/1/46 Aiea Hts, HI, die 2a	150.00
UC11	5¢ on 6¢ Orange 10/1/46 Aiea Hts, HI die 2b	200.00
UC12	5¢ on 6¢ Orng. 10/1/46 Aiea Hts, HI, APO & NY, NY die 2c	100.00
UC13	5¢ on 6¢ Orng. 10/1/46 Aiea Hts, HI, die 3	100.00
UC14	5¢ Skymaster 9/25/46 DC	2.25
UC16	10¢ Air Letter 4/29/47 DC	5.00
UC17	5¢ CIPEX, Type 1 5/21/47 New York, NY	2.50
UC17a	5¢ CIPEX, Type 2 5/21/47 New York, NY	2.50
UC18	6¢ Skymaster 9/22/50 Philadelphia, PA	1.75
UC20	6¢ on 5¢ 9/17/51 U.S. Navy Cancel .... (uncacheted)	400.00
UC22	6¢ on 5¢ die 2 (UC15) 8/29/52 Norfolk, VA .. (uncacheted)	35.00
	Cacheted	30.00
UC25	6¢ FIPEX 5/2/56 New York, NY, "short clouds"	1.75
	"Long clouds"	1.75
UC26	7¢ Skymaster 7/31/58 Dayton, OH, "straight left wing"	1.75
	"Crooked left wing"	3.00
	Size 8 ....(uncacheted)	35.00
UC32a	10¢ Jet Air Letter 9/12/58 St. Louis, MO	2.00
UC33	7¢ Jet, blue 11/21/58 New York, NY	1.75
UC34	7¢ Jet, red 8/18/60 Portland, OR	1.75
UC35	11¢ Jet Air Letter 6/16/61 Johnstown, PA	1.75
UC36	8¢ 11/17/62 Chantilly, VA	1.75
UC37	8¢ Jet Triangle 1/7/65 Chicago, IL	1.75
	Size 10	15.00
UC37a	8¢ Jet Triangle, tagged 8/15/67 DC	15.00
	Dayton, OH	15.00
	Size 10	7.50
UC38	11¢ Kennedy Air Letter 5/29/65 Boston, MA	1.75
UC39	13¢ Kennedy Air Letter 5/29/67 Chic., IL	1.75
UC40	10¢ Jet Triangle 1/8/68 Chicago, IL	1.75
	1/9/68 DC, size 10	7.50
UC41	8 + 2¢ revalued UC37 2/5/68 DC	10.00
	Size 10	10.00
UC42	13¢ Human Rights Air Letter 12/3/68 DC	1.75
UC43	11¢ Jet & Circles 5/6/71 Williamsburg, PA	1.75
	Size 10	6.00

POSTAL CARD FIRST DAY COVERS

Scott #	Description 1971-99	Cacheted
UC44	15¢ Birds Air Letter 5/28/71 Chicago, IL	1.75
UC44a	15¢ Birds AEROGRAMME 12/13/71 Phila., PA	1.75
UC45	10¢+1¢ revalued UC40 6/28/71 DC	5.00
	Size 10	10.00
UC46	15¢ Balloon Air Letter 2/10/73 Albuquerque, NM	1.75
UC47	13¢ Dove 12/1/73 Memphis, TN	1.75
	1/5/74, size 10, earliest known use	5.00
UC48	18¢ USA Air Letter 1/4/74 Atlanta, GA	1.75
UC49	17¢ NATO Air Letter 4/4/74 DC	1.75
UC50	22¢ USA Air Letter 1/16/76 Tempe, AZ	1.75
UC51	22¢ USA Air Letter 11/3/78 St. Petersburg, FL	1.75
UC52	22¢ Olympics 12/5/79 Bay Shore, NY	1.75
UC53	30¢ USA 12/29/80 San Francisco, CA	1.75
UC54	30¢ USA 9/21/81 Honolulu, HI	1.75
UC55	30¢ USA & Globe 9/16/82 Seattle, WA	1.75
UC56	30¢ Communications 1/7/83 Anaheim, CA	1.75
UC57	30¢ Olympics 10/14/83 Los Angeles, CA	1.75
UC58	30¢ Landsat Sat. 2/14/85 Goddard Flight Ctr., MD	1.75
UC59	36¢ Travel 5/21/85 DC	1.75
UC60	36¢ Twain / Halley's Comet 12/4/85 DC	1.75
UC61	39¢ Stylized Aerogramme 5/9/88 Miami, FL	1.75
UC62	39¢ Montgomery Blair 11/20/89 DC	1.75
UC63	45¢ Eagle White paper	2.00
UC63	45¢ Eagle 5/17/91 Denver, CO	2.00
UC64	50¢ Thaddeus Lowe – Aerogramme 9/23/95 Tampa, FL	2.25
UC65	60¢ Voyager National Park – Aerogramme 5/15/99	2.50

OFFICIAL POSTAL STATIONERY

Scott #	Description 1983-01	Cacheted
UO73	20¢ Eagle 1/12/83 DC, size 10	2.00
	Window	3.00
UO74	22¢ Eagle 2/26/85 DC, size 10	1.75
UO75	22¢ Savings Bond Env. Window 3/2/87 DC	4.00
UO76	(25¢) Official "E" Savings Bond Env. Window 3/22/52 DC .	2.00
UO77	25¢ Official Mail 4/11/88 DC	1.75
	Window	2.00
UO78	25¢ Savings Bond Env. 4/14/88 DC	1.75
	Window	2.00
UO79	45¢ Passport Envelope (2 oz.) 3/17/90 Springfield, VA	2.00
UO80	65¢ Passport Envelope (3 oz.) 3/17/90 Springfield, VA	2.50
UO81	45¢ "Stars" clear, "Official" 14.5 mm long, 8/10/90 DC	2.00
UO82	65¢ "Stars" clear, "Official" 14.5 mm long, 8/10/90 DC	2.50
UO83	(29¢) "F" Savings Bond Env. 1/22/91 DC	1.75
UO84	29¢ Official Mail 4/6/91 Oklahoma City, OK	1.75
UO85	29¢ Savings Bond Env. 4/17/91 DC	1.75
UO86	52¢ U.S. Consular Service, Passport Env. 7/10/92 DC	2.25
UO87	75¢ U.S. Consular Service, Passport Env. 7/10/92 DC	2.75
UO88	32¢ Eagle (Legal size only) 5/9/95 DC	2.00
UO89	33¢ Eagle 2/22/99 DC	2.00
UO90	34c Eagle size 10, 2/27/01, Washington, DC	2.25

POSTAL CARD FIRST DAY COVERS

Scott #	Description 1873-1966	Uncacheted	Cacheted
UX1	1¢ Liberty 5/13/1873 Boston, NY, or DC	3000.00	...
UX37	3¢ McKinley 2/1/26 DC	250.00	...
UX38	2¢ Franklin 11/16/51 New York, NY	...	1.75
UX39	2¢ on 1¢ Jefferson (UX27) 1/1/52 DC	12.50	25.00
UX40	2¢ on 1¢ Lincoln (UX28) 3/22/52 DC	100.00	250.00
UX43	2¢ Lincoln 7/31/52 DC	...	1.75
UX44	2¢ FIPEX 5/4/56 New York, NY	...	1.75
UX45	4¢ Liberty 11/16/56 New York, NY	...	1.75
UX46	3¢ Liberty 8/1/58 Philadelphia, PA	...	1.75
UX46a	Missing "I"/"N God We Trust"	175.00	250.00
UX46c	Precancelled 9/15/61	50.00	...
UX48	4¢ Lincoln 11/19/62 Springfield, IL	...	1.75
UX48a	4¢ Lincoln, tagged 6/25/66 Bellevue, OH	35.00	50.00
	7/6/66 DC	4.50	10.00
	Bellevue, OH	20.00	35.00
	Cincinnati, OH	15.00	20.00
	Cleveland, OH	18.00	30.00
	Columbus, OH	20.00	35.00
	Dayton, OH	10.00	18.00
	Indianapolis, IN	20.00	35.00
	Louisville, KY	20.00	35.00
	Overlook, OH	15.00	20.00
	Toledo, OH	20.00	35.00

Scott #	Description 1963-87	Cacheted
UX49	7¢ USA 8/30/63 New York, NY	1.75
UX50	4¢ Customs 2/22/64 DC	1.75
UX51	4¢ Social Security 9/26/64 DC	1.75
	Official Gov't. Printed Cachet	12.00
	Blue hand cancel and gov't. cachet	20.00
UX52	4¢ Coast Guard 8/4/65 Newburyport, MA	1.75
UX53	4¢ Census Bureau 10/21/65 Phila, PA	1.75
UX54	8¢ USA 12/4/67 DC	1.75
UX55	5¢ Lincoln 1/4/68 Hodgenville, KY	1.75
UX56	5¢ Women Marines 7/26/68 San Fran., CA	1.75
UX57	5¢ Weathervane 9/1/70 Fort Myer, VA	1.75
UX58	6¢ Paul Revere 5/15/71 Boston, MA	1.75
UX59	10¢ USA 6/10/71 New York, NY	1.75
UX60	6¢ America's Hospitals 9/16/71 NY, NY	1.75
UX61	6¢ US Frigate Constellation 6/29/72 Any City	1.75
UX62	6¢ Monument Valley 6/29/72 Any City	1.75
UX63	6¢ Gloucester, MA 6/29/72 Any City	1.75
UX64	6¢ John Hanson 9/1/72 Baltimore, MD	1.75
UX65	6¢ Liberty Centenary 9/14/73 DC	1.75
UX66	8¢ Samuel Adams 12/16/73 Boston, MA	1.75
UX67	12¢ Ship's Figurehead 1/4/74 Miami, FL	1.75
UX68	7¢ Charles Thomson 9/14/75 Bryn Mawr, PA	1.75
UX69	9¢ J. Witherspoon 11/10/75 Princeton, NJ	1.75
UX70	9¢ Caeser Rodney 7/1/76 Dover, DE	1.75
UX71	9¢ Galveston Court House 7/20/77 Galveston, TX	1.75
UX72	9¢ Nathan Hale 10/14/77 Coventry, CT	1.75
UX73	10¢ Music Hall 5/12/78 Cincinnati, OH	1.75

U.S. First Day Covers

UX220

1963-87 (cont.)

Scott #	Description	Cacheted
UX74	(10¢) John Hancock 5/19/78 Quincy, MA	1.75
UX75	10¢ John Hancock 6/20/78 Quincy, MA	1.75
UX76	14¢ Coast Guard Eagle 8/4/78 Seattle, WA	1.75
UX77	10¢ Molly Pitcher 9/8/78 Freehold, NJ	1.75
UX78	10¢ George R. Clark 2/23/79 Vincennes, IN	1.75
UX79	10¢ Casimir Pulaski 10/11/79 Savannah, GA	1.75
UX80	10¢ Olympics 9/17/79 Eugene, OR	1.75
UX81	10¢ Iolani Palace 10/1/79 Honolulu, HI	2.00
UX82	14¢ Olympic Skater 1/15/80 Atlanta, GA	1.75
UX83	10¢ Mormon Temple 4/5/80 Salt Lake City, UT	1.75
UX84	10¢ Count Rochambeau 7/11/80 Newport, RI	1.75
UX85	10¢ King's Mountain 10/7/80 King's Mountain, NC	1.75
UX86	19¢ Golden Hinde 11/21/80 San Rafael, CA	1.75
UX87	10¢ Battle of Cowpens 1/17/81 Cowpens, SC	1.75
UX88	(12¢) "B" Eagle 3/15/81 Memphis, TN	1.75
UX89	12¢ Isaiah Thomas 5/5/81 Worcester, MA	1.75
UX90	12¢ Nathaniel Greene 9/8/81 Eutaw Springs, SC	1.75
UX91	12¢ Lewis & Clark 9/23/81 St. Louis, MO	1.75
UX92	(13¢) Robert Morris 10/11/81 Memphis, TN	1.75
UX93	13¢ Robert Morris 11/10/81 Phila., PA	1.75
UX94	13¢ Frances Marion 4/3/82 Marion, SC	1.75
UX95	13¢ LaSalle 4/7/82 New Orleans	1.75
UX96	13¢ Philadelphia Academy 6/18/82 Philadelphia, PA	1.75
UX97	13¢ St. Louis P.O. 10/14/82 St. Louis, MO	1.75
UX98	13¢ Oglethorpe 2/12/83 Savannah, GA	1.75
UX99	13¢ Old Washington P.O. 4/19/83 DC	1.75
UX100	13¢ Olympics - Yachting 8/5/83 Long Beach, CA	1.75
UX101	13¢ Maryland 3/25/84 St. Clemente Island, MD	1.75
UX102	13¢ Olympic Torch 4/30/84 Los Angeles, CA	1.75
UX103	13¢ Frederic Baraga 6/29/84 Marquette, MI	1.75
UX104	13¢ Rancho San Pedro 9/16/84 Compton, CA	1.75
UX105	(14¢) Charles Carroll 2/1/85 New Carrollton, MD	1.75
UX106	14¢ Charles Carroll 2/1/85 Annapolis, MD	1.75
UX107	25¢ Flying Cloud 2/27/85 Salem, MA	1.75
UX108	14¢ George Wythe 6/20/85 Williamsburg, VA	1.75
UX109	14¢ Settling of CT 4/18/86 Hartford, CT	1.75
UX110	14¢ Stamp Collecting 5/23/86 Chicago, IL	1.75
UX111	14¢ Frances Vigo 5/24/86 Vincennes, IN	1.75
UX112	14¢ Rhode Island 6/26/86 Providence, RI	1.75
UX113	14¢ Wisconsin Terr. 7/3/86 Mineral Point, WI	1.75
UX114	14¢ National Guard 12/12/86 Boston, MA	1.75
UX115	14¢ Steel Plow 5/22/87 Moines, IL	1.75
UX116	14¢ Constitution Convention 5/25/87 Philadelphia, PA	1.75
UX117	14¢ Flag 6/14/87 Baltimore, MD	1.75
UX118	14¢ Pride in America 9/22/87 Jackson, WY	1.75
UX119	14¢ Historic Preservation 9/28/87 Timberline, OR	1.75

1988-91

Scott #	Description	Cacheted
UX120	15¢ America the Beautiful 3/28/88 Buffalo, NY	1.75
UX121	15¢ Blair House 5/4/88 DC	1.75
UX122	28¢ Yorkshire 6/29/88 Mystic, CT	1.75
UX123	15¢ Iowa Territory 7/2/88 Burlington, IA	1.75
UX124	15¢ Northwest/Ohio Territory 7/15/88 Marietta, OH	1.75
UX125	15¢ Hearst Castle 9/20/88 San Simeon, CA	1.75
UX126	15¢ Federalist Papers 10/27/88 New York, NY	1.75
UX127	15¢ The Desert 1/13/89 Tucson, AZ	1.75
UX128	15¢ Healy Hall 1/23/89 DC	1.75
UX129	15¢ The Wetlands 3/17/89 Waycross, GA	1.75
UX130	15¢ Oklahoma Land Run 4/17/89 Guthrie, OK	1.75
UX131	21¢ The Mountains 5/5/89 Denver, CO	1.75
UX132	15¢ The Seashore 6/19/89 Cape Hatteras, NC	1.75
UX133	15¢ The Woodlands 8/26/89 Cherokee, NC	1.75
UX134	15¢ Hull House 9/16/89 Chicago, IL	1.75
UX135	15¢ Independence Hall 9/25/89 Philadelphia, PA	1.75
UX136	15¢ Baltimore Inner Harbor 10/7/89 Baltimore, MD	1.75
UX137	15¢ Manhattan Skyline 11/8/89 New York, NY	1.75
UX138	15¢ Capitol Dome 11/26/89 DC	1.75
UX139-42	15¢ Cityscapes sheet of 4 diff.views,rouletted 12/1/89 DC	7.00
UX139-42	Cityscapes, set of 4 different, rouletted	8.00
UX143	(15¢) White House, Picture PC (cost 50¢) 11/30/89 DC	1.75
UX144	(15¢) Jefferson Mem. Pict. PC (cost 50¢) 12/2/89 DC	1.75
UX145	15¢ American Papermaking 3/13/90 New York, NY	1.75
UX146	15¢ Literacy 3/22/90 DC	1.75
UX147	(15¢) Geo. Bingham Pict.PC (cost 50¢) 5/4/90 St. Louis, MO	1.75
UX148	15¢ Isaac Royall House 6/16/90 Medford, MA	1.75
UX150	15¢ Stanford University 9/30/90 Stanford, CA	1.75
UX151	15¢ DAR Mem., Continental/Constitution Hall 10/11/91 DC	1.75

1988-91 (cont.)

Scott #	Description	Cacheted
UX152	15¢ Chicago Orchestra Hall 10/19/91 Chicago, IL	1.75
UX153	19¢ Flag 1/24/91 DC	1.75
UX154	19¢ Carnegie Hall 4/1/91 New York, NY	1.75
UX155	19¢ "Old Red" Bldg., U.of Texas 6/14/91 Galveston, TX	1.75
UX156	19¢ Bill of Rights Bicent. 9/25/91 Notre Dame, IN	1.75
UX157	19¢ Notre Dame Admin. Bldg. 10/15/91 Notre Dame, IN	1.75
UX158	30¢ Niagara Falls 8/21/91 Niagara Falls, NY	1.75
UX159	19¢ Old Mill, Univ. of Vermont 10/29/91 Burlington, VT	1.75

1992-01

Scott #	Description	Cacheted
UX160	19¢ Wadsworth Atheneum 1/16/92 Hartford, CT	1.75
UX161	19¢ Cobb Hall, Univ. of Chicago 1/23/92 Chicago, IL	1.75
UX162	19¢ Waller Hall 2/1/92 Salem, OR	1.75
UX163	19¢ America's Cup 5/6/92 San Diego, CA	1.75
UX164	19¢ Columbia River Gorge 5/9/92 Stevenson, WA	1.75
UX165	19¢ Great Hall, Ellis Island 5/11/92 Ellis Island, NY	1.75
UX166	19¢ National Cathedral 1/6/93 DC	1.75
UX167	19¢ Wren Building 2/8/93 Williamsville, VA	1.75
UX168	19¢ Holocaust Memorial 3/23/93 DC	2.25
UX169	19¢ Ft. Recovery 6/13/93 Fort Recovery, OH	1.75
UX170	19¢ Playmaker's Theater 9/14/93 Chapel Hill, NC	1.75
UX171	19¢ O'Kane Hall 9/17/93 Worcester, MA	1.75
UX172	19¢ Beecher Hall 10/9/93 Jacksonville, IL	1.75
UX173	19¢ Massachusetts Hall 10/14/93 Brunswick, ME	1.75
UX174	19¢ Lincoln Home 2/12/94 Springfield, IL	1.75
UX175	19¢ Myers Hall 3/11/94 Springfield, OH	1.75
UX176	19¢ Canyon de Chelly 8/11/94 Canyon de Chelly, AZ	1.75
UX177	19¢ St. Louis Union Station 9/1/94 St. Louis, MO	1.75
UX178-97	19¢ Legends of the West, set of 20 10/18/94 Tucson, AZ Lawton, OK or Laramie, WY	35.00
	19¢ Legends of the West, Combo w/2689a-t	50.00
UX198	20¢ Red Barn 1/3/95 Williamsburg, PA	1.75
UX199	(20¢) "G" Old Glory, 12/13/94 cancel, released 1/12/95	1.75
UX200-19	20¢ Civil War Set of 20 6/29/95 Gettysburg, PA	35.00
	20¢ Civil War, combo w/2975a-t	50.00
UX220	20¢ Clipper Ship 9/23/95 Hunt Valley, MD	1.75
UX221-40	20¢ Comic Strips Set of 20 10/1/95 Boca Raton, FL	35.00
UX241	20¢ Winter Farm Scene 2/23/96 Watertown, NY	1.75
UX242-61	20¢ Olympics, Set of 20 5/2/96 DC	35.00
UX262	20¢ McDowell Hall, Hist.Pres.Series 6/1/96, Anapolis, Md	1.75
UX263	20¢ Alexander Hall, Hist.Pres.Series 9/20/96, Princeton, NJ	1.75
UX264-78	20¢ Endangered Species, Set of 15, 10/2/96, San Diego, Ca.	35.00
UX279	20¢ Love Swan Stamp 2/4/97, L.A., Ca.	1.75
UX280	20¢ City College of NY, Hist.Pres.Series, NY,NY 5/7/97	1.75
UX281	32¢ Bugs Bunny, 5/22/97, Burbank, CA	2.00
UX282	20¢ Pacific '97, Golden Gate in Daylight 6/2/97 S.F.,Ca.	1.75
UX283	40¢ Pacific '97, Golden Gate at Sunset 6/2/97 S. F., Ca.	1.75
UX284	20¢ Fort McHenry, Hist. Pres. Series 9/97	1.75
UX285-89	20¢ Classic Movie Monsters, 9/30/97, Set of 5, Universal City, CA	9.00
UX290	20¢ University of Mississippi, 4/20/98, Univ. of Ms	1.75
UX291	20¢ Tweety & Sylvester, 4/27/98 NY, NY	2.00
UX292	20¢ Girard College, 5/1/98. Phil. PA	1.75
UX293–96	20¢ Tropical Birds, Set of 4, 7/29/98, Ponce, PR	8.50
UX297	20¢ Ballet, 9/16/98, NY, NY	2.00
UX298	20¢ Northeastern Univ., 10/3/98, Boston, MA	1.90
UX299	20¢ Brandies Univ. 10/17/98, Waltham, MA	1.90
UX300	20¢ Love, 1/28/99, Loveland, CO	2.25
UX301	20¢ Univ. of Wisconsin, 2/5/99, Madison, IW	1.90
UX302	20¢ Washington & Lee Univ., 2/11/99, Lexington, VA	1.90
UX303	20¢ Redwood Library & Anthenaeum, 3/11/99	1.90
UX304	20¢ Daffy Duck, 4/16/99	2.25
UX305	20¢ Mount Vernon, 5/14/99, Mount Vernon, VA	1.75
UX306	20¢ Block Island Lighthouse, 7/24/99, Block Is., RI	1.75
UX307-11	20¢ All Aboard!, set of 5, 8/26/99, Cleveland, OH	10.00
UX307-11	Combo w/#3333-7	15.00
UX312	20¢ Univ. of Utah, 2/28/00, Salt Lake City, UT	1.75
UX313	20¢ Ryman Auditorium, 3/18/00, Nashville, TN	1.75
UX314	20¢ Wile E. Coyote & Roadrunner	2.25
UX314	20¢ Coyote & Roadrunner combo w/stamp	3.00
UX315	20¢ Adoption picture card, 5/10/00	2.25
	20¢ Adoption combo w/stamp	3.00
UX316	20¢ Middlebury College 5/19/00	1.75
UX317-36	20c Stars & Stripes, 6/14/00, Baltimore, MD set of 20	45.00
	Combo w/3403a-t, set of 20	55.00
UX337-56	20c Legends of Baseball, 7/6/00, Atlanta, GA set of 20	50.00
	Combo w/3408a-t, set of 20	60.00
UX357-60	20c Holiday Deer, 10/12/00, Rudolph, WI set of 4	10.00
	Combo w/3356-59 set of 4	12.00
UX361	20c Yale University,, 3/30/01, New Haaven, CT	2.00
	20c University ofSouth Carolina, 4/26/01, Columbia, SC	2.00
	20c Northwestern University, 4/28/01, Evanston, IL	2.00
	20c University of Portland, 5/1/01, Portland, OR	2.00

AIRMAIL POST CARDS
1949-01

Scott #	Description	Cacheted
UXC1	4¢ Eagle 1/10/49 DC, round "O" in January 10	2.00
	Oval "O" in January 10	5.00
UXC2	5¢ Eagle 7/31/58 Wichita, KS	2.00
UXC3	5¢ Eagle w/border 6/18/60 Minneapolis, MN	2.00
	"Thin dividing line" at top	5.00
UXC4	6¢ Bald Eagle 2/15/63 Maitland, FL	2.00
UXC5	11¢ Visit the USA 5/27/66 DC	1.75
UXC6	6¢ Virgin Islands 3/31/67 Charlotte Amalie, VI	1.75
UXC7	6¢ Boy Scouts 8/4/67 Farragut State Park, ID	1.75
UXC8	13¢ Visit the USA 9/8/67 Detroit, MI	1.75

U.S. First Day Covers

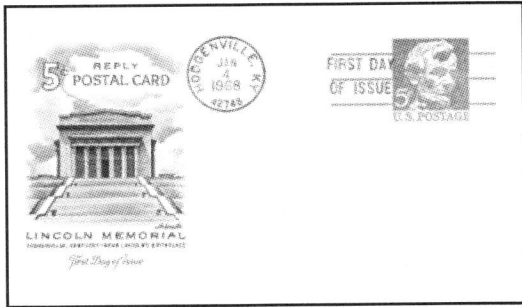

UY21

CHRISTMAS SEAL FIRST DAY COVERS

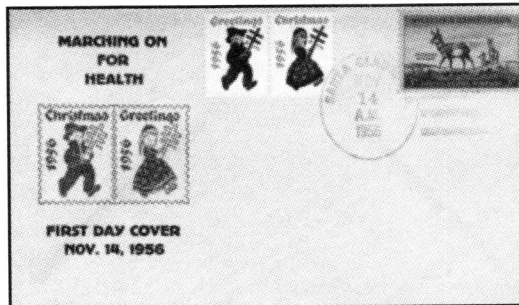

Beginning in 1936, Santa Claus, Indiana has been used as the First Day City of U.S. National Christmas Seals. In 1936 the Postmaster would not allow the seal to be tied to the front of the cover and seals for that year are usually found on the back. Since 1937, all seals were allowed to be tied on the front of the FDC's. **All prices are for cacheted FDC's.**

AIRMAIL POST CARDS
1949-01 (cont.)

Scott #	Description	Cacheted
UXC9	8¢ Eagle 3/1/68 New York, NY	1.75
UXC9a	8¢ Eagle, tagged 3/19/69 DC	15.00
UXC10	9¢ Eagle 5/15/71 Kitty Hawk, NC	1.75
UXC11	15¢ Visit the USA 6/10/71 New York, NY	1.75
UXC12	9¢ Grand Canyon 6/29/72 any city	1.75
UXC13	15¢ Niagara Falls 6/29/72 any city	1.75
UXC13a	Address side blank .... (uncacheted)	600.00
UXC14	11¢ Modern Eagle 1/4/74 State College, PA	1.75
UXC15	18¢ Eagle Weathervane 1/4/74 Miami, FL	1.75
UXC16	21¢ Angel Weathervane 12/17/75 Kitty Hawk, NC	1.75
UXC17	21¢ Jenny 9/16/78 San Diego, CA	1.75
UXC18	21¢ Olympic-Gymnast 12/1/79 Fort Worth, TX	1.75
UXC19	28¢ First Transpacific Flight 1/2/81 Wenatchee, WA	1.75
UXC20	28¢ Soaring 3/5/82 Houston, TX	1.75
UXC21	28¢ Olympic-Speedskating 12/29/83 Milwaukee, WI	1.75
UXC22	33¢ China Clipper 2/15/85 San Fran., CA	1.75
UXC23	33¢ AMERIPEX '86 2/1/86 Chicago, IL	1.75
UXC24	36¢ DC-3 5/14/88 San Diego, CA	2.00
UXC25	40¢ Yankee Clipper 6/28/91	2.00
UXC26	50¢ Eagle 8/24/95 St. Louis, MO	2.25
UXC27	55¢ Mt. Ranier, 5/15/99	2.25
UXC28	70c Badlands National Park, 2/22/01, Wall, SD	2.50

POSTAL REPLY CARDS
1892-1956

Scott #	Description	Uncacheted	Cacheted
UY1	1¢ + 1¢ U.S. Grant 10/25/1892 any city	350.00	...
UY12	3¢ + 3¢ McKinley 2/1/26 any city	250.00	...
UY13	2¢ + 2¢ Washington 12/29/51 DC	...	1.75
UY14	2¢ on 1¢ + 2¢ G. Wash. 1/1/52 any city	50.00	75.00
UY16	4¢ + 4¢ Liberty 11/16/56 New York, NY	...	1.75
UY16a	Message card printed on both halves	75.00	100.00
UY16b	Reply card printed on both halves	50.00	75.00

POSTAL CARD FIRST DAY COVERS
1958-75

UY17	3¢ + 3¢ Liberty 7/31/58 Boise, ID	1.75
UY18	4¢ + 4¢ Lincoln 11/19/62 Springfield, IL	1.75
UY18a	4¢ + 4¢ Lincoln, Tagged 3/7/67 Dayton, OH	500.00
UY19	7¢ + 7¢ USA 8/30/63 New York, NY	1.75
UY20	8¢ + 8¢ USA 12/4/67 DC	1.75
UY21	5¢ + 5¢ Lincoln 1/4/68 Hodgenville, KY	1.75
UY22	6¢ + 6¢ Paul Revere 5/15/71 Boston, MA	1.75
UY23	6¢ + 6¢ John Hanson 9/1/72 Baltimore, MD	1.75
UY24	8¢ + 8¢ Samuel Adams 12/16/73 Boston, MA	1.75
UY25	7¢ + 7¢ Charles Thomson 9/14/75 Bryn Mawr, PA	1.75
UY26	9¢ + 9¢ John Witherspoon 11/10/75 Princeton, NJ	1.75

1976-95

UY27	9¢ + 9¢ Caeser Rodney 7/1/76 Dover, DE	1.75
UY28	9¢ + 9¢ Nathan Hale 10/14/77 Coventry, CT	1.75
UY29	(10¢ + 10¢) John Hancock 5/19/78 Quincy, MA	2.50
UY30	10¢ + 10¢ John Hancock 6/20/78 Quincy, MA	1.75
UY31	(12¢ + 12¢) "B" Eagle 3/15/81 Memphis, TN	1.75
UY32	12¢ + 12¢ Isaiah Thomas 5/5/81 Worcester, MA	1.75
UY32a	"Small die"	5.00
UY33	(13¢ + 13¢) Robert Morris 10/11/81 Memphis, TN	1.75
UY34	13¢ + 13¢ Robert Morris 11/10/81 Philadelphia, PA	1.75
UY35	(14¢ + 14¢) Charles Carroll 2/1/85 New Carrollton, MD	1.75
UY36	14¢ + 14¢ Charles Carroll 3/6/85 Annapolis, MD	1.75
UY37	14¢ + 14¢ George Wythe 6/20/85 Williamsburg, PA	1.75
UY38	14¢ + 14¢ American Flag 9/1/87 Baltimore, MD	1.75
UY39	15¢ + 15¢ America the Beautiful 7/11/88 Buffalo, NY	1.75
UY40	19¢ + 19¢ American Flag 3/27/91 DC	2.00
UY41	20¢+20¢ Red Baron 1/3/95 Williamsburg, PA	2.25
UY42	20¢+20¢ Block Island, 11/10/99, Block Island, RI	2.25

OFFICIAL POSTAL CARDS
1983-95

UZ2	13¢ Eagle 1/12/83 DC	1.75
UZ3	14¢ Eagle 2/26/85 DC	1.75
UZ4	15¢ Eagle (4 colors) 6/10/88 New York, NY	1.75
UZ5	19¢ Eagle 5/24/91 Seattle, WA	1.75
UZ6	20¢ Eagle 5/9/95 DC	1.75

"POSTAL BUDDY" CARDS

PB1	15¢ 7/5/90 Merriifield, VA	2.50
PB2	19¢ 2/3/91 Any city	...
PB3	19¢ Stylized Flag 11/13/92 Any city	27.50

YEAR	PRICE	YEAR	PRICE
1936 (500 processed) ...	55.00	1968	10.00
1937	35.00	1969	10.00
1938	35.00	1970	6.00
1939	35.00	1971	6.00
1940	35.00	1972	6.00
1941	30.00	1973	6.00
1942	40.00	1974	6.00
1943	25.00	1975	7.00
1944	30.00	1976	10.00
1945	12.00	1977	6.00
1946	12.00	1978	10.00
1947	12.00	1979	6.00
1948	20.00	1980	5.00
1949	12.00	1981	5.00
1950	12.00	1982	5.00
1951	15.00	1983	10.00
1952	12.00	1984	5.00
1953	10.00	1985	5.00
1954	10.00	1986	5.00
1955	10.00	1987	5.00
1956	10.00		

YEAR	PERF	IMPERF
1957	10.00	
1958	10.00	
1959	10.00	
1960	20.00	
1961	10.00	
1962	10.00	
1963	10.00	
1964	40.00	
1965	10.00	
1966	10.00	
1967	20.00	
1968	10.00	

YEAR	PERF	IMPERF
1988	7.50	30.00
1989	7.50	30.00
1990	5.00	20.00
1991	5.00	20.00
1991-Foil	10.00	...
1992	7.50	35.00
1993	5.00	20.00
1994	5.00	20.00
1995	5.00	20.00
1996	5.00	20.00
1997	5.00	20.00
1998	5.00	20.00
1999	5.00	20.00

World War II & Korean War Patriotic Covers

3/8/45

The listing below features the dates of significant patriotic events of World War II. The values listed are for standard size covers bearing related, printed cachets, and cancelled on the appropriate date.

Cachets produced by Minkus and others, which feature general patriotic themes such as "Win the War" are valued at 75¢ unused and $2.00 used.

Covers with Naval cancels, when available, usually sell for twice the listed prices.

WORLD WAR II EVENT	CACHETED COVER
Pearl Harbor 12/7/41	100.00
U.S. Declares War on Japan 12/8/41	75.00
Germany and Italy Declare War on U.S. 12/11/41	75.00
U.S. Declares War on Germany and Italy 12/11/41	75.00
Churchill Arrives at the White House 12/22/41	60.00
Manila and Cavite Fall 1/2/42	60.00
Roosevelt's Diamond Jubilee Birthday 1/30/42	60.00
Singapore Surrenders 2/15/42	60.00
Japan Takes Java 3/10/42	60.00
Marshall Arrives in London 4/8/42	60.00
Dedication of MacArthur Post Office 4/15/42	60.00
Doolittle Air Raid on Tokyo 4/18/42	60.00
Fort Mills Corregidor Island Surrenders 5/6/42	60.00
Madagascar Occupied by U.S. 5/9/42	60.00
Mexico at War with Axis 5/23/42	60.00
Bremen Bombed 6/30/42	60.00
Bombing of Cologne 6/6/42	60.00
Japan Bombs Dutch Harbor, AK 6/3/42	60.00
Six German Spies Sentenced to Death 8/7/42	60.00
Brazil at War 8/22/42	60.00
Battle of El Alamein 10/23/42	70.00
Operation Torch (Invasion of North Africa) 11/8/42	50.00
Gas Rationing in U.S. 12/1/42	50.00
The Casablanca Conference 1/14/43	50.00
The Casablanca Conference (You must remember this!) 1/22/43	40.00
Russia takes Rostov 2/14/43	35.00
Point Rationing 3/1/43	50.00
Restoration Day, Honolulu 3/10/43	50.00
Battle of the Bismarck Sea 3/13/43	40.00
U.S. Planes Bomb Naples 4/5/43	50.00
Bizerte & Tunis Occupied 5/8/43	40.00
Invasion of Attu 5/11/43	40.00
U.S. Invades Rendova Island 6/30/43	35.00
Allies Occupy Tobriand + Woodlark 7/1/43	35.00
Siciliy Invaded 7/14/43	35.00
Yanks Bomb Rome 7/19/43	35.00
Mussolini Kicked Out 7/25/43	35.00
Fascist Regime is Dissolved 7/28/43	40.00
The Quebec Conference 8/14/43	35.00
Sicily Encircled 8/17/43	35.00
Japanese Flee From Kiska 8/21/43	40.00
Italy Invaded 9/3/43	40.00
Italy Surrenders 9/8/43	40.00
3rd War Loan Drive 9/9/43	35.00
Mussolini Escapes 9/18/43	50.00
Naples Captured 10/1/43	35.00
U.S. Drives Germans out of Naples 10/2/43	35.00
Italy Declares War on Germany 10/13/43	35.00
Hull, Eden, Stalin Conference 10/25/43	35.00
U.S. Government takes over Coal Mines 11/3/43	40.00
The Cairo Meeting 11/25/43	40.00
The Teheran Meeting 11/28/43	40.00
Roosevelt, Churchill, Kai-Shek at Cairo 12/2/43	40.00
FDR, Stalin, Churchill Agree on 3 fronts 12/4/43	40.00
2nd Anniversary of Pearl Harbor 12/7/43	40.00
US Runs the Railroads 12/28/43	40.00
UN Declaration Signed in Washington 1/1/44	35.00
Soviets Reach Polish Border 1/4/44	35.00
Marshalls Invaded 2/4/44	35.00
Yanks Take Over Kwajalein 2/5/44	35.00
Truk Attacked 2/18/44	35.00
U.S. Captures Cassino 3/16/44	35.00
Last Day of 2 Cent Rate 3/25/44	
Last Day of 2 Cent Rate and First	
Day of 3 cent Rate-Honolulu 3/26/44	35.00
Title of Military Governor	

WORLD WAR II EVENT	CACHETED COVER
Invasion of Dutch New Guinea 4/24/44	35.00
Sevastopol Seige 5/11/44	35.00
Yanks Finally Capture Cassino 5/18/44	40.00
Rome Falls 6/4/44	35.00
D-Day Single Face Eisenhower 6/6/44	100.00
D-Day Double Face Eisenhower 6/6/44	35.00
D-Day: Invasion of Normandy 6/6/44	35.00
5th War Loan Drive 6/12/44	40.00
B29's Bomb Japan 6/15/44	35.00
Yanks Land on Siepan 6/17/44	35.00
Cherbourg Surrenders 6/27/44	40.00
Paris Revolts 6/23/44	35.00
Caen Falls to Allies 7/10/44	35.00
Relinquished Territory of Hawaii 7/21/44	50.00
Marines Invade Guam 7/21/44	35.00
Waikiki Conference-Honolulu 7/28/44	40.00
Yanks Enter Brest, etc. 8/7/44	35.00
Yanks Capture Guam 8/10/44	40.00
Roosevelt and Mac Aruther in Hawaii 8/10/44	40.00
U.S. Bombs Phillipines 8/10/44	35.00
Alies Invade Southern France 8/15/44	40.00
Invasion of Southern France 8/16/44	25.00
Liberation of Paris 8/23/44	30.00
Romania Joins Allies 8/23/44	35.00
Florence Falls to Allies 8/23/44	30.00
Liberation of Brussels 9/4/44	25.00
Antwerp Liberated 9/4/44	40.00
We Invade Holland, Finland Quits 9/5/44	30.00
Soviets Invade Yugoslavia 9/6/44	30.00
Russians Enter Bulgaria 9/9/44	30.00
We Invade Luxembourg 9/9/44	30.00
Liberation of Luxembourg 9/10/44	25.00
U.S. First Army Invades Germany 9/11/44	30.00
Lights Go On Again in England 9/17/44	30.00
Albania Invaded 9/27/44	35.00
Phillipines, We Will Be Back 9/27/44	25.00
Greece Invaded 10/5/44	35.00
Liberation of Athens 10/14/44	25.00
Liberation of Belgrade 10/16/44	25.00
Flying Tigers Raid Hong Kong 10/16/44	35.00
Russia Invades Czechoslovakia 10/19/44	30.00
Invasion of the Philippines 10/20/44	25.00
The Pied Piper of Leyte-Philippine Invasion 10/21/44	35.00
Martial Law Abolished-Honolulu 10/24/44	40.00
Invasion of Norway 10/25/44	25.00
Cairo Meeting 11/2/44	50.00
Liberation of Tirana 11/18/44	25.00
France Joins UN 1/10/45	50.00
100,000 Yanks Land on Luzon 1/10/45	25.00
Liberation of Warsaw 1/17/45	30.00
Warsaw Recaptured 1/17/45	30.00
Russians Drive to Oder River 2/2/45	25.00
Liberation of Manila 2/4/45	25.00
Yalta Conference 2/12/45	25.00
Liberation of Budapest 2/13/45	25.00
Corregidor Invaded 2/16/45	25.00
Bataan Falls 2/16/45	25.00
Corregidor is Ours 2/17/45	25.00
Turkey Wars Germany and Japan 2/23/45	25.00
US Flag Flies Over Iwo Jima 2/23/45	35.00
Egypt at War 2/25/45	25.00
Palawan Captured 2/28/45	40.00
Yanks Enter Cologne 3/5/45	25.00
Cologne is Taken 3/6/45	20.00
Historical Rhine Crossing 3/8/45	20.00
Mindanao Invaded 3/8/45	40.00
Bombing of Tokyo 3/10/45	25.00
Russia Crosses Oder River 3/13/45	25.00
Capture of Iwo Jima 3/14/45	20.00
Panay Invaded 3/18/45	20.00
Honshu Invaded 3/19/45	20.00
Battle of the Inland Sea 3/20/45	20.00
Crossing of the Rhine 3/24/45	20.00
Kerama Falls 3/26/45	30.00
Danzig Invaded 3/27/45	25.00
Okinawa Invaded 4/1/45	20.00
Vienna Invaded 4/5/45	25.00
Masbate Invaded 4/5/45	30.00
Russia Denounces Jap Treaty 4/5/45	25.00
Japanese Cabinet Resigns 4/7/45	20.00
6 japanese Warships Sunk 4/7/45	25.00
Liberation of Vienna 4/10/45	20.00
We Invade Bremen, etc. 4/10/45	25.00
FDR Dies - Truman becomes President 4/12/45	50.00
Liberation of Vienna 4/13/45	25.00
Patton Invades Czechoslovakia 4/18/45	25.00
Ernie Pyle Dies 4/18/45	25.00
Berlin Invaded 4/21/45	25.00
UN Conference 4/25/45	20.00
Berlin Encircled 4/25/45	20.00
"GI Joe" and "Ivan" Meet at Torgau-Germany 4/26/45	20.00
Patton Enters Austria 4/27/45	25.00
Yanks Meet Reds 4/27/45	25.00
Mussolini Executed 4/28/45	35.00
Hitler Dead 5/1/45	35.00
Liberation of Italy 5/2/45	20.00
Berlin Falls 5/2/45	25.00
Liberation of Rangoon 5/3/45	20.00

World War II & Korean War Patriotic Covers

WORLD WAR II EVENT	CACHETED COVER
5th and 7th Armies Meet at Brenner Pass 5/4/45	20.00
Liberation of Copenhagen 5/5/45	20.00
Liberation of Amsterdam 5/5/45	25.00
Over a Million Nazis Surrender 5/5/45	25.00
Liberation of Oslo 5/8/45	25.00
Liberation of Prague 5/8/45	25.00
V-E Day 5/8/45	35.00
Atomic Bomb Test 5/16/45	25.00
Invasion of Borneo 6/11/45	25.00
Eisenhower Welcomed Home 6/19/45	20.00
Okinawa Captured 6/21/45	25.00
United Nations Conference 6/25/45	25.00
American Flag Raised over Berlin 7/4/45	25.00
Gen. Spatts Made Commander of Strategic Air Force in Pacific 7/5/45	20.00
Italy Declares War on Japan 7/15/45	25.00
Potsdam Conference Opens 7/17/45	25.00
3rd Fleet Hits Tokyo Bay 7/19/45	25.00
Churchill Defeated 7/26/45	25.00
Chineses Armies Retake Kweilin 7/28/45	25.00
Big Three Meet at Potsdam 8/1/45	25.00
Atomic Bomb Dropped on Hiroshima 8/6/45	65.00
Russia Declares War on Japan 8/8/45	25.00
Japan Offers To Surrender 8/10/45	25.00
Japan Capitulates 8/14/45	25.00
Hirohito Broadcasts News of Surrender 8/15/45	40.00
Hirohito Orders Cease Fire 8/16/45	25.00
Japan Signs Peace Treaty 9/1/45	50.00
Liberation of China 9/2/45	35.00
V-J Day 9/2/45	35.00
Liberation of Korea 9/2/45	35.00
MacArthur in Tokyo 9/7/45	25.00
Flag Raising over Tokyo - Gen. MacArthur Takes Over 9/8/45	25.00
Gen. Wainright Rescued from the Japanese 9/10/45	25.00
Nimitz Post Office 9/10/45	25.00
Wainright Day 9/10/45	25.00
Marines Land in Japan 9/23/45	40.00
Nimitz Day-Washington 10/5/45	25.00
War Crimes Commission 10/18/45	25.00
Premier Laval Executed as Traitor 10/15/45	25.00
Fleet Reviewed by President Truman 10/27/45	35.00
De Gaulle Wins Election 10/27/45	25.00
Atomic Bomb and Energy Conference Opens 11/10/45	25.00
Eisenhower Named Chief of Staff 11/20/45	25.00
End of Meat and Fat Rations 11/24/45	25.00
Big 3 Conferencxe at Moscow 12/15/45	25.00
Trygue Lie Elected 1/21/46	25.00
Big 4 Meet in Paris 4/25/46	20.00
Tojo and 24 others Indicated 4/30/46	25.00
1st Anniversary of V-E Day 5/8/46	25.00
2nd Anniversary of D-Day 6/6/46	25.00
Operation Crossroads 6/30/46	100.00
Bikini Atomic Bomb Able Test 7/1/46	125.00
Philippine Republic Independence 7/3/46	25.00
Atomic Age 7/10/46	25.00
Bikini Atomic Bomb Baker Test 7/25/46	125.00
Victory Day 8/14/46	25.00
Opening of UN Post Office at Lake Success 9/23/46	25.00
Goering Commits Suicide 10/16/46	40.00
Opening Day of UN in Flushing, NY 10/23/46	25.00
Marshall is Secretary of State 1/21/47	25.00
Moscow Peace Conference 3/10/47	25.00

KOREAN WAR

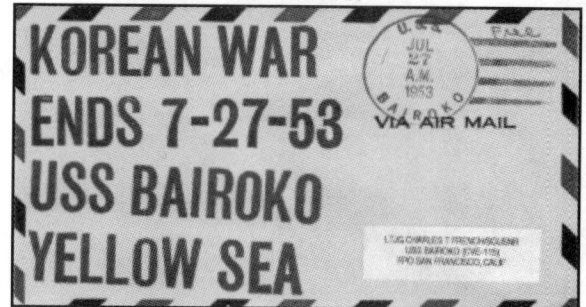

KOREAN WAR EVENT	CACHETED COVER
MacArthur Takes Command of Our Army to Repel the Reds 6/27/50	40.00
US Forces From Japan go into Action in Korea 7/1/50	35.00
MacArthur Takes Supreme Command of All Land and Sea Forces in Korea Under the UN Flag 7/8/50	35.00
Red Korean Chief of Staff, Gen. Kam, Killed 9/8/50	40.00
UN Naval Ships Shell Inchon 9/14/50	40.00
US Marines Land at Inchon 9/15/50	40.00
US Flag Raised Over Seoul 9/27/50	40.00
Liberation of Seoul Completed 9/28/50	40.00
Seoul Restored as Capital of Korea 9/29/50	40.00
South Korean Troops Drive Reds Back North Across the 38th Parallel 10/1/50	40.00
UN Troops Capture Pyongyang, Capital of North Korea 10/20/50	40.00
UN Forces Recapture Seoul 3/15/51	40.00
Truman Removes MacArthur From Command of the UN Troops 4/11/51	40.00
MacArthur Departs From the Far East for USA 4/16/51	40.00
MacArthur Arrives at San Francisco, CA 4/17/51	40.00
MacArthur Addresses the Joint Session of Congress at Washington, DC 4/19/51	40.00
Operation Atomic Nevada 5/14/51	60.00
UN and Communists Meet at Kaesong to Open Formal Cease Fire Talks 7/10/51	40.00
Communists Break Off Truce Talks 8/23/51	40.00
USS New Jersey Bombarding Chansangot Region of Korea 11/13/51	40.00
1st H-Bomb Explosion 11/18/52	50.00
General Taylor Takes Command of the 8th Army with Teixeira Cachet 2/11/53	75.00
Operation Little Switch with Teixeira Cachet 4/20/53	75.00

U.S. Inauguration Covers

Korean War Ends, USS Bairoko – Yellow Sea 7/27/53 .... 60.00

Values listed below from 1901 thru 1925 are for Picture Postcards with Washington DC Cancels with or without content relating to the Inauguration or Washington DC related items.

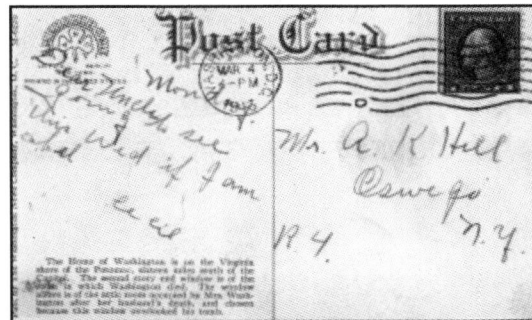

1913 WILSON WITHOUT CONTENT

		Without Content	With Content
1901	McKinley, 3/4/01	1000.00	1500.00
1901	McKinley, 9/7/01, Assignment Day on cover with add-on cachet	...	650.00
1901	McKinley, 9/14/01, Day of Death with add-on cachet	...	1500.00
1905	Teddy Roosevelt, 3/4/05	350.00	500.00
1909	Taft, 3/4/09	200.00	250.00
1913	Wilson, 3/4/13	300.00	400.00
1917	Wilson, 3/4/17	400.00	500.00
1921	Harding, 3/4/21	350.00	450.00
1925	Coolidge, 3/4/25	300.00	400.00

1937 FRANKLIN D. ROOSEVELT

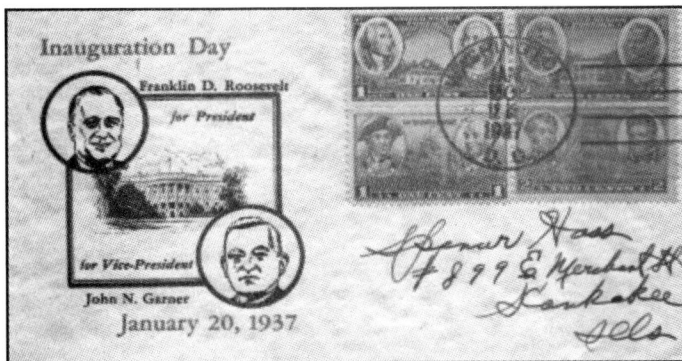

1969 RICHARD NIXON

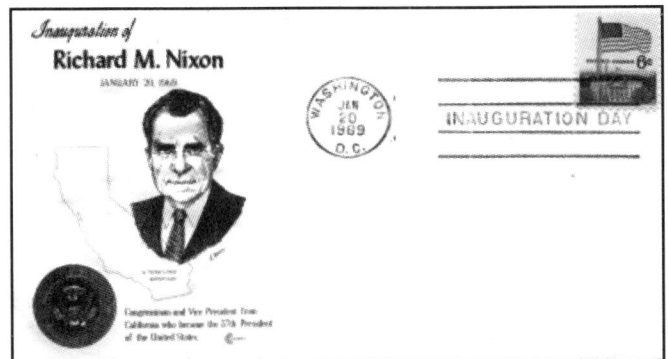

Prices are for covers with PRINTED CACHETS and Wash, D.C. cancels. Covers with cancels from other cities, except as noted, sell for somewhat less.

1929	Hoover 3/4/29	250.00
1929	Hoover 3/4/29 (Rubber Stamp Cachet)	150.00
1933	Roosevelt 3/4/33	60.00
1937	Roosevelt 1/20/37	225.00
1941	Roosevelt 1/20/41	225.00
1945	Roosevelt 1/20/45	225.00
1945	Truman 4/12/45	250.00
1949	Truman 1/20/49	70.00
1953	Eisenhower 1/20/53	16.00
1957	Eisenhower 1/21/57	12.00

1961	Kennedy 1/20/61	20.00
1963	Johnson 11/22/63 Any City	100.00
1965	Johnson 1/20/65	8.00
1969	Nixon 1/20/69	10.00
1973	Nixon 1/20/73	8.00
1974	Ford 8/9/74	6.00
1977	Carter 1/20/77	4.00
1981	Reagan 1/20/81	4.00
1985	Reagan 1/20/85	3.50
1989	Bush 1/20/89	3.50
1993	Clinton 1/20/93	3.00
1997	Clinton 1/20/97	3.00

UNITED STATES SOUVENIR CARDS

UNITED STATES POSTAL SERVICE

EXPOSICIÓN FILATÉLICA INTERNACIONAL
EFIMEX 68
MEXICO, D. F.   1-9 NOVIEMBRE, 1968

EL SELLO TRANS-MISSISSIPI DE $1.00 "GANADO DEL OESTE DURANTE UNA TORMENTA", DETALLE DE LA PINTURA POR J. A. MacWHIRTER CON EL TÍTULO "LA VANGUARDIA"

OBSEQUIO DEL DEPARTAMENTO DE CORREOS DE LOS ESTADOS UNIDOS DE NORTEAMÉRICA

PS2

SCCS Number	Event and Description	First Day Show/Issue	Mint Card	Cancelled Card
FPS1939Aa	Philatelic Truck with Gum	1939	50.00	..
FPS1939Ab	Philatelic Truck without Gum	1939	9.50	..
PS1	Barcelona'60-Columbus Landing ($) (2)	3/26/60	450.00	425.00
PS2	Efimex'68-#292 (4)	11/1/68	2.50	7.50
1970-1975				
PS3	Philympia - #548-550 (9)	9/18/70	1.50	sc/12.00
PS4	Exfilima'71 - #1110, 1125, Peru (15)	11/6/71	1.25	50.00
PS5	Belgica'72 - #914, 1026, 1104 (20)	6/24/72	1.25	sc/22.50
PS6	Olympia Philatelie Munchen'72 - #1460, 1461, 1462, C85 (21)	8/18/72	1.25	25.00
PS7	Exfilbra'72 - #C14, Brazil (22)	8/26/72	1.25	45.00
PS8	Postal Forum VI - #1396 Block (23)	8/28/72	1.25	20.00
PS9	Postal People - #1489-98 (11"x14")	1973	110.00	200.00
PS10	Ibra'73 - #C13, Germany (28)	5/11/73	1.50	10.00
PS11	Apex'73 - #C3a, Newfld., Honduras (30)	7/4/73	1.50	20.00
PS12	Polska'73 - #1488 (31)	8/19/73	1.50	150.00
PS13	Hobby Show Chicago - #1456-59 (35)	2/3/74	1.75	15.00
PS14	Internaba'74 - #1530-37 (37)	6/6/74	2.75	12.00
PS15	Stockholmia'74 - #836, Sweden (38)	9/21/74	2.75	15.00
PS15	Swedish First Day Cancel			22.50
PS16	Exfilmex'74 - #1157, Mexico (39)	10/26/74	2.75	sc/37.50
PS17	Espana'75 - #233, 1271, Spain (40)	4/4/75	1.50	35.00
PS17	Spanish First Day Cancel			75.00
PS18	Arphila'75 - #1187, 1207, France (42)	6/6/75	2.35	35.00
1976-1980				
PS19	Weraba'76 - #1434-35 (45)	4/1/76	2.75	4.00
PS20	Science & Technology - #C76 (48)	5/30/76	3.25	3.50
PS21	Colorado Centennial - #288, 743, 1670 (50)	8/1/76	2.75	3.50
PS22	Hafnia'76 - #5, Denmark (51)	8/20/76	2.50	3.50
PS23	Italia'76 - #1168, Italy (52)	10/14/76	2.50	3.50
PS23	Italian First Day Cancel			40.00
PS24	Nordposta'76 - #689, Germany, Hamburg(53)	10/30/76	2.25	3.50
PS25	Amphilex'77 - #1027, Netherlands (56)	5/26/77	2.75	3.50
PS26	San Marino'77 - #1, 2, San Marino (57)	8/27/77	2.75	3.50
PS27	Rocpex'78 - #1706-9, Taiwan (60)	3/20/78	2.75	100.00
PS28	Naposta'78 - $555, 563, Germany (61)	5/20/78	2.50	4.00
PS28	German First Day Cancel			22.50
PS29	Brasiliana'79 - #C91-92, Brazil (63)	9/15/79	3.25	4.50
PS30	Japex'79 - #1158, Japan (64)	11/2/79	3.25	4.50
PS31	London'80 - #329 (65)	5/6/80	3.25	75.00
PS32	Norwex'80 - #620-21, Norway (66)	6/13/80	3.25	4.50
PS33	Essen'80 - #1014, German (69)	11/15/80	3.25	4.50
1981-1985				
PS34	Wipa'81 - #1252, Austria (71)	5/22/81	3.25	4.50
PS35	Stamp Collecting Month - #245, 1913 (72)	10/1/81	2.75	4.50
PS36	Philatokyo'81 - #1531, Japan (73)	10/9/81	2.75	4.50
PS37	Nordposta'81 - #923, Germany (74)	11/7/81	3.00	4.50
PS38	Canada'82 - #116, Canada #15 (76)	5/20/82	3.25	4.50
PS39	Philexfrance'82 - #1753, France (77)	6/11/82	3.25	4.50
PS40	Stamp Collecting Month - #C3a (78)	10/1/82	3.25	4.50
PS41	Espamer'82 - #801, 1437, 2024 (80)	10/12/82	3.25	5.00
PS42	U.S.-Sweden - #958, 2036, Sweden (81)	3/24/83	3.00	4.50
PS43	Concord, German Settlers - #2040, Germany (82)	4/29/83	3.00	4.50
PS44	Tembal'83 - #C71, Switzerland (83)	5/21/83	3.00	4.50

BRASILIANA 83

Rio de Janeiro, Brasil   29 de julho a 7 de agosto

O Serviço Postal dos Estados Unidos se compraz em render homenagem a BRASILIANA 83 com o lançamento deste cartão postal filatélico.

Assinalando tão importante exposição filatélica internacional, realizada no Rio de Janeiro por ensejo do 140º aniversário de lançamento dos primeiros selos postais brasileiros. Este cartão comemorativo traz uma reprodução do famoso "Olho-de-Boi" de 30 réis, um dos três valores emitidos a 1º de julho de 1843. Foram estes os primeiros selos emitidos no Hemisfério Ocidental.

Em BRASILIANA 83 figura também uma réplica do primeiro selo emitido pelos Estados Unidos da América, em 1847, em homenagem a George Washington.

William F. Bolger
Postmaster General

PS45

SCCS Number	Event and Description	First Day Show/Issue	Mint Card	Cancelled Card
1981-1985 (cont.)				
PS45	Brasiliana'83 - #2, Brazil (85)	7/29/83	3.00	4.50
PS46	Bangkok'83 - #210, Siam (86)	8/4/83	3.00	4.50
PS47	Philatelic Memento'83 - #1387 (87)	8/19/83	2.75	3.50
PS48	Stamp Collecting Month - #293 (88)	10/4/83	3.75	6.00
PS49	Espana'84 - #233, Spain (92)	4/27/84	3.00	5.00
PS50	Hamburg'84 - #C66, Germany (95)	6/19/84	3.00	5.00
PS51	St. Lawrence Seaway - #1131, Canada #387 (96)	6/26/84	3.25	4.50
PS52	Ausipex'84 - #290, Australia (97)	9/21/84	3.00	4.50
PS53	Stamp Collecting Month - #2104 (98)	10/1/84	2.75	4.50
PS54	Philakorea'84 - #741, Korea (99)	10/22/84	3.00	5.00
PS55	Philatelic Memento'85 - #2 (101)	2/26/85	3.00	4.50
PS56	Olymphilex'85 - #C106, Switzerland (102)	3/18/85	3.00	5.00
PS57	Israphil'85 - #566, Israel (103)	5/14/85	3.00	5.00
PS58	Argentina'85 - #1737, Argentina (107)	7/5/85	3.00	5.00
PS59	Mophila'85 - #296, Germany (108)	9/11/85	3.75	5.00
PS60	Italia'85 - #1107, Italy (109)	10/25/85	3.00	5.00
PS61	Statue of Liberty - #2147	7/18/85	32.50	25.00
1986-1992				
PS62	Statue of Liberty - #C87 (110)	2/21/86	5.00	5.50
PS62v	Stampex Overprint - #2204, Australia	8/4/86	15.00	25.00
PS63	Stockholmia'86 - #113, Sweden (113)	8/28/86	5.00	5.50
PS64	Capex'87 - #569, Canada #883 (117)	6/13/87	5.00	7.00
PS65	Hafnia'87 - #299, Denmark (118)	10/16/87	5.00	7.00
PS66	Monte Carlo - #2286, 2300, Monaco (121)	11/13/87	5.00	7.00
PS67	Finlandia'88 - #836, Finland (122)	6/1/88	5.00	7.00
PS68	Philexfrance'89 - #C120, France (125)	7/7/89	9.00	12.00
PS69	World Stamp Expo'89 - #2433 (127)	11/17/89	8.00	9.00
PS70	Stamp World London - #1, G.B. #1 (130)	5/3/90	8.00	9.00
PS71	Olymphilex'92 - #2619, 2637-41		60.00	125.00

BUREAU OF ENGRAVING AND PRINTING

SCCS Number	Event and Description	First Day Show/Issue	Mint Card	Cancelled Card
1954-1970				
F1954A	National Philatelic Museum, DC (1)	3/13/54	1875.00	..
F1966A	Sipex Scenes'66 - Washington D.C. Scenes (3)	5/21/66	150.00	160.00
B1	Sandipex - 3 Washington D.C. Scenes(5)	7/16/69	50.00	150.00
B2	ANA'69 - Eagle "Jackass" Notes (N1)	8/12/69	75.00	..
B3	Fresno Fair - 3 Wash. D.C. Scenes (N2)	10/2/69	400.00	..
B4	ASDA'69 - #E4 Block (6)	11/21/69	22.50	85.00
B5	Interpex'70 - #1027, 1035, C35, C38 (7)	3/13/70	50.00	150.00
B6	Compex'70 - #C18 Block (8)	5/29/70	12.50	175.00
B7	ANA'70 - Currency Collage ($) (N3)	8/18/70	75.00	..
B8	Hapex APS'70 - #799, C46, C55 (10)	11/5/70	10.00	..
1971-1973				
B9	Interpex'71 - #1193 Block,1331-32, 1371,C76 (11)	3/12/71	1.75	50.00
B10	Westpex San Francisco - #740,852,966,997 (12)	4/23/71	1.75	130.00
B11	Napex'71 - #990-92 (13)	5/12/71	2.00	125.00
B12	ANA'71- 80th Anniv. Convention ($) (N4)	8/10/71	5.95	..
B13	Texanex'71 - #938, 1043, 1242 (14)	8/26/71	1.75	250.00
B14	ASDA'71 - #C13-15 (16)	11/19/71	2.65	37.50
B15	Anphilex, Collectors Club - #1-2 (17)	11/26/71	1.00	..
B16	Interpex'72 - #1173 Block,976,1434-35 (18)	3/17/72	1.00	10.00
B17	Nopex, New Orleans - #1020 (19)	4/6/72	1.00	150.00
B18	ANA'72 - $2 Science Allegory ($) (N5)	8/15/72	6.50	135.00
B19	Sepad'72, SPA - #1044 Block (24)	10/20/72	1.00	30.00
B20	ASDA'72 - #863, 868, 883, 888 (25)	11/17/72	1.00	10.00
B21	Stamp Expo'72 - #C36 Block (26)	11/24/72	2.00	25.00
B22	Interpex'73 - #976 Block (27)	3/9/73	1.25	10.00
B23	Compex'73 - #245 Block (29)	5/25/73	2.50	30.00
B24	ANA'73 - $5 "America" ($) (N6)	8/23/73	9.00	25.00
B25	Napex'73 - #C3 Block, C4-6 (32)	9/14/73	2.00	35.00
B26	ASDA'73 - #908 Block, 1139-44 (33)	11/16/73	1.00	8.00
B27	Stamp Expo'73 - #C20 Block (34)	12/7/73	2.00	20.00

BUREAU OF ENGRAVING AND PRINTING

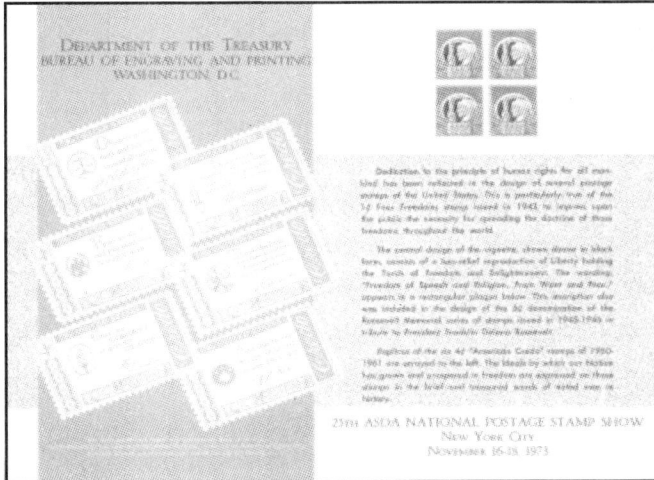

B26

SCCS Number	Event and Description	First Day Show/Issue	Mint Card	Cancelled Card
	1974-1976			
B28	Milcopex'74 - #C43 Block (36)	3/8/74	1.50	6.50
B29	ANA'74 - $10 Education ($) (N7)	8/13/74	11.00	40.00
B30	Napex'75 - #708 Block (41)	5/9/75	5.75	18.50
B31	Women's Year (with folder) - #872, 878, #959, $1 Martha Washington ($) (43)	5/2/75	22.50	250.00
B32	ANA'75 -$1 George & Martha Wash. ($)(N8)	8/19/75	9.00	40.00
B33	ASDA'75 - #1003 Block, Washington (44)	11/21/75	27.50	50.00
B34	Interphil'76 - #120 Block, Jefferson (46)	5/29/76	5.00	15.00
B35	Card from Interphil program - #1044	5/29/76	5.50	100.00
B36	Bicentennial Expo on Science and Technology, Kitty Hawk/Space	5/30/76	5.50	150.00
B37	Stamp Expo'76, Citizen Soldier - #1348, #1348, 51, 52 (49)	6/11/76	5.50	40.00
B38	ANA'76 - $2 Fulton & Morse ($) (N9)	8/24/76	8.00	32.50
	1977-1980			
B39	Milcopex'77, Polar Theme - #733, 1128 (54)	3/4/77	2.00	15.00
B40	Rompex'77, Mountains - #1001 Block (55)	5/20/77	2.00	9.50
B41	ANA'77 - $5 Indian Chief ($) (N10)	8/23/77	8.00	10.00
B42	Puripex'77 - #801 Block, San Juan Gate(58)	9/2/77	1.50	6.00
B43	ASDA'77 - #C45 Block, Wright Bros (59)	11/16/77	2.25	6.00
B44	Paper Money Show'78 -De Soto Vign.(N11)	6/2/78	3.75	8.00
B45	Cenjex'78 - #785 Block, 646, 680, 689, #1086, 1716 (62)	6/23/78	2.00	6.00
B46	ANA'80 - $5 Grant & Sheridan ($) (N12)	2/15/80	15.00	40.00
B47	Paper Money Show'80 - 2 $10 Lewis-Clark ($) (N13)	6/6/80	15.00	20.00
B48	Napex'80 - #573 Block, Capitol (67)	7/4/80	8.50	30.00
B49	Visitor Center - Eagle & Freedom	9/8/80	4.75	15.00
B50	ASDA Stamp Festival - #962 Block, Francis S.Key (68)	9/25/80	9.50	35.00
	1981-1983			
B51	Stamp Expo'81 South - #1287 Block, 1331-32 (70)	3/20/81	10.75	37.50
B52	Visitor Center - G.Wash. & D.C.Views	4/22/81	6.50	12.00
B53	Paper Money Show'81-$20 G.Wash.($)(N14)	6/19/81	12.50	15.00
B54	ANA'81 - $5 Silver Certificate ($) (N15)	7/27/81	9.00	18.00
B55	Milcopex'82 - #1136 Block, Reuter (75)	3/5/82	8.75	17.50
B56	Paper Money Show'82 - "Brown Backs"($)(N16)	6/18/82	9.50	20.00
B57	ANA'82 - $1 Great Seal ($) (N17)	8/17/82	9.50	17.00
B58	Espamer'82 - #244 Block, Isabella (79)	10/12/82	25.00	35.00
B59	FUN'83 - $100 "Watermelon" ($) (N18)	1/5/83	18.00	18.00
B60	Texanex-Topex'83 - #776 Block, 1660 (84)	6/17/83	18.00	20.00
B61	ANA'83 - $20 1915 Note ($) (N19)	8/16/83	14.50	15.00
B62	Philatelic Show'83, Boston - #718-19 (89)	10/21/83	10.00	25.00
B63	ASDA'83 - #881, Metropolitan Opera (90)	11/17/83	10.00	20.00
	1984			
B64	FUN'84 - $1 1880 Note ($) (N20)	1/4/84	18.50	15.00
B65	Spider Press, Intaglio, Brown Eagle	1/4/84	350.00	425.00
B66	Espana'84 - #241 Block (91)	4/27/84	16.50	18.00
B67	Stamp Expo'84 - #1791-94, Torch (93)	4/27/84	15.00	18.00
B68	Compex'84 - #728 (94)	5/25/84	20.00	22.50
B69	Money Show'84, Memphis - $10,000 1878 Note ($) (N21)	6/15/84	22.50	22.50
B70	Spider Press, Intaglio, Blue Eagle	6/15/84	350.00	450.00
B71	ANA'84 - $500 1882 Gold Certificate($)(N22)	7/28/84	12.50	15.00
B72	Spider Press, Intaglio, Green Eagle	7/28/84	350.00	425.00
B73	ASDA'84 - #1470 Block, Youth (100)	11/15/84	13.00	25.00
B74	Spider Press, Intaglio, Green Eagle	11/15/84	140.00	200.00

SCCS Number	Event and Description	First Day Show/Issue	Mint Card	Cancelled Card
	1985			
B75	Long Beach'85 #954, $20 1865 Note $(104)	1/31/85	10.00	11.00
B76	Milcopex'85 - #880 Block, Sousa (105)	3/1/85	11.00	15.00
B77	Coin Club of El Paso-$50 1902 Note ($)(N23)	4/19/85	12.50	15.00
B78	Spider Press, Maroon Statue of Liberty	4/19/85	150.00	180.00
B79	Pacific NW Numismatics -$50 1914 ($)(N24)	5/17/85	13.50	15.00
B80	Napex'85 - #2014 Block, Peace Garden(106)	6/7/85	10.00	22.50
B81	Paper Money Show, Memphis - $10,000 1878 Note ($) (N25)	6/14/85	15.00	15.00
B82	ANA'85 - $500 1882 Gold Cert. ($) (N26)	8/20/85	13.00	15.00
B83	Spider Press, Green Statue of Liberty	8/20/85	175.00	200.00
B84	Paper Money Show, Cherry Hill - $10 1882 ($) (N27)	11/14/85	13.50	23.50
B85-86	Spider Press,Blue Liberty Bell with card	11/14/85	175.00	200.00
	1986-1987			
B87	FUN'86 - $100 1890 Treasury ($) (N28)	1/2/86	12.50	18.00
B88	ANA Midwinter,Salt Lake C.-$10 1901($)(N29)	2/19/86	12.50	12.50
B89	Garfield-Perry - #306 Block,Martha Wash.(111)	3/21/86	10.00	25.00
B90	Ameripex'86-#134,2052,1474, Franklin(112)	5/22/86	10.00	20.00
B91-92	Spider Press, Green Liberty Bell with card	5/22/86	65.00	100.00
B93	Paper Money Show'86 - $5 1902 ($)(N30)	6/20/86	11.00	17.50
B94	ANA'86, Milwaukee - 5¢ Fractional ($) (N31)	8/5/86	11.00	17.50
B95-96	Spider Press, Brown Liberty Bell with card	8/5/86	65.00	100.00
B97	Houpex'86 - #1035, 1041, 1044A (114)	9/5/86	12.00	25.00
B98	Lobex'86 - $10 1907 Gold Cert. ($) (115)	10/2/86	13.00	22.50
B99	NW Paper Money-Fractional Currency($)(N32)	11/13/86	13.00	22.50
B100	Dallas Expo-#550 Block,$10,000 1918($)(116)	12/11/86	14.00	22.50
B101	BEP 125th Anniv. - Cherry Blossoms	1/7/87	45.00	70.00
B101A	same, "FUN" Embossed	1/7/87	75.00	100.00
B101B	same, ANA Midwinter Seals	2/27/87	75.00	90.00
B101C	same, BEP & WMPG Seals	4/9/87	85.00	135.00
B101D	same, BEP & IPMS Seals	6/19/87	85.00	100.00
B101E	same, BEP & ANA'87 Seals	8/26/87	80.00	95.00
B101F	same, BEP & GENA Seals	9/18/87	50.00	75.00
B102	FUN'87 -$1 1874 Columbus,Wash. ($)(N33)	1/7/87	14.00	18.50
B103	ANA Midwinter'87 - $500,000,000 Treasury Note ($) (N34)	2/27/87	15.00	18.50
B104	BEP 125th Anniv., Fort Worth - $5 1902 Harrison ($) (N35)	4/25/87	18.00	115.00
B105	Paper Money Show'87-$20 1922 Seal($)(N36)	6/19/87	11.00	15.00
B106	ANA'87, Atlanta - $2 1886 ($) (N37)	8/26/87	11.00	15.00
B108	GENA'87 Numismatics - $10 1907 ($)(N38)	9/18/87	15.00	18.00
B109	Spider Press, Brown State Shields, Intaglio	9/18/87	85.00	150.00
B110	Sescal'87 - #798 Constitution (119)	10/16/87	12.50	22.50
B111	Hawaii Numismatist -$5 1923($),#C55(120)	11/12/87	19.50	26.50
	1988-1989			
B112	FUN'88 - 50¢ Fractional Currency ($) (N39)	1/7/88	12.00	17.50
B113	Spider Press, Green State Shields, Intaglio	1/7/88	85.00	125.00
B114	ANA Midwinter, Little Rock, $10,000 1882 Jackson, Gold Certificate ($) (N40)	3/11/88	13.50	16.50
B115	Paper Money Show'88 - $5 1899 ($) (N41)	6/24/88	13.00	16.00
B116	ANA'88,Cincinnati -$2 1918 Battleship($)(N42)	7/20/88	14.50	18.00
B117	Spider Press, Blue State Shields, Intaglio	7/20/88	85.00	140.00
B118	APS Stampshow,Detroit-#835 Constitution(123)	8/25/88	11.00	20.00
B119	Illinois Numismatist - $10 1915 ($) (N43)	10/6/88	10.00	15.00
B120	Midaphil'88 - #627, Steamboat (124)	11/18/88	10.00	22.50
B121	FUN'89 - $50 1891 Seward ($) (N44)	1/5/89	10.00	15.00
B122	FUN, Indian Mourning Civilization, Intaglio	1/5/89	45.00	75.00
B124	ANA Midwinter, Colorado Springs - $5,000 1878 ($) (N45)	3/3/89	11.50	17.50
B125	Texas Numismatics, El Paso - $5,000 1918 ($) (N46)	4/28/89	11.50	15.00
B126	Paper Money Show - $5 1907 U.S. Note ($) (N47)	6/23/89	10.00	15.00
B127	Paper Money S., Agriculture Scene, Intag.	6/23/89	45.00	70.00
B129	ANA'89, Pittsburgh - $10 1891 ($) (N48)	8/9/89	15.00	17.50
B130	ANA, Declaration of Independence, Intag.	8/9/89	45.00	75.00
B132	APS Stampshow, Anaheim - #565, Indians (126)	8/24/89	10.00	18.00
	1990-1991			
B133	FUN'90 - $5 1897 Silver ($) (N49)	1/4/90	10.00	16.00
B134	FUN, Brown Eagle & Ships, Intaglio	1/4/90	35.00	70.00
B135	ANA Midwinter, San Diego - $2 1897 ($)(N50)	3/2/90	10.00	16.00
B136	Central States Numismatics, Milwaukee - $1 1897 Silver ($) (N51)	4/6/90	10.00	16.00
B137	CSNS, Blue Eagle & Ships, Intaglio	4/6/90	35.00	70.00
B138	Aripex'90 - #285 Trans-Mississippi (128)	4/20/90	10.00	17.50
B139	DCSE'90, Dallas -$10 1890 Note ($) (N52)	6/14/90	12.50	18.00
B140	ANA Seattle - $1,000 1891 Silver ($) (N53)	8/22/90	12.50	18.00
B141	ANA, Green Eagle & Ships, Intaglio	8/22/90	35.00	70.00
B142	APS Stampshow - #286 Trans-Mississippi (129)	8/23/90	10.00	18.00
B143	Westex Numismatic, Denver - $2 1890 ($) (N54)	9/21/90	12.50	16.00
B144	Hawaii Numis. - $50 1874 Legal Tender($) (N55)	11/1/90	15.00	25.00
B145	FUN - $20 1875 Legal Tender ($)(N49)	1/3/91	11.50	16.00
B146	FUN, Green "Freedom & Capitol, Intaglio	1/3/91	39.50	70.00
B147	ANA Midwinter - $2 1917 Legal Tender ($) (N50)	3/1/91	11.50	16.00
B148	Paper Money Show, Memphis - $20 1890 ($) (N58)	6/14/91	11.50	16.00

BUREAU OF ENGRAVING AND PRINTING

B119

SCCS Number	Event and Description	First Day Show/Issue	Mint Card	Cancelled Card
	1991 (continued)			
B149	ANA, Chicago - $5,000 1878 Legal T. ($) (N59)	8/13/91	16.50	19.50
B150	ANA, Gray "Freedom" & Capitol, Intaglio	8/13/91	42.50	70.00
B151	APS Stampshow, Philadelphia - #537 (131)	8/22/91	15.00	20.00
B152	Fort Worth, Five BEP Buildings	4/26/91	40.00	160.00
	1992-1993			
B153	FUN - $1 1862 Legal Tender ($) (N60)	1/9/92	10.00	16.00
B154	FUN, Blue Columbus Voyage, Intaglio	1/9/92	35.00	70.00
B155	Central States Numis. - $1,000 1875 Legal Tender ($) (N61)	4/30/92	13.00	18.50
B156	World Columbian Stamp Expo - #118 (132)	5/22/92	11.00	18.00
B157	WCSE, Red Columbus Voyage, Intaglio	5/22/92	35.00	80.00
B158	Paper Money Show - $5 1914 ($) (N62)	6/19/92	10.00	16.00
B159	ANA, Orlando - $5 1865 Note ($) (N63)	8/12/92	12.50	16.00
B160	ANA, Green Columbus Voyage, Intaglio	8/12/92	35.00	85.00
B161	APS, Oakland - #118 Block (134)	8/27/92	10.00	17.00
B162	Savings Bonds - #WS7, $25 Sav. Bond (133)	6/15/92	15.00	30.00
B163	Green Fleet of Columbus 1492, Intaglio	10/13/92	35.00	75.00
B164	CFC, Red Cross - #1016 + 1155, 1263, 1385, 1425, 1438, 1549 (135)	1/13/93	11.50	30.00
B165	FUN - $1,000 1890 Treasury Note Back ($) (N64)	1/7/93	12.50	16.00
B166	FUN, 3 National Parks Scenes, Intaglio	1/7/93	35.00	65.00
B167	ANA, Colorado Springs - $2 1880 Legal Tender Back($) (N65)	3/11/93	12.00	16.00
B168	ASDA'93 - #859, 864, 869, 874, 879, 884, 889, 893 1¢ Famous Americans (136)	5/5/93	10.00	16.00
B169	Texas Numismatics - $500 1902 Back ($)(N66)	5/6/93	12.50	16.00
B170	Georgia Numism.-$1,000 1878 Back($)(N67)	5/13/93	12.50	16.00
B171	Paper Money Show-$500 1918 Back ($)(N69)	6/18/93	12.50	16.00
B172	IPMS, 3 National Parks Scenes,Purple, Int.	6/18/93	35.00	55.00
B173	ANA, Baltimore - $100 1914 Back ($)	7/28/93	12.50	16.00
B174	ANA, 3 National Parks Scenes, Green, Int.	7/28/93	35.00	60.00
B175	Savings Bond - #WS8, $200 Bond (137)	8/2/93	11.50	25.00
B176	Omaha Philatelic - #QE4, JQ5, E7, Newspaper (138)	9/3/93	12.00	20.00
B178	ASDA - Unfinished Masterpieces,Wash(139)	10/28/93	10.00	16.00
	1994-1995			
B179	FUN'94 - $20 1923 Proposed ($) (N70)	1/6/94	10.00	16.00
B180	FUN, Justice Orlando, Intaglio	1/6/94	35.00	50.00
B181	SANDICAL - #E1 Block (140)	2/11/94	10.00	17.50
B182	ANA, New Orleans -$10 1899 Proposed($) (N71)	3/3/94	12.50	17.50
B183	European Paper Money Show, Netherlands - $100 1908 Proposed Note (N72)	4/16/94	13.50	37.50
B184	Paper Money Show - $10 Proposed Note ($) (N73)	6/17/94	12.50	16.00
B185	IPMS, Justice Memphis, Intaglio	6/17/94	33.50	50.00
B186	BEP Stamp Centennial -#246/263 Black(13)	7/1/94	150.00	175.00
B187	ANA, Detroit - $10 1915 Prop. Back ($)(N74)	7/27/94	12.50	16.00
B188	ANA, 1915 3 Female Figures Allegory, Int	7/27/94	70.00	90.00
B189	Savings Bonds - #S1-5, Minuteman (141)	8/1/94	15.00	25.00
B190	APS, Pittsburgh - #J31, J32, J35 (142)	8/18/94	10.00	16.00
B191	ASDA, N.Y. - 1894 Newspaper Stamps(143)	11/3/94	10.00	16.00
B192	FUN'95 - $1 1899 Silver Certificate ($)(N75)	1/5/95	12.50	16.50
B193	FUN, Red-Brown Seated Eagle, Intaglio	1/5/95	32.50	45.00
B194	COLOPEX,Columbus,OH - #261 Block(144)	4/7/95	10.00	16.50
B195	New York Numismatics - $1 1917 ($) (N76)	5/5/95	11.50	22.50

SCCS Number	Event and Description	First Day Show/Issue	Mint Card	Cancelled Card
	1995 (continued)			
B196	Paper Money Show, Memphis - $1 1880 ($) (N77)	6/16/95	11.50	18.00
B197	BEP Stamp Centennial - #246/263, Blue (13) (145)	6/30/95	90.00	115.00
B198	Savings Bond - #905, 908, 940 WWII (146)	8/16/95	10.00	25.00
B199	ANA, Anaheim - $1 1918 Back ($) (N78)	8/16/95	12.50	20.00
B200	ANA, Blue Eagle & Flag, Intaglio	8/16/95	35.00	45.00
B201	Long Beach Numism. - $1 1923 Back ($) (N79)	10/4/95	10.00	18.00
B202	ASDA, N.Y. - #292 Block and background (147)	11/2/95	10.00	18.00
	1996-1997			
B203	FUN'96 - $500 1878 Silver Cert. ($) (N80)	1/4/96	10.00	18.00
B204	FUN, Miners Panning for Gold, Brown Int	1/4/96	35.00	45.00
B205	Suburban Washington / Baltimore Coin Show - $500 1878 Back Silver Cert. ($) (N81)	3/22/96	10.00	18.00
B206	Central States Numism.-$1,000 1907($)(N82)	4/25/96	10.00	18.00
B207	CAPEX'96, Toronto - #291 Block (148)	6/8/96	10.00	20.00
B208	Olymphilex, Atlanta - #718 Block (149)	7/19/96	10.00	18.00
B209	Olymphiles, Miners Panning Gold, Green Intaglio	7/19/96	35.00	45.00
B210	Savings Bond - Brown Eagle in Flight	8/12/96	11.50	25.00
B211	ANA, Denver - $1,000 1907 Back ($) (N83)	8/14/96	10.00	18.00
B212	ANA, Miners Panning for Gold, Blue Int	8/14/96	35.00	45.00
B213	Billings Stamp Club (150)	10/19/96	10.00	24.00
B214	FUN'96 20 1886 Silver Cert. ($) (N84)	1/9/97	12.00	20.00
B215	Long Beach C&C, Lock Seal (151)	2/19/97	12.00	20.00
B216	Bay State Coin Show, $20 1882 BN (N85)	4/17/97	12.00	20.00
B217	Pacific '97, Butter Revenue	5/29/97	12.00	20.00
B218	Pacific '97 Handprint	5/29/97	...	...
B219	1PMS, Memphis, TN, $10 1902 ($) (N86)	6/20/97	12.00	20.00
B220	1PMS, intaglio	6/20/97	40.00	50.00
B221	ANA 106th, $100 1874 LT ($) (N87)	7/30/97	12.00	20.00
B222	Milcopex, Newspaper Stamps (153)	9/17/97	12.00	20.00
	1998-1999			
B224	FUN'98 (N88)	1/8/98	12.00	20.00
B225	Okpex'98 #922 Block (154)	5/1/98	12.00	20.00
B226	IPMS, Memphis ($) (N89)	6/19/98	12.00	20.00
B227	ANA, Portland, OR ($) (N90)	8/5/98	12.00	20.00
B228	Long Beach C&C ($) (N91)	9/23/98	12.00	20.00
B229	Long Beach C&C, Trans-Mississippi (155)	9/23/98	40.00	50.00
B230	Savings Bond, Washington, DC	12/21/98	12.00	20.00
B231	FUN'99 ($) (N92)	1/7/99	12.00	20.00
B232	Bay State Coin ($) (N93)	2/26/99	12.00	20.00
B233	1PMS, Memphis ($) (N94)	6/18/99	12.00	20.00
B234	Savings Bonds, DC	8/9/99	12.00	20.00
B235	ANA, Rosemont, IL ($) (N95)	8/11/99	12.00	20.00
B236	ANA, Intaglio	8/11/99	40.00	50.00
B237	National, King of Prussia, PA (156)	10/1/99	12.00	20.00
	2000-2001			
B238	Progress, DC	1/3/00	12.00	20.00
B239	Wright Brothers, DC	2/1/00	12.00	20.00
B240	Panama Canal, DC	3/1/00	12.00	20.00
B241	Engineering, DC	4/3/00	12.00	20.00
B242	Mt. Rushmore, Perkins, DC	5/1/00	12.00	20.00
B243	Eagle & Ships, DC	6/1/00	12.00	20.00
B244	Nuclear Sub, DC	7/3/00	12.00	20.00
B245	M.L.King, Jr., DC	8/1/00	12.00	20.00
B246	Vietnam Soldier, DC	9/1/00	12.00	20.00
B247	Banking & Commerce #1577-78, DC	10/2/00	12.00	20.00
B248	Space Shuttle, DC	11/1/00	12.00	20.00
B249	Information Highway, DC	12/1/00	12.00	20.00
B250	FUN, 2001 Orlando, FL($)	1/4/01	12.00	20.00
B251	IPMS, Memphis, TN	6/15/01	12.00	20.00
B252	ANA, Atlanta,GA ($)	8/8/01	12.00	20.00
B253	LBC & CEC, Long Beach, CA	10/4/01	12.00	20.00

UNITED STATES SOUVENIR CARDS

AMERICAN BANK NOTE COMPANY

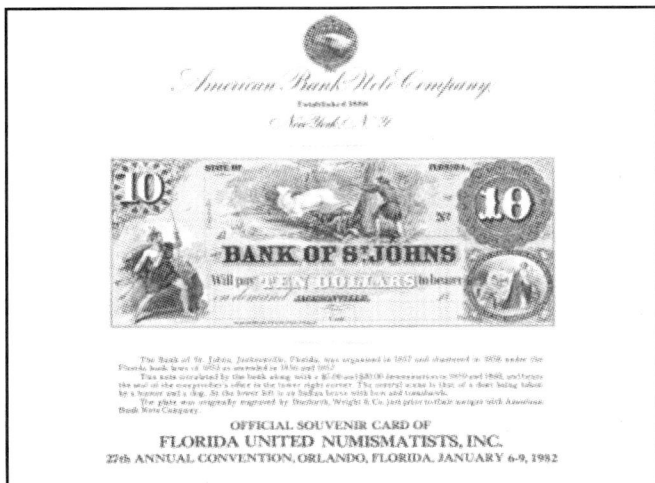

OFFICIAL SOUVENIR CARD OF
FLORIDA UNITED NUMISMATISTS, INC.
27th ANNUAL CONVENTION, ORLANDO, FLORIDA, JANUARY 6-9, 1982

2nd Annual National and World Paper Money Convention
8th National Silver Dollar Convention
St. Louis, Missouri, October 29 - November 1, 1987

SO22

SCCS Number	Event and Description	First Day Show/Issue	Mint Card	Cancelled Card
	1966-1980			
SO1	SIPEX Miner - United States Bank Note Company	5/21/66	10.00	(sc)95.00
SO2	Interphil "America 1776-1976"	5/29/76	50.00	100.00
SO3	Interphil "Lincoln's Gettysburg Address"	5/29/76	60.00	100.00
SO4	Interphil "Awards Banquet, Scenes"	6/5/76	135.00	300.00
SO5	Interphil "Awards Banquet Menu"	6/5/76	175.00	400.00
SO9	Paper Money Show - $2 Liberty Bank of Providence, RI ($)	6/15/79	35.00	50.00
SO10	ANA'79 - $10 Exchange Bank, St.Louis ($)	7/28/79	8.00	35.00
SO11	Paper Money Show - $100 Bank of Lebanon, NH ($)	6/6/80	20.00	35.00
SO12	ANA'80 - $3 Bank of the Ohio Valley ($)	8/13/80	8.00	50.00
SO13	Bank Note Reporter - $3 Bank of the State of Kansas ($)	9/9/80	7.00	500.00
	1981-1984			
SO14	ANA Midyear, Honolulu - $5 Republic of Hawaii Silver Certificate ($)	2/5/81	15.00	85.00
SO15	Paper Money Show - $50 Bank of Selma,AL($)	6/19/81	13.50	20.00
SO16	INTERPAM - $1 Grenville County Bank of Prescott, ON & $2 Cataract City Bank of Paterson, NJ ($)	6/15/81	9.00	100.00
SO17	ANA'81 - $5,000 Canal Bank of New Orl.($)	7/28/81	12.50	22.50
SO18	ANA Building Fund - $10 Artisan Bank of Trenton, NJ ($)	7/28/81	18.50	150.00
SO20	Chester County, PA - 4 Vignettes, Green	12/10/81	9.00	95.00
SO21	Chester County, PA - 4 Vignettes, Brown	21/10/81	9.00	95.00
SO22	FUN'82 - $10 Bank of St. Johns, FL ($)	1/6/82	10.00	300.00
SO23	ANA Midyear, Colorado Springs - Certificate of Deposit, Bank of Ruby, CO	2/18/82	9.50	20.00
SO24	Paper Money Show - $1 Baton Rouge ($)	6/18/82	17.50	20.00
SO25	ANA'82 - $3 Tremont Bank of Boston ($)	8/17/82	11.00	20.00
SO32	ANA Midwinter, Tucson - $1 Lord & Williams Arizona Territory ($)	1/5/83	11.50	17.00
SO33	Paper Money Show - $2 White Mountains Bank of Lancaster, NH ($)	1/5/83	14.00	18.00
SO34	ANA'83 - $1,000 Felix Argenti & Co. ($)	8/16/83	14.00	18.00
SO35	ANA Midwinter, Colorado Springs - Colorado National Bank Advertising Card	2/23/84	17.50	35.00
SO37	Paper Money Show - $100 Bank of the State of Indiana ($)	6/15/84	16.50	25.00
SO38	Statue of Liberty, Black	7/4/84	7.75	18.00
SO39	ANA'84 - $10 Michigan State Bank ($)	7/28/84	25.00	32.50
	1985-1988			
SO40	FUN'85 - $10 Bank of Commerce at Fernandina, FL ($)	1/3/85	9.00	45.00
SO41	ANA Midwinter, San Antonio - $3 Commercial and Agricultural Bank of Galveston ($)	2/21/85	27.50	40.00
SO42	Natl. Assoc. of Tobacco Distributors	3/27/85	9.00	..
SO43	SPMC & IBNS - Hologram with Statue of Liberty		50.00	..
SO53	INS'87 - Statue of Liberty	2/6/87	30.00	95.00
SO54	200th Anniv.-Constitution - Independence Hall	6/19/87	10.00	20.00
SO56	AFL-CIO Trade Show - Eagle	6/19/87	125.00	175.00
SO57	ANA'87 - $10 Republic of Hawaii ($)	8/26/87	16.00	20.00

SO58

SCCS Number	Event and Description	First Day Show/Issue	Mint Card	Cancelled Card
	1985-1988 (cont.)			
SO58	NWPMC, St.Louis - $20 Rep. of Hawaii ($)	10/29/87	17.00	20.00
SO59	200th Anniv.-Constitution - 8 States & Eagle	1988	9.00	..
SO60	Paper Money Show - $50 Rep.of Hawaii($)	6/24/88	17.50	20.00
SO61	ANA'88 - $100 Republic of Hawaii ($)	7/20/88	15.00	20.00
	1989-1991			
SO62	FUN'89 - $5 Republic of Hawaii ($)	1/5/89	15.00	20.00
SO63	Miami Stamp Expo - 3 Railroad Vignettes	1/27/89	24.00	35.00
SO64	ANA'89 - #SO34 with Museum Overprint on Back($)	3/3/89	20.00	25.00
SO65	Washington Inauguration - $20 Bank of Pittsylvania ($)	3/15/89	12.00	..
SO66	200th Anniv.-Constitution - 3 States	..	12.00	..
SO67	Paper Money Show - $10 Rep. Hawaii ($)	6/23/89	15.00	20.00
SO68	ANA'89 - $20 Republic of Hawaii ($)	8/9/89	18.00	22.50
SO69	200th Anniv.-N.Carolina - $5 Bank of North Carolina ($)	11/2/89	13.50	....
SO71	Miami Stamp Expo - Native Americans	1/12/90	20.00	35.00
SO72	200th Anniv.-Rhode I. - $100 Bank-America($)	6/15/90	14.00	20.00
SO73	ANA'90 - #SO12 overprinted on back ($)	..	15.00	18.00
SO74	Paper Money Show -$5 City of Memphis($)	6/14/91	15.00	20.00
SO75	IPMS - America, American Flag Hologram	6/14/91	15.00	20.00
SO76	ANA'91 - $3 Marine Bank of Chicago ($)	8/13/91	15.00	20.00
SO77	Souvenir Card Collectors Soc.10th Anniv.	8/13/91	15.00	20.00
SO78	APS'91 - #114 and Railroad Scene	8/22/91	12.50	25.00
SO79	APS - William Penn Treaty with Indians	8/22/91	115.00	175.00
SO80	Baltimore Phil.Soc.- #120 Decl.of Indep.	8/31/91	15.00	25.00
SO81	ASDA - #117 and S.S.Adriatic	11/7/91	12.50	25.00
SO82	ASDA - Brooklyn Bridge Harbor Scene	11/7/91	110.00	175.00
SO83	PSNE - #118 and Landing of Columbus	11/15/91	15.00	25.00
	1992-1994			
SO84	FUN'92 - Cuban 50 Centavo Note ($)	1/9/92	15.00	25.00
SO85	FUN - Columbus with Globe Hologram	1/9/92	17.00	30.00
SO86	ANA - Costa Rica 100 Colones Gold Ct.($)	2/27/92	18.00	25.00
SO87	Interpex - Venezuela 25¢ Land.-Columbus	3/12/92	15.00	25.00
SO88	World Columbian Stamp Expo - Costa Rica 12¢ Christopher Columbus	5/22/92	12.50	25.00
SO89	WCSE - #230 1¢ Columbian	5/22/92	15.00	25.00
SO90	WCSE - 1921 El Salvador & Statue (Red)	5/22/92	110.00	165.00
SO90A	WCSE - 1921 El Salvador & Statue (Blue)	5/22/92	250.00	375.00
SO91-96	WCSE - set of 6 1893 Columbian Exposition Tickets	5/22/92	165.00	275.00
SO97	WCSE - Folder for #2624-29 with insert bearing "Landing of Columbus"	5/22/92	35.00	45.00
SO102	Paper Money Show -$10 City -Memphis($)	6/19/92	15.00	25.00
SO103	ANA, Orlando - $4 Bank of Florida ($)	8/12/92	15.00	27.50
SO104	APS, Oakland - #234, Costa Rica #122	8/27/92	15.00	25.00
SO105	APS, 3 El Salvador stamps in brown	8/27/92	70.00	100.00
SO105A	same as SO105 in Green, Purple, Orge.	8/27/92	250.00	375.00
SO106	ASDA - 2 El Salvador stamps plus vignette of Columbus	10/28/92	15.00	25.00
SO107	ASDA, Historic Event, Dominican Rep. 50 Pesos Columbus Note ($)	10/28/92	15.00	25.00
SO108	ASDA, Grey Columbus Vignette	10/28/92	100.00	175.00
SO108A	same, Maroon Hand Pulled Proof	10/28/92	250.00	375.00
SO109	Orcoexpo, Anaheim - Hawaii #79 Block	1/8/93	15.00	25.00
SO110	Orcoexpo, Iron-Horse Hologram	1/8/93	15.00	25.00
SO111	Milcopex - Hawaii #76 Block	3/5/93	15.00	25.00

UNITED STATES SOUVENIR CARDS

AMERICAN BANK NOTE COMPANY

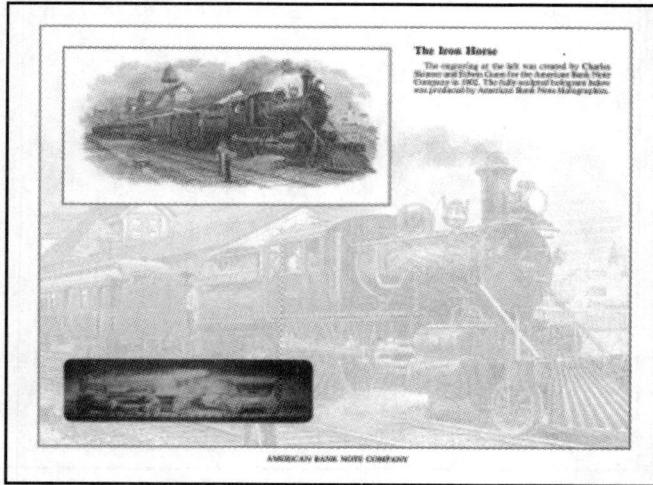

The Iron Horse

SO112

PLATE PRINTERS UNION

F1973B

SCCS Number	Event and Description	First Day Show/Issue	Mint Card	Cancelled Card
	1992-1994(cont.)			
SO112	ANA - 50 Peso Banco de Minero,Mexico($)	3/11/93	15.00	25.00
SO113	Plymouth, MI - Hawaii #75 Block	4/24/93	15.00	60.00
SO114	ASDA Mega Event - Hawaii #77 Block	5/5/93	15.00	25.00
SO115	Paper Money Show - $20 City-Memphis($)	6/18/93	15.00	25.00
SO116	ANA, Baltimore - $20 Peoples' Bank of Baltimore ($)	7/28/93	14.00	25.00
SO117	ANA, $100 Chesepeake Bank Proof ($)	7/28/93	80.00	120.00
SO118	APS, Houston - Hawaii #74 Block	8/19/93	14.00	22.50
SO119	APS, $1 Hawaii Revenue Blue Proof	8/19/93	70.00	110.00
SO119A	same, Black Hand pulled Proof	8/19/93	250.00	375.00
SO120	ASDA Mega Event - Hawaii #78 Block	10/28/93	13.50	22.50
SO121	ASDA - Holiday, Bank Draft for the Shetucket Bank of Norwich, CT	10/28/93	13.50	22.50
SO122	ASDA, 3 Hawaii Foreign Affairs, Green	10/28/93	80.00	120.00
SO122A	same, Green, Blue, Red Proof	10/28/93	250.00	375.00
SO123	Aripex, Mesa,AZ - U.S. #1 Franklin	1/7/94	16.00	25.00
SO124	ANA, New Orleans - 1 Peso Medellin, Colombia ($)	3/3/94	16.00	25.00
SO125	Milcopex - #73, 2¢ Andrew Jackson	3/4/94	16.00	25.00
SO126	Garfield-Perry - #13, 10¢ Washington	3/18/94	16.00	25.00
SO127	Central States Numism. - $2 Indiana's Pioneer Association ($)	4/8/94	16.00	25.00
SO128	Paper Money Show - $100 Union Bank ($)	6/17/94	16.00	25.00
SO129	ANA, Detroit - $5 Bank of the Capitol, Lansing, Michigan ($)	7/27/94	16.00	25.00
SO130	ANA - Winged Majesty / Eagle Hologram	7/27/94	20.00	30.00
SO131	ANA - $1 White Mountain Bank 0f NH ($)	7/27/94	80.00	120.00
SO132	APS, Pittsburgh - #39, 90¢ Washington	8/18/94	16.00	25.00
SO133	APS - #1 Proof of 5¢ Franklin	8/18/94	80.00	120.00
SO134	Balpex'94 - #226, 10¢ D. Webster	9/3/94	16.00	25.00
SO135	ASDA Mega Event - #122, 90¢ Lincoln	11/3/94	16.00	25.00
SO136	ASDA - #2 Proof of 10¢ Washington	11/3/94	80.00	120.00
SO137	Paper Money Show - 100 Peso El Banco of Uruguay ($)	11/11/94	16.00	25.00

Note: From 1995 on, ABNC Souvenir Cards were limited editions.

SCCS celled Number Card	Event and Description	First Day Show/Issue	Mint Card	Can-celled Card
F1973B	Four Statues with IPP Text line	5/21/73	9.50	70.00
F1981B	$2 Embarkation of the Pilgrims ($)	5/17/81	35.00	95.00
F1982A	Napex'82 - Flag with Pledge of Allegiance	7/2/82	10.00	20.00
F1982B	Balpex'82 - Great Seal	9/4/82	15.00	40.00
F1983A	IPPDS & EU - $1 North Berwick Bank($)	1983	10.00	40.00
F1983C	Napex'83 - "Medal of Honor"	6/10/83	10.00	25.00
F1983F	Balpex'83 - George Washington	9/3/83	10.00	15.00
F1984A	Napex'84 - G.Washington & U.S. Capitol	6/24/84	10.00	20.00
F1984C	"Men in Currency" 11 faces	1984	250.00	275.00
F1985D	IPPDS & EU - Eagle resting on Rock	5/12/85	30.00	..
F1987A-B	IPPDS & EU - 6 Train Vignettes on 2 cards	5/3/87	35.00	90.00
F1987G	IPPDS & EU - 6 Train Vignettes on 1 card	5/3/87	70.00	150.00
F1988C	IPPDS & EU - Canadian Parliament, Statue of Liberty, Indep.Hall, U.S. Capitol	1988	30.00	..
F1990D	Napex'90 - #F1983C with 60th Ann. Ovpt.	6/1/90	80.00	100.00
F1991F	GENA'91 - "1000" Breakfast Card	9/27/91	125.00	..
F1992A	SCCS Annual Meeting - Trolley Scene	1992	25.00	..
F1993A	GENA'93 - Woman with Sword & Shield	3/5/93	9.50	..
F1993F	ANA'93 - SCCS "$" Card	7/28/93	10.00	12.00
F1993G	SCCS'93 - Farming Scene	1993	25.00	28.50
F1993J	MANA'93 - SCCS, Eagle & Shield	1993	11.50	..

STAMP VENTURES SOUVENIR CARDS

SO98	World Columbian Stamp Expo - Vignette of Columbus by Canadian Bank Note Co.	5/22/92	42.50	90.00
SO99	WCSE - Czeslae Slania, Engraver	5/22/92	75.00	80.00
SO100	WCSE - Bonnie Blair Olympic Champion	5/22/92	70.00	80.00
SO101	WCSE - Eagle in Flight Hologram	5/22/92	50.00	90.00

OFFICIAL SOUVENIR PAGES

1453

Since March 1, 1972 the U.S. Postal Service has offered, by subscription, Souvenir Pages with first day cancels. They are known as "Official" Souvenir Pages. These were issued flat and unfolded.

Scott No.	Subject	Price
1972-78 Regular Issues		
1297	3¢ Francis Parkman	5.00
1305C	$1 O'Neill coil	17.50
1305E	15¢ O.W. Holmes	6.00
1393D	7¢ Benjamin Franklin	6.00
1397	14¢ LaGuardia	110.00
1399	18¢ Eliz. Blackwell	3.00
1400	21¢ A. Giannini	4.50
1972 Commemoratives		
1448-51	2¢ Cape Hatteras	85.00
1452	6¢ Wolf Trap Farm	35.00
1453	8¢ Yellowstone Park	100.00
1454	15¢ Mt. McKinley	25.00
1455	8¢ Family Planning	750.00
1456-59	8¢ Colonial Craftsmen	16.00
1460-62	C85 Olympics	12.00
1463	8¢ PTA	6.50
1464-67	8¢ Wildlife	7.50
1468	8¢ Mail Order	6.00
1469	8¢ Osteopathic Med	6.00
1470	8¢ Tom Sawyer	10.00
1471-72	8¢ Christmas 1972	7.50
1473	8¢ Pharmacy	7.50
1474	8¢ Stamp Collecting	6.00
1973 Commemoratives		
1475	8¢ Love	7.50
1476	8¢ Pamphleteers	6.00
1477	8¢ Broadside	6.00
1478	8¢ Post Rider	6.00
1479	8¢ Drummer	4.00
1480-83	8¢ Boston Tea Party	7.50
1484	8¢ George Gershwin	7.50
1485	8¢ Robinson Jeffers	5.50
1486	8¢ Henry O. Tanner	6.50
1487	8¢ Willa Cather	6.00
1488	8¢ Copernicus	7.00
1489-98	8¢ Postal People	7.00
1499	8¢ Harry S. Truman	6.00
1500-02,C86	Electronics	9.50
1503	8¢ Lyndon B. Johnson	5.75
1504	8¢ Angus Cattle	4.50
1505	10¢ Chautauqua	4.00
1506	10¢ Kansas Wheat	3.75
1507-08	8¢ Christmas 1973	6.50
1973-74 Regular Issues		
1509	10¢ Crossed Flags	3.50
1510	10¢ Jeff. Memorial	3.50
1511	10¢ Zip Code	4.50
1518	6.3¢ Bulk Rate coil	4.00

Scott No.	Subject	Price
1974 Commemoratives		
1525	10¢ VFW	3.50
1526	10¢ Robert Frost	5.50
1527	10¢ Expo '74	7.50
1528	10¢ Horse Racing	7.50
1529	10¢ Skylab	7.00
1530-37	10¢ Univ. Postal Un	7.50
1538-41	10¢ Mineral Heritage	7.50
1542	10¢ Fort Harrod	3.50
1543-46	10¢ Cont. Congress	6.50
1547	10¢ Energy Conserv	3.75
1548	10¢ Sleepy Hollow	5.50
1549	10¢ Retarded Children	3.50
1550-52	10¢ Christmas 1974	5.50
1975 Commemoratives		
1553	10¢ Benjamin West	4.50
1554	10¢ Paul L. Dunbar	6.00
1555	10¢ D.W. Griffith	5.50
1556	10¢ Pioneer – Jupiter	7.50
1557	10¢ Mariner 10	7.50
1558	10¢ Coll. Bargaining	3.50
1559	8¢ Sybil Ludington	4.00
1560	10¢ Salem Poor	5.00
1561	10¢ Haym Salomon	4.50
1562	18¢ Peter Francisco	4.50
1563	10¢ Lexington-Con.	4.50
1564	10¢ Bunker Hill	4.50
1565-68	10¢ Military Uniforms	7.50
1569-70	10¢ Apollo Soyuz	8.75
1571	10¢ Women's Year	3.50
1572-75	10¢ Postal Bicent	5.00
1576	10¢ Peace thru Law	3.50
1577-78	10¢ Bank /Commerce	4.75
1579-80	10¢Christmas 1975	5.25
1975-81 Americana Issues		
1581-82,84-85	1¢-4¢ Issues	3.50
1591	9¢ Rt. to Assemble	3.50
1592	10¢ Petit./Redress	3.50
1593	11¢ Free./Press	3.50
1594,1816	12¢ Conscience	3.75
1596	13¢ Eagle/Shield	4.00
1597,1618C	15¢ Ft. McHenry	4.00
1599,1619	16¢ Liberty	3.00
1603	24¢ Old No. Church	3.50
1604	28¢ Remote Outpost	3.00
1605	29¢ Lighthouse	3.75
1606	30¢ Am. Schools	4.00
1608	50¢ "Betty" Lamp	5.25
1610	$1 Rush Lamp	5.75
1611	$2 Kerosene Lamp	7.50
1612	$5 R.R. Lantern	13.50

Scott No.	Subject	Price
1975-81 Americana Issues (cont.)		
1613	3.1¢ Non Profit coil	8.00
1614	7.7¢ Bulk Rate coil	4.00
1615	7.9¢ Bulk Rate coil	3.00
1615C	8.4¢ Bulk Rate coil	4.00
1616	9¢ Assembly coil	3.00
1617	10¢ Redress coil	4.00
1618	13¢ Libty. Bell coil	3.50
1622,25	13¢ Flag/Ind. Hall	3.50
1623c	$1 Vending bk. p. 10	21.50
1976 Commemoratives		
1629-31	13¢Spirit of '76	5.00
1632	13¢ Interphil'76	4.50
1633-82	13¢ State Flags(5 pgs)	47.50
1683	13¢ Telephone Cent.	3.00
1684	13¢ Comm.Aviation	3.25
1685	13¢ Chemistry	3.25
1686-89	Bicentennial SS (4)	42.50
1690	13¢ Ben Franklin	3.00
1691-94	13¢ Decl.of Indep.	5.75
1695-98	13¢ Olympics	5.75
1699	13¢ Clara Maass	5.00
1700	13¢ Adolphe Ochs	4.25
1701-3	13¢ Christmas 1976	4.50
1977 Commemoratives		
1704	13¢ Wash./Princeton	3.00
1705	13¢ Sound Recording	4.00
1706-9	13¢ Pueblo Art	6.00
1710	13¢ Lindbergh Flight	4.00
1711	13¢ Colorado	3.50
1712-15	13¢ Butterflies	4.50
1716	13¢ Lafayette	3.00
1717-20	13¢ Skilled Hands	4.00
1721	13¢ Peace Bridge	3.25
1722	13¢ Herkimer/Oriskany	3.00
1723-24	13¢ Energy	3.00
1725	13¢ Alta California	3.00
1726	13¢ Art. of Confed.	3.00
1727	13¢ Talking Pictures	4.00
1728	13¢ Saratoga	4.00
1729-30	13¢ Christmas,Omaha	3.00
1729-30	13¢ Valley Foige	3.00
1978 Issues		
1731	13¢ Carl Sandburg	3.75
1732-33	13¢ Cook, Anchorage	4.00
1732-33	13¢ Cook, Honolulu	4.00
1734	13¢ Indian Head Penny	4.00
1735,43	(15¢)"A" Stamp (2)	5.00
1737	15¢ Roses Bklt.single	3.75
1742a	15¢ Windmills Booklet Pane of 10 (1980)	7.50
1744	13¢ Harriet Tubman	5.75
1745-48	13¢ Quilts	4.75
1749-52	13¢ Dance	5.50
1753	13¢ French Alliance	3.00
1754	13¢ Dr.Papenicolaou	3.75
1755	13¢ Jimmie Rodgers	5.25
1756	15¢ George M. Cohan	3.75
1757	13¢ CAPEX'78	9.50
1758	15¢ Photography	4.50
1759	15¢ Viking Missions	6.25
1760-63	15¢ American Owls	4.75
1764-67	15¢ American Trees	4.00
1768	15¢ Madonna & Child	3.00
1769	15¢ Hobby Horse	3.00
1979 Commemoratives		
1770	15¢ Robert F. Kennedy	4.25
1771	15¢ Martin L.King,Jr.	5.00
1772	15¢ Year of the Child	3.25
1773	15¢ John Steinbeck	5.00
1774	15¢ Albert Einstein	5.75
1775-78	15¢ PAToleware	4.50
1779-82	15¢ Architecture	4.25
1783-86	15¢ Endang.Flora	4.50
1787	15¢ Seeing Eye Dogs	3.00
1788	15¢ Special Olympics	3.00
1789	15¢ John Paul Jones	3.85
1790	10¢ Olympics	4.25
1791-94	15¢ Summer Olympics	6.25
1795-98	15¢ Winter Olympics(80)	6.50
1799	15¢ Virgin & Child	3.50
1800	15¢ Santa Claus	3.50
1801	15¢ Will Rogers	4.00
1802	15¢ Vietnam Vets	5.00
1980-81 Issues		
1803	15¢ W.C.Fields	4.75
1804	15¢ Ben.Banneker	4.75
1805-10	15¢ Letter Writing	4.00
1811	1¢ Quill Pen Coil	3.00
1813	3.5¢ Non Profit Coil	4.00
1818,20	(18¢) "B" Stamps	3.50
1821	15¢ Frances Perkins	4.00
1822	15¢ Dolly Madison	3.00
1823	15¢ Emily Bissell	3.00
1824	15¢ Keller/Sullivan	3.50
1825	15¢ Veterans Admin.	3.00

Scott No.	Subject	Price
1826	15¢ B. de Galvez	3.25
1827-30	15¢ Coral Reefs	5.00
1831	15¢ Organized Labor	4.50
1832	15¢ Edith Wharton	4.50
1833	15¢ Education	4.25
1834-37	15¢ Indian Masks	5.00
1838-41	15¢ Architecture	4.00
1842	15¢ St.Glass Windows	3.75
1843	15¢ Antique Toys	4.25
1980-85 Great Americans		
1844	1¢ Dorothea Dix	4.00
1845	2¢ Igor Stravinsky	3.50
1846	3¢ Henry Clay	3.00
1847	4¢ Carl Shurz	3.00
1848	5¢ Pearl S. Buck	3.00
1849	6¢ Walter Lippmann	3.00
1850	7¢ A. Baldwin	3.75
1851	8¢ Henry Knox	3.00
1852	9¢ Sylvanus Thayer	3.50
1853	10¢ Richard Russell	3.00
1854	11¢ A. Partridge	3.00
1855	13¢ Crazy Horse	4.00
1856	14¢ Sinclair Lewis	3.00
1857	17¢ Rachel Carson	3.00
1858	18¢ George Mason	3.00
1859	19¢ Sequoyah	3.00
1860	20¢ Ralph Bunche	6.50
1861	20¢ T. Gallaudet	3.50
1862	20¢ Truman	3.00
1863	22¢ Audubon	3.50
1864	30¢ Dr. Laubach	3.00
1865	35¢ Dr. C. Drew	3.00
1866	37¢ R. Millikan	3.50
1867	39¢ G. Clark	3.00
1868	40¢ L. Gilbreth	3.00
1869	50¢ C. Nimitz	4.00
1981-82 Issues		
1874	15¢ Everett Dirksen	3.00
1875	15¢ Whitney Young	5.25
1876-79	18¢ Flowers	4.00
1889a	18¢ Wildlife bk/10	6.50
1890-91	18¢ Flag	4.00
1893a	6¢ & 18¢ Flag & Stars bklt. pn	3.50
1894-95	20¢ Flag	5.00
1896a	20¢ Flag bklt. pn./6	4.50
1896b	20¢ Flag bkt. pn./10	4.50
1981-84 Transportation Coils		
1897	1¢ Omnibus	4.00
1897A	2¢ Locomotive	5.00
1898	3¢ Handcar	4.50
1898A	4¢ Stagecoach	5.25
1899	5¢ Motorcycle	6.75
1900	5.2¢ Sleigh	6.00
1901	5.9¢ Bicycle	8.00
1902	7.4¢ Baby Buggy	5.00
1903	9.3¢ Mail Wagon	5.25
1904	10.9¢ Hansom Cab	5.50
1905	11¢ Caboose	4.75
1906	17¢ Electric Car	4.00
1907	18¢ Surrey	4.00
1908	20¢ Pumper	6.00
1981-83 Regulars & Commem.		
1909	$9.35 Eagle bklt. sgl.	110.00
1909a	$9.35 Bklt.pane of 3	175.00
1910	18¢ Red Cross	3.00
1911	18¢ Savings & Loan	3.00
1912-19	18¢ Space Achieve	10.00
1920	18¢ Prof. Manage	3.00
1921-24	18¢ Wildlife Habitats	4.00
1925	18¢ Disable Person	3.00
1926	18¢ St. Vincent Millay	3.75
1927	18¢ Alcoholism	4.25
1928-31	18¢ Architecture	4.25
1932	18¢ Babe Zaharias	12.50
1933	18¢ Bobby Jones	15.00
1934	18¢ Fred. Remington	3.00
1935-36	18¢ & 20¢ J. Hoban	3.00
1937-38	18¢ Yrktwn/V Capes	4.00
1939	20¢ Madonna/Child.	4.00
1940	20¢ "Teddy Bear"	5.00
1941	20¢ John Hanson	3.00
1942-45	20¢ Desert Plants	3.75
1946-47	"C" sht./coil stamps	4.50
1948a	"C" bklt. pane/10	4.25
1949a	20¢ Sheep bk pn/10	5.00
1982 Commemoratives		
1950	20¢ F.D. Roosevelt	3.00
1951	20¢ Love	3.00
1952	20¢ G. Washington	5.00
1953/2002	20¢ State Birds & Flowers (5)	65.00
2003	20¢ Netherlands	3.00
2004	20¢ Library-Congress	3.00

Scott No.	Subject	Price
1982 Issues		
2005	20¢ Consumer Coil .	4.75
2006-09	20¢ World's Fair	3.00
2010	20¢ Horatio Alger ...	3.00
2011	20¢ Aging	3.00
2012	20¢ Barrymores	5.00
2013	20¢ Dr. Mary Walker	3.00
2014	20¢ Int'l Peace Garden	3.00
2015	20¢ Libraries	3.00
2016	20¢ Jackie Robinson	15.00
2017	20¢ Touro Synagogue	3.00
2018	20¢ Wolf Trap	3.00
2019-22	20¢ Architecture	3.00
2023	20¢ Francis of Assisi	2.75
2024	20¢ Ponce de Leon	2.75
2025	13¢ Kitten & Puppy	3.50
2026	20¢ Madonna	3.50
2027-30	20¢ Snow Scene	3.50
1983 Commemoratives		
2031	20¢ Science & Industry	3.00
2032-35	20¢ Balloons	3.00
2036	20¢ Sweden/US	3.00
2037	20¢ Civ.Conservation	3.00
2038	20¢ Joseph Priestley	3.00
2039	20¢ Volunteerism ...	3.00
2040	20¢ German Immigr	3.00
2041	20¢ Brooklyn Bridge	3.75
2042	20¢ Tenn. Valley Auth	3.00
2043	20¢ Physical Fitness	3.00
2044	20¢ Scott Joplin	4.00
2045	20¢ Medal of Honor	8.00
2046	20¢ Babe Ruth	15.00
2047	20¢ Hawthorne	3.00
2048-51	13¢ Olympics	4.50
2052	20¢ Treaty of Paris	3.00
2053	20¢ Civil Service	3.00
2054	20¢ Metropolitan Opera	3.75
2055-58	20¢ Inventors	3.50
2059-62	20¢ Streetcars	4.50
2063	20¢ Madonna	3.00
2064	20¢ Santa Claus	3.00
2065	20¢ Martin Luther ...	4.50
1984 Commemoratives		
2066	20¢ Alaska Statehood	3.00
2067-70	20¢ Winter Olympics	4.00
2071	20¢ FDIC	3.00
2072	20¢ Love	3.00
2073	20¢ Carter G. Woodson	4.50
2074	20¢ Soil/Water Con	3.00
2075	20¢ Credit Un.Act ..	3.00
2076-79	20¢ Orchids	4.50
2080	20¢ Hawaii Statehood	4.00
2081	20¢ Nat'l. Archives	3.00
2082-85	20¢ Summer Olympics	4.75
2086	20¢ LA World Expo	3.00
2087	20¢ Health Research	3.00
2088	20¢ Douglas Fairbanks	5.00
2089	20¢ Jim Thorpe	10.00
2090	20¢ John McCormack	5.00
2091	20¢ St. Lawren. Seaway	3.00
2092	20¢ Mig. Bird Stamp Act	6.50
2093	20¢ Roanoke Voyages	3.00
2094	20¢ Herman Melville	3.50
2095	20¢ Horace Moses .	3.00
2096	20¢ Smokey Bear ..	10.00
2097	20¢ Roberto Clemente	14.00
2098-2101	20¢ Dogs	5.00
2102	20¢ Crime Prevention	3.00
2103	20¢ Hispanic Americans	2.50
2104	20¢ Family Unity	3.75
2105	20¢ Eleanor Roosevelt	5.00
2106	20¢ Nation of Readers	3.75
2107	20¢ Xmas Traditional	3.75
2108	20¢ Xmas Santa Claus	3.75
2109	20¢ Vietnam Vets Mem	5.00
1985-87 Issues		
2110	22¢ Jerome Kern ...	3.75
2111-12	"D" sht./coil stamps	3.00
2113a	22¢ "D" bklt. pane/10	4.50
2114-15	22¢ Flag	3.75
2115b	22¢ Flag "T" coil	4.00
2116a	22¢ Flag bklt. bk./5	4.00
2121a	22¢ Seashells bk/10	6.00
2122	$10.75 Eagle bklt.sgl.	47.50
2122a	$10.75 Bklt. pane/3	100.00
1985-89 Transportation Coils		
2123	3.4¢ School Bus	4.75
2124	4.9¢ Buckboard	4.50
2125	5.5¢ Star Rt. Truck	4.75
2126	6¢ Tricycle	4.00
2127	7.1¢ Tractor	3.75
2127a	7.1¢ Tractor Zip+4 .	3.00
2128	8.3¢ Ambulance	4.50

Scott No.	Subject	Price
1985-89 Transportation Coils (cont.)		
2129	8.5¢ Tow Truck	3.00
2130	10.1¢ Oil Wagon	3.75
2130a	10.1¢ Red Prec	3.50
2131	11¢ Stutz Bearcat ..	4.50
2132	12¢ Stanley Stmr ...	4.25
2133	12.5¢ Pushcart	4.50
2134	14¢ Iceboat	5.00
2135	17¢ Dog Sled	3.50
2136	25¢ Bread Wagon ..	4.75
1985 Issues (cont.)		
2137	22¢ Mary Bethune .	4.50
2138-41	22¢ Duck Decoys ..	6.00
2142	22¢ Winter Special Olympics.	3.00
2143	22¢ Love	4.25
2144	22¢ Rural Electr	3.00
2145	22¢ AMERIPEX '86	3.25
2146	22¢ Abigail Adams .	3.00
2147	22¢ Fred Bartholdi .	4.50
2149	18¢ G. Wash. coil ..	3.00
2150	21.1¢ Zip+4 coil	4.25
2152	22¢ Korean War Vets	3.75
2153	22¢ Social Security	3.00
2154	22¢ W War I Vets ..	4.50
2155-58	22¢ Horses	6.00
2159	22¢ Public Education	3.00
2160-63	22¢ Youth Year	5.75
2164	22¢ End Hunger	3.25
2165	22¢ Madonna	3.00
2166	22¢ Poinsettia	4.00
1986 Issues		
2167	22¢ Arkansas Statehd	3.00
1986-94 Great Americans		
2168	1¢ M. Mitchell	4.50
2169	2¢ Mary Lyon	3.00
2170	3¢ Dr. P.D. White ...	3.00
2171	4¢ Fr. Flanagan	3.00
2172	5¢ Hugo Black	3.50
2173	5¢ Munoz Marin	3.00
2175	10¢ Red Cloud	4.50
2176	14¢ Julia W. Howe .	2.50
2177	15¢ Buffalo Bill	3.00
2178	17¢ B. Lockwood ...	3.50
2179	20¢ Virginia Agpar .	5.50
2180	21¢ C. Carlson	3.00
2181	23¢ M. Cassatt	3.00
2182	25¢ Jack London ...	3.00
2182a	Bklt. pn./10	5.75
2183	28¢ Sitting Bull	3.00
2184	29¢ Earl Warren	4.50
2185	29¢ T. Jefferson	4.00
2186	35¢ Dennis Chavez	4.25
2187	40¢ C.L. Chennault	3.75
2188	45¢ Cushing	3.00
2189	52¢ H. Humphrey ..	3.75
2190	56¢ John Harvard ..	3.75
2191	65¢ H. Arnold	4.50
2192	75¢ Wendell Wilkie .	4.50
2193	$1 Dr. B. Revel	3.00
2194	$1 Johns Hopkins ..	4.00
2195	$2 W.J. Bryan	5.00
2196	$5 B. Harte	12.50
2197a	25¢ London, bk/6 ..	4.00
1986 Issues		
2201a	22¢ Stamp Collect .	5.50
2202	22¢ Love	4.00
2203	22¢ Sojourner Truth	4.25
2204	22¢ Republic Texas	3.00
2209a	22¢ Fish bklt. pane/5	6.00
2210	22¢ Public Hospitals	3.00
2211	22¢ Duke Ellington .	6.00
2216-19	US Pres. shts.,4 pgs.	25.00
2220-23	22¢ Polar Explorers	4.50
2224	22¢ Statue of Liberty	4.00
2226	2¢ Locom. re-engr .	3.00
2235-38	22¢ Navajo Art	4.75
2239	22¢ T.S. Elliot	4.50
2240-43	22¢ Woodcarv Figs	4.75
2244	22¢ Madonna	4.00
2245	22¢ Christmas Trees	3.00
1987 Issues		
2246	22¢ Michigan	3.50
2247	22¢ Pan-Am. Games	3.50
2248	22¢ Love	3.50
2249	22¢ J. Baptiste Pointe du Sable	6.75
2250	22¢ Enrico Caruso .	3.75
2251	22¢ Girl Scouts	6.50
1987-88 Transportation Coils		
2252	3¢ Con. Wag	3.50
2253,62	5¢,17.5¢	3.75

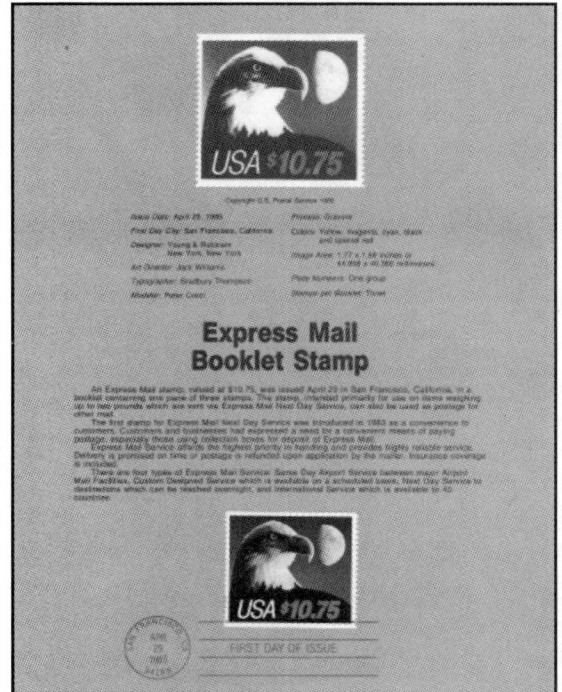

2122

Scott No.	Subject	Price
1987-88 Transportation Coils (cont.)		
2254	5.3¢ Elevator, Prec.	3.75
2255	7.6¢ Carretta, Prec.	3.75
2256	8.4¢ Wheelchair, Prec.	3.75
2257	10¢ Canal Boat	3.00
2258	13¢ Police Wag,Prec.	4.50
2259	13.2¢ RR Car, Prec	4.00
2260	15¢ Tugboat	3.50
2261	16.7¢ Pop.Wag,Prec.	3.50
2263	20¢ Cable Car	3.50
2264	20.5¢ Fire Eng, Prec	4.50
2265	21¢ RR Mail Car,Pre	4.75
2266	24.1¢ Tand. Bike,Pr	3.75
1987-89 Issues		
2274a	22¢ Sp. Occ. Bk	5.50
2275	22¢ United Way	3.00
2276a	222¢ Flag/Fireworks	3.00
2276a	Bklt. pair	4.00
2277,79	(25¢) "E" sheet/coil	4.25
2278	25¢ Flag/Clouds	3.00
2280	25¢ Flag/Yosem. coil	3.00
2280var	Pre-phos. paper	3.00
2281	25¢ Honeybee coil ..	4.75
2282a	(25¢) "E" Bklt. Pane/10	5.00
2283a	25¢ Pheasant Bk/10	5.00
2284-85	25¢ Owl/Grosbeak. Bk	4.25
2285Ac	25¢ Flag/Clouds Bk	4.50
2286-2335	22¢ Wildlife (5) ...	35.00
1987-90 Bicentennial Issues		
2336	22¢ Delaware	3.75
2337	22¢ Penn	3.00
2338	22¢ New Jersey	3.50
2339	22¢ Georgia	3.50
2340	22¢ Conn	3.50
2341	22¢ Mass	4.00
2342	22¢ Maryland	3.00
2343	25¢ S. Carolina	3.00
2344	25¢ New Hampshire	3.00
2345	22¢ Virginia	3.50
2346	25¢ New York	3.50
2347	25¢ North Carolina .	3.50
2348	25¢ Rhode Island ..	3.50
1987-88 Issues		
2349	22¢ U.S.-Moroc. Rel.	3.00
2350	22¢ Faulkner	5.00
2351-54	22¢ Lacemaking	6.50
2359a	22¢ Const. Bklt. ...	5.00
2360	22¢ Sign. Const	3.00
2361	22¢ CPA	5.75
2366a	22¢ Loco. Bklt	9.00
2367	22¢ Madonna	3.00
2368	22¢ Ornament	3.00

Scott No.	Subject	Price
1987-88 Issues (continued)		
2369	22¢ '88 Wnt. Olym .	3.00
2370	22¢ Australia Bicent.	3.50
2371	22¢ J.W. Johnson .	4.00
2372-75	22¢ Cats	6.00
2376	22¢ Knute Rockne .	10.00
2377	25¢ F. Ouimet	13.50
2378	25¢ Love	3.50
2379	45¢ Love	3.00
2380	25¢ Sum. Olym	3.00
2385a	25¢ Classic Cars bk	6.50
2386-89	25¢ Ant. Expl	4.00
2390-93	25¢ Carousel Anim	5.00
2394	$8.75 Express Mail	27.50
2396a-98a	25¢ Occas.bk.(2)	45.00
2399	25¢ Madonna	3.00
2400	25¢ Village Scene ..	3.00
1989-90 Issues		
2401	25¢ Montana Sthd .	3.00
2402	25¢ A.P. Randolph .	4.25
2403	25¢ N.Dakota Sthd	3.00
2404	25¢ Washington sthd.	3.00
2409a	25¢ Steamboats bklt.	6.00
2410	25¢ Wld. Stamp Exp	3.00
2411	25¢ A. Toscanini ...	4.50
2412	25¢ House of Reps	3.00
2413	25¢ U.S. Senate	3.00
2414	25¢ Exec.Branch/GW	3.00
2415	25¢U.S.Sup.Ct.('90)	3.00
2416	25¢ S.Dakota sthd.	3.00
2417	25¢ Lou Gehrig	15.00
2418	25¢ E. Hemingway .	6.00
2419	$2.40 Moon Landing	18.00
2420	25¢ Letter Carriers .	3.00
2421	25¢ Bill of Rights ...	3.00
2422-25	25¢ Prehis. Animals	10.00
2426/C121	25¢/45¢ Pre-Columbian Customs	3.50
2427,27a	25¢ Christmas Art, Sht. & Bklt. Pn	6.75
2428,29a	25¢ Christmas Sleigh, Sht. & Bklt. Pn	6.75
2431	25¢ Eagle, self-adhes	3.00
2433	90¢ WSE S/S of 4 .	11.50
2434-37	25¢ Classic Mail	5.00
2438	25¢ Cl.Mail S/S of 4	7.00
2439	25¢ Idaho Sthd	3.00
2440,41a	25¢ Love, sht. & bklt.	5.00
2442	25¢ Ida B. Wells	5.00
2443a	15¢ Bch. Umbr., bklt.	5.00
2444	25¢ Wyoming Sthd .	4.00
2445-48	25¢ Classic Films .	7.50
2449	25¢ Marianne Moore	3.75

OFFICIAL SOUVENIR PAGES

2522

Scott No.	Subject	Price
	1992 Commemoratives	
2611-15	29¢ Winter Olympics	5.50
2616	29¢ World Columbian	3.50
2617	29¢ W.E.B. DuBois	6.00
2618	29¢ Love	3.50
2619	29¢ Olympic BB	17.50
2620-23	29¢ Columb. Voyages	5.50
2624-29	1¢-$5 Columbus S/S	55.00
2630	29¢ NY Stock Exchg	3.75
2631-34	29¢ Space Accomp	7.00
2635	29¢ Alaska Hwy	4.00
2636	29¢ Kentucky Sthd	3.75
2637-41	29¢ Summer Olymp	5.50
2646a	29¢ Hummingbird Pn	8.50
2647-96	29¢ Wildflowers (5)	45.00
2697	29¢ WW II S/S	9.50
2698	29¢ Dorothy Parker	4.00
2699	29¢ Dr. von Karman	6.00
2700-03	29¢ Minerals	7.00
2704	29¢ Juan Cabrillo	3.75
2709a	29¢ Wild Animals Bklt.	7.00
2710,10a	29¢ Christmas Trad. Sheet & Bklt.	11.00
2711-14,18a,19	29¢ Toys, sheet bklt.& Die Cut	7.50
2720	29¢ Chinese New Yr	11.00
	1993 Commemoratives	
2721	29¢ Elvis Presley	17.50
2722	29¢ Oklahoma	3.50
2723	29¢ Hank Williams	6.00
2724/30,2737a	29¢ Rock 'n Roll Bklt. & Single	30.00
2745a	29¢ Space Fantasy, Bklt. Pane of 5	12.00
2746	29¢ Perry L. Julian	6.50
2747	29¢ Oregon Trail	4.00
2748	29¢ World Games	4.00
2749	29¢ Grace Kelly	11.00
2750-3	29¢ Circus	7.50
2754	29¢ Cherokee Strip	6.00
2755	29¢ Dean Acheson	4.00
2756-9	29¢ Sports Horses	8.50
2764a	29¢ Garden Flowers, Bklt. Pane of 5	6.50
2765	29¢ WW II S/S	11.00
2766	29¢ Joe Louis	14.50
2770a	29¢ Broadway, Booklet of 4	8.00
2771/4,2778a	Country Music, Booklet & Single	18.00
2779-82	29¢ Postal Museum	5.50
2783-4	29¢ Deaf Commun	4.00
2785-8	29¢ Youth Classics	5.25
2789,2790a	29¢ Madonna	8.50
2791/4,2798b,2799/2802,2803	29¢ Christmas	22.00
2804	29¢ Nthn. Marianas	4.00
2805	29¢ Columbus Landing in Puerto Rico	5.00
2806,2806b	29¢ AIDS	8.00
	1994 Issues	
2807-11	29¢ Winter Olympics	8.25
2812	29¢ Edward R.Murrow	5.25
2813	29¢ Sunrise Love	5.25
2814a,15	29¢-52¢ Love	11.00
2814C	29¢ Love	5.00
2816	29¢ Dr. Allison Davis	8.00
2817	29¢ Chinese New Year	6.00
2818	29¢ Buffalo Soldiers	8.50
2819-28	29¢ Silent ScreenStars	10.00
2833a	29¢ Garden Flowers, Bklt. Pane of 5	8.50
2834-36	29¢-50¢ Soccer	10.00
2837	Soccer Sv. Sheet	10.00
2838	29¢ WW II S/S	9.00
2839-40	29¢ Rockwell Stamp & S/S	16.50
2841-42	29¢/$9.95 Moon	30.00
2847a	29¢ Locomotive Pn.	10.75
2848	29¢ George Meany	5.25
2849-53	29¢ Pop Singers	10.00
2854-61	29¢ Blues/Jazz	13.00
2862	29¢ J. Thurber	6.00
2863-66	29¢ Wonders-Sea	8.00
2867-68	29¢ Cranes	5.00
2869	29¢ Legends-West	26.50
2871,71b	29¢ Madonna	12.00
2872,72a	29¢ Stocking	8.50
2873-74	29¢ Santa/Cardinal	10.00
2875	$2 BEP S/S	22.50
2876	29¢ Happy New Year	8.50
2877,84,90,93	"G" ABNC	6.00
2878,80,82,85	"G" SVS	6.00
2879,81,83,89	"G" BEP	6.00

Scott No.	Subject	Price
2886-87	"G" Self. Adh.	12.50
	1995-99 Issues	
2897/2916	32¢ Flag-Porch	8.00
2902	(5¢)Butte Coil	7.00
2902B,4A, 6,10,12A,15B Coils		8.00
2903-4	(5¢) Mountain Coil	6.50
2905	(10¢) Automobile Coil	6.50
2907,20d,21 Regulars		6.50
2908-9	(15¢) Tail Fin Coil	6.50
2911-12	(25¢) Juke Box Coil	5.25
2912B/15	Self Adhesives	8.00
2919	32¢ Flag - Field, S.A.	4.00
2933	32¢ M. Hershey	5.00
2934	32¢ Cal Farley	5.00
2935	32¢ Henry R. Luce	9.00
2936	32¢ Wallaces	9.00
2938	46¢ Ruth Benedict	5.00
2940	55¢ A. Hamilton	4.00
2941	55¢ Justin S. Morrill	9.00
2942	77¢ M. Breckenridge	7.00
2943	78¢ Alice Paul	4.00
	1995 Commemoratives	
2948-49	(32¢) Love	5.00
2950	32¢ Florida	4.00
2951-54	32¢ Kids Care	5.00
2955	32¢ Richard Nixon	5.00
2956	32¢ Bessie Coleman	6.50
2957-60	32¢ - 55¢ Angel	5.00
2961-65	32¢ Rec. Sports	12.50
2966	32¢ POW/MIA	5.00
2967	32¢ Marilyn Monroe	15.00
2968	32¢ Texas	6.00
2973a	32¢ Lighthouses Pn.	12.00
2974	32¢ U.N. Nations	4.00
2975	32¢ Civil War	20.00
2976-79	32¢ Carousel	8.50
2980	32¢ Suffrage	4.00
2981	32¢ World War II	10.00
2982	32¢ L. Armstrong	6.00
2983-92	32¢ Jazz	11.00
2997a	32¢ Garden Flowers, Pane of 5	10.00
2998	60¢ E. Rickenbacker	6.00
2999	32¢ Republic-Palau	5.00
3000	32¢ Comic Strips	20.00
3001	32¢ Naval Academy	6.00
3002	32¢ Tenn. Williams	6.00
3003,3b	32¢ Madonna	8.50
3004-7,8-11	32¢ Christmas	7.50
3012	32¢ Midnight Angel	6.50
3013	32¢ Children Sledding	6.50
3019-23	32¢ Antique Autos	8.50
	1996 Commemoratives	
3024	32¢ Utah Statehood	5.00
3029a	32¢ Garden Flowers, Pane of 5	8.50
3030	32¢ Love	6.50
	1996-2000 Regulars	
3031	1¢ Kestrel, SA	9.00
3032	2¢ Woodpeckers	5.00
3033	3¢ Bluebird	5.00
3036	$1 Red Fox	10.75
3048,53	20¢ Bluejay	7.00
3050,55	20¢ Pheasant	9.00
3052	33¢ Coral Pink Rose	9.00
3052E	33¢ Coral Pink Rose	9.00
3054	32¢ Yellow Rose Coil(97)	9.00
	1996 Commemoratives (cont.)	
3058	32¢ Ernest Just	7.50
3059	32¢ Smithsonian	5.00
3060	32¢ Chinese New Year	8.50
3061-64	32¢ Communications	6.50
3065	32¢ Fulbright	5.00
3066	50¢ J Cochran	5.00
3067	32¢ Marathon	5.00
3068	32¢ Atlanta Games	21.50
3069	32¢ Georgia O'Keefe	6.50
3070	32¢ Tennessee	5.00
3072-76	32¢ American Indian Dances	6.50
3077-80	32¢ Prehist. Animals	6.50
3081	32¢ Breast Cancer	6.50
3082	32¢ James Dean	9.00
3083-86	32¢ Folk Heroes	7.00
3087	32¢ Olympic Games	7.00
3088-89	32¢ Iowa	7.00
3090	32¢ Rural Free Delivery	5.50
3091-95	32¢ Riverboats	80.00
3096-99	32¢ Big Band Leaders	9.00
3100-3	32¢ Songwriters	9.00
3104	32¢ F.Scott Fitzgerald	5.50
3105	32¢ Endangered Species	22.50
3106	32¢ Computer Tech	5.50

Scott No.	Subject	Price
	1990-95 Transportation Coils	
2451	4¢ Steam Carriage	3.75
2452	5¢ Circus Wagon	4.00
2452B	5¢ Wagon, gravure	6.00
2452D	5¢ Circus Wagon, (c)Sign	5.25
2453,57	5¢/10¢ Canoe/Trailer	3.75
2454	5¢ Canoe, gravure	4.50
2458	10¢ Tractor Trailer	4.00
2463	20¢ Cog Railway	5.00
2464	23¢ Lunch Wagon	3.75
2466	32¢ Ferryboat	5.00
2468	$1.00 Seaplane coil	8.00
	1990-95 Issues	
2474a	25¢ Lighthouse bklt	7.50
2475	25¢ ATM Plastic Flag	4.50
2476,78,80	1¢/30¢ Birds	3.75
2477	1¢ Kestrel	4.00
2479	19¢ Fawn	3.75
2481	45¢ Pumpkinseed	4.50
2482	$2 Bobcat	6.50
2483	29¢ Blue Jay	4.00
2484a,85a	29¢ Wood Duck bklts. BEP & KCS	15.00
2486a	29¢ African Violet, booklet pane of 10	6.00
2487-88,93-94	Peach & Pear	6.00
2489	29¢ Red Squirrel	4.50
2490	29¢ Rose	4.00
2491	29¢ Pine Cone	4.00
2492	32¢ Pink Rose	6.50
2493-94	32¢ Peach/Pear	12.50
2496-2500	29¢ Olympics	7.00
2505a	25¢ Indian Headress	8.00
2506-07	25¢ Marsh Is. & Micro. Joint Issue	4.00
2508-11	25¢ Sea Creatures	7.00
2512/C127	25¢,45¢ America	4.00
2513	25¢ D.D. Eisenhower	4.00
2514,14a	25¢ Christmas sht. & Bklt. Pn./10	7.50
2515,16a	25¢ Christmas Tree sht. & Bklt. Pn./10	7.50
	1991-94 Issues	
2517,18	(29¢) "F" Flower, sht. & Coil pr	3.75
2519,20a	(29¢) "F" Flower, Bklt. Pns. of 10	11.00
2521	(4¢) Make-up rate	3.50
2522	(29¢) "F" Self Adh	3.75
2523	29¢ Flag/Rushmore	4.00
2523A	29¢ Mt. Rush, grav.	3.50
2524,27a	29¢ Flower,sht./bklt	8.00
2525	29¢ Flwr. coil,roulette	3.00

Scott No.	Subject	Price
	1991-94 Issues (continued)	
2526	29¢ Flower coil,perf.	4.00
2528a	29¢ Flag/Olympic Rings Bklt. pane	8.00
2529	19¢ Fishing Boat coil	5.00
2529C	19¢ Fishing Boat III	5.00
2530a	19¢ Balloons, bklt	5.50
2531	29¢ Flags on Parade	3.75
2531A	29¢ Liberty, ATM	3.75
	1991 Commemoratives	
2532	50¢ Switzerland	3.50
2533	29¢ Vermont	3.75
2534	29¢ Savings Bonds	3.00
2535,36a,37	29¢,52¢ Love, shts. & Bklt.	7.50
2538	29¢ William Saroyan	6.00
	1991-95 Regular Issues	
2539	$1.00 USPS & Olym	4.75
2540	$2.90 Priority Mail	12.50
2541	$9.95 Express Mail	30.00
2542	$14.00 Express Mail	42.50
2543	$2.90 Space P.M.	13.00
2544	$3 Challenger	16.00
2544A	$10.75 Endeavor	30.00
	1991 Commemoratives	
2549a	29¢ Fishing Flies bklt.	12.50
2550	29¢ Cole Porter	3.75
2551	29¢ Desert Storm/ Shield	10.00
2553-57	29¢ Summer Olympic	7.00
2558	29¢ Numismatics	5.00
2559	29¢ WW II S/S	10.75
2560	29¢ Basketball	10.00
2561	29¢ Washington, D.C.	3.50
2566a	29¢ Comedians bklt.	9.00
2567	29¢ Jan Matzeliger	6.00
2577a	29¢ Space bklt	9.00
2578,78a	29¢ Madonna,sht/bklt	11.00
2579,80,	29¢ Santa Claus	
	or 81,82-85 sht./bklt	17.50
	1992-95 Regulars	
2587	32¢ James Polk	6.50
2590	$1.00 Burgoyne	6.00
2592	$5.00 Washington	16.00
2593a	29¢ Pledge bklt.	6.00
2595-97	29¢ Eagle & Shield/ Die Cut (3 Pgs.)	5.50
2598	29¢ Eagle S/A	4.00
2599	29¢ Liberty	4.00
2602	(10¢)Eagle&Shld. coil	5.00
2603-4	(10¢) BEP & SV	5.25
2605	23¢ Flag/Pre-sort	3.50
2606	23¢ USA/Pre-sort	4.00
2607	23¢ Same, BEP	4.00
2608	23¢ Same, SV	3.75
2609	29¢ Flag/W.H. Coil	3.75

Scott No.	Subject	Price
1996 Issues (continued)		
3107/12	32¢ Madonna	9.00
3108/16	32¢ Family Scenes	9.00
3117	32¢ Skaters	9.00
3118	32¢ Hanukkah	7.00
3119	50¢ Cycling S.S.	9.00
1997 Issues		
3120	32¢ Chinese New Year	9.00
3121	32¢ B.O. Davis, Jr.	9.00
3122	32¢ Liberty	8.00
3123-24	32¢-55¢ Love	8.00
3125	32¢ Children Learn .	7.00
3126-29	32¢ Merian Prints ..	8.00
3130-31	32¢ PAC-97 Triangles	9.00
3132-33	Linerless Coils	8.00
3134	32¢ Thorton Wilder .	7.00
3135	32¢ R. Wallenberg .	7.00
3136	32¢ Dinosaurs	22.50
3137a	32¢ Bugs Bunny	19.50
3139	50¢ B. Franklin Sh.	18.00
3140	60¢ G.Washington Sh	18.00
3141	32¢ Marshall Plan ..	7.00
3142	32¢ Aircraft	22.50
3143-46	32¢ Football Coaches	19.50
3147	32¢ Vince Lombardi	13.00
3148	32¢ Bear Bryant	13.00
3149	32¢ Pop Warner	13.00
3150	32¢ George Halas ..	13.00
3151	32¢ Dolls ....:........	18.50
3152	32¢ Humphry Bogart	9.00
3153	32¢ Stars & Stripes	9.00
3154-57	32¢ Opera Singers .	13.00
3158-65	32¢ Composers	
	& Conductors	15.00
3166	32¢ Felix Varela	9.00
3167	32¢ Air Force	12.50
3168-72	32¢ Movie Monsters	15.00
3173	32¢ Supersonic Flight	13.00
3174	32¢ Women in Military	9.00
3175	32¢ Kwanza	11.00
3176	32¢ Madonna	11.00
3177	32¢ Holly	11.00
3178	$3 Mars Pathfinder	21.00
1998 Issues		
3179	32¢ Chinese New Yr	10.00
3180	32¢ Alpine Skiing ...	10.00
3181	32¢ Mdm. CJ Walker	10.00
3182	32¢ 1900's	20.00
3183	32¢ 1910's	20.00
3184	32¢ 1920's	20.00
3185	32¢ 1930's	20.00
3186	33¢ 1940's (1999) ..	20.00
3187	33¢ 1950's (1999) ..	20.00
3188	33¢ 1960's (1999) ..	20.00
3189	33¢ 1970's (1999) ..	20.00
3190	33¢ 1980's (2000) ..	20.00
3191	33¢ 1990's (2000) ..	20.00
3192	32¢ Remember-Maine	10.00
3193-97	32¢ Flowering Trees	12.00
3198-3202	32¢ A. Calder	12.00
3203	32¢ Cinco de Mayo	9.00
3204a	32¢ Sylvester & Tweety	12.00
3206	32¢ Wisconsin	10.00
3207-8	Wetlands, Diner Coils	9.00
3207A,70-71	Wetlands,	
	Eagle & Shield Coils	10.00
3208A	Diner Coil	9.00
3211	32¢ Berlin Airlift	9.00
3212-15	32¢ Folk Musicians	12.00
3216-19	32¢ Gospel Singers	11.00
3220	32¢ Spanish Sett. ...	9.00
3221	32¢ Stephen Benet	9.00
3222-25	32¢ Tropical Birds ..	12.00
3226	32¢ Alfred Hitchcock	10.00
3227	32¢ Organ & Tissue	9.00
3229	(10¢) Green Bicycle	9.00
3230-34	32¢ Bright Eyes	12.00
3235	32¢ Klondike Gold .	10.00
3236	32¢ American Art ...	20.00
3237	32¢ Ballet	10.00
3238-42	32¢ Space Discovery	12.00
3243	32¢ Giving & Sharing	9.00
3244	32¢ Madonna & Child	9.00
3245-52	32¢ Wreaths	12.00
3257-58,60	1¢ W.Vane, 33¢ Hat	10.00
3259,63	22¢ Uncle Sam	9.00
3261	$3.20 Shuttle	18.00
3262	$11.75 Shuttle	27.50
3264,66	33¢ Hat, Coils	10.50
3267-69	33¢ Hat,	
	Booklet Singles ...	11.00

Scott No.	Subject	Price
1999 Issues		
3272	33¢ Year of the Rabbit	9.00
3273	33¢ Malcolm X	9.00
3274	33¢ Love	12.00
3275	55¢ Love	10.00
3276	33¢ Hospice Care ..	9.00
3279,80,82	33¢ Flag and City	10.00
3283	33¢ Flag-Chalkboard	9.00
3286	33¢ Irish Immigration	9.00
3287	33¢ Lunt & Fontaine	9.00
3288-92	33¢ Arctic Animals .	12.00
3293	33¢ Sonoran Desert	19.50
3294-97	33¢ Berries	11.00
3294a-96a,97c	Berries (2000)	18.00
3306a	33¢ Daffy Duck	12.00
3308	33¢ Ayn Rand	10.00
3309	33¢ Cinco de Mayo	9.00
3310-13	33¢ Tropical Flowers	11.00
3314	33¢ J & W Bertram	9.00
3315	33¢ Prostrate Cancer	9.00
3316	33¢ Calif.Gold Rush	9.00
3317-20	33¢ Aquarium Fish .	11.00
3321-24	33¢ Xtreme Sports .	11.00
3325-28	33¢ American Glass	11.00
3329	33¢ James Cagney	11.00
3330	55¢ Billy Mitchell	11.00
3331	33¢ Those Who Served	9.00
3332	45¢ Univ.Postal Union	9.00
3333-37	33¢ All Aboard,Trains	12.00
3338	33¢ F.L.Olmstead ..	9.00
3339-44	33¢ Hollwd.Composers	15.00
3345-50	33¢ Bdwy.Songwriters	15.00
3351	33¢ Insects-Spiders	18.50
3352	33¢ Hanukkah	9.00
3353	22¢ Uncle Sam	9.00
3354	33¢ N.A.T.O.	9.00
3355	33¢ Madonna & Child	9.00
3356-59	33¢ Christmas Deer	11.00
3368	33¢ Kwanzaa	9.00
3369	33¢ Year 2000	9.00
2000 Commemoratives		
3370	33¢ Year of the Dragon	9.00
3371	33¢ P.R.Harris	9.00
3372	33¢ Submarine	10.00
3378	33¢ Pacific Coast R.F.	18.00
3379-83	33¢ Louise Nevelson	11.50
3384-88	33¢ Hubble Telescope	11.50
3389	33¢ American Samoa	9.00
3390	33¢ Library of Congress	9.00
3391a	33¢ Road Runner &	
	Wile E. Coyote	11.00
3393-96	33¢ Dist.Soldiers ...	12.00
3397	33¢ Summer Sports	9.00
3398	33¢ Adoption	9.00
3399-3402	33¢ Team Sports	10.00
3403	33¢ Stars & Stripes	17.50
3408	33¢ Legends-Baseball	21.00
3414-17	33¢ Stampin-Future	10.00
2000 Distinguished Americans		
3420	10¢ J.W. Stilwell	9.00
3426	33¢ Claude Pepper .	9.00
2000 Commemoratives (continued)		
3438	33¢ California	9.00
3439-43	33¢ Sea Creatures .	11.50
3444	33¢ Thomas Wolfe ..	9.00
3445	33¢ The White House	9.00
3446	33¢ Edward G. Robinson	9.00
2000 Regular Issues		
3447	(10¢) N.Y.Library Lion	9.00

25-cent and 31-cent International Airmail Stamps

C89-90

Scott No.	Subject	Price
1998 Semi-Postal		
B1	32¢+8¢ Breast Cancer	10.00
1973-85 Airmails		
C79	13¢ Winged Envelope	3.50
C83	13¢ Winged Env. Coil	3.50
C84	11¢ City of Refuge .	85.00
C87	18¢ Stat. of Liberty	7.00
C88	26¢ Mt. Rushmore .	5.50
C89-90	25¢ & 31¢ Airmails .	4.00
C91-92	31¢ Wright Brothers	4.00
C93-94	21¢ Octave Chanute	4.25
C95-96	25¢ Wiley Post	4.00
C97	31¢ Olympic Games	5.50
C98	40¢ Philip Mazzei ..	4.50
C99	28¢ Blanche Scott .	3.00
C100	35¢ Glenn Curtiss ..	3.00
C101-04	28¢ Olympics	5.00
C105-08	40¢ Olympics	4.00
C109-12	35¢ Olympics	4.50
C113	33¢ Alfred Verville .	3.00
C114	39¢ L.& E. Sperry ..	3.75
C115	44¢ Transpacific Flight	3.00
C116	44¢ Father J. Serra	3.00
1988-2000 Airmails		
C117	44¢ New Sweden ...	3.00
C118	45¢ S.P. Langley ...	3.00
C119	36¢ Sikorsky	3.50
C120	45¢ French Rev	5.00
C122-25	45¢ Future Mail	6.50
C126	$1.80 Future Mail S/S	6.50
C128	50¢ Harriet Quimby	3.50
C129	40¢ William Piper ..	3.50
C130	50¢ Antarctic Treaty	4.00
C131	50¢ America	3.50
C133	48¢ Niagara Falls ...	10.00
C134	40¢ Rio Grande	9.00
C135	60¢ Grand Canyon .	9.00

Scott No.	Subject	Price
1983-95 Official Issues		
O127-29,30-35	1¢/$5 (5 pgs)	22.50
O129A,136	14¢&22¢ Issues	4.00
O138-39	(14¢&22¢)"D" Sht.&Coil	3.00
O138A,141	15¢,25¢ Coils ..	3.50
O138B	20¢ Coil	3.00
O140	(25¢) "E" Coil	3.50
O143	1¢ Offset	3.50
O144	(29¢) "F" Coil	4.00
O145,47-48	19¢,23¢,29¢	
	Sgls. & Coil	3.75
O146	4¢ Make-up rate	3.75
O146A	10¢ Official	4.25
O153/56	1¢/32¢ Officials	4.50
O157	33¢ Official Coil	9.00
1992-94 Variable Rate Coils		
CV31	29¢ Variable Rate ..	5.00
CV32	29¢ Vert. Design	6.00
CV33	32¢ Variable Rate ..	6.75

AMERICAN COMMEMORATIVE PANELS

1480-83

1706-09

The U.S. Postal Service has provided panels for commemorative and Christmas issues since Scott #1464-67 (Sept. 20, 1972). Each panel features mint stamps along with appropriate steel engravings and interesting stories about the subject. Prices are for with or without the original sleeves. Please add 20% if you require sleeves.

Scott No.	Subject	Price
1972 Commemoratives		
1464-67	8¢ Wildlife	6.00
1468	8¢ Mail Order	6.00
1469	8¢ Osteopathic Med	10.00
1470	8¢ Tom Sawyer	9.00
1471	8¢ Christmas 1972	10.00
1472	8¢ 'Twas Night...	10.00
1473	8¢ Pharmacy	10.00
1474	8¢ Stamp Collecting	7.50
1973 Commemoratives		
1475	8¢ Love	9.00
1476	8¢ Pamphleteers	8.00
1477	8¢ Posting Broadside	8.00
1478	8¢ Post Rider	9.00
1479	8¢ Drummer	11.50
1480-83	8¢ Boston Tea Party	27.50
1484	8¢ George Gershwin	10.00
1485	8¢ Robinson Jeffers	7.50
1486	8¢ Henry O. Tanner	8.00
1487	8¢ Willa Cather	8.00
1488	8¢ Copernicus	8.00
1489-98	8¢ Postal People ...	8.00
1499	8¢ Harry S Truman .	10.00
1500-02,C86	Electronics	10.00
1503	8¢ Lyndon B. Johnson	9.50
1504	8¢ Angus Cattle	9.50
1505	10¢ Chautauqua (74)	8.00
1506	10¢ Kansas Wheat(74)	8.00
1507	8¢ Christmas (73) ..	12.00
1508	8¢ Needlepoint	11.00
1974 Commemoratives		
1525	10¢ Vet. Foreign Wars	7.00
1526	10¢ Robert Frost	7.00
1527	10¢ Expo '74	8.00
1528	10¢ Horse Racing ..	11.00
1529	10¢ Skylab	12.00
1530-37	10¢ Univ. Postal Un	9.00
1538-41	10¢ Mineral Heritage	10.00
1542	10¢ Fort Harrod	7.00
1543-46	10¢ Cont. Congress	9.00
1547	10¢ Energy Conserv	6.50
1548	10¢ Sleepy Hollow .	8.00
1549	10¢ Retarded Children	7.00
1550	10¢ Angel	10.00
1551	10¢ Currier R Ives .	10.00
1975 Commemoratives		
1553	10¢ Benjamin West	9.00
1554	10¢ Paul L. Dunbar	8.00
1555	10¢ D.W. Griffith	10.00
1556	10¢ Pioneer	12.00
1557	10¢ Mariner	14.00
1558	10¢ Coll Bargaining	6.00
1559-62	10¢ Contrib. to Cause	9.00
1563	10¢ Lexing. & Concord	7.00
1564	10¢ Bunker Hill	9.00

Scott No.	Subject	Price
1975 Commemoratives (cont.)		
1565-68	10¢ Military Uniforms	8.50
1569-70	10¢ Apollo Soyuz ..	14.00
1571	10¢ Women's Year .	7.00
1572-75	10¢ Postal Bicent ..	7.00
1576	10¢ Peace thru Law	7.00
1577-78	10¢ Bank/Commerce	8.50
1579	10¢ Madonna	9.00
1580	10¢ Christmas Card	9.00
1976 Commemoratives		
1629-31	13¢ Spirit of '76 ...	11.00
1632	13¢ INTERPHIL '76	9.00
1633/82	State Flags,Blk.4 .	22.50
1683	13¢ Telephone Cent.	9.00
1684	13¢ Commer. Aviation	11.00
1685	13¢ Chemistry	9.00
1690	13¢ Benj Franklin ...	9.00
1691-94	13¢ Dec. of Indepen	9.00
1695-98	13¢ Olympics	11.50
1699	13¢ Clara Maass	13.50
1700	13¢ Adolph S. Ochs	13.00
1701	13¢ Copley Nativity	12.00
1702	13¢ Currier Winter Past	11.00
1977 Commemoratives		
1704	13¢ Wash. Princeton	13.00
1705	13¢ Sound Recording	25.00
1706-09	13¢ Pueblo Art	90.00
1710	13¢ Lindbergh Flight	90.00
1711	13¢ Colorado	15.00
1712-15	13¢ Butterflies	17.50
1716	13¢ Lafayette	13.00
1717-20	13¢ Skilled Hands ..	13.00
1721	13¢ Peace Bridge ..	13.00
1722	13¢ Herkimer	13.00
1723-24	13¢ Energy	14.00
1725	13¢ Alta California .	13.50
1726	13¢ Art. of Confed .	20.00
1727	13¢ Talking Pictures	17.50
1728	13¢ Saratoga	19.50
1729	13¢ Valley Forge	22.50
1730	13¢ Rural Mailbox ..	30.00
1978 Commemoratives		
1731	13¢ Carl Sandburg .	8.50
1732-33	13¢ Captain Cook ..	15.00
1744	13¢ Harriet Tubman	13.00
1745-48	13¢ Quilts	17.50
1749-52	13¢ Dance	12.00
1753	13¢ French Alliance	13.00
1754	13¢ Dr. Papanicolaou	11.00
1755	13¢ Jimmie Rodgers	15.00
1756	15¢ George M. Cohan	15.00
1757	15¢ Photography ...	12.00
1758	15¢ Viking Missions	39.50
1760-63	15¢ Owls	39.50
1764-67	15¢ Trees	30.00

Scott No.	Subject	Price
1978 Commemoratives (cont.)		
1768	15¢ Madonna	14.00
1769	15¢ Hobby Horse ...	14.00
1979 Commemoratives		
1770	15¢ Robert Kennedy	11.00
1771	15¢ Martin L. King, Jr.	10.00
1772	15¢ Year of the Child	8.00
1773	15¢ John Steinbeck	7.50
1774	15¢ Albert Einstein	9.50
1775-78	15¢ Toleware	11.00
1779-82	15¢ Architecture	9.50
1783-86	15¢ Endang. Flora .	9.50
1787	15¢ Seeing Eye Dogs	8.00
1788	15¢ Special Olympics	10.00
1789	15¢ John Paul Jones	9.50
1790/C97	Olympic Games ...	11.00
1791-94	15¢ Summ.Olympics	12.00
1795-98	15¢ Winter Olym (80)	11.00
1799	15¢ Virgin & Child .	11.00
1800	15¢ Santa Claus	11.00
1801	15¢ Will Rogers	11.00
1802	15¢ Vietnam Vets ..	10.00
1980 Commemoratives		
1803	15¢ W.C. Fields	14.00
1804	15¢ Benj. Banneker	9.00
1821	15¢ Frances Perkins	7.00
1823	15¢ Emily Bissell ...	10.00
1824	15¢ Keller/Sullivan .	7.00
1825	15¢ Vet. Admin	7.00
1826	15¢ Gen. B. de Galvez	7.00
1827-30	15¢ Coral Reefs	9.00
1831	15¢ Organized Labor	7.00
1832	15¢ Edith Wharton .	6.50
1833	15¢ Amer. Education	7.00
1834-37	15¢ Indian Masks ..	13.00
1838-41	15¢ Architecture	7.50
1842	15¢ St. Glass Window.	10.00
1843	15¢ Antique Toys ...	10.00
1981 Commemoratives		
1874	15¢ Everett Dirksen	8.00
1875	15¢ Whitney Young	10.00
1876-79	18¢ Flowers	10.00
1910	18¢ Red Cross	9.00
1911	18¢ Savings & Loan	9.00
1912-19	18¢ Space Achieve	14.00
1920	18¢ Prof. Manage ..	7.00
1921-24	18¢ Wildlife Habitats	10.00
1925	18¢ Yr. Disable Per.	7.00
1926	18¢ Vincent Millay .	7.50
1928-31	18¢ Architecture	8.50
1932-33	18¢ Jones/Zaharias	32.50
1934	18¢ Fred Remington	10.00
1935-36	18¢ & 20¢ J. Hoban	7.00
1937-38	18¢ Yorktown Capes	7.00
1939	20¢ Madonna.	9.00
1940	20¢ "Teddy Bear" ...	10.00
1941	20¢ John Hanson ...	7.00
1942-45	20¢ Desert Plants ..	10.00

Scott No.	Subject	Price
1982 Commemoratives		
1950	20¢ Roosevelt	11.00
1951	20¢ Love	12.00
1952	20¢ G. Washington	13.00
1953/2002	20¢ State Birds & Flowers Blk	35.00
2003	20¢ Netherlands	13.00
2004	20¢ Library Congress	13.00
2006-09	20¢ World's Fair	11.00
2010	20¢ Horatio Alger ...	12.00
2011	20¢ Aging	12.00
2012	20¢ Barrymores	13.50
2013	20¢ Mary Walker	10.00
2014	20¢ Peace Garden .	12.00
2015	20¢ Libraries	10.00
2016	20¢ J.Robinson	35.00
2017	20¢ Touro Synag ...	12.00
2018	20¢ Wolf Trap	12.00
2019-22	20¢ Architecture	13.00
2023	20¢ Francis Assisi .	12.00
2024	20¢ Ponce de Leon	12.00
2025	20¢ Kitten & Puppy	18.50
2026	20¢ Madonna	17.00
2027-30	20¢ Snow Scene	17.00
1983 Commemoratives		
2031	20¢ Science/Industry	7.00
2032-35	20¢ Balloons	8.50
2036	20¢ Sweden/US	7.00
2037	20¢ Conserv.Corps	7.00
2038	20¢ Priestley	7.00
2039	20¢ Voluntarism	10.00
2040	20¢ German Immigr	7.00
2041	20¢ Brooklyn Bridge	8.00
2042	20¢ Tenn. Valley Auth	7.00
2043	20¢ Physical Fitness	7.00
2044	20¢ Scott Joplin	9.00
2045	20¢ Medal of Honor	10.00
2046	20¢ Babe Ruth	27.50
2047	20¢ Nath. Hawthorne	6.50
2048-51	13¢ Olympics	9.50
2052	20¢ Treaty of Paris	8.00
2053	20¢ Civil Service ...	7.50
2054	20¢ Met. Opera	9.00
2055-58	20¢ Inventors	9.00
2059-62	20¢ Streetcars	10.00
2063	20¢ Madonna	10.00
2064	20¢ Santa Claus	10.00
2065	20¢ Martin Luther ..	9.00
1984 Commemoratives		
2066	20¢ Alaska Statehood	7.00
2067-70	20¢ Winter Olympics	8.50
2071	20¢ FDIC	7.00
2072	20¢ Love	7.00
2073	20¢ Carter Woodson	6.00
2074	20¢ Soil/Water Cons.	6.00
2075	20¢ Credit Un.Act ..	6.00
2076-79	20¢ Orchids	7.00
2080	20¢ Hawaii Statehood	6.50
2081	20¢ Nat'l. Archives	6.00
2082-85	20¢ Summer Olympics	6.50

2381-85

2505a

Scott No.	Subject	Price
1984 Commemoratives (cont.)		
2086	20¢ Louisiana Expo	7.50
2087	20¢ Health Research	7.00
2088	20¢ Doug Fairbanks	8.00
2089	20¢ Jim Thorpe	9.00
2090	20¢ J McCormack	8.00
2091	20¢ St. Lawr. Seaway	8.50
2092	20¢ Migratory Bird	12.00
2093	20¢ Roanoke	7.00
2094	20¢ Herman Melville	8.00
2095	20¢ Horace Moses	7.00
2096	20¢ Smokey Bear	25.00
2097	20¢ Clemente	40.00
2098-2101	20¢ Dogs	10.00
2102	20¢ Crime Prevent	7.00
2103	20¢ Hispanic Amer.	7.00
2104	20¢ Family Unity	7.00
2105	20¢ E. Roosevelt	13.00
2106	20¢ Nation Readers	7.00
2107	20¢ Madonna	8.50
2108	20¢ Santa Claus	8.50
2109	20¢ Vietnam Vets	11.00
1985 Commemoratives		
2110	22¢ Jerome Kern	8.00
2137	22¢ Mary M. Bethune	8.00
2138-41	22¢ Duck Decoys	16.50
2142	22¢ Winter Special Olympics.	7.00
2143	22¢ Love	7.00
2144	22¢ Rural Electrific	7.00
2145	22¢ AMERIPEX '86	8.50
2146	22¢ Abigail Adams	7.00
2147	22¢ Bartholdi	10.00
2152	22¢ Korean War Vets	10.00
2153	22¢ Social Security	7.00
2154	22¢ World War I Vets	7.50
2155-58	22¢ Horses	13.50
2159	22¢ Public Education	7.00
2160-63	22¢ Youth Year	13.50
2164	22¢ Help End Hunger	7.50
2165	22¢ Madonna	9.00
2166	22¢ Poinsettias	9.00
1986 Commemoratives		
2167	22¢ Arkansas Statehd.	7.00
2201a	22¢ Stamp Col.	8.50
2202	22¢ Love	10.00
2203	22¢ Sojourner Truth	10.00
2204	22¢ Republic Texas	8.00
2209a	22¢ Fish booklet	11.00
2210	22¢ Public Hospitals	7.00
2211	22¢ Duke Ellington	10.00
2216-19	22¢ US Pres.4 panels	35.00
2220-23	22¢ Polar Explorers	10.00
2224	22¢ Statue of Liberty	10.00
2235-38	22¢ Navajo Art	11.50
2239	22¢ T.S. Elliot	8.50
2240-43	22¢ Woodcarved	10.00
2244	22¢ Madonna	8.00
2245	22¢ Village	8.00

Scott No.	Subject	Price
1987 Commemoratives		
2246	22¢ Michigan	8.00
2247	22¢P-Am. Games	7.00
2248	22¢ Love	8.00
2249	22¢ J.Bap. Sable	9.00
2250	22¢ Enrico Caruso	9.00
2251	22¢ Girls Scouts	11.00
2274a	22¢ Sp. Occ. Bk	7.00
2275	22¢ United Way	7.00
2286-2335	22¢ Am.Wildlife(5)	42.50
1987-90 Bicentennial Issues		
2336	22¢ Delaware	9.50
2337	22¢ Pennsylvania	8.00
2338	22¢ New Jersey	8.00
2239	22¢ Georgia	8.00
2340	22¢ Connecticut	8.00
2341	22¢ Massachusetts	8.00
2342	22¢ Maryland	8.00
2343	25¢ South Carolina	8.00
2344	25¢ New Hampshire	8.00
2345	25¢ Virginia	8.00
2346	25¢ New York	8.00
2347	25¢ North Carolina	8.00
2348	25¢ Rhode Island	8.00
1987 Commemoratives (cont)		
2349	22¢ U.S.-Morocco	7.00
2350	22¢ Faulkner	7.00
2351-54	22¢ Lacemaking	10.00
2359a	22¢ Const. Bklt.	8.50
2360	22¢ Const. Signing	8.00
2361	22¢ CPA	25.00
2366a	22¢ Locom. Bklt.	10.00
2367	22¢ Madonna	8.00
2368	22¢ Ornaments	7.00
1988 Commemoratives		
2369	22¢ '88 Wint. Olympics	8.00
2370	22¢ Australia Bicent.	9.00
2371	22¢ J.W. Johnson	8.50
2372-75	25¢ Cats	10.00
2376	22¢ K. Rockne	15.00
2377	25¢ F. Ouimet	21.50
2378-79	25¢-45¢ Love	8.50
2380	25¢ Sum. Olympics	8.00
2385a	25¢ Classic Cars bk	10.00
2386-89	25¢ Ant. Explorers	8.50
2390-93	25¢ Carousel	10.00
2395-98	25¢ Occasions bk.	8.50
2399-2400	25¢ Christmas	8.50
1989 Commemoratives		
2401	25¢ Montana	8.00
2402	25¢ Randolph	10.00
2403	25¢ North Dakota	8.00
2404	25¢ Washington	8.00
2409a	25¢ Steamboats bklt.	10.00
2410	25¢ Wld. Stamp Expo	7.00
2411	25¢ Arturo Toscanini	10.00
2412	25¢ House of Reps	10.00
2413	25¢ U.S. Senate	10.00
2414	25¢ Exec./GW Inaug.	10.00
2415	25¢ Supr Court(1990)	8.50

Scott No.	Subject	Price
1989 Commemoratives (cont.)		
2416	25¢ South Dakota	8.50
2417	25¢ Lou Gehrig	35.00
2418	25¢ E. Hemingway	12.00
2420	25¢ Letter Carriers	8.50
2421	25¢ Bill of Rights	8.00
2422-25	25¢ Prehis. Animals	20.00
2426/C121	25¢/45¢ Pre-Columbian Customs	9.00
2427-28	25¢ Christmas	11.00
2434-37	25¢ Classic Mail	8.00
1990 Commemoratives		
2439	25¢ Idaho Sthd	7.00
2440,41a	25¢ Love	8.50
2442	25¢ Ida B. Wells	15.00
2444	25¢ Wyoming Sthd	8.50
2445-48	25¢ Classic Films	18.00
2449	25¢ Marianne Moore	8.00
2474a	25¢ Lighthouse bklt	16.50
2496-2500	25¢ Olympians	13.00
2505a	25¢ Headress Bklt.	12.00
2506-07	25¢ Marshalls & Micronesia Joint Issue	9.00
2508-11	25¢ Sea Creatures	15.00
2512/C127	25¢,45¢ America	11.00
2513	25¢ D.D. Eisenhower	11.00
2514,15	25¢ Christmas	10.00
1991 Commemoratives		
2532	50¢ Switzerland	10.00
2533	29¢ Vermont	8.00
2534	29¢ Savings Bonds	8.50
2535,37	29¢ Love	11.00
2538	29¢ William Saroyan	12.50
2549a	29¢ Fishing Flies bk	13.00
2550	29¢ Cole Porter	10.00
2551	29¢ Desert Shield	35.00
2553-57	29¢ Summer Olymp	11.00
2558	29¢ Numismatics	9.50
2559	29¢ WW II	15.00
2560	29¢ Basketball	16.50
2561	29¢ Dist.of Columbia	9.00
2566a	29¢ Comedians bklt.	14.00
2567	29¢ Jan Matzeliger	9.50
2577a	29¢ Space bklt	14.00
2578-79	29¢ Christmas	12.00
2587	32¢ J. S. Polk(1995)	11.50
1992 Commemoratives		
2611-15	29¢ Winter Olympics	11.00
2616	29¢ World Columbian	11.00
2617	29¢ W.E.B. DuBois	15.00
2618	29¢ Love	12.00
2619	29¢ Olympic Baseball	40.00
2620-23	29¢ Columb.Voyages	12.00
2624-29	1¢/$5 Columbus S/S Set of 3 Panels	200.00
2630	29¢ Stock Exchange	15.00
2631-34	29¢ Space Accomp	14.00
2635	29¢ Alaska Highway	9.50
2636	29¢ Kentucky Sthd	8.50
2637-41	29¢ Summer Olympic	11.00
2646a	29¢ Hummingbird B.Pn	13.00

Scott No.	Subject	Price
1992 Commemoratives (cont.)		
2647-96	29¢ Wildflowers (5)	175.00
2697	29¢ WW II S/S	13.00
2698	29¢ Dorothy Parker	8.50
2699	29¢ Dr. von Karman	13.50
2700-03	29¢ Minerals	13.50
2704	29¢ Juan Cabrillo	11.00
2709a	29¢ Wild Animals Pn.	14.00
2710,14a	29¢ Christmas	15.00
2720	29¢ Chinese New Yr	25.00
1993 Commemoratives		
2721	29¢ Elvis Presley	25.00
2722	29¢ Oklahoma	10.00
2723	29¢ Hank Williams	20.00
2737b	29¢ Rock 'n Roll	25.00
2745a	29¢ Space Fantasy	15.00
2746	29¢ Percy L. Julian	13.00
2747	29¢ Oregon Trail	11.00
2748	29¢ World Games	11.00
2749	29¢ Grace Kelly	22.50
2750-3	29¢ Circus	12.00
2754	29¢ Cherokee Strip	11.00
2755	29¢ Dean Acheson	14.00
2756-9	29¢ Sports Horses	13.00
2764a	29¢ Garden Flowers	11.00
2765	29¢ WW II S/S	15.00
2766	29¢ Joe Louis	35.00
2770a	29¢ Broadway Musicals, Booklet Pane	15.00
2775-8	29¢ Country-Western	22.50
2779-82	29¢ Postal Museum	12.50
2783-4	29¢ Deaf Commun	11.00
2785-8	29¢ Youth Classics	13.50
2789,91-4	29¢ Christmas	14.00
2804	29¢ Nthn.Marianas	11.00
2805	29¢ Columbus Lands in Puerto Rico	14.00
2806	29¢ AIDS	12.00
1994 Commemoratives		
2807-11	29¢ Winter Olympics	20.00
2812	29¢ Edward R.Murrow	12.00
2814a	29¢ Love, Bklt Pane	13.00
2816	29¢ Allison Davis	15.00
2817	29¢ Chinese New Year	18.00
2818	29¢ Buffalo Soldiers	16.00
2819-28	29¢ Silent Screen Stars	18.00
2833a	29¢ Garden Flowers, Pane of 5	14.00
2837	29¢,40¢,50¢ World Cup Soccer, S/S of 3	15.00
2838	29¢ WWII S/S	18.00
2839	29¢ Norman Rockwell	25.00
2841	29¢ Moon Landing	22.50
2847a	29¢ Locomotives, Pane of 5	16.00
2848	29¢ George Meany	11.00
2849-53	29¢ Pop. Singers	16.00
2854-61	29¢ Jazz/Blues	20.00
2862	29¢ J. Thurber	10.00
2863-66	29¢ Wonders - Sea	15.00
2867-68	29¢ Cranes	15.00

AMERICAN COMMEMORATIVE PANELS

2967

C105-08

Scott No.	Subject	Price
1994 commemoratives (cont.)		
2871	29¢ Madonna	11.00
2872	29¢ Stocking	11.00
2876	29¢ Year of Boar	16.00
1995 Commemoratives		
2950	32¢ Florida	12.00
2951-54	32¢ Kids Care	12.00
2955	32¢ R. Nixon	18.00
2956	32¢ B. Coleman	17.00
2957-58	32¢-55¢ Love	17.00
2961-65	32¢ Rec. Sports	17.00
2966	32¢ POW/MIA	14.00
2967	32¢ M. Monroe	30.00
2968	32¢ Texas	15.00
2973a	32¢ Lighthouses	17.00
2974	32¢ Un. Nations	13.00
2976-79	32¢ Carousel	17.00
2980	32¢ Women's Suffrage	13.00
2981	32¢ WWII S/S	19.50
2982	32¢ L. Armstrong	20.00
2983-92	32¢ Jazz Musicians.	21.50
2997a	32¢ Garden Flowers	
	Pane of 5	13.00
2999	32¢ Palau	13.00
3001	32¢ Naval Academy	17.00
3002	32¢ Tennessee Williams	15.00
3003	32¢ Madonna	17.00
3004-7	32¢ Christmas	17.00
3019-23	32¢ Antique Autos	22.50
1996 Commemoratives		
3024	32¢ Utah	13.00
3029a	32¢ Garden Flowers	13.00
3058	32¢ Ernest E. Just	18.00
3059	32¢ Smithsonian	13.00
3060	32¢ Chinese New Year	22.00
3061-4	32¢ Communications	17.00
3065	32¢ Fulbright Scholar.	13.00
3067	32¢ Marathon	17.00
3068	32¢ Olympics Sheet	45.00
3069	32¢ Georgia O'Keeffe	13.00
3070	32¢ Tennessee	13.00
3071-6	32¢ Indian Dances	21.50
3077-80	32¢ Prehistoric Animals	21.50
3081	32¢ Breast Cancer	13.00
3082	32¢ James Dean	21.50
3083-86	32¢ Folk Heroes	21.50
3087	32¢ Olympic Games	15.00
3088	32¢ Iowa	13.00
3090	32¢ Rural Free	
	Delivery	13.00
3091-95	32¢ Riverboats	21.50
3096-99	32¢ Big Band Leaders	21.50
3100-3	32¢ Songwriters	21.50
3104	32¢ Scott Fitzgerald	25.00
3105	32¢ Endangered Spec	35.00
3106	32¢ Computer Tech	25.00
3107	32¢ Madonna	17.00
3108-11	32¢ Family	18.00
3118	32¢ Hanukkah	25.00
3119	50¢ Cycling Sv. Sheet	25.00

Scott No.	Subject	Price
1997 Commemoratives		
3120	32¢ Chinese New Year	27.50
3121	32¢ Benjamin Davis	17.00
3124	55¢ Love	15.00
3125	32¢ Children Learn	13.00
3130-31	32¢ Triangles	17.00
3134	32¢ Thorton Wilder	15.00
3135	32¢ R. Wallenberg	15.00
3136	32¢ Dinosaurs	27.50
3137c	32¢ Bugs Bunny	25.00
3139	50¢ B. Franklin Sh	75.00
3140	60¢ G.Washington Sh	75.00
3141	32¢ Marshall Plan	13.00
3142	32¢ Aircraft Sheet	36.50
3143-46	32¢ Football Coaches	23.50
3151	32¢ Dolls Sheet	35.00
3152	32¢ Humphrey Bogart	18.00
3153	32¢ Stars and Stripes	16.00
3154-57	32¢ Opera Singers	18.00
3158-65	32¢ Comp/Conductors	18.50
3166	32¢ Felix Varela	16.00
3167	32¢ Air Force	19.00
3168-72	32¢ Movie Monsters	20.00
3173	32¢ Supersonic Flight	20.00
3174	32¢ Women in Military	16.00
3175	32¢ Kwanza	18.50
3176a	32¢ Madonna	23.50
3177a	32¢ Holly	23.50
1998 Commemoratives		
3179	32¢ Chinese New Yr	16.00
3180	32¢ Alpine Skiing	16.00
3181	32¢ Mdm. CJ Walker	16.00
1998-2000 Celebrate the Century		
3182	32¢ 1900's	25.00
3183	32¢ 1910's	25.00
3184	32¢ 1920's	25.00
3185	32¢ 1930's	25.00
3186	33¢ 1940's (1999)	25.00
3187	33¢ 1950's (1999)	25.00
3188	33¢ 1960's (1999)	25.00
3189	33¢ 1970's (1999)	25.00
3190	33¢ 1980's (2000)	25.00
3191	33¢ 1990's (2000)	25.00
1998 Commemoratives (cont.)		
3192	32¢ Remember-Maine	16.00
3193-97	32¢ Flowering Trees	19.50
3198-3202	32¢ A. Calder	19.50
3203	32¢ Cinco de Mayo	16.00
3204c	32¢ Sylvester/Tweety	20.00
3206	32¢ Wisconsin	16.00
3209-10	Trans-Mississippi (2)	27.50
3211	32¢ Berlin Airlift	16.00
3212-15	32¢ Folk Musicians	18.00
3216-19	32¢ Gospel Singers	16.00
3220	32¢ Spanish Settlem.	18.00
3221	32¢ Stephen V. Benet	16.00
3222-25	32¢ Tropical Birds	16.00
3226	32¢ Alfred Hitchcock	16.00
3227	32¢ Organ & Tissue	16.00
3230-34	32¢ Bright Eyes	17.00

Scott No.	Subject	Price
1998 Commemoratives (cont.)		
3235	32¢ Klondiike Gold	16.00
3236	32¢ Art	25.00
3237	32¢ Ballet	16.00
3238-42	32¢ Space Discovery	17.00
3243	32¢ Giving/Sharing	16.00
3244a	32¢ Madonna	21.00
3249-52	32¢ Wreaths	16.00
1999 Commemoratives		
3272	33¢ Year of the Rabbit	16.00
3273	33¢ Malcolm X	16.00
3274a	33¢ Love, Pane	25.00
3275	55¢ Love	18.00
3276	33¢ Hospice Care	16.00
3286	33¢ Irish Immigration	16.00
3287	33¢ Lunt & Fontaine	16.00
3288-92	33¢ Arctic Animals	17.00
3293	33¢ Sonoran Desert	25.00
3306	33¢ Daffy Duck	25.00
3308	33¢ Ayn Rand	22.50
3309	33¢ Cinco de Mayo	16.00
3314	33¢ J & W Bartram	16.00
3315	33¢ Prostrate Cancer	16.00
3316	33¢ Calif. Gold Rush	16.00
3317-20	33¢ Aquarium Fish	16.00
3321-24	33¢ Xtreme Sports	16.00
3325-28	33¢ American Glass	16.00
3329	33¢ James Cagney	16.00
3331	33¢ Those who Served	16.00
3333-37	33¢ All Aboard,Trains	20.00
3338	33¢ F.L.Olmstead	16.00
3339-44	33¢ Hollywd.Composers	17.50
3345-50	33¢ Bdwy.Songwriters	17.50
3351	33¢ Insects-Spiders	25.00
3352	33¢ Hanukkah	16.00
3354	33¢ N.A.T.O.	16.00
3355	33¢ Madonna and Child	16.00
3356-59	33¢ Christmas Deer	16.00
3368	33¢ Kwanzaa	16.00
2000 Commemoratives		
3370	33¢ Year of the Dragon	20.00
3371	33¢ Patricia R. Harris	18.00
3372	33¢ Submarine	18.00
3378	33¢ Pacific Rain Forest	25.00
3379-83	33¢ Lousie Nevelson	18.00
3384-88	33¢ Space Telescope	18.00
3389	33¢ American Samoa	16.00
3390	33¢ Library of Congress	16.00
3391	33¢ Road Runner &	
	Wile E. Coyote	25.00
3393-96	33¢ Disting.Soldiers	20.00
3397	33¢ Summer Sports	16.00
3398	33¢ Adoption	16.00
3399-3402	33¢ Team Sports	16.00
3403	33¢ Stars & STripes	25.00
3408	33¢ Legends- Baseball	25.00
3414-17	33¢ Stampin'the Future	16.00
3438	33¢ California	16.00
3439-43	33¢ Deep Sea Creatures	18.00
3444	33¢ Thomas Wolfe	16.00

Scott No.	Subject	Price
2000 Commemoratives (cont.)		
3445	33¢ Whtie House	16.00
3446	33¢e Edward G. Robinson	
		16.00
1998 Semi-Postal		
B1	32¢+8¢ Breast Cancer	22.50
Airmails		
C101-04	28¢ Olympics	8.50
C105-06	40¢ Olympics	8.50
C109-12	35¢ Olympics	9.50
C117	44¢ New Sweden	8.50
C120	45¢ French Revolution	8.00
C122-25	45¢ Future Mail	10.00
C130	50¢ Antarctic Treaty	8.00
C131	50¢ America	8.00

CONFEDERATE STATES OF AMERICA

1,4   6   7   8

9   11   12   13

1861-62 (OG + 40%) (C)

Scott's No.		Unused Fine	Unused Ave.	Used Fine	Used Ave.
1	5¢ Jefferson Davis, Green	165.00	95.00	140.00	85.00
2	10¢ T. Jefferson, Blue	210.00	130.00	175.00	110.00
3	2¢ Andrew Jackson, Green (1862) ..	465.00	275.00	600.00	350.00
4	5¢ Jefferson, Rose (1862)	125.00	75.00	95.00	55.00
5	10¢ T. Jefferson, Rose (1862)	825.00	500.00	450.00	275.00
6	5¢ J. Davis, London Print, Clear ('62)	7.50	4.50	25.00	16.00
7	5¢ J. Davis, Local Print, Coarse ('62)	10.75	6.50	17.50	11.00

1862-63 (OG + 30%) (C)

Scott's No.		Unused Fine	Unused Ave.	Used Fine	Used Ave.
8	2¢ A. Jackson, Brown Red (1863) ...	49.50	29.50	300.00	180.00
9	10¢ J. Davis, Blue "TEN CENTS" ('63)	575.00	335.00	475.00	280.00
10	10¢ Blue "10 CENTS", Frame Line ..	2750.00	1600.00	1150.00	675.00
11	10¢ same, No Frame Line, Die A ..	8.50	5.50	13.00	7.75
12	10¢ same, Filled in Corners, Die B ..	10.00	6.00	15.00	9.00
13	20¢ Washington, Green (1863)	27.50	17.00	350.00	210.00
14	1¢ J.C. Calhoun, Orange (unissued)	65.00	42.50	...	...

CANAL ZONE

1904 U.S. 1902-03 Issue Ovptd. "CANAL ZONE" "PANAMA" VF Used + 50% ©

Scott's No.		NH VF	NH F-VF	Unused VF	Unused F-VF	Used F-VF
4	1¢ Frank., Bl. Grn. (#300)	79.50	52.50	48.50	32.50	22.50
5	2¢ Wash., Carmine (#319)	72.50	47.50	42.50	27.50	23.50
6	5¢ Lincoln, Blue (#304)	240.00	160.00	145.00	95.00	60.00
7	8¢ M. Wash., V.Blk. (#306) ...	400.00	265.00	240.00	160.00	80.00
8	10¢ Webster,Red Brn.(#307) ..	425.00	280.00	265.00	175.00	100.00

70   71   96   100

1924-25 U.S. Stamps of 1923-25 Overprinted "CANAL ZONE" (Flat Top "A") Flat Press, Perf. 11 VF Used + 30% (B)

Scott's No.		NH VF	NH F-VF	Unused VF	Unused F-VF	Used F-VF
70	½¢ N. Hale (#551)	2.10	1.50	1.30	.95	.65
71	1¢ Franklin (#552)	2.40	1.80	1.60	1.20	.80
71e	1¢ Bklt. Pane of 6 (#552a)	285.00	200.00	185.00	135.00	...
72	1½¢ Harding (#553)	3.75	2.65	2.35	1.75	1.50
73	2¢ Washington (#554)	14.50	10.50	9.50	7.00	1.65
73a	2¢ Bklt. Pane of 6 (#554c)	400.00	300.00	275.00	200.00	...
74	5¢ T. Roosevelt (#557)	36.50	27.50	24.00	18.00	7.50
75	10¢ Monroe (#562)	82.50	61.50	53.50	40.00	21.50
76	12¢ Cleveland (#564)	77.50	55.00	47.50	35.00	30.00
77	14¢ Indian (#565)	57.50	41.50	37.50	27.50	21.00
78	15¢ Liberty (#566)	100.00	77.50	65.00	50.00	32.50
79	30¢ Buffalo (#569)	60.00	45.00	40.00	30.00	21.50
80	50¢ Amphitheater (#570)	135.00	100.00	87.50	65.00	42.50
81	$1 Lincoln Mem. (#571)	500.00	380.00	330.00	250.00	90.00

1925-28 Same as Preceding but with Pointed "A", VF Used + 30% (B)

Scott's No.		NH VF	NH F-VF	Unused VF	Unused F-VF	Used F-VF
84	2¢ Washington (#554)	60.00	45.00	38.50	28.50	7.50
84d	2¢ Bklt. Pane of 6 (#554c)	395.00	275.00	285.00	195.00	...
85	3¢ Lincoln (#555)	8.25	6.25	5.35	3.95	3.25
86	5¢ T. Roosevelt (#557)	8.35	6.25	5.25	3.95	2.10
87	10¢ Monroe (#562)	65.00	46.50	40.00	30.00	11.00
88	12¢ Cleveland (#564)	50.00	35.00	30.00	22.50	13.00
89	14¢ Indian (#565)	41.50	30.00	26.50	19.50	16.50
90	15¢ Liberty (#566)	13.50	10.00	8.50	6.50	4.25
91	17¢ Wilson (#623)	7.50	5.50	4.85	3.65	2.85
92	20¢ Golden Gate (#567)	13.00	10.00	8.50	6.50	3.25
93	30¢ Buffalo (#569)	10.50	7.75	6.25	5.00	3.75
94	50¢ Amphitheater (#570)	500.00	385.00	325.00	250.00	210.00
95	$1 Lincoln Mem (#571)	250.00	185.00	160.00	120.00	60.00

1926 Sesquicentennial Issue Overprinted "CANAL ZONE" VF Used + 30%

96	2¢ Liberty Bell (#627)	7.50	5.50	5.25	4.00	3.00

1926-27 Rotary Press, Perf. 10, Overprinted "CANAL ZONE" VF Used + 60% (B)

97	2¢ Washington (#583)	100.00	60.00	65.00	42.50	11.50
98	3¢ Lincoln (#584)	19.50	11.50	12.50	7.50	4.35
99	10¢ Monroe (#591)	32.50	19.50	21.50	13.00	7.25

CANAL ZONE

1927-31 Rotary Press, Perf. 11x10½, Overprinted "CANAL ZONE" VF Used + 30% (B)

Scott's No.		NH VF	NH F-VF	Unused VF	Unused F-VF	Used F-VF
100	1¢ Franklin (#632)	3.85	2.85	2.80	2.10	1.35
101	2¢ Washington (#634)	4.50	3.20	3.15	2.30	.85
101a	2¢ Bklt. Pane of 6 (#634d) ...	450.00	300.00	300.00	200.00	...
102	3¢ Lincoln (#635) (1931)	8.50	6.25	5.75	4.25	2.75
103	5¢ T. Roosevelt (#637)	50.00	37.50	33.50	25.00	10.75
104	10¢ Monroe (#642) (1930)	35.00	26.75	23.75	18.00	11.50

105   107   110   112

1928-40 Flat Plate Printing VF Used + 20% (B)

Scott's No.		NH VF	NH F-VF	Unused VF	Unused F-VF	Used F-VF
105-14	Set of 10	10.75	8.25	7.75	6.25	4.25
105	1¢ General Gorgas	.30	.25	.25	.20	.15
105	Plate Block of 6	1.00	.70	.70	.50	...
106	2¢ General Goethels	.30	.25	.25	.20	.15
106	Plate Block of 6	3.25	2.40	2.35	1.75	...
106a	2¢ Booklet Pane of 6	36.50	28.00	26.50	20.00	...
107	5¢ Gaillard Cut (1929)	1.60	1.15	1.15	.90	.50
107	Plate Block of 6	16.00	12.00	11.75	8.75	...
108	10¢ General Hodges (1932)	.35	.25	.25	.20	.20
108	Plate Block of 6	9.50	7.00	6.75	5.00	...
109	12¢ Colonel Gaillard (1929)	1.35	1.00	.95	.75	.65
109	Plate Block of 6	14.50	10.75	10.50	8.00	...
110	14¢ Gen. W.L. Sibert (1937)	1.50	1.15	1.10	.85	.85
110	Plate Block of 6	17.00	12.50	12.00	9.50	...
111	15¢ Jackson Smith (1932)	.70	.55	.50	.40	.40
111	Plate Block of 6	11.00	8.00	7.75	6.00	...
112	20¢ Adm. Rousseau (1932)	1.00	.80	.75	.60	.20
112	Plate Block of 6	11.75	8.50	8.25	6.50	...
113	30¢ Col. Williamson (1940)	1.50	1.15	1.10	.90	.75
113	Plate Block of 6	19.00	13.75	13.00	9.50	...
114	50¢ J. Blackburn (1929)	2.50	1.90	1.85	1.50	.65
114	Plate Block of 6	25.00	19.00	18.50	15.00	...

1933 Rotary Press, Perf. 11x10½ VF Used + 30% (B)

115	3¢ Washington (#720)	5.15	3.95	3.65	2.75	.25
115	Plate Block of 4	65.00	50.00	47.50	35.00	...
116	14¢ Indian (#695)	8.75	6.25	6.00	4.50	3.50
116	Plate Block of 4	100.00	75.00	70.00	50.00	...

1934-39 Issues VF Used + 30% (B)

117   118   120

117	3¢ General Goethals	.35	.25	.30	.20	.15
117	Plate Block of 6	2.10	1.60	1.55	1.25	...
117a	3¢ Booklet Pane of 6	110.00	72.50	75.00	52.50	...
118	½¢ Franklin (#803) (1939)	.35	.25	.30	.20	.15
118	Plate Block of 4	5.00	3.75	3.65	2.75	...
119	1½¢ M. Wash. (#805) (1939)	.35	.25	.30	.20	.15
119	Plate Block of 4	4.65	3.50	3.35	2.50	...

1939 25th Anniversary Series VF + 30%

Scott's No.		Plate Blocks F-VF NH	Plate Blocks F-VF Unus.	F-VF NH	F-VF Unus.	F-VF Used
120-35	Set of 16			120.00	85.00	72.50
120	1¢ Balboa, before .... (6)	13.50	10.00	.75	.55	.35
121	2¢ Balboa, after .... (6)	13.50	10.00	.75	.55	.40
122	3¢ Gaillard Cut, before .... (6)	13.50	10.00	.75	.55	.25
123	5¢ Gaillard Cut, after .... (6)	22.00	16.00	1.75	1.25	1.15
124	6¢ Bas Obispo, before .... (6)	47.50	35.00	3.25	2.35	2.75
125	7¢ Bas Obispo, after .... (6)	47.50	35.00	3.50	2.50	2.75
126	8¢ Gatun Locks, before ...... (6)	60.00	45.00	5.25	3.75	3.25
127	10¢ Gatun Locks, after .... (6)	60.00	45.00	3.75	2.85	2.65
128	11¢ Canal Channel, before .. (6)	130.00	100.00	9.00	6.50	8.00
129	12¢ Canal Channel, after .... (6)	110.00	80.00	8.50	6.00	7.50
130	14¢ Gamboa, before .... (6)	130.00	100.00	8.50	6.00	7.50
131	15¢ Gamboa, after .... (6)	165.00	125.00	11.50	8.00	5.50
132	18¢ P. Miguel Locks, before . (6)	160.00	120.00	11.50	8.00	7.50
133	20¢ P. Miguel Locks, after .. (6)	200.00	150.00	14.00	10.00	6.75
134	25¢ Gatun Spillway, before . (6)	335.00	250.00	20.00	14.00	16.00
135	50¢ Gatun Spillway, after ... (6)	365.00	275.00	25.75	18.00	5.50

137   141   142   145

Scott's No.		Plate Blocks NH	Plate Blocks Unus.	F-VF NH	F-VF Unus.	F-VF Used
	1946-51 Issues VF + 25%					
136-40	**Set of 5**	**18.50**	**15.00**	**2.50**	**1.95**	**1.50**
136	½¢ General Davis (1948) ... (6)	3.00	2.50	.45	.35	.25
137	1½¢ Gov. Magoon (1948) .. (6)	3.00	2.50	.45	.35	.25
138	2¢ T. Roosevelt (1949) .... (6)	.95	.75	.25	.20	.15
139	5¢ J. Stevens, 19x22 mm .. (6)	3.50	2.75	.45	.35	.20
140	25¢ J.F. Wallace (1948) ..... (6)	9.50	7.50	1.00	.80	.75
141	10¢ Biological Area (1948) . (6)	11.00	8.50	1.35	1.15	.85
142-45	**Gold Rush (1949)**	**52.50**	**43.50**	**4.75**	**3.75**	**3.35**
142	3¢ "Forty Niners" .... (6)	6.50	5.00	.65	.50	.35
143	6¢ Journey to Las Cruces .. (6)	7.00	5.50	.75	.60	.45
144	12¢ Las Cruces Trail .... (6)	19.50	16.50	1.30	1.00	.90
145	18¢ To San Francisco .... (6)	22.50	18.50	2.50	1.90	1.80
146	10¢ W. Indian Labor(1951) (6)	27.50	21.50	2.75	2.10	1.50

1955-58 Commemoratives

148

149

150

Scott's No.		Plate Blocks NH	F-VF NH	F-VF Used
147	3¢ Panama Railroad .... (6)	7.50	.75	.45
148	3¢ Gorgas Hospital (1957)	4.35	.50	.40
149	4¢ S.S. Ancon (1958)	3.75	.50	.35
150	4¢ T. Roosevelt (1958)	4.00	.55	.40

1960-62 Issues

151

152

153

157

151	4¢ Boy Scouts	4.50	.55	.45
152	4¢ Administration Bldg	1.10	.20	.20
		Line Pairs		
153	3¢ Goethals, Coil, Perf.10 Vert.	1.10	.20	.15
154	4¢ Admin. Bldg., Coil, Perf.10 Horiz. ...	1.15	.20	.15
155	5¢ Stevens, Coil, Perf.10 Vert. (1962) .	1.50	.30	.25
		Plate Blocks		
156	4¢ Girl Scouts (1962)	2.75	.45	.35
157	4¢ Thatcher Ferry Bridge ('62)	3.75	.40	.30

1968-78 Issues

158

159

163

165

158	6¢ Goethals Monument Balboa	2.25	.35	.30
159	8¢ Fort San Lorenzo (1971)	2.95	.45	.25
		Line Pairs		
160	1¢ Gorgas,Coil,Pf.10 Vert.(1975)	1.10	.20	.20
161	10¢ Hodges,Coil,Pf.10 Vert.(1975)	5.50	.85	.50
162	25¢ Wallace,Coil,Pf.10 Vert.(1975)	21.50	3.00	2.85
		Plate Blocks		
163	13¢ Dredge Cascadas (1976)	2.35	.40	.30
163a	13¢ Booklet Pane of 4	...	3.50	...
164	5¢ Stevens, Rotary, 19x22½mm (1977)	4.25	.65	.75
164a	5¢ Stevens, Tagged	...	11.00	...
165	15¢ Towing Locomotive (1978)	2.75	.50	.40

AIR MAIL STAMPS

C1

C3

C5

C6

CANAL ZONE

Scott's No.		NH VF	NH F-VF	Unused VF	Unused F-VF	Used F-VF
	1929-31 Surcharges on Issues of 1928-29 VF Used + 30% (B)					
C1	15¢ on 1¢ Gorgas T.I (#105) ...	16.00	12.00	9.75	7.50	5.75
C2	15¢ on 1¢ Gorgas T.II (1931)	210.00	155.00	130.00	87.50	90.00
	Type I: Flag "5" points up. Type II: Flag of "5" is curved up.					
C3	25¢ on 2¢ Goethals (#106)	7.50	5.25	4.75	3.50	2.10
C4	10¢ on 50¢ Blackburn (#114) ..	15.00	11.00	9.75	7.50	7.00
C5	20¢ on 2¢ Goethals (#106)	11.00	7.50	6.75	5.00	1.85
	1931-49 Series Showing "Gaillard Cut" VF Used + 25% (B)					
C6-14	**Set of 9**	**32.75**	**24.50**	**22.50**	**18.00**	**6.75**
C6	4¢ Red Yellow (1949)	1.10	.90	.85	.70	.75
C6	Plate Block of 6	8..50	6.75	6.75	5.50	...
C7	5¢ Yellow Green	.90	.65	.65	.50	.45
C7	Plate Block of 6	6.50	5.00	4.95	4.00	...
C8	6¢ Yellow Brown (1946)	1.20	.95	.90	.70	.35
C8	Plate Block of 6	8.50	6.75	6.65	5.50	...
C9	10¢ Orange	1.50	1.20	1.15	.90	.35
C9	Plate Block of 6	15.75	12.00	11.75	9.50	...
C10	15¢ Blue	1.85	1.50	1.40	1.10	.30
C10	Plate Block of 6	16.75	12.75	12.50	10.00	...
C11	20¢ Red Violet	3.25	2.50	2.40	1.90	.30
C11	Plate Block of 6	28.00	21.50	21.00	16.50	...
C12	30¢ Rose Lake (1941)	5.25	4.00	3.75	2.95	1.10
C12	Plate Block of 6	45.00	36.50	35.00	27.50	...
C13	40¢ Yellow	5.25	4.00	3.75	2.95	1.25
C13	Plate Block of 6	45.00	36.50	35.00	27.50	...
C14	$1 Black	13.50	10.00	9.50	7.50	2.25
C14	Plate Block of 6	125.00	97.50	95.00	75.00	...

1939 25th Anniversary of Canal Opening VF + 30%

Scott's No.		Plate Blocks NH	Plate Blocks Unused	F-VF NH	F-VF Unused	F-VF Used
C15-20	**Set of 6**	**...**	**...**	**79.50**	**58.75**	**42.50**
C15	5¢ Plane over Sosa Hill ..... (6)	45.00	33.50	4.75	3.50	2.65
C16	10¢ Map of Central America(6)	55.00	40.00	4.00	3.00	2.60
C17	15¢ Fort Amador .... (6)	59.50	45.00	5.50	4.00	1.40
C18	25¢ Cristobal Harbor .... (6)	235.00	175.00	15.00	11.00	8.50
C19	30¢ Gaillard Cut .... (6)	170.00	125.00	13.75	10.00	7.00
C20	$1 Clipper Landing .... (6)	535.00	400.00	40.00	30.00	23.50

C21

C32

C33

Scott's No.		Plate Blocks NH	Plate Blocks Unused	F-VF NH	F-VF Unused	F-VF Used
	1951 "Globe and Wing" Issue VF + 25%					
C21-26	**Set of 6**	**210.00**	**160.00**	**24.50**	**18.50**	**11.00**
C21	4¢ Red Violet .... (6)	7.50	5.75	.80	.60	.40
C22	6¢ Brown .... (6)	5.75	4.25	.75	.55	.35
C23	10¢ Red Orange .... (6)	9.50	7.50	1.15	.90	.50
C24	21¢ Blue .... (6)	75.00	57.50	8.50	6.50	4.25
C25	31¢ Cerise .... (6)	75.00	57.50	8.50	6.50	4.25
C26	80¢ Gray Black .... (6)	42.50	33.75	5.25	4.00	1.75

1958 "Globe and Wing" Issue

Scott's No.		Plate Blocks F-VF NH	F-VF NH	F-VF Used
C27-31	**Set of 5**	**180.00**	**25.75**	**9.50**
C27	5¢ Yellow Green	7.00	1.25	.75
C28	7¢ Olive	6.00	1.15	.60
C29	15¢ Brown	40.00	5.00	2.50
C30	25¢ Orange Yellow	90.00	10.75	3.25
C31	35¢ Dark Blue	55.00	9.00	3.25
	1961-63 Issues			
C32	15¢ U.S. Army Carib. School	15.00	1.50	.95
C33	7¢ Anti-Malaria (1962)	3.25	.55	.50
C34	8¢ Globe & Wing (1963)	5.00	.65	.35
C35	15¢ Alliance for Progress (1963)	14.00	1.30	1.00
	1964 50th Anniversary of Canal Opening			
C36-41	**Set of 6**	**60.00**	**10.95**	**8.75**
C36	6¢ Jet over Cristobal	2.25	.45	.40
C37	8¢ Gatun Locks	2.75	.50	.45
C38	15¢ Madden Dam	8.00	1.20	.80
C39	20¢ Gaillard Cut	10.50	2.00	1.10
C40	30¢ Miraflores Lock	16.50	2.70	2.50
C41	80¢ Balboa	25.00	4.50	3.75
	1965 Seal & Jet Plane			
C42-47	**Set of 6**	**29.50**	**5.75**	**2.65**
C42	6¢ Green & Black	2.25	.40	.30
C43	8¢ Rose Red & Black	2.50	.45	.20
C44	15¢ Blue & Black	3.00	.55	.35
C45	20¢ Lilac & Black	3.50	.80	.45
C46	30¢ Reddish Brown & Black	5.50	1.10	.50
C47	80¢ Bistre & Black	15.00	2.75	1.00
	1968-76 Seal & Jet Plane			
C48-53	**Set of 6**	**24.95**	**4.65**	**4.50**
C48	10¢ Dull Orange & Black	2.00	.40	.20
C48a	10¢ Booklet Pane of 4 (1970)	...	5.25	...
C49	11¢ Olive & Black (1971)	2.25	.45	.25
C49a	11¢ Booklet Pane of 4	...	4.25	...
C50	13¢ Emerald & Black (1974)	5.50	1.10	.35
C50a	13¢ Booklet Pane of 4	...	7.00	...
C51	22¢ Violet & Black (1976)	5.50	1.10	1.75
C52	25¢ Pale Yellow Green & Black	4.25	.85	.75
C53	35¢ Salmon & Black (1976)	7.00	1.15	1.75

CANAL ZONE

1941-47 OFFICIAL AIRMAIL STAMPS VF Used + 30%
Issue of 1931-46 Overprinted OFFICIAL PANAMA CANAL "PANAMA CANAL" 19-20 mm long

Scott's No.		NH VF	NH F-VF	Unused VF	Unused F-VF	Used F-VF
CO1-7,14	Set of 8	165.00	140.00	125.00	100.00	43.50
CO 1	5¢ Yellow Green (#C7)	7.50	6.00	5.50	4.50	2.00
CO 2	10¢ Orange (#C9)	14.50	11.50	10.50	8.75	2.50
CO 3	15¢ Blue (#C10)	18.00	13.50	12.50	10.00	3.00
CO 4	20¢ Rose Violet (#C11)	21.00	17.00	15.50	13.00	5.50
CO 5	30¢ Rose Lake (#C12) (1942)	25.50	21.50	20.00	16.50	6.50
CO 6	40¢ Yellow (#C13)	27.50	22.50	21.00	17.00	9.00
CO 7	$1 Black (#C14)	40.00	30.00	27.50	22.50	13.50
CO 14	6¢ Yel. Brown (#C8) (1947)	21.00	16.50	14.75	11.75	5.00

1941 OFFICIAL AIRMAIL STAMPS
Issue of 1931-46 Overprinted OFFICIAL PANAMA CANAL "PANAMA CANAL" 17 mm long

		Used VF	Used F-VF
CO 8	5¢ Yellow Green (#C7)	175.00	135.00
CO 9	10¢ Orange (#C9)	290.00	225.00
CO 10	20¢ Red Violet (#C11)	215.00	165.00
CO 11	30¢ Rose Lake (#C12)	70.00	55.00
CO 12	40¢ Yellow (#C13)	225.00	175.00

NOTE: ON #CO1-CO14 AND O1-9, USED PRICES ARE FOR CANCELLED-TO-ORDER. POSTALLY USED COPIES SELL FOR MORE.

POSTAGE DUE STAMPS

1914 U.S. Dues Ovptd. "CANAL ZONE", Perf. 12 VF Used + 50% (C)

Scott' No.		NH VF	NH F-VF	Unused VF	Unused F-VF	Used F-VF
J1	1¢ Rose Carmine (#J45a)	170.00	115.00	110.00	75.00	1.00
J2	2¢ Rose Carmine (#J46a)	515.00	340.00	335.00	225.00	50.00
J3	10¢ Rose Carmine (#J49a)	...	975.00	...	750.00	45.00

1924 U.S. Dues Ovptd. "CANAL ZONE", Flat "A" VF Used + 40% (B)

J12	1¢ Carmine Rose (#J61)	275.00	195.00	180.00	130.00	26.50
J13	2¢ Claret (#J62b)	140.00	100.00	85.00	60.00	12.00
J14	10¢ Claret (#J65b)	575.00	390.00	350.00	250.00	55.00

1925 U.S. Ovptd. "CANAL ZONE POSTAGE DUE" VF Used + 40% (B)

J15	1¢ Franklin (#552)	215.00	150.00	140.00	100.00	15.00
J16	2¢ Washington (#554)	47.50	35.00	31.50	22.50	7.00
J17	10¢ Monroe (#562)	120.00	80.00	75.00	52.50	11.50

1925 U.S. Dues Ovptd. "CANAL ZONE", Sharp "A" VF Used + 40% (B)

J18	1¢ Carmine Rose (#J61)	17.00	11.50	10.50	7.50	4.25
J19	2¢ Carmine Rose (#J62)	3.00	22.50	21.50	15.00	4.50
J20	10¢ Carmine Rose (#J65)	295.00	215.00	195.00	140.00	23.50

1929-30 Issue of 1928 Surcharged "POSTAGE DUE" VF Used + 30% (B)

J21	1¢ on 5¢ Gaillard Cut (#107)	9.25	6.25	5.50	4.25	2.00
J22	2¢ on 5¢ Blue	14.00	10.50	9.25	7.00	3.00
J23	5¢ on 5¢ Blue	14.00	10.50	9.25	7.00	3.50
J24	10¢ on 5¢ Blue	14.00	10.50	9.25	7.00	3.50

1932-41 Canal Zone Seal VF Used + 30% (B)

J25-29	Set of 5	5.95	4.35	4.50	3.15	3.25
J25	1¢ Claret	.35	.25	.30	.20	.20
J26	2¢ Claret	.35	.25	.30	.20	.20
J27	5¢ Claret	.75	.50	.55	.40	.30
J28	10¢ Claret	2.50	1.85	1.80	1.35	1.50
J29	15¢ Claret (1941)	2.50	1.85	1.80	1.35	1.25

1941-47 OFFICIAL STAMPS VF Used + 30% (B)
Issues of 1928-46 Overprinted "OFFICIAL PANAMA CANAL"

O1	1¢ Gorgas, Type 1 (#105)	4.00	3.00	2.80	2.10	.50
O2	3¢ Goethals, T. 1 (#117)	7.50	5.50	5.00	3.75	.75
O3	5¢ Gaillard Cut, T. 2 (#107)	...	...	...	...	35.00
O4	10¢ Hodges, Type 1 (#108)	11.75	8.75	8.85	6.50	2.00
O5	15¢ Smith, Type 1 (#111)	23.00	17.00	16.50	12.00	2.25
O6	20¢ Rousseau, T. 1 (#112)	24.75	18.75	18.50	13.75	3.00
O7	50¢ Blackburn, T. 1 (#114)	70.00	50.00	50.00	37.50	6.00
O8	50¢ Blackburn, T. 1A (#114)	...	...	...	...	625.00
O9	5¢ Stevens, T. 1 (#139) ('47)	14.50	10.75	10.75	7.75	4.25

Type 1: Ovptd. "10mm", Type 1A: Ovptd. "9mm", Type 2: Ovptd. "19½mm".

CUBA #222   CUBA #224   CUBA #226

CUBA VF + 50% (C)

1899 U.S. Stamps of 1895-98 Surcharged for Use in Cuba

Scott's No.		NH Fine	Unused Fine	Unused Ave.	Used Fine	Used Ave.
221	1¢ on 1¢ Franklin (#279)	8.00	5.00	3.25	.50	.30
222	2¢ on 2¢ Wash. T. III (#267)	13.00	8.00	4.75	.75	.45
222A	2¢ on 2¢ Wash. T. IV (#279B)	10.75	6.50	4.00	.50	.30
223	2½¢ on 2¢ Wash. (#267)	7.00	4.50	2.75	.85	.55
223A	2½¢ on 2¢ Wash. (#279B)	5.75	3.75	2.25	.60	.35
224	3¢ on 3¢ Jackson (#268)	17.00	11.00	7.00	1.65	1.00
225	5¢ on 5¢ Grant (#281a)	17.00	11.00	7.00	2.00	1.25
226	10¢ on 10¢ Webster (#282C)	38.50	25.00	15.00	8.75	5.25

CUBA

Scott's No.		NH Fine	Unused Fine	Unused Ave.	Used Fine	Used Ave.

1899 Issues of Republic under U.S. Military Rule, Wtmk. "US-C"

227	1¢ Statue of Columbus	7.00	4.25	2.50	.30	.20
228	2¢ Royal Palms	7.00	4.25	2.50	.30	.20
229	3¢ Allegory "Cuba"	7.00	4.25	2.50	.35	.25
230	5¢ Ocean Liner	10.00	6.25	3.75	.35	.25
231	10¢ Cane Field	21.50	13.50	8.00	.75	.45

NOTE: A RE-ENGRAVED SET WAS ISSUED BY THE REPUBLIC OF CUBA IN 1905-07. THEY ARE UN-WATERMARKED.

1899 SPECIAL DELIVERY

E1	10¢ on 10¢ Blue (#E5)	185.00	120.00	80.00	95.00	60.00
E2	10¢ Messenger, Orange	75.00	50.00	32.50	15.00	9.00

#E2 IS INSCRIBED "IMMEDIATE". THE REPUBLIC OF CUBA ISSUED A CORRECTED VERSION IN 1902 INSCRIBED "INMEDIATA".

1899 POSTAGE DUE

J1	1¢ on 1¢ Claret (#J38)	65.00	42.50	25.00	5.75	3.50
J2	2¢ on 2¢ Claret (#J39)	65.00	42.50	25.00	5.75	3.50
J3	5¢ on 5¢ Claret (#J41)	65.00	42.50	25.00	5.75	3.50
J4	10¢ on 10¢ Claret (#J42)	55.00	35.00	21.50	3.25	1.95

GUAM VF + 60% (C)

GUAM #2   GUAM #5

1899 U.S. Stamps of 1895-98 Overprinted "GUAM"

1	1¢ Franklin (#279)	35.00	20.50	14.00	27.50	16.00
2	2¢ Wash., Red (#279B)	26.50	17.50	10.50	26.50	16.00
2a	2¢ Rose Carmine (#279Bc)	32.50	20.00	13.50	35.00	22.50
3	3¢ Jackson (#268)	170.00	110.00	65.00	160.00	95.00
4	4¢ Lincoln (#280a)	195.00	125.00	75.00	160.00	95.00
5	5¢ Grant (#281a)	45.00	28.50	18.00	45.00	27.50
6	6¢ Garfield (#282)	180.00	115.00	70.00	175.00	110.00
7	8¢ Sherman (#272)	180.00	115.00	70.00	175.00	110.00
8	10¢ Webster (#282C)	62.50	40.00	25.00	55.00	35.00
10	15¢ Clay (#284)	210.00	135.00	85.00	160.00	95.00
11	50¢ Jefferson (#275)	425.00	275.00	165.00	350.00	215.00
12	$1 Perry, Type I (#276)	575.00	375.00	225.00	425.00	240.00
13	$1 Perry, Type II (#276A)	...	3250.00	2250.00	...	...

1899 SPECIAL DELIVERY

E1	10¢ Blue (on U.S. #E5)	220.00	140.00	85.00	190.00	10.00

HAWAII

1857-68 Issues (OG + 30%) (C)

Scott's No.		Unused Fine	Unused Ave.	Used Fine	Used Ave.
8	5¢ Kamehameha III, Blue	550.00	325.00	525.00	315.00
9	5¢ Blue, Bluish Paper	325.00	195.00	225.00	135.00
10	5¢ Blue, Reissue	22.50	13.75	...	...
11	13¢ Dull Rose, Reissue	225.00	140.00	...	...
15	1¢ Numeral, Black, Grayish	425.00	275.00	...	...
16	2¢ Black, Grayish Paper	700.00	450.00	550.00	350.00
19	1¢ Black	400.00	250.00	...	...
20	2¢ Black	575.00	350.00	...	...
21	5¢ Blue, Bluish Paper	675.00	425.00	475.00	300.00
22	5¢ Blue, Interisland	450.00	275.00	700.00	425.00
23	1¢ Black, Laid Paper	230.00	140.00	...	...
24	2¢ Black, Laid Paper	230.00	140.00	...	...
25	1¢ Dark Blue	230.00	140.00	...	...
26	2¢ Dark Blue	230.00	140.00	...	...

35, 38, 43   37, 42   40, 44-45   52

1861-86 Issues (OG + 20%, NH + 100) (VF + 50%) (C)

27	2¢ Kamehameha IV, Pale Rose	250.00	150.00	225.00	135.00
28	2¢ Pale Rose, Vert. Laid Paper	250.00	150.00	135.00	85.00
29	2¢ Red, Thin Wove Paper Reprint	40.00	25.00	...	...
30	1¢ Victoria Kamamalu, Purple	8.50	5.00	7.00	4.25
31	2¢ Kamehameha IV, Vermilion	14.50	9.00	8.25	4.75
32	5¢ Kamehameha V, Blue	140.00	95.00	27.50	16.50
33	6¢ Kamehameha V, Green	23.00	14.00	8.50	5.25
34	18¢ Kekuanaoa, Dull Rose, Gum	75.00	42.50	32.50	18.75
34v	18¢ Without Gum	19.50	13.50	...	...
35	2¢ Kalakaua, Brown	7.50	4.75	2.75	1.60
36	12¢ Leleiohoku, Black	47.50	28.50	25.00	15.00

HAWAII

1882 Issues (OG + 20%) (VF + 50%) (C)

Scott's No.		NH Fine	Unused Fine	Unused Ave.	Used Fine	Used Ave.
37	1¢ Likelike, Blue	9.00	5.75	3.50	10.00	6.50
38	2¢ Kalakaua, Lilac Rose	170.00	110.00	67.50	40.00	25.00
39	5¢ Kamehameha V, Ultra ...	22.50	14.50	9.00	3.00	1.85
40	10¢ Kalakaua, Black	50.00	32.50	20.00	18.50	11.00
41	15¢ Kapiolani, Red Brown ..	77.50	50.00	30.00	25.00	15.00

1883-86 Issues (OG + 20%) (VF + 50%) (C)

42	1¢ Likelike, Green	3.85	2.50	1.50	1.75	1.00
43	2¢ Kalakaua, Rose	6.50	4.25	2.50	.90	.55
44	10¢ Kalakaua, Red Brown .	42.50	27.50	16.50	9.00	5.50
45	10¢ Kalakaua, Vermilion	45.00	29.75	18.00	12.00	7.50
46	12¢ Leleiohoku, Red Lilac .	125.00	80.00	50.00	31.50	19.50
47	25¢ Kamehameha I, Dk. Viol.	190.00	120.00	75.00	50.00	30.00
48	50¢ Lunalilo, Red	230.00	150.00	90.00	75.00	46.50
49	$1 Kaleleonalani, Rose Red	350.00	225.00	140.00	130.00	80.00

1886-91 Issues (OG + 20%) (VF + 50%) (C)

50	2¢ Orange Verm., Imperf, Reprint...	150.00	95.00	...	...	
51	2¢ Carmine, Imperf, Reprint	...	30.00	17.50	...	...
52	2¢ Liliuokalani, Dull Violet ..	9.75	6.00	3.75	1.75	1.10
52C	5¢ Kamehameha, V.D. Ind.	170.00	110.00	65.00	125.00	75.00

1893 Issues of 1864-91 Overprinted "Provisional Government 1893" VF + 40% (C)

53   55   58   66

Red Overprints

53	1¢ Purple (#30)	11.00	7.00	4.25	11.00	6.50
54	1¢ Blue (#37)	8.50	5.50	3.35	11.00	6.50
55	1¢ Green (#42)	2.30	1.50	.90	2.50	1.50
56	2¢ Brown (#35)	14.00	9.00	5.50	17.50	10.75
57	2¢ Dull Violet (#52)	4.00	2.50	1.50	1.75	1.10
58	5¢ Deep Indigo (#52C)	15.75	10.00	6.25	22.50	14.50
59	5¢ Ultramarine (#39)	8.75	5.75	3.50	3.00	1.85
60	6¢ Green (#33)	21.00	13.50	8.25	22.75	14.50
61	10¢ Black (#40)	13.50	8.75	5.25	13.75	8.75
62	12¢ Black (#36)	13.50	8.75	5.25	16.00	10.00
63	12¢ Red Lilac (#46)	215.00	140.00	85.00	225.00	135.00
64	25¢ Dark Violet (#47)	35.00	22.50	13.50	35.00	22.00

Black Overprint

65	2¢ Rose Vermilion (#31)	95.00	60.00	37.50	65.00	40.00
66	2¢ Rose (#43)	2.15	1.40	.85	2.25	1.35
67	10¢ Vermilion (#45)	21.50	13.50	8.25	26.50	17.50
68	10¢ Red Brown (#44)	11.50	7.50	4.50	12.00	7.50
69	12¢ Red Lilac (#46)	385.00	250.00	155.00	450.00	275.00
70	15¢ Red Brown (#41)	28.50	18.50	11.50	27.50	16.50
71	18¢ Dull Rose (#34)	35.00	22.50	14.00	31.00	18.75
72	50¢ Red (#48)	90.00	57.50	35.00	85.00	50.00
73	$1 Rose Red	160.00	100.00	60.00	160.00	95.00

74,80   76   78   O1

1894 Issues VF + 40% (B)

74	1¢ Coat of Arms, Yellow	2.70	1.80	1.10	1.25	.75
75	2¢ Honolulu, Brown	3.25	2.10	1.25	.70	.40
76	5¢ Kameha I, Rose Lake	6.50	4.25	2.60	2.00	1.35
77	10¢ Star & Palms, Yel. Grn.	8.50	5.50	3.75	4.50	2.75
78	12¢ S.S. "Arawa", Blue	21.00	13.50	8.00	20.00	13.50
79	25¢ Dole, Deep Blue	18.50	12.00	7.25	20.00	13.50

1899 Issues VF + 40% (B)

80	1¢ Coat of Arms, Green	2.25	1.50	.90	1.20	.75
81	2¢ Honolulu, Rose	2.25	1.50	.90	1.20	.75
82	5¢ Kamehameha I, Blue	8.00	5.25	3.25	3.00	1.80

1896 OFFICIALS VF + 40% (B)

O1	2¢ Thurston, Green	57.50	37.50	23.00	20.00	12.50
O2	5¢ Black Brown	57.50	37.50	23.00	20.00	12.50
O3	6¢ Deep Ultramarine	57.50	37.50	23.00	20.00	12.50
O4	10¢ Bright Rose	57.50	37.50	23.00	20.00	12.50
O5	12¢ Orange	80.00	50.00	30.00	20.00	12.50
O6	25¢ Gray Violet	100.00	60.00	40.00	20.00	12.50

===

PHILIPPINE ISLANDS VF + 50% (C)

214   216   227

1899 U.S. Stamps of 1894-98 Overprinted "PHILIPPINES"

Scott's No.		NH Fine	Unused Fine	Unused Ave.	Used Fine	Used Ave.
212	50¢ Jefferson (#260)	650.00	400.00	250.00	250.00	160.00
213	1¢ Franklin (#279)	5.75	3.75	2.25	1.00	.60
214	2¢ Wash., Red (#279)	2.75	1.75	1.20	.75	.45
215	3¢ Jackson (#268)	10.00	6.50	4.00	1.95	1.15
216	5¢ Grant (#281)	10.00	6.50	4.00	1.50	.90
217	10¢ Webster Ty. I (#282C) ..	33.50	21.50	13.00	4.25	2.75
217A	10¢ Webster, Ty. II (#283) ..	325.00	210.00	130.00	40.00	25.00
218	15¢ Clay (#284)	60.00	38.00	25.00	8.25	4.95
219	50¢ Jefferson (#275)	230.00	145.00	90.00	40.00	25.00

1901 U.S. Stamps of 1895-98 Overprinted "PHILIPPINES"

220	4¢ Lincoln (#280b)	36.50	23.50	15.00	5.25	3.00
221	6¢ Garfield (#282)	45.00	28.50	17.50	7.50	4.50
222	8¢ Sherman (#272)	52.50	32.50	21.00	7.50	4.50
223	$1 Perry, Ty. I (#276)	700.00	450.00	280.00	250.00	160.00
223A	$1 Perry, Ty. II (#276A)	3,200.00	2,000.00	1,375.00	1,050.00	650.00
224	$2 Madison (#277a)	825.00	525.00	350.00	300.00	185.00
225	$5 Marshall (#278)	1500.00	950.00	625.00	650.00	425.00

1903-04 U.S. Stamps of 1902-03 Overprinted "PHILIPPINES"

226	1¢ Franklin (#300)	7.00	4.50	2.75	.45	.30
227	2¢ Wash. (#301)	12.50	8.00	5.00	1.85	1.10
228	3¢ Jackson (#302)	115.00	75.00	47.50	16.00	9.00
229	4¢ Grant (#303)	130.00	80.00	52.50	24.00	14.50
230	5¢ Lincoln (#304)	19.00	12.50	7.50	1.40	.85
231	6¢ Garfield (#305)	140.00	90.00	55.00	23.50	13.75
232	8¢ M. Wash. (#306)	77.50	50.00	30.00	15.00	9.00
233	10¢ Webster (#307)	38.75	25.00	15.00	3.25	1.95
234	13¢ Harrison (#308)	57.50	37.50	23.00	18.00	11.00
235	15¢ Clay (#309)	100.00	65.00	40.00	17.00	10.50
236	50¢ Jefferson (#310)	275.00	175.00	110.00	40.00	27.50
237	$1 Farragut (#311)	725.00	450.00	290.00	275.00	175.00
238	$2 Madison (#312)	...	1,050.00	700.00	825.00	500.00
239	$5 Marshall (#313)	...	1,250.00	850.00	950.00	550.00
240	2¢ Wash. (#319)	10.00	6.50	4.00	3.00	1.85

1901 SPECIAL DELIVERY U.S. #E5 Ovptd. "PHILIPPINES"

E1	10¢ Messenger, Dark Blue	180.00	115.00	75.00	110.00	65.00

1899-1901 POSTAGE DUES U.S. Dues Ovptd. "PHILIPPINES"

J1	1¢ Deep Claret (#J38)	9.50	6.00	3.75	2.25	1.40
J2	2¢ Deep Claret (#J39)	9.75	6.25	3.90	2.25	1.40
J3	5¢ Deep Claret (#J41)	26.00	16.50	10.00	3.75	2.30
J4	10¢ Deep Claret (#J42)	31.50	20.00	13.00	7.50	4.50
J5	50¢ Deep Claret (#J44)	300.00	190.00	120.00	110.00	70.00
J6	3¢ Deep Claret (#J40)	27.50	17.50	11.00	9.50	5.65
J7	30¢ Deep Claret (#J43)	335.00	215.00	135.00	100.00	65.00

===

PUERTO RICO VF + 50% (C)

215   216

1899 U.S. Stamps of 1895-98 Overprinted "PORTO RICO"

210	1¢ Franklin (36° Angle)	11.00	7.00	4.25	2.25	1.40
210a	1¢ (#279) (25° Angle)	15.00	9.50	5.75	2.75	1.70
211	2¢ Wash. (36° Angle)	11.00	7.00	4.25	2.50	1.60
211a	2¢ (#279Bf) (25° Angle)	15.00	9.50	5.75	2.75	1.70
212	5¢ Grant, Blue (#281a)	15.00	9.50	5.75	2.35	1.45
213	8¢ Sherman (36° Angle)	55.00	35.00	21.50	18.00	13.00
213a	8¢ (#272) (25° Angle)	65.00	40.00	25.00	18.50	13.50
214	10¢ Webster (#282C)	35.00	22.50	14.00	5.75	3.50

1900 U.S. Stamps of 1895-98 Overprinted "PUERTO RICO"

215	1¢ Franklin (#279)	11.00	7.00	4.25	1.95	1.20
216	2¢ Wash. (#279B)	12.50	8.00	5.00	2.25	1.40

1899 Postage Dues; U.S. Dues Overprinted "PORTO RICO"

J1	1¢ (#J38) (36° Angle)	36.50	23.50	14.00	7.50	4.50
J1a	1¢ Claret (25° Angle)	40.00	26.50	16.00	9.00	5.50
J2	2¢ (#J39) (36° Angle)	27.50	17.50	11.00	7.50	4.50
J2a	2¢ Claret (25° Angle)	35.00	22.50	14.00	9.00	5.50
J3	10¢ (#J42) (36° Angle)	260.00	165.00	100.00	55.00	32.50
J3a	10¢ Claret (25° Angle)	315.00	200.00	120.00	70.00	42.50

201

U.S. TRUST TERRITORY OF THE PACIFIC

THE MARSHALL ISLANDS, MICRONESIA, AND PALAU WERE PART OF THE U.S. TRUST TERRITORY OF THE PACIFIC. THE MARSHALL'S BECAME INDEPENDENT IN 1986.

MARSHALL ISLANDS

31

35

50

1984 Commemoratives

Scott's No.		Mint Sheetlet	Plate Block	F-VF NH
31-34	20¢ Postal Service Inaugural, attd	...	4.00	3.00
50-53	40¢ U.P.U., attd	...	4.50	3.50
54-57	20¢ Ausipex '84, Dolphins, attd	...	3.00	2.25
58	20¢ Christmas, 3 Kings, Strip of 4, attd	(16) 11.75	(8) 6.75	3.00
58	Christmas with tabs, attd.		(8) 7.00	4.50
59-62	20¢ Marshalls Constitution, attd	...	3.50	2.35

1984-85 Maps and Navigational Instruments

35-49A	1¢-$1 Definitives (16)		49.50	11.95
39a	13¢ Booklet Pane of 10	...		12.75
40a	14¢ Booklet Pane of 10	...		12.50
41a	22¢ Booklet Pane of 10	...		12.75
41b	13¢/20¢ Bklt. Pane of 10 (5 #39, 5 #41)	...		13.50
42a	22¢ Booklet Pane of 10	...		12.50
42b	14¢/22¢ Bklt. Pane of 10 (5 #40, 5 #42)	...		13.50

63-64

1985 Commemoratives

63-64	22¢ Audubon, attd	...	3.35	1.60
65-69	22¢ Sea Shells, strip of 5 attd	(10)	5.50	2.40
70-73	22¢ Decade for Women, attd	...	3.00	2.25
74-77	22¢ Reef and Lagoon Fish, attd	...	3.25	2.40
78-81	22¢ International Youth Year, attd	...	3.00	2.25
82-85	14¢,22¢,33¢,44¢ Christmas, Missions (4)	...	15.00	2.75
86-90	22¢ Halley's Comet, strip of 5 attd	(15) 45.00	(10) 15.00	6.25
86-90	Halley's Comet with tabs, attd	...		35.00
91-94	22¢ Medicinal Plants, attd	...	3.00	2.30

1986-87 Maps and Navigational Instruments

107	$2 Wotje & Erikub, 1871 Terrestrial Globe	...	27.50	5.95
108	$5 Bikini, Stick Chart	...	65.00	14.75
109	$10 Stick Chart (1987)	...	95.00	21.50

110

163

1986-87 Commemoratives

110-13	14¢ Marine Invertebrates, attd	...	3.35	2.75
114	$1 Ameripex S/S (C-54 Globemaster) .	...	...	4.00
115-18	22¢ Operation Crossroads, attd	...	2.85	2.35
119-23	22¢ Seashells, strip of 5, attd	(10)	6.50	2.95
124-27	22¢ Game Fish, attd	...	3.00	2.35
128-31	22¢ Christmas / Year of Peace, attd	...	4.25	3.25
132-35	22¢ Whaling Ships, attd (1987)	...	3.00	2.50
136-41	33¢,39¢,44¢ Pilots (3 pairs)	(12) 13.50		6.00
142	$1.00 Amelia Earhart / CAPEX S/S	...		3.25
143-51	14¢,22¢,44¢ U.S. Const. Bicent (3)	(15) 32.50	...	6.50
152-56	22¢ Seashells, strip of 5, attd	(10)	6.95	3.00
157-59	44¢ Copra Industry, strip of 3, attd	(6)	6.00	2.75
160-63	14¢,22¢,33¢,44¢ Christmas, Bible Verses (4)	...	12.00	2.50

164

184

MARSHALL ISLANDS (continued)

1988 Commemoratives

Scott's No.		Mint Sheetlet	Plate Block	F-VF NH
164-67	44¢ Marine Birds, attd	...	5.25	4.50
188	15¢ Olympics, Javelin, Strip of 5	...	(10) 5.00	2.25
189	25¢ Olympics, Runner, Strip of 5	...	(10) 6.75	3.15
190	25¢ Robt. Louis Stevenson S/S of 9 ..	...		6.50
191-94	25¢ Colonial Ships and Flags, attd	...	3.50	3.00
195-99	25¢ Christmas, strip of 5	...	(10) 7.25	3.25
200-04	25¢ John F. Kennedy, Strip of 5	(15) 17.50		3.95
205-08	25¢ Space Shuttle, Strip of 4	(12) 8.95	(8) 6.75	3.00
205-08	Space Shuttle Tab Strip	...	...	3.75

1988-89 Fish Definitives

168-83	1¢-$5.00 Fish (16)	...	125.00	26.50
170a	14¢ Booklet Pane of 10	...		5.75
171a	15¢ Booklet Pane of 10	...		7.50
173a	22¢ Booklet Pane of 10	...		7.75
173b	14¢ & 22¢ Bklt. Pane of 10 (5 ea.)	...		6.00
174a	25¢ Booklet Pane of 10	...		7.75
174b	15¢ & 25¢ Booklet Pane of 10	...		8.00
184	$10 Fish Definitive ('89)	...	105.00	23.75

1989 Commemoratives

209

222

209-12	45¢ Links to Japan, attd	...	5.00	4.50
213-15	45¢ Alaska State 30th Anniv., Strip of 3	(9) 12.75		3.50
216-20	25¢ Seashells, Strip of 5	...	(10) 5.95	2.75
221	$1.00 Hirohito Memorial S/S	...		2.25
222-25	45¢ Migrant Birds, attd	...	5.50	4.50
226-29	45¢ Postal History, attd	...	5.75	4.75
230	25¢ Postal History, S/S of 6	...	...	12.75
231	$1.00 PHILEXFRANCE, S/S	...	...	12.50
232-38	25¢ (6)$1 Moon Landing, 20th Ann., Bklt. sgls	...	...	21.75
238a	$2.50 Booklet Pane of 7 (6x25¢,$1)	...	...	21.75
	Also See #341-45			

239

298

* WW II Anniversaries 1939-1989

239	25¢ Invasion of Poland	(12) 13.50	4.50	.90
240	45¢ Sinking of HMS Royal Oak	(12) 24.50	8.00	1.65
241	45¢ Invasion of Finland	(12) 24.50	8.00	1.65
242-45	45¢ Battle of River Platte, attd	(16) 32.50	8.00	6.75

* WW II Anniversaries 1940-1990

246-47	25¢ Invas. of Norway & Denmark, attd	(12) 20.75	4.00	1.85
248	25¢ Katyn Forest Massacre	(12) 12.50	4.50	.95
249-50	25¢ Invasion of Belgium, attd	(12) 13.50	4.50	1.80
251	45¢ Churchill Becomes Prime Minister	(12) 24.50	8.00	1.65
252-53	45¢ Evacuation at Dunkirk, attd	(12) 23.50	7.95	3.50
254	45¢ Occupation of Paris	(12) 25.00	8.00	1.65
255	25¢ Mers-el-Kebir	(12) 13.00	4.35	.90
256	25¢ Burma Road	(12) 13.00	4.35	.90
257-60	45¢ U.S. Destroyers for G.B., atd	(16) 32.50	8.00	6.50
261-64	45¢ Battle of Britain, attd	(16) 32.50	8.00	6.50
265	45¢ Tripartite Pact, 1940	(12) 24.50	8.00	1.65
266	25¢ FDR Elected to Third Term	(12) 13.50	4.50	.90
267-70	25¢ Battle of Taranto, attd	(16) 17.75	5.00	4.25

* WW II Anniversaries 1941-1991

271-74	30¢ Four Freedoms, attd	(16) 23.50	5.50	4.50
275	30¢ Battle of Beda Fomm	(12) 13.50	4.50	.90
276-77	29¢ German Invasion of Greece & Yugoslavia, attd	(12) 16.50	5.50	2.25
278-81	50¢ Sinking of the Bismarck, attd	(16) 29.50	10.00	7.50
282	30¢ Germany Invades Russia	(12) 16.50	5.50	1.10
283-84	29¢ Atlantic Charter, attd. pair	(12) 14.50	4.75	2.25
285	29¢ Siege of Moscow	(12) 16.50	5.50	1.10
286-87	30¢ Sinking of the USS Reuben James, attd	(16) 19.50	4.75	2.25
288-91	50¢ Japanese Attack Pearl Harbor, attd	(16) 35.00	8.95	7.50
288a-91a	50¢ Pearl Harbor Reprint,attd.	(16) 75.00	19.50	15.75
292	29¢ Japanese Capture Guam	(12) 16.50	5.50	1.10
293	29¢ Fall of Singapore	(12) 16.50	5.50	1.10
294-95	50¢ Flying Tigers, attd	(16) 26.50	8.95	3.75
296	29¢ Fall of Wake Island	(12) 16.50	5.50	1.10

* WW II Anniversaries 1942-1992

297	29¢ FDR & Churchill at Arcadia Conference	(12) 16.50	5.50	1.10
298	50¢ Japanese enter Manila	(12) 27.75	9.25	1.85
299	29¢ Japanese take Rabaul	(12) 16.50	5.50	1.10
300	29¢ Battle of Java Sea	(12) 16.50	5.50	1.10
301	50¢ Fall of Rangoon	(12) 27.75	9.25	1.85
302	29¢ Battle for New Guinea	(12) 16.50	5.50	1.10
303	29¢ MacArthur Leaves Corregidor	(12) 16.50	5.50	1.10

Scott's No.		Mint Sheetlet	Plate Block	F-VF NH
WW II Anniversaries 1942-1992 (continued)				
304	29¢ Raid on Saint-Nazaire .... (12)	16.50	5.50	1.10
305	29¢ Surrender of Bataan .... (12)	16.50	5.50	1.10
306	50¢ Doolittle Raid on Tokyo .... (12)	27.75	9.25	1.85
307	29¢ Fall of Corregidor .... (12)	16.50	5.50	1.10
308-11	50¢ Battle of the Coral Sea, attd .... (16)	35.00	8.95	7.50
308a-11a	50¢ Coral Sea Reprint, attd. .... (16)	95.00	24.75	19.75
312-15	50¢ Battle of Midway, attd .... (16)	35.00	8.95	7.50
316	29¢ Village of Lidice Destroyed .... (12)	16.50	5.50	1.10
317	29¢ Fall of Sevastopol .... (12)	16.50	5.50	1.10
318-19	29¢ Convoy, attd .... (12)	18.50	6.00	2.50
320	29¢ Marines Land on Guadalcanal .... (12)	16.50	5.50	1.10
321	29¢ Battle of Savo Island .... (12)	16.50	5.50	1.10
322	29¢ Dieppe Raid .... (12)	16.50	5.50	1.10
323	50¢ Battle of Stalingrad .... (12)	27.50	9.25	1.85
324	29¢ Battle of Eastern Solomons .... (12)	16.50	5.50	1.10
325	50¢ Battle of Cape Esperance .... (12)	27.50	9.25	1.85
326	29¢ Battle of El Alamein .... (12)	16.50	5.50	1.10
327-28	29¢ Battle of Barents Sea, attd. pair .... (12)	16.50	5.50	2.25
* WW II Anniversaries 1943-1993				
329	29¢ Casablanca Conference .... (12)	16.50	5.50	1.10
330	29¢ Liberation of Kharkov .... (12)	16.50	5.50	1.10
331-34	50¢ Battle of Bismarck Sea, attd .... (16)	35.00	8.95	7.50
335	50¢ Interception of Yamamoto .... (12)	27.50	9.25	1.85
336-37	29¢ Battle of Kursk .... (16)	24.00	6.00	2.50

364

382

383

1989 Commemoratives (cont.)				
341-44	25¢ Christmas 1989, attd		6.00	5.00
345	45¢ Milestones in Space, Sheet of 25 diff. designs ...		...	43.50
1990-92 Birds Definitives				
346-65A	1¢-$2 Birds (21)		175.00	29.50
361a	95¢ Essen '90 Min. Sht. of 4 (#347,350,353,361) ...		...	5.75
1990 Commemoratives				
366-69	25¢ Children's Games, attd		6.00	5.00
370-76	25¢, (6)$1 Penny Black, 150th Anniv., Booklet Singles		...	17.75
376a	Booklet Pane of 7 (6x25¢,$1)		...	18.50
377-80	25¢ Endangered Sea Turtles, attd		7.00	6.00
381	25¢ Joint Issue with Micronesia & U.S.		11.75	1.30
382	45¢ German Reunification		6.75	1.50
383-86	25¢ Christmas, attd		4.75	4.00
387-90	25¢ Breadfruit, attd		4.50	3.75
1991 Commemoratives				

399

411

391-94	50¢ US Space Shuttle Flights, 10th Anniv., attd	...	6.00	4.75
395-98	52¢ Flowers, attd	...	8.50	6.75
398a	52¢ Phila Nippon, min. sht. of 4	...	...	6.95
399	29¢ Operation Desert Storm	...	8.75	1.45
400-06	29¢, (6)$1 Birds, set of 7 booklet singles	...	...	28.75
406a	Booklet Pane of 7 (6x29¢,$1)	...	...	29.50
407-10	12¢,29¢,50¢ (2) Air Marshall Island Aircraft (4)	21.75	...	5.00
411	29¢ Admission to United Nations	...	11.00	1.10
412	30¢ Christmas, Peace Dove	...	5.75	1.20
413	29¢ Peace Corps in Marshall Islands	...	6.50	1.20

425

426

427

428

THE MARSHALL ISLANDS

Scott's No.		Mint Sheetlet	Plate Block	F-VF NH
1992 Commemoratives				
414-17	29¢ Ships, Strip of 4	...	(8) 11.75	5.00
418-24	50¢, (6) $1 Voyages of Discovery, set of 7 booklet sgls	...	...	18.50
424a	Booklet Pane of 7 (6x50¢,$1)	...	...	19.50
425-28	29¢ Traditional Handcrafts, attd	...	(8) 8.00	3.50
429	29¢ Christmas	...	5.50	1.00
1992 Birds Definitives				
430-33	9¢,22¢,28¢,45¢ Birds		30.00	4.95
1993 Commemoratives				
434-40	50¢, (6) $1 Reef Life, 7 booklet sgls ..	...	...	19.75
440a	Booklet Pane of 7 (6x50¢,$1)	...	...	20.00

441

464

1993-95 Ship Definitives				
441/65	10¢-$3.00 Ships (24)		170.00	35.00
463	$1.00 Canoe	...	17.50	3.25
464	$2.00 Canoe	...	25.00	5.25
466A	$5.00 Canoe (1994)	...	70.00	12.50
466B	$10.00 Canoe (1994)	...	125.00	25.00
466C	15¢-75¢ Sailing Vessels, S/S of 4 (1994)	...	...	4.75

476

477

* WW II Anniversaries 1943-1993 (continued)				
467-70	52¢ Invasion of Sicily, attd. blk. of 4 ..	(16) 36.50	9.25	7.95
471	50¢ Bombing Raids on Schweinfurt ..	(12) 27.50	9.25	1.85
472	29¢ Liberation of Smolensk	(12) 16.50	5.50	1.10
473	29¢ Landing at Bougainville	(12) 16.50	5.50	1.10
474	50¢ US Invasion of Tarawa	(12) 27.50	9.25	1.85
475	52¢ Tehran Conference	(12) 27.50	9.25	1.85
476-77	29¢ Battle of North Cape, attd. pair ...	(12) 18.75	6.25	2.60
* WW II Anniversaries 1944-1994				
478	29¢ Eisenhower Commands SHAEF	(12) 16.50	5.50	1.10
479	50¢ Invasion of Anzio	(12) 27.50	9.25	1.85
480	52¢ Siege of Leningrad Ends	(12) 27.50	9.25	1.85
481	29¢ U.S. Frees Marshall Islands	(12) 16.50	5.50	1.10
482	29¢ Japanese Defeat at Truk	(12) 16.50	5.50	1.10
483	52¢ Bombing of Germany	(12) 27.50	9.25	1.85
484	50¢ Rome Falls to Allies	(12) 27.50	9.25	1.85
485-88	75¢ D-Day Landings, attd	(16) 52.50	13.00	11.50
485a-88a	75¢ D-Day, Reprint, attd.	(16) 110.00	29.50	24.95
489	50¢ V-1 Bombs Strike England	(12) 27.50	9.25	1.85
490	29¢ Landing on Saipan	(12) 16.50	5.50	1.10
491	50¢ Battle of Philippine Sea	(12) 27.50	9.25	1.85
492	29¢ U.S. Liberates Guam	(12) 16.50	5.50	1.10
493	50¢ Warsaw Uprising	(12) 27.50	9.25	1.85
494	50¢ Liberation of Paris	(12) 27.50	9.25	1.85
495	29¢ Marines Land on Peliliu	(12) 16.50	5.50	1.10
496	52¢ MacArthur Returns to Philippines	(12) 27.50	9.25	1.85
497	52¢ Battle of Leyte Gulf	(12) 27.50	9.25	1.85
498-99	50¢ Battleship "Tirpitz" Sunk, attd	(16) 38.50	10.75	4.50
500-3	50¢ Battle of the Bulge	(16) 45.00	12.50	10.75
WWII Anniversaries 1945-1995				
504	32¢ Yalta Conference	(12) 22.50	7.00	1.40
505	55¢ Bombing of Dresden	(12) 31.50	16.00	3.50
506	$1 Iwo Jima Invaded	(12) 57.50	19.75	4.50
507	32¢ Remagen Bridge Taken	(12) 22.50	7.00	1.40
508	55¢ Marines Invade Okinawa	(12) 36.50	11.75	2.60
509	50¢ Death of F.D. Roosevelt	(12) 45.00	11.00	2.50
510	32¢ US/USSR Troops Link	(12) 23.50	7.00	1.50
511	60¢ Soviet Troops Conquer Berlin	(12) 45.00	11.50	2.50
512	55¢ Allies liberate concentration camps	(12) 45.00	11.50	2.50
513-16	75¢ V.E. Day, Block of 4	(16) 75.00	19.50	17.75
517	32¢ United Nations Charter	(12) 22.50	7.00	1.50
518	55¢ Postdam Conference	(12) 45.00	11.00	2.50
519	60¢ Churchill's Resignation	(12) 45.00	11.50	2.50
520	$1 Atomic Bomb dropped on Hiroshima	(12) 75.00	21.75	4.85
521-24	75¢ V.J. Day, Block of 4	(16) 87.50	19.50	17.75

* WW II Anniversary Issues are are available in Tab singles, Tab pairs and Tab blocks for an additional 25%.

1994-95 WWII Anniversary Souvenir Sheets

562	50¢ MacArthur Returns to Philippines, Souvenir Sheet of 2			4.75
563	$1 U.N. Charter Souvenir Sheet (1995)	...	...	3.95

1993 Commemoratives (cont.)

567   **572**   **576**

Scott's No.		Mint Sheetlet	Plate Block	F-VF NH
567-70	29¢ Capitol Complex	...	18.50	3.00
571	50¢ Mobil Oil Tanker, Eagle Souv. Sheet		...	1.20
572-75	29¢ Life in 1800's, attd		3.85	3.00
576	29¢ Christmas		5.25	1.00

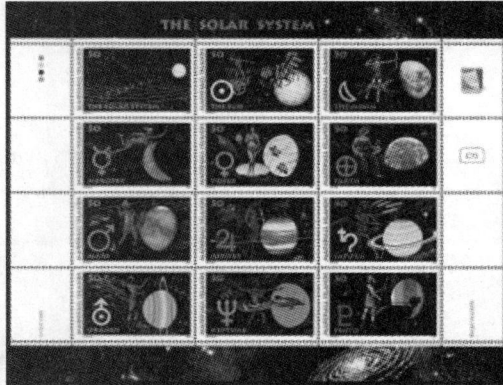

582

1994 Commemoratives

577	$2.90 15th Anniv. Constitution Souv. Sht (94)	...	...	6.50
578	29¢ 10th Anniv. Postal Service Souv. Sht (94)	...	...	.95
579-80	50¢ Soccer Cup, Attd.	...	14.00	6.25
582	50¢ Solar System, sheet of 12	...	...	18.95
583-86	75¢ Moon Landing, 25th Anniv. attd.	...	9.00	7.50
586b	75¢ Moon Landing, Souv. Sheet of 4	...	...	7.50
587	29¢, 52¢, $1 Butterflies, Souv. Sheet of 3	...	...	5.25
588	29¢ Christmas	...	5.75	1.00

1995 Commemoratives

592 Part   **596 Part**   **599**

589	50¢ Year of the Boar, Souv. Sheet	...	...	2.10
590	55¢ Underseas Glory, Block of 4	...	12.00	9.50
591	55¢ John F. Kennedy, Strip of 6	...(12)	19.50	8.75
592	75¢ Marilyn Monroe, Block of 4	(12) 23.75	9.75	7.95
593	32¢ Cats, Block of 4	...	5.75	3.95
594	75¢ Mir-Shuttle Docking, Block of 4	...	8.75	7.75
595	60¢ Game Fish, Block of 8	...	(8) 21.50	16.75
596	32¢ Island Legends, Block of 4	...	4.00	3.50
597	32¢ Singapore '95 Orchids Souv. Sheet of 4	...	...	3.35
598	50¢ Beijing '95, Suzhou Gardens, Souv. Sheet	...	...	1.25
599	32¢ Christmas	...	4.25	.85
600	32¢ Jet Fighter Planes, Min.Sheet of 25	...	...	19.75
601	32¢ Yitzhak Rabin	(8) 8.50	6.00	1.00

604 Part   **608**   **616**

1996 Commemoratives

Scott's No.		Mint Sheetlet	Plate Block	F-VF NH
602	50¢ Year of the Rat Souvenir Sheet	...	...	1.25
603	32¢ Local Birds, Block of 4	...	9.00	7.50
604	55¢ Wild Cats, Block of 4	...	8.00	6.50
605	32¢ Millennium of Navigation, Mini Sht of 25 .	...	...	19.75
606	60¢ Modern Olympics, Block of 4	...	7.25	6.00
607	55¢ Marshall Island Chronology, Shtlt of 12 ..	...	...	16.50
608	32¢ Elvis Presley	(20) 65.00	(6)21.50	2.00
609	50¢ China '96 Palace Museum Souv. Sheet ..	...	...	1.50
610	32¢ James Dean	(20) 52.50	(6) 19.50	1.75
611	60¢ Ford Motor 100th Anniv., S/S of 8	...	...	11.75
612	32¢ Island Legends, Block of 4	...	4.25	3.25
613	55¢ Steam Locomotives, sheetlet of 12	...	...	16.50
614	32¢ Taipei 1996 Souvenir Sheet of 4	...	...	3.25
615	$3 Compact with U.S.	...	40.00	7.95
616	32¢ Christmas Angels	(16) 14.95	...	.85
617	32¢ Biplanes Sheetlet of 25	...	...	19.75

621   **638**

1997 Commemoratives

618	32¢ Handicrafts, Block of 4	...	4.00	3.25
619	60¢ Year of the Ox, Souvenir Sheet .	...	...	1.50
620-21	32¢-60¢ Amata Kabua (2)	(8) 18.00	4.75	2.30
622	32¢ Elvis Presley, Strip of 3	(15) 13.50	(6)5.95	2.75
623-24	32¢ Hong Kong '97, Souvenir Sheets of 2 (2)	...	...	2.80
625	60¢ Twelve Apostles, Sheetlet of 12	...	...	18.50
626	$3 Last Supper, Souvenir Sheet	...	...	7.50
627	60¢ 20th Century, 1900-1909, Sheetlet of 15 ...	...	...	22.50
628	60¢ Deng Xiaoping	...	7.50	1.50
629	32¢ Traditional Crafts, Self-adhesive block of 4 (2x10 design)	(20) 19.95	4.75	3.85
630	32¢ Traditional Crafts, Self-adhesive strip of 4 (4x5 design)	(20) 20.75	(8) 8.95	3.95
631-37	50¢, (6) $1 Pacific '97, 1st Marshall Is. and U.S. stamps, set of 7 singles	...	...	9.85
636a,37a	50¢-$1 Pacific '97 Booklet (6-50¢, 1-$1 Souvenir Sheet)	...	...	9.95
638	16¢ World Wildlife Fund, Birds (4)	(16) 6.35	...	1.60
639	50¢ Bank of China, Hong Kong S/S ..	...	...	1.85

640

647-48

640	32¢ Canoes, 4 designs	...	3.75	3.25
641	32¢ Air Force, Sheetlet of 25	...	...	19.95
642	32¢ Old Ironsides	(15) 12.00	3.75	.80
643	32¢ Folklore, 4 designs	(8) 6.50	3.75	3.25
644	60¢ Underseas Glory, 4 designs	(24) 35.00	7.00	6.00
645	60¢ Princess Diana, 3 designs	(15) 22.50	...	4.50
646	60¢ 20th Century, 1910-1919,Sheetlet of 15 ...	...	...	22.50
647-648	32¢ Christmas, Raphael's Angel, Pair	(16) 12.75	(8) 7.50	1.60

1997 Commemoratives (continued)

Scott's No.		Mint Sheetlet	Plate Block	F-VF NH
649	20¢ U.S. Warships of 50 States .... (50)	...	...	24.75
650	50¢ Shanghai '97 Souvenir Sheet	...	...	1.40

1998 Commemoratives

651	60¢ Year of the Tiger Souvenir Sheet	...	...	1.50
652	32¢ Elvis Presley TV Special,Strip of 3 (15)	11.95	...	2.40
653	32¢ Seashells, 4 Designs .... (20)	15.75	3.85	3.25

654

654	60¢ 20th Century, 1920-29, Sheetlet of 15 ..	...	...	22.50
655	32¢ Canoes of the Pacific, Sheetlet of 8	...	...	6.50
656	60¢ Berlin Airlift 4 Designs .... (16)	23.00	7.00	5.95
657	60¢ 20th Century, 1930-39, Sheetlet of 15 ..	...	...	22.50
664a	60¢-$3 Czar Nicholas II Booklet (6-60¢ ,1-$3)	...	...	16.50
658-64	60¢-$3 Czar Nicholas, set of 7 singles (6-60¢, 1-$3 Souvenir Sheet)	...	...	16.25
665	32¢ Babe Ruth .... (15)	11.75	4.00	.80
666	32¢ Legendary Aircraft of the U.S. Navy Sheetlet of 25	...	...	19.50
667	60¢ Chevrolet Automobiles, Sheetlet of 8	...	...	11.75
668	33¢ Alphabet & Language, Sheetlet of 24	...	...	19.50
669	33¢ New Buildings, Strip of 3 .... (12)	9.75(6)	5.50	2.50
670	32¢ Christmas Angel	...	4.00	.80
677a	60¢-3$ John Glenn, Hero in Space Booklet (6-60¢, $3 Souvenir Sheet)	...	...	16.50
671-77	60¢-$3 John Glenn, set of 7 singles	...	...	16.25

678

678	$3 Drought Relief Priority Mail Souvenir Sheet	...	...	7.50
679	60¢ 20th Century, 1940-49, Sheetlet of 15 ...	...	...	22.50
680	33¢ History's Greatest Fighting Ships, Shtlt of 25	...	...	19.75
681	60¢ Year of the Rabbit Souvenir Sheet	...	...	1.50

1999 Birds of the Marshall Islands Regular Issue

682-89	1¢, 3¢, 20¢, 22¢, 33¢, 55¢, $1, $10 (8)	...	115.00	26.75

1999 Commemoratives

690	33¢ Canoes of the Pacific, Sheetlet of 8	...	...	6.25
691-98	33¢ Canoes of the Pacific, Self-adhesive ..... 8 designs .... (20)	15.75	...	6.25
699	60¢ Great American Indian Chiefs, Sheetlet of 12	...	...	17.50
700	33¢ Marshallese Flag .... (16)	12.00	3.75	.80
701	33¢ Flowers of the Pacific, 6 designs .... (12)	10.00	...	4.75
702	60¢ 20th Century, 1950-59, Sheetlet of 15 ...	...	...	21.50
703	$1.20 Australia '99 Souvenir Sheet	...	...	2.80
704	33¢ Elvis Presley, Artist of the Century .... (20)	15.75	3.75	.80

1999 Commemoratives (continued)

705

Scott's No.		Mint Sheetlet	Plate Block	F-VF NH
705	60¢ IBRA '99 Stamp Exhibition Souvenir Sheet of 4 ...	...	...	5.75
706	33¢ RMI Constitution 20th Anniversary .... (6)4.75		...	.80
707	33¢ 15th Anniversary RMI Postal Service (4) (24)18.50		3.95	3.25
708	33¢ Legendary Aircraft, Sheetlet of 25	...	...	19.50
709	$1 Philexfrance '99, Transportation on the Moon, Souvenir Sheet	...	...	2.40
710	60¢ Marshall Is. Ship Registry	...	...	1.50
711	60¢ 20th Century, 1960-69, Sheetlet of 15 ..	...	...	21.50

712

712	33¢ 30th Anniversary of First Men on the Moon Souvenir Sheet	...	...	2.40
713	33¢ Early European Navigation,4 designs(16) 12.50		3.75	3.25

1999 Birds of the Marshall Islands Regular Issue

714-21	5¢,40¢,45¢,75¢,$1.20,$2,$3.20,$5 (8)	...	120.00	27.50

1999 Commemoratives (continued)

722	33¢ Traditional Christmas .... (20) 15.50		3.75	.80
723	60¢ 20th Century, 1970-79, Sheetlet of 15	...	...	21.50
724-25	33¢ End/Beginning of Millennium,Pr.. (16) 12.50 1.60		3.75	3.25

2000 Commemoratives

726	60¢ 20th Century, 1980-89, Sheetlet of 15 . .	...	...	21.50
727	60¢ Year of the Dragon Souvenir Sheet . .	...	...	1.40
728	33¢ Legendary Aircraft II Sheetlet of 25	...	...	18.50
729	33¢ Garden Roses, Block of 6 .... (12) 8.95		...	4.50
730	60¢ 20th Century, 1990-99, Sheetlet of 15 .	...	...	19.50
731	33¢ China Panda, Block of 6 .... (12) 8.95		...	4.50
732-38	1¢-42¢ American Presidents, set of 7 sheetlets of 6 depicting each president plus White House...	...	...	19.75
739	33¢ Graf Zeppelin, Block of 4 .... (16) 1.85		3.50	3.00
746a	60¢ - $1 Winston Churchill Booklet (6-60¢, 1-$1 Souvenir Sheet)	..	...	9.75
740-46	60¢-$1 Winston Churchill, set of 7 singles	..	...	9.65

747

747	33¢ 225th Anniv. of U.S. Military (3) . (12) 3.50	(6) 4.50		2.15

2000 Commemoratives (cont.)

Scott's No.		Mint Sheetlet	Plate Block	F-VF NH
748	33¢ Marshall Island Capitol, Nitijela Flag and Seal (4) .... (16)	11.00	3.25	2.80
749	60¢ Ships of Discovery (6) .... (12)	15.25	8.25	7.75
750	60¢ Queen Mother's Birthday .... (16)	20.75	5.95	5.25
751	33¢ Reef Life Sheetlet of 8	...	...	5.50
752	60¢ Butterflies Sheetlet of 12	...	...	15.50
753	33¢ Germany United 10th Anniversary (16)	11.00	3.25	.70
754	33¢ U.S. Submarines, block of 4 ...... (8)	5.50	3.00	2.80
755	33¢ Christmas - Palm Trees .... (20)	13.75	3.25	.70
756	60¢-$1 Sun Yat-Sen Booklet of 7	...	...	9.75
756a-g	60¢-$1 Sun Yat-Sen set of 7 singles	...	...	9.65

2001 Commemoratives

757	80¢ Year of the Snake Souvenir Sheet	...	...	1.75

2001 Flower of the Month

758	34¢ January - Carnation .... (8)	5.50	3.25	.70
759	34¢ February - Violet .... (8)	5.50	3.25	.70
760	34¢ March - Jonquil .... (8)	5.50	3.25	.70
761	34¢ April - Sweet Pea .... (8)	5.50	3.25	.70
762	34¢ May - Lily of the Valley .... (8)	5.50	3.25	.70
763	34¢ June - Rose .... (8)	5.50	3.25	.70
764	34¢ July - Larkspur .... (8)	5.50	3.25	.70
765	34¢ August - Poppy .... (8)	5.50	3.25	.70

2001 Sailing Canoes Regular Issue

770	$5 Walap of Jaluit	...	43.95	9.95
771	$10 Walap of Enewetak	...	87.50	19.75

2001 Commemoratives (continued)

Great Marshallese

...	34¢,55¢,80¢,$1 Great Marshallese (4)	...	25.00	5.75
...	80¢ Butterflies Sheetlet of 12 II	...	...	20.75
...	34¢ Fairy Tales, strip of 7 .... (28)	20.75	...	5.25

Watercraft Racing

...	34¢ Watercraft Racing, block of 4 .... (16)	11.85	...	3.00
...	80¢ Manned Space Flight - 4 .... (8)	13.85	...	6.95

B1

Scott's No.		Mint Sheetlet	Plate Block	F-VF NH
	1996 Semi-Postals			
B1	32¢ + 8¢ Operations Crossroads, Sheetlet of 6	...	...	5.75

C8   **C9-12**

	1985-89 Airmails			
C1-2	44¢ Audubon, attd	...	6.95	3.35
C3-6	44¢ Ameripex - Planes, attd (1986)	...	6.75	5.50
C7	44¢ Operation Crossroads, S/S (1986)	...	...	5.75
C8	44¢ Statue of Liberty/Peace Year (1986)	...	6.25	1.40
C9-12	44¢ Girl Scouts, attd (1986)	...	5.25	4.50
C13-16	44¢ Marine Birds, attd (1987)	...	4.85	4.25

C17   **C22**

C17-20	44¢ Amelia Earhart/CAPEX attd (1987)	...	5.50	4.50
C21	45¢ Astronaut and Space Shuttle (1988)	...	5.75	1.30
C22-25	12¢,36¢,39¢,45¢ Aircraft (1989) (4)	...	17.50	3.75
C22a	12¢ Bklt. Pane of 10	...	...	4.85
C23a	36¢ Bklt. Pane of 10	...	...	13.00
C24a	39¢ Bklt. Pane of 10	...	...	13.75
C25a	45¢ Bklt. Pane of 10	...	...	15.75
C25b	36¢-45¢ Bklt. Pane of 10 (5 each)	...	...	14.75

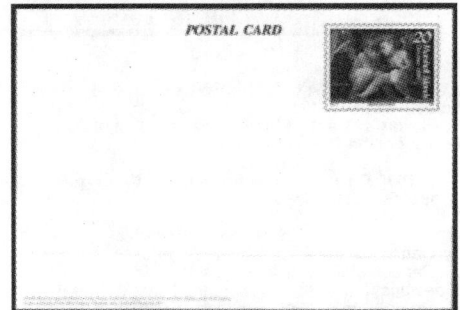

UX6

Postal Cards

UX1	20¢ Elvis Presley (1996)	...	...	2.50
UX2-5	20¢ Canoes, Set of 4	...	...	4.75
UX6	20¢ Heavenly Angels, Christmas (1996)	...	...	1.35
UX7	32¢ Turtle (1997)	...	...	1.25

MICRONESIA
MICRONESIA BECAME INDEPENDENT IN 1986

1	21	22

1984 Commemoratives

Scott's No.		Mint Sheetlet	Plate Block	F-VF NH
1-4	20¢ Postal Service Inaugural, attd	...	3.00	2.50
21,C4-6	20¢,28¢,35¢,40¢ AUSIPEX (4)	17.50	3.75	
22,C7-9	20¢,28¢,35¢,40¢ Christmas (4)	27.50	5.75	

1984 Explorers and Views Definitives

5-20	1¢-$5 Definitives (16)		110.00	25.75

23	24	C36

1985 Commemoratives

23,C10-12	22¢,33¢,39¢,44¢ Ships (4)	...	21.50	3.75
24,C13-14	22¢,33¢,44¢ Christmas (3)		23.50	3.75
25-28,C15	22¢,44¢ Audubon (5)		10.00	4.50
45,C16-18	22¢,33¢,39¢,44¢ Ruins (4)		22.50	4.50

1985-88 Definitives

31-39,C34-36	3¢-$10 Definitives & Airs (12)	...	140.00	29.50
33a	15¢ Booklet Pane of 10		...	9.95
36a	25¢ Booklet Pane of 10		...	9.95
36b	15¢ & 25¢ Booklet Pane of 10 (5 ea.)		...	11.75

52	C31	63

1986 Commemoratives

46,C19-20	22¢, 44¢ Int'l Peace Year (3)	...	25.00	5.25
48-51	22¢ on 20¢ Postal Service (#1-4), attd	...	2.85	2.50
52,C21-24	22¢,33¢,39¢,44¢ AMERIPEX (4) ..	...	28.50	6.00
53	22¢ Passport	...	3.95	.85
54-5,C26-7	5¢,22¢,33¢,44¢ Christmas Paintings (4)	...	22.95	4.75

1987 Commemoratives

56,C28-30	22¢,33¢,39¢,44¢ Homeless, Events (4)	...	24.50	4.75
57	$1.00 CAPEX Souvenir Sheet	...	...	4.75
58,C31-33	22¢,33¢,39¢,44¢ Christmas (4) .... (25)130.00	21.75	4.25	

1988 Commemoratives

59-62,C37-8	22¢,44¢ Colonial Flags, attd (6)	...	10.75	5.75
59-62,C37-8	Center Blocks of 8		...	22.50
63-66	25¢ Olympics, attd., two pair		7.75	3.25
67-70	25¢ Christmas Tree, attd		2.95	2.65
71	25¢ Truk Lagoon S/S of 18		...	12.50

1989 Commemoratives

72-75	45¢ Flowers, attd		5.25	4.50
76	$1.00 Hirohito Memorial S/S		...	2.50
77-80	25¢-45¢ Sharks, attd. two pair		8.50	3.50
81	25¢ Moon Landing, 20th Anniv., S/S of 9		...	6.95
82	$2.40 Moon Landing, 20th Anniv		26.50	5.75
103	25¢ WSE, Fruits & Flowers, Sht. of 18...		...	11.75
104-05	25¢,45¢ Christmas (2)		9.75	1.95

1989 Seashells Definitives

83-102	1¢/$5 Seashell definitives (12)		105.00	24.75
85a	15¢ Booklet Pane of 10 (1990)		...	10.00
88a	25¢ Booklet Pane of 10 (1990)		...	15.00
88b	15¢ & 25¢ Booklet Pane of 10 (5 ea.)(1990) ...		...	15.00

FEDERATED STATES OF MICRONESIA
1990 Commemoratives

Scott's No.		Mint Sheetlet	Plate Block	F-VF NH
106-09	10¢,15¢,20¢,25¢ World Wildlife Fund (4)	...	26.50	4.95
110-113	45¢ Stamp World London '90 Whalers, attd	...	5.75	4.50
114	$1.00 S.W. London '90, Whalers, S/S	...	...	2.75
115	$1.00 Penny Black, 150th Anniv., S/S	...	...	2.75
116-20	25¢ Pohnpei Agric. & School, Strip of 5 (15)	9.75	...	3.25
121	$1.00 Int'l. Garden Expo, Osaka, Japan S/S	...	...	2.50
122-23	25¢,45¢ Loading Mail, Airport & Truk Lagoon (2)		7.25	2.25
124-26	25¢ Joint issue w/Marsh. Isl. & U.S. (12) 10.00	(6)	5.75	2.50
127-30	45¢ Moths, attd	...	5.25	4.50
131	25¢ Christmas, S/S of 9	...	...	5.75

1991 Commemoratives

134-35	142

132	25¢,45¢ New Capital of Micronesia, S/S	...	...	1.85
133	$1 New Capital, S/S	...	...	2.50
134-37	29¢-50¢ Turtles, attd. two pairs		15.75	6.75
138-41	29¢ Operation Desert Storm, Block of 4		4.00	3.25
142	$2.90 Frigatebird, Flag		...	6.95
142a	$2.90 Frigatebird, S/S		...	7.25
143	29¢ Phila Nippon '91, min. sht. of 3 ..		...	2.95
144	50¢ Phila Nippon '91, min. sht. of 3 ..		...	4.25
145	$1 Phila Nippon S/S		...	2.85
146-48	29¢,40¢,50¢ Christmas (3)		...	2.95
149	29¢ Pohnpei Rain Forest, min. sht. of 18	...	...	16.75

1992 Commemoratives

150	29¢ Peace Corps, strip of 5	(15)12.75	...	3.50
151	29¢ Discovery of America, strip of 3 ..		(6) 12.75	5.95
152-53	29¢,50¢ U.N. Membership Anniv (2) .		...	4.75
153a	Same, S/S of 2		...	4.50
154	29¢ Christmas		12.50	2.50

160	172	179

1993 Commemoratives

155	29¢ Pioneers of Flight, se-ten. Blk. Of 8	...	7.50	6.25
168	29¢ Golden Age of Sail, min. sht. Of 12	...	...	19.95
172	29¢ Thomas Jefferson		5.75	1.10
173-76	29¢ Pacific Canoes, attd		4.50	3.95
177	29¢ Local Leaders, strip of 4	(8)	7.50	3.50
178	50¢ Pioneers of Flight, block of 8 .	(8)	11.50	9.75
179-80	29¢-50¢ Pohnpei		11.95	2.85
181	$1 Pohnpei Souvenir Sheet		...	2.60
182-83	29¢-50¢ Butterflies, two pairs		10.00	4.25
184-185	29¢-50¢ Christmas		11.95	2.60
186	29¢ Yap Culture, sheet of 18		...	16.50

1993-94 Fish Definitives

156-67	10¢-$2.90 Fish, set of 16	...	115.00	23.95

1994 Commemoratives

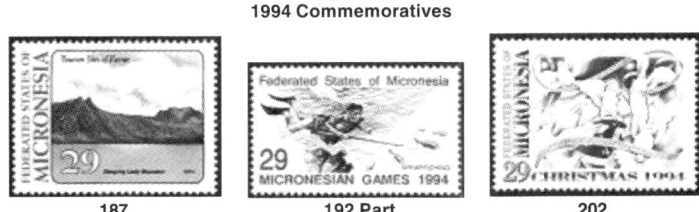

187	192 Part	202

187-89	29¢,40¢,50¢ Kosrae		13.00	2.95
190	29¢-50¢ Butterflies, Hong Kong, sheet of 4	...	...	5.50
191	29¢ Pioneers of Flight, block of 8		8.00	7.00
192	29¢ Micronesian Games, block of 4 ...		4.25	3.50
193	29¢ Native Costumes, block of 4		4.25	3.50
194	29¢ Anniversary of Constitution		8.50	1.95
195	29¢ Flowers, Strip of 4	(8)	7.75	3.50
196-97	50¢ World Cup Soccer, attd		11.50	4.75
198	29¢ Postal Service, 10th Anniv., Block of 4		7.75	5.95

Note: From #151 to date, Plate Blocks have Logos instead of Plate Numbers

Scott's No.		Mint Sheetlet	Plate Block	F-VF NH
199	29¢, 52¢, $1 Philakorea Dinosaurs, Souvenir Sheet of 3	...	...	6.95
200	50¢ Pioneers of Flight, Block of 8	...	11.50	9.95
201	29¢ Migratory Birds, Block of 4	...	7.75	5.75
202-3	29¢-50¢ Christmas (2)	...	18.00	3.75
204-7	32¢ Local Leaders (4)	...	30.00	7.25

211

236

1995 Commemoratives

208	50¢ Year of the Boar Souvenir Sheet	...	...	1.50
209	32¢ Chuuk Lagoon, underwater scenes, Blk/4	...	8.50	6.95
210	32¢ Pioneers of Flight, block of 8	...	6.25	5.75
211	32¢ Dogs of the World, block of 4	...	4.25	3.65
228	32¢ Hibiscus, Strip of 4	(8)	7.50	3.15
229	$1 United Nations 50th Anniv. Souv. Sheet	...	...	2.40
230	32¢ Singapore '95, Orchids S/S of 4	...	...	3.25
231	60¢ End of World War II, Block of 4 .	...	6.95	5.75
232	50¢ Beijing '95 Souvenir Sheet	...	...	1.40
233	60¢ Pioneers of Flight, Block of 8	...	13.50	12.00
234-35	32¢-60¢ Christmas (2)	...	11.95	2.20
236	32¢ Yitzhak Rabin	(8) 13.95	...	1.10

1995-96 Fish Definitives

213-26	23¢-$5.00 Fish Set of 9	...	115.00	23.95
227	32¢ Native Fish Shtlt of 25 (96)	...	...	23.50

1996 Commemoratives

239

237	50¢ Year of the Rat Souvenir Sheet ..	...	...	1.60
238	32¢ Pioneers of Flight, Block of 8	...	8.25	6.95
239	32¢ Tourism in Yap, Block of 4	...	4.35	3.65
240	55¢ Starfish, Block of 4	...	7.50	6.25
241	60¢ Modern Olympics, Block of 4	...	8.75	7.50
242	50¢ China '96 Souvenir Sheet	...	...	1.75
243-44	32¢ Patrol Boats, Pair	...	5.75	2.50
245	55¢ Ford Motor 100th Anniversary, S/S of 8	...	...	11.75
247	32¢ Officer Reza, Police Dog	...	7.50	1.25
248	50¢ Citrus Fruits, strip of 4	(8) 15.00	...	6.75
249	60¢ Pioneers of Flight, Block of 8	...	17.00	15.00
250	32¢ Taipei '96, Souvenir sheet of 4 ...	...	...	4.00
251-52	32¢-60¢ Christmas (2)	...	17.50	2.75
253	$3 Compact with US	...	39.50	8.25

1997 Commemoratives

254	60¢ Deng Xiaoping, Sheetlet of 4	...	...	5.95
255	$3 Deng Xiaoping, Souvenir Sheet	...	...	7.50
256	$2 Hong Kong, Souvenir Sheet	...	...	5.75
57	32¢ Year of the Ox	...	4.75	1.00
258	$2 Year of the Ox, Souvenir Sheet ...	...	...	4.95
259	60¢ Hong Kong return to China, Sheet of 6	...	...	8.95
260	$3 Hong Kong return to China, S/S ...	...	...	7.50
261	32¢ Pacific '97, Goddesses of the Sea, sheetlet of 6	...	...	4.75
262-64	20¢,50¢,60¢ Hiroshige Sheetlets of 3	...	...	9.75
265-66	$2 Hiroshige Souvenir Sheets (2)	...	...	9.95

1997 Commemoratives (continued)

267

273

Scott's No.		Mint Sheetlet	Plate Block	F-VF NH
267	32¢ Pre-Olympics, 4 designs	(16) 12.95	3.95	3.25
268	50¢ Elvis Presley, Sheetlet of 6	...	...	8.25
269	32¢ Underwater Exploration, Sheetlet of 9	...	...	7.25
270-72	$2 Underwater Exploration, Souv. Shts (3)	...	...	14.95
273	60¢ Diana, Princess of Wales, ...	(6) 8.75	...	1.50
274	50¢ WWF, Butterfly Fish, 4 designs ..	(16) 19.75	5.95	4.95
275-76	32¢ Christmas, Fra Angelico, 2 designs	(16) 12.75	3.95	1.60
277-78	60¢ Christmas, Simon Marmion, 2 des.	(16) 23.50	7.50	2.95

1998 Commemoratives

279

287

279-80	50¢ Year of the Tiger Souvenir Sheets	(2)	...	2.75
281	$1 Micronesia's admission to the United Nations Souvenir Sheet	...	...	2.50
282	32¢ Disney "Winnie the Pooh" Sheetlet of 8	...	...	8.50
283-84	$2 Disney "Winnie the Pooh" Souvenir Sheets (2)	...	...	11.50
285	32¢ Soccer, Sheetlet of 8	...	...	6.50
286-87	$2 Soccer, Souvenir Sheets (2)	...	...	9.75
288	$3 Olympics, Souvenir Sheet	...	...	7.50
289-91	32¢, 40¢, 60¢ Israel '98 Sheetlets of 3 (3)	...	...	9.50
292-94	$2 Israel '98, Souvenir Sheets (3)	...	...	14.50
295	32¢ Year of the Ocean, Deep-Sea Research, Sheetlet of 9	...	...	7.25
296-98	$2 Year of the Ocean, Souvenir Sheets (3)	...	...	14.75
299	50¢ Native Birds, Block of 4	(16) 18.00	...	4.85
300	$3 Native Birds, Souvenir Sheet	...	...	7.50

1998-99 Definitives

301-19	1¢-$5 Fish (19)	...	120.00	27.50
319A	$10.75 Fish Definitive	...	95.00	22.75
328-32	33¢-$3.20 Fish, Part II (5)	...	47.50	11.50
333	$11.75 Fish Definitive	...	100.00	23.75

1998 Commemoratives (continued)

320	32¢ F.D. Roosevelt Memorial, Fala, Sheetlet of 6...	...	...	4.75
321-22	32¢-60¢ Christmas, Madonna in 20th Century Art, Sheetlet-3...	...	...	6.25
323	$2 Christmas Souvenir Sheet	...	...	4.75
324-25	60¢ John Glenn's Return to Space Sheetlets of 8 (2)	...	...	23.50
326-27	$2 John Glenn's Return to Space Souvenir Sheets (2)	...	...	9.75

1999 Commemoratives

340-41

1999 Commemoratives (continued)

Scott's No.		Mint Sheetlet	Plate Block	F-VF NH
334	33¢ Russian Space Accomplishments, Sheetlet of 20	...	...	14.95
335-36	$2 Russian Space Souvenir Sheets (2)	...	...	9.50
337-38	33¢ Romance of the Three Kingdoms, Sheetlets of 5 (2)	...	...	7.75
339	$2 Romance of Three Kingdoms, Souvenir Sheet	...	...	4.75
340-41	55¢ IBRA'99, Caroline Is. Stamps (2)	...	5.65	2.65
342	$2 IBRA'99, Caroline Is. Stamps, Souvenir Sheet	...	...	4.75
343	33¢ Australia '99 WSE, Voyages of the Pacific, Sheetlet of 20	...	...	14.95
344	33¢ United States Space Achievements Sheetlet of 20	...	...	14.95
345-46	$2 U.S. Space Achievements Souvenir Sheets (2)	...	...	9.50
347	33¢ Earth Day: Endangered, Extinct and Prehistoric Species, Sheetlet of 20	...	...	14.95
348-49	$2 Earth Day, Souvenir Sheets (2)	...	...	9.50
350-51	33¢ Hokusai, Sheetlets of 6 (2)	...	...	9.50
352-53	$2 Hokusai, Souvenir Sheets (2)	...	...	9.50
354	50¢ Faces of the Millennium, Princess Diana Sheetlet of 8 ...	...	...	9.50
355	20¢ Millennium, 12th Century, Sheetlet of 17	...	...	8.00
356	33¢ Millennium, Science & Technology of Ancient China Sheetlet of 17	...	...	12.75
357	33¢ Costumes of the World Sheetlet of 20 ...	...	...	14.95
358-60	33¢, 60¢, $2 Christmas, Van Dyck (3)	...	32.50	7.25
361	$2 Christmas Souvenir Sheet	...	...	4.75
362	33¢ First Century of Flight ..... Sheetlet of 15	...	...	11.75

2000 Commemoratives

363-64	$2 Flight Souvenir Sheets (2)	...	...	9.50
365-67	33¢ Orchids Sheetlets of 6 (3)	...	...	13.50
368-69	$2 Orchids Souvenir Sheets (2)	...	...	9.00
370	33¢ Religious Leaders Sheetlet of 12	...	...	8.85
371	$2 Year of the Dragon Souvenir Sheet	...	...	4.50
372-73	20¢-55¢ Butterflies Sheetlets of 6 (2)	...	...	10.00
374-76	$2 Butterflies Souvenir Sheets (2)	...	...	13.50
377	20¢ 20th Century 1920-29 Sheetlet of 17	...	...	7.75
378	33¢ Millennium 2000	...	...	.70

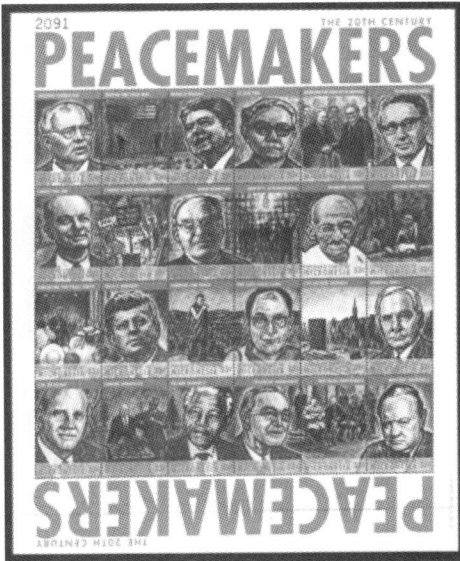

379

379	33¢ Peacemakers Sheetlet of 24	...	...	16.75
380	33¢ 20th Century Philanthropists Shtlt of 16	...	...	11.50
381-82	33¢ Mushrooms Sheetlets of 6 (2)	...	...	8.50
383-84	$2 Mushrooms Souvenir Sheets (2)	...	...	8.50
385	33¢ Flowers of the Pacific Sheetlet of 6	...	...	4.25
386	33¢ Wildflowers Sheetlet of 6	...	...	4.25
387	$2 Flowers of the Pacific Souvenir Sheet	...	...	4.25
388	$2 Wildflowers Souvenir Sheet	...	...	4.25
389	33¢ Sydney Olympics Sheet of 4	...	...	2.75
390	33¢ Zeppelin Sheetlet of 6	...	...	4.25
391-92	$2 Zeppelin Souvenir Sheet (2)	...	...	8.50
393	33¢ Queen Mother Photomosiac Sheetlet of 8	...	...	5.50
394	33¢, $1 Olymphilex 2000 Sheetlet of 3	...	...	3.50
395-98	33¢ Coral Reef set of 4	...	...	2.75
399-400	33¢ Coral Reef Sheetlets of 9 (2)	...	...	12.50
401-2	$2 Coral Reef Souvenir Sheets (2)	...	...	8.50
403	50¢ Pope John Paul II Photomosaic Sheetlet of 8	...	...	8.50
404-7	20¢, 33¢, 60¢, $3.20 Christmas (4)	...	...	8.95

2001 Commemoratives

Scott's No.		Mint Sheetlet	Plate Block	F-VF NH
408	33¢ Dogs Sheetlet of 6	...	...	4.25
409	33¢ Cats Sheetlet of 6	...	...	4.25
410	$2 Dogs Souvenir Sheet	...	...	4.25
411	$2 Cats Souvenir Sheet	...	...	4.25
412-13	60¢ Year of the Snake Souvenir Sheets (2) ..	...	...	2.65
416-17	50¢-60¢ Whales Sheetlets of 6 (2)	...	...	14.50
418-19	$2 Whales Souvenir Sheets (2)	...	...	8.50

Enviroment Sheet of 6

...	33¢ Environment-One Earth Sheetlets of 6, 4(2)	...	...	9.25
...	$2 Environment-One Earth Souvenir Sheet 3(2)	...	...	8.50
414	50¢ Pokemon Sheetlet of 6	...	...	6.50
415	$2 Pokemon Souvenir Sheet	...	...	4.25

2001 Fish Definitives

...	11¢,34¢,70¢,80¢,$3.50 set of 5	...	49.50	11.50

2001 Commemoratives (continued)

...	60¢ Queen Elizabeth 75th Birthday Sheetlet of 6	...	...	7.75
...	$2 Queen Elizabeth 75th Birthday Souvenir Sheet	...	...	4.25
...	60¢ Queen Victoria Sheetlet of 6	...	...	7.75
...	$2 Queen Victoria Souvenir Sheet	...	...	4.25
...	34¢ Philanippon '01 Sheetlet of 6	...	...	4.25
...	34¢ Philanippon '01 (6)	...	...	4.25
...	$2 Philanippon '01 Souvenir Sheets (2)	...	...	8.50

Airmails

C39-42

1984-94

C1-3	28¢,35¢,40¢ Aircraft (1984)	...	14.75	3.00
C25	$1.00 Ameripex S/S (1986)	...	...	4.75
C39-42	45¢ Federated State Flags, attd (1989)	...	4.85	4.50
C43-46	22¢,36¢,39¢,45¢ Aircraft Serving Micronesia ('90)	...	23.75	5.75
C47-48	40¢,50¢ Aircraft (1992)	...	18.75	4.25
C49	$2.90 Moon Landing Souvenir Sheet (1994) .	...	...	7.25

Postal Stationary Entires

U1	20¢ National Flag (1984)	...	...	18.50
U2	22¢ Tall Ship Senyavin (1986)	...	...	10.75
U3	29¢ on 30¢ New Capital (1991)	...	...	4.95

Postal Cards

UX1-4	20¢ Scenes, Set of 4 (1997)	...	...	5.95

REPUBLIC OF PALAU
PALAU BECAME INDEPENDENT IN 1994.

1983 Commemoratives

1   5   9   21

Scott's No.		Mint Sheetlet	Plate Block	F-VF NH
1-4	20¢ Postal Service Inaugural, attd	...	3.95	3.00
5-8	20¢ Birds, attd	...	2.75	2.25
24-27	20¢ Whales, attd	...	4.25	3.25
28-32	20¢ Christmas, Strip of 5	...	(10) 7.50	3.50
33-40	20¢ Henry Wilson, Block of 8	...	6.75	5.25

1983-84 Marine Definitives

9-21	1¢-$5 Definitives, Set of 13	...	125.00	25.75
13a	13¢ Booklet Pane of 10	...	...	12.75
13b	13¢/20¢ Bklt. Pane of 10 (5 #13, 5 #14)	...	...	14.75
14b	20¢ Booklet Pane of 10	...	...	13.75

59   95   99

1984 Commemoratives

41-50	20¢ Seashells, Block of 10, attd)	...	6.50	5.50
51-54	40¢ 19th UPU Congress	...	5.95	4.95
55-58	20¢ Ausipex, attd	...	3.00	2.35
59-62	20¢ Christmas, attd	...	3.00	2.35

1985 Commemoratives

63-66	22¢ Audubon, attd	...	5.50	4.75
67-70	22¢ Shipbuilding, attd	...	4.25	3.50
86-89	44¢ International Youth Yr., attd	...	5.25	4.50
90-93	14¢,22¢,33¢,44¢ Christmas	...	23.50	3.75
94	$1.00 Trans-Pacific Air Anniv. S/S	...	...	3.25
95-98	44¢ Halley's Comet, attd	...	5.00	4.25

1985 Marine Definitives

75-85	14¢/$10 Marine Life (7)	...	140.00	30.75
75a	14¢ Booklet Pane of 10	...	...	10.75
76a	22¢ Booklet Pane of 10	...	...	13.50
76b	14¢/22¢ Bklt. Pane of 10 (5 #75, 5 #76)	...	...	14.75

1986 Commemoratives

99-102	44¢ Songbirds, attd	...	5.25	4.65
103	14¢ AMERIPEX Sea & Reef, Sht of 40 ...	...	...	50.00
104-08	22¢ Seashells, attd	(10)	8.35	3.85
109-12	22¢ Int'l. Peace Year, attd	...	10.00	4.85
113-16	22¢ Reptiles, attd	...	4.25	3.35
117-21	22¢ Christmas,Strip of 5, attd	(15) 10.50	(10) 5.95	2.75
117-21	Christmas with Tabs	...	(10) 7.50	3.50

122   141   164

1987 Commemoratives

121B-E	44¢ Butterflies, attd	...	5.95	4.85
122-25	44¢ Fruit Bats, attd	...	5.50	4.75
146-49	22¢ CAPEX, attd	...	3.25	2.65
150-54	22¢ Seashells, Strip of 5 attd	...	(10) 7.95	3.50
155-63	14¢,22¢,44¢ U.S. Constitution Bicentennial, attd. (3 strips of 3)	(15) 28.50	...	6.25
164-67	14¢,22¢,33¢,44¢ Japanese Links (4)	...	14.50	2.95
168	$1 S/S Japanese Links to Palau	...	...	2.95
173-77	22¢ Christmas, Strip of 5 attd	...	(10) 8.50	3.35
178-82	22¢ "Silent Spring" Symb. Species,attd	(15) 12.50	(10) 8.95	3.65

REPUBLIC OF PALAU

Scott's No.		Mint Sheetlet	Plate Block	F-VF NH

1987-88 Indigenous Flowers Definitives

126-42	1¢ - $10 Flowers (17)	...	250.00	52.50
130a	14¢ Bklt. Pane of 10	...	...	5.25
131a	15¢ Bklt. Pane of 10 (1988)	...	...	4.25
132a	22¢ Bklt. Pane of 10	...	...	8.25
132b	14¢/22¢ Bklt. Pane of 10 (5 ea.)	...	...	8.25
133a	25¢ Bklt. Pane of 10 (1988)	...	...	7.00
133b	15¢/25¢ Bklt. Pane of 10 (5 ea.) (1988)	...	...	6.75

191-95

1988 Commemoratives

183-86	44¢ Butterflies & Flowers, attd	...	5.00	4.35
187-90	44¢ Ground Dwelling Birds, attd	...	5.25	4.50
191-95	25¢ Seashells, Strip of 5, attd	...	(10) 8.00	3.25
196	25¢ Postal Indep. S/S of 6 (FINLANDIA)	...	...	3.75
197	45¢ USPPS S/S of 6 (PRAGA '88)	...	...	6.50
198-202	25¢ Christmas, strip of 5	(15) 9.50	(10) 7.00	3.35
198-202	Christmas with Tabs	...	(10) 8.75	4.35
203	25¢ Palauan Nautilus, S/S of 5	...	...	4.15

1989 Commemoratives

204-07	45¢ Endangered Birds, attd	...	5.25	4.50
208-11	45¢ Exotic Mushrooms, attd	...	5.50	4.75
212-16	25¢ Seashells, strip of 5	...	(10) 6.75	3.25
217	$1 Hirohito Memorial S/S	...	...	2.75
218	25¢ Moon Landing, 20 Anniv., S/S of 25	...	...	14.95
219	$2.40 Moon Landing, 20th Anniv	...	26.75	5.85
220	25¢ Literacy, block of 10	...	6.95	5.95
221	25¢ World Stamp Expo, Fauna, Min. sheet of 25	...	...	15.75
222-26	25¢ Christmas, Strip of 5, attd	(15)10.00	(10) 7.00	3.25
222-26	25¢ Christmas with Tabs	...	(10) 9.50	3.95

258

1990 Commemoratives

227-30	25¢ Soft Coral, attd	...	3.25	2.85
231-34	45¢ Forest Birds, attd	...	4.85	4.50
235	25¢ Stamp World London '90, S/S of 9 ..	...	...	5.75
236	$1.00 Penny Black, 150th Anniv. S/S ...	...	...	2.65
237-41	45¢ Orchids, strip of 5	(15) 17.50	(10) 12.00	5.75
237-41	45¢ Orchids with Tabs	...	...	6.50
242-45	45¢ Butterflies & Flowers, attd	...	5.25	4.50
246	25¢ Lagoon Life, Sheetlet of 25	...	...	16.50
247-48	45¢ Pacifica/Mail Delivery, attd	(10) 19.75	9.00	3.95
249-53	25¢ Christmas, Strip of 5, attd	(15) 9.75	(10)7.25	3.25
249-53	Christmas with Tabs	...	...	3.75
254-57	45¢ U.S. Forces in Palau, 1944, attd ...	...	5.95	5.25
258	$1 U.S. Forces in Palau, 1944, S/S ..	...	...	3.50

259   266   291

1991 Commemoratives

Scott's No.		Mint Sheetlets	Plate Block	F-VF NH
259-62	30¢ Coral, attd	...	4.25	3.50
263	30¢ Angaur, The Phospate Island, Sheet/16	...	...	12.50
288	29¢ Cent. of Christianity in Palau, Sheet of 6	...	...	4.25
289	29¢ Marine Life, Sheet of 20	...	...	16.95
290	20¢ Desert Shield/Desert Storm, min. Sheet/9	...	...	4.75
291	$2.90 Fairy tern, Yellow/Ribbon	...	...	7.25
292	$2.90 Same, S/S	...	...	7.25
293	29¢ Women's Conf. & Palau,10th Anniv,min sht of 8	...	...	5.95
294	50¢ Giant Clam Cultivation, S/S of 4	...	...	5.50
295	29¢ Japanese Heritage, Phila Nippon,Shtlt of 6	...	...	4.50
296	$1.00 Pearl Harbor	...	...	3.25
297	29¢ Peace Corps in Palau, min. sht. of 6	...	...	4.50
298	29¢ Christmas, strip of 5, attd	(15) 10.50	(10) 7.50	3.50
298	Christmas with Tabs	...	...	4.25
299	29¢ WWII in the Pacific, min. sht. of 10	...	...	9.75

1991-92 Birds Definitives

266-83	1¢-$10 Birds (18)	...	230.00	49.75
269b	19¢ Palau Fantail, Bklt. Pane of 10	...	...	4.50
272a	29¢ Fruit Dove, Bklt. Pane of 10	...	...	6.75
272b	19¢ Fantail & 29¢ Fruit Dove, Bklt. Pane/10(5 ea)	...	...	5.75

300

312 part

1992 Commemoratives

300	50¢ Butterflies, Block of 4	...	5.75	5.00
301	29¢ Shells, strip of 5	...	(10) 9.50	3.75
302	29¢ Columbus & Age of Discovery, min. sht/20	...	...	14.75
303	29¢ Biblical Creation/Earth Summit, min sht/24	...	...	16.95
304-09	50¢ Summer Olympics, Souvenir Sheets (6)	...	...	7.50
310	29¢ Elvis Presley, min. sht. of 9	...	...	8.50
311	50¢ WWII, Aircraft - Pacific Theater, min sht/10	...	...	14.95
312	29¢ Christmas, strip of 5	(15) 11.50	(10) 8.25	3.95
312	Christmas with Tabs	...	...	4.35

313 Part

315 Part

1993 Commemoratives

313	50¢ Animal Families, block of 4	...	5.00	4.50
314	29¢ Seafood, block of 4	...	...	3.00
315	50¢ Sharks, block of 4	...	...	4.50
316	29¢ WWII, Pacific Theater, min. sheet of 10	...	...	9.75
317	29¢ Christmas, strip of 5	(15) 10.00	(10) 7.75	3.65
317	29¢ Christmas with Tabs	...	...	4.25
318	29¢ Prehistoric & Legendary Sea Creatures, Sheet of 25	...	...	16.50
319	29¢ Indigenous People, sheet of 4	...	...	2.95
320	$2.90 Indigenous People, Souvenir Sheet	...	...	7.50
321	29¢ Jonah and the Whale, sheet of 25 ..	...	...	17.95

323

Scott's No.		Mint Sheetlets	Plate Block	F-VF NH
	1994 Commemoratives			
322	40¢ Palau Rays, block of 4	...	...	3.95
323	20¢ Crocodiles, block of 4	...	3.25	2.95
324	50¢ Seabirds, block of 4	...	...	5.00
325	29¢ WWII, Pacific Theater, min. sheet of 10	...	...	9.50
326	50¢ WWII, D-Day, min. sheet of 10	...	...	13.50
327	29¢ Baron Pierre de Coubertin	...	...	.90
328-33	50¢, $1, $2 Coubertin and Winter Olympics Stars, Set of 6 Souv. Sheets	...	...	15.95
334-36	29¢, 40¢, 50¢ Philakorea '94 Philatelic Fantasies, Wildlife, 3 Souv. Sheets of 8 .	...	...	29.50
337	29¢ Apollo XI Moon Landing 25th Anniv., Miniature Sheet of 20	...	...	14.75
338	29¢ Independence Day Strip of 5	(15) 10.75	...	3.65
339	$1 Invasion of Peleliu Souvenir Sheet	...	...	2.95
340	29¢ Disney Tourism Sheetlet of 9	...	...	7.50
341-43	$1, $2.90 Disney Tourism, 3 Souv. Sheets ...	...	...	13.50
344	20¢ Year of the Family, Min. Sheet of 12	...	...	5.95
345	29¢ Christmas '94 Strip of 5	(15) 10.00	...	3.75
345	Christmas with Tabs	...	...	4.25
346-48	29¢, 50¢ World Cup of Soccer, Set of 3 Sheetlets of 12	...	...	29.95

364

365

384

Scott's No.		Mint Sheetlets	Plate Block	F-VF NH
	1995 Commemoratives			
350	32¢ Elvis Presley, Sheetlet of 9	...	...	7.50
368	32¢ Tourism, Lost Fleet, Sheetlet of 18 .	...	...	14.50
369	32¢ Earth Day '95, Dinosaurs, Shtlt of 18	...	...	13.95
370	50¢ Jet Aircraft, Sheetlet of 12	...	...	14.50
371	$2 Jet Aircraft, Souvenir Sheet	...	...	4.85
372	32¢ Underwater Ships, Sheetlet of 18	...	...	14.50
373	32¢ Singapore '95 Hidden Treasures, Blk of 4	...	3.75	3.25
374	60¢ U.N., FAO 50th Anniv., Block of 4 ...	...	6.85	6.00
375-76	$2 U.N. FAO 50th Anniv., Souv. Sheets .	...	...	9.75
377	20¢ Independence, Block of 4	...	2.60	2.10
378	32¢ Independence, Marine Life	...	3.95	.85
379	32¢ End of World War II, Sheetlet of 12 ..	...	...	10.75
380	60¢ End of World War II, Sheetlet of 5	...	...	9.75
381	$3 End of World War II Souvenir Sheet ...	...	...	7.75
382	32¢ Christmas Strip of 5	(15) 11.50	(10) 8.50	3.75
382	32¢ Christmas with Tabs	...	...	4.25
383	32¢ Life Cycle of the Sea Turtle, Shtlt/12	...	...	12.75
384	32¢ John Lennon	(16) 23.95	...	1.25

1995 Fish Definitives

351-64	1¢-$5 Fish Definitives (14)	...	125.00	25.95
365	$10 Fish Definitive	...	100.00	22.50
366	20¢ Fish, Booklet Single	...	...	.55
366a	20¢ Fish, Booklet Pane of 10	...	...	4.75
367	32¢ Fish, Booklet Single	...	...	.85
367a	32¢ Fish, Booklet Pane of 10	...	...	7.75
367b	20¢, 32¢ Fish, Bklt. Pane of 10 (5 each)	...	...	6.50

1996 Commemoratives

385	10¢ Year of the Rat Strip of 4	(8) 4.50	...	2.25
386	60¢ Year of the Rat Souvenir Sheet	...	...	2.85
387	32¢ 50th Anniversary of UNICEF Blk/4 ..	(16) 11.50	3.50	2.85
388	32¢ China '96 Underwater Strip of 5	(15) 11.00	...	3.60
389	32¢ Capex '96 Circumnavigators Shtlt/9	...	...	6.50
390	60¢ Capex '96 Air & Space Sheetlet of 9	...	...	12.95
391	$3 Capex '96 Air & Space Souvenir Sheet	...	...	7.50
392	$3 Capex '96 Circumnavigators S/S	...	...	7.50
393	60¢ Disney Sweethearts Sheetlet of 9 ...	...	...	14.95
394-95	$2 Disney Sweethearts Souv. Sheets (2)	...	...	11.00
392A-F	1¢ - 6¢ Disney Sweethearts (6)	...	...	1.00

1996 Commemoratives (continued)

Scott's No.		Mint Sheetlets	Plate Block	F-VF NH
396	20¢ 3000th Anniversary of Jerusalem Shtlt/30	...	...	14.95

399-400

397-400	40¢-60¢ Atlanta '96, 2 Pairs	(20)	65.00	11.50	5.50
401	32¢ Atlanta '96, Sheetlet of 20		...	...	15.95
402	50¢ Lagoon Birds, Sheetlet of 20		...	...	25.00
403	40¢ "Spies in the Sky", Sheetlet of 12		...	...	12.50
404	60¢ Oddities of the Air, Sheetlet of 12		...	...	17.75
405	$3 Stealth Bomber, Souvenir Sheet		...	...	7.50
406	$3 Martin Marietta X-24B, Souv. Sheet		...	...	7.50
407-8	20¢ Independence	(16)	7.95	...	1.00
409	32¢ Christmas, Strip of 5	(15)	12.00	...	3.95
409	32¢ Christmas with Tabs		...	...	4.25
410	32¢ Voyages to Mars, Sheetlet of 12		...	...	9.95
411-12	$3 Voyages to Mars, Souvenir Sheet	(2)	...	...	15.00

1997 Commemoratives

412A	$2 Year of the Ox, Souvenir Sheet		...	5.00
413	$1 South Pacific Commission, 50th Anniv., Souvenir Sheet	...	...	2.50

414   **425**

1997 Pacific '97, Flowers

414-19	1¢-$3 Flowers (6)		37.50	7.95
420-21	32¢-50¢ Shoreline Plants, 2 Blocks of 4	(16) 32.50	9.75	8.25

1997 Commemoratives (continued)

422-23	32¢-60¢ Parachutes, Sheetlets of 8 (2)		...	17.95
424-25	$2 Parachutes, Souvenir Sheets (2)		...	9.75
426	20¢ Avian Environment, Sheetlet of 12		...	5.95
427-28	32¢-60¢ UNESCO, 50th Anniversary, Sheetlets of 8 and 5 (2)		...	13.50
429-30	$2 UNESCO, Souvenir Sheets (2)		...	9.75
431	32¢ Hiroshige Poetic Prints, Sheetlet of 5		...	3.95
432-33	$2 Hiroshige Souvenir Sheets (2)		...	9.75
434	32¢ Volcano Goddesses of the Pacific, Pacific '97, Sheetlet of 6		...	4.75

435   **440**

435	32¢ 3rd Anniv. of Independence	(12)	9.50	3.95	.80
436	32¢ Underwater Exploration, Sheetlet of 9		...	6.95
437-39	$2 Underwater Exploration, Souvenir Sheets (3)		...	14.75
440	60¢ Diana, Princess of Wales,	(6)	8.95	...	1.50
441-46	1¢-10¢ Disney "Let's Read (6)		...	1.00
447	32¢ Disney "Let's Read" Sheetlet of 9		...	7.00
448-49	$2-$3 Disney "Let's Read" Souvenir Sheets (2)		...	13.00
450	32¢ Christmas song, 5 designs	(15) 11.75	...	3.95

1998 Commemoratives

Scott's No.		Mint Sheetlets	Plate Block	F-VF NH
451-52	50¢ Year of the Tiger Souvenir Sheets (2)	...	...	2.50
453	32¢ Hubble Space Telescope Sheetlet of 6	...	...	4.75
454-56	$2 Hubble, Souvenir Sheets (3)	...	...	14.50

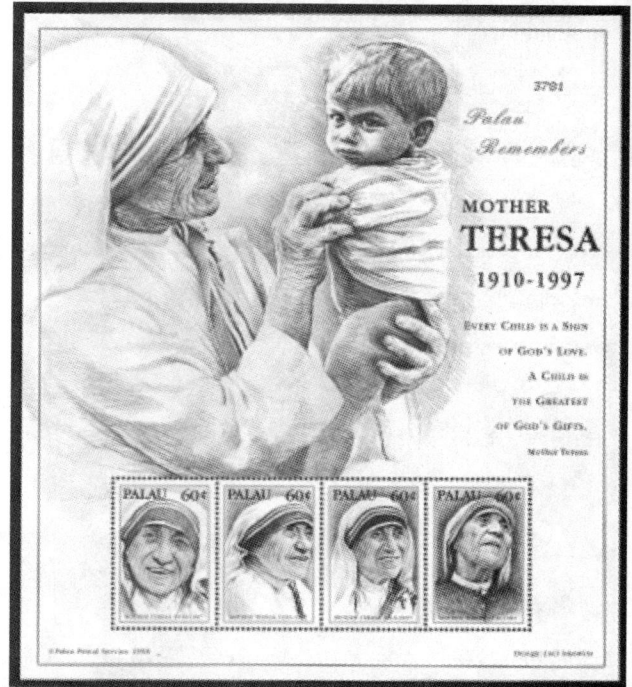

457

457	60¢ Mother Teresa, Souvenir Sheet of 4	...	...	5.95
458	32¢ Deep Sea Robots Sheetlet of 18	...	...	13.95
459-60	$2 Deep Sea Robots, Souvenir Sheets (2)	...	...	9.75
461	20¢ "Israel 98" Overprint on Jerusalem Sheetlet of 30 (#396)	...	...	15.00
462	40¢ Legend of Orachel, Sheetlet of 12	...	...	13.00
463	50¢ World Cup Soccer, Sheetlet of 8	...	...	9.75
464	$3 World Cup Soccer, Souvenir Sheet	...	...	7.50
465	32¢ 4th Micronesian Games, Sheetlet of 9	...	...	7.25
466	32¢ Christmas, Rudolph, Strip of 5	(15) 10.50	...	3.95
467-70	20¢, 32¢, 50¢, 60¢ Disney's "A Bug's Life" Sheetlets of 4 (4)	...	...	18.00
471-74	$2 Disney's "A Bug's Life" Souvenir Sheets (4)	...	...	22.50

1999 Commemoratives

475-76	60¢ John Glenn's Return to Space Sheetlets of 8 (2)	...	21.95
477-78	$2 John Glenn's Return to Space Souvenir Sheets (2)	...	9.75
479	33¢ Environmental Heroes of 20th Century Sheetlet of 16	...	11.50
480	33¢ Mir and the Space Shuttles Sheetlet of 6	...	4.75
481-84	$2 Mir and the Space Shuttles Souvenir Sheets (4)	...	19.50

1999 Famous Persons Regular Issues

485-94 (Ex)

485-94	1¢,2¢,20¢,22¢,33¢,50¢,55¢,60¢.77¢,$3.20 set of 10	59.50	13.50

1999 Commemoratives (continued)

495	33¢ Vanishing Turtles, Frogs and Amphibians, Sheetlet of 12	...	9.50
496-97	$2 Vanishing Turtles, etc. Souvenir Sheets (2)	...	...	9.75
498-99	55¢ IBRA '99, Caroline Is. Stamps (2)	...	11.50	2.65
500	$2 IBRA '99, Caroline Is. Stamps, Souv. Sht	...	...	4.75
501	33¢ Exploring Mars, Sheetlet of 6	...	...	4.75
502-5	$2 Exploring Mars, Souvenir Sheets (4)	...	...	19.00
506	33¢ Earth Day, Pacific Insects, Sheetlet of 20	...	...	16.50
507	33¢ Space Station, Sheetlet of 6	...	...	4.75
508-11	$2 Space Station, Souvenir Sheets (4)	...	...	19.50
512	33¢ Information Age, Visionaries of the 20th Century, Sheetlet of 25	...	...	19.50
513-14	33¢ Hokusai Paintings Sheetlets of 6 (2)	...	...	9.50
515-16	$2 Hokusai Paintings Souvenir Sheets (2)	...	...	9.75
517	33¢ Apollo 11 Sheetlet of 6	...	...	4.75
518-21	$2 Apollo ii Souvenir Sheets (4)	...	...	19.00
522	60¢ Queen Mother 100th Birthday Sheetlet of 4	...	...	5.75
523	$2 Queen Mother 100th Birthday Souvenir Sheet	...	...	4.75

1998 Commemoratives

Scott's No.		Mint Sheetlets	Plate Block	F-VF NH
524	33¢ Hubble Images from Space Sheetlet of 6	...	...	4.75
525-28	$2 Hubble Images from Space Souvenir Sheets (4)			19.00
529	20¢ Christmas, Strip of 5	(15) 7.50	...	2.50
530	33¢ Love your Dog Sheetlet of 10	...	...	7.95
531-32	$2 Love your Dog Souvenir Sheets (2)			9.50

2000 Commemoratives

533	33¢ Space Probes Sheetlet of 6	...	...	4.75
534-37	$2 Space Probes Souvenir Sheets (4)	...	...	18.50
538	20¢ Millennium 1800-1850 Sheetlet of 17	...	...	7.25
539	20¢ Millennium 1980-89 Sheetlet of 17	...	...	7.25
540	$2 Year of the Dragon Souvenir Sheet	...	...	4.50

2000 Famous Persons Regular Issue

541-44	$1, $2, $3, $5 set of 4	...	97.50	22.50
545	$11.75 J.F. Kennedy	...	...	23.75

2000 Commemoratives (cont.)

546	20¢ 20th Century Discoveries about PreHistoric Life Sheetlet of 20	...	...	8.50
547	33¢ Olympics Sheetlet of 4	...	...	2.85
548	33¢ Unmanned Space Craft Sheetlet of 6	...	...	4.25
549-52	$2 Unmanned Space Craft Souvenir Sheets (4)	...	...	17.00
553-54	20¢-33¢ Native Birds Sheetlets of 6 (2)	...	...	6.95
555-56	$2 Native Birds Souvenir Sheets (2)	...	...	8.50
557	33¢ Visionaries of the 20th Century Sheetlet of 20	...	...	14.50
558-61	33¢ Science & Medicine Sheetlets of 5 (4)	...	...	14.00
562-63	$2 Sciences & Medicine Souvenir Sheets (2)	...	...	8.50
564-65	33¢ Marine Life Sheetlet of 6 (2)	...	...	8.50
566-67	$2 Marine Life Souvenir Sheet (2)	...	...	8.50
568-69	20¢-55¢ New & Recovering Species Sheetlets of 6 (2)	...	...	9.50
570-71	33¢ New & Recovering Species Souvenir Sheets (2)	...	...	8.50
572-73	$2 New & Recovering Species Souvenir Sheets (2)	...	...	8.50
574-75	20¢-33¢ Dinosaurs Sheetlet of 4 and 6 (2)	...	...	6.75
576-77	$2 Dinosaurs Souvenir Sheet (2)	...	...	8.50
578-79	55¢ Queen Mother, Pair	(4) 9.50	...	4.95
580	$2 Queen Mother Souvenir Sheet	...	...	4.25
581	55¢ Zeppelin Sheetlet of 6	...	...	7.00
582-83	$2 Zeppelin Souvenir Sheets (2)	...	...	8.50
585	50¢ Pope John Paul II Photomosaic Sheetlet of 8	...	...	6.50
586-87	60¢ Year of the Snake Souvenir Sheets (2)	...	...	2.65
588	55¢ Marine Life Sheetlet of 6	...	...	6.95
589	20¢ Atlantic Fishes Sheetlet of 6	...	...	2.65
590-91	$2 Atlantic Fishes Souvenir Sheets (2)	...	...	8.50
592	33¢ Arts Festival Sheetlet of 9	...	...	2.95
593	33¢ Belau Museum Sheetlet of 12	...	...	8.50
594-97	33¢ Butterflies, set of 4	...	...	2.95
598-99	33¢ Butterflies Sheetlets of 6 (2)	...	...	8.50
600-01	$2 Butterflies Souvenir Sheets (2)	...	...	8.50
602-03	33¢ Fauna and Flora Sheetlets of 6 (2)	...	...	8.50
604-05	$2 Fauna and Flora Souvenir Sheets(2)	...	...	8.50

2001 Famous Persons Regular Issue

...	1¢,11¢,60¢ set of 3	...	...	1.60

2001 Commemoratives

607-08	$2 Year of the Snake Souvenir Sheets (2)	...	...	8.50

592

Scott's No.		Mint Sheetlets	Plate Block	F-VF NH

1988 Semi-Postals

B1-2

B1-4	25¢ + 5¢,45¢ + 5¢ Olympic Sports, 2 pairs	...	10.00	4.85

Airmails

C5   C10

1984-95

C1-4	40¢ Birds, attd (1984)	...	4.75	3.95
C5	44¢ Audubon (1985)	...	7.50	1.50
C6-9	44¢ Palau-Germany Exchange Cent., attd	...	6.00	4.95
C10-13	44¢ Trans-Pacific Anniv., attd	...	5.50	4.50
C14-16	44¢ Remelik Memorial, Strip of 3 (1986)	(9) 16.50	(6) 9.50	4.50
C14-16	Remelik Mem., with tabs, attd	...	(6) 12.00	5.95

C17   C18-20

C17	44¢ Peace Year, St. of Liberty	...	7.00	1.35
C18-20	36¢,39¢,45¢ Aircraft (1989)	...	15.75	3.25
C18a	36¢ Bklt. Pane of 10	...	...	8.75
C19a	39¢ Bklt. Pane of 10	...	...	9.50
C20a	45¢ Bklt. Pane of 10	...	...	10.50
C20b	36¢/45¢ Bklt. Pane of 10 (5 each)	...	...	9.50
C21	50¢ Palauan Bai (#293a), self adh (1991)	...	9.75	1.90
C22	50¢ Birds, Block of 4 (1995)	...	...	4.95

Postal Stationery

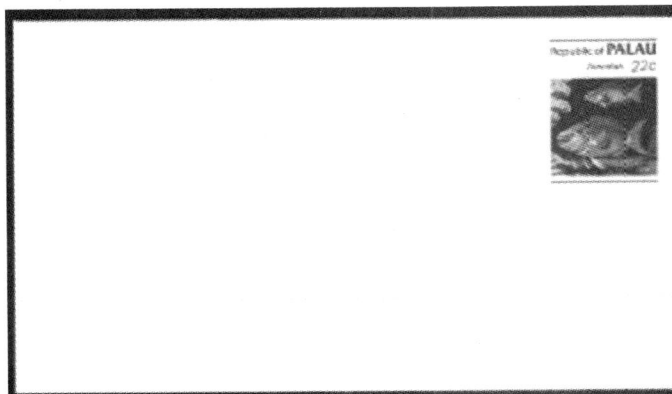

U1

U1	22¢ Parrotfish (1989)	...	...	4.50
U2	22¢ Spearfishing	...	...	7.95
U3	25¢ Chambered Nautilus (1991)	...	...	4.25
UC1	36¢ Birds (1985)	...	...	11.95
UX1	14¢ Giant Clam (1985)	...	...	3.50

1951 Regular Issue

Scott's No.		MI Block of 4	F-VF NH	F-VF Used
1-11	1¢-$1 Regular Issue	32.50	7.00	6.75
1	1¢ Peoples, Magenta	.60	.20	.15
2	1½¢ U.N. Hdqtrs. Blue Green	.60	.20	.15
2p	1½¢ Precancelled	...	...	50.00
3	2¢ Peace, Justice, Sec. Purple	.60	.20	.15
4	3¢ Flag, Magenta & Blue	.60	.20	.15
5	5¢ UNICEF, Blue	.60	.20	.15
6	10¢ Peoples, Chocolate	1.25	.25	.20
7	15¢ Flag, Violet & Blue	1.35	.30	.20
8	20¢ World Unity, Dark Brown	3.50	.75	.50
9	25¢ Flag, Olive Gray & Blue	2.75	.60	.50
10	50¢ U.N. Hdqtrs., Indigo	19.50	4.25	4.00
11	$1 Peace, Justice Sec., Red	8.00	1.80	1.50

1952

12-14	set of 3	2.50	.55	...
12	5¢ War Memorial Building, U.N. Charter	.85	.20	.20
13-14	3¢-5¢ Human Rights, Flame	1.85	.40	.30

1953

15-22	set of 8	19.50	4.25	...
15-16	3¢-5¢ Refugee Family	3.25	.70	.55
17-18	3¢-5¢ Universal Postal Union	5.65	1.25	1.15
19-20	3¢-5¢ Technical Assistance	3.50	.75	.70
21-22	3¢-5¢ Human Rights, Hands	7.75	1.75	1.00

1954

23-30	set of 8	69.50	15.75	...
23-24	3¢-8¢ Food & Agriculture Org	8.00	1.70	1.25
25-26	3¢-8¢ Int'l. Labor Organization	10.00	2.25	1.25
27-28	3¢-8¢ U.N. European Office, Geneva	15.00	3.25	2.00
29-30	3¢-8¢ Human Rights, Mother and Child	40.00	9.00	3.50

1955

31/40	#31-37,39-40 set of 9	33.75	7.25	...
31-32	3¢-8¢ Int'l Civil Aviation Organization	16.50	3.50	2.25
33-34	3¢-8¢ UNESCO Emblem	4.00	.85	.70
35-37	3¢, 4¢, 8¢ 10th Anniversary United Nations	11.75	2.50	1.75
38	3¢, 4¢, 8¢ 10th Anniv. Souv. Sheet of 3	...	140.00	50.00
38v	3¢, 4¢, 8¢ Second Print, Retouched	...	150.00	60.00
39-40	3¢-8¢ Human Rights, Torch	3.15	.70	.65

1956

41-48	set of 8	8.15	1.90	...
41-42	3¢-8¢ Telecommunications	3.15	.70	.65
43-44	3¢-8¢ World Health Organ	3.15	.70	.65
45-46	3¢-8¢ General Assembly, U.N. Day	1.25	.30	.25
47-48	3¢-8¢ Human Rights, Flame and Globe	1.00	.30	.25

1957

Scott's No.		MI Block of 4	F-VF NH	F-VF Used
49-58	set of 10	5.95	1.60	...
49-50	3¢-8¢ Meteorological, Weather Balloon	1.00	.30	.25
51-52	3¢-8¢ U.N. Emergency Force	1.00	.30	.25
53-54	3¢-8¢ Same, re-engraved	2.50	.60	.30
#53-54	The area around the circles is shaded, giving a halo effect.			
55-56	3¢-8¢ Security Council, Emblem and Globe	1.00	.30	.25
57-58	3¢-8¢ Human Rights, Flaming Torch	1.00	.30	.25

1958

59-68	set of 10	4.65	1.40	...
59-60	3¢-8¢ Atomic Energy Agency	1.10	.30	.25
61-62	3¢-8¢ Central Hall, London	.90	.30	.25
63-64	4¢-8¢ Regulars, U.N. Seal	.90	.30	.25
65-66	4¢-8¢ Economic & Social Council	1.10	.30	.25
67-68	4¢-8¢ Human Rights, Hands and Globe	.90	.30	.25

1959

69-76	set of 8	4.50	1.10	...
69-70	4¢-8¢ Flushing Meadows, Gen. Assembly	1.10	.30	.25
71-72	4¢-8¢ Economic Comm. - Europe	1.20	.30	.25
73-74	4¢-8¢ Trusteeship Council	1.30	.30	.25
75-76	4¢-8¢ World Refugee Year	1.15	.30	.25

1960

77/87	#77-84.86-87 set of 10	5.50	1.40	...
77-78	4¢-8¢ Chaillot Palace Paris	1.15	.30	.25
79-80	4¢-8¢ Economic Council - Asia & Far East	1.15	.30	.25
81-82	4¢-8¢ World Forestry Congress	1.15	.30	.25
83-84	4¢-8¢ 15th Anniversary, United Nations	1.15	.30	.25
85	4¢-8¢ 15th Anniv. Souvenir Sheet	...	1.10	1.10
85v	Same broken "v" Variety	...	60.00	55.00
86-87	4¢-8¢ Bank for Reconstruction & Develop.	1.15	.30	.25

1961

88-99	set of 12	10.75	2.50	...
88-89	4¢-8¢ Int'l Court of Justice	1.15	.30	.25
90-91	4¢-7¢ Monetary Fund	1.15	.30	.25
92	30¢ Regular, Flags	3.15	.70	.55
93-94	4¢-11¢ Economic Council - Latin America	2.25	.50	.45
95-96	4¢-11¢ Economic Comm. - Africa	1.60	.35	.25
97-99	3¢, 4¢, 13¢ Children's Fund, UNICEF	2.30	.50	.45

1962

100-13	set of 14	10.75	2.50	...
100-01	4¢-7¢ Housing & Urban Development	1.15	.30	.25
102-03	4¢-11¢ World Health Org., Anti-Malaria	1.70	.40	.35
104-07	1¢, 3¢, 5¢, 11¢ Regulars	2.75	.60	.50
108-09	5¢-15¢ Dag Hammarskjold	2.15	.50	.45
110-11	4¢-11¢ Operations in Congo	1.90	.45	.45
112-13	4¢-11¢ Peaceful Uses of Outer Space	1.85	.40	.30

NOTE : "MI" REFERS TO MARGINAL INSCRIPTION BLOCKS FROM THE CORNERS OF U.N. MINT SHEETS.

NOTE: PRICES THROUGHOUT THIS LIST ARE SUBJECT TO CHANGE WITHOUT NOTICE IF MARKET CONDITIONS REQUIRE. MINIMUM MAIL ORDER MUST TOTAL AT LEAST $20.00.

115 **119** **133** **136**

192 **197** **201** **209**

1963

Scott's No.		MI Block of 4	F-VF NH	F-VF Used
114-22	set of 9	9.25	2.10	...
114-15	5¢-11¢ Science & Technology	1.75	.40	.30
116-17	5¢-11¢ Freedom from Hunger	1.75	.40	.30
118	25¢ UN in West New Guinea (UNTEA)	2.65	.60	.50
119-20	5¢-11¢ General Assembly Bldg.,N.York	1.75	.40	.30
121-22	5¢-11¢ Human Rights, Flame	1.75	.40	.30

1964

123-36	set of 14	14.75	3.75	...
123-24	5¢-11¢ Maritime Consultative Org	1.75	.40	.30
125-28	2¢,7¢,10¢,50¢ Regulars	7.25	1.60	1.25
129-30	5¢-11¢ Trade & Development	1.75	.40	.30
131-32	5¢-11¢ Control Narcotics	1.75	.40	.35
133	5¢ Ending Nuclear Tests	.60	.20	.15
134-36	4¢,5¢,11¢ Education Progress	2.25	.50	.45

1969

Scott's No.		MI Block of 4	F-VF NH	F-VF Used
192-202	set of 11	10.50	2.40	...
192-93	6¢-13¢ Training & Research Inst.	1.75	.40	.35
194-95	6¢-15¢ U.N. Building, Santiago	1.95	.45	.35
196	13¢ Regular "U.N." & Emblem	1.20	.30	.25
197-98	6¢-13¢ Peace Through Law	1.75	.40	.30
199-200	6¢-20¢ Labor & Development	2.50	.55	.40
201-02	6¢-13¢ Art, Tunisian Mosaic	1.75	.40	.30

1970

203/14	#203-11,213-14 set of 11	11.75	2.50	...
203-04	6¢-25¢ Art, Japanese Peace Bell	2.85	.65	.50
205-06	6¢-13¢ Mekong Basin Development.	1.75	.40	.30
207-08	6¢-13¢ Fight Against Cancer	1.75	.40	.30
209-11	6¢,13¢,25¢ 25th Anniversary of U.N.	4.25	.90	.80
212	6¢,13¢,25¢ 25th Anniv. Souv. Sheet of 3 ...	...	.90	.85
213-14	6¢-13¢ Peace, Justice & Progress	1.85	.40	.35

1971

137 **140** **154** **163**

215 **216** **220** **224**

1965

137/53	#137-44,146-53 set of 16	25.00	5.50	...
137-38	5¢-11¢ Development Fund	1.75	.40	.30
139-40	5¢-11¢ Peace Keeping Force - Cyprus	1.75	.40	.30
141-42	5¢-11¢ Telecommunications Union	1.75	.40	.30
143-44	5¢-15¢ 20th Anniv. Cooperation Year.	1.95	.45	.35
145	5¢-12¢ 20th Anniv. Souvenir Sheet of 2	...	.55	.55
146-50	1¢,15¢,20¢,25¢,$1 Regulars	17.50	3.65	3.00
151-53	4¢,5¢,11¢ Population Trends	2.10	.45	.40

215-25	set of 11	15.65	3.50	...
215	6¢ Peaceful Uses of the Sea Bed	.70	.20	.15
216-17	6¢-13¢ Support for Refugees	1.75	.40	.30
218	13¢ World Food Program	1.40	.30	.25
219	20¢ U.P.U. Headquarters, Bern	1.75	.40	.35
220-21	8¢-13¢ Racial Discrimination	2.00	.45	.35
222-23	8¢-60¢ Regulars	6.25	1.35	1.00
224-25	8¢-21¢ U.N. Int'l. School	2.75	.60	.45

1966

154-63	set of 10	8.50	1.95	...
154-55	5¢-15¢ Fed. of U.N. Associations	1.95	.45	.30
156-57	5¢-11¢ W.H.O. Headqtrs. Geneva	1.75	.40	.30
158-59	5¢-11¢ Coffee Agreement	1.75	.40	.30
160	15¢ Peacekeeping - Observers	1.65	.35	.30
161-63	4¢,5¢,11¢ UNICEF 20th Anniv.	1.85	.45	.35

228 **233** **236** **243**

1972

226-33	set of 8	16.50	3.65	...
226	95¢ Regular, Letter	8.50	1.90	1.50
227	8¢ No More Nuclear Weapons	.75	.20	.15
228	15¢ World Health Day, Man.	1.40	.30	.25
229-30	8¢-15¢ Human Environment, Stockholm	2.35	.50	.40
231	21¢ Economic Comm. - Europe	2.10	.45	.40
232-33	8¢-15¢ Art, Jose Maria Sert Mural	2.25	.50	.45

166 **170** **185** **190**

1967

164/80	#164-78, 180 set of 16	12.75	2.95	...
164-65	5¢-11¢ Development Program	1.75	.40	.30
166-67	1½¢-5¢ Regulars	.90	.30	.20
168-69	5¢-11¢ Independent Nations, Fireworks	1.75	.40	.30
170-74	4¢,5¢,8¢,10¢,15¢ Expo '67, Montreal	4.50	.95	.80
175-76	5¢-15¢ Tourist Year	1.95	.45	.30
177-78	6¢-13¢ Disarmament	1.95	.45	.35
179	6¢ Chagall Souvenir Sheet of 6	...	.75	.70
180	6¢ Chagall Window Stamp	.70	.20	.15

1973

234-43	set of 10	11.75	2.50	...
234-35	8¢-15¢ Disarmament Decade	2.25	.50	.45
236-37	8¢-15¢ Against Drug Abuse	2.25	.50	.45
238-39	8¢-21¢ Volunteer Program	2.75	.60	.50
240-41	8¢-15¢ Namibia, Map of Africa	2.25	.50	.50
242-43	8¢-21¢ Human Rights, 25th Anniv.	2.75	.60	.50

1968

181-91	set of 11	15.95	3.50	...
181-82	6¢-13¢ Secretariat	1.95	.45	.35
183-84	6¢-75¢ Art, Starcke Statue	7.75	1.65	1.40
185-86	6¢-13¢ Industrial Development	1.75	.40	.30
187	6¢ Regular, U.N. Headquarters	.70	.20	.15
188-89	6¢-20¢ World Weather Watch	2.50	.55	.35
190-91	6¢-13¢ Human Rights, Flame	1.95	.45	.35

1974

| 244 | 252 | 256 | 263 |

Scott's No.		MI Block of 4	F-VF NH	F-VF Used
244-55	**set of 12**	**15.50**	**3.35**	...
244-45	10¢-21¢ Labor Organization Headquarters	2.95	.65	.60
246	10¢ U.P.U. Centenary	1.10	.25	.20
247-48	10¢-18¢ Art, Brazil Peace Mural	2.75	.60	.60
249-51	2¢,10¢,18¢ Regulars	2.75	.60	.60
252-53	10¢-18¢ Population Year	3.25	.70	.70
254-55	10¢-25¢ Law of the Sea	3.75	.80	.75

1975

256/66	**#256-61,263-66 set of 10**	**16.50**	**3.60**	...
256-57	10¢-26¢ Peaceful Use of Outer Space	3.75	.80	.70
258-59	10¢-18¢ Women's Year	3.25	.70	.65
260-61	10¢-26¢ 30th Anniversary of U.N.	3.65	.80	.75
262	10¢-26¢ 30th Anniv. Souv. Sheet of 2	...	.85	.85
263-64	10¢-18¢ Namibia, Hand	2.95	.65	.55
265-66	13¢-26¢ Peacekeeping Operations	3.85	.85	.80

| 273 | 278 | 283 | 289 |

1976

267-80	**set of 14**	**31.75**	**7.00**	...
267-71	3¢,4¢,9¢,30¢,50¢ Regulars	8.75	1.95	1.50
272-73	13¢-26¢ U.N. Associations(WFUNA)	3.75	.80	.60
274-75	13¢-31¢ Trade & Development	4.25	.90	.70
276-77	13¢-25¢ Human Settlement, Habitat	3.75	.80	.65
278-79	13¢-31¢ 25th Postal Anniversary	12.00	2.75	2.25
278-79	Sheetlets of 20	...	52.50	...
280	13¢ World Food Council	1.35	.30	.25

1977

281-90	**set of 10**	**17.75**	**3.75**	...
281-82	13¢-31¢ Intellectual Property(WIPO)	4.15	.90	.75
283-84	13¢-25¢ Water Conference	3.75	.80	.65
285-86	13¢-31¢ Security Council	4.15	.90	.75
287-88	13¢-25¢ Racial Discrimination	3.75	.80	.65
289-90	13¢-18¢ Peaceful - Atomic Energy	3.00	.65	.65

| 296 | 299 | 310 | 312 |

| 299 | 300 | 302 |

1978

291-303	**set of 13**	**28.75**	**6.15**	...
291-93	1¢,25¢,$1 Regulars	11.50	2.50	1.95
294-95	13¢-31¢ Smallpox-Eradication	4.15	.90	.75
296-97	13¢-18¢ Namibia, Open Handcuff	3.00	.65	.60
298-99	13¢-25¢ Civil Aviation Organ (ICAO)	3.75	.80	.70
300-01	13¢-18¢ General Assembly	3.25	.70	.70
302-03	13¢-31¢ Technical Cooperation	4.50	.95	.85

UNITED NATIONS - Offices in New York

1979

Scott's No.		MI Block of 4	F-VF NH	F-VF Used
304-15	**set of 12**	**19.50**	**4.15**	...
304-07	5¢,14¢,15¢,20¢ Regulars	5.00	1.10	1.00
308-09	15¢-20¢ Disaster Relief (UNDRO)	3.25	.70	.60
310-11	15¢-31¢ Year of the Child	4.50	.95	.85
310-11	Sheetlets of 20	...	18.50	...
312-13	15¢-31¢ Namibia, Olive Branch	4.50	.95	.80
314-15	15¢-20¢ Court of Justice, The Hague	3.25	.70	.70

| 316 | 325 | 344 | 346 |

1980

316/42	**#316-23,341-42 set of 10**	**19.75**	**4.15**	...
316-17	15¢-31¢ New Economic Order	4.50	.95	.85
318-19	15¢-31¢ Decade for Women	3.50	.75	.65
320-21	15¢-31¢ Peacekeeping Operations	4.50	.95	.85
322-23	15¢-31¢ 35th Anniversary of U.N.	4.50	.95	.80
324	15¢-31¢ 35th Anniv. - Souv. Sheet of 2	...	.95	.95
*325-40	15¢ World Flag Series of 16	19.00	4.75	4.50
325-40	Se-Tenant Block of 4(4)	...	9.50	...
341-42	15¢-20¢ Economic & Social Council	3.75	.80	.70

1981

343/67	**#343-49,366-67 set of 9**	**20.75**	**4.65**	...
343	15¢ Palestinian People	1.50	.30	.25
344-45	20¢-35¢ Disabled Persons	4.95	1.10	1.0
346-47	20¢-31¢ Art, Bulgarian Mural	4.95	1.10	.95
348-49	20¢-40¢ Energy Conference	5.50	1.20	1.10
*350-65	20¢ World Flag Series of 16	26.00	6.50	5.00
350-65	Se-Tenant Blocks of 4(4)	...	10.75	...
366-67	18¢-28¢ Volunteers Program	4.95	1.10	.95

| 371 | 390 | 394 | 397 |

1982

368/91	**#368-73,390-91 set of 8**	**21.50**	**4.65**	...
368-70	17¢,28¢,40¢ Regulars	8.75	1.90	1.75
371-72	20¢-40¢ Human Environment	5.75	1.25	1.15
373	20¢ Peaceful Use of Outer Space	2.75	.60	.55
*374-89	20¢ World Flag Series of 16	26.00	6.50	5.00
374-89	Se-Tenant Blocks of 4(4)	...	10.75	...
390-91	20¢-28¢ Nature Conservation	5.25	1.15	1.00

1983

392/416	**#392-98,415-16 set of 9**	**25.00**	**5.50**	...
392-93	20¢-40¢ Communications Year	5.75	1.25	1.00
394-95	20¢-37¢ Safety at Sea	5.50	1.20	1.15
396	20¢ World Food Program	2.80	.60	.50
397-98	20¢-28¢ Trade & Development	6.00	1.35	1.20
*399-414	20¢ World Flag Series of 16	26.00	6.50	5.25
399-414	Se-Tenant Blocks of 4(4)	...	12.50	...
415-16	20¢-40¢ Human Rights, 35th Anniv.	6.50	1.40	1.15
415-16	Same, Sheetlets of 16	...	21.75	...

1984

| 417 | 419 | 421 |

417/42	**#417-24,441-42 set of 10**	**36.00**	**7.95**	...
417-18	20¢-40¢ Population Conference	6.25	1.35	1.10
419-20	20¢-40¢ FAO Food Day	7.00	1.50	1.10
421-22	20¢-50¢ UNESCO World Heritage	7.50	1.65	1.20
423-24	20¢-50¢ Refugee Futures	8.50	1.85	1.50
*425-40	20¢ World Flag Series of 16	42.50	10.50	10.00
425-40	Se-Tenant Blocks of 4(4)	...	19.50	...

NOTE: WORLD FLAGS ARE ISSUED IN SHEETS OF 16, EACH WITH 4 DIFFERENT BLOCKS. SHEETS OF 16 WILL BE SUPPLIED AT MI BLOCK PRICE.

| 441-42 | 20¢-35¢ Youth Year | 8.75 | 1.95 | 1.70 |

466   468   473

1985

Scott's No.		MI Block of 4	F-VF NH	F-VF Used
443/67	#443-48,466-67 set of 8	50.00	10.95	...
443	23¢ ILO-Turin Centre	3.50	.75	.60
444	50¢ U.N. University in Japan	6.50	1.40	1.40
445-46	22¢-$3 Regulars	28.50	6.25	4.50
447-48	22¢-45¢ 40th Anniversary of U.N.	8.50	1.80	1.75
449	22¢-45¢ 40th Anniv. Souvenir Sheet of 2 ...		2.25	2.10
*450-65	22¢ World Flag Series of 16	43.50	10.75	10.00
450-65	Se-Tenant Blocks of 4(4)	...	21.50	...
466-67	22¢-33¢ UNICEF Child Survival	6.50	1.40	1.15

1986

468-76	set of 9 .... (6)	29.00	12.50	...
468	22¢ Africa in Crisis, Against Hunger	2.75	.60	.55
469-72	22¢ UN Development Program, attd.	9.50	8.50	7.50
469-72	Sheet of 40	...	95.00	...
473-74	22¢-44¢ Philately, Stamp Collecting	7.00	1.50	1.25
475-76	22¢-33¢ International Peace Year	11.50	2.50	2.25
*477-92	22¢ World Flag Series of 16	45.00	11.00	10.75
477-92	Se-Tenant Blocks of 4(4)	...	20.75	...
493	22¢,33¢,39¢,44¢ WFUNA S/S of 4	...	5.25	5.00

1987

502   517

494/518	#494-98,515-18 set of 9	44.50	9.75	...
494	22¢ Trygve Lie, Secretary-General	5.00	1.10	.95
495-96	22¢-44¢ Shelter for the Homeless	9.50	2.10	1.85
497-98	22¢-33¢ Life Yes/Drugs No	9.50	2.10	1.85
*499-514	22¢ 1987 World Flag Series of 16	47.50	11.50	10.50
499-514	Se-Tenant Blocks of 4 (4)	...	20.75	...
515-16	22¢-39¢ U.N. Day, Multinational	6.75	1.50	1.50
515-16	Miniature Sheets of 12	...	20.75	...
517-18	22¢-44¢ Child Immunization	16.00	3.50	2.00

519   524   544

1988

519/44	#519-27, 544 set of 10 .... (9)	50.75	14.50	...
519-20	22¢-33¢ World Without Hunger(IFAO)	9.75	2.15	1.85
521	3¢ Regular, UN For a Better World	.70	.20	.15
522-23	25¢-44¢ Forestry, pair	17.00	7.50	6.25
522-23	Miniature Shelter of 12	...	42.50	...
524-25	25¢-50¢ Int'l. Volunteers Day	11.00	2.25	2.00
526-27	25¢-38¢ Health in Sports	11.50	2.35	2.10
*528-43	25¢ World Flag Series of 16	47.50	11.50	10.75
528-43	Se-Tenant Blocks of 4 (4)	...	20.75	...
544	25¢ Human Rights 40th Anniv.	3.65	.85	.75
545	$1 Human Rights Anniv. S/S	...	2.25	2.10

1989

546/71	#546-53,570-71 set of 10 .... (8)	58.95	14.50	...
546-47	25¢-45¢ World Bank	12.75	2.75	2.35
548	25¢ UN Peace Keeping, Nobel Prize	4.00	.80	.70
549	45¢ Regular UN Headquarters	4.50	.90	.90
550-51	25¢-36¢ World Weather Watch	13.50	3.00	2.75
552-53	25¢-90¢ UN Offices Vienna, 10th Anniv	27.50	6.00	5.25
552-53	Sheets of 25	...	195.00	...
*554-69	25¢ World Flags Series of 16	51.50	12.50	11.00
554-69	Se-Tenant Blocks of 4 (4)	...	21.75	...
570-71	25¢-45¢ Declaration of Human Rights	...	1.75	1.60
570-71	Strips of 3 with Tabs at Bottom	...	5.25	...
570-71	Miniature Sheets of 12	...	26.50	...

577   592   593

1990

Scott's No.		MI Block of 4	F-VF NH	F-VF Used
572/83	#572-78,580-83 set of 11 .... (9)	66.50	16.50	...
572	25¢ International Trade Center	9.00	1.90	1.60
573-74	25¢-40¢ Fight Against AIDS	11.50	2.50	2.25
575-76	25¢-90¢ Medicinal Plants	13.50	3.00	2.75
577-78	25¢-45¢ UN 45th Anniversary	19.50	4.25	3.75
579	25¢-45¢ UN 45th Anniversary S/S of 2	...	10.75	9.50
580-81	25¢-36¢ Crime Prevention	17.50	3.75	3.25
582-83	25¢-45¢ Declaration of Human Rights	...	1.95	1.85
582-83	Strips of 3 with Tabs at Bottom	...	5.85	...
582-83	Miniature Sheets of 12	...	27.50	...

1991

584-600	set of 17 .... (12)	110.00	29.75	...
584-87	30¢ Europe Econ. Commission attd.	6.50	5.50	5.00
588-89	30¢-50¢ Namibia Independence	16.50	3.50	2.75
590-91	30¢-50¢ Regulars	13.75	2.75	2.40
592	$2 Regular U.N. Headquarters	18.50	3.95	3.25
593-94	30¢-70¢ Children's Rights	21.75	4.75	4.25
595-96	30¢-90¢ Chemical Weapons Ban	26.50	5.95	5.50
597-98	30¢-40¢ UNPA 40th Anniv.	13.50	3.00	2.75
599-600	30¢-50¢ Declaration of Human Rights	...	2.40	2.25
599-600	Strips of 3 with Tabs at Bottom	...	7.20	...
599-600	Miniature Sheets of 12	...	30.00	...

601   617   623

1992

601-17	set of 17 .... (10)	51.75	19.75	...
601-02	30¢-50¢ World Heritage, UNESCO	11.00	2.40	2.25
603-04	29¢ Clean Oceans attd	6.75	1.50	1.25
603-04	Miniature Sheet of 12	...	13.00	...
605-08	29¢ UNICED: Earth Summit attd.	3.50	3.00	3.00
605-08	UNICED Sheet of 40	...	32.50	...
609-10	29¢ Mission to Planet Earth attd.	18.50	8.00	7.95
609-10	Miniature Sheet of 10	...	50.00	...
611-12	29¢-50¢ Science & Technology	8.50	1.85	1.50
613-15	4¢,29¢,40¢ Regulars	7.75	1.80	1.60
616-17	29¢-50¢ Declaration of Human Rights	...	2.50	2.50
616-17	Strips of 3 with Tabs at Bottom	...	7.50	...
616-17	Miniature Sheet of 12	...	37.50	...

1993

618-36	set of 19 .... (8)	49.50	25.50	...
618-19	29¢-52¢ Aging with Dignity	16.00	3.50	3.50
620-23	29¢ Endangered Species attd	3.65	3.25	3.00
620-23	Miniature sheet of 16	...	14.50	...
624-25	29¢-50¢ Healthy Environments	11.00	2.40	2.25
626	5¢ Regular	.85	.20	.18
627-28	29¢-35¢ Human Rights	...	2.75	2.75
627-28	Strips of 3 with Tabs at Bottom	...	8.25	...
627-28	Miniature Sheets of 12	...	40.00	...
629-32	29¢ Peace Day, attd.	12.00	11.00	9.50
629-32	Sheet of 40	...	115.00	...
633-36	29¢ Environment - Climate .... (8)	8.25	3.75	3.25
633-36	Miniature Sheet of 24	...	25.00	...

1994

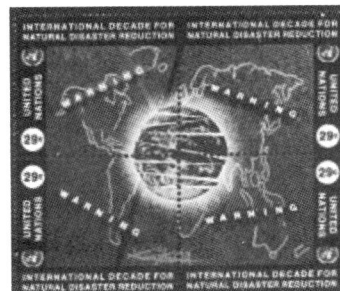

647-50   651

1994

Scott's No.		MI Block of 4	F-VF NH	F-VF Used
637-54	set of 18 .... (12)	72.50	24.50	...
637-38	29¢-45¢ Year of the Family	18.75	3.95	3.50
639-42	29¢ Endangered Species, attd	3.95	3.25	3.00
639-42	Miniature Sheets of 16	...	13.50	...
643	50¢ Refugees	7.50	1.60	1.25
644-46	10¢,19¢,$1 Regulars	14.50	2.95	2.75
647-50	29¢ Natural Disaster, block of 4	11.00	9.75	8.75
647-50	Sheet of 40	...	95.00	...
651-52	29¢-52¢ Population Development	11.50	2.50	2.40
653-54	29¢-50¢ Development Partnership	8.75	1.90	1.75

1995

656

661

663

655/68	#655-64,666-68 set of 13 .... (10)	63.50	16.00	...
655	32¢ U.N. 50th Anniversary	9.00	1.90	1.50
656	50¢ Social Summit, Copenhagen	6.00	1.35	1.15
657-60	32¢ Endangered Species, attd	3.75	3.25	3.00
657-60	Miniature Sheet of 16	...	15.00	...
661-62	32¢-55¢ Youth: Our Future	15.00	3.25	3.00
663-64	32¢-50¢ 50th Anniv. of U.N.	19.50	4.25	3.50
665	82¢ 50th Anniversary Souv. Sheet of 2	...	4.50	3.75
666-67	32¢-40¢ Conference on Women	11.50	2.50	2.00
668	20¢ Regular Issue, U.N. Headquarters	2.35	.50	.45
669	32¢ U.N. 50th Anniv. Sheetlet - 12	...	17.75	...
670	32¢ U.N. 50th Anniversary Souvenir Booklet of 12	...	18.00	...

1996

672

673

671/89	#671-84,686-89 set of 18 .... (9)	55.00	20.00	...
671	32¢ WFUNA 50th Anniv.	3.65	.75	.65
672-73	32¢-60¢ Regular Issues	10.50	2.15	1.75
674-77	32¢ Endangered Species, attd.	3.35	2.85	2.50
674-77	Miniature Sheet of 16	...	13.50	...
678-82	32¢ City Summit, Strip of 5 .... (10)	16.50	7.50	6.00
678-82	Miniature Sheet of 25	...	37.50	...
683-84	32¢-50¢ Sport & Environment	14.00	3.25	2.75
685	32¢-50¢ Sport & Environment Souv. Sheet ...	2.95	2.50	...
686-87	32¢-60¢ Plea For Peace	10.50	2.25	1.75
688-89	32¢-60¢ UNICEF 50th Anniv.	...	2.50	2.00
688-89	Miniature Sheet of 8 .... (2)	...	24.50	...

1997

698

699

708

718

Scott's No.		MI Block of 4	F-VF NH	F-VF Used
690-97	32¢ Flags of New Countries (8)	...	6.95	5.75
690-97	Sheetlets of 16 (2)	...	27.50	...
690-97	Se-Tenant Blocks of 4	...	12.50	...
	690 Tadjikistan 692 Armenia 694 Liechtenstein 696 Kazakhstan			
	691 Georgia 693 Namibia 695 Rep. Of Korea 697 Latvia			
698/717	**#698-707,709-16 set of 19 .... (9)**	**42.00**	**15.65**	...
698-99	8¢-55¢ Regulars, Flowers	7.00	1.50	1.30
700-3	32¢ Endangered Species	3.50	2.95	2.50
700-3	Miniature Sheets of 16	...	13.75	...
704-7	32¢ Earth Summit	4.25	3.50	3.00
704-7	Miniature Sheet of 16	...	21.75	...
708	$1 Earth Summit, Souvenir Sheet	...	2.95	2.85
708a	$1 Pacific "97 Overprint on #708	...	21.95	20.95
709-13	32¢ Transportation, 5 designs	(10)7.95	3.75	3.75
709-13	Sheetlet of 20	...	14.75	...
714-15	32¢-50¢ Tribute to Philately, set of 2	10.50	2.25	2.10
716-17	32¢-60¢ Heritage, Terracotta Warriors	11.00	2.50	2.25
718	$1.92 Terracotta Warriors Prestige Booklet with 6 8¢ Blocks of 4	...	6.75	...
718a-f	Set of Singles From #718(6)	...	2.50	2.25

1998

727

728

729

735

737

738

719-26	32¢ Flags of New Countries (8)	...	6.50	5.00
719-26	Sheetlet of 16 (2)	...	25.95	...
719-26	Se-Tenant Blocks of 4	...	11.50	...
	719 Micronesia 721 Dem. Rep. Korea 723 Uzbekistan 725 Czech Rep.			
	720 Slovakia 722 Azerbaijan 724 Monaco 726 Estonia			
727/42	**#727-33,735,737-42 set of 14 .... (11)**	**35.50**	**9.85**	...
727-29	1¢, 2¢, 21¢ Regulars	2.85	.60	.50
730-33	32¢ Endangered Species	3.50	2.95	2.10
730-33	Miniature Sheet of 16	...	13.75	...
734	32¢ Year of the Ocean, Min. Sheet of 12 ...	...	8.25	...
735	32¢ Rainforests	3.50	.75	.65
735	Rainforests, Sheet of 20	...	14.50	...
736	$2 Rainforests, Souvenir Sheet	...	4.75	4.25
737-38	33¢-40¢ Peacekeeping (2)	8.75	1.90	1.75
737-38	Peacekeeping, Sheets of 20	...	37.50	...
739-40	32¢-55¢ Human Rights (2)	9.00	2.00	1.85
739-40	Human Rights, Sheets of 20	...	39.00	...
741-42	33¢-60¢ Schonbrunn Palace (2)	10.00	2.25	2.10
741-42	Schonbrunn Palace, Sheets of 20	...	44.00	...
743	Schonbrunn Palace, Prestige Booklet with Six Booklet Panes of 3 or 4	...	6.50	...
743a-f	11¢-15¢ Set of 6 Singles from booklet	...	2.25	2.25

1999

754

755

764-67

768

Scott's No.		MI Block of 4	F-VF NH	F-VF Used
744-51	33¢ Flags of New Countries (8)	...	5.75	4.75
744-51	Flags, Sheetlets of 16 (2)	...	22.75	...
744-51	Se-Tenant Blocks of 4	...	10.50	...
744 Lithuania	745 San Marino	746 Turkmenistan		
748 Moldova	749 Kyrgyzstan	750 Bosnia & Herzegovina		747 Marshall Is. 751 Eritrea
752/71	#752-55,57-62,64-68,70-71 set of 17 ... (10)	70.00	24.50	...
752	33¢ Banner of Flags Regular Issue	3.35	.70	.65
753	$5 Roses Regular Issue	43.50	9.95	7.95
754-55	33¢-60¢ World Heritage-Australia (2)	8.75	1.90	1.75
754-55	Australia, Sheetlets of 20 (2)	...	37.50	...
756	Australia, Prestige Booklet with Six Bk. Panes of 4	...	5.75	...
756a-f	5¢-15¢ Set of 6 singles from booklet	...	1.95	1.95
757-60	33¢ Endangered Species (4)	3.35	2.80	2.50
757-60	Endangered Species, Sheetlet of 16	...	11.75	...
761-62	33¢ UNISPACE III, Pair	3.35	1.40	1.40
761-62	UNISPACE III, Miniature Sheet of 10	...	6.95	...
763	$2 UNISPACE III, Souvenir Sheet	...	4.75	4.25
763a	$2 "Stamp Expo 2000"	...	5.75	...
764-67	33¢ Universal Postal Union (4)	3.35	2.80	2.50
764-67	33¢ U.P.U., Sheetlet of 20	...	13.75	...
768	33¢ In Memoriam Fallen in Cause of Peace	3.35	.70	.65
768	33¢ In Memoriam Sheetlet of 20	...	13.75	...

769

769	$1 In Memoriam Souvenir Sheet	...	2.15	...
770-71	33¢-60¢ Education (2)	8.95	1.95	1.85
770-71	33¢-60¢ Education Sheetlets of 20	...	38.50	...

773-76

Scott's No.		MI Block of 4	F-VF NH	F-VF Used
772/87	#772-80,82,84-85,87 set of 13 .... (10)	38.50	10.25	...
772	33¢ Year of Thanksgiving	3.25	.70	.65
772	33¢ Thanksgiving Sheetlet of 20	...	13.75	...
773-76	33¢ Endangered Species, Block	3.35	2.80	2.50
773-76	33¢ Endangered Species Sheetlet of 16	...	11.75	...
777-78	33¢-60¢ Our World 2000 (2)	8.95	1.95	1.85
777-78	33¢-60¢ Our World Sheetlets of 20 (2)	...	38.50	...
779-80	33¢-55¢ U.N. 55th Anniversary (2)	8.50	1.85	1.75
779-80	33¢-55¢ 55th Anniv. Sheetlets of 20 (2)	...	36.50	...
781	88¢ U.N. 55th Anniversary Souvenir Sheet	...	1.85	1.75
782	33¢ International Flag of Peace	3.35	.70	.65
782	33¢ Flag of Peace Sheetlet of 20	...	13.75	...
783	33¢ United Nations in 21st Century Sheetlet of 6	...	4.15	4.00
784-85	33¢-60¢ World Heritage-Spain (2)	8.95	1.95	1.85
784-85	33¢-60¢ Spain Sheetlets of 20 (2)	...	38.50	...
786	5¢-15¢ World Heritage - Spain Prestige Booklet of 6 Panes of 4	...	4.95	...
786a-f	5¢-15¢ set of singles from Prestige Booklet (6)	...	1.60	1.60
787	33¢ Respect for Refugees	3.35	.70	.65
787	33¢ Respect for Refugees Sheetlet of 20 ..	...	13.75	...

788

| 788 | $1 Respect for Refugees Souvenir Sheet .. | ... | 2.10 | 2.00 |

2001 Issues

| 789-92 | 34¢ Endangered Species (4) .... | 3.35 | 2.80 | 2.65 |
| 789-92 | 34¢ Endangered Species Sheetlet of 16 .... | ... | 11.75 | ... |

793-94

793-94	34¢-80¢ Year of Volunteers (2)	11.00	2.50	2.40
793-94	34¢-80¢ Volunteers Sheetlets of 20 (2)	...	48.50	...
...	34¢ Flags of New Countries (8)	...	5.95	5.75
...	Flags, Sheetlets of 16 (2)	...	23.50	...
...	Flags, Se-Tenant Blocks of 4 (2)	...	10.50	...
	Slovenia, Palau, Tonga, Croatia			
	Macedonia, Kiribati, Andorra, Nauru			

UNITED NATIONS - Offices in New York

AIRMAILS

C1

C5

C7

Scott's No.		MI Block of 4	F-VF NH	F-VF Used
C1-23	1951-77 Airmails set of 23	33.50	7.35	...

1951 First Airmail Issue

C1-4	6¢,10¢,15¢,25¢ Airmail Issue	6.75	1.50	1.25

1957-59

C5-7	4¢,5¢,7¢ Airmails	1.85	.45	.40

C8

C11

C14

1963-69

C8-10	6¢,8¢,13¢ Airmails	2.75	.60	.50
C11-12	15¢ & 25¢ Airmails (1964)	4.50	.95	.85
C13	20¢ Jet Plane (1968)	2.10	.45	.40
C14	10¢ Wings & Envelopes (1969)	1.10	.25	.25

C15

C19

C22

1972-77

C15-18	9¢,11¢, 17¢, 21¢ Airmails	5.75	1.25	.90
C19-21	13¢, 18¢, 26¢ Airmails (1974)	5.25	1.15	.95
C22-23	25¢ & 31¢ Airmails (1977)	5.25	1.15	.95

UNITED NATIONS IN NEW YORK 1951-2000

1-788,C1-23	.... Complete	...	715.00	...
1/788,C1-23	.... Without Souvenir Sheet #38	...	585.00	...

**FOR VERY FINE, ADD 20% TO PRICE LISTED.
MINIMUM-10¢ PER STAMP**

UNITED NATIONS (IN NY) POSTAL STATIONERY

U8

UC5

Scott's No.		Mint Entire
ENVELOPE ENTIRES		
U1	3¢ Emblem (1953)	.75
U1	Large Envelope	.85
U2	4¢ Emblem (1958)	.65
U2	Large Envelope	.90
U3	5¢ Wthr. Vane (1963)	.30
U3	Large Envelope	.90
U4	6¢ Wthr. Vane (1969)	.25
U4	Large Envelope	.45
U5	8¢ Hdqtrs (1973)	.70
U5	Large Envelope	.65
U6	10¢ Hdqtrs (1975)	.50
U6	Large Envelope	.60
U7	22¢ Bouquet (1985)	10.75
U8	25¢ NY Headqtrs ('89) ..	3.50
U8	Large Envelope	3.75
U9	25¢+4¢ Schg on U8 (91)	3.50
U9	Large Envelope	3.75
U9A	25¢+7¢ Surcharge on #U9 (1995)	3.75
U9A	Large Envelope	4.00
U10	32¢ Cripticondina small design (1997)	2.50
U11	32¢ Cripticondina, larger design (1997)	2.50
U12	32¢+1¢ Cripticondina, small design ("U10)('99)	2.25
U13	32¢+1¢ Cripticondina, larger design(U11)('99) .	2.25
...	34¢ U.N.Building(2001) .	.90
AIRMAIL ENVELOPE ENTIRES		
UC3	7¢ Flag (1959)	1.95
UC3	Large Envelope	2.00
UC6	8¢ Emblem (1963)	.60
UC6	Large Envelope	.80
UC8	10¢ Emblem (1969)	.45
UC8	Large Envelope	.50
UC10	11¢ Birds (1973)	.75
UC10	Large Envelope	.90
UC11	13¢ Globe (1975)	.45
UC11	Large Envelope	.60
AIRLETTER SHEETS		
UC1	10¢ Air Letter (1952)	27.95
UC2	10¢ "Air Letter/Aero..." White Border (1954)	8.50
UC2a	10¢ Same, No White Border (1958)	7.75
UC4	10¢ Flag (1960)	.80
UC5	11¢ Gull, blue (1961)	.75
UC5a	11¢ Greenish (1965)	1.75

Scott's No.		Mint Entire
AIRLETTER SHEETS (continued)		
UC7	13¢ Plane (1968)	.40
UC9	15¢ Globe (1972)	.70
UC12	18¢ Hdqtrs (1975)	.70
UC13	22¢ Birds (1977)	.85
UC14	30¢ Paper Airplane (82)	1.95
UC15	30¢+6¢ Surcharge (87)	55.00
UC16	39¢ NY Headqrts (89) ..	4.25
UC17	39¢+6¢ Surcharge on UC16 (1991)	19.50
UC18	45¢ Winged Hand ('92) ..	3.25
UC19	45¢+5¢ Surcharge on UC18 (95)	6.50
UC20	50¢ Cherry Blossom ('97)	2.65
UC21	50¢+10¢ Cherry Blossom (UC20) (1999)	1.75
UC22	50¢+20¢ Cherry Blossom (UC20) (2001)	1.60
...	70¢ Airletter (2001)	1.60
POSTAL CARDS		
UX1	2¢ Hdqtrs (1952)	.25
UX2	3¢ Hdqtrs (1958)	.25
UX3	4¢ Map (1963)	.25
UX4	5¢ Post Horn (1969)	.25
UX5	6¢ "UN" (1973)	.30
UX6	8¢ "UN" (1975)	.65
UX7	9¢ Emblem (1977)	.75
UX8	13¢ Letters (1982)	.55
UX9-13	15¢ NY HQ Views(89) .	9.50
UX14-18	36¢ NY HQ Views (1989)	11.50
UX19	40¢ UN HQ (1992)	4.25
UX20	21¢ Rose Garden(1998)	.60
UX21	50¢ NY Skyline (1998) ..	1.40
...	70¢ U.N.Building (2001)	1.50
AIRMAIL POSTAL CARDS		
UXC1	4¢ Wing (1957)	.30
UXC2	4¢ + 1¢ Surch (1959)	.55
UXC3	5¢ Wing (1959)	.95
UXC4	6¢ Space (1963)	.85
UXC5	11¢ Earth (1966)	.50
UXC6	13¢ Earth (1968)	.45
UXC7	8¢ Planes (1969)	.60
UXC8	9¢ Wings (1972)	.45
UXC9	15¢ Planes (1972)	.50
UXC10	11¢ Clouds (1975)	.45
UXC11	18¢ Pathways ('75)	.50
UXC12	28¢ Flying Mailman(82)	.65

UNITED NATIONS - Offices in Geneva, Switzerland
DENOMINATIONS ARE GIVEN IN SWISS CURRENCY
MOST DESIGNS ARE SIMILAR TO U.N. NEW YORK ISSUES

1   4   8   14

1969-70

Scott's No.		MI Block of 4	F-VF NH	F-VF Used
1-14	5¢,10¢,20¢,30¢,50¢,60¢,70¢,75¢, 80¢,90¢,1fr.,2fr.,3fr.,10 fr. Regular Issue ..	42.50	9.75	9.75

16   18   22

1971

15-21	set of 7	14.50	3.15	...
15	30¢ Peaceful Use of Sea Bed	1.15	.25	.25
16	50¢ Support for Refugees	1.75	.40	.40
17	50¢ World Food Program	2.10	.45	.40
18	75¢ U.P.U. Headquarters	2.75	.60	.60
19-20	30¢-50¢ Racial Discrimination	3.25	.70	.50
21	1.10 fr. U.N. Int'l. School	4.25	.90	.90

1972

22-29	set of 8	23.75	4.95	...
22	40¢ Palace of Nations,Geneva	1.35	.30	.30
23	40¢ No Nuclear Weapons	2.35	.50	.50
24	80¢ World Health Day, Man	3.00	.65	.65
25-26	40¢-80¢ Human Environment	5.75	1.25	1.10
27	1.10 fr. Economic Comm. - Europe	5.95	1.30	1.20
28-29	40¢-60¢ Art, Jose Maria Sert Mural	6.50	1.40	1.30

36   37   43   45

1973

30-36	set of 7	19.00	4.15	...
30-31	60¢-1.10 fr. Disarmament Decade	7.00	1.50	1.50
32	60¢ Against Drug Abuse	2.50	.55	.55
33	80¢ Volunteer Program	2.75	.60	.60
34	60¢ Namibia, Map of Africa	2.50	.55	.55
35-36	40¢-80¢ Human Rights, Flame	5.25	1.15	.85

1974

37-45	set of 9	27.50	5.95	...
37-38	60¢-80¢ ILO Headquarters,Geneva	5.50	1.20	1.10
39-40	30¢-60¢ U.P.U. Centenary	4.75	1.00	.90
41-42	60¢-1 fr. Art, Brazil Peace Mural	6.25	1.30	1.15
43-44	60¢-80¢ Population Year	7.00	1.50	1.45
45	1.30 fr. Law of the Sea	5.75	1.20	1.10

50   55   59   61

1975

46/56	#46-51,53-56 set of 10	30.75	6.60	...
46-47	60¢-90¢ Peaceful Use of Outer Space ..	6.25	1.35	1.30
48-49	60¢-90¢ Women's Year	6.50	1.40	1.40
50-51	60¢-90¢ 30th Anniversary of U.N.	6.25	1.35	1.30
52	60¢-90¢ 30th Anniv. - Souv. Sheet of 2 .	...	1.30	1.20
53-54	50¢-1.30 fr. Namibia, Hand	7.00	1.50	1.40
55-56	60¢-70¢ Peacekeeping Operations	5.75	1.25	1.25

UNITED NATIONS - Offices in Geneva

1976

Scott's No.		MI Block of 4	F-VF NH	F-VF Used
57-63	set of 7	32.75	7.65	...
57	90¢ U.N. Association (WFUNA)	4.50	.95	.95
58	1.10 fr. Trade & Development (UNCTAD)	4.50	.95	.95
59-60	40¢-1.50 fr. Human Settlements,Habitat	6.65	1.40	1.40
61-62	80¢-1.10 fr. 25th Postal Anniversary	18.50	4.00	3.85
61-62	Sheetlets of 20	...	75.00	...
63	70¢ World Food Council	3.25	.70	.65

65   69   76   79

1977

64-72	set of 9	28.75	6.25	...
64	80¢ Intellectual Property (WIPO)	3.25	.70	.70
65-66	80¢-1.10 fr. Water Conference	7.00	1.50	1.40
67-68	80¢-1.10 fr. Security Council	7.00	1.50	1.40
69-70	40¢-1.10 fr. Racial Discrimination	6.00	1.30	1.30
71-72	80¢-1.10 fr. Peaceful - Atomic Energy	7.00	1.50	1.40

1978

73-81	set of 9	28.00	6.00	...
73	35¢ Regular, Tree of Doves	1.65	.35	.35
74-75	80¢-1.10 fr. Smallpox Eradication	7.00	1.50	1.45
76	80¢ Namibia, Handcuffs	3.75	.85	.80
77-78	70¢-80¢ Civil Aviation Organ (ICAO)	5.75	1.25	1.20
79-80	70¢-1.10 fr. General Assembly	7.50	1.60	1.50
81	80¢ Technical Cooperation	4.25	.90	.80

82   86   93   96

1979

82-88	set of 7	24.50	5.25	...
82-83	80¢-1.50 fr. Disaster Relief(UNDRO)	8.50	1.85	1.75
84-85	80¢-1.10 fr. Year of the Child	7.50	1.60	1.35
84-85	Sheetlets of 20	...	29.75	...
86	1.10 fr. Namibia, Map	3.65	.80	.80
87-88	80¢-1.10 fr. Court of Justice, The Hague ...	6.50	1.40	1.35

1980

89/97	#89-94,96-97 set of 8	23.00	4.85	...
89	80¢ New Economic Order	4.00	.85	.80
90-91	40¢-70¢ Decade for Women	5.25	1.10	1.00
92	1.10 fr. Peacekeeping Operations	4.50	.95	.90
93-94	40¢-70¢ 35th Anniversary of U.N.	5.25	1.10	1.00
95	40¢-70¢ 35th Anniv. - Souv. Sheet of 2	...	1.20	1.15
96-97	40¢-70¢ Economic & Social Council	5.25	1.10	1.10

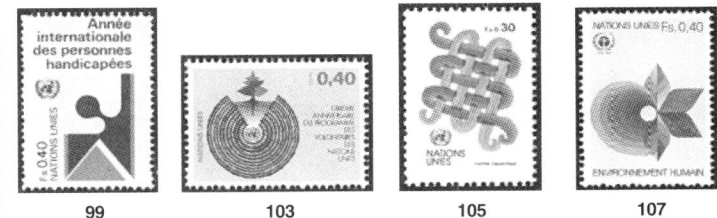

99   103   105   107

1981

98-104	set of 7	25.00	5.25	...
98	80¢ Palestinian People	3.75	.80	.70
99-100	40¢-1.50 fr. Disabled Persons	7.50	1.60	1.50
101	80¢ Art, Bulgarian Mural	4.00	.85	.85
102	1.10 fr. Energy Conference	4.50	.95	.95
103-04	40¢-70¢ Volunteers Program	6.75	1.50	1.50

1982

105-12	set of 8	28.00	6.00	...
105-06	30¢-1 fr. Regulars	5.75	1.25	1.20
107-08	40¢-1.20 fr. Human Environment	7.50	1.60	1.50
109-10	80¢-1 fr. Peaceful Use of Outer Space ...	7.75	1.65	1.65
111-12	40¢-1.50 fr. Nature Conservation	8.50	1.80	1.75

1983

113   114   116

Scott's No.		MI Block of 4	F-VF NH	F-VF Used
113-20	set of 8	33.50	7.25	...
113	1.20 fr. Communications Year	6.75	1.45	1.40
114-15	40¢-80¢ Safety at Sea	6.00	1.30	1.25
116	1.50 fr. World Food Program	6.95	1.50	1.40
117-18	80¢-1.10 fr. Trade & Development	7.75	1.65	1.50
119-20	40¢-1.20 fr. Human Rights, 35th Anniv.	8.00	1.75	1.70
119-20	Sheetlets of 16	...	27.50	...

121   131   135

1984

121-28	set of 8	32.50	7.00	...
121	1.20 fr. Population Conference	5.75	1.25	1.20
122-23	50¢-80¢ FAO Food Day	6.25	1.40	1.30
124-25	50¢-70¢ UNESCO, World Heritage	9.25	2.00	1.80
126-27	35¢-1.50 fr. Refugee Futures	9.25	2.00	1.85
128	1.20 fr. Youth Year	8.00	1.70	1.60

1985

129/39	#129-36,38-39 set of 10	43.50	9.35	...
129-30	80¢-1.20 fr. ILO - Turin Centre	10.50	2.25	1.80
131-32	50¢-80¢ U.N. Univ. in Japan	7.75	1.70	1.65
133-34	20¢-1.20 fr. Regulars	9.00	1.95	1.90
135-36	50¢-70¢ 40th Anniversary of U.N.	8.00	1.75	1.70
137	50¢-70¢ 40th Anniv. Souvenir Sheet of 2	...	2.50	2.25
138-39	50¢-1.20 fr. UNICEF Child Survival	10.75	2.35	2.25

140   145   151   154

1986

140-49	set of 10 (7)	42.75	15.50	...
140	1.40 fr. Africa in Crisis, Anti-Hunger	8.00	1.90	1.80
141-44	35¢ UN Development Program, attd	11.00	10.00	9.50
141-44	Sheet of 40	...	100.00	...
145	5¢ Regular, Dove & Sun	.70	.20	.15
146-47	50¢-80¢ Philately, Stamp Collecting	7.75	1.70	1.65
148-49	45¢-1.40 fr. Int'l. Peace Year	16.75	2.50	2.25
150	35¢,45¢,50¢,70¢ WFUNA S/S	...	5.00	4.75

1987

151-61	set of 11	59.50	12.95	...
151	1.40 fr. Trygve Lie, Secretary-General	8.00	1.75	1.65
152-53	90¢-1.40 fr. Bands/Sphere Regulars	10.00	2.25	2.20
154-55	50¢-90¢ Shelter for the Homeless	8.50	1.85	1.80
156-57	80¢-1.20 fr. Life Yes/Drugs No	8.50	1.85	1.80
158-59	35¢-50¢ U.N. Day	7.00	1.50	1.50
158-59	Miniature Sheets of 12	...	19.50	...
160-61	90¢-1.70 fr. Child Immunization	21.75	4.50	4.50

164   167   173   178

Scott's No.		MI Block of 4	F-VF NH	F-VF Used
1988				
162-71	set of 10 (8)	59.50	17.75	...
162-63	35¢-1.40 fr. World Without Hunger	11.50	2.50	2.35
164	50¢ Regular, UN for a Better World	4.50	.95	.85
165-66	50¢-1.10 fr. Forest Conservation, pair	20.00	9.25	8.75
165-66	Miniature Sheet of 12	...	47.50	...
167-68	80¢-90¢ Int'l. Volunteers Day	10.50	2.25	2.20
169-70	50¢-1.40 fr. Health in Sports	11.75	2.50	2.25
171	90¢ Human Rights 40th Anniv	5.75	1.20	1.15
172	2 fr. Human Rights 40th Anniv. S/S	...	3.25	3.15
1989				
173-81	set of 9 (7)	63.50	15.50	...
173-74	80¢-1.40 fr. World Bank	17.50	3.75	3.75
175	90¢ Peace Keeping, Nobel Prize	5.85	1.25	1.25
176-77	90¢-1.10 fr. World Weather Watch	20.00	4.25	4.00
178-79	50¢-2 fr. UN Offices in Vienna, 10th Anniv	23.50	5.00	4.50
178-79	Miniature Sheets of 25	...	130.00	...
180-81	35¢-80¢ Declaration of Human Rights	...	2.25	2.25
180-81	Strips of 3 with Tabs at Bottom	...	6.75	...
180-81	Miniature Sheets of 12	...	27.50	...

188   202   204

1990				
182/94	#182-89,191-94 set of 12 (10)	105.00	25.00	...
182	1.50 fr. International Trade Center	15.00	3.15	2.75
183	5 fr. Regular	25.00	5.50	5.50
184-85	50¢-80¢ Fight Against AIDS	16.00	3.50	3.25
186-87	90¢-1.40 fr. Medicinal Plants	16.50	3.70	3.50
188-89	90¢-1.10 fr. UN 45th Anniversary	18.75	4.00	3.75
190	90¢-1.10 fr. UN 45th Anniv. S/S of 2	...	7.75	6.50
191-92	50¢-2 fr. Crime Prevention	18.75	4.00	3.85
193-94	35¢-90¢ Declaration of Human Rights	...	2.50	2.50
193-94	Strips of 3 with Tabs at Bottom	...	7.50	...
193-94	Miniature Sheets of 12	...	30.75	...
1991				
195-210	set of 16 (11)	102.00	29.50	...
195-98	90¢ Eur. Econ. Commission, attd	7.50	6.50	6.00
195-98	Sheet of 40	...	62.50	...
199-200	70¢-90¢ Namibia, Independence	19.50	4.25	4.00
201-02	80¢-1.50 fr. Regulars	19.50	4.25	4.00
203-04	80¢-1.10 fr. Children's Rights	18.50	4.00	3.95
205-06	80¢-1.40 fr. Chemical Weapons Ban	22.00	4.75	4.50
207-08	50¢-1.60 fr. UNPA 40th Anniv	21.00	4.50	4.25
207-08	Miniature Sheets of 12	...	90.00	...
209-10	50¢-90¢ Human Rights	...	3.00	2.75
209-10	Strips of 3 with Tabs at Bottom	...	9.00	...
209-10	Miniature Sheets of 12	...	36.50	...

220-221

1992				
211-25	set of 15 (8)	83.50	28.75	...
211-12	50¢-1.10 fr. World Heritage	20.75	4.50	4.00
213	3 fr. Regular	16.50	3.75	3.75
214-15	80¢ Clean Oceans, attd	6.25	2.75	2.50
214-15	Miniature Sheet of 12	...	19.50	...
216-19	75¢ UNICED: Earth Summit, attd	6.25	5.25	4.95
216-19	Sheet of 40	...	55.00	...
220-21	1.10 fr. Mission to Planet Earth, attd	14.50	6.00	5.00
220-21	Miniature Sheet of 10	...	30.00	...
222-23	90¢-1.60 fr. Science & Technology	21.00	4.50	4.25
224-25	50¢-90¢ Human Rights	...	2.75	2.50
224-25	Strips of 3 with Tabs at Bottom	...	8.25	...
224-25	Miniature Sheets of 12	...	35.00	...
1993				
226-43	set of 18 (7)	71.50	31.75	...
226-27	50¢-1.60 fr. Aging with Dignity	20.75	4.25	3.75
228-31	80¢ Endangered Species, attd	5.75	5.00	5.00
228-31	Miniature Sheet of 16	...	22.50	...
232-33	60¢-1 fr. Healthy Environments	18.50	3.75	3.50
234-35	50¢-90¢ Declaration of Human Rights	...	2.90	2.75
234-35	Strips of 3 with Tabs at Bottom	...	8.70	...
234-35	Miniature Sheets of 12	...	40.00	...
236-39	60¢ Peace Day, attd	11.00	10.00	9.00
236-39	Sheet of 40	...	100.00	...
240-43	1.10 fr. Environment - Climate, attd (8)	18.00	8.00	7.75
240-43	Miniature Sheet of 24	...	57.50	...

1994

255

258

260

Scott's No.		MI Block of 4	F-VF NH	F-VF Used
244-61	set of 18 .... (12)	105.00	32.50	...
244-45	80¢-1 fr. Year of the Family	17.50	3.75	3.25
246-49	80¢ Endangered Species,attd	6.50	5.50	5.00
246-49	Miniature Sheet of 16	...	22.75	...
250	1.20 fr. Refugees	14.75	3.00	2.75
251-54	60¢ Natural Disaster, Block of 4	9.50	8.25	7.95
251-54	Sheet of 40	...	80.00	...
255-57	60¢,80¢,1.80 fr. Regulars	24.50	5.25	4.75
258-59	60¢-80¢ Population Development	21.00	4.50	4.25
260-61	80¢-1 fr. Development Partnership	16.50	3.50	3.50

1995

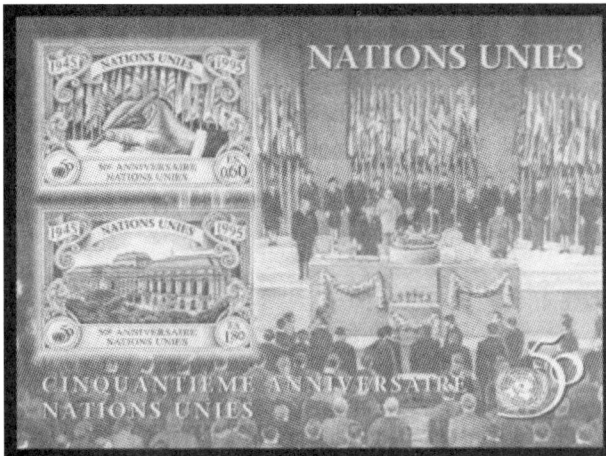

272

262/74	#262-71,273-74 set of 12 .... (9)	85.00	22.75	...
262	80¢ U.N. 50th Anniversary	7.50	1.60	1.50
263	1 fr Social Summit	8.75	1.85	1.85
264-67	80¢ Endangered Species, attd	6.75	5.95	5.95
264-67	Miniature Sheet of 16	...	23.50	...
268-69	80¢ 1 fr Youth: Our Future	22.50	4.95	4.75
270-71	60¢-180 fr 50th Anniv. of U.N.	22.50	4.95	4.75
272	2.40 fr 50th Anniv. Souv. Sheet of 2	...	5.95	5.95
273-74	60¢-1 fr Conference on Women	21.50	4.75	4.50
275	30¢ U.N. 50th Anniv. Sheetlet - 12	...	21.50	21.50
276	30¢ U.N. 50th Anniv. Souvenir, Booklet of 12	...	24.50	...

1996

277/95	#277-90,292-95 set of 18 .... (9)	74.50	27.75	...
277	80¢ WFUNA 50th Anniversary.	8.25	1.80	1.65
278-79	40¢-70¢ Regular Issues	8.75	1.90	1.70
280-83	80¢ Endangered Species,attd	6.00	5.25	4.50
280-83	Miniature Sheet of 16	...	20.75	...
284-88	70¢ City Summit, Strip of 5 .... (10)	19.00	8.50	7.95
284-88	Miniature Sheet of 25	...	42.50	...
289-90	70¢-1.10 fr Sport & Environment	17.50	3.75	3.75
291	70¢-1.10 fr Sport & Environment,Souv.Sheet	...	3.75	3.75
292-93	90¢-1.10 fr Plea for Peace	19.50	4.25	4.15
294-95	70¢-1.80 fr UNICEF 50th Anniversary	...	4.00	3.95
294-95	Miniature Sheets of 8	...	30.00	...

1997

297

298-301

1997 (continued)

302-5

312-13

307-11

Scott's No.		MI Block of 4	F-VF NH	F-VF Used
296/315	#296-305,307-15 set of 19 .... (9)	62.50	23.50	...
296-97	10¢-1.10 fr Regulars	10.75	2.25	2.10
298-301	80¢ Endangered Species, attd	6.95	5.95	4.95
298-301	Miniature Sheet of 16	...	23.75	...
302-5	45¢ Earth Summit, attd	5.00	4.25	3.75
302-5	Miniature Sheet of 24	...	25.00	...
306	1.10fr Earth Summit, Souvenir Sheet	...	3.50	3.25
307-11	70¢ Transportation, 5 designs .... (10)	10.75	5.00	5.00
307-11	70¢ Transportation, Sheetlet of 20	...	19.95	...
312-13	70¢-1.10fr Tribute to Philately, set of 2	18.95	4.25	4.00
314-15	45¢-70¢ Terracotta Warriors	14.50	3.25	3.15
316	fr. 240 Terracotta Warriors Prestige Booklet with 6 10¢ Blocks of 4	...	5.50	...
316a-f	Set of singles from #316 (6)	...	2.75	2.75

1998

318-21

317/30	#317-21,323,325-30 set of 12 .... (9)	70.00	18.75	...
317	2 fr. Palais des Nations, Geneva, Regular Issue	14.50	2.95	2.75
318-21	80¢ Endangered Species	5.75	4.95	4.50
318-21	Miniature Sheet of 16	...	19.75	...
322	45¢ Year of the Ocean, Miniature Sheet of 12	...	9.95	...
323	70¢ Rainforest	5.95	1.25	1.15
323	Rainforest, Sheet of 20	...	24.50	...
324	2 fr.Rainforest, Souvenir Sheet	...	5.25	5.00
325-26	70¢ 90¢ Peacekeeping (2)	11.00	2.50	2.30
325-26	Peacekeeping, Sheets of 20	...	47.50	...
327-28	90¢ - 1.80fr Human Rights (2)	20.75	4.50	4.25
327-28	Human Rights, Sheets of 20	...	86.50	...
329-30	70¢-1.10fr Schonnbrun Palace (2)	15.75	3.50	3.25
329-30	Schonnbrun Palace, Sheets of 20	...	68.50	...
331	Schonnbrun Palace, Prestige Booklet with Six Booklet Panes of 3 or 4	...	6.50	...
331a-f	10¢-30¢ Set of Singles from booklet	...	2.85	...

1999

332    333    334

340-41

Scott's No.		MI Block of 4	F-VF NH	F-VF Used
332/50	#332-34,36-41,43-47,49-50 set of 16 ..... (9)	65.00	22.50	...
332	1.70fr Palais de Wilson Regular Issue	12.75	2.75	2.35
333-34	90¢-1.10fr World Heritage-Australia	18.75	4.25	3.75
333-34	Australia, Sheetlets of 20 (2)	...	82.50	...
335	Australia, Prestige Bklt with Six Bk. Panes of 4	...	5.75	...
335a-f	10¢-20¢ Set of singles from booklet	...	2.50	...
336-39	90¢ Endangered Species, (4)	6.35	5.50	4.75
336-39	Endangered Species, Sheetlet of 16	...	21.50	...
340-41	45¢ UNISPACE III, Pair	3.35	1.40	...
340-41	45¢ UNISPACE III, Miniature Sheet of 10 ...	...	6.85	...
342	2 fr UNISPACE III, Souvenir Sheet	...	3.35	...
343-46	70¢ Universal Postal Union (4)	4.95	4.25	2.75
343-46	70¢ UPU, Sheetlet of 20	...	20.95	...
347	1.10fr In Memoriam Fallen in Cause of Peace	8.25	1.80	1.65
347	1.10fr In Memoriam Sheetlet of 20	...	35.00	...
348	2fr In Memoriam Souvenir Sheet	...	4.75	...

349    350

349-50	90¢-1.80fr Education (2)	18.00	4.25	3.95
349-50	90¢-1.80fr Education Sheetlets of 20	...	82.50	...

2000 Commemoratives

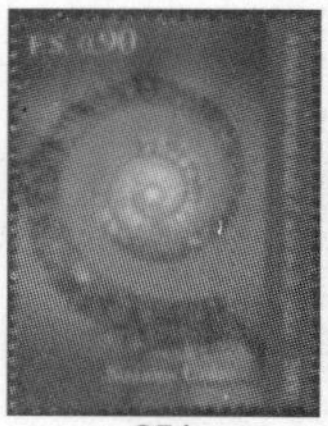

351 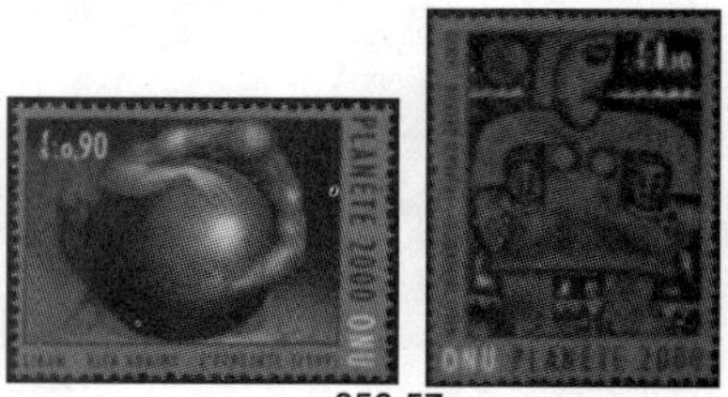   356-57

Scott's No.		MI Block of 4	F-VF NH	F-VF Used
351/65	#351-59,62-63,65 set of 12 .... (9)	51.50	16.50	...
351	90¢ Year of Thanksgiving	6.75	1.40	1.35
351	90¢ Thanksgiving Sheetlet of 20	...	27.00	...
352-55	90¢ Endangered Species, Block	6.00	5.25	4.75
352-55	90¢ Endangered Species Sheetlet of 16	...	20.75	...
356-57	90¢-1.10fr Our World 2000 (2)	12.50	2.75	2.50
356-57	90¢-1.10fr Our World 2000 Sheetlets of 20 (2)	...	52.50	...
358-59	90¢-1.40fr U.N. 55th Anniversary (2)	14.50	3.25	3.00
358-59	90¢-1.40fr U.N. 55th Anniv. Sheetlets of 20 (2)	...	62.50	...
360	2.30fr U.N. 55th Anniversary Souvenir Sheet	...	3.25	3.00
361	50¢ United Nations in 21st Century Sheetlet of 6 ...	...	4.15	4.00
362-63	1fr-1.20fr World Heritage - Spain (2)	13.00	3.00	2.50
362-63	1fr-1.20fr Spain Sheetlets of 20 (2)	...	59.50	...
364	10¢-20¢ World Heritage - Spain Prestige Booklet of 6 Panes of 4	...	4.95	...
364a-f	10¢-20¢ set of singles from Prestige Booklet (6)	...	1.60	1.60
365	80¢ Respect for Refugees	5.25	1.15	1.10
365	80¢ Refugees Sheetlet of 20	...	22.75	...
366	1.80fr Respect for Refugees Souvenir Sheet	...	2.50	2.40

2001 Commemoratives

367-70

Scott's No.		MI Block of 4	F-VF NH	F-VF Used
367-70	90¢ Endangered Species (4)	5.50	4.95	4.50
367-70	90¢ Endangered Species Sheetlet of 16	...	19.50	...
371-72	90¢-1.30fr Year of Volunteers (2)	13.00	2.95	2.85
371-72	90¢-1.30fr Volunteers Sheetlets of 20 (2) ..	...	58.50	...

UN. NATIONS OFFICES IN GENEVA 1969-2000

1-366	Complete	...	510.00	...

UNITED NATIONS GENEVA POSTAL STATIONERY

UC1

Scott's No.		Mint Entire
	GENEVA AIRLETTER SHEET	
UC1	65¢ Plane (1969)	1.25
	GENEVA POSTAL CARDS	
UX1	20¢ Post Horn (1969) ...	.45
UX2	30¢ Earth (1969)	.50
UX3	40¢ Emblem (1977)	.50
UX4	70¢ Ribbons (1977)	1.00
UX5	50¢ "UN" Emblm (85) ..	4.50
UX6	70¢ Peace Dove(85) ..	4.00
UX7	70¢ + 10¢ Surch (86) .	3.50
UX8	90¢ Gen Offices (92) .	3.00

Scott's No.		Mint Entire
	GENEVA POSTAL CARDS	
UX9	50¢+10¢ Surch (93)	2.25
UX10	80¢ Palais des Nations (1993)	3.00
UX11	50¢ + 20¢ Surcharge on #UX5 (1996)	3.00
UX12	80¢ + 30¢ Surcharge on #UX10.(1996)..	3.00
UX13	70¢ Assembly Hall (1998)	2.25
UX14	1.10 fr.Palais des Nations	2.95

DENOMINATIONS ARE GIVEN IN AUSTRIAN CURRENCY

Scott's No.		MI Block of 4	F-VF NH	F-VF Used
	1979 Regular Issue			
1-6	50g,1s,4s,5s,6s,10s Regulars	9.00	2.00	2.00
	1980			
7/16	#7-13,15-16 set of 9	28.75	5.25	...
7	4s New Economic Order .... 19.50 (TP)	9.50 (B)	.75	.75
	(TP)= Top Position, (B)=Bottom			
8	2.50s Regular, Dove	1.50	.35	.35
9-10	4s-6s Decade for Women	5.25	1.10	1.10
11	6s Peacekeeping Operations	3.75	.80	.80
12-13	4s-6s 35th Anniversary of U.N.	5.25	1.15	1.15
14	4s-6s 35th Anniv. - Souv. Sheet of 2	...	.95	.95
15-16	4s-6s Economic & Social Council	5.25	1.15	1.10
	1981			
17-23	set of 7	21.75	4.50	...
17	4s Palestinian People	2.95	.65	.60
18-19	4s-6s Disabled Persons	6.00	1.25	1.20
20	6s Art, Bulgarian Mural	4.00	.85	.80
21	7.50s Energy Conference	3.75	.80	.80
22-23	5s-7s Volunteers Program	6.25	1.35	1.35
	1982			
24-29	set of 6	20.00	4.25	...
24	3s Regular, Better World	2.30	.50	.50
25-26	5s-7s Human Environment	8.75	1.70	1.70
27	5s Peaceful Use of Outer Space	3.50	.75	.70
28-29	5s-7s Nature Conservation	7.00	1.50	1.50
	1983			
30-38	set of 9	29.50	6.25	...
30	4s Communications Year	2.95	.65	.65
31-32	4s-6s Safety at Sea	5.75	1.25	1.25
33-34	5s-7s World Food Program	6.75	1.40	1.40
35-36	4s-8.50s Trade & Development	8.00	1.65	1.60
37-38	5s-7s Human Rights, 35th Anniversary.	7.50	1.60	1.50
37-38	Sheetlets of 16	...	24.50	...
	1984			
39-47	set of 9	34.50	7.50	...
39	7s Population Conference	4.00	.85	.85
40-41	4.50-6s FAO Food Day	5.75	1.25	1.20
42-43	3.50-15s UNESCO, World Heritage	9.25	2.00	2.00
44-45	4.50-8.50s Refugee Futures	9.75	2.10	2.10
46-47	3.50-6.50s Youth Year	8.00	1.75	1.65
	1985			
48/56	#48-53,55-56 set of 8	48.50	10.50	...
48	7.50s ILO - Turin Centre	5.25	1.15	1.10
49	8.50s U.N. Univ. in Japan	5.75	1.25	1.20
50-51	4.50-15s Regulars	13.50	2.95	2.95
52-53	6.50-8.50s 40th Anniversary of U.N.	13.00	2.85	2.80
54	6.50-8.50 40th Anniv. Souvenir Sht of 2	...	3.50	3.50
55-56	4s-6s UNICEF, Child Survival	13.50	2.85	2.75

Scott's No.		M Block of 4	F-VF NH	F-VF Used
	1986			
57-65	set of 9 .... (6)	33.50	14.00	...
57	8s Africa in Crisis, Anti-Hunger	4.85	1.25	1.25
58-61	4.50s UN Dev. Program, attd	11.00	9.75	9.25
58-61	Sheet of 40	...	100.00	...
62-63	3.5s-6.5s Philately, Stamp Collecting	8.50	1.80	1.70
64-65	5s-6s Int'l. Peace Year	11.00	2.25	2.25
66	4s,5s,6s,7s WFUNA S/S of 4	...	5.00	4.95
	1987			
67-77	set of 11	62.50	13.50	...
67	8s Trygve Lie	6.00	1.25	1.20
68-69	4s-9.50s Shelter for Homeless	10.75	2.25	2.25
70-71	5s-8s Life Yes/Drugs No	8.95	1.90	1.85
72-73	2s-17s Regulars	12.00	2.65	2.50
74-75	5s-6s U.N. Day	10.75	2.25	2.25
74-75	Miniature Sheet of 12	...	27.50	...
76-77	4s-9.50s Child Immunization	17.50	3.75	3.50
	1988			
78-86	set of 9 .... (8)	59.75	17.25	...
78-79	4s-6s World Without Hunger	9.00	1.95	1.90
80-81	4s-5s Forest Conservation, pair	21.75	9.50	8.75
80-81	Miniature Sheet of 12	...	50.00	...
82-83	6s-7s Int'l. Volunteers Day	13.50	2.75	2.50
84-85	6s-8s Health in Sports	14.00	3.00	2.75
86	5s Human Rights 40th Anniv	5.25	1.10	1.00
87	11s Human Rights 40th Anniv. S/S	...	2.50	2.40
	1989			
88-96	set of 9 .... (7)	69.50	17.75	...
88-89	5.50s-8s World Bank	17.50	3.75	3.50
90	6s Peace Keeping, Nobel Prize	5.35	1.15	1.10
91-92	4s-9.50s World Weather Watch	20.75	4.50	4.00
93-94	5s-7.50s UN Offices in Vienna, 10th Anniv.	29.50	6.75	5.75
93-94	Miniature Sheets of 25	...	195.00	...
95-96	4s-6s Human Rights 40th Anniv	...	2.50	2.50
95-96	Strips of 3 with Tabs at Bottom	...	7.50	...
95-96	Miniature Sheets of 12	...	32.50	...
	1990			
97/109	#97-104,106-9 set of 12 .... (10)	83.50	20.00	...
97	12s International Trade Center	9.50	2.00	2.00
98	1.50s Regular	1.95	.40	.35
99-100	5s-11s Fight Against AIDS	18.75	4.00	3.75
101-02	4.5s-9.5s Medicinal Plants	18.75	4.00	4.00
103-04	7s-9s UN 45th Anniversary	20.75	4.35	5.50
105	7s-9s UN 45th Anniversary S/S of 2	...	6.00	3.75
106-07	6s-8s Crime Prevention	18.75	4.00	2.50
108-09	4.5s-7s Human Rights	...	2.50	3.00
108-09	Strips of 3 with Tabs at Bottom	...	7.50	...
108-09	Miniature Sheets of 12	...	32.50	...
	1991			
110-24	set of 15 .... (10)	100.00	28.75	...
110-13	5s Europe Econ. Commission, attd	7.50	6.25	6.00
110-13	Sheet of 40	...	60.00	...
114-15	6s-9.50s Namibia Independence	23.75	5.00	4.75
116	20s Regular	17.50	3.75	3.50
117-18	7s-9s Children's Rights	19.50	4.25	3.75
119-20	5s-10s Chemical Weapons Ban	20.75	4.50	4.25
121-22	5s-8s UNPA 40th Anniv	16.50	3.50	3.25
121-22	Miniature Sheets of 25	...	65.00	...
123-24	4.50s-7s Human Rights	...	3.00	3.00
123-24	Strips of 3 with Tabs at Bottom	...	9.00	...
123-24	Miniature Sheets of 12	...	39.50	...

UNITED NATIONS - Offices in Vienna

129-132

Scott's No.		MI Block of 4	F-VF NH	F-VF Used
	1992			
125-40	**set of 16** .... (9)	**73.50**	**29.00**	...
125-26	5s-9s World Heritage	20.75	4.50	4.00
127-28	7s Clean Oceans, attd	7.25	3.25	3.00
127-28	Miniature Sheet of 12	...	25.00	...
129-32	5.5s UNICED: Earth Summit, attd	7.25	6.50	6.00
129-32	Sheet of 40	...	65.00	...
133-34	10s Mission to Planet Earth, attd	14.00	6.25	6.00
133-34	Miniature Sheet of 10	...	39.50	...
135-36	5.5s-7s Science & Technology	13.50	2.85	2.75
137-38	5.5s-7s Regulars	15.00	3.25	3.00
139-40	6s-10s Human Rights	...	4.00	3.75
139-40	Strips of 3 with Tabs at Bottom ...	...	12.00	...
139-40	Miniature Sheets of 12	...	50.00	...
	1993			

143-146

		MI Block of 4	F-VF NH	F-VF Used
141-59	**set of 19** .... (8)	**78.50**	**35.00**	...
141-42	5.5s-7s Aging with Dignity	15.00	3.25	3.00
143-46	7s Endangered Species, attd	6.50	5.75	5.50
143-46	Miniature Sheet of 16	...	24.50	...
147-48	6s-10s Healthy Environments	20.75	4.50	3.95
149	13s Regular, Globe	13.00	2.75	2.50
150-51	5s-6s Human Rights	...	3.50	3.25
150-51	Strips of 3 with Tabs at Bottom ...	...	10.50	...
150-51	Miniature Sheets of 12	...	42.50	...
152-55	5.5s Peace Day, attd	11.00	9.75	8.75
152-55	Sheet of 40	...	100.00	...
156-59	7s Environment - Climate, attd .... (8)	16.50	7.50	7.00
156-59	Miniature Sheet of 24	...	42.50	...
	1994			
160-77	**set of 18** .... (12)	**110.00**	**34.00**	...
160-61	5.5s-8s Year of the Family	16.50	3.50	3.25
162-65	7s Endangered Species, attd	8.00	6.75	6.25
162-65	Miniature Sheet of 16	...	27.50	...
166	12s Refugees	14.50	2.75	2.50
167-69	50g,4s,30s Regulars	29.75	6.25	5.50
170-73	6s Natural Disaster, Block of 4 ...	10.00	9.00	8.50
170-73	Sheet of 40	...	90.00	...
174-75	5.50s-7s Population Development ...	18.50	3.95	3.75
176-77	6s-7s Development Partnership	18.00	3.65	3.50
	1995			

180-83

Scott's No.		MI Block of 4	F-VF NH	F-VF Used
178/90	#178-87,189-90 set of 12 ..... (9)	87.50	22.50	...
178	7s U.N. 50th Anniversary	9.50	1.95	1.75
179	14s Social Summit	15.75	3.25	3.00
180-83	7s Endangered Species, attd	6.75	5.75	5.75
180-83	Miniature Sheet of 16	...	25.00	...
184-85	6s-7s Youth: Our Future	18.50	4.00	3.75
186-87	7s-10s 50th Anniv. of U.N.	24.50	4.75	4.50
188	17s 50th Anniv. Souv. Sheet of 2 ..	...	8.00	7.50
189-90	5-50s-6s Conference on Women	17.50	3.75	3.50
191	3s U.N. 50th Anniv. Sheetlet - 12 .	...	23.50	23.50
192	3s U.N. 50th Anniv. Souvenir Booklet of 12	...	25.00	...
	1996			

193

194

195

		MI Block of 4	F-VF NH	F-VF Used
193/211	#193-206,208-11 set of 18 ..... (9)	85.00	29.50	...
193	7s WFUNA 50th Anniv.	8.50	1.75	1.50
194-95	1s-10s Regular Issues	12.00	2.50	2.25
196-99	7s Endangered Species	7.95	6.50	5.75
196-99	Miniature Sheet of 16	...	26.00	...
200-4	6s City Summit, Strip of 5 .... (10)	26.50	9.75	8.75
200-4	Miniature Sheet of 25	...	48.50	...
205-6	6s-7s Sport & Environment	14.50	2.95	2.75
207	6s-7s Sport & Environment Souv Sheet	...	2.95	2.75
208-9	7s-10s Plea for Peace	19.75	4.25	4.25
210-11	5.50s-8s UNICEF 50th Anniversary ..	...	3.25	3.00
210-11	Miniature Sheets of 8	...	30.00	...
	1997			

212	213		218-21

228	229	230	231

		MI Block of 4	F-VF NH	F-VF Used
212/31	#212-21,23-31 set of 19 .... (9)	66.75	25.65	...
212-13	5s-6s Regulars	10.50	2.30	2.15
214-17	7s Endangered Species	7.75	6.50	5.75
214-17	Miniature Sheet of 16	...	25.75	...
218-21	3.50s Earth Surnmit	3.85	3.25	3.00
218-21	Miniature Sheet of 24	...	19.50	...
222	11s Earth Summit, Souvenir Sheet ..	...	2.50	2.25
223-27.	7s Transportation, 5 designs ..... (10)	16.50	7.95	7.95
223-27	7s Transportation, Sheetlet of 20 .	...	31.50	...
228-29	6.50s-7s Tribute to Philately, set of 2 ...	17.00	3.75	3.50
230-31	3s-6s Terracotta Warriors	14.75	3.25	3.15
232	24s Terracotta Warriors, Prestige Booklet with 6 1s Blocks of 4 ...	...	5.75	...
232a-f	Set of singles from #232 (6)	...	2.75	2.75

1998

235-38

240

Scott's No.		MI Block of 4	F-VF NH	F-VF Used
233/47	#233-38,240,242-47 set of 13 .... (10)	52.50	14.75	...
233-34	6.50s-9s Regulars	12.95	2.75	2.65
235-38	7s Endangered Species	5.75	4.95	4.75
235-38	Miniature Sheet of 16	...	19.75	...
239	3.50 Year of the Ocean Miniature Sht of 12	...	8.25	...
240	6.50s Rainforests	6.25	1.35	1.25
240	Rainforests, Sheet of 20	...	24.95	...
241	22s Rainforests, Souvenir Sheet	...	4.50	...
242-43	4s-7 .50s Peacekeeping (2)	10.50	2.25	2.15
242-43	Peacekeeping, Sheets of 20	...	43.50	...
244-45	4.50s-7s Human Rights (2)	10.50	2.25	2.15
244-45	Human Rights, Sheets of 20	...	43.50	...
246-47	3.50's-7's Schonbrunn Palace (2)	8.95	1.95	1.85
246-47	Schonbrunn Palace, Sheets of 20	...	38.50	...
248	Schonbrunn Palace, Prestige Booklet with Six Booklet Panes of 3 or 4	...	5.95	...
248a-f	1s-2s Set of 6 singles from booklet	...	2.50	2.50
	1999			
249/67	#249-51,53-58,60-64,66-67 set of 16 ..... (9)	51.50	18.50	...
249	8s Volcanic Landscape, Regular Issue	7.50	1.60	1.50
250-51	4.50s-6.50s World Heritage-Australia	12.00	2.60	2.40
250-51	Australia, Sheetlets of 20 (2)	...	51.50	...
252	Australia, Prestige Booklet w/6 B. Panes of 4	...	6.75	...
252a-f	1s-2s Set of 6 singles from booklet	...	2.75	2.75
253-56	7s Endangered Species (4)	5.65	4.75	4.25
253-56	Endangered Species, Sheetlet of 16	...	18.75	...
257-58	3.50s UNISPACE III, Pair	3.50	1.50	...
257-58	UNISPACE III, Miniature Sheet of 10	...	7.50	...

259

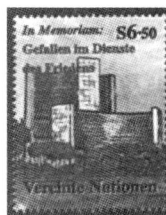

264

259	13s UNISPACE III, Souvenir Sheet	...	2.75	...
260-63	6.50's Universal Postal Union(4)	5.15	4.30	3.75
260-63	UPU, Sheetlet of 20	...	20.95	...
264	6.50s In Memoriam Fallen in Cause of Peace	5.65	1.30	1.20
264	In Memoriam Sheetlet of 20	...	25.75	...
265	14s In Memoriam Souvenir Sheet	...	2.75	...
266-67	7s-13s Education (2)	15.00	3.50	3.25
266-67	Education Sheetlets of 20	...	67.50	...

269-72

UNITED NATIONS - Offices in Vienna

2000 Commemoratives

Scott's No.		MI Block of 4	F-VF NH	F-VF Used
268/82	#268-76,79-80,82 set of 12 .... (9)	46.50	13.50	...
268	7s/Euro 0,51 Year of Thanksgiving	5.75	1.25	1.15
268	7s/Euro 0'51 Thanksgiving Sheetlet of 20 ...	...	24.50	...
269-72	7s/Euro 0'51 Endangered Species, Block ..	5.65	4.75	4.25
269-72	7s/Euro 0'51 Endangered Species, Sheetlet of 16...	...	18.75	...
273-74	7s/0'51-8s/0'58 Our World 2000 (2)	10.75	2.35	2.15
273-74	7s/0'51-8s/0'58 Our World Sheetlets of 20 (2)	...	45.00	...
275-76	7s/0'51-9s/0'65 U.N. 55th Anniversary .. (2)	11.75	2.60	2.50
275-76	7s/0'51-9s/0'65 U.N. 55th Anniv. Sheetlets of 20 (2)	...	51.00	...
277	16s/Euro 1.16 U.N. 55th Anniv. Souvenir Sht	...	2.60	2.50
278	3.50s United Nations in 21st Century Sheetlet of 6...	...	3.35	3.25
279-80	4.50s-6.50s World Heritage - Spain (2)	8.50	1.80	1.75
279-80	4.50s-6.50s Spain Sheetlets of 20 (2)	...	34.50	...
281	1s-2s World Heritage - Spain Prestige Booklet of 6 Panes of 4	...	5.75	...
281a-f	1s-2s set of singles from Prestige Booklet (6)	...	1.90	1.85
282	7s Respect for Refugees	5.25	1.15	1.10
282	7s Respect for Refugees Sheetlet of 20	...	22.75	...
283	25s Respect for Refugees Souvenir Sheet	...	3.85	...
	2001 Commemoratives			
284-87	7s Endangered Species (4)	4.95	4.50	4.00
284-87	7s Endangered Species Sheetlet of 16	...	17.50	...
288-89	10s-12s Year of Volunteers (2)	14.50	3.35	3.25
288-89	10s-12s Volunteers Sheetlets of 20 (2)	...	65.00	...

U.N. OFFICES IN VIENNA 1979-2000

1-283	Complete	...	470.00	...

UNITED NATIONS VIENNA POSTAL STATIONERY

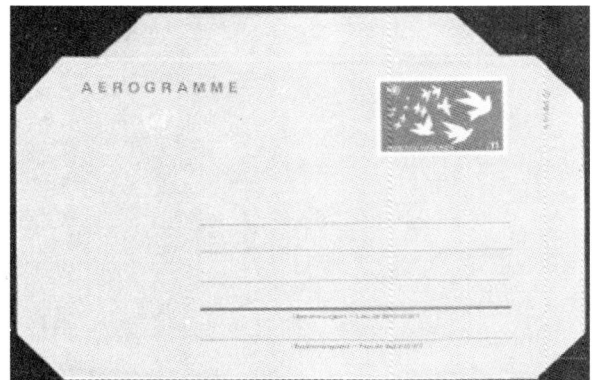

UC3

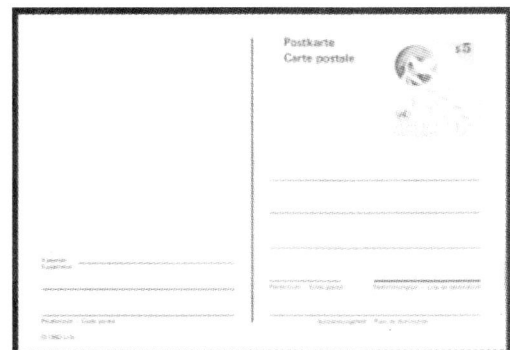

UX2

Scott's No.		Mint Entire
	VIENNA ENVELOPE ENTIRES	
U1	6s Vienna Centre (95) ...	3.95
U2	7s Landscape (1995)	1.95
U3	13s Lake Scene (1998) .	3.50
	VIENNA AIRLETTER SHEET	
UC1	9s Bird (1982)	3.50
UC2	9s + 2s Surchrg (86)	47.50
UC3	11s Birds in Flight (87) .	3.25
UC4	11s + 1s Surchrg (92) ...	52.50
UC5	12s Vienna Offices (92)	4.75

Scott's No.		Mint Entire
	VIENNA POSTAL CARDS	
UX1	3s Branch (1982)	1.50
UX2	5s Glove (1982)	1.00
UX3	4s Emblem (1985)	3.75
UX4	5s + 1s Surch (1992)	21.75
UX5	6s Regschek Paint(92) .	3.75
UX6	5s Peoples (1993)	12.75
UX7	6s Donaupark (1993)	3.75
UX8	5s + 50g (1994)	4.75
UX9	6.50s (Revalued 1992 6s Postal Card (1997)	2.50
UX10	7s (Revalued 1993 6s Postal Card) (1997)	2.85
UX11	6.50s Vienna International Center (1998)	1.50
UX12	7s Gloriette (1999)	2.00
UX13	7s,0'51s WIPA 2000 (2000)	1.60

15

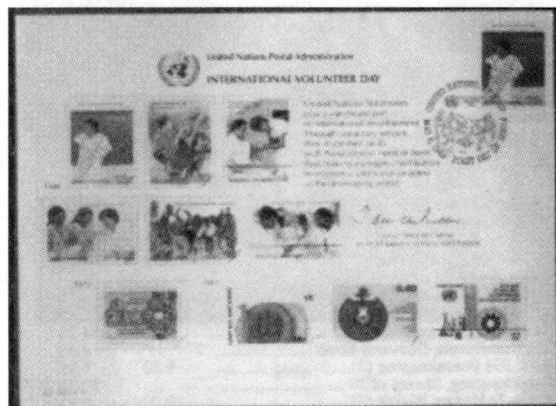

33 New York Cancel

		Mint Card	First Day of Issue N.Y.	Geneva	Vienna
1	World Health Day 1st Print 4/7/72	1.00	18.50	175.00	...
1A	World Health Day 2nd Print 4/7/72	3.75	25.00	165.00	...
2	UN Art 11/17/72	.65	.55	.55	...
3	Disarmament 3/9/73	.75	.60	.60	...
4	Human Rights 11/16/73	.90	.55	.60	...
5	Univ. Postal Union 3/22/74	.95	.65	.65	...
6	Population Year 10/18/74	10.75	1.50	1.50	...
7	Outer Space 3/14/75	2.75	1.20	1.20	...
8	Peacekeeping 11/21/75	2.65	1.50	1.40	...
9	WFUNA 3/12/76	4.95	2.25	2.25	...
10	Food Council 11/19/76	2.75	1.50	1.50	...
11	WIPO 3/11/77	2.00	1.15	1.15	...
12	Combat Racism 9/19/77	2.15	1.25	1.25	...
13	NAMIBIA 5/5/78	1.25	1.20	1.20	...
14	Civil Aviation 6/12/78	2.00	1.10	1.10	...
15	Year of the Child 5/4/79	.75	.60	.60	...
16	Court of Justice 11/9/79	.95	1.00	1.00	...
17	Decade of Women 3/7/80	15.00	5.75	5.00	5.75
18	Econ. & Social Council 11/7/80	1.10	.80	.80	1.00
19	Disabled Persons 3/6/81	1.00	.90	.90	.90
20	Energy Sources 5/29/81	1.50	1.10	1.00	1.00
21	Environment 3/19/82	1.75	1.25	1.25	1.25
22	Outer Space 6/11/82	1.80	1.25	1.25	1.25
23	Safety at Sea 3/18/83	1.60	1.50	1.50	1.50
24	Trade & Development 6/6/83	2.35	1.75	1.60	1.60
25	Population 2/3/84	2.50	2.25	2.00	2.00
26	Youth Year 11/15/84	3.75	2.75	2.75	3.25
27	ILO - Turin Centre 2/1/85	4.75	3.50	3.50	3.50
28	UNICEF 11/22/85	5.00	2.75	2.50	2.50
29	Stamp Collecting 5/22/86	9.50	4.25	4.25	4.25
30	Int'l. Peace Year 6/20/86	5.00	3.25	3.00	3.00
31	Shelter for Homeless 3/13/87	4.50	3.50	3.50	3.50
32	Child Immunization 11/20/87	5.25	4.25	4.25	4.25
33	Int'l. Volunteers Day 5/6/88	8.25	5.25	5.00	5.25
34	WHO/Sports Health 6/17/88	8.25	5.25	5.00	5.25
35	World Bank 1/27/89	8.25	4.50	5.00	5.50
36	World Weather Watch 4/21/89	8.50	6.00	6.00	6.50
37	Fight Against AIDS 3/16/90	10.75	6.00	6.00	6.25
38	Crime Prevention 9/13/90	11.00	7.50	7.50	7.75
39	European Econ. Commission 3/15/91	11.00	7.50	7.50	7.75
40	Children's Rights 6/14/91	14.00	6.50	6.25	6.25
41	Mission to Planet Earth 9/4/92	23.50	12.50	12.50	12.50
42	Science And Technology 10/2/92	19.50	10.75	10.75	10.75
43	Healthy Environments 5/7/93	19.50	12.75	12.75	12.75
44	Peace 9/21/93	17.50	13.50	12.50	12.50
44A	Peace - Gold Hong Kong overprint	20.00	...	...	...
45	Year of the Family 2/4/94	16.00	11.75	11.75	10.75
46	Population - Development 9/1/94	13.50	10.00	10.75	9.75
47	Social Summit 2/3/95	12.50	9.50	9.75	9.75
48	Youth: Our Future 5/26/95	13.50	10.00	9.50	9.50
49	WFUNA 50th Anniversary 2/2/96	11.75	9.00	9.50	9.50
50	UNICEF 50th Anniversary 9/27/96	9.75	8.25	8.25	8.25
51	Philately 1997 .... 10/14/97	11.50	7.50	7.50	7.50
52	Peacekeeping 9/15/98	9.50	7.50	7.50	7.50
53	Human Rights 10/27/98	9.50	7.50	7.50	7.50
54	Universal Postal Union 8/23/99	8.75	7.50	7.50	7.50
55	Respect for Refugees 11/9/00	8.75	7.50	7.50	7.50
56	Volunteers Year 3/29/01	7.75	7.50	7.50	7.50

29-30

Scott #	Description	Separate Covers	One Cover
	NEW YORK		
	1951		
1-11	1¢-$1 Regular Issue 10/24+11/16	70.00	60.00
	1952		
12	5¢ Charter 10/24/52	...	1.25
13-14	3¢-5¢ Human Rights 12/10/52	3.00	4.00
	1953		
15-16	3¢-5¢ Refugee Family 4/24/53	4.50	5.00
17-18	3¢-5¢ Univ. Postal Union 6/12/53	5.00	6.00
19-20	3¢-5¢ Tech. Assistance 10/24/53	6.00	7.00
21-22	3¢-5¢ Human Rights 12/10/54	6.00	7.00
	1954		
23-24	3¢-8¢ F.A.O. 2/11/54	5.00	4.50
25-26	3¢-8¢ Int'l. Labor Organ. 5/10/54	4.50	4.00
27-28	3¢-8¢ U.N. Euro. Office 10/25/54	4.00	3.50
29-30	3¢-8¢ Human Rights 12/10/54	6.00	6.50
	1955		
31-32	3¢-8¢ Int'l. Civil Aviat. 2/9/55	4.50	3.00
33-34	3¢-8¢ UNESCO Emblem 5/11/55	4.50	4.00
35-37	3¢-8¢ 10th Anniv. 10/24/55	6.00	5.00
38	3¢-8¢ 10th Anniversary S/S 10/24/55	...	50.00
39-40	3¢-8¢ Human Rights 12/9/55	2.50	3.00
	1956		
41-42	3¢-8¢ I.T.U 2/17/56	2.50	2.00
43-44	3¢-8¢ W.H.O. 4/6/56	2.50	2.00
45-46	3¢-8¢ General Assembly 10/24/56	2.50	2.00
47-48	3¢-8¢ Human Rights 12/10/56	2.50	2.00
	1957		
49-50	3¢-8¢ Meteor Org. 1/28/57	2.50	2.00
51-52	3¢-8¢ U.N. Emerg. Force 4/8/57	2.50	2.00
55-56	3¢-8¢ Security Council 10/24/57	2.50	2.00
57-58	3¢-8¢ Human Rights 12/10/57	2.50	1.50
	1958		
59-60	3¢-8¢ Atomic Ener. Agency 2/10/58	2.50	1.50
61-62	3¢-8¢ Central Hall London 4/14/58	2.50	2.00
63-64	4¢-8¢ Reg. U.N. Seal 6/2 & 10/24	2.50	1.50
65-66	4¢-8¢ Economic & Social C. 10/24	2.50	1.50
67-68	4¢-8¢ Human Rights 12/10/58	2.50	1.50
	1959		
69-70	4¢-8¢ Flushing Meadows 3/30/59	2.50	1.50
71-72	4¢-8¢ Econ. Comm. Europe 5/18/59	2.50	1.50
73-74	4¢-8¢ Trusteeship Coun. 10/23/59	2.50	1.50
75-76	4¢-8¢ World Refugee Year 12/10/59	2.50	1.50
	1960		
77-78	4¢-8¢ Chalot Palace Paris 2/29/60	2.50	1.50
79-80	4¢-8¢ ECAFE 4/11/90	2.50	1.50
81-82	4¢-8¢ World Forestry Cong. 8/29/60	2.50	1.50
83-84	4¢-8¢ 15th Anniversary 10/24/60	2.50	1.50
85	4¢-8¢ 15th Anniv. S/S 10/24/60	...	2.75
85v	Same broken "v" 10/24	...	120.00
86-87	4¢-8¢ International Bank 12/9/60	2.50	1.50
	1961		
88-89	4¢-8¢ Court of Justice 2/13/61	2.50	1.50
90-91	4¢-7¢ Monetary Fund 4/17/61	2.50	1.50
92	30¢ Regular Flags 6/5/61	...	1.50
93-94	4¢-11¢ Econ. C. Lat. Am. 9/18/61	2.50	1.50
95-96	4¢-11¢ Econ. Comm. Africa 10/24/61	2.50	1.50
97-99	3¢-13¢ Children's Fund 12/14/61	2.75	1.75

Scott #	Description	Separate Covers	One Cover
	NEW YORK		
	1962		
100-01	4¢-7¢ House & Urban Dev. 2/28/62	2.50	1.50
102-03	4¢-11¢ Wld. Health Organ. 3/30/62	2.50	1.50
104-07	1¢-4¢ Regulars 5/25/62	5.00	4.00
108-09	5¢-15¢ Hammarskjold 9/17/62	2.50	1.50
110-11	4¢-11¢ Oper. in Congo 10/24/62	2.50	1.50
112-13	4¢-11¢ Outer Space 12/3/62	2.50	1.50
	1963		
114-15	5¢-11¢ Science & Tech. 2/4/63	2.50	1.50
116-17	5¢-11¢ Freedom from Hung. 3/22/63	2.50	1.50
118	25¢ UNTEA 10/1/63	...	1.50
119-20	5¢-11¢ General Assembly 11/4/63	2.50	1.50
121-22	5¢-11¢ Human Rights 12/10/63	2.50	1.50
	1964		
123-24	5¢-11¢ Maritime Organ. 1/13/64	2.50	1.50
125-27	2¢-10¢ Regulars 5/29/64	3.75	4.00
128	50¢ Reg. Weather Vane 3/6/64	...	2.00
129-30	5¢-11¢ Trade & Develop. 6/15/64	2.50	1.50
131-32	5¢-11¢ Control Narcotics 9/21/64	2.50	1.50
133	5¢ End Nuclear Tests 10/23/64	...	1.25
134-36	4¢-11¢ Education Prog. 12/7/64	3.75	1.75
	1965		
137-38	5¢-11¢ Development Fund 1/25/65	2.50	1.50
139-40	5¢-11¢ Peace Force Cyprus 3/4/65	2.50	1.50
141-42	5¢-11¢ Telecomm. Union 5/17/65	2.50	1.50
143-44	5¢-15¢ 20th Anniv. ICY 6/26/65	2.50	1.75
145	5¢-12¢ 20th Anniv. S/S 6/26/65	...	1.75
146-49	1¢-25¢ Regulars 9/20 & 10/25/65	3.75	2.25
150	$1 Regular Emblem 3/25/65	...	3.00
151-53	4¢-11¢ Population 11/29/65	3.75	1.75
	1966		
154-55	5¢-15¢ Fed. U.N. Assoc. 1/31/66	2.50	1.50
156-57	5¢-11¢ W.H.O. Headqtrs. 5/26/66	2.50	1.50
158-59	5¢-11¢ Coffee Agreement 9/19/66	2.50	1.50
160	15¢ Peacekpg. Obsrv. 10/24/66	...	1.75
161-63	4¢-11¢ UNICEF 11/28/66	3.75	1.50
	1967		
164-65	5¢-11¢ Develop. Program 1/23/67	2.50	1.50
166-67	1½¢-5¢ Regulars 3/17 & 1/23/67	2.50	1.50
168-69	5¢-11¢ Independ. Nations 3/17/67	2.50	1.50
170-74	4¢-15¢ Expo '67 Montreal 4/28/67	5.00	4.00
175-76	5¢-15¢ Tourist Year 6/19/67	2.50	1.50
177-78	6¢-13¢ Disarmament 10/24/67	2.50	1.50
179	6¢ Chagall S/S 11/17/67	...	1.75
180	6¢ Chagall Window 11/17/67	...	1.50
	1968		
181-82	6¢-13¢ Secretariat 1/16/68	2.50	1.00
183-84	6¢-75¢ Art, Starcke Stat. 3/1/68	4.50	5.00
185-86	6¢-13¢ Industrial Dev. 4/18/68	2.50	1.00
187	6¢ Regular, U.N. Hdqtrs. 5/31/68	...	.75
188-89	6¢-20¢ Wld. Weather Watch 9/19/68	2.50	1.00
190-91	6¢-13¢ Human Rights 11/22/68	2.50	1.00
	1969		
192-93	6¢-13¢ Train. & Res. Inst. 2/10/69	2.50	1.50
194-95	6¢-13¢ U.N. Bldg., Chile 3/14/69	2.50	1.50
196	13¢ Regular U.N. & Emblem 3/14/69	...	1.25
197-98	6¢-13¢ Peace Through Law 4/21/69	2.50	1.50
199-200	6¢-20¢ Labor & Dev. 6/5/69	2.50	1.50
201-02	6¢-13¢ Tunisian Mosaic 11/21/69	2.50	1.50

131-131

224-225

Scott #	Description NEW YORK	Separate Covers	One Cover
	1970		
203-04	6¢-25¢ Art, Peace Bell 3/13/70	2.50	1.50
205-06	6¢-13¢ Mekong Basin Dev. 3/13/70	2.50	1.50
207-08	6¢-13¢ Fight Cancer 5/22/70	2.50	1.50
209-11	6¢-25¢ 25th Anniversary 6/26/70	3.75	1.75
212	6¢-25¢ 25th Anniv. S/S 6/26/70	...	1.50
213-14	6¢-13¢ Peace, Just. & Pro. 5/20/70	2.50	1.50
	1971		
215	6¢ Peaceful Uses of the Sea 1/25/71	...	1.25
216-17	6¢-13¢ Support Refugees 3/2/71	2.50	1.50
218	13¢ World Food Program 4/13/71	...	1.25
219	20¢ U.P.U. Headquarters 5/28/71	...	1.25
220-21	8¢-13¢ Racial Discrim. 9/21/71	2.50	1.50
222-23	8¢-60¢ Regulars 10/22/71	3.00	2.00
224-25	8¢-21¢ U.N. Int'l. School 11/19/71	2.50	1.50
	1972		
226	95¢ Regular, Letter 1/5/72	...	2.50
227	8¢ No Nuclear Weapons 2/14/72	...	1.25
228	15¢ World Health Day, Man. 4/7/72	...	1.25
229-30	8¢-15¢ Human Environment 6/5/72	2.50	1.50
231	21¢ Economic Comm. Europe 9/11/72	...	1.75
232-33	8¢-15¢ Maria Sert. Mural 11/17/72	2.50	1.50
	1973		
234-35	8¢-15¢ Disarmament Decade 3/9/73	2.50	1.50
236-37	8¢-15¢ Against Drug Abuse 4/13/73	2.50	1.50
238-39	8¢-21¢ Volunteer Program 5/25/73	2.50	1.50
240-41	8¢-15¢ Namibia 10/1/73	2.50	1.50
242-43	8¢-21¢ Human Rights 11/16/73	2.50	1.50
	1974		
244-45	10¢-21¢ ILO Headquarters 1/11/74	2.50	1.50
246	10¢ U.P.U. Centenary 3/22/74	...	1.25
247-48	10¢-18¢ Art, Brazil Mural 5/6/74	2.50	1.25
249-51	2¢-18¢ Regualrs 6/10/74	3.75	1.75
252-53	10¢ Population Year 10/18/74	2.50	1.50
254-55	10¢-25¢ Law of the Sea 11/22/74	2.50	1.50
	1975		
256-57	10¢-26¢ Peaceful-O. Space 3/14/75	2.50	1.50
258-59	10¢-18¢ Women's Year 5/9/75	2.50	1.50
260-61	10¢-26¢ 30th Anniversary 6/26/75	2.50	1.50
262	10¢-26¢ 30th Anniv. S/S 6/26/75	...	1.75
263-64	10¢-18¢ Namibia 9/22/75	2.50	1.50
265-66	13¢-26¢ Peacekpg. Force 11/21/75	2.50	1.50
	1976		
267-71	3¢-50¢ Regulars 1/6 & 11/19/76	4.00	2.50
272-73	13¢-26¢ U.N. Assoc. 3/12/76	2.50	1.50
274-75	13¢-31¢ Trade & Dev. 4/23/76	2.50	1.50
276-77	13¢-25¢ Human Settlement 5/28/76	2.50	1.50
278-79	13¢-31¢ 25th Postal Ann. 10/8/76	7.75	6.75
280	13¢ World Food Council 11/18/76	...	1.25
	1977		
281-82	13¢-31¢ Intellect Prop. 3/11/77	2.50	1.50
283-84	13¢-25¢ Water Conference 4/22/77	2.50	1.50
285-86	13¢-31¢ Security Council 5/27/77	2.50	1.50
287-88	13¢-25¢ Racial Discrim. 9/19/77	2.50	1.50
289-90	13¢-18¢ Atomic Energy 11/18/77	2.50	1.50
	1978		
291-93	1¢-$1 Regulars 1/27/78	3.75	3.00
294-95	13¢-31¢ Smallpox-Erad. 3/31/78	2.50	1.50
296-97	13¢-18¢ Namibia 5/5/78	2.50	1.50
298-99	25¢ ICAO 6/12/78	2.50	1.50
300-01	13¢-18¢ General Assembly 9/15/78	2.50	1.50
302-03	13¢-31¢ Technical Coop. 11/17/78	2.50	1.50

Scott #	Description NEW YORK	Separate Covers	One Cover
	1979		
304-07	5¢-20¢ Regulars 1/19/79	3.75	1.75
308-09	15¢-20¢ Disaster Relief 3/9/79	2.50	1.50
310-11	15¢-31¢ Yr. of the Child 5/4/79	3.50	2.85
312-13	15¢-31¢ Namibia 10/5/79	2.50	1.50
314-15	15¢-20¢ Court of Justice 11/9/79	2.50	1.50
	1980		
316-17	15¢-31¢ New Econ. Order 1/11/80	2.50	1.75
318-19	15¢-20¢ Decade for Women 3/7/80	2.50	1.75
320-21	15¢-31¢ Peacekpg. Oper. 5/16/80	2.50	1.75
322-23	15¢-31¢ 35th Anniversary 6/26/80	2.75	1.75
324	15¢-31¢ 35th Anniv. S/S 6/26/80	...	1.30
325-40	15¢ 1980 Flag Series 9/26/80	14.00	...
341-42	15¢-20¢ Econ. & Soc. 11/21/80	1.50	1.50
	1981		
343	15¢ Palestinian People 1/30/81	...	1.50
344-45	20¢-35¢ Disabled Persons 3/6/81	2.50	1.50
346-47	20¢-31¢ Bulgarian Mural 4/15/81	2.50	1.50
348-49	20¢-40¢ Energy Conf. 5/29/81	2.50	1.50
350-65	20¢ 1981 Flag Series 9/25/81	14.00	...
366-67	18¢-28¢ Volunteers 11/13/81	...	1.50
	1982		
368-70	17¢-40¢ Definitives 1/22/82	3.75	2.25
371-72	20¢-40¢ Human Environ. 3/19/82	2.50	2.25
373	20¢ Peaceful, Use of Space 6/11/82	...	1.50
374-89	20¢ 1982 Wld. Flag Series 9/24/82	14.00	...
390-91	20¢-28¢ Nature Conserv. 11/19/82	2.50	2.25
	1983		
392-93	20¢-40¢ Commun. Year 1/28/83	3.00	2.00
394-95	20¢-37¢ Safety at Sea 3/18/83	3.00	2.00
396	20¢ World Food Program 4/22/83	...	1.75
397-98	20¢-28¢ Trade & Develop. 6/6/83	3.00	2.00
399-414	20¢ 1983 Flag Series 9/23/83	16.00	...
415-16	20¢-40¢ Human Rights 12/9/83	3.00	2.25
	1984		
417-18	20¢-40¢ Population Conf. 2/3/84	2.50	1.75
419-20	20¢-40¢ FAO Food Day 3/15/84	2.50	1.75
421-22	20¢-50¢ UNESCO 4/18/84	2.50	2.00
423-24	20¢-50¢ Refugee Futures 5/29/84	2.50	1.85
425-40	20¢ 1984 Flag Series 9/20/84	18.00	...
441-42	20¢-35¢ Youth Year 11/15/84	2.50	1.75
	1985		
443	23¢ ILO-Turin Centre 2/1/85	...	1.75
444	50¢ U.N. Univ. in Japan 3/15/85	...	2.25
445-46	22¢-$3 Definitives 5/10/85	7.00	6.00
447-48	22¢-45¢ 40th Anniv. 6/26/85	3.50	3.00
449	22¢-45¢ 40th Anniv. S/S 6/26/85	...	3.00
450-65	22¢ 1985 Flag Series 9/20/85	20.00	...
466-67	22¢-33¢ UNICEF 11/22/85	2.50	1.75
	1986		
468	22¢ Africa in Crisis 1/31/86	...	1.75
469-72	22¢ UN Dev. & Prog. attd. 3/14/86	...	6.00
469-72	UN Dev. & Prog., set of 4 singles	7.00	...
473-74	22¢-44¢ Philately 5/22/86	3.00	2.00
475-76	22¢-33¢ Int'l. Year of Peace 6/20/86	2.75	1.75
477-92	22¢ 1986 World Flag Series 9-19-86	20.00	...
493	22¢,33¢,39¢,44¢ WFUNA S/S 11/14/86	...	5.50
	1987		
494	22¢ Trygve Lie 1/30/87	...	2.00
495-96	22¢-44¢ Shelter for the Homeless 3/13/87	2.75	2.00
497-98	22¢-33¢ Life Yes/Drugs No 6/12/87	2.50	1.75
499-514	22¢ 1987 World Flag Series 9/18/87	24.00	...
515-16	22¢-39¢ U.N. Day 10/23/87	2.75	2.00
517-18	22¢-44¢ Child Immunization 11/20/87	2.75	2.00

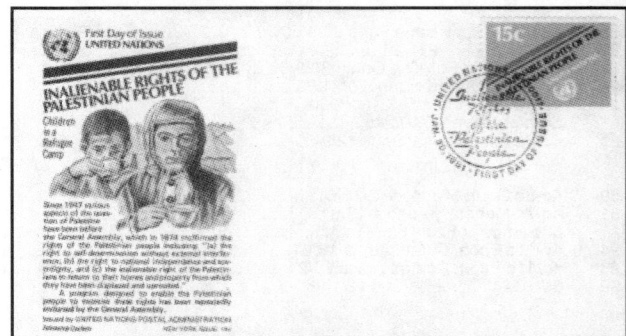

493

UNITED NATIONS FIRST DAY COVERS

C19-21

Scott #	Description NEW YORK	Separate Covers	One Cover
	1988		
519-20	22¢-33¢ World Without Hunger 1/29/88	2.50	1.75
521	3¢ UN For a Better World 1/29/88		2.00
522-23	25¢-50¢ Forest Conservation 3/18/88	10.00	8.00
524-25	25¢-50¢ Int'l. Volunteers Day 5/6/88	2.50	2.00
526-27	25¢-38¢ Health in Sports 6/17/88	2.50	2.15
528-43	25¢ World Flag Series of 16 9/19/88	24.00	...
544-45	25¢,$1 S/S Human Rights Anniv. 12/9/88	5.00	...
	1989		
546-47	25¢-45¢ World Bank 1/27/89	4.00	3.00
548	25¢ UN Peace Force, Nobel Prize 3/17/89	...	2.50
549	45¢ UN Headquarters 3/17/89		2.50
550-51	25¢-36¢ World Weather Watch 4/21/89	2.50	2.00
552-53	25¢-90¢ UN Of. in Vienna Anniv. 8/23/89	3.50	2.50
554-69	25¢ World Flags Series of 16 9/22/89	24.00	...
570-71	25¢-45¢ Human Rights 11/17/89	2.50	2.00
570-71	Strips of 3 with tabs on bottom	8.50	...
	1990		
572	25¢ International Trade Center 2/2/90	...	2.25
573-74	25¢-40¢ Fight Against AIDS 3/16/90	4.00	4.00
575-76	25¢-90¢ Medicinal Plants 5/4/90	3.50	5.50
577-78	25¢-45¢ UN 45th Anniversary 6/26/90	3.50	3.50
579	25¢-45¢ UN Anniversary S/S	...	3.50
580-81	25¢-36¢ Crime Prevention 9/13/90	4.00	3.50
582-83	25¢-45¢ Human Rights 11/16/90	2.50	3.00
582-83	Strips of 3 with tabs on bottom	8.50	...
	1991		
584-87	30¢ Eur. Econ. Commission attd. 3/15/91	8.00	6.00
588-89	30¢-50¢ Namibia 5/10/91	3.00	3.00
590-91	30¢-50¢ Definitives 9/11/91	3.00	3.00
592	$2 UN Headquarters Definitive 5/10/91	...	5.00
593-94	30¢-70¢ Children's Rights 6/14/91	3.50	3.50
595-96	30¢-90¢ Chemical Weapons Ban 9/11/91	4.00	3.25
597-98	30¢-40¢ UNPA 40th Anniv. 10/24/91	3.00	2.25
599-600	30¢-50¢ Human Rights 11/20/91	3.00	2.50
599-600	Strips of 3 with tabs on bottom	8.00	...
	1992		
601-02	30¢-50¢ World Heritage 1/24/92	3.50	4.00
603-04	29¢ Clean Oceans attd. 3/13/92	5.00	4.00
605-08	29¢ UNICED: Earth Summit attd. 5/22/92	8.00	4.00
609-10	29¢ Mission to Planet Earth attd. 9/4/92	4.50	4.00
611-12	29¢-50¢ Science & Technology 10/2/92	3.00	6.00
613-15	4¢,29¢,40¢ Definitives 10/2/92	5.50	2.50
616-17	29¢-50¢ Human Rights S/S 12/10/92	3.50	4.50
616-17	Strips of 3 with tabs on bottom	7.00	...
	1993		
618-19	29¢-52¢ Aging 2/5/93	3.00	3.50
620-23	29¢ Endangered Species attd. 3/3/93	8.00	4.50
624-25	29¢-50¢ Healthy Environments 5/7/93	3.00	3.50
626	5¢ Definitive 5/7/93	...	2.00
627-28	29¢-35¢ Human Rights 6/11/93	3.00	5.00
627-28	Strips of 3 with tabs on bottom	7.50	...
629-32	29¢ Peace attd. 9/21/93	8.00	4.00
633-36	29¢ Environment - Climate 10/29/93	8.00	4.50
	1994		
637-38	29¢-45¢ Year of the Family 2/4/94	3.00	2.50
639-42	29¢ Endangered Species 3/18/94	5.00	4.00
643	50¢ Refugees 4/29/94	...	2.50
644-46	10¢,19¢,$1 Definitives 4/29/94	6.00	5.00
647-50	29¢ Natural Disaster 5/27/94	5.00	4.00
651-52	29¢-52¢ Population-Development 9/1/94	3.00	2.50
653-54	29¢-50¢ Development Partnership 10/28/94	3.00	2.50
	1995		
655	32¢ U.N. 50th Anniversary 1/195	...	6.00
656	50¢ Social Summit 2/3/95	...	2.25
657-60	32¢ Endangered Species 3/24/95	5.00	4.00
661-62	32¢-55¢ Youth: Our Future 5/26/95	4.00	3.00
663-64	32¢-50¢ 50th Anniv. of U.N. 6/26/95	4.00	3.00
665	82¢ 50th Anniv. Souv. Sheet 6/26/95	...	4.00
666-67	32¢-40¢ Conference on Women 9/5/95	3.00	2.50
668	20¢ Definitive 9/5/95	...	1.50
669	32¢ U.N. 50th Anniv. Souv. Sheet 10/24/95	35.00	25.00
670	32¢ U.N. 50th Anniv. Souv. Bklt. of 12 10/24/95	40.00	29.00
671	WFUNA 50th Anniv. 2/2/96	...	1.50
672-73	32¢-60¢ Regular Issues 2/2/96	3.00	2.50
674-77	32¢ Endangered Species 3/14/96	5.00	4.00

NOTE:"HUMAN RIGHTS" ALL CAN COME AS 6 ON 1, 2 W/STRIP OF 3 EACH, 3 W/2 STAMPS EACH

Scott #	Description NEW YORK	Separate Covers	One Cover
	1996		
678-82	32¢ City Summit, Strip of 5 6/3/96	7.50	3.25
683-84	32¢-50¢ s/s Sports&Envir.,7/19/96 Atlanta, GA.	3.45	2.75
683-84	32¢-50¢ s/s Sport & Environment, NY, 7/19/96 .	3.10	2.40
686-87	32¢-60¢ Plea For Peace, 9/17/96	3.75	2.50
688-89	32¢ - 60¢ UNICEF 50th Anniv., 11/20/96	3.75	2.50
	1997		
690-97	32¢ Flags of New Countries (8) 2/12/97	14.00	14.00(2)
698-99	8¢ - 55¢ Regulars, Flowers 2/12/97	3.00	2.75
700-3	32¢ Endangered Species 3/13/97	5.00	3.50
704-7	32¢ Earth Summit 5/30/97	6.75	3.50
708	$1 Earth Summit, S/S 5/30/97	...	4.00
708a	$1 Pacific '97 Overprint on #708 5/30/97	...	4.50
709-713	32¢ Transportation (strips of 5) 8/29/97	10.00	4.50
714-715	32¢,50¢ Tribute to Philately,10/14/97	4.00	3.00
716-717	32¢,60¢ Terracotta Warriors,11/19/97	4.00	3.00
	1998		
719-726	32¢ Flags of New Countries (8),2/13/98	14.00	12.00(2)
727-729	1¢,2¢,21¢ Regulars, 2/13/98	4.75	3.50
730-733	32¢ Endangered Species, 3/13/98	3.20	3.00
734	32¢ Year of the Ocean, Sheet of 12, 5/20/98	...	10.00
735	32¢ Rain Forest, 4 designs, 6/19/98	5.50	3.00
736	$2 Rain Forest, S/S, 6/19/98	...	3.50
737-38	33¢-40¢ Peacekeeping 9/15/98	3.00	2.50
739-40	32¢-55¢ Human Rights 10/27/98	3.25	2.75
741-42	33¢-60¢ Schonbrunn Castle 12/4/98	5.00	4.00
	1999		
744-51	33¢Flags of New Countries (8) 2/5/99	16.00	12.00(2)
752-56	33c-$5.00 Definitives 2/5/99	12.00	10.00
754-55	33c-60c World Heritage/Australia 3/19/99	4.50	3.50
757-60	33c Endangered Species 4/22/99	8.00	5.50
761-62	33c UnispaceIII 7/7/99	...	3.50
762	$2.00 Unispace III s/s 7/7/99	...	6.00
764-67	33c Universal Postal Union 8/23/99	8.00	5.50
765	33c In Memoriam 9/21/99	...	3.00
766	$1.00 In Memoriam s/s 9/21/99	...	4.50
770-71	33c-60c Education 11/18/99	4.50	3.50
	2000		
772	33c Year of Thanksgiving 1/1/00	...	2.50
773-76	33c Endangered species 4/6/00	8.00	5.50
777-78	33c-60c Our World 2000 5/30/00	4.00	3.00
779-80	33c-55c Anniversary of UN 7/7/00	4.00	3.00
781	88c Anniversary of UN s/s 7/7/00	...	4.00
782	33c Int. Flag of Peace 9/15/00	...	8.00
783a-f	33c UN in the 21st Century 9/15/00	15.00	
784-85	33c-60c World Heritage Spain 10/6/00	4.00	3.00
787	33c Respect for Refugees 11/9/00	...	2.00
788	$1.00 Respect for Refugees s/s 11/9/00	...	3.50
	Airmail Issues		
	1951-59		
C1-4	6¢-25¢ 1st Airmail Issue 12/14/51	22.00	25.00
C5-7	4¢-7¢ Airmail 5/27/57 & 2/9/59	2.50	12.50
	1963-69		
C8-10	6¢-13¢ Airmail 6/17/63	3.75	6.00
C11-12	15¢ & 25¢ Airmail 5/1/64	2.50	5.00
C13	20¢ Jet Plane 4/18/68	...	1.50
C14	10¢ Wings & Envelopes 4/21/69	...	1.50
	1972-77		
C15-18	9¢-21¢ Airmail 5/1/72	3.00	3.00
C19-21	13¢-26¢ Airmail 9/16/74	3.00	2.00
C22-23	25¢ & 31¢ Airmail 6/27/77	3.00	2.00

U.N. Postal Stationery
Stamped Envelopes

Scott #	Description		One Cover
U1	3¢ Emblem 9/15/53	...	3.50
U2	4¢ Emblem 9/22/58	...	1.50
U3	5¢ Weather Vane 4/26/63	...	1.50
U4	6¢ Weather Vane 4/26/63	...	1.50
U5	8¢ Headquarters 1/12/73	...	1.50
U6	10¢ Headquarters 1/10/75	...	1.50
U7	22¢ Bouquet 5/10/85	...	4.00
U8	25¢ UN Headquarters 3/17/89	...	4.00
U9	25¢ + 4¢ Surcharge on U8 4/15/91	...	4.00
U10	32¢ Cripticondia (97), 2/12/97 (#63/4 env.)	...	4.00
U10	32¢ Cripticondia (97), 2/12/97 (#10 env.)	...	2.50
UC3	7¢ Flag and Plane 9/21/59	...	1.50
UC6	8¢ Emblem 4/26/63	...	1.50
UC8	10¢ Emblem 1/8/69	...	1.50
UC10	11¢ Birds 1/12/73	...	1.50
UC11	13¢ Globe 1/10/75	...	1.50

Airletter Sheets

Scott #	Description		One Cover
UC1	10¢ Air Letter 8/29/52	...	6.00
UC2	10¢ Air Letter/Aerogramme 9/14/54(white border)	...	80.00
UC2a	10¢ same, no white border, 1958	...	...
UC4	10¢ Flag 1/18/60	...	1.50
UC5	11¢ Gull, Blue 6/26/61	...	1.50
UC5a	11¢ Gull (greenish) (1965)	...	...
UC7	13¢ Plane 5/31/68	...	1.50
UC9	15¢ Globe 10/16/72	...	1.50
UC12	18¢ Headquarters 1/10/75	...	1.50
UC13	22¢ Birds 6/27/77	...	1.50
UC14	30¢ Airplane 4/28/82	...	3.25
UC15	30¢ + 6¢ Surcharge on UC14 7/7/87	...	16.00
UC16	39¢ UN Headquarters 3/17/89	...	9.00
UC17	39¢ + 6¢ Surcharge on UC16 2/12/91	...	6.00
UC18	45¢ Winged Hand 9/4/92	...	6.00
UC19	45¢,5¢ Surcharge on UC18 (95)	...	...
UC20	50¢ Cherry Blossom Airletter 3/13/97	...	4.00

Scott #	Description	Separate Covers	One Cover
	Postal Cards		
UX1	2¢ Headquarters 7/18/52	...	1.50
UX2	3¢ Headquarters 9/22/58	...	1.50
UX3	4¢ Map 4/26/63	...	1.50
UX4	5¢ Post Horn 1/8/69	...	1.50
UX5	6¢ "UN" 1/12/73	...	1.50
UX6	8¢ "UN" 1/10/75	...	1.50
UX7	9¢ Emblem 6/27/77	...	1.50
UX8	13¢ Letters 4/28/82	...	1.50
UX9-13	15¢ UN Headquarters, 5 Diff. Views 3/17/89	...	16.00
UX14-18	36¢ UN Headquarters, 5 Diff. Views 3/17/89	...	18.00
UX19	40¢ U.N. Headquarters 9/4/92	...	7.50
UX20	21c Regular Issue 5/20/98	2.50	...
UX21	50c Regular Issue 5/20/98	3.00	...
	Airmail Postal Cards		
UXC1	4¢ Wing 5/27/57	...	1.50
UXC2	4¢ + 1¢ 6/8/59 (first day of public use)	...	150.00
UXC3	5¢ Wing 9/21/59	...	1.50
UXC4	6¢ Space 4/26/63	...	1.50
UXC5	11¢ Earth 6/9/66	...	1.50
UXC6	13¢ Earth 5/31/68	...	1.50
UXC7	8¢ Plane 1/8/69	...	1.50
UXC8	9¢ Wing 10/16/72	...	1.50
UXC9	15¢ Planes 10/16/72	...	1.50
UXC10	11¢ Clouds 1/10/75	...	1.50
UXC11	18¢ Pathways 1/10/75	...	1.50
UXC12	28¢ Flying Mailmen 4/28/82	...	1.75

30-31

GENEVA

Scott #	Description	Separate Covers	One Cover
	1969-70		
1-14	5¢-10¢ fr. Regular 10/4 + 9/22	35.00	...
	1971		
15	30¢ Peaceful Use of Sea 1/25/71	...	1.50
16	50¢ Support for Refugees 3/12/71	...	1.50
17	50¢ World Food Program 4/13/71	...	1.50
18	75¢ U.P.O. Headquarters 5/28/71	...	1.75
19-20	30¢-50¢ Racial Discrim. 9/21/71	2.50	2.00
21	1.10 fr. Int'l. School 11/19/71	...	2.00
	1972		
22	40¢ Palace of Nations 1/15/72	...	1.50
23	40¢ No Nuclear Weapons 2/14/72	...	2.00
24	80¢ World Health Day 4/7/72	...	1.50
25-26	40¢-80¢ Human Environment 6/5/72	3.50	2.50
27	1.10 fr. Econ. Comm. Europe 9/11/72	...	2.75
28-29	40¢-80¢ Sert Mural 11/17/72	3.00	2.50
	1973		
30-31	60¢-1.10 Disarm. Decade 3/9/73	3.00	2.50
32	60¢ Against Drug Abuse 4/13/73	...	1.50
33	80¢ Volunteer Program 5/25/73	...	1.75
34	60¢ Namibia 10/1/73	...	1.75
35-36	40¢-80¢ Human Rights 11/16/73	2.50	2.00
	1974		
37-38	60¢-80¢ ILO Headqtrs. 1/11/74	2.65	2.15
39-40	30¢-60¢ UPU Centenary 3/22/74	2.50	1.85
41-42	60¢-1 fr. Brazil Mural 5/6/74	2.75	2.40
43-44	60¢-80¢ Population Year 10/18/74	2.40	2.15
45	1.30 fr. Law of the Sea 11/22/74	...	2.15
	1975		
46-47	60¢-90¢ Peace - Out. Space 3/14/75	2.50	2.00
48-49	60¢-90¢ Women's Year 5/9/75	2.65	2.40
50-51	60¢-90¢ 30th Anniv. 6/26/75	2.50	2.00
52	30¢ Anniv. S/S 6/26/75	...	2.50
53-54	50¢-1.30 fr. Namibia 9/22/75	2.75	2.25
55-56	60¢-70¢ Peacekpg. Force 11/21/75	2.50	2.00
	1976		
57	90¢ U.N. Association 3/12/76	...	1.75
58	1.10 fr. Trade & Develop. 4/23/76	...	1.90
59-60	40¢-1.50 fr. Human Settle. 5/28/76	2.75	2.40
61-62	80¢-1.10 fr. 25th Post Ann. 10/8/76	8.00	5.00
63	70¢ World Food Council 11/19/76	...	1.75

Scott #	Description	Separate Covers	One Cover
	GENEVA		
	1977		
64	80¢ Intellect Prop. 3/11/77	...	1.75
65-66	80¢-1.10 fr. Water Conf. 4/22/77	2.75	2.40
67-68	80¢-1.10 fr. Sec. Count. 5/29/77	2.75	2.40
69-70	40¢-1.10 fr. Racial Disc. 9/19/77	2.50	2.10
71-72	80¢-1.10 fr. Atom. Energy 11/18/77	2.80	2.45
	1978		
73	35¢ Regular 1/27/78	...	1.50
74-75	80¢-1.10 fr. Smallpox 3/31/78	2.75	2.40
76	80¢ Namibia 5/5/78	...	1.50
77-78	70¢-80¢ Civil Aviat. Org. 6/12/78	2.50	1.90
79-80	70¢-1.10 fr. Gen. Assem 9/15/78	2.85	2.50
81	80¢ Technical Coop. 11/19/78	...	1.50
	1979		
82-83	80¢-1.50 fr. Disaster Relief 3/9/79	2.95	2.60
84-85	80¢—1.10 fr. Year of Child 5/4/79	4.50	3.50
86	1.10 fr. Namibia 10/5/79	...	1.75
87-88	80¢-1.10 fr. Court of Just. 11/9/79	2.85	2.50
	1980		
89	80¢ New Econ. Organ. 1/11/80	...	1.50
90-91	40¢-70¢ Dec. for Women 3/7/80	2.50	1.60
92	1.10 fr. Peacekpg. Force 5/16/80	...	1.70
93-94	40¢-70¢ 35th Anniv. 6/26/80	2.50	1.60
95	40¢-70¢ 35th Anniv. S/S 6/26/80	...	2.50
96-97	40¢-70¢ Econ. & Social Co. 11/21/80	2.50	1.50
	1981		
98	80¢ Palestinian People 1/30/81	...	1.50
99-100	40¢-1.50 fr. Disabled Persons 3/6/81.	2.50	2.25
101	80¢ Bulgarian Mural 4/15/81	...	1.50
102	1.10 fr. Energy Conf. 5/29/81	...	1.50
103-04	40¢-70¢ Volunteers 11/13/81	1.85	1.60
	1982		
105-06	30¢-1 fr. Definitives 1/22/82	1.95	1.70
107-08	40¢-1.20 fr. Human Environ. 3/19	2.25	2.00
109-10	80¢-1 fr. Peac. Use of Space 6/11	2.50	2.25
111-12	40¢-1.50 fr. Nat. Cons. 11/19/82	2.85	2.50
	1983		
113	1.20 fr. Commun. Year 1/28/33	...	2.00
114-15	40¢-80¢ Safety at Sea 3/28/83	1.60	1.50
116	1.50 fr. World Food Prog. 4/22/83	...	2.50
117-18	80¢-1.10 fr. Trade & Dev. 6/6/83	3.00	2.75
119-20	40¢-1.20 fr. Human Rights 12/9	3.25	2.90
	1984		
121	1.20 fr. Population Conf. 2/3/84	...	2.00
122-23	50¢-80¢ FAO Food Day 3/15/84	2.00	1.75
124-25	50¢-70¢ UNESCO 4/18/84	2.35	2.10
126-27	35¢-1.50 fr. Refugee 5/29/84	2.75	2.40
128	1.20 fr. Youth Year 11/15/84	...	2.00
	1985		
129-30	80¢-1.20 fr. ILO-Turin Centre 2/1	3.25	2.50
131-32	50¢-80¢ UN Univ. of Japan 3/15/85	3.00	2.00
133-34	20¢-1.20 fr. Definitives 5/10/85	3.00	2.50
135-36	50¢-70¢ 40th Anniversary 6/26/85	3.00	2.50
137	50¢-70¢ 40th Anniv. S/S 6/26/85	...	3.00
138-39	50¢-4 fr. UNICEF 11/22/85	4.00	3.00
	1986		
140	1.40 fr. Africa in Crisis 1/31	...	2.75
141-44	35¢ UN Dev. attd. 3/14/86	...	7.50
141-44	UN Dev. set of 4 singles	8.50	...
145	5¢ Definitive 3/14/86	...	1.50
146-47	50¢-80¢ Philately 5/22/86	3.00	2.00
148-49	45¢-1.40 fr. Int. Peace 6/20/86	3.25	2.50
150	35¢,45¢,50¢,70¢ WFUNA S/S 11/14/86	...	4.00

135-136

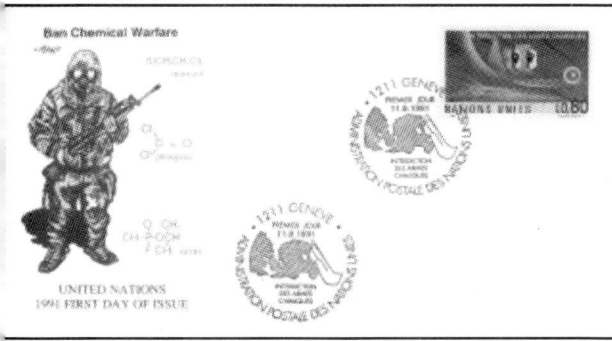

205

Scott #	Description	Separate Covers	One Cover
	GENEVA		
	1987		
151	1.40 fr. Trygve Lie 1/30/87	...	3.00
152-53	90¢-1.40 fr. Bands/Sphere Definitives 1/30/87	3.00	2.75
154-55	50¢-90¢ Shelter for the Homeless 3/13/87	3.00	2.50
156-57	80¢-1.20 fr. Life Yes/Drugs No 6/12/87	3.00	2.50
158-59	50¢-1.70 fr. U.N. Day 10/23/87	3.25	2.75
160-61	35¢-90¢ Child Immunization 11/20/87	3.00	2.75
	1988		
162-63	35¢-1.40 fr. World Without Hunger 1/29/88	3.00	2.50
164	50¢ UN For a Better World 1/29/88	...	2.00
165-66	50¢-1.40 fr. Forest Conservation 3/18/88	10.50	9.50
167-68	80¢-90¢ Int'l. Volunteers Day 5/6/88	3.50	3.00
169-70	50¢-1.40 fr. Health in Sports 6/17/88	3.50	3.00
171-72	90¢,2 fr. S/S Human Rts. Decl. Anniv. 12/9/88	5.00	3.75
	1989		
173-74	80¢-1.40 fr. World Bank 1/27/89	3.00	2.50
175	90¢ UN Peace Force, Nobel Prize 3/17/89	...	2.00
176-77	90¢-1.10 fr. World Weather Watch 4/21/89	3.00	2.50
178-79	50¢-2 fr. UN Offices in Vienna Anniv. 8/23/89	3.50	3.00
180-181	35¢-80¢ Human Rights 11/17/89	3.50	3.00
180-181	Strips of 3 with tabs on bottom	8.00	...
	1990		
182	1.50 fr. International Trade Center 2/2/90	...	3.25
183	5 fr. Definitive 2/2/90	...	7.00
184-85	50¢-80¢ Fight Against AIDS 3/16/90	3.00	2.50
186-87	90¢-1.40 fr. Medicinal Plants 5/4/90	3.25	3.00
188-89	90¢-1.10 fr. UN 45th Anniversary 6/26/90	3.00	2.50
190	90¢-1.10 fr. UN 45th Anniversary S/S 6/26/90	...	8.50
191-92	50¢-2 fr. Crime Prevention 9/13/90	4.50	4.00
193-94	35¢-90¢ Human Rights 11/16/90	3.50	3.00
,...	Strips of 3 with tabs on bottom	7.75	...
	1991		
195-98	90¢ Eur. Econ. Commission attd. 3/15/91	8.00	5.00
199-200	70¢-90¢ Namibia 5/10/91	4.00	4.00
201-02	80¢-1.50 fr. Definitives 5/10/91	4.50	3.75
203-04	80¢-1.10 fr. Children's Rights 6/14/91	4.00	3.25
205-06	80¢-1.40 fr. Chemical Weapons Ban 9/11/91	4.50	3.75
207-08	50¢-1.60 fr. UNPA 40th Anniv. 10/24/91	4.25	3.50
209-10	50¢-90¢ Human Rights 11/20/91	7.00	5.75
209-10	Strips of 3 with tabs on bottom	8.00	...
	1992		
211-12	50¢-1.10 fr. World Heritage 1/24/92	3.50	3.00
213	3 fr. Definitive 1/24/92	...	7.00
214-15	80¢ Clean Oceans attd. 3/13/92	3.50	3.00
216-19	75¢ UNICED: Earth Summit attd. 5/22/92	8.00	5.00
220-21	1.10 fr. Mission to Planet Earth attd. 9/4/92	4.75	4.50
222-23	90¢-1.60 fr. Science & Technology 10/2/92	6.00	4.25
224-25	50¢-90¢ Human Rights 12/10/92	6.00	3.25
224-225	Strips of 3 with tabs on bottom	7.00	...
	1993		
226-27	50¢-1.60 fr. Aging 2/5/93	4.25	3.50
228-31	80¢ Endangered Species, block of 4 3/3/93	7.00	4.75
232-33	60¢-1 fr. Healthy Environments 5/7/93	3.75	3.00
234-35	50¢-90¢ Human Rights 6/11/93	6.00	3.50
234-235	Strips of 3 with tabs on bottom	7.00	...
236-39	60¢ Peace, block of 4, attd. 9/21/93	8.00	5.00
240-43	1.10 fr. Environment - Climate 10/29/93	8.00	5.00
	1994		
244-45	80¢-1 fr. Year of the Family 2/4/94	4.00	3.00
246-49	80¢ Endangered Species 3/18/94	8.00	5.50
250	1.20 fr. Refugees 4/29/94	...	2.50
251-54	60¢ Natural Disaster 5/24/94 (4)	6.00	4.50
255-57	60¢,80¢,1.80 fr. Definitives 9/1/94	8.00	6.25
258-59	60¢-80¢ Population Development 9/1/94	3.50	2.75
260-61	60¢-1 fr. Development Partnership 10/28/94	4.00	3.25
262	80¢ U.N. 50th Anniversary 1/1/95	...	2.00
263	1 fr Social Summit 2/3/95	...	2.25
	1995		

Scott #	Description	Separate Covers	One Cover
	GENEVA		
264-67	80¢ Endangered Species 3/24/95	6.95	4.50
268-69	80¢-1 fr Youth: Our Future 5/26/95	4.00	3.25
270-71	60¢-1.80 fr 50th Anniv. of U.N. 6/26/95	5.25	4.25
272	2.40 fr 50th Anniv. Souv. Sheet 6/26/95	...	5.00
273-74	60¢-1 fr Conference on Women 9/5/95	4.00	3.50
275	30¢ U.N. 50th Anniv. Souv. Sheet 10/24/95	40.00	30.00
276	30¢ U.N. 50th Anniv. Souv. Bklt. of 12 10/24/95	42.50	30.00
	1996		
277	80¢ WFUNA 50th Anniversary 2/2/96	...	2.00
278-79	40¢-70¢ Definitives 2/2/96	3.75	3.00
280-83	80¢ Endangered Species 3/14/96	8.00	5.50
284-88	70¢ City Summit Strip of 5 6/3/96	...	6.75
289-90	70¢ - 1.10fr Sport & Environment 7/19/96	4.25	3.50
291	70¢ - 1.10fr Sport & Environment s/s 7/19/96	...	4.25
292-93	90¢ - 1.10fr Plea For Peace 9/17/96	4.00	3.50
294-95	70¢ - 1.80fr UNICEF 50th Anniversary 11/20/96	4.25	3.75
	1997		
296-97	10¢ - 1.10fr Regulars 2/12/97	3.25	2.75
298-301	80¢ Endangered Species 3/13/97	8.00	5.00
302-5	45¢ Earth Summit 5/30/97	8.75	3.50
306	1.10fr Earth Summit, S/S 5/30/97	...	2.50
307-11	70¢ Transportation , 5 designs 8/29/97	10.00	6.00
312-13	70¢ 1.10fr Tribute to Philately 10/14/97	4.75	4.50
314-15	45¢,70¢ Terracotta Warriors 11/19/97	3.75	3.25
	1998		
317	2fr Definitive, 2/13/98	...	4.50
318-21	80¢ Endangered Species, 4/22/99	5.75	5.00
322	45¢ Year of the Ocean	...	12.00
323	70¢ Rain Forest	...	2.50
324	3 Fr Rainforest s/s	...	7.50
327-28	90¢ 1.80 Fr Peacekeeping (2), 9/15/98	4.00	2.25
329-30	70¢ 1.10 Fr Schonburn Palace, 12/4/98	3.00	2.75
	1999		
332	1.70 Fr. Definitive 2/5/99	...	2.50
333-34	90¢-1.10 Fr. World Heritage/Australia 3/19/99	4.00	3.00
336-39	90¢ Endangered species 4/22/99	8.00	6.00
340	45¢ Unispace III 7/7/99	...	2.50
341	2 Fr. Unispace III s/s 7/7/99	...	5.00
343-46	70¢ Universal Postal Union 8/23/99	8.00	5.50
347	70¢ In Memoriam 9/21/99	...	2.50
348	2 Fr. In Memoriam s/s 9/21/99	...	5.00
349-350	90¢-1.80 Fr. Education 11/9/99	4.50	3.50
	2000		
351	90¢ Year of Thanksgiving 1/1/00	...	3.00
352-55	90¢ Endangered species 4/22/00	8.00	6.00
356-57	90¢-1.10 Fr. Our World 2000 5/30/00	4.00	3.00
358-59	90¢-1.40 Fr. Anniversary of UN 7/7/00	4.50	3.50
360	2.30 Fr. Anniversary of UN s/s 7/7/00	...	4.00
361a-f	50¢ UN in the 21st Century 9/15/00	15.00	7.50
362-63	1 Fr.-1.20 Fr. World Heritage/Spain 10/6/00	5.00	4.00
365	80¢ Respect for Refugees 11/9/00	...	2.50
366	1.80 Fr, Respect for Refugees s/s 11/9/00	...	4.50
	GENEVA AIRLETTER SHEETS		
UC1	65¢ Plane 10/4/69	...	4.75
	GENEVA POSTAL CARDS		
UX1	20¢ Post Horn 10/4/69	...	1.85
UX2	30¢ Earth 10/4/69	...	2.00
UX3	40¢ Emblem 6/27/77	...	1.90
UX4	70¢ Ribbons 6/27/77	...	2.00
UX5	50¢ "UN" Emblem 5/10/85	...	3.75
UX6	70¢ Peace Dove 5/10/85	...	4.00
UX7	70¢ + 10¢ Surcharge on UX6 1/2/86	...	12.00
UX8	90¢ Letters 9/4/92	...	4.50
UX9	50¢ + 10¢ Surcharge on UX5 5/7/93	...	17.50
UX10	80¢ Palais des Nations 5/7/93	...	4.00

Scott #	Description	Separate Covers	One Cover
	GENEVA POSTAL CARDS (cont.)		
UX11	50¢ + 20¢ Surcharge on UX5	...	10.00
UX12	80¢ + 30¢ Surcharge on UX10	...	10.00
UX13	70¢ Assembly Hall	...	2.00
UX14	$1.10 Fr Palaisdes Nations	...	2.25

11

Scott #	Description	Separate Covers	One Cover
	VIENNA		
1-6	50g-10s Regular Issue 8/24/79	6.00	5.00
	1980		
7	4s Economic Order 1/11/80	...	3.35
8	2.50s Regular, Dove 1/11/80	...	1.50
9-10	4s-6s Decade for Women 3/7/80	2.75	2.50
11	6s Peacekeeping Forces 5/16/80	...	1.75
12-13	4s-6s 35th Anniversary 6/26/80	2.85	2.60
14	4s-6s 35th Anniv. S/S 6/26/80	...	3.50
15-16	5s-6s Econ. & Soc. Coun. 11/21/80	2.10	1.85
	1981		
17	4s Palestinian People 1/30/81	...	1.40
18-19	4s-6s Disabled Persons 3/6/81	2.50	2.25
20	6s Art, Bulgarian Mural 4/15/81	...	1.50
21	7.50s Energy Conference 5/29/81	...	1.75
22-23	5s-7s Volunteers 11/13/81	2.75	2.50
	1982		
24	3s Definitive 1/22/81	...	1.50
25-26	5s-7s Human Environment 3/19/82	2.25	2.00
27	5s Peaceful Use of Space 6/11/82	...	1.75
28-29	5s-7s Nature Conserv. 11/16/82	2.25	2.00
	1983		
30	4s Communications Yr. 1/28/83	...	1.50
31-32	4s-6s Safety at Sea 3/18/83	2.50	2.25
33-34	5s-7s World Food Prog. 4/22/83	2.50	2.25
35-36	4s-8.50s Trade & Dev. 6/6/83	2.50	2.25
37-38	5s-7s Human Rights 12/9/83	2.85	2.50
	1984		
39	7s Population Conf. 2/3/84	...	1.75
40-41	4.50s-6s FAO Food Day 3/15/84	2.50	2.00
42-43	4.50s-8.50s UNESCO 3/15/84	3.00	2.75
44-45	4.50s-8.50s Refugee 3/29/84	2.50	2.00
46-47	3.50s-6.50s Youth Year 11/15/84	2.50	2.00
	1985		
48	7.50s ILO-Turin Centre 2/1/85	...	2.00
49	8.50s UN Univ. of Japan 3/15/85	...	2.00
50-51	4.50s-15s Definitives 5/10/85	2.85	2.50
52-53	6.50s-8.50s 40th Anniv. 6/26/85	2.50	2.25
54	6.50s-8.50s 40th Anniv. S/S 6/26/85	...	3.50
55-56	4s-6s UNICEF 11/22/85	2.25	2.00
	1986		
57	8s African Crisis 1/31/86	...	1.50
58-61	4.50s UN Dev. attd. 3/14/86	...	2.75
58-61	UN Dev. set of 4 singles	5.00	...
62-63	3.50s-6.50s Philately 5/22	2.50	2.00
64-65	6s-7s Int. Year 6/20/86	3.00	2.50
66	4s-7s WFUNA S/S 11/14/86	...	7.00
	1987		
67	8s Trygve Lie 1/30/87	...	2.00
68-69	4s-9.50s Shelter for Homeless 3/13/87	3.50	3.00
70-71	5s-8s Life Yes/Drugs No 6/12/87	3.50	3.00
72-73	2s-17s Definitives 6/12/87	3.75	3.25
74-75	5s-6s U.N. Day 10/23/87	3.50	3.00
76-77	4s-9.50s Child Immunization 11/20/87	3.50	3.00
	1988		
78-79	4s-6s World Without Hunger 1/29/88	3.00	3.00
80-81	4s-5s Forest Conservation 3/18/88	9.50	8.00
82-83	6s-7.50s Int'l Volunteers Day 5/6/88	3.00	2.50
84-85	6s-8s Health in Sports 6/17/88	3.00	3.00
86-87	5s-11s Human Rights Decl. Anniv. 12/9/88	7.00	...
	1989		
88-89	5.5s-8s World Bank 1/27/89	3.75	3.00
90	6s UN Peace Force, Nobel Prize 3/17/89	...	2.00
91-92	4s-9.5s World Weather Watch 4/21/89	3.50	3.00
93-94	5s-7.5s UN Offices in Vienna Anniv. 8/23/89	4.50	4.00
95-96	4s-6s Human Rights 11/17/89	5.00	4.50
95-96	Strips of 3 with tabs on bottom	7.00	...
	1990		
97	12s International Trade Center 2/2/90	...	3.00
98	1.50s Definitive 2/2/90	...	2.00
99-100	5s-11s Fight Against AIDS 3/16/90	3.50	3.00
101-02	4.5s-9.5s Medicinal Plants 5/4/90	3.50	3.00
103-04	7s-9s UN 45th Anniversary 6/26/90	3.50	3.00
105	7s-9s UN 45th Anniversary S/S	...	6.00

Scott #	Description	Separate Covers	One Cover
	VIENNA		
106-07	6s-8s Crime Prevention 9/13/90	3.75	3.25
108-09	4.5s-7s Human Rights 11/16/90	6.75	6.00
108-09	Strips of 3 with tabs on bottom	7.50	...
	1991		
110-13	5s Eur. Econ. Commission attd. 3/15/91	7.00	6.00
114-15	6s-9.50s Namibia 5/10/91	4.75	3.75
116	20s Definitive 5/10/91	...	4.25
117-18	7s-9s Children's Rights 6/14/91	4.00	3.25
119-20	5s-10s Chemical Weapons Ban 9/11/91	4.25	3.50
121-22	5s-8s UNPA 40th Anniv. 10/24/91	3.75	3.00
123-24	4.50s-7s Human Rights 11/20/91	7.00	6.00
123-24	Strips of 3 with tabs on bottom	8.00	...
	1992		
125-26	5s-9s World Heritage 1/24/92	4.50	4.00
127-28	7s Clean Oceans attd. 3/13/92	3.75	3.25
129-32	5.5s UNICED: Earth Summit 5/22/92	8.00	5.50
133-34	10s Mission to Planet Earth attd. 9/4/92	4.95	4.50
135-36	5.5s-7s Science & Technology 10/2/92	3.40	3.00
137-38	5.5s-7s Definitives 10/2/92	3.40	3.00
139-40	6s-10s Human Rights 12/10/92	4.50	3.75
139-40	Strips of 3 with tabs on bottom	7.75	...
	1993		
141-42	5.5s-7s Aging 2/5/93	3.40	3.00
143-46	7s Endangered Species, block of 4 3/3/93	7.00	5.75
147-48	6s-10s Healthy Environments 5/7/93	4.00	3.75
149	13s Definitive 5/7/93	...	2.75
150-51	5s-6s Human Rights 6/11/93	6.50	5.00
150-511	Strips of 3 with tabs on bottom	7.25	...
152-55	5.5s Peace, block of 4, attd. 9/21/93	12.00	6.00
156-59	7s Environment - Climate 10/29/93	14.00	7.00
	1994		
160-61	5.5s-8s Year of the Family 2/4/94	4.25	3.50
162-65	7s Endangered Species 3/18/94	8.00	6.00
166	12s Refugees 4/29/94	...	3.00
167-69	50g,4s,30s Definitives 4/29/94	8.25	6.75
170-73	6s Natural Disaster 5/24/94 (4)	18.00	8.00
174-75	5.50s-7s Population Development 9/1/94	3.65	2.85
176-77	6s-7s Development Partnership 10/28/94	3.75	2.95
	1995		
178	7s U.N. 50th Anniversary 1/195	...	2.75
179	14s Social Summit 2/3/95	...	3.75
180-83	7s Endangered Species 3/24/95	8.00	5.50
184-85	6s-7s Youth: Our Future 5/26/95	3.75	2.95
186-87	7s-10s 50th Anniv. of U.N. 6/26/95	3.75	3.00
188	17s 50th Anniv. Souv. Sheet 6/2/65	...	4.75
189-90	5.50s-6s Conference on Women 9/5/95	3.75	3.25
191	3s U.N. 50th Anniv. Sheetlet of 12 10/24/95	40.00	27.50
192	3s U.N. 50th Anniv. Souv. Booklet of 12 10/24/95	47.00	42.00
	1996		
193	7s WFUNA 50th Anniversary 2/2/96	...	2.00
194-95	1s – 10¢ Regular Issues 2/2/96	3.50	3.00
196-99	7s Endangered Species 3/14/96	8.00	5.50
200-4	6s City Summit, Strip of 5 6/3/96	...	5.25
205-6	6s - 7s Sport & Environment 7/19/96	3.75	3.50
207	6s - 7s Sport & Environment S/S 7/19/96	...	4.75
208-9	7s - 10s Plea For Peace 9/17/96	4.25	3.75
210-11	5.50s - 8s UNICEF 50th Anniversary 11/20/96	3.00	2.60
	1997		
212-13	5s - 6s Regulars 2/12/97	3.00	2.75
0214-17s	Endangered Species 3/13/97	8.00	5.25
218-21	3.50s Earth Summit 5/30/97	8.00	5.25
222	11s Earth Summit, S/S, 5/30/97	...	3.00
223-27	7s Transportation, 5 designs, 8/29/97	10.00	6.00
228-29	6.50s – 7s Tribute to Philately, 10/14/97	4.75	4.50
230-31	3s-6s Terracotta Warriors, 11/19/97	3.75	3.25
	1998		
233-34	6.50s – 9s Definitives, 2/13/98	3.50	3.00
235-238	7s Endangered Species 3/13/98	8.00	5.50
239	3.50s Year of Ocean, Mini-sheet	...	10.00
240	6.50s Rain Forests, 6/19/98	...	1.50
241	22s Rainforest s/s, 6/19/98	...	5.50
242-43	4s – 7.50s Peacekeeping, 9/15/98	3.00	2.50
244-45	4.50s – 7s Human Rights, 10/27/98	3.00	2.50
246-47	3.50s – 7s Schonbrun Palace, 12/4/98	3.00	2.50
	1999		
235-38	7s Endangered Species, 4/22/99	8.00	5.50
249	8s Definitive 2/5/99	...	2.50
250-51	4.50s-6.50s World Heritage/Australia 3/19/99	4.00	3.00
253-56	7s Endangered species 4/22/99	8.00	6.00
257	3.50s Unispace III 7/7/99	...	2.50
258	13s Unispace III s/s 7/7/99	...	5.00
260-63	6.50s Universal Postal Union 8/23/99	8.00	5.50
264	6.50s In Memoriam 9/21/99	...	2.50
265	14s In Memorians/s 9/21/99	...	5.00
266-67	7s-13s Education 11/18/99	4.50	3.50
	2000		
268	7s Year of Thanksgiving 1/1/00	...	3.00
269-72	7s Endangered species 4/6/00	8.00	6.00
273-74	7s-8s Our World 2000 5/30/00	4.00	3.00
275-76	7s-9s Anniversary of UN 7/7/00	4.50	3.50
277	16s Anniversary of UN s/s 7/7/00	...	4.00
278a-f	3.50s UN in the 21st Century 9/15/00	15.00	7.50
279-80	4.50s-6.50s World Heritage/Spain 10/6/00	5.00	4.00
282	7.50s Respect for Refugees 11/19/00	...	2.50
283	25s Respect for Refugees 11/19/00	...	4.50

UNITED NATIONS FIRST DAY COVERS

Scott #	Description	Separate Covers	One Cover
	VIENNA ENVELOPE ENTIRES		
U1	6s Vienna Centre	...	5.95
U2	7s Landscape	...	6.50
	VIENNA AIRLETTER SHEETS		
UC1	9s Bird 4/28/82	...	6.50
UC2	9s + 2s Surcharge on UC1 2/3/86	...	30.00
UC3	11s Birds in Flight 1/30/87	...	11.00
UC4	11s+1s Surcharge (1992)	...	25.00
UC5	12s Donaupark 9/4/92	...	25.00
	VIENNA POSTAL CARDS		
UX1	3s Branch 4/28/82	...	3.50
UX2	5s Globe 4/28/82	...	6.00
UX3	4s Emblem 5/10/85	...	6.75
UX4	5s + 1s Surcharge on UX2 1/1/92	...	13.00
UX5	6s Regschek Painting 9/4/92	...	12.00
UX6	5s Peoples 5/7/93	...	12.00
UX7	6s Donaupark 5/7/93	...	11.00
UX8	5s+50g (1994)	...	...

CANANDA

1,4    2,5,10    8

PROVINCE OF CANADA
1851 Laid Paper, Imperforate (OG + 75%) (C)

Scott's No.		Unused		Used	
		Fine	Ave.	Fine	Ave.
1	3p Beaver, Red	…	…	550.00	325.00
2	6p Albert, Grayish Purple	…	…	900.00	500.00

1852-1857 Wove Paper, Imperforate (OG + 75%) (C)

		Fine	Ave.	Fine	Ave.
4	3p Beaver, Red, Thick Paper	875.00	525.00	130.00	80.00
4d	3p Thin Paper	900.00	550.00	140.00	90.00
5	6p Albert, Slate Gray	…	…	775.00	425.00
7	10p Cartier, Blue	…	…	850.00	500.00
8	½p Victoria, Rose	450.00	265.00	300.00	190.00
9	7½p Victoria, Green	…	…	1400.00	750.00
10	6p Albert, Reddish Purple, Thick	…	…	…	1500.00

1858-59 Wove Paper, Perforated 12 (OG + 75%) (C)

		Fine	Ave.	Fine	Ave.
11	½p Victoria, Rose	…	950.00	700.00	375.00
12	3p Beaver, Red	…	1650.00	400.00	250.00
13	6p Albert, Brown Violet	…	…	…	1650.00

14   17   18   19   20

1859-64 (OG + 50%) VF + 80% (C)

		Fine	Ave.	Fine	Ave.
14	1¢ Victoria, Rose	175.00	110.00	32.50	19.00
15	5¢ Beaver, Vermilion	210.00	130.00	18.00	11.00
16	10¢ Albert, Black Brown	…	…	…	1100.00
17	10¢ Red Lilac	475.00	290.00	50.00	30.00
18	12½¢ Victoria, Yellow Green	425.00	250.00	50.00	30.00
19	17¢ Cartier, Blue	500.00	275.00	80.00	45.00
20	2¢ Victoria, Rose (1864)	265.00	175.00	140.00	90.00

CANADA
DOMINION OF CANADA
1868-1876 Large "Cents" Issue, Perf. 12 (OG + 30%) VF + 80% (C)

21   22   26   27   28

Scott's No.		Unused		Used	
		Fine	Ave.	Fine	Ave.
21	½¢ Victoria, Black	40.00	23.50	27.50	15.00
21a	½¢ Perf. 11½ x 12	45.00	26.50	30.00	16.50
21c	½¢ Thin Paper	45.00	27.00	37.50	21.50
22	1¢ Brown Red	325.00	195.00	55.00	35.00
22a	1¢ Watermarked	…	…	180.00	105.00
22b	1¢ Thin Paper	335.00	200.00	55.00	35.00
23	1¢ Yellow Orange (1869)	550.00	325.00	80.00	45.00
24	2¢ Green	300.00	180.00	30.00	16.50
24a	2¢ Watermarked	…	1000.00	175.00	115.00
24b	2¢ Thin Paper	425.00	275.00	40.00	23.50
25	3¢ Red	500.00	280.00	16.00	10.00
25a	3¢ Watermarked	2000.00	1150.00	175.00	115.00
25b	3¢ Thin Paper	600.00	350.00	20.00	12.50
26	5¢ Olive Green, Perf. 11½ x 12(1875)	650.00	375.00	110.00	65.00
27	6¢ Dark Brown	800.00	500.00	50.00	30.00
27b	6¢ Watermarked	…	1800.00	800.00	450.00
27c	6¢ Thin Paper	1000.00	600.00	100.00	60.00
28	12½¢ Blue	425.00	250.00	55.00	31.50
28a	12½¢ Watermarked	1400.00	800.00	140.00	90.00
28b	12½¢ Thin Paper	575.00	350.00	75.00	45.00
29	15¢ Gray Violet	40.00	26.50	18.50	11.50
29a	15¢ Perf. 11½ x 12	600.00	375.00	110.00	67.50
29b	15¢ Red Lilac	450.00	300.00	60.00	32.50
29c	15¢ Gray Violet Wmkd	…	1400.00	475.00	275.00
29e	15¢ Gray Violet, Thin Paper	375.00	235.00	75.00	45.00
30	15¢ Gray	42.50	25.00	19.50	11.50
30a	15¢ Perf. 11½ x 12	575.00	350.00	110.00	65.00

1868 Laid Paper, Perf. 12 VF +80% (C)

		Fine	Ave.	Fine	Ave.
31	1¢ Brown Red	…	…	2500.00	1350.00
33	3¢ Bright Red	…	…	525.00	275.00

CANADA

| 34 | 37, 41 | 38 | 44 | 47 |

Scott's No.	NH Fine	Unused Fine	Ave.	Used Fine	Ave.
1870-1889 Small "Cents" Issue, Perf. 12 (OG + 20%) VF + 80% (C)					
34	½¢ Victoria Black (1882) 12.50	4.75	2.75	4.25	2.40
35	1¢ Yellow 40.00	16.50	9.50	.60	.35
35a	1¢ Orange 130.00	50.00	32.50	5.25	3.15
35d	1¢ Orange, Pf. 11½ x 12 ...... 300.00	125.00	75.00	12.50	7.00
36	2¢ Green (1872) 55.00	22.50	14.50	1.00	.60
36d	2¢ Blue Green 100.00	40.00	22.50	2.50	1.50
36e	2¢ Green, Pf. 11½ x 12 .... 375.00	150.00	85.00	15.00	9.25
37	3¢ Dull Red 125.00	50.00	30.00	1.65	.90
37a	3¢ Rose 650.00	250.00	150.00	7.50	4.25
37b	3¢ Copper Red	675.00	375.00	30.00	17.50
37c	3¢ Orange Red 100.00	40.00	22.50	1.15	.65
37d	3¢ Cop. Red 12½ x 12	...	...	625.00	400.00
37e	3¢ Red, Perf. 11½ x 12 .... 325.00	135.00	75.00	7.50	4.50
38	5¢ Slate Green (1876) 575.00	235.00	130.00	11.75	7.75
38a	5¢ Ol. Gr., Pf. 11½ x 12 .... 750.00	295.00	180.00	30.00	18.75
39	6¢ Yellow Brown (1877) 475.00	195.00	110.00	11.00	7.00
39b	6¢ Brown, 11½ x 12 .... 750.00	300.00	185.00	20.00	13.50
40	10¢ Dull Rose Lilac (1877) 700.00	280.00	165.00	32.50	20.00
40c	10¢ Rose Ll., 11½ x 12 .... 650.00	375.00	225.00	130.00	
1888-1893 Small "Cents" Issue, Perf. 12 (OG + 20%) VF + 80% (C)					
41	3¢ Bright Vermilion 46.50	19.50	11.00	.40	.25
41a	3¢ Rose Carmine 575.00	225.00	120.00	6.50	4.15
42	5¢ Gray 120.00	55.00	32.50	2.75	1.65
43	6¢ Red Brown 100.00	45.00	27.50	7.50	4.15
43a	6¢ Chocolate 295.00	120.00	65.00	19.50	12.00
44	8¢ Gray (1893) 120.00	52.50	27.50	2.95	1.75
45	10¢ Brown Red (1891) 350.00	150.00	90.00	22.50	12.50
46	20¢ Vermilion (1893) 425.00	185.00	110.00	52.50	30.00
47	50¢ Deep Blue (1893) 425.00	185.00	110.00	45.00	25.00

1897 Jubilee Issue VF Used + 60% (B)

| 56 | 58 | 61 |

Scott's No.	VF	NH F-VF	Unused VF	F-VF	Used F-VF
50	½¢ Victoria, Black 210.00	125.00	85.00	50.00	52.50
51	1¢ Orange 35.00	22.50	15.00	9.00	6.00
52	2¢ Green 47.50	27.50	18.00	11.75	8.00
53	3¢ Bright Rose 27.50	17.00	11.00	7.00	1.35
54	5¢ Deep Blue 90.00	55.00	35.00	22.50	14.50
55	6¢ Yellow Brown 425.00	250.00	185.00	110.00	100.00
56	8¢ Dark Violet 100.00	60.00	40.00	25.00	20.00
57	10¢ Brown Violet 190.00	115.00	85.00	50.00	45.00
58	15¢ Steel Blue 425.00	275.00	175.00	110.00	100.00
59	20¢ Vermillion 425.00	270.00	185.00	115.00	100.00
60	50¢ Ultramarine 525.00	325.00	190.00	120.00	100.00
61	$1 Lake 1450.00	900.00	650.00	400.00	400.00
62	$2 Dark Purple 2500.00	1500.00	1100.00	675.00	350.00
63	$3 Yellow Bistre 2950.00	1850.00	1300.00	800.00	650.00
64	$4 Purple 2950.00	1850.00	1300.00	800.00	650.00
65	$5 Olive Green 2950.00	1850.00	1300.00	800.00	650.00

| 73 | 84 | 85-86 | 88 |

1897-1898 Issue, Maple Leaves in Four Corners, VF Used + 60% (B)

66	½¢ Victoria, Black 14.75	9.50	6.50	4.25	3.50
67	1¢ Blue Green 35.00	22.50	14.50	9.00	.65
68	2¢ Purple 35.00	22.00	15.00	9.50	1.00
69	3¢ Carmine (1898) 60.00	37.50	23.50	15.00	.25
70	5¢ Dark Blue 225.00	140.00	85.00	55.00	3.50
71	6¢ Brown 150.00	90.00	67.50	42.50	15.75
72	8¢ Orange 425.00	275.00	160.00	100.00	5.50
73	10¢ Brown Violet (1898) 475.00	300.00	195.00	125.00	45.00

Scott's No.	VF	NH F-VF	Unused VF	F-VF	Used F-VF
1898-1902 Issue, Numerals in Lower Corners VF Used + 60% (B)					
74	½¢ Victoria, Black 7.50	4.65	2.75	1.75	1.00
75	1¢ Gray Green 41.50	26.50	17.00	10.75	.20
76	2¢ Purple 41.50	26.50	16.50	10.50	.20
77	2¢ Carmine, Die I (1898) 42.50	27.50	17.50	11.00	.20
77a	2¢ Carmine, Die II 47.50	30.00	19.00	12.00	.25
78	3¢ Carmine 75.00	47.50	27.50	17.50	.40
79	5¢ Blue 300.00	180.00	120.00	75.00	1.00
80	6¢ Brown 225.00	140.00	95.00	57.50	26.50
81	7¢ Olive Yellow (1902) 180.00	110.00	82.50	50.00	12.00
82	8¢ Orange 275.00	170.00	135.00	85.00	12.75
83	10¢ Brown Violet 425.00	250.00	190.00	120.00	12.50
84	20¢ Olive Green (1900) 875.00	550.00	350.00	225.00	55.00
1898 Imperial Penny Post VF Used + 50% (B)					
85	2¢ Map, Blk. Lav. Carm. 47.50	30.00	26.50	17.50	4.35
86	2¢ Black, Blue, Carmine 47.50	30.00	26.50	17.50	4.35
1899 Surcharges VF Used + 60% (B)					
87	2¢ on 3¢ Carmine (on #69) 23.50	15.00	9.25	6.00	3.85
88	2¢ on 3¢ Carmine (on #78) 35.00	21.50	15.00	9.50	2.75

| 94 | 100 | 103 |

1903-1908 King Edward VII VF Used + 60% (B)					
89	1¢ Edward VII, Green 47.50	30.00	18.50	12.00	.20
90	2¢ Carmine 47.50	30.00	18.50	12.00	.20
90a	2¢ Imperforate Pair 55.00	40.00	35.00	25.00	...
91	5¢ Blue 230.00	145.00	95.00	60.00	2.00
92	7¢ Olive Bistre 190.00	115.00	77.50	50.00	2.00
93	10¢ Brown Lilac 350.00	200.00	140.00	90.00	4.00
94	20¢ Olive Green 950.00	595.00	375.00	240.00	18.00
95	50¢ Purple (1908) 1175.00	750.00	515.00	325.00	65.00
1908 Quebec Tercentenary VF + 65% (B)					
96-103	Set of 8 .... 1300.00	795.00	535.00	335.00	255.00
96	½¢ Prince & Princess 8.25	5.00	4.00	2.50	2.50
97	1¢ Cartier & Champlain 23.50	14.00	10.50	6.50	2.60
98	2¢ Alexandria & Edward 40.00	25.00	15.00	9.50	.80
99	5¢ Champlain's Home 95.00	60.00	40.00	25.00	20.00
100	7¢ Montcalm & Wolfe 235.00	150.00	95.00	60.00	40.00
101	10¢ 1700 View of Quebec 235.00	150.00	95.00	60.00	45.00
102	15¢ Champlain Heads West .. 285.00	170.00	130.00	80.00	62.50
103	20¢ Cartier Arrival 425.00	250.00	180.00	110.00	95.00

| 104-105 | 122 | 131 | 140 |

1912-1925 "Admiral Issue" Perf. 12 VF Used + 50% (B)					
104-22	Set of 18 .... 1475.00	985.00	595.00	395.00	25.50
104	1¢ George V. Green 19.50	12.50	8.25	5.50	.15
104a	1¢ Booklet Pane of 6 .... 35.00	23.50	23.75	15.00	...
105	1¢ Yellow (1922) 19.50	12.50	8.25	5.50	.15
105a	1¢ Booklet Pane of 4 .... 85.00	55.00	50.00	35.00	...
105b	1¢ Booklet Pane of 6 .... 70.00	47.50	45.00	30.00	...
106	2¢ Carmine 17.50	11.75	6.75	4.50	.15
106a	2¢ Booklet Pane of 6 .... 45.00	29.50	26.50	17.50	...
107	2¢ Yellow Green (1922) 13.75	8.50	5.75	3.75	.15
107a	2¢ Thin Paper 13.00	8.00	6.00	4.00	1.75
107b	2¢ Booklet Pane of 4 .... 95.00	62.50	57.50	37.50	...
107c	2¢ Booklet Pane of 6 .... 425.00	290.00	300.00	200.00	...
108	3¢ Brown (1918) 22.50	14.50	9.25	6.00	.15
108a	3¢ Booklet Pane of 4 .... 115.00	75.00	77.50	52.50	...
109	3¢ Carmine (1923) 12.50	8.25	5.25	3.50	.15
109a	3¢ Booklet Pane of 4 .... 80.00	53.50	52.50	35.00	...
110	4¢ Olive Bistre (1922) 55.00	36.50	22.00	14.50	1.90
111	5¢ Dark Blue 185.00	125.00	80.00	52.50	.35
112	5¢ Violet (1922) 35.00	23.50	14.75	9.75	.35
112a	5¢ Thin Paper 30.00	20.00	15.00	10.00	4.50
113	7¢ Yellow Ochre 70.00	47.50	27.50	18.50	1.80
113a	7¢ Olive Bistre 70.00	47.50	27.50	18.50	1.95
114	7¢ Red Brown (1924) 35.00	23.50	15.00	10.00	5.25
115	8¢ Blue (1925) 55.00	37.50	22.50	15.00	4.75
116	10¢ Plum 415.00	280.00	135.00	90.00	.90
117	10¢ Blue (1922) 67.50	45.00	30.00	20.00	1.10
118	10¢ Bister Brown (1925) 65.00	42.50	27.50	18.50	1.00
119	20¢ Olive Green 135.00	90.00	55.00	37.50	.85
120	50¢ Black Brown (1925) 135.00	90.00	60.00	40.00	1.50
120a	50¢ Black 280.00	190.00	120.00	80.00	4.50
122	$1 Orange (1923) 185.00	125.00	85.00	55.00	5.35
1912 Coil Stamps, Perf. 8 Horizontally VF Used + 50% (B)					
123	1¢ Dark Green 165.00	110.00	75.00	50.00	35.00
124	2¢ Carmine 165.00	110.00	75.00	50.00	35.00

1912-1924 Coil Stamps, Perf. 8 Vertically VF Used + 50% (B)

Scott's No.		NH VF	NH F-VF	Unused VF	Unused F-VF	Used F-VF
125-30	**Set of 6**	**215.00**	**140.00**	**115.00**	**77.50**	**10.50**
125	1¢ Green	27.50	18.00	14.00	9.50	.65
126	1¢ Yellow (1923)	16.50	11.00	9.00	6.00	4.25
126a	1¢ Block of four	70.00	47.50	45.00	30.00	...
127	2¢ Carmine	32.50	21.50	18.00	12.00	.55
128	2¢ Green (1922)	22.50	15.00	11.50	7.75	.55
128a	2¢ Block of four	70.00	47.50	45.00	30.00	...
129	3¢ Brown (1918)	16.50	11.00	9.00	6.00	.55
130	3¢ Carmine (1924)	110.00	70.00	60.00	40.00	4.50
130a	3¢ Block of four	935.00	625.00	635.00	425.00	...

#126a,128a,130a are from Part.-Perf. Sheets - Pairs are at half block prices.

1915-1924 Coil Stamps, Perf. 12 Horizontally VF Used + 50% (B)

Scott's No.		NH VF	NH F-VF	Unused VF	Unused F-VF	Used F-VF
131-34	**Set of 4**	**165.00**	**110.00**	**95.00**	**63.50**	**53.75**
131	1¢ Dark Green	10.50	7.00	6.00	4.00	5.00
132	2¢ Carmine	32.50	21.50	18.00	12.00	7.50
133	2¢ Yellow Green (1924)	115.00	75.00	67.50	45.00	40.00
134	3¢ Brown (1921)	12.50	8.25	7.25	4.75	4.00

1917 Confederation VF Used + 100% (B)

Scott's No.		NH VF	NH F-VF	Unused VF	Unused F-VF	Used F-VF
135	3¢ "Fathers of Confed."	75.00	40.00	35.00	17.50	.60

1924 Imperforate VF Used + 30% (B)

Scott's No.		NH VF	NH F-VF	Unused VF	Unused F-VF	Used F-VF
136	1¢ Yellow	65.00	47.50	37.50	28.50	28.50
137	2¢ Green	65.00	47.50	37.50	28.50	28.50
138	3¢ Carmine	33.50	25.00	19.50	15.00	15.00

1926 Surcharges on #109 VF Used + 50% (B)

Scott's No.		NH VF	NH F-VF	Unused VF	Unused F-VF	Used F-VF
139	2¢ on 3¢ - One Line	87.50	52.50	53.50	35.00	35.00
140	2¢ on 3¢ - Two Lines	37.50	25.00	25.00	16.50	16.50

141

143

146

148

1927 Confederation Issue VF Used + 30% (B)

Scott's No.		NH VF	NH F-VF	Unused VF	Unused F-VF	Used F-VF
141-45	**Set of 5**	**49.50**	**36.50**	**28.00**	**20.75**	**8.25**
141	1¢ John A. MacDonald	4.50	3.25	2.60	1.95	.65
142	2¢ "Fathers of Confed."	2.70	1.95	1.60	1.20	.20
143	3¢ Parliament Building	10.75	8.00	7.00	5.25	3.25
144	5¢ Sir Wilfrid Laurier	6.25	4.50	3.75	2.75	1.75
145	12¢ Map of Canada	28.50	21.00	15.00	11.50	3.00

1927 Historical Issue VF Used + 30% (B)

Scott's No.		NH VF	NH F-VF	Unused VF	Unused F-VF	Used F-VF
146-48	**Set of 3**	**47.50**	**35.00**	**27.50**	**20.75**	**8.50**
146	5¢ Thomas d'Arcy McGee	5.95	4.50	3.25	2.50	1.75
147	12¢ Laurier & MacDonald	13.50	10.00	8.25	6.25	3.00
148	20¢ Baldwin & Lafontaine	30.00	22.50	17.00	13.00	4.25

1928-29 Scroll Series VF Used + 40% (B)

149

154

156

158

Scott's No.		NH VF	NH F-VF	Unused VF	Unused F-VF	Used F-VF
149-59	**Set of 11**	**915.00**	**665.00**	**525.00**	**370.00**	**110.00**
149	1¢ George V, Orange	4.50	3.15	2.25	1.60	.25
149a	1¢ Booklet Pane of 6	28.50	20.00	18.50	13.50	...
150	2¢ Green	1.85	1.30	1.10	.80	.15
150a	2¢ Booklet Pane of 6	28.50	20.00	18.00	13.00	...
151	3¢ Dark Carmine	31.50	22.50	16.50	11.75	7.00
152	4¢ Bistre (1929)	32.50	22.50	16.00	11.50	3.25
153	5¢ Deep Violet	15.75	11.50	7.50	5.50	1.70
153a	5¢ Booklet Pane of 6	165.00	115.00	110.00	75.00	...
154	8¢ Blue	22.50	16.00	10.50	7.50	3.75
155	10¢ Mt. Hurd	22.50	16.00	10.50	7.50	.70
156	12¢ Quebec Bridge (1929)	35.00	25.00	17.50	12.50	4.00
157	20¢ Harvest Wheat (1929)	55.00	40.00	26.50	19.00	7.00
158	50¢ "Bluenose" (1929)	350.00	240.00	200.00	145.00	40.00
159	$1 Parliament (1929)	400.00	285.00	250.00	175.00	45.00

1929 Coil Stamps, Perf. 8 Vertically VF Used + 40% (B)

Scott's No.		NH VF	NH F-VF	Unused VF	Unused F-VF	Used F-VF
160	1¢ George V, Orange	47.50	33.50	22.75	16.50	13.75
161	2¢ Green	35.00	25.00	17.50	12.50	1.75

1930-31 King George V & Pictorials VF Used + 40% (B)

171

173

176

177

1930-31 George V & Pictorials (continued)

Scott's No.		NH VF	NH F-VF	Unused VF	Unused F-VF	Used F-VF
162-77	**Set of 16**	**650.00**	**460.00**	**360.00**	**260.00**	**39.50**
162	1¢ George V. Orange	1.75	1.25	.85	.60	.35
163	1¢ Deep Green	2.00	1.40	1.20	.85	.15
163a	1¢ Booklet Pane of 4	170.00	115.00	110.00	75.00	...
163c	1¢ Booklet Pane of 6	32.00	23.00	21.00	15.00	...
164	2¢ Dull Green	1.40	1.00	.90	.65	.15
164a	2¢ Booklet Pane of 6	50.00	35.00	32.50	22.50	...
165	2¢ Deep Red, Die I	2.10	1.45	1.35	.95	.15
165a	2¢ Deep Red, Die II	2.30	1.65	1.60	1.15	.20
165b	2¢ B. Pane of 6, Die I	35.00	24.00	22.75	16.00	...
166	2¢ Dark Br., Die II (1931)	2.15	1.50	1.40	1.00	.15
166a	2¢ B. Pane of 4, Die II	140.00	100.00	105.00	75.00	...
166b	2¢ Dark Brown, Die I	6.25	4.50	4.25	3.00	2.75
166c	2¢ B. Pane of 6, Die I	47.50	33.50	31.50	22.50	...
	Die I: Small Dot of Color in "P" of Postage. Die II: Large Dot in "P".					
167	3¢ Deep Red (1931)	3.50	2.50	2.10	1.50	.15
167a	3¢ Booklet Pane of 4	55.00	38.50	35.00	25.00	...
168	4¢ Yellow Bistre	16.50	10.75	8.50	6.00	3.50
169	5¢ Dull Violet	8.75	6.25	5.00	3.50	2.25
170	5¢ Dull Blue	5.50	4.00	2.75	2.00	.20
171	8¢ Dark Blue	27.50	19.00	15.00	10.50	5.50
172	8¢ Red Orange	8.75	6.00	5.00	3.50	2.50
173	10¢ Library of Parliament	14.50	10.50	7.50	5.50	.70
174	12¢ Citadel at Quebec	26.50	18.00	13.50	9.75	3.35
175	20¢ Harvesting Wheat	39.50	27.50	21.00	15.00	.35
176	50¢ Museum-Grand Pre	275.00	190.00	150.00	110.00	7.75
177	$1 Mt. Edith Cavell	280.00	195.00	150.00	110.00	16.50

1930-31 Coil Stamps, Perf. 8½ Vertically VF Used + 40% (B)

Scott's No.		NH VF	NH F-VF	Unused VF	Unused F-VF	Used F-VF
178-83	**Set of 6**	**107.50**	**72.50**	**57.50**	**41.50**	**13.75**
178	1¢ George V,Orange	20.00	14.00	11.50	8.00	7.00
179	1¢ Green	10.75	7.50	6.00	4.25	3.25
180	2¢ Dull Green	8.00	5.50	4.35	3.35	1.85
181	2¢ Carmine	31.50	22.50	17.50	12.50	1.65
182	2¢ Dark Brown (1931)	14.75	10.50	9.75	7.00	.45
183	3¢ Deep Red (1931)	25.00	17.50	14.00	10.00	.45

1931 Design of 1912, Perf. 12 x 8 VF Used + 30% (B)

Scott's No.		NH VF	NH F-VF	Unused VF	Unused F-VF	Used F-VF
184	3¢ George V Carmine	8.75	6.00	3.65	2.75	2.35

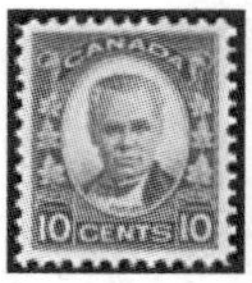
190

192

194

199

1931 Cartier Issue VF + 30% (B)

Scott's No.		NH VF	NH F-VF	Unused VF	Unused F-VF	Used F-VF
190	10¢ Sir Georges Cartier	15.00	11.50	7.25	5.50	.20

1932 Surcharges VF + 30% (B)

Scott's No.		NH VF	NH F-VF	Unused VF	Unused F-VF	Used F-VF
191	3¢ on 2¢ Deep Red, Die II	1.40	1.10	.95	.75	.15
191a	3¢ on 2¢ Deep Red, Die I	3.50	2.50	2.25	1.65	1.50

1932 Imperial Conference VF + 30% (B)

Scott's No.		NH VF	NH F-VF	Unused VF	Unused F-VF	Used F-VF
192-94	**Set of 3**	**17.00**	**12.50**	**11.95**	**8.50**	**5.15**
192	3¢ George V	1.00	.75	.65	.50	.20
193	5¢ Prince of Wales	8.00	5.75	5.25	4.00	1.50
194	13¢ Allegory	9.00	6.75	6.00	4.50	3.75

1932 George V, Medallion, VF Used + 30% (B)

Scott's No.		NH VF	NH F-VF	Unused VF	Unused F-VF	Used F-VF
195-201	**Set of 7**	**140.00**	**100.00**	**79.50**	**62.50**	**7.50**
195	1¢ George V. Dark Green	1.00	.75	.70	.55	.15
195a	1¢ Booklet Pane of 4	120.00	90.00	85.00	65.00	...
195b	1¢ Booklet Pane of 6	30.75	23.75	21.50	16.50	...
196	2¢ Black Brown	1.40	1.00	.95	.70	.15
196a	2¢ Booklet Pane of 4	120.00	90.00	85.00	65.00	...
196b	2¢ Booklet Pane of 6	31.50	24.50	22.50	17.00	...
197	3¢ Deep Red	1.75	1.30	1.20	.90	.15
197a	3¢ Booklet Pane of 4	45.00	32.50	31.50	23.50	...
198	4¢ Ocher	55.00	40.00	32.50	25.00	3.75
199	5¢ Dark Blue	9.75	7.00	5.95	4.50	.20
200	8¢ Red Orange	31.50	23.50	18.50	14.00	2.35
201	13¢ Citadel at Quebec	55.00	41.50	30.00	22.50	1.75

203

208

209

1933 Pictorials VF + 30%

Scott's No.		NH VF	NH F-VF	Unused VF	Unused F-VF	Used F-VF
202	5¢ U.P.U. Meeting	9.75	7.75	6.25	4.75	2.00
203	20¢ Grain Exhib. (on #175)	40.00	30.00	26.00	20.00	8.00
204	5¢ "Royal William"	10.00	7.50	6.50	5.00	2.00

CANADA

1933 Coil Stamps, Perf. Vertically VF + 30% (B)

Scott's No.		VF	NH F-VF	Unused VF	F-VF	Used F-VF
205	1¢ George V. Dark Green	21.50	16.00	12.50	9.50	1.50
206	2¢ Black Brown	23.50	17.50	13.00	10.00	.55
207	3¢ Deep Red	21.50	16.00	11.50	8.50	.25

1934 Commemoratives VF + 30%

208	3¢ Cartier at Quebec	4.75	3.50	2.60	2.00	.85
209	10¢ Loyalists Monument	31.50	24.00	18.50	14.00	4.75
210	2¢ Seal of New Brunswick	3.00	2.25	1.85	1.40	1.10

==

1935 Silver Jubilee VF + 25%

211   213   214   216

Scott's No.		Plate Blocks NH	Unused	F-VF NH	F-VF Unused	F-VF Used
211-16	Set of 6	...	...	20.75	15.00	7.35
211	1¢ Princess Elizabeth .... (6)	8.00	6.50	.45	.30	.25
212	2¢ Duke of York .... (6)	7.50	6.25	.60	.45	.20
213	3¢ George V and Mary .... (6)	17.50	13.50	1.90	1.30	.15
214	5¢ Prince of Wales .... (6)	47.50	35.00	5.00	3.50	1.80
215	10¢ Windsor Castle .... (6)	57.50	45.00	6.25	4.25	1.65
216	13¢ Royal Yacht "Brittania" (6)	75.00	55.00	9.00	6.25	3.50

1935 George V & Pictorials VF + 25%

217   222   225   227

217-27	Set of 11	...	...	140.00	105.00	13.75
217	1¢ George V Green .... (8)	3.75	3.00	.25	.20	.15
217a	1¢ Booklet Pane of 4	...	...	60.00	45.00	...
217b	1¢ Booklet Pane of 6	...	...	24.50	18.00	...
218	2¢ Brown .... (8)	3.75	3.00	.35	.25	.15
218a	2¢ Booklet Pane of 4	...	...	60.00	45.00	...
218b	2¢ Booklet Pane of 6	...	...	21.50	16.00	...
219	3¢ Dark Carmine .... (8)	7.00	5.50	.50	.40	.15
219a	3¢ Booklet Pane of 4	...	...	20.00	15.00	...
220	4¢ Yellow .... (6)	35.00	27.50	2.50	1.75	.35
221	5¢ Blue .... (6)	35.00	27.50	2.50	1.70	.15
222	8¢ Deep Orange .... (6)	35.00	27.50	3.00	2.00	1.30
223	10¢ Mounted Police .... (6)	55.00	42.50	7.50	5.25	.15
224	13¢ Confederation Conf .... (6)	62.50	47.50	7.75	5.75	.50
225	20¢ Niagara Falls .... (6)	180.00	135.00	21.50	16.00	.35
226	50¢ Parliament, Victoria ..... (6)	235.00	175.00	27.50	20.00	3.25
227	$1 Champlain Monument ... (6)	575.00	425.00	75.00	55.00	7.75

1935 Coil Stamps, Perf. 8 Vertically VF + 25% (B)

228	1¢ George V, Green	...	...	15.00	9.75	1.75
229	2¢ Brown	...	...	12.00	7.50	.60
230	3¢ Dark Carmine	...	...	12.00	7.50	.35

231   237   241   244

1937 George VI VF + 25% (B)

231-36	Set of 6	...	...	8.95	6.50	.85
231	1¢ George VI, Green	2.25	1.85	.35	.25	.15
231a	1¢ Booklet Pane of 4	...	...	11.75	8.50	...
231b	1¢ Booklet Pane of 6	...	...	2.30	1.70	...
232	2¢ Brown	2.75	2.25	.45	.35	.15
232a	2¢ Booklet Pane of 4	...	...	15.00	10.75	...
232b	2¢ Booklet Pane of 6	...	...	8.75	6.50	...
233	3¢ Carmine	3.50	2.75	.60	.50	.15
233a	3¢ Booklet Pane of 6	...	...	2.75	2.10	...
234	4¢ Yellow	18.00	13.50	2.70	2.00	.20
235	5¢ Blue	18.00	13.50	3.00	2.25	.20
236	8¢ Orange	18.00	13.50	2.70	2.00	.30

1937 Coronation Issue VF + 25% (B)

237	3¢ George VI and Elizabeth ..	2.25	1.75	.25	.20	.20

CANADA

1937 Coil Stamps, Perf. 8 Vertically VF + 25% (B)

Scott's No.		Plate Blocks NH	Unused	F-VF NH	F-VF Unused	F-VF Used
238	1¢ George VI, Green	...	...	1.60	1.10	.70
239	2¢ Brown	...	...	2.25	1.60	.25
240	3¢ Carmine	...	...	4.25	2.90	.20

1938 Pictorials VF + 25%

241-45	Set of 5	...	...	115.00	79.50	7.95
241	10¢ Memorial Hall	35.00	27.50	5.50	4.25	.20
242	13¢ Halifax Harbor	35.00	25.00	7.50	5.25	.35
243	20¢ Ft. Garry Gate, Winnipeg	90.00	65.00	12.00	8.50	.25
244	50¢ Vancouver Harbor	175.00	120.00	24.50	16.50	3.25
245	$1 Chateau de Ramezay	400.00	275.00	72.50	50.00	4.75

1939 Royal Visit VF + 25%

246   247   248

246-48	Set of 3	3.65	2.90	.65	.50	.45
246	1¢ Elizabeth & Margaret Rose	1.65	1.35	.25	.20	.20
247	2¢ War Memorial, Ottawa	1.65	1.35	.25	.20	.20
248	3¢ George VI and Elizabeth ..	1.65	1.35	.25	.20	.20

1942-43 War Set VF +25%

249   250   257   262

249-62	Set of 14	...	...	127.50	90.00	10.75
249	1¢ George VI, Green	1.75	1.25	.30	.20	.15
249a	1¢ Booklet Pane of 4	...	...	7.00	5.25	...
249b	1¢ Booklet Pane of 6	...	...	1.50	1.10	...
249c	1¢ Booklet Pane of 3	...	...	1.65	1.25	...
250	2¢ Brown	2.35	1.75	.45	.35	.15
250a	2¢ Booklet Pane of 4	...	...	7.50	5.50	...
250b	2¢ Booklet Pane of 6	...	...	6.50	4.75	...
251	3¢ Dark Carmine	2.35	1.75	.40	.30	.15
251a	3¢ Booklet Pane of 4	...	...	1.95	1.40	...
252	3¢ Rose Violet (1943)	2.35	1.75	.40	.30	.15
252a	3¢ Booklet Pane of 4	...	...	1.85	1.35	...
252b	3¢ Booklet Pane of 3	...	...	3.35	2.50	...
252c	3¢ Booklet Pane of 6	...	...	3.50	2.50	...
253	4¢ Grain Elevators	8.50	6.25	1.25	.90	.55
254	4¢ George VI. Carm.(1943)	2.35	1.75	.40	.30	.15
254a	4¢ Booklet Pane of 6	...	...	2.25	1.50	...
254b	4¢ Booklet Pane of 3	...	...	3.00	2.25	...
255	5¢ George VI, Deep Blue ..	7.50	5.50	1.15	.90	.15
256	8¢ Farm Scene	12.50	9.00	1.60	1.10	.35
257	10¢ Parliament Buildings ...	25.00	17.50	4.00	2.75	.20
258	13¢ "Ram" Tank	27.50	20.00	4.75	3.50	2.75
259	14¢ "Ram" Tank (1943)	40.00	30.00	7.00	5.00	.25
260	20¢ Corvette	42.00	30.00	8.50	5.75	.20
261	50¢ Munitions Factory	175.00	120.00	36.50	25.00	1.65
262	$1 Destroyer	430.00	295.00	77.50	52.50	6.00

1942-43 Coil Stamps, Perf. 8 Vertically VF + 25%

263-67	Set of 5	...	...	10.00	6.85	2.25
263	1¢ George VI, Green	...	...	1.00	.70	.35
264	2¢ Brown	...	...	1.50	1.10	.80
265	3¢ Dark Carmine	...	...	1.50	1.10	.80
266	3¢ Rose Violet (1943)	...	...	2.60	1.75	.25
267	4¢ Dark Carmine (1943)	...	...	4.00	2.75	.20

1946 Reconversion "Peace" Issue VF + 25%

268   272   273

268-73	Set of 6	...	...	63.50	43.50	4.35
268	8¢ Farm Scene	7.75	6.00	1.35	1.00	.45
269	10¢ Great Bear Lake	8.25	6.50	1.75	1.30	.20
270	14¢ Hydroelectric Station ..	17.50	13.75	3.00	2.25	.20
271	20¢ Combine	22.00	16.50	3.75	2.75	.20
272	50¢ Logging	100.00	70.00	17.50	13.00	1.35
273	$1 Train Ferry	225.00	165.00	40.00	28.50	2.25

274   275   276   283

1947-48 Commemoratives

Scott's No.		Plate Blocks NH	F-VF NH	F-VF Used
274-77,282-83	Set of 6	...	.90	.70
274	4¢ Alexander Graham Bell	.85	.20	.15
275	4¢ Citizenship	.85	.20	.15
276	4¢ Royal Wedding (1948)	.85	.20	.15
277	4¢ Parliament (1948)	.75	.20	.15

1948 Coils, Perf. 9½ Vertically

278-81	Set of 4	...	27.00	11.00
278	1¢ George VI, Green		3.25	1.50
279	2¢ George VI, Brown		10.75	6.25
280	3¢ George VI, Rose Violet		6.00	1.85
281	4¢ George VI, Dark Carmine		8.50	2.25

1949 Commemoratives

282	4¢ Founding of Newfoundland	.95	.20	.15
283	4¢ Halifax Anniversary	.95	.20	.15

284   289   294   302

1949 George VI with "Postes-Postage" In Design

284-88	Set of 5	...	2.50	.55
284	1¢ George VI, Green	.85	.20	.15
284a	1¢ Book. Pane of 3 (1950)	...	1.40	...
285	2¢ Sepia	1.50	.30	.15
286	3¢ Rose Violet	1.70	.35	.15
286a	3¢ Book. Pane of 3 (1950)	...	1.65	...
286b	3¢ Booklet Pane of 4	...	1.75	...
287	4¢ Dark Carmine	2.50	.55	.15
287a	4¢ Book. Pane of 3 (1950)	...	12.50	...
287b	4¢ Book. Pane of 6 (1951)	...	14.00	...
288	5¢ Deep Blue	6.00	1.25	.15

1950 George VI without "Postes-Postage" In Design

289-93	Set of 5	...	2.15	1.25
289	1¢ George VI, Green	.65	.20	.15
290	2¢ Sepia	2.25	.40	.15
291	3¢ Rose Violet	1.20	.25	.15
292	4¢ Dark Carmine	1.50	.30	.15
293	5¢ Deep Blue	5.75	1.25	.85

1950 Regular Issue

294	50¢ Oil Wells, Alberta	55.00	11.75	1.20

1949-50 Coil Stamps, Perf. 9½ Vertically

295-300	Set of 6	...	16.75	2.95
	(without "Postes-Postage")			
295	1¢ George VI, Green	...	.60	.30
296	3¢ Rose Violet	...	.90	.50
	(with "Postes-Postage")			
297	1¢ George VI, Green (1950)	...	.35	.25
298	2¢ Sepia (1950)	...	2.50	1.35
299	3¢ Rose Violet (1950)	...	1.60	.20
300	4¢ Dark Carmine (1950)	...	12.50	.65

1950-1951 Regular Issue

301	10¢ Fur Resources	4.50	.85	.20
302	$1 Fishing (1951)	300.00	65.00	10.75

303   311   314   315

1951-52 Commemoratives

303-4,11-15,17-19	Set of 10		5.00	2.65

1951 Commemoratives

303	3¢ Robert L. Borden	1.40	.25	.15
304	4¢ William L. Mackenzie King	1.50	.25	.15

1951 Color Changes (with "Postes-Postage")

Scott's No.		Plate Blocks NH	F-VF NH	F-VF Used
305	2¢ George VI, Olive Green	.70	.20	.15
306	4¢ Orange Vermillion	1.10	.25	.15
306a	4¢ Booklet Pane of 3	...	2.75	...
306b	4¢ Booklet Pane of 6	...	3.00	...
309	2¢ Ol. Gr., Coil Pf. 9½ Vert	...	1.25	.60
310	4¢ Or. Verm., Coil Pf. 9½ Vert	...	2.75	.70

1951 Int'l. Philatelic Exhibition "CAPEX"

311-14	Set of 4	...	3.95	1.95
311	4¢ Trains of 1851 & 1951	2.30	.50	.20
312	5¢ Steamships	8.75	1.75	1.35
313	7¢ Plane & Stagecoach	5.00	1.00	.30
314	15¢ 1st Canada Stamp	5.75	1.00	.30

1951 Commemoratives

315	4¢ Royal Visit to Canada and U.S.	.95	.20	.15

316   317   320

1952 Regular Issue

316	20¢ Paper Industry	7.50	1.50	.20

1952 Commemoratives

317	4¢ Red Cross Conference	1.15	.20	.15
318	3¢ John J.C. Abbott	1.00	.20	.15
319	4¢ Alexander Mackenzie	1.25	.25	.15

1952-53 Regular Issues

320	7¢ Canada Goose	1.70	.35	.15
321	$1 Totem Pole (1953)	50.00	10.00	.80

322   327   330   334

1953-54 Commemoratives

322-24,35-36,49-50	Set of 7	...	1.35	.95

1953 Wildlife Commemoratives

322	2¢ Polar Bear	1.00	.20	.15
323	3¢ Moose	1.10	.20	.15
324	4¢ Bighorn Sheep	1.25	.20	.15

1953 Queen Elizabeth II Issue

325-29	Set of 5	...	.95	.60
325	1¢ Elizabeth II, Brown	.50	.20	.15
325a	1¢ Booklet Pane of 3	...	2.25	...
326	2¢ Green	.60	.20	.15
327	3¢ Carmine Rose	.75	.20	.15
327a	3¢ Booklet Pane of 3	...	2.00	...
327b	3¢ Booklet Pane of 4	...	1.25	...
328	4¢ Violet	1.15	.25	.15
328a	4¢ Booklet Pane of 3	...	2.25	...
328b	4¢ Booklet Pane of 6	...	1.75	...
329	5¢ Ultramarine	1.40	.30	.15

1953 Coronation Issue

330	4¢ Elizabeth II	.85	.20	.15

1953 Queen Elizabeth II Coils, Perf. 9½ Vertically

331	2¢ Elizabeth II, Green	...	1.35	.90
332	3¢ Carmine Rose	...	1.30	.90
333	4¢ Violet	...	2.95	1.40

1953 Regular Issue

334	50¢ Textile Industry	21.00	3.75	.20

336   339   349   351

1954 Wildlife Commemoratives

335	4¢ Walrus	1.40	.25	.15
336	5¢ Beaver	1.40	.25	.15
336a	5¢ Booklet Pane of 5	...	2.00	...

FROM 1947 TO PRESENT, ADD 20% FOR VERY FINE QUALITY
Minimum of 10¢ per stamp

1954 Queen Elizabeth II Issue

Scott's No.		Plate Blocks NH	F-VF NH	F-VF Used
337-43	Set of 7	...	2.25	.75
337	1¢ Elizabeth II, V. Brown	.50	.20	.15
337a	1¢ Booklet Pane of 5 (1956)	...	1.25	...
338	2¢ Green	.60	.20	.15
338a	2¢ Min. Pane of 25 (1961)	...	4.50	...
338a	Pack of 2	...	9.00	...
339	3¢ Carmine Rose	.75	.20	.15
340	4¢ Violet	.90	.20	.15
340a	4¢ Booklet Pane of 5 (1956)	...	1.75	...
340b	4¢ Booklet Pane of 6 (1955)	...	7.75	...
341	5¢ Bright Blue	1.10	.20	.15
341a	5¢ Booklet Pane of 5	...	1.65	...
341b	5¢ Min. Pane of 20 (1961)	...	8.75	...
342	6¢ Orange	1.70	.35	.15
343	15¢ Gannet, Gray	5.25	1.10	.15

1954 Elizabeth II Coil Stamps, Perf. 9½ Vertically

345	2¢ Elizabeth II, Green	...	.50	.20
347	4¢ Violet	...	1.50	.20
348	5¢ Bright Blue	...	2.25	.20

1954 Commemoratives

349	4¢ J.S.D. Thompson	1.40	.25	.15
350	5¢ M. Bowell	1.40	.25	.15

1955 Regular Issue

351	10¢ Eskimo in Kayak	1.70	.35	.15

352   356   359   360

1955 Commemoratives

352-58	Set of 7	...	1.90	.85
352	4¢ Wildlife - Musk Ox	1.40	.30	.15
353	5¢ Whooping Cranes	1.50	.30	.15
354	5¢ Civil Aviation Org	1.65	.30	.15
355	5¢ Alberta - Saskatchewan	1.65	.30	.15
356	5¢ Boy Scout Jamboree	1.65	.30	.15
357	4¢ Richard B. Bennett	1.50	.30	.15
358	5¢ Charles Tupper	1.50	.30	.15

1956 Commemoratives

359-61,364	Set of 4	...	1.05	.50
359	5¢ Ice Hockey	1.50	.30	.15
360	4¢ Wildlife - Caribou	1.60	.30	.15
361	5¢ Mountain Goat	1.60	.30	.15

362   364   370   374

1956 Regular Issues

362	20¢ Paper Industry	6.00	1.25	.15
363	25¢ Chemistry Industry	7.50	1.50	.15

1956 Commemoratives

364	5¢ Fire Prevention	1.25	.25	.15

1957 Commemoratives

365-74	Set of 10	...	4.15	2.75
365-68	5¢ Outdoor Recreation, attd	2.00	1.50	1.45
365-68	Set of 4 Singles	...	1.40	.80
369	5¢ Wildlife - Loon	1.40	.25	.15
370	5¢ David Thompson	1.40	.25	.15
371	5¢ U.P.U. - Parliament	1.40	.25	.15
372	15¢ U.P.U. - Post Horn	9.00	1.80	1.50
373	5¢ Mining Industry	1.25	.25	.15
374	5¢ Royal Visit	1.25	.25	.15

1958 Commemoratives

376   378   380   382

CANADA

Scott's No.		Plate Blocks NH	F-VF NH	F-VF Used
375-82	Set of 8	...	1.85	1.00
375	5¢ Newspaper Industry	(Blank) 2.50	.25	.15
376	5¢ Int'l. Geophysical Year	(Blank) 2.50	.25	.15
377	5¢ British Columbia Cent	2.25	.25	.15
378	5¢ Explorer La Verendrye	1.95	.25	.15
379	5¢ Quebec Anniversary	4.00	.25	.15
380	5¢ National Health	1.60	.25	.15
381	5¢ Petroleum Industry	1.60	.25	.15
382	5¢ 1st Elected Assembly	1.50	.25	.15

1959 Commemoratives

383   385   388

383-88	Set of 6	...	1.35	.75
383	5¢ Golden Anniv. of Flight	1.75	.25	.15
384	5¢ 10th Anniv. of N.A.T.O.	1.60	.25	.15
385	5¢ Country Women of the World	1.40	.25	.15
386	5¢ Royal Tour	1.40	.25	.15
387	5¢ St. Lawrence Seaway	4.25	.25	.15
388	5¢ Plains of Abraham	1.40	.25	.15

1960-1961 Commemoratives

390   391   393   395

389-95	Set of 7	...	1.60	.85
389	5¢ Girl Guides Association	1.40	.25	.15
390	5¢ Battle of Long Sault	1.40	.25	.15
391	5¢ Northland Development (1961)	1.40	.25	.15
392	5¢ E. Pauline Johnson (1961)	1.40	.25	.15
393	5¢ P. Minister A. Meighen (1961)	1.40	.25	.15
394	5¢ Colombo Plan (1961)	1.40	.25	.15
395	5¢ Resources for Tomorrow (1961)	1.40	.25	.15

396   398   400   402

1962 Commemoratives

396-400	Set of 5	...	1.10	.65
396	5¢ Education	1.40	.25	.15
397	5¢ Red River Settlement, Lord Selkirk ...	1.40	.25	.15
398	5¢ Jean Talon	1.40	.25	.15
399	5¢ Victoria B.C. Centenary	1.40	.25	.15
400	5¢ Trans-Canadian Highway	1.40	.25	.15

1962-63 Queen Elizabeth "Cameo" Issue

401-05	Set of 5	...	.85	.60
401	1¢ Deep Brown (1963)	.50	.20	.15
401a	1¢ Booklet Pane of 5	...	3.75	...
402	2¢ Green (1963)	2.95	.20	.15
402a	2¢ Miniature Pane of 25 .... (pack of 2)	17.50	8.75	...
403	3¢ Purple (1963)	.70	.20	.15
404	4¢ Carmine (1963)	.90	.20	.15
404a	4¢ Booklet Pane of 5	...	3.50	...
404b	4¢ Miniature Pane of 25	...	9.75	...
405	5¢ Violet Blue	1.10	.20	.15
405a	5¢ Booklet Pane of 5 (1963)	...	5.25	...
405b	5¢ Miniature Pane of 20 (1963)	...	12.75	...

1962-63 Coil Stamps, Perf. 9½ Horizontally

406-9	Set of 4	...	14.50	4.85
406	2¢ Elizabeth, Green (1963)	...	4.25	1.75
407	3¢ Purple (1963)	...	2.75	1.35
408	4¢ Carmine (1963)	...	4.25	1.50
409	5¢ Violet Blue	...	4.25	.60

| 410 | 411 | 412 |

1963 Commemoratives

Scott's No.		Plate Block	F-VF NH	F-VF Used
410,412-13	Set of 3	...	.70	.35
410	5¢ Sir Casimir S. Gzowski	1.20	.25	.15

1963 Regular Issues

411	$1 Export Trade, Crate & Map	65.00	13.00	2.00

1963 Commemoratives

412	5¢ Explorer M. Frobisher	1.15	.25	.15
413	5¢ First Post Route	1.15	.25	.15

1963-1964 Regular Issues

414	7¢ Jet at Ottawa Airport (1964)	1.65	.35	.35
415	15¢ Canada Geese (1963)	9.75	1.95	.15

1964 Commemoratives

416,431-35	Set of 6	...	1.25	.75
416	5¢ "Peace on Earth"	1.15	.25	.15

| 418 | 431 | 433 |

1964-1966 Coat of Arms & Flowers

417-29A	Set of 14	14.75	2.75	1.75
417	5¢ Canadian Unity, Maple Leaf	1.00	.20	.15
418	5¢ Ontario, White Trillium	1.00	.20	.15
419	5¢ Quebec, White Garden Lily	1.00	.20	.15
420	5¢ Nova Scotia, Mayflower/1965	1.00	.20	.15
421	5¢ New Brunswick, Purple Violet ('65) ..	1.00	.20	.15
422	5¢ Manitoba, Prairie Crocus ('65)	1.75	.20	.15
423	5¢ British Columbia, Dogwood ('65)	1.00	.20	.15
424	5¢ Pr. Edward I., Lady's Slipper ('65) ..	1.00	.20	.15
425	5¢ Saskatchewan, Prairie Lily ('66)	1.00	.20	.15
426	5¢ Alberta, Wild Rose ('66)	1.00	.20	.15
427	5¢ Newfoundland, Pitcher Plant ('66)	1.75	.20	.15
428	5¢ Yukon, Firewood ('66)	1.00	.20	.15
429	5¢ Northwest Terr., Mountain Avens ('66) ..	1.00	.20	.15
429A	5¢ Canada, Maple Leaf ('66)	1.00	.20	.15

1964 Regular Issue

430	8¢ on 7¢ Jet Aircraft (on #414)	(Blank) 1.65	.35	.30

1964 Commemoratives

431	5¢ Charlottestown Conference	1.15	.25	.15
432	5¢ Quebec Conference	1.00	.20	.15
433	5¢ Queen Elizabeth Visit	1.00	.20	.15
434	3¢ Christmas, Family & Star	.75	.20	.15
434a	3¢ Miniature Pane of 25 ...... (pack of 2)	16.00	8.00	...
435	5¢ Christmas, Family & Star	1.15	.20	.15

1964 Regular Issue

436	8¢ Jet at Ottawa Airport	1.75	.35	.20

1965 Commemoratives

| 438 | 440 | 441 | 443 |

437-44	Set of 8	...	1.50	1.00
437	5¢ International Cooperation Year	.90	.20	.15
438	5¢ Sir Wilfred Grenfell	.90	.20	.15
439	5¢ National Flag	.90	.20	.15
440	5¢ Sir Winston Churchill	.90	.20	.15
441	5¢ Interparliamentary Union	.90	.20	.15
442	5¢ Ottawa Centennial	.90	.20	.15
443	3¢ Christmas, Gifts of Wise Men	.70	.20	.15
443a	3¢ Miniature Pane of 25 .... (pack of 2)	14.00	7.00	...
444	5¢ Christmas, Gifts of Wise Men	1.25	.20	.15

1966 Commemoratives

| 445 | 448 | 450 | 451 |

Scott's No.		Plate Block	F-VF NH	F-VF Used
445-52	Set of 8	...	1.50	1.00
445	5¢ Satellite Alouette II	1.00	.20	.15
446	5¢ LaSalle Arrival Tercentary	1.00	.20	.15
447	5¢ Highway Safety	1.00	.20	.15
448	5¢ London Conf. Centenary	1.00	.20	.15
449	5¢ Atomic Energy	1.00	.20	.15
450	5¢ Parliamentary Association	1.00	.20	.15
451	3¢ Christmas, Praying Hands	.70	.20	.15
451a	3¢ Miniature Pane of 25 .... (pack of 2)	7.50	3.75	...
452	5¢ Christmas, Praying Hands	1.00	.20	.15

1967 Commemoratives

453,469-77	Set of 10		1.90	1.30
453	5¢ Canadian Centenary	1.00	.20	.15

1967-72 Centennial Regular Issue, Perf. 12

| 459,460 | 465A | 465B |

454-65B	Set of 14	...	14.95	2.40
454	1¢ Elizabeth & Dog Team, Brown	.70	.20	.15
454a	1¢ Booklet Pane of 5	...	1.25	...
454b	B. Pane of 5 (1 #454 & 4 #459), Perf. 10(1968)	...	3.50	...
454c	B. Pane of 10 (5 #454 & 5 #457) Perf.10(1968)	...	2.50	...
454d	1¢ Booklet Single, Perf. 10 (1968)	...	.35	.20
454e	1¢ Booklet Single, Perf. 12½ x 12 (1969)	...	.65	.20
455	2¢ Elizabeth & Totem Pole, Green	.75	.20	.15
455a	B. Pane of 8 (4 #455, 4 #456)	...	1.90	...
456	3¢ Elizabeth & Combine, Purple	1.50	.20	.15
456a	3¢ Booklet Single, Perf. 12½ x 12 (1971)	...	4.50	2.00
457	4¢ Elizabeth & Seaway Lock, Carmine ..	1.50	.20	.15
457a	4¢ Booklet Pane of 5	...	1.75	...
457b	4¢ Miniature Pane of 25	...	25.00	...
457c	4¢ B. Pane of 25, Perf. 10 (1968)	...	9.50	...
457d	4¢ Booklet Single, Perf. 10(1968)	...	.70	.25
458	5¢ Elizabeth & Fishing Port, Blue	1.25	.20	.15
458a	5¢ Booklet Pane of 5	...	7.95	...
458b	5¢ Miniature Pane of 20	...	32.50	...
458c	5¢ B. Pane of 20, Perf. 10 (1968)	...	8.25	...
458d	5¢ Booklet Single, Perf. 10 (1968)	...	.65	.25
459	6¢ Elizabeth & Trans, Orange, Perf. 10 (1968)	3.50	.35	.15
459a	6¢ Booklet Pane of 25, Perf. 10 (1968)..	...	10.75	...
459b	6¢ Orange, Perf. 12½ x 12 (1968)	2.75	.30	.15
460	6¢ Black, Die I, Perf. 12½ x 12 (1970) ...	1.75	.20	.15
460a	6¢ Die I, B. Pane of 25, Perf. 10 (1970) .	...	13.50	...
460g	6¢ Die I, Booklet Single, Perf. 10 (1970)	...	1.80	.35
460b	6¢ Die I, B.Pane of 25, Perf. 12½x12 (1970)	...	19.50	...
460c	6¢ Black, Die II. Perf. 12½ x 12 (1970)	2.00	.25	.15
460d	6¢ Die II, B. Pane of 4, Perf. 12½ x 12 (1970)	...	4.50	...
460e	6¢ Die II, B. Pane of 4, Perf. 10 (1970) ..	...	11.75	...
460h	6¢ Die II, Booklet Single, Perf. 10	...	5.00	3.75
460f	6¢ Die II, Perf. 12 (1973)	3.25	.65	.60

#460 Die I has weak shading lines around "6"; #460c Die II has lines strengthened.

461	8¢ "Alaska Highway"	3.00	.30	.20
462	10¢ "The Jack Pine"	1.65	.30	.20
463	15¢ "Bylot Island"	2.75	.40	.20
464	20¢ "The Ferry, Quebec"	3.25	.55	.20
465	25¢ "The Solemn Land"	5.75	1.00	.20
465A	50¢ "Summer's Stores"	16.50	3.50	.20
465B	$1 "Oilfield, Edmonton"	40.75	8.25	.50

1967-70 Coil Stamps, Perf. 9½ or 10 Horiz.

466-68B	Set of 5	...	4.15	2.85
466	3¢ Elizabeth & Oil Rig	...	1.50	1.25
467	4¢ Elizabeth & Canal Lock	...	.80	.70
468	5¢ Elizabeth & Fishing Port	...	1.50	.80
468A	6¢ Elizabeth, Orange (1969)	...	.30	.15
468B	6¢ Elizabeth, Black (1970)	...	.30	.15

1967 Commemoratives (See also #453)

| 469 | 471 | 473 |

1967 Commemoratives (continued)

Scott's No.		Plate Block	F-VF NH	F-VF Used
469	5¢ Expo '67, Montreal	1.00	.20	.15
470	5¢ Women's Franchise	1.00	.20	.15
471	5¢ Royal Visit, Elizabeth II	1.00	.20	.15
472	5¢ Pan American Games	1.00	.20	.15
473	5¢ Canadian Press	1.00	.20	.15
474	5¢ Georges P. Vanier	1.00	.20	.15
475	5¢ Toronto Centennial	1.00	.20	.15
476	3¢ Christmas, Singing Children	.80	.20	.15
476a	3¢ Miniature Pane of 25 (pack of 2)	7.50	3.75	...
477	5¢ Christmas, Singing Children	.85	.20	.15

1968 Commemoratives

479   485   486   488

478-89	Set of 12	...	3.95	2.50
478	5¢ Wildlife - Gray Jays	3.75	.40	.15
479	5¢ Meteorological Readings	1.00	.20	.15
480	5¢ Wildlife - Narwhal	1.00	.20	.15
481	5¢ Int'l. Hydrological Decade	1.00	.20	.15
482	5¢ Voyage of "Nonsuch"	1.25	.25	.20
483	5¢ Lacrosse Players	1.25	.25	.20
484	5¢ George Brown and "Globe"	1.25	.25	.20
485	5¢ Henry Bourassa - Journalist	1.15	.20	.15
486	15¢ World War I Armistice	8.00	1.65	1.20
487	5¢ John McCrae - Poet	1.15	.20	.15
488	5¢ Christmas - Eskimo Carving	.75	.20	.15
488a	5¢ Booklet Pane of 10	...	3.25	...
489	6¢ Christmas - Mother & Infant	1.00	.20	.15

1969 Commemoratives

493   496   498

490-504	Set of 15	...	9.75	6.85
490	6¢ Sports - Curling	1.25	.25	.15
491	6¢ Vincent Massey	1.00	.20	.15
492	50¢ Aurele de Fey Suzor-Cote	16.00	3.25	2.25
493	6¢ Int'l. Labor Organization	1.25	.25	.15
494	15¢ Non-Stop Atlantic Flight	8.75	1.85	1.50
495	6¢ Sir William Osler	1.25	.25	.15
#496-98	Canadian Birds			
496	6¢ White-Throated Sparrow	1.65	.35	.20
497	10¢ Ipswich Sparrow	3.25	.70	.45
498	25¢ Hermit Thrush	8.50	1.75	1.50
499	6¢ Charlottetown Bicentennial	1.25	.25	.15
500	6¢ Canada Summer Games	1.00	.20	.15
501	6¢ Sir Isaac Brock	1.00	.20	.15
502	5¢ Christmas, Children Praying	.85	.20	.15
502a	5¢ Booklet Pane of 10	...	3.50	...
503	6¢ Christmas, Children Praying	.85	.20	.15
504	6¢ Stephen Leacock	1.25	.25	.15

NOTE: STARTING IN 1967, MANY PLATE BLOCKS HAVE IMPRINTS WITHOUT PLATE NUMBERS.

1970 Commemoratives

505   507   513

505-18,531	Set of 15	...	11.50	9.75
505	6¢ Manitoba Centenary	.95	.20	.15
506	6¢ Northwest Territory	.90	.20	.15
507	6¢ Biological Program	1.15	.25	.15
508-11	25¢ Expo '70, Osaka, Japan, attd	9.50	8.50	8.50
508-11	Set of 4 Singles	...	7.75	7.75
512	6¢ Henry Kelsey - Explorer	1.15	.25	.15

1970 Commemoratives (continued)

Scott's No.		Plate Block	F-VF NH	F-VF Used
513	10¢ 25th Anniv. of United Nations	2.95	.60	.50
514	15¢ 25th Anniv. of United Nations	4.50	.90	.70
515	6¢ Louis Riel, Metis Leader	1.15	.25	.15
516	6¢ Sir A. Mackenzie - Explorer	.90	.20	.15
517	6¢ Sir Oliver Mowat	1.15	.25	.15
518	6¢ Group of Seven	.95	.20	.15

Note: Prices are for stamps without straight edges.

1970 Christmas - Children's Designs

529   530   531

519-30	Set of 12 Singles	...	4.35	2.40
519-23	5¢ Christmas, attached	(10) 6.75	2.75	2.50
519-23	Set of 5 Singles		1.50	.75
524-28	6¢ Christmas, attached	(10) 7.25	3.00	2.75
524-28	Set of 5 Singles		1.95	.75
529	10¢ Christ Child in Manger	1.95	.40	.30
530	15¢ Snowmobile & Trees	3.85	.75	.75

1970 Commemoratives (continued)

531	6¢ Donald Alexander Smith	.90	.20	.15

532   533   535   539

1971 Commemoratives

532-42,552-58	Set of 18	...	5.50	3.95
532	6¢ Emily Carr - Painter	.85	.20	.15
533	6¢ Discovery of Insulin	.85	.20	.15
534	6¢ Sir Ernest Rutherford	.85	.20	.15
535	6¢ Maple Leaf - Spring	1.15	.25	.15
536	6¢ Maple Leaf - Summer	1.15	.25	.15
537	7¢ Maple Leaf - Autumn	1.15	.25	.15
538	7¢ Maple Leaf - Winter	1.15	.25	.15
539	6¢ Louis Papineau	.85	.20	.15
540	6¢ Samuel Hearne	.85	.20	.15
541	15¢ Radio Canada Int'l	7.00	1.50	1.10
542	6¢ Census Centennial	.85	.20	.15

1971-72 Regular Issue

543	7¢ Elizabeth & Transportation, Green	3.00	.25	.15
543a	B. Pane of 5 (1 #454,1 #456,3 #543)	...	5.95	...
543b	B. Pane of 20 (4 #454,4 #456,12 #543)	...	11.00	...
544	8¢ Elizabeth & Parliament, Slate	2.50	.20	.15
544a	B. Pane of 6 (3 #454,1 #460c,2 #544)	...	1.80	...
544b	B. Pane of 18 (6 #454,1 #460c,11 #544)	...	7.25	...
544c	B. Pane of 10 (4 #454,1 #460c,5 #544) (1972)	...	2.50	...
549	7¢ Green, Coil, Perf. 10 Horiz	...	.35	.15
550	8¢ Slate, Coil, Perf. 10 Horiz	...	.45	.15

1971 Commemoratives (continued)

552   556   561

552	7¢ British Columbia Centenary	.85	.20	.15
553	7¢ Paul Kane - Painter	2.50	.35	.20
554	6¢ Christmas, Snowflake	.85	.20	.15
555	7¢ Christmas, Snowflake	1.00	.20	.15
556	10¢ Christmas, Snowflake	1.60	.35	.30
557	15¢ Christmas, Snowflake	3.00	.65	.60
558	7¢ Pierre Laporte	2.25	.25	.15

1972 Commemoratives

559-61,582-85,606-10	Set of 12	...	9.95	8.75
559	8¢ Figure Skating	1.15	.25	.15
560	8¢ World Health Day	1.40	.30	.15
561	8¢ Frontenac Anniversary	1.15	.25	.15

CANADA

1972-76 Canadian Indians

564-65   568-69

1972-76 Canadian Indians (continued)

Scott's No.		Plate Block	F-VF NH	F-VF Used
1972 Indians of the Plains				
562-63	8¢ Plains Indians, attached	1.65	.65	.60
562-63	Set of 2 Singles, Horizontal Design	...	.60	.30
564-65	8¢ Plains Indians, attached	1.65	.65	.60
564-65	Set of 2 Singles, Vertical Design	...	.60	.30
1973 Algonkian Indians				
566-67	8¢ Algonkians, attached	1.65	.65	.60
566-67	Set of 2 Singles, Horizontal Design	...	.60	.30
568-69	8¢ Algonkians, attached	1.65	.65	.60
568-69	Set of 2 Singles, Vertical Design	...	.60	.30
1974 Pacific Coast Indians				
570-71	8¢ Pacific Indians, attached	1.50	.60	.55
570-71	Set of 2 Singles, Horizontal Design	...	.55	.30
572-73	8¢ Pacific Indians, attached	1.50	.60	.55
572-73	Set of 2 Singles, Vertical Design	...	.55	.30

576-77   580-81

1975 Subarctic Indians				
574-75	8¢ Subarctic, attached	1.20	.50	.45
574-75	Set of 2 Singles, Horizontal Design	...	.45	.30
576-77	8¢ Subarctic, attached	1.20	.50	.45
576-77	Set of 2 Singles, Vertical Design	...	.45	.30
1976 Iroquois Indians				
578-79	10¢ Iroquois, attached	1.20	.50	.45
578-79	Set of 2 Singles, Horizontal Design	...	.45	.30
580-81	10¢ Iroquois, attached	1.20	.50	.45
580-81	Set of 2 Singles, Vertical Design	...	.45	.30
562-81	**Canadian Indians, set of 20**	...	5.15	2.65
1972 Earth Sciences				
582-85	15¢ Sciences, attached (16)	33.50	8.00	7.75
582-85	Set of 4 Singles		7.50	7.25

1972-1977 Regular Issue, Perf. 12 x 12½ or 12½ x 12

586    591    593   599

586-601	**Set of 17**	...	16.00	5.75
#586-92 Famous People				
586	1¢ Sir John A. MacDonald	.40	.20	.15
586a	B. Pane of 6 (3 #586,1 #591,2 #593) ('74)	...	1.20	...
586b	B. Pane of 18 (6 #586,1 #591,11 #593)('75)	...	3.25	...
586c	B. Pane of 10 (2 #586,4 #587,4 #593c)('76)	...	1.40	...
587	2¢ Sir Wilfred Laurier ('73)	.50	.20	.15
588	3¢ Sir Robert L. Borden ('73)	.50	.20	.15
589	4¢ W.L. Mackenzie King ('73)	.60	.20	.15
590	5¢ Richard B. Bennett ('73)	.80	.20	.15
591	6¢ Lester B. Pearson ('73)	.80	.20	.15
592	7¢ Louis St. Laurent ('74)	.90	.20	.15
593	8¢ Queen Elizabeth II, Perf. 12 x 12½ ('73)	1.00	.20	.15
593b	8¢ Queen Elizabeth II, Perf. 13 x 13½ ('76)	4.95	.95	.75
593A	10¢ Queen Elizabeth II, Perf. 13 x 13½ ('76)	1.20	.25	.15
593Ac	10¢ Booklet Single, Perf. 12 x 12½ ('76)	...	.45	.25
#594-601 Scenic Pictorials				

CANADA

1972 Commemoratives (continued)

Scott's No.		Plate Block	F-VF NH	F-VF Used
594	10¢ Forests, Tagged, Narrow Side Bars	1.40	.30	.15
594a	10¢ Redrawn, Perf. 13½ ('76)	1.50	.30	.15
595	15¢ Mountain Sheep, Tagged Narrow Bars	1.60	.35	.15
595a	15¢ Redrawn, Perf. 13½ ('76)	2.15	.50	.15
596	20¢ Prairie Mosaic, Tagged Narrow Bars	2.10	.45	.15
596a	20¢ Redrawn, Perf. 13½ ('76)	2.40	.50	.15
597	25¢ Polar Bears, Tagged Narrow Bars	2.70	.55	.15
597a	25¢ Redrawn, Perf. 13½ ('76)	3.00	.65	.15
598	50¢ Seashore	5.00	1.10	.15
598a	50¢ Redrawn, Perf. 13½ ('76)	8.00	1.70	.20
599	$1 Vancouver, Revised ('73)	13.50	2.50	.45
599a	$1 Redrawn, Perf. 13½ ('77)	12.50	2.50	.30
600	$1 Vancouver, Original, Perf. 11	25.00	5.50	1.75
601	$2 Quebec Buildings, Perf. 11	21.00	4.50	2.25
604	8¢ Elizabeth II, Coil, Perf. 10 Vert (1974)	...	.25	.15
605	10¢ Elizabeth II, Coil, Perf. 10 Vert(1976)	...	.30	.15

606   608   610

606	6¢ Christmas, Candles	.90	.20	.15
607	8¢ Christmas, Candles	1.00	.20	.15
608	10¢ Christmas, Candles & Fruit	2.15	.45	.35
609	15¢ Christmas, Candles & Prayer Book	3.25	.70	.70
610	8¢ C. Krieghoff, Painter	1.80	.25	.15

1973 Commemoratives

615   616   617

611-28	**Set of 18**	...	5.15	4.25
611	8¢ Monsignor de Laval	.90	.20	.15
612	8¢ Mounties - G.A. French	.95	.20	.15
613	10¢ Mounties - Spectograph	1.60	.35	.35
614	15¢ Mounties - Municipal Rider	3.15	.65	.60
615	8¢ Jeanne Mance - Nurse	.90	.20	.15
616	8¢ Joseph Howe - Journalist	.90	.20	.15
617	15¢ J.E.H. MacDonald - Painter	2.50	.50	.45
618	8¢ Prince Edward I Centenary	.90	.20	.15
619	8¢ Scottish Settlers Bicentenary	.90	.20	.15
620	8¢ Royal Visit, Elizabeth II	.90	.20	.15
621	15¢ Royal Visit, Elizabeth II	2.75	.60	.50
622	8¢ Nellie McClung, Suffragette	.90	.20	.15
623	8¢ 21st Olympics Publicity	.90	.20	.15
624	15¢ 21st Olympics Publicity	2.25	.50	.45
625	6¢ Christmas - Ice Skate	.70	.20	.15
626	8¢ Christmas - Dove	.90	.20	.15
627	10¢ Christmas - Santa Claus	1.25	.25	.25
628	15¢ Christmas - Shepherd and Star	2.25	.50	.50

NOTE: STARTING IN 1973, ALL CANADIAN STAMPS ARE TAGGED.

1974 Commemoratives

655   644   645
                646   647

CANADA

1974 Commemoratives

Scott's No.		Plate Block	F-VF NH	F-VF Used
629-55	**Set of 27**	...	**8.85**	**5.65**
629-32	8¢ Summer Olympics, attd	1.50	1.25	.95
629-32	Set of 4 Singles	...	1.20	.70
633	8¢ Winnipeg Centenary	.90	.20	.15
634-39	8¢ Letter Carriers, attached (6)	4.00	3.25	3.25
634-39	Set of 6 Singles	...	2.25	2.00
640	8¢ Agriculture Education	.90	.20	.15
641	8¢ Telephone Centenary	.90	.20	.15
642	8¢ World Cycling Champs	.90	.20	.15
643	8¢ Mennonite Settlement	.90	.20	.15
644-47	8¢ Winter Olympics, attached	1.50	1.25	.95
644-47	Set of 4 Singles	...	1.20	.70
648	8¢ Universal Postal Union	.90	.20	.15
649	15¢ Universal Postal Union	3.50	.75	.65
650	6¢ Christmas "Nativity"	.70	.20	.15
651	8¢ Christmas "Skaters in Hull"	.85	.20	.15
652	10¢ Christmas "The Ice Cone"	1.45	.30	.25
653	15¢ Christmas "Village"	2.75	.55	.50
654	8¢ Marconi Centenary	.90	.20	.15
655	8¢ William H. Merritt, Welland Canal ...	.90	.20	.15

1975 Commemoratives

657

658-59

664

680

Scott's No.		Plate Block	F-VF NH	F-VF Used
656-80	**Set of 25**	...	**15.50**	**10.95**
656	$1 Olympics "The Sprinter"	12.00	2.50	2.10
657	$2 Olympics "The Plunger"	23.00	5.00	4.50
658-59	8¢ Writers,Montgomery,Hemon attached	1.10	.45	.35
658-59	Set of 2 Singles	...	.40	.30
660	8¢ Marguerite Bourgeoys	.90	.20	.15
661	8¢ Alphonse Desjardins	.90	.20	.15
662-63	8¢ Religious Leaders,Chown,Cook att ..	1.10	.45	.40
662-63	Set of 2 Singles	...	.40	.35
664	20¢ Olympics - Pole Vaulting	2.75	.55	.50
665	25¢ Olympics - Marathon Running	3.15	.65	.55
666	50¢ Olympics - Hurdling	5.50	1.25	1.00
667	8¢ Calgary Centennial "Untamed"	1.00	.20	.15
668	8¢ Women's Year	1.00	.20	.15
669	8¢ Supreme Court Centenary	1.00	.20	.15
670-73	8¢ Canadian Coastal Ships, attached ...	2.25	1.80	1.70
670-73	Set of 4 Singles	...	1.75	1.20
674-75	6¢ Christmas, attached	.85	.45	.35
674-75	Set of 2 Singles	...	.40	.30
676-77	8¢ Christmas, attached	1.00	.45	.35
676-77	Set of 2 Singles	...	.40	.30
678	10¢ Christmas, Gift Box	1.20	.25	.25
679	15¢ Christmas, Tree	1.85	.40	.40
680	8¢ Royal Canadian Legion	1.00	.20	.15

1976 Commemoratives

684

692-93

CANADA

1976 Commemoratives (continued)

687

Scott's No.		Plate Block	F-VF NH	F-VF Used
681-703	**Set of 23**	...	**17.50**	**13.75**
681	8¢ Olympic Torch	.95	.20	.15
682	20¢ Olympic Opening Ceremonies	2.75	.60	.50
683	25¢ Olympic Medal Ceremonies	3.50	.75	.70
684	20¢ Olympics - Communication Arts ...	5.00	1.10	.65
685	25¢ Olympics - Handcraft Tools	5.75	1.20	.70
686	50¢ Olympics - Performing Arts	9.00	2.00	1.20
687	$1 Olympic Site - Tower and Church ...	12.00	2.50	2.35
688	$2 Olympic Site - Olympic Stadium	26.50	5.75	4.75
689	20¢ Winter Olympic Games	3.35	.75	.65
690	20¢ HABITAT - U.N. Conference	2.00	.45	.45
691	10¢ U.S. Bicentennial - B. Franklin	1.40	.30	.20
692-93	8¢ Royal Military College, attd.	1.00	.45	.40
692-93	Set of 2 Singles	...	.40	.30
694	20¢ Olympiad for Physically Disabled .	2.85	.60	.55
695-96	8¢ Authors,R. Service, G. Guevremont att	1.00	.45	.35
695-96	Set of 2 Singles	...	.40	.30
697	8¢ Xmas - Stained Glass Window	.75	.20	.15
698	10¢ Xmas - Stained Glass Window	1.10	.25	.15
699	20¢ Xmas - Stained Glass Window	2.15	.45	.40
700-03	10¢ Canadian Inland Ships, attached ..	1.60	1.25	1.25
700-03	Set of 4 Singles	...	1.20	1.10

1977 Commemoratives

704,732-51	**Set of 21**	...	**5.95**	**3.95**
704	25¢ Queen Elizabeth II Silver Jubilee ..	2.75	.60	.50

1977-1979 Definitive Issues, Perf. 12 x 12½

Scott's No.		Plate Block	F-VF NH	F-VF Used
705-27	**Set of 22**	...	**14.75**	**5.25**
705	1¢ Wildflower - Bottle Gentian	.40	.20	.15
707	2¢ Wildflower - W. Columbine	.45	.20	.15
708	3¢ Wildflower - Canada Lily	.50	.20	.15
709	4¢ Wildflower - Hepatica	.50	.20	.15
710	5¢ Wildflower - Shooting Star	.60	.20	.15
711	10¢ Wildflower - Lady's Slipper	1.10	.25	.15
711a	10¢ Same (1978), Perf. 13)	1.10	.25	.15
712	12¢ Wildflower - Jewelweed, Pf. 13 x 13½ (1978)	1.50	.30	.20
713	12¢ Elizabeth II, Perf. 13 x 13½	1.20	.25	.15
713a	12¢ Booklet Single., Perf. 12 x 12½	...	.35	.25
714	12¢ Houses of Parliament, Perf. 13 ('78)	1.20	.25	.15
715	14¢ Houses of Parliament, Perf. 13 ('78)	1.40	.30	.15
716	14¢ Eliz. II, 13 x 13½ ('78)	1.40	.30	.15
716a	14¢ Bklt. Sgl., Perf. 12 x 12½ ('78)	...	.40	.15
716b	14¢ B. Pane of 25, Perf. 12 x 12½ ('78)	...	6.50	...
717	15¢ Tree - Trembling Aspen, Perf. 13½ .	1.85	.40	.15
718	20¢ Tree - Doug. Fir, Perf. 13½	1.85	.40	.15
719	25¢ Trees - Sugar Maple, Perf. 13½	2.25	.50	.15
720	30¢ Trees - Red Oak, Perf. 13½ ('78) ..	2.75	.60	.20
721	35¢ Trees - Winter Pine, Perf. 13½ ('79)	3.25	.70	.25
723	50¢ Streets-Prairie Town, Perf.13½ ('78)	5.25	1.15	.25
723A	50¢ Same, "1978" on License Plate	4.75	1.00	.20
724	75¢ Streets-Row Houses, Perf.13½ ('78)	7.00	1.50	.40
725	80¢ Streets-Maritime, Perf. 13½ ('79) ..	7.00	1.50	.45
726	$1 Bay of Fundy, Perf. 13½ ('79)	8.75	1.95	.50
726a	$1 Untagged(1981)	9.00	2.00	.65
727	$2 Kluane National Park, Perf.13½ ('79)	18.00	3.95	1.10
729	12¢ Parliament, Coil, Perf. 10 Vert	...	.25	.15
730	14¢ Parliament, Coil, Perf. 10 Vert. ('78)	...	.30	.15

NOTE: Also see #781-806

1977 Commemoratives (continued)

704

733-34

736

738-39

732	12¢ Wildlife - Eastern Cougar	1.20	.25	.15
733-34	12¢ Thomson Paintings, attd	1.20	.50	.40
733-34	Set of 2 Singles	...	.50	.30
735	12¢ Canadian-born Gov. Generals	1.20	.25	.15

1977 Commemoratives (continued)

Scott's No.		Plate Block	F-VF NH	F-VF Used
736	12¢ Order of Canada 10th Anniv	1.20	.25	.15
737	12¢ Peace Bridge - 50th Anniv	1.20	.25	.15
738-39	12¢ Pioneers,Bernier,Fleming att	1.20	.50	.40
738-39	Set of 2 Singles	...	.50	.30
740	25¢ Parliamentary Conference	3.00	.65	.65
741	10¢ Christmas - Christmas Star	.95	.20	.15
742	12¢ Christmas - Angelic Choir	1.20	.25	.15
743	25¢ Christmas - Christ Child	2.40	.50	.40
744-47	12¢ Sailing Ships, attached	1.20	1.00	.90
744-47	Set of 4 Singles	...	.95	.75
748-49	12¢ Inuit Hunting, attached	1.20	.50	.40
748-49	Set of 2 Singles, Seal, Spear Fishing ..	...	.50	.30
750-51	12¢ Inuit Hunting, attached	1.20	.50	.40
750-51	Set of 2 Singles, Caribou, Walrus	...	.50	.30

1978 Commemoratives

Scott's No.		Plate Block	F-VF NH	F-VF Used
752-56,757-79	**Set of 28**	...	**11.25**	**6.75**
752	12¢ Peregrine Falcon	1.20	.25	.15
753-56	12¢ -$1.25 Capex, Set of 4	16.50	3.50	1.75
753	12¢ CAPEX, 12p Queen Victoria	1.20	.25	.15
754	14¢ CAPEX, 10p Cartier	1.40	.30	.15
755	30¢ CAPEX, ½p Queen Victoria	2.75	.60	.40
756	$1.25 CAPEX, 6p Prince Albert	11.50	2.50	1.10
756a	$1.69 CAPEX Souvenir Sheet	...	3.25	3.15
757	14¢ Commonwealth Games, Symbol ..	1.40	.30	.15
758	30¢ Commonwealth Games, Badminton	2.75	.60	.40
759-60	14¢ Commonwealth Games, attd	1.35	.60	.40
759-60	Set of 2 Singles, Stadium,Running	...	.55	.30
761-62	30¢ Commonwealth Games, attd	2.75	1.25	1.25
761-62	Set of 2 Singles, Edmonton, Bowls	...	1.20	1.10
763-64	14¢ Captain Cook, attached	1.35	.60	.40
763-64	Set of 2 Singles	...	.55	.30
765-66	14¢ Resource Development, attd	1.35	.60	.40
765-66	Set of 2 Singles	...	.55	.30
767	14¢ Canadian National Exhibition	1.35	.30	.15
768	14¢ Mere d'Youville, Beatified	1.35	.30	.15

769-70

Scott's No.		Plate Block	F-VF NH	F-VF Used
769-70	14¢ Travels of Inuit, attached	1.35	.60	.40
769-70	Set of 2 Singles, Woman Walking,Migration	...	.55	.30
771-72	14¢ Travels of Inuit, attached	1.35	.60	.40
771-72	Set of 2 Singles, Plane, Dogteam & Sled .	...	.55	.30
773	12¢ Christmas, Madonna	1.15	.25	.15
774	14¢ Christmas, Virgin & Child	1.35	.30	.15
775	30¢ Christmas, Virgin & Child	2.60	.60	.45
776-79	14¢ Sailing Ice Vessels, attd	1.50	1.30	1.10
776-79	Set of 4 Singles	...	1.20	.90

1979 Commemoratives

Scott's No.		Plate Block	F-VF NH	F-VF Used
780,813-20,833-46	**Set of 23**	...	**7.85**	**4.75**
780	14¢ Quebec Winter Carnival	1.35	.30	.15

1977-1983 Definitives, Perf. 13 x 13½
Designs of #705-730 plus new designs

Scott's No.		Plate Block	F-VF NH	F-VF Used
781-792	**Set of 11**	...	**2.90**	**1.45**
781	1¢ Wildflower, Bottle Gentian ('79)	.40	.20	.15
781a	1¢ Bklt. Sgl., Perf. 12 x 12½	...	.45	.20
781b	B. Pane of 6 (2 #781a & 4 #713a)	...	1.25	...
782	2¢ Wildflower, W. Columbine (1979)	.40	.20	.15
782a	B. Pane of 7 (4 #782b, 3 #716a) ('78)	...	1.25	...
782b	2¢ B. Sgl. Perf. 12 x 12½ ('78)	...	.25	.15
783	3¢ Wildflower-Canada Lily ('79)	.45	.20	.15
784	4¢ Wildflower-Hepatica ('79)	.50	.20	.15
785	5¢ Wildflower-Shooting Star ('79)	.60	.20	.15
786	10¢ Wildflower-Lady's Slipper (1979)	.80	.20	.15
787	15¢ Wildflower-Canada Violet ('79)	1.40	.30	.15
789	17¢ Elizabeth II ('79)	1.35	.30	.15
789a	B. Sgl. Perf. 12 x 12½ ('79)	...	.35	.25
789b	B. Pane of 25, Perf. 12 x 12½ ('79)	...	8.50	...
790	17¢ Houses of Parliament / 1979	1.35	.30	.15
791	30¢ Elizabeth II (1982)	2.25	.50	.15
792	32¢ Elizabeth II (1983)	2.50	.55	.15
797	1¢ Parl. B. Sgl. Perf. 12 x 12½ ('79)	...	.35	.20
797a	B. Pane/6 (1 #797,3 #800,2 #789a)	...	1.15	...
800	5¢ Parl. B. Sgl. Perf. 12 x 12½ ('79)	...	.20	.15
806	17¢ Parl. Coil, Perf. 10 Vert	...	.40	.15

1979 Commemoratives (continued)

780

817-18

1979 Commemoratives (continued)

839   **840**   **841**

Scott's No.		Plate Block	F-VF NH	F-VF Used
813	17¢ Wildlife, Turtle	1.35	.30	.15
814	35¢ Wildlife, Whale	3.25	.70	.60
815-16	17¢ Postal Code, attached	1.50	.60	.55
815-16	Set of 2 Singles	...	.60	.30
817-18	17¢ Writer F. Grove & Poet E. Nelligan att	1.50	.60	.55
817-18	Set of 2 Singles	...	.60	.30
819-20	17¢ Colonels, De Salaberry & By att	1.50	.60	.55
819-20	Set of 2 Singles	...	.60	.40
821-32	17¢ Provincial Flags, Set of 12 Singles	...	3.80	2.40
832a	Sheetlet of Twelve Flags	...	3.95	3.75
833	17¢ Canoe-Kayak Meet	1.35	.30	.15
834	17¢ Women's Field Hockey	1.35	.30	.15
835-36	17¢ Inuit, attached	1.45	.60	.55
835-36	Set of 2 Singles, Summer Tent, Igloo	...	.60	.30
837-38	17¢ Inuit, attached	1.45	.60	.55
837-38	Set of 2 Singles, Dance, Two Figures	...	.60	.30
839	15¢ Christmas - Antique Toy Train	1.40	.30	.15
840	17¢ Christmas - Antique Toy Horse	1.40	.30	.15
841	35¢ Christmas - Antique Knitted Doll	2.90	.65	.45
842	17¢ Int'l. Year of the Child	1.35	.30	.15
843-44	17¢ Flying Boats, attached	1.45	.60	.55
843-44	Set of 2 Singles	...	.60	.30
845-46	35¢ Flying Boats, attached	3.20	1.35	1.25
845-46	Set of 2 Singles	...	1.30	1.20

1980 Commemoratives

847   **848**   **855**

859   **860-61**

Scott's No.		Plate Block	F-VF NH	F-VF Used
847-77	**Set of 31**	...	**11.65**	**7.50**
847	17¢ Arctic Islands	1.35	.30	.15
848	35¢ Winter Olympics, Skier	2.85	.60	.55
849-50	17¢ Artists,Harris,Hebert attached	1.45	.60	.55
849-50	Set of 2 Singles	...	.60	.30
851-52	35¢ Artists, Fuller, O'Brien attached	2.95	1.30	1.25
851-52	Set of 2 Singles	...	1.20	1.20
853	17¢ Wildlife Atlantic Whitefish	1.60	.35	.15
854	17¢ Wildlife Greater Prairie Chicken	1.60	.35	.15
855	17¢ Montreal Flower Show	1.35	.30	.15
856	17¢ Rehabilitation Congress	1.35	.30	.15
857-58	17¢ "O Canada" Centenary, attd	1.45	.60	.55
857-58	Set of 2 Singles	...	.60	.30
859	17¢ John George Diefenbaker	1.35	.30	.15
860-61	17¢ Musicians, Albani, Willan attached	1.45	.60	.55
860-61	Set of 2 Singles	...	.55	.35
862	17¢ Ned Hanlan, Oarsman	1.35	.30	.15
863	17¢ Saskatchewan, Wheat Field	1.35	.30	.15
864	17¢ Alberta, Strip Mining	1.35	.30	.15
865	35¢ Uranium Resources	3.00	.65	.50
866-67	17¢ Inuit Spirits, attached	1.45	.60	.55
866-67	Set of 2 Singles, Sedna, Return-Sun	...	.60	.30
868-69	35¢ Inuit Spirits, attached	2.95	1.30	1.25
868-69	Set of 2 Singles, Bird Spirit, Shaman	...	1.20	1.20
870	15¢ Christmas, "Christmas Morning"	1.30	.30	.15
871	17¢ Christmas, "Sleigh Ride"	1.35	.30	.15
872	35¢ Christmas, "McGill Cab Stand"	2.90	.60	.45
873-74	17¢ Military Aircraft, attached	1.50	.65	.55
873-74	Set of 2 Singles	...	.60	.30
875-76	35¢ Military Aircraft, attached	2.95	1.30	1.25
875-76	Set of 2 Singles	...	1.20	1.20
877	17¢ E.P. Lachapelle, Physician	1.35	.30	.15

CANADA

1981 Commemoratives

879-82

Scott's No.		Plate Block	F-VF NH	F-VF Used
878-906	**Set of 29**	...	**9.70**	**5.60**
878	17¢ 18th Century Mandora	1.35	.30	.15
879-82	17¢ Feminists, attached	1.65	1.40	1.35
879-82	Set of 4 Singles	...	1.35	.90
883	17¢ Endangered Wildlife, Marmot	1.35	.30	.15
884	35¢ Endangered Wildlife, Wood Bison	3.25	.75	.70
885-86	17¢ Beatified Women, attached	1.45	.60	.55
885-86	Set of 2 Singles	...	.60	.30
887	17¢ Marc-Aurele Fortin, Painter	1.35	.30	.15
888	17¢ Frederic H. Varley, Painter	1.35	.30	.15
889	35¢ Paul-Emile Borduas, Painter	2.95	.60	.60
890-93	17¢ Historic Maps, attached strip	(8) 3.25	1.35	1.30
890-93	Set of 4 Singles	...	1.30	.90
894-95	17¢ Botanists Marie-Victorin, Macoun, att	1.45	.60	.55
894-95	Set of 2 Singles	...	.60	.30
896	17¢ Montreal Rose	1.35	.30	.15
897	17¢ Niagara-on-the-Lake	1.35	.30	.15
898	17¢ Acadian Congress Centenary	1.35	.30	.15
899	17¢ Aaron Mosher Labor	1.35	.30	.15
900	15¢ 1781 Christmas Tree	1.15	.25	.15
901	15¢ 1881 Christmas Tree	1.15	.25	.15
902	15¢ 1981 Christmas Tree	1.15	.25	.15
903-04	17¢ Aircraft, attached	1.50	.65	.55
903-04	Set of 2 Singles	...	.60	.30
905-06	35¢ Aircraft, attached	2.95	1.25	1.20
905-06	Set of 2 Singles	...	1.20	1.10

907

914

915

1981 "A" Interim Definitives

907	(30¢) "A" and Maple Leaf, Perf. 13 x 13½	2.50	.55	.15
908	(30¢) "A" and Maple Leaf, Coil	...	1.10	.20

1982 Commemoratives

909-13,914-16,954,967-75	**Set of 18**	...	**11.85**	**6.65**
909-13	30¢-60¢ Youth Exhibition, Set of 5	...	3.35	2.25
909	30¢ 1851 3d Beaver	2.60	.55	.20
910	30¢ 1908 15¢ Champlain	2.60	.55	.20
911	35¢ 1935 10¢ Mountie	3.00	.65	.60
912	35¢ 1928 10¢ Mt. Hurd	3.00	.65	.60
913	60¢ 1929 50¢ Bluenose	5.75	1.15	.90
913a	$1.90 Exhibition Souvenir Sheet	...	4.50	4.50
914	30¢ Jules Leger, Governor-Gen'l	2.60	.55	.15
915	30¢ Marathon of Hope - Terry Fox	2.60	.55	.15
916	30¢ New Constitution	2.60	.55	.15

1982-89 Regular Issue

917    **923**

927   **929**

917-37	**Set of 23**	...	**29.95**	**9.50**
#917-22,927-30,932-33 Artifacts				
917	1¢ Decoy, Perf. 14 x 13½	.40	.20	.15
917a	1¢ Perf. 13 x 13½ (1985)	.40	.20	.15
918	2¢ Fishing Spear, Perf. 14 x 13½	.40	.20	.15
918a	2¢ Perf. 13 x 13½ (1984)	.40	.20	.15
919	3¢ Stable Lantern, Perf. 14 x 13½	.40	.20	.15
919a	3¢ Perf. 13 x 13½ (1985)	.40	.20	.15
920	5¢ Bucket, Perf. 14 x 13½	.60	.20	.15
920a	5¢ Perf. 13 x 13½ (1985)	.60	.20	.15
921	10¢ Weathercock, Perf. 14 x 13½	.90	.20	.15
921a	10¢ Perf. 13 x 13½ (1985)	1.30	.30	.15
922	20¢ Ice Skates	1.85	.40	.15

CANADA

Scott's No.		Plate Block	F-VF NH	F-VF Used
923	30¢ Maple Leaf, Red & Blue Pf.13x13½	2.50	.55	.15
923a	Bklt. Pane of 20, Pf. 12 x 12½	...	11.75	...
923b	Bklt. Sgl., Pf. 12 x 12½	...	.75	.20
924	32¢ Maple Leaf, Red & Brown on Beige, Pf. 13 x 13½ ('83)	2.30	.55	.15
924a	Bklt. Pane of 25, Pf. 12 x 12½ ('83)	...	14.50	...
924b	Bklt. Sgl. Pf. 12 x 12½ ('83)	...	.75	.35
925	34¢ Parliament Library ('85)	2.50	.60	.15
925a	Parl. Bklt. Pane of 25 ('85)	...	14.75	...
925b	Bluer sky, Pf. 13½ x 14, bklt. sgl('86)	...	.95	.20
925c	Same, Bklt. Pane of 25 (1986)	...	14.95	...
926	34¢ Queen Elizabeth II ('85)	2.50	.60	.15
926A	36¢ Queen Elizabeth II ('85)	19.50	3.75	1.75
926B	36¢ Parliamentary Library ('87)	2.75	.60	.15
926Bc	Booklet Pane of 10 ('87)	...	6.50	...
926Bd	Booklet Pane of 25 ('87)	...	16.50	...
926Be	Bklt. Sgl., Perf. 13½ x 14 ('87)	...	.85	.25
927	37¢ Wooden Plow ('83)	3.00	.65	.20
928	39¢ Settle Bed ('85)	3.25	.70	.20
929	48¢ Hand Hewn Cradle ('83)	4.25	.90	.25
930	50¢ Sleigh (1985)	4.00	.85	.20
931	60¢ Ontario Street Scene	5.50	1.20	.25
932	64¢ Wood Burning Stove ('83)	5.25	1.10	.35
933	68¢ Spinning Wheel (1985)	5.25	1.15	.35
934	$1.00 Glacier National Park ('84)	8.00	1.75	.45
935	$1.50 Waterton Lakes Nat'l. Park	13.50	3.00	.70
936	$2.00 Banff National Park ('85)	16.00	3.50	.90
937	$5.00 Point Pelee Nat'l. Park ('83)	39.50	9.00	2.00
NOTE: Also see #1080-84				

Booklet Stamps

938-48	**Set of 11**	...	**4.95**	**3.35**
938	1¢ Parl. East, Bklt. Sgl. ('87)	...	.20	.15
939	2¢ West Parl. Bldg., Booklet Sgl. ('85)	...	.20	.15
939a	Slate Green, bklt. sgl. ('89)	...	.20	.15
940	5¢ Maple Leaf, Booklet Single	...	.20	.15
941	5¢ East Parl. Bldg., Booklet Sgl. ('85)	...	.30	.20
942	6¢ Parl., West B. Sgl. ('87)	...	.25	.15
943	8¢ Maple Leaf, Bklt. Single ('83)	...	.45	.40
944	10¢ Maple Leaf, Booklet Single	...	.45	.35
945	30¢ Maple Leaf, Red, Bklt. Sgl	...	.80	.60
945a	Bklt. Pane of 4 (2 #940,#944,#945) Pf. 12 x 12½	...	1.30	...
946	32¢ Maple Leaf, Brown, Bklt. Sgl. ('83)	...	.70	.50
946b	Bklt. Pane of 4 (2 #941, #943, #946, Pf. 12 x 12½)	...	1.25	...
947	34¢ Center Parl. Bldg., Bklt. Sgl. ('85)	...	1.10	.60
947a	B. Pane of 6 (3 #939,2 #941, #947)	...	1.50	...
948	36¢ Parl. Library, Bklt. Sgl. ('87)	...	.95	.60
948a	Vend Bklt. of 5 (2 #938,2 #942, #948)	...	1.50	...

Coil Stamps

950-53	**Set of 4**	...	**2.65**	**.55**
950	30¢ Maple Leaf, Red	...	.80	.20
951	32¢ Maple Leaf, Brown ('83)	...	.65	.15
952	34¢ Parliament Red Brown ('85)	...	.65	.15
953	36¢ Parliament Dark Red ('87)	...	.65	.15

1982 Commemoratives (continued)

954

967

973

954	30¢ Salvation Army	2.60	.55	.15

1982 Canada Day Paintings

955-66	30¢ Canada Day Paintings, Set of 12 Sgls	...	8.75	6.25
966a	Sheetlet of 12 Paintings	...	9.00	9.00

1982 Commemoratives (continued)

967	30¢ Regina Centennial	2.60	.55	.15
968	30¢ Henley Rowing Regatta	2.60	.55	.15
969-70	30¢ Bush Aircraft, attached	2.60	1.20	.90
969-70	Set of 2 Singles	...	1.10	.40
971-72	60¢ Bush Aircraft, attached	5.50	2.20	2.10
971-72	Set of 2 Singles	...	2.10	1.90
973	30¢ Christmas, Nativity	2.60	.55	.15
974	35¢ Christmas, Shepherds	2.95	.65	.55
975	60¢ Christmas, Wise Men	5.25	1.10	.80

1983 Commemoratives

976-82,993-1008	**Set of 23**	...	**20.75**	**9.95**
976	32¢ Communications Year	2.60	.55	.20
977	$2 Commonwealth Day	39.50	8.50	3.50
978-79	32¢ Poet L. Conan, Author E. Pratt attached	2.60	1.15	1.00
978-79	Set of 2 Singles	...	1.10	.40

CANADA

1983 Commemoratives (continued)

977   980   981

Scott's No.		Plate Block	F-VF NH	F-VF Used
980	32¢ St. John Ambulance	2.80	.55	.20
981	32¢ World University Games	2.80	.55	.20
982	64¢ World University Games	5.50	1.10	.75

1983 Historic Forts Commemorative Booklet

983-92	32¢ Historic Forts, Set of 10 Bklt.Singles	...	6.75	6.50
992a	Booklet Pane of 10	...	7.00	7.00

993   995   996

1005   1007-08

1983 Commemoratives (continued)

993	32¢ Boy Scout Jamboree	2.50	.55	.20
994	32¢ World Council of Churches	2.50	.55	.20
995	32¢ Sir Humphrey Gilbert	2.50	.55	.20
996	32¢ Discovery of Nickel	2.75	.60	.20
997	32¢ Josiah Henson	2.50	.55	.20
998	32¢ Antoine Labelle	2.50	.55	.20
999-1000	32¢ Steam Locomotives, attd	2.50	1.15	1.10
999-1000	Set of 2 Singles	...	1.10	.50
1001	37¢ Locomotive Samson 0-6-0, ...	3.00	.65	.65
1002	64¢ Locomotive Adam Brown 4-4-0, ...	5.50	1.10	.95
1003	32¢ Dalhousie Law School	2.50	.55	.20
1004	32¢ Christmas, Urban Church	2.50	.55	.20
1005	37¢ Christmas, Family	2.95	.65	.50
1006	64¢ Christmas, Rural Church	5.50	1.10	.95
1007-08	32¢ Army Regiment Uniforms, attd	2.50	1.15	1.00
1007-08	Set of 2 Singles	...	1.10	.40

1984 Commemoratives

1013   1028   1043

1009-15,1028-39,1040-44 Set of 24		...	14.95	7.95
1009	32¢ Yellowknife	2.50	.55	.20
1010	32¢ Montreal Symphony	2.50	.55	.20
1011	32¢ Cartier Landing in Quebec	2.50	.55	.20
1012	32¢ Voyage of Tall Ships	2.50	.55	.20
1013	32¢ Red Cross Society	2.50	.55	.20
1014	32¢ New Brunswick	2.50	.55	.20
1015	32¢ St. Lawrence Seaway	2.50	.55	.20

1984 Provincial Landscapes

1016-27	32¢ Canada Day Paintings, Set of 12 Sgls.	...	9.75	4.75
1027a	Sheetlet of Twelve Paintings	...	9.95	9.95

1984 Commemoratives (continued)

1028	32¢ United Empire Loyalists	2.50	.55	.20
1029	32¢ Catholic Church in Newfoundland .	2.50	.55	.20
1030	32¢ Papal Visit	2.50	.55	.20

CANADA

1984 Commemoratives (continued)

Scott's No.		Plate Block	F-VF NH	F-VF Used
1031	64¢ Papal Visit	5.25	1.10	.80
1032-35	32¢ Lighthouses, attd	3.15	2.75	1.20
1032-35	Set of 4 Singles	...	2.60	.90
1036-37	32¢ Steam Locomotives, attd	2.50	1.20	1.00
1036-37	Set of 2 Singles	...	1.10	.40
1038	37¢ Locomotive Grand Trunk 2-6-0	3.15	.65	.65
1039	64¢ Locomotive Canadian Pacific 4-6-0 .	5.75	1.20	1.00
1039a	$1.65 Locomotive Souvenir Sheet	...	3.95	3.95
1040	32¢ Christmas, Annunciation	2.50	.55	.20
1041	37¢ Christmas, Three Kings	3.10	.65	.60
1042	64¢ Christmas, Snow in Bethlehem	5.25	1.10	.90
1043	32¢ Royal Canadian Air Force	2.50	.55	.20
1044	32¢ Newspaper, La Presse	2.50	.55	.20

1985 Commemoratives

1045   1062   1075   1076

1045-49,1060-66,1067-70,1071-76 Set of 22		...	14.50	6.75
1045	32¢ Int'l. Youth Year	2.50	.55	.20
1046	32¢ Canadian Astronaut	2.75	.60	.20
1047-48	32¢ Decade of Women T. Casgrain, E. Murphy, attd	2.50	1.20	1.00
1047-48	Set of 2 Singles	...	1.10	.40
1049	32¢ Gabriel Dumont, Metis	2.50	.55	.20

1985 Historic Forts Commemorative Booklet

1050-59	34¢ Historic Forts, Set/10 Bklt Sgls	...	8.75	6.75
1059a	Booklet Pane/10	...	9.00	9.00

1985 Commemoratives (continued)

1060	34¢ Louis Hebert	2.75	.60	.20
1061	34¢ Interparliamentary Union	2.75	.60	.20
1062	34¢ Girl Guides 7th Anniv	2.75	.60	.20
1063-66	34¢ Lighthouses, attd	3.65	3.25	3.00
1063-66	Set of 4 Singles	...	3.15	1.10
1066b	$1.36 Lighthouse Souvenir Sheet of 4	...	3.25	3.15
1067	34¢ Christmas, Santa Claus	2.75	.60	.20
1068	39¢ Christmas, Coach	3.40	.70	.60
1069	68¢ Christmas, Tree	5.95	1.25	.85
1070	32¢ Christmas,Polar Float Bklt. Sgl	...	.90	.40
1070a	Christmas Bklt. Pane/10	...	8.50	8.50
1071-72	34¢ Locomotives, attd	2.75	1.20	.50
1071-72	Set of 2 Singles	...	1.15	.40
1073	39¢ Locomotives #010a	3.25	.70	.70
1074	68¢ Locomotives #H4D	5.95	1.25	1.00
1075	34¢ Royal Canadian Navy	2.75	.60	.20
1076	34¢ Montreal Fine Arts Museum	2.75	.60	.20

1986 Commemoratives

1078   1084   1117

1077-79,1090-1107,1108-21 Set of 32		...	25.00	10.50
1077	34¢ 1988 Calgary Winter Olympics, Map	2.75	.60	.20
1078	34¢ EXPO '86 Pavilion	2.75	.60	.20
1079	39¢ EXPO '86 Communications	3.25	.70	.55

1986-87 Regular Issues

1080-84	Set of 5	...	13.50	3.35
1080	25¢ Artifact Butter Stamp (1987)	2.30	.50	.25
1081	42¢ Artifact Linen Chest (1987)	4.15	.85	.25
1082	55¢ Artifact Iron Kettle (1987)	6.25	1.35	.35
1083	72¢ Artifact Cart (1987)	8.00	1.70	.50
1084	$5 La Maurice Nat'l. Park	42.50	9.50	2.25

1986 Commemoratives (continued)

1090	34¢ Philippe Aubert de Gaspe	2.75	.60	.20
1091	34¢ Molly Brant, Iroquois	2.75	.60	.20
1092	34¢ EXPO '86, Expo Center	2.75	.60	.20
1093	68¢ EXPO '86, Transportation	6.00	1.25	.55
1094	34¢ Canadian Forces Postal Serv	2.75	.60	.20
1095-98	34¢ Indigenous Birds, attd	5.00	4.25	3.75
1095-98	Set of 4 Singles	...	4.00	1.20
1099-1102	34¢ Canada Day,Inventions attd	3.50	3.00	2.75
1099-1102	Set of 4 Singles	...	2.90	1.10
1103	34¢ Canadian Broadcasting Corp	2.75	.60	.20

FROM 1947 TO PRESENT, ADD 20% FOR VERY FINE QUALITY
Minimum of 10¢ Per Stamp

1986 Commemoratives (cont.)

Scott's No.		Plate Block	F-VF NH	F-VF Used
1104-07	34¢ Canada Exploration, attd	3.50	3.00	2.75
1104-07	Set of 4 Singles	...	2.90	1.20
1107b	$1.36 CAPEX '87, Exploration Souv. Sheet	...	3.25	3.00
1108-09	34¢ Frontier Peacemakers, attd	2.75	1.20	1.00
1108-09	Set of 2 Singles	...	1.15	.50
1110	34¢ International Peace Year	2.75	.60	.20
1111-12	34¢ Calgary Winter Olympics, attd	2.75	1.20	.90
1111-12	Set of 2 Singles, Ice Hockey, Biathlon	...	1.15	.40
1113	34¢ Christmas, Angels	2.75	.60	.25
1114	39¢ Christmas, Angels	3.00	.65	.50
1115	68¢ Christmas, Angels	5.50	1.15	.75
1116	29¢ Christmas, Bklt. Sgl. Perf. 13½	...	1.20	.60
1116a	Bklt. Pane of 10, Perf. 13½	...	11.00	...
1116b	Bklt. Sgl., Perf. 12½	...	8.00	2.50
1116c	Bklt. Pane of 10, Perf. 12½	...	80.00	...
1117	34¢ John Molson	2.75	.60	.20
1118-19	34¢ Locomotives, attd	4.25	1.50	.90
1118-19	Set of 2 Singles	...	1.40	.40
1120	39¢ Locomotive CN U2a	4.75	1.10	.80
1121	68¢ Locomotive CP H1c	7.50	1.65	1.40

1987 Commemoratives

1122

1130

1134

1122-25,1126-54	**Set of 33**	...	**24.50**	**11.50**
1122-25	34¢-72¢ CAPEX '87 Set of 4	...	3.25	2.25
1122	34¢ 1st Toronto P.O.	2.75	.60	.20
1123	36¢ Nelson-Miramichi P.O.	3.10	.65	.25
1124	42¢ Saint Ours P.O.	4.25	.90	.80
1125	72¢ Battleford P.O.	6.75	1.60	1.35
1125A	$1.84 CAPEX S/S	...	3.95	3.95
1126-29	34¢ Exploration,New France, attd	4.25	3.75	3.50
1126-29	Set of 4 Singles	...	3.60	1.40
#1130-31 1988 Calgary Winter Olympics				
1130	36¢ Speed Skating	2.95	.65	.20
1131	42¢ Bobsledding	3.95	.90	.80
1132	36¢ Volunteer Week	3.00	.65	.20
1133	36¢ Law Day	3.00	.65	.20
1134	36¢ Engineering Institute	3.00	.65	.20
1135-38	36¢ Canada Day, Communications, attd	3.25	2.75	2.50
1135-38	Set of 4 Singles	...	2.65	1.10
1139-40	36¢ Steamships, attd	3.15	1.35	1.10
1139-40	Set of 2 Singles	...	1.30	.60
1141-44	36¢ Underwater Archaeology, attd	3.65	3.15	3.00
1141-44	Set of 4 Singles	...	3.10	1.20

1145

1148

1152-53

1145	36¢ Air Canada 50th Anniv	3.00	.65	.20
1146	36¢ Francophone Int'l. Summit	3.00	.65	.20
1147	36¢ Commonwealth Heads of Gov't	3.00	.65	.20
1148	36¢ Christmas, Poinsettia	3.00	.65	.15
1149	42¢ Christmas, Holly Wreath	3.95	.90	.80
1150	72¢ Christmas, Mistletoe	6.75	1.50	1.10
1151	31¢ Christmas Gifts Bklt. Sgl	...	.75	.60
1151a	Christmas Bklt. Pane of 10	...	6.50	...
1152-53	36¢ Calgary Winter Olympics, attd	3.00	1.30	1.00
1152-53	Set of 2 Singles Skiing, Ski Jumping	...	1.25	.50
1154	36¢ Grey Cup 75th Anniv	3.00	.65	.20

1987-91 Regular Issues

1155-83	**Set of 30**	...	**34.95**	**12.00**
#1155-61, 1170-80 Mammals				
1155	1¢ Flying Squirrel, Pf. 13 x 13½ (1988)	.40	.20	.15
1155a	1¢ Perf 13 x 12½ (1991) (Blank)	14.75	3.50	1.95
1156	2¢ Porcupine (1988)	.40	.20	.15
1157	3¢ Muskrat (1988)	.50	.20	.15
1158	5¢ Hare (1988)	.60	.20	.15
1159	6¢ Red Fox (1988)	.70	.20	.15
1160	10¢ Skunk, Pf. 13 x 13½ (1988)	.85	.20	.15
1160a	10¢ Perf. 13 x 12½ (1991) (Blank)	24.50	5.25	.50
1161	25¢ Beaver (1988)	2.10	.45	.15
1162	37¢ Elizabeth II	3.50	.75	.15
1163	37¢ Parliament Perf. 13½ x 13	3.50	.75	.15
1163a	Booklet Pane of 10 (1163c) ('88)	...	7.50	...
1163b	Booklet Pane of 25 (1163c) ('88)	...	18.50	...
1163c	37¢ Bklt. sgl., Pf. 13½ x 14 ('88)	...	1.10	.20
1164	38¢ QE II pf. 13 x 12½ ('88)	3.25	.70	.15
1164a	38¢ Bklt. sgl., pf. 13 x 13½ ('88)	...	1.25	.60
1164b	Bklt. Pane of 10 + 2 labels (1988)	...	8.25	...

1987-91 Regular Issues (cont.)

1165

1166

1167

1173

Scott's No.		Plate Block	F-VF NH	F-VF Used
1165	38¢ Parliament Clock Tower ('88)	3.25	.70	.15
1165a	Bklt. Pane of 10 + 2 labels (1988)	...	8.50	...
1165b	Bklt. Pane of 25 + 2 labels (1988)	...	21.50	...
1166	39¢ Flag & Clouds ('89)	3.50	.75	.15
1166a	Bklt. Pane of 10 (1989)	...	8.50	...
1166b	Bklt. Pane of 25 (1989)	...	21.75	...
1166c	39¢ Perf. 12½ x 13 ('90) (Blank)	65.00	13.50	.95
1167	39¢ Elizabeth II, Perf. 13 x 13½ ('90)	3.25	.70	.15
1167a	Bklt. Pane of 10 (1990)	...	10.50	...
1167b	39¢ Perf. 13 ('90) (Blank)	80.00	17.50	.50
1168	40¢ Elizabeth II ('90)	3.25	.70	.15
1168a	Bklt. Pane of 10 + 2 labels (1990)	...	8.75	...
1169	40¢ Flag & Mountains ('90)	3.25	.70	.15
1169a	Bklt. Pane of 25 + 2 labels	...	26.50	...
1169b	Bklt. Pane of 10 + 2 labels	...	8.75	...
1170	43¢ Lynx ('88)	5.35	1.10	.35
1171	44¢ Walrus Perf. 14½ x 14 ('89)	8.50	1.85	.25
1171a	44¢ Bklt. Sgl. Perf. 12½ x 13 (1989)	...	3.25	1.20
1171b	Perf. 12½ x 13, Bklt. Pane of 5+label	...	13.95	...
1171c	44¢ Perf. 13½ x 13 ('89) (Blank)	1650.00	375.00	45.00
1172	45¢ Pronghorn ('90) Perf. 14½ x 14 ('90)	4.25	.95	.30
1172f	Bklt. Sgl. Perf. 12½ x 13 ('90)	...	3.25	.65
1172b	Bklt. Pane of 5 + label, Perf. 12½ x 13	...	13.75	...
1172d	45¢ Perf. 13 ('90) (Blank)	95.00	19.75	.95
1172A	46¢ Wolverine, Perf. 13 ('90)	3.95	.85	.30
1172Ac	46¢ Wolverine,Bklt. Sgl. Perf. 12½ x 13 ('90)	...	1.60	.60
1172Ae	Bklt. pn. of 5 + label, Perf. 12½x13 ('91)	...	8.75	...
1172Ag	46¢ Wolverine, Perf. 14½ x 14 ('90)	27.50	5.50	.60
1173	57¢ Killer Whale ('88)	6.75	1.00	.30
1174	59¢ Musk-ox Perf. 14½ x 14 ('89)	5.75	1.25	.35
1174a	59¢ Perf. 13 ('89) (Blank)	45.00	10.75	5.75

1175

1183

1185

1175	61¢ Timber Wolf Perf. 14½ x 14 ('90)	5.00	1.10	.40
1175a	61¢ Perf. 13 ('90) (Blank)	375.00	75.00	3.50
1176	63¢ Harbor Porpoise Perf. 14½ x 14 ('90)	12.00	1.85	.40
1176a	63¢ Perf. 13 (1990) (Blank)	37.50	6.50	3.50
1177	74¢ Wapiti ('88)	7.75	1.60	.60
1178	76¢ Grizzly Bear, Perf. 14½ x 14 ('89)	7.75	1.60	.50
1178a	76¢ Bklt sgl. perf. 12½ x 13 (1989)	...	2.75	2.25
1178b	Bklt. pane of 5 + label, Perf. 12½x13	...	18.50	...
1178c	Perf. 13 (Blank)	275.00	57.50	11.75
1179	78¢ Beluga ('90) Perf. 14½ x 14 ('90)	8.00	1.65	.65
1179a	Bklt. Pane of 5, Perf. 12½ x 13	...	15.00	...
1179b	78¢ Perf. 13 ('90) (Blank)	225.00	47.50	6.50
1179c	78¢ Blklt. Sgl. Perf. 12½ x 13 (1990)	...	2.95	1.50
1180	80¢ Peary Caribou, Perf. 13 ('90)	9.50	2.10	.85
1180a	80¢ Bklt. Sgl. Perf 12½ x 13 ('90)	...	2.50	1.25
1180b	Bklt. Pane of 5+label, Perf. 12½x13 ('91)	...	19.50	...
1180c	80¢ Perf. 14½ x 14 ('91)	29.50	7.00	2.25
1181	$1 Runnymede Library ('89)	7.75	1.75	.60
1182	$2 McAdam Train Station ('89)	15.50	3.50	1.10
1183	$5 Bonsecours Market ('90)	38.50	8.50	2.50

1988-90 Booklet Singles and Panes

1184-90	**Set of 7**	**5.15**	**1.70**
1184	1¢ Flag, Perf. 13½ x 14 (1990)	.20	.20
1184a	1¢ Perf. 12½ x 13 (1990)	16.50	14.75
1185	5¢ Flag, Perf. 13½ x 14 (1990)	.20	.20
1185a	5¢ Perf. 12½ x 13 (1990)	13.50	13.50
1186	6¢ Parliament (1988)	.85	.30
1187	37¢ Parl. Library ('88)	.85	.50
1187a	Bklt. Pane of 4 (#938,2 #942,#1187)	1.65	...
1188	38¢ Parliament Center, ('89)	.85	.35
1188a	Bklt. pane of 5 (3 #939a, 1186, 1188)	1.65	...
1189	39¢ Canadian Flag, ('90)	1.75	.35
1189a	Bklt. pn. of 4 (#1184,2 #1185,#1189)	2.15	...
1189b	39¢ Perf. 12½ x 13	27.50	23.50
1189c	Same, Bklt. pn. of 4 (#1184a,2 #1185a,#1189b)	82.50	...
1190	40¢ Canadian Flag ('90)	2.10	.60
1190a	Bklt. pane of 4 (2 #1184,1185,1190)	2.75	...

1193 1203 1204

1229 1241 1249

1989-91 Self-Adhesive Stamps

Scott's No.		Plate Block	F-VF NH	F-VF Used
1191	38¢ National Flag, bklt. sgl.		1.10	.50
1191a	Booklet of 12		12.75	...
1192	39¢ Flag & Landscape, bklt. sgl. ('90)		1.10	.50
1192a	Booklet of 12		12.75	...
1193	40¢ Flag & Seacoast, bklt. sgl. ('91)		1.10	.50
1193a	Booklet of 12		12.75	...

1988-90 Coil Stamps, Perf. 10 Horizontal

1194-94C	Set of 4		3.70	.90
1194	37¢ Parliament Library ('88)		.95	.25
1194A	38¢ Parliament Library ('89)		.95	.25
1194B	39¢ Canadian Flag (1990)		.95	.25
1194C	40¢ Canadian Flag (1990)		.95	.25

1988 Commemoratives

1195-1228	Set of 34	...	27.50	11.25
1195-96	37¢ Winter Olympics, attd	3.25	1.50	1.10
1195-96	Set of 2 Singles Alpine Skiing, Curling		1.45	.50
1197	43¢ Winter Olympics, Figure Skating	3.75	.80	.60
1198	74¢ Winter Olympics, Luge	6.25	1.40	.95
1199-1202	37¢ 18th Century Explorers, attd	3.50	3.00	2.25
1199-1202	Set of 4 Singles	...	2.90	1.40
1203	50¢ Canadian Art, The Young Reader	5.00	1.10	.95
1204-05	37¢ Wildlife Conservation., attd	3.15	1.40	.90
1204-05	Set of 2 Singles, Duck, Moose	...	1.35	.60

1214 1215 1216

1221 1223 1226 1228

1206-09	37¢ Science & Technology, attd	4.00	3.50	2.25
1206-09	Set of 4 Singles	...	3.40	1.20
1210-13	37¢ Butterflies, attd	4.50	3.95	2.50
1210-13	Set of 4 Singles	...	3.85	1.40
1214	37¢ St. John's Newfld. City Cent	3.00	.65	.20
1215	37¢ 4-H Clubs Anniversary	3.00	.65	.20
1216	37¢ Les Forges du Saint-Maurice	3.00	.65	.20
1217-20	37¢ Kennel Club Cent. (Dogs) attd	5.50	4.95	2.95
1217-20	Set of 4 Singles	...	4.85	1.40
1221	37¢ Canadian Baseball Sesqui	3.25	.70	.20
#1222-25	Icons of the Eastern Church			
1222	37¢ Christmas, Conception	2.95	.65	.20
1223	43¢ Christmas, Virgin and Child	3.95	.85	.65
1224	74¢ Christmas, Virgin and Child	5.75	1.35	.95
1225	32¢ Christmas Nativity, bklt. single	...	.80	.60
1225a	Booklet Pane of 10	...	7.75	...
1226	37¢ Bishop Charles Inglis	3.00	.65	.20
1227	37¢ Frances Ann Hopkins	3.00	.65	.20
1228	37¢ Angus Walters	3.25	.70	.20

Scott's No.		Plate Block	F-VF NH	F-VF Used
1229-63	Set of 34	...	27.95	13.75
1229-32	38¢ Small Craft Series, attd	4.00	3.50	2.50
1229-32	Set of 4 Singles, Canoes and Kayak	...	3.40	1.40
1233-36	38¢ Explorers/Canadian North, attd	4.00	3.50	2.50
1233-36	Set of 4 Singles	...	3.40	1.40
1237-40	38¢ Canada Day Photography, attd	4.00	3.50	2.50
1237-40	Set of 4 Singles	...	3.40	1.40
1241	50¢ Art, Ceremonial Frontlet	5.95	1.30	.85
1243-44	38¢ Poets, Frechette, Lampman attd	2.95	1.35	.75
1243-44	Set of 2 Singles	...	1.30	.50
1245-48	38¢ Mushrooms, attd	4.00	3.50	2.50
1245-48	Set of 4 Singles	...	3.40	1.40
1249-50	38¢ Canadian Infantry Regiments, attd	*225.00	1.65	1.20
1249-50	Set of 2 Singles	...	1.60	.70

* Printing difficulties caused a severe shortage of inscription blocks.

1251 1252 1260

1251	38¢ International Trade	2.95	.65	.20
1252-55	38¢ Performing Arts, attd	4.00	3.50	2.50
1252-55	Set of 4 Singles	...	3.40	1.40
1256	38¢ Christmas Landscape, pf. 13 x 13½	3.00	.65	.20
1256a	Bklt. pane of 10, perf. 13 x 12½	...	45.00	...
1256b	38¢ Bklt. sgl., perf. 13 x 12½	...	4.50	4.25
1257	44¢ Christmas Landscape	4.75	1.00	.90
1257a	Bklt. pane of 5 + label	...	22.50	...
1258	76¢ Christmas Landscape	7.50	1.65	1.15
1258a	Bklt. pane of 5 + label	...	32.50	...
1259	33¢ Christmas Landscape bklt. sgl	...	1.35	1.20
1259a	Bklt. Pane of 10	...	12.75	...
1260-63	38¢ WWII, 1939 Events, attd	4.25	3.50	3.25
1260-63	Set of 4 Singles	...	3.35	2.00

1990 Commemoratives

1264 1270 1271

1264-71,1274-1301	Set of 36	...	30.95	16.50
1264-65	39¢ Norman Bethune, attd	3.95	2.10	1.25
1264-65	Set of 2 Singles	...	2.00	.80
1266-69	39¢ Small Work Crafts, attd	4.00	3.50	2.50
1266-69	Set of 4 Singles	...	3.40	1.40
1270	39¢ Multicultural Heritage of Canada	3.25	.70	.25
1271	50¢ Canadian Art, The West Wind	5.75	1.25	1.10

1272-73 1278

1990 Regular Issue Prestige Booklet

Scott's No.		Plate Block	F-VF NH	F-VF Used
1272-73	39¢ Postal Truck bklt. singles	...	1.70	1.00
1273a	Bk. pn. of 8 (4 Eng. + 4 Fr. Inscriptions)...	...	7.50	...
1273b	Bk. pn. of 9 (4 Eng. + 5 Fr. Inscriptions)	...	9.75	...

1990 Commemoratives (continued)

		Plate Block	F-VF NH	F-VF Used
1274-77	39¢ Dolls, attd	4.50	3.75	2.50
1274-77	Set of 4 Singles	...	3.65	1.40
1278	39¢ Canada Day, 25 Anniv. of Flag	3.25	.70	.25
1279-82	39¢ Prehistoric Life, attd	4.50	3.75	2.50
1279-82	Set of 4 Singles	...	3.65	1.40
1283-86	39¢ Forests, World Congress, attd	4.25	3.60	2.25
1283-86	Set of 4 Singles	...	3.50	1.20
1283a-86b	Miniature sheets of 4 (Set of 4)	...	37.50	30.00

1287 1288 1293 1294

		Plate Block	F-VF NH	F-VF Used
1287	39¢ Weather Observations Sesqui	3.25	.70	.20
1288	39¢ International Literacy Year	3.25	.70	.20
1289-92	39¢ Canadian Lore and Legend, attd ..	4.65	4.00	3.75
1289-92	Set of 4 Singles, Perf. 12½ x 13	...	3.90	3.50
1289a-92a	39¢ Lore, Perf. 12½ x 12, attd..........	...	27.50	20.00
1289a-92a	Set of 4 Singles, Perf. 12½ x 12	...	27.00	19.00
1293	39¢ Agnes Macphail, 1st Woman MP ..	3.25	.70	.20
1294	39¢ Christmas, Virgin Mary	3.25	.70	.20
1294a	Booklet Pane of 10	...	11.00	...
1295	45¢ Christmas, Mother & Child	5.25	1.20	.85
1295a	Booklet Pane of 5 + label	...	10.00	...
1296	78¢ Christmas, Children/Raven	8.50	1.85	1.20
1296a	Booklet Pane of 5 + label	...	16.50	...
1297	34¢ Christmas, Rebirth, bklt. sgl	...	.70	.50
1297a	Bklt. Pane of 10	...	8.00	...
1298-1301	39¢ World War II, 1940 Events, attd .	5.25	4.50	4.25
1298-1301	Set of 4 Singles	...	4.35	3.75

1991 Commemoratives

1302 1310 1316

		Plate Block	F-VF NH	F-VF Used
1302-43,1345-48	Set of 45	...	39.95	15.95
1302-05	40¢ Physicians, attd	4.00	3.50	2.75
1302-05	Set of 4 Singles	...	3.40	1.40
1306-09	40¢ Prehistoric Life in Canada, attd	4.25	3.60	3.00
1306-09	Set of 4 Singles	...	3.50	1.40
1310	50¢ Canadian Art, Emily Carr	4.75	1.00	.85
1311-15	40¢ Public Gardens, bklt. sgls, strip of 5	...	4.50	3.25
1311-15	Set of 5 Singles	...	4.40	1.75
1315b	Booklet Pane of 10	...	8.75	...
1316	40¢ Canada Day	3.75	.80	.20
1317-20	40¢ Small Craft, attd	4.00	3.50	2.75
1317-20	Set of 4 Singles	...	3.40	1.40
1321-25	40¢ River Heritage, bklt. sgls., strip of 5...	...	4.50	3.25
1321-25	Set of 5 Singles	...	4.40	1.75
1325b	River Booklet Pane of 10	...	8.75	...
1326-29	40¢ Ukrainian Migration to Canada, attd	4.00	3.50	2.75
1326-29	Set of 4 Singles	...	3.40	1.40
1330-33	40¢ Dangerous Public Service orgs,attd	5.25	4.50	2.75
1330-33	Set of 4 Singles	...	4.35	1.40
1334-37	40¢ Canadian Folktales, attd	4.25	3.75	2.75
1334-37	Set of 4 Singles	...	3.65	1.40

1338 1339 1345

1991 Commemoratives (continued)

Scott's No.		Plate Block	F-VF NH	F-VF Used
1338	40¢ Queen's University, bklt. single	...	.90	.25
1338a	Booklet Pane of 10	...	8.75	...
1339	40¢ Christmas, Santa at Fireplace	4.00	.85	.20
1339a	Booklet Pane of 10	...	8.50	...
1340	46¢ Christmas,Santa with Tree	3.75	.80	.70
1340a	Booklet Pane of 5	...	5.75	...
1341	80¢ Christmas, Sinterklass & Girl	7.75	1.75	1.20
1341a	Booklet Pane of 5	...	9.50	...
1342	35¢ Greet More, Santa Claus, bklt. sgl.	...	.95	.25
1342a	Bklt. Pane of 10	...	8.95	...
1343	40¢ Basketball Centennial	4.25	.95	.30
1344	40¢, 46¢, 80¢ Basketball S/S of 3	...	5.75	5.50
1345-48	40¢ World War II, 1941 Events, attd.	4.25	3.50	2.75
1345-48	Set of 4 Singles	...	3.35	1.60

1991-98 Regular Issues

1349 1358 1359 1361

		Plate Block	F-VF NH	F-VF Used
1349-78	Set of 29	...	35.95	10.00
	#1349-55, 1361-74 Edible Berries			
1349	1¢ Blueberry (1992)	.40	.20	.15
1350	2¢ Strawberry (1992)	.40	.20	.15
1351	3¢ Crowberry (1992)	.50	.20	.15
1351v	3¢ Crowberry, reprint (1998)	.50	.20	...
1352	5¢ Rose Hip (1992)	.50	.20	.15
1353	6¢ Black Raspberry (1992)	.60	.20	.15
1354	10¢ Kinnikinnick (1992)	.80	.20	.15
1355	25¢ Saskatoon Berry (1992)	1.95	.45	.20
1358	42¢ Canadian Flag & Rolling Hills	3.25	.70	.15
1358a	Booklet Pane of 10	...	7.50	...
1358b	Booklet Pane of 50	...	95.00	...
1358c	Booklet Pane of 25	...	18.95	...
1359	42¢ QE II, Karsh Portrait	3.25	.70	.15
1359a	Booklet Pane of 10	...	7.50	...
1360	43¢ QE II Karsh Portrait (1992)	4.00	.85	.15
1360a	Booklet Pane of 10	...	8.50	...
1360B	43¢ Flag & Prairie, Perf. 13½ x 13 (1992)	3.50	.75	.15
1360Bc	Booklet Pane of 10, Perf. 13½ x 13	...	7.50	...
1360Bd	Booklet Pane of 25, Perf. 13½ x 13	...	20.95	...
1360Be	43¢ Flag & Prairie Perf. 14½ (1994)	5.50	1.10	.20
1360Bf	Booklet Pane of 10, Perf. 14½	...	8.95	...
1360Bg	Booklet Pane of 25, Perf. 14½	...	25.00	...
1360H	45¢ Elizabeth II ('95)	3.50	.75	.15
1360Hi	Booklet Pane of 10	...	8.50	...
1360J	45¢ Flag Perf. 14½ ('95)	3.50	.75	.15
1360Jk	Booklet Pane of 10, Perf 14½	...	8.50	...
1360Jl	Booklet Pane of 25, Perf 14½	...	25.00	...
1360Jm	45¢ Bklt. Single, Perf. 13½ x 13	...	.80	.20
1360Jn	Booklet Pane of 10, Perf 13½ x 13	...	8.50	...
1360Jo	Booklet Pane of 25, Perf 13½ x 13	...	21.50	...
1360P	45¢ Flag, smaller 16 x 20mm size, Perf. 13 x 13½ (1998)	...	.75	.20
1360Pq	Booklet Pane of 10, 13 x 13½	...	7.50	...
1360Pr	Booklet Pane of 30, 13 x 13½	...	21.95	...
1361	48¢ McIntosh Apple Tree, Perf. 13	4.25	.90	.20
1361a	48¢ Bklt. single, Perf. 14½x14 on 3 sides	...	1.30	.30
1361b	Booklet Pane of 5	...	6.50	...
1362	49¢ Delicious Apple, Perf. 13 (1992)	4.75	1.00	.20
1362a	49¢ Perf. 14½ x 14	...	1.35	.30
1362b	Booklet Pane of 5, Perf. 14½ x 14	...	6.75	...
1362c	Booklet Pane of 5, Perf. 13	...	13.95	...
1363	50¢ Snow Apple, Perf. 13 (1994)	4.75	1.00	.25
1363a	Booklet Pane of 5, Perf. 13	...	6.75	...
1363b	50¢ Bklt. Single Perf. 14½ x 14 (1995)	...	2.50	1.50
1363c	Booklet Pane of 5, Pf. 14½ x 14	...	12.50	...
1364	52¢ Gravenstein Apple Perf. 13 ('95)	9.50	1.85	.30
1364a	Booklet Pane of 5, Perf. 13	...	9.50	...
1364b	52¢ Bklt. Single, Perf. 14½ x 14	...	2.75	.70
1364c	Booklet Pane of 5, Perf 14½ x 14	...	12.50	...
1366	65¢ Black Walnut Tree	7.25	1.45	.50
1367	67¢ Beaked Hazelnut (1992)	7.00	1.40	.45
1368	69¢ Shagbark Hickory (1994)	5.95	1.30	.40
1369	71¢ American Chestnut ('95)	5.95	1.30	.45
1369a	71¢ Perf. 14½ x 14	27.50	5.50	1.50
1371	84¢ Stanley Plum Tree, Perf. 13	9.50	1.90	.50
1371a	84¢ Bklt. single, Perf. 14½x14	...	2.40	.70
1371b	Booklet Pane of 5	...	12.00	...
1372	86¢ Bartlett Pear, Perf. 13 (1992)	9.95	2.25	.60
1372a	86¢ Bklt. Single, Perf. 14½ x 14	...	3.75	1.50
1372b	Booklet Pane of 5, Perf. 14½ x 14	...	16.50	...
1372c	Booklet Pane of 5, Perf. 13	...	22.50	...
1373	88¢ Westcot Apricot, Perf. 13(1994)	8.50	1.75	.50
1373a	Booklet Pane of 5, Perf. 13	...	9.00	...
1373b	88¢ Bklt. Single, Perf. 14½ x 14 (1995)	...	3.95	.85
1373c	Booklet Pane of 5, Pf. 14½ x 14	...	19.50	...
1374	90¢ Elberta Peach, Perf. 13 ('95)	7.95	2.35	.45
1374a	Booklet Pane of 5, Perf. 13	...	12.50	...
1374ii	90¢ Elberta Peach, Perf.14½x14	87.50	17.50	...
1374b	90¢ Bklt. Single, Perf 14½ x 14	...	3.75	.85
1374c	Booklet Pane of 5, Perf. 14½ x 14	...	14.75	...

1991-96 Regular Issues (continued)

1375

1388

1395

Scotts No.		Plate Block	F-VF NH	F-VF Used
1375	$1 Yorkton Court House Perf. 14½ x 14 (1994)	8.75	1.90	.50
1375b	$1 Yorkton, Perf. 13½ x 13	8.95	1.95	.60
1376	$2 Truro Normal School (1994) Perf. 14½ x 14	15.75	3.50	1.10
1376c	$2 Truro, Perf 13½ x 13	16.75	3.65	1.10
1378	$5 Victoria Public Library (1996)	40.75	8.75	2.75

1992 Self-Adhesive Stamps

1388	42¢ Flag & Mountains, booklet single.	...	1.00	.50
1388a	Booklet of 12		11.50	...
1389	43¢ Flag & Seashore,booklet.single.	...	1.00	.50
1389a	Booklet of 12		11.50	...

1991-95 Coil Stamps, Perf. 10 Horizontal

1394	42¢ Canadian Flag & Rolling Hills	...	.80	.25
1395	43¢ Canadian Flag (1992)	...	.80	.25
1396	45¢ Canadian Flag (1995)	...	.80	.20

1992 Commemoratives

1407

1413

1419

1399-1407,1408-19,1432-55 Set of 45			38.50	17.25
1399-1403	42¢ Winter Olympics, strip of 5 bklt. stamps ...		4.75	3.50
1399-1403	Set of 5 Singles	...	4.65	1.75
1403b	Olympics Booklet Pane of 10		9.50	...
#1404-7a Canada Day, Explorers and Montreal				
1404-05	42¢ 350th Anniv. of Montreal, attd. pair ..	3.50	1.50	.80
1404-05	Set of 2 Singles	...	1.45	.60
1406	48¢ Jacques Cartier	3.95	.85	.80
1407	84¢ Christopher Columbus	6.95	1.50	.95
1407a	$2.16 Explorers S/S of 4, special edition		4.50	4.50
1407a var	Same, special ed., w/Maisonneuve signature...		160.00	...
1408-12	42¢ Rivers, strip of 5 booklet stamps	...	4.75	3.25
1408-12	Set of 5 Singles	...	4.65	1.75
1412b	Rivers Booklet Pane of 10	...	9.50	...
1413	42¢ Alaska Highway	3.50	.75	.20
1414-18	42¢ Summer Olympics,strip of 5 bklt.stamps	...	4.75	3.75
1414-18	Set of 5 Singles	...	4.65	1.75
1418b	Olympics Booklet Pane of 10	...	9.50	...
1419	50¢ Art, Red Nasturtiums	4.50	.95	.85
1431a	42¢ Canada Day, min.sht.of 12 paintings	...	25.95	24.75
1420-31	Set of 12 Singles, Provincial Views	...	24.95	18.50

1436

1441-42

1432-35	42¢ Legendary Heroes, attd	4.35	3.75	2.25
1432-35	Set of 4 Singles	...	3.65	1.20
1436-40	42¢ Minerals, strip of 5 booklet stamps ..	...	5.00	4.50
1436-40	Set of 5 Singles	...	4.85	1.75
1440b	Minerals Booklet Pane of 10	...	9.75	...
1441-42	42¢ Space Exploration, Pair	3.95	1.80	1.50
1441-42	Set of 2 Singles	...	1.70	1.40

1992 Commemoratives (continued)

1445

1446-47

1453

Scott's No.		Plate Block	F-VF NH	F-VF Used
1443	42¢ Hockey, Early Years	...	.75	.25
1443a	Skates, sticks, booklet pane of 8	...	5.95	...
1444	42¢ Hockey, Six-Team Years	...	.75	.25
1444a	Team emblems, booklet pane of 8	...	5.95	...
1445	42¢ Hockey, Expansion Years	...	.75	.25
1445a	Goalie's mask, booklet pane of 9	...	7.50	...
1446-47	42¢ Order of Canada & R. Michener, pair	4.25	1.80	1.30
1446	42¢ Order of Canada	...	.75	.25
1447	42¢ Roland Michener		1.10	.35
1448-51	42¢ WWII, 1942 Events, attd	4.35	3.75	2.50
1448-51	Set of 4 Singles	...	3.65	1.60
1452	42¢ Christmas, Jouluvana, perf. 12½ ...	3.50	.75	.15
1452a	42¢ Bklt. Single Perf. 13½	...	.85	.20
1452b	Booklet Pane of 10, Perf. 13½	...	7.50	...
1453	48¢ Christmas, La Befana	4.00	.85	.75
1453a	Booklet Pane of 5	...	5.25	...
1454	84¢ Christmas, Weihnachtsmann	7.25	1.50	.80
1454a	Booklet Pane of 5	...	8.50	...
1455	37¢ Christmas, Santa Claus, Bklt. Sgl ...	...	.85	.60
1455a	Booklet Pane of 10	...	8.25	...

1993 Commemoratives

1460

1466

1484

1456-71,1484-89,1491-1506 Set of 38		...	34.75	13.75
1456-59	43¢ Canadian Woman, attd	4.35	3.75	2.25
1456-59	Set of 4 Singles		3.65	1.20
1460	43¢ Stanley Cup Centennial	3.50	.75	.20
1461-65	43¢ Hand-crafted Textiles, strip of 5	...	4.50	3.00
1461-65	Set of 5 Singles	...	4.40	1.75
1465b	Textiles, Booklet Pane of 10	...	8.75	...
1466	86¢ Art, Drawing for the Owl	7.00	1.50	1.00
1467-71	43¢ Historic Hotels, Strip of 5 bklt. sgls ..	...	4.50	3.00
1467-71	Set of 5 Singles	...	4.40	1.75
1471b	Historic Hotels, Booklet Pane of 10	...	8.75	...
1483a	43¢ Canada Day, Provincial & Territorial Parks, miniature sheet of 12 ...	...	18.95	15.95
1472-83	Set of 12 Singles	...	17.95	8.75
1484	43¢ Founding of Toronto	3.50	.75	.20

1485-89

1491-94

1495-98

1485-89	43¢ Rivers, Strip of 5 bklt. sgls.	...	4.50	3.00
1485-89	Set of 5 Singles	...	4.40	1.75
1489b	Rivaers, Booklet Pane of 10	...	8.75	...
1490	$3.56 Motor Vehicles, Souv. Sheet of 6 ..	...	8.50	8.25
1490a-f	Set of 6 Singles, 2-43¢,2-49¢,2-86¢	...	8.35	7.50
1491-94	43¢ Folk Songs, attd	4.35	3.75	2.75
1491-94	Set of 4 Singles	...	3.65	1.20
1495-98	43¢ Dinosaurs, attd	4.65	3.95	3.00
1495-98	Set of 4 Singles	...	3.85	1.20
1499	43¢ Christmas, Swiety Mikolaj	4.00	.85	.15
1499a	Booklet Pane of 10	...	8.25	...
1500	49¢ Christmas, Ded Moroz	4.15	.90	.80
1500a	Booklet Pane of 5	...	4.50	...
1501	86¢ Christmas, Father Christmas	7.50	1.60	1.00
1501a	Booklet Pane of 5	...	7.95	...

1993 Commemoratives (continued)

Scott's No.		Plate Block	F-VF NH	F-VF Used
1502	38¢ Christmas, Santa Claus, bklt. sgl	...	.75	.50
1502a	Booklet Pane of 10	...	7.35	...
1503-06	43¢ World War II, 1943 Events, attd.	4.35	3.75	2.50
1503-06	Set of 4 Singles	...	3.65	1.60

1509   **1510**   **1511**

1994 Regular Issues

1507-08	43¢ Greetings, Self-adhesive	...	2.25	1.20
1508a	Booklet Pane of 10 (5 each) w/stickers ..	...	10.95	...

1994 Commemoratives

1509-22,1525-26,1528-40 Set of 29		...	26.85	12.95
1509	43¢ Jeanne Sauve with Tab	...	.90	.30
1509	Block of 4 w/4 different tabs	4.25	3.75	2.25
1510	43¢ T. Eaton Company.	...	.85	.30
1510a	Prestige Booklet of 10	...	7.95	...
1511-15	43¢ Rivers, Strip of 5 bklt. sgls.	...	6.50	5.00
1511-15	Set of 5 Singles	...	6.40	2.75
1515b	Rivers, Booklet Pane of 10	...	12.50	...
1516	88¢ Canadian Art, Vera	8.50	1.80	1.25

1522   **1529-32**

1517-22	43¢-88¢ Commonwealth Games(6)	15.00	4.95	1.95
1517-18	43¢ Lawn Bowl and Lacrosse, Pair	3.50	1.50	.90
1517-18	Set of 2 Singles	...	1.45	.50
1519-20	43¢ High Jump and Wheelchair Marathon, Pair	3.50	1.50	.90
1519-20	Set of 2 Singles	...	1.45	.50
1521	50¢ Diving	5.25	1.10	.95
1522	88¢ Cycling	7.50	1.60	.85
1523	43¢ Year of the Family, Souv. Sht. of 5 ..	...	5.25	4.50
1523a-e	Set of 5 Singles	...	5.15	2.25
1524	43¢ Canada Day, Maple Trees, Miniature Sheet of 12	...	12.75	10.95
1524a-l	Set of 12 Singles	...	12.50	7.50
1525-26	43¢ Billy Bishop and Mary Travers, Pair	3.50	1.50	.80
1525-26	Set of 2 Singles	...	1.45	.60
1527	$3.62 Public Service Vehicles, Souvenir Sheet of 6	...	8.50	7.25
1527a-f	Set of 6 Singles, 2-43¢,2-50¢,2-88¢	...	8.35	5.75
1528	43¢ Civil Aviation, ICAO	3.50	.75	.20
1529-32	43¢ Prehistoric Life, attd.	4.35	3.75	2.50
1529-32	Set of 4 Singles	...	3.65	1.40
1533	43¢ Christmas, Singing Carols	3.50	.75	.15
1533a	Booklet Pane of 10	...	7.50	...
1534	50¢ Christmas, Choir	4.25	.90	.70
1534a	Booklet Pane of 5	...	4.50	...
1535	88¢ Christmas, Caroling	7.50	1.60	1.00
1535a	Booklet Pane of 5	...	7.75	...
1536	38¢ Christmas, Soloist, booklet single ...	...	.95	.50
1536a	Booklet Pane of 10	...	9.25	...
1537-40	43¢ World War II, 1944 Events, attd.	4.50	4.00	3.25
1537-40	Set of 4 Singles	...	3.95	1.60

1995 Commemoratives

1541-51,1553-58,1562-66,1570-90 Set of 46		...	39.50	13.85
1541-44	43¢ World War II, 1995 Events, attd.	4.65	4.00	3.25
1541-44	Set of 4 Singles	...	3.95	1.60
1545	88¢ Art, "Floraison"	7.50	1.60	.85
1546	(43¢) Canada Flag 30th Anniv.	3.50	.75	.25
1547-51	(43¢) Fortress of Louisbourg, Strip of 5 Bklt. Singles	...	4.50	3.50
1547-51	Set of 5 singles	...	4.40	1.75
1551b	Louisbourg, Booklet Pane of 10	...	8.75	...

1552

1558   **1536-66**   **1562**

Scott's No.		Plate Block	F-VF NH	F-VF Used
1552	$3.62 Farm and Frontier Vehicles, Souvenir Sheet of 6	...	8.50	6.95
1552a-f	Set of 6 Singles, 2-43¢,2-50¢,2-88¢	...	8.25	5.75
1553-57	43¢ Golf, Strip of 5 Bklt. Sgls.	...	4.50	3.25
1553-57	Set of 5 Singles	...	4.40	1.75
1557b	Golf, Booklet Pane of 10	...	8.75	...
1558	43¢ Lunenburg Academy	3.50	.75	.25
1559-61	43¢ Canada Day, Set of 3 Souvenir Sheets bearing 10 different stamps	...	11.95	11.50
1559a-c,1560a-d,1561a-c Set of 10 Singles		...	11.75	10.75
1562	43¢ Manitoba	3.50	.75	.30
1563-66	43¢ Migratory Wildlife,"Aune" Block of 4	5.50	4.75	2.25
1563-66	Set of 4 singles	...	4.50	1.20
1563/67	43¢ Migratory Wildlife revised Inscribed "Faune", Block of 4	6.00	5.25	2.50
1567	43¢ Belted Kingfisher Single "Faune"	...	2.50	2.25

1568-69

1995 Greetings Booklets

1568-69	45¢ Greetings, Self-adhesive	...	2.50	1.10
1569a	Booklet Pane of 10 (5 Each) w/ labels	...	11.50	...
1569c	Booklet Pane of 10 w/ "Canadian Memorial Chiropractic College", covers and labels	...	11.50	...

1579   **1584**   **1585**

1995 Commemoratives (continued)

Scott's No.		Plate Block	F-VF NH	F-VF Used
1570-73	45¢ Bridges, Block of 4	4.35	3.75	2.25
1570-73	Set of 4 Singles	...	3.65	1.20
1574-78	45¢ Canadian Arctic, Strip of 5 Bklt.Sgls.	...	4.50	3.25
1574-78	Set of 5 Singles	...	4.40	1.60
1578b	Arctic, Booklet Pane of 10	...	8.75	...
1579-83	45 Comic Books, Strip of 5 Bklt. Singls. ..	...	4.50	3.25
1579-83	Set of 5 Singles	...	4.40	1.60
1583b	Comic Books, Booklet Pane of 10	...	8.75	...
1584	45¢ U.N. 50th Anniversary	3.95	.80	.25
1585	45¢ Christmas, The Nativity	3.95	.80	.20
1585a	Booklet Pane of 10	...	8.00	...
1586	52¢ Christmas, The Annunciation	4.75	1.00	.80
1586a	Booklet Pane of 5	...	4.75	...
1587	90¢ Christmas, Flight to Egypt	7.95	1.60	.90
1587a	Booklet Pane of 5	...	8.25	...
1588	40¢ Christmas, Holly, booklet single	...	.80	.60
1588a	Booklet Pane of 10	...	7.95	...
1589	45¢ La Francophonie	3.95	.80	.25
1590	45¢ End of Holocaust	3.95	.80	.25

1996 Commemoratives

1595-98

1591-98,1602-3,1606-14,1617-21,1622-29 Set of 36		...	36.00	14.25
1591-94	45¢ Birds, Strip of 4	...	3.50	2.50
1591-94	Set of 4 singles	...	3.40	1.10
1591-94d	Diamond Pane of 12	...	12.95	...
1591-94r	Rectangular Pane of 12	...	16.95	...
1595-98	45¢ High Technology Industries, Block of 4 Booklet singles	...	5.00	4.00
1595-98	Set of 4 singles	...	4.95	1.40
1598b	Technology, Booklet Pane of 12	...	14.75	...

1996 Greetings Booklets

1600-1	45¢ Greetings, Self-adhesive	...	2.75	1.80
1601a	Booklet Pane of 10 (5 each) with labels .	...	12.95	...

NOTE: #1600-1 are slightly larger than #1568-69.

1996 Commemoratives (continued)

1602	90¢ Art "The Spirit of Haidi Gwali"	7.00	1.50	.90
1603	45¢ Aids Awareness	4.15	.85	.25
1604	$3.74 Industrial and Commercial Vehicles Souvenir Sheet of 6	...	8.75	8.50
1604a-f	Set of 6 singles, 2-45¢,2-52¢,2-90¢	...	8.50	6.75
1605	5¢ (10), 10¢ (4), 20¢ (10), 45¢ Canadian Vehicles Souvenir Pane of 25	...	9.75	...
1605a-y	Set of 25 Singles	...	9.65	7.75

NOTE: The above pane pictures all 24 stamps shown on the Vehicles series souvenir sheets of 6 plus one additional vehicle.

1607 **1613** **1614**

1606	45¢ Yukon Gold Strip of 5	...	5.25	3.25
1606a-e	Yukon Set of 5 Singles	...	5.15	1.75
1606	Yukon Miniature Pane of 10	...	10.50	...
1607	45¢ Canada Day, Maple Leaf in stylized Quilt Design, self-adhesive	...	1.20	.40
1607a	Canada Day Pane of 12	...	13.50	...
1608-12	45¢ Canadian Olympic Gold Medalist, Strip of 5 Booklet Singles	...	5.65	3.75
1608-12	Set of 5 Singles	...	5.50	2.75
1612b	Olympics, Booklet Pane of 10	...	11.00	...
1613	45¢ British Columbia	3.75	.80	.25
1614	45¢ Canadian Heraldry	3.75	.80	.25
1615-16	45¢ 100 Years of Cinema, Self-adhesive Souvenir Sheets of 5 (2)	...	9.75	...
1615a-16a	Set of 10 Singles	...	9.65	7.50

CANADA

1617 **1627** **1628**

Scott's No.		Plate Block	F-VF NH	F-VF Used
1617	45¢ Edouard Montpetit	3.50	.75	.25
1618-21	45¢ Winnie the Pooh, Block of 4	...	7.00	6.50
1618-21	Set of 4 Singles	...	6.95	1.60
1618-21	Booklet of 16 (4 each design)	...	28.00	...
1621b	45¢ Winnie the Pooh, Souvenir Sheet of 4	...	7.00	6.50
1622-26	45¢ Authors, Booklet Strip of 5	...	5.00	4.00
1622-26	Set of 5 Singles	...	4.90	1.50
1626b	Authors, Booklet Pane of 10	...	9.75	...
1627	45¢ Christmas, Snowshoes, Sled	3.75	.80	.20
1627a	Booklet Pane of 10	...	8.00	...
1628	52¢ Christmas, Skiing	4.75	1.00	.75
1628a	Booklet Pane of 5	...	5.00	...
1629	90¢ Christmas, Skating	7.35	1.60	1.25
1629a	Booklet Pane of 5	...	8.00	...

1997 Commemoratives

1630, 1631-36, 1637-38, 1639-48, 1649-60, 1661-69, 1670, 1671, 1672, Set of 43			36.75	22.95
1630	45¢ Chinese New Year, Year of the Ox ..	4.25	.90	.30
1630a	New Year Souvenir Sheet of 2	...	2.25	2.10
1630v	Hong Kong '97 Overprint SS of 2	...	8.75	...
1631-34	45¢ Birds, Block or Strip of 4	4.00	3.50	1.85
1631-34	Set of 4 Singles	...	3.40	1.10
1635	90¢ Art, "York Boat on Lake Winnipeg" ..	7.50	1.65	1.25
1636	45¢ Canadian Tire, 75th Anniversary	...	.85	.40
1636a	Tire, Booklet of 12	...	9.95	...

1637 **1638** **1639**

1640 **1641-44**

1647 **1649** **1655**

1637	45¢ Father Charles-Emile Gadbois	3.75	.80	.25
1638	45¢ Quebec Floral Festival, Blue Poppy	...	.85	.25
1638a	Blue Poppy, Booklet Pane of 12	...	9.95	...
1639	45¢ Victorian Order of Nurses	3.75	.80	.25
1640	45¢ Law Society of Upper Canada	3.75	.80	.25
1641-44	45¢ Ocean Water Fish, Block of 4	4.00	3.50	1.85
1641-44	Fish, Set of 4 Singles	...	3.40	1.10
1645-46	45¢ Confederation Bridge, Pair	3.75	1.65	1.10
1645-46	Bridge, Set of 2 Singles	...	1.60	.50
1647	45¢ Gilles Villeneuve	3.75	.80	.25
1648	90¢ Gilles Villeneuve	8.95	1.95	1.50
1648b	45¢-90¢ Gilles Villeneuve, S/S of 8	...	11.75	...
1649	45¢ John Cabot	3.75	.80	.25
1650-53	45¢ Scenic Highways, Block of 4	4.00	3.50	1.85
1650-53	Highways, Set of 4 Singles	...	3.40	1.10

1997 Commemoratives (continued)

Scott's No.		Plate Block	F-VF NH	F-VF Used
1654	45¢ Canadian Industrial Designers	3.75	.80	.25
1654	45¢ Industrial, Sheet of 24 w/12 diff. labels	...	17.75	...
1655	45¢ Highland Games	3.75	.80	.25
1656	45¢ Knights of Columbus	3.75	.80	.25
1657	45¢ World Congress PTTI	3.75	.80	.25
1658	45¢ Year of Asia-Pacific	3.75	.80	.25
1659-60	45¢ Hockey Series of Century, bklt. single	...	1.70	.60
1660a	45¢ Hockey, Booklet Pane of 10 (5 ea.) .	...	8.50	...
1661-64	45¢ Prominent Canadians, block or strip	4.00	3.50	1.85
1661-64	45¢ Prominent Canadians, set of 4 singles	...	3.40	1.10

1665-68

1669

1672

1665-68	45¢ Supernatural, block of 4	4.00	3.50	1.85
1665-68	45¢ Supernatural, set of 4 singles	...	3.40	1.10
1665-68	45¢ Supernatural, sheetlet of 16	...	13.75	...
1669	45¢ Christmas, Stained Glass Windows	3.75	.80	.20
1669a	45¢ Christmas, Booklet Pane of 10	...	8.00	...
1670	52¢ Christmas, Stained Glass Windows	4.85	1.00	.85
1670a	52¢ Christmas, Booklet Pane of 5	...	4.95	...
1671	90¢ Christmas, Stained Glass Windows	7.75	1.60	.95
1671a	90¢ Christmas, Booklet Pane of 5	...	8.00	...
1672	45¢ Royal Agricultural Winter Fair	3.75	.80	.25

1997-2000 Regular Issues

1673	1682	1687	1692	1698

1673-1700 1¢-S8 set of 17		...	24.50	15.95
1673	1¢ Bookbinding (1999)	.40	.20	.15
1674	2¢ Decorative Ironwork (1999)	.40	.20	.15
1675	3¢ Glass-blowing (1999)	.40	.20	.15
1676	4¢ Oyster Farming (1999)	.45	.20	.15
1677	5¢ Weaving (1999)	.45	.20	.15
1678	9¢ Quilting (1999)	.70	.20	.15
1679	10¢ Artistic Woodworking (1999)	.75	.20	.15
1680	25¢ Leatherworking (1999)	1.75	.40	.20
1682	46¢ Queen Elizabeth II (1998)	3.50	.75	.15
1683	47¢ Elizabeth II (2000)	3.25	.70	.20
1687	46¢ Flag over Mountains (1998)	3.50	.75	.15
1687a	Flag, Booklet Pane of 10	...	7.50	...
1692	55¢ Maple Leaf, (1998)	4.75	1.00	.60
1692a	Maple Leaf, Booklet Pane of 5	...	5.00	...
1694	73¢ Maple Leaf (1998)	5.75	1.25	.70
1696	95¢ Maple Leaf (1998)	7.00	1.55	1.00
1696a	Maple Leaf, Booklet Pane of 5	...	7.65	...
1697	$1 Loon (1998)	7.50	1.65	1.00
1698	$2 Polar Bear (1998)	13.95	3.25	2.00
1700	$8 Grizzly Bear, ...	62.50	13.50	9.95
1703	46¢ Canadian Flag Coil, Perf. 10 Horiz. (1998) ...		.75	.20
1705	46¢ Flag over Mountains, S.A. Booklet Single	...	1.10	.60
1705a	Flag, Self-adhesive Booklet Pane of 30 (1998) ...		25.00	...
1706	46¢ Maple Leaf, Self-adhesive Booklet Single	...	.95	.70
1706a	Maple Leaf, S.A. Booklet Pane of 18 (1998)	...	15.00	...
1707	47¢ Flag & Inunshuk, SA Booklet Single (2000)	...	.70	.25
1707a	Flag, Booklet of 10	...	6.85	...
1707b	Flag, Booklet of 30	...	19.95	...

CANADA

1998 Commemoratives

1708

1710-13

Scott's No.		Sheet-lets	Plate Block	F-VF NH	FVF Used
1708,1710-13, 1715-20, 1721-24, 1735-37, 1738-42,					
1750-54, 1756-60, 1761-66 Set of 40		...	...	35.00	14.75
1708	45¢ Year of the Tiger	(25) 19.75	3.75	.80	.25
1708a	45¢ Year of the Tiger S/S of 2		...	1.75	1.65
1708i	same, Overprinted Souvenir Sheet		...	3.25	...
1709	45¢ Provincial Prime Ministers				
	Souvenir Sheet of 10		...	8.75	8.50
1709a-j	Set of 10 Singles		...	8.65	5.50
1710-13	45¢ Birds, Strip or Block of 4	(20) 17.50	4.00	3.50	2.95
1710-13	45¢ Birds, Set of 4 Singles		...	3.40	1.20

1714,14B	1721	1722	1735

1998 Self-Adhesive Stamps

1714	45¢ Maple Leaf, die-cut		...	2.25	1.35
1714a	Sheetlet of 18		...	29.50	...
1714B	45¢ Maple Leaf Coil, die-cut		...	1.75	1.10

1998 Commemoratives (continued)

1715-20	45¢ Fishing Flies, Strip of 6 Bklt. Stamps		...	7.00	4.25
1715-20	Flies, Set of 6 Singles		...	6.75	3.50
1720a	Flies, Bklt. Pane of 12		...	13.85	...
1721	45¢ Institute of Mining, Metallurgy				
	and Petroleum	(20) 19.75	3.75	.80	.25
1722	45¢ Imperial Penny Postage				
	Centennial	(14) 12.95	4.50	.95	.35
1723-24	45¢ Sumo Wrestling, 2 designs ..	(20) 16.50	4.00	1.70	1.25
1723-24	Sumo, Set of 2 Singles		...	1.65	.60
1724b	45¢ Sumo, Souvenir Sheet of 2 .		...	1.85	1.60
1734a	45¢ Canals, Booklet of 10 Stamps		...	11.75	...
1725-34	Canals, Set of 10 Singles		...	11.50	5.75
1735	45¢ Health Professionals	(16) 12.50	3.75	.80	.25

1737b

1736-37	45¢ Royal Canadian Mounted				
	Police	(20) 16.75	4.00	1.70	1.40
1736-37	Mounties, Set of 2 Singles		...	1.65	.60
1737b	45¢ Mounties, Souvenir Sheet of 2		...	2.50	2.25
1737c	Same, "French" Overprint		...	4.25	4.25
1737d	Same, "Portugal" Overprint		...	4.95	4.75
1737e	Same, "Italia," "98" Overprint		...	4.95	4.75

1998 Commemoratives (continued)

1738

1761

1750-53

Scott's No.		Sheet-lets	Plate Block	F-VF NH	FVF used
1738	45¢ William J. Roue, "Bluenose"	(25) 19.75	3.75	.80	.25
1739-42	45¢ Scenic Highways, Block or Strip of 4	(20) 16.75	4.00	3.50	3.00
1739-42	Highways, Set of 4 Singles	...		3.40	1.20
1743-49	45¢ Montreal Painters, Set of 7 Singles			6.85	4.95
1749a	45¢ Montreal Painters "The Automatistes Booklet of 7	...		6.95	...
1750-53	45¢ Legendary Canadians, Block/Strip of 4	(20) 16.75	4.00	3.50	3.00
1750-53	Canadians, Set of 4 Singles			3.40	1.20
1754	90¢ Canadian Art, "The Farmers Family"	(16) 24.75	7.50	1.60	1.25
1755	45¢ Housing in Canada, Sheetlet of 9	...		8.75	...
1755a-i	45¢ Housing, Set of 9 Singles	...		8.65	6.25
1756	45¢ University of Ottawa	(20) 15.75	3.75	.80	.25
1757-60	45¢ Circus, Set of 4 Singles	...		4.20	1.50
1760a	45¢ Circus, Booklet of 12	...		12.50	...
1760b	45¢ Circus, Souvenir Sheet of 4 .	...		4.50	4.35
1761	45¢ John Humphrey	(20) 15.75	3.75	.80	.25

1762-63

1762-63	45¢ Naval Vessels, attd.	(20) 16.25	3.85	1.70	1.40
1762-63	45¢ Naval Vessels, set of 2 singles	...		1.65	.60
1764	45¢ Christmas Angel		3.75	.80	.20
1764a	45¢ Christmas Booklet Pane of 10	...		8.00	...
1765	52¢ Christmas Angel		4.85	1.00	.85
1765a	52¢ Christmas Booklet Pane of 5	...		4.95	...
1766	90¢ Christmas Angel		8.00	1.65	1.15
1766a	90¢ Christmas Booklet Pane of 5	...		8.25	...

1999 Commemoratives

1767

1769

1779

1767, 1769-79, 1780-1806, 1809-10, 1812-17					
	set of 47	...		33.50	21.95
1767	46¢ Year of the Rabbit	(25) 17.00	3.25	.70	.30
1768	95¢ Year of the Rabbit Souvenir Sheet	...		1.40	1.35
1768i	same, China'99 Logo Overprint .	...		2.75	2.50
1769	46¢ Theatre du Rideau Vert	(16) 10.95	3.25	.70	.30
1770-73	46¢ Birds of Canada, attd.	(20) 13.95	3.25	2.80	2.70
1770-73	Birds, set of 4 singles			2.75	1.60
1774-77	46¢ Birds of Canada, Self-adhesive singles			2.80	2.00
1777a	Birds, Booklet Pane, 2-1774-5, 1-1776-7	...		4.25	...
1777b	Birds, Booklet Pane, 1-1774-5, 2-1776-7	...		4.25	...
1777v	Birds, Booklet of 12, Self-adhesive	...		8.35	...
1778	46¢ UBC Museum of Anthropology	(16) 10.95	3.25	.70	.30

1999 Commemoratives (continued)

1780-83

Scott's No.		Sheet-lets	Plate Block	F-VF NH	F-VF Used
1779	46¢ "Marco Polo", 19th Century Ship	(16) 10.95	3.25	.70	.30
1779a	46¢"Marco Polo" on Souvenir Sheet with 85¢ Australian Joint Issue	...		2.35	2.25
1780-83	46¢ Scenic Highways , attd.	(20) 13.95	3.25	2.80	2.70
1780-83	Highways, Set of 4 singles	...		2.75	1.60
1784	46¢ Nunavit	(20) 13.95	3.25	.70	.30
1785	46¢ Year of Older Person	(16) 10.95	3.25	.70	.30
1786	46¢ Sikh Canadians	(16) 10.95	3.25	.70	.30
1787-90	46¢ Orchids, 4 Booklet Singles ..	...		2.80	2.00
1790a	Orchids, Booklet of 12	...		8.35	...
1790b	Orchids, Souvenir Sheet of 4	...		3.50	...
1791-94	46¢ Canadian Horses, attd	(20) 13.95	3.25	2.80	2.00
1791-94	Horses, Set of 4 singles	...		2.75	1.60
1795-98	Horses, Booklet Singles, SA	...		2.80	2.00
1798a	Horses, Booklet of 12	...		8.35	...
1799	46¢ Barreau du Quebec	(16) 10.95	3.25	.70	.30
1800	95¢ Canadian Art. "Cog Licorne"	(16) 22.75	6.75	1.45	1.25
1801-4	46¢ Pan-American Games, attd .	(16) 10.95	3.25	2.80	2.00
1801-4	Games, Set of 4 singles	...		2.75	1.60
1805	46¢ World Rowing Championship	(20) 13.95	3.25	.70	.30
1806	46¢ Universal Postal Union	(20) 13.95	3.25	.70	.30
1807	46¢ Canadian Air Show, Sheet of 4	...		2.80	2.70
1807a-d	Air Show, Set of 4 singles	...		2.75	1.80
1808	46¢ Canadian Air Force 75th Anniv. Sheet of 16	...		11.00	...
1808a-p	Air Force, Set of 16 singles	...		10.75	9.50
1809	46¢ NATO 50th Anniversary	(16) 10.95	3.25	.70	.30

1810

1813

1814

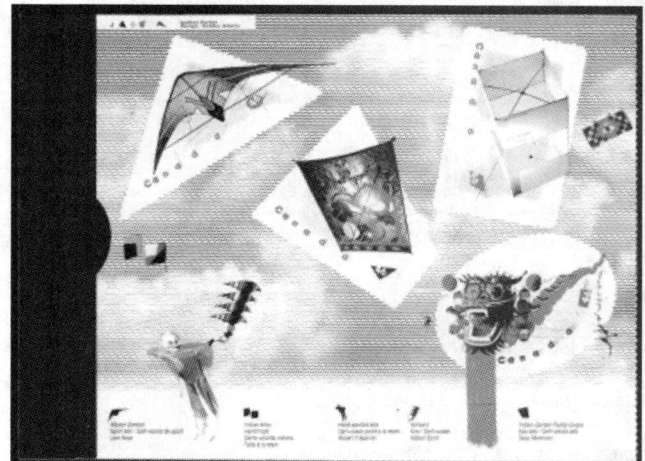

1811a-d

1810	46¢ Frontier College	(16) 10.95	3.25	.70	.30
1811a-d	46¢ Kites, set of 4 designs, SA ..	...		2.80	2.60
1811	46¢ Kites, Complete Booklet of 8, SA	...		5.50	...
1812	46¢ Millennium Hologram, Dove	(4) 2.80		.70	.50
1813	55¢ Millennium Lithog., Girl & Dove	(4) 3.40		.85	.80
1814	95¢ Millennium Engraved, Dove on Branch	(4) 5.80		1.45	1.40

1999 Commemoratives (continued)

Scott's No.		Sheet-lets	Plate Block	F-VF NH	FVF Used
1815	46¢ Christmas Angels		3.25	.70	.30
1815a	46¢ Angels Booklet Pane of 10 ..		...	6.95	...
1816	55¢ Christmas Angels		3.85	.85	.75
1816a	55¢ Angels Booklet Pane of 5		...	4.25	...
1817	95¢ Christmas Angels		6.50	1.45	1.40
1817a	95¢ Angels Booklet Pane of 5		...	7.25	...

1999-2000 Millennium Collection Souvenir Sheets of 4

1820

1818-34	Set of 17 Souvenir Sheets	...	44.75	...
1818	46¢ Media Technologies: IMAX, Softimage, William Stephenson, Ted Rogers Jr.	...	2.75	2.75
1818a-d	46¢ Media, set of 4 singles	...	2.75	2.40
1819	46¢ Canadian Entertainment: Calgary Stampede, Cirque du Soleil, Hockey-forum, Hockey Night	...	2.75	2.75
1819a-d	46¢ Entertainment, set of 4 singles	...	2.75	2.40
1820	46¢ Extraordinary Entertainers: Portia White, Glenn Gould, Felix Leclerc, Guy Lombardo	...	2.75	2.75
1820a-d	46¢ Entertainers, set of 4 singles	...	2.75	2.40
1821	46¢ Fostering Canadian Talent: Academy of Arts, Canada Council, Canadian Broadcasting Corp., National Film Board	...	2.75	2.75
1821a-d	46¢ Talent, set of 4 singles	...	2.75	2.40
1822	46¢ Medical Innovators: Frederick Banting, Armand Frappier, Maude Abbott, Dr. Hans Selye	...	2.75	2.75
1822a-d	46¢ Medical, set of 4 singles	...	2.75	2.40
1823	46¢ Social Progress: Les Hospitalieres, Women are Persons, Desjardins, Moses Coady	...	2.75	2.75
1823a-d	46¢ Social, set of 4 singles	...	2.75	2.40
1824	Hearts of Gold: CIDA, Lucille Teasdale, Meals and Friends on Wheels, Marathon of Hope	...	2.75	2.75
1824a-d	46¢ Hearts of Gold, set of 4 singles	...	2.75	2.40
1825	46¢ Humanitarians and Peacekeepers: Raoul Dandurand, Vanier and Smellie, Banning Land Mines, Lester B. Pearson	...	2.75	2.75
1825a-d	46¢ Humanitarians, set of 4 singles	...	2.75	2.40
1826	46¢ First Peoples: Pontiac, Tom Longboat, Healing from Within, Inuit Shamans	...	2.75	2.75
1826a-d	46¢ First Peoples, set of 4 singles	...	2.75	2.40
1827	46¢ Cultural Fabric: L'Anse Aux Meadows, Welcome to Canada, Stratford Festival, Neptune Story	...	2.75	2.75
1827a-d	46¢ Cultural, set of 4 singles	...	2.75	2.40
1828	46¢ Literary Legends: W.O.Mitchell, Gratien Gelinas, Harlequin, Pierre Tisseyre	...	2.75	2.75
1828a-d	46¢ Literary, set of 4 singles	...	2.75	2.40
1829	46¢ Great Thinkers: Marshal McLuhan, Northrop Frye, Hilda Marion Neatby, Roger Lemelin	...	2.75	2.75
1829a-d	46¢ Thinkers, set of 4 singles	...	2.75	2.40
1830	46¢ Tradition of Generosity: Massey Foundation, Killam Legacy, Macdonald Stewart Foundation, Eric Lafferty Harvie	...	2.75	2.75
1830a-d	46¢ Generosity, set of 4 singles .	...	2.75	2.40
1831	46¢ Engineering and Technological Marvels: Locomotive & Tunnel, Manic Dams, Canadian Satellites, CN Tower	...	2.75	2.75
1831a-d	46¢ Engineering, set of 4 singles ...	...	2.75	2.40
1832	46¢ Fathers of Invention: George Klein, Abraham Geiner, Alexander Graham Bell, Joseph-Armand Bombardier	...	2.75	2.75
1832a-d	46¢ Invention, set of 4 singles	...	2.75	2.40
1833	46¢ Food: Marquis Wheat, Pablum, Frozen Fish, McCain Foods	...	2.75	2.75
1833a-d	46¢ Food, set of 4 singles	...	2.75	2.40
1834	46¢ Enterprising Giants: Hudson's Bay Company, Bell Canada, Vachon Co., George Weston Ltd.	...	2.75	2.75
1834a-d	46¢ Giants, set of 4 singles	...	2.75	2.40

Note: These sheets depict stamps that are included in the limited edition Millennium Collection hard-cover book that is available for $79.50. There are slight differences between the stamps in the book and the souvenir sheets.

2000 Commemoratives

1835

1836

1837

Scott's No.		Sheet-lets	Plate Block	F-VF NH	F-VF Used
1835-36,39-48,49-52,54-57 set of 48				39.50	...
1835	46¢ Millennium Partnership	(16) 10.95	3.25	.70	.30
1836	46¢ Year of the Dragon	(25) 17.00	3.25	.70	.30
1837	95¢ Year of the Dragon Souvenir Sheet	...		1.45	1.40
1838	46¢ 50th National Hockey League All-Start Game Souvenir Sheet of 6	...		4.15	3.95
1839-42	46¢ Canadian Birds	(20) 13.75	3.25	2.80	2.65
1839-42	46¢ Birds, set of 4 singles			2.75	1.60
1843-46	46¢ Canadian Birds, Booklet Singles			2.80	1.80
	Note: 1843-Canada Warbler,1844-Osprey, 1845-Loon, 1846 Blue Jay				
1846a	46¢ Birds Bklt.Pane of 6 (2each 1843-4, 1 each 1845-6)			4.20	...
1846b	46¢ Birds Bklt.Pane of 6 (1each 1843-4, 2 each 1845-6)			4.20	...
1846a-b	46¢ Birds Booklet of 12 with 2 Bklt.Panes of 6			8.35	...
1847	46¢ Supreme Court	(16) 10.95	3.25	.70	.30
1848	46¢ Ritual of the Calling of an Engineer, Pair	(16) 10.95	3.25	.70	.30
1848a	46¢ Engineer, Tete-Beche Pair ...	...		1.40	1.30
1849-52	46¢ Rural Mailboxes, block	...		2.85	2.60
1849-52	46¢ Mailboxes, set of 4 singles ..	...		2.80	1.80
1852a	46¢ Mailboxes, Booklet of 12	...		8.35	...

2000 Greetings Booklet

1853	46¢ Greetings, Self-adhesive	...		.75	.65
1853a	46¢ Booklet of 5 + 5 stickers	...		3.50	...

2000 Commemoratives (continued)

1856

1858

1854	55¢ Fresh Waters, Booklet of 5, SA	...		4.25	...
1854a-e	55¢ Fresh Waters, set of 5 singles ...	...		4.20	4.00
1855	95¢ Fresh Waters, Booklet of 5, SA	...		7.25	...
1855a-e	95¢ Fresh Waters, set of 5 singles ...	...		7.20	7.00
1856	95¢ Queen Mother's 100th Birthday	(9) 12.75		1.45	1.25
1857	46¢ Boys and Girls Clubs	(16) 10.95	3.25	.70	.30
1858	46¢ Seventh-Day Adventists	(16) 10.95	3.25	.70	.30
1859-62	46¢ Stampin' the Future, attd	(16) 10.95	3.25	2.80	...
1859-62	46¢ Stampin' set of 4 singles			2.75	1.60
1862b	46¢ Stampin' the Future, Souvenir Sheet of 4			2.80	...
1863	95¢ Art "Artist et Niagara"	(16) 22.75	6.75	1.45	1.25
1864-65	46¢ Tall Ships visit Halifax, 2 designs, SA			1.45	.80
1864b	46¢ Tall Ships Booklet of 10	...		7.15	...
1866	46¢ Labour	(16) 10.95	3.25	.70	.30
1867	46¢ Petro-Canada			.70	.30
1867a	46¢ Petro-Canada	...		8.35	...
1868-71	46¢ Whales, block of 4	(16) 10.95	3.25	2.80	2.75
1868-71	46¢ Whales, set of 4 singles			2.75	1.60
1872	46¢ Christmas Greetings Single .			.70	.70
1872a	46¢ Christmas Greetings Booklet of 5	...		3.50	...
1873	46¢ Christmas Nativity		3.25	.70	.30
1873a	46¢ Christmas Nativity Booklet of 10	...		6.95	...
1874	55¢ Christmas Nativity		3.85	.85	.75
1874a	55¢ Christmas Nativity Booklet of 6	...		5.00	...
1875	95¢ Christmas Nativity		6.50	1.45	1.40
1875a	95¢ Christmas Nativity Booklet of 6	...		8.50	...
1876-77	46¢ Horse Regiments, Pair	(10) 10.95	3.25	1.40	1.35
1876-77	46¢ Regiments, set of 2 singles ...	...		1.40	.80

CANADA

2000 Regular Issues, Self-Adhesive

1878	1879	1880	1881

Scott's No.		Sheet-lets	Plate Block	F-VF NH	FVF Used
1878	47¢ Maple Leaf, Coil		...	.70	.20
1879	60¢ Red Fox, Coil		...	.90	.60
1879v	60¢ Red Fox, Booklet Single		...	.90	.60
1879a	60¢ Red Fox, Booklet Pane of 6		...	5.25	...
1880	75¢ Grey Wolf, Coil		...	1.10	.90
1881	$1.05 White-Tailed Deer, Coil		...	1.55	1.10
1881v	$1.05 White-Tailed Deer, Booklet Single		...	1.55	1.00
1881a	$1.05 White-Tailed Deer, Booklet Pane of 6		...	9.15	...

2000 Greetings Booklet

| 1882 | 47¢ Booklet of 5 + 5 Stickers .... | | ... | 3.50 | ... |

2001 Commemoratives

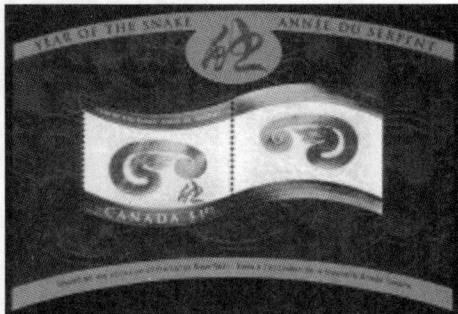

1884

1883	47¢ Year of the Snake .... (25) 17.00	3.15	.70	.30
1884	47¢ Year of the Snake Souvenir Sheet	...	1.40	...
1885	47¢ National Hockey League Legends Souvenir Sheet of 6	...	4.25	...

1886-89

1886-89	47¢ Birds of Canada, Water-Activated (4) .... (20) 13.50	3.25	2.80	1.60
1890-93	47¢ Birds, SA Block of 4	...	2.80	1.60
1893a	47¢ Birds, Booklet Pane of 6 (2-Auila Chrysaetos)...		4.20	...
1893b	47¢ Birds, Booklet Pane of 6 (2-Calcarius Lapponicus)		4.20	...
1893v	47¢ Birds, SA Booklet of 12	...	8.35	...
1894-95	47¢ Games of La Francophone(2)(16) 10.95	3.25	1.40	.80

1896-99

1896-99	47¢ Figure Skating (4) .... (16) 10.95	3.25	2.80	1.60
1900	47¢ 150th Anniversary of First Canadian Stamp, 3p Beaver, Booklet Single	...	.70	.30
1900v	47¢ First Canadian Stamp Booklet of 8	...	5.50	...
...	47¢ Toronto Blue Jays, Booklet Single	...	.70	.30
...	47¢ Toronto Blue Jays Booklet of 8	...	5.50	...
...	47¢ Summit of the Americas (16) 10.95	3.25	.70	.30
...	60¢ Tourist Attractions, Booklet of 5, SA	...	4.50	...
...	60¢ Tourist Attractions, Booklet Singles	...	4.40	3.50
...	$1.05 Tourist Attractions, Booklet of 5, SA	...	7.75	...
...	$1.05 Tourist Attractions, Booklet Singles	...	7.65	6.00
...	47¢ Armenian Apostolic Church(16) 10.95	3.25	.70	.30
...	47¢ Royal Military College .... (16) 10.95	3.25	.70	.30

MINT CANADA COMMEMORATIVE YEAR SETS
All Fine To Very Fine, Never Hinged

Year	Scott Nos.	Qty.	F-VF NH
1947-49	274-77,82-83	6	.90
1951-52	303-04,11-15,17-19	10	5.00
1953-54	322-24,35-36,49-50	7	1.35
1955	352-58	7	1.90
1956	359-61,64	4	1.05
1957	365-74	10	4.15
1958	375-82	8	1.85
1959	383-88	6	1.35
1960-61	389-95	7	1.60
1962	396-400	5	1.10
1963	410,12-13	3	.70
1964	416,431-35	6	1.25
1964-66	417-29A (Coats of Arms & Flowers)	14	2.75
1965	437-44	8	1.50
1966	445-52	8	1.50
1967	453,469-77	10	1.90
1968	478-89	12	3.95
1969	490-504	15	9.75
1970	505-18,531	15	12.50
1970	519-30 (Christmas)	12	4.35
1971	532-42,552-58	18	5.50
1972	559-61,582-85,606-10	12	9.95
1972-76	562-81 (Indians)	20	5.15
1973	611-28	18	5.15
1974	629-55	27	8.85
1975	656-80	25	15.50
1976	681-703	23	17.50

Year	Scott Nos.	Qty.	F-VF NH
1977	704,732-51	21	5.95
1978	752-56,757-79	28	11.25
1979	780,813-20,833-46	23	7.85
1980	847-77	31	11.65
1981	878-906	29	9.70
1982	909-13,914-16,954,967-75	18	11.85
1983	976-82,993-1008	23	20.75
1984	1009-15,1028-39,1040-4444	24	14.95
1985	1045-49,1060-66,1067-70,1071-76	22	14.50
1986	1077-79,1090-1107,1108-15,1116b,1117-21	32	25.00
1987	1122-25,1126-54	33	24.50
1988	1195-1228	34	27.50
1989	1229-63	34	27.95
1990	1264-71,1274-1301	36	30.95
1991	1302-43,1345-48	45	39.95
1992	1399-1407,1408-19,1432-55	45	38.50
1993	1456-71,1484-89,1491-1506	38	34.75
1994	1509-22,1525-26,1528-40	29	26.85
1995	1541-51,1553-58,1562-67,1570-90	47	39.50
1996	1591-98,1602-3,1606-14,1617-21,1622-29	36	36.00
1997	1630, 1631-36, 1637-38, 1639-48, 1649-60 1661-69, 1670, 1671, 1672	43	36.75
1998	1708, 1710-13, 1715-20, 1721-24, 1735-37, 1738-42, 1750-54, 1756-60, 1761-66	40	35.00
1999	1767, 1769-79, 1780-1806, 1809-10, 1812-17	47	33.50
2000	1835-36,39-48,49-52,54-57	48	39.50

CANADA "TAGGED" ISSUES

(A) = Wide Side Bars
(B) = Wide Bar in Middle
(C) = Bar at Left or Right
(D) = Narrow Bar in Middle
(E) = Narrow Side Bars - General

Scott's No.		F-VF NH
1962-63 Elizabeth II		
337-41p	1¢-5¢, Set of 5	10.75
337p	1¢ Violet Brown (A)	1.30
338p	2¢ Green (A)	1.30
339p	3¢ Carmine Rose (A)	1.30
340p	4¢ Violet (B)	3.50
341p	5¢ Blue (A)	3.75
401-5p	1¢-5¢, Set of 5	1.90
401p	1¢ Brown (A)	.20
402p	2¢ Green (A)	.20
403p	3¢ Purple (A)	.25
404p	4¢ Carmine (C)	.90
404pa	4¢ Carmine (D)	.90
404pb	4¢ Carmine (B)	4.00
405p	5¢ Violet Blue (A)	.55
405q	5¢ Min. Pane of 20	49.50
1964-67		
434p	3¢ Brown (A)	.75
434q	3¢ Min. Pane of 25	12.00
435p	5¢ 1964 Xmas (A)	1.20
443p	3¢ 1965 Xmas (A)	.25
443q	3¢ Min. Pane of 25	10.00
444p	5¢ 1965 Xmas (A)	.35
451p	3¢ 1966 Xmas (A)	.25
451q	3¢ Min. Pane of 25	5.50
452p	5¢ 1966 Xmas (A)	.45
453p	5¢ Flag over Globe (A)	.45

Scott's No.		F-VF NH
1967-72 Definitives, Pf. 12		
454p	1¢ Brown (A)	.30
454pa	1¢ Brown (B)	.30
454pb	1¢ Brown (E)	.20
454ep	1¢ Booklet single, Perf. 12½ x 12 (E)	.60
455p	2¢ Green (A)	.25
455pa	2¢ Green (B)	.25
455pb	2¢ Green (E)	.20
456p	3¢ Purple (A)	.25
456pa	3¢ Purple (E) precan	1.00
457p	4¢ Carmine (C)	.55
457pa	4¢ Carmine (B)	.50
457pb	4¢ Carmine (E)	.20
458p	5¢ Blue (A)	.60
458bp	5¢ Min. Pane of 20	62.50
458pa	5¢ Blue (B)	.45
459p	6¢ Orange, Pf. 10 (A)	.65
459bp	6¢ Orange, Perf. 12½ x 12 (A)	.65
460p	6¢ Black, Die I, Perf. 12½ x 12 (A)	.50
460cp	6¢ Black, Die II, Perf. 12½ x 12 (B)	1.25
460cpa	6¢ Black, Bklt. Sgl., Die II (E)	5.50
460fp	6¢ Black, Die I (B)	.30
460fpa	6¢ Black, Die I (E)	.65
462p	10¢ Jack Pine (A)	1.00
462pa	10¢ Jack Pine (E)	.85
463p	15¢ Bylot Island (A)	1.00
463pa	15¢ Bylot Island (E)	1.00
464p	20¢ Ferry (A)	1.50
465p	25¢ Solemn Land (A)	3.25

Scott's No.		F-VF NH
1967-69		
476p	3¢ 1967 Xmas (A)	.25
476q	3¢ Min. Pane of 25	4.95
477p	5¢ 1967 Xmas (A)	.30
488p	5¢ 1968 Xmas (B)	.25
488q	5¢ B. Pane of 10	3.75
489p	6¢ 1968 Xmas (A)	.30
502p	5¢ 1969 Xmas (B)	.25
502q	5¢ B. Pane of 10	3.95
503p	6¢ 1969 Xmas (A)	.30
1970		
505p	6¢ Manitoba (A)	.35
508-11p	25¢ Expo '70 (A)	11.75
513p	10¢ UN (A)	1.10
514p	15¢ UN (A)	1.75
519-30p	5¢-15¢ Set of 12 sngls	6.95
519-23p	5¢ Strip of 5 (B)	4.50
524-28p	6¢ Strip of 5 (B)	4.95
529p	10¢ Manger (B)	.55
530p	15¢ Snowmobile (B)	1.00
1971-72		
541p	15¢ Radio Canada (A)	2.75
543p	7¢ Green (A)	.60
544p	8¢ Slate (A)	.35
544pa	8¢ Slate (E)	.30
544q	B.Pn.of 6 [#454pb (3), 460cpa (1),544pa (2)]	2.25
544r	B.Pn.of 18 [#454pb (6), 460cpa (1),544pa (11)]	5.95

Scott's No.		F-VF NH
544s	B.Pn.of 10 [#454pb (4), 460cpa (1),544pa (5)]	2.75
550p	8¢ Coil, Slate (E)	.35
554p	6¢ Snowflake (B)	.25
555p	7¢ Snowflake (A)	.35
556p	10¢ Snowflake (A)	.50
557p	15¢ Snowflake (A)	.95
560p	8¢ World Health (E)	.60
561p	8¢ Fronterac (E)	.85
562-63p	8¢ Indians (E)	1.25
564-65p	8¢ Indians (E)	1.25
582-85p	15¢ Sciences (E)	11.00
1972 Pictorials		
594	10¢ Forests (E)	.30
594p	10¢ Forests (A)	1.10
595	15¢ Mountain Sheep (E)	.35
595p	15¢ Mountain Sheep (A)	1.35
596	20¢ Prairie Mosaic (E)	.45
596p	20¢ Prairie Mosaic (A)	1.75
597	25¢ Polar Bears (E)	.55
597p	25¢ Polar Bears (A)	1.85
1972 Commemoratives		
606p	6¢ Christmas (E)	.25
606pa	6¢ Christmas (A)	.30
607p	8¢ Christmas (E)	.30
607pa	8¢ Christmas (A)	.35
608p	10¢ Christmas (E)	.65
608pa	10¢ Christmas (A)	.70
609p	15¢ Christmas (E)	1.20
609pa	15¢ Christmas (A)	1.25
610p	8¢ Krieghoff (E)	.35

SEMI-POSTALS

B3	B4	B7	B10

Scott's No.		Plate Block	F-VF NH	F-VF Used
B1-12	Montreal Olympics, Set of 12	...	5.75	5.75

1974 Olympic Games

B1	8¢+2¢ Olympic Emblem, Bronze	1.80	.40	.40
B2	10¢+5¢ Olympic Emblem, Silver	2.00	.45	.45
B3	15¢+5¢ Olympic Emblem, Gold	3.00	.65	.65

1975 Olympic Games - Water Sports

B4	8¢+2¢ Swimming	1.40	.30	.30
B5	10¢+5¢ Rowing	2.00	.45	.45
B6	15¢+5¢ Sailing	3.00	.65	.65

1975 Olympic Games - Combat Sports

B7	8¢+2¢ Fencing	1.40	.30	.30
B8	10¢+5¢ Boxing	2.00	.45	.45
B9	15¢+5¢ Judo	3.00	.65	.65

1976 Olympic Games - Team Sports

B10	8¢+2¢ Basketball	1.40	.30	.30
B11	10¢+5¢ Vaulting	2.00	.45	.45
B12	20¢+5¢ Soccer	3.50	.75	.75

1996 Literacy Issue

B13

B13	45¢ + 5¢ Literacy Singles	...	1.10	.75
B13a	Booklet Pane of 10	...	10.75	...

AIR MAIL STAMPS

C1	C2	C5

1928-1932 Airmail Issues VF + 30% (B)

Scott's No.		NH VF	NH F-VF	Unused VF	Unused F-VF	Used F-VF
C1	5¢ Allegory (1928)	14.75	10.75	9.00	6.75	2.50
C2	5¢ Globe, Brown (1930)	55.00	41.50	36.50	27.50	16.50
C3	6¢ on 5¢ Allegory (1932)	9.75	7.25	6.75	5.00	2.50
C4	6¢ on 5¢ Ottawa (1932)	27.50	19.75	16.00	11.75	8.50

1935-46 Airmail Issues VF + 25%

C6	C7	C9

Scott's No.		Plate Blocks NH	Plate Blocks Unused	F-VF NH	F-VF Unused	F-VF Used
C5-9	Set of 5	...	...	9.25	7.25	1.85
C5	6¢ Daedalus, Red Brown ..... (6)	16.50	12.50	2.25	1.75	.75
C6	6¢ Steamer (1938)	16.00	13.50	3.00	2.25	.25
C7	6¢ Student Flyers (1942)	18.50	14.00	3.50	2.75	.75
C8	7¢ Student Flyers (1943)	3.50	2.75	.70	.55	.20
C9	7¢ Canada Geese (1946)	4.00	3.00	.80	.65	.15
C9a	7¢ Booklet Pane of 4	...	...	3.35	2.75	...

CE1	E1

AIRMAIL SPECIAL DELIVERY 1942-1947 VF + 25%

Scott's No.		Plate Blocks NH	Plate Blocks Unused	F-VF NH	F-VF Unused	F-VF Used
CE1-4	Set of 4			12.95	9.50	9.15
CE1	16¢ Aerial View	14.00	10.75	1.90	1.40	1.35
CE2	17¢ Aerial Veiw (1943)	15.00	11.75	2.70	1.95	1.85
CE3	17¢ Plane, Original Die (1946) ...	23.00	18.00	4.50	3.25	3.15
CE4	17¢ Corrected Die (1947)	23.00	18.00	4.50	3.25	3.15

CE3 has circumflex (^) over second "E" of "EXPRES". CE4 has an accent (`).

CO1	7¢ Ovptd. "O.H.M.S." (C9)	47.50	35.00	10.75	7.95	3.85
CO2	7¢ Ovptd. "G" (#C9) (1950)	75.00	58.50	15.00	12.00	11.00

SPECIAL DELIVERY STAMPS
1898 First Issue VF + 50% (B)

Scott's No.		NH VF	NH F-VF	Unused VF	Unused F-VF	Used F-VF
E1	10¢ Blue Green (1898)	165.00	110.00	65.00	42.50	6.75

1922-1933 Special Delivery VF Used +30% (B)

E2	E3	E4

E2	20¢ Carmine (1922)	130.00	90.00	57.50	42.50	6.00
E3	20¢ Mail Transport (1927)	27.50	20.00	12.75	9.50	9.50
E4	20¢ "TWENTY" (1930)	82.50	55.00	42.50	30.00	10.75
E5	20¢ "20 CENTS" (1933)	77.50	51.50	38.50	27.50	13.00

SPECIAL DELIVERY 1935-1946 VF + 25%

E6	E7

E10	E11

Scott's No.		Plate Blocks NH	Plate Blocks Unused	F-VF NH	F-VF Unused	F-VF Used
E6-11	Set of 6	...		41.50	29.50	27.50
E6	20¢ Progress .... (6)	65.00	45.00	7.50	5.00	4.50
E7	10¢ Arms, Green (1939)	24.00	17.50	4.25	3.00	2.50
E8	20¢ Arms, Carm. (1938)	210.00	140.00	28.50	19.50	19.50
E9	10¢ on 20¢ (#E8) (1939)	33.50	24.00	4.50	3.25	3.25
E10	10¢ Arms & Flags (1942)	12.00	8.75	2.25	1.65	1.40
E11	10¢ Arms (1946)	8.75	6.50	1.65	1.25	.75

SPECIAL DELIVERY OFFICIAL STAMPS 1949-1950 VF + 20%

EO1	10¢ Ovptd. "O.H.M.S." (#E11) ..	75.00	55.00	13.00	9.50	9.50
EO2	10¢ Ovptd. "G" (#E11) (1950) .	140.00	110.00	22.50	17.50	17.50

F2   J1   J6   J11

REGISTRATION STAMPS 1875-1888 (OG + 20%) VF + 80% (C)

Scott's No.		NH Fine	Unused Fine	Ave.	Used Fine	Ave.
F1	2¢ Orange, Perf. 12	130.00	50.00	30.00	2.25	1.40
F1a	2¢ Vermillion, Perf. 12	140.00	57.50	35.00	6.50	3.75
F1b	2¢ Rose Carmine, Perf. 12	...	150.00	90.00	75.00	42.50
F1d	2¢ Orange, Perf. 12 x 11½	...	250.00	150.00	75.00	42.50
F2	5¢ Dark Green, Perf. 12	200.00	80.00	45.00	2.75	1.60
F2a	5¢ Blue Green, Perf. 12	210.00	85.00	47.50	3.00	1.75
F2b	5¢ Yellow Green, Perf. 12	295.00	120.00	70.00	4.25	2.50
F2d	5¢ Green, Perf. 12 x 11½	...	850.00	500.00	140.00	85.00
F3	8¢ Blue (1876)	...	250.00	150.00	200.00	125.00

POSTAGE DUE STAMPS

1906-1928 VF Used + 40% (B)

Scott's No.		NH VF	F-VF	Unused VF	F-VF	Used F-VF
J1-5	Set of 5	190.00	135.00	102.50	73.50	26.75
J1	1¢ Violet	20.00	13.50	12.00	8.50	2.75
J1a	1¢ Thin Paper (1924)	35.00	24.50	20.00	14.50	5.00
J2	2¢ Violet	20.00	13.50	12.00	8.50	.65
J2a	2¢ Thin Paper (1924)	39.50	27.50	23.00	16.50	6.50
J3	4¢ Violet (1928)	82.50	60.00	45.00	32.50	13.50
J4	5¢ Violet	20.00	13.50	12.00	8.50	1.10
J4a	5¢ Thin Paper (1928)	16.00	11.00	9.00	6.25	4.75
J5	10¢ Violet (1928)	60.00	42.50	30.00	21.50	10.75

1930-1932 VF Used + 40% (B)

J6-10	Set of 5	185.00	135.00	102.50	75.00	16.95
J6	1¢ Dark Violet	16.50	11.75	9.00	6.50	2.65
J7	2¢ Dark Violet	10.50	7.25	5.65	4.00	.65
J8	4¢ Dark Violet	25.00	17.50	13.50	9.50	2.75
J9	5¢ Dark Violet (1931)	19.50	13.75	12.00	8.50	6.50
J10	10¢ Dark Violet (1932)	130.00	95.00	70.00	50.00	5.50

1933-1934 VF Used + 40% (B)

J11-14	Set of 4	61.50	42.75	36.50	25.00	11.95
J11	1¢ Dark Violet (1934)	16.00	11.50	9.50	6.50	3.95
J12	2¢ Dark Violet	6.50	4.50	3.85	2.75	.80
J13	4¢ Dark Violet	15.00	10.75	8.50	6.00	4.75
J14	10¢ Dark Violet	27.50	19.50	16.50	11.75	3.50

J15   J23   J28   MR1   MR3

POSTAGE DUE STAMPS
1935-1965 VF + 20%

Scott's No.		Plate Block	F-VF NH	F-VF Used
J15-20	Set of 7	...	4.75	3.15
J15	1¢ Dark Violet	1.75	.20	.15
J16	2¢ Dark Violet	1.75	.20	.15
J16B	3¢ Dark Violet ('65)	15.00	2.00	1.10
J17	4¢ Dark Violet	2.25	.25	.15
J18	5¢ Dark Violet ('48)	3.00	.40	.30
J19	6¢ Dark Violet ('57)	12.50	1.65	1.35
J20	10¢ Dark Violet	3.00	.40	.15

POSTAGE DUE STAMPS (cont.)

Scott's No.		Plate Block	F-VF NH	F-VF Used
1967 Centennial Issue Regular Size 20 x 17 mm., Perf. 12				
J21-27	Set of 7	...	3.10	3.10
J21	1¢ Carmine Rose	7.00	.20	.20
J22	2¢ Carmine Rose	1.40	.25	.25
J23	3¢ Carmine Rose	1.60	.30	.30
J24	4¢ Carmine Rose	2.75	.40	.40
J25	5¢ Carmine Rose	8.75	1.40	1.40
J26	6¢ Carmine Rose	2.75	.40	.40
J27	10¢ Carmine Rose	2.50	.35	.35
1969-1970 Modular Size 20 x 15¾ mm., Perf. 12 Dextrose (Yellow Gum)				
J28,J31,J32a,J34,J35,J36 (6)		...	21.50	21.50
J28	1¢ Carmine Rose (1970)	2.75	.50	.45
J31	4¢ Carmine Rose	2.25	.45	.45
J32a	5¢ Carmine Rose	95.00	19.50	19.50
J34v	8¢ Carmine Rose	2.10	.35	.30
J35	10¢ Carmine Rose	2.75	.60	.50
J36	12¢ Carmine Rose	3.95	.70	.60
1973-74 Modular Size 20 x 15¾ mm., Perf.12 White Gum				
J28v,J29-30,J31v,J33,J34v,J35v,J36v,J37 (9)		...	2.30	2.15
J28v	1¢ Carmine Rose (1974)	1.65	.35	.35
J29	2¢ Carmine Rose (1974)	1.50	.20	.20
J30	3¢ Carmine Rose (1974)	1.65	.25	.20
J31v	4¢ Carmine Rose (1974)	1.20	.25	.25
J33	6¢ Carmine Rose	1.20	.25	.25
J34	8¢ Carmine Rose (1974)	1.25	.25	.25
J35v	10¢ Carmine Rose	1.25	.25	.25
J36v	12¢ Carmine Rose	1.50	.25	.25
J37	16¢ Carmine Rose (1974)	2.25	.40	.35
1977-78 Modular Size 20 x 15¾mm.,Perf. 12½ x 12				
J28a-40 Set of 9		...	4.15	3.60
J28a	1¢ Carmine Rose	.50	.20	.15
J31a	4¢ Carmine Rose	.60	.20	.20
J32	5¢ Carmine Rose	.75	.20	.20
J34a	8¢ Carmine Rose (1978)	2.10	.35	.30
J35a	10¢ Carmine Rose	1.10	.25	.25
J36a	12¢ Carmine Rose	9.75	1.20	.95
J38	20¢ Carmine Rose .	2.25	.45	.40
J39	24¢ Carmine Rose .	2.75	.60	.55
J40	50¢ Carmine Rose .	4.75	.95	.90

WAR TAX STAMPS 1915-1916 VF Used + 50% (B)

Scott's No.		NH VF	F-VF	Unused VF	F-VF	Used F-VF
MR1	1¢ George V, Green	25.00	16.50	12.50	8.25	.20
MR2	2¢ Carmine	25.00	16.50	12.50	8.25	.25
MR3	2¢ + 1¢ Carm., T.1 ('16)	28.50	18.75	16.50	11.00	.20
MR3a	2¢ + 1¢ Carm., Type II	215.00	135.00	120.00	75.00	3.50
MR4	2¢ + 1¢ Brown, Type II	24.00	16.00	13.50	9.00	.20
MR4a	2¢ + 1¢ Brown, Type I	...	...	240.00	160.00	7.50
MR5	2¢ + 1¢ Carm., Perf. 12 x 8	67.50	45.00	37.50	25.00	20.00
MR6	2¢ + 1¢ Carm., P.8 Vert. Coil .	180.00	120.00	100.00	65.00	5.75
MR7	2¢ + 1¢ Br.,T.II P.8 Vt. Coil ...	35.00	23.50	20.00	13.50	.85
MR7a	2¢ + 1¢ Br.,T.I P.8 Vt. Coil	235.00	155.00	135.00	90.00	5.75

O2 **O15A** **O19**

O28 **O36** **O40** **O46**

1949-50 Issues of 1942-46 Overprinted O.H.M.S. VF + 25%

Scott's No.		Plate Blocks NH	Unused	F-VF NH	F-VF Unused	F-VF Used
O1-10	Set of 9	...	...	245.00	180.00	150.00
O1	1¢ George VI, Green (249)	9.50	7.25	1.85	1.40	1.35
O2	2¢ George VI, Brown (250)	110.00	90.00	9.50	7.00	6.50
O3	3¢ George VI, Violet (252)	9.75	7.25	1.85	1.40	1.00
O4	4¢ George VI, Carmine (254)	19.00	13.50	2.50	1.80	.60
O6	10¢ Great Bear Lake (269)	23.75	20.00	3.00	2.40	.55
O7	14¢ Hydroelectric Sta. (270)	30.00	23.75	4.50	3.50	2.10
O8	20¢ Reaper (271)	80.00	60.00	11.50	9.00	2.85
O9	50¢ Lumbering (272)	1000.00	750.00	175.00	125.00	115.00
O10	$1 Train Ferry (273)	395.00	295.00	42.50	31.50	32.50

1950 Issues of 1949-50 Overprinted O.H.M.S. VF + 20%

O11	50¢ Development (294)	135.00	100.00	25.00	19.50	16.50
O12-15A	Set of 5	...	...	4.65	3.75	2.50
O12	1¢ George VI, Green (284)	3.65	3.00	.30	.25	.25
O13	2¢ George VI, Sepia (285)	4.50	3.50	.95	.75	.65
O14	3¢ G. VI, Rose Violet (286)	5.75	4.50	1.00	.80	.45
O15	4¢ G. VI, Carmine (287)	5.75	4.50	1.00	.80	.15
O15A	5¢ G. VI, Deep Blue (288)	10.75	8.00	1.80	1.35	1.20

1950 Issues of 1948-50 Overprinted G VF + 20%

O16-25	Set of 10	...	...	105.00	80.00	65.00
O16	1¢ George VI, Green (284)	2.50	2.00	.35	.25	.15
O17	2¢ George VI, Sepia (285)	5.00	4.00	1.20	.90	.70
O18	3¢ G. VI, Rose Violet (286)	6.25	5.00	1.20	.90	.20
O19	4¢ G. VI, Carmine (287)	6.25	5.00	1.20	.90	.15
O20	5¢ G. VI, Deep Blue (288)	13.00	10.75	1.40	1.10	.75
O21	10¢ Great Bear Lake (269)	14.00	11.00	2.35	1.80	.40
O22	14¢ Hydroelectric Sta. (270)	33.50	26.50	5.75	4.50	2.10
O23	20¢ Reaper (271)	87.50	65.00	12.75	9.75	.90
O24	50¢ Oil Development (294)	52.50	40.00	9.00	7.00	5.50
O25	$1 Train Ferry (273)	375.00	300.00	80.00	60.00	60.00
O26	10¢ Fur Trading (301)	5.95	4.75	1.10	.90	.20

NOTE: NUMBER IN ( ) INDICATES CATALOG NUMBER OF BASIC STAMP WHICH HAS NOT BEEN OVERPRINTED.

1951-53 Issues of 1951-53 Overprinted G VF + 20%

Scott's No.		Plate Blocks NH	Unused	F-VF NH	F-VF Unused	F-VF Used
O27	$1 Fisheries (302)	375.00	300.00	75.00	60.00	60.00
O28	2¢ G. VI, Olive Green (305)	2.40	1.95	.50	.40	.15
O29	4¢ George VI, Orange (306)	4.50	3.25	.80	.60	.15
O30	20¢ Forestry Products (316)	12.00	9.00	2.25	1.65	.20
O31	7¢ Canada Goose (320)	16.00	12.00	3.65	2.75	1.10
O32	$1 Totem Pole (321)	85.00	65.00	16.50	12.00	10.50

1953-55 Issues of 1953-55 Overprinted G VF + 20%

O33-37	Set of 5	...	...	1.70	1.35	.65
O33	1¢ Queen Elizabeth (325)	1.70	1.40	.30	.25	.15
O34	2¢ Queen Elizabeth (326)	1.70	1.40	.30	.25	.15
O35	3¢ Queen Elizabeth (327)	1.70	1.40	.30	.25	.15
O36	4¢ Queen Elizabeth (328)	2.40	1.95	.45	.35	.15
O37	5¢ Queen Elizabeth (329)	2.40	1.95	.45	.35	.15
O38	50¢ Textile (334)	24.00	19.50	4.25	3.25	1.10
O38a	50¢ Textile, Flying G (1961)	23.50	18.75	4.25	3.25	1.70
O39	10¢ Eskimo (351)	4.75	3.75	.85	.65	.15
O39a	10¢ Eskimo, Flying G (1962)	12.50	10.00	1.75	1.40	.85

1955-56 Issues of 1955-56 Overprinted G VF + 20%

O40-45	Set of 5	...	...	3.35	2.75	.80
O40	1¢ Queen Elizabeth (337)	1.50	1.30	.30	.25	.25
O41	2¢ Queen Elizabeth (338)	1.85	1.60	.30	.25	.15
O43	4¢ Queen Elizabeth (340)	4.50	3.75	.95	.80	.15
O44	5¢ Queen Elizabeth (341)	2.75	2.25	.55	.45	.15
O45	20¢ Paper Industry (362)	8.25	6.75	1.50	1.20	.20
O45a	20¢ Paper, Flying G (1962)	43.50	35.00	6.50	5.25	.45

===

1963 Issue of 1962-63 Overprinted G

Scott's No.		Plate Block	F-VF NH	F-VF Used
O46-49	Set of 4	...	2.75	2.75
O46	1¢ Queen Elizabeth (401)	(Blank) 3.75	.80	.80
O47	2¢ Queen Elizabeth (402)	(Blank) 3.75	.80	.80
O48	4¢ Queen Elizabeth (404)	(Blank) 7.50	.80	.80
O49	5¢ Queen Elizabeth (405)	(Blank) 2.75	.50	.50

CANADA HUNTING PERMIT STAMPS

AB1

BC1   **MAN1**

No.	Description	F-VF NH
	CANADA	
CN 1	'85 $4 Mallards Bklt	12.00
CN 2	'86 $4 Canvasbks Bklt	12.00
CN 2B	'86 Min. Sheet of 16	165.00
CN 3	'87 $6.50 Can. G'se Bklt	11.00
CN 3B	'87 Min. Sheet of 16	275.00
CN 4	'88 $6.50 Pintails Bklt	14.00
CN 4B	'88 Min. Sheet of 16	275.00
CN 5	'89 $7.50 Snow G'se Bklt	14.50
CN 5B	'89 Min. Sheet of 16	275.00
CN 6	'90 $7.50 Wood Duck Bklt	14.00
CN 6B	'90 Min. Sheet of 16	225.00
CN 7	'91 $8.50 Blk. Duck Bklt	13.00
CN 7B	'91 Min. Sheet of 16	225.00
CN 7J	'91 Joint Issue w/US	31.50
CN 7JI	'91 J'nt Issue w/US, Impf	72.50
CN 8	'92 $8.50 Cmn Elders Bklt	13.00
CN 8B	'92 Min. Sheet of 16	225.00
CN 9	'93 $8.50 Hd'd Mergans'r	13.00
CN 9B	'93 Min. Sheet of 16	195.00
CN 10	'94 $8.50 Ross' Geese	13.00
CN10B	'94f Min. Sheet of 16	195.00
CN 11	'95 $8.50 Redheads	13.00
CN11B	'95 Min. Sheet of 16	195.00
CN12	'96 $8.50 Goldeneyes	13.00
CN12B	'96 Min. Sheet of 16	195.00
CN13	'97 $8.50 Gadwalls	13.00
CN13B	'97 Min. sheet of 16	195.00
CN14	'98 $8.50 Ring Necked Duck	12.00
CN14B	'98 Mini Sheet of 16	195.00

No.	Description	F-VF NH
	CANADA (continued)	
CN15	'99 $8.50 Buffleheads	12.00
CN15B	'99 Mini Sheet of 16	175.00
CN16	'00 $8.50 Sandhill Crane	12.00
CN16B	'00 Mini Sheet of 16	175.00
CN17	'01 $8.50	12.00
CN17B	'01 Mini Sheet of 16	175.00
Canada Complete 1985-2000(16)		190.00
	ALBERTA	
AB 1	'89 $6.00 Canada Geese	25.00
AB 2	'90 $7.00 Mallards	20.00
AB 3	'91 $7.71 Pintails	18.00
AB 4	'92 $7.90 Snow Geese	17.00
AB 5	'93 $7.90 Canvasbacks	15.00
AB 6	'94 $8.36 Redheads	13.00
AB 7	'95 $8.36 Wh. Fronted Geese	13.00
AB 8	'96 $8.36 Goldeneyes	13.00
AB 9	'97 $8.36 Harlequin	13.00
Alberta Complete 1989-97 (9)		140.00
	ALBERTA HABITAT	
ABH 1	'96 $6.00 Big Horn Sheep	8.00
ABH 1B	'96 Same-Booklet	10.00
ABH 1M	'96 $6.00 Same-Mini Sheet	34.00
ABH 2	'97 $6.00 Rocky Mnt. Goat	8.00
ABH 2B	'97 Same-Booklet	10.00
ABH 2M	'97 $6.00 Same-Mini Sheet.	34.00
ABH 3	'98 $6.00 Cougar	8.00
ABH 3B	'98 $6.00 Same, Booklet	10.00

No.	Description	F-VF NH
	ALBERTA HABITAT (continued)	
ABH 3M	'98 $6.00 Mini Sheet	34.00
ABH 4	'99 $6.00 Elk	8.00
ABH 4B	'99 Same, Booklet	10.00
ABH 4M	'99 Same, Mini Sheet	34.00
ABH 5	'00 $6 Bald Eagle	8.00
ABH 5B	'00 Same, Booklet	10.00
ABH 5M	'00 Same, Mini Sheet	34.00
	BRITISH COLUMBIA	
BC 1	'95 $6 Bighorn Sheep	8.00
BC 1B	'95 Same, Booklet	10.00
BC 1M	'95 Same, Mini Sheet	34.00
BC 2	'96 $6 Elk	8.00
BC 2B	'96 Same, Booklet	10.00
BC 2M	'96 Same, Mini Sheet	34.00
BC 3	'97 $6 Grizzly Bear	8.00
BC 3B	'97 Same, Booklet	10.00
BC 3M	'97 Same, Mini Sheet	34.00
BC 4	'98 $6 Tufted Puffins	8.00
BC 4B	'98 Same, Booklet	10.00
BC 4M	'98 Same, Mini Sheet	34.00
BC 5	'99 $6 Bald Eagle	8.00
BC 5B	'99 Same, Booklet	10.00
BC 5M	'99 Same, Mini Sheet	34.00
BC 6	'00 $6 Mule Deer	8.00
BC 6B	'00 Same, Booklet	10.00
BC 6M	'00 Same, Mini Sheet	34.00

No.	Description	F-VF NH
	MANITOBA	
	Winnipeg Duck Stamp	13.00
	Winnipeg Duck,Flourescent Paper	13.00
MAN 1	'94 $6 Polar Bear	8.00
MAN 1B	'94 Same, Booklet	10.00
MAN 1M	'94 Same, Mini Sheet 4	34.00
MAN 2	'95 $6 Whitetailed Deer	8.00
MAN 2B	'95 Same, Booklet	10.00
MAN 2M	'95 Same, Mini Sheet 4	34.00
MAN 3	'96 $6 Lynx	8.00
MAN 3B	'96 Same, Booklet	10.00
MAN 3M	'96 Same, Mini Sheet	34.00
MAN 4	'97 $6 Falcon	8.00
MAN 4B	'97 Same, Booklet	10.00
MAN 4M	'97 Same, Mini Sheet	34.00
MAN 5	'98 $6 Moose	8.00
MAN 5B	'98 Same, Booklet	10.00
MAN 5M	'98 Same, Mini Sheet	34.00
MAN 6	'99 $6 Buffalo	8.00
MAN 6B	'99 Same, Booklet	10.00
MAN 6M	'99 Same, Mini Sheet	34.00
MAN 7	'00 $6 Canada Geese	8.00
MAN 7B	'00 Same, Booklet	10.00
MAN 7M	'00 Same, Mini Sheet	34.00

CANADA HUNTING PERMIT STAMPS

NB1

NF1

NWT1

NS1

ON1

PE1

SK1

YT1

No.	Description	F-VF NH
NEW BRUNSWICK		
NB 1 '94	$6 White Tail Deer ..	8.00
NB 1B '94	Same, Booklet	10.00
NB 1M '94	Same, Mini Sheet of 4	34.00
NB 2 '95	$6 Cougar	8.00
NB 2B '95	Same, Booklet	10.00
NB 2M '95	Same, Mini Sheet of 4	34.00
NB 3 '96	$6 Moose	8.00
NB 3B '96	Same, Booklet	10.00
NB 3M '96	Same, Mini Sheet ...	34.00
NB 4 '97	$6 Pheasant	8.00
NB 4B '97	Same, Booklet	10.00
NB 4M '97	Same, Mini Sheet ...	34.00
NB 5 '98	$6 Rainbow Trout ...	8.00
NB 5B '98	Same, Booklet	10.00
NB 5M '98	Same, Mini Sheet ...	34.00
NB 6 '99	$6 Wood Ducks	8.00
NB 6B '99	Same, Booklet	10.00
NB 6M '99	Same, Mini Sheet ...	34.00
NB 7 '00	$6 King Eider	8.00
NB 7B '00	Same, Booklet	10.00
NB 7M '00	Same, Mini Sheet ...	34.00
NEWFOUNDLAND		
NF 1 '94	$6 Woodland Caribou	8.00
NF 1B '94	Same, Booklet	10.00
NF 1M '94	Same, Mini Sht. 4	34.00
NF 2 '95	$6 Goldeneyes	8.00
NF 2B '95	Same, Booklet	10.00
NF 2M '95	Same, Mini Sheet ...	34.00
NF 3 '96	$6 Moose	8.00
NF 3B '96	Same, Booklet	10.00
NF 3M '96	Same, Mini Sheet ...	34.00
NF 4 '97	$6 Harlequin Duck ...	8.00
NF 4B '97	Same, Booklet	10.00
NF 4M '97	Same, Mini Sheet ...	34.00
NF 5 '98	$6 Bear	8.00
NF 5B '98	Same, Booklet	10.00
NF 5M '98	Same, Mini Sheet ...	34.00
NF 6 '99	$6 Fox	8.00
NF 6B '99	Same, Booklet	10.00
NF 6M '99	Same, Mini Sheet	34.00
NF 7 '00	$6 King Eider	8.00
NF 7B '00	Same, Booklet	10.00
NF 7M '00	Same, Mini Sheet ...	34.00
NORTHWEST TERRITORIES		
NWT 1 '97	$6 Arctic Hare	8.00
NWT 1B '97	Same, Booklet	10.00
NWT 1M '97	Same, Mini Sheet	34.00
NWT 2 '98	$6 Snowy Owl	8.00
NWT 2B '98	Same, Booklet	10.00
NWT 2M '98	Same, Mini Sheet	34.00
NWT 3 '99	$6 Arctic Locn	8.00
NWT 3B '99	Same, Booklet	10.00
NWT 3M '99	Same, Mini Sheet	34.00
NWT 4 '00	$6 Caribou	8.00
NWT 4B '00	Same, Booklet	10.00
NWT 4M '00	Same, Mini Sheet	34.00

No.	Description	F-VF NH
NOVA SCOTIA		
NS 1 '92	$6 Whitetail Deer	12.00
NS 1B '92	$6 Wh'tail Deer Bklt	35.00
NS 1M '92	$6 Mini Sheet of 4 ..	50.00
NS 2 '93	$6 Summer Pheasant	10.00
NS 2B '93	$6 Pheasant Bklt ...	12.50
NS 2M '93	$6 Mini Sheet of 4 ..	34.00
NS 3 '94	$6 Wood Duck	8.00
NS 3B '94	Same, Booklet	10.00
NS 3M '94	Same,Mini Sheet-4 .	34.00
NS 4 '95	$6 Coyote	8.00
NS 4B '95	Same, Booklet	10.00
NS 4M '95	Same, Mini Sheet-4	34.00
NS 5 '96	$6 Osprey	8.00
NS 5B '96	Same, Booklet	10.00
NS 5M '96	Same, Mini Sheet ...	34.00
NS 6 '97	$6 Woodpecker	8.00
NS 6B '97	Same, Booklet	10.00
NS 6M '97	Same, Mini Sheet ...	34.00
NS 7 '98	$6 Blue Winged Teal	8.00
NS 7B '98	Same, Booklet	10.00
NS 7M '98	Same, Mini Sheet ...	34.00
NS 8 '99	$6 Moose	8.00
NS 8B '99	Same, Booklet	10.00
NS 8M '99	Same, Mini Sheet ...	34.00
NS 9 '00	$6 Bald Eagle	8.00
NS 9B '00	Same, Booklet	10.00
NS 9M '00	Same, Mini Sheet ...	34.00
NUNAVUT TERRITORY		
NU 1 '99	$6 Polar Bear	8.00
NU 1B '99	Same, Booklet	10.00
NU 1M '99	Same, Mini Sheet	34.00
NU 2 '00	$6 Arctic Loon	8.00
NU 2B '00	Same, Booklet	10.00
NU 2M '00	Same, Mini Sheet	34.00
ONTARIO		
ON 1 '93	$6 Ruffled Grouse ..	11.00
ON 1B '93	$6 Grouse Bklt	10.00
ON 1M '93	$6 Mini Sheet of 4 ..	34.00
ON 2 '94	$6 Deer	8.00
ON 2B '94	Same, Booklet	10.00
ON 2M '94	Same, Mini Sheet of 4	34.00
ON 3 '95	$6 Fish	8.00
ON 3B '95	Same, Booklet	10.00
ON 3M '95	Same, Mini Sheet/4	34.00
ON 4 '96	$6 Blue Wing Teal ..	8.00
ON 4B '96	Same, Booklet	10.00
ON 4M '96	Same, Mini Sheet ...	34.00
ON 5 '97	$6 Lesser Scaup	8.00
ON 5B '97	Same, Booklet	10.00
ON 5M '97	Same, Mini Sheet ...	34.00
ON 6 '98	$6 River Otter	8.00
ON 6B '98	Same, Booklet	10.00
ON 6M '98	Same, Mini Sheet ...	34.00
ON 7 '99	$6 Buffleheads	8.00
ON 7B '99	Same, Booklet	10.00
ON 7M '99	Same, Mini Sheet	34.00
ON 8 '00	$6 Cardinals	8.00

No.	Description	F-VF NH
ONTARIO (continued)		
ON 8B '00	Same, Booklet	10.00
ON 8M '00	Same, Mini Sheet	34.00
PRINCE EDWARD ISLAND		
PEI 1 '95	$6 Canada Geese ..	8.00
PEI 1B '95	Same, Booklet	10.00
PEI 1M '95	Same, Mini Sheet of 4	34.00
PEI 2 '96	$6 Woodcock	8.00
PEI 2B '96	Same, Booklet	10.00
PEI 2M '96	Same, Mini Sheet	34.00
PEI 3 '97	$6 Red Fox	8.00
PEI 3B '97	Same, Booklet	10.00
PEI 3M '97	Same, Mini Sheet	34.00
PEI 4 '98	$6 Wigeon	8.00
PEI 4B '98	Same, Booklet	10.00
PEI 4M '98	Same, Mini Sheet	34.00
PEI 5 '99	$6 Mallard	8.00
PEI 5B '99	Same, Booklet	10.00
PEI 5M '99	Same, Mini Sheet	34.00
PEI 6 '00	$6 Wood Ducks ...	8.00
PEI 6B '00	Same, Booklet	10.00
PEI 6M '00	Same, Mini Sheet	34.00
QUEBEC		
QU 1 '88	$6 Ruffled Grouse	120.00
QU 1M '88	$6 Mini Sheet of 4	225.00
QU 1MI '88	Imperf. Sheet of 4	POR
QU 2 '89	$6 Black Ducks	37.50
QU 2M '89	$6 Mini Sheet of 4	140.00
QU 2MI '89	Imperf. Sheet of 4	350.00
QU 3 '90	$6 Common Loons	22.00
QU 3M '90	$6 Mini Sheet of 4	135.00
QU 3MI '90	Imperf. Sheet of 4	350.00
QU 4 '91	$6 Cmn Gldneyes	16.00
QU 4M '91	$6 Mini Sheet of 4	83.40
QU 4MI '91	Imperf. Sheet of 4	350.00
QU 5 '92	$6.50 Lynx	12.50
QU 5A '92	$10 Lynx Surcharge	25.00
QU 5M '92	$6 Mini Sheet of 4	90.00
QU 5MI '92	Imperf. Sheet of 4	280.00
QU 6 '93	$6.50 Pergrn Falcon	12.50
QU 6M '93	$6.50 Mini Sheet of 4	60.00
QU 6MI '93	$6.50 Impf Sht. of 4	225.00
QU 7 '94	$7 Beluga Whale ..	13.00
QU 7M '94	Same, Mini Sheet of 4	445.00
QU 7MI '94	Same, Imperf. Sht.4	225.00
QU 8 '95	$7 Moose	12.00
QU 8M '95	Same, Mini Sht of 4	45.00
QU 8MI '95	Same, Imperf.Sht/4	225.00
QU 9 '96	$7 Blue Heron	12.00
QU 9A '96	Same,OvrpntedWWF	18.00
QU 9M '96	Same, Mini Sheet of 4	445.00
QU 9MI '96	Same, Imperf. Sht.4	225.00
QU 10 '97	$8.50 Snowy Owl ..	14.00
QU 10A '97	Same,OvrprintedWWF	18.00
QU 10M '97	Same, Mini Sheet of	55.00
QU 10MI '97	Same, Imperf. Sht.4	225.00
QU 11 '98	$10 Snow Goose .	14.00
QU 11A '98	Same,Overprint.WWF	18.00
QU 11M '98	Same, Mini Sheet of4	55.00
QU 11MI '98	Same,Impf.Sheet4	225.00
QU 12 '99	$10 River Otter	14.00

No.	Description	F-VF NH
QUEBEC (continued)		
QU 12A '99	Same,Overprint.WWF	18.00
QU 12M '99	Same,Mini Sheet of 4	55.00
QU 12MI '99	Same,Impf Sheet-4	225.00
QU 13 '00	$10 Puffin/Turtle ..	14.00
QU 13A '00	Same,Overprint.WWF	18.00
QU 13M '00	Same,Mini Sheet-4	55.00
QU 13MI '00	Same,Impf.Sheet4	225.00
QU 14 '01	$10 Blue Jay	14.00
QU 14A '01	Same,Overprint WWF	18.00
QU 14M '01	Same, Mini Sheet-4	55.00
QU 14MI '01	Same,Impf.Sheet-4	225.00
SASKATCHEWAN		
SK 1 '88	$5 American Widgeon	40.00
SK 2 '89	$5 Bull Moose	40.00
SK 3 '90	$5 Shp Tail'd Grouse	50.00
SK 4 '93	$6 Mallards	8.00
SK 4B '93	$6 Mallards Bklt ...	10.00
SK 4M '93	$6 Mini Sht. of 4 .	34.00
SK 5 '94	$6 Wood Ducks	8.00
SK 5B '94	Same, Booklet	10.00
SK 5M '94	Same, Mini Sheet/4	34.00
SK 6 '95	$6 Antelope	8.00
SK 6B '95	Same, Booklet	10.00
SK 6M '95	Same, Mini Sheet/4	34.00
SK 7 '96	$6 Ruddy Duck	8.00
SK 7B '96	Same, Booklet	10.00
SK 7M '96	Same, Mini Sheet	34.00
SK 8 '97	$6 Wigeon	8.00
SK 8B '97	Same, Booklet	10.00
SK 8M '97	Same, Mini Sheet	34.00
SK 9 '98	$6 Swans	8.00
SK 9B '98	Same, Booklet	10.00
SK 9M '98	Same, Mini Sheet	34.00
SK 10 '99	$6 Moose	8.00
SK 10B '99	Same, Booklet	10.00
SK 10M '99	Same, Mini Sheet	34.00
SK 11 '00	$6 Pheasants	8.00
SK 11B '00	Same, Booklet	10.00
SK 11M '00	Same, Mini Sheet	34.00
YUKON TERRITORY		
YT 1 '96	$6 Bald Eagle	8.00
YT 1B '96	Same, Booklet	10.00
YT 1M '96	Same, Mini Sheet	34.00
YT 2 '97	$6 Moose	8.00
YT 2B '97	Same, Booklet	10.00
YT 2M '97	Same, Mini Sheet	34.00
YT 3 '98	$6 Polar Bear	8.00
YT 3B '98	Same, Booklet	10.00
YT 3M '98	Same, Mini Sheet	34.00
YT 4 '99	$6 Rocky Mnt Goat	8.00
YT 4B '99	Same, Booklet	10.00
YT 4M '99	Same, Mini Sheet	34.00
YT 5 '00	$6 Snowy Owl	8.00
YT 5B '00	Same, Booklet	10.00
YT 5M '00	Same, Mini Sheet	34.00

NEWFOUNDLAND

3,11A

23

1857 Imperf. Thick Wove Paper, Mesh (OG + 50%) (C)

Scott's No.		Unused Fine	Unused Ave.	Used Fine	Used Ave.
1	1p Crown & Flowers, Brn. Violet	60.00	35.00	150.00	95.00
3	3p Triangle, Green	450.00	275.00	425.00	275.00
5	5p Crown & Flowers, Vlt. Brown	150.00	90.00	325.00	200.00
8	8p Flowers, Scarlet Vermillion	175.00	110.00	225.00	150.00

1860 Imperf. Thin Wove Paper, No Mesh (OG + 50%) (C)

11	2p Flowers, Orange	200.00	130.00	300.00	190.00
11A	3p Triangle, Green	45.00	27.00	125.00	75.00
12	4p Flowers, Orange	...	...	750.00	500.00
12A	5p Crown & Flowers, Vlt. Brown	65.00	40.00	180.00	110.00
13	6p Flowers, Orange	...	...	500.00	350.00

1861-62 Imperforate Thin Wove Paper (OG + 50%) (C)

15A	1p Crown & Flowers, Vlt. Brown	120.00	70.00	225.00	135.00
17	2p Flowers, Rose	110.00	65.00	300.00	185.00
18	4p Flowers, Rose	26.75	16.50	80.00	50.00
19	5p Crown & Flowers, Red Brown	35.00	20.00	150.00	95.00
20	6p Flowers, Rose	15.00	10.00	80.00	52.50
21	6½ Flowers, Rose	50.00	27.50	325.00	195.00
22	8p Flowers, Rose	55.00	37.50	450.00	270.00
23	1sh Flowers, Rose	25.00	13.75	250.00	150.00

24

31

32-32A

33, 34

1865-1894 Perf. 12 (OG + 40%, NH + 150%) (C)

24	2¢ Codfish, Green, White Paper	45.00	30.00	25.00	15.00
24a	2¢ Green, Yellow Paper	65.00	40.00	30.00	19.00
25	5¢ Harp Seal, Brown	350.00	225.00	225.00	150.00
26	5¢ Harp Seal, Black (1868)	170.00	110.00	85.00	55.00
27	10¢ Prince Albert, Black, White Paper	115.00	75.00	37.50	22.50
27a	10¢ Black, Yellow Paper	175.00	110.00	65.00	40.00
28	12¢ Victoria, Red Brown, Yel.Paper	32.50	17.00	27.50	15.00
28a	12¢ Red Brown, White Paper	275.00	150.00	110.00	70.00
29	12¢ Brown, Yellow Paper (1894)	35.00	21.50	35.00	21.50
30	13¢ Fishing Ship, Orange	75.00	45.00	55.00	33.50
31	24¢ Victoria, Blue	22.50	14.00	25.00	15.00

1868-1894 Perf. 12 (OG + 40%, NH + 150%) (C)

32	1¢ Prince of Wales, Violet	35.00	21.50	40.00	25.00
32A	1¢ Brown Lilac (1871)	55.00	35.00	45.00	27.00
33	3¢ Victoria, Vermillion (1870)	170.00	100.00	90.00	55.00
34	3¢ Blue (1873)	195.00	115.00	18.00	10.00
35	6¢ Victoria, Dull Rose (1870)	9.50	6.00	14.00	8.75
36	6¢ Carmine Lake (1894)	11.75	7.25	13.50	8.50

1876-1879 Rouletted (OG + 30%, NH + 150%) (C)

37	1¢ Prince of Wales, Brn. Lilac (1877)	70.00	45.00	30.00	18.50
38	2¢ Codfish, Green (1879)	90.00	55.00	35.00	21.50
39	3¢ Victoria, Blue (1877)	175.00	110.00	7.75	5.25
40	5¢ Harp Seal, Blue	125.00	80.00	7.75	5.25

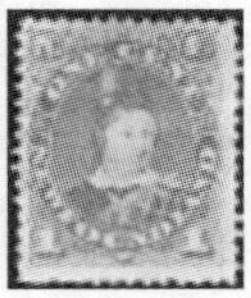
41-45

46-48

56-58

59

1880-1896 Perf. 12 (OG + 20%) VF + 50% (C)

Scott's No.		NH Fine	Unused Fine	Unused Ave.	Used Fine	Used Ave.
41	1¢ Prince, Vlt. Brown	40.00	19.50	12.00	7.50	4.25
42	1¢ Gray Brown	37.50	18.50	11.00	7.50	4.25
43	1¢ Brown (1896)	80.00	40.00	25.00	40.00	25.00
44	1¢ Deep Green (1887)	10.00	5.50	3.50	2.75	1.65
45	1¢ Green (1897)	18.75	10.00	6.00	6.50	4.00
46	2¢ Codfish, Yellow Green	75.00	35.00	21.50	18.00	11.00
47	2¢ Green (1896)	110.00	55.00	32.50	35.00	21.50
48	2¢ Red Orange (1887)	23.50	12.00	7.00	5.25	3.00
49	3¢ Victoria, Blue	100.00	50.00	30.00	3.50	1.95
51	3¢ Umber Brown (1887)	80.00	40.00	25.00	3.00	1.65
52	3¢ Violet Brown (1896)	125.00	65.00	40.00	60.00	35.00
53	5¢ Harp Seal, Pale Blue	300.00	170.00	100.00	7.00	4.25
54	5¢ Dark Blue (1887)	140.00	75.00	45.00	5.25	3.25
55	5¢ Bright Blue (1894)	77.50	40.00	25.00	4.25	2.50

NEWFOUNDLAND

1887-1896 (OG + 20%) VF + 50% (C)

Scott's No.		NH Fine	Unused Fine	Unused Ave.	Used Fine	Used Ave.
56	½¢ Dog, Rose Red	12.75	7.00	4.25	6.00	3.75
57	½¢ Orange Red (1896)	65.00	35.00	21.50	35.00	21.50
58	½¢ Black (1894)	14.00	7.50	4.50	4.00	2.25
59	10¢ Schooner, Black	85.00	45.00	27.50	45.00	27.50

1890 Issue (OG + 20%) VF + 50% (C)

60	3¢ Victoria, Slate	35.00	18.50	11.00	1.35	.80

1897 John Cabot Issue VF Used + 30% (B)

61

63

67

74

Scott's No.		NH VF	NH F-VF	Unused VF	Unused F-VF	Used F-VF
61-74	**Set of 14**	**550.00**	**425.00**	**275.00**	**210.00**	**160.00**
61	1¢ Queen Victoria	4.50	3.50	2.30	1.75	3.50
62	2¢ Cabot	3.95	3.00	1.95	1.50	2.00
63	3¢ Cape Bonavista	6.00	4.50	2.95	2.25	1.00
64	4¢ Caribou Hunting	19.00	14.00	9.50	7.00	2.75
65	5¢ Mining	25.00	18.50	12.75	9.50	2.75
66	6¢ Logging	17.00	12.75	8.75	6.50	3.00
67	8¢ Fishing	35.00	26.50	18.00	13.50	6.75
68	10¢ Ship "Matthew"	70.00	55.00	36.50	27.50	5.25
69	12¢ Willow Ptarmigan	65.00	50.00	33.50	25.00	6.25
70	15¢ Seals	35.00	26.00	17.50	13.00	12.50
71	24¢ Salmon Fishing	47.50	37.50	25.00	18.50	15.00
72	30¢ Colony Seal	95.00	70.00	47.50	35.00	50.00
73	35¢ Iceberg	160.00	110.00	80.00	55.00	55.00
74	60¢ King Henry VII	32.50	25.00	16.50	12.50	10.00

1897 Surcharges VF Used + 50% (C)

75	1¢ on 3¢ Type a (#60)	105.00	70.00	55.00	36.50	15.00
76	1¢ on 3¢ Type b (#60)	300.00	200.00	150.00	100.00	110.00
77	1¢ on 3¢ Type c (#60)	1075.00	700.00	525.00	350.00	335.00

78

79-80

81-82

86

1897-1901 Royal Family Issue VF Used + 30% (B)

78-85	**Set of 8**	**180.00**	**130.00**	**95.00**	**72.50**	**15.95**
78	½¢ Edward VII as Child	4.00	3.10	2.25	1.70	1.65
79	1¢ Victoria, Carm. Rose	6.75	4.75	3.75	2.65	2.65
80	1¢ Yellow Green (1898)	11.00	8.50	6.00	4.50	.20
81	2¢ Prince, Orange	7.35	5.35	4.00	3.00	2.75
82	2¢ Vermillion (1898)	24.00	17.50	13.00	9.50	.45
83	3¢ Princess (1898)	25.75	19.50	14.00	10.75	.45
84	4¢ Duchess (1901)	44.00	31.50	23.50	17.50	3.95
85	5¢ Duke of York (1899)	67.50	50.00	36.50	27.50	2.50

1908 Map Stamp VF Used + 30% (B)

86	12¢ Map of Newfoundland	55.00	40.00	30.00	22.50	1.00

88

91

94,100

96, 102

1910 Guy Issue (Lithographed) Perf. 12 except as noted VF Used + 30% (B)

87-97	**#87-91,92A,93-97 Set of 11**	**685.00**	**500.00**	**340.00**	**245.00**	**450.00**
87	1¢ James I,Pf. 12 x 11	3.15	2.35	1.60	1.20	.80
87a	1¢ Perf. 12	11.00	8.50	6.25	4.75	2.00
87b	1¢ Perf. 12 x 14	7.00	5.50	4.00	3.00	5.00
88	2¢ Company Arms	17.50	13.50	9.75	7.50	1.50
88a	2¢ Perf. 12 x 14	9.00	7.00	4.75	3.75	.65
88c	2¢ Perf. 12 x 11½	...	...	300.00	225.00	225.00
89	3¢ John Guy	20.00	15.00	10.50	7.75	12.50
90	4¢ The "Endeavor"	29.00	21.00	15.00	11.00	9.50
91	5¢ Cupids, Perf. 14 x 12	22.00	16.00	11.50	8.25	2.50
91a	5¢ Perf. 12	42.00	31.00	23.50	17.50	5.25
92	6¢ Lord Bacon Claret (Z Reversed)	135.00	100.00	70.00	52.50	95.00
92A	6¢ Claret (Z Normal)	46.50	35.00	24.00	18.00	45.00
93	8¢ Mosquito, Pale Brown	100.00	75.00	50.00	37.50	70.00
94	9¢ Logging, Olive Green	100.00	75.00	50.00	37.50	60.00

1910 Guy Issue (Lithographed) Perf. 12 except as noted VF Used + 30% (B) (continued)

Scott's No.		NH VF	NH F-VF	Unused VF	Unused F-VF	Used F-VF
95	10¢ Paper Mills, Black	120.00	90.00	60.00	45.00	80.00
96	12¢ Edward VII, L. Brown	120.00	90.00	60.00	45.00	65.00
97	15¢ George V, Gray Black	150.00	110.00	75.00	55.00	80.00

1911 Guy Issue (Engraved) Perf. 14 VF Used + 30% (B)

Scott's No.		NH VF	NH F-VF	Unused VF	Unused F-VF	Used F-VF
98-103	**Set of 6**	**660.00**	**470.00**	**340.00**	**250.00**	**375.00**
98	6¢ Lord Bacon Brown Violet	47.50	34.00	25.00	18.00	35.00
99	8¢ Mosquito, Bistre Brn	110.00	75.00	55.00	40.00	55.00
100	9¢ Logging, Ol. Grn	95.00	70.00	50.00	37.50	75.00
101	10¢ Paper Mills, Vi. Black	180.00	130.00	95.00	70.00	95.00
102	12¢ Edward VII, Red Brn	130.00	95.00	66.50	50.00	50.00
103	15¢ George V, Slate Gr	130.00	95.00	66.50	50.00	90.00

104

105

111

124

1911 Royal Family Coronation Issue VF Used + 30% (B)

Scott's No.		NH VF	NH F-VF	Unused VF	Unused F-VF	Used F-VF
104-14	**Set of 11**	**435.00**	**335.00**	**235.00**	**180.00**	**295.00**
104	1¢ Queen Mary	9.50	7.00	5.25	4.00	.25
105	2¢ George V	5.75	4.50	3.25	2.50	.25
106	3¢ Prince of Wales	40.00	30.00	22.00	16.50	22.50
107	4¢ Prince Albert	33.00	25.00	18.00	13.50	20.00
108	5¢ Princess Mary	16.00	12.00	8.75	6.50	1.25
109	6¢ Prince Henry	31.50	23.50	17.50	13.00	20.00
110	8¢ George (color paper)	105.00	80.00	57.50	42.50	60.00
110a	8¢ White Paper	110.00	85.00	60.00	45.00	70.00
111	9¢ Prince John	42.50	31.50	23.00	17.00	30.00
112	10¢ Queen Alexandra	55.00	41.50	30.00	22.50	30.00
113	12¢ Duke of Connaught	55.00	41.50	30.00	22.50	30.00
114	15¢ Seal of Colony	55.00	41.50	30.00	22.50	35.00

1919 Trail of the Caribou Issue VF Used + 30% (B)

Scott's No.		NH VF	NH F-VF	Unused VF	Unused F-VF	Used F-VF
115-26	**Set of 12**	**350.00**	**260.00**	**190.00**	**140.00**	**180.00**
115	1¢ Suvla Bay	5.25	3.95	2.95	2.25	.20
116	2¢ Ubigue	5.85	4.50	3.25	2.50	.45
117	3¢ Gueudecourt	8.50	6.25	4.75	3.50	.20
118	4¢ Beaumont Hamel	8.50	6.25	4.75	3.50	.85
119	5¢ Ubigue	8.95	6.75	4.85	3.75	1.10
120	6¢ Monchy	31.50	24.00	18.00	13.50	25.00
121	8¢ Ubigue	31.50	24.00	18.00	13.50	30.00
122	10¢ Steenbeck	16.50	12.50	9.00	6.75	3.50
123	12¢ Ubigue	87.50	67.50	50.00	36.50	37.50
124	15¢ Langemarck	55.00	40.00	30.00	22.50	45.00
125	24¢ Cambral	65.00	47.50	34.00	26.00	30.00
126	36¢ Combles	53.50	40.00	28.75	21.50	21.50

1920 Stamps of 1897 Surcharged VF Used + 30% (B)

Scott's No.		NH VF	NH F-VF	Unused VF	Unused F-VF	Used F-VF
127	2¢ on 30¢ Seal (#72)	9.00	6.75	5.00	3.75	12.00
128	3¢ on 15¢ Bars 10½ mm	350.00	270.00	195.00	150.00	150.00
129	3¢ on 15¢ Bars 13½ mm	23.00	17.50	13.00	10.00	10.00
130	3¢ on 35¢ Iceberg (#73)	17.00	12.50	9.50	7.00	8.50

1923-1924 Pictorial Issue VF Used + 30% (B)

131

132

133

139

Scott's No.		NH VF	NH F-VF	Unused VF	Unused F-VF	Used F-VF
131-44	**Set of 14**	**205.00**	**150.00**	**115.00**	**85.00**	**115.00**
131	1¢ Twin Hills, Tor's Cove	2.50	1.80	1.50	1.10	.20
132	2¢ South West Arm, Trinity	2.50	1.80	1.50	1.10	.20
133	3¢ War Memorial	2.75	2.00	1.60	1.20	.20
134	4¢ Humber River	3.35	2.50	1.95	1.50	1.40
135	5¢ Coast of Trinity	5.75	4.25	3.35	2.50	2.25
136	6¢ Upper Steadies, Humber R.	6.75	5.25	4.00	3.00	3.00
137	8¢ Quidi Vidi	6.00	4.25	3.50	2.50	2.40
138	9¢ Caribou Crossing Lake	41.50	30.00	25.00	18.00	24.00
139	10¢ Humber River Canyon	7.50	5.75	4.25	3.25	2.50
140	11¢ Shell Bird Island	11.50	8.50	6.75	5.00	11.50
141	12¢ Mt. Moriah	11.50	8.50	6.75	5.00	7.50
142	15¢ Humber River	14.50	10.50	8.50	6.25	10.00
143	20¢ Placentia (1924)	15.00	11.50	8.75	6.75	7.50
144	24¢ Topsail Falls (1924)	95.00	67.50	55.00	40.00	60.00

NEWFOUNDLAND

145,163,172

146,164,173

148,166,175

155

1928 Publicity Issue - Unwatermarked - Thin Paper VF Used + 30% (B)

Scott's No.		NH VF	NH F-VF	Unused VF	Unused F-VF	Used F-VF
145-59	**Set of 15**	**157.50**	**115.00**	**95.00**	**72.50**	**135.00**
145	1¢ Map, Deep Green	3.35	2.50	1.95	1.50	1.10
146	2¢ "Caribou", Deep Carmine	5.00	3.75	3.00	2.25	.45
147	3¢ Mary & George V, Brown	3.70	2.75	2.20	1.65	.75
148	4¢ Prince, Lilac Rose	9.95	7.50	5.95	4.50	1.85
149	5¢ Train, Slate Green	21.00	16.00	12.50	9.50	3.50
150	6¢ Newfld. Hotel, Ultramarine	8.00	5.85	4.75	3.50	13.50
151	8¢ Heart's Content, Lt. Red Brn	8.00	6.00	5.00	3.75	17.50
152	9¢ Cabot Tower Myrtle Green	10.00	7.50	6.00	4.50	8.50
153	10¢ War Mem., Dark Violet	10.00	7.50	6.00	4.50	9.00
154	12¢ P.O., Brown Carmine	8.50	6.25	5.00	3.75	13.75
155	14¢ Cabot Tower, Red Brown	10.00	7.50	6.00	4.50	6.50
156	15¢ Nonstop Flight, Dark Blue	12.00	8.75	7.00	5.25	19.50
157	20¢ Colonial Bldg, Gray Blk	10.00	7.50	6.00	4.50	5.25
158	28¢ P.O., Gray Green	41.50	32.50	25.00	19.50	35.00
159	30¢ Grand Falls, Olive Brown	12.00	8.75	7.00	5.25	12.00

1929 Stamp of 1923 Surcharged VF Used + 30% (B)

Scott's No.		NH VF	NH F-VF	Unused VF	Unused F-VF	Used F-VF
160	3¢ on 6¢ Upper Steadies(#136)	4.95	3.75	2.95	2.25	3.75

1929-31 Publicity Issue Re-engraved - Like Preceding but Thicker Paper VF Used + 30% (B) (See your favorite Specialized catalog for details)

Scott's No.		NH VF	NH F-VF	Unused VF	Unused F-VF	Used F-VF
163-71	**Set of 9**	**167.50**	**125.00**	**107.50**	**77.50**	**110.00**
163	1¢ Green	5.75	3.95	3.25	2.50	.35
164	2¢ Deep Carmine	2.25	1.80	1.40	1.10	.30
165	3¢ Deep Red Brown	2.35	1.80	1.50	1.15	.20
166	4¢ Magenta	4.95	3.65	2.95	2.25	.75
167	5¢ Slate Green	7.95	6.25	4.95	3.75	1.50
168	6¢ Ultramarine	18.50	13.50	11.50	8.50	9.75
169	10¢ Dark Violet	6.00	4.50	3.75	2.75	2.25
170	15¢ Deep Blue (1930)	53.50	40.00	37.50	25.00	65.00
171	20¢ Gray Black (1931)	80.00	57.50	47.50	35.00	35.00

1931 Publicity Issue - Re-engraved - Wmk. Arms VF Used + 30% (B)

Scott's No.		NH VF	NH F-VF	Unused VF	Unused F-VF	Used F-VF
172-82	**Set of 11**	**310.00**	**230.00**	**190.00**	**140.00**	**140.00**
172	1¢ Green	8.75	6.75	5.50	4.25	2.50
173	2¢ Red	8.75	6.75	5.50	4.25	2.75
174	3¢ Red Brown	4.25	3.15	2.60	1.95	1.25
175	4¢ Rose	5.50	4.00	3.35	2.50	1.10
176	5¢ Greenish Gray	12.50	9.25	7.75	5.75	7.50
177	6¢ Ultramarine	28.00	21.00	16.75	12.75	17.50
178	8¢ Red Brown	37.50	27.50	23.50	17.50	22.50
179	10¢ Dark Violet	19.50	14.00	11.50	8.75	7.75
180	15¢ Deep Blue	53.50	42.50	32.50	25.00	40.00
181	20¢ Gray Black	92.50	72.50	58.50	45.00	11.50
182	30¢ Olive Brown	59.50	45.00	36.50	27.50	35.00

1932-1937 Pictorial Set, Perf. 13½ or 14 VF Used + 25%

183-84,253

190-91,257

199,266

210,264

Scott's No.		NH VF	NH F-VF	Unused VF	Unused F-VF	Used F-VF
183-99	**Set of 17**	**100.00**	**82.50**	**73.50**	**57.50**	**49.75**
183	1¢ Codfish, Green	2.65	2.10	1.85	1.50	.30
183a	1¢ Booklet Pane of 4	85.00	70.00	60.00	50.00	...
184	1¢ Gray Black	.90	.70	.65	.50	.15
184a	1¢ Bk. Pane of 4, Pf. 13½	65.00	52.50	45.00	37.50	...
184b	1¢ Bk. Pane of 4, Pf. 14	80.00	65.00	55.00	45.00	...
185	2¢ George V, Rose	1.85	1.50	1.35	1.10	.20
185a	2¢ Bk. Pane of 4	52.50	42.50	36.50	30.00	...
186	2¢ Green	2.25	1.75	1.60	1.25	.20
186a	2¢ Bk. Pane of 4, Pf. 13½	26.00	21.50	20.00	16.50	...
186b	2¢ Bk. Pane of 4, Pf. 14	37.50	29.50	26.00	21.00	...
187	3¢ Queen Mary	2.25	1.75	1.60	1.25	.20
187a	3¢ Bk. Pane of 4, Pf. 13½	70.00	55.00	47.50	37.00	...
187b	3¢ Bk. Pane of 4, Pf. 14	85.00	67.50	57.50	45.00	...
187c	3¢ Bk. Pane of 4, Pf. 13	85.00	70.00	60.00	50.00	...
188	4¢ Prince, Deep Violet	7.75	6.25	5.50	4.50	1.75
189	4¢ Rose Lake	1.75	1.40	1.25	1.00	.30
190	5¢ Caribou V. Brown (I)	7.00	5.50	5.00	4.00	1.10
191	5¢ Deep Violet (II)	1.25	1.00	.90	.70	.25
191a	5¢ Deep Violet (I)	11.50	9.50	8.25	6.75	1.25
	#191 Antler under "T" higher, #190,191a Antlers are even height.					
192	6¢ Elizabeth, Dull Blue	11.50	9.00	8.00	6.50	10.75
193	10¢ Salmon, Olive Black	1.50	1.15	1.10	.85	.60
194	14¢ Dog, Intense Black	5.25	4.15	3.75	3.00	3.75
195	15¢ Seal Pup, Magenta	3.30	2.60	2.35	1.85	1.75

1932-37 Pictorial Set, Perf.13½ or 14 VF Used + 25% (continued)

Scott's No.		NH		Unused		Used
		VF	F-VF	VF	F-VF	F-VF
196	20¢ Cape Race, Gray Green	3.30	2.60	2.35	1.85	.85
197	25¢ Sealing Fleet, Gray	3.65	3.15	2.85	2.25	2.00
198	30¢ Fishing Fleet, Ultra	39.50	31.50	28.00	22.50	22.50
199	48¢ Fishing Fleet					
	Red Brown (1937)	13.50	10.50	9.50	7.50	8.00

1932 New Values VF Used + 25%

208	7¢ Duchess, Red Brown	3.15	2.50	2.20	1.75	2.50
209	8¢ Corner Brook, Or. Red	3.95	3.15	2.80	2.25	1.50
210	24¢ Bell Island, Light Blue	4.00	3.15	2.85	2.25	2.75

1933 "L & S Post" Overprinted on C9 VF + 20%

211	15¢ Dog Sled & Plane	10.50	8.50	8.00	6.50	8.25

1933 Sir Humphrey Gilbert Issue VF + 25%

212-25	Set of 14	210.00	167.50	142.50	110.00	135.00
212	1¢ Sir Humphrey Gilbert	1.25	1.00	.85	.70	1.00
213	2¢ Compton Castle	1.60	1.25	1.10	.85	.50
214	3¢ Gilbert Coat of Arms	2.95	2.35	2.00	1.60	1.00
215	4¢ Eton College	2.30	1.90	1.60	1.30	.45
216	5¢ Token from Queen	3.15	2.50	2.15	1.70	.85
217	7¢ Royal Patents	25.00	20.00	17.00	13.50	14.50
218	8¢ Leaving Plymouth	14.00	11.00	9.25	7.25	10.00
219	9¢ Arriving St. John's	15.00	12.00	10.00	8.00	9.00
220	10¢ Annexation	15.00	12.00	10.00	8.00	7.50
221	14¢ Coat of Arms	27.50	21.50	18.50	14.50	25.00
222	15¢ Deck of "Squirrel"	26.00	20.00	17.50	13.75	13.00
223	20¢ 1626 Map of Nwfld	18.50	14.50	12.50	9.75	11.50
224	24¢ Queen Elizabeth I	33.50	26.50	22.50	18.00	20.00
225	32¢ Gilbert Statue at Truro	36.50	29.50	25.00	20.00	35.00

1935 Silver Jubilee Issue VF + 20%

Scott's No.		F-VF NH	Unused	F-VF Used
226-29	Set of 4	13.00	9.25	12.75
226	4¢ George V, Bright Rose	1.10	.85	1.25
227	5¢ Violet	1.30	1.00	1.25
228	7¢ Dark Blue	3.50	2.50	4.50
229	24¢ Olive Green	7.75	5.75	6.50

1937 Coronation Issue VF + 25%

230-32	Set of 3	4.95	3.85	4.50
230	2¢ Elizabeth & George VI Deep Green	1.00	.75	1.50
231	4¢ Carmine Rose	1.40	1.10	1.75
232	5¢ Dark Violet	2.95	2.25	1.75

1937 Coronation Issue (Long Set) VF + 30%

233-43	Set of 11	36.50	26.75	27.50
233	1¢ Codfish	1.25	.95	.20
234	3¢ Map of Newfoundland (I), Fine	3.85	3.00	2.25
234a	3¢ Map (II), Coarse	2.90	2.25	2.25
235	7¢ Caribou	2.25	1.65	1.50
236	8¢ Corner Brook Paper Mills	2.25	1.65	2.00
237	10¢ Salmon	3.65	2.75	5.00
238	14¢ Newfoundland Dog	3.25	2.50	2.40
239	15¢ Harp Seal Pup	6.00	4.50	3.00
240	20¢ Cape Race	2.85	2.10	4.00
241	24¢ Loading Iron Ore	3.65	2.70	2.50
242	25¢ Sealing Fleet	3.65	2.70	2.50
243	48¢ Fishing Fleet	6.25	4.75	3.50

1938 Royal Family, Perf. 13½ VF + 25%

Scott's No.		F-VF NH	Unused	F-VF Used
245-48	Set of 4	6.25	4.80	3.25
245	2¢ George VI, Green	1.50	1.20	.40
246	3¢ Queen Elizabeth, Dark Carmine	1.50	1.20	.45
247	4¢ Princess Elizabeth, Light Blue	1.95	1.50	.20
248	7¢ Queen Mother, Ultramarine	1.50	1.20	2.50

1939 Royal Visit VF + 20%

Scott's No.		Plate Blocks NH	Unused	NH	Unused	F-VF Used
249	5¢ George VI - Elizabeth	10.50	8.50	1.25	1.00	.65

1939 Royal Visit Surcharge VF + 20%

250	2¢ on 5¢ (#249)	11.75	9.50	1.35	1.10	.85
251	4¢ on 5¢ (#249)	10.50	8.50	1.10	.85	.65

1941 Grenfell Issue VF + 20%

252	5¢ Wilfred Grenfell	2.75	2.25	.30	.25	.35

1941-1944 Pictorial Set, Perf. 12½ VF + 25%

253-66	Set of 14	...	...	29.50	22.75	29.50
253	1¢ Codfish, Dark Gray	3.00	2.40	.30	.25	.25
254	2¢ George VI, Deep Green	3.00	2.40	.30	.25	.20
255	3¢ Elizabeth, Rose Carm	3.75	2.95	.30	.25	.15
256	4¢ Princess Elizabeth, Blue	8.75	7.00	1.60	1.25	.20
257	5¢ Caribou, Violet (I)	10.00	8.00	1.75	1.40	.25
258	7¢ Queen Mother (1942)	...	...	3.15	2.50	3.75
259	8¢ Corner Brook, Red	8.75	7.00	1.25	1.00	1.25
260	10¢ Salmon, Brown Black	10.00	8.00	1.40	1.10	.75
261	14¢ Dog, Black	19.00	15.00	2.50	2.00	3.50
262	15¢ Seal Pup, Rose Violet	32.50	25.00	4.50	3.50	4.50
263	20¢ Cape Race, Green	32.50	25.00	4.50	3.50	3.50
264	24¢ Bell Island, Deep Blue	21.00	16.50	2.85	2.25	6.50
265	25¢ Sealing Fleet, Slate	32.50	25.00	4.50	3.50	5.00
266	48¢ Fishing, Red Br. (1944)	19.00	15.00	2.75	2.15	4.00

1943 University Issue VF + 20%

267	30¢ Memorial University	8.00	6.50	1.25	1.00	1.25

1946 Two Cent Provisional VF + 20%

268	2¢ on 30¢ (#267)	3.50	3.00	.30	.25	.45

1947 Issues VF + 20%

269	4¢ Princess Elizabeth	2.35	2.00	.30	.25	.35
270	5¢ Cabot in the "Matthew"	2.75	2.25	.30	.25	.50

NEWFOUNDLAND

AIRMAIL STAMPS

1919-21 Overprint Issues VF Used + 40% (B)

Scott's No.		NH		Unused		Used
		VF	F-VF	VF	F-VF	F-VF
C2	$1 on 15¢ "Trans-Atlantic" AIRPOST,1919.					
'	ONE DOLLAR (#70)	295..00	215.00	190.00	135.00	135.00
C2a	$1 on 15¢ Without Comma after "Post"'	325.00	235.00	210.00	150.00	165.00
C3	35¢ "AIR MAIL to Halifax, N.S. 1921"(#73)	215.00	150.00	135.00	95.00	100.00
C3a	35¢ Period after "1921"	250.00	175.00	155.00	110.00	120.00

C7,C10 C6,C9 C8,C11

1931 Airs, Unwatermarked VF Used + 30% (B)

Scott's No.		NH VF	NH F-VF	Unused VF	Unused F-VF	Used F-VF
C6-8	Set of 3	137.50	105.00	90.00	67.50	90.00
C6	15¢ Dog Sled & Airplane	11.50	8.75	7.50	5.75	8.25
C7	50¢ Trans-Atlantic Plane	39.50	30.00	26.50	19.50	30.00
C8	$1 Flight Routes	92.50	70.00	59.50	45.00	60.00

1931 Airs, Watermarked "Coat of Arms" VF Used + 30% (B)

C9-11	Set of 3	195.00	140.00	125.00	90.00	155.00
C9	15¢ Dog Sled & Airplane	11.50	8.75	7.50	5.75	10.75
C10	50¢ Trans-Atlantic Plane	50.00	37.50	33.00	25.00	45.00
C11	$1 Flight Routes	145.00	100.00	90.00	67.50	110.00

NOTE: PRICES THROUGHOUT THIS LIST ARE SUBJECT TO CHANGE WITHOUT NOTICE IF MARKET CONDITIONS REQUIRE. MINIMUM ORDER MUST TOTAL AT LEAST $20.00.

NEWFOUNDLAND

C13 C19 J5

1932 DO-X Trans-Atlantic Surcharge VF Used + 30% (B)

Scott's No.		NH VF	NH F-VF	Unused VF	Unused F-VF	Used F-VF
C12	$1.50 on $1 Routes (#C11)	385.00	300.00	250.00	195.00	225.00

1933 Labrador Issue VF Used + 25%

C13-17	Set of 5	225.00	175.00	150.00	117.50	170.00
C13	5¢ "Put to Flight"	20.00	16.00	13.50	10.75	12.50
C14	10¢ "Land of Heart's Delight" .	24.00	19.00	16.00	12.50	18.50
C15	30¢ "Spotting the Herd"	45.00	35.00	30.00	23.50	30.00
C16	60¢ "News from Home"	75.00	60.00	50.00	40.00	60.00
C17	75¢ "Labrador, Land of Gold" .	75.00	60.00	50.00	40.00	55.00

1933 General Balbo Flight VF Used + 25%

C18	$4.50 on 75¢ (#C17)	495.00	385.00	330.00	260.00	295.00

1943 St. John's VF + 20%

Scott's No.		Plate Blocks NH	Plate Blocks Unused	F-VF NH	F-VF Unused	F-VF Used
C19	7¢ View of St. John's	3.00	2.50	.35	.30	.35

POSTAGE DUE STAMPS 1939-1949 VF + 25%
Unwatermarked, Perf. 10 x 10½ Unless Otherwise Noted

Scott's No.		F-VF NH	F-VF Unused	F-VF Used
J1-6	Set of 6	39.75	29.50	...
J1	1¢ Yellow Green, Perf.11 (1949)	4.50	3.25	7.50
J1a	1¢ Perf. 10x10½	5.25	4.25	6.50
J2	2¢ Vermillion	11.75	8.75	6.00
J2a	2¢ Perf. 11 x 9 (1946)	11.75	8.75	13.50
J3	3¢ Ultramarine	7.00	5.25	13.00
J3a	3¢ Perf. 11 x 9 (1949)	11.00	8.25	22.50
J3b	3¢ Perforated 9	450.00	325.00	...
J4	4¢ Yellow Orange Perf. 11x9	10.50	7.75	35.00
J4a	4¢ Perf. 10x10½ (1949)	12.75	9.50	13.50
J5	5¢ Pale Brown	5.00	3.75	15.00
J6	10¢ Dark Violet	5.75	4.25	12.50
J7	10¢ Watermarked, Perf. II	18.00	13.50	50.00

BRITISH COLUMBIA AND VANCOUVER ISLAND

1860 British Columbia & Vancouver I (C)

Scott's No.		Unused Fine	Unused Ave.	Used Fine	Used Ave.
2	2½p Victoria, Dull Rose	225.00	110.00	165.00	85.00

1865 Vancouver Island (OG + 50%) (C)

		Fine	Ave.	Fine	Ave.
4	10¢ Victoria, Blue, Imperf	1400.00	950.00	850.00	550.00
5	5¢ Victoria, Rose, Perf. 14	250.00	145.00	170.00	100.00
6	10¢ Victoria, Blue, Perf. 14	250.00	145.00	170.00	100.00

1865 British Columbia (OG + 50%) (C)

		Fine	Ave.	Fine	Ave.
7	3p Seal, Blue, Perf. 14	80.00	50.00	80.00	50.00

1867-1869 Surcharges on #7 Design, Perf. 14 (OG + 40%) (C)

		Fine	Ave.	Fine	Ave.
8	2¢ on 3p Brown (Black Surch)	100.00	60.00	100.00	60.00
9	5¢ on 3p Bright Red (Black)	170.00	100.00	170.00	100.00
10	10¢ on 3p Lilac Rose (Blue)	1250.00	750.00	...	...
11	25¢ on 3p Orange (Violet)	165.00	100.00	165.00	100.00
12	50¢ on 3p Violet (Red)	625.00	375.00	625.00	375.00
13	$1 on 3p Green (Green)	1100.00	600.00	...	...

1869 Surcharges on #7 Design, Perf. 12½ (OG + 40%) (C)

		Fine	Ave.	Fine	Ave.
14	5¢ on 3p Bright Red (Black)	1250.00	800.00	1000.00	600.00
15	10¢ on 3p Lilac Rose (Blue)	825.00	500.00	825.00	500.00
16	25¢ on 3p Orange (Violet)	500.00	300.00	500.00	300.00
17	50¢ on 3p Green (Green)	675.00	400.00	675.00	400.00
18	$1 on 3p Green (Green)	1250.00	750.00	1250.00	750.00

NEW BRUNSWICK

Scott's No.		Unused Fine	Unused Ave.	Used Fine	Used Ave.
	1851 Imperforate - Blue Paper - Unwatermarked (OG + 50%) (C)				
1	3p Crown & Flowers, Red	1050.00	595.00	275.00	165.00
2	6p Olive Yellow	2500.00	1400.00	500.00	300.00
3	1sh Bright Red Violet	...	...	...	1400.00
4	1sh Dull Violet	...	...	...	1800.00

1860-1863 - Perf. 12 - White Paper (VF + 50%, OG + 30%, NH + 100%) (C)

6	**7-9**	**10**	**11**

		Fine	Ave.	Fine	Ave.
6	1¢ Locomotive, Red Lilac	19.50	11.00	19.50	11.00
6a	1¢ Brown Violet	32.50	18.50	30.00	17.00
7	2¢ Victoria, Orange (1863)	7.00	4.15	7.00	4.15
8	5¢ Victoria, Green	8.00	4.75	8.00	4.75
8b	5¢ Olive Green	70.00	42.50	15.00	9.50
9	10¢ Victoria, Vermillion	27.50	16.50	27.50	16.50
10	12½¢ Steam & Sailing Ship, Blue	35.00	21.50	35.00	21.50
11	17¢ Prince of Wales, Black	27.50	16.50	27.50	16.50

NOTE: PRICES THROUGHOUT THIS LIST ARE SUBJECT TO CHANGE WITHOUT NOTICE IF MARKET CONDITIONS REQUIRE. MINIMUM ORDER MUST TOTAL AT LEAST $20.00.

NOVA SCOTIA

1851-1853 - Imperforate - Blue Paper (OG + 50%) (C)

2,3

Scott's No.		Unused Fine	Unused Ave.	Used Fine	Used Ave.
1	1p Victoria, Red Brown	1500.00	900.00	325.00	210.00
2	3p Crown & Flowers, Blue	435.00	250.00	110.00	70.00
3	3p Dark Blue	750.00	450.00	140.00	85.00
4	6p Crown & Flowers,, Yellow Green ..	...	1500.00	350.00	210.00
5	6p Dark Green	...	3000.00	625.00	375.00
6	1sh Crown & Flowers, Reddish Violet	...	...	...	1500.00
7	1sh Dull Violet	...	...	...	2575.00

1860-1863 - Perforated 12
(VF + 50%, OG + 20%, NH + 60%)

8	**10**	**11**	**13**

		Fine	Ave.	Fine	Ave.
8	1¢ Victoria, Black, Yellow Paper	4.50	2.75	8.50	5.00
8a	1¢ White Paper	4.50	2.75	8.50	5.00
9	2¢ Lilac, White Paper	4.75	3.00	9.00	5.50
9a	2¢ Yellowish Paper	4.75	3.00	9.00	5.50
10	5¢ Blue, White Paper	210.00	130.00	11.00	7.00
10a	5¢ Yellowish Paper	210.00	130.00	11.00	7.00
11	8½¢ Green, Yellowish Paper	4.25	2.60	25.00	16.00
11a	8½¢ White Paper	10.00	6.50	30.00	20.00
12	10¢ Vermillion, White Paper	5.50	3.50	15.00	10.00
12a	10¢ Yellowish Paper	8.50	5.25	16.50	11.00
13	12½¢ Black, Yellowish Paper	18.50	11.00	17.50	11.00
13a	12½¢ White Paper	27.50	16.50	23.50	14.50

PRINCE EDWARD ISLAND

1,5	**2,6**	**3,7**	**9**

1861 - Perf. 9 - Typographed (OG + 50%)

Scott's No.		Unused Fine	Unused Ave.	Used Fine	Used Ave.
1	2p Victoria, Dull Rose	285.00	180.00	140.00	90.00
2	3p Blue	625.00	375.00	300.00	185.00
3	6p Yellow Green	1000.00	650.00	600.00	375.00

1862-1865 - Perf. 11,11½,12 and Compound - Typographed
(VF + 50%, OG + 30%, NH + 80%)

		Fine	Ave.	Fine	Ave.
4	1p Victoria, Yellow Orange	16.50	10.50	30.00	20.00
5	2p Rose, White Paper	6.00	3.25	7.00	4.00
5a	2p Yellowish Paper	6.00	3.25	7.00	4.00
6	3p Blue, White Paper	5.50	3.25	8.50	5.00
6a	3p Yellowish Paper	8.50	5.00	8.50	5.00
7	6p Yellow Green	52.50	31.50	52.50	31.50
8	9p Violet	42.50	25.00	42.50	25.00

1868-1870 Issues (VF + 50%, OG + 30%, NH + 80%)

		Fine	Ave.	Fine	Ave.
9	4p Victoria, Black, White Paper	5.25	3.15	20.00	13.00
9a	4p Yellowish Paper	11.00	7.00	17.50	11.50
10	4½p Brown (1870)	35.00	22.50	37.50	24.50

1872 Issue, Perf. 12,12½ (VF + 50%, OG + 20%, NH + 60%)

11	**12**	**15**	**16**

		Fine	Ave.	Fine	Ave.
11	1¢ Victoria, Brown Orange	3.35	2.10	9.00	5.50
12	2¢ Ultramarine	9.00	5.75	25.00	16.50
13	3¢ Rose	13.50	8.00	16.00	9.00
14	4¢ Green	3.75	2.40	11.00	7.50
15	6¢ Black	3.75	2.40	11.00	7.50
16	12¢ Violet	3.75	2.40	19.50	12.00

Welcome to
Brookman's Autograph Section

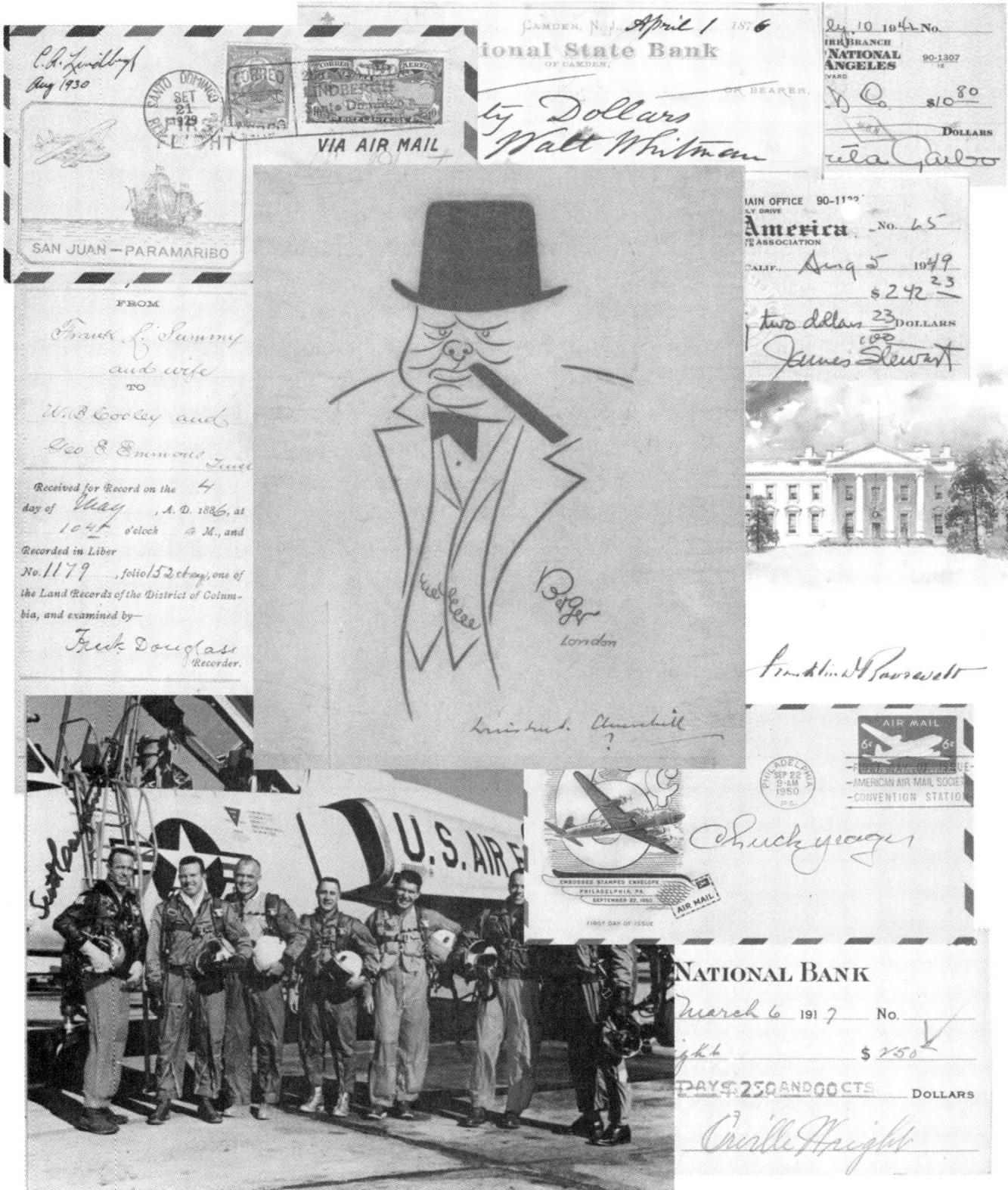

Welcome to the Wonderful World of Autograph Collecting!

We are very excited about the response to our 2001 edition, which inaugurated the Autograph section. As we suspected, there is a very significant cross-over of autograph collectors to philately and vice-versa. As we have previously mentioned, a collector interested in collecting certain famous individuals on the stamps and covers, might also want to have their autograph as well. In addition, autograph collectors, now have an opportunity to have all this information in one price guide. No other price guide offers stamps, covers and autographs all in one guide, and no other autograph guide prices autographs on cover.

This was a massive project to begin with, from which we have created a huge database. We have tried to correct many of the misspelled names and as this new venture is a work in progress, it should be noted that we will continue to clean up our database. Several hundred new names were added this year in addition to the hundreds of price changes.

We wish to thank our current editors, Scott Winslow of Scott Winslow Associates, who specializes in early historical figures as well as Presidents, government figures and war and military leaders; Phillip J. Marks, who has over 20 years experience in sports autographs including cards and sports memorabilia; and, I. Michael Orenstein of Superior Galleries, a leading expert in astronaut autographs and memorabilia. We also welcome our newest contributing editor Greg Tucker who is a specialist in movie stars, celebrities and sports. A special thanks to Alexander Autographs, a premier auction house, for the use of their autograph database.

ABBREVIATIONS USED IN THE AUTOGRAPH SECTION

ALS : Autograph Letter Signed (written and signed by the same person.)

LS : Letter Signed (body of letter written by another person.)

TLS : Typed Letter Signed

DS : Document Signed

SIG : Signature on paper or card

WH CARD : White House Card signed

COVER : Depending on the time period, can be franked envelope, stamped envelope, event or First Day of Issue

HOF : Hall of Fame

D : Deceased

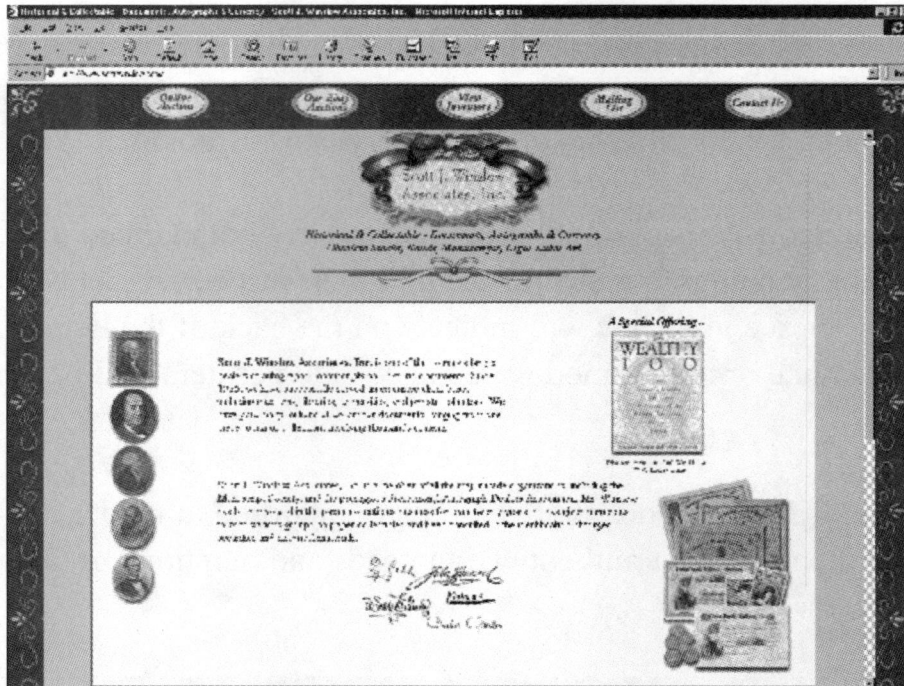

PROFILES IN HISTORY CELEBRATES
15 YEARS IN COLLECTING

PROFILES IN HISTORY is the nation's leading dealer of original historical autographs. Founded in 1986 by Joseph Maddalena, Profiles in History is dedicated to the acquisition and selling of the highest quality autographed original historical letters and manuscripts.

We offer autograph materials including:

- American Presidents and statesmen
- Revolutionary and Civil War soldiers
- Scientists, inventors and business leaders
- Celebrated authors, artists and composers
- Aviators, explorers and Wild West adventurers
- Sports heroes and Hollywood legends

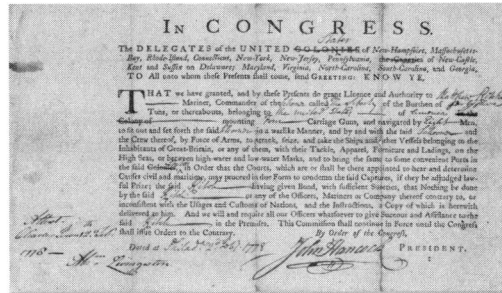

Profiles in History has been seen in the pages of:

- *Forbes, Business Week, Newsweek and Worth*
- *People, Millionaire and Hollywood Reporter*
- *The New York Times, The Los Angeles Times*
- *The Wall Street Journal, The Washington Post, The New York Post*

Feature segments on the company have appeared on:

- *The Discovery Channel and The Incurable Collector on A&E*
- *Entertainment Tonight and E! Entertainment Television*
- *CNN, ABC, CBS, NBC & Fox News*

Hollywood Entertainment Memorabilia Auctions

- Live auction w/bidding in person, by phone, fax and internet
- Memorabilia from film, television and the music industry, including
- Props, costumes, photographs, sketches and posters
- Previews open to the public

Catalogs

- Historical document catalogs ($20 U.S.)
- Hollywood auction catalogs ($30 U.S.)
- Catalogs on-line at www.profilesinhistory.com

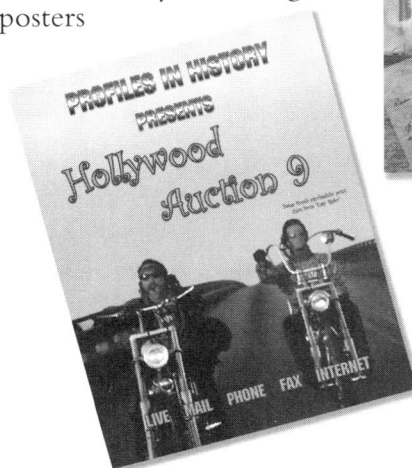

For more information, please call 1-800-942-8856 or visit us @
www.profilesinhistory.com

Profiles in History 345 N. Maple Drive, Suite 202, Beverly Hills, California 90210
Phone (310) 859-7701 ● (800) 942-8856 in U.S. ● Fax (310) 859-3842.

PRESIDENTIAL - SIGNED AS PRESIDENT

	PHOTO	ALS	LS/TLS	DS	SIG.	COVER
John Adams		15000	4900	4000	2000	4000
John Quincy Adams		1750		650	375	750
Chester A. Arthur		1500		750	350	700
*** David R. Atchison (Pres. only one day)		1400		850	375	750
James Buchanan	750	900		650	300	600
George Bush	275	900		900	150	200
George W. Bush	475	1050		850	315	525
Jimmy Carter	150	575		250	50	350
Grover Cleveland	900	750		500	225	450
William J. Clinton	400	900		750	275	450
Calvin Coolidge	400	750		400	200	400
Dwight D. Eisenhower	650	1500		850	400	650
Millard Fillmore		2500		750	325	650
Gerald R. Ford	200	900		600	125	200
James A. Garfield	2500	900		650	250	500
Ulysses S. Grant	2500	1500		1250	525	1050
Warren G. Harding	550	950		400	250	500
Benjamin Harrison	950	750		600	300	600
William Henry Harrison		1500		950	500	1000
Rutherford B. Hayes	950	650		750	250	500
Herbert Hoover	350	900		275	195	350
Andrew Jackson		3500		1750	750	1500
Thomas Jefferson		12500		5500	3500	7000
Andrew Johnson	3000	2000	1200	1500	575	1150
Lyndon B. Johnson	550	2500		950	275	500
John F. Kennedy	2500	3500		1750	900	1800
Abraham Lincoln	75000	12500		7500	3500	7000
James Madison		2500		1400	550	1100
William McKinley	950	2500		500	325	650
James Monroe		2900		900	400	800
Richard M. Nixon	450	2500		750	250	450
Franklin Pierce		950		750	375	750
James Polk		3000		1750	500	1000
Ronald Reagan	375	1500		575	225	400
Franklin D. Roosevelt	900	1200		900	375	750
Theodore Roosevelt	1250	950		750	450	900
William Taft	450	750		400	225	450
Zachary Taylor		4000		3500	900	1800
Harry S. Truman	450	2000		1200	300	600
John Tyler		1500		900	375	750
Martin VanBuren		900		900	325	650
George Washington		15000		10000	5000	10000
Woodrow Wilson	400	750		575	300	600

VICE PRESIDENTS

	PHOTO	ALS	LS/TLS	DS	SIG.	COVER
Spiro T. Agnew	95	575		150	35	75
Alben W. Barkley	75	150		75	25	75
John C. Calhoun	375	350		275	125	250
Richard Cheney	90				30	60
George Clinton		300		175	125	250
Schuyler Colfax	250			125	75	150
Charles Curtis	90	150		125	50	100
George M. Dallas		300		200	75	150
Charles G. Dawes	275	225		150	35	70
William Eustis		175		125	35	70
Charles Fairbanks	150	275		100	50	100
John N. Garner	175	250		175	65	200

	PHOTO	ALS	LS/TLS	DS	SIG.	COVER
Elbridge Gerry		2500		750	275	550
Alexander Hamilton		4500		3500	900	1800
Hannibal Hamlin		350		200	90	180
Thomas Hendricks		175		150	50	100
Garrett Hobart	200	225		200	75	150
Hubert H. Humphrey	65			125	45	100
Richard M. Johnson	400	350		200	100	200
William King				340	200	400
Thomas R. Marshall	175	350		175	75	150
Walter Mondale	45			35	25	75
Levi P. Morton	240	240		85	60	120
Dan Quayle	45	45			35	70
Nelson Rockefeller	50	90		75	25	50
James S. Sherman	200	275		175	75	150
Adlai E. Stevenson	150	200		150	50	100
Daniel D. Tompkins		150		125	100	200
Henry A. Wallace	100	150		125	50	200
William A. Wheeler				225	75	150
Henry Wilson		125		125	75	150
Al Gore	80				25	50

FIRST LADIES

	PHOTO	ALS	LS/TLS	DS	SIG.	COVER
Abigal Adams		4900		2500	500	1000
Louisa Catherine Adams		750		575	250	500
Ellen Lewis Arthur		1200			600	1200
Barbara Bush	75	125		100	50	100
Laura Bush	300			300	200	250
Rosalynn Carter	50	90		65	25	75
Francis Flosom Cleveland	225	200		75	50	100
Hillary Clinton						
Grace Coolidge	150	150		125	75	150
Mamie Eisenhower	50	150		125	50	125
Caroline Fillmore		1200		900	500	1000
Betty Ford	50			90	35	75
Lucretia R. Garfield		225		175	95	190
Julia Dent Grant		750		375	150	300
Florence Harding	75			125	75	150
Anna Harrison		2000		950	750	1500
Caroline S. Harrison	750	950		250	150	300
Mary Lord Harrison	125	175		125	75	150
Lucy W. Hayes	750	400		300	225	450
Lou Henry Hoover		200		100	75	150
Rachel Jackson					575	1150
Lady Bird Johnson	125	100		275	60	150
Eliza M. Johnson				1500	750	1500
Jacqueline Kennedy	1250	1500		950	450	900
Harriet Lane (acting First Lady for James Buchanan)	375			250	100	200
Mary Lincoln		1500		900	350	700
Dolly Payne Madison		2500		1500	900	1800
Ida Saxton McKinley	500	950		600	375	750
Patricia Nixon	175	250		75	50	200
Jane M. Pierce		950		500	250	500
Sarah Polk	1200	900		500	300	600
Nancy Reagan	75	100		75	35	200
Edith K. Roosevelt	350	225		200	75	150
Eleanor Roosevelt	250	325		200	75	175
Helen M. Taft	750	325		200	90	180
Bess Truman	175	175		125	75	150

	PHOTO	ALS	LS/TLS	DS	SIG.	COVER
Julia G. Tyler	650			450	200	400
Martha Washington					8500	17000
Edith Bolling Wilson	200	175		200	90	180
Ellen Louise Wilson		500		300	125	250
William Benjamin Jr.	60				40	80
Hugo Black	95	225		120	45	90
Harry Blackman	75	270		225	40	80
John Blair	48	1200		775	150	300
Samuel Blatchford		150		125	45	90
Joseph P. Bradley		200		100	55	110
Louis D. Brandeis	1200	650		400	150	300
William J. Brennan	90	155		105	65	130
David J. Brewer		160		95	75	150
Henry A. Brown		250		175	60	120
Warren E. Burger	75	195		175	50	100
Harold E. Burton	85			170	40	80
Pierce Butler	45	275		90	35	70
James F. Byrnes	55	235		125	30	60
Benjamin Cardozo	650	600		350	160	320
John A. Cambell		200		150	100	200
Tom Clark	125	125		100	40	80
Nathan Clifford	150	200		175	75	150
Benjamin R. Curtis		200		150	35	70
David Davis		225		200	75	150
William O. Douglas	200	150		175	75	150
Gabriel Duval		245		115	45	90
Oliver Ellsworth		575		275	100	200
Stephen J. Field	225	250		150	75	150
Abe Fortas		200		150	25	100
Felix Frankfurter	750	1195		1250	145	290
Melville Fuller	175	275		150	50	100
Arthur J. Goldberg	115			145	50	150
John M. Harlan		175		95	55	110
Oliver W. Holmes	600	550		300	250	500
Charles E. Hughes	250			150	45	90
Robert H. Jackson	125			295	50	100
John Jay		2250		1750	550	1100
Lucius Lamar	200	150		100	75	150
Thurgood Marshall	175			200	115	230
John Marshall		2500		1200	600	1200
Stanley Matthews		275		150	50	100
John McLean		285		200	55	110
J.C. McReynolds	100	145		125	30	60
Samuel F. Miller		250		185	95	190
Sherman Minton	100	250		150	50	100
William H. Moody	100	175		125	50	100
Alfred Moore	RARE				3000	6000
Frank Murphy	150	250		195	65	130
Samuel Nelson		200		150	50	100
Sandra Day O'Connor	45	200		125	25	50
Rufus Peckham	125	250		125	65	130
Lewis F. Powell Jr.				100	30	60
William H. Rehnquist	100	175		150	50	100
Owen J. Roberts	100	200		150	50	100
John Rutledge	50	250		100	30	60
Edward Shippin		150			50	100
George Shiras		350		250	100	200

SUPREME COURT JUSTICES (cont)

	PHOTO	ALS	LS/TLS	DS	SIG.	COVER
John Paul Stevens	150			90	40	80
Potter Stewart	90				35	70
Harlan Fiske Stone	225	250		200	75	150
Joseph Story		250		175	100	200
George Sutherland	250			150	75	150
Roger B. Taney		350		275	100	200
Clarence Thomas	40				25	50
Smith Thompson		175		150	75	150
Frederick M. Vinson	300	300		75	75	150
Morrison R. Waite	65			40	40	80
Earl Warren	250			75	75	150
Bushrod Washington		700		350	125	250
James Wayne		350		200	100	200
Byron R. White	75	150		125	55	110
Edward D. White	150	200		150	50	100
Levi Woodbury		250		150	65	130

SIGNERS OF THE CONSTITUTION

	PHOTO	ALS	LS/TLS	DS	SIG.	COVER
Abraham Baldwin		100		40	25	50
Richard Bassett				700	350	700
Gunning Bedford				700	350	700
John Blair	48	1200		775	150	300
William Blount				900	320	640
David Brearly				800	375	750
Jacob Broom		2000		900	350	700
Pierce Butler	45	275		90	35	70
Daniel Carroll		710		685	175	350
George Clymer		900		505	125	250
Jonathan Dayton		657		450	175	350
John Dickinson				575	200	400
William Few		750		450	200	400
Thomas Fitzsimons		400		315	200	400
Benjamin Franklin					4300	8600
Nicholas Gilman		500		300	100	200
Nathaniel Gorham		1200		425	375	750
Alexander Hamilton		3500		3000	800	1600
Jared Ingersoll		400		250	100	200
William S. Johnson		675		375	130	260
Rufus King		450		475	250	500
John Langdon		1200		400	210	420
William Livingston		1600		900	300	600
James Madison	2500	3000		1100	550	1100
James McHenry		RARE		275	200	400
Thomas Mifflin		600		450	150	300
Gouverneur Morris		625		585	190	380
Robert Morris		750		750	325	650
Charles Pinckney Jr.		1200			450	900
Charles C. Pickney		650			175	350
George Read		1250		450	350	700
John Rutledge		1200		600	200	400
Roger Sherman		900		600	200	400
Richard Dobbs Spaight				250	100	200
George Washington		14000		10000	4500	9000
James Wilson		1400		900	700	1400

SIGNERS OF THE DECLARATION OF INDEPENDENCE

	PHOTO	ALS	LS/TLS	DS	SIG.	COVER
John Adams						
Samuel Adams		3500		2000	750	1500

	PHOTO	ALS	LS/TLS	DS	SIG.	COVER
Josiah Bartlett		750		555	250	500
Charter Braxton		1200		550	275	550
Charles Carroll		765		679	275	550
Samuel Chase		1550		775	275	550
Abraham Clark				800	320	640
George Clymer		900		505	125	250
William Ellery		785		360	175	350
William Floyd		1600		1250	450	900
Elbridge Gerry		2880		675	265	530
Button Gwinnett	RARE			150000	85000	170000
Lyman Hall		3500		2950	2200	4400
John Hancock		6000		4500	2200	4400
Benjamin Harrison		1800		675	450	900
John Hart		1300		644	320	640
Joseph Hewes		8500		7250	2500	5000
Thomas Heyward		1800		1300	600	1200
William Hooper	SCARCE				3000	6000
Stephen Hopkins		900		600	250	500
Francis Hopkinson		900		450	250	500
Samuel Huntington		1200		750	250	500
Thomas Jefferson	(Covered under Presidents)					
Francis Lightfoot Lee		3000		1050	660	1320
Richard Henry Lee		2250		1600	450	900
Francis Lewis		2500		1250	400	800
Philip Livingston		1175		1080	288	576
Thomas Lynch, Jr.	RARE			35000	20000	40000
Thomas McKean		800		475	250	500
Arthur Middleton		25000		12000	5000	10000
Lewis Morris		1500		950	675	1350
Robert Morris		750		750	325	650
John Morton		1400		1200	500	1000
Thomas Nelson Jr.		2500		1400	550	1100
William Paca		2500		1500	750	1500
Robert Treat Paine		900		450	250	500
John Penn	RARE			1500	750	1500
George Read		1250		450	350	700
Caesar Rodney		2000		900	500	1000
George Ross		950		450	250	500
Benjamin Rusk		2250			750	1500
Edward Rutledge		750		500	200	400
James Smith		1600		750	250	500
Richard Stockton	RARE			1000	500	1000
Thomas Stone		1400		775	500	1000
George Taylor		45000		20000	7500	15000
Matthew Thorton		1650		1400	625	1250
George Walton		950		650	350	700
William Whipple		1500			750	1500
William Williams		600		450	300	600
James Wilson		1400		900	700	1400
John Witherspoon				1500	600	1200
Oliver Wolcott		1200		450	200	400
George Wythe				650	450	900

HEADS OF STATE

	PHOTO	ALS	LS/TLS	DS	SIG.	COVER
Behangi Aljere						
Alexander II (Russia)	200				125	250
Alfonso XIII (Spain)	500	550			175	350
Arthur J. Balfour	90	125		100	50	100

HEADS OF STATE

	PHOTO	ALS	LS/TLS	DS	SIG.	COVER
Menachem Begin	150	250			80	160
David Ben-Gurion	600	1200			300	500
Jean B. Bernadotte		650		575	150	300
Simon Bolivar		4975		3075	500	1000
Joseph Bonaparte (Spain)		350		245	120	240
Willy Brandt	85	210		175	35	100
Fidel Castro	950			750	675	1350
Catherine the Great		2400		1200	600	1200
Neville Chamberlain	165	400		400	75	150
Charles I		4000		1750	625	1250
Charles II (England)		2500		2000	900	1800
Charles IV (England)				1100	245	490
Charles V (Spain)		4000		2100	580	1160
Charles VI				1200	375	750
Charles X		725		450	150	300
John Charles XIV		880		675	145	290
Charles Prince	600	1500			400	800
Chou En-Lai	2500				1250	2500
Henry Christophe (Haiti)					1200	2400
Sarah Churchill	35	30		35	20	40
Winston S. Churchill	2750	2750		1600	800	1600
George Clemenceau		175		150	150	300
Hernando Cortes				20000	6000	12000
Charles de Gaulle	2500	1500		1000	375	750
Grace de Monaco	300	450		300	165	330
Porfirio Diaz	225	250		200	100	200
Duke & Duchess of Windsor	650				400	800
Duke of Wellington		375		250	175	350
Duke of Windsor (Edward)	655			600	200	400
Sir Anthony Eden	90	200		150	50	200
Edward VII (England)				200		
Edward VIII (England)	750	650		900	300	600
Elizabeth I		30000		12000	5500	11000
Elizabeth II	775	800		775	350	700
Empress Josephine		2500		1500	750	1500
Levi Eshkol		560		250	295	590
Francisco Franco				750	500	1000
Ferdinand VIII				475	125	250
Frederick I				95	25	50
Frederick V		500		270	90	180
Frederick II (The Great)		2000		1200	400	800
Indira Gandhi		350		350	150	300
Giuseppe Garibaldi	650			370	155	310
George I (England)		2500		1000	225	450
George II (England)		1200		550	400	800
George III (England)				400	200	400
George IV (England)		550		275	125	250
George V (England)		750		475	125	250
George VI (England)	450	300		400	200	400
Mikhail Gorbachev	575	900			300	600
Gregory XIV (Pope)				1200		
Gustaf V	275					
Gustavus II (Sweden)		985		700	115	230
Henry III (France)		1250		675	250	500
Henry IV (France)				700	200	400
Henry VII (England)					1200	2400
Henry VIII				15000	3500	7000
Hirohito	12000				2000	4000

	PHOTO	ALS	LS/TLS	DS	SIG.	COVER
Adolf Hitler	2500			2250	1500	3000
Isabella I		5000		2500	850	1700
Isabella II (Spain)		600		400	175	350
James I				1200	800	1600
James II (England)		1700		1200	530	1060
Anson Jones		1200			350	700
Joseph II (King of Germany)		875		350	125	250
Franz Joseph (Austria)	45	140		75	40	80
Josephine (Napoleon)		2500		1500	750	1500
Juan II	150	245		120	55	110
Benito Juarez	1500	1500		1200	425	850
Chaing Kai-Shek	700	450		220	100	225
Kalakaua (Hawaiin Chief & King)	1500	850		425	100	200
King Hussein	75	300		135	75	150
A. Kihito (Emperor of Japan)		650			400	800
Lajos Kossuth	90	475		825	125	250
Leopold I (Belgium)				475	105	210
Leopold II		625		375	100	200
Louis XII (France)				1750	800	1600
Louis XIII (France)				900	500	1000
Louis XVI				600	375	750
Louis XVIII		1250		400	200	400
Ferdinand Marcos	125			125	50	100
Maximilian (Mexico)		1250		675	400	800
Golda Meir	300	550		250	125	200
Benito Mussolini	1200			450	300	600
Napoleon I				2200	700	1400
Napoleon III		2000		700	300	600
Gamal Abdel Nasser	275	350		400	75	150
Jawaharlai Nehru	400	700		350	130	260
Nicholas I		1200				
Nicholas II (Russia)		2500				
Manuel A. Noriega		100		100	75	150
M.R. Pahlavi (Shah of Iran)	300	300		200	125	250
Tomas Estrsda Palma		45		35	20	40
Juan Peron	600	500		300	125	250
Peter I (The Great)		7500		5500		
Philip II (Spain)					250	500
Philip III (France)				750	250	500
Philip IV (Spain)		900		550	250	500
Pope John XXIII	650				500	1000
Pope Paul III				1200		
Pope Paul VI	600	900		475	300	600
Pope Pius X				700		
Pope Pius XI				950	450	900
Prince Albert					25	50
Prince Rainier III	125	200			75	150
Queen Alexandra (England)					150	300
Queen Anne (Great Britian)		2000		1500	500	1000
Quenn Victoria	900	550		350	175	350
Rudolf I (Austria)		750				
Anwar Sadat	500	300			100	200
Haile Selassie	750	550		300	200	400
Margaret Thatcher	135	225		150	50	100
Leon Trotsky	950	2250		1500	650	1300
Arthur W. Wellington		375		250	175	350
William III (England)		2250		1400	650	1300
William IV (England)		400		300	100	200

	PHOTO	ALS	LS/TLS	DS	SIG.	COVER
Dean Acheson	90				35	75
Edward Bates	450	250		125	35	70
Jonathan Belcher		650		325	225	450
Francis Bernard		750		522	175	350
William Jennings Bryan	375	375			125	250
Dewitt Clinton		500		300	100	200
Henry Clinton		2200		925	425	850
Henry Clay		950		300	125	250
Benjamin Curtis		200		150	35	70
David Davis		225		200	75	150
HenryM. Dearborn		550		400	100	200
Joseph Dudley		1000		800	400	800
John Foster Dulles	75	150		120	30	100
Miriam A. Ferguson		175		150	60	120
William P. Fessenden				65	40	80
Hamilton Fish		100		95	20	40
John B. Floyd		400		320	175	350
James Forrestal	25			100	45	100
John W. Foster	140	65			25	50
Albert Gallatin		390		275	75	150
Alexander Hamilton		3500		3000	800	1600
W. Averell Harriman	50	100		70	25	50
Cordell Hull	125			135	50	150
John Jay		2250		1750	550	1100
Robert F. Kennedy	675			800	200	400
Henry Kissinger	60			125	35	100
Henry Knox		650		300	150	300
Paul Kruger	175			350	75	150
Robert T. Lincoln		325		200	100	200
Robert R. Livingston		900		400	200	400
Henry Cabot Lodge	95	200		160	45	90
William L. Marcy		225		150	50	100
John Marshall	20	35		20	10	20
James McHenry				275	200	400
Robert S. McNamara	30			45	15	30
Andrew W. Mellon	400	1200		900	250	500
John Mitchell		125		50	30	60
Timothy Pickering					10	20
William Pinkney		200		100	100	200
Caesar Rodney		2000		900	500	1000
Elihu Root	140				65	130
Dean Rusk	50			60	25	50
John Sevier		700			600	1200
William H. Seward		150		125	75	150
George P. Shultz	30	55		25	10	20
Caleb B. Smith		250		150	50	100
Hoke Smith	30			35	10	20
Edwin M. Stanton		300		160	100	200
Henry L. Stimson		50		125	40	80
Charles Thomas				600		
Daniel Webster	475	350		250	100	200
Gideon Welles	675	300		200	100	200
Edward D. White	150	200		150	50	100
Oliver Wolcott JR		350		250	75	150

	PHOTO	ALS	LS/TLS	DS	SIG.	COVER
Samuel Adams		3500	2500	1700	750	1500
Lord Jefferry Amherst		1000		575	400	800
Joseph Anderson		350		225	75	150
John Andre		7500		3500	1250	2500
John Armstrong		450		250	75	150
Benedict Arnold		4500		3250	1500	3000
Moses Austin		2250		1500	575	1150
Daniel Boone		17500		11000	5000	10000
Elias Boudinot		950		750	275	550
James Bowdoin		275		200	125	250
William Bradford		450		250	125	250
William Clark		3500		2500	1000	2000
Henry Clinton		2000		950	400	800
Elias Dayton		375		200	125	250
Jonathan Dayton		650		400	175	350
Marquis de Lafayette		1100		900	375	750
Thomas Gage		950		875	225	450
Horatio Gates		1250		750	275	550
Nathaniel Green		3250		2500	900	1800
Edward Hand		1250		575	225	450
Willaim Heath		1250		250	150	300
Patrick Henry		3500		1750	850	1700
Nicholas Herkimer				3700		
Sir William Howe		750		450	200	400
David Humphreys		250		175	75	150
Jedediah Huntington		250		125	75	150
James Irvine		250		125	75	150
Henry Knox		650		450	125	250
John Langdon		950		375	200	400
Tobias Lear		300		200	75	150
Charles Lee		2000		1500	750	1500
Henry Lee		625		575	200	400
Benjamin Lincoln		500		225	100	200
George Mason				4500		
Lachlan Mcintosh		1250		950	550	1100
Samuel Meredith		275		175	100	200
John Morton		1500		1200	450	900
William Moultrie		750		475	250	500
Gen. John Nixon		325		275	125	250
James Otis		750		475	250	500
Thomas Paine		12500		5500	3500	7000
John Paterson		300		200	75	150
William Penn		7500		3000	1500	3000
William Phillips		750		500	200	400
Oliver Prescott		450		175	75	150
Rufus Putman		425		300	175	350
Edmund Randolph		750		400	200	400
Paul Revere		20000		8500	4000	8000
Robert Rogers				900	400	800
Philip Schuyler		750		450	200	400
Charles Scott		300		200	100	200
Isaac Shelby		500		300	200	400
John Stark		2000		1250	650	1300
Arthur St. Clair		950		300	175	350
Baron Von Stueben		1250		900	450	900
Gen. John Sullivan		500		375	150	300
Thomas Sumter		950		750	400	800
Charles Thomas		600				

	PHOTO	ALS	LS/TLS	DS	SIG.	COVER
Charles Thompson		750		450	125	250
Jonathan Trumbull		750		500	300	600
Thomas Truxton		550		300	125	250
Richard Varick		200		125	75	150
James Wadsworth		225		125	50	100
Seth Warner		1500		950	250	500
Anthony Wayne		1750		1250	750	1500
Gen. Samuel B. Webb		450		275	125	250
Jamees Wilkinson		350		275	125	250
Marinus Willett		250		125	75	150
William Williams		575		350	275	550
David Wooster				650	250	500

CIVIL WAR-CONFEDERATE STATES OF AMERICA

	PHOTO	ALS	LS/TLS	DS	SIG.	COVER
William W. Allen		550			175	350
Robert H. Anderson	1500	500		300	125	250
J.R. Anderson		3000		400		
Turner Ashby		1600			450	900
William Barksdale		1500			450	900
W.N.R. Beall		600		300	175	350
P.G.T. Beauregard	900	950		850	350	700
Barnard Elliott Bee		1600		700	300	600
Judah P. Benjamin		1200		800	300	600
Braxton Bragg	900	900		600	365	730
John C. Breckinridge				40	25	50
Simon B. Bucker		375			200	400
William L. Cabell				405	175	350
Bwn F. Cheatham				400	225	450
Charles Clark		350		275	110	220
Pat Cleburne				1650	1050	2100
Howell Cobb		400		200	100	200
Francis Marion Cockrell		200		110	70	140
Samuel Cooper		445		230	120	240
Jefferson Davis	2500	1750		1500	500	1000
Varian Davis	700	500		250	150	300
G.G. Dibrell		300		300	150	300
Jubal A. Early		1000		800	500	1000
Samuel W. Ferguson		550		350	180	360
Nathan Bedford Forrest	RARE	SCARCE			575	1150
Frankllin Gardner		850		215	225	450
Randall L. Gibson		600		300	100	200
S.R. Gist		1250		900	450	900
John Brown Gordon		400		200	150	300
Wade Hampton		900		550	270	540
William J. Hardee	950	1110		875	300	600
Harry T. Hays				900	300	600
Henry Heth		3500		3000	750	1500
Ambrose Powell Hill	SCARCE	SCARCE		3000	2000	4000
Ddaniel Harvey Hill		600		500	320	640
Thomas Carmichael Hindman					320	640
Robert F. Hoke		300			100	200
Theophilus H. Holms				245	205	410
John B. Hood	1000	1600		1500	800	1600
Benjamin Huger		300		250	90	180
W.Y.C. Humes		435		235	140	280
T. J. "Stonewall" Jackson	RARE	20000		10000	4000	8000
Bushrood Johnson				300	115	230
Albert S. Johnston		2000		1500	290	580

	PHOTO	ALS	LS/TLS	DS	SIG.	COVER
Joseph E. Johnston	1600	750		600	300	600
John Marshall Jones				650	225	450
Samuel Jones				300	95	190
William E. Jones		600		250	140	280
Thomas Jordan		350		255	80	160
John H. Kelly					475	950
Joseph Brevard Kershaw		900			200	400
James H. Lane	950	335		200	100	200
Evander M. Law		500		250	100	200
Danville Leadbetter				450	150	300
Fitzhugh Lee	500	300		200	150	300
George W. C. Lee		410			155	310
Mary Lee	475	690			150	300
Robert E. Lee	6500			3500	2000	4000
Stephen Dill Lee		400		325	125	250
Lunsford L. Lomax		370		270	100	200
James Longstreet	900	1200		900	400	800
Francis R. Lubbock	350	295		185	150	300
John B. Magruder		475		525	275	550
William Mahone		365		252	120	240
Will T. Martin		400		250	100	200
Abney H. Maury		350			100	200
Samuel Bell Maxey		250		225	125	250
Henry McCulloch				350	145	290
Fayette McLaws		400		300	175	350
Christopher Memminger		550		480	165	330
George Meade				400	300	600
Samuel P. Moore		800		725	595	1190
John T. Morgan		350		200	125	250
John S. Mosby	2750	2000		900	450	900
Johm C. Pemberton	500	400		350	150	300
William Dorsey Pender					400	800
George J. Pillow		350			100	200
Leonidas Polk					300	600
Elisha F. Paxton	RARE	RARE		RARE	750	1500
Sterling Price				350	200	400
William A. Quarles				225	75	150
George W. Randolph		550		400	250	500
John H. Reagan		600		450	150	300
Robert Emmet Rodes	RARE	RARE		RARE	1000	2000
John Ross		1000		600	350	700
Thomas L. Rosser	350	350		250	125	250
Daniel Ruggles		600		300	90	180
James A. Seddon	RARE	RARE		500	250	500
Raphael Semmens	1500	1400		750	300	600
Paul Semmes		900		900	700	1400
J.O. Shelby	2000	1200			300	600
E. Kirby Smith		600			300	600
Martin Luther Smith		200		125	75	150
G.W. Smith		550		250	125	250
Alexandeer H. Stephens		500			250	500
C.L. Stevenson		400		200	100	200
J.E.B. Stuart	RARE	RARE		4500	2500	5000
Richard Taylor				675	225	450
Walter H. Taylor				100	50	100
Robert Toombs		200		200	125	250
Isaac R. Trimble		1200			400	800
David Emanuel Twiggs		750		300	150	300

CIVIL WAR-CONFEDERATE STATES OF AMERICA (cont)

	PHOTO	ALS	LS/TLS	DS	SIG.	COVER
Robert C. Tyler		800		500	250	500
Earl Van Dorn		700			250	500
L.P. Walker			1100	1100		
Richard Waterhouse		550	320	320	150	300
Joseph Wheeler	950	475	225	225	80	160
William Henry Whiting					200	400
Marcus Wright		200	160	160	125	250
Felix K. Zolllicoffer		540	350	350	175	350

CIVIL WAR-UNION ARMY

	PHOTO	ALS	LS/TLS	DS	SIG.	COVER
R.A. Alger	75	85	55	55	30	60
Daniel Ammen	175	85	60	60	32	64
Robert Anderson	1950	300	325	325	115	230
Christopher C. Auger		170	125	125	50	100
Addam Badeau		125	60	60	35	70
Nathaniel P. Banks		145	100	100	70	140
John Beatty		80	55	55	27	54
William Belknap		175	160	160	50	100
H.W. Benham		135	50	50	35	70
Frederick W. Benteen	2500		3500	3500		
Thomas H. Benton Jr.		205	95	95	50	100
J.D. Bingham		185	140	140	45	90
James G. Blunt			75	75	46	92
John Wilkes Booth	4500	4000	3050	3050	1500	3000
C.R. Brayton		100	65	65	40	80
John Brown	8500	3450	1700	1700	775	1550
Don C. Buell	150	175	155	155	70	140
John N. Burns	1250				350	700
Ambrose E. Burnside	725	405	375	375	110	220
Benjamin F. Butler		255	125	125	90	180
Daniel Butterfiled	450	315	260	260	55	110
Edward Canby		370	310	310	55	110
Samuel P. Chase	300	325	150	150	90	180
Cassius m. Clay		450	220	220	80	160
James B. Coit		125			25	50
P. Edward Connor			58	58	35	70
S.W. Crawford		210	85	85	48	96
George Crook	400	375	275	275	125	250
George A. Custer	13000	15000	12500	12500	3380	6760
John A. Dahlgren		415	295	295	85	170
J.J. Dana			140	140	40	80
Gustavus A. DeRussy			250	250	45	90
John A. Dix	500	170-600	110	110	60-115	120-230
Abner Doubleday		1670	675	675	285	570
Ephriam Elmer Ellsworth		2500	1500	1500	540	1080
Richard E. Ewell			395	395	190	380
Thomas Ewing		245	110	110	40	80
David G. Farragut	1500	750	290	290	100	200
James W.M. Forsyth		175	105	105	35	70
John C. Fremont		1025	700	700	230	460
John Gibbon		330	185	185	50	100
Gordon Granger		145	95	95	45	90
Benjamin Grierson		330	235	235	125	250
Henry W. Halleckk	200	530	300	300	150	300
Winfield Scott Hancock		250	245	245	150	300
James A. Hardie		245	205	205	55	110
Joseph Henry		245	130	130	55	110
Ethan A. Hitchcock		200	150	150	50	100

	PHOTO	ALS	LS/TLS	DS	SIG.	COVER
Joseph Hooker		675	400	400	180	360
Oliver O. Howard	270	285	185	185	120	240
David Hunter	250	170	130	130	55	110
Fred S. Hutchinson		130			35	70
Philip Kearney		850	650	650	360	720
Erasmus D. Keyes		275	120	120	47	94
Rufus King		355			250	500
Samuel P. Lee		275	210	210	60	120
Joseph K.F. Mansfield		410	330	330	150	300
George B. McClellan		395	275	275	200	400
Irvin McDowell	1250	595	235	235	125	250
James B. McPherson		1125			150	300
George G. Meade	350	765	345	345	245	490
Wesley Merritt		175	250	250	80	160
Nelson A. Miles		230	160	160	85	170
John G. Mitchell		140	50	50	30	60
John Newton		325			50	100
Richard James Oglesby	150	95	60	60	40	80
Edward H.C. Ord	750	210	145	145	50	100
John M. Palmer		225	140	140	80	160
John G. Parke		150	75	75	45	90
Ely S. Parker			195	195	300	600
M.R.Patrick		205	50	50	35	70
John S. Phelps		100	65	65	25	50
Alfred Pleasanton			185	185	75	150
Fitz John Porter	750	155	100	100	40	80
David Dixon Porter		410	285	285	105	210
Horace Porter		85	190	190	45	90
William Radford		30	15	15	10	20
Joseph Jones Reynolds		190	110	110	45	90
James W. Ripley		210	185	185	55	110
William S. Rosecrans		365	270	270	160	320
Lovell H. Rousseau			165	165	50	100
Eliakia P. Scammon					125	250
Winfield Scott Hancock	450	430	330	330	125	250
John Sedgwick			350	350	135	270
Truman Seymour		205	110	110	75	150
Daniel Sickles	175	290	225	225	110	220
Franz Sigel		200	115	115	45	90
Henry W. Slocum		150	75	75	50	100
William Sprague		105	90	90	75	150
George Stoneman		195	155	155	60	120
Henry D. Terry		160	100	100	45	90
George H. Thomas		435	195	195	100	200
Lorenzo Thomas		270	140	140	90	180
Henry VanRensselaer					225	450
Mary E. Walker		575			215	430
Joseph Wheeler	950	475	225	225	80	160
George Williams		40	25	25	10	20
Thomas J. Wood			105	105	45	90
John Wool		375	210	210	85	170
Marcus J. Wright		200	160	160	125	250
Horatio G. Wright		200	75	75	40	80

MILITARY

	PHOTO	ALS	LS/TLS	DS	SIG.	COVER
William Alexander		1200		600	300	600
Ethan Allen		3000		1500	750	1500
Juan N. Almonte		250			60	120

	PHOTO	ALS	LS/TLS	DS	SIG.	COVER
William Bainbridge		550		300	150	300
Sir John Barron		325		170	75	150
W.A. "Billy" Bishop	220	300		225	150	300
Cpt. William Bligh		7500		3500	1500	3000
Omar Bradley	185	300		250	100	200
Lloyd Bucher	90	150		90	35	90
Arleigh Burke	100	110		60	35	70
Aaron Burr		750		650	400	800
Guy (Aaron) Carleton		800		645	250	500
Mark W. Clark	100	275		190	35	70
Lucius Clay	100	145		125	30	60
Sir Henry Clinton		2200		925	425	850
Robert Clive		1200		600	250	500
Charles Cornwallis		1200		650	175	350
Moshe Dayan	250	275		235	125	250
Stephen Decatur		4500		2700	1000	2000
Jeff Deblanc	40	45			15	30
George Dewey	300	200		150	100	200
Hugo Eckner	550	550		400	200	400
Adolf Eichmann	750	1250		500	275	550
Mariano Escobedo				225	50	100
Thomas Ferebee	100	250		125	50	100
Ferninand Foch	235	280		125	50	100
Eugene B. Fluckey	90	110			45	90
Mitsuo Fuchida		500		350	300	600
Frances Gabreski	72	125		95	35	70
James Gavin	125	275		100	45	100
Joseph Goebbels	1250	1250		1025	350	700
Charles G. Gordon	600	1217		350	110	220
Hermann Goering	1475	2425		2044	450	900
Natnanael Greene		3000		2400	900	1800
Otto Gunsche	55	85			50	100
Alexander Haig	45	50		45	20	40
William Bull-Halsey	200	225		175	75	150
Frank Hamer					110	220
Albert H. Heinrich		120			35	70
Erich Hartmann	300				125	250
Rudolf Hess	750	750		450	155	310
Heinrich Himmler	750	1500		750	250	500
Kurt Caesar Hoffman	65				25	50
Sam Houston		2200		1500	600	1200
William Howe				850	200	400
Isaac Hull		565		570	190	380
Alfred Jodl	250	550		500	150	300
J. Joffre	225	250		155	75	150
Johnny Johnson	95	120		65	30	60
Robert Johnson	80	45			25	50
John Paul Jones	RARE	65000		25000	8000	16000
Ernst Kaltenbrunner	175			500	150	300
Richard Kane	75				25	50
Mike Kawato	150				50	100
Wilhelm Keitel	650			575	350	700
Albert Kesselring	175				100	200
Ernest J. King	125			100	30	125
Otto Kretschmer	185			140	45	90
Marquis De Lafayette		1600		850	400	800
Ernest Lehmann		365			100	200
Curtis Lemay	75			75	30	60

	PHOTO	ALS	LS/TLS	DS	SIG.	COVER
Erich Ludendorff	275	350		225	100	200
Douglas MacArthur	500	750		600	225	450
George C. Marshall	400	550		300	200	400
Anthony McAuliffe	350	175		175	85	170
David McCampbell	75	45		25	15	30
George G. Meade	450			400	300	600
Frank D. Merrill		325			225	450
Erhard Milch	175	400		250	80	160
Gen. Nelson Miles		350		285	130	260
William Mitchell	1495	975		900	200	400
Sir Bernard Montgomery	350			225	75	300
Horatio Nelson		3000		1900	800	1600
Chester Nimitz	400	350		300	125	300
Oliver North	65	175		100	35	70
George S. Patton	5000	3500		2000	950	1900
Robert Peary	600	450			150	300
Matthew Calbraitte Perry		1400		775	450	900
John J. Pershing	400	300			100	200
Philippe Petain	50			90	35	70
Colin Powell	100			100	35	70
William C. Quantrill		3500			900	1800
Erich Raeder	125	400		175	65	130
Gunther Rall	90	125		65	40	80
Hyman C. Rickover	250	350		200	100	200
Matthew B. Ridgeway	125	175		195	90	180
John Rogers		350		350	150	300
Erwin Rommel	1500	RARE		1150	750	1500
Alfred Rosenberg				350	175	350
Joe Rosenthal	250	250		200	75	150
Hams Ulrich Rudel	350	RARE		300	150	300
Ftitz Sauckel				200	75	150
Norman Schwarzkoff	75	125			35	70
Winfield Scott		675		400	175	350
Otto Skorzeny	500	450			250	500
Albert Speer	150	225		150	50	100
H.R. Stark	40	75		45	15	30
Joseph Stilwell	400				175	350
Maxwell D. Taylor	65	100		75	25	75
Lorenzo Thomas		250		140	75	150
Hideki Tojo	1500	1500		550	250	500
Hoyt Vandenberg	75				25	50
James Vanfleet	45	75		65	25	50
Franz Vonpapen	175	250		150	100	200
Joachim Von Ribbentrop	325	550		450	200	400
Jonathan Wainwright	225	250		225	100	200
William Westmoreland	65	75			25	75
Earle Wheeler	50				20	40
Charles Wilkes		200		100	50	100
Katsumari Yamashiro	300				100	200
Sgt. Alvin York	425	450		250	175	350
Elmo Zumwalt	50	125		75	25	50

ARTISTS

	PHOTO	ALS	LS/TLS	DS	SIG.	COVER
Ansel Adams	200	350		200	100	200
John J. Audobon		3000			750	1500
Fabian Bacharach	75	125			50	100
Frederic A. Bartholdi	900	600		750	400	800
Albert Bierstadt		540		220	125	250

	PHOTO	ALS	LS/TLS	DS	SIG.	COVER
Karl Bitter	100	155		75	25	50
Rosa Bonheur		325		155	110	220
Gutzon Borgulm	800	550		375	225	450
Matthew B. Brady		2000		1000	350	700
Benvenuto Cellini				4800	1000	2000
Marc Chagall	350			350	185	370
Giorgio Giulio Clovio		2000		1400	650	1300
John Singleton Copley				710	350	700
George Cruikshank	375	345		115	160	320
E.E. Cummings	690	500		350	200	400
Salvador Dali	850	650		450	200	400
Edgar Degas		2000			650	1300
Gustave Dore		550		150	50	100
Raqul Dufy	500	750		450	300	600
Albrecht Durer					3000	6000
Sir Jacob Epstein		392		210	150	300
Max Ernst		575		300	200	400
Erte		450		275	125	250
Paul Gauguin		3600		1250	585	1170
Charles Dana Gibson	300	200		200	80	160
Francisco Goya					2500	5000
Kate Greenaway				1500	1000	2000
George Grosz		250		250	55	110
Kieth Haring	200	95		40	25	50
William Hart	425	235		180	130	260
Childe Hassam		500		350	150	300
Herman Hesse	400	550		500	100	200
William Hogarth		3500		1665	450	900
William Morris Hunt		500		215	50	100
Peter Hurd		300		200	100	200
George Inness		425		225	75	150
William H. Jackson				110	40	80
Will James	600	400		250	75	150
John Barthold Jongkind		750		450	200	400
Wasily Kandinsky				500	200	400
Rockwell Kent	75				40	80
Dong Kingman		100		50	25	50
Marie Laurencin		590			125	250
Sir Thomas Lawrence		200		225	150	300
Sal Lewitt	50				25	50
Rene Magritte		900		350	200	400
Aristide Maillol		800		460	200	400
Edouard Manet				2000		
Henri Matisse		1200		750	550	1100
Jean Francois Millet				450	200	400
Juan Miro	310	700		575	200	400
Claude Monet		1500		1200	450	900
Henry Moore	100	450		200	50	100
A.M.R. Moses (Grandma)	600	860		500	175	350
Thomass Nast	RARE	300		350	125	250
Leroy Neiman	75	150		150	40	80
Georgia O'Keefe		950			350	700
Maxfield Parrish		800		500	175	350
Charles Wilson Peale		750		450	250	500
Pablo Picasso	1500			1500	750	1500
Camille Pissarro		1200			250	500
Alexander Pope		600		300	150	300
Hiram Powers	150	250		150	50	100

	PHOTO	ALS	LS/TLS	DS	SIG.	COVER
Raphael	RARE			9000	3500	7000
Frederic Remington	1750	1750		800	575	1150
Pierre Auguste Renoir	RARE	2100		700	300	600
Diego Rivera	1200	800		550	300	600
Norman Rockwell	250			300	125	400
Auguste Rodin		475		450	250	500
George Romney		450		375	150	300
Georges Roualt	900	750		475	200	400
Theodore Rousseau		475		175	75	150
Thomas Rowlandson		800		500	250	500
Charles M. Russell		1500		750	250	500
Augustus Saint-Gaudens	1200	900			200	400
John Singer Sargent		350		250	100	200
Thomas Scully		550		375	200	400
Paul Signac		300		150	75	150
Alfred Sisley		1200		400	175	350
Alfred Stieglitz		600		450	200	400
Gilbert Stuart		750		500	200	400
Louis C. Tiffany	1500			750	400	800
Henry Toulousse-Lautrec					1200	2400
John Trumbull		750		300	100	200
Vincent Van Gogh					4000	8000
Alberto Vargas	250	350			150	300
Andy Warhol	275	475		250	150	300
George Frederic Watts		300		150	75	150
Benjamin West		1250		700	200	400
Edward H. Weston					35	70
James M. Whistler		600		450	300	600
Olaf Wieghorst	200	250		225	75	150
Grant Wood		550		400	150	300
Andrew Wyeth	950	650		450	250	500
N.C. Wyeth		800		400	150	300

ASTRONAUTS

	PHOTO	ALS	LS/TLS	DS	SIG.	COVER
Edwin Aldrin	200	300	225	75	150	150
Bill Anders	700					175
Apollo I (ALL THREE)	6000					
Apollo II (ALL THREE)	3000					950
Neil A. Armstrong	1500		550	175		350
Charles Bassett II						400
Alan L. Bean	100		150	40		80
Frank Borman	125			30		60
John Bull	125			15		30
Scott Carpenter	100	125	75	25		100
Eugene A. Cernan	200			35		70
Roger Chaffee	400			200		400
Michael Collins	500	250	150	100		200
Charles Conrad Jr.	175			35		50
Walter Cunningham	75					35
Charlie Duke	75					35
Donn F. Eisele	75					75
Ronald Evans	150			50		100
Yuri Gagarin	1000			400		400
John Glenn	75		150	40		125
Dick Gordon	30					
David Griggs	140		150	60		120
Virgil "Gus" Grissom	900		725	275		550
Fred Haise	35			10		35

ASTRONAUTS (cont.)

	PHOTO	ALS	DS	SIG.	SIG. CHK	COVER
James B. Irwin	1100	800				
Gregory B. Jarvis	1200					350
Vladamir Kumarov	250					200
Alexei Leonov	100					
James A. Lovell	100					175
Christa McAuliffe	800	1250	1000	450		700
James A. McDivitt	100			30		60
Ronald E. McNair	100			100		200
Ed Mitchell	85	150		20		40
Ellison S. Onizuka	225					
Mercury 7 Astronauts	7500					2500
Robert Overmyer	65			20		40
Judith A. Resnick	250		250	100		200
Sally K. Ride	65		45	15		30
Stuart Roosa	125			15		30
Walter M.Schirra	150	150	75	25		50
Harrison H. Schmitt	175		125	20		40
Dick Scobee	350			50		100
Dave Scott	200			50		100
Elliot M. See Jr.	650			175		350
Alan B. Shepard	195		150	60		90
Donald K. Slayton	55		150	35		70
Michael Smith	250			200		400
Thomas P. Stafford	35					60
John L. Swigert Jr.	125		75	40		80
Valentina Tereshkova	150	75				100
Wernher Von Braun	2200	200				475
Edward H. White II	400	550	250	200		400
Al M. Worden						40
John Young	250			75		125

AUTHORS & POETS

Edward Albee	80				30	60
Louisa May Alcott		450			250	500
Horatio Alger	250	250			125	250
W.H. Auden	550	500			200	400
Hans Christian Andersen	1650	1250			450	900
Gertrude Atherton	75	150			30	60
John James Audubon		3000			750	1500
Francis Bacon		20000		12000	5500	11000
Sabine Baring Gould	60	200			20	40
James M. Barrie		250		250	85	170
John Barth	40	85		40	30	60
Katherine Lee Bates		300			75	150
Charles Baudelaire		1600		900	300	600
Frank L. Baum	RARE	4500		2750	1750	3500
Samuel Beckett		400			150	300
Stephen V. Benet	150	175		140	80	160
Sir Walter Besant		190		125	35	70
Ambrose Bierce		588		670	275	550
Earl Derr Biggers	350	400			150	300
Vincent Blasco-Ibanez	450				100	200
William Cullen Bryant	750	375		250	100	200
Pearl S. Buck	65	198		145	40	100
Ned Buntline	750	250			140	280
Robert Burns		2750		1450	500	1000
Edgar Rice Burroughs	600	750		450	225	450
John Burroughs	525	200			100	200

	PHOTO	ALS	LS/TLS	DS	SIG.	COVER
Lord Geo G. Byron		2750			1600	3200
Erskine Caldwell	75	210		150	35	70
Albert Camus		600		250	75	150
Truman Capote	250			225	125	250
Edgar Cayce				225	70	140
Robert W. Chambers		20		15	10	20
Paddy Chayefsky	125	250		150	75	150
John Cheever	100	250		125	45	90
Agatha Christie				400	150	300
Samuel Clemens (Mark Twain)		2000		1500	750	1500
Irvin S. Cobb	95	150		45	25	50
Jean Cocteau	600	600			125	250
Samuel Taylor Coleridge		1250		575	325	650
Wilkie Collins	1380	530		309	100	200
Joseph Conrad	1250	1450		1125	230	460
Alistair Cooke	75	140		95	20	40
James Fenimore Cooper				180	90	180
Noel Coward	275	340		200	100	200
Hart Crane	350	1500		600	130	260
Stephen Crane	RARE	4500			1500	3000
E.E. Cummings	690	500		350	200	400
Richard H. Dana Jr.		215		200	50	100
Daniel Defoe					1500	3000
Theodore Dreiser	300	300		200	75	150
Dr. Suess	250	400			75	150
Alexander Dumas	750	550		225	110	220
T.S. Eliot	750			400	175	350
Ralph Waldo Emerson		450		300	200	400
John Erskine		175		125	35	70
Mary Ann Evans (George Eliot)		1250		595	160	320
William Faulkner		2500		1500	350	700
Eugene Field	200	400		230	110	220
F. Scott Fitzgerald	SCARCE			1500	450	900
Gustave Flaubert		1500		635	175	350
Ian Fleming	1800			1500	575	1150
Robert Frost	750	1000		600	150	300
Erle Stanley Gardner	200	300		200	75	150
Andre Gide		600		350	175	350
Allen Ginsberg	75	225		200	35	70
Johann W. Goethe				2550	1200	2400
Nikolai Gogol		6500		3350	750	1500
Maksim Gorky	1200	1200		900	400	800
Horace Greeley	750	300		275	65	130
Zane Grey	400	450		200	75	150
Jacob Grimm		3760		1840	565	1130
Edward Everett Hale	225	250		200	75	150
Sarah J. Hale		225		150		
Alex Haley	140	150		125	40	80
Dashiell Hammett	RARE			1500	550	1100
Thomas Hardy	1400	1425		1000	275	550
Nathaniel Hawthorne		1750		950	400	800
Lillian Hellman				145	50	100
Ernest Hemingway	2500	3000		2000	1000	2000
John Hersey	25	125		75	20	40
Herman Hessse	400	550		500	100	200
Oliver Wendall Holmes		350		200	75	150
A.E. Housmat		600		225	75	150
Julia Ward Howe		300		150	100	200

	PHOTO	ALS	LS/TLS	DS	SIG.	COVER
William Dean Howells				195	75	150
Elbert Hubbard	145	275		160	50	100
Thomas Hughs		125			40	80
Victor Hugo	975	650		375	200	400
Washington Irving		550		385	150	300
James Jones				150	50	100
James Joyce		2500		590	400	800
Emanuel Kant					1000	2000
Helen Keller	875			400	200	400
Francis Scott Key		950		650	450	900
Joyce Kilmer				550	200	400
Stephen King	100	400		150	60	120
Charles Kinsley		160		95	45	90
Rudyard Kipling	900	700		550	200	400
Charles Lamb		550		399	125	250
Louis L'Amour	200	RARE		200	90	180
Sidney Lanier		900		590	300	600
D.H. Lawrence		2500		590	300	600
T.E. Lawrence	RARE			1250	650	1300
Edward Lear		450			150	300
Harper Lee	250			250	100	200
Mikhail Lermontov	RARE				750	1500
Sinclair Lewis	300	550		325	100	200
Vachel Lindsay	125	450		185	50	100
John Locke	RARE			1950	700	1400
Jack London				750	400	800
Henry W. Longfellow	950	600			175	350
J.H. Lowell	350	225		145	75	150
Clare Boothe Luce	40	175		100	30	75
Niccolo Machiavelli				1250	500	1000
Vladimir V. Maiakovski	RARE			795	300	600
Maurice Maeterlinck	425	205		115	35	70
Norman Mailer	75	175		125	35	70
Thomas Mann	1100	900		450	200	400
Marcel Marceau	95			70	25	50
Edwin Markham	65	140		125	35	70
Karl Marx	RARE			1500	750	1500
Edgar Lee Masters	65	250		150	50	100
W.S. Maugham	400	350		250	85	170
Herman Melville	RARE			2000	750	1500
Henry Mencken	450	350		225	100	200
James A. Mitchner	115	340		265	40	80
Edna St. Vincent Millay	1265	800		325	140	280
Arthur Miller	100	200		100	50	100
Henry Miller	150	350		160	85	170
A.A. Milne	550	750		450	225	450
Margaret Mitchell	RARE	2500		1750	750	1500
George Moore		125		150	45	90
Frank Norris	450			275	125	250
Sean O'Casey	300	400		275	100	200
John O'Hara		600		450	150	300
Eugene O'Neill	RARE			350	200	400
Thomas Paine	RARE				3500	7000
Dorothy Parker	45	75			30	60
Boris Pasternak		1600		750	400	800
Albert Pike		250		175	100	200
Luigi Pirandello	375	300		175	75	150
Edgar Allan Poe	RARE			15000		

	PHOTO	ALS	LS/TLS	DS	SIG.	COVER
Alexander Pope	RARE				600	1200
William S. Porter (O. Henry)		1717		850	350	700
Emily Post		125			65	130
Beatrix Potter		750			250	500
Ezra Pound		900		675	250	500
Marcel Proust		1600		875	500	1000
Joseph Pulizter		500		350	125	250
Alexander Pushkin				2600	825	1650
Mario Puzo	55			75	25	50
Ernie Pyle	350	450		300	200	400
Ayn Rand	750				500	1000
John Reed	300				200	400
James Whitcomb Riley	225	450		150	85	170
Harold Robbins	35	100		75	20	40
Dante Rossetti		550		225	150	300
Ramon Runyon	225	350		275	125	250
Jerome David Salinger		4000		3000		
Carl Sandberg	400	300		225	100	200
George Sand		600	250		250	250
Dorothy Sayers		475		350	200	400
Arthur Schopenhauer	RARE				1500	3000
Sir Walter Scott		900		500	150	300
Rod Serling				200	125	250
George Bernard Shaw	1500	800		650	400	800
Neil Simon	50			50	25	50
Upton Sinclair	125	150			50	100
Betty Smith	75				40	80
Samuel Francis Smith	450				200	400
Mickey Spillane	125	100		75	40	80
Elizabeth Cody Stanton		400		225	150	300
Richard Steele		1200		600	200	400
Gertrude Stein	675	750		550	400	800
John Steinbeck	1250	2250		1450	400	800
Robert Louis Stevenson	RARE	1400		750	300	600
Irving Stone	40	100		45	20	40
Rex Stout	45	200		100	35	70
Harriet Stowe		550			275	550
Rabindranath Tagore	350	350		250	100	200
Ida M. Tarbell	30	75		45	20	40
Allen Tate		75		30	10	20
Bayard Taylor		125		75	25	50
Lord Alfred Tennyson	950	700			200	400
Dylan Thomas	1500	1500			500	1000
Henry David Thoreau	RARE	8500		6000	3000	6000
Leo Tolstoy	2200	RARE			1200	2400
John Updike	45	125		75	25	50
S.S. Vandine (William H. Huntington)				650		
Jules Verne	RARE	900		1400	250	500
Francois Voltaire	RARE			225	500	1000
Edgar Wallace	350	300		100	75	150
Irving Wallace	75	150		100	25	50
Robert Penn Warren	75	125		750	35	70
Noah Webster		1400			500	1000
H.G. Welles	750	400		125	175	350
E.B. White				2000	35	70
Walt Whitman	2750	2400			1200	2400
John Greenleaf Whittier		350		250	100	200
Oscar Wilde	2250	2500		1500	675	1350

	PHOTO	ALS	LS/TLS	DS	SIG.	COVER
William Carlos Williams	300				275	550
Tennessee Williams	350	475		300	150	300
Thomas Wolfe	RARE			2000	500	1000
Virginia Woolf		1500			450	900
Herman Wouk	125	150		100	45	90
William Butler Yeats	1500	900		600	200	400
Emile Zola		450			200	400

AVIATION

	PHOTO	ALS	LS/TLS	DS	SIG.	COVER
John W. Alcock	600			500	300	600
Hap Arnold	175	350		175	55	150
Italo Balbo	200	200			125	250
Gerhard Barkhorn	125				60	120
Floyd Bennett	500	750		370	300	600
Jacob Beser	100			100	50	100
Louis Bleriot	500	595		500	250	500
Gregory "Pappy" Boyington	175	200		150	75	150
Arthur W. Brown	575	575		400	300	600
Richard Byrd	325	450		275	75	250
Clarence D. Chamberlin	250	375		250	50	200
Claire L. Chenault	525	600			500	1000
Jacquelince Cochran	150			175	45	100
Everett R. Cook	50			30	10	40
Douglas Corrigan				80	65	130
Dieudonne Coste	275	385		235	125	300
Glenn Curtiss	850	650		500	300	600
F.L. Dobehoff	75				25	50
Joseph Doerflinger	45	50			15	30
James H. Doolittle	75	200		150	50	100
Donald W. Douglas Sr.	360	450		295	150	300
Amelia Earhart	1500			1750	400	1200
Ira Eaker	150	100		75	35	70
Hugo Eckener	550	550		400	200	400
Ruth Elder	350	310		190	100	200
Thomas Ferebee	100	250		125	50	100
Anthony Fokker	500	530		295	200	400
Joe Foss	55	85		75	30	60
Mitzuo Fuchida		500		350	300	600
Harold Gatty	175	450		275	75	150
Francis Gabreski	72	125		95	35	70
Claude Grahame-White	125	250		100	75	150
Frank Hawks	250	325		135	80	160
Herman Hesse	400	550		500	100	200
Amy Johnson	200	135		85	75	150
George C. Kennedy	200				40	80
Samuel Langley		600			250	500
Hubert Latham	75	90		35	25	50
Ruth Law	100				35	75
Pierre Charles L'Enfant		1200		850	400	800
Charles A. Lindbergh	2500	2400		1250	575	1400
Alan Lockheed	150	250		150	75	200
Gunther Lutzow	450	445			175	350
Glenn L. Martin	250	265		170	75	250
Dick Merrill	75	105		55	35	70
Henry T. Merrill	100	100		45	30	60
Willy Messerschmitt	395			275	125	200
Billy Mitchell	1495	975		900	200	400
Edwin C. Musick	150	300	200	175	100	150

	PHOTO	ALS	LS/TLS	DS	SIG.	COVER
Ruth R. Nichols	250			250	125	250
Charles Nungesser	275					
Walter Oesau	200	400			150	300
Earle Ovington	250	200			45	100
Clyde Pangborn				150	75	150
William T. Piper	750			350	175	350
Wiley Post	275	650			350	900
Edward Rickenbacker		450		200	100	350
W. Roedel	200					
Charles Rosendahl		200		160	75	150
Claude Ryan	225				100	200
A. Santos-Dumont	750	600			300	600
William E. Scripps	40			50	15	30
Boris Sergievsky	150				75	150
Paul W. Tibbetts	75	100			25	100
Juan T. Trippe	40	200	125	100	30	40
Roscoe Turner	125				75	150
Ermst Udet	500	450		375	225	450
Theodore Van Kirk	100			85	50	100
Wolfgang VonGronau	500				200	400
Ferdinand VonZeppelin	1000	775	1045		375	750
Leigh Wade	45	100		75	30	60
Frank Whittle	45				15	30
Orville Wright	2000	1750		1250	500	1000
Wilbur Wright	4500	5000		2000	775	1550
Jeanne Yeager	35				15	50
Chuck Yeager	50	65		50	25	100

BUSINESS

	PHOTO	ALS	LS/TLS	DS	SIG.	COVER
John Jacob Astor III		800		550	200	400
William B. Astor		1200		800	250	500
Phineas T. Barnum	900	550		750	200	400
Bernard Baruch	250	550		300	75	150
Clyde Beatty	150	150		100	50	100
Nicholas Biddle		800		600	150	300
William Bingham		340		315	120	240
"Diamond" Jim Brady	650	1500		1250		2500
J.M. Browning		575				
Luther Burbank	165	298		275		550
August A. Busch	50	175		90		200
Andrew Carnegie	1110	1250		1250		2500
Auguste Chouteau		900		600		1200
Walter P. Chrysler	900	1500		1000		2000
Andre Citreon	700			350		700
Jay Cooke		2250		1250		2500
W.K. Coors	50	95		60		125
Erastas Corning		295		175		350
Cyrus Curtis	95	140		55		100
John Deere		1500		1500		3000
Sanford B. Dole	100	350		250		500
Frank W. Doubleday		375		185		400
Frederick S. Duesenberg				1250		2500
Charles E. Duryea	RARE SCARCE			450		900
J. Eberhard Faber		725		500		1000
Max Factor	60	175		125		250
William G. Fargo				900		1800
Enzo Ferrari	550			550		1100
Marshall Field Jr.	75	170		110		220

	PHOTO	ALS	LS/TLS	DS	SIG.	COVER
Cyrus W. Field		1500		550		1100
Harvey S. Firestone	35	85		50		100
Malcolm Forbes	75	150		75	35	70
Edsel Ford	500			550	250	500
Henry Ford	2550	5000		3500	900	1800
Henry Ford II	55	30		15	10	20
Alfred C. Fuller	150	195			125	250
J. Paul Getty	375	1500		750	185	500
A.P.M Giannini		500		290	150	300
Bernard F. Gimbel	90	375		175	60	120
Stephen Girard		325		350	125	250
Charles Goodyear	RARE	RARE		2000	400	800
Jay Gould	1200	1500		550	250	500
W.T. Grant	275	350		125	50	100
Armand Hammer	150	275		535	50	100
William Randolph Hearst	695	950		600	150	300
Henry John Heinz	350	550			150	300
Leona Hemsley	35				10	20
Conrad Hilton	110	190		90	60	120
Ben Holladay		450		250	125	250
Johns Hopkins				500	175	350
Howard Hughes	2750	3500		2000	1250	2500
Henry E. Huntington		200		125	75	150
Lee A. Iaccoca	35			50	15	50
Robert H. Ingersoll	225	300		175	80	160
John Jay		2250		1750	550	1100
Howard Johnson	35			30	15	30
Henry J. Kaiser	375			900	200	400
W.K. Kellogg	250	400		250	125	250
Joeseph P. Kennedy	150				75	150
James C. Kraft	50	175		95	30	60
Ray Kroc	100	150			40	80
Alfred Krupp		500		450	180	360
Carl Laemmle	700	600		250	100	200
William P. Lear Sr.	100	150		100	30	60
Louis K. Liggett		350		170	90	180
Peter Lorillard		450		250	125	250
Frederick L. Maytag	200	600		275	100	200
Richard McDonald	250			275	75	150
Andrew Mellon	400	1200		900	250	500
J.P. Morgan Sr.	1200	2500		900	300	600
J.S.G. Morton	75	145		50	25	50
John K. Northrop	100	250		125	45	90
Ransom E. Olds				1200	300	600
Aristotle Onassis	225			300	175	350
Fred Pabst	400			450	150	300
J.C. Penny	300	400		300	100	200
Allen Pinkerton	RARE	1200		750	300	600
Dr. Ferdinand Porsche	550			450	225	450
Joseph Pulitzer		500		350	125	250
George M. Pullman		500		450	225	450
Orville Redenbacker	30	30		30	10	20
R.J. Reynolds				600	250	500
Albert Ringling				400	150	300
Charles Ringling				300	125	250
Henry Ringling				350	125	250
John Ringling				600	125	250
John D. Rockerfeller	1500	2250		1650	500	1000

	PHOTO	ALS	LS/TLS	DS	SIG.	COVER
John D. Rockerfeller Jr.	75	175		125	35	70
Washington A. Roebling		400		225	100	200
Charles S. Rolls		600			300	600
Nathan Meyer Rothschild				850	275	550
Sir Henry Royce		1200			600	1200
Russel Sage		1500		750	200	400
David Sarnoff	150	750		400	75	150
Harry Sinclair	200	300		175	125	250
Leland Stanford	400	2500		1750	225	450
F.O. Stanley		1200			350	700
Clement Studebaker		650		500	200	400
Seth E. Thomas		400		250	125	250
Charles L. Tiffany	1500	RARE		400	200	400
Donald J. Trump	40	75		50	15	30
Ted Turner	30	40			10	20
Cornelius Vanderbilt	3000	3500		2000	600	1200
William H. Vanderbilt	500	1500		750	250	500
Jack L. Warner	150			175	75	150
Wells & Fargo				1250	850	1700
Henry Wells		1500		750	300	600
George Westinghouse				1500	500	1000
Frank W. Woolworth	RARE	RARE		2500	550	1100
William J. Wrigley	350	400		350	150	300

CELEBRITIES

	PHOTO	ALS	LS/TLS	DS	SIG.	COVER
Ralph Abernathy	75	125			30	60
Abigail Adams		5500		2000	550	1100
Louisa C. Adams		750		500	250	500
Jane Addams	250				75	150
Susan B. Anthony	1200	600			175	350
Stephen Austin		5000		2000	800	1600
Clara Barton	800	675		450	155	310
Judge Roy Bean		7500		5000	2000	4000
Henry Ward Beecher		200			75	150
William W. Belknap		175			75	150
David Berkowitz		250			75	150
Harry Blackstone	250	450			120	240
Letizia Bonaparte		2700		1500		
Lizzie Borden	RARE	RARE		RARE	1800	3600
Margaret Bourke-White		200		75	75	150
Belle Boyd	10000	RARE		10000	2000	4000
Joseph Brant	RARE	5000		RARE	RARE	
Eva Braun		2750			1000	2000
Harry Bridges	140			125	70	140
Chief John F. Brown		350		175	100	200
John Brown	2500	2500		1600	775	1550
Ralph Bunche	125	225		130	50	100
David G. Burnet		1200		635	275	550
Al Capone	RARE	RARE		8000	3000	6000
Clementine S. Churchill	150	200		150	75	150
William Clark		2000		1500	400	800
William F. Cody	4500	2000		1500	750	1500
Capt. James Cook	RARE	RARE		8850	3800	7600
Peter Cooper		750		500	150	300
Hernando Cortez	RARE	RARE		20000	6000	12000
Davy Crockett		20000		9000	6000	12000
George Croghan		800		400	200	400
Emmett Dalton	SCARCE	3500		1600	800	1600

	PHOTO	ALS	LS/TLS	DS	SIG.	COVER
Clarence Darrow	1300	2200		1600	400	800
Varina H. Davis	750	500		250	150	300
James W. Denver		450		210	100	200
Thomas E. Dewey	100	150		75	40	80
Mahlon Dickerson		150		75	25	50
Jacob M. Dickinson		125		50	25	50
Dorothea L. Dix	25	45		30	15	30
Stephen A. Douglas	270	450		225	100	200
Allen W. Dulles	75	225		165	30	60
Virgil Earp		7500		4500	2000	4000
Wyatt Earp		30000		15000	5000	10000
Mary Baker Eddy	SCARCE	SCARCE		2500	1250	2500
Muhammad Elijah	425			275	175	350
Brian Epstein		750		600	350	700
James A. Farley	25	70		40	15	30
Father Flanagan	250			125	45	90
Nathan Bedford Forrest	RARE	RARE		SCARCE	750	1500
Otto Frank				550	300	600
Sir John Franklin		610		320	125	250
James Gadsden		550		350	175	350
Gandhi	SCARCE	1500		1200	550	1100
Pat Garrett		3000		2500	SCARCE	
Geronimo	RARE	RARE		RARE	5000	10000
Joseph Goebbels	1250			1025	350	700
Samuel Gompers		450		225	150	300
Robert K. Gray	100	250		150	50	100
Horace Greeley	750	300		275	65	130
Charles J. Guiteau	SCARCE	2500		900	400	800
John N. Griggs		110		45	15	30
John Wesley Hardin	RARE	9000		3750	1800	3600
Mata Hari	RARE	RARE		1100	400	800
Lucy Webb Hayes	700	400			230	460
Patty Hearst					325	650
John Hinckley Jr.		200		150	35	70
Alger Hiss		200		65	40	80
James R. Hoffa	400				275	550
J. Edgar Hoover	145	220		160	60	120
L. Ron Hubbard	SCARCE	SCARCE		900	200	400
Robert G. Ingersoll	40	85		60	30	60
Jessie Jackson	35	45			15	30
Frank James		2750		1600	975	1950
Marshall Jewell		195		75	40	80
Anson Jones		1200			350	700
Alvin Karpis	100				75	150
Emmett Kelly	275			150	65	130
Ethel Kennedy	35			45	15	30
Rose Kennedy	100			150	100	200
Sister Elizabeth Kenny	275				175	350
Simon Kenton					400	800
Alexander F. Ferensky	400				200	400
Martin Luther King Jr.	3000	3500		2750	1500	3000
Frederick West Lander		375		225	150	300
Marcy C. Lee	475	690			150	300
Meriwether Lewis	RARE	11500		6000	RARE	
G. A. "Pawnee Bill" Lillie	500	750		550	275	550
David Livingstone		1600		750	225	450
Martin Luther	RARE	550000		40000	15000	30000
Cotton Mather				4000		

	PHOTO	ALS	LS/TLS	DS	SIG.	COVER
Malcom X	RARE	14000		900	1250	2500
Thomas Robert Malthus				250	300	600
Charles Manson	200	350		175	75	150
Luther Martin		360		RARE	70	140
Bat Masterson	RARE	RARE		400	5000	10000
John Stuart Mill		850			150	300
Maria Montessori					295	590
John Montagu (Earl of Sandwich)		400		200	75	150
Lola Montez		500			200	400
Mother Teresa	275	RARE		250	125	250
Elijah Muhammad				250	100	200
Edward R. Murrow	250			300	130	260
Eliot Ness	RARE	RARE		800	375	750
Annie Oakley	7500	9000		6000	2500	5000
Judge Isaac Parker				1500	500	1000
Rosa Parks	100			100	40	80
Eva Peron		600			400	800
Jane M. Pierce		900		500	200	400
William A. Pinkerton				200	100	200
Peter B. Porter		175		150	75	150
John Profumo	100			65	40	80
Melvin Purvis	100	150		100	25	50
Buford Pusser				250	125	250
Ernie Pyle	350	450		300	200	400
James Earl Ray		200			75	150
Hiram R. Revels					500	1000
John Ross		1000		600	350	700
Jack Ruby	RARE	RARE		400	200	400
Harland (Col) Sanders		125		150	45	90
John Scopes	1500	RARE			300	600
John Selman				2500	1200	2400
Samuel Sewall	60				25	50
Sitting Bull	RARE	RARE		RARE	5750	11500
Alfred E. Smith	125				50	100
Joseph Smith				1500	750	1500
Ashrel Smith		450			150	300
Sir Henry M. Stanley	750	550			275	550
Elizabeth C. Stanton		400		225	150	300
Edwin M. Stanton		300		160	100	200
William Stratton (Tom Thumb)	450	375			250	500
John A. Sutter	RARE	2700		RARE	1200	2400
Henretta Szold		600		450	150	300
Isiah Thomas		750		300	150	300
William M. Tilghman		1250		850	200	400
Donald Trump	40	75		50	15	30
William M. "Boss" Tweed	750	350		200	125	250
Bartolomeo Vanzetti	RARE	RARE		1500	600	1200
Booker T. Washington	1500	700		450	300	600
Francis E. Willard		125		65	40	80
Wendell L. Willkie	125			75	35	70
Christopher Wren	RARE	RARE		RARE	1500	3000
Frank Lloyd Wright	RARE	RARE		1550	900	1800
Brigham Young	RARE	RARE		1500	650	1300
Cole Younger		7500			2000	4000
Emiliano Zapate	RARE	RARE		1500	500	1000

COMPOSERS, CONDUCTORS, OPERA & BALLET DANCERS

Antonio Annalord	40	35			10	20

	PHOTO	ALS	LS/TLS	DS	SIG.	COVER
Edmond Audran		175	85	85	45	90
Joann Sebastion Bach	50				20	40
George Balanchine	200	250			125	250
Mikhail Baryshnikov	150	130	85	85	65	130
Harold Bauer			80	80	45	90
Alan Berg		1425	485	485	135	270
Irving Berlin	1100	1420	1060	1060	230	460
Hector Berlioz		2190	785	785	245	490
Leonard Bernstein	255	525	350	350	200	400
Georges Bizet		2100	890	890	350	700
Eubie Blake	125	175	105	105	60	120
Sir Arthur Bliss		175			25	50
Arrigo Boita		325	110	110	45	90
Alexander Borodin		1100	450	450	250	500
Joannes Brahms	6200	5375	1350	1350	1000	2000
Benjamin Britten	195	650	405	405	115	230
Anton Bruckner	2500	5500	2500	2500	1200	2400
Ferruccio Busoni	425	340			120	240
John Cage	190	250	125	125	95	190
Sammy Cahn	50	125	80	80	15	30
Maria Callas	825	976	850	850	300	600
Hoagy Carmichael	110		200	200	45	90
Enrico Caruso	1265	1250	625	625	275	550
Pablo Casals	285	245	150	150	100	200
Cecile Chaminade	270	300	195	195	85	170
Gustave Charpentier	300	370	250	250	100	200
Ernest Chausson		345	145	145	50	100
Luigi Cherubini		595	375	375	175	350
George M. Cohan	280	275	185	185	85	170
Florencio Constantino	365				75	150
Aaron Copland	155	285	165	165	75	150
Peter Cornelius		325			55	110
Noel Coward	375	380	210	210	165	330
George Crumb		375			25	50
Cesar Cui		450	200	200	95	190
Walter J. Damrosch	200	115	75	75	50	100
Felicien David			500	500	100	200
Claude Debussy		1375	1000	1000	350	700
Manuel Defalla			1200	1200	425	850
Mario Delmonaco	175	125	65	65	45	90
Erno Dohnanyi		220	135	135	50	100
Gaetano Donnizetti		2150	800	800	500	1000
Isadora Duncan	825	1150			400	800
Antonin Dvorak		2500	895	895	400	800
Duke Ellington	400		325	325	125	250
Daniel D. Emmett		600	425	425	300	600
Geraldine Farrar	130	120			65	130
Margot Fonteyn	200	135	45	45	40	80
Arthur Foote		195	85	85	30	60
Stephen Foster		10000	3500	3500	1000	2000
Cesar Franck		890	1100	1100	340	680
Rudolf Friml	250	325	250	250	100	200
Amelita Galli-Curci	200	385	190	190	85	170
Mary Garden	85	45	30	30	20	40
George Gershwin	4075	4650	1700	1700	900	1800
Ira Gershwin	180	1375	250	250	85	170
Beniamino Gigli	275	300	90	90	50	100
Umberto Giordano	400		400	400	250	500

	PHOTO	ALS	LS/TLS	DS	SIG.	COVER
Alexander Glazunov		675	365	365	225	450
Louis M. Gottschalk	SCARCE	1600		1200	500	1000
Charles Gounod	550	500		365	150	300
Edward Grieg	1095	1125		600	350	700
Ferde Grofe	125	245		200	100	200
Oscar Hammerstein	250			250	125	250
George Frederick Handel	RARE	RARE		5800	1000	2000
W.C. Handy	450	SCARCE		475	275	550
Joseph Hayon	RARE	RARE		RARE	3500	7000
Roland Hayes	250				100	200
Jascha Heifetz	585				130	260
Hans Werner Henze	150				45	90
Victor Herbert	350	375		200	100	200
Paul Hindemith		425		295	100	200
Earl K. "Father" Hines	30				125	250
Josef C. Hofmann	150	140		100	40	80
Arthur Honegger	50	290		130	45	90
Englebert Humperdinck	250	375		225	100	200
Jacques Ibert		325			75	150
Charles E. Ives	500	1500		750	250	500
Joseph Joachim	220	337		150	95	190
Scott Joplin		2000		1200	750	1500
Walter Kent	65				40	80
Jerome Kern	2000	SCARCE		650	250	500
Zoltan Kodaly	450	450		250	125	250
Erich Korngold	100	350		200	75	150
D.J. "Nick" LaRocca	200				75	150
Franz Lehar	350	550		200	85	170
Ruggierro Leoncavallo	675	500		500	175	350
Lydia Lipkowska	325				100	200
Franz Liszt	1600	950		650	450	900
Anna Magnani	450				275	550
Gustav Mahler	RARE	3500		1200	550	1100
Henry Mancini	75			60	30	60
Pietro Mascagni	600	500		375	165	330
Jules Massenet	295	255		145	65	130
Jimmy McHugh				75	25	50
Johnny Mercer	135				50	100
Olivier Messiaen				200	70	140
Giacomo Meyerbeer	300	400		250	175	350
Julia Migenes	35				15	30
Darius Milhaud	450	300		250	150	300
Glenn Miller	450	600		400	200	400
Wolfgang A. Mozart	RARE	75000		RARE	RARE	
Ethelbert Nevin	100	300		150	75	150
Jacques Offenbach	275	450		250	145	290
Eugene Ormandy	80	90		45	25	50
Ignace J. Paderewski	450	550			175	350
Nicolo Paganini	RARE	RARE		RARE	450	900
Luciano Pavarotti	65	100			35	70
Anna Pavlona	550	450			350	700
Aureliano Pertile	125				40	80
Lily Pons	125				50	100
Cole Porter	650			450	225	450
Andre Previn	75	80		40	20	40
William Primrose	225				75	150
Serge Prokofieff	950	1200		750	400	800
Serge Rachmaninoff	475	775		600	225	450

	PHOTO	ALS	LS/TLS	DS	SIG.	COVER
Maurice Ravel	1600	1400			450	900
Hans Richter		450			150	300
Nikolai Rimsky-Korsakov	1500	2500		1500	600	1200
Richard Rodgers	225			250	75	150
Sigmund Romberg	225	300		200	75	150
Gioacchino Rossini	RARE	1750		1000	RARE	
Anton Rubinstein	400	300		200	75	150
Camille Saint Saens	400	400		300	150	300
Alessandro Scarlatti	RARE	20000		RARE	RARE	
Ernestine Schumann-Heink	150				50	100
Robert Schumann	RARE	RARE		RARE	1000	2000
Franz Schubert	RARE	RARE		5000	2500	5000
Sara Scuderi	85				35	70
Neil Sedaka	20			20	10	20
Pete Seeger		75		50	20	40
Marcella Sembrich	200	200			100	200
Roger Sessions		90			15	30
George B. Shaw	1500	800		650	400	800
John Philip Sousa	900	400		400	125	250
William Grant Still	250	300			125	250
Leoplod Stokowski	150	150		125	65	130
Oscar Straus	200	250			150	300
Joann Strauss Jr.	RARE	900		750	450	900
Richard Strauss	700	750		450	225	450
Igor Stravinsky	750	750		550	325	650
Arthur Sullivan	1000	650		400	175	350
Set Svanholm	45				20	40
Gladys Swarthout	75			75	25	50
Marie Taglioni	RARE	RARE			300	600
Peter Tchaikovsky	RARE	RARE		3000	2000	4000
John Charles Thomas	45	55		45	25	50
Virgil Thomson	125	150		75	50	100
Arturo Toscanini	700	750		550	300	600
Ludwig Van Beethoven	RARE	50000		27500	RARE	
Guiseppe Verdi	RARE	2400		1500	1200	2400
Hans Von Bulow		65			20	40
Richard Wagner	3000	2500		1600	1200	2400
Thomas "Fats" Waller	400	RARE		275	125	250
Bruno Walter	375	150			75	150
Kurt Weil	375	900		500	250	500
John Williams	50			75	20	40

	PHOTO	SIG.	COVER
F. Murray Abraham	30	15	25
Isabelle Adjani	30	15	25
Ben Affleck	40	20	25
Christina Aguilera	50	25	35
Dan Akyrod	20	10	20
Alan Alda	40	20	25
Kim Alexis	30	15	25
Karen Allen	20	10	20
Woody Allen	35	15	20
Kirstie Ally	20	10	20
Carol Alt	25	17	20
Gillian Anderson	40	20	25
Loni Anderson	20	10	20
Pamela Anderson	50	25	35
Ursula Andress	40	20	25
Julie Andrews	40	17.5	25
Ann Margaret	40	15	18
Christina Applegate	40	20	25
Roseanne Arquette	20	10	20
Armand Assante	20	10	20
Lauren Bacall	20	10	20
Catherine Bach	20	10	20
Kevin Bacon	25	10	20
Max Baer	40	20	30
Carroll Baker	40	20	30
Alec Baldwin	35	17.5	25
Anne Bancroft	30	15	20
Brigitte Bardot	50	25	40
Roseanne Barr	25	12.5	25
Drew Barrymore	50	25	35
Chuck Berry	75	40	60
Kim Basinger	50	25	40
Kathy Bates	30	15	25
Justine Bateman	20	10	20
Stephanie Beacham	10	5	15
Jennifer Beals	15	7.5	15
Amanda Bearse	10	5	20
Warren Beatty	50	25	25
Milton Berle	50	17.5	35
Corbin Bernsen	20	10	20
Valerie Bertinelli	20	10	20
Jacqueline Bisset	25	12.5	20
Shirley Temple Black	60	25	40
Linda Blair	20	10	20
Tommy "Butch" Bond	35	17.5	25
Lisa Bonet	20	10	20
Jon Bon Jovi	60	30	40
Shirley Booth	35	17.5	25
Ernest Borgnine	30	15	25
David Bowie	75	40	60
Marlon Brando	400	200	275
Lloyd Bridges	35	17.5	30
Christie Brinkley	40	20	35
Morgan Brittany	10	5	20
Matthew Broderick	25	12.5	25
Charles Bronson	40	20	40
Mel Brooks	35	17.5	30
Garth Brooks	50	25	35

	PHOTO	SIG.	COVER
Pierce Brosnan	50	15	25
Blair Brown	20	10	20
Julie Budd	10	5	15
Jimmy Buffett	40	20	25
Gary Burghoff	20	10	20
Carol Burnett	10	5	20
George Burns	50	25	50
Raymond Burr	40	20	40
Nicholas Cage	35	17.5	30
Michael Caine	35	17.5	30
Kirk Cameron	10	5	20
Dyan Cannon	10	5	20
Kate Capshaw	10	5	20
Jean Carmen	10	5	15
Art Carney	30	15	25
Jim Carrey	40	20	25
Johnny Carson	40	15	25
Linda Carter	20	10	20
Johnny Cash	50	25	35
David Cassidy	20	10	20
Phoebe Cates	35	17.5	25
Marilyn Chambers	35	17.5	30
Richard Chamberlain	20	10	20
Chevy Chase	40	20	25
Cher	40	20	30
Julie Christie	35	17.5	30
Andrew Dice Clay	20	10	20
Eric Clapton	75	40	60
Glenn Close	25	12.5	25
Joan Collins	20	10	20
Jennifer Connelly	40	20	25
Sean Connery (James Bond)	75	40	65
Sean Connery (Portrait)	75	40	65
Alice Cooper	50	25	35
Jackie Cooper	35	17.5	30
Bill Cosby	30	15	25
Kevin Costner	50	25	35
Courtney Cox	40	20	30
Yvonne Craig	25	17.5	25
Fred Crane	25	17.5	25
Cindy Crawford	50	25	40
Michael Crawford	40	20	30
Billy Crystal	30	15	25
Cathy Lee Crosby	35	17.5	25
Russell Crowe	50	25	35
Tom Cruise	95	40	50
Macaulay Culkin	35	17.5	25
Jamie Lee Curtis	40	20	35
John Cusack	20	10	20
Timothy Dalton	40	20	25
Matt Damon	40	20	25
Ted Danson	20	10	20
Tony Danza	20	10	20
Geena Davis	25	12.5	20
Pam Dawber	20	10	20
Daniel Day-Lewis	30	15	20
Yvonne DeCarlo	35	20	20
Dana Delaney	35	17.5	25

	PHOTO	SIG.	COVER
Peter DeLuise	10	5	15
Rebecca DeMornay	25	12.5	25
Robert DeNiro	75	35	50
Johnny Depp	40	20	35
Bo Derek	50	25	50
Curly Joe DeRita	75	40	60
Danny Devito	40	20	30
Neil Diamond	50	25	35
Leonardo Dicaprio	60	30	40
Angie Dickinson	35	15	25
Matt Dillon	35	15	25
Celine Dion	40	20	25
Donna Dixon	35	15	25
Shannon Doherty	40	15	25
Kirk Douglas	40	20	25
Michael Douglas	40	20	35
Leslie Anne Down	25	12	20
Robert Downey Jr.	25	12	20
Richard Dreyfuss	30	12	20
Olympia Dukakis	20	10	15
Faye Dunaway	40	20	30
Robert Duvall	40	20	30
Clint Eastwood	60	30	40
Barbara Eden	35	15	20
Buddy Ebsen	35	15	20
Anita Ekberg	50	25	30
Britt Ekland	50	25	30
Robert Englund	30	15	20
Melissa Ethrige	40	20	25
Peter Falk	35	15	20
David Faustino	20	10	15
Farrah Fawcett	45	22	30
Sally Fields	35	15	20
Carrie Fisher	40	20	25
Louise Fletcher	15	5	15
Linda Fiorintino	15	5	15
Jane Fonda	30	20	25
Peter Fonda	35	15	20
Joan Fontaine	35	15	20
Glenn Ford	35	15	25
Harrison Ford	75	35	50
John Forsythe	25	12	20
Jodie Foster	75	35	50
Michael J. Fox	50	25	40
Samantha Fox	50	25	35
Morgan Freeman	35	15	25
Janine Furner	25	15	20
Megan Gallagher	20	10	15
Teri Garber	25	15	20
Andy Garcia	35	20	25
James Garner	35	20	30
Teri Garr	30	15	20
Greer Garson	50	25	35
Richard Gere	50	25	35
Mel Gibson	75	40	60
John Gielgud	40	20	25
Melissa Gilbert	25	10	20
Mark Goddard	20	10	20

PHOTO		SIG.	COVER
Whoopie Goldberg	30	15	30
Jeff Goldblum	30	15	25
John Goodman	30	15	20
Louis Gossett Jr.	35	20	30
Stewart Granger	35	20	30
Jennifer Grey	35	20	25
Richard Grieco	20	20	25
Andy Griffith	50	20	30
Melanie Griffith	50	25	30
Charles Grodin	20	10	15
Fred Gwynn (as Herman)	150	75	90
Shelley Hack	15	5	15
Gene Hackman	35	20	25
Jessica Hahn	20	10	15
Fawn Hall	20	10	15
Jerry Hall	25	10	15
Huntz Hall	50	20	25
Harry Hamlin	20	10	20
Tom Hanks	50	30	50
Daryl Hannah	30	20	35
Neil Patrick Harris	25	15	20
Lisa Hartman	35	15	25
Rutger Hauer	30	15	25
Ethan Hawke	35	15	20
Goldie Hawn	40	20	30
Don Henly	60	30	40
Barbara Hershey	35	15	25
Charlton Heston	35	15	30
Dustin Hoffman	50	25	40
Paul Hogan	25	10	20
Kane Hooder	25	10	20
Bob Hope	60	30	75
Anthony Hopkins	40	20	30
Dennis Hopper	40	20	30
Bob Hoskins	20	10	20
Helen Hunt	50	25	30
Holly Hunter	30	15	25
Isabelle Huppert	30	15	20
William Hurt	45	25	40
Anjelica Huston	25	15	25
Lauren Hutton	25	15	25
Timothy Hutton	25	10	20
Jeremy Irons	30	15	25
Glenda Jackson	20	10	20
Janet Jackson	125	75	100
Kate Jackson	50	20	35
Michael Jackson			
Mick Jagger	125	75	100
Billy Joel	50	25	35
Don Johnson	35	15	25
Janet Jones	30	15	20
James E. Jones	30	15	20
Michael Keaton (Portrait)	35	25	35
Michael Keaton (Batman)	65	25	35
Diane Keaton	40	20	30
Marthe Keller	25	10	20
Deforest Kelly	50	25	30
George Kennedy	20	25	30

PHOTO	SIG.	COVER	
Persis Khambatta	50	25	30
Margot Kidder	40	20	30
Val Kilmer	60	35	40
B.B. King	50	25	35
Cammie King	50	25	30
Ben Kingsley	40	20	25
Natassia Kinski	75	45	50
Ertha Kitt	50	25	30
Werner Klempereer	50	25	30
Don Knotts	25	10	15
Sylvia Kristel	50	25	30
Kris Kristofferson	40	20	30
Cheryl Ladd	40	20	25
Burt Lancaster	75	35	45
Diane Lane	45	25	30
Jessica Lange	45	25	30
Angela Lansbury	35	20	25
Kelly LeBrock	35	20	25
Gordon "Porky" Lee	40	20	25
Spike Lee	30	15	20
Janet Leigh	35	20	25
Jack Lemmon	40	20	25
Jay Leno	30	15	20
David Letterman	40	20	25
Emily Lloyd	25	12	15
Heather Locklear	50	25	30
Robert Loggia	20	10	15
Gina Lollobrigida	50	25	30
Shelley Long	35	15	20
Jennifer Lopez	40	20	35
Sophia Loren	45	20	25
Rob Lowe	45	20	25
George Lucas	60	35	40
Kelly Lynch	25	12	20
Carol Lynley	35	20	30
Ralph Macchio	25	15	25
Andie MacDowell	30	15	20
Ali McGraw	25	12	20
Marion Mack	35	15	20
Shirley MacLaine	45	20	30
Virginia Madsen	35	15	20
Pamela Sue Martin	30	15	20
Ricky Martin	50	25	35
Steve Martin	40	20	30
Mary S. Masterson	30	15	20
Marlee Matlin	30	15	25
David McCallum	30	15	20
Roddy McDowell	50	25	30
Reba McEntire	35	15	20
Kelly McGillis	30	20	25
Elizabeth McGovern	30	15	20
Tim McGraw	35	15	20
Nancy Mckeon	25	12	20
Kyle McLachlin	25	12	20
Butterfly McQueen	50	25	30
Robert Merrill	30	15	25
Mike Meyers	40	20	25
Bette Midler	50	25	50

	PHOTO	SIG.	COVER
Alyssa Milano	35	15	20
Vera Miles	25	12	25
Donna Mills	25	12	20
Liza Minnelli (Full Name)	40	20	30
Liza Minnelli (First Name)	30	15	25
Robert Mitchum	60	30	40
Richard Moll	20	10	20
Dudley Moore	50	20	25
Mary Tyler Moore	35	20	30
Roger Moore (Portrait)	50	25	35
Roger Moore (007)	65	35	50
Demi Moore	75	40	50
Rick Moranis	20	10	20
Morgana	25	12	20
Pat Morita	20	10	20
Kate Mulgrew	40	20	25
Bill Munn	35	15	20
Caroline Munro	75	35	40
Eddie Murphy	75	40	50
Jim Nabors	35	20	25
Patricia Neal	35	15	25
Julie Newman	35	15	20
Paul Newman	100	50	75
Olivia Newton John	35	15	25
Michelle Nichols	35	15	20
Jack Nicholson (Joker)	75	40	60
Jack Nicholson (Portrait)	65	35	50
Bridgette Nielson	25	15	25
Stevie Nicks	60	30	40
Leonard Nimoy	60	30	40
Nick Nolte	30	15	25
Chuck Norris	25	12	20
Jay North	30	15	20
Kim Novak	35	15	25
Rosie O'Donnell	40	20	25
Tatum O'Neal	35	15	20
Ed O'Neill	20	10	20
Maureen O'Sullivan	40	20	25
Lena Olin	25	12	20
Ozzy Osborne	60	30	40
Al Pacino	60	35	40
Debra Paget	50	25	30
Gwyneth Paltrow	40	20	25
Butch Patrick	30	15	20
Paulina	30	15	20
Gregory Peck	50	25	35
Sean Penn	40	20	25
Elizabeth Perkins	20	10	20
Tom Petty	60	30	40
Michelle Pfeiffer	60	35	40
Lou Diamond Phillips	30	15	20
Brad Pitt	50	25	35
Susanne Pleshette	25	12	20
Michelle Phillips	25	12	20
Martha Plimpton	25	12	20
Christopher Plummer	30	15	20
Sidney Poiter	35	15	25
Markie Post	30	15	20

	PHOTO	SIG.	COVER
Jane Powell	35	15	25
Priscilla Presley	40	20	25
Kelly Preston	25	12	25
Jan Provost	35	15	20
Dennis Quaid	30	15	20
Anthony Quinn	50	25	35
Martha Raye	30	15	25
Vanessa Redgrave	40	20	25
Robert Redford	75	35	40
Christopher Reeve(Portrait)	75	35	40
Christopher Reeve (Superman)	100	50	60
Keanu Reeves	50	25	30
Burt Reynolds	35	15	25
Cynthia Rhodes	25	12	20
Donna Rice	25	12	20
Keith Richards	75	40	60
Molly Ringwald	30	15	20
John Ritter	20	10	20
Joan Rivers	20	10	25
Julia Roberts	75	35	25
Tanya Roberts	40	20	30
Cliff Robertson	25	12	25
Mimi Rogers	25	15	25
Gilbert Roland	40	20	30
Cesar Romero	40	20	30
Micky Rooney	40	20	30
S.O. Roselline	35	15	20
Mickey Rourke	35	15	25
Jane Russell	35	15	25
Kurt Russell	40	20	25
Rene Russo	40	20	25
Ann Rutherford	40	20	25
Meg Ryan	75	35	40
Winona Ryder	75	35	40
Katey Sagal	20	10	20
Emma Samms	20	10	20
Adam Sandler	35	15	20
Laura Sangiacomo	30	15	20
Carlos Santana	50	25	35
Susan Sarandon	30	15	25
Fred Savage	25	12	20
Maximillian Schell	45	22	30
Claudia Schiffer	50	25	30
Arnold Schwarzenegger	100	50	60
Paul Scofield	45	22	35
Tracy Scoggins	30	15	20
Gordon Scott	35	15	20
Steven Segal	40	20	30
Jerry Seinfeld	50	25	35
Connie Sellecca	30	15	20
Tom Selleck	40	20	25
Joan Severance	20	10	20
Jane Seymour	40	20	30
William Shatner (Star Trek)	75	40	45
Ally Sheedy	35	17	25
Charles Sheen	35	17	25
John "Boy" Sheffield	35	15	20
Cybil Shepherd	40	20	35

	PHOTO	SIG.	COVER
Nicollette Sheridan	40	20	25
Red Skelton	75	35	50
Brooke Shields	40	20	30
Christian Slater	45	22	30
Jaclyn Smith	40	20	30
Maggie Smith	35	17	25
Suzanne Somers	40	20	25
Elke Sommer	35	20	25
Sissy Spacek	35	17	40
Kevin Spacey	35	15	20
Britney Spears	50	25	35
Steven Spielberg	100	50	60
Bruce Springsteen	75	40	60
Robert Stack	25	12	20
Sylvester Stallone	75	35	40
John Stamos	30	15	20
Ringo Starr	125	75	100
Rod Steiger	40	20	25
Trish Sterling	25	12	20
Stella Stevens	25	12	20
James Stewart (Portrait)	75	35	50
James Stewart (Rabbit sketch)	400	200	240
Patrick Stewart	40	20	25
Rod Stewart	50	25	35
Sting	50	25	35
Dean Stockwell	25	12	20
Sharon Stone	75	35	50
Meryl Streep	75	35	50
Donald Sutherland	40	20	30
Hillary Swank	40	20	25
Patrick Swayze	40	20	25
George Takei	35	17	20
Elizabeth Taylor	250	125	150
Heather Thomas	40	20	25
Lea Thompson	35	17	20
Cheryl Tiegs	35	17	25
Meg Tilly	35	15	20
Kathleen Turner	35	15	25
Lana Turner	75	35	50
Tina Turner	40	20	25
Shania Twain	40	20	25
Shannon Tweed	35	15	25
Tracy Ullman	20	10	20
Mamie VanDoren	40	20	25
Jon Voight	35	17	25
Robert Wagner	35	17	30
Ken Wahl	30	15	20
Christopher Walken	45	25	30
Burt Ward	45	22	25
Rachel Ward	40	20	30
Jack Warden	20	10	20
Denzel Washington	50	25	35
David Wayne	30	15	20
Shawn Weatherly	20	10	20
Sigourney Weaver	35	17	25
Raquel Welch	50	25	35
Adam West	45	25	30
Diane West	30	15	20

CURRENT ENTERTAINERS (cont)

	PHOTO	SIG.	COVER
Joanne Whalley-Kilmer	30	15	20
Gene Wilder	35	17	25
Esther Williams	50	25	40
Van Williams	45	22	30
Bruce Willis	75	40	50
Debra Winger	30	15	25
Joanne Woodward	30	15	25
Fay Wray	75	40	50
Teresa Wright	50	25	30
Sean Young	30	15	20
Daphne Zuniga	30	15	20

	PHOTO	ALS	LS/TLS	DS	SIG.	COVER
Abbott & Costello	1500			1000	500	600
Bud Abbot	350	450	420	350	150	200
Maude Adams	100	125	110	100	50	60
Nick Adams	200	250	220	220	75	100
Brian Aherne	35	45	38	35	20	25
Fred Allen	75	95	85	80	25	30
Grace Allen	150	195	180	165	50	60
Don Ameche	75	97	90	80	25	65
Heather Angel	50	65	60	50	20	30
Roscoe Arbuckle	950	1200	1100	1050	400	480
Richard Arlen	75	95	85	75	35	40
George Arliss	100	125	115	100	30	35
Robert Armstrong	200	255	225	200	100	110
Desi Arnez (full name)	200	260	240	220	100	120
Edward Arnold	100	125	110	100	30	40
Jean Arthur	200	260	240	210	100	120
Mary Astor	75	95	90	85	25	30
Roscoe Ates	100	115	110	100	25	30
Agnes Ayres	100	115	110	100	25	30
Lew Ayres	50	65	57	55	20	25
Fay Bainter	125	160	145	125	45	55
Josephine Baker	350	450	420	385	125	150
Lucille Ball (first name)	200	260	240	230	75	100
Lucille Ball (full name)	400	520	480	460	125	150
Tallulah Bankhead	150	195	180	165	50	60
John Banner	200	255	225	200	75	85
Theda Bara	250	325	300	275	100	120
Diana Barrymore	100	130	120	110	35	40
Freddie Bartholomew	100	130	120	110	35	40
Clara Bow	400	520	480	440	125	150
Lex Barker	200	260	240	220	75	100
Warner Baxter	125	160	145	125	45	55
Scotty Beckett	100	110	110	100	50	60
Noah Beery	75	100	90	80	35	40
Wallace Beery	200	260	240	220	75	100
Ed Begley Sr.	125	160	140	125	50	60
Ralph Bellamy	50	65	60	50	20	30
John Belushi	400	450	360	320	250	300
William Bendix	125	160	145	135	50	60
Joan Bennett	50	65	60	50	20	45
Jack Benny	150	195	160	175	50	75
Gertrude Berg	65	80	75	65	20	25
Edgar Bergen	125	160	140	135	50	75
Ingrid Bergman	225	260	240	220	100	150
Busby Berkeley	350	450	420	400	100	120
Sarah Bernhardt	250	320	300	275	100	120
Joe Besser	100	110	110	100	50	60
Turhan Bey	75	100	90	80	25	30
Amanda Blake	100	130	120	110	25	35
Clara Blandick	2500	3200	2900	2750	700	840
Joan Blondell	100	130	110	100	25	30
Ben Blue	50	65	60	55	20	25
Humphrey Bogart	2000	2600	2400	2300	900	900
Mary Boland	50	60	55	50	20	25
Ray Bolger	100	130	120	110	50	60
Ward Bond	125	160	150	135	50	60
Edwin Booth	200	260	240	240	75	90
Clara Bow	400	520	480	450	125	150

	PHOTO	ALS	LS/TLS	DS	SIG.	COVER
Charles Boyer	100	130	120	110	35	40
Eddie Bracken	50	60	55	50	20	25
Walter Brennen	150	190	170	160	50	60
Fanny Brice	150	195	180	175	50	60
Bruce Bennett(Tarzan)	100	130	120	120	50	60
Clive Brook	75	80	80	75	25	30
Louise Brooks	400	520	480	440	200	240
Rand Brooks(GWTW)	75	100	90	90	30	40
Lenny Bruce	500	650	600	600	250	300
Nigel Bruce	350	435	400	400	225	265
Yul Brynner	75	100	90	85	35	40
Frank Buck	75	90	85	75	30	35
Billie Burke	200	260	240	220	100	120
Burns & Allen	250				100	120
Richard Burton	125	160	150	140	50	60
Francis X. Bushman	200	260	240	220	50	60
Bruce Cabot	150	195	180	165	50	60
Sebastian Cabot	150	195	180	165	75	90
James Cagney	100	130	120	110	50	75
Eddie Cantor	100	130	120	110	50	75
Frank Capra	75	100	90	85	30	35
Capucine	75	100	90	75	30	35
Harry Carey Sr.	100	130	120	100	50	60
Mary Carlise	50	60	55	50	20	25
John Carradine	100	130	120	110	50	60
Leo Carrillo (Portrait)	100	130	120	120	40	50
Earl Carroll	75	90	85	75	30	35
Madeleine Carroll	100	120	110	110	35	40
Ted Cassidy	200	260	240	220	100	120
Joan Caulfield	50	60	55	50	25	35
Jeff Chandler	100	120	110	100	35	40
Lon Chaney Jr.	750	975	900	900	275	330
Lon Chaney Sr.	1500	1950	1800	1800	750	900
Charles Chaplin	1000	1300	1200	1200	400	420
Ruth Chalterton	200	250	225	220	50	60
Maurice Chevalier	100	130	120	110	35	40
Rene Clair	100	110	110	100	40	45
Mae Clark	50	55	55	55	25	30
Montgomery Clift	300	390	360	360	100	120
Lee J. Cobb	100	120	110	110	35	50
Charles Coburn	50	60	55	50	20	25
Steve Cochran	75	85	85	75	25	30
Claudette Colbert	75	95	85	85	25	30
Ronald Colman	200	260	240	230	50	60
Walter Connolly	75	85	85	75	25	30
Jerry Colonna	75	85	85	75	20	25
Gary Cooper	250	325	300	300	100	125
Wendell Corey	75	95	90	80	25	30
Katherine Cornell	50	60	60	55	20	25
Dolores Costello	50	60	55	50	20	25
Lou Costello	350	425	400	400	150	180
Joseph Cotton	50	60	55	55	20	40
Buster Crabbe (As Tarzan)	100	125	120	120	25	40
Jeanne Crain	100	120	110	100	25	30
Bob Crane	200	250	225	225	75	90
Broderick Crawford	100	125	110	110	50	70
Joan Crawford	200	250	225	225	50	70
Laura Hope Crews(GWTW)	250	300	275	275	75	90

	PHOTO	ALS	LS/TLS	DS	SIG.	COVER
Bob Cummings	50	60	55	55	20	30
Dan Dailey	75	90	85	75	20	25
Dorothy Dandridge	250	320	300	275	100	120
Bebe Daniels	75	90	85	75	20	25
Linda Darnell	100	120	110	100	50	70
Marion Davies	100	120	115	100	50	60
Jim Davis	75	90	85	75	25	30
Sammy Davis Jr.	125	160	150	140	75	100
Bette Davis	75	100	90	90	50	60
James Dean	4500	5750	5400	5250	2000	2400
Olivia DeHavilland	50	60	55	55	20	30
Dolores Del Rio	50	60	55	50	20	30
Cecil B. DeMille	200	260	250	240	50	60
Andy Devine	200	250	225	225	50	60
Marlene Dietrich	75	90	85	85	50	60
Robert Donat	100	120	110	110	25	30
Diana Dors	100	100	110	100	35	40
Melvyn Douglas	50	60	55	55	20	25
Billie Dove	75	95	90	80	35	40
Marie Dresser	350	450	420	400	75	90
Eddie Duchin	75	90	85	85	35	40
Howard Duff	50	60	55	50	20	25
Irene Dunne	50	60	55	50	20	25
Jimmy Durante	125	125	120	110	50	50
Douglas Fairbanks Sr.	200	250	240	220	75	90
Frances Farmer	250	320	300	275	100	120
Dustin Farnum	75	90	85	80	35	40
Marty Feldman	150	150	165	150	75	90
Edith Fellows	50	55	55	50	20	25
Jose Ferrer	50	60	55	50	20	25
W.C. Fields	1250	1600	1500	1600	500	600
Peter Finch	250	300	275	275	75	90
Larry Fine	450	550	500	475	200	240
Barry Fitzgerald	300	360	330	340	100	120
Eric Fleming	250	300	275	260	100	120
Victor Fleming	1000	1300	1200	1150	400	500
Joe Flynn	200	250	225	225	75	100
Errol Flynn	500	650	600	600	300	360
Henry Fonda	95	100	90	85	50	75
Joan Fontaine	50	65	60	55	20	30
Lynn Fontaine	85	40	40	35	20	30
John Ford	250	325	300	300	100	120
William Frawley	350	375	350	350	250	300
Clark Gable	950	1200	1150	1100	350	420
Greta Garbo	7500	9750	9000	9000	2000	2400
Ava Gardner	75	110	90	85	50	60
John Garfield	300	375	360	350	100	120
Judy Garland	800	975	900	900	500	550
Janet Gaynor	75	90	85	80	25	30
Gladys George	75	90	85	75	25	30
Billy Gilbert	75	95	85	80	25	30
John Gilbert	150	185	165	165	75	90
William Gillette	75	90	85	75	40	45
Lillian Gish	50	65	60	55	30	35
Jackie Gleason	225	260	240	240	100	150
Paulette Goddard	75	95	90	85	30	40
Arthur Godfrey	50	65	60	55	20	35
Betty Grable	200	260	240	240	50	75

	PHOTO	ALS	LS/TLS	DS	SIG.	COVER
Cary Grant	400	520	480	440	150	200
Bonita Granville	50	65	60	55	20	25
Sid Grauman	100	125	110	100	50	60
Gilda Gray	75	90	85	80	25	30
Sydney Greenstreet	450	575	540	525	200	240
D.W. Griffith	750	975	900	900	200	240
Alec Guiness	40				20	30
Alan Hale Jr.	200	250	240	240	75	90
Jack Haley (Portrait)	150	195	180	180	75	90
Jack Haley (Tin Man)	300	390	360	360	75	90
Billy Halop(Dead End Kids)	200	260	240	240	50	60
Oliver Hardy	500	650	600	600	200	240
Margaret Hamilton (Wiz. Oz)	200	260	240	240	75	90
Jean Harlow	2500	3250	3000	2750	1000	1200
Rex Harrison	50	65	60	55	25	40
Laurence Harvey	100	120	110	110	50	60
Helen Hayes	50	60	55	55	20	30
Will H. Hays	100	100	110	100	25	30
Susan Hayward	250	325	300	300	100	150
Rita Hayworth	250	325	300	275	100	150
Margaux Hemingway	100				50	75
Sonja Henie	100	125	120	110	40	50
Audrey Hepburn	250	325	300	300	100	120
Kathryn Hepburn	750	975	900	900	125	120
Jon-Erik Hexum	200	240	230	220	100	120
Alfred Hitchcock	500	650	600	600	250	300
John Hodiak	100	120	110	110	35	50
William Holden	100	120	110	110	50	75
Judy Holliday	200	260	240	240	75	100
Meriam Hopkins	100	110	110	110	25	30
Harry Houdini	2500	3250	3000	2750	1000	1200
Leslie Howard	350	450	425	375	100	120
Moe Howard	450	585	540	525	200	240
Shemp Howard	750	975	900	850	350	420
Rock Hudson	200	250	220	220	50	75
Josephine Hull	200	240	220	220	50	60
John Huston	100	110	110	110	25	40
Jeffrey Hunter	100	110	110	100	35	50
Walter Huston	100	110	110	110	35	50
Thomas Ince	400	480	440	440	200	240
Jill Ireland	50	55	55	55	20	30
Henry Irving	250	265	265	265	100	120
Emil Jannings	250	300	300	275	75	90
David Janssen	200	240	220	220	50	75
Al Jolson (Black Face)	1500	1950	1800	1800		
Al Jolson (Portrait)	500	650	600	600	100	120
Jennifer Jones	250	300	275	275	100	120
Boris Karloff	500	650	600	600	250	300
Roscoe Karns	100	110	110	110	25	30
Andy Kaufman	200	260	240	220	100	120
Danny Kaye	100	110	110	110	50	75
Buster Keaton	500	650	600	550	200	
Harry Kellar	500	600	550	550	250	300
Cecil Kellaway	100	110	110	100	50	60
Gene Kelly	75				35	50
Grace Kelly	450	585	540	525	200	250
Emmett Kelly Sr.	200	260	240	220	75	100
Paul Kelly	100	110	110	100	25	30

	PHOTO	ALS	LS/TLS	DS	SIG.	COVER
Edgar Kennedy	100	100	110	100	30	35
Deborah Kerr	50	60	55		20	30
Alan Ladd	100	110	110	100	50	75
Bert Lahr (as Cowardly Lion)	5000	6500	6000	6000		7200
Arthur Lake (Dagwood)	150	190	180	180	50	60
Veronica Lake	300	375	360	360	100	120
Hedy Lamarr	75				35	40
Dorothy Lamour	50				25	30
Elsa Lanchester	100	110	110	110	50	60
Elissa Landi	100	100	110	100	25	30
Carole Landis	200	240	220	220	50	75
Michael Landon	100	125	120	120	50	60
Harry Langdon	250	300	290	275	100	120
Lillie Langtry	450	585	540	540	250	300
Charles Laughton	250	300	290	290	75	100
Laurel & Hardy	1500				500	1000
Stan Laurel	500	650	600	600	200	
Peter Lawford	200	240	230	230	50	75
Gertrude Lawrence	100	130	120	110	25	40
Bruce Lee	2000	2600	2400	2400	650	1200
Gypsy Rose Lee	200	260	240	220	50	60
Lila Lee	50	55	55	50	20	25
Vivien Leigh	750	975	900	900	350	420
Elmo Lincoln (Tarzan)	1000	1300	1200	1200	300	360
Jenny Lind	400	500	450	450	100	120
Mary Livingston	100	120	110	110	50	60
Harold Lloyd	350	450	400	375	100	120
Carole Lombard	750	975	900	900	300	360
Peter Lorre	350	450	400	400	200	240
Anita Louise	50	60	55	50	20	25
Bessie Love	75	85	80	75	25	30
Myrna Loy	50	60	55	50	20	25
Bella Lugosi (Dracula)	2000	2600	2400	2400		
Bella Lugosi (Portrait)	1000	1300	1200	1200	400	480
Paul Lukas	150	180	165	165	30	35
Alfred Lunt	50	60	55	55	20	25
Bert Lytell	50	55	55	50	20	25
Fred MacMurray	50	60	55	55	20	25
Anna Magnani	300	390	360	360	100	120
Jock Mahoney (Tarzan)	100	130	120	120	40	50
Marjorie Main	200	260	240	240	75	90
Jayne Mansfield	400	520	480	450	200	240
Frederic March	100	120	110	110	50	60
Enid Markey (First Jane)	250	325	300	275	100	120
Mae Marsh	100	110	110	100	25	30
Dean Martin	100				50	75
Mary Martin	50	60	55	50	20	25
Lee Marvin	125	120	110	110	60	75
Chico Marx	350	420	400	420	200	240
Groucho Marx	350	450	420		200	240
Harpo Marx	400	520	480	480	200	240
Zeppo Marx	250	325	300	325	100	120
Marx Brothers	2500				1000	1200
James Mason	75	90	85	80	25	30
Raymond Massey	50	60	55	55	20	25
Victor Mature	50				25	30
Louis Mayer	250	325	300	300	100	120
Hattie Mcdaniel (Portrait)	1000	1300	1200	1200	450	550

	PHOTO	ALS	LS/TLS	DS	SIG.	COVER
Hattie Mcdaniel (Portrait)	750	975	900	900		
Victor Mclaglen	200	250	225	225	75	90
Steve McQueen	350	450	425	375	200	240
Adolph Menjou	75	90	85	80	20	25
Una Menkel	75	90	85	80	20	25
Burgess Meredith (Penquin)	75				35	40
Burgess Meredith (Portrait)	35				20	30
Ethel Merman	75	100	90	80	25	30
Ray Milland	50	60	55	55	20	25
Marilyn Miller	125	150	140	130	50	60
Denny Miller (Tarzan)	50	60	55	60	20	25
Sal Mineo	200	260	240	240	75	90
Carmen Miranda	200	260	240	240	100	120
Cameron Mitchell	50	60	55	50	20	25
Marilyn Monroe	5000	6500	6000	6000	1500	1800
Maria Montez	250	325	300	300	75	90
Robert Montgomery	50	60	55	55	20	25
Colleen Moore	50	60	55	50	20	25
Grace Moore	50	60	55	55	20	25
Antonio Moreno	75	85	80	75	25	30
Frank Morgan (Portrait)	450	585	540	525	250	300
Chester Morriss	50	60	55	50	20	25
Vic Morrow	200	240	225	230	75	90
Audie Murphy	300	390	360	360	200	240
George Murphy	50	60	55	55	10	12
Conrad Nagel	75	90	85	80	15	18
Nita Naldi	100	120	110	110	25	30
J. Carrol Naish	100	115	110	110	20	25
Alla Nazimova	200	240	225	225	75	90
Pola Negri	200	260	240	240	75	90
Ozzie Nelson	200	240	230	230	50	75
David Niven	50	60	55	55	25	30
Mabel Normand	500	625	600	600	250	300
Edmond O'Brien	100	115	110	110	35	40
Pat O'Brien	50	60	55	55	20	25
Carroll O'Connor	40				20	25
Maureen O'Sullivan (as Jane)	50	65	60	60	25	30
Peter O'Toole	75	90	85	80	25	30
Merle Oberon	100	120	110	110	50	60
Warner Oland	250	325	300	300	100	120
Lawrence Olivier	100	100	90	90	50	60
Maria Ouspenskaya	375	485	450	425	200	240
Geraldine Page	50	60	55	55	20	25
Larry Parks	200	260	240	240	50	60
George Peppard	40				20	35
River Pheonix	200				100	125
Mary Pickford	75	90	85	85	25	35
Walter Pidgeon	75	90	85	85	20	30
James Pierce (Tarzan)	100	130	120	110	20	25
Lily Pons	100	120	110	110	20	30
Dick Powell	100	120	110	110	20	30
William Powell	150	195	175	165	50	60
Tyrone Power	200	260	240	230	75	90
Otto Preminger	75	100	90	90	20	30
Elvis Presley	1200	2000	1000	1000	600	1000
Robert Preston	50	60	55	55	20	30
Vincent Price	75	100	90	90	35	40
Freddie Prinz	250	325	300	300	100	120

	PHOTO	ALS	LS/TLS	DS	SIG.	COVER
Gilda Radner	200	240	220	220	100	120
George Raft	100	130	120	110	25	35
Luise Rainer	75	100	90	90	20	25
Claude Raines	250	325	300		100	120
Esther Ralston	65	75	70	70	20	25
Vera Ralston	50	60	55	55	20	30
Sally Rand	65	75	70	70	20	25
Basil Rathbone (S.H.)	2000	2600	2400	2400		
Basil Rathbone (Portrait)	500	650	600	600	150	100
Donna Reed	125	160	150	135	50	75
George Reeves (as Superman)	3000	3900	3600	3600		
George Reeves (Portrait)	1000	1300	1200	1200	500	600
Wallace Reid	300	350	330	300	100	120
Thelma Ritter	150	180	165	160	50	60
Hal Roach	100	110	110	100	50	50
Marty Robbins	100	110	110	100	50	60
Paul Robeson	300	390	360	360	100	120
Edward G. Robinson	175	180	165	165	75	100
May Robson	50	55	55	50	20	25
Rochester (Eddie Anderson)	200	260	240	220	75	90
Ginger Rogers	95	95	85	80	60	60
Will Rogers	400	520	480	480	200	240
Alma Rubens	100	110	110	100	50	60
John Russell	50	55	55	50	20	25
Lillian Russell	200	240	220	220	75	90
Rosalind Russell	100	110	110	100	25	30
Ann Rutherford (GWTW)	75	95	90	90	20	25
Irene Ryan (as Granny)	200	260	240	240	100	120
Robert Ryan	100	110	110	100	20	35
Sabu	200	260	240	240	50	60
S.Z. Sakall	150	180	165	160	50	60
George Sanders	150	180	165	160	50	60
Zachary Scott	125	150	140	135	35	40
Peter Sellers	200	250	240	225	100	120
David O. Selznick	250	320	300	275	75	90
Mack Sennett	500	650	600	600	200	240
Norma Shearer	100	120	110	110	35	50
Ann Sheridan	150	180	165	160	50	60
Simone Signoret	100	120	110	110	20	40
Jay Silverheels	400	520	480	480	200	240
Phil Silvers	100	110	110	100	50	60
Red Skelton	75	90	85	85	40	60
Barbara Stanwyck	75	90	85	85	25	40
Inger Stevens	200	240	220	210	75	90
Dorothy Stratten	750	920	900	900	500	600
Ed Sullivan	100	110	110	100	25	30
Slim Summerville	75	85	75	75	20	25
Frank Sutton	100	110	100	100	35	40
Gloria Swanson	100	130	120	110	35	40
Jessica Tandy	40				20	30
Lilyan Tashman	50	55	50	50	25	30
Sharon Tate	1000	1300	1200	1200	500	600
Robert Taylor	100	110	100	100	45	60
Shirley Temple (Pre 1950's)	250	325	300	300	100	125
Irving Thalberg	500	650	600	600	200	240
Three Stooges (W/ Curley)	2500				1250	1500
Howard Thurston	450	550	500	500	100	120
Gene Tierney	75	90	85	85	30	50

	PHOTO	ALS	LS/TLS	DS	SIG.	COVER
Thelma Todd	400	480	440	440	200	240
Sidney Toler (as Chan)	400	520	480	480	200	240
Spencer Tracy	400	520	480	480	200	250
Lana Turner	75	95	85	80	25	50
Ben Turpin	300	390	360	360	100	120
Rudolph Valentino	1500	1950	1800	1800	500	600
Vivian Vance	300	390	360	360	200	240
Conrad Veidt	200	250	225	225	50	60
Lupe Velez	250	325	275	275	50	60
Erich Von Stroheim	400	520	480	440	75	90
Jack Warner	200	260	220	220	35	40
John Wayne (Portrait)	800	1000		800	400	450
Carol Wayne	150	125			35	120
Charles Weaver						60
Jack Webb	100			75	45	60
Johnny Weissmuller (Tarzan)	400			300	150	200
Orson Welles	350			450	125	150
Mae West	250			115	55	70
Roland Winters (as Chan)	75	75		45	30	60
Anna May Wong	175	150		150	75	60
Natalie Wood						120
Fay Wray (King Kong)	50				25	30
Jane Wyman	35				15	25
Ed Wynn	45			35	25	30
Gig Young	75	75		50	30	50
Loretta Young	50				25	30
Florence Ziegfield Jr.	300	500		350	200	250

GROUP AUTOGRAPHS

	PHOTO
Don Adams & B. Feldon	75
Addams Family, The	500
All In The Family	100
Andy Griffith Show (Complete)	500
Andy Griffith Show (3)	200
Fred Astaire/Ginger Rogers	350
Barnaby Jones	75
Barney Miller	350
Batman & Joker (Nicholson, Keaton)	75
Batman & Robin (West, Ward)	75
Beverely Hillbillies (4)	200
Big Valley	400
Bob Cummings Show	75
Bonanza	600
Charles Bronson/Jill Ireland	75
Cagney & Lacey	75
Charlies Angels (Original)	200
Crosby & Rashad	75
Dallas (Original)	300
Designing Women (4) (Original)	100
Family Ties	100
Father Knows Best	200
Gilligan's Island (Original)	500
Golden Girls	100
Gone With the Wind (DeHavilland, Brooks, McQueen, & Rutherford)	200
Grease (Travolta, Olivia Newton-John)	100

GROUP AUTOGRAPHS

	PHOTO
Happy Days (Howard & Winkler)	75
Honeymooners, The	400
I Dream of Jeannie	150
Knot's Landing (6)	100
LA Law (3)	75
Laugh In (Rowan & Martin)	100
Leave it to Beaver	200
Lost in Space	350
Lucy & Desi (First Name)	250
Lucy & Desi (Full Names)	450
Dean Martin/Jerry Lewis	275
Mash	500
Midnight Caller (5)	100
Moonlighting	100
"Munsters, The"	500
Nabors & Knotts	100
Odd Couple	75
Perfect Strangers	75
Psycho (Perkins & Leigh)	200
Shatner & Nimoy	100
Smothers Brothers	50
Star Trek (3)	125
Star Trek (6)	500
Steel Magnolias	100
Jessica Tandy & Morgan Freeman	75
Three Amigos	100
Young Guns	250

	PHOTO	ALS	LS/TLS	DS	SIG.	COVER
Louis J.R. Agassiz	600	250			100	200
George Airy	50	250				
Andre Marie Ampere		1000			250	500
Charles Babbage		550			200	400
John Logie Baird	450			300	150	300
Frederick S. Banting	900	1500		1000	600	1200
Alexander Graham Bell	2500	1800		1200	500	1000
Jons Jakob Berzelius		475		165	75	150
Theodor Billroth		295		225	75	150
Aage Niels Bohr	55				25	50
William Bond		350		190	45	90
Max Born		575		350	175	350
William Henry Bragg				95	45	90
Robert W. Bunsen	1250	900		400	175	350
Luther Burbank	165	290		275	115	230
David Bushnell		1250		750	250	500
Richard E. Byrd	325	450		275	75	150
Rachel Carson	275	285		205	70	140
George Washington Carver	1750	700			200	400
Edith Cavell		750		375	225	450
Dr. Charles A. Cheever	75			100	40	80
Robert A. Chesebrough		50		30	15	30
Samul Colt		2750		2000	500	1000
George W. Corner	100			150	75	150
Marie Curie	SCARCE	2600		1550	1050	2100
Harvey Cushing		675		475	165	330
Louis J. Daguerre		1250		490	250	500
Charles Darwin	RARE	1750		1600	750	1500
Dr. Lee Dubridge	50	145		100	30	60
Charles Duryea	RARE	SCARCE		450	150	300
James Buchanan Eads		450		300	100	200
George Eastman	1500	3000		1200	800	1200
Arthur Eddington		150		125	25	50
Alexandre G. Eiffel	1250	900		600	300	600
Albert Einstein	2750	3500		1800	900	1800
Havelock Ellis	275	155			35	70
John Ericson		400		195	75	150
Michael Faraday	650	450			175	350
John Flamstead				975	800	1600
John Ambrose Fleming		145		65	25	50
Sir Alexander Fleming	900	750		600	225	450
Sigmund Freud	6000	4500		3500	1650	3300
Robert Fulton	RARE	2500		1300	325	650
Richard J. Gatling		2500		1200	400	800
Robert H. Goddard	SCARCE	1425		1750	450	900
Joseph Guillotin	SCARCE	SCARCE		SCARCE	275	550
Johannes Hagen		100		40	15	30
Otto Hahn	350	SCARCE		300	150	300
George Hale				100	25	50
Joseph Henry		250		200	55	110
John Herschel		675		475	150	300
William Herschel		675		475	150	300
Werner Heisenberg		650		225	75	150
Elias Howe	SCARCE	SCARCE		SCARCE	400	800
Edwin Hubble				60	20	40
Thomas H. Huxley		235		150	65	130
Edward Jenner	SCARCE	SCARCE		850	450	900
Sir William Jenner		295		110	35	70

	PHOTO	ALS	LS/TLS	DS	SIG.	COVER
Karl Gustav Jung		3500		1500	600	1200
Hogo Junker		300			50	100
Dr. Alfred Kinsey	250	350		225	150	300
Robert Koch	1500	2200		1200		
Simon Lake		450		150	60	120
Antoine Lavoisier	RARE	RARE		RARE	750	1500
Carolus Linnaeus	RARE	RARE		RARE	925	1850
Joseph Lister		600		400	225	450
Sir Oliver J. Lodge	250	225		130	90	180
Nevil Maskelyne		405		250	85	170
Hudson Maxim	175	175		150	60	120
Sir Hiram S. Maxim	300	375		190	95	190
Dr. Charles H. Mayo	475	380		290	140	280
Dr. William J. Mayo	475	380		290	105	210
Cyrus H. McCormick		2000		850	350	700
Gregor Mendel		2000		850	400	800
Karl Menninger	60	75		65	30	60
Albert Michelson		450			120	240
Robert Millikan	200	400		200	100	200
Maria Montessori		900			295	590
Samuel F.B. Morse	RARE	1250			550	1100
John Muir		1950		1450	600	1200
Sir Isaac Newton	RARE	25000		12000	4000	8000
Florence Nightingale		750		750	450	900
Alfred Nobel	450	400			250	500
John H. Northrop	100			150	50	100
Herman Oberth	250			200	72	144
Louis Pasteur	RARE	1750		900	500	1000
Linus Pauling	125	400		250	60	120
Emile Picard		400		200	75	150
Julian Pond		300			100	200
Joseph Priestly		1400		900	350	700
George M. Pullman		500		450	225	450
Sir William Ramsey		450		300	150	300
Otto Rank		400			200	400
Walter Reed	675	RARE		750	400	800
David Rittenhouse	RARE	RARE		1100	850	1700
Wilhelm Roentgen		2400		1300	650	1300
Dr. Jonas Salk	200	250		150	45	90
Dr. Albert Schweitzer	750	550			150	300
Glenn Seaborg	75	150		75	40	80
Ignaz Semmelweis	RARE	RARE		900	500	1000
Herlow Shapley		150		150	50	100
William Shockley	100	150		100	45	90
Igor Sikorsky	275	300		225	85	170
Herbert Spencer		200		125	50	100
Dr. Benjamin Spock	50	100		75	35	70
Charles Steinmetz		300		150	75	150
George Stephenson		750		350	225	450
William Talbot		900			300	600
Edward Teller	90	250		125	35	70
Nikola Tesla	1250	1250		850	400	800
James VanAllen	100	200		100	40	80
Alessandro Volta	RARE	2500		1400	600	1200
Dr. Hugo Voneckener	550	550		400	200	400
Werner Vonbraun	400	550		400	150	300
Mary E. Walker	RARE	550			300	600
Benjamin Waterhouse		1650		600	250	500

SCIENCE (cont)

	PHOTO	ALS	LS/TLS	DS	SIG.	COVER
James Watt		1400		750	400	800
Eli Whitney	RARE	3500		2500	750	1500

WESTERN - BUSINESS & FINANCIAL FIGURES

		ALS		DS	SIG.	COVER
James G. Fair		110		145	30	60
John Mackay		200		100	50	100
D.O. Mills		2000		750	250	500
William Sharon		200		100	50	100
Francis M. "Borax" Smith		75		60	30	60
Adolph Sutro		150		90	35	70
Orion Clemens		200			125	250
James W. Nye		75		125	75	150
William M. Stewart		65		45	30	60

WESTERN-VINTAGE & DECEASED

	PHOTO				SIG.	COVER
Buddy Allen	100				50	60
Gene Autry	100				50	75
Don "Red" Berry	75				25	30
Dan Blocker (Bonanza)	300				100	125
Richard Boone (Paladin)	200				100	125
Bill Boyd	275				100	115
Johnny Mack Brown	200				50	60
Smiley Burnette	200				50	60
Rod Cameron	100				35	40
Yakima Canutt	100				35	40
Leo Carrillo (Pancho)	250				50	60
Sunset Carson	75				25	30
Chuck Connors	75				25	35
Jim Davis	75				25	30
Andy Devine	200				50	60
Wild Bill Elliott	250				50	60
Hoot Gibson	300				100	125
Kirby Grant	75				25	30
Lorne Greene	75				25	30
William S. Hart	225				50	60
Russell Hayden	75				25	30
Gabby Hayes	350				100	115
Jack Holt	75				50	55
Tim Holt	200				75	85
Buck Jones	400				125	140
Bob Livingston	75				25	30
Ken Maynard	200				50	55
Tim McCoy	200				50	60
Joel McCrea	50				25	30
Tom Mix	450				200	225
Slim Pickens	75				25	30
Duncan Renaldo (Cisco Kid)	125				50	60
Tex Ritter	100				40	50
Randolph Scott	100				25	35
Jay Silverheels	400				200	250
Charles Durango Starrett	50				25	30
Bob Steele	75				25	35
Tom Tyler	250				100	115
Lee Van Cleef	75				30	35
Jimmy Wakely	75				30	35
John Wayne	750				400	450
Chill Wills	50				25	30

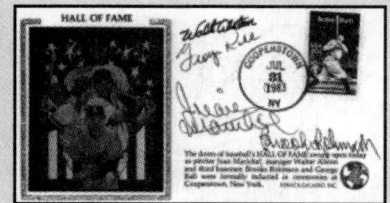

		SIG.(CUT)	3X5 CARD	PHOTO	SIG BBC	DS/TLS	* PLAK	SIG. CHK	COVER	BALL
*	Hank Aaron	20	35	40	40	100	45	45	40	60
	Roberto Alomar	5	10	25	10					35
*-D	Grover C. Alexander	300	500	100		2000	2000		600	8000
*-D	Walt Alston	20	35	100	40	100	175	75	50	750
*	Sparky Anderson	5	10	25	10		35		25	35
*-D	Cap Anson	1250	2000			2500		5000		
*	Luis Aparicio	12	20	25	15	75	20	300	25	30
*-D	Luke Appling	5	10	30	20	50	20		35	75
*-D	Richie Ashburn	5	10	25	15	75	30	75	30	50
*-D	Earl Averill Sr.	10	15	75	20	100	25	275	50	450
	Jeff Bagwell	5	12	30	10					35
*-D	Franklin "Home Run" Baker	200	300	750	500	1200	1250	2000	500	4000
*-D	Dave Bancroft	75	150	400	250	400	1000		200	3250
*	Ernie Banks	10	15	25	25	75	20	45	30	40
*-D	Al Barlick	5	10	25	20	75	20	40	25	50
*-D	Ed Barrow	50	125	300		300		150	150	3000
*-D	Jake Beckley	2000				4000				
*-D	James "Cool Papa" Bell	10	20	50	30	300	40	400	50	250
	Albert Belle	10	25	35	25					50
*	Johnny Bench	15	25	30	15	50	30	500	30	40
*-D	Chief Bender	150	275	500		750		800	350	3500
D	Moe Berg	100	200	500	300	1500		275		1500
*-D	Yogi Berra	10	15	25	20	50	25		30	40
	Wade Boggs	10	20	25	15				35	45
	Barry Bonds	15	40	75	50				75	75
*-D	Jim Bottomley	125	200	650	400	750		2500	400	4000
D	Ken Boyer	25	50	150	125	250			125	500
*	Lou Boudreau	5	10	25	10	50	12	45	25	30
*-D	Roger Breshnahan	400	750			1500			1500	12500
*	George Brett	15	30	40	25	100	100		40	75
*	Lou Brock	5	12	20	15	50	15	250	25	30
*-D	Dan Brouthers	4000				7500				
*-D	Mordecai Brown (3 finger)	250	500	1250		1500			750	5000
*-D	Morgan Bulkeley	2500				5000		3000		
*	Jim Bunning	5	10	20	15	50	25		25	35
*-D	Jesse Burkett	450	750	2500	1250	1000	2000	2500	800	5000
*-D	Roy Campanella (Pre Accid.)	300	500	1500	800	1500			800	4500
*-D	Roy Campanella (Post Accid.)	150	250	500	300		500		500	
	Jose Canseco	10	20	30	20				40	45
*	Rod Carew	10	25	30	15	50	25		25	35
*-D	Max Carey	15	25	150	50	125	75	50	75	500
	Gary Carter	5	10	25	15				25	30
*-D	Alexander Cartwright	1200				2000		3000		
D	Norm Cash	25	50	125	50				100	500
*	Orlando Cepeda	5	10	20	15	50	30		25	30
*-D	Henry Chadwick	1750				3500				
*-D	Frank Chance	700	1000			3000				
*-D	Albert "Happy" Chandler	12	25	50	25	100	25	150	40	75
*-D	Oscar Charleston	1250	2000			5000				
*-D	Jack Chesbro	1250	2000			4000		15000		
*-D	Nestor Chylak	150	350	800	500	500			750	2500

HOF= *

		SIG.(CUT)	3X5 CARD	PHOTO	SIG BBC	DS/TLS	* PLAK	SIG. CHK	COVER	BALL
D	Eddie Cicotte (1919 CWS)	200	300			2500			500	2000
	Will Clark	5	10	25	15				25	30
*-D	Fred Clarke	150	250	500	500	1000	800		300	2500
*-D	John Clarkson	2500				4000				
	Roger Clemens	15	35	50	30				75	85
*-D	Roberto Clemente	250	500	800	600	2000		1000	750	4000
*-D	Ty Cobb	300	550	2500	1000	2500	2000	1000	900	7500
*-D	Mickey Cochrane	100	150	500	350	1500	600	250	250	4000
	Rocky Colavito	5	10	25	15			30	30	40
*-D	Eddie Collins	150	350	600		350	1500	2000	400	4000
*-D	Jimmy Collins	800	1500			3000				5000
*-D	Earle Combs	35	75	250	75	500	150	125	100	1500
*-D	Charles Comiskey	600	900	2000		2000		6500		
	David Cone	5	10	20	10				25	30
D	Tony Conigliaro	50	100	250	100				175	500
*-D	Jocko Conlan	10	15	35	20	75	25		35	100
*-D	Thomas Connolly	300	500			750	1750		1500	4000
*-D	Roger Connor	4000				7500				
*-D	Stan Coveleski	10	15	75	30	100	35		40	400
*-D	Sam "Wahoo" Crawford	100	200	500	400	1500	300		200	2500
*-D	Joe Cronin	15	30	75	50	100	50	150	75	500
*-D	Candy Cummings	4000				10000				
*-D	Hazen "Kiki" Cuyler	250	400	800		2000		2500	500	5000
*-D	Ray Dandridge	8	15	30	25	150	25	50	50	75
	Alvin Dark		5	25	10	50			25	35
*-D	George Davis	5000				20000				
	Eric Davis	5	10	20	10				25	30
D	Jake Daubert	1000	2000			4000				
D	Andre Dawson	5	10	20	10			30	20	30
*-D	Leon Day	10	25	50	25	200		100	50	100
*-D	"Dizzy" Dean	75	125	250	275	500	175		200	800
*-D	Ed Delehanty	4000				10000				
*-D	Bill Dickey	20	30	50	40	150	50	150	75	200
*-D	Martin DiHigo	500	1000			3000				6000
	Dom DiMaggio	5	15	25	20			50	35	50
*-D	Joe Dimaggio	75	150	175	150	500	200	1500	175	250
D	Vince DiMaggio	30	50	100	100				100	250
*	Larry Doby	5	15	20	20	75	30	100	30	35
*	Bobby Doerr		5	12	10	40	10	30	20	25
*-D	Don Drysdale	10	25	45	25	100	40	300	40	100
*-D	Hugh Duffy	250	500	1000		2500	1500		800	3500
*-D	Leo Durocher	10	25	45	35	200		300	50	150
*-D	Billy Evans	175	300	1000		500			500	4000
*-D	John Evers	400	600	1750		3000		2500	1250	5000
*-D	Buck Ewing	4000				10000				
*-D	Urban "Red" Faber	30	45	150	75	150	75		100	1500
*	Bob Feller		5	10	10	40	10	200	20	25
*-D	Rick Ferrell	5	10	25	20	75	15	35	35	50
	Cecil Fielder	5	10	25	15				25	35
*	Rollie Fingers	5	10	20	10	50	15	40	20	25
*	Carlton Fisk	10	20	30	25	50	50		45	50
*-D	Elmer Flick	40	75	200	250	300	400		175	1000
*	Whitey Ford	10	20	30	25	1075	25	35	30	35
*-D	Rube Foster	3000				7500				
*-D	Willie Foster	1500	2500	3500	2500	5000				
*-D	Nellie Fox	75	150	350	175	1500		1000	300	1500
*-D	Jimmy Foxx	250	400	800	600	2500	1000		1000	6000

		SIG.(CUT)	3X5 CARD	PHOTO	SIG BBC	DS/TLS	* PLAK	SIG. CHK	COVER	BALL
*-D	Ford Frick	35	60	250	100	500	175		150	1500
*-D	Frankie Frisch	50	75	200	200	300	250	250	150	1500
D	Carl Furillo	20	40	75	100				100	250
	Andre Gallaraga	5	10	25	10				25	30
*-D	"Pud" Galvin	3000				5000				
	Nomar Garciaparra	5	15	30	20				30	40
*-D	Lou Gehrig	1250	2000	7500	5000	15000		12500	3500	15000
*-D	Charles Gehringer	10	20	50	30	150	25	250	50	125
D	Bart Giamatti	20	40	100		150			75	500
*	Bob Gibson	5	10	25	15	50	20		25	30
*-D	Josh Gibson	1000				5000				7500
*-D	Warren Giles	30	50	100	75	250		750	100	400
D	Jim Gilliam(55BKN)	45	75	200	75					600
	Tom Glavine	5	10	25	10				25	30
*-D	"Lefty" Gomez	10	20	50	35	100	30	150	50	150
	Juan Gonzalez	5	15	30	15				30	35
	Dwight Gooden	5	10	25	15				25	30
*-D	"Goose" Goslin	75	150	250	250	750	750		300	1500
	Mark Grace		5	20	10				20	25
*-D	Hank Greenberg	35	60	200	75	250	100	1000	125	1000
	Ken Griffey JR.	10	35	60	50				60	75
	Ken Griffey SR.	5	10	20	10				25	25
*-D	Clark Griffith	100	200	500		1500	1000	1500	400	4000
*-D	Burleigh Grimes	10	20	60	30	100	25	75	50	250
*-D	Robert "Lefty" Grove	25	50	250	125	500	125	175	100	1500
	Tony Gwynn	5	15	25	15				25	35
*-D	Chick Hafey	30	50	200	100	200	300		100	1500
*-D	Jessie "Pop" Haines	20	30	150	75	250	125	100	75	1000
*-D	Billy Hamilton	2000	3500			7500			3000	7500
*-D	Ned Hanlon	2500				4000				
*-D	William Harridge	50	100	250	125	200			200	3000
*-D	Bucky Harris	50	75	200	100	200	150		125	1200
*-D	Gabby Hartnett	50	80	200	125	350	250	300	150	1500
*-D	Harry Heilmann	250	400	1000		5000		1500	750	4000
	Ricky Henderson	10	25	30	25				35	50
*-D	Billy Herman	10	15	35	20	75	15	75	40	75
D	Gil Hodges	125	250	400	300	500			500	2500
*-D	Harry Hooper	20	30	100	75	125	150	100	75	600
*-D	Rogers Hornsby	200	400	1000	500	3500	800	7000	600	5000
D	Elston Howard	50	100	250	125	350			250	1000
*-D	Waite Hoyt	10	20	75	40	100	35	150	50	250
*-D	Cal Hubbard(Also FB *)	50	75	200	200	250	1000	200	200	800
*-D	Carl Hubbell (Pre Stroke)	10	20	50	35	150	35	100	75	200
*-D	Carl Hubbell (Post Stroke)	5	10	25	20	75	20		35	100
*-D	Miller Huggins	900	1250	2500		7500				5000
*-D	William Hulbert	7500				10000				
*-D	Jim "Catfish" Hunter	10	25	40	25	150	45	250	50	75
*	Monte Irvin	5	10	20	15	50	15	40	25	30
	Bo Jackson	10	20	35	25				50	50
D	Joe Jackson (1919 CWS)	7500				17500				40000
*	Reggie Jackson	25	40	40	25	100	60	200	50	50
*-D	Travis Jackson	20	30	100	40	250	50	500	50	350
*	Ferguson Jenkins		5	15	10	50	20	25	20	25
*-D	Hugh Jennings	1000	2200	2500		7500				7500
D	Jackie Jensen	15	25	75	75			100	75	200

		SIG.(CUT)	3X5 CARD	PHOTO	SIG BBC	DS/TLS	* PLAK	SIG. CHK	COVER	BALL
	Derek Jeter	10	25	40	45				50	50
*-D	Ban Johnson	300				800		3000		
*-D	Judy Johnson	15	30	75	40	250	40	400	50	200
	Randy Johnson	5	10	30	25				30	40
*-D	Walter Johnson	350	500	2000		3500		1000	1000	6000
	Chipper Jones	5	10	25	20				25	30
*-D	Addie Joss	10000								
*	Al Kaline	5	15	25	15	50	15		30	35
*-D	Tim Keefe	5000				7500				10000
*-D	Willie Keeler	4000				7500				
*	George Kell		5	20	10	40	10	35	25	30
*-D	George "Highpockets" Kelly	10	20	40	40	150	35	75	50	200
*-D	Joe Kelley	1500	2500			7500			4000	10000
*-D	Mike "King" Kelly	7000				25000				
*	Harmon Killebrew	10	20	25	20	75	20	250	30	40
*-D	Chuck Klein	400	600	1250	400	5000		7500	1250	4000
*-D	Bill Klem	350	500	1000		1000			1000	3500
D	Ted Kluszewski	15	30	60	50				75	150
*	Sandy Koufax	25	50	60	60	350	75		50	100
	Tony Kubek	10	25	50	50				50	100
*-D	Nap Lajoie	350	500	1500		5000	1250		1000	5000
*-D	Kenesaw Landis	250	400	800		2500		3000	1000	4000
	Barry Larkin	5	10	25	10				25	30
*	Tommy Lasorda	5	12	25	10	100	50	250	30	40
*-D	Anthony Lazzeri	600	800	1250		5000		3000	1250	5000
*-D	Bob Lemon	5	10	25	15	75	15	250	30	50
*-D	Buck Leonard	10	20	50	20	150	35	50	50	75
*-D	Fred Lindstrom	20	30	125	75	150	60	500	75	500
*-D	John H."Pops" Lloyd	2500	5000							10000
*	Al Lopez	5	15	40	25	100	35		40	75
*-D	Ted Lyons	10	15	75	30	150	35	75	50	250
*-D	Connie Mack	200	400	750	500	750	1000		600	2500
*-D	Larry MacPhail	75	150	250		500		1000	250	1250
*	Lee MacPhail	15	30	50		75	50	250	75	100
	Greg Maddux	5	15	30	20				30	40
*-D	Mickey Mantle	75	150	175	150	750	175	1500	175	250
*-D	Heinie Manush	40	75	250	150	250	250	350	200	1750
*-D	"Rabbit" Maranville	250	400	750	500	1000	1250		800	3000
*	Juan Marichal	10	25	35	20	100	25	250	35	50
*-D	"Rube" Marquard	20	30	100	50	125	50		75	500
D	Roger Maris	100	225	500	250				350	1250
D	Billy Martin	25	60	100	75				100	200
D	Pepper Martin	40	75	300	150	250			250	1000
	Tino Martinez	5	15	30	15				30	40
	Pedro Martinez	5	15	40	25				30	40
*-D	Eddie Mathews	5	20	35	25	100	30		35	55
*-D	Christy Mathewson	1500				10000		10000		20000
	Don Mattingly	10	25	40	20				40	50
*	Bill Mazeroski	5	15	25	15	50		250	30	40
*	Willie Mays	20	50	50	35	500	50	750	50	60
*-D	Joe McCarthy	25	40	150	50	150	100	500	75	1000
*-D	Thomas McCarthy	1500				7500				
*	Willie McCovey	10	20	30	25	100	25	50	35	50
*-D	"Bid" McPhee	5000	10000			25000				
*-D	Joseph McGinnity	1500				5000				
*-D	Wiilliam McGowan	400	500			3500			1000	5000
*-D	John McGraw	500	800			10000		7500		7500

		SIG.(CUT)	3X5 CARD	PHOTO	SIG BBC	DS/TLS	* PLAK	SIG. CHK	COVER	BALL
	Fred McGriff	5	10	25	10				25	35
	Mark McGwire	25	50	100	100	500			150	250
*-D	William McKechnie JR.	100	200	500	250	2500			500	2500
*-D	Joe Medwick	35	60	200	100	200	150		150	1000
*-D	Johnny Mize	5	15	25	15	100	20	150	30	50
	Paul Molitor	10	20	35	15				35	40
*	Joe Morgan	10	20	30	15	50	30	250	35	40
D	Thurman Munson	200	400	750	450				750	3000
*	Stan Musial	10	20	30	25	75	25	75	40	40
*-D	Hal Newhouser	5	15	25	15	100	20	50	35	50
*-D	Charles"Kid" Nichols	350	500	1000		3500	1500	5000	1000	10000
*	Phil Niekro	5	10	20	10	75	25			
*-D	Mel Ott	250	450			1750	2000			
*-D	Satchel Paige	75	125	300	150	750	150		250	
	Rafael Palmeiro	5	10	25	10					
*	Jim Palmer	5	15	25	15	100	30	250	30	40
*-D	Herb Pennock	250	500	750		750		900	750	4000
*	Tony Perez	5	15	25	15	75	35		30	40
*	Gaylord Perry		5	20	10	50	15	25	25	30
	Mike Piazza	10	15	35	30					50
*-D	Eddie Plank	2500								12500
*	Kirby Puckett	5	20	35	25	125			40	50
	Manny Ramirez	5	10	30	25				30	45
*-D	Pee Wee Reese	20	35	50	25	150	50	500	50	75
*-D	Sam Rice	40	60	250	100	200	175	500	125	1250
	Bobby Richardson		5	20	10				20	30
*-D	Branch Rickey	100	200	1000	350	400			400	2500
	Cal Ripken JR.	20	50	50	35				75	75
D	Swede Risberg (1919 CWS)	300	500	2000						
*-D	Eppa Rixey	125	250	500		500		250	500	2500
*	Phil Rizzuto	10	20	30	20	100	30	250	35	35
*	Robin Roberts	5	10	20	10	75	15		20	30
*	Brooks Robinson	5	10	20	10	75	15	25	25	30
*	Frank Robinson	5	15	30	20	100	25	100	30	45
*-D	Jackie Robinson	250	450	1250	450	3500	900	500	750	3500
*-D	Wilbert Robinson	1000				2500				
	Alex Rodriguez	5	25	45	35				65	65
	Ivan Rodriguez	5	15	30	20				30	35
*-D	"Bullett" Joe Rogan	2500								
	Scott Rolen	5	15	30	15				30	35
	Pete Rose	10	20	30	25	250			35	40
*-D	Edd Roush	5	10	50	25	100	25	175	40	200
*-D	Red Ruffing	20	35	75	35	200	60		100	600
*-D	Amos Rusie	2500	4000			10000				
*-D	Babe Ruth	1500	2500		4000	6000				8000
*-D	G.H. Ruth (Legal Sig)	1000	1750			4000		2000	3000	5000
*	Nolan Ryan	20	40	50	35	250	60		50	60
*-D	Ray Schalk(1919 CWS)	75	125	200		250	275		150	2000
*	Mike Schmidt	20	40	50	35	100	60		50	60
*	Red Schoendienst	5	15	25	10	50	15	250	25	30
*	Tom Seaver	10	30	35	20	150	50	300	45	50
*-D	Frank Selee	5000								
*-D	Joe Sewell	5	10	30	15	75	20	25	30	75
D	Urban Shocker	3000								
*-D	Al Simmons	175	350	700	500	1000	1000	1250	600	3500
*-D	George Sisler	40	75	150	100	400	150	300	125	2000
*	Enos Slaughter		5	20	10	50	10	25	25	30

		SIG.(CUT)	3X5 CARD	PHOTO	SIG BBC	DS/TLS	* PLAK	SIG. CHK	COVER	BALL
	Ozzie Smith	5	10	25	10				30	35
	John Smoltz	5	10	25	10				25	30
*	Duke Snider	5	15	25	15	75	15	50	30	40
	Sammy Sosa	20	40	75	50				75	100
*	Warren Spahn	5	10	20	10	75	10	75	25	30
*-D	Albert Spalding	1250				5000		5000		
*-D	Tris Speaker	250	400	1000		750	1000		800	7000
*-D	Willie Stargell	5	20	35	20	150	35	300	45	60
*-D	Casey Stengel	75	125	300	125	375	200	750	250	1000
	Darryl Strawberry	10	20	40	20				40	45
*	Don Sutton		5	20	10	100	30		20	30
*-D	Bill Terry	10	20	50	25	100	25	125	50	175
	Frank Thomas	5	10	30	20				30	45
*-D	Sam Thompson	3500				7500				
	Bobby Thomson (The Shot)	5	10	20	10			35	25	30
*-D	Joe Tinker	350	500	2000		3000		5000	1000	5000
	Alan Trammel		5	20	10				20	30
*-D	Harold"Pie" Traynor	200	300	600	400	750	500	750	400	2000
*-D	Dizzy Vance	150	300	500	400	1000	1500		500	2500
D	Johnny Vandermeer	5	15	40	15			45	30	50
*-D	Arky Vaughan	250	400	750		2500			800	4000
	Mo Vaughn	5	10	25	10				25	35
*-D	Bill Veeck SR.	65	125	200		150		250	175	600
*-D	Rube Waddell	2000				7500				
*-D	Honus Wagner	300	500	1500	600	5000	2000	1750	800	3500
	Larry Walker		5	20	15				20	30
*-D	R.J."Bobby" Wallace	200	400	1250	500	3500	1750		800	3500
*-D	Ed Walsh (Sr.)	200	350	1000	500	1000	750		800	3500
*-D	Lloyd Waner	10	20	150	30	200	40		50	350
*-D	Paul Waner	100	175	400	300	750	1000			5000
*-D	John M. Ward	4000				10000				
*-D	Willie Wells	200	500	750		1000				
*-D	Zack Wheat	50	75	200	150	250	300	700	150	2500
*	Hoyt Wilhelm	5	10	20	10	75	25	100	25	35
	Bernie Williams	10	20	40	25				40	50
*	Billy Williams	5	10	20	15	75	15	300	25	35
*-D	"Smokey" Joe Williams	7500	12500							
*	Ted Williams	50	125	150	100	750	150	2000	150	175
*-D	Vic Willis	4000	5000			10000				
*-D	Hack Wilson	350	750	2000		5000		1000		7500
*	Dave Winfield	5	20	30	20	150			35	45
D	"Smokey Joe" Wood	10	20	75	35			25	50	400
*-D	George Wright	1000				3000				
*-D	Harry Wright	2500				5000				
*-D	Early Wynn	10	25	40	25	150	30	125	40	50
*	Carl Yastrzemski	10	25	35	25	150	35	250	40	50
*-D	Thomas Yawkey	50	150	300		250			250	1500
*-D	Cy Young	275	500	1500		2500	1250		800	7500
*-D	Ross Youngs	3000	6000			7500				
*	Robin Yount	15	30	45	25	200	50		40	50

		3X5 CARD	PHOTO	COVER	SIGN.BSKB
*	Kareem Abdul Jabbar	40	50	75	150
*	Lew Alcindor	150	400	300	500
*	Nate Archibald	5	15	15	75
*	Paul Arizin	10	20	15	75
	Charles Barkley	25	35	40	100
*	Rick Barry	10	25	25	100
*	Elgin Baylor	15	30	25	100
*	Walt Bellamy	5	15	15	75
*	Dave Bing	10	15	15	75
	Larry Bird	40	75	75	175
*	Bill Bradley	50	100	75	175
*	Carl Braun	10	25	15	75
	Kobe Bryant	35	50	50	125
	Lou Carneseca	10	20	20	75
	Vince Carter	30	50	50	125
*-D	Wilt Chamberlain	100	275	250	750
*	John Cheyney	10	25	20	75
	Doug Collins	10	20	20	75
*	Bob Cousey	10	25	20	100
*	Dave Cowens	10	25	20	100
*	Billy Cunningham	15	25	25	100
*	Bob Davies	25	50	50	200
*	Dave DeBusschere	15	30	25	125
	Clyde Drexler	20	30	30	100
	Tim Duncan	25	40	40	125
*	Julius "dr.J" Erving	30	50	50	150
	Patrick Ewing	50	125	100	275
*	Walt Frazier	10	20	15	100
*-D	Joe Fulks	50	125	100	1000
	Kevin Garnett	25	40	40	125
*-D	"Pop" Gates	10	15	15	100
*	George Gervin	10	20	20	100
	Artis Gilmore	10	15	20	75
*	Tom Gola	5	15	15	75
	Gail Goodrich	5	15	15	75
*	Hal Greer	10	20	20	100
*	Clifford Hagan	5	15	15	75
	Anfernee Hardaway	15	25	25	100
*	John Havlicek	15	25	30	150
*	Connie Hawkins	10	20	20	100
*	Elvin Hayes	10	20	20	100
	Spencer Haywood	10	20	20	75
	Walt Hazzard	5	15	15	75
*	Tommy Heinsohn	15	30	25	125
	Grant Hill	20	35	35	100
*	Nat Holman	20	40	35	125
	Red Holzman	15	30	25	75
	"Hot Rod" Hundley	15	35	35	100
*	Henry Iba	30	75	60	250
*	Dan Issel	10	20	20	100
	Alan Iverson	35	50	50	150
	Phil Jackson	35	50	50	250
*	Buddy Jeannette	5	15	15	75
	Irvin "Magic" Johnson	50	75	75	250
	Kevin Johnson	20	30	30	125
	Bobby Jones	10	20	20	75
	Eddie Jones	10	20	25	100
*	K.C. Jones	10	20	15	100
*	Sam Jones	10	20	15	125

		3X5 CARD	PHOTO	COVER	SIGN.BSKB
	Michael Jordan	125	300	250	400
	Johnny "Red" Kerr	10	20	15	75
	Jason Kidd	20	30	30	100
	Bobby Knight	15	30	25	125
*	Mike Krzyzewski(Duke)				
	Toni Kukoc	20	35	35	125
*	Bob Lanier	10	20	20	125
*	Clyde Lovellette	5	15	15	75
*	Jerry Lucas	5	15	15	75
	Maurice Lucas	10	20	20	75
*	Ed MacCauley	10	20	15	75
	Karl Malone	25	40	40	150
*	Moses Malone	10	25	25	100
*	"Pistol Pete" Maravich (Full)	250	500	400	1000
*	"Pistol Pete"	100	250	200	500
	Stephon Marbury	20	30	30	125
*	Slater Martin	10	20	15	75
	Bob McAdoo	10	20	20	100
*	Dick McGuire	5	15	15	75
	Kevin McHale	20	30	25	100
*	George Mikan	20	40	40	150
*	Vernon Mikkelsen	5	15	15	75
	Reggie Miller	20	35	35	150
*	Earl "The Pearl" Monroe	5	15	20	100
	Alonzo Mourning	25	40	40	150
	Chris Mullin	20	35	35	125
*	Calvin Murphy	10	20	20	100
*	"Stretch" Murphy	20	50	40	200
	Shaq O'Neal	40	75	75	200
	(H)Akeem Olajuwon	25	40	40	150
	Gary Payton	25	35	35	125
*	Bob Pettit	5	15	15	75
*	Andy Phillip	10	20	15	75
	Scottie Pippen	40	50	50	200
*-D	James Pollard	40	75	50	250
*	Frank Ramsey	5	15	15	75
*	Willis Reed	10	20	20	125
*	Oscar Robertson "Big O"	25	40	40	150
	David Robinson	25	40	40	150
	Dennis Rodman	50	75	75	250
*	Bill Russell	75	125	100	350
	Cazzie Russell	5	15	15	75
*	Dolph Schayes	10	20	15	100
*	William Sharman	10	25	20	150
	John Stockton	25	40	35	150
	Isiah Thomas	25	40	40	150
*	Nate Thurmond	5	15	15	100
	Rudy Tomjanovich	10	15	15	75
*	Jack Twyman	5	15	15	75
*	Wes Unseld	5	15	15	100
*	Bill Walton	20	40	35	175
	Chris Webber	20	35	35	125
*	Jerry West	20	40	40	150
	Paul Westphal	10	20	15	100
	Dominique Wilkins	20	35	30	125
*	Lenny Wilkins	10	25	20	100
*-C	John Wooden	20	40	40	150
	James Worthy	20	35	35	125
	Max Zaslofsky	20	35	35	125

		3X5 CARD	PHOTO	DS/TLS	SIG FBC	GL ART	COVER
*	Herb Adderly	5	10		10	25	15
	Troy Aikman	30	40		30		50
	Marcus Allen	20	30		20		35
*	Lance Alworth	10	20		15	25	25
D	Lyle Alzado	50	100		100		150
D	Alan Ameche	40	100		100		150
*	Doug Atkins	5	10		10	20	15
*-D	Red Badgro	10	25		20	45	30
*	Lem Barney	10	15		15	25	20
*-D	Cliff Battles	50	250		100		150
*	Sammy Baugh	25	50		50	45	50
*	Chuck Bednarik	8	15		15	25	15
*-D	Bert Bell	200	500	500			
*	Bobby Bell	10	15		10	25	20
*	Raymond Berry	10	15		10	25	20
*-D	Charles Bidwill	500		2500			
*	Fred Biletnikoff	10	15		10	25	20
*	George Blanda	10	20		15	35	25
	Drew Bledsoe	20	30		15		40
*	Mel Blount	12	20		15	25	20
*	Terry Bradshaw	30	50		25	60	50
	John Brodie	15	25		20		25
*	Jim Brown	35	60		30	40	75
*-D	Paul Brown	50	100	200	60		150
*	Roosevelt Brown	10	20		10	25	20
	Tim Brown (Raiders)	10	20		15		20
*	Willie Brown	5	12		10	20	15
	Mark Brunell	25	35		25		40
*-D	Buck Buchanan	25	50		50	75	50
*	Nick Buoniconti	5	15		10		20
*	Dick Butkus	20	25		15	40	30
*	Earl Campbell	10	20		20	30	25
*	Tony Canadeo	5	12		10	20	15
*-D	Joe Carr	600		1500			
	Chris Carter	15	25		20		30
*-D	Guy Chamberlin	200	350	500			
*-D	Jack Christensen	50	150		75		150
*-D	"Dutch" Clark	65	200		150		150
D	Charles Conerly	25	75		50		50
*	George Connor	5	12		10	20	15
*-D	Jim Conzelman	300	750	1000			
	Tim Couch	20	40		20		40
*	Lou Creekmur	5	12		10	20	15
*	Larry Csonka	15	30		15	40	35
	Randall Cunningham	20	30		15		35
*	Al Davis	150	300	500	100	500	250
	Terrell Davis	20	35		25		40
*	Willie Davis	10	20		10	25	20
*	Lenny Dawson	10	20		20	25	25
*	Eric Dickerson	20	30		20	40	30
*	Dan Dierdorf (Also MNF)	20	35		20	40	35
*	Mike Ditka	12	20		20	25	25
*	Art Donovan	15	25		20	30	25
*	Tony Dorsett	15	30		25	30	35
*-D	"Paddy" Driscoll	275	500	500			
	Fred Dryer (Also Actor)	15	30		15		30
*	Bill Dudley	5	12		10	20	15

		3X5 CARD	PHOTO	DS/TLS	SIG FBC	GL ART	COVER
*-D	Al "Turk" Edwards	150	350	400			250
	Carl Eller	10	15		10		15
	John Elway	40	75		35		75
*-D	Weeb Ewbank	25	40		35	50	40
	Marshall Faulk	20	35		25		40
	Brett Favre	30	50		40		50
*-D	Tom Fears	5	12		10	20	15
*-D	Jim Finks	150	300	500	350		50
*-D	Ray Flaherty	25	50		40	75	20
*-D	Lenny Ford	500	1000	1000	500		750
	Doug Flutie	20	35		25		40
*-D	Dan Fortmann	30	50		75	75	50
*	Dan Fouts	15	25		25	30	30
	Roman Gabriel	5	12		10		15
*	Frank Gatski	5	12		10	20	15
*-D	Bill George	100	250		100		200
	Eddie George	20	35		25		30
	Jeff George	25	40		20		40
*	Joe Gibbs	20	30		25	35	30
*	Frank Gifford	30	50		35	50	50
*	Sid Gillman	5	12		10	25	15
*	Otto Graham	10	25		15	40	25
*-D	"Red" Grange	75	200	250	125	200	175
*	Bud Grant	10	20		15	40	20
	Darrell Green	10	25		15		20
*	Joe Greene	10	20		15	30	25
*	Forrest Gregg	5	12		10	20	15
*	Rosie Grier	15	25		15	30	30
*	Bob Griese	20	35		25	50	40
*-D	Lou Groza	10	20		15	30	20
	Ray Guy	10	15		10		15
*-D	Joe Guyon	50	250	100			200
	Pat Haden	15	25		10		30
	John Hadl	10	20		10		15
*-D	George Halas	50	200	100	100		150
	Charles Haley	10	20		15		20
*	Jack Ham	10	20		10	30	25
*	Franco Harris	15	30		15	40	40
	Bob Hayes	15	25		15		25
*-D	Ed Healy	100	350	300			250
*-D	Mel Hein	15	40		25	200	20
*	Ted Hendricks	15	25		10	40	30
*-D	Pete Henry	350	1000	750			
*-D	Bill Hewitt	250	1000	800			
*-D	Clark Hinkle	50	90	225			50
*	Elroy Hirsch	5	12		12	20	15
*	Paul Hornung	20	30		20	35	30
*	Ken Houston	10	20		10	20	20
*-D	Cal Hubbard	75	250		200		200
*	Sam Huff	10	20		15	25	20
*-D	Don Hutson	25	75		40	75	50
	Bo Jackson	25	50		25		50
	Jimmy Johnson	15	35		20		35
*	John Henry Johnson	5	12		10	20	15
	Keyshawn Johnson	20	35		20		30
*	Charlie Joiner	5	15		10	20	15
*	Deacon Jones	10	20		10	25	20
*	Stan Jones	10	15		10	20	15

		3X5 CARD	PHOTO	DS/TLS	SIG FBC	GL ART	COVER
*-D	Henry Jordan	350	600	1000	450		500
*	Lee Roy Jordan	5	15		10	20	15
*	Sonny Jurgensen	10	20		20	25	25
	Alex Karras	15	25		20		25
	Jim Kelly	20	35		25		40
*	Leroy Kelly	10	20		15	25	25
	Jack Kemp	50	100		75		100
*-D	Walter Kiesling	150	800	400			
*-D	Frank Kinard	100	500	300			
	Jerry Kramer	10	15		10		20
*	Paul Krause	10	15		10	25	15
*-D	Curly Lambeau	250	1000	1000			
*	Jack Lambert	10	20		10	25	20
*-D	Tom Landry	25	50	100	25	75	50
*	Dick Lane	10	15		10	25	20
*	Jim Langer	5	15		10	20	15
*	Willie Lanier	10	15		10	25	20
*	Steve Largent	10	20		15	35	25
*	Yale Lary	10	20		10	25	15
*	Dante Lavelli	5	15		10	20	15
*-D	Bobby Layne	50	200		100		150
*-D	"Tuffy" Leemans	125	500	300	125		250
*	Marv Levy	5	10		15		
*	Bob Lilly	5	15		15	20	15
	Gene Lipscomb	150	300	400	250		350
*	Larry Little	10	15		15	20	20
*-D	Vince Lombardi	250	500	400			500
*	Howie Long (TV)	20	35		35		40
*	Ronnie Lott	15	30		15		30
*-D	Sid Luckman	25	50		40	60	40
*-D	Link Lyman	125	500	400			250
*	Tom Mack	5	12		10	20	15
*	John Mackey	5	12		10	20	15
	John Madden	30	50		30		50
*	Geno Marchetti	10	15		10	20	20
	Peyton Manning	25	40		25		40
	Ed Marinaro(Also Actor)	25	40		20		35
*-D	Tim Mara	400		1500			
*	Wellington Mara	10	25				
	Dan Marino	40	50		30		75
*-D	George P. Marshall	250	800	1000			
	Jim Marshall	10	15		10		15
*	Olle Matson	10	20		15	20	20
*	Dan Maynard	10	20		15	20	20
*	George McAfee	5	12		10	20	15
*	Mike McCormack	5	12		10	20	15
*	Tommy McDonald	5	12		10	20	15
*	Hugh McElhenney	10	15		15	25	15
	Jim McMahon	20	35		20		40
	Steve McNair	15	35		15		30
*-D	John McNally	50	125				125
	Don Meredith	15	25		25		30
*-D	Mike Michalske	50	200				100
*-D	Wayne Millner	75	300	250	150		150
*	Bobby Mitchell	5	12		10	20	15
*	Ron Mix	10	15		15	20	15
	Art Monk	15	25		15		20
*	Joe Montana	40	75		40		75

		3X5 CARD	PHOTO	DS/TLS	SIG FBC	GL ART	COVER
	Warren Moon	15	25		20		30
*	Lenny Moore	10	20		15	20	15
	Craig Morton	10	15		10		15
	Randy Moss	20	40		35		40
*-D	Marion Motley	20	30		40	40	40
*	Mike Munchak	5	10		10		
*	Anthony Munoz	10	15		15	25	20
*-D	George Musso	10	20		25	35	25
*-D	Bronko Nagurski	50	200		100		125
*-D	Earle "Greasy" Neale	150	750	400			275
*	Joe Namath	45	60		40	75	75
*-D	Ernie Nevers	50	250				100
*	Ozzie Newsome	10	20		15	25	20
*-D	Ray Nitschke	15	30		25	50	30
*	Chuck Noll	10	25		15	25	30
*-D	Leo Nomellini	10	20		25	30	25
*	Merlin Olsen	10	25		15	25	25
*	Jim Otto	10	15		10	20	20
*-D	Steven Owen	400	1500	1500			
*	Alan Page	15	25		15	35	25
	Jack Pardee	10	20		15		20
*	Clarence "Ace" Parker	5	12		10	20	15
*	Jim Parker	5	12		10	20	15
	"Babe" Parilli	10	15		15		15
*-D	Walter Payton	75	150		75	125	150
*	Joe Perry	10	20		10	25	20
D	Brian Piccolo	500	1000		750		1000
*	Pete Pihos	5	12		10	20	15
	Jim Plunkett	10	20		15		25
*-D	Hugh Ray	500	1500	2000			
	Andre Reed	10	20		15		25
*-D	Daniel Reeves	100	500	400			300
*	Mel Renfro	10	20		10	20	15
	Jerry Rice	25	50		30		50
*	John Riggins	25	75		75	50	75
*	Jim Ringo	10	20		10	30	20
*	Andy Robustelli	5	12		10	20	15
*-D	Knute Rockne	500	2000	1500			
*-D	Art Rooney	50	150				125
D	Kyle Rote	10	15		25		20
*-D	Pete Rozelle	40	100		75	150	75
*	Bob St.Clair	5	12		10	20	15
	Barry Sanders	30	50		25		40
	Deion Sanders	25	40		25		40
	Warren Sapp	10	20		15		15
*	Gale Sayers	15	30		25	35	35
*	Joe Schmidt	5	12		10	20	15
*	Tex Schramm	5	12		10	20	15
	Junior Seau	10	25		15		25
*	Leroy Selmon	10	20		15	25	25
	Shannon Sharpe	15	30		25		30
*	Billy Shaw	5	12		10	20	15
*	Art Shell	15	25		20	30	25
*	Don Shula	15	25		25	45	40
	Phil Simms	15	30		15		35
*	O.J. Simpson	75	125		75	125	150
*	Mike Singletary	10	20		15	30	25
*	Jackie Slater	5	12		10		20

		3X5 CARD	PHOTO	DS/TLS	SIG FBC	GL ART	COVER
	Bruce Smith	20	30		20		35
	Bubba Smith	10	20		15		20
	Emmitt Smith	25	40		25		40
*	Jackie Smith	5	12		10	20	15
	Steve Spurrier	20	25		25		35
	Ken Stabler	15	25		25		25
*	Bart Starr	20	30		35	75	35
*	Roger Staubach	15	30		25	50	35
*	Ernie Stautner	5	12		10	20	15
*	Jan Stenerud	10	20		12	20	20
*	Dwight Stephenson	10	15		15	25	15
*-D	Ken Strong	75	200	250	100		150
*-D	Joe Stydahar	65	250	250	150		150
*	Lynn Swann	20	35		25		35
	George Taliaferro	5	12		10		15
*	Fran Tarkenton	20	35		20	40	40
*	Charlie Taylor	10	20		15	25	20
*	Jim Taylor	10	20		15	25	20
*	Lawrence Taylor	25	35		25	50	50
	Vinny Testaverde	15	25		15		30
	Joe Theismann	15	35		15		40
D	Derrick Thomas	25	75		60		75
	Thurman Thomas	15	30		15		40
*-D	Jim Thorpe	750	2000	5000			1500
*	Y.A. Tittle	10	25		15	30	25
*-D	George Trafton	200	500	500			400
*	Charley Trippi	5	12		10	20	15
*-D	Emlen Tunnell	100	200	300	125		200
*-D	"Bulldog" Turner	20	40		40	60	50
*	Johnny Unitas	15	30		30	50	40
*	Gene Upshaw	10	20		15	25	25
*-D	Norman Van Brocklin	60	250	200	150		200
*	Steve VanBuren	12	25		15	20	25
*-D	Doak Walker	15	35		25	25	35
	Herschel Walker	20	30		20		35
*	Bill Walsh	25	40		25	50	40
*	Paul Warfield	10	20		15	20	20
	Kurt Warner	20	40		35		40
*-D	Bob Waterfield	50	175		100		150
	Ricky Watters	10	25		15		25
*	Mike Webster	10	20		15	25	20
*	Arnie Weinmeister	10	20		10	25	20
	Danny White	10	20		12		20
*	Randy White	10	20		15	25	20
	Reggie White	15	30		20		30
*	Bill Willis	10	15		10	20	15
*	Larry Wilson	10	15		10	25	15
*	Kellen Winslow	10	25		15	25	25
*-D	Alex Wojciechowicz	15	40		20	1000	40
*	Willie Wood	10	20		10	25	20
	Rob Woodson	10	20		15		25
*	Ron Yary	5	12		10		20
	Steve Young	25	45		35		50
*	Jack Youngblood	10	15		10		15

COLLEGE FOOTBALL	3x5 CARD	PHOTO	COVER
D Harry Agganis	100	500	500
"Reds" Bagnell	10	25	20
Angelo Bertelli	15	30	25
"Doc" Blanchard	20	30	35
Bobby Bowden	10	20	20
Frank Broyles	10	20	20
D Paul Bear Bryant	50	300	200
John Cappellitti	20	30	35
Hopalong Cassady	10	25	20
D Ernie Davis	500	1500	
Glenn Davis	10	25	20
Dan Devine	20	30	30
D George Gipp			
"The Gipper"	1000		
D Tom Harmon	25	75	75
D Woody Hayes	100	250	200
D John Heisman	2000		
D Vic Janowicz	20	50	40
D Johnny Lattner	15	30	25
D Elmer Layden	50	125	100
D Frank Leahy	60	150	125
Johnny Lujack	10	20	25
Tom Osborne	15	25	30
Ara Parseghian	10	20	20
Joseph Paterno	25	50	50
D Fritz Pollard	100	250	
Mike Reid	10	25	20
Eddie Robinson			
(Grambling)	20	30	40
Darrell Royal	10	20	20
Bo Schembechler	15	25	30
D Amos Alonzo Stagg	100	400	
D "Pop" Warner	150	400	
D Bud Wilkinson	25	50	50

BOXING	3x5 CARD	PHOTO	COVER
Muhammad Ali	50	75	75
Ray Arcel	10	25	25
Alexis Arguello	15	35	25
D Henry Armstrong	100	200	
Bob Arum			
D Abe Attel	100	250	
D Max Baer	150	500	
Wilfredo Benitez	10	25	20
Riddick Bowe	10	25	25
D James J. Braddock	300	600	
D Tommy Burns	400	1000	
Hector Macho			
Man Camacho	15	35	30
D Tony Canzoneri	75	200	
D Primo Carnera	200	400	
D Marcel Cerdan	500	1500	
D Ezzard Charles	150	300	
Julio"Cesar"Chavez	20	40	40
D "Kid" Chocolate	200	400	
Gil Clancy			
Cassius Clay	100	250	200
D Billy Conn	35	100	
Gerry Cooney	10	15	15

BOXING (cont.)	3x5 CARD	PHOTO	COVER
D James J. Corbett	500	1000	
D Cus D'Amato			
Oscar De Lahoya	25	50	50
D Jack Dempsey	100	250	150
Angelo Dundee	10	20	20
D Johnny Dundee			
Roberto Duran	20	45	40
D Bob Fitzsimmons	3000		
George Foreman	25	40	40
Joe Frazier	10	25	25
Eddie Futch			
D Kid Galivan	20	40	40
D Joe Gans	1000		
Joey Giardello	10	25	25
D Rocky Graziano	40	100	75
Marvin Hagler	15	30	25
D Marvin Hart	2000		
Thomas Hearns	15	35	30
Larry Holmes	15	35	30
Evander Holyfield	25	50	40
D James J. Jeffries	500	1250	
Ingemar Johansson	20	40	40
D Jack Johnson	1000	2000	
Roy Jones Jr.	20	40	40
Don King	15	35	30
Jake Lamotta	15	30	30
"Sugar Ray" Leonard	20	40	35
Lennox Lewis	15	35	30
D Sonny Liston	500	1250	
D Joe Louis	250	500	
D Rocky Marciano	500	1250	
D Joey Maxim	10	30	25
D "Kid"McCoy(The Real)			
Arthur Mercante			
D Carlos Monzon	75	200	150
Archie Moore	15	35	30
Ken Norton	15	35	30
Floyd Patterson	15	35	30
Eusebio Pedroza	10	25	20
Willie Pep	10	25	20
Aaron Pryor	15	35	30
D Jerry Quarry	25	50	50
D Tex Rickard	225	500	
D Sugar Ray Robinson	75	200	125
Luis Rodriquez	15	35	30
D Maxie Rosenbloom	50	100	75
D Barney Ross	50	100	75
Mike Rossman	10	25	20
D Salvador Sanchez	50	125	
D Max Schmeling	25	50	50
Jack Sharkey	40	75	60
Michael Spinks	20	45	35
Leon Spinks	10	25	20
Emanuel Steward			
D John L. Sullivan	1500		
D Lew Tendler			
Gene Tunney	100	250	150
Mike Tyson	40	75	60
D Pancho Villa	50	125	75

BOXING (cont.)		3x5 CARD	PHOTO	COVER
D	Jersey Joe Walcott	40	100	75
D	Mickey Walker	60	175	
D	Jess Willard	300	750	
	Ike Williams	15	35	30
D	Tony Zale	15	30	25

GOLF		3x5 CARD	PHOTO	COVER
D	Tommy Armour	400	800	
	Paul Azinger	10	25	20
	Seve Ballestros	10	25	20
	Jerry Barber	5	20	20
	Miller Barber	10	25	20
LPGA	Patty Berg	10	20	20
LPGA	Pat Bradley	10	20	20
*	Jack Burke JR	20	40	50
LPGA	Donna Caponi	10	20	20
LPGA	JoAnne Carner	10	20	20
	Billy Casper	10	20	20
*	Harry Cooper	20	40	30
	Fred Couples	20	35	35
	Ben Crenshaw	15	35	30
LPGA	Beth Daniel	10	20	20
*	Jimmy Demaret	175	500	
	David Duval	25	40	50
	Lee Elder	10	20	20
	Ernie Els	10	25	25
	Nick Faldo	20	30	35
	Ray Floyd	20	30	35
	Sergio Garcia	20	50	40
*-D	Ralph Guldahl	175	350	
*-D	Walter Hagen	750	2000	
LPGA	Sandra Haynie	10	20	20
*-D	Ben Hogan	75	250	150
LPGA	Julie Inkster	10	20	20
	Hale Irwin	10	25	25
D	Tony Jacklin	15	30	30
LPGA	Betty Jameson	10	20	20
*-D	Bobby Jones	1500	3000	
	Robert Trent Jones	35	75	50
LPGA	Betsy King	10	20	20
	Tom Kite	10	25	25
	Tom Lehman	10	25	25
	Justin Leonard	10	35	30
D	Lawson Little	75	200	150
*	Gene Littler	15	30	20
*-D	Bobby Locke	200	500	
LPGA	Nancy Lopez-Knight	20	35	40
	Davis Love III	10	25	25
LPGA	Carol Mann	10	20	20
	Phil Mickelson	15	30	30
	Johnny Miller	10	25	25
	Dr. Gil Morgan	5	20	20
*	Byron Nelson	20	40	50
*	Jack Nicklaus	50	75	75
	Greg Norman	35	50	50
	Jose Maria Olazabel	10	25	25
	Mark O'Meara	10	25	25
*-D	Francis Ouimet	500	1250	
	Arnie Palmer	40	75	75

GOLF (cont.)		3x5 CARD	PHOTO	COVER
	Gary Player	15	30	30
	Nick Price	10	25	25
LPGA	Judy Rankin	10	20	20
LPGA	Betsy Rawls	10	20	20
	Chi Chi Rodriguez	15	25	25
*	Gene Sarazen	15	30	30
LPGA	Patti Sheehan	10	20	20
	Charlie Sifford	5	20	20
	Vijay Singh	10	25	25
D	Horton Smith	500	1000	750
	Sam Snead	20	40	40
LPGA	Annika Sorenstam	10	25	25
	Craig Stadler	10	20	25
LPGA	Jan Stephenson	15	40	30
D	Payne Stewart	50	150	125
	Curtis Strange	10	25	25
	Hal Sutton	10	25	25
	Lee Travino	20	40	35
*-D	Harry Vardon	1000	2500	
	Ken Venturi	15	30	30
	Lanny Wadkins	10	20	20
	Tom Watson	20	30	30
	Tom Weiskopf	5	20	20
LPGA	Kathy Whitworth	10	20	20
	Tiger Woods	300	500	450
LPGA	Mickey Wright	25	50	50
*-D	Babe Zaharias(L)	1000	2000	
	Fuzzy Zoeller	10	20	20

HOCKEY		3X5 CARD	PHOTO	COVER
*-D	Syl Apps	15	40	30
*-D	Ace Bailey	75	275	
*	Bill Barber	5	20	15
*	Jean Beliveau	10	25	25
*-D	Toe Blake	75	150	150
*-D	Mike Bossy	10	25	25
	Ray Bourque	25	35	35
*	Scotty Bowman	30	50	40
	Martin Brodeur	15	35	30
*	Johnny Bucyk	5	15	20
*-D	Clarence Campbell	400		
*-D	King Clancy	125	400	
*-D	Bobby Clarke	15	20	30
	Paul Coffey	20	35	35
*	Yvan Cournoyer	10	25	25
	John Davidson	10	25	25
*	Marcel Dionne	10	25	20
*	Ken Dryden	25	40	50
*	Phil Esposito	20	25	35
*	Tony Esposito	15	25	25
	Sergei Federov	25	40	50
	Grant Fuhr	20	35	40
*	Rod Gilbert	10	25	25
*	Ed Giacomin	10	25	25
*	Wayne Gretzky	75	75	250
*-D	Gene Hart	15	30	25
*-D	Doug Harvey	150	275	
	Dominik Hasek	25	40	50
*-D	Bryan Hextall	50	100	125

HOCKEY (cont.)

		3X5 CARD	PHOTO	COVER
*-D	Tim Horton	250	500	500
*	Gordie Howe	35	50	50
*	Bobby Hull	25	40	40
	Brett Hull	15	30	40
*-D	Punch Imlach	30	75	
	Jaromir Jagr	25	40	40
*	Dave Keon	10	25	25
	Guy Lafleur	15	25	25
*	Mario Lemieux	30	50	75
	Eric Lindros	30	50	50
	Mark Messier	40	75	75
*	Stan Mikita	10	20	20
*-D	Howie Morenz	1000		
*	Bobby Orr	30	50	50
*	Bernie Parent	10	15	20
*	Brad Park	10	20	20
*-D	Frank Patrick	100		
*-D	Lester Patrick	250		
*-D	Jacques Plante	150	500	300
*	Maurice Richard	15	25	25
	Patrick Roy	25	35	35
	Joe Sakic	15	25	25
*	Glenn Sather	10	25	25
*-D	Terry Sawchuk	250	500	500
*-D	Eddie Shore	125	300	250
*	Darryl Sittler	15	25	25
*	Billy Smith	10	25	25
*-D	Conn Smythe	250		
*	Allan Stanley	10	25	25
*-D	Lord Stanley of Preston	1500		
*	Peter Stastny	15	30	25
*	Vladislav Tretiak	20	40	40
*	Bryan Trottier	10	20	20
*-D	Georges Vezina	600	2000	
*	Gump Worsley	10	25	25
	Steve Yzerman	20	30	30

TENNIS

		3X5 CARD	PHOTO	COVER
	Andre Agassi	50	75	75
D	Arthur Ashe	100	250	200
	Boris Becker	25	40	40
	Bjorn Borg	20	40	40
	Don Budge	20	35	40
	Jennifer Capriati	10	25	25
	Michael Chang	15	30	30
	Jimmy Connors	30	50	45
	Margaret Court	15	30	25
	Lindsay Davenport	15	30	30
	Chris Evert	15	30	30
D	Vitas Gerulaitis	50	125	100
	Althea Gibson	30	75	50
	Steffi Graf	30	50	50
	Martina Hingis	20	40	40
	Helen Jacobs	35	75	50
	Billy Jean King	15	30	30
	Anna Kournikova	25	50	50
	Rod Laver	10	25	25
	Ivan Lendl	25	40	40
	John McEnroe	30	50	50

TENNIS (cont.)

		3X5 CARD	PHOTO	COVER
	Ile Nastase	25	40	40
	Martina Navratilova	25	40	40
	John Newcombe	10	25	25
	Pat Rafter	10	25	25
D	Bobby Riggs	40	100	100
	Gabriella Sabatini	20	35	30
	Peter Sampras	40	65	50
	Monica Seles	25	45	35
*-D	Bill Tilden	300	600	500
	Mats Wilander	5	20	25
	Serena Williams	25	50	40
	Venus Williams	25	50	40

MISC. SPORTS

		3X5 CARD	PHOTO	COVER
	Bobby Allison	10	25	20
	Mario Andretti	20	40	30
	Roger Bannister	10	25	20
D	Dale Earnhardt	40	100	75
	Peggy Fleming	25	40	30
	A.J. Foyt	15	35	25
	Curt Gowdy	20	40	30
	Andy Granatelli	20	40	30
	Sonja Henie	75	200	125
D	Graham Hill	75	125	100
D	Willie Hoppe	125	300	
	Bruce Jenner	25	40	35
	Rafer Johnson	15	35	25
	Parnelli Jones	15	30	20
	Evel Knievel	40	75	50
	Carl Lewis	40	75	50
	Greg Louganis	25	50	40
	Bob Mathias	15	35	30
	Jim Mckay	10	30	20
	Minnesota Fats	50	125	75
	Willie Mosconi	25	50	35
	Brent Musburger	15	35	25
D	Barney Oldfield	300	750	
D	Jessie Owens	125	500	200
D	Johnny Parsons	50	100	75
	Pele	40	100	75
	Richard Petty	25	50	35
	Cathy Rigby	10	25	20
	Jim Ryun	10	25	20
	Alberto Salazar	10	25	20
	Vin Scully	25	50	40
	Willie Shoemaker	50	100	75
	Mark Spitz	20	40	30
	Danny Sullivan	15	25	20
	Al Unser	20	35	30
	Bobby Unser	20	35	30

Looking For Those Missing Stamps, Covers & Supplies
And At Bargain Prices Too !!!
Do You Enjoy Great Articles From The Leading Philatelic Writers?
You'll Find The Answer In The

BROOKMAN TIMES

"The Brookman Times" is published 6 times a year and has ads from leading stamp dealers and aticles from leading Philatelic writers, such as Les Winick, Marjory Sente & George Griffenhagen. There are bargains galore and of particular note is that only dealers who advertise in the Brookman Price Guide can advertise in "The Brookman Times". We feel these dealers are the "cream of the crop" and can heartily endorse them.

SOME OF THE LEADING DEALERS YOU WILL FIND IN "THE BROOKMAN TIMES"

Alexander Autographs
American First Day Cover Society
American Philatelic Society
American Stamp Dealer Assoc.
American Topical Assoc.
Artmaster, Incorporated
BJ's Stamps
Brookman/Barrett & Worthen
Brookman Cover Co.
Brookman Stamp Co.
Champion Stamp Co., Inc.
Dale Enterprises, Inc.
Eric Jackson
Greg Tucker
Henry Gitner Philatelists, Inc.
Michael Jaffe Stamps, Inc.
Kenmore Stamp Co.

Krause Publications
Linn's Stamp News
James T. McCusker, Inc.
Alan Miller Stamps
Mystic Stamp Co.
Phillip Marks
Plate Block Stamp Co.
Gary Posner, Inc.
Profiles in History
Regency Stamps, Ltd.
R & R Enterprises
Scott Publishing
Scott Winslow Assoc.
Stamp Collector
Superior Galleries
Vidiforms Co., Inc.

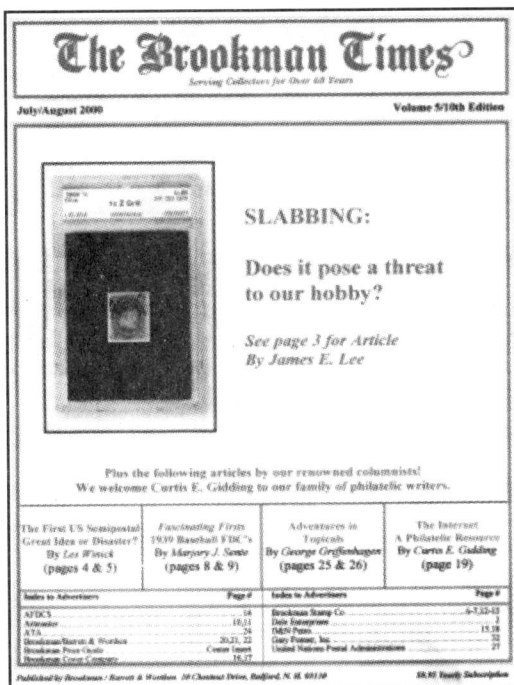

Now You Can Get This $11.95 Value FREE !!!

Everyone who purchases a Brookman Price Guide can receive the **"Brookman Times" FREE**.
All you have to do is fill out the coupon below (or a copy of the coupon).
(If you purchased your copy directly from Brookman/Barrett & Worthen you will automatically receive the "Brookman Times".)

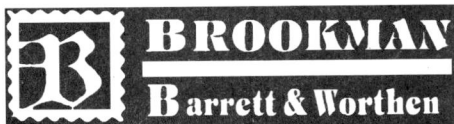

BROOKMAN
Barrett & Worthen

Dept. - PG
10 Chestnut Drive
Bedford, NH 03110

E-mail: sales@coverspecialist.com
www.coverspecialist.com

☐ Please send me 6 issues of the "Brookman Times".
(I am enclosing $3.00 for Postage & Handling)

Name : _____

Address : _____

_____

NO PHONE ORDERS PLEASE - MAIL ONLY

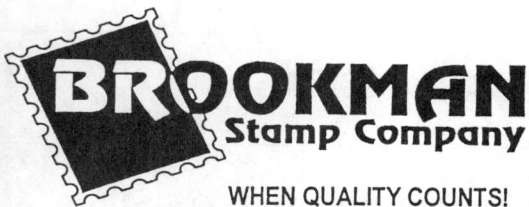

340

$5 THIS COUPON **$5**
IS WORTH
$5.00
Towards any First Day Cover order over
$55.00 from this
2002 Brookman Price Guide

ONE COUPON PER ORDER

Brookman Cover Company

P.O. Box 6208
Louisville, KY 40206

$5 **$5**

$10 THIS COUPON **$10**
IS WORTH
$10.00
Towards any First Day Cover order over
$110.00 from this
2002 Brookman Price Guide

ONE COUPON PER ORDER

Brookman Cover Company

P.O. Box 6208
Louisville, KY 40206

$10 **$10**

$10 THIS COUPON **$10**
IS WORTH
$10.00
Towards any First Day Cover order over
$110.00 from this
2002 Brookman Price Guide

ONE COUPON PER ORDER

Brookman Cover Company

P.O. Box 6208
Louisville, KY 40206

$10 **$10**

$10 THIS COUPON **$10**
IS WORTH
$10.00
Towards any First Day Cover order over
$110.00 from this
2002 Brookman Price Guide

ONE COUPON PER ORDER

Brookman Cover Company

P.O. Box 6208
Louisville, KY 40206

$10 **$10**

$25 THIS COUPON **$25**
IS WORTH
$25.00
Towards any First Day Cover order over
$275.00 from this
2002 Brookman Price Guide

ONE COUPON PER ORDER

Brookman Cover Company

P.O. Box 6208
Louisville, KY 40206

$25 **$25**

$40 THIS COUPON **$40**
IS WORTH
$40.00
Towards any First Day Cover order over
$450.00 from this
2002 Brookman Price Guide

ONE COUPON PER ORDER

Brookman Cover Company

P.O. Box 6208
Louisville, KY 40206

$40 **$40**

HOW TO WRITE YOUR COVER ORDER—PLEASE USE THE ORDER BLANK

Please send the items listed below for which I enclose: $ __128.00__   Date: __8/2/2001__

SHIP TO: **CREDIT CARD BILLING ADDRESS:**

Name: __Rebecca Ryan__

Address: __PO Box 77__

City: __Franklin__   City: _____

State: __MA__   Zip: __01842__   State: _____ Zip: _____

Phone: __(999)555-1234__   Please charge my: Visa _____ MasterCard _____ __✓__ Check Enclosed.

Card#: _____   Expiration Date: _____

From Page	Qty. Wanted	Country and items ordered: Specify Scott Numbers plus first day cover, souvenir card, plate block, mint sheet or other description	Quality Wanted	Unused	Used	Price Each	Leave Blank
153	1	1030-53 FDC Set of 27, Cacheted				100.00	
156	1	1381 FDC Cacheted				12.00	
171	1	3499 Convertible Booklet					
		Pane of 20 Cacheted				20.00	

1. Fill out date, phone#.

2. Print name and address, information including ZIP CODE. Please make sure to include your credit card billing address.

3. Note Minimum order of $20.00.

4. If ordering by Visa or Mastercard, please indicate charge # and expiration date.

5. If paying by check, please make payments in U.S. Funds.

6. Example of how to write up your orders above.

PAY SHIPPING/INSURANCE AS FOLLOWS:

Stamps only - $ 4.00

Other orders:

$20.00 to $49.99 - $ 4.00
$50.00 to $199.99 - $ 6.00
$200.00 & over - $ 8.00

Total this page	132 00
Total from reverse	
Shipping/Insurance (see chart at left)	6 00
SUBTOTAL	138 00
Sales Tax (if any)	
Less any discounts, refund checks, coupons etc.	- (10 00)
TOTAL ENCLOSED	128 00

SATISFACTION GUARANTEED
MINIMUM ORDER MUST TOTAL AT LEAST $20.00
On orders outside the U.S. additional postage will be billed if necessary

$5 THIS COUPON **$5**
IS WORTH $5.00
Towards any stamp order over $55.00 from
this 2002 Brookman Price Guide

ONE COUPON PER ORDER

Available from:

Brookman Stamp Co.
Vancouver, WA
98666-0090

$5 **$5**

$10 THIS COUPON **$10**
IS WORTH $10.00
Towards any stamp order over $110.00 from
this 2002 Brookman Price Guide

ONE COUPON PER ORDER

Available from:

Brookman Stamp Co.
Vancouver, WA
98666-0090

$10 **$10**

$10 THIS COUPON **$10**
IS WORTH $10.00
Towards any stamp order over $110.00 from
this 2002 Brookman Price Guide

ONE COUPON PER ORDER

Available from:

Brookman Stamp Co.
Vancouver, WA
98666-0090

$10 **$10**

$10 THIS COUPON **$10**
IS WORTH $10.00
Towards any stamp order over $110 from
this 2002 Brookman Price Guide

ONE COUPON PER ORDER

Available from:

Brookman Stamp Co.
Vancouver, WA
98666-0090

$10 **$10**

$25 THIS COUPON **$25**
IS WORTH $25.00
Towards any stamp order over $275.00 from
this 2002 Brookman Price Guide

ONE COUPON PER ORDER

Available from:

Brookman Stamp Co.
Vancouver, WA
98666-0090

$25 **$25**

$40 THIS COUPON **$40**
IS WORTH $40.00
Towards any stamp order over $450.00 from
this 2002 Brookman Price Guide

ONE COUPON PER ORDER

Available from:

Brookman Stamp Co.
Vancouver, WA
98666-0090

$40 **$40**

HOW TO WRITE YOUR STAMP ORDER—PLEASE USE THE ORDER BLANK

Please send the items listed below for which I enclose: $ _____   Date: 6/15/2001

SHIP TO:

Name: JEFFREY Roberts

Address: 42 EVERGREEN ROAD

City: WEST HARTFORD

State: CT   Zip: 06321

Phone: (999) 444-7777

Card#: 4432-998-321-640

CREDIT CARD BILLING ADDRESS:

City: _____

State: _____ Zip: _____

Please charge my: Visa _____ MasterCard ✓ _____ Check Enclosed.

Expiration Date: 11/03

From Page	Qty. Wanted	Country and items ordered: Specify Scott Numbers plus first day cover, souvenir card, plate block, mint sheet or other description	Quality Wanted	Unused	Used	Price Each	Leave Blank
21	1	803-34 set of 32	FVFNH			185.00	
21	1	855 PLATE BLOCK	FVFNH			11.00	
188	1	B253 SOUVENIR CARD	MINT			12.00	

1. Fill out date, phone#.
2. Print name and address, information including ZIP CODE. Please make sure to include your credit card billing address.
3. Note Minimum order of $20.00.

4. If ordering by Visa or Mastercard, please indicate charge # and expiration date.
5. If paying by check, please make payments in U.S. Funds.
6. Example of how to write up your orders above.

PAY SHIPPING/INSURANCE AS FOLLOWS:

Stamps only - $ 4.00

Other orders:

$20.00 to $49.99 - $ 4.00
$50.00 to $199.99 - $ 6.00
$200.00 & over - $ 8.00

Total this page	208.00
Total from reverse	
Shipping/Insurance (see chart at left)	8.00
SUBTOTAL	216.00
Sales Tax (if any)	
Less any discounts, refund checks, (coupons) etc.	- (10.00)
TOTAL ENCLOSED	206.00

SATISFACTION GUARANTEED
MINIMUM ORDER MUST TOTAL AT LEAST $20.00
On orders outside the U.S. additional postage will be billed if necessary

EASY ORDER FORM – 2002 EDITION

Please send the items listed below for which I enclose: $_____ Date:_____

SHIP TO:

Name: _____

Address: _____

City:_____

State: _____ Zip:_____

Phone: _____

Card#:_____

CREDIT CARD BILLING ADDRESS:

_____

_____

City:_____

State: _____ _____ Zip:_____

Please charge my: Visa_____ MasterCard_____ _____Check Enclosed.

Expiration Date:_____

MINIMUM ORDER MUST BE $20.00

From Page #	Quantity Wanted	Country and items ordered: Specify Scott Numbers plus first day cover, souvenir card, plate block, mint sheet or other description	Quality Wanted	Unused	Used	Price Each	Leave Blank

PAY SHIPPING/INSURANCE AS FOLLOWS:

Stamps only - $ 4.00
Other orders:
$20.00 to $49.99 - $ 4.00
$50.00 to $199.99 - $ 6.00
$200.00 & over - $ 8.00

Total this page

Total from reverse

Total from reverse

Shipping/Insurance (see chart at left)

SUBTOTAL

Sales Tax (if any)

Less any discounts, refund checks, coupons, etc.

TOTAL ENCLOSED

SATISFACTION GUARANTEED
MINIMUM ORDER MUST TOTAL AT LEAST $20.00
On orders outside the U.S. additional postage will be billed if necessary

Easy Order Form (continued)

From Page #	Quantity Wanted	Country and items ordered: Specify Scott Numbers plus first day cover, souvenir card, plate block, mint sheet or other description	Quality Wanted	Unused	Used	Price Each	Leave Blank
				Total This Page			

EASY ORDER FORM – 2002 EDITION

Please send the items listed below for which I enclose: $_____ Date:_____

SHIP TO: **CREDIT CARD BILLING ADDRESS:**

Name: _____   _____

Address: _____   _____

City:_____   City:_____

State: _____ Zip:_____   State: _____ _____ Zip:_____

Phone: _____ Please charge my: Visa_____ MasterCard_____ _____Check Enclosed.

Card#:_____   Expiration Date:_____

MINIMUM ORDER MUST BE $20.00

From Page #	Quantity Wanted	Country and items ordered: Specify Scott Numbers plus first day cover, souvenir card, plate block, mint sheet or other description	Quality Wanted	Unused	Used	Price Each	Leave Blank

PAY SHIPPING/INSURANCE AS FOLLOWS:

Stamps only - $ 4.00
Other orders:
$20.00 to $49.99 - $ 4.00
$50.00 to $199.99 - $ 6.00
$200.00 & over - $ 8.00

Total this page _____

Total from reverse _____

Total from reverse _____

Shipping/Insurance (see chart at left _____

SUBTOTAL _____

Sales Tax (if any) _____

Less any discounts, refund checks, coupons, etc. _____

TOTAL ENCLOSED

SATISFACTION GUARANTEED
MINIMUM ORDER MUST TOTAL AT LEAST $20.00
On orders outside the U.S. additional postage will be billed if necessary

347

From Page #	Quantity Wanted	Country and items ordered: Specify Scott Numbers plus first day cover, souvenir card, plate block, mint sheet or other description	Quality Wanted	Unused	Used	Price Each	Leave Blank
			Total This Page				

EASY ORDER FORM – 2002 EDITION

Please send the items listed below for which I enclose: $_____   Date:_____

SHIP TO: **CREDIT CARD BILLING ADDRESS:**
Name: _____   _____
Address: _____   _____
City:_____   City:_____
State: _____ Zip:_____   State: _____ _____ Zip:_____

Phone: _____ Please charge my: Visa_____ MasterCard_____ _____Check Enclosed.
Card#:_____   Expiration Date:_____

MINIMUM ORDER MUST BE $20.00

From Page #	Quantity Wanted	Country and items ordered: Specify Scott Numbers plus first day cover, souvenir card, plate block, mint sheet or other description	Quality Wanted	Unused	Used	Price Each	Leave Blank

PAY SHIPPING/INSURANCE AS FOLLOWS:

Stamps only - $ 4.00
Other orders:
$20.00 to $49.99 - $ 4.00
$50.00 to $199.99 - $ 6.00
$200.00 & over - $ 8.00

Total this page _____
Total from reverse _____
Total from reverse _____
Shipping/Insurance (see chart at left _____
SUBTOTAL
Sales Tax (if any) _____
Less any discounts, refund checks, coupons, etc. _____
TOTAL ENCLOSED

SATISFACTION GUARANTEED
MINIMUM ORDER MUST TOTAL AT LEAST $20.00
On orders outside the U.S. additional postage will be billed if necessary

From Page #	Quantity Wanted	Country and items ordered: Specify Scott Numbers plus first day cover, souvenir card, plate block, mint sheet or other description	Quality Wanted	Unused	Used	Price Each	Leave Blank
			Total This Page				

The Brookman Post Dispatch Subscription Offer

Here's your chance to see photos of the best covers in the comfort of your home.

<u>Subscribe Now!</u> to Brookman's newest publication used to highlight only very recent cover purchases. It goes to a limited number of collectors before they are seen by thousands of buyers. This is your chance to get the first shot at buying that special cover you've been hunting for. Featured areas of collecting are: *Zeppelins, Akron-Macons, Patriotics, Flights (including Clipper Flights), Autograph Covers and better FDC's.*

All subscribers will receive their issues via <u>First Class Mail.</u>

ORDER TODAY AND RECIEVE A GIFT CERTIFICATE FOR $20.00
GOOD TOWARDS YOUR FIRST ORDER

- -

The Brookman Post Dispatch Order Form
(10 Issues for $19.95 - Refundable With First Order)

Name:_____

Address:_____

City:_____ State:_____ Zip:_____

Daytime Phone:_____

OR Charge: Visa:_____Mastercard:_____ Card #_____ Expires_____

Check enclosed for $19.95 _____

BROOKMAN
Barrett & Worthen
10 Chestnut Drive   Phone: 1-800-332-3383   email: sales@coverspecialist.com
Bedford, NH 03110   Fax 1-603-472-8795   www.coverspecialist.com

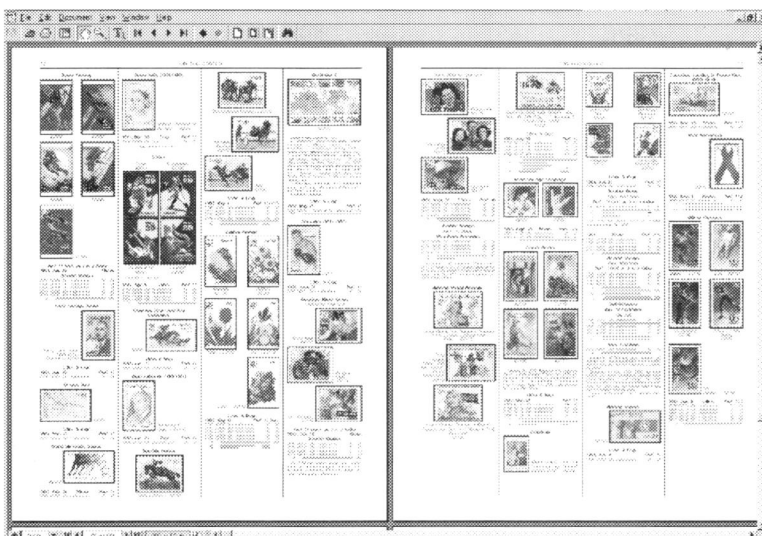

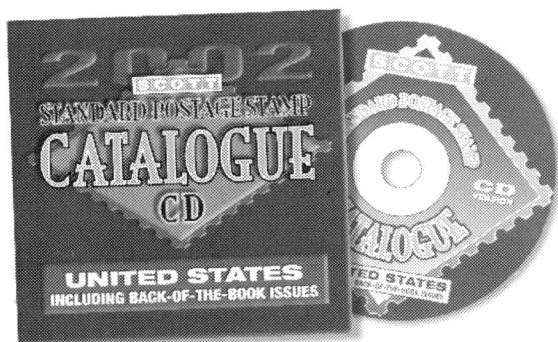

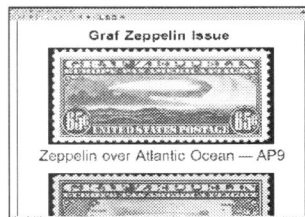

THE BROOKMAN HERITAGE SERIES!

Our Albums are fully illustrated on heavy, artstock pages printed on one side only, showing spaces for singles, plate blocks and first day covers. The 3-ring album binders are elegant, luxuriously padded and lettered in gold. In addition, periodic supplements will keep your albums to date.

BROOKMAN HONORS "AMERICA IN SPACE"

Brookman's America in Space Album pay tribute to America's contribution to the exploration of space.

Volume 1
Complete thru
1994
With Binder
ONLY $39.95
1995-97
SUPPLEMENT
ONLY $5.95

AMERICA IN SPACE

PAYING TRIBUTE TO AMERICA'S CONTRIBUTION IN THE EXPLORATION OF SPACE.

Extra Binders Only $14.95
Blank Pages (20) $5.95

JUST RELEASED!
1998-99 SUPPLEMENT
ONLY $6.95

BROOKMAN'S CHRISTMAS IN AMERICA

Brookman's Christmas in America Album features US stamps issued for the Yuletide Season.
VOLUME I 1962-1979
with binder ONLY $45.95
VOLUME II 1980-1993
with binder ONLY $45.95
1994 SUPPLEMENT
ONLY $6.95
1995 SUPPLEMENT
ONLY $12.95
1996-97 SUPPLEMENT
ONLY $19.95
1998 SUPPLEMENT
ONLY $11.95

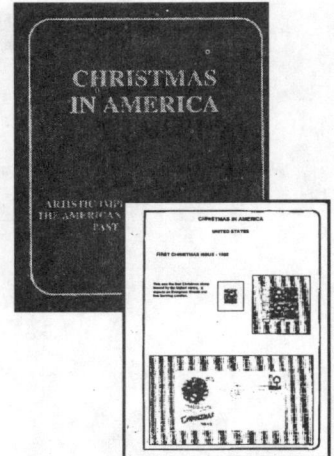

CHRISTMAS IN AMERICA

ARTISTICALLY THE AMERICAS PAST

CHRISTMAS IN AMERICA
UNITED STATES
FIRST CHRISTMAS ISSUE - 1962

Extra Binder $ 14.95
Blank Pages (20) $ 5.95

JUST RELEASED!
1999 SUPPLEMENT
ONLY $6.95

HONORING AMERICA'S BLACK HERITAGE

The Only Catalog of it's kind for this Important and Popular Topic

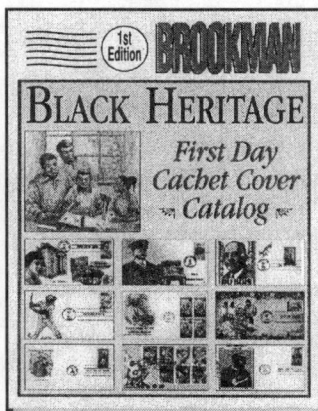

1st Edition BROOKMAN

BLACK HERITAGE
First Day
Cachet Cover
Catalog

(Perfect Bound Only)
$29.95

- ◆ **176 pages** perfect bound with index by Scott number and individual
- ◆ Over **1700 Cachet Illustrations**
- ◆ **Priced by experts** with over 60 years of First Day Cover Experience
- ◆ **$100 in redeemable coupons** toward the purchase of covers from the catalog

Purchase your copy of the **Black Heritage First Day Cachet Cover Catalog** and you can order **Volume I of Brookman's Black Heritage Album** series for only $10.

Brookman's Black Heritage Stamp Album honors the contributions of Black Americans to the development of the nation.

Album thru 1993 with binder
ONLY $39.95
1994 SUPPLEMENT
ONLY $6.95
1995 SUPPLEMENT
ONLY $11.95
1996-97 SUPPLEMENT
ONLY $5.95
1998 SUPPLEMENT
ONLY $11.95
1999 SUPPLEMENT
ONLY $6.95

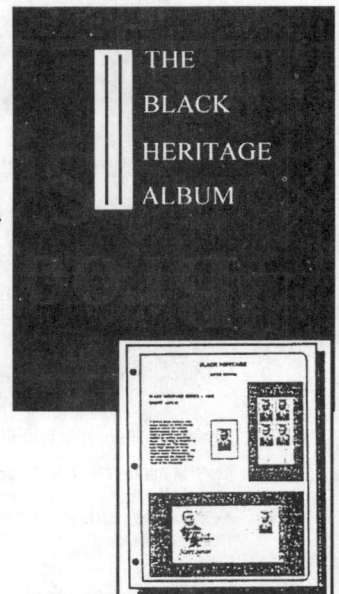

THE BLACK HERITAGE ALBUM

BLACK HERITAGE

Extra Binder $ 14.95
Blank Pages (20) $ 5.95

see ordering info on next page

GREAT PHILATELIC RESOURCES

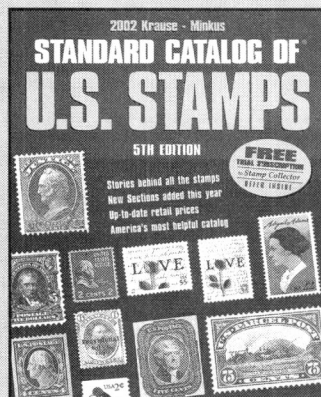

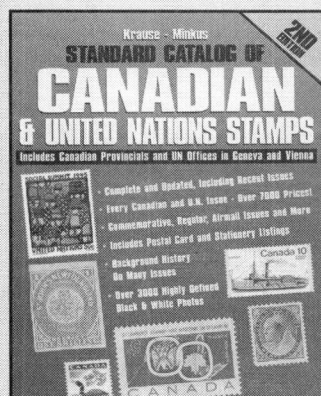

Brookman's Classifieds

Support our Advertisers
Please mention The Brookman Price Guide
when contacting them.

Brookman's Classifieds

Why go elsewhere?

For 85 years philatelists have always turned to our members for Integrity, Honesty, Expertise, Dedication, and Reliability in the stamp business. Whenever you are buying or selling anything philatelic, be sure to look for the familiar ASDA emblem.

Integrity-Honesty
Expertise-Dedication
Hobby Builders-Reliabilty

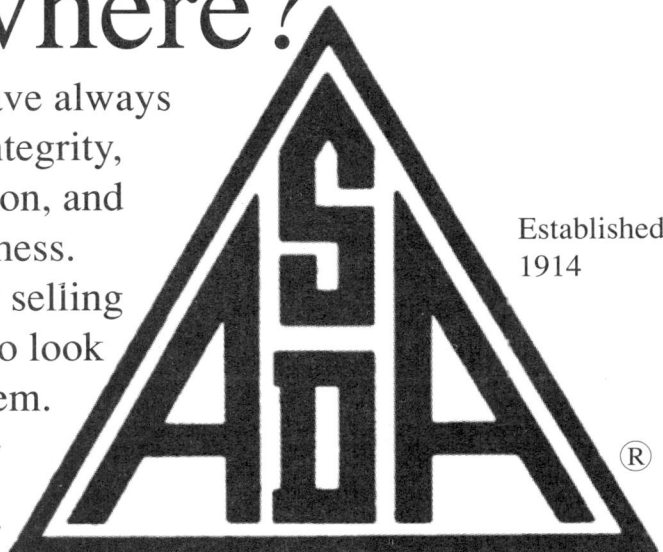

Established 1914

ASDA®

www.asdabourse.com
Our mainsite--find the dealer near you.

Visit us on the Web at:
www.asdaonline.com
1,000's of stamps & covers for sale everyday!

SHOWGARD ®

THE STAMP MOUNTING SPECIALISTS

Item #	QTY	Descripton	Pcs. in Pkg	Price $	Total	Item #	QTY	Descripton	Pcs. in Pkg	Price $	Total
		CUT STYLE				105		UK Blocks, Covers, Cards	10	10.25	
C 50/31		US Jumbo Singles-Horizontal	40	2.95		107		US Plate # Strips (20)	10	10.25	
CV31/50		Same-Vertical	40	2.95		111		US Floating Plate # Strips (20)	5	6.75	
J40/25		US Comm-Horizontal	40	2.95		127		US Modern Definitive Sheets (20)	5	7.75	
JV 25/40		Same-Vertical	40	2.95		137		US SS UK Coronation	5	8.50	
E 22/25		US Regular issues	40	2.95		158		Miniature Sheets, Apollo Soyuz PB	5	9.75	
EH 22/25		Same-Horizontal	40	2.95		175		US Sheets-Pan American reissues	5	10.75	
T 25/27		US Famous Americans	40	2.95		188		US Miniature Shts-Hollywood, etc.	5	11.40	
U 33/27		UN and Germany	40	2.95		198		US Miniature Sheets	5	11.60	
N 40/27		United Nations	40	2.95				**MISCELLANEOUS**			
AH 41/31		US Semi-Jumbo, Horizontal	40	2.95		MPK		Assortment #22-#41	12	4.95	
DH 52/36		US Duck Stamps	40	2.95		MPKII		Assortment #76-#171	15	19.95	
		SETS				Group AB		US SS to 1975, except W. Plains	11	5.50	
US 2		Cut Style with Tray	320	17.75		265/231		Full Sheets and Souvenir Cards	5	14.95	
US 3		Strip Style with Tray	75	26.50				**BLOCKS**			
		PLATE BLOCKS & COVERS				260/25		Plate # Coil Strips	25	8.75	
67/25		US Coil Strips of 3	40	4.95		260/40		US Postal People Full Strip	10	6.95	
57/55		Regular Issue US	25	4.95		260/46		US Vending Booklets	10	6.95	
106/55		US 3 cent, 4 cent Commems	20	4.95		260/55		US 13 cent Eagle Full Strip	10	6.95	
105/57		US Giori Press, Modern	20	4.95		260/59		US Double Press Reg.			
127/70		US Jumbo Issues	10	4.95				Issue Strip (20)	10	6.95	
140/89		Postal Cards, Souvenir Sheets	10	4.95		111/91		Columbian Souvenir Shts	6	3.15	
165/94		First Day Covers	10	4.95		229/131		WWII Souvenir Shts	5	7.40	
		STRIPS 215mm Long				187/144		UN Flag Sheetlets	10	13.00	
20		Mini Stamps US, etc.	22	6.25		204/153		US Commem Sheets, Bicent.	5	7.40	
22		Narrow US Airs	22	6.25		120/207		Ameripex Presidential Shtlets	4	5.00	
24		UK and Canada, early US	22	6.25				**ACCESSORIES**			
25		US Commem & Reg. Issue	22	6.25		506		Desert Magic Drying			
27		US Famous Americans & UN	22	6.25				Book 8 1/2x5 3/4	1	5.25	
28		Switzerland & Liechtenstein	22	6.25		507		Desert Magic II Like 506 dbl height	1	7.25	
30		US Jamestown Foreign	22	6.25		602		Guillotine "EXCAL" mini	1	19.95	
31		US Squares & Semi-Jumbos	22	6.25		604		Guillotine "ORTHOMATIC" major	1	39.95	
33		UK Issues, Misc. Foreign	22	6.25		790		"At Home" Organizer	1	13.95	
36		Duck Stamps, Misc. Foreign	15	6.25		793		Modular Drawing Set	1	24.75	
39		US Magsaysay, Misc. Foreign	15	6.25		894		FDC Album US size, Blk, Tan, Red	1	19.95	
41		US Vertical Comm., Israel Tabs	15	6.25		894C		Close End Slip Case for #894 Blk	1	9.50	
44		Booklet Panes Hatteras Quartet	15	6.25		895		FDC Album GB & Canada size,			
48		Canada Reg. Issue & Comm Blks.	15	6.25				Blk, Tan, Red	1	20.95	
50		US Plain Blocks of 4	15	6.25		896		FDC Album #10 size Blk, Tan, Red	1	21.95	
52		France Paintings, Misc. Foreign	15	6.25		901		Tongs, Point Tip	1	5.50	
57		US Comm Plate Blocks (4)	15	6.25		902		Tongs, Point Tip, Professional	1	6.95	
61		Souvenir Sheets, Tab Singles	15	6.25		907		Tongs, Angled Tip, Professional	1	6.95	
		STRIPS 240mm Long				908		Tongs, Sharp Point, Professional	1	6.95	
63		US Semi Jumbo Blocks	10	7.25		909		Tongs, Spade Tip, Professional	1	6.95	
66		ATM Panes, SA Duck Panes	10	7.25							
68		Canadian Plate Blks., etc.	10	7.25							
74		UN Inscription Blocks (4)	10	7.25							
80		US Comm., Plate Blocks (4)	10	7.25							
82		UN Chagell SS, Canada, Plt Blks.	10	7.25							
84		Israel Tab Blocks, etc.	10	7.25							
89		UN Insription Blocks (6)	10	7.25							
100		US Squares-Plate Blocks	7	7.25							
120		Miniature Sheets	7	7.25							
		STRIPS 264mm Long									
70		US Jumbo Plate Blocks	10	10.25							
91		UK Souvenir Sheets	10	10.25							

Showgard Dark Background - All Strips 264 mm Long

$1.50	#76 #109 #115 #117 #121 #129 #131 #135 #143 #149	$1.75 each	#147 #151 #163 #167 #171 #201